Baseball America

2023

PROSPECT
HANDBOOK

BASEBALL AMERICA INC. DURHAM, N.C.

Baseball America
2023
PROSPECT
HANDBOOK

Editors
CARLOS COLLAZO, J.J. COOPER, MATT EDDY,
CHRIS HILBURN-TRENKLE AND JOSH NORRIS

Assistant Editors
BEN BADLER, TEDDY CAHILL,
KYLE GLASER, SAVANNAH MCCANN AND
GEOFF PONTES

Database and Application Development
MARK TAYLOR

Contributing Writers
MARK CHIARELLI, JON MEOLI,
BILL MITCHELL, NICK PIECORO,
JEFF SANDERS, ALEX SPEIER,
EMILY WALDON
AND TAYLOR BLAKE WARD

Design & Production
SETH MATES AND NEVILLE HARVEY

Cover Photo
GUNNAR HENDERSON BY
MIKE JANES/FOUR SEAM IMAGES

FOR ADDITIONAL COPIES
VISIT OUR WEBSITE AT BASEBALLAMERICA.COM
OR CALL 1-800-845-2726 TO ORDER.

US $39.95, PLUS SHIPPING AND HANDLING PER ORDER.
EXPEDITED SHIPPING AVAILABLE.

DISTRIBUTED BY SIMON & SCHUSTER
ISBN: 978-1-932391-93-0

STATISTICS PROVIDED BY MAJOR LEAGUE BASEBALL
ADVANCED MEDIA AND COMPILED BY
BASEBALL AMERICA

Baseball America

ESTABLISHED 1981 • P.O. Box 12877, Durham, NC 27709 • (800) 845-2726

PRESIDENT Tom Dondero
EDITOR IN CHIEF J.J. Cooper @jjcoop36
EXECUTIVE EDITOR Matt Eddy @MattEddyBA
CHIEF INNOVATION OFFICER Ben Badler @benbadler
DIRECTOR OF FINANCE AND REVENUE Mike Stewart

EDITORIAL
SENIOR EDITOR Josh Norris @jnorris427
NATIONAL WRITERS Teddy Cahill @tedcahill
Carlos Collazo @CarlosACollazo
Kyle Glaser @KyleAGlaser
PROSPECT WRITER Geoff Pontes @GeoffPontesBA
ASSOCIATE EDITOR Chris Hilburn-Trenkle @ChrisTrenkle
WEB EDITOR Kayla Lombardo @KaylaLombardo11
CONTENT PRODUCER Savannah McCann @savjaye
SPECIAL CONTRIBUTOR Tim Newcomb @tdnewcomb

PRODUCTION
DIRECTOR, MARKETING & DESIGN Seth Mates @SethMates

ADVERTISING
DIRECTOR OF SALES, WESTERN REGION Penn Jones
DIRECTOR OF SALES,
MIDWEST & EASTERN REGIONS Joe Martin

BUSINESS
CHIEF TECHNOLOGY OFFICER Mark Taylor
MARKETING/OPERATIONS COORDINATOR Angela Lewis
CUSTOMER SERVICE Melissa Sunderman

STATISTICAL SERVICE
MAJOR LEAGUE BASEBALL ADVANCED MEDIA

BASEBALL AMERICA ENTERPRISES

ALLIANCE
— SPORTS —

CHAIRMAN & CEO Gary Green
PRESIDENT Larry Botel
GENERAL COUNSEL Matthew Pace
DIRECTOR OF OPERATIONS Joan Disalvo
PARTNERS Stephen Alepa
Jon Ashley
Martie Cordaro
David Geaslen
Glenn Isaacson
Sonny Kalsi
Peter G. Riguardi
Ian Ritchie
Brian Rothschild
Beryl Snyder
Tom Steiglehner

FOREWORD

This foreword may be at the front of the book, but it's always one of the last things we write. It gets created at a time of both relief and exhaustion, at the end of the lengthy and taxing—but rewarding—process of building the latest Prospect Handbook.

We want every Prospect Handbook to be better than the last. Our goal is continual improvement. We hope that you agree that this book has cleared that bar.

The first Prospect Handbook in 2001 was 446 pages in length—and printed on a smaller page size. Now, the book spans more than 500 pages. Over the years, the book's presentation has steadily changed. Most significantly, we've added BA Grades and scouting tools grades for the Top 10 Prospects. In return, some charts and statistical components have been removed to handle the steadily growing length of the reports. We've consistently felt that the quality of reports is the most important aspect of the Handbook.

This year, we've taken things a step further. For years, readers have asked us to include tools grades for all 30 prospects for all 30 teams. We have been hesitant because we wanted to be confident that those grades would be as accurate as the ones we've listed for the Top 10 Prospects.

We now feel comfortable enough with the information we have gathered to take on that challenge. We promise you that there are tools grades in this book that are wrong, but that's the nature of attempting to predict what will happen with players five and even 10 years into the future. We can, however, feel confident that these grades are as accurate as they can be.

It's also worth noting that as you read this year's book, you may believe we have become harsher in our assessments.

We've heard from some in the baseball industry about how it's best to "use the entire scale" when it comes to the 20-to-80 scouting grades.

Too often, we have ended up defaulting to the middle. It's something the baseball industry as a whole has battled with for years. It's safer and easier to project most minor leaguers in a range of 45 to 55 hitters with 45 to 55 power and 50 defense. We are looking ahead, so we project that a hitter will get to being an average hitter with average power. As we look back as well as forward, we have come to the decision that this is not the best way to approach these grades.

When you read in this book that a player has 20 power or a 30 hit tool, it's not meant as a withering rebuke. It's meant to be a more accurate attempt at projecting the player. Martin Maldonado, for instance, is a catcher with a long and successful MLB career that spans nearly 3,000 at-bats. With a career .209 batting average and .285 on-base percentage, he's also a 20 hitter by the scouting scale.

If our 2012 Handbook had included full tools grades for Maldonado, it would have been accurate to project him as a 20 hitter with 40 power, but also a 70 defender with a 70 arm. That may have seemed harsh, but it would have been an accurate projection of a player with a long MLB career ahead. So when you read that a player has 30 control, a 20 hit tool or 80 power, please understand that we're trying to better show differences between players. By using the entire scale we are trying to give you an improved book.

The book is the same size as it has been for years, which means the decision to add full tools grades means something had to be removed. We added thumbnail reports for teams' Nos. 31-40 prospects in the 2021 Handbook. We hoped to do so again this year but have found that the room needed for the tools grades, as well as our continually growing scouting reports, meant that something had to give. This year's reports are the longest and most detailed we've had in the book, so we hope you agree with our decision to give you longer reports on the Top 30 Prospects, even if it means those 31-40 prospects are relegated this year to being on the depth chart and an online extra.

If you have any further thoughts, feel free to email me at jj.cooper@baseballamerica.com.

J.J. COOPER
EDITOR IN CHIEF, BASEBALL AMERICA

EDITOR'S NOTE: The transactions deadline for this book was Dec. 11, 2022. You can find players who changed organizations by using the index in the back.

>> For the purposes of Baseball America rankings, a prospect is any player who is signed with a major league organization and who has not exceeded 130 at-bats, 50 innings or 30 pitching appearances in the major leagues, regardless of major league service time. This leads to rare instances in which a player is prospect eligible for BA but *not* eligible for the 2023 American or National league Rookie of the Year awards because he has exceeded the MLB service time threshold of 45 days. Notable examples of prospects who are not ROY eligible in this year's book: the Rays' **Shane Baz**, the Padres' **Luis Campusano** and the Blue Jays' **Gabriel Moreno**.

TABLE OF CONTENTS

CHICAGO WHITE SOX

STARTS ON PAGE 98

No.Player, Pos.	BA Grade/Risk	No.Player, Pos.	BA Grade/Risk	No.Player, Pos.	BA Grade/Risk
1. Colson Montgomery, SS	60/H	11. Jonathan Cannon, RHP	50/H	21. Jonathan Stiever, RHP	45/H
2. Oscar Colas, OF	50/M	12. Matthew Thompson, RHP	45/H	22. Jason Bilous, RHP	45/H
3. Bryan Ramos, 3B	50/H	13. Kohl Simas, RHP	45/H	23. Ryan Burrowes, SS	50/X
4. Noah Schultz, LHP	55/X	14. Jared Kelley, RHP	50/X	24. Yolbert Sanchez, 2B	40/M
5. Sean Burke, RHP	50/H	15. Tanner McDougal, RHP	50/X	25. Terrell Tatum, OF	45/H
6. Cristian Mena, RHP	50/H	16. Yoelqui Cespedes, OF	45/H	26. Erick Hernandez, OF	50/X
7. Peyton Pallette, RHP	55/X	17. Wilfred Veras, OF/3B	50/X	27. Loidel Chapelli, 2B	50/X
8. Norge Vera, RHP	55/X	18. Wes Kath, 3B	50/X	28. Tyler Schweitzer, LHP	45/V
9. Jose Rodriguez, SS	45/M	19. Jordan Sprinkle, SS	45/H	29. Andrew Dalquist, RHP	45/V
10. Lenyn Sosa, SS	45/M	20. Luis Mieses, OF	45/H	30. Adam Hackenberg, C	45/V

CINCINNATI REDS

STARTS ON PAGE 114

No.Player, Pos.	BA Grade/Risk	No.Player, Pos.	BA Grade/Risk	No.Player, Pos.	BA Grade/Risk
1. Elly De La Cruz, SS	70/V	11. Andrew Abbott, LHP	45/M	21. Ariel Almonte, OF	50/X
2. Noelvi Marte, 3B	55/H	12. Matt McLain, SS	45/M	22. Ricky Karcher, RHP	45/H
3. Edwin Arroyo, SS	55/H	13. Ricardo Cabrera, SS	55/X	23. Logan Tanner, C	40/M
4. Cam Collier, 3B	60/X	14. Jay Allen, OF	50/H	24. Hector Rodriguez, OF	45/H
5. Christian Encarnacion-Strand, 3B	55/V	15. Levi Stoudt, RHP	50/H	25. Justin Boyd, OF	45/H
6. Chase Petty, RHP	50/H	16. Carlos Jorge, 2B	45/H	26. Cade Hunter, C	45/H
7. Spencer Steer, 3B	45/M	17. Victor Acosta, SS	50/X	27. Lyon Richardson, RHP	50/X
8. Sal Stewart, 3B	55/X	18. Michael Siani, OF	45/M	28. Yerlin Confidan, OF	50/X
9. Connor Phillips, RHP	50/H	19. Leonardo Balcazar, SS	45/H	29. Casey Legumina, RHP	45/H
10. Brandon Williamson, LHP	50/H	20. Joe Boyle, RHP	50/X	30. Rece Hinds, OF	45/X

CLEVELAND GUARDIANS

STARTS ON PAGE 130

No.Player, Pos.	BA Grade/Risk	No.Player, Pos.	BA Grade/Risk	No.Player, Pos.	BA Grade/Risk
1. Daniel Espino, RHP	70/V	11. Tyler Freeman, 2B/SS	45/M	21. Gabriel Rodriguez, 3B	50/V
2. Gavin Williams, RHP	65/H	12. Gabriel Arias, SS	45/M	22. Xzavion Curry, RHP	45/H
3. Bo Naylor, C	55/H	13. Justin Campbell, RHP	50/H	23. Angel Genao, SS	50/X
4. George Valera, OF	55/H	14. Jose Tena, SS	50/H	24. Richie Palacios, OF/2B	45/H
5. Brayan Rocchio, SS	55/H	15. Jake Fox, 2B/OF	50/H	25. Petey Halpin, OF	45/H
6. Logan Allen, LHP	55/H	16. Juan Brito, 2B	50/H	26. Hunter Gaddis, RHP	45/H
7. Tanner Bibee, RHP	55/H	17. Cody Morris, RHP	50/H	27. Doug Nikhazy, LHP	45/H
8. Angel Martinez, SS	55/H	18. Joey Cantillo, LHP	50/H	28. Tanner Burns, RHP	45/H
9. Chase DeLauter, OF	55/H	19. Parker Messick, LHP	50/H	29. Will Benson, OF	45/H
10. Will Brennan, OF	50/M	20. Jhonkensy Noel, OF/3B	50/V	30. Bryan Lavastida, C	45/H

COLORADO ROCKIES

STARTS ON PAGE 146

No.Player, Pos.	BA Grade/Risk	No.Player, Pos.	BA Grade/Risk	No.Player, Pos.	BA Grade/Risk
1. Ezequiel Tovar, SS	65/H	11. Jackson Cox, RHP	55/X	21. Brenton Doyle, OF	45/H
2. Zac Veen, OF	55/H	12. Victor Juarez, RHP	50/V	22. Juan Guerrero, OF	45/H
3. Drew Romo, C	55/H	13. Yanquiel Fernandez, OF	50/V	23. Dyan Jorge, SS	50/X
4. Adael Amador, SS	55/H	14. Hunter Goodman, C	45/H	24. Carson Palmquist, LHP	45/H
5. Gabriel Hughes, RHP	50/H	15. Jaden Hill, RHP	50/X	25. Gavin Hollowell, RHP	40/H
6. Benny Montgomery, OF	55/X	16. Michael Toglia, 1B	40/M	26. Alberto Pacheco, LHP	45/X
7. Warming Bernabel, 3B	50/H	17. Jeff Criswell, RHP	45/H	27. Bryant Betancourt, C/1B	45/X
8. Sterlin Thompson, 3B/OF	50/H	18. Julio Carreras, SS	45/H	28. Ryan Ritter, SS	40/X
9. Jordy Vargas, RHP	55/X	19. Nolan Jones, OF	40/M	29. Connor Staine, RHP	40/H
10. Jordan Beck, OF	50/H	20. Angel Chivilli, RHP	50/X	30. Michael Prosecky, LHP	40/H

DETROIT TIGERS

STARTS ON PAGE 162

No.Player, Pos.	BA Grade/Risk	No.Player, Pos.	BA Grade/Risk	No.Player, Pos.	BA Grade/Risk
1. Jackson Jobe, RHP	60/H	11. Reese Olson, RHP	45/H	21. Troy Melton, RHP	45/H
2. Jace Jung, 2B	55/H	12. Parker Meadows, OF	45/H	22. Josh Crouch, C	45/H
3. Wilmer Flores, RHP	55/H	13. Cristian Santana, SS	50/X	23. Manuel Sequera, SS/3B	50/X
4. Ty Madden, RHP	50/H	14. Roberto Campos, OF	45/H	24. Abel Bastidas, SS	50/X
5. Colt Keith, 3B	50/H	15. Izaac Pacheco, 3B	45/H	25. Adinso Reyes, SS	50/X
6. Peyton Graham, SS	50/H	16. Joey Wentz, LHP	45/H	26. Brant Hurter, LHP	40/H
7. Dillon Dingler, C	45/H	17. Dylan Smith, RHP	45/H	27. Gage Workman, 3B	45/X
8. Kerry Carpenter, OF	45/M	18. Andre Lipcius, 2B/3B	40/M	28. Javier Osorio, SS	45/X
9. Ryan Kreidler, SS	45/M	19. Wenceel Perez, 2B	45/H	29. Jose De La Cruz, OF	45/X
10. Justyn-Henry Malloy, OF/3B	45/H	20. Mason Englert, RHP	45/H	30. Eliezer Alfonzo, C	40/H

TABLE OF CONTENTS

MILWAUKEE BREWERS
STARTS ON PAGE 258

No.Player, Pos.	BA Grade/Risk	No.Player, Pos.	BA Grade/Risk	No.Player, Pos.	BA Grade/Risk
1. Jackson Chourio, OF	70/H	11. Robert Gasser, LHP	45/M	21. Daniel Guilarte, SS	45/X
2. Sal Frelick, OF	55/H	12. Robert Moore, 2B	45/H	22. Gregory Barrios, SS	45/X
3. Joey Wiemer, OF	55/H	13. Luis Lara, OF	50/X	23. Matt Wood, C	40/H
4. Brice Turang, SS	50/M	14. Abner Uribe, RHP	45/H	24. Cam Robinson, C	40/H
5. Garrett Mitchell, OF	50/H	15. Carlos Rodriguez, RHP	45/H	25. Dylan O'Rae, SS	45/X
6. Jeferson Quero, C	50/H	16. Logan Henderson, RHP	45/V	26. Luke Adams, 3B	45/X
7. Jacob Misiorowski, RHP	55/X	17. Ethan Small, LHP	40/H	27. Victor Castaneda, RHP	40/H
8. Esteury Ruiz, OF	45/M	18. Felix Valerio, 2B/SS/3B	40/H	28. Jadher Areinamo, 2B/SS/3B	40/H
9. Tyler Black, 2B/OF	50/H	19. Hendry Mendez, OF	45/X	29. Eduardo Garcia, SS	40/H
10. Eric Brown, SS	50/H	20. Hedbert Perez, OF	40/H	30. Freddy Zamora, SS	40/H

MINNESOTA TWINS
STARTS ON PAGE 274

No.Player, Pos.	BA Grade/Risk	No.Player, Pos.	BA Grade/Risk	No.Player, Pos.	BA Grade/Risk
1. Royce Lewis, SS/OF	60/H	11. Matt Canterino, RHP	50/H	21. Bryan Acuña, SS	50/X
2. Brooks Lee, SS	60/H	12. Yasser Mercedes, OF	55/X	22. Ronny Henriquez, RHP	40/M
3. Emmanuel Rodriguez, OF	60/V	13. Austin Martin, 2B/OF	45/H	23. Blayne Enlow, RHP	40/M
4. Edouard Julien, 2B	55/H	14. Jose Rodriguez, OF	50/X	24. Cole Sands, RHP	40/H
5. Connor Prielipp, LHP	55/X	15. Noah Miller, SS	45/H	25. Tanner Schoebel, SS/2B	45/H
6. Matt Wallner, OF	50/H	16. Jordan Balazovic, RHP	45/H	26. Michael Helman, 2B/OF	40/M
7. Marco Raya, RHP	55/X	17. Danny De Andrade, SS	45/H	27. Sean Mooney, RHP	40/H
8. Louie Varland, RHP	45/M	18. Brent Headrick, LHP	45/H	28. Steven Cruz, RHP	40/H
9. David Festa, RHP	50/H	19. Misael Urbina, OF	50/X	29. Jaylen Nowlin, LHP	40/H
10. Simeon Woods Richardson, RHP	45/M	20. Alejandro Hidalgo, RHP	45/H	30. Aaron Sabato, 1B	40/H

NEW YORK METS
STARTS ON PAGE 290

No.Player, Pos.	BA Grade/Risk	No.Player, Pos.	BA Grade/Risk	No.Player, Pos.	BA Grade/Risk
1. Francisco Alvarez, C	65/M	11. Matt Allan, RHP	55/X	21. Nick Morabito, OF	50/X
2. Kodai Senga, RHP	55/M	12. Dominic Hamel, RHP	50/H	22. Dangelo Sarmiento, SS	50/X
3. Brett Baty, 3B	55/M	13. Mike Vasil, RHP	50/H	23. Jacob Reimer, 3B	45/H
4. Kevin Parada, C	60/H	14. Jesus Baez, SS	50/X	24. Luis Moreno, RHP	45/H
5. Alex Ramirez, OF	55/H	15. Joel Diaz, RHP	50/X	25. Javier Atencio, LHP	45/H
6. Jett Williams, SS	55/X	16. Jordany Ventura, RHP	50/X	26. Zach Greene, RHP	40/M
7. Mark Vientos, 3B	45/M	17. Layonel Ovalles, RHP	50/X	27. Christian Scott, RHP	45/H
8. Ronny Mauricio, SS	50/H	18. Jose Butto, RHP	40/M	28. Eric Orze, RHP	45/H
9. Blade Tidwell, RHP	50/H	19. Luis Rodriguez, LHP	50/X	29. William Lugo, 3B	45/H
10. Calvin Ziegler, RHP	50/H	20. Junior Santos, RHP	45/H	30. Grant Hartwig, RHP	40/M

NEW YORK YANKEES
STARTS ON PAGE 306

No.Player, Pos.	BA Grade/Risk	No.Player, Pos.	BA Grade/Risk	No.Player, Pos.	BA Grade/Risk
1. Anthony Volpe, SS	65/M	11. Luis Gil, RHP	45/M	21. Clayton Beeter, RHP	45/H
2. Oswald Peraza, SS	50/M	12. Luis Serna, RHP	55/V	22. Omar Gonzalez, RHP	50/X
3. Jasson Dominguez, OF	55/H	13. Roderick Arias, SS	55/X	23. Angel Benitez, RHP	50/X
4. Everson Pereira, OF	55/H	14. Trey Sweeney, SS	45/H	24. Greg Weissert, RHP	40/L
5. Austin Wells, C	55/H	15. Elijah Dunham, OF	45/H	25. Antonio Gomez, C	45/H
6. Spencer Jones, OF	55/V	16. Engelth Ureña, C	50/X	26. Yoendrys Gomez, RHP	45/H
7. Will Warren, RHP	50/H	17. Tyler Hardman, 3B	45/H	27. Carson Coleman, RHP	40/H
8. Drew Thorpe, RHP	50/H	18. Richard Fitts, RHP	45/H	28. Jhony Brito, RHP	40/H
9. Randy Vasquez, RHP	50/H	19. Anthony Hall, OF	45/H	29. Jared Serna, 2B	40/H
10. Estevan Florial, OF	45/M	20. Trystan Vrieling, RHP	45/H	30. Juan Carela, RHP	40/H

OAKLAND ATHLETICS
STARTS ON PAGE 322

No.Player, Pos.	BA Grade/Risk	No.Player, Pos.	BA Grade/Risk	No.Player, Pos.	BA Grade/Risk
1. Tyler Soderstrom, C/1B	60/H	11. Henry Bolte, OF	55/X	21. Garrett Acton, RHP	45/H
2. Zack Gelof, 2B/3B	50/H	12. Gunnar Hoglund, RHP	50/H	22. Colin Peluse, RHP	45/H
3. Mason Miller, RHP	55/X	13. J.T. Ginn, RHP	50/H	23. Brayan Buelvas, OF	45/H
4. Ken Waldichuk, LHP	50/H	14. Hogan Harris, LHP	45/H	24. Jefferson Jean, RHP	50/X
5. Max Muncy, SS	50/H	15. Brett Harris, 3B	45/H	25. Jorge Juan, RHP	45/H
6. Daniel Susac, C	50/H	16. Joey Estes, RHP	45/H	26. Pedro Pineda, OF	50/X
7. Lawrence Butler, OF/1B	50/H	17. Ryan Cusick, RHP	45/H	27. Logan Davidson, SS/3B	40/H
8. Denzel Clarke, OF	55/X	18. Clark Elliott, OF	45/H	28. Junior Perez, OF	40/H
9. Luis Medina, RHP	50/H	19. Euribiel Angeles, 2B/SS	45/H	29. Kyle Virbitsky, RHP	40/H
10. Jordan Diaz, 2B/1B	45/M	20. Ryan Noda, 1B	40/M	30. Cooper Bowman, 2B	40/H

TABLE OF CONTENTS

SEATTLE MARINERS
STARTS ON PAGE 418

No. Player, Pos.	BA Grade/Risk	No. Player, Pos.	BA Grade/Risk	No. Player, Pos.	BA Grade/Risk
1. Harry Ford, C	55/H	11. Jonatan Clase, OF	50/V	21. Spencer Packard, OF	40/H
2. Cole Young, SS	55/X	12. Zach DeLoach, OF	45/H	22. Tyler Gough, RHP	45/X
3. Bryce Miller, RHP	50/H	13. Walter Ford, RHP	50/X	23. Travis Kuhn, RHP	40/H
4. Gabriel Gonzalez, OF	55/X	14. Lazaro Montes, OF	50/X	24. Kaden Polcovich, 2B	40/H
5. Emerson Hancock, RHP	50/H	15. Cade Marlowe, OF	40/M	25. Josh Hood, SS	40/H
6. Taylor Dollard, RHP	50/H	16. Axel Sanchez, SS	45/H	26. Alberto Rodriguez, OF	40/H
7. Bryan Woo, RHP	50/H	17. Robert Perez Jr., 1B	45/H	27. Victor Labrada, OF	40/H
8. Michael Arroyo, SS	55/X	18. Michael Morales, RHP	45/H	28. Joseph Hernandez, RHP	40/H
9. Tyler Locklear, 3B	50/H	19. Isaiah Campbell, RHP	40/H	29. Starlin Aguilar, 3B	45/X
10. Prelander Berroa, RHP	50/H	20. Ashton Izzi, RHP	45/X	30. Juan Pinto, LHP	45/X

TAMPA BAY RAYS
STARTS ON PAGE 434

No. Player, Pos.	BA Grade/Risk	No. Player, Pos.	BA Grade/Risk	No. Player, Pos.	BA Grade/Risk
1. Shane Baz, RHP	65/X	11. Osleivis Basabe, 2B/3B	50/H	21. Ryan Cermak, OF	45/H
2. Curtis Mead, 2B/3B	55/M	12. Brock Jones, OF	50/H	22. Chandler Simpson, OF	45/H
3. Taj Bradley, RHP	55/M	13. Xavier Isaac, 1B	55/X	23. Carlos Colmenarez, SS	50/X
4. Carson Williams, SS	55/H	14. Rene Pinto, C	40/L	24. Shane Sasaki, OF	45/H
5. Kyle Manzardo, 1B	55/H	15. Willy Vasquez, 3B	50/H	25. Marcus Johnson, RHP	45/H
6. Jonathan Aranda, 2B	50/M	16. Kameron Misner, OF	45/H	26. Calvin Faucher, RHP	40/M
7. Mason Auer, OF	55/H	17. Santiago Suarez, RHP	45/H	27. Kevin Kelly, RHP	40/M
8. Junior Caminero, 3B	50/H	18. Heriberto Hernandez, OF	45/H	28. Austin Vernon, RHP	45/H
9. Mason Montgomery, LHP	50/H	19. Greg Jones, SS	45/H	29. Austin Shenton, 3B	40/H
10. Cole Wilcox, RHP	55/X	20. Colby White, RHP	50/X	30. Ian Seymour, LHP	45/X

TEXAS RANGERS
STARTS ON PAGE 450

No. Player, Pos.	BA Grade/Risk	No. Player, Pos.	BA Grade/Risk	No. Player, Pos.	BA Grade/Risk
1. Evan Carter, OF	60/H	11. Justin Foscue, 2B	50/H	21. Cody Bradford, LHP	45/H
2. Owen White, RHP	55/H	12. Cole Winn, RHP	50/H	22. Thomas Saggese, 2B	45/H
3. Josh Jung, 3B	55/H	13. Yeison Morrobel, OF	55/X	23. Chandler Pollard, SS	45/V
4. Luisangel Acuña, SS/2B	55/H	14. Mitchell Bratt, LHP	50/H	24. Marcos Torres, OF	50/X
5. Anthony Gutierrez, OF	60/X	15. Cameron Cauley, SS	50/V	25. Jonathan Ornelas, SS/OF	45/H
6. Aaron Zavala, OF	55/V	16. Gleider Figuereo, 3B	50/V	26. Luis Ramirez, RHP	45/H
7. Jack Leiter, RHP	55/V	17. Zak Kent, RHP	45/H	27. Tekoah Roby, RHP	45/H
8. Brock Porter, RHP	55/X	18. Danyer Cueva, SS	50/X	28. Tommy Specht, OF	55/X
9. Dustin Harris, OF/1B	50/H	19. Cole Ragans, LHP	40/M	29. Echedry Vargas, 3B	45/X
10. Kumar Rocker, RHP	55/X	20. Emiliano Teodo, RHP	45/H	30. JoJo Blackmon, OF	45/X

TORONTO BLUE JAYS
STARTS ON PAGE 466

No. Player, Pos.	BA Grade/Risk	No. Player, Pos.	BA Grade/Risk	No. Player, Pos.	BA Grade/Risk
1. Gabriel Moreno, C	65/M	11. Adam Macko, LHP	50/V	21. Kendry Rojas, LHP	50/X
2. Ricky Tiedemann, LHP	60/H	12. Josh Kasevich, SS	45/H	22. Manuel Beltre, SS	50/X
3. Yosver Zulueta, RHP	55/H	13. Dahian Santos, RHP	50/X	23. Alejandro Melean, RHP	40/M
4. Brandon Barriera, LHP	55/X	14. Dasan Brown, OF	50/X	24. Adrian Pinto, SS/2B	50/X
5. Addison Barger, SS/3B	50/H	15. Gabriel Martinez, OF	45/H	25. Zach Britton, OF	40/H
6. Orelvis Martinez, SS/3B	55/X	16. Otto Lopez, 2B/OF/SS	40/M	26. Damiano Palmegiani, OF	40/H
7. Tucker Toman, SS/3B	55/X	17. Sem Robberse, RHP	45/H	27. Rainer Nuñez, 1B	40/H
8. Cade Doughty, 2B/3B	50/H	18. Hagen Danner, RHP	45/H	28. Yondrei Rojas, RHP	45/X
9. Hayden Juenger, RHP	50/H	19. Spencer Horwitz, 1B/OF	40/M	29. C.J. Van Eyk, RHP	45/X
10. Nate Pearson, RHP	50/V	20. Leonardo Jimenez, SS	50/X	30. Trent Palmer, RHP	45/X

WASHINGTON NATIONALS
STARTS ON PAGE 482

No. Player, Pos.	BA Grade/Risk	No. Player, Pos.	BA Grade/Risk	No. Player, Pos.	BA Grade/Risk
1. James Wood, OF	65/H	11. Jake Bennett, LHP	50/H	21. Zach Brzykcy, RHP	45/H
2. Robert Hassell III, OF	60/H	12. Armando Cruz, SS	50/X	22. Jake Irvin, RHP	40/H
3. Elijah Green, OF	65/X	13. Cole Henry, RHP	50/X	23. Evan Lee, LHP	40/H
4. Cade Cavalli, RHP	60/H	14. Mitchell Parker, LHP	45/H	24. Trey Lipscomb, 3B	40/H
5. Brady House, SS	55/X	15. Andry Lara, RHP	45/H	25. Drew Millas, C	40/H
6. Cristhian Vaquero, OF	55/X	16. Thad Ward, RHP	45/M	26. Gerardo Carrillo, RHP	40/H
7. Jarlin Susana, RHP	55/X	17. Roismar Quintana, OF	50/X	27. Daylen Lile, OF	45/X
8. Jeremy De La Rosa, OF	50/H	18. Matt Cronin, LHP	45/H	28. Tim Cate, LHP	40/H
9. Jackson Rutledge, RHP	50/H	19. Israel Pineda, C	45/H	29. Aldo Ramirez, RHP	40/H
10. TJ White, OF	50/H	20. Jose Ferrer, LHP	45/H	30. Will Frizzell, 1B	40/H

For the 12th year, Baseball America has assigned Grades and Risk Factors for each of the 900 prospects in the Prospect Handbook. For the BA Grade, we used a 20-to-80 scale, similar to the scale scouts use, to keep it familiar. However, most major league clubs put an overall numerical grade on players, called the Overall Future Potential or OFP. Often the OFP is merely an average of the player's tools.

The BA Grade is not an OFP. It's a measure of a prospect's value, and it attempts to gauge the player's realistic ceiling. We've continued to adjust our grades to try to be more realistic, and less optimistic, and keep refining the grade-vetting process. The majority of the players in this book rest in the 50 High/45 Medium range, because the vast majority of worthwhile prospects in the minors are players who either have a chance to be everyday regulars but are far from that possibility, or players who are closer to

> **BA GRADE**
> **50** Risk: High

the majors but who are likely to be role players and useful contributors. Few future franchise players or perennial all-stars graduate from the minors in any given year. The goal of the Grade/Risk system is to allow readers to take a quick look at how strong their team's farm system is, and how much immediate help the big league club can expect from its prospects. Got a minor leaguer who was traded from one organization to the other after the book went to press? Use the player's Grade/Risk and see where he would rank in his new system.

It also helps with our Organization Rankings, but those will not simply flow, in formulaic fashion, from the Grade/Risk results because we incorporate a lot of factors into our talent rankings including the differences in risk between pitchers and hitters. Hitters have a lower injury risk and therefore are safer bets.

BA Grade Scale

GRADE	HITTER ROLE	PITCHER ROLE	EXAMPLES
75-80	Franchise Player	No. 1 starter	Mike Trout, Justin Verlander, Aaron Judge
65-70	Perennial All-Star	No. 2 starter	Brandon Woodruff, Manny Machado, JT Realmuto
60	Occasional All-Star	No. 3 starter, Game's best reliever	George Springer, Jose Abreu, Edwin Diaz
55	First-Division Regular	No. 3/No. 4 starter, Elite closer	Randy Arozarena, Rhys Hoskins, Liam Hendriks
50	Solid-Average Regular	No. 4 starter, Elite set-up reliever	Alex Verdugo, Kolten Wong, Marco Gonzales
45	Second-Division Regular/Platoon	No. 5 starter, Middle reliever	Chad Pinder, Jordan Lyles, Shawn Armstrong
40	Reserve	Fill-in starter, Low-leverage reliever	Dylan Moore, Austin Pruitt, Elieser Hernandez

RISK FACTORS

LOW: Likely to reach realistic ceiling, certain big league career barring injury.

MEDIUM: Some work left to refine their tools, but a polished player.

HIGH: Most top draft picks in their first seasons, players with plenty of projection left, players with a significant flaw left to correct or players whose injury history is worrisome.

VERY HIGH: Recent draft picks with a limited track record of success or injury issues.

EXTREME: Teenagers in Rookie ball, players with significant injury histories or players whose struggle with a key skill (especially control for pitchers or strikeout rate for hitters).

Explaining The 20-80 Scouting Scale

None of the authors of the Prospect Handbook is a scout, but we all have spoken to plenty of scouts to report on the prospects and scouting reports enclosed. So we use their lingo, including the 20-80 scouting scale. Many of these grades are measurable data, such as fastball velocity and speed (usually timed from home to first or in workouts over 60 yards). A fastball grade doesn't stem solely from its velocity—command and life are crucial elements as well. A 100 mph fastball with poor movement characteristics may grade below a 97 mph fastball with elite movement. Secondary pitches are graded in a similar fashion. The more swings and misses a pitch induces from hitters and the sharper the bite of the movement, the better the grade.

Velocity steadily has increased over the past decade. Not all that long ago an 88-91 mph fastball was considered major league average, but current data show it is now below-average. Big league starting pitchers now sit 93 mph on average. You can reduce the scale by 1 mph for lefthanders, whose velocities are usually slightly lower. Fastballs earn their grades based on the average range of the pitch over the course of a typical outing, not their peak velocity.

A move to the bullpen complicates in another direction. Pitchers airing it out for one inning should throw harder than someone trying to last six or seven innings, so add 1-2 mph for relievers.

Hitting ability is as much a skill as it is a tool, but the physical elements—hand-eye coordination, swing mechanics, bat speed—are key factors in how it is graded. Raw power generally is measured by how far a player can hit the ball, but game power is graded by how many home runs the hitter projects to hit in the majors, preferably an average over the course of a career. We have tweaked our power grades based on the recent rise in home run rates.

Arm strength can be evaluated by observing the velocity and carry of throws, measured in workouts with radar guns or measured in games for catchers with pop times—the time it takes from the pop of the ball in the catcher's mitt to the pop of the ball in the fielder's glove at second base. Defense takes different factors into account by position but starts with proper footwork and technique, incorporates physical attributes such as hands, short-area quickness and fluid actions, then adds subtle skills such as instincts and anticipation.

Not every team uses the wording below. Some use a 2-to-8 scale without half-grades, and others use above-average and plus synonymously. For the Handbook, consider this BA's 20-80 scale.

20: As bad as it gets for a big leaguer. Think Billy Hamilton's power or Miguel Cabrera's speed.

30: Poor, but not unplayable, such as Miguel Sano's hitting ability.

40: Below-average, such as Rafael Devers' defense or Blake Snell's control.

45: Fringe-average. Joe Musgrove's fastball and Mike Zunino's arm qualify.

50: Major league average. Carlos Correa's speed.

55: Above-average. Will Smith's power.

60: Plus. Marcus Semien's defense or Lance Lynn's control.

70: Plus-Plus. Among the best tools in the game, such as Manny Machado's arm, Freddie Freeman's hitting ability and Charlie Morton's curveball.

80: Top of the scale. Some scouts consider only one player's tool in all of the major leagues to be 80. Think of Aaron Judge's power, Trea Turner's speed or Shohei Ohtani's splitter.

20-80 Measurables

HIT	POWER	SPEED		FASTBALL	ARM STRENGTH
Grade Batting Avg	**Grade Home Runs**	**Home-First (In Secs.)**		**Velocity (Starters)**	**Catcher: Pop**
		RHH	**LHH**	**Grade Velocity**	**Times To Second**
80 .... .315+	80 .... 40+	80 .... 4.00	3.90	80 ..... 98+ mph	**Base (In Seconds)**
70 ..... .295-.314	70 34-39	70 .... 4.10	4.00	70 97	80 .... < 1.90
60 .... .275-.294	60 28-33	65 .... 4.15	4.05	65 96	70 ...... 1.90-1.94
55 .... .265-.274	55 23-27	60 .... 4.20	4.10	60 95	60 ...... 1.95-1.99
50 .... .255-.264	50 19-22	55 .... 4.25	4.15	55 94	50 ..... 2.00-2.04
45 .... .245-.254	45 14-18	50 .... 4.30	4.20	50 93	40 ..... 2.05-2.09
40 .... .235-.244	40 10-13	45 .... 4.35	4.25	45 92	30 ..... 2.10-2.14
30 .... .215-.234	30 5-9	40 .... 4.40	4.30	40 90-91	20 .... > 2.15
20 .... <.215	20 0-4	30 .... 4.50	4.40	30 88-89	
		20 .... 4.60	4.50	20 ..... 87 or less	

AN OVERVIEW

Another feature of the Prospect Handbook is a depth chart of every organization's minor league talent. This shows you at a glance what kind of talent a system has and provides even more prospects beyond the Top 30.

Players are usually listed on the depth charts where we think they'll ultimately end up. To help you better understand why players are slotted at particular positions, we show you here what scouts look for in the ideal candidate at each spot, with individual tools ranked in descending order.

LF	CF	RF
Power	Fielding	Power
Hitting	Hitting	Hitting
Fielding	Speed	Arm Strength
Arm Strength	Power	Fielding
Speed	Arm Strength	Speed

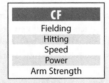

3B	SS	2B	1B
Power	Fielding	Hitting	Power
Hitting	Arm Strength	Fielding	Hitting
Fielding	Hitting	Power	Fielding
Arm Strength	Power	Speed	Arm Strength
Speed	Speed	Arm Strength	Speed

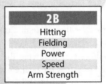

C
Fielding
Hitting
Arm Strength
Power
Speed

STARTING PITCHERS

No. 1 starter	No. 2 starter	No. 3 starter	No. 4-5 starters
• Two plus pitches	• Two plus pitches	• One plus pitch	• Command of two major league pitches
• Average third pitch	• Average third pitch	• Two average pitches	• Average velocity
• Plus-plus command	• Average command	• Average command	• Consistent breaking ball
• Plus makeup	• Average makeup	• Average makeup	• Decent changeup

CLOSER
- One dominant pitch
- Second plus pitch
- Plus command
- Plus-plus makeup

SETUP MAN
- Plus fastball
- Second above-average pitch
- Average command

POSITION RANKINGS

Context is crucial to prospect evaluations. So to provide yet another layer of context, we rank prospects at all eight field positions plus righthanded and lefthanded starting pitchers. The rankings go deeper at the glamour positions, i.e. shortstop, center field and righthanded starter.

We grade players' tools on the 20-80 scouting scale, where 50 is average. The tools listed for position players are ability to hit for average (HIT), hit for power (POW), speed (SPD), fielding ability (FLD) and throwing arm (ARM). The tools listed for pitchers are fastball (FB), curveball (CB), slider (SL), changeup (CHG), other (OTH) and control (CTL). The "other" category can be a splitter, cutter or screwball.

Included as the final categories are BA Grades and Risk levels on a scale ranging from low to extreme.

CATCHER

No	Player	Org	HIT	POW	RUN	FLD	ARM	BA Grade	Risk
1.	Francisco Alvarez	Mets	50	70	30	45	50	65	Medium
2.	Gabriel Moreno	Blue Jays	70	45	40	60	60	65	Medium
3.	Endy Rodriguez	Pirates	60	60	45	50	55	65	High
4.	Diego Cartaya	Dodgers	50	70	30	45	60	65	High
5.	Logan O'Hoppe	Angels	50	50	30	55	60	55	Medium
6.	Bo Naylor	Guardians	40	50	50	55	55	55	High
7.	Drew Romo	Rockies	50	40	50	70	60	55	High
8.	Henry Davis	Pirates	55	60	45	40	60	55	High
9.	Harry Ford	Mariners	55	50	60	45	60	55	High
10.	Luis Campusano	Padres	50	55	30	45	55	50	Medium

FIRST BASE

No	Player	Org	HIT	POW	RUN	FLD	ARM	BA Grade	Risk
1.	Triston Casas	Red Sox	55	65	30	55	50	60	Medium
2.	Tyler Soderstrom	Athletics	60	60	40	40	55	60	High
3.	Kyle Manzardo	Rays	65	55	20	50	50	55	High
4.	Matt Mervis	Cubs	50	60	30	40	70	50	Medium
5.	D. De Los Santos	D-backs	45	65	45	40	50	55	High
6.	Jacob Berry	Marlins	55	60	40	30	45	55	High
7.	C. Encarnacion-Strand	Reds	40	70	40	45	70	55	Very High
8.	Xavier Isaac	Rays	50	65	40	30	45	55	Extreme
9.	Ivan Melendez	D-backs	55	60	30	50	50	50	High
10.	Jordan Diaz	Athletics	60	50	30	40	55	45	Medium

SECOND BASE

No	Player	Org	HIT	POW	RUN	FLD	ARM	BA Grade	Risk
1.	Termarr Johnson	Pirates	70	60	50	50	50	60	High
2.	Michael Busch	Dodgers	50	60	45	40	40	55	Medium
3.	Connor Norby	Orioles	55	55	50	50	45	55	High
4.	Jace Jung	Tigers	55	55	40	45	50	55	High
5.	Edouard Julien	Twins	60	50	45	30	40	55	High
6.	Jonathan Aranda	Rays	60	50	30	40	50	50	Medium
7.	Luisangel Acuña	Rangers	40	55	55	50	40	55	High
8.	Zack Gelof	Athletics	50	55	55	50	50	50	High
9.	Nick Gonzales	Pirates	55	50	55	45	50	50	High
10.	Tyler Black	Brewers	55	40	55	40	40	50	High

THIRD BASE

No	Player	Org	HIT	POW	RUN	FLD	ARM	BA Grade	Risk
1.	Jordan Walker	Cardinals	50	70	55	50	60	70	High
2.	Miguel Vargas	Dodgers	65	50	60	40	55	60	Medium
3.	Curtis Mead	Rays	70	60	40	45	40	55	Medium
4.	Brett Baty	Mets	60	55	45	45	60	55	Medium
5.	Noelvi Marte	Reds	45	65	50	45	50	55	High
6.	Josh Jung	Rangers	55	60	40	45	50	55	High
7.	Cam Collier	Reds	60	55	40	50	65	60	Extreme
8.	Casey Schmitt	Giants	55	50	50	65	70	55	High
9.	Colt Keith	Tigers	55	50	45	50	60	50	High
10.	Bryan Ramos	White Sox	55	55	40	50	55	50	High

SHORTSTOP

No	Player	Org	HIT	POW	RUN	FLD	ARM	BA Grade	Risk
1.	Gunnar Henderson	Orioles	60	70	60	60	70	70	Medium
2.	Elly De La Cruz	Reds	40	70	70	55	70	70	Very High
3.	Jordan Lawlar	D-backs	60	55	60	55	60	65	High
4.	Ezequiel Tovar	Rockies	55	55	60	70	60	65	High
5.	Marcelo Mayer	Red Sox	60	55	40	60	60	65	High
6.	Anthony Volpe	Yankees	60	60	55	50	45	65	High
7.	Jackson Holliday	Orioles	60	55	60	60	60	65	Extreme
8.	Royce Lewis	Twins	50	60	65	55	55	60	High
9.	Jackson Merrill	Padres	60	55	50	55	55	60	High
10.	Colson Montgomery	White Sox	55	55	50	55	55	60	High
11.	Marco Luciano	Giants	60	60	40	50	60	60	High
12.	Brooks Lee	Twins	70	50	40	50	55	60	High
13.	Masyn Winn	Cardinals	55	45	60	55	80	55	High
14.	Zach Neto	Angels	60	50	55	55	60	55	High
15.	Edwin Arroyo	Reds	55	45	55	65	60	55	High
16.	Brayan Rocchio	Guardians	50	50	60	60	50	55	High
17.	Carson Williams	Rays	40	60	55	60	70	55	High
18.	Adael Amador	Rockies	65	45	45	50	45	55	High
19.	Jordan Westburg	Orioles	50	55	55	55	50	50	Medium
20.	Brice Turang	Brewers	55	40	60	50	50	50	Medium
21.	Oswald Peraza	Yankees	55	45	55	60	55	50	Medium
22.	Angel Martinez	Guardians	50	50	50	55	60	55	High
23.	Cole Young	Mariners	60	45	55	50	55	55	Extreme
24.	Brady House	Nationals	50	65	50	55	60	55	Extreme
25.	Cristian Hernandez	Cubs	50	60	40	55	60	55	Extreme

CENTER FIELD

No	Player	Org	HIT	POW	RUN	FLD	ARM	BA Grade	Risk
1.	Jackson Chourio	Brewers	60	70	70	55	50	70	High
2.	Corbin Carroll	D-backs	60	60	80	60	45	65	Medium
3.	Druw Jones	D-backs	60	55	70	70	60	65	Very High
4.	Evan Carter	Rangers	60	50	60	55	50	60	High
5.	Pete Crow-Armstrong	Cubs	60	45	60	80	55	60	High
6.	Robert Hassell III	Nationals	60	45	55	55	55	60	High
7.	Elijah Green	Nationals	50	70	70	55	60	65	Extreme
8.	Sal Frelick	Brewers	70	40	70	50	45	55	Medium
9.	Colton Cowser	Orioles	60	55	55	50	55	55	Medium
10.	Emmanuel Rodriguez	Twins	60	60	50	50	60	60	Very High
11.	Ceddanne Rafaela	Red Sox	50	50	60	70	60	55	High
12.	Jasson Dominguez	Yankees	55	60	55	50	55	55	High
13.	Miguel Bleis	Red Sox	50	65	60	60	60	60	Extreme
14.	Chase DeLauter	Guardians	50	60	55	50	60	55	High
15.	Everson Pereira	Yankees	50	55	55	50	55	55	High

CORNER OUTFIELD

No	Player	Org	HIT	POW	RUN	FLD	ARM	BA Grade	Risk
1.	James Wood	Nationals	55	65	55	50	55	65	High
2.	George Valera	Guardians	50	55	50	50	50	55	High
3.	Zac Veen	Rockies	50	50	60	50	50	55	High
4.	Joey Wiemer	Brewers	30	70	60	55	80	55	High
5.	Brennen Davis	Cubs	45	55	55	50	55	55	High
6.	Oscar Colas	White Sox	55	60	40	50	60	50	Medium
7.	Alex Ramirez	Mets	50	55	55	55	60	55	High
8.	Kevin Alcantara	Cubs	45	60	55	55	50	55	High
9.	Gavin Cross	Royals	55	55	50	50	55	55	High
10.	Alec Burleson	Cardinals	60	50	40	45	50	50	Medium
11.	Masataka Yoshida	Red Sox	55	45	40	40	40	50	Medium
12.	Andy Pages	Dodgers	40	70	30	50	70	50	High
13.	Samuel Zavala	Padres	55	50	45	55	55	55	Extreme
14.	Aaron Zavala	Rangers	55	40	50	50	50	55	Very High
15.	Gabriel Gonzalez	Mariners	45	60	40	45	70	55	Extreme

RIGHTHANDER

No	Pitcher	Team	FB	CB	SL	CHG	OTH	CTL	BA Grade	Risk
1.	Grayson Rodriguez	Orioles	60	70	60	60	—	70	70	Medium
2.	Andrew Painter	Phillies	70	50	60	55	—	70	70	High
3.	Eury Perez	Marlins	70	60	60	60	—	65	70	High
4.	Hunter Brown	Astros	70	55	55	45	—	50	65	High
5.	Bobby Miller	Dodgers	70	50	70	60	—	50	65	High
6.	Daniel Espino	Guardians	80	55	70	50	—	55	70	Very High
7.	Gavin Williams	Guardians	70	60	55	50	—	50	65	High
8.	Kodai Senga	Mets	60	50	45	—	70*	50	55	Medium
9.	Brandon Pfaadt	D-backs	60	45	60	55	—	60	55	Medium
10.	Cade Cavalli	Nationals	70	65	55	55	—	50	60	High
11.	Shane Baz	Rays	80	45	60	50	—	60	65	Extreme
12.	Ryan Pepiot	Dodgers	70	—	50	60	—	40	55	Medium
13.	Gavin Stone	Dodgers	60	45	50	70	—	60	55	Medium
14.	Dylan Lesko	Padres	70	60	—	70	—	60	65	Extreme
15.	Mick Abel	Phillies	60	50	60	55	—	50	60	High
16.	Jackson Jobe	Tigers	60	50	70	60	—	55	60	High
17.	Tink Hence	Cardinals	60	60	55	55	—	50	60	Very High
18.	Tanner Bibee	Guardians	60	50	60	50	—	55	55	High
19.	Owen White	Rangers	55	55	60	50	—	60	55	High
20.	Max Meyer	Marlins	60	—	70	55	—	55	55	High
21.	Gordon Graceffo	Cardinals	55	50	60	55	—	65	55	High
22.	Luis Ortiz	Pirates	70	—	60	50	—	45	55	High
23.	Wilmer Flores	Tigers	55	55	—	—	50†	60	55	High
24.	Quinn Priester	Pirates	50	60	50	50	—	55	55	High
25.	Ryne Nelson	D-backs	60	50	55	45	—	55	50	Medium
26.	Yosver Zulueta	Blue Jays	60	50	60	50	—	40	55	High
27.	Drey Jameson	D-backs	65	50	70	50	—	50	50	Medium
28.	Chase Silseth	Angels	60	55	50	—	45*	45	50	Medium
29.	Griff McGarry	Phillies	70	50	60	55	60†	40	55	Very High
30.	Cade Horton	Cubs	70	50	60	45	—	50	55	Very High
31.	Ben Brown	Cubs	60	60	55	30	—	50	55	Very High
32.	Jack Leiter	Rangers	55	50	60	45	—	40	55	Very High
33.	Jarlin Susana	Nationals	70	45	55	45	—	45	55	Extreme
34.	Bryce Miller	Mariners	70	45	55	50	—	50	50	High
35.	AJ Smith-Shawver	Braves	70	—	70	45	—	50	55	Extreme
36.	Mason Miller	Athletics	70	—	60	50	—	55	55	Extreme
37.	Mason Black	Giants	60	—	60	40	—	55	50	High
38.	Nick Nastrini	Dodgers	65	45	55	50	—	40	50	High
39.	Marco Raya	Twins	65	55	60	50	—	50	55	Extreme
40.	Owen Murphy	Braves	60	60	50	45	—	55	55	Extreme

LEFTHANDER

No	Pitcher	Team	FB	CB	SL	CHG	OTH	CTL	BA Grade	Risk
1.	Kyle Harrison	Giants	70	—	60	50	—	45	60	High
2.	Ricky Tiedemann	Blue Jays	65	—	60	70	—	55	60	High
3.	Matthew Liberatore	Cardinals	50	60	50	45	—	50	50	Medium
4.	DL Hall	Orioles	80	60	70	60	—	40	55	High
5.	Logan Allen	Guardians	50	—	50	60	55†	60	55	High
6.	Kyle Muller	Braves	60	55	60	40	—	45	50	Medium
7.	Cooper Hjerpe	Cardinals	60	40	55	55	—	55	55	High
8.	Blake Walston	D-backs	50	50	55	60	—	50	55	High
9.	Brandon Barriera	Blue Jays	60	50	65	50	—	50	55	Extreme
10.	Ken Waldichuk	Athletics	55	45	60	55	—	50	50	High
11.	Mason Montgomery	Rays	60	—	45	40	—	55	50	High
12.	Connor Prielipp	Twins	60	—	70	55	—	55	55	Extreme
13.	Brandon Williamson	Reds	55	55	50	45	—	45	50	High
14.	Ky Bush	Angels	55	45	60	50	—	50	50	High
15.	Noah Schultz	White Sox	65	—	60	50	—	50	55	Extreme

* Splitter. † Cutter

Organization	2022	2021	2020	2019	2018
1. Baltimore Orioles	4	7	12	22	17

Baltimore boasts the No. 1 overall prospect in Gunnar Henderson and one of the best pitching prospects in the game in Grayson Rodriguez. Both should make an impact at Camden Yards in 2023, and there's plenty of upper-level depth with outfielder Colton Cowser and infielders Jordan Westburg, Connor Norby and Joey Ortiz.

2. Arizona Diamondbacks	10	17	10	21	26

The prospect trio of Corbin Carroll, Jordan Lawlar and Druw Jones might be the best in baseball and is backed by a stable of talented, upper-level pitchers like Brandon Pfaadt, Ryne Nelson and Drey Jameson. With three potential stars, plenty of arms and talented players in the upper levels, Arizona has a competitive core on the way.

3. Los Angeles Dodgers	8	9	3	10	9

Miguel Vargas is arguably the best pure hitting prospect in the game, while the hard-throwing trio of Bobby Miller, Ryan Pepiot and Gavin Stone should make an MLB impact in 2023. Add in Diego Cartaya and 2022 acquisitions Dalton Rushing (draft) and Josue De Paula (international), and the Dodgers are loaded with potential stars.

4. Cleveland Guardians	12	11	19	15	21

Led by two of the top pitching prospects in baseball in Daniel Espino and Gavin Williams, the Guardians boast a deep and talented group of close-to-the-majors prospects. With Bo Naylor, Will Brennan, Tyler Freeman and Gabriel Arias already seeing time in the majors, the youngest team in baseball is set to get younger.

5. New York Mets	16	19	25	19	27

The system's top three prospects—Francisco Alvarez, NPB import Kodai Senga and Brett Baty—will impact the big leagues this season, while 2022 top draft picks Kevin Parada, Jett Williams and Blade Tidwell provide depth and upside to supplement up-the-middle talents like Alex Ramirez and Ronny Mauricio.

6. Tampa Bay Rays	2	1	1	2	5

Though Tampa Bay's system has taken a step back in recent years, it's still pretty good. No. 1 prospect Shane Baz is a wild card, but hitters like Curtis Mead, Carson Williams and Kyle Manzardo offer a range of upside, and righthander Taj Bradley is one of the game's best pitching prospects.

7. Washington Nationals	26	30	23	16	15

Trading outfielder Juan Soto to the Padres netted the Nats one of the biggest prospect hauls in recent memory, headlined by James Wood, Robert Hassell III and Jarlin Susana. Add that trio to high-upside outfielder Elijah Green and big league-ready righthander Cade Cavalli, and brighter days might be ahead in D.C.

8. Cincinnati Reds	7	18	29	7	10

The Reds went into full rebuild mode in 2022 and it's reflected in the fact that seven of their top 10 prospects—led by Noelvi Marte and Edwin Arroyo—were acquired via trades. Others, like dynamic power-speed shortstop Elly De La Cruz as well as 2022 draft picks Cam Collier and Sal Stewart, offer exciting upside and projection.

9. St. Louis Cardinals	18	12	14	11	13

Few teams have consistently developed big leaguers like the Cardinals. With a talented group at the top led by Jordan Walker, Tink Hence and Masyn Winn, the pipeline doesn't look likely to dry up any time soon. In the 2022 draft, the Cardinals added another group of college strike-throwers, a successful archetype for the organization.

10. Boston Red Sox	11	21	22	30	23

Boston's prospect group isn't deep, but it's led by MLB-ready first baseman Triston Casas and talented shortstop Marcelo Mayer. Breakout prospect Ceddanne Rafaela and toolsy wunderkind Miguel Bleis add upside to the system, and Japanese import Masataka Yoshida gives Boston a plug-and-play outfielder for its new-look lineup.

11. Pittsburgh Pirates	3	15	24	18	16

After winning the first ever MLB draft lottery, the Pirates will choose from the top spot once again in 2023. The player Pittsburgh selects will join an intriguing talent base at the top of the system that includes top-of-the-board picks Henry Davis and Termarr Johnson as well as Pirates top prospect Endy Rodriguez.

12. Texas Rangers	9	24	20	24	22

As an amateur, Evan Carter flew under the radar. Now, he's one of the game's elite prospects. Fireballing righthander Owen White has emerged as the team's top pitching prospect, and third baseman Josh Jung overcame a shoulder injury to make his MLB debut. High-end outfielder Anthony Gutierrez could be poised for a breakout.

13. Milwaukee Brewers	25	28	30	26	6

Any system led by Jackson Chourio is going to rank fairly high, but the Brewers have an exciting group of tooled-up talents and variety at the top with outfielders Sal Frelick, Joey Wiemer and Garrett Mitchell offering a little bit of everything. Shortstop Brice Turang offers safety, while righthander Jacob Misiorowski offers excitement.

14. Colorado Rockies	24	25	28	23	19

The 2022 season was a very good one in the Rockies' system. Ezequiel Tovar established himself as one of the top 20 prospects in baseball, reaching MLB by season's end. A young crop of international signees—highlighted by infielder Adael Amador and righthander Jordy Vargas—flashed immense upside in the lower levels.

15. Toronto Blue Jays	19	4	6	3	8

After trading first-round picks Austin Martin and Gunnar Hoglund in consecutive seasons, the Blue Jays' farm ranking was poised to slide. But thanks to the breakouts by Ricky Tiedemann and flamethrower Yosver Zulueta and a talented draft class led by lefthander Brandon Barriera, the Blue Jays have rebuilt the farm on the fly.

Organization	2022	2021	2020	2019	2018
16. New York Yankees	13	16	17	20	2

Anthony Volpe and Oswald Peraza give the Yankees a dynamic duo of high-upside middle infielders with proximity. Jasson Dominguez ascended from Low-A to Double-A, while New York popped uber-athletic Vanderbilt outfielder Spencer Jones in the first round and got an excellent season from catcher Austin Wells.

17. Chicago Cubs	15	22	21	29	28

Pete Crow-Armstrong leads a strong group of outfield prospects, and the Cubs continue to add intriguing pitchers such as 2022 first-rounder Cade Horton and trade pickups Ben Brown and Hayden Wesneski. The Cubs' system is light on middle infielders and many of its top prospects have concerning injury histories, adding volatility.

18. San Francisco Giants	17	14	13	28	25

Shortstop Marco Luciano and lefty Kyle Harrison form one of the game's better one-two duos, while third baseman Casey Schmitt showed tons of potential. Righthanders Mason Black and Eric Silva showed promise, and San Francisco chased upside with college lefties Reggie Crawford and Carson Whisenhunt in the 2022 draft.

19. Philadelphia Phillies	23	27	26	12	7

Philadelphia's system is extremely top-heavy, but Andrew Painter, Mick Abel and Griff McGarry make for an excellent trio of righthanders. Add in first-rounder Justin Crawford and his big league bloodlines and you have the start of an intriguing group that could supplement the reigning NL champions' roster in the coming years.

20. Miami Marlins	20	10	9	25	24

A great deal of this system's value rests on the recoveries of three injured pitchers—Max Meyer, Jake Eder and Sixto Sanchez. Skyscraper righthander Eury Perez is one of the game's best pitching prospects, and polished first-rounder Jacob Berry could add a much-needed injection of offense.

21. Minnesota Twins	14	8	7	8	12

With four position players leading the way in Royce Lewis, Brooks Lee, Emmanuel Rodriguez and Edouard Julien, the Twins have a nice group of up-the-middle players with above-average hitting potential. After that, the Twins' system runs heavy with risky pitching prospects like Connor Prielipp, Marco Raya and Matt Canterino.

22. Seattle Mariners	1	2	5	17	30

The graduations of Julio Rodriguez and George Kirby and trades of Noelvi Marte, Edwin Arroyo and others helped lead the Mariners to their first playoff appearance in 21 years last season, so it's no concern that the system has thinned out. Recent first-round picks Harry Ford and Cole Young will help replenish the prospect stock.

23. San Diego Padres	21	3	2	1	3

The Padres nearly emptied their farm system to acquire Juan Soto from the Nationals at the 2022 trade deadline. Shortstop Jackson Merrill has potential and catcher Luis Campusano is ready for a big league shot, but top pitching prospects Dylan Lesko, Robby Snelling and Victor Lizarraga are all teenagers who are years away.

24. Houston Astros	28	26	27	5	11

The Astros didn't pick in the first round in 2020 and 2021 as punishment for the sign-stealing scandal. Despite the restrictions, Houston has managed to churn out MLB contributors year after year. The song remains the same in 2023 with righthander Hunter Brown, catcher Yainer Diaz and infielder David Hensley all likely to contribute.

25. Los Angeles Angels	29	23	16	13	14

Logan O'Hoppe, Zach Neto and Edgar Quero give the Angels a promising trio of up-the-middle position players, while Chase Silseth and Ky Bush have emerged as promising arms from their 2021 all-pitcher draft. There is little behind them, with righthander Sam Bachman looking like yet another first-round whiff.

26. Detroit Tigers	6	5	11	14	20

The rebuild needs to be rebuilt in Detroit. After graduating top position prospects Spencer Torkelson and Riley Greene in 2022, the Tigers' system is once again spearheaded by pitchers, such as Jackson Jobe, Wilmer Flores and Ty Madden. A group of smooth-hitting infielders in Jace Jung, Colt Keith and Peyton Graham offers promise.

27. Oakland Athletics	27	29	15	9	18

The A's have traded Matt Olson, Matt Chapman, Frankie Montas, Chris Bassitt and Sean Manaea from the 2021 team and have little to show for it. The club has few hitters of note outside of recent draftees Tyler Soderstrom and Zack Gelof. This has all the hallmarks of a failed rebuild effort, and the A's may not be good again for a long time.

28. Chicago White Sox	30	20	8	6	4

This system is led by a strong top two in shortstop Colson Montgomery and outfielder Oscar Colas but then falls off quickly. There's a deep corps of pitchers inside the top 10 who offer upside profiles, like 2022 first-round lefthander Noah Schultz as well as righthanders Sean Burke, Cristian Mena and Peyton Pallette.

29. Kansas City Royals	5	13	18	27	29

The Royals graduated 10 players from their Top 30 Prospects list last year, so the system was bound to tumble. The Royals lack the depth to cushion the fall. The organization's remaining prospect group is headlined by three in-season acquisitions—draftees Gavin Cross and Cayden Wallace and trade pickup Drew Waters.

30. Atlanta Braves	22	6	4	4	1

The Braves have a good reason to rank last in these rankings. Over the last two years, the Braves effectively used their farm system depth and pitching development prowess to turn ponies on the farm into horses on the major league team. There's little left in the cupboard, but Braves fans should be satisfied.

Arizona Diamondbacks

BY NICK PIECORO

Corbin Carroll's major league debut took place on Aug. 29, 2022. The evening had the feel of an unofficial Diamondbacks holiday.

Down on the field for batting practice, standing near Carroll's family and friends, were his coaches from Double-A and Triple-A. Over near the dugout were the scouts who had recommended him as an amateur. And scattered about was a contingent of club officials who had crossed paths with Carroll along the way.

The D-backs, who had arranged for many of those people to fly in for the game, were in no way downplaying what they felt was an important day for the franchise—one they hope will serve as a mile marker for an organization on the upswing.

Carroll is the club's best position prospect in years and one of its best ever, ranking among the likes of Justin Upton and Stephen Drew.

The D-backs are hoping not just that he will be a good player who can help them win, but that he will be in the vanguard of a wave of prospects who can help them enjoy sustained success for the first time since the early days of the franchise.

The last several D-backs playoff teams—in 2007, 2011 and 2017—were one-offs. They created excitement one year only to disappoint the next. Mix in a handful of ill-fated trades and it is easy to see why fans have viewed the franchise with skepticism in recent years.

But the D-backs are setting themselves up to change that with a rebuild that is steadily gaining momentum.

In addition to Carroll, they have two other prospects—shortstop Jordan Lawlar and center fielder Druw Jones—whom scouts believe could one day rank among the better players in baseball. The D-backs are developing well-rounded prospects as well. Carroll, Lawlar and Jones should all contribute offensively and defensively, something that is also true with recent MLB graduates like Daulton Varsho and Alek Thomas.

They also have the makings of their best pitching pipeline in more than a decade, with many prospects, led by Brandon Pfaadt, having reached Double-A or Triple-A, meaning they should be ready to help before long. Righthanders Ryne Nelson and Drey Jameson have already reached Arizona.

They have a collection of talented young outfielders already in MLB with others not far behind.

They have potential sluggers and, finally, they have some power-armed relievers working their way to the majors.

With a big league club that improved by 22

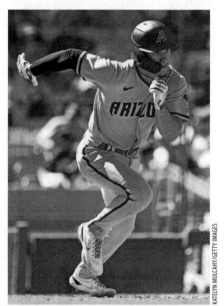

Top prospects Alek Thomas (pictured) and shortstop Geraldo Perdomo graduated in 2022.

PROJECTED 2026 LINEUP

Catcher	Carson Kelly	31
First Base	Deyvison De Los Santos	23
Second Base	Ketel Marte	32
Third Base	A.J. Vukovich	24
Shortstop	Jordan Lawlar	23
Left Field	Corbin Carroll	25
Center Field	Druw Jones	22
Right Field	Jake McCarthy	28
Designated Hitter	Daulton Varsho	29
No. 1 Starter	Zac Gallen	30
No. 2 Starter	Brandon Pfaadt	27
No. 3 Starter	Ryne Nelson	28
No. 4 Starter	Drey Jameson	28
No. 5 Starter	Blake Walston	25
Closer	Landon Sims	25

games from the previous year and a front office that seems fully committed to building from within, the D-backs' near- and long-term outlook feels as promising as it has in a long time.

Much of that hope was on display that night in August. After falling behind 7-0, they rallied for a 13-7 win against the eventual National League-champion Phillies. Carroll was in the middle of it all: His tie-breaking, two-run double put the D-backs ahead for good.

For much of the second half, the D-backs showed reasons to believe their core has promise. Beginning in 2023, they will need to show that promise can deliver them to October—more than just every once in a while. ∎

ARIZONA DIAMONDBACKS

TOP 2023 MLB CONTRIBUTORS	RANK
Corbin Carroll, OF	1
Brandon Pfaadt, RHP	4
Ryne Nelson, RHP	6
BREAKOUT PROSPECTS	**RANK**
Ruben Santana, 3B	17
Cristofer Torin, SS	20
Yu-Min Lin, LHP	18

SOURCE OF TOP 30 TALENT			
Homegrown	29	Acquired	1
College	13	Trade	1
Junior college	0	Rule 5 draft	0
High school	6	Independent league	0
Nondrafted free agent	0	Free agent/waivers	0
International	10		

LF
Corbin Carroll (1)
Dominic Canzone (24)
Junior Franco

CF
Druw Jones (3)
Jorge Barrosa (15)
Dominic Fletcher (16)
Alvin Guzman

RF
A.J. Vukovich (10)
Wilderd Patino (14)
Kristian Robinson (30)

3B
Deyvison De Los Santos (5)
Ruben Santana (17)
Johan Benitez
Gavin Conticello

SS
Jordan Lawlar (2)
Blaze Alexander (11)
Cristofer Torin (20)

2B
Manuel Peña (21)
Andrew Pintar (25)
Jansel Luis
Ryan Bliss

1B
Ivan Melendez (12)
Tristin English

C
Adrian Del Castillo
Kenny Castillo
Caleb Roberts

LHP

LHSP	LHRP
Blake Walston (8)	Andrew Saalfrank
Yu-Min Lin (18)	Tyler Holton
Nate Savino (27)	Kyle Backhus
Diomede Sierra	Liam Norris

RHP

RHSP	RHRP
Brandon Pfaadt (4)	Justin Martinez (22)
Ryne Nelson (6)	Carlos Vargas (23)
Drey Jameson (7)	Conor Grammes (29)
Landon Sims (9)	Christian Montes De Oca
Slade Cecconi (13)	Luis Frias
Dylan Ray (19)	Mitchell Stumpo
Yilber Diaz (26)	Listher Sosa
Bryce Jarvis (28)	Edgar Isea
Joe Elbis	
Jameson Hill	
Abel Fuerte	

1 CORBIN CARROLL, OF

Born: August 21, 2000. **B-T:** L-L. **HT:** 5-10. **WT:** 165.
Drafted: HS—Seattle, 2019 (1st round).
Signed by: Dan Ramsay.

TRACK RECORD: Carroll dominated the high school showcase circuit the summer before his draft year, then performed well in his senior season, all the while showing an advanced approach, surprising power and a well-rounded skill set. He was seen as a surefire first-round selection when the D-backs drafted him No. 16 overall and signed him away from a UCLA commitment with a $3.75 million bonus. The pandemic wiped out Carroll's 2020 season, other than time spent at the alternate training site, and he played in just seven games in 2021 before suffering a season-ending shoulder injury that required surgery to repair labrum and capsule tears. The D-backs kept their expectations for his 2022 season in check, unsure how his shoulder would respond or if he would need to knock off rust, but Carroll got off to a red-hot start with Double-A Amarillo and never slowed down, mashing his way first to Triple-A Reno then to a major league callup in late August. He performed well in the majors over the final six weeks of the season despite arriving with just 142 career games of MiLB experience under his belt.

SCOUTING REPORT: Carroll has a powerful swing, excellent bat-to-ball skills and a discerning eye, a combination of traits often found in baseball's premier hitters. Though small in size, Carroll gets the most out of his elite, quick-twitch athletic ability at the plate. He loads into his back side before driving forward, efficiently transferring energy from his core and into his swing. His tendency to offer at the right pitches and square them up leads to a heavy dose of exit velocities at 100 mph and higher. He uses the whole field well, including going the other way with power; his first two career homers in the majors were hit to center and left field. Carroll is an explosive runner with elite speed. His top sprint speed during his brief time in the majors was the second-fastest ever recorded in the eight-year history of Statcast data. He is aggressive on the bases with excellent instincts. Carroll's speed plays well in the outfield, where he can let loose his athleticism to make rangy catches. He rated as one of the best left fielders in the majors in his brief debut. His fringe-average arm is his only subpar tool.

THE FUTURE: The D-backs kept Carroll's at-bat total low in the majors in order to keep his rookie

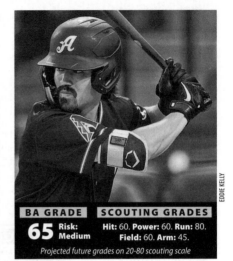

EDDIE KELLY

BA GRADE	SCOUTING GRADES
65 Risk: Medium	**Hit:** 60. **Power:** 60. **Run:** 80. **Field:** 60. **Arm:** 45.

Projected future grades on 20-80 scouting scale

BEST TOOLS

BATTING

Best Hitter for Average	Corbin Carroll
Best Power Hitter	Deyvison De Los Santos
Best Strike-Zone Discipline	Corbin Carroll
Fastest Baserunner	Corbin Carroll
Best Athlete	Drey Jameson

PITCHING

Best Fastball	Ryne Nelson
Best Curveball	Conor Grammes
Best Slider	Drey Jameson
Best Changeup	Blake Walston
Best Control	Brandon Pfaadt

FIELDING

Best Defensive Catcher	Alberto Barriga
Best Defensive Infielder	Blaze Alexander
Best Infield Arm	Blaze Alexander
Best Defensive Outfielder	Jorge Barrosa
Best Outfield Arm	Alvin Guzman

status intact and potentially make a push for Rookie of the Year honors—and the accompanying extra draft pick. As such, he received only semi-regular playing time and never seemed to get locked in at the plate. And yet he still managed to hit an impressive .260/.330/.500. Carroll exhibited some areas that could use polish. He showed more chase and swing-and-miss than he had in the minors and struggled in limited looks against lefthanders. Still, evaluators are unanimous in their excitement about his future, with questions only about how many all-star appearances he is expected to make. He figures to be a mainstay in Arizona's lineup for years, starting with Opening Day 2023.

Year	Age	Club (League)	Lvl	AVG	G	AB	R	H	2B	3B	HR	RBI	BB	SO	SB	OBP	SLG
2022	21	D-backs Red (ACL)	R	.500	2	6	2	3	0	0	1	1	2	3	0	.625	1.000
2022	21	Amarillo (TL)	AA	.313	58	227	62	71	11	8	16	39	41	68	20	.430	.643
2022	21	Reno (PCL)	AAA	.287	33	129	25	37	11	0	7	22	24	36	11	.408	.535
2022	21	Arizona (NL)	MLB	.260	32	104	13	27	9	2	4	14	8	31	2	.330	.500
Major League Totals				.260	32	104	13	27	9	2	4	14	8	31	2	.330	.500
Minor League Totals				.310	142	539	134	167	32	17	28	87	102	155	52	.426	.588

2 JORDAN LAWLAR, SS

Born: July 17, 2002. **B-T:** R-R. **HT:** 6-2. **WT:** 190.
Drafted: HS—Dallas, 2021 (1st round). **Signed by:** J.R. Salinas.
TRACK RECORD: Lawlar was a well-regarded prep player who won Gatorade's Texas player of the year honors and performed well on the showcase circuit. His well-rounded skill set had him in the mix to go No. 1 overall in 2021 but he slid to sixth, where the D-backs swooped in and signed him for $6.7 million, the third-highest bonus in the draft. That summer, just two games into his pro career, Lawlar suffered a labrum injury that required season-ending surgery, but he made the issue look like just a speed bump by turning in a terrific 2022 season in which he reached Double-A. His time in the AFL was cut short by a fractured left scapula on a hit by pitch.
SCOUTING REPORT: Lawlar has plus bat speed and power, and last season he showed an approach at the plate that was well beyond that of most players his age, thus allowing him to tap into that power on a regular basis. He uses a controlled leg kick to start an efficient swing, producing hard-hit balls to all fields. He has good feel for the barrel, the ability to catch up to velocity and is able to make adjustments at the plate, sometimes within at-bats. His walk and chase rates were above-average, while his whiff and strikeout rates were roughly average. He has some things to iron out defensively—he committed 29 errors in 87 games, many on throws—but has the skill set to not only stick at shortstop but to play it at an above-average level, showing range, quickness, arm strength and smooth actions. Lawlar has plus speed and is an excellent baserunner.
THE FUTURE: Lawlar may have as much upside as anyone in the organization, looking like a potential middle-of-the-lineup, middle-of-the-diamond star not unlike Carlos Correa.

BA GRADE
65 Risk: High

SCOUTING GRADES	Hitting: 60	Power: 55	Speed: 60	Fielding: 55	Arm: 60

Year	Age	Club (League)	Lvl	AVG	G	AB	R	H	2B	3B	HR	RBI	BB	SO	SB	OBP	SLG
2022	19	D-backs Red (ACL)	R	.368	6	19	5	7	1	1	0	2	4	6	0	.500	.526
2022	19	Visalia (CAL)	LoA	.351	44	174	44	61	9	4	9	32	27	48	24	.447	.603
2022	19	Hillsboro (NWL)	HiA	.288	30	111	31	32	8	2	3	17	16	33	13	.385	.477
2022	19	Amarillo (TL)	AA	.212	20	85	18	18	0	0	4	11	10	28	2	.299	.353
Minor League Totals				.305	102	394	98	120	19	7	16	63	58	116	40	.402	.510

3 DRUW JONES, OF

Born: November 28, 2003. **B-T:** R-R. **HT:** 6-4. **WT:** 180.
Drafted: HS—Peachtree Corners, Ga., 2022 (1st round). **Signed by:** Hudson Belinsky.
TRACK RECORD: Andruw Jones won 10 Gold Gloves in center field and slammed 434 career home runs—and his son Druw is a chip off the old block. After an impressive run on the showcase circuit, Jones went on to win Gatorade's Georgia player of the year award in 2022. His combination of tools, skills and projection put him at the top of the D-backs' draft board—and most other teams'—and they were ecstatic when he fell to them at No. 2 overall. He signed for a bonus just shy of $8.2 million. He hit an obstacle when he tore his left labrum during batting practice on his first day at Arizona's spring training complex and needed season-ending surgery.
SCOUTING REPORT: Jones has a simple, repeatable swing and an advanced approach that the D-backs believe will allow him to hit for both average and power. He times pitches with a small leg kick that leads to a short, compact stroke. His bat stays through the zone well and allows him to take aim at the middle of the field. He can handle both velocity and spin, and he showed improvement last year at laying off breaking balls out of the zone. Jones should have an impact bat, but time will tell whether he produces gaudy home run totals like his father or is more about using his plus speed to produce loads of doubles and triples. He is a graceful defender in center field who gets good reads and glides to where the ball will be. He has a plus arm and gets good carry on his throws.
THE FUTURE: Jones provided little to nitpick during his amateur career, and he enters pro ball with sky-high expectations of a potential franchise-altering player. Once his shoulder is fully healthy—which could happen in time for Opening Day—he should open in Low-A Visalia to make his official pro debut.

BA GRADE
65 Risk: Very High

SCOUTING GRADES	Hitting: 60	Power: 55	Speed: 70	Fielding: 70	Arm: 60

Year	Age	Club (Lge)	Level	AVG	G	AB	R	H	2B	3B	HR	RBI	BB	SO	SB	OBP	SLG
2022	18	Did not play—Injured															

4 BRANDON PFAADT, RHP

Born: October 15, 1998. **B-T:** R-R. **HT:** 6-4. **WT:** 230.
Drafted: Bellarmine, 2020 (5th round). **Signed by:** Jeremy Kehrt.
TRACK RECORD: Pfaadt turned in a solid performance in the Cape Cod League the summer before his draft year, then followed it up with an impressive five-start run before the pandemic ended his junior season. It was enough to prompt the D-backs to select him in the fifth round in 2020. In two seasons, Pfaadt has risen to become the most well-regarded pitcher in the organization. He was the D-backs' pitcher of the year in 2022 and his 218 strikeouts were the most in a minor league season since 2001.
SCOUTING REPORT: Pfaadt's fastball averages 93-94 mph and tops out at 96-97. The pitch is unique in that it acts almost like a cut fastball with carry, allowing him to pitch up in the zone. His putaway pitch is his slider, which sits 80-84 mph with heavy sweep, and he made big strides last year with his changeup, which has a different movement profile—running armside—from his other pitches. Pfaadt also has a curveball he uses early in counts. He instinctively pounds the strike zone, attacking hitters even after giving up a home run, but last year improved at working the fringes of the zone, leading to more strikeouts. Pfaadt repeats his delivery well, with every pitch coming out of the same slot. He is a hard worker with an inquisitive nature.
THE FUTURE: Pfaadt did enough to earn a callup last year but did not receive one in part because he didn't need to be added to Arizona's 40-man roster until after the season. He projects as a midrotation starter, but his combination of stuff, command, work ethic and pitching acumen has the D-backs hopeful he might become more than that. He is expected to debut in 2023.

BA GRADE
55 Risk: Medium

SCOUTING GRADES:	Fastball: 60	Curveball: 45	Slider: 60	Changeup: 55	Control: 60

Year	Age	Club (League)	Lvl	W	L	ERA	G	GS	IP	H	HR	BB	SO	BB/9	SO/9	WHIP	AVG
2022	23	Amarillo (TL)	AA	6	6	4.53	19	19	105	113	19	19	144	1.6	12.3	1.25	.274
2022	23	Reno (PCL)	AAA	5	1	2.63	10	10	62	47	9	14	74	2.0	10.8	0.99	.210
Minor League Totals				19	14	3.56	51	51	299	265	50	61	378	1.8	11.4	1.09	.234

5 DEYVISON DE LOS SANTOS, 3B

Born: June 21, 2003. **B-T:** R-R. **HT:** 6-1. **WT:** 225.
Signed: Dominican Republic, 2019. **Signed by:** Cesar Geronimo/Wil Tejada.
TRACK RECORD: The D-backs were drawn to De Los Santos' ability to impact the baseball when they signed him for $200,000 in 2019. So far, their hulking prospect has lived up to expectations. His pro debut was delayed until 2021 by the pandemic, but he looked at ease as he climbed to Low-A Visalia as an 18-year-old. Despite being young for the level at every stop, De Los Santos has done nothing but hit. In 2022 he not only hit for power and drove in runs but also finished eighth in the minors in hits.
SCOUTING REPORT: De Los Santos' strong frame produces explosive bat speed and his high-end exit velocities lead the D-backs' system. When his swing is right, he keeps it tight and compact, getting his bat in the zone early and exiting late. De Los Santos has a tendency to tinker with his mechanics and his swing can get long. His aggressiveness at the plate can also be an issue. So, too, is his inability to recognize spin, particularly sliders breaking away from him. Still, De Los Santos has continued to hit at every stop, including for power despite still having strides to make toward pulling the ball with authority. He has good hands and enough arm to handle third base, but there are questions about his footwork, throwing accuracy and both present and future range, depending on how his body matures. Those factors could necessitate a move to first base. He is an average runner who could slow down as he develops physically.
THE FUTURE: De Los Santos has immense upside, but his willingness to expand the zone raises questions. If it comes together, he could be a masher in the mold of a peak Miguel Sano.

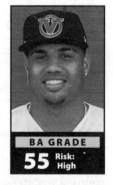

BA GRADE
55 Risk: High

SCOUTING GRADES	Hitting: 50	Power: 65	Speed: 45	Fielding: 40	Arm: 50

Year	Age	Club (League)	Lvl	AVG	G	AB	R	H	2B	3B	HR	RBI	BB	SO	SB	OBP	SLG
2022	19	Visalia (CAL)	LoA	.329	78	316	43	104	18	2	12	67	22	84	4	.370	.513
2022	19	Hillsboro (NWL)	HiA	.278	38	158	24	44	9	0	9	33	7	54	1	.307	.506
2022	19	Amarillo (TL)	AA	.231	10	39	5	9	2	0	1	6	5	9	0	.333	.359
Minor League Totals				.303	188	740	117	224	45	4	30	143	60	214	8	.355	.496

6 RYNE NELSON, RHP

Born: February 1, 1998. **B-T:** R-R. **HT:** 6-4. **WT:** 190.
Drafted: Oregon, 2019 (2nd round). **Signed by:** Dan Ramsay.
TRACK RECORD: Nelson was a two-way player at Oregon before becoming a full-time pitcher in 2019. An unrefined power arm when the D-backs drafted him, Nelson showed up at instructional league in the fall of 2020 looking far more polished. Last year, he grinded through the hitter-friendly Pacific Coast League, reached the majors late in 2022 and pitched well before his year ended due to a minor shoulder issue.
SCOUTING REPORT: Nelson averaged 93 mph with his fastball at Triple-A Reno, but he sat closer to 95 during his time in the majors. The pitch has excellent life, which allows him to throw it up in the zone. Nelson has total confidence in his fastball, leaning on it in tight situations and using it to over-

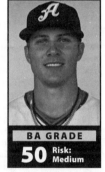

BA GRADE
50 Risk: Medium

power hitters even in fastball counts. He throws a firm slider and a slower curveball, both of which have good downward action. The two can alternate between being his best secondary pitch. His changeup, his fourth-best pitch, is inconsistent but flashes plus. Nelson has a clean, repeatable delivery that allows him to throw quality strikes with consistency. He is a good competitor who maintains an even-keeled demeanor. He impressed teammates in the majors with his ability to process information and develop a game plan.
THE FUTURE: After his three dazzling starts in the big leagues in September, Nelson is well-positioned to compete for a rotation spot in spring training. Failing that, he could be one of the first reinforcements if help is needed. Still lacking a wipeout secondary pitch, he continues to best profile as a midrotation starter, but his fastball is dominant enough to allow the D-backs to hope he is even more.

SCOUTING GRADES:	Fastball: 60	Curveball: 50	Slider: 55	Changeup: 45	Control: 55

Year	Age	Club (League	Lvl	W	L	ERA	G	GS	IP	H	HR	BB	SO	BB/9	SO/9	WHIP	AVG
2022	24	Reno (PCL)	AAA	10	5	5.43	26	26	136	142	25	47	128	3.1	8.5	1.39	.264
2022	24	Arizona (NL)	MLB	1	1	1.47	3	3	18	9	2	6	16	2.9	7.9	0.82	.145
Major League Totals				1	1	1.47	3	3	18	9	2	6	16	2.9	7.9	0.82	.145
Minor League Totals				17	10	4.28	58	55	271	244	42	97	317	3.2	10.5	1.26	.238

7 DREY JAMESON, RHP

Born: August 17, 1997. **B-T:** R-R. **HT:** 6-0. **WT:** 165.
Drafted: Ball State, 2019 (1st round supplemental). **Signed by:** Jeremy Kehrt.
TRACK RECORD: A multi-sport athlete in high school and initially a two-way player at Ball State, Jameson focused his attention solely on pitching during his draft-eligible sophomore year and took off. He was named the 2019 Mid-American Conference pitcher of the year, setting a conference record with 146 strikeouts in 91.2 innings. He steadily climbed Arizona's system, reached the majors in 2022 and turned in four impressive starts.
SCOUTING REPORT: Jameson has a big fastball that averages close to 97 mph and can occasionally reach triple-digits. Hitters can square it up on occasion, prompting him to adopt a two-seamer that has turned into a weapon. It sits closer to 94 mph with late, boring action that gets both ground balls and

BA GRADE
50 Risk: Medium

whiffs. His slider is a swing-and-miss pitch with sharp, late life, but he can also vary the speed and shape on it depending on the desired outcome. His curveball and changeup are average at best, pitches he uses primarily early in counts. Jameson has more control than command, but both have improved, as has his willingness to attack hitters with more than just his fastball. He is undersized, but he has a lightning-quick arm and is a terrific athlete. He is one of the fastest runners in the organization.
THE FUTURE: Jameson's performance in MLB at least temporarily put to rest questions about a move to the bullpen, but he still might need to refine his command to remain a starter. He figures to come to camp with a chance to win a rotation spot or put himself in position to claim one when a need arises.

SCOUTING GRADES:	Fastball: 60	Curveball: 50	Slider: 70	Changeup: 50	Control: 50

Year	Age	Club (League)	Lvl	W	L	ERA	G	GS	IP	H	HR	BB	SO	BB/9	SO/9	WHIP	AVG
2022	24	Amarillo (TL)	AA	2	1	2.41	4	4	19	13	0	4	23	1.9	11.1	0.91	.197
2022	24	Reno (PCL)	AAA	5	12	6.95	22	21	114	139	21	42	109	3.3	8.6	1.59	.299
2022	24	Arizona (NL)	MLB	3	0	1.48	4	4	24	20	2	7	24	2.6	8.9	1.11	.222
Major League Totals				3	0	1.48	4	4	24	20	2	7	24	2.6	8.9	1.11	.222
Minor League Totals				12	19	5.29	55	53	255	264	37	91	289	3.2	10.2	1.39	.266

8 BLAKE WALSTON, LHP

Born: June 28, 2001. **B-T:** L-L. **HT:** 6-5. **WT:** 195.
Drafted: HS—Wilmington, N.C., 2019 (1st round). **Signed by:** George Swain.

TRACK RECORD: A standout two-sport star at New Hanover High in Wilmington, N.C., where he was a decorated quarterback who helped lead his school to a state championship, Walston was seen as a projectable starting pitching prospect when the D-backs bought him out of a North Carolina State commitment in 2019 with a $2.45 million bonus. Though he has had some success while advancing through the system, his outlook is still based on some projectability, with the potential still there for continued development in both his body and stuff.

SCOUTING REPORT: Walston averaged 91-92 mph with his fastball last season and topped out at 95-96. As has been the case since his amateur days, his velocity fluctuated both within games and from start to start, and finding a way to harness the top-end fastball more consistently was an emphasis as he entered the offseason. He still has a lot of room to add strength to his frame, making his fastball more projectable than most Double-A pitchers' heat. Walston made big strides with his changeup, turning it into his best secondary pitch in part thanks to pregame work he did throwing a football, which he said had a similar feel to what he wanted from his changeup. His slider was more consistent than his curveball, but while neither was a plus pitch, he does have a feel for both, giving him the potential for a legit four-pitch mix. Walston's athleticism allows him to repeat his delivery with ease, leading to him being a consistent strike-thrower.

THE FUTURE: Evaluators more willing to project still have Walston as the best or the second-best pitching prospect in the organization. For now, his stuff fits a profile of No. 4 starter, though with his athleticism and potential to put on weight, his upside remains significant.

BA GRADE
55 Risk: High

SCOUTING GRADES:	Fastball: 50	Curveball: 50	Slider: 55	Changeup: 60	Control: 50

Year	Age	Club (League)	Lvl	W	L	ERA	G	GS	IP	H	HR	BB	SO	BB/9	SO/9	WHIP	AVG
2022	21	Hillsboro (NWL)	HiA	1	0	2.55	4	4	18	13	0	7	27	3.6	13.8	1.13	.200
2022	21	Amarillo (TL)	AA	7	3	5.16	21	21	106	115	16	39	110	3.3	9.3	1.45	.280
Minor League Totals				12	8	4.25	50	49	231	222	32	81	271	3.2	10.6	1.31	.251

9 LANDON SIMS, RHP

Born: January 3, 2001. **B-T:** R-R. **HT:** 6-2. **WT:** 227.
Drafted: Mississippi State, 2022 (1st round supplemental). **Signed by:** Stephen Baker.

TRACK RECORD: Sims was well-regarded out of high school in Georgia for his explosive fastball, but many projected him as a future reliever and he wound up on campus at Mississippi State. As a sophomore he put together one of the more dominant relief seasons in the country, logging a 1.44 ERA while striking out 16 per nine innings. He shined at the 2021 College World Series, allowing one run in four appearances while striking out 15 and walking one in 10 one-run innings for the national champions. Sims maintained his dominance as a starter in 2022, but he tore the ulnar collateral ligament in his right elbow during his third start, requiring season-ending Tommy John surgery. Still, the D-backs saw enough to take him with the 34th overall pick and sign him for $2.3 million.

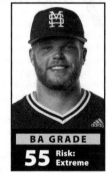

BA GRADE
55 Risk: Extreme

SCOUTING REPORT: Prior to his injury, Sims possessed an elite fastball in every way. He sat in the mid 90s and touched 97-98 mph, even as a starter, and his fastball had characteristics that gave it tremendous life and carry through the zone. He also had the ability to locate his heater to the parts of the zone where it is most effective. Sims had another plus pitch in his power slider with late tilt. His changeup was below-average with some fade. He has good deception, hiding the ball and tunnels his pitches well. His high-octane delivery with recoil gives him the look of a reliever. He has excellent makeup, including a terrific work ethic and good pitching acumen, suggesting he could have the intangibles to start.

THE FUTURE: Before his injury, Sims was on his way to showing his future might be in the rotation. The D-backs plan to give him every chance to start, though his rehab is likely to push beyond the start of 2023. If he is destined for the bullpen, he has the makings of a shutdown, late-inning reliever.

SCOUTING GRADES:	Fastball: 65	Slider: 60	Changeup: 45	Control: 55

Year	Age	Club (League)	Lvl	W	L	ERA	G	GS	IP	H	HR	BB	SO	BB/9	SO/9	WHIP	AVG
2022	21	Did not play—Injured															

10 AJ VUKOVICH, 3B/OF

Born: July 20, 2001. **B-T:** R-R. **HT:** 6-5. **WT:** 230.
Drafted: HS—East Troy, Wisc., 2020 (4th round). **Signed by:** Nate Birtwell.

TRACK RECORD: Vukovich was a two-sport star in high school and a final-ist for Wisconsin's Mr. Basketball honors. Intrigued by his athleticism, the D-backs chose him and bought him out of a Louisville baseball scholarship with a $1.25 million bonus in the fourth round of the five-round 2020 draft. In each of his two full seasons, he has started slow before finishing strong.

SCOUTING REPORT: Vukovich employs a closed stance then strides open to get back to neutral. While he has a clean swing, it can appear stiff, and his bat speed is only average. Still, he has a knack for getting the bat to the ball and possesses plus raw power. He has an extremely aggressive approach, seemingly trying to cover all parts of the zone and often making contact on pitches he can't hit hard. Vukovich rarely walks, striking out more than five times as often. When he is locked in, he can do damage to all fields. He does not always look smooth but is an excellent athlete. While he showed improvement at third base, Vukovich's arm action created issues with throwing accuracy, making a move to the outfield increasingly likely. In fact, he began getting reps at all three outfield positions in July. He is an average runner who runs the bases extremely well, with good instincts and a feel for stealing bases.

THE FUTURE: Vukovich's supporters believe his history as a plus athlete from a cold-weather state means he has plenty of development to come. Not many players can thrive with such an aggressive approach, but that might matter less if he can learn to tap into his latent power more consistently.

BA GRADE
50 Risk: High

| SCOUTING GRADES | | Hitting: 50 | | Power: 60 | | Speed: 50 | | Fielding: 40 | | Arm: 50 | |

Year	Age	Club (League)	Lvl	AVG	G	AB	R	H	2B	3B	HR	RBI	BB	SO	SB	OBP	SLG
2022	20	Hillsboro (NWL)	HiA	.274	106	424	55	116	26	2	15	69	18	105	35	.308	.450
2022	20	Amarillo (TL)	AA	.295	11	44	6	13	0	0	2	9	1	13	1	.311	.432
Minor League Totals				.274	209	836	116	229	45	5	30	140	41	223	52	.314	.447

11 BLAZE ALEXANDER, SS

Born: June 11, 1999. **B-T:** R-R. **HT:** 6-0. **WT:** 175.
Drafted: HS—Bradenton, Fla., 2018 (11th round). **Signed by:** Luke Wrenn.

TRACK RECORD: Alexander had a strong showing on the summer circuit, but swing-and-miss concerns arose the following spring of his draft year. As an older senior who was said to have a high asking price, he slipped to the 11th round. He had a loud pro debut but struggled to replicate that success until 2022, when he posted a .928 OPS, the second-best mark in the organization among regulars.

SCOUTING REPORT: Alexander is at his best when he is taking aim at the right-center field gap. He showed an improved approach last year, swinging less often at pitchers' pitches, and wound up making loads of loud contact. His profile still has significant risk. Though his data suggest he hits offspeeds well, questions remain as to whether that will translate to the majors. More alarmingly, his in-zone swing-and-miss rate of 29.7% ranked fourth-worst in the system. He is a flashy defender with smooth, easy actions. He still boots routine balls, but he showed more consistency last year and erased concerns about his ability to play at least an average shortstop. His plus-plus arm is his loudest tool.

THE FUTURE: Having shown he can handle short, Alexander's floor has been raised, but his ceiling depends on his bat. If he can tap into his power often enough, he could be a Chris Taylor-type hitter with multi-positional versatility.

| BA GRADE: 50/High | | Hitting: 45 | | Power: 55 | | Speed: 50 | | Fielding: 55 | | Arm: 70. | |

Year	Age	Club (League)	Lvl	AVG	G	AB	R	H	2B	3B	HR	RBI	BB	SO	SB	OBP	SLG
2022	23	D-backs Black (ACL)	R	.250	3	8	1	2	0	0	1	1	1	2	0	.333	.625
2022	23	Amarillo (TL)	AA	.306	88	317	48	97	17	3	17	54	33	92	10	.388	.539
2022	23	Reno (PCL)	AAA	.259	7	27	8	7	1	0	2	4	4	8	0	.412	.519
Minor League Totals				.273	342	1244	225	339	65	15	42	186	155	369	51	.364	.450

12 IVAN MELENDEZ, 1B

Born: Jan. 24, 2000. **B-T:** R-R. **HT:** 6-3. **WT:** 225.
Drafted: Texas, 2022 (2nd round). **Signed by:** J.R. Salinas.

TRACK RECORD: Melendez played two seasons at Odessa (Texas) JC before transferring to Texas, where he immediately became one of the better hitters in the Big 12. A DH-only his first year there, he went to the Marlins in the 16th round in 2021 but did not sign. He returned to Texas and not only played a solid first base but also improved as a hitter. He had a monster year, capturing the Golden Spikes Award and slugging 32 home runs, the most since the NCAA adopted bat restrictions in 2011.

SCOUTING REPORT: Melendez uses his lower half well to generate and transfer energy before uncorking his powerful swing. His all-fields power is his calling card, but he also demonstrates a feel to hit. He cut down on his strikeouts last year, in part thanks to a quicker swing that made it easier to shore up his approach and chase less. He also improved his walk rate. Those strides helped convince the D-backs they were taking a hitter on the rise despite him having played all last year at age 22. He is a below-average runner but his feet work well on defense and he has a chance to be an average first baseman. He also played a passable third base in his pro debut, which proved a pleasant surprise to club officials. He has an average arm.

THE FUTURE: Melendez's batted-ball data suggest his debut was better than his subpar numbers would make it seem, but he is going to need to hit a ton—and quickly, given his age—for his prospect value to remain intact.

BA GRADE: 50/High		Hitting: 55		Power: 60		Speed: 40		Fielding: 50		Arm: 50						

Year	Age	Club (League)	Lvl	AVG	G	AB	R	H	2B	3B	HR	RBI	BB	SO	SB	OBP	SLG
2022	22	D-backs Black (ACL)	R	.000	1	1	1	0	0	0	0	0	2	0	0	.750	.000
2022	22	D-backs Red (ACL)	R	.222	3	9	1	2	0	0	0	0	1	5	0	.300	.222
2022	22	Visalia (CAL)	LoA	.207	25	87	11	18	3	1	3	8	10	20	0	.349	.368
Minor League Totals				.206	29	97	13	20	3	1	3	8	13	25	0	.358	.351

13 SLADE CECCONI, RHP

Born: June 24, 1999. **B-T:** R-R. **HT:** 6-4. **WT:** 224.
Drafted: Miami, 2020 (1st round supplemental). **Signed by:** Eric Cruz.

TRACK RECORD: Cecconi shined on the summer circuit before his senior year, but a triceps injury limited his time on the mound the following spring. He wound up landing at Miami, where he pitched parts of two seasons before the D-backs took him at 34th overall. He impressed observers that year at the team's alternate site and in instructional league, showcasing elite stuff in short stints. He was nagged by injuries and never found his best stuff in 2021, but he showed flashes of dominance in a solid 2022 season.

SCOUTING REPORT: Cecconi averaged 93.7 mph with his fastball last year, allowing hard contact and struggling to miss bats. He can sit around 95-96 mph with carry through the zone early in starts but it tapers off in the middle innings. His slider is his best secondary offering. It's a sharp, late-breaking weapon when he throws it in the 84-87 mph range. He got good results with his 70-75 mph curveball, though it is unclear if it will play as effectively in the majors. His changeup improved but remains inconsistent. He threw strikes and logged innings. Coaches believe Cecconi can hold his top-end stuff longer by maintaining better direction down the mound, and that while his work habits improved he can dig deeper to take it to another level.

THE FUTURE: If he can learn to maintain his stuff, Cecconi has all the ingredients to be a midrotation starter. If not, his fastball-slider combo should work well in short bursts in relief.

BA GRADE: 50/High		Fastball: 55		Curveball: 45		Slider: 60		Changeup: 40		Control: 55						

Year	Age	Club (League)	Lvl	W	L	ERA	G	GS	IP	H	HR	BB	SO	BB/9	SO/9	WHIP	AVG
2022	23	Amarillo (TL)	AA	7	6	4.37	26	25	130	139	22	32	127	2.2	8.8	1.32	.266
Minor League Totals				11	8	4.29	38	37	189	192	27	52	190	2.5	9.1	1.29	.258

14 WILDERD PATIÑO, OF

Born: July 18, 2001. **B-T:** R-R. **HT:** 6-1. **WT:** 195.
Signed: Venezuela, 2017. **Signed by:** Cesar Geronimo/Kristians Pereira.

TRACK RECORD: Patiño's $1.3 million agreement with the Rangers was nixed when he hurt his elbow prior to the July 2 signing period in 2017, opening the door for the D-backs to swoop in and sign him for $985,000. Patiño had flashed his tooled-up game for stretches in the past while climbing through the system, but last year he put together his most consistent season yet, hitting a combined .290 with 67 steals, tied for the sixth-most in the minors.

SCOUTING REPORT: Patiño has the kind of tools and physique that give him the potential to be an impact player. He has terrific bat speed and the ability to make hard contact to all fields, and his easy plus speed allows him to leg out extra bases. He remains a high-risk prospect because of his propensity to chase and swing and miss, particularly when it comes to spin, though he showed improvement in both categories last year. He also more than doubled his walk rate. He has steadily improved defensively to the point he is now viewed as a future center fielder. He gets high marks for his aptitude and makeup and is considered one of the best athletes in the system.

THE FUTURE: Patiño still seems to be coming into an approach and figuring out who he is at the plate, but if it all comes together he could have a profile—speedy center fielder with double-digit home run potential—similar to a young Starling Marte.

BA GRADE: 50/Very High	Hitting: 50	Power: 55	Speed: 65	Fielding: 55	Arm: 45

Year	Age	Club (League)	Lvl	AVG	G	AB	R	H	2B	3B	HR	RBI	BB	SO	SB	OBP	SLG
2022	20	Visalia (CAL)	LoA	.290	75	293	54	85	16	2	8	42	23	84	54	.370	.440
2022	20	Hillsboro (NWL)	HiA	.288	19	73	14	21	5	0	1	11	4	25	13	.342	.397
Minor League Totals				.277	206	765	126	212	35	9	12	96	61	237	93	.357	.393

15 JORGE BARROSA, OF

Born: Feb. 17, 2001. **B-T:** B-L. **HT:** 5-9. **WT:** 165.
Signed: Venezuela, 2017. **Signed by:** Alfonso Mora/Cesar Geronimo.

TRACK RECORD: Despite being undersized, Barrosa was well-liked as an amateur for his ability to consistently hit while showing an advanced approach, including in looks against older competition. The D-backs signed him for $415,000, and Barrosa has steadily climbed through the system, playing good defense at every stop and showing incremental improvements offensively. He turned in his best season last year, earning a spot on the D-backs' 40-man roster.

SCOUTING REPORT: Barrosa is a switch-hitter with a controlled swing from both sides, but he shows more natural strength through the zone from the right side. He improved last year at limiting his chase, drawing more walks and cutting down his swing-and-miss. His home run power could be limited, but he is a steady hitter with good bat-to-ball skills and is a plus runner, all of which could enable him to rack up doubles and triples. Still, his physical projection is limited and his overall offensive impact remains a question. He is a plus defensive outfielder who gets terrific reads and jumps, seemingly moving in the right direction before the ball is hit.

THE FUTURE: Though the D-backs are loaded with outfielders, Barrosa distinguishes himself as a switch-hitter. Given that he played all of last season at 21, he could still have room to develop. He figures to open next season at Triple-A Reno.

BA GRADE: 40/Medium	Hitting: 55	Power: 40	Speed: 60	Fielding: 65	Arm: 45

Year	Age	Club (League)	Lvl	AVG	G	AB	R	H	2B	3B	HR	RBI	BB	SO	SB	OBP	SLG
2022	21	Hillsboro (NWL)	HiA	.300	10	40	5	12	3	0	1	6	2	5	4	.349	.450
2022	21	Amarillo (TL)	AA	.276	110	434	85	120	30	2	12	51	65	80	22	.374	.438
Minor League Totals				.276	341	1351	250	373	79	13	24	143	146	241	102	.361	.407

16 DOMINIC FLETCHER, OF

Born: Sept. 2, 1997. **B-T:** L-L. **HT:** 5-9. **WT:** 185.
Drafted: Arkansas, 2019 (2nd round supplemental). **Signed by:** Nate Birtwell.

TRACK RECORD: The younger brother of Angels infielder David Fletcher, Dominic was a well-regarded recruit when he landed at Arkansas. During his three years there, he made a habit of turning in highlight-reel catches and was a reliable offensive performer, connecting for at least 10 home runs each season. The D-backs took him with the 75th overall pick in 2019. After spending 2020 at the alternate site, Fletcher turned in a so-so 2021 season at Double-A before rebounding with an impressive 2022 that finished at Triple-A Reno.

SCOUTING REPORT: Fletcher has a line-drive swing with average bat speed. He has surprising power for his size and is capable of generating loud exit velocities, but he is at his best when he is driving balls to the gaps. He toned down his aggressiveness after a disappointing 2021 season, and last year he walked more, struck out less and hit more balls hard. He is at least a plus defensive outfielder, with some believing he might be as good as Gold Glove finalists Alek Thomas and Daulton Varsho. Fletcher has average speed but makes up for it with excellent routes and reads.

THE FUTURE: With so many other lefthanded-hitting outfielders ahead of him, Fletcher is in a tough spot.

It might take a trade—either of him or someone in front of him—to open up a big league opportunity. As it stands, Fletcher looks likely to return to Triple-A Reno to wait for his chance.

BA GRADE: 40/Medium		Hitting: 50		Power: 45		Speed: 50		Fielding: 65		Arm: 45					
Year	Age	Club (League)	Lvl	AVG	G	AB	R	H	2B	3B	HR	RBI	BB	SO	SB	OBP	SLG
2022	24	Amarillo (TL)	AA	.346	32	127	28	44	6	2	7	34	13	25	4	.408	.591
2022	24	Reno (PCL)	AAA	.301	101	396	70	119	29	8	5	38	42	88	5	.368	.452
Minor League Totals				.296	290	1139	191	337	67	16	32	156	102	272	13	.358	.467

17 RUBEN SANTANA, 3B

Born: Feb. 16, 2005. **B-T:** R-R. **HT:** 6-0. **WT:** 190.
Signed: Dominican Republic, 2022. **Signed by:** Cesar Geronimo/Pedro Meyer.
TRACK RECORD: The D-backs had already been tracking Santana when the pandemic hit, and when they saw him again after scouting restrictions had been lifted they were taken aback by how much he had improved. Intrigued by his tools and advanced offensive approach, they wound up signing him to a $750,000 deal. Santana put together an impressive debut in the Dominican Summer League, showing flashes of the powerful offensive profile on which the D-backs are betting.
SCOUTING REPORT: Santana gets good extension on his quick, aggressive swing, generating hard contact to all fields. He goes to the plate looking to do damage but shows good plate discipline relative to his age and experience level. His power projects to be at least plus. He recognizes and has shown an ability to hit breaking balls. He has some swing and miss concerns, but his ability to make adjustments helped him limit his strikeouts. He has plus speed, a surprise given his muscular build. He has good hands and footwork and a plus arm, giving him a chance to be at least an average defender at third.
THE FUTURE: Though he has yet to play outside the DSL, Santana has D-backs officials excited in the same way Deyvison De Los Santos did a few years ago. Santana will make his stateside debut in 2023 and will try to show he is the organization's next big power-hitting infield prospect.

BA GRADE: 50/Extreme		Hitting: 50		Power: 60		Speed: 60		Fielding: 55		Arm: 60					
Year	Age	Club (League)	Lvl	AVG	G	AB	R	H	2B	3B	HR	RBI	BB	SO	SB	OBP	SLG
2022	17	D-backs Red (DSL)	R	.316	43	133	35	42	5	4	1	17	25	33	15	.436	.436
Minor League Totals				.316	43	133	35	42	5	4	1	17	25	33	15	.436	.436

18 YU-MIN LIN, LHP

Born: July 12, 2003. **B-T:** L-L. **HT:** 5-11. **WT:** 160.
Signed: Taiwan, 2021. **Signed by:** Tzu-Yao Wei/Peter Wardell.
TRACK RECORD: Lin was an accomplished amateur on the international stage whom the D-backs had been following for years, but his performance for Chinese Taipei in a tournament in the fall of 2021 pushed the organization over the top to sign him. Pitching at 18, he carved through a Venezuelan lineup filled with pros three or four years his senior. He received a $525,000 bonus, then had a dominant pro debut, leading the organization (minimum 50 innings) with a 40% strikeout rate.
SCOUTING REPORT: Lin's fastball sits 89-91 mph with good carry, touching 92-93. He confounds hitters with his array of offerings and his pitching acumen. He generates elite spin with his curveball and slider; at their best, the former is a downer with bite and the latter is a harder, slashing option. The slider might have the most upside, but his best current pitch is his changeup, which drops off the table with armside run. He also has tinkered with a two-seamer, a cutter and a variation of his changeup that behaves like a screwball. He is athletic and repeats his delivery well, allowing him to project for plus control. Lin could still add weight to his slender frame, which could help him eke out another couple of ticks of velocity.
THE FUTURE: Though not overpowering, Lin has some starter characteristics. The D-backs took things slowly with him in 2022, but they figure to let his performance dictate his progression in 2023. The highly competitive lefthander should begin the season at High-A.

BA GRADE: 50/Exteme		Fastball: 50		Curveball: 50		Slider: 60		Changeup: 60		Control: 60				
Year	Age	Club (League)	Lvl	W	L	ERA	G	GS	IP	H	HR	BB	SO	BB/9	SO/9	WHIP	AVG
2022	18	D-backs Red (ACL)	R	0	2	2.35	7	7	23	9	0	6	41	2.3	16.0	0.65	.118
2022	18	Visalia (CAL)	LoA	2	0	2.97	7	7	33	31	2	16	50	4.3	13.5	1.41	.254
Minor League Totals				2	2	2.72	14	14	56	40	2	22	91	3.5	14.5	1.10	.202

19 DYLAN RAY, RHP

Born: May 9, 2001. **B-T:** R-R. **HT:** 6-3. **WT:** 230.
Drafted: Alabama, 2022 (4th round). **Signed by:** Stephen Baker.
TRACK RECORD: Ray is a big-bodied righthander whose amateur career was derailed by a pair of significant surgeries, but he showed glimpses of his upside last summer, prompting the D-backs to take a chance on him. Ray tore his ACL in a football injury his junior year of high school, then needed Tommy John surgery shortly after arriving at Alabama. He logged just 31 innings in 2022, all of it in relief, for the Crimson Tide, then pitched another 11 innings in the Cape Cod League, where the draft-eligible redshirt freshman's performance ultimately won over D-backs scouts.
SCOUTING REPORT: Ray was up to 96 mph with his fastball on the Cape, complementing that with a power slider that has a chance to be plus and a curveball that projects to be average. He is working on incorporating a changeup. His stuff was up across the board on the Cape, and his ability to throw three pitches for strikes helped convince the D-backs he had the potential to start. Ray's injuries appeared to take a toll on his athleticism, but the D-backs saw glimpses of it returning and hope he will look even better the further he gets from his surgeries. He has relatively low mileage on his arm, which could translate into more potential for development.
THE FUTURE: Ray worked strictly in relief at Alabama, but the D-backs plan to give him a chance to start. With a loose arm, functional delivery and prototypical pitcher's frame, they see a potential innings-eater if it all comes together.

BA GRADE: 50/Extreme		Fastball: 55	Curveball: 50	Slider: 60	Changeup: 45	Control: 50

Year	Age	Club (League)	Lvl	W	L	ERA	G	GS	IP	H	HR	BB	SO	BB/9	SO/9	WHIP	AVG
2022	21	D-backs Red (ACL)	R	0	0	0.00	2	2	2	0	0	1	3	4.5	13.5	0.50	.000
2022	21	Visalia (CAL)	LoA	0	3	7.71	6	6	12	16	5	3	14	2.3	10.8	1.63	.314
Minor League Totals				0	3	6.59	8	8	14	16	5	4	17	2.6	11.2	1.46	.281

20 CRISTOFER TORIN, SS

Born: May 26, 2005. **B-T:** R-R. **HT:** 5-10. **WT:** 175.
Signed: Venezuela, 2022. **Signed by:** Cesar Geronimo/Didimo Bracho.
TRACK RECORD: The D-backs were drawn to Torin's advanced defensive profile when they signed him for $240,000 in January 2022 but were unsure what sort of hitter they would be getting. Questions remain about his long-term offensive impact, but Torin surprised his new organization with his knack for finding the barrel. He was one of the organization's better performers in the DSL, hitting .333 with gap power and nearly twice as many walks (37) as strikeouts (20).
SCOUTING REPORT: Torin's bat speed is just average, but he sees the ball well and is seemingly on every pitch. He has advanced hand-eye coordination evidenced by his 10% overall whiff rate and 5% in-zone whiff rate. His swing decisions are good; he chases only 20% of the time. He does not safely project for even average power, but with his age and contact skills, more strength and pop could come in time. He is a flashy defender with soft hands, a plus arm and good instincts, with relatively few questions about his ability to stick at shortstop. He carries himself in the field with the flair of Javier Baez, his favorite player.
THE FUTURE: The D-backs are impressed with how polished Torin's game is for his age and club officials wouldn't be surprised to see him reach multiple levels next season. They envision him becoming a middle-of-the-diamond leader on defense and the kind of hitter a team wants at the plate in big situations.

BA GRADE: 50/Extreme		Hitting: 55	Power: 40	Speed: 50	Fielding: 60	Arm: 60

Year	Age	Club (League)	Lvl	AVG	G	AB	R	H	2B	3B	HR	RBI	BB	SO	SB	OBP	SLG
2022	17	D-backs Black (DSL)	R	.333	50	159	45	53	12	2	0	26	37	20	21	.465	.434
Minor League Totals				.333	50	159	45	53	12	2	0	26	37	20	21	.465	.434

21 MANUEL PEÑA, 2B

Born: December 5, 2003. **B-T:** L-R. **HT:** 6-1. **WT:** 170.
Signed: Dominican Republic, 2021. **Signed by:** Cesar Geronimo/Omar Rogers/Ronald Rivas.
TRACK RECORD: The D-backs made Peña the highest-paid player ($1.2 million) in their international class in 2021 because they liked his loose, easy swing, his disciplined approach and his likelihood of sticking on the infield. He has held his own through two seasons, including reaching full-season ball at 18, opening eyes with his offensive potential and standout work ethic.
SCOUTING REPORT: Peña has a controlled but aggressive swing with plus bat speed and the ability to

spray line drives to all fields. He has good hands and feel to hit. He has gap power now but should grow into more as he matures. He has no trouble timing up fastballs. He can get overly aggressive and pull happy. Still, he has the makings of a good approach thanks to his ability to recognize balls from strikes. He is a fringy runner and his lack of speed and quickness make him a better fit at second than short. He has the pregame routine of a big leaguer and impresses coaches with his diligence. Peña profiles as an average defender at second with an above-average arm.

THE FUTURE: The D-backs hope to see Peña add more strength to his frame, further refine his approach and show continued improvement as a hitter. They foresee a regular or semi-regular infielder with offensive impact. He will be 19 in 2023 and figures to open the season at Low-A Visalia.

BA GRADE: 45/High		Hitting: 50		Power: 45		Speed: 45		Fielding: 50		Arm: 55							
Year	Age	Club (League)	Lvl	AVG	G	AB	R	H	2B	3B	HR	RBI	BB	SO	SB	OBP	SLG
2022	18	D-backs Red (ACL)	R	.284	32	116	25	33	3	3	4	28	10	30	4	.336	.466
2022	18	Visalia (CAL)	LoA	.248	36	137	17	34	7	1	0	17	20	41	1	.344	.314
Minor League Totals				.260	125	447	72	116	15	6	8	75	56	117	22	.341	.374

22 JUSTIN MARTINEZ, RHP

Born: July 30, 2001. **B-T:** R-R. **HT:** 6-3. **WT:** 195.
Signed: Dominican Republic, 2018. **Signed by:** Cesar Geronimo/Jose Ortiz.

TRACK RECORD: Martinez had recently converted from outfielder to pitcher when the D-backs signed him for $50,000 in March 2018. Athletic with a strong arm, he quickly showed all the makings of a raw but intriguing, high-end pitching prospect, but his career hit a roadblock when he needed Tommy John surgery in 2021. He returned last year and raced through four levels as a reliever, finishing his season with an impressive Arizona Fall League showing.

SCOUTING REPORT: Martinez sits in the mid-to-upper 90s with his fastball, occasionally touching triple-digits. He has average rise and carry through the zone. His slider is sweepy and sharp and flashes plus, but his best weapon is his split-change, an 85-89 mph dive-bombing pitch that elicits loads of swings and misses. Martinez came back from surgery throwing better strikes and pitching with more confidence. He is still an inconsistent strike-thrower, but his clean, repeatable delivery allows projection for average future control.

THE FUTURE: Martinez had been seen as a possible starter, but his injury led to the shift to relief—and possibly to a fast-tracking of his big league arrival. His impressive year prompted the D-backs to add him to their 40-man roster in November, and he will come to major league camp looking to make an impression in hopes of debuting sometime in 2023.

BA GRADE: 45/High		Fastball: 65		Slider: 55		Changeup: 65		Control: 50							
Year	Age	Club (League)	Lvl	W	L	ERA	G	GS	IP	H	HR	BB	SO	BB/9	SO/9	WHIP	AVG
2022	20	D-backs Black (ACL)	R	0	1	18.00	1	0	1	2	1	0	1	0.0	9.0	2.00	.400
2022	20	D-backs Red (ACL)	R	0	0	0.00	1	0	1	0	0	1	1	9.0	9.0	1.00	.000
2022	20	Hillsboro (NWL)	HiA	1	2	2.67	13	0	27	21	1	14	44	4.7	14.7	1.30	.216
2022	20	Amarillo (TL)	AA	1	0	4.15	2	0	4	6	0	2	8	4.2	16.6	1.85	.316
2022	20	Reno (PCL)	AAA	1	0	3.86	3	0	5	3	0	5	8	9.6	15.4	1.71	.167
Minor League Totals				5	14	4.81	60	29	161	150	6	112	194	6.3	10.8	1.63	.243

23 CARLOS VARGAS, RHP

Born: October 13, 1999. **B-T:** R-R. **HT:** 6-4. **WT:** 210.
Signed: Dominican Republic, 2016. **Signed by:** Rafael Espinal (Guardians).

TRACK RECORD: Vargas was Cleveland's highest-dollar international signee when he received $275,000 in 2016. The organization bet on his projectable frame and quick arm, and within two years, his fastball had climbed from the low 90s to touching 100 mph. He was added to the 40-man roster in the fall of 2020, then blew out his arm in the spring of 2021, ultimately having Tommy John surgery. He got back on the mound last year and performed well in a relief role, then was shipped to the D-backs for pitcher Ross Carver in November.

SCOUTING REPORT: Vargas sits 98 mph with his fastball, routinely reaching triple-digits. Because his four-seamer does not get good ride consistently, the Guardians introduced a sinker, eliciting better results. His slider is a legitimate weapon. He can throw it for strikes early in the count or bury it as a putaway pitch. It averages 90-91 mph and Vargas can occasionally dial it up into the 93-94 mph range. Vargas walked too many batters but it is possible that was due to his long layoff from competition. He is comfortable working down in the zone but needs to learn to better command up in the zone.

THE FUTURE: Vargas joins an organization starved for power bullpen arms, putting him in position to claim a job with a strong spring. If he sharpens his command and control, his stuff could play in a high-leverage role.

BA GRADE: 45/High		Fastball: 60		Slider: 70			Control: 45							
Year	Age	Club (League)	Lvl	W	L	ERA	G	GS	IP	H	HR	BB	SO	BB/9	SO/9	WHIP	AVG
2022	22	Akron (EL)	AA	3	3	4.81	19	0	24	25	1	12	21	4.4	7.8	1.52	.269
2022	22	Columbus (IL)	AAA	1	0	0.90	8	0	10	8	1	5	16	4.5	14.4	1.30	.222
Minor League Totals				11	9	4.18	52	24	146	139	8	65	149	4.0	9.2	1.39	.253

24 DOMINIC CANZONE, OF

Born: August 16, 1997. **B-T:** L-R. **HT:** 6-1. **WT:** 190.
Drafted: Ohio State, 2019 (8th round). **Signed by:** Jeremy Kehrt.
TRACK RECORD: Canzone reached base in 59 consecutive games in his junior year at Ohio State, hitting .345 with 16 homers and leading the Big Ten in hits, total bases and slugging. His limited profile likely caused him to slip to the eighth round, but he has done little but make consistent hard contact since getting into the D-backs' system.
SCOUTING REPORT: Canzone's swing has never done much for scouts, who describe a rigid, sometimes stiff-looking cut that can be in and out of the zone quickly. But he produces good bat speed and has a knack for finding the barrel. He ranks near the top of the organization in percentage of balls hit 95 mph or harder (40.2) and average exit velocity (89.5 mph), doing so while carrying decent walk (8.5%) and strikeout (19.5%) rates. He puts together consistently tough at-bats. All of which is good because his bat will need to be his carrying tool; he grades as fringe-average or below with his defense, arm and speed.
THE FUTURE: Canzone's bat might be good enough to carve out a role, perhaps as a Corey Dickerson type. His path to Arizona is complicated by the Diamondbacks' logjam of outfielders, especially considering Canzone's defensive limitations, plus the fact he was left off the 40-man in the winter.

BA GRADE: 40/Medium		Hitting: 50		Power: 60		Speed: 40			Fielding: 45		Arm: 40				
Year	Age	Club (League)	Lvl	AVG	G	AB	R	H	2B	3B	HR	RBI	BB	SO	SB	OBP	SLG
2022	24	D-backs Black (ACL)	R	.250	3	8	2	2	0	1	0	1	1	3	0	.333	.500
2022	24	Amarillo (TL)	AA	.400	15	55	18	22	7	0	6	20	8	6	1	.476	.855
2022	24	Reno (PCL)	AAA	.284	88	331	61	94	18	1	16	68	28	74	14	.349	.489
Minor League Totals				.297	231	880	160	261	60	8	44	179	78	183	39	.360	.533

25 ANDREW PINTAR, 2B/CF

Born: March 23, 2001. **B-T:** R-R. **HT:** 6-2. **WT:** 190.
Drafted: Brigham Young, 2022 (5th round). **Signed by:** Mark Ross.
TRACK RECORD: Pintar was an undersized walk-on when he arrived at BYU from nearby Spanish Fork (Utah) High, but he became the first player under then-coach Mike Littlewood's tenure to subsequently earn a scholarship. A blue-collar type whose work ethic was forged on the family farm, Pintar gained size and strength and by the end of his redshirt freshman year had turned into one of the better offensive players in the West Coast Conference. His college career was derailed by a capsule injury in his right shoulder that needed multiple surgeries, leading him to fall in the draft.
SCOUTING REPORT: Pintar has a line-drive swing and the ability to make consistent, hard contact. He has a disciplined approach, rarely swings and misses and uses the whole field well. He could have latent plus power if he can learn to hit the ball in the air more often. He is a terrific athlete with plus speed. Defensively, he has the hands and footwork to play shortstop, but how his arm bounces back from the surgeries will determine his position, with second base and center field as the most likely possibilities.
THE FUTURE: Before his injury, the D-backs saw in Pintar a player in the mold of A.J. Pollock. They were willing to roll the dice on his upside, though time will tell how he looks once he is back on the field.

BA GRADE: 50/Extreme		Hitting: 55		Power: 50		Speed: 60			Fielding: 50		Arm: 45				
Year	Age	Club (League)	Lvl	AVG	G	AB	R	H	2B	3B	HR	RBI	BB	SO	SB	OBP	SLG
2022	21	Did not play—Injured															

26 YILBER DIAZ, RHP

Born: August 19, 2000. **B-T:** R-R. **HT:** 6-0. **WT:** 190.
Signed: Venezuela, 2021. **Signed by:** Cesar Geronimo/Ronald Salazar.

TRACK RECORD: Unsigned at 16, Diaz quit baseball for a year or so before giving it one last try. The D-backs saw him hit 92 mph and brought him to the Dominican Republic in early 2020 to work out. The pandemic hit, stranding him there, but he had access to the team's facility, allowing him to eat well and train regularly. Within months, he was up to 95 mph and the D-backs signed the then-20-year-old for $10,000. He enjoyed a breakout 2022 season, reaching High-A and seeing his velocity approach triple-digits.

SCOUTING REPORT: At his best, Diaz has a fastball that can sit at 96 and touch 99 mph. The pitch has good carry and he uses it well at the top of the zone. His curveball is his most trusted secondary pitch, but it can get loopy at 76-78 mph. He began throwing a slider last season and it flashed plus with tight, lateral action. It could become his best weapon after his fastball. He also has a changeup that he throws with good arm speed and conviction. It projects to be an average pitch. Diaz has below-average control that could get to fringe-average in time.

THE FUTURE: Diaz has some characteristics that could allow him to develop into a starter, but the club's newfound depth in that area—and Diaz's subpar command—could push him into a relief role sooner than later.

BA GRADE: 45/Very High   **Fastball:** 70   **Curveball:** 50   **Slider:** 55   **Changeup:** 50   **Control:** 45

Year	Age	Club (League)	Lvl	W	L	ERA	G	GS	IP	H	HR	BB	SO	BB/9	SO/9	WHIP	AVG
2022	21	Visalia (CAL)	LoA	4	2	3.56	11	9	48	34	4	21	70	3.9	13.1	1.15	.199
2022	21	Hillsboro (NWL)	HiA	0	1	4.85	8	8	30	22	1	17	29	5.2	8.8	1.31	.204
Minor League Totals				6	6	4.33	38	18	104	80	6	56	116	4.8	10.0	1.31	.216

27 NATE SAVINO, LHP

Born: January 24, 2002. **B-T:** L-L. **HT:** 6-3. **WT:** 210.
Drafted: Virginia, 2022 (3rd round). **Signed by:** Rick Matsko.

TRACK RECORD: Seen as a possible first-round pick entering his senior year of high school, Savino instead enrolled early at Virginia, where he performed well but did not develop the way many scouts hoped. He did show signs of progress in 2022, particularly with a late-season uptick in stuff, displaying better velocity on both his fastball and slider.

SCOUTING REPORT: At his best, Savino can sit around 93-94 mph with his fastball. He gets good sink and armside run with the pitch and is at his best when working at the bottom of the zone. As a result, he is more about inducing ground balls than hunting swings and misses. He can get whiffs with his slider, which shows depth and lateral movement and ranges between 80-86 mph. His changeup, perhaps his best secondary pitch in high school, projects to be average despite being used sparingly last year. He is a consistent strike-thrower whose command flashes plus. He throws from a low three-quarters arm slot and from a delivery that looked looser and more athletic last season.

THE FUTURE: Savino has all the ingredients to have a future as a back-of-the-rotation starter. If he can maintain the bump in stuff he displayed last season and find it more consistently, perhaps he could be more. If not, he could project as an effective reliever.

BA GRADE: 45/Very High   **Fastball:** 50   **Slider:** 50   **Changeup:** 50   **Control:** 55

Year	Age	Club (League)	Lvl	W	L	ERA	G	GS	IP	H	HR	BB	SO	BB/9	SO/9	WHIP	AVG
2022	20	Did not play															

28 BRYCE JARVIS, RHP

Born: December 26, 1997. **B-T:** L-R. **HT:** 6-2. **WT:** 195.
Drafted: Duke, 2020 (1st round). **Signed by:** George Swain.

TRACK RECORD: Jarvis opted against pitching in the Cape Cod League after his sophomore season at Duke and instead spent the summer adding strength and refining his stuff. The work paid off. He enjoyed a dominant four-start run in the pandemic-shortened 2020 season, and the D-backs made him the highest-selected (18th overall) player in Duke history. Jarvis' stuff hasn't played as well in pro ball, and he entered this past offseason open to making a variety of possible changes.

SCOUTING REPORT: Jarvis averages close to 95 mph with his four-seam fastball, but because he gets just 5.2 feet of extension and lacks deception, hitters tee off on it. The D-backs are hoping changes to Jarvis' mechanics can get his fastball to play better, and there has been thought of committing more to a two-seamer. The good news is he has two plus pitches in his changeup and slider and a curveball that flashes plus. Those pitches are good for inducing chases, but he struggles to throw them in the zone. Moreover, there's some concern that he telegraphs his secondary stuff, prompting hitters to wait out fastballs.

THE FUTURE: Jarvis still has the ingredients to start, but if he can't get his mechanics in order and salvage his fastball, his future might be in relief, where he can lean heavily on his secondary stuff.

| BA GRADE: 45/Very High | | Fastball: 45 | | Curveball: 50 | | Slider: 60 | | Changeup: 60 | | Control: 50 | | |

Year	Age	Club (League)	Lvl	W	L	ERA	G	GS	IP	H	HR	BB	SO	BB/9	SO/9	WHIP	AVG
2022	24	Amarillo (TL)	AA	3	6	8.27	25	25	107	141	27	60	110	5.1	9.3	1.88	.325
Minor League Totals				5	10	6.68	41	41	182	204	39	90	199	4.5	9.8	1.62	.286

29 CONOR GRAMMES, RHP

Born: July 13, 1997. **B-T:** R-R. **HT:** 6-2. **WT:** 205.
Drafted: Xavier, 2019 (5th round). **Signed by:** Jeremy Kehrt.

TRACK RECORD: Grammes was a two-way player at Xavier with a spotty track record of strike-throwing, but the D-backs rolled the dice on his athleticism, betting on the possibility of significant improvement given his limited experience on the mound. He arrived at instructional league in the fall of 2020 looking like he had turned a corner. Unfortunately, he needed Tommy John surgery the following year. All told, he has thrown just 60 innings in three professional seasons—eight fewer than he logged his junior year at Xavier.

SCOUTING REPORT: Grammes returned from surgery and still had the same explosive stuff as before, starting with a fastball that averages 97.5 mph and touches 100 with life through the zone. He also has a pair of plus breaking balls—a sharp-breaking slider that can touch the upper 80s and a hammer curveball in the low-to-mid 80s. Unfortunately, his mechanics were out of whack after the long layoff, and he ended the year needing to clean up his direction and the length of his arm action.

THE FUTURE: Few, if any, pitchers in the D-backs system have stuff on par with Grammes, and if he can smooth out his mechanics he could move fast as a power-armed reliever. He will need to find a level of consistency he has yet to show as a professional.

| BA GRADE: 45/Extreme | | Fastball: 70 | | Curveball: 60 | | Slider: 60 | | | Control: 45 | | |

Year	Age	Club (League)	Lvl	W	L	ERA	G	GS	IP	H	HR	BB	SO	BB/9	SO/9	WHIP	AVG
2022	24	D-backs Black (ACL)	R	0	0	0.00	1	0	1	1	0	0	3	0.0	27.0	1.00	.250
2022	24	D-backs Red (ACL)	R	0	1	40.50	1	0	1	4	1	1	1	13.5	13.5	7.50	.667
2022	24	Hillsboro (NWL)	HiA	1	1	8.50	12	0	18	14	2	13	33	6.5	16.5	1.50	.209
Minor League Totals				1	5	7.16	31	13	60	65	8	34	89	5.1	13.3	1.64	.272

30 KRISTIAN ROBINSON, OF

Born: December 11, 2000. **B-T:** R-R. **HT:** 6-3. **WT:** 215.
Signed: Bahamas, 2017. **Signed by:** Cesar Geronimo/Craig Shipley.

TRACK RECORD: The D-backs were so enamored by Robinson's athleticism and potential upside—particularly after seeing him play well against older and more experienced competition—they signed him at age 16 for $2.5 million, the fourth-highest bonus of his signing class. He quickly delivered on that upside and performed well in the lower minors as a teenager. However, he has been stuck in limbo after a confrontation with a law enforcement officer in April 2020. A felony assault charge has left him unable to secure a proper work visa and he has not played in an official game since 2019.

SCOUTING REPORT: Robinson was once seen as a potential multi-tool prospect with massive upside, though it is unclear how much that has changed after missing three seasons. He generated loud contact with a simple, compact swing, doing so with a sound approach and limited chase. He was seen as a possible center fielder given his plus speed and instincts but would likely need to move to a corner as his body matures.

THE FUTURE: Robinson has been on the restricted list since November 2021 but has been limited to informal game action and at-bats due to his visa status. Once that is cleared up, he should be able to resume his career. He may still have one of the highest ceilings of anyone in the system.

| BA GRADE: 45/Extreme | | Hitting: 50 | | Power: 60 | | Speed: 60 | | Fielding: 55 | | Arm: 50 | |

Year	Age	Club (League)	Lvl	AVG	G	AB	R	H	2B	3B	HR	RBI	BB	SO	SB	OBP	SLG
2022	21	Did not play															

Atlanta Braves

BY CARLOS COLLAZO

While the Braves lost to the Phillies in the National League Division Series and failed to defend their 2021 World Series championship, the organization won 101 games and secured a fifth consecutive National League East division title.

On June 1, the Braves were 10.5 games behind the Mets for the division lead, but from that day forward went 78-34 (.696), including a pivotal three-game series sweep against the Mets in the penultimate series of the regular season.

While Atlanta failed to become the first team since the 1998-2000 Yankees to win consecutive World Series, general manager Alex Anthopoulos has turned the Braves into one of the model franchises in the game.

In all areas, the Braves have proven to be a well-run organization: from savvy scouting and development, to aggressive trading, to extending a competitive window by extending the contracts of much of the team's young core.

Prior to the 2022 season, the Braves moved on from face of the franchise first baseman Freddie Freeman and immediately found his replacement in a trade for Matt Olson. The team shipped out top prospects Shea Langeliers and Cristian Pache as well as righthanders Ryan Cusick and Joey Estes in what has been Anthopoulos' most aggressive trade with Atlanta.

The Braves immediately extended Olson with an eight-year, $168 million deal. Then in August, Atlanta extended third baseman Austin Riley with a 10-year, $212 million contract to lock down the team's top power source.

It wasn't just veterans who secured big deals with the Braves in 2022. In late August, eventual NL Rookie of the Year Michael Harris II signed an eight-year, $72 million extension. In October, flamethrowing rookie righthander Spencer Strider signed a six-year, $75 million contract.

Both Harris and Strider are the latest examples of Atlanta's productive scouting and player development. Harris played like a Gold Glove center fielder while coming one homer shy of a 20-20 season in 114 games. Strider posted a 2.67 ERA over 131.2 innings in the rotation and bullpen.

Now the Braves are looking at a young player core of Riley, Olson, Harris, Strider, Ronald Acuña Jr. and Ozzie Albies through the 2027 season.

It's good that the Braves have such a strong MLB core, because the farm system is as barren as it's been in years. With both Harris and second baseman Vaughn Grissom graduating from prospect status in 2022, there are few impact hitters to be found in the minor leagues.

Strong seasons from Justyn-Henry Malloy and

Michael Harris II required just 43 games above Class A before he was big league ready.

PROJECTED 2026 LINEUP

Position	Player	Age
Catcher	William Contreras	28
First Base	Matt Olson	32
Second Base	Ozzie Albies	29
Third Base	Austin Riley	29
Shortstop	Vaughn Grissom	25
Left Field	Jesse Franklin	27
Center Field	Michael Harris II	25
Right Field	Ronald Acuña Jr.	28
Designated Hitter	Ignacio Alvarez	23
No. 1 Starter	Max Fried	32
No. 2 Starter	Kyle Wright	30
No. 3 Starter	Ian Anderson	28
No. 4 Starter	Spencer Strider	27
No. 5 Starter	Kyle Muller	28
Closer	AJ Smith-Shawver	23

Cal Conley gave the organization solid depth pieces, but there are no Harris types to feel confident in—especially once Malloy was traded to the Tigers for reliever Joe Jimenez during the Winter Meetings

As ever, the organization is still capable of pumping out big league arms, with lefthander Kyle Muller leading the pack.

There's upside potential and plenty of firepower in lower-level arms—most notably righthanders AJ Smith-Shawver, Owen Murphy and JR Ritchie—and a few exciting Latin American hitters, including Ignacio Alvarez and Ambioris Tavarez, but Atlanta will need to be patient with those players' development paths. ∎

ATLANTA BRAVES

TOP 2023 MLB CONTRIBUTORS	RANK
Kyle Muller, LHP	1
Jared Shuster, LHP	4
BREAKOUT PROSPECTS	**RANK**
Spencer Schwellenbach, RHP	12
Ignacio Alvarez, 3B	17
Ambioris Tavarez, SS	21

SOURCE OF TOP 30 TALENT

Homegrown	29	Acquired	1
College	15	Trade	0
Junior college	2	Rule 5 draft	1
High school	8	Independent league	0
Nondrafted free agent	0	Free agent/waivers	0
International	4		

LF
Jesse Franklin (17)

CF
Kadon Morton (28)
Douglas Glod
Tyler Collins
Justin Dean

RF
Brandol Mezquita
Greyson Jenista

3B
Ignacio Alvarez (17)

SS
Braden Shewmake (13)
Cal Conley (14)
Ambioris Tavarez (21)

2B
Geraldo Quintero (23)
Luke Waddell (26)

1B
David McCabe (27)
Mahki Backstrom (29)

C
Drake Baldwin (20)
Logan Brown
Tyler Tolve

LHP

LHSP	LHRP
Kyle Muller (1)	Adam Shoemaker
Jared Shuster (4)	Samuel Strickland
Dylan Dodd (9)	
Luis De Avila (22)	

RHP

RHSP	RHRP
AJ Smith-Shawver (2)	Royber Salinas (6)
Owen Murphy (3)	Blake Burkhalter (10)
JR Ritchie (5)	Freddy Tarnok (8)
Darius Vines (7)	Victor Vodnik (16)
Cole Phillips (11)	Brooks Wilson (18)
Spencer Schwellenbach (12)	Roddery Munoz (24)
Adam Maier (19)	Justin Yeager (25)
Tanner Gordon	Austin Smith (30)
Ian Mejia	Seth Keller
Alan Rangel	Daysbel Hernandez
Nolan Kingham	Rolddy Muñoz
Allan Winans	Indigo Diaz
	Cedric De Grandpre
	Landon Harper
	Jared Johnson

1 KYLE MULLER, LHP

Born: Oct. 7, 1997. **B-T:** R-L. **HT:** 6-7. **WT:** 250.
Drafted: HS—Dallas, 2016 (2nd round).
Signed by: Nate Dion.

TRACK RECORD: The Braves have had plenty of success developing former two-way players, and like graduated homegrown prospects Austin Riley and Michael Harris II, Muller was a standout two-way prospect in high school. Muller showed improved velocity during his 2016 draft year and leapt up draft boards after he struck out 24 straight batters over two starts in a competitive Dallas region. The Braves eventually signed Muller for $2.5 million in the second round of the 2016 draft and watched him continue to improve his stuff—to the point where he had some of the best pure arm talent in the system. Harnessing that stuff has always held Muller back, though with Triple-A Gwinnett in 2022 he posted his lowest walk rate (7.4%) since the 2018 season and pitched well in two of his three big league starts.

SCOUTING REPORT: Muller has a four-pitch mix headlined by a fastball that sits in the 93-95 mph range and tops out around 97-98. While the pitch has ordinary life and shape, it does play up a bit thanks to his extension—a product of an extra-large, 6-foot-7, 250-pound frame. The Braves have encouraged Muller to attack the zone aggressively with his fastball, both to get ahead in counts and to make hitters swing. He did just that in the minors, throwing his fastball for strikes more than 70% of the time, which should allow him to use his secondaries more effectively to get hitters to chase. Muller throws a firm, upper-80s slider that averaged nearly 87 mph in the majors and put him among the top 25 hardest-thrown lefthanded sliders. The pitch is his go-to secondary offering, and analytically it is his best pitch overall, with impressive chase rates and a whiff rate around 40% in the minors. Muller's slider has earned plus scouting grades, while his low-80s curveball is another quality breaking pitch with horizontal and vertical bite. His curve spin rate is in the 2,400 rpm range, though he threw the pitch in the zone less frequently than any of his offerings. Muller's firm, upper-80s changeup is his fourth pitch and was exclusively used against righthanded hitters in his major league time. It's a non-fastball to use against opposite-hand hitters for Muller in a starting role, though the movement and velocity separation on his changeup don't suggest it'll be anything more than a fourth offering.

BEST TOOLS

BATTING

Best Hitter for Average	Luke Waddell
Best Power Hitter	Drew Lugbauer
Best Strike-Zone Discipline	Luke Waddell
Fastest Baserunner	Cal Conley
Best Athlete	AJ Smith-Shawver

PITCHING

Best Fastball	AJ Smith-Shawver
Best Curveball	Kyle Muller
Best Slider	AJ Smith-Shawver
Best Changeup	Darius Vines
Best Control	Dylan Dodd

FIELDING

Best Defensive Catcher	Drake Baldwin
Best Defensive Infielder	Ambiorvis Tavarez
Best Infield Arm	Ignacio Alvarez
Best Defensive Outfielder	Kadon Morton
Best Outfield Arm	Greyson Jenista

THE FUTURE: Muller has one more minor league option remaining, and he graduates from prospect eligibility with just four more outs. He took a solid step forward with his fastball command at Triple-A Gwinnett in 2022. While Muller has been developed as a starter, the Braves have plenty of rotation options, and scouts have long believed his pure stuff could play up in the bullpen, where he could pitch in a high-leverage capacity and scrap his changeup. Entering his age-25 season, Muller doesn't have much left to prove. He just needs an MLB opportunity, which may come somewhere other than Atlanta.

Year	Age	Club (League)	Lvl	W	L	ERA	G	GS	IP	H	HR	BB	SO	BB/9	SO/9	WHIP	AVG
2022	24	Gwinnett (IL)	AAA	6	8	3.41	23	23	135	119	14	40	159	2.7	10.6	1.18	.240
2022	24	Atlanta (NL)	MLB	1	1	8.03	3	3	12	13	2	8	12	5.8	8.8	1.70	.260
Major League Totals				3	5	5.14	12	11	49	39	4	28	49	5.1	9.0	1.37	.218
Minor League Totals				31	22	3.18	108	107	541	449	41	226	588	3.8	9.8	1.25	.227

2 AJ SMITH-SHAWVER, RHP

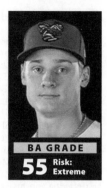

Born: November 20, 2002. **B-T:** R-R. **HT:** 6-3. **WT:** 205.
Drafted: HS—Colleyville, Texas, 2021 (7th round). **Signed by:** Trey McNickle.

TRACK RECORD: Smith-Shawver was a quick-twitch, multi-sport athlete in high school who was a college prospect as a hitter and pitcher, but the Braves loved his arm enough to sign him for just under $1 million in the seventh round in 2021. Smith-Shawver spent 2022 with Low-A Augusta, where he showed perhaps the highest upside in Atlanta's farm system.

SCOUTING REPORT: Smith-Shawver is a powerful and athletic righthander who has shown legitimate frontline starter stuff, according to scouts both inside and outside the organization. It all starts with his four-seam fastball, a beast of a pitch that averaged nearly 95 mph and peaked at 98. It has excellent life, with 20 inches of induced vertical break and both cutting and running action at times. He's still developing his command of the pitch, but when

BA GRADE

55 Risk: Extreme

he's hitting the zone, it can be overpowering. Similarly, Smith-Shawver's slider has the potential to be a wipeout offering. It's an upper-80s pitch with short and hard biting action that disappears at the bottom of the strike zone when it's on. Smith-Shawver throws a changeup in the same velocity range that remains a work in progress. The pitch flashes solid fading life, but he has below-average feel for it presently. Smith-Shawver has reduced the violence of his delivery since high school, but there are still needed refinements. His arm speed is electric, but it's such that he's not often synced up, and he also features plenty of cross-fire action and a heavy fall-off to the first base side—all of which will limit his control and command.

THE FUTURE: The Braves will likely prioritize fastball command and slider consistency with Smith-Shawver. If his command doesn't improve, his stuff could play in a big league bullpen.

SCOUTING GRADES:	Fastball: 70	Slider: 70	Changeup: 45	Control: 50

Year	Age	Club (League)	Lvl	W	L	ERA	G	GS	IP	H	HR	BB	SO	BB/9	SO/9	WHIP	AVG
2022	19	Augusta (CAR)	LoA	3	4	5.11	17	17	69	54	4	39	103	5.1	13.5	1.35	.215
Minor League Totals				3	5	5.49	21	21	77	58	6	49	119	5.7	13.9	1.39	.208

3 OWEN MURPHY, RHP

Born: September 27, 2003. **B-T:** R-R. **HT:** 6-1. **WT:** 190.
Drafted: HS—Brookfield, IL, 2022 (1st round). **Signed by:** Jeremy Gordon.

TRACK RECORD: Murphy ranked as the No. 45 prospect in the 2022 draft class thanks to his impressive pure stuff and natural athleticism. He was also a star football player and legitimate prospect as a shortstop. The Braves drafted Murphy 20th overall and signed him to a bonus just over $2.5 million—hoping he would follow in their long line of successfully developed former two-way players. Murphy pitched in Rookie ball and with Low-A Augusta for 12 combined innings after signing.

SCOUTING REPORT: A 6-foot-1, 190-pound righthander, Murphy has a strong foundation as a strike-thrower and a four-pitch mix, though the Braves will likely have him focus on his fastball, curveball and slider during his first full sea-

BA GRADE

55 Risk: Extreme

son as a pitcher. His fastball sits in the low 90s and touches 94-95 mph at peak velocity, with high spin rates of 2,500-2,600 rpm and impressive carry. He had more than 19 inches of induced vertical break on the pitch in his brief pro debut. Murphy throws a hammer curveball in the upper 70s that earned plus grades from amateur scouts, and he also throws a hard, slider/cutter in high school in the mid 80s. The Braves are turning that slider into more of a gyro-slider—the same slider Spencer Strider employed to great effect—and will have him scrap an infrequently used but promising 80 mph changeup, at least initially. Atlanta has praised Murphy's makeup and control, and believe he has a good chance to profile as a starter.

THE FUTURE: Murphy will likely begin the 2023 season at Low-A Augusta. He has the stuff and polish to move relatively quickly—particularly given his multi-sport and two-way background—and has No. 3 or 4 starter upside.

SCOUTING GRADES:	Fastball: 60	Curveball: 60	Slider: 50	Changeup: 45	Control: 55

Year	Age	Club (League)	Lvl	W	L	ERA	G	GS	IP	H	HR	BB	SO	BB/9	SO/9	WHIP	AVG
2022	18	Braves (FCL)	R	0	0	0.00	2	2	5	2	0	0	7	0.0	12.6	0.40	.118
2022	18	Augusta (CAR)	LoA	0	1	7.71	3	3	7	5	0	6	10	7.7	12.9	1.57	.192
Minor League Totals				0	1	4.50	5	5	12	7	0	6	17	4.5	12.8	1.08	.163

4 JARED SHUSTER, LHP

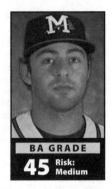

Born: August 3, 1998. **B-T:** L-L. **HT:** 6-3. **WT:** 210.
Drafted: Wake Forest, 2020 (1st round). **Signed by:** Billy Best.

TRACK RECORD: The 2020 draft has proved to be an exceptional one for the Braves, who drafted Shuster in the first round at No. 25 overall as well as Jesse Franklin, Spencer Strider and Bryce Elder. Strider and Elder have already established themselves as big leaguers just two years later. Shuster could be knocking on the door after a strong overall 2022 season.

SCOUTING REPORT: Shuster has impressive feel for a solid three-pitch mix. During his final college season, Shuster showed improved fastball velocity and was touching 96-97 mph, but that velocity has never carried over to pro ball. In 2022, Shuster sat around 90-92 mph with solid carry and cut, with a max velocity around 94-95. His changeup remains his best offering and is go-to secondary, a plus pitch that averages around

BA GRADE

45 Risk: Medium

80 mph. The pitch generates whiffs at a high rate, as well as ugly swings as it falls below the zone. Shuster's changeup features double-digit velocity separation from his fastball. Shuster tried throwing his slider harder during the 2022 season, and Braves officials were happy with the progress of the pitch—which sat in the 82-87 mph range—though external scouts view it as a fringy pitch that will play up with good command. Shuster is an above-average strike-thrower with a career minor league walk rate of 6.8%. In 2022 he threw all three of his pitches for strikes more than 64% of the time.

THE FUTURE: Shuster's upside is limited if he cannot rediscover the power he showed in flashes as an amateur, but he's one of the most probable big leaguers in the system, with back-end starter or middle reliever upside.

SCOUTING GRADES:	Fastball: 50	Slider: 45	Changeup: 60	Control: 55

Year	Age	Club (League)	Lvl	W	L	ERA	G	GS	IP	H	HR	BB	SO	BB/9	SO/9	WHIP	AVG
2022	23	Mississippi (SL)	AA	6	7	2.78	17	16	91	65	8	22	106	2.2	10.5	0.96	.198
2022	23	Gwinnett (IL)	AAA	1	3	4.25	10	9	49	43	10	16	39	3.0	7.2	1.21	.239
Minor League Totals				9	10	3.69	45	42	212	174	33	58	235	2.5	10.0	1.09	.220

5 JR RITCHIE, RHP

Born: June 26, 2003. **B-T:** R-R. **HT:** 6-2. **WT:** 185.
Drafted: HS—Bainbridge Island, WA, 2022 (1st round supp). **Signed by:** Cody Martin.

TRACK RECORD: Ritchie was the back-to-back Washington Gatorade player of the year and worked with the same pitching coach as 2021 Phillies first-rounder Mick Abel. Ritchie ranked as the No. 52 prospect in the 2022 draft and signed with the Braves for $2.4 million in the supplemental first round. Atlanta acquired the 35th overall pick Ritchie was selected with when it traded Drew Waters, Andrew Hoffmann and CJ Alexander to the Royals about a week before the 2022 draft.

SCOUTING REPORT: Ritchie is nearly physically maxed out at 6-foot-2, 185 pounds, but he requires less projection than most prep pitching prospects thanks to an advanced three-pitch mix and solid command. Ritchie sits in the low 90s with his fastball but touched 97-98 mph during the

BA GRADE

50 Risk: Extreme

spring and got into the mid 90s during his pro debut, which culminated in three starts for Low-A Augusta. His fastball has just modest life and carry, though he has shown an ability to locate the pitch to both sides of the plate and change eye levels. Ritchie's secondaries are a low-to-mid 80s slider and a changeup in the same velocity band. Both are at least solid-average pitches that—like his fastball—he's shown impressive feel for. His slider has flashed above-average or plus potential in the past, though the shape of the pitch comes and goes depending on the start. Ritchie's slider generated a ton of whiffs in his brief pro debut and will likely be his most reliable out pitch moving forward. The Braves rave about his advanced pitchability and mentality

THE FUTURE: Ritchie could start 2023 at Low-A or High-A and it wouldn't be surprising to see him push to Double-A. He has back-of-the-rotation upside and a clear path as a starter.

SCOUTING GRADES: .	Fastball: 55	Slider: 55	Changeup: 50	Control: 55

Year	Age	Club (League)	Lvl	W	L	ERA	G	GS	IP	H	HR	BB	SO	BB/9	SO/9	WHIP	AVG
2022	19	Braves (FCL)	R	0	0	0.00	2	2	4	2	0	1	4	2.1	8.3	0.69	.125
2022	19	Augusta (CAR)	LoA	0	0	2.70	3	3	10	7	1	4	10	3.6	9.0	1.10	.212
Minor League Totals				0	0	1.88	5	5	14	9	1	5	14	3.1	8.8	0.98	.184

6 ROYBER SALINAS, RHP

Born: April 10, 2001. **B-T:** R-R. **HT:** 6-3. **WT:** 205.
Signed: Venezuela, 2018. **Signed by:** Carlos Sequera.

TRACK RECORD: Salinas was an under-the-radar signing in 2018, but he flashed bat-missing potential in the Dominican Summer League in 2019 and in domestic leagues in 2021, when he whiffed 67 batters in 39.1 innings. He fully broke out in 2022 at Low-A Augusta and High-A Rome by striking out 175 batters in 109 innings. It was the most strikeouts in the Braves system and fourth-most among all minor league pitchers.

SCOUTING REPORT: Salinas is a big-bodied righthander listed at 6-foot-3, 205 pounds, though he's quite a bit heavier than that listed weight. He attacks hitters with a powerful three-pitch mix headlined by one of the best fastballs in the system. Salinas sat 93-95 mph with his four-seam fastball and touched 98 in 2022. The pitch has plus carry in the top of

BA GRADE

50 Risk: Extreme

the zone, with high spin (2,400 rpm) and more than 18 inches of induced vertical break. He pairs his fastball up with multiple breaking balls that have improved significantly during the 2022 season. Salinas previously threw his slider and curveball with slower, loopier shape. By the end of the season, he was throwing a gyro slider around 87 mph that touched 90 as well as a hammer, downer curveball in the 80-82 mph range. Scouts are mixed on which breaking pitch they prefer, though both were bat-missing pitches at a high level. Salinas' slider was thrown for a strike more frequently and was used more often, while his curve could pair nicely as a north-south complement to his fastball, with more velocity separation. Salinas currently has below-average control.

THE FUTURE: Salinas has midrotation stuff, but scouts wonder if his control will limit him to a high-leverage bullpen role. They also note that he will need to stay on top of maintaining his body.

SCOUTING GRADES: Fastball: 65   Curveball: 60   Slider: 60   Control: 40

Year	Age	Club (League)	Lvl	W	L	ERA	G	GS	IP	H	HR	BB	SO	BB/9	SO/9	WHIP	AVG
2022	21	Augusta (CAR)	LoA	0	1	1.52	5	5	24	10	1	12	52	4.6	19.8	0.93	.127
2022	21	Rome (SAL)	HiA	5	7	4.11	20	20	85	63	6	51	123	5.4	13.0	1.34	.202
Minor League Totals				10	14	3.33	55	34	181	128	11	109	279	5.4	13.8	1.31	.197

7 DARIUS VINES, RHP

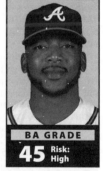

Born: April 30, 1998. **B-T:** R-R. **HT:** 6-1. **WT:** 190.
Drafted: Cal State Bakersfield, 2019 (7th round). **Signed by:** Kevin Martin.

TRACK RECORD: The Braves signed Vines for $130,000 in the seventh round of the 2019 draft after he transferred from junior college and established himself as one of the best pitchers in the Western Athletic Conference. Vines impressed with his feel for secondary stuff in 2021 and continued to perform against upper-minors competition in 2022

SCOUTING REPORT: Vines isn't a hard thrower, but he has excellent feel for a pitch mix that previously included four different options and is now down to three. The Braves had Vines remove a curveball from his arsenal in 2022 to focus on his fastball, changeup and slider. He pitches off a 90-92 mph fastball that touches 94 with above-average carry, but his go-to

BA GRADE

45 Risk: High

secondary is a low-80s changeup that has developed into the best such pitch in the system. While Vines' curveball was his bread-and-butter offering as an amateur, he didn't throw it much for strikes in pro ball. The opposite is true of his changeup. He has exceptional command of the pitch and threw it for strikes more than 70% of the time in 2022, with excellent whiff rates, chase rates and analytical and traditional scouting grades. Vines' changeup is at least a plus offering, and some scouts have put 70-grade evaluations on the pitch. He also throws a slider in the low-to-mid 80s with solid spin that should be an average breaking ball. Vines has consistently been a good strike-thrower and his exceptional feel to land his changeup indicates above-average or better control moving forward.

THE FUTURE: Scouts previously wondered if Vines had the sort of stuff to miss upper-level bats. He proved he could in 2022. He profiles as a back-end starter given his command of three pitches.

SCOUTING GRADES: Fastball: 55   Slider: 50   Changeup: 65   Control: 55

Year	Age	Club (League)	Lvl	W	L	ERA	G	GS	IP	H	HR	BB	SO	BB/9	SO/9	WHIP	AVG
2022	24	Mississippi (SL)	AA	7	4	3.95	20	20	107	100	16	30	127	2.5	10.7	1.21	.244
2022	24	Gwinnett (IL)	AAA	1	0	3.21	7	5	34	29	1	14	29	3.7	7.8	1.28	.228
Minor League Totals				14	13	3.77	61	58	284	252	36	83	320	2.6	10.1	1.18	.233

8 FREDDY TARNOK, RHP

Born: November 24, 1998. **B-T:** R-R. **HT:** 6-3. **WT:** 185.
Drafted: HS—Riverview, FL, 2017 (3rd round). **Signed by:** Justin Clark.
TRACK RECORD: Tarnok was a two-way player in high school in Florida, but the Braves signed him for $1.4 million as a pitcher in the 2017 third round after taking Kyle Wright in the first and Drew Waters in the second. Tarnok's progress was slow initially, before a breakout 2021 season when he reached the upper minors. In 2022, Tarnok made his MLB debut by pitching two-thirds of an inning in relief on Aug. 17 against the Mets.
SCOUTING REPORT: In his age-23 season, Tarnok mostly pitched between Double-A Mississippi and Triple-A Gwinnett, where he showed flashes of dominance and periods of inconsistency. Tarnok has a four-pitch mix, headlined by a four-seam fastball that sits 93-95 mph and touches 98 with

BA GRADE
45 **Risk:** High

good spin and carry. His go-to secondary is a 12-to-6 curveball in the upper 70s that was previously the best such pitch in the system, but evaluators inside and outside the system noted it took a step backward in 2022. Tarnok showed some progress with a mid-80s changeup, and the Braves have continued to try to help him develop a low-80s slider, though it has been slow going. External evaluators view his changeup and slider as fringe-average offerings. At times, Tarnok showed the ability to dominate with his fastball, but he has also struggled to sync his delivery and navigate a lineup multiple times with consistency.
THE FUTURE: The Braves have committed to developing Tarnok as a starter, but plenty of scouts think he could excel in shorter stints as a reliever where he can focus on dominating with two pitches.

SCOUTING GRADES:	Fastball: 60	Curveball: 55	Slider: 45	Changeup: 45	Control: 45

Year	Age	Club (League)	Lvl	W	L	ERA	G	GS	IP	H	HR	BB	SO	BB/9	SO/9	WHIP	AVG
2022	23	Mississippi (SL)	AA	2	2	4.31	15	15	63	54	8	27	75	3.9	10.8	1.29	.228
2022	23	Gwinnett (IL)	AAA	2	1	3.68	10	8	44	38	7	17	49	3.5	10.0	1.25	.228
2022	23	Atlanta (NL)	MLB	0	0	0.00	1	0	1	1	0	0	1	0.0	13.5	1.50	.333
Major League Totals				0	0	0.00	1	0	1	1	0	0	1	0.0	13.5	1.50	.333
Minor League Totals				18	23	4.05	98	78	377	337	35	153	417	3.6	9.9	1.30	.236

9 DYLAN DODD, LHP

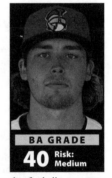

Born: June 6, 1998. **B-T:** L-L. **HT:** 6-2. **WT:** 210.
Drafted: Southeast Missouri State, 2021 (3rd round). **Signed by:** JD French.
TRACK RECORD: The Braves signed Dodd to an under-slot bonus of $125,000 in the third round of the 2021 draft, and used the savings there to go over slot to sign players such as seventh-rounder AJ Smith-Shawver and 11th-rounder Adam Shoemaker. The organization liked Dodd's talent, and he moved from High-A Rome to Triple-A Gwinnett in 2022, while posting a 5.4% walk rate.
SCOUTING REPORT: Dodd is regarded more for his pitchability than pure stuff, but his standout command of four-seam and two-seam fastballs sets up the rest of his arsenal. Dodd throws in the 91-92 mph range with his fastball and touches 95, with modest four-seam carry, but he threw each

BA GRADE
40 **Risk:** Medium

variant of his fastball for strikes more than 73% of the time in 2022. He uses his fastball to set up a slider and a changeup that are both in the low-to-mid 80s. Both pitches flash solid-average to above-average grades, though scouts think the slider is more of a gradual breaking pitch that will play up thanks to his ability to command it and mix it with his other offerings. Dodd's changeup could be a tick ahead, though he throws the slider for strikes more often. If he can add more power to his breaking pitch, Dodd could improve his upside. But his stuff was good enough to miss bats even as he progressed to higher levels of the minors where he was more age-appropriate as a prospect.
THE FUTURE: Dodd has pitched just 53 innings in the upper minors, but at 25 he could make his MLB debut in 2023. He has the command and stuff to serve as a swingman or middle reliever.

SCOUTING GRADES:	Fastball: 50	Slider: 50	Changeup: 50	Control: 60

Year	Age	Club (League)	Lvl	W	L	ERA	G	GS	IP	H	HR	BB	SO	BB/9	SO/9	WHIP	AVG
2022	24	Rome (SAL)	HiA	9	5	3.44	16	16	89	85	6	17	91	1.7	9.2	1.15	.245
2022	24	Mississippi (SL)	AA	2	4	3.11	9	9	46	46	3	13	55	2.5	10.7	1.27	.258
2022	24	Gwinnett (IL)	AAA	1	0	4.05	1	1	7	5	1	1	7	1.4	9.5	0.90	.200
Minor League Totals				12	11	3.87	30	30	156	155	14	34	173	2.0	10.0	1.21	.255

10 BLAKE BURKHALTER, RHP

Born: September 19, 2000. **B-T:** R-R. **HT:** 6-0. **WT:** 204.
Drafted: Auburn, 2022 (2nd round). **Signed by:** Travis Coleman.
TRACK RECORD: Burkhalter was one of the most effective college relievers in 2022 for Auburn. His 16 saves were second most in the country, and he posted a 3.69 ERA over 46.1 innings while striking out 71 batters (38.6%) and walking just seven (3.8%). The Braves selected him with the 76th overall pick in the supplemental second round and signed him for $650,000. He ramped up later in the year and threw just 4.2 innings in pro ball, but his final appearance was dominant—a three-inning outing on Sept. 11 where he struck out six batters and allowed no hits and no walks.
SCOUTING REPORT: Burkhalter is going to be developed—at least initially—as a starter with the Braves. He didn't start a game in college, but

BA GRADE

45 Risk: **High**

the control he showed in 2022 is more than enough for the role, with loud pure stuff to go with it. He throws a flat-plane fastball in the 93-96 mph range that has touched 98, with the sort of characteristics that should allow him to rack up buckets of whiffs at the top of the zone. He also throws a hard cutter/slider that the Braves are attempting to make a true slider and a mid-80s changeup that looks like a viable third pitch. His slider earns plus grades, while his changeup could be solid-average.
THE FUTURE: Burkhalter will attempt to get acclimated to a starting role during the 2023 season, where attacking with his fastball/slider combination will be prioritized.

SCOUTING GRADES:	Fastball: 60	Slider: 60	Changeup: 50	Control: 50

Year	Age	Club (League)	Lvl	W	L	ERA	G	GS	IP	H	HR	BB	SO	BB/9	SO/9	WHIP	AVG
2022	21	Braves (FCL)	R	0	0	54.00	1	0	0	3	0	1	0	27.0	0.0	12.00	.750
2022	21	Augusta (CAR)	LoA	1	0	0.00	2	1	4	1	0	0	7	0.0	14.5	0.23	.071
Minor League Totals				1	0	3.86	3	1	5	4	0	1	7	1.9	13.5	1.07	.222

11 COLE PHILLIPS, RHP

Born: May 26, 2003. **B-T:** R-R. **HT:** 6-3. **WT:** 200.
Drafted: HS—Boerne, Texas, 2022 (2nd round). **Signed by:** Darin Vaughan.
TRACK RECORD: Phillips was one of the most prominent helium prospects in the 2022 draft class during the spring after he showed increased physicality and velocity that boosted his draft stock into first round territory. That helium deflated a bit after Tommy John surgery ended his season, but the Braves still signed him for $1.5 million in the second round.
SCOUTING REPORT: After pitching in the low 90s during the 2021 summer, Phillips was routinely in the mid 90s and touching upper-90s velocity during the 2022 spring before his injury. That improved power translated to his breaking ball as well—a mid-80s slider with traditional downward, three-quarters bite that was sharp and late, giving him an above-average secondary. Phillips also flashed a firm, mid-to-upper-80s changeup that looks like a serviceable third pitch, though he rarely needed to use it. Phillips still needed to sharpen his command, but his control around the zone was also improved in the spring, and he earned comparisons with Rays righthander Shane Baz thanks to his frame and the shape of his fastball/slider combination. He showed a clean and loose delivery and should have more than enough athleticism and control to begin his pro career as a starter.
THE FUTURE: Phillips spent the offseason rehabbing, but the Braves think he has a chance to start pitching at some point in the second half of the 2023 season.

BA GRADE: 50/Extreme	Fastball: 70	Slider: 55	Changeup: 45	Control: 55

Year	Age	Club (League)	Lvl	W	L	ERA	G	GS	IP	H	HR	BB	SO	BB/9	SO/9	WHIP	AVG
2022	19	Did not play—Injured															

12 SPENCER SCHWELLENBACH, RHP

Born: May 31, 2000. **B-T:** R-R. **HT:** 6-1. **WT:** 200.
Drafted: Nebraska, 2021 (2nd round). **Signed by:** JD French.
TRACK RECORD: Schwellenbach was one of the best two-way prospects in the 2021 draft class and ranked as the No. 51 overall prospect after hitting .284/.403/.459 and playing shortstop for Nebraska. He also showed 99 mph velocity as a reliever. The Braves' scouting staff loved his upside potential as a two-way player and his phenomenal pure arm talent, with relatively little experience

pitching, and signed him for $1 million.

SCOUTING REPORT: Schwellenbach needed Tommy John surgery after the 2021 draft and was still in the recovery process. He hasn't pitched yet in pro ball, leaving scouts to look back on what he did in college and hope he returns as the same player. With Nebraska, he sat 94-95 mph with a fastball that touched 98-99. He had a good feel for a low-80s slider and low-80s changeup as well. Despite being a primary shortstop at the time, Schwellenbach threw all three pitches for strikes 67-68% of the time and scouts viewed each as potentially above-average—while Braves officials think they could be plus. Atlanta initially planned to stretch Schwellenbach out as a starter, where they believe his athleticism, easy operation and three-pitch mix could serve him nicely. There's no reason to think that course has changed just yet.

THE FUTURE: Atlanta expects Swchellenbach to be ready for spring training in 2023, where he'll look to make up for lost time and remove some of the uncertainty from his profile.

BA GRADE: 50/Extreme   **Fastball:** 60   **Slider:** 50   **Changeup:** 50   **Control:** 55

Year	Age	Club (League)	Lvl	W	L	ERA	G	GS	IP	H	HR	BB	SO	BB/9	SO/9	WHIP	AVG
2022	22	Did not play—Injured															

13 BRADEN SHEWMAKE, SS

Born: Nov. 19, 1997. **B-T:** L-R. **HT:** 6-4. **WT:** 190.
Drafted: Texas A&M, 2019 (1st round). **Signed by:** Darin Vaughan.

TRACK RECORD: The Braves signed Shewmake for just over $3 million in the first round of the 2019 draft after three seasons with Texas A&M. He pushed to Double-A in his first pro season in 2019 but has been a below-league average hitter with Double-A Mississippi and Triple-A Gwinnett. In 2022, Shewmake spent the season at the Triple-A level, where he hit .259/.316/.399 with seven home runs.

SCOUTING REPORT: Shewmake has tinkered with his swing throughout his pro career and has solid pure bat-to-ball skills but an approach that has held him back. He expands the zone too frequently and struggled to do damage on velocity 93 mph or higher. Shewmake has below-average power potential. Some scouts are optimistic he has more coming offensively, while others are skeptical of his swing. It's a flat path and that combined with a tendency to drop his hands in his load leads to popped balls and high infield fly rates in each of the last two seasons. Scouts who are higher point to solid top-end exit velocities that could indicate more power on the way. Shewmake has continued to get most of his innings at shortstop, where he remains a solid defender with good instincts and hands, as well as above-average arm strength.

THE FUTURE: Shewmake will need to improve his approach and impact ability to become an everyday player, and currently profiles as a utility infield type.

BA GRADE: 45/High   **Hit:** 45   **Power:** 40   **Speed:** 50   **Fielding:** 50   **Arm:** 55

Year	Age	Club (League)	Lvl	AVG	G	AB	R	H	2B	3B	HR	RBI	BB	SO	SB	OBP	SLG
2022	24	Gwinnett (IL)	AAA	.259	76	278	37	72	14	2	7	25	23	57	9	.316	.399
Minor League Totals				.259	224	849	121	220	46	7	22	105	65	172	26	.316	.408

14 CAL CONLEY, SS/2B

Born: July 17, 1999. **B-T:** B-R. **HT:** 5-10. **WT:** 185.
Drafted: Texas Tech, 2021 (4th round). **Signed by:** Trey McNickle.

TRACK RECORD: The son of former pro player and coach Brian Conley, Cal was signed for $425,000 in the fourth round of the 2021 draft after serving as the spark plug for Texas Tech. He had signed with Miami out of high school, but transferred to Texas Tech before he ever played a game. After a modest pro debut in 2021, Conley improved on both sides of the ball in 2022, where he played at both Class A affiliates and showed impressive on-base ability and speed in the Arizona Fall League.

SCOUTING REPORT: While Conley remains a prospect who impresses more for his collection of his solid tools, grinder mentality and high baseball IQ, scouts in 2022 saw a player with plus speed and above-average defensive potential at shortstop. He has solid actions at the position and is one of the more polished and reliable defensive infielders in Atlanta's system. Offensively, he'll have to rely on plate discipline and speed more than power. While his in-game power production was up significantly year-over-year, Conley has modest exit velocity numbers and below-average raw power. He might have to cut down his chase rate at higher levels to sustain solid offensive production. He showed impressive baserunning ability and went 36-for-44 (82%) in stolen base attempts.

THE FUTURE: The 2022 season was a step forward for Conley, who now has a better chance to provide big league value thanks to his defensive ability. His next test will be proving his bat against upper-minors pitching.

BA GRADE: 45/High		Hit: 45			Power: 30			Speed: 60			Fielding: 55			Arm: 50		

Year	Age	Club (League)	Lvl	AVG	G	AB	R	H	2B	3B	HR	RBI	BB	SO	SB	OBP	SLG
2022	22	Augusta (CAR)	LoA	.246	75	309	62	76	10	6	10	40	25	59	23	.307	.414
2022	22	Rome (SAL)	HiA	.260	44	177	32	46	10	1	6	25	19	50	13	.337	.429
Minor League Totals				.243	154	626	115	152	25	8	18	74	58	142	44	.315	.395

15 JESSE FRANKLIN, OF

Born: Dec. 1, 1998. **B-T:** L-L. **HT:** 6-1. **WT:** 215.
Drafted: Michigan, 2020 (3rd round). **Signed by:** Jeremy Gordon.
TRACK RECORD: A third-round pick in 2020 who signed for $500,000, Franklin impressed in his 2021 debut season with the Braves when he led the system with 24 home runs while playing at High-A Rome. Franklin started the 2022 season at Double-A Mississippi but played just 15 games before his season ended with Tommy John surgery. The surgery adds to a reasonable injury history for Franklin, who also missed the 2020 season at Michigan with a broken collarbone.
SCOUTING REPORT: Franklin has some of the best raw power in Atlanta's system and in his first pro season he showed a tweaked setup and pull-oriented approach that yielded impressive in-game power. His exit velocity numbers were solid in his 15-game sample at Double-A, where he hit .236/.333/.400 before his season ended in late April. Contact could prevent Franklin from being an average hitter in the big leagues, but his swing decisions are solid, and he doesn't expand the zone at a worrying rate. Franklin has played all three outfield positions, though he mostly played right field in 2022. Scouts believe he's more of a corner outfielder who can play center in a pinch—with left field being most likely thanks to fringy arm strength even before his Tommy John surgery.
THE FUTURE: Franklin should be ready early in 2023. He will get another chance to test his bat against upper-level pitching and profiles as a lefty-hitting platoon power bat and fourth outfielder.

BA GRADE: 45/High		Hit: 40			Power: 60			Speed: 50			Fielding: 55			Arm: 40		

Year	Age	Club (League)	Lvl	AVG	G	AB	R	H	2B	3B	HR	RBI	BB	SO	SB	OBP	SLG
2022	23	Mississippi (SL)	AA	.236	15	55	6	13	1	1	2	9	6	18	2	.333	.400
Minor League Totals				.243	116	415	61	101	25	3	26	70	40	133	21	.322	.506

16 VICTOR VODNIK, RHP

Born: Oct. 9, 1999. **B-T:** R-R. **HT:** 6-0. **WT:** 200.
Drafted: HS—Rialto, Calif., 2018 (14th round). **Signed by:** Kevin Martin.
TRACK RECORD: The Braves liked Vodnik's natural arm strength in high school and signed him for $200,000 as a day three pick in the 14th round in 2018. He showed flashes in the lower minors but struggled in 2021 in his first challenge at Double-A, where control and injuries, including a forearm strain and blisters, limited him. He moved to a full-time reliever role in 2022 and had the best pro season of his career, posting a 2.34 ERA between Double-A Mississippi and Triple-A Gwinnett.
SCOUTING REPORT: Vodnik primarily worked with a two-pitch mix in 2022 as a reliever. He throws a plus fastball around 95-96 mph that touched 99 and has earned plus or better grades internally and externally. The pitch comes at hitters with a flat approach angle, though it is a lower-spin fastball with below-average carry and 12.5 inches of induced vertical break. His firm, upper-80s changeup has terrific, plus-plus movement with sink and run and was a bonafide swing-and-miss pitch during the 2022 season (33% whiffs). He will tip the pitch at times with a different arm slot, and he also needs to learn how to throw it more consistently for a strike. Feel for spin has been a challenge for Vodnik dating back to his prep days, but the Braves are working to establish a short slider/cutter for him to have a third pitch that can be thrown for strikes and offer a different look.
THE FUTURE: Vodnik is more stuff-over-pitchability and how his command improves will determine whether he becomes a high-leverage reliever or not.

BA GRADE: 40/High		Fastball: 65			Slider: 35			Changeup: 60			Control: 40		

Year	Age	Club (League)	Lvl	W	L	ERA	G	GS	IP	H	HR	BB	SO	BB/9	SO/9	WHIP	AVG
2022	22	Mississippi (SL)	AA	0	0	0.00	7	0	7	4	0	3	14	3.9	18.0	1.00	.160
2022	22	Gwinnett (IL)	AAA	2	0	2.93	24	0	28	26	2	16	33	5.2	10.7	1.52	.252
Minor League Totals				5	8	3.59	69	14	140	125	9	66	166	4.2	10.6	1.36	.239

17 IGNACIO ALVAREZ, 3B/SS

Born: April 11, 2003. **B-T:** R-R. **HT:** 6-0. **WT:** 190.
Drafted: Riverside (Calif.) JC, 2022 (5th round). **Signed by:** Ryan Dobson.

TRACK RECORD: Alvarez helped lead Riverside (Calif.) JC to a state championship in 2022, while hitting .370/.494/.582 with five home runs and establishing himself as one of the top junior college players in the draft class. Amateur scouts were split on him, with some believing he was a top 10 rounds talent and others believing he didn't have a carrying tool for pro ball. The Braves were one of the former clubs and signed "Nacho" for $500,000 in the fifth round.

SCOUTING REPORT: Alvarez displayed his strike-zone discipline in junior college by walking 36 times compared to 16 strikeouts, and that keen batting eye translated to the pro game during his debut season as well. His chase rate was among the lowest of any Braves hitter, and he walked at a 21% clip compared to a 12% strikeout rate in 30 games between the Florida Complex League and Low-A Augusta. Alvarez has pure bat-to-ball skills and a high contact rate, with above-average raw power, though he still needs to learn how to elevate more frequently to tap into that power consistently in game. Some Atlanta officials compare him with Vaughn Grissom offensively, though his defensive game is better at the same age at all three infield positions. Alvarez could be an above-average third baseman with above-average arm strength and he also played 10 games at shortstop in his pro debut.

THE FUTURE: Alvarez's well-rounded tool set and excellent makeup and work ethic make him one of the more interesting sleepers in the lower levels of Atlanta's system.

| BA GRADE: 45/Extreme | | Hit: 50 | | Power: 50 | | Speed: 45 | | Fielding: 55 | | Arm: 55 | |

Year	Age	Club (League)	Lvl	AVG	G	AB	R	H	2B	3B	HR	RBI	BB	SO	SB	OBP	SLG
2022	19	Braves (FCL)	R	.279	15	43	11	12	1	1	1	5	7	6	4	.392	.419
2022	19	Augusta (CAR)	LoA	.294	15	51	14	15	2	1	0	6	19	9	4	.493	.373
Minor League Totals				.287	30	94	25	27	3	2	1	11	26	15	8	.451	.394

18 BROOKS WILSON, RHP

Born: March 15, 1996. **B-T:** L-R. **HT:** 6-2. **WT:** 205.
Drafted: Stetson, 2018 (7th round). **Signed by:** Justin Clark.

TRACK RECORD: Wilson was a two-way player at Stetson and signed for $80,000 as a seventh-round senior sign with the Braves in 2018. Wilson's minor league career has been superb. He has posted a 2.24 ERA over 165 total innings, with the bulk of that work coming out of the bullpen. The Braves placed him on the 40-man roster following the 2021 season. His 2022 season was cut short before it began thanks to Tommy John surgery.

SCOUTING REPORT: Wilson found success with a three-pitch mix that featured a four-seam fastball with solid carry, a devastating split-changeup and a get-me-over curveball in the upper 70s. In 2021, Wilson sat in the 92-94 mph range and touched 96, but his fastball featured plus riding life with nearly 19 inches of induced vertical break. His low-80s split-change was his go-to secondary and his best bat-misser, generating whiffs over 50% of the time. The pitch falls out of the bottom of the zone, has around 10 mph separation from his fastball and an 18–19-inch gap in IVB. Wilson's split-change was the primary reason he set a career-high strikeout rate in the upper minors in 2021. His curveball is more of a below-average offering he can land in the strike zone as a change-of-pace pitch.

THE FUTURE: Wilson likely would've gotten a chance to make his MLB debut in 2022 if he was healthy. The Braves have been impressed with his work ethic throughout the rehab process. He profiles as a multi-inning or low-leverage reliever if he comes back with the same stuff.

| BA GRADE: 45/Extreme | | Fastball: 50 | | Curveball: 40 | Changeup: 60 | | Control: 50 | |

Year	Age	Club (League)	Lvl	W	L	ERA	G	GS	IP	H	HR	BB	SO	BB/9	SO/9	WHIP	AVG
2022	26	Did not play—Injured															

19 ADAM MAIER, RHP

Born: Nov. 26, 2001. **B-T:** R-R. **HT:** 6-0. **WT:** 203.
Drafted: Oregon, 2022 (7th round). **Signed by:** Cody Martin.

TRACK RECORD: Maier was one of the most heavily anticipated college pitchers in the 2022 class after a stellar 25.2 innings in the Cape Cod League in 2021. He transferred from British Columbia to Oregon for the 2022 season and stepped into the team's Friday night role but threw just 15.2 innings before his season ended with an elbow injury. Maier didn't have Tommy John surgery; instead, he had a brace surgery to stabilize his ulnar collateral ligament and the Braves signed him for $1.2 million in the seventh round.

SCOUTING REPORT: As his price tag likely suggests, Maier flashed exciting pure stuff when healthy. He generated almost a 70% groundball rate with a sinking, low-90s fastball that touched 97 mph at peak, and he has a pair of secondaries that have plus potential. The first is a high-spin slider in the low 80s that gets to 2,900 rpm and both misses bats and generates weak, groundball contact. The second is a mid-80s changeup with impressive run and tumbling action that he did a nice job keeping at the bottom of the zone. Maier's stuff could play up thanks to a lower-than-average release point and he has been a solid strike-thrower in his admittedly brief college career—just 34.2 total innings between British Columbia, the Cape and Oregon.

THE FUTURE: Given the timeline of Maier's injury, he has a chance to start his pro career early in 2023. As a Canadian-born player who began college early, he will be in just his age-21 season.

BA GRADE: 45/Extreme	Fastball: 50	Slider: 55	Changeup: 55	Control: 50

Year	Age	Club (League)	Lvl	W	L	ERA	G	GS	IP	H	HR	BB	SO	BB/9	SO/9	WHIP	AVG
2022	20	Did not play—Injured															

20 DRAKE BALDWIN, C

Born: March 28, 2001. **B-T:** L-R. **HT:** 6-1. **WT:** 210.
Drafted: Missouri State, 2022 (3rd round). **Signed by:** JD French.

TRACK RECORD: Baldwin ranked as the No. 7 college catcher and No. 143 draft prospect in the 2022 class after a 19-homer season with Missouri State and a long track record as a strong on-base percentage player. The Braves made him their first hitter selected in the 2022 class when they signed him for $633,300 in the third round.

SCOUTING REPORT: Baldwin has an athletic background as a multi-sport athlete who was also a standout hockey player during high school in Wisconsin. He turned into a bat-first catching prospect with Missouri State, where he showed strong swing decisions throughout the course of his college career, with power showing up during his 2022 junior campaign. Baldwin derives his power from strength more than bat speed, but he posted impressive exit velocities (89.3 average) during his pro debut, and continued to show a patient and selective approach at the plate, with most of his games coming at Low-A Augusta. Baldwin earned fringy grades for his defensive ability behind the plate in college, but the Braves are high on his aptitude at the position and believe he will do enough to stick at the position. Amateur scouts thought he had adequate hands, with average arm strength and blocking ability that needed more consistency.

THE FUTURE: Baldwin will look to be another catcher who exceeds his amateur defensive evaluations, a la the Twins' Ryan Jeffers or the Mariners' Cal Raleigh, while bringing a strong lefthanded bat to the plate.

BA GRADE: 40/High	Hit: 45	Power: 50	Speed: 30	Fielding: 45	Arm: 50

Year	Age	Club (League)	Lvl	AVG	G	AB	R	H	2B	3B	HR	RBI	BB	SO	SB	OBP	SLG
2022	21	Braves (FCL)	R	.375	3	8	2	3	2	0	0	3	1	3	0	.400	.625
2022	21	Augusta (CAR)	LoA	.247	21	81	13	20	3	0	0	6	18	22	1	.396	.284
Minor League Totals				.258	24	89	15	23	5	0	0	9	19	25	1	.396	.315

21 AMBIORVIS TAVAREZ, SS

Born: Nov. 12, 2003. **B-T:** R-R. **HT:** 6-0. **WT:** 168.
Signed: Dominican Republic, 2021. **Signed by:** Jonathan Cruz/Luis Santos.

TRACK RECORD: Tavarez was the centerpiece of the Braves' 2021 international class, and the first prominent international prospect the organization signed since its international sanctions. Atlanta signed the power-hitting shortstop for $1.5 million. He made his pro debut in 2022 but played just 17 games in the Florida Complex League.

SCOUTING REPORT: Tavarez was praised for his raw power and bat speed as an amateur, and his 88.5 mph average exit velocity was one of the system's best at the Rookie level. While his power is encouraging, Tavarez needs plenty of refinement as a hitter. He struck out 28 times compared to just three walks, and his 40% whiff rate was one of the highest in the system. He employs a large leg kick to start his swing and brings the barrel through the zone with plenty of speed and force. Tavarez played all his innings in the field at shortstop, where he impressed Braves officials with his defensive actions and arm strength. He's been called a no-doubt shortstop in 2022, which is a significant uptick from his previous defensive evaluations, where scouts thought he might fit best at third base or corner outfield, where an easy plus arm would fit nicely. Atlanta currently views him as the organization's best defensive shortstop and best infield arm.

THE FUTURE: Tavarez likely would have reached Low-A Augusta in 2022 if it weren't for his injury. He'll likely play at the Low-A level in 2023, where he'll need to log more at-bats and continue improving his offensive approach.

BA GRADE: 45/Extreme		Hit: 40		Power: 55		Speed: 50			Fielding: 60			Arm: 60	

Year	Age	Club (League	Lvl	AVG	G	AB	R	H	2B	3B	HR	RBI	BB	SO	SB	OBP	SLG
2022	18	Braves (FCL)	R	.277	17	65	12	18	4	0	1	8	3	28	3	.304	.385
Minor League Totals				.277	17	65	12	18	4	0	1	8	3	28	3	.304	.385

22 LUIS DE AVILA, LHP

Born: May 29, 2001. **B-T:** L-L. **HT:** 5-9. **WT:** 215.
Signed: Colombia, 2017. **Signed by:** Rafael Miranda (Royals).

TRACK RECORD: Originally signed by the Rockies out of Colombia for $250,000, De Avila has already played for three organizations before turning 22 or reaching Double-A. The Rockies released him following the 2019 season, and the Royals signed him about a month later. The Braves selected De Avila in the minor league phase of Rule 5 draft in 2021 based on solid strike throwing for a 20-year-old.

SCOUTING REPORT: Atlanta immediately converted De Avila to a starting role after he pitched in the bullpen for the Royals' Low-A affiliate in 2021. He posted a 3.49 ERA over 126.1 innings at High-A Rome—good for his best pro season in his age-21 season. De Avila is not a power-oriented pitcher. He throws a three-pitch mix that features a two-seam fastball, curveball and changeup. Some days he will throw his fastball around 93-94 mph, but others it will be more 90-91. Overall, he averaged 91 mph and peaked at 95 during the 2022 season. His curveball is around 80 mph and his changeup checks in around the mid 80s, though scouts describe both pitches as just fringy at the moment. His success has mostly come from the fact that he locates both his secondaries well and induced a lot of weak groundball contact with a 61% groundball rate.

THE FUTURE: De Avila has a short and squatty frame without much physical projection left, so his upside is limited barring big steps forward with his curveball and changeup. Being lefthanded and young with feel for a three-pitch mix keeps him alive as an interesting depth starter.

BA GRADE: 40/High		Fastball: 45		Curveball: 45	Changeup: 45		Control: 55				

Year	Age	Club (Leag	Lvl	W	L	ERA	G	GS	IP	H	HR	BB	SO	BB/9	SO/9	WHIP	AVG
2022	21	Rome (SAL)	HiA	6	8	3.49	24	24	126	115	11	45	129	3.2	9.2	1.27	.241
Minor League Totals				13	14	4.28	59	31	215	219	17	81	220	3.4	9.2	1.40	.262

23 GERALDO QUINTERO, 3B/2B

Born: October 10, 2001. **B-T:** B-R. **HT:** 5-8. **WT:** 155.
Signed: Venezuela, 2019. **Signed by:** Chris Roque.

TRACK RECORD: Quintero signed with the Braves out of Venezuela in 2019 and made his U.S. debut in 2021, when he struggled to a .207/.312/.273 slash line in 40 games in the Florida Complex League. The 2022 season was a better showing for the 20-year-old infielder, who started showing flashes offensively, while playing multiple infield positions.

SCOUTING REPORT: Listed at 5-foot-8, 155 pounds, Quintero is a small grinder type who began making more contact and showing a solid offensive approach at Low-A Augusta. Quintero has above-average bat-to-ball skills, but his power is below-average, and he doesn't look like the sort of player who will grow into much more in the future. A switch-hitter, Quintero hit for better average, got on base more and showed more power from the left side in 2022, though his offensive value will be driven by contact and speed more than impact. He was second in Atlanta's system with 34 stolen bases and is a plus runner. Defensively, some scouts think Quintero could be an above-average shortstop, but he played third base and second base in 2022 in deference to Cal Conley, and most evaluators think he is a good enough defender at enough positions to provide super utility value.

THE FUTURE: Quintero will struggle to profile as an everyday player without showing more power, though his speed, contact ability and defensive versatility could give him major league value in a reserve role with continued improvement.

| BA GRADE: 40/High | | Hit: 40 | | Power: 30 | | Speed: 60 | | Fielding: 55 | | Arm: 50 | |

Year	Age	Club (League)	Lvl	AVG	G	AB	R	H	2B	3B	HR	RBI	BB	SO	SB	OBP	SLG
2022	20	Augusta (CAR)	LoA	.262	91	362	61	95	22	9	6	47	48	69	26	.358	.423
2022	20	Rome (SAL)	HiA	.238	22	80	12	19	4	0	2	12	10	22	8	.347	.363
Minor League Totals				.251	211	760	131	191	38	15	10	87	105	145	67	.355	.380

24 RODDERY MUNOZ, RHP

Born: April 14, 2000. **B-T:** R-R. **HT:** 6-2. **WT:** 210.
Signed: Dominican Republic, 2018. **Signed by:** Jonathan Cruz.
TRACK RECORD: Munoz signed with the Braves out of the Dominican Republic in 2018, then spent his first two years in the Dominican Summer League as a teenager. After the Covid pandemic, Munoz came to the U.S. and made his domestic debut with Low-A Augusta where he showed solid stuff in a brief stint. The 2022 season was a strong one for Munoz. He racked up plenty of strikeouts with High-A Rome and was promoted to Double-A Mississippi for three starts at the end of the season.
SCOUTING REPORT: Munoz has a solid, 6-foot-2 frame with a strong lower half and has explosive pure stuff out of a longer arm action that isn't always synced up. Munoz mostly pitched off a loud two-pitch combo: a 95-mph fastball that gets up to 98-99 mph with average carry and a potentially wipeout slider in the 88-91 mph range. His slider is his best pitch currently and had heavy usage during the 2022 season with solid spin in the 2,400-2,500 rpm range with power and bite that led to a 45% whiff rate. It's a plus or better offering now. Munoz has also used a firm changeup in the 89-91 mph range, but it's a distant third pitch that doesn't have enough separation from his fastball—in either velocity or shape.
THE FUTURE: Munoz has pitched well as a starter to this point in his career, but he has the sort of power arm and scattered control that could lead to a better role in the bullpen, where he could scrap his changeup and add more power to his fastball in shorter outings.

| BA GRADE: 40/High | | Fastball: 60 | | Slider: 65 | | Changeup: 30 | | Control: 40 | |

Year	Age	Club (League)	Lvl	W	L	ERA	G	GS	IP	H	HR	BB	SO	BB/9	SO/9	WHIP	AVG
2022	22	Rome (SAL)	HiA	8	4	4.03	19	19	89	85	9	37	105	3.7	10.6	1.37	.244
2022	22	Mississippi (SL)	AA	0	0	9.82	3	3	11	12	3	5	14	4.1	11.5	1.55	.261
Minor League Totals				10	13	4.87	54	42	209	200	17	96	236	4.1	10.2	1.42	.248

25 JUSTIN YEAGER, RHP

Born: January 20, 1998. **B-T:** L-R. **HT:** 6-4. **WT:** 215.
Drafted: Southern Illinois, 2019 (33rd round). **Signed by:** Kevin Barry.
TRACK RECORD: Yeager was a productive reliever with Southern Illinois for three seasons before the Braves signed him in the 33rd round of the 2019 draft for just $140,000. He continued pitching as a reliever in pro ball, generating plenty of strikeouts while dealing with below-average control. That remained the case in 2022, when Yeager pushed to Double-A Mississippi, where he served as a late-inning reliever and managed a 37% strikeout rate that was one of the best in Atlanta's system.
SCOUTING REPORT: Yeager is a reliever all the way, with a high effort and violent delivery that inhibits his control and the consistency of his strikes. But with his arm strength and pure stuff, he could potentially find success without precision. He throws two pitches that grade out as plus: a 95-96 mph four-seam fastball that touches 99 and has great vertical life with 19 inches of induced vertical break and an 87-91 mph hard-breaking slider with short and tight, three-quarters shape. He used the latter to generate nearly a 40% whiff rate, and his fastball is a bat-missing pitch as well thanks to power and shape. To be trusted in any sort of leveraged big league role, Yeager will need to improve his control. He has a 13% career minor league walk rate and didn't seem to take any steps forward in that area in 2022.
THE FUTURE: With plenty of stuff to miss bats, Yeager just needs to put his fastball and slider over the plate more frequently to find himself in a big league bullpen.

| BA GRADE: 40/High | | Fastball: 65 | | Slider: 60 | | Control: 30 | |

Year	Age	Club (League)	Lvl	W	L	ERA	G	GS	IP	H	HR	BB	SO	BB/9	SO/9	WHIP	AVG
2022	24	Rome (SAL)	HiA	0	0	0.75	11	0	12	3	1	9	27	6.8	20.2	1.00	.077
2022	24	Mississippi (SL)	AA	1	0	3.79	38	0	40	26	5	23	54	5.1	12.0	1.21	.181
Minor League Totals				10	5	3.21	94	0	118	81	12	66	178	5.0	13.6	1.25	.188

26 LUKE WADDELL, SS/2B

Born: July 13, 1998. **B-T:** L-R. **HT:** 5-9. **WT:** 180.
Drafted: Georgia Tech, 2021 (5th round). **Signed by:** Chris Lionetti.

TRACK RECORD: Waddell spent four years with Georgia Tech and was draft eligible in three straight years beginning in 2019 before signing with the Braves as a fifth-rounder in 2021. Waddell stood out for his contact ability and zone control skills as an amateur, and after two pro seasons, those remain his calling cards.

SCOUTING REPORT: Waddell has the best pure bat-to-ball ability in Atlanta's system, with a miniscule 13.5% miss rate. He connects with virtually everything in the zone. On top of his excellent hand-eye, Waddell makes good swing decisions and walked more than he struck out for the first time in his pro career in 2022. What holds the middle infielder back is his lack of power. Waddell is mostly a singles hitter who lacks raw power—his 90th percentile exit velocity was 99 mph—and doesn't project to add much in the future. He's a reliable defender at multiple infield positions, with good game awareness and baseball IQ but isn't the sort of player who will threaten to win Gold Gloves.

THE FUTURE: Waddell's season ended in late May due to injury, but he'll look to get more upper-level time in 2023 and could be an emergency infielder who will grind out at-bats at the plate if necessary.

| BA GRADE: 40/High | | Hit: 50 | | Power: 30 | | Speed: 40 | | Fielding: 50 | | Arm: 50 | |

Year	Age	Club (League)	Lvl	AVG	G	AB	R	H	2B	3B	HR	RBI	BB	SO	SB	OBP	SLG
2022	23	Mississippi (SL)	AA	.272	41	162	20	44	10	0	2	29	23	22	3	.364	.370
Minor League Totals				.267	70	262	38	70	11	0	8	44	32	39	5	.349	.401

27 DAVID MCCABE, 1B/3B

Born: March 25, 2000. **B-T:** B-R. **HT:** 6-4. **WT:** 230.
Drafted: UNC Charlotte, 2022 (4th round). **Signed by:** Billy Best.

TRACK RECORD: McCabe signed with the Braves as a fourth-rounder in 2022 for $476,400. He dealt with plenty of injuries throughout college that limited his playing time, but when he was on the field, he always hit well and in 2022 finished the season with more extra-base hits (29) than strikeouts (28). McCabe struggled in his pro debut and slashed .245/.336/.330, mostly with Low-A Augusta.

SCOUTING REPORT: McCabe is a physically imposing switch-hitter with a big frame and huge raw power to go with it. Internal evaluators have put double-plus raw power on McCabe, and amateur scouts thought his power production was much better from the left side. McCabe produced more offense batting lefty in his pro debut but didn't produce much impact. McCabe has a solid understanding of the strike zone and will take his walks when necessary while also making contact at a solid clip. Mostly a first baseman in college, the Braves played McCabe at third base in 2022 and he has a huge arm that would be more than enough for the position. However, his size, agility and glovework might end up pushing him back to first.

THE FUTURE: McCabe has big tools with his arm strength and raw power, but he faces a high offensive bar to clear and will look to hit for more game-power in a full 2023 season.

| BA GRADE: 40/High | | Hit: 40 | | Power: 55 | | Speed: 30 | | Fielding: 40 | | Arm: 65 | |

Year	Age	Club (League)	Lvl	AVG	G	AB	R	H	2B	3B	HR	RBI	BB	SO	SB	OBP	SLG
2022	22	Braves (FCL)	R	.000	2	6	1	0	0	0	0	0	1	0	0	.143	.000
2022	22	Augusta (CAR)	LoA	.260	26	100	14	26	6	0	1	23	15	27	0	.347	.350
Minor League Totals				.245	28	106	15	26	6	0	1	23	16	27	0	.336	.330

28 KADON MORTON, OF

Born: November 19, 2000. **B-T:** R-R. **HT:** 6-2. **WT:** 195.
Drafted: HS—Seguin, Texas, 2019 (19th round). **Signed by:** Darin Vaughan.

TRACK RECORD: Morton was a standout athlete in the 2019 draft class, with upside as a pitcher who threw a low-90s fastball and as a hitter with raw power. The Braves bought into his upside and signed him for $500,000 in the 19th round, and he's now one of the best defensive outfielders in the system.

SCOUTING REPORT: Morton's offensive game hasn't quite kept pace with his defense. He's a career .207/.322/.351 hitter in the lower minors and has consistently struggled to make enough contact. There is raw power in his lean frame, with solid exit velocity numbers to back it up, but he hasn't yet been able to find the barrel enough to access it. Morton struck out at a 33.5% clip between Low-A Augusta and High-A Rome, and he has never gotten his strikeout rate below 30% in any season.

Morton draws walks, but he is often too passive or simply doesn't have much of a plan at the plate. Defensively, Morton resembles BJ Upton in center field with above-average defensive ability and one of the best arms in the system. He could also fit in right field.

THE FUTURE: It would be easier to be optimistic about Morton if he were younger, but he'll enter his age-22 season in 2023 and has yet to be tested at Double-A. If he can find a way to make more contact, he has interesting power, speed and defensive tools.

BA GRADE: 45/Extreme		Hit: 30			Power: 40		Speed: 55			Fielding: 60		Arm: 60	

Year	Age	Club (League)	Lvl	AVG	G	AB	R	H	2B	3B	HR	RBI	BB	SO	SB	OBP	SLG
2022	21	Augusta (CAR)	LoA	.227	107	352	57	80	11	4	12	47	56	139	12	.341	.384
2022	21	Rome (SAL)	HiA	.188	5	16	1	3	0	0	1	4	1	6	0	.235	.375
Minor League Totals				.207	189	615	95	127	26	9	15	77	94	252	27	.322	.351

29 MAHKI BACKSTROM, OF

Born: October 10, 2001. **B-T:** L-L. **HT:** 6-5. **WT:** 220.
Drafted: HS—Gardena, Calif., 2019 (18th round). **Signed by:** Kevin Martin.
TRACK RECORD: One of the youngest players in the 2019 draft, Backstrom had impressive bat speed and raw power but lacked refinement in all phases of the game. The Braves signed him for $400,000 in the 18th round, and in three years he's struggled to make contact but shown impressive impact.
SCOUTING REPORT: Backstrom is a large and physical, lefthanded-hitting first baseman listed at 6-foot-5, 220 pounds. The power that comes from that build is Backstrom's calling card, and he can boast some of the best raw power in the minor leagues, evidenced by a near 110 mph 90th percentile exit velocity mark that was the best in Atlanta's system in 2022. His contact ability is at the opposite end of the spectrum with his 45.9% whiff rate among the worst for Braves minor leaguers. He has a career 37.5% strikeout rate in Rookie ball and Low-A. Backstrom still managed to be an above-average hitter with a 117 wRC+ with Augusta, thanks to a 17% walk rate and solid eye. He provides little value defensively and on the bases, with a first base-only profile and well below-average speed.
THE FUTURE: Backstrom has eye-popping power potential, but it's hard to see him finding a way to access that power against upper-level arms without significantly improving his bat-to-ball skills.

BA GRADE: 45/Extreme		Hit: 25			Power: 60		Speed: 30		·	Fielding: 40		Arm: 50	

Year	Age	Club (League)	Lvl	AVG	G	AB	R	H	2B	3B	HR	RBI	BB	SO	SB	OBP	SLG
2022	20	Augusta (CAR)	LoA	.205	79	263	48	54	15	5	10	48	56	124	8	.355	.414
Minor League Totals				.211	143	455	75	96	25	7	15	68	90	207	10	.348	.396

30 AUSTIN SMITH, RHP

Born: June 22, 1999. **B-T:** R-R. **HT:** 6-3. **WT:** 210.
Drafted: Arizona, 2021 (18th round). **Signed by:** Ted Lekas.
TRACK RECORD: Smith was a standout starter for Division III Southwestern (Texas), but after transferring to Arizona his struggles with control limited him in a split starter/reliever role. The Braves took a chance on him and signed him for $80,000 in the 18th round in 2021. Smith closed games for High-A Rome in 2022 and showed swing-and-miss stuff in the Arizona Fall League after the season.
SCOUTING REPORT: Smith has a solid pitching frame at 6-foot-3, 210 pounds, but he's a straight reliever who pitches with a high-effort, violent delivery that features plenty of head whack and recoil. He pitches with a fastball and slider, and both offerings have plus potential. His fastball sits in the 94-95 mph range and touches 97, with solid riding life. His slider is a firm, upper-80s breaking ball that features tight and hard sweeping shape at the bottom of the zone and generated whiffs more than 35% of the time in 2022. His stuff is good enough to miss bats, and he has pitched to nearly a 30% strikeout rate overall with Low-A Augusta and High-A Rome in two seasons. That remained the case against AFL hitters when he struck out 14 of the 47 batters he faced.
THE FUTURE: Smith improved his walk rate from 14.7% in 2021 to 8.7% in 2022 and will need to sustain that sort of control moving forward to get a shot in a big league bullpen.

BA GRADE: 35/High		Fastball: 55		Slider: 60		Control: 35	

Year	Age	Club (Leag	Lvl	W	L	ERA	G	GS	IP	H	HR	BB	SO	BB/9	SO/9	WHIP	AVG
2022	23	Rome (SAL)	HiA	2	3	4.62	45	0	49	38	4	18	61	3.3	11.3	1.15	.209
Minor League Totals				2	3	4.61	51	0	57	43	5	23	71	3.7	11.3	1.16	.204

Baltimore Orioles

BY JON MEOLI

The Orioles entered 2022 with one of the league's lowest payrolls and traded two top bullpen pieces away on the eve of Opening Day, so it goes without saying that their 31-win improvement from 2021 to 2022 and resulting winning season came as a surprise both inside and outside the organization.

The team was more competitive on the mound early, particularly with their bullpen full of second-chancers and some improved starting pitchers, but the arrival of top prospect Adley Rutschman was clearly a turning point. Baltimore went 67-55 after his May 21 callup, an 89-win pace.

It was thought to be a year in which Rutschman would be one of several top prospects to graduate. In reality, progress on that front was slower. Righthander Kyle Bradish, acquired after the 2019 season for Dylan Bundy, broke into the rotation early but took until the last two months of the year to truly take off. Gunnar Henderson took over top prospect status from Rutschman both in the organization and in the game and debuted in August. The 21-year-old was Minor League Player of the Year and is poised for a regular MLB role in 2023.

But the Orioles got only one start from their top pitching prospects Grayson Rodriguez and DL Hall, with Rodriguez never making the big leagues thanks to a midseason lat strain and Hall starting once before moving to the bullpen to manage his innings.

Baltimore's turnaround and the convergence of two waves of top prospects in the high minors has created an enviable talent collection at the top of their farm system, and the club owes that to its success in the early rounds of the draft. Rutschman, Henderson and Kyle Stowers—the first three picks in 2019, the first under executive vice president Mike Elias—made the majors this year.

Their first-day picks in ensuing drafts, including Jordan Westburg in 2020, Colton Cowser and Connor Norby in 2021, and top pick Jackson Holliday plus 33rd overall pick Dylan Beavers in 2022, make for a collection of hitting potential on the farm few clubs can match, and the organization's challenging hitting practices have made that group and countless others better since signing.

Outside Rodriguez and Hall, the Orioles' pitching program lacks star power. There's always been a plan in place to target specific pitch mixes and traits, specifically later in the draft and in trades, and develop them in a way the organization knows it can.

That's meant longer development lead time overall, but effective, modern-day pitchers with

The Orioles played at an 89-win pace with Adley Rutschman in tow—and better days are ahead.

PROJECTED 2026 LINEUP

Catcher	Adley Rutschman	28
First Base	Ryan Mountcastle	29
Second Base	Jordan Westburg	27
Third Base	Gunnar Henderson	25
Shortstop	Jackson Holliday	22
Left Field	Cedric Mullins	31
Center Field	Colton Cowser	26
Right Field	Kyle Stowers	28
Designated Hitter	Coby Mayo	24
No. 1 Starter	Grayson Rodriguez	26
No. 2 Starter	John Means	33
No. 3 Starter	DL Hall	27
No. 4 Starter	Kyle Bradish	29
No. 5 Starter	Dean Kremer	30
Closer	Felix Bautista	31

hoppy fastballs and sweepy sliders are pitching well in the high minors.

Those hitter-heavy drafts, a focus on developing a specific kind of pitcher, and tens of millions of dollars invested internationally under Elias has created a prospect base deep enough to both develop stars for the major league team and trade players away to help improve in that avenue.

While the Orioles had not swung any major trades as of mid December, that appears to be the next step for the club as it looks to take the next step toward competing for an American League playoff spot. The foundation for Baltimore's next contender has already been built from strong drafts and effective player development plans. ■

BALTIMORE ORIOLES

TOP 2023 MLB CONTRIBUTORS	RANK
Gunnar Henderson, SS	1
Grayson Rodriguez, RHP	2
DL Hall, LHP	5
BREAKOUT PROSPECTS	**RANK**
Dylan Beavers, OF	11
Samuel Basallo, C	13
Jud Fabian, OF	18

SOURCE OF TOP 30 TALENT

Homegrown	26	Acquired	4
College	14	Trade	4
Junior college	0	Rule 5 draft	0
High school	7	Independent league	0
Nondrafted free agent	1	Free agent/waivers	0
International	4		

LF
Hudson Haskin (26)
John Rhodes (27)

CF
Colton Cowser (4)
Dylan Beavers (11)
Jud Fabian (14)
Braylin Tavera

RF
Kyle Stowers (9)
Heston Kjerstad (12)

3B
Coby Mayo (10)
Max Wagner (20)
Cesar Prieto (25)
Anderson De Los Santos (30)

SS
Gunnar Henderson (1)
Jackson Holliday (3)
Jordan Westburg (6)
Joey Ortiz (8)
Darell Hernaiz (18)
Frederick Bencosme (29)
Maikol Hernandez
Carter Young

2B
Terrin Vavra (17)
Greg Cullen

1B
Andrew Daschbach
TT Bowens

C
Samuel Basallo (15)
Silas Ardoin

LHP

LHSP	LHRP
DL Hall (5)	Nick Vespi
Cade Povich (13)	Easton Lucas
Drew Rom (24)	
Antonio Velez	
Alexander Wells	
Zac Lowther	

RHP

RHSP	RHRP
Grayson Rodriguez (2)	Logan Gillaspie
Seth Johnson (16)	Kade Strowd
Mike Baumann (19)	Xavier Moore
Justin Armbruester (21)	
Noah Denoyer (22)	
Chayce McDermott (23)	
Carlos Tavera (28)	
Carter Baumler	
Ryan Watson	
Chris Vallimont	
Garrett Stallings	
Jean Pinto	
Ignacio Feliz	

1 GUNNAR HENDERSON, SS

Born: June 29, 2001. **B-T:** L-R. **HT:** 6-3. **WT:** 195.
Drafted: HS—Selma, Ala., 2019 (2nd round).
Signed by: David Jennings.

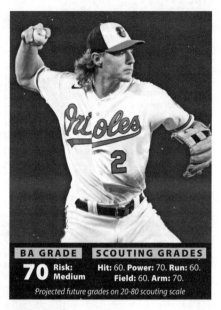

TRACK RECORD: When the pandemic shut down minor league baseball in 2020, the Orioles worried high school hitters like Henderson—whom they signed for an over-slot $2.3 million as the 42nd overall pick in 2019—would be most impacted by the loss of development time. Instead, Henderson flourished. Two years after being the youngest player at Baltimore's alternate training site and exposed to the challenging and, at times, overwhelming Orioles hitting practices, Henderson forced his MLB debut at 21 years old. The Orioles wouldn't have thought Henderson would be in the majors by September when they didn't invite him to big league camp in 2022, but he walked more than he struck out (41 to 38) with a 1.025 OPS in two months at Double-A Bowie before continuing to produce at Triple-A Norfolk, becoming the top prospect in baseball and earning Baseball America's Minor League Player of the Year honors.

SCOUTING REPORT: The talent to put together such a season has always been within Henderson. His offseason work meant it came faster than the team expected. He added a little rhythm to his swing to get himself moving early, flattened out his bat path to be able to combat riding fastballs up in the zone, and most importantly improved his plate discipline in his return to Double-A Bowie in 2022. He showed immediate gains with swing decisions and contact rates. Henderson's swing has always been a powerful one, and him growing into his body over the last year made it more so. His strength and explosiveness allow him to get away with having a smaller move—where he doesn't need to generate much momentum to produce all-fields power—and his approach allows him to stay up the middle consistently. Henderson was exposed to plenty of outer-half spin in 2022 as pitchers tried to avoid the heart of the plate against him. That gave him plenty of looks at one of the few areas where he's continuing to search for solutions. Otherwise, his plus hit tool and plus-plus power showed up in the majors. Henderson had a 92.4 mph average exit velocity and a 53.7% hard-hit rate—ranking 17th and seventh, respectively, among big leaguers with at least 50 plate appearances. Defensively, Henderson hasn't outgrown shortstop and has the potential to be at least above-average there with elite capabilities at

third base thanks to his plus-plus arm and range. He's a plus runner as well and impressed the big league staff with his speed on his callup late in the season. Henderson is an intensely driven player who constantly seeks improvement.

THE FUTURE: Henderson reaching the majors this quickly and succeeding in the manner he has puts his career on a steep upward trajectory. The Orioles believe he can be an MVP-caliber player. Even if doesn't reach those heights, he has a solid path to being a a cornerstone in the Orioles turnaround.

BA GRADE	SCOUTING GRADES
70 Risk: Medium	Hit: 60. Power: 70. Run: 60. Field: 60. Arm: 70.

Projected future grades on 20-80 scouting scale

BEST TOOLS

BATTING

Best Hitter for Average	Gunnar Henderson
Best Power Hitter	Gunnar Henderson
Best Strike-Zone Discipline	Jackson Holliday
Fastest Baserunner	Luis Valdez
Best Athlete	Jordan Westburg

PITCHING

Best Fastball	DL Hall
Best Curveball	DL Hall
Best Slider	Grayson Rodriguez
Best Changeup	Grayson Rodriguez
Best Control	Grayson Rodriguez

FIELDING

Best Defensive Catcher	Silas Ardoin
Best Defensive Infielder	Joey Ortiz
Best Infield Arm	Gunnar Henderson
Best Defensive Outfielder	Jud Fabian
Best Outfield Arm	Kyle Stowers

Year	Age	Club (League)	Lvl	AVG	G	AB	R	H	2B	3B	HR	RBI	BB	SO	SB	OBP	SLG
2022	21	Bowie (EL)	AA	.312	47	157	41	49	11	3	8	35	41	38	12	.452	.573
2022	21	Norfolk (IL)	AAA	.288	65	250	60	72	13	4	11	41	38	78	10	.390	.504
2022	21	Baltimore (AL)	MLB	.259	34	116	12	30	7	1	4	18	16	34	1	.348	.440
Major League Totals				.259	34	116	12	30	7	1	4	18	16	34	1	.348	.440
Minor League Totals				.276	246	914	190	252	57	13	37	161	146	287	40	.378	.488

2 GRAYSON RODRIGUEZ, RHP

Born: Nov. 16, 1999. **B-T:** L-R. **HT:** 6-5. **WT:** 220.
Drafted: HS—Nacogdoches, Texas, 2018 (1st round). **Signed by:** Thom Dreier.

TRACK RECORD: Rodriguez, a pop-up prospect signed for $4.3 million as the 11th pick in the 2018 draft, has done nothing but dominate since joining the Orioles. He shared the organization's pitcher of the year honors in 2019, won it on his own in 2021 and was on the cusp of an MLB debut as the May Triple-A International League pitcher of the month before a lat strain in early June kept him out for two months. He returned to the mound in September but wasn't summoned to the majors before the season ended.

SCOUTING REPORT: Rodriguez's stuff remained similar to that which made him the game's top pitching prospect entering the season. His fastball sat 95-99 mph and topped out at 100 with above-average hop, and he showed the ability to spot it in every part of the strike zone. He executed his development

BA GRADE

70 Risk: High

goal of achieving more consistent top-end spin in 2022, because in past years the consistency of his pitch action could waver. His plus-plus slider remains his top secondary pitch, sitting 79-85 mph with late bite, and he uses different shapes depending on the situation. Rodriguez's changeup, a pitch he learned in pro ball, is a plus pitch as well, with screwball-like action that works to both sides of the plate. His curveball has above-average potential, and Rodriguez ramped up usage of his new low-90s cutter as the season went on, especially against lefthanded hitters. His lat injury was his first major setback, but Rodriguez otherwise has the makings of a physical, innings-eating workhorse with a durable, repeatable delivery.

THE FUTURE: Rodriguez has top-of-the-rotation potential and a midrotation floor based on his stuff and mentality. The Orioles expect him to compete for a major league rotation job in spring training.

SCOUTING GRADES:	Fastball: 70	Curveball: 55	Slider: 70	Changeup: 60	Control: 65

Year	Age	Club (League)	Lvl	W	L	ERA	G	GS	IP	H	HR	BB	SO	BB/9	SO/9	WHIP	AVG
2022	22	Aberdeen (SAL)	HiA	0	0	0.00	1	1	1	1	0	2	1	13.5	6.8	2.25	.250
2022	22	Bowie (EL)	AA	0	1	9.64	2	2	5	2	0	5	11	9.6	21.2	1.50	.125
2022	22	Norfolk (IL)	AAA	6	1	2.20	14	14	70	44	2	21	97	2.7	12.5	0.93	.178
Minor League Totals				25	9	2.47	69	68	292	179	16	98	419	3.0	12.9	0.95	.173

3 JACKSON HOLLIDAY, SS

Born: Dec. 4, 2003. **B-T:** L-R. **HT:** 6-1. **WT:** 175.
Drafted: HS—Stillwater, Okla., 2022 (1st round). **Signed by:** Ken Guthrie.

TRACK RECORD: The son of MLB all-star Matt Holliday was drafted first overall by the Orioles in 2022. Holliday took classes from home the winter of his senior year of high school to work on adding strength and further refining his picturesque lefthanded swing, and he elevated himself to the top of the draft by doing so. He broke JT Realmuto's national high school hits record in the process and was recognized as BA High School Player of the Year. Holliday signed for $8.19 million—a record for a high school player—and had an impressive pro debut. He walked 25 times against 12 strikeouts, primarily in full-season ball.

BA GRADE

65 Risk: Extreme

SCOUTING REPORT: Holliday's draft-year improvement only made what could be an elite offensive future even clearer. He has a smooth, fluid swing that doesn't require maximum effort to create maximum bat speed, with good body awareness to make him adjustable and keep the barrel through the zone well. Holliday already boasts advanced strike-zone discipline, and the continued physical development his frame suggests is imminent could give him above-average power to go along with his potential plus hit tool. He handled velocity well in his pro debut, but the Orioles want him to continue overcoming expected challenges with velocity and advanced pitch shapes as he climbs the minors. Holliday is a true shortstop with all the skills and instincts to play the position at a plus level, with a plus arm and plus speed as well.

THE FUTURE: If Holliday ends up being the Orioles' last high first-round pick in a while, they'll be glad to have his all-star potential in the organization. He has the talent, mindset and work ethic to get there, and could be back in Low-A Delmarva to begin the 2023 season.

SCOUTING GRADES	Hitting: 60	Power: 55	Speed: 60	Fielding: 60	Arm: 60

Year	Age	Club (League)	Lvl	AVG	G	AB	R	H	2B	3B	HR	RBI	BB	SO	SB	OBP	SLG
2022	18	Orioles (FCL)	R	.409	8	22	6	9	1	0	1	3	10	2	3	.576	.591
2022	18	Delmarva (CAR)	LoA	.238	12	42	8	10	4	0	0	6	15	10	1	.439	.333
Minor League Totals				.297	20	64	14	19	5	0	1	9	25	12	4	.489	.422

4 COLTON COWSER, OF

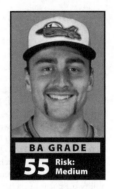

Born: March 20, 2000. **B-T:** L-R. **HT:** 6-3. **WT:** 195.
Drafted: Sam Houston State, 2021 (1st round). **Signed by:** Thom Dreier.

TRACK RECORD: The Orioles believed Cowser to be the best hitter in the 2021 draft, even if signing him for a below-slot $4.9 million as the fifth overall pick skewed that impression. Cowser backed that up in his first full season in 2022, overcoming some early challenges at High-A Aberdeen before taking off and dominating Double-A Bowie with a 1.037 OPS in 49 games there. He was one of a handful of 2021 draftees to reach Triple-A.

SCOUTING REPORT: Cowser's special bat-to-ball skills showed up as he climbed through the minors. His potential plus hit tool impressed the Orioles with the amount of line drives and hard contact he produced even as there was a bit more in-zone whiff than they expected. Cowser's preferred opposite-field approach came into conflict with the team's damage-oriented swing decision mantra at times, but Cowser got better at tapping into his pull-side pop as the season went on, showing at least above-average power potential. His offensive path seems unsettled, though. There's a belief that he can both maintain a gap-based, on-base strategy at the top of a lineup or gear his approach toward more power and succeed at either. Cowser might not be more than an average center fielder, but he can handle the position well thanks to his smooth motions and range as an above-average runner. He could be above-average in a corner spot, with at least an above-average arm.

THE FUTURE: Cowser could become a solid-average regular, though his advanced bat could make him a first-division starter with continued refinement. He will return to Triple-A to begin 2023, with the hopes of playing himself into a major league debut.

BA GRADE

55 Risk: Medium

SCOUTING GRADES	Hitting: 60	Power: 55	Speed: 55	Fielding: 50	Arm: 55

Year	Age	Club (League)	Lvl	AVG	G	AB	R	H	2B	3B	HR	RBI	BB	SO	SB	OBP	SLG
2022	22	Aberdeen (SAL)	HiA	.258	62	229	42	59	19	2	4	22	45	79	16	.385	.410
2022	22	Bowie (EL)	AA	.341	49	176	49	60	10	0	10	33	36	57	2	.469	.568
2022	22	Norfolk (IL)	AAA	.219	27	105	23	23	7	0	5	11	13	38	0	.339	.429
Minor League Totals				.297	170	630	144	187	44	2	21	100	119	197	25	.422	.473

5 DL HALL, LHP

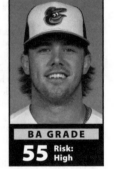

Born: Sept. 19, 1998. **B-T:** L-L. **HT:** 6-0. **WT:** 180.
Drafted: HS—Valdosta, Ga., 2017 (1st round). **Signed by:** Arthur McConnehead.

TRACK RECORD: Hall was one of the best prep lefthanders in the 2017 class and signed with the Orioles for $3 million to begin a pro career that has often tantalized and finally included an MLB debut in 2022. He made just seven starts in 2021 due to a stress reaction in his elbow and was eased back onto the mound in 2022 by the Orioles. Hall continued to show flashes of dominance—36% strikeout rate in Triple-A—but also control issues as he walked 14% of the batters he faced. The Orioles gave him a start for his MLB debut in August, then moved him to the bullpen to control his innings.

SCOUTING REPORT: Few lefthanders can match Hall's raw stuff. His four-seam fastball sits in the mid-to-upper 90s and has touched 100 mph with above-average hop. His 85-89 mph slider features bat-missing sweep and is his best secondary pitch, though his mid-80s changeup plays extremely well off his fastball and has plus potential. So does his curveball, a slower offering in the high 70s and low 80s. Hall's extension in the big leagues was exceptional, which makes his one shortfall—repeating his delivery and consistently commanding around the strike zone—a point of concern. But with his fastball velocity, extension and pitch mix, Hall only needs his pitches to look like strikes out of his hand to force bad swings.

THE FUTURE: Hall has a No. 2 starter ceiling, but a high-leverage relief role is more likely at this point in his career. The Orioles will continue to develop him as a starter, with a realistic midrotation goal.

BA GRADE

55 Risk: High

SCOUTING GRADES:	Fastball: 80	Curveball: 60	Slider: 70	Changeup: 60	Control: 40

Year	Age	Club (League)	Lvl	W	L	ERA	G	GS	IP	H	HR	BB	SO	BB/9	SO/9	WHIP	AVG
2022	23	Aberdeen (SAL)	HiA	0	0	0.00	1	1	4	2	0	0	6	0.0	13.5	0.50	.154
2022	23	Bowie (EL)	AA	0	1	4.91	1	1	4	3	0	1	6	2.5	14.7	1.09	.214
2022	23	Norfolk (IL)	AAA	3	7	4.70	22	18	77	62	10	49	125	5.8	14.7	1.45	.212
2022	23	Baltimore (AL)	MLB	1	1	5.93	11	1	14	17	0	6	19	4.0	12.5	1.68	.298
Major League Totals				1	1	5.93	11	1	14	17	0	6	19	4.0	12.5	1.68	.298
Minor League Totals				11	20	3.40	77	69	301	214	24	172	421	5.1	12.6	1.28	.198

6 JORDAN WESTBURG, SS/3B

Born: Feb. 18, 1999. **B-T:** R-R **HT:** 6-3. **WT:** 200.
Drafted: Mississippi State, 2020 (1st round supplemental). **Signed by:** David Jennings.

BA GRADE
50 Risk: Medium

TRACK RECORD: Westburg went 30th overall in the 2020 draft and signed for $2.37 million on the belief that his improved performance in the summer and abbreviated spring before his draft year was legitimate. Nothing he's done as a pro has made the Orioles question that. Westburg climbed to Double-A in 2021, his first full pro season, and spent most of 2022 at Triple-A Norfolk. His 69 extra-base hits were fifth-most in the minors, and Westburg's continued improvement earned him the organization's Brooks Robinson minor league player of the year award.
SCOUTING REPORT: Recognizing Westburg for his improvement the way the Orioles did only highlights all his skills. He doesn't have a plus tool but has spent his career maximizing what he has. Westburg has become more aggressive in all counts as he has matured, and he used the team's challenging practice to address deficiencies with hoppy fastballs up in the zone and sliders away. At every level, he's adjusted back to the league and gone on to excel. Westburg has a clean, simple swing that still generates plenty of bat speed and could allow him to be an average hitter with above-average power thanks to his ability to pull the ball and drive it to the opposite-field gap. Consistency in his at-bat quality has been an issue, leading to two prolonged slumps in 2022. Westburg is an above-average runner who can play shortstop but may be stretched to be average there, with above-average potential at second base. He plays third base, too.
THE FUTURE: Westburg's versatility may be key to his future in what's shaping up to be a loaded Orioles infield. His ability to play up the middle and potentially hit for power make him a future solid-average regular, and he'll compete for a major league job in spring training.

SCOUTING GRADES	Hitting: 50	Power: 55	Speed: 55	Fielding: 55	Arm: 50

Year	Age	Club (League)	Lvl	AVG	G	AB	R	H	2B	3B	HR	RBI	BB	SO	SB	OBP	SLG
2022	23	Bowie (EL)	AA	.247	47	182	32	45	14	0	9	32	26	57	3	.344	.473
2022	23	Norfolk (IL)	AAA	.273	91	362	64	99	25	3	18	74	44	90	9	.361	.508
Minor League Totals				.274	250	968	170	265	66	8	42	185	131	274	29	.371	.489

7 CONNOR NORBY, 2B

Born: June 8, 2000. **B-T:** R-R **HT:** 5-10. **WT:** 190.
Drafted: East Carolina, 2021 (2nd round). **Signed by:** Quincy Boyd.

BA GRADE
55 Risk: High

TRACK RECORD: Norby was a first-team All-America selection for East Carolina in 2021 as he led Division I with 102 hits and impressed against top-level starters in the NCAA Tournament. The Orioles drafted him in the second round at No. 41 overall and signed him for $1.7 million—slightly below slot. He began 2022 at High-A Aberdeen and saw a significant burst in production in the second half, hitting 21 home runs in the high minors for an organization-leading 29 and ending the year at Triple-A Norfolk.
SCOUTING REPORT: Norby's breakout came as he found comfortable lower-body patterning by recommitting to a toe-tap he abandoned in the winter and moving his hands to allow him to be less vertical through the hitting areas and better combat sliders away and fastballs up. The adjustments allowed Norby to take off. His extreme feel for hitting and high-level ability to execute his plan continued to put him in good positions to do damage, as did his acceptable strike-zone control. Norby showed the capabilities of an above-average hitter with potentially above-average power, with his ability to drive the ball the other way and overall consistency in elevating hard contact key factors in that. Defensively, Norby is limited to second base or maybe left field due to a fringe-average arm.
THE FUTURE: Bat-first second basemen are tricky propositions, but Norby's offensive profile is one that is increasingly hard to doubt at this point. He can hit enough to be a first-division regular. He will start at Triple-A Norfolk in 2023 with an eye toward pushing for a major league debut.

SCOUTING GRADES	Hitting: 55	Power: 55	Speed: 50	Fielding: 50	Arm: 45

Year	Age	Club (League)	Lvl	AVG	G	AB	R	H	2B	3B	HR	RBI	BB	SO	SB	OBP	SLG
2022	22	Aberdeen (SAL)	HiA	.237	48	186	27	44	7	2	8	20	18	50	6	.311	.425
2022	22	Bowie (EL)	AA	.298	64	252	58	75	14	2	17	46	34	59	10	.389	.571
2022	22	Norfolk (IL)	AAA	.359	9	39	7	14	2	0	4	7	3	5	0	.405	.718
Minor League Totals				.276	154	598	112	165	29	5	32	92	77	149	22	.364	.502

8 JOEY ORTIZ, SS/2B

Born: July 14, 1998. **B-T:** R-R. **HT:** 5-11. **WT:** 175.
Drafted: New Mexico State, 2019 (4th round). **Signed by:** John Gillette.

TRACK RECORD: Drafted out of the friendly offensive environment of New Mexico State, Ortiz was an early second-day pick in 2019 mostly because of his elite traits at shortstop. The pandemic allowed him to address his offensive shortcomings. He added nearly 30 pounds to his frame and leveraged his swing toward elevated contact. His breakout was cut short in 2021 due to a torn left labrum that required surgery, and he struggled in the first half of 2022 before a breakout that brought him to Triple-A Norfolk. From July 1 to the end of the season, Ortiz hit .352/.416/.610 and led the minor leagues with 101 hits, 68 runs and 175 total bases.

BA GRADE

50 Risk: High

SCOUTING REPORT: Ortiz always boasted exceptional contact ability—he only whiffed 7.4% of the time in 2022, best in the organization—but the quality of contact wavered early in the year as he struggled to come back from his lead shoulder injury. By adjusting his hand placement to allow him to get to a better launch position and focusing more on the areas where he can drive the ball as opposed to just making contact, Ortiz started producing elite exit velocities. His adjustments and improvements raised his offensive capabilities to potentially an above-average hitter with average power. He drives the ball well to all fields but could improve his pull-side power. Considering he is a true shortstop with plus capabilities at the position thanks to his range, play-making ability and arm, that makes for quite an intriguing tool set.

THE FUTURE: Ortiz's defensive versatility and ability to play shortstop give him a utility floor, but his offensive progress makes an everyday role likely if he can sustain it. Ortiz likely needs more time at Triple-A before a major league debut, but not much time if he continues hitting.

SCOUTING GRADES	Hitting: 55	Power: 50	Speed: 50	Fielding: 60	Arm: 55

Year	Age	Club (League	Lvl	AVG	G	AB	R	H	2B	3B	HR	RBI	BB	SO	SB	OBP	SLG
2022	23	Bowie (EL)	AA	.269	111	435	69	117	28	4	15	71	41	81	2	.337	.455
2022	23	Norfolk (IL)	AAA	.346	26	104	22	36	7	2	4	14	9	17	6	.400	.567
Minor League Totals				.271	228	870	139	236	46	8	24	119	96	167	14	.349	.425

9 KYLE STOWERS, OF

Born: Jan. 2, 1998. **B-T:** L-L. **HT:** 6-3. **WT:** 200.
Drafted: Stanford, 2019 (2nd round supplemental). **Signed by:** Scott Walter.

TRACK RECORD: Stowers spent his college career searching for a balance of contact and power, and the Orioles believed in his potential for both. He used the 2020 shutdown to get stronger and hit a system-high 27 home runs in his first full minor league season in 2021. Stowers spent most of 2022 at Triple-A Norfolk, where he cut down his strikeout rate while hitting for consistent power. He was in the big leagues for good by mid August.

SCOUTING REPORT: Part of Stowers' year-over-year improvement came down to him flattening his swing a bit to help him defend against velocity at the top of the zone, and otherwise being adjustable to hit offspeed pitches as higher-level pitchers grew wary of giving him anything in his red zones. The resulting

BA GRADE

45 Risk: Medium

season featured lower whiff rates, showing he was able to meet his goals without losing power. Stowers' power will always be his calling card as an easy plus and potentially better tool thanks to his aggressive, naturally lofted swing. He was challenged when it came to whiffs and strikeouts in the majors, but that would be enough along with continued plate discipline gains to help him access his power. Stowers' power is imperative to his future, because he can be a fringe-average center fielder but is better suited for a corner outfield spot, where he can potentially be solid-average with a plus arm and above-average speed.

THE FUTURE: Stowers' power potential and all the drawbacks that come with it make him a high-ceiling proposition, but his progress makes it possible he becomes a first-division regular.

SCOUTING GRADES	Hitting: 40	Power: 65	Speed: 55	Fielding: 50	Arm: 60

Year	Age	Club (League)	Lvl	AVG	G	AB	R	H	2B	3B	HR	RBI	BB	SO	SB	OBP	SLG
2022	24	Norfolk (IL)	AAA	.264	95	349	54	92	29	3	19	78	45	104	3	.357	.527
2022	24	Baltimore (AL)	MLB	.253	34	91	11	23	4	1	3	11	5	29	0	.306	.418
Major League Totals				.253	34	91	11	23	4	1	3	11	5	29	0	.306	.418
Minor League Totals				.260	274	1002	146	261	65	5	52	186	138	328	16	.356	.491

10 COBY MAYO, 3B

Born: Dec. 10, 2001. **B-T:** R-R. **HT:** 6-5. **WT:** 215.
Drafted: HS—Parkland, Fla., 2020 (4th round). **Signed by:** Brandon Verley.

BA GRADE

50 Risk: High

TRACK RECORD: Mayo was the first of two significantly over-slot high school draftees for the Orioles from the 2020 draft. He signed for $1.75 million in the fourth round thanks to his impressive raw power. As a professional, Mayo has been assigned aggressively and reached Double-A Bowie at 20 years old. Back spasms forced him to miss some time upon arriving there, but he finished well after a slow start and his expected stats paint a more optimistic picture of his season than his actual ones.

SCOUTING REPORT: Mayo's carrying tool is his plus-plus raw power, and his ability to turn on inside pitches while driving balls over the heart of the plate gives him significant in-game power potential. Upper-minors pitchers exposed his issues with outer-third channeling and spin away, but the Orioles feel another offseason of adding strength can help Mayo control his body and the moving parts of his aggressive swing better to be more adjustable to those pitches and cover more of the plate. He might only be an average hitter and needs to control his bat path to keep the ball elevated to maximize the contact he does make. If he does so, his game power can flourish. Defensively, Mayo's peers may save the Orioles from having to make a call on him staying at third base. He could be fringe-average there and has a plus arm that fits at the position, but the expectation that the 6-foot-5 third baseman gets bigger could make him better suited for first base or a corner outfield spot.

THE FUTURE: This is a big winter for Mayo, who with the right training and adjustments could break out on his way to becoming a first-division regular.

SCOUTING GRADES	Hitting: 50	Power: 60	Speed: 45	Fielding: 45	Arm: 60

Year	Age	Club (League)	Lvl	AVG	G	AB	R	H	2B	3B	HR	RBI	BB	SO	SB	OBP	SLG
2022	20	Orioles (FCL)	R	.000	2	5	1	0	0	0	0	0	1	2	0	.167	.000
2022	20	Aberdeen (SAL)	HiA	.251	68	255	50	64	16	2	14	49	27	62	5	.326	.494
2022	20	Bowie (EL)	AA	.250	34	128	21	32	4	0	5	20	12	50	0	.331	.398
Minor League Totals				.270	157	570	118	154	34	3	28	110	69	154	16	.359	.488

11 DYLAN BEAVERS, OF

Born: Aug. 11, 2001. **B-T:** L-R. **HT:** 6-4. **WT:** 205.
Drafted: California, 2022 (1st round supplemental). **Signed by:** Scott Walter.

TRACK RECORD: Beavers was a two-way player coming to California, but was rewarded for his commitment to hitting by a pair of first-team all-Pacific-12 Conference honors and a spot on USA Baseball's Collegiate National Team in 2021. His power potential, toolset and Pac-12 performance meant many teams had first-round grades on Beavers, but issues with his swing dropped him to No. 33 overall where the Orioles signed him for slightly below slot at $2.2 million.

SCOUTING REPORT: Their hitting department was on-board with taking Beavers and working with him to get his bat on a better and less steep path through the zone, and so was the player. Quick alterations including his hand placement and torso angle after signing allowed Beavers to lower his in-zone whiff rate and make more contact from college to pro ball. Beavers is a quick-twitch athlete who has taken to instruction well, but still has several aspects of his swing overhaul ahead of him and will be undertaking those as he deals with consistent velocity and challenging pitch shapes in pro ball. Even moderate swing improvements can make him a fringe-average hitter with plus power, though there's way more upside here. He's a plus runner who is even quicker underway and has a plus arm, with the potential to adequately handle either center or right in the majors.

THE FUTURE: Beavers landed in a perfect program for his developmental needs, but has a long road to his first-division everyday role. Most of that relies on his swing changes, and early returns show it's possible. He'll begin his first full season at High-A Aberdeen.

BA GRADE: 55/Extreme	Hit: 45	Power: 60	Speed: 60	Fielding: 50	Arm: 60

Year	Age	Club (League)	Lvl	AVG	G	AB	R	H	2B	3B	HR	RBI	BB	SO	SB	OBP	SLG
2022	20	Orioles (FCL)	R	.111	3	9	1	1	1	0	0	0	2	2	0	.333	.222
2022	20	Delmarva (CAR)	LoA	.359	16	64	13	23	7	2	0	13	12	11	6	.468	.531
2022	20	Aberdeen (SAL)	HiA	.286	4	14	0	4	0	0	0	2	2	5	0	.375	.286
Minor League Totals				.322	23	87	14	28	8	2	0	15	16	18	6	.438	.460

12 HESTON KJERSTAD, OF

Born: Feb. 12, 1999. **B-T:** L-R. **HT:** 6-3. **WT:** 205.
Drafted: Arkansas, 2020 (1st round). **Signed by:** Ken Guthrie.
TRACK RECORD: Kjerstad was considered the best lefthanded power bat in the shortened 2020 draft when the Orioles took him second overall and signed him to a below-slot $5.2 million bonus. Shortly after signing, he was diagnosed with myocarditis and missed all of 2021. A spring training hamstring injury delayed his pro debut until June, and he dominated Low-A Delmarva before finishing at High-A Aberdeen.
SCOUTING REPORT: His layoff obviously impacted his development. Kjerstad makes a lot of quality contact with a unique swing that features an aggressive leg-lift, but issues with his approach have led to elevated strikeout numbers due to chase. The Orioles believe consistent game action can help him improve that, with exposure to high-level pitching a priority in Kjerstad's development. The club also believes Kjerstad will continue to regain the strength he lost from his time away to recapture his power stroke as time goes on. Kjerstad will be limited to a corner outfield spot due to his range, but has at least an above-average arm that will play in right field. Considering power was meant to be his carrying tool, maximizing that through swing decisions and physical development will determine his major league future.
THE FUTURE: The Orioles view his return to action in 2022 a success on its own, and acknowledge the challenge Kjerstad's time away from the game has presented. His ceiling remains that of a bat-first slugging outfielder on a winning team, but Kjerstad's pending introduction to the high minors in 2023 will show how realistic reaching that will be.

BA GRADE: 50/Very high		Hit: 45		Power: 55		Speed: 45		Fielding: 50		Arm: 55							
Year	Age	Club (League)	Lvl	AVG	G	AB	R	H	2B	3B	HR	RBI	BB	SO	SB	OBP	SLG
2022	23	Delmarva (CAR)	LoA	.463	22	80	17	37	9	0	2	17	13	17	0	.551	.650
2022	23	Aberdeen (SAL)	HiA	.233	43	163	28	38	8	2	3	20	16	47	1	.312	.362
Minor League Totals				.309	65	243	45	75	17	2	5	37	29	64	1	.394	.457

13 CADE POVICH, LHP

Born: April 12, 2020. **B-T:** L-L. **HT:** 6-3. **WT:** 185.
Drafted: Nebraska, 2021 (3rd round). **Signed by:** Joe Bisenius (Twins).
TRACK RECORD: Povich made the kind of gains teams hope for when drafting pitchability lefties in his first pro season, as he went from consistently sitting in the high 80s to comfortably pitching in the low 90s and topping out at 97 mph. The Twins unlocked some of his potential in his full-season debut, then traded him as part of a four-pitcher package to bring back Orioles closer Jorge Lopez at the deadline. Povich finished the season at Double-A Bowie.
SCOUTING REPORT: His ability to fill up the strike zone with an impressive pitch mix was evident from early on in his time with the Orioles. The fastball has riding life and late bore, making it hard for hitters to square up, perhaps because they have so many other pitches to consider. Povich features a 1-7 curveball that sits in the mid-70s with big shape; it's used interchangeably with his sweepy slider—a low-80s plus sweeper that plays to hitters on both sides of the plate. Both pitches can drive swings and misses, as well as chases. Povich re-introduced his high-80s cutter after the trade with immediate success. His average changeup gives him another look against righthanded-heavy lineups.
THE FUTURE: The diversity of his pitch mix as well as his ability to throw strikes makes Povich an effective starting candidate provided he sustains the gains he made on his fastball. The Orioles will likely have him back at Bowie to begin 2023 in an effort to get him to the big leagues in the rotation quickly.

BA GRADE: 50/Very high		Fastball: 50		Curveball: 55		Slider: 60		Changeup: 50		Cutter: 45		Control: 55					
Year	Age	Club (League)	Lvl	W	L	ERA	G	GS	IP	H	HR	BB	SO	BB/9	SO/9	WHIP	AVG
2022	22	Aberdeen (SAL)	HiA	2	0	0.00	2	2	12	4	0	2	15	1.5	11.2	0.50	.103
2022	22	Cedar Rapids (MWL)	HiA	6	8	4.46	16	16	79	71	9	26	107	3.0	12.2	1.23	.234
2022	22	Bowie (EL)	AA	2	2	6.94	6	5	23	21	5	11	26	4.2	10.0	1.37	.231
Minor League Totals				10	10	4.21	28	26	124	103	14	41	167	3.0	12.1	1.16	.219

14 JUD FABIAN, OF

Born: Sept. 27, 2000. **B-T:** R-L. **HT:** 6-1. **WT:** 195.
Drafted: Florida, 2022 (2nd round supplemental). **Signed by:** Eric Robinson.
TRACK RECORD: Fabian entered 2021 as a potential top pick candidate but struggled to make contact, forcing him out of the first round. The Orioles were connected to him for an above-slot deal in the second round, and when Boston took him one pick ahead of Baltimore and didn't meet his bonus demands,

Fabian returned to Florida for his senior season to play with his younger brother Deric. Fabian cut down on his strikeouts in 2022 and ultimately ended up with the Orioles anyway, signing for slot at $1.03 million.

SCOUTING REPORT: As a pro, he destroyed Low-A Delmarva thanks to his ability to recognize spin and pound fastballs, and High-A Aberdeen in September proved a more appropriate challenge. Overall, however, the Orioles saw an exciting skillset that features at least plus power, an advanced approach at the plate, and the potential for plus defense in center field. Fabian was among the organizational leaders with 41.8% of his batted balls above 95 mph. While the Orioles appreciate how he managed his strikeouts and continued to slug in college, they understand that will be part of his game thanks to some natural swing-and-miss that they believe is manageable. He made immediate gains in terms of formulating plans at the plate, and showed he can cover the high fastball well in his pro debut, with the next step being defending against righthanded spin.

THE FUTURE: If Fabian can make enough contact to be a fringe-average hitter, his power and defensive tools can support an everyday role on a winning club. He'll likely start his first full season back at Aberdeen, but could move quickly.

BA GRADE: 50/Very high	Hit: 45	Power: 60	Speed: 60	Fielding: 60	Arm: 50

Year	Age	Club (League)	Lvl	AVG	G	AB	R	H	2B	3B	HR	RBI	BB	SO	SB	OBP	SLG
2022	21	Orioles (FCL)	R	.500	4	10	2	5	1	0	0	3	6	4	1	.647	.600
2022	21	Delmarva (CAR)	LoA	.386	10	44	16	17	7	2	3	9	8	9	0	.481	.841
2022	21	Aberdeen (SAL)	HiA	.167	8	24	1	4	1	0	0	4	5	8	0	.300	.208
Minor League Totals				.333	22	78	19	26	9	2	3	16	19	21	1	.455	.615

15 SAMUEL BASALLO, C

Born: Aug. 13, 2004. **B-T:** L-R. **HT:** 6-3. **WT:** 180.
Signed: Dominican Republic, 2021 **Signed by:** Micheal Cruz/Geraldo Cabrera.

TRACK RECORD: The Orioles' renewed commitment to Latin America in recent years meant Basallo, their top signee in January 2021, signed for a club-record $1.3 million bonus. Basallo hit a team-high five home runs in the Dominican Summer League in 2021, then played most of the Florida Complex League season at age 17 and tied for the league lead with six home runs.

SCOUTING REPORT: At this stage in Basallo's pro career, the potential for plus-plus power is real. While he might only be a fringe-average hitter and maintains a high chase rate, he dealt with being pitched tough better as the season went on and hit a third of his balls in play over 95 mph during the FCL season. He also kept his strikeout rate manageable and walked at a decent clip, leading the Orioles to believe he can continue to manage that aspect of his game and keep the slugging ability accessible by bringing pitchers into his damage zones. Basallo signed with a plus arm and despite being big for his age showed improved flexibility and movement behind the plate that keeps the position in play for him long-term.

THE FUTURE: As long as he's catching, Basallo's profile is an attractive one with middle-of-the-lineup slugging potential at a premium position. His bat makes it so he could still be valuable at first base or a corner outfield spot, too. He'll likely make his affiliated debut at age-18 at Low-A Delmarva in 2023.

BA GRADE: 50/Extreme	Hit: 45	Power: 60	Speed: 40	Fielding: 50	Arm: 60

Year	Age	Club (League)	Lvl	AVG	G	AB	R	H	2B	3B	HR	RBI	BB	SO	SB	OBP	SLG
2022	17	Orioles (FCL)	R	.278	43	158	22	44	5	0	6	32	15	37	1	.350	.424
Minor League Totals				.260	84	292	40	76	13	0	11	51	34	69	2	.344	.418

16 SETH JOHNSON, RHP

Born: Sept. 19, 1998. **B-T:** R-R. **HT:** 6-1. **WT:** 200.
Drafted: Campbell, 2019 (1st round supplemental). **Signed by:** Joe Hastings (Rays).

TRACK RECORD: Johnson was as a shortstop at Louisburg (N.C.) JC but showed impressive aptitude once he converted to the mound and pitched his way up draft boards in his one season at Campbell. The Rays selected him 40th overall in 2019 and traded him to the Orioles as part of a three-team deal that sent Trey Mancini to Houston and outfielder Jose Siri to Tampa Bay. Johnson had an elbow injury that required Tommy John surgery at the time of the trade, which made such a talented arm available at the deadline.

SCOUTING REPORT: Before his injury, Johnson boasted the kind of hoppy fastball the Orioles favor, one that regularly sat in the mid-90s and topped out at 98 mph. He generated that velocity from an easy, effortless delivery. His slider was at least a plus pitch with tight, late break, and he also boasts a slower curveball and developing changeup. Johnson showed an ability to miss bats with that arsenal, with a 17.7% swinging-strike rate helping him strike out 13.7 batters per nine innings in seven starts for High-A

Bowling Green without an elevated walk rate.

THE FUTURE: The injury, however, means Johnson likely won't pitch a meaningful amount until 2024. The Orioles added Johnson to the 40-man roster in November to protect him from the Rule 5 draft, and hope he recovers quickly enough to warrant the long-term roster spot. It stands to reason he will, however, considering Johnson's stuff comfortably profiles to the back half of a major league rotation with the potential to otherwise end up in a high-leverage relief role should he come back healthy.

| BA GRADE: 50/Extreme | | Fastball: 60 | | Curveball: 45 | | Slider: 60 | | Changeup: 45 | | Control: 50 | |

Year	Age	Club (League)	Lvl	W	L	ERA	G	GS	IP	H	HR	BB	SO	BB/9	SO/9	WHIP	AVG
2022	23	Bowling Green (SAL)	HiA	1	1	3.00	7	7	27	23	4	11	41	3.7	13.7	1.26	.232
Minor League Totals				7	8	2.81	39	32	138	126	11	47	172	3.1	11.2	1.26	.243

17 TERRIN VAVRA, 2B

Born: May 12, 1997. **B-T:** L-R. **HT:** 6-1. **WT:** 185.
Drafted: Minnesota, 2018 (3rd round). **Signed by:** Brett Baldwin (Rockies).
TRACK RECORD: All three of former Twins hitting coach Joe Vavra's sons played professional baseball, but the youngest, Terrin, was the first to make the majors. The 2019 South Atlantic League MVP in 2019 with the Rockies' affiliate in Asheville, Vavra came to the Orioles in the 2020 trade for reliever Mychal Givens and made his major league debut in July 2022.
SCOUTING REPORT: Vavra has always been a productive minor leaguer thanks to his advanced bat-to-ball skills and strike zone control, but the Orioles believe he made significant strides in both the amount of contact he made and the quality of that contact in the minors in advance of his debut. Vavra has shown the ability to handle high-end velocity and now consistently makes high-quality contact, spraying line drives all over the field. He can be an above-average hitter with fringe-average power at the highest level. He played second base and left field in the big leagues, and might only be average at both spots, but he can provide cover all over the infield and outfield to keep his unique skill set in the lineup.
THE FUTURE: As long as Vavra continues to embrace his offensive profile, he can be a borderline regular who provides a platoon advantage and plays all over the field for a winning team. The Orioles could give him a chance to play every day at second base in 2023.

| BA GRADE: 40/Medium | | Hit: 55 | | Power: 45 | | Speed: 55 | | Fielding: 50 | | Arm: 45 | |

Year	Age	Club (League)	Lvl	AVG	G	AB	R	H	2B	3B	HR	RBI	BB	SO	SB	OBP	SLG
2022	25	Aberdeen (SAL)	HiA	.188	5	16	5	3	0	0	1	4	3	1	.333	.375
2022	25	Norfolk (IL)	AAA	.324	45	173	34	56	14	1	2	18	28	36	5	.435	.451
2022	25	Baltimore (AL)	MLB	.258	40	89	14	23	2	1	1	12	12	19	0	.340	.337
Major League Totals				.258	40	89	14	23	2	1	1	12	12	19	0	.340	.337
Minor League Totals				.305	244	910	174	278	69	8	21	118	154	189	40	.410	.468

18 DARELL HERNAIZ, SS

Born: Aug. 3, 2001. **B-T:** R-R. **HT:** 6-1. **WT:** 170.
Drafted: HS—El Paso, Texas, 2019 (5th round). **Signed by:** John Gillette.
TRACK RECORD: Young hitters like Hernaiz, who signed for $400,000 in 2019, were among Orioles general manager Mike Elias' chief concerns from a developmental standpoint during the canceled 2020 season. Hernaiz's uneven path through the low minors showed why as he needed to repeat Low-A Delmarva in 2022. He went back to dominate the level, and performed well at High-A Aberdeen as well, meaning he finished the year at age-21 at Double-A Bowie.
SCOUTING REPORT: After learning to be more consistent in his preparation and getting a feel for full-season baseball in 2021, Hernaiz was better able to show his strong contact skills and line-drive approach that could make him an average hitter with at best average power by better controlling the zone. Hernaiz hit the ball harder with more consistency without losing any of his contact ability at the lower levels. He finds the sweet spot consistently. However, exposure to Double-A pitching where secondaries are better commanded proved challenging for Hernaiz, especially when it came to swing decisions. Defensively, Hernaiz has the athleticism and actions to play shortstop but the arm to play third and the overall ability to handle second base as well if he's pushed off shortstop. He's also one of the organization's most instinctive and effective basestealers, swiping 32 bases in 2022 thanks to his plus speed.
THE FUTURE: Hernaiz has the potential to be more than an athletic utility player, something that seems much more reachable after his impressive 2022, and there's upside for him to exceed that outcome if he continues to develop offensively. He'll be back at Bowie to open 2023.

BA GRADE: 45/High		Hit: 50		Power: 45		Speed: 60		Fielding: 55		Arm: 50	

Year	Age	Club (League)	Lvl	AVG	G	AB	R	H	2B	3B	HR	RBI	BB	SO	SB	OBP	SLG
2022	20	Delmarva (CAR)	LoA	.283	32	127	25	36	7	2	6	25	8	22	9	.341	.512
2022	20	Aberdeen (SAL)	HiA	.305	60	226	41	69	13	3	5	29	22	43	22	.376	.456
2022	20	Bowie (EL)	AA	.113	13	53	6	6	1	0	1	8	5	16	1	.186	.189
Minor League Totals				.274	228	877	153	240	35	6	20	122	80	177	59	.341	.396

19 MIKE BAUMANN, RHP

Born: Sept. 10, 1995. **B-T:** R-R. **HT:** 6-4. **WT:** 225.
Drafted: Jacksonville, 2017 (3rd round). **Signed by:** Arthur McConnehead.

TRACK RECORD: The Orioles invested multiple high draft picks on starting pitching candidates in the draft in the last years of the Dan Duquette era. Baumann, signed for $500,000, may be the last hope at one of them panning out in a major league rotation. The 2019 Orioles' minor league pitcher of the year was slowed by an elbow injury in 2020 and took a while to get to his best form in 2021. Baumann started the year riding the Triple-A shuttle between stints in the major league bullpen, but the team recommitted to him starting in the second half and he pitched well in Norfolk in that role.

SCOUTING REPORT: His fastball is still plus as he averaged 96 mph in the big leagues, and started to get swinging strikes on his above-average low-90s slider as the season went on. The Orioles believe his fringe-average curveball may end up as his best secondary pitch as it has elite traits at its best, but Baumann is still learning to be consistent with the pitch and throw it well more often. He also has a fringe-average changeup. In general, that's the prescription for Baumann overall—to continue to find consistency with his delivery to make it more repeatable, and more frequently achieve the top-end spins and directions for his pitches.

THE FUTURE: Even if those gains don't materialize, Baumann still has the stuff to stick in a major league bullpen. However, he's a third pitch away from being able to compete as a back-end starter.

BA GRADE: 40/Medium		Fastball: 60		Curveball: 45		Slider: 55		Changeup: 45		Control: 45	

Year	Age	Club (League)	Lvl	W	L	ERA	G	GS	IP	H	HR	BB	SO	BB/9	SO/9	WHIP	AVG
2022	26	Norfolk (IL)	AAA	2	6	4.20	20	9	60	54	6	25	81	3.8	12.2	1.32	.231
2022	26	Baltimore (AL)	MLB	1	3	4.72	13	4	34	43	3	9	23	2.4	6.0	1.51	.314
Major League Totals				2	4	5.89	17	4	44	56	5	15	28	3.0	5.7	1.60	.311
Minor League Totals				30	22	3.11	97	83	428	318	27	176	443	3.7	9.3	1.16	.205

20 MAX WAGNER, 3B

Born: Aug. 19, 2001. **B-T:** R-R. **HT:** 6-0. **WT:** 215.
Drafted: Clemson, 2022 (2nd round). **Signed by:** Quincy Boyd.

TRACK RECORD: Wagner saw limited action as a freshman at Clemson and wasn't even projected to be a starter as a sophomore. He hit his way into their third base job early, and finished as the ACC Player of the Year with the nation's second-highest slugging percentage (.852) and tied for third in the country with 27 home runs. The Orioles took him 42nd overall as a draft-eligible sophomore and signed him for $1.9 million. He finished his season in the playoffs with High-A Aberdeen.

SCOUTING REPORT: The club believed at draft time that Wagner had consistently strong at-bats to help get to his power, which they believe can be above-average to pair a potential average hit tool. He drove the ball consistently to all fields in college, and found that more challenging to do against higher-level pitching in pro ball. The expectation is Wagner is fundamentally sound enough to identify and get his barrel on pitches he can drive, even if his limited college experience might mean it takes time. Wagner is a physical player with an above-average arm and actions at third base, with no reason to move him from there or obvious alternatives if that was required.

THE FUTURE: Wagner will need to slug the way he did at Clemson to justify an everyday role in the big leagues, but a fringe-average starter or bench role seems realistic at this early stage. He'll start back at Aberdeen in 2023.

BA GRADE: 45/High		Hit: 45		Power: 50		Speed: 40		Fielding: 50		Arm: 55	

Year	Age	Club (League)	Lvl	AVG	G	AB	R	H	2B	3B	HR	RBI	BB	SO	SB	OBP	SLG
2022	20	Orioles (FCL)	R	.500	1	4	0	2	1	0	0	2	0	0	1	.500	.750
2022	20	Delmarva (CAR)	LoA	.250	13	48	9	12	2	2	1	8	9	13	0	.403	.438
2022	20	Aberdeen (SAL)	HiA	.167	5	18	3	3	0	0	0	1	0	5	1	.158	.167
Minor League Totals				.243	19	70	12	17	3	2	1	11	9	18	2	.353	.386

21 JUSTIN ARMBRUESTER, RHP

Born: Oct. 21, 1998. **B-T:** R-R. **HT:** 6-4. **WT:** 235.
Drafted: New Mexico, 2021 (12th round). **Signed by:** Logan Schuemann.
TRACK RECORD: Armbruester has the unique distinction of two different conference pitcher of the year awards on his collegiate resume—he won that honor in the Northwest Conference for Division III Pacific Lutheran in 2019, then transferred to New Mexico and was the Mountain West's top pitcher in 2021. He began his first full season in High-A Aberdeen and finished at Double-A Bowie, with his success coming from elite zone rates and the ability to miss bats with multiple pitches.
SCOUTING REPORT: Armbruester has a hoppy low-to-mid-90s fastball that he elevates well at the top of the zone from a deceptive arm slot. He improved the sweep on his low-80s slider to give it plus traits, and added an 88-90 mph cutter during the season as another weapon. The cutter generated his highest swinging strike rate of any pitch during the season, and it showed at least average potential. While he used the pitch effectively to righties and lefties alike, it's more suited for righties at the highest level, and Armbruester's work-in-progress changeup will need improvement to give him a weapon against lefties.
THE FUTURE: Armbruester's repertoire at present almost assures a major league future as a relief weapon, but his strike-throwing and ability to develop as he climbs the levels leaves a legitimate starter possibility in his future. He'll likely be back at Bowie to begin 2023.

BA GRADE: 45/High   **Fastball:** 55   **Cutter:** 55   **Slider:** 60   **Changeup:** 30   **Control:** 55

Year	Age	Club (League)	Lvl	W	L	ERA	G	GS	IP	H	HR	BB	SO	BB/9	SO/9	WHIP	AVG
2022	23	Aberdeen (SAL)	HiA	2	1	4.02	12	12	54	42	8	18	63	3.0	10.6	1.12	.215
2022	23	Bowie (EL)	AA	4	1	3.69	14	10	63	49	13	16	63	2.3	9.0	1.03	.210
Minor League Totals				6	2	3.70	34	23	126	95	22	40	142	2.8	10.1	1.07	.207

22 NOAH DENOYER, RHP

Born: Feb. 17, 1998. **B-T:** S-R. **HT:** 6-5. **WT:** 225.
Signed: San Joaquin Delta (Calif.) JC, 2019 (NDFA). **Signed by:** Ryan Carlson.
TRACK RECORD: Denoyer missed most of his time at San Joaquin Delta due to Tommy John surgery, and the Orioles signed him out of the Northwoods League to keep him from an Oklahoma State commitment after the 2019 draft. He was limited by a sore elbow at times in 2022, but struck out 12.4 batters per nine with a 0.93 WHIP in a swingman role High-A Aberdeen and Double-A Bowie.
SCOUTING REPORT: In the Orioles' measurements of pitch quality based on movement and command, every one of Denoyer's pitches jumped a full grade this season. His size and over-the-top delivery help his hoppy mid-90s fastball be an above-average offering up in the zone, and help his vertical low-80s curveball play as a plus pitch at times as well. His sweeping slider and cutter each have at least fringe-average potential, and his high-80s splitter gives him a weapon to attack lefties with. The pitch mix helped Denoyer achieve a 17.4% swinging strike rate on the season, putting him in elite company in the Orioles' system.
THE FUTURE: Denoyer remains in the Orioles' starter program and has the pitch mix to maintain a back-end profile, but roster and workload considerations could make him an impact reliever.

BA GRADE: 45/High   **Fastball:** 55   **Curveball:** 60   **Slider:** 45   **Cutter:** 45   **Splitter:** 45   **Control:** 50

Year	Age	Club (League)	Lvl	W	L	ERA	G	GS	IP	H	HR	BB	SO	BB/9	SO/9	WHIP	AVG
2022	24	Orioles (FCL)	R	0	0	0.00	1	1	2	1	0	0	3	0.0	13.5	0.50	.143
2022	24	Aberdeen (SAL)	HiA	4	0	4.00	6	1	18	19	0	6	27	3.0	13.5	1.39	.268
2022	24	Bowie (EL)	AA	1	2	2.61	14	3	52	30	8	11	69	1.9	12.0	0.79	.167
Minor League Totals				10	5	2.87	44	17	147	108	15	48	185	2.9	11.3	1.06	.203

23 CHAYCE McDERMOTT, RHP

Born: Aug. 22, 1998. **B-T:** L-R. **HT:** 6-3. **WT:** 197.
Drafted: Ball State, 2021 (4th round). **Signed by:** Scott Oberhelman (Astros).
TRACK RECORD: McDermott's brother played in the NBA with the Memphis Grizzlies but Chayce's path in pro sports has come on the mound. A senior sign out of Ball State, McDermott went to an Astros organization that valued his fastball velocity and pitch traits before they traded him to Baltimore in a 2022 deadline deal that sent Trey Mancini to Houston.
SCOUTING REPORT: The Orioles targeted him for his diverse repertoire of high-octane pitches on the belief they can help keep him in the strike zone and make his offerings more dynamic. His whole arsenal is based off his above-average mid-90s fastball with high-quality vertical life, and he has separation in all four directions otherwise. His sweeper slider had a 39% chase rate, and he also has a harder cutter

that challenged hitters in that same direction. McDermott has a vertical curveball and made strides on a changeup after the trade. All the pitches can be at least average, but McDermott will need to iron out inconsistencies in his delivery and more regularly throw his pitches in the zone, as higher-level hitters will be able to recognize balls out of hand.

THE FUTURE: The Orioles are planning to help him achieve that starting at Double-A Bowie next year, where they'll work to help him reach the big league rotation ceiling his stuff gives him.

| BA GRADE: 45/Very High | | Fastball: 55 | Curveball: 50 | Slider: 50 | Changeup: 40 | Cutter: 50 | Control: 40 |

Year	Age	Club (League)	Lvl	W	L	ERA	G	GS	IP	H	HR	BB	SO	BB/9	SO/9	WHIP	AVG
2022	23	Aberdeen (SAL)	HiA	0	1	3.60	2	2	5	3	1	1	10	1.8	18.0	0.80	.167
2022	23	Asheville (SAL)	HiA	6	1	5.50	19	10	72	57	9	43	114	5.4	14.2	1.39	.210
2022	23	Bowie (EL)	AA	1	1	6.08	6	6	27	17	7	20	36	6.8	12.2	1.39	.179
Minor League Totals				7	3	5.11	34	22	125	89	20	75	200	5.4	14.4	1.31	.194

24 DREW ROM, LHP

Born: December 15, 1999. **B-T:** L-L. **HT:** 6-2. **WT:** 170.
Drafted: HS—Fort Thomas, Ky., 2018 (4th round). **Signed by:** Adrian Dorsey.

TRACK RECORD: Rom was signed away from a commitment to Michigan in the last draft before the Orioles' rebuild began and has benefited from the improved pitching development program that came with it. He spent most of 2022 at Double-A Bowie before a promotion to finish at Triple-A Norfolk, and led the organization with 144 strikeouts while fanning 10.8 batters per nine.

SCOUTING REPORT: Rom was consistently in the low 90s with his fastball in 2022, and he could have an average slider with the potential for an average splitter as well. He is a different pitcher to lefties than righties, though. Against same-side hitters, Rom will drop down and throw sinkers and sliders, and he'll attack more vertically from a higher arm slot against righties. Rom is at his best when he's aggressive in the strike zone, but needs to come into the zone with his secondaries more often to establish the ability to throw those pitches for strikes and force hitters to honor that instead of just assuming they'll tail out of the zone.

THE FUTURE: That, and maintaining or improving his low-90s velocity, will keep Rom on a back-end rotation track. He could put himself in the big league mix next summer with a strong showing at Norfolk.

| BA GRADE: 40/High | | Fastball: 45 | Slider: 45 | Splitter: 50 | Control: 50 |

Year	Age	Club (League	Lvl	W	L	ERA	G	GS	IP	H	HR	BB	SO	BB/9	SO/9	WHIP	AVG
2022	22	Bowie (EL)	AA	7	2	4.37	19	18	82	92	9	29	101	3.2	11.0	1.47	.280
2022	22	Norfolk (IL)	AAA	1	1	4.54	7	7	38	38	1	18	43	4.3	10.3	1.49	.268
Minor League Totals				25	9	3.41	80	69	354	328	28	112	414	2.9	10.5	1.24	.243

25 CESAR PRIETO, 3B

Born: May 10, 1999. **B-T:** L-R. **HT:** 5-9. **WT:** 175.
Signed: Cuba, 2022. **Signed by:** Koby Perez.

TRACK RECORD: Prieto was one of the top young players in Cuba when he defected on an Olympic qualifying trip to Miami in May 2021. The following January, he signed with the Orioles for $650,000, as he still at age 22 had to fit within teams' international bonus pools. Prieto had a strong month to begin his pro career at High-A Aberdeen, but struggled through the rest of the season a level up at Double-A Bowie.

SCOUTING REPORT: The advanced bat-to-ball skills that were Prieto's calling card in Cuba and give him an above-average hit tool ultimately led to his most significant challenges in his first pro season. Prieto struggled to adapt his approach and learn to lay off pitches on the fringes, even if he could get his bat to them, and pitchers started coaxing him into swings on the edges and low-quality contact as the season went on. While he went on a power run in April thanks to some added strength, Prieto might never have better than below-average pop, and will need to improve his strength and swing decisions to help him maximize his gap power. He proved adequate at third base and second base during the season.

THE FUTURE: The infield is well populated with talent on the Orioles' farm. Prieto has the contact skills to make the big leagues with further refinement, but it might be in a bench role.

| BA GRADE: 40/High | | Hit: 50 | Power: 40 | Speed: 50 | Fielding: 50 | Arm: 50 |

Year	Age	Club (League)	Lvl	AVG	G	AB	R	H	2B	3B	HR	RBI	BB	SO	SB	OBP	SLG
2022	23	Aberdeen (SAL)	HiA	.340	25	97	13	33	6	0	7	20	5	16	3	.381	.619
2022	23	Bowie (EL)	AA	.255	90	368	44	94	22	0	4	37	15	58	2	.296	.348
Minor League Totals				.273	115	465	57	127	28	0	11	57	20	74	5	.314	.404

26 HUDSON HASKIN, OF

Born: Dec. 31, 1998. **B-T:** R-R. **HT:** 6-2. **WT:** 200.
Drafted: Tulane, 2020 (2nd round). **Signed by:** David Jennings.
TRACK RECORD: The Orioles started a recent trend of taking an eligible sophomore early in the draft by picking Haskin 39th in 2020 and signing him for $1.91 million based on how he improved before that season was shut down. He spent all of 2022 at Double-A Bowie, where he had a 126 wRC+ at age 23.
SCOUTING REPORT: Haskin's pre-draft reports of a unique swing that could be on the flat side still haunt him as a player, but he made strides to be a bit more consistent with it and still has room to grow there. He made a decent amount of contact and improved at controlling the strike zone, which led to some good on-base ability, but his is an average hit tool at this point. He might only ever have average power as well, though the hope is that he can add some strength and give his bat more juice in the offseason to allow it to play at a corner outfield spot and make him more versatile. His speed was his carrying tool in 2021 and didn't disappear, but Haskin stole just five bases in 2022.
THE FUTURE: The fact that he does everything well enough but has no elite skill makes his a lower major league ceiling at this point, though he could be a fine platoon player on a good team. He'll likely start at Triple-A Norfolk in 2023.

BA GRADE: 40/High		Hit: 50		Power: 45		Speed: 55		Fielding: 50		Arm: 50					
Year	Age	Club (Leag	Lvl	AVG	G	AB	R	H	2B	3B	HR	RBI	BB	SO	SB	OBP	SLG
2022	23	Bowie (EL)	AA	.264	109	387	58	102	23	3	15	56	43	101	5	.367	.455
Minor League Totals				.269	192	695	117	187	42	6	20	98	75	179	27	.373	.433

27 JOHN RHODES, OF

Born: Aug. 15, 2000. **B-T:** R-R. **HT:** 6-0. **WT:** 200.
Drafted: Kentucky, 2021 (3rd round). **Signed by:** Trent Friedrich.
TRACK RECORD: Rhodes signed for an above-slot $1.38 million in 2021 after the draft moving from June to July made him eligible as a sophomore. He was more of a projection pick than one based on production after an uneven draft summer, and injuries to his wrist, toe, and knee limited him to 83 games in 2022. He started well when healthy at High-A Aberdeen before struggling to end the year at Double-A Bowie.
SCOUTING REPORT: At his best, Rhodes showed advanced control of the strike zone and made a lot of contact in the air. His swing deteriorated as his health did later in the year. The key to his offensive output will be to maximize his athleticism and impact the baseball more often. Rhodes is physical, but the Orioles believe he can hit like a corner outfielder through improved movements and efficiency to help the ball jump off his bat better. He can still be a fringe-average outfielder with average speed.
THE FUTURE: Those physical gains, however, will be the difference between Rhodes being an everyday outfielder and more of a bench player. A healthy 2023 back at Bowie with a productive offseason behind him could be the recipe for Rhodes bringing his ceiling into play.

BA GRADE: 40/High		Hit: 50		Power: 45		Speed: 50		Fielding: 45		Arm: 50					
Year	Age	Club (League)	Lvl	AVG	G	AB	R	H	2B	3B	HR	RBI	BB	SO	SB	OBP	SLG
2022	21	Aberdeen (SAL)	HiA	.259	58	201	43	52	15	2	5	35	35	50	16	.389	.428
2022	21	Bowie (EL)	AA	.189	25	90	12	17	3	2	0	9	12	22	0	.288	.267
Minor League Totals				.243	112	399	78	97	22	4	7	67	59	91	22	.357	.371

28 CARLOS TAVERA, RHP

Born: Oct. 6, 1998. **B-T:** R-R. **HT:** 6-1. **WT:** 195.
Drafted: Texas-Arlington, 2021 (5th round). **Signed by:** Ken Guthrie.
TRACK RECORD: Tavera signed for a below-slot $375,000 but looked like he'd be a fast-mover in his full-season debut at High-A Aberdeen. He allowed one earned run in four May starts to earn organizational pitcher of the month honors. Tavera entered June striking out 12.1 batters per nine with a 17% swinging strike rate and 0.98 WHIP before non-baseball medical issues that eventually ended his season materialized. Even with two months where he wasn't at his best, Tavera still struck out 32.9% of batters he faced.
SCOUTING REPORT: Tavera has a compact, repeatable delivery with a quick arm action that makes him hard for hitters to get comfortable against. His fastball was in the low-to-mid 90s with great hop, and played well off a slider that he can locate for strikes or bury for chase. Over the course of the season, he began to vary his slider to separate a sweeper and a cutter, the latter in the upper 80s and quite effective. Tavera has a changeup that's an effective way to attack lefties as well, though it worked against both sides

in High-A. The command is still poor, as he walked 13.8% of batters in 2022.

THE FUTURE: He might have moved quickly were he healthy in 2022, but as it stands, Tavera will look to re-establish his backend rotation future if he's healthy in 2023, likely at Double-A Bowie.

| BA GRADE: 45/Extreme | | Fastball: 60 | | Curveball: 55 | | Slider: 55 | | Changeup: 50 | | Control: 30 | | |

Year	Age	Club (League)	Lvl	W	L	ERA	G	GS	IP	H	HR	BB	SO	BB/9	SO/9	WHIP	AVG
2022	23	Aberdeen (SAL)	HiA	3	3	4.40	16	16	57	43	8	34	81	5.3	12.7	1.34	.205
Minor League Totals				3	3	4.02	22	19	69	47	8	46	94	6.0	12.2	1.34	.190

29 FREDERICK BENCOSME, SS

Born: May 11, 2005. **B-T:** R-R. **HT:** 6-0. **WT:** 160.

Signed: Dominican Republic, 2020. **Signed by:** Francisco Rosario/Geraldo Cabrera.

TRACK RECORD: Bencosme signed for $10,000 late in 2020 as an 18-year-old and ended up progressing faster than any of his classmates through the Orioles' system. He was so above the competition in extended spring training that he played in just two Florida Complex League games before he was promoted to Low-A Delmarva, where he had an .842 OPS with 27 strikeouts against 31 walks.

SCOUTING REPORT: High-A Aberdeen proved more challenging in September, but he continued to show extremely advanced bat-to-ball skills and good strike zone control with a smooth lefthanded swing that could make him an above-average hitter at the highest level. The power potential may not be very high, but he could add strength as he physically matures to maximize his line-drive stroke and add that dimension to his game. Continued focus on swing decisions and not settling for weak contact will help that as he progresses through the minors. Bencosme has the athleticism for shortstop but didn't always consistently make the expected plays in full-season ball.

THE FUTURE: Bencosme's offensive capabilities, however, likely mean he'll have a long runway to continue developing at shortstop as at least a platoon role in the majors seems possible at this early stage of his career. He'll get a chance to apply his September lessons back in Aberdeen to start 2023.

| BA GRADE: 45/Extreme | | Hit: 55 | | Power: 40 | | Speed: 50 | | Fielding: 40 | | Arm: 50 | | |

Year	Age	Club (League)	Lvl	AVG	G	AB	R	H	2B	3B	HR	RBI	BB	SO	SB	OBP	SLG
2022	19	Orioles (FCL)	R	.375	2	8	2	3	0	1	0	0	0	0	0	.444	.625
2022	19	Delmarva (CAR)	LoA	.336	59	220	29	74	8	2	3	29	27	31	8	.410	.432
2022	19	Aberdeen (SAL)	HiA	.154	12	39	5	6	2	1	0	2	2	9	0	.195	.256
Minor League Totals				.311	117	409	54	127	16	8	5	47	40	58	18	.376	.425

30 ANDERSON DE LOS SANTOS, 3B

Born: Jan. 11, 2004. **B-T:** R-R. **HT:** 5-11. **WT:** 185.

Signed: Dominican Republic, 2021. **Signed by:** Geraldo Cabrera/Rafael Belen.

TRACK RECORD: A $350,000 signee in the Orioles' heralded international signing class from January 2021, De Los Santos was one of a handful of 17-year-olds with an OPS over .900 in the Dominican Summer League in 2021 before coming stateside for a solid domestic debut in the Florida Complex League in 2022. He had 13 extra-base hits in 39 games and has as many walks (23) as strikeouts at age 18. The control of the strike zone was most encouraging at this young stage in his career, as De Los Santos hit the ball hard in the DSL but was a free swinger.

SCOUTING REPORT: That kind of continued progress will make him a potential average hitter. De Los Santos projects to at least fringe-average power if he continues to bring pitchers into his red zones and, more importantly, if he continues to gear his swing toward line drives and elevated contact as opposed to ground balls. His progress to this point is encouraging given the challenges some of his peers have had embracing the Orioles' offensive practices geared around swing decisions. Defensively, De Los Santos has an impressive arm fit for third base and he profiles to stay there.

THE FUTURE: He'll likely being 2023 at Low-A Delmarva, where his ability to reach a second-division major league ceiling will be in focus.

| BA GRADE: 45/Extreme | | Hit: 50 | | Power: 45 | | Speed: 45 | | Fielding: 45 | | Arm: 55 | | |

Year	Age	Club (League)	Lvl	AVG	G	AB	R	H	2B	3B	HR	RBI	BB	SO	SB	OBP	SLG
2022	18	Orioles (FCL)	R	.242	39	124	20	30	11	0	2	17	23	23	5	.373	.379
Minor League Totals				.281	75	235	38	66	17	2	5	34	38	41	8	.389	.434

Boston Red Sox

BY ALEX SPEIER

While the Red Sox endured a deeply disappointing 78-84 season and last-place finish in the American League East, the 2022 season represented a milestone in the team's quest to identify the next building blocks of a sustainable contender.

For the first time since the arrival of Rafael Devers in Boston in 2017, the Red Sox had potential future cornerstones emerge in the big leagues.

Righthander Brayan Bello had a breakthrough development year thanks to the development of an elite sinker, and he now looks like a potential midrotation fixture. And at the end of the year, first baseman Triston Casas reached the big leagues and offered a glimpse of the mature approach and power that could give him a home in the middle of the lineup.

The arrivals of Bello and Casas suggested progress in rebuilding a farm system that was all but empty at the upper levels prior to 2021. Further, Bello and Casas represent important players in the blueprint for a sustainable future. The Red Sox organization likewise has a number of arms who either reached the majors in 2022 or are likely to do so in 2023 that suggest a chance to feature the sort of internal pitching options that are necessary to end the team's cycle of volatility.

Still, behind Bello and Casas, the Red Sox prospects with the best chances to emerge as true cornerstones remain years away from the big leagues. It's a reflection of the fact that the team's highest-ceiling players have been acquired in recent years as either high school draftees—Boston hasn't taken a college first-rounder since 2017—or international signees.

Shortstop Marcelo Mayer showed all-star potential in his first full pro season, with a polished all-around game that validated his selection out of high school with the No. 4 overall pick in the 2021 draft. Meanwhile, in his first season in the States, 18-year-old Dominican center fielder Miguel Bleis showed true five-tool talent in Rookie ball.

But it will be years until Mayer, who will be 20 in 2023, and Bleis, who will be 19, have the opportunity to raise the ceiling of their major league team. In the meantime, chief baseball officer Chaim Bloom must continue to navigate the same challenging tightrope from which the Red Sox have plummeted with last-place finishes in 2020 and 2022 sandwiched around a surprise run to the AL Championship Series in 2021.

The farm system is improved but not yet fully formed. That leaves the Red Sox to address numerous big league holes from outside the organization, especially after homegrown shortstop Xander

Brayan Bello rounded into form with a 3.12 ERA and 40 strikeouts in his final 40.1 innings.

PROJECTED 2026 LINEUP

Catcher	Connor Wong	30
First Base	Triston Casas	26
Second Base	Trevor Story	33
Third Base	Rafael Devers	29
Shortstop	Marcelo Mayer	23
Left Field	Masataka Yoshida	32
Center Field	Ceddanne Rafaela	25
Right Field	Miguel Bleis	22
Designated Hitter	Nick Yorke	24
No. 1 Starter	Brayan Bello	27
No. 2 Starter	Garrett Whitlock	30
No. 3 Starter	Brandon Walter	29
No. 4 Starter	Bryan Mata	27
No. 5 Starter	Wikelman Gonzalez	24
Closer	Tanner Houck	30

Bogaerts signed an 11-year, $280 million deal with the Padres, while buying time for the maturation of a player development system that is nearly ready to supply the big league team with depth.

As much as Bloom was brought in after the 2019 season to strike that long-term balance, the results of his first three years at the helm of the Red Sox create pressure on the organization to pair its big league performance with growth in the farm system.

If that doesn't happen in 2023, Bloom's position could become tenuous in his fourth season in Boston—the same season in which predecessors Ben Cherington and Dave Dombrowski were pushed aside in their tenures. ∎

BOSTON RED SOX

TOP 2023 MLB CONTRIBUTORS	RANK
Triston Casas, 1B	2
Bryan Mata, RHP	7
BREAKOUT PROSPECTS	**RANK**
Luis Perales, RHP	16
Nathan Hickey, C	14

SOURCE OF TOP 30 TALENT

Homegrown	24	Acquired	6
College	6	Trade	4
Junior college	0	Rule 5 draft	0
High school	10	Independent league	0
Nondrafted free agent	0	Free agent/waivers	2
International	8		

LF
Masataka Yoshida (4)
Allan Castro

CF
Ceddanne Rafaela (3)
Miguel Bleis (5)

RF
Roman Anthony (9)
Wilyer Abreu (22)
Gilberto Jimenez

3B
Matthew Lugo (18)
Cutter Coffey (21)

SS
Marcelo Mayer (1)
Mikey Romero (6)
Luis Ravelo (29)

2B
Nick Yorke (7)
Eddinson Paulino (11)
Brainer Bonaci (16)
Enmanuel Valdez (19)
Chase Meidroth (26)
David Hamilton (30)
Jeter Downs

1B
Triston Casas (2)
Blaze Jordan (14)
Niko Kavadas (23)

C
Nathan Hickey (15)
Connor Wong (20)
Brooks Brannon (24)

LHP

LHSP	LHRP
Brandon Walter (10)	Dalton Rogers (28)
Chris Murphy (13)	Noah Dean
Shane Drohan	

RHP

RHSP	RHRP
Wikelman Gonzalez (12)	Bryan Mata (8)
Luis Perales (17)	Zack Kelly (27)
Elmer Rodriguez-Cruz (25)	Franklin German
Juan-Daniel Encarnacion	Ryan Fernandez
Connor Seabold	Wyatt Olds
	Angel Bastardo
	Jacob Webb
	A.J. Politi
	Taylor Broadway
	Jacob Wallace

1 MARCELO MAYER, SS

Born: Dec. 12, 2002. **B-T:** L-R. **HT:** 6-3. **WT:** 205.
Drafted: HS—Chula Vista, Calif., 2021 (1st round).
Signed by: J.J. Altobelli.

TRACK RECORD: In 2019, Red Sox area scout J.J. Altobelli made several trips to Eastlake High to see eventual first-rounder Keoni Cavaco, but it was Mayer—then a sophomore—who repeatedly commanded his attention. Mayer's consistent excellence in high school and a stint on Team USA's 17U development team in 2019 established him as a clear top talent entering the 2021 season. He was the sort of player who would almost never be available to the Red Sox in the draft, but Boston's awful performance in the Covid-compressed 2020 campaign netted the organization's highest pick since 1967. While Mayer was a candidate to go to the Pirates with the top pick after a dominant senior year—he hit .397/.555/.886 with 14 homers, 31 walks and eight strikeouts—he remained on the board when the Red Sox picked at No. 4. They jumped at the chance to take him, and signed him to a $6.64 million bonus. After the first two months of Mayer's first full pro season in 2022 were disrupted by a right wrist sprain, he excelled as a 19-year-old against more experienced competition with Low-A Salem and High-A Greenville. He showed impressive maturity and polish both in the field and at the plate.

SCOUTING REPORT: Mayer's smooth lefthanded swing is the stuff of instructional videos. His ability to manipulate the barrel and adapt his swing plane to pitches of varying types and locations at a young age is captivating. He produces easy loft to left field—a trait that should eventually serve him well at Fenway Park—and has the ability to hit rockets to his pull side. It's a combination that suggests a doubles machine with 20-plus homer upside. Though his 25% strikeout rate—and tendency to swing and miss on pitches below the zone—proved higher than expected, his 16% walk rate pointed to both good pitch recognition and swing decisions. Mayer showed the ability to respond to struggles in 2022. He bounced back after a tough start to his time in High-A Greenville—he hit .179 through 17 games—with a blistering .452/.553/.710 stretch to close the year. While his lack of speed limits his raw range, Mayer has excellent hands, a strong, accurate arm with the ability to vary his throwing angle, and the anticipation and well-calibrated clock of an above-average to plus shortstop. Some evaluators still wonder if he'll outgrow the position as he adds strength into his 20s, but such a move is

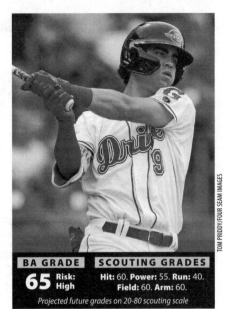

TOM PRIDDY/FOUR SEAM IMAGES

BA GRADE	SCOUTING GRADES
65 Risk: High	Hit: 60. Power: 55. Run: 40. Field: 60. Arm: 60.

Projected future grades on 20-80 scouting scale

BEST TOOLS

BATTING

Best Hitter for Average	Nick Yorke
Best Power Hitter	Niko Kavadas
Best Strike-Zone Discipline	Masataka Yoshida
Fastest Baserunner	David Hamilton
Best Athlete	Miguel Bleis

PITCHING

Best Fastball	Luis Perales
Best Curveball	A.J. Politi
Best Slider	Brandon Walter
Best Changeup	Zack Kelly
Best Control	Brandon Walter

FIELDING

Best Defensive Catcher	Connor Wong
Best Defensive Infielder	Marcelo Mayer
Best Infield Arm	Marcelo Mayer
Best Defensive Outfielder	Ceddanne Rafaela
Best Outfield Arm	Gilberto Jimenez

unlikely to be considered as he moves through the minors. Though Mayer has below-average speed, his instincts allow him to play faster than his foot speed. He was 17-for-17 on stolen base attempts.

THE FUTURE: Mayer will likely open 2023 back in High-A but should remain on an accelerated track that will bring him to the upper levels by the end of the year, with a potential big league ETA of late 2024. His first full pro season reinforced the sense that he's a potential cornerstone player. "From what I've seen, he's going to be a superstar," Salem hitting coach Nelson Paulino said.

Year	Age	Club (League)	Lvl	AVG	G	AB	R	H	2B	3B	HR	RBI	BB	SO	SB	OBP	SLG
2022	19	Salem (CAR)	LoA	.286	66	252	46	72	26	1	9	40	51	78	16	.406	.504
2022	19	Greenville (SAL)	HiA	.265	25	98	15	26	4	1	4	13	17	29	1	.379	.449
Minor League Totals				.279	117	441	86	123	34	3	16	70	83	134	24	.394	.478

2 TRISTON CASAS, 1B

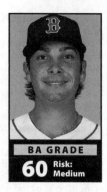

Born: January 15, 2000. **B-T:** L-R. **HT:** 6-4. **WT:** 255.
Drafted: HS—Plantation, Fla., 2018 (1st round). **Signed by:** Willie Romay.

TRACK RECORD: Neighbors of Casas' American Heritage High program were notified to move their cars during batting practice to shield property from a hail of tape-measure homers. Yet raw power was only part of Casas' game. He impressed both in high school and for 16U and 18U Team USA squads with an advanced, all-fields approach en route to being the 26th overall pick in 2018. He signed for a slot bonus of $2.55 million. In 2022, despite a high ankle sprain that sidelined him for two months with Triple-A Worcester, Casas tapped into increased power and made his MLB debut.

BA GRADE

60 Risk: Medium

SCOUTING REPORT: Casas is a formidable presence in the batter's box, with long levers that allow him to obliterate baseballs. Whereas in 2021 he focused foremost on contact and getting on base—often widening his stance and choking up significantly—in 2022, he hunted pitches to damage. He became more upright even with two strikes. While he maintained his characteristic plate discipline, he swung with bad intentions, showing significant jumps in exit velocities. In his MLB debut, he hit .197/.358/.408 but showed a sophisticated ability to game-plan and control the zone (20% walk rate) with considerable opposite-field power. There's some platoon risk with Casas, though he had quality left-on-left at-bats in the big leagues. Defensively, he moved well around the bag and showed a good arm.

THE FUTURE: Casas will either open 2023 in the big leagues or get there by early to midseason. He could emerge as a middle-of-the-order force who takes aim at the Green Monster for years to come.

SCOUTING GRADES		Hitting: 55		Power: 65		Speed: 30			Fielding: 55		Arm: 50			
Year	Age	Club (League)	Lvl	AVG	G	AB	R	H	2B	3B	HR	RBI	BB	SO	SB	OBP	SLG
2022	22	Red Sox (FCL)	R	.429	4	14	3	6	3	0	1	3	3	2	0	.529	.857
2022	22	Worcester (IL)	AAA	.273	72	264	45	72	20	1	11	38	46	68	0	.382	.481
2022	22	Boston (AL)	MLB	.197	27	76	11	15	1	0	5	12	19	23	1	.358	.408
Major League Totals				.197	27	76	11	15	1	0	5	12	19	23	1	.358	.408
Minor League Totals				.269	284	1019	177	274	64	9	46	181	165	261	10	.374	.485

3 CEDDANNE RAFAELA, OF/SS

Born: September 18, 2000. **B-T:** R-R. **HT:** 5-9. **WT:** 165.
Signed: Curacao, 2017. **Signed by:** Dennis Neuman/Rollie Pino/Todd Claus.

TRACK RECORD: As an undersized amateur in Curacao, Rafaela caught the attention of Red Sox scouts with dynamic defense, a knack for getting the barrel to the ball—with surprising flashes of pop—and incredible on-field energy. Boston signed him for $10,000, hoping he would develop into a utility player. Rafaela's career transformed in 2021 when he made a fish-to-water move from shortstop to center field and also raised his hands to smooth a hitch in his swing. He started smoking balls in the air rather than beating them into the ground. A strong second half for Low-A Salem in 2021 served as a prelude to a breakout campaign in 2022 in which Rafaela had 63 extra-base hits and 28 steals for High-A Greenville and Double-A Portland while delivering frequent web gems.

BA GRADE

55 Risk: High

SCOUTING REPORT: Rafaela's stance has visual similarities to that of Mookie Betts. He rests his bat on his shoulder before moving it overhead as the pitcher starts his delivery, then draws it back like a slingshot as the ball is released. Despite an incredibly aggressive approach, his hand-eye coordination has always yielded a high contact rate, and in 2022 he barreled balls regularly. Walks will likely be a rarity, but if Rafaela can improve his swing decisions, he possesses average or better hit and power potential. That's a tantalizing package given his show-stopping defense. Rafaela's great jumps placed him as one of the best defensive center fielders in pro ball, and he also shows above-average potential at short. His plus speed is also an asset.

THE FUTURE: Even with modest offense, Rafaela's defense gives him a floor in the mold of outfielders such as Jose Siri, Harrison Bader or Jackie Bradley Jr. He should finish 2023 in the big leagues.

SCOUTING GRADES		Hitting: 50		Power: 50		Speed: 60			Fielding: 70		Arm: 60			
Year	Age	Club (League)	Lvl	AVG	G	AB	R	H	2B	3B	HR	RBI	BB	SO	SB	OBP	SLG
2022	21	Greenville (SAL)	HiA	.330	45	197	37	65	17	4	9	36	10	51	14	.368	.594
2022	21	Portland (EL)	AA	.278	71	284	45	79	15	6	12	50	16	62	14	.324	.500
Minor League Totals				.272	316	1242	216	338	62	25	40	185	79	262	79	.324	.459

4 MASATAKA YOSHIDA, OF

Born: July 15, 1993. **B-T:** L-R. **HT:** 5-8. **WT:** 176.
Signed: Japan, 2022. **Signed by:** Brett Ward/Kento Matsumoto.

TRACK RECORD: Yoshida debuted for Orix in 2016 and quickly blossomed into one of Japan's top pure hitters, making four all-star games and leading the Pacific League in batting average and OPS in 2020 and 2021. He progressively added power without sacrificing contact ability and led the Buffaloes to their first Japan Series championship in 26 years. Orix posted him after the season and the Red Sox signed him for a five-year, $90 million deal and paid Orix a $15.4 million posting fee.

BA GRADE

50 Risk: Medium

SCOUTING REPORT: Yoshida is undersized at 5-foot-8, but he's strong in his frame. He has a quick, flat swing from the left side and consistently barrels balls with his elite hand-eye coordination. He has good rhythm and balance in the batter's box and is able to hit multiple pitch types, including the high-velocity fastballs he'll see in MLB. Yoshida is an aggressive hitter who attacks pitches early in counts and mostly hits hard line drives from gap to gap. He rarely strikes out despite that aggressiveness and had more walks than strikeouts each of his last four seasons. Yoshida shows plus raw power in batting practice and had three 20-home run seasons in Japan, but his power projects to be fringy in MLB. He will have to add loft to his swing and learn to hit the ball out front better to access more power against big league pitching. Yoshida's value is tied almost exclusively to his bat. He's a below-average runner and below-average defender in left field whose range is severely limited. He plays hard and catches what is hit to him, but he struggles to reach balls in the gap or down the line. He has below-average arm strength that limits him to left field.

THE FUTURE: Yoshida projects to hit for average in MLB but will have to access more power to be an average everyday left fielder. If he doesn't, his on-base skills should still make him a solid contributor.

SCOUTING GRADES	Hitting: 55	Power: 45	Speed: 40	Fielding: 40	Arm: 40

Year	Age	Club (League)	Lvl	AVG	G	AB	R	H	2B	3B	HR	RBI	BB	SO	SB	OBP	SLG
2022	28	Orix (PL)	NPB	.335	119	412	56	138	28	1	21	88	80	41	4	.447	.561
Japanese League Totals				.327	762	2703	418	884	161	7	133	467	421	300	21	.421	.539

5 MIGUEL BLEIS, OF

Born: March 1, 2004. **B-T:** R-R. **HT:** 6-2. **WT:** 180.
Signed: Dominican Republic, 2021. **Signed by:** Eddie Romero/Manny Nanita.

TRACK RECORD: Bleis stood out as a five-tool talent who possessed what the Red Sox considered "extreme bat life" when they signed him for $1.5 million in January 2021. That was Boston's highest bonus amount for a player out of the Dominican Republic since signing Rafael Devers for the same amount in 2013. Bleis made a solid pro debut in the Dominican Summer League in 2021, then delivered an electrifying performance as the top prospect in the Florida Complex League in 2022. He would have been promoted to Low-A Salem had it not been for lower back tightness in mid August.

BA GRADE

55 Risk: Extreme

SCOUTING REPORT: Bleis mesmerized scouts with his tremendous talent in every facet of the game. When he barrels balls, he makes resounding contact, resulting in huge exit velocities that ranked atop the FCL, and he showed the ability to handle fastballs of any velocity. His strikeout rate was high at nearly 27%—a red flag for some organizations—largely due to swings and misses on breaking balls, and his 6% walk rate likewise points to a free-swinger. But Bleis is young enough that he has a chance to improve his swing decisions and emerge as an average or better hitter, with work he did to clean up a barrel drop in 2022 offering optimism about his adaptability. His speed is currently plus or better, giving him a buffer even as he continues to fill out. He's a glider in center field, with instincts to become an above-average defender at the position or a standout in right.

THE FUTURE: Bleis has electrifying all-star potential. His hit tool will determine how close he comes to scraping it. He's so far from the big leagues that no solid floor is apparent, but his upside is immense.

SCOUTING GRADES	Hitting: 50	Power: 65	Speed: 60	Fielding: 60	Arm: 60

Year	Age	Club (League)	Lvl	AVG	G	AB	R	H	2B	3B	HR	RBI	BB	SO	SB	OBP	SLG
2022	18	Red Sox (FCL)	R	.301	40	153	28	46	14	4	5	27	10	45	18	.353	.542
Minor League Totals				.279	76	272	45	76	20	5	9	44	22	70	25	.343	.489

6 MIKEY ROMERO, SS/2B

Born: January 12, 2004. **B-T:** L-R. **HT:** 6-1. **WT:** 180.
Drafted: HS—Orange, Calif., 2022 (1st round). **Signed by:** J.J. Altobelli.

TRACK RECORD: One year after drafting Marcelo Mayer, the Red Sox used their 2022 first-round pick at No. 24 overall on another high school shortstop from Southern California. Romero displayed a mature, well-rounded game at Orange Lutheran High, hitting .372/.419/.659 and playing solid defense at short. While his hit tool was the primary driver of his prospect status, he grew into power as the season progressed, convincing the Red Sox to take him earlier than most mock drafts forecasted. Romero signed for a below-slot $2.3 million. In his pro debut, he performed well in the Florida Complex League and then finished with an excellent showing in Low-A Salem, hitting .349/.364/.581 with seven extra-base hits in nine games.

BA GRADE	
55	Risk: **Extreme**

SCOUTING REPORT: Romero has a sweet lefthanded swing with little stride or wasted motion. His barrel is a magnet for pitches all over the zone, and he produces gap-to-gap, line-drive contact. While Romero was viewed as having limited power projection by many scouts, he added strength throughout his senior year. By the time he turned pro, he was able to clear the right field bullpens at Fenway Park in batting practice, suggesting an average power ceiling. At shortstop, he possesses good instincts and clean actions but has limited range. There's a chance he stays at shortstop as an average defender, but more likely he becomes an average second baseman with the ability to provide fringe defense on the other side of second. He's a slightly below-average runner.

THE FUTURE: Romero should start 2023 in Low-A Salem, and his strong showing at the end of 2022 offers a glimpse of a teenager who could move quickly up the ladder. He projects as a table-setting everyday middle infielder who could reach the big leagues by late 2025 or early 2026.

SCOUTING GRADES	Hitting: 55	Power: 45	Speed: 45	Fielding: 50	Arm: 45

Year	Age	Club (League)	Lvl	AVG	G	AB	R	H	2B	3B	HR	RBI	BB	SO	SB	OBP	SLG
2022	18	Red Sox (FCL)	R	.250	10	36	5	9	3	0	1	6	7	4	1	.372	.417
2022	18	Salem (CAR)	LoA	.349	9	43	6	15	4	3	0	11	1	11	1	.364	.581
Minor League Totals				.304	19	79	11	24	7	3	1	17	8	15	2	.368	.506

7 NICK YORKE, 2B

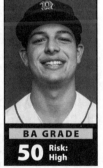

Born: April 2, 2002. **B-T:** R-R. **HT:** 6-0. **WT:** 210.
Drafted: HS—San Jose, 2020 (1st round). **Signed by:** Josh Labandeira.

TRACK RECORD: The Red Sox stunned the industry when they selected Yorke—a projected second- or third-round pick—with the 17th overall pick in 2020. After signing for a below-slot $2.7 million, Yorke quieted skeptics with a .325/.412/.516 batting line at two Class A levels in 2021. But in 2022, a succession of injuries—turf toe, back stiffness, wrist soreness—contributed to inconsistency with his mechanics, approach and ultimately his performance.

SCOUTING REPORT: At his best, Yorke's compact, quick swing affords him the extra time needed to handle velocity while spitting on pitches out of the zone and attacking those he can drive. In 2021, he produced line drives to all fields

BA GRADE	
50	Risk: **High**

and showed plenty of easy pull-side power. But Yorke's struggles with health and performance in 2022 left him tinkering with his swing throughout the season—with poor results. His groundball rate spiked, his previous all-fields approach became too pull-heavy, and his strikeout rate jumped from 15.6% to 25.2%. Yorke and the Red Sox are hopeful that with health, he'll reclaim his status as one of the best pure hitting prospects in the minors. There's a lot of pressure on Yorke's bat given that his range is limited—a growing concern given the shift restrictions coming to MLB in 2023. But while Yorke isn't rangy, he proved reliable in the field. He committed only one error in 68 games at second base in 2022. He has a chance to stick at second with fringy defense.

THE FUTURE: The 2023 campaign should clarify whether Yorke is the standout hitting prospect of 2021. A rebound campaign would put him on track to reach the big leagues by late 2024, with the potential to hit toward the top of the lineup with high on-base percentages, loads of doubles and 20-homer potential. He'll open 2023 back at High-A Greenville or, with a strong spring, potentially at Double-A Portland.

SCOUTING GRADES	Hitting: 55	Power: 45	Speed: 45	Fielding: 45	Arm: 45

Year	Age	Club (League)	Lvl	AVG	G	AB	R	H	2B	3B	HR	RBI	BB	SO	SB	OBP	SLG
2022	20	Greenville (SAL)	HiA	.231	80	337	48	78	10	1	11	45	33	94	8	.303	.365
Minor League Totals				.281	177	715	124	201	30	6	25	107	85	163	21	.362	.445

8 BRYAN MATA, RHP

BA GRADE

50 Risk: High

Born: May 3, 1999. **B-T:** R-R. **Ht.:** 6-3. **Wt.:** 230.
Signed: Venezuela, 2016. **Signed by:** Alex Requena/Eddie Romero.

TRACK RECORD: Mata signed with the Red Sox for $25,000 in January 2016 and projection quickly became reality as he gained size and strength. Though Mata entered pro ball with a four-seam fastball, curveball and changeup, the Red Sox felt his natural arm slot was better suited for a sinker and slider. The shift resulted in growing pains—particularly difficulties working in the strike zone—but also considerable promise in 2018 and 2019. After the lost 2020 Covid season, Mata blew out his elbow in spring training, which required Tommy John surgery that sidelined him until mid 2022. He advanced across four levels in 2022, striking out 30% of batters and recording 53% ground balls.

SCOUTING REPORT: Mata is a formidable presence on the mound, a powerful righthander whose stuff may be unrivaled in the Red Sox system. He sits at 97 mph with his sinker, and his plus slider tunnels well off of it. He has topped out at 102 mph on his four-seamer, and his changeup has the action of a solid-average offering or better. In a vacuum, Mata's arsenal could be that of a midrotation starter with two caveats. First, his swing-and-miss numbers are below what might be expected given his underlying pitch traits, though he did make gains in his slider depth in late 2022, resulting in more whiffs. Secondly, he lacks a starter's control—he walked 13% of batters in 2022—likely capping his potential innings load.

THE FUTURE: If Mata makes control gains—possible as he gets further from Tommy John surgery—he could emerge as a depth starter in 2023 with a long-term future as a No. 4 with fringy command.

SCOUTING GRADES:	Fastball: 55	Slider: 60	Changeup: 50	Control: 40

Year	Age	Club (League)	Lvl	W	L	ERA	G	GS	IP	H	HR	BB	SO	BB/9	SO/9	WHIP	AVG
2022	23	Salem (CAR)	LoA	0	0	0.00	1	1	2	0	0	2	2	9.0	9.0	1.00	.000
2022	23	Greenville (SAL)	HiA	0	1	4.00	3	3	9	6	1	6	15	6.0	15.0	1.33	.182
2022	23	Portland (EL)	AA	5	2	1.85	10	9	49	35	4	23	58	4.3	10.7	1.19	.202
2022	23	Worcester (IL)	AAA	2	0	3.47	5	5	23	19	0	15	30	5.8	11.6	1.46	.224
Minor League Totals				29	23	3.21	88	87	398	339	18	191	412	4.3	9.3	1.33	.233

9 ROMAN ANTHONY, OF

BA GRADE

55 Risk: Extreme

Born: May 13, 2004. **B-T:** L-R. **HT:** 6-3. **WT:** 200.
Drafted: HS—Parkland, FL, 2022 (2nd round supplemental). **Signed by:** Willie Romay.

TRACK RECORD: Anthony was a force at South Florida power Stoneman Douglas High, hitting .520/.589/.980 with 10 homers in 32 games as a senior and showing plus power potential combined with a sound approach at the plate. The Red Sox drafted him 79th overall in 2022 and signed him for $2.5 million—roughly triple slot value—to pass on a scholarship to Mississippi. Anthony had consistently impressive at-bats in his brief pro debut, and hit .429/.475/.486 in the Florida Complex League.

SCOUTING REPORT: While Anthony shows plus to double-plus raw power and can clear fences with ease, he controls at-bats in impressive fashion, particularly for a player with his stout frame. While his raw power is obvious, there's less consensus around Anthony's pure hitting ability. He showed swing-and-miss tendencies during the showcase circuit in high school but made adjustments during the spring and also performed well in a brief pro debut. He already has size and strength but projects to get bigger. Anthony's ability to maintain mobility in his next 15 pounds represents a key that will determine whether he stays in center field, though the safest bet would be an eventual move to right field. Still, his bat projects well in a corner, as does his arm.

THE FUTURE: In a system deep in up-the-middle athletes with balanced skill sets, Anthony stands out for his middle-of-the-order potential that could slot him as a run-producer, if his mature approach as a young hitter remains intact as he moves up and fills out. He most likely will become a power-hitting corner down the road, though the Red Sox won't rush him off center field. Anthony will open 2023 in Low-A Salem, with the possibility of a 2025 or 2026 big league ETA.

SCOUTING GRADES	Hitting: 45	Power: 55	Speed: 50	Fielding: 50	Arm: 50

Year	Age	Club (League)	Lvl	AVG	G	AB	R	H	2B	3B	HR	RBI	BB	SO	SB	OBP	SLG
2022	18	Red Sox (FCL)	R	.429	10	35	5	15	2	0	0	7	4	4	1	.475	.486
2022	18	Salem (CAR)	LoA	.189	10	37	2	7	2	0	0	5	5	4	0	.279	.243
Minor League Totals				.306	20	72	7	22	4	0	0	12	9	8	1	.373	.361

10 BRANDON WALTER, LHP

Born: September 8, 1996. **B-T:** L-L. **HT:** 6-2. **WT:** 215.
Drafted: Delaware, 2019 (26th round). **Signed by:** Reed Gragnani.

BA GRADE

45 Risk: Medium

TRACK RECORD: When Walter returned from Tommy John surgery in his 2019 draft year, his fastball peaked in the high 80s, but his movement, command and ability to change speeds impressed area scout Reed Gragnani and convinced the Red Sox to draft him in the 26th round. He built strength during the Covid shutdown, and in the spring of 2021, the Red Sox were floored when Walter threw mid-90s sinkers. His bullpen dominance led to a shift to the rotation, and he struck out 36% of batters in 2021. Walter opened 2022 in the Double-A Portland rotation before a May promotion to Triple-A. His season ended in early June due to a bulging cervical disk.

SCOUTING REPORT: Walter creates an extreme angle with a whippy, cross-body delivery from a low three-quarters arm slot. He confuses hitters with a three-pitch mix that generates grounders and whiffs. Walter works relentlessly in the strike zone with his sinker—mostly 88-90 mph in 2022, down from 92-94 mph in 2021—to set up a devastating low-80s slider that has elite plate-wide sweep, as well as an above-average changeup with depth and fade. Even at his lower 2022 velocity, Walter beat hitters in the strike zone with three pitches, suggesting a rotation profile so long as he can stay healthy. Walter enters 2023 as a 26-year-old with just 180 career innings, making his ability to handle a starter's workload unknown.

THE FUTURE: Walter will likely open 2023 in the Triple-A Worcester rotation, but if he's healthy he may be Boston's best depth starting option. His mix profiles as that of a No. 4 starter if he can handle the workload. Otherwise, he could be a nasty multi-inning reliever for one time through the order.

SCOUTING GRADES:	Fastball: 50	Slider: 70	Changeup: 55	Control: 60

Year	Age	Club (League)	Lvl	W	L	ERA	G	GS	IP	H	HR	BB	SO	BB/9	SO/9	WHIP	AVG
2022	25	Portland (EL)	AA	2	2	2.88	9	9	50	36	6	3	68	0.5	12.2	0.78	.191
2022	25	Worcester (IL)	AAA	1	1	8.22	2	2	8	9	0	4	7	4.7	8.2	1.70	.281
Minor League Totals				12	8	3.09	49	25	180	138	14	35	246	1.7	12.3	0.96	.203

11 EDDINSON PAULINO, SS/3B

Born: July 2, 2002. **B-T:** L-R. **HT:** 5-9. **WT:** 170.
Signed: Dominican Republic, 2018. **Signed by:** Esau Medina/Eddie Romero.

TRACK RECORD: Paulino's hand-eye coordination stood out when the Red Sox signed him for $205,000 in 2018. In pro ball, that trait has been evident in tandem with a discerning eye and impressive bat life that permits him to generate steady, hard contact to the gaps. Paulino has had strong performances in each of his three minor league stops. He put up a .985 OPS in the Dominican Summer League in 2021. He had 58 extra-base hits for Low-A Salem in 2022 and ranked top 10 with a .203 isolated slugging percentage among qualified full-season players in their age-19 seasons or younger. Signed as a shortstop, Paulino has moved all over the field in pro ball, and played short, second base, third base and center field in 2022.

SCOUTING REPORT: Though physically unimposing at 5-foot-9, Paulino is live-bodied, controls the strike zone well (12% walk rate), makes reliable contact (19.5% strikeout rate) and has a good sense for those pitches that he can hit hard. He produces lots of well-struck line drives interspersed with occasional pull-side pop. Paulino is a good athlete who plays solid defense at second and third base with the ability to fill in as a starter at shortstop with fringy defense. Paulino started getting time in center field in 2022. While he's at a very early stage of his development there, he has the athleticism to have a true super-utility profile. Paulino shows solid speed on the bases, contributing to a well-rounded profile.

THE FUTURE: Paulino has a future as a solid, bottom-of-the-order super-utility player. He should open 2023 in High-A Greenville, with a likely big league ETA of 2025. Boston's depth of middle infield options could make Paulino a trade candidate, but his versatility makes that something other than a foregone conclusion.

BA GRADE: 45/Medium	Hitting: 55	Power: 40	Speed: 50	Fielding: 50	Arm: 50

Year	Age	Club (Leagu	Lvl	AVG	G	AB	R	H	2B	3B	HR	RBI	BB	SO	SB	OBP	SLG
2022	19	Salem (CAR)	LoA	.266	114	463	96	123	35	10	13	66	64	105	27	.359	.469
Minor League Totals				.281	185	684	138	192	53	18	13	89	97	149	34	.377	.468

12 WIKELMAN GONZALEZ, RHP

Born: March 25, 2002. **B-T:** R-R. **HT:** 6-0. **WT:** 195.
Signed: Venezuela, 2018. **Signed by:** Wilder Lobo/Rollie Pino.

TRACK RECORD: As a slender amateur in Venezuela, Gonzalez impressed by shaping three pitches while exuding physical projection. After the Covid shutdown year of 2020, Gonzalez emerged with a mid-90s fastball that overpowered hitters in 2021. But a lack of strength and suboptimal conditioning left Gonzalez with wildly inconsistent mechanics through much of 2022 in Low-A Salem, resulting in a 5.28 ERA and 14.8% walk rate through 17 starts. He responded well to a mid-year challenge to take ownership of his career. Added strength helped him harness his delivery to finish with a 2.43 ERA, 30.4% strikeout rate, and 8.6% walk rate in his last eight starts, split between Salem and High-A Greenville.

SCOUTING REPORT: One evaluator described Gonzalez as a "freaky mover," a hyper-mobile pitcher who generates incredible length in his delivery. His ability to stay on his back leg yields a low, down-the-mound release point that allows his fastball, which sits 94-96 mph and tops out at 99, to jump on hitters and get above bats, a potentially elite fastball. His curveball and changeup show average or better potential, and he developed a cutter/slider at the end of 2022 that will be part of his mix in 2023.

THE FUTURE: Gonzalez has midrotation upside if he can throw enough strikes to get there, with plenty of fastball to be a late-innings arm if his starter development stalls. Gonzalez will start 2023 in High-A Greenville.

BA GRADE: 50/Very high	Fastball: 65	Curveball: 50	Slider: 50	Changeup: 50	Control: 40

Year	Age	Club (League)	Lvl	W	L	ERA	G	GS	IP	H	HR	BB	SO	BB/9	SO/9	WHIP	AVG
2022	20	Salem (CAR)	LoA	4	3	4.54	21	21	81	63	2	48	98	5.3	10.8	1.36	.212
2022	20	Greenville (SAL)	HiA	0	0	2.65	4	4	17	13	0	6	23	3.2	12.2	1.12	.213
Minor League Totals				8	8	3.65	51	50	197	152	7	94	231	4.3	10.5	1.25	.213

13 CHRIS MURPHY, LHP

Born: June 5, 1998. **B-T:** L-L. **HT:** 6-1. **WT:** 175.
Drafted: San Diego, 2019 (6th round). **Signed by:** J.J. Altobelli.

TRACK RECORD: The Red Sox scouted Murphy at San Diego as a pitcher with untapped potential. He was a lefty with a good fastball who they felt was using it in the wrong part of the zone—down instead of up—and who had putaway stuff but tended to nibble with two strikes. In his 2019 pro debut in short-season Lowell, Murphy immediately showed an eagerness to embrace data-driven tweaks to his plan of attack. In two years since the lost 2020 campaign, Murphy has advanced to Triple-A while pitching 253.1 innings, fifth most in the minors.

SCOUTING REPORTS: Murphy features a three-pitch mix anchored by a fastball that sits 92-94 mph and tops out at 96, complemented by an above-average changeup and an average slider. He's delivered occasionally dominant outings but has mostly shown an ability to work to gameplans while offering a steady supply of five- to six-inning outings. He seemed to lose steam as the 2022 season progressed, with his velocity ticking down and his ERA rising in each month of the year.

THE FUTURE: Murphy has shown the building blocks of a potential No. 5 starter, and after being placed on the 40-man roster, he's likely to open 2023 in Triple-A as a depth option for the Red Sox. It's possible his stuff could play up in a multi-innings relief role.

BA GRADE: 45/Medium	Fastball: 50	Curveball: 45	Slider: 50	Changeup: 55	Control: 45

Year	Age	Club (League)	Lvl	W	L	ERA	G	GS	IP	H	HR	BB	SO	BB/9	SO/9	WHIP	AVG
2022	24	Portland (EL)	AA	4	5	2.58	15	13	77	46	6	31	91	3.6	10.7	1.00	.170
2022	24	Worcester (IL)	AAA	3	6	5.50	15	15	75	77	8	41	58	4.9	6.9	1.57	.266
Minor League Totals				15	17	3.89	61	58	287	238	36	115	311	3.6	9.8	1.23	.225

14 BLAZE JORDAN, 1B/3B

Born: December 19, 2002. **B-T:** R-R. **HT:** 6-2. **WT:** 220.
Drafted: HS—Southaven, Miss., 2020 (3rd round). **Signed by:** Danny Watkins.

TRACK RECORD: Jordan showed prodigious power on the amateur showcase circuit before he started shaving. That carrying tool made him one of the top high school talents in 2020—particularly given that he was still 17 at the time of the draft after reclassifying from the 2021 class. But questions about his hitting as well as his asking price left him on the board for the Red Sox in the third round, with the team signing the No. 89 overall pick away from Mississippi State with a $1.75 million bonus. Jordan had a strong age-19 season at the dish with Low-A Salem and High-A Greenville in 2022, hitting .289/.363/.445 with 12 homers, 45 extra-base hits and an 18% strikeout rate.

SCOUTING REPORT: Though Jordan has 70-grade raw power with the ability to clear the fences to all fields, the trait made only occasional appearances in 2022. Instead he maintained a more controlled swing that allowed him to cover the plate with an approach geared from center field to right-center. While that yielded a high batting average and on-base percentage, Jordan had a high groundball rate and did little damage against good fastballs. Still, he showed athleticism and strength in his swing to suggest a future ability to take chances and drive the ball with more frequency. While Jordan played both infield corners, his lack of speed and range suggest a future at first base or DH.

THE FUTURE: Jordan should open 2023 back in Greenville but stands an excellent chance of advancing to Double-A. If his approach evolves to tap into his power, that could eventually yield a middle-of-the-order slugger.

BA GRADE: 50/Very High	Hit: 50	Power: 65	Speed: 40	Fielding: 45	Arm: 60

Year	Age	Club (League)	Lvl	AVG	G	AB	R	H	2B	3B	HR	RBI	BB	SO	SB	OBP	SLG
2022	19	Salem (CAR)	LoA	.286	95	370	48	106	29	3	8	57	37	67	4	.357	.446
2022	19	Greenville (SAL)	HiA	.301	25	93	12	28	1	0	4	11	11	27	1	.387	.441
Minor League Totals				.296	148	568	79	168	38	4	18	94	56	115	6	.364	.472

15 NATHAN HICKEY, C

Born: November 23, 1999. **B-T:** L-R. **HT:** 6-0. **WT:** 210.
Drafted: Florida, 2021 (5th round). **Signed by:** Dante Ricciardi.

TRACK RECORD: After shifting around the infield in high school, Hickey moved behind the dish full time at Florida. Though raw defensively, Hickey showed enough while hitting .316/.436/.539 in 2021 during his one full college season to convince the Red Sox to sign the draft-eligible redshirt freshman to an above-slot $1 million bonus as a fifth-round pick. In his first full pro season, Hickey hit .263/.415/.522 between Low-A Salem and High-A Greenville.

SCOUTING REPORT: Hickey features little wasted motion in the batter's box, staying balanced through a short stride before unloading on pitches with a powerful hip turn to produce plus raw power. His calm initial move buys time to recognize pitches and contributes to an excellent approach in the lower minors, punishing pitches in all quadrants. Defensively, Hickey remains raw behind the plate with plenty of cleanup to do in his blocking, receiving and framing, though an automated strike zone could lower the bar. He has average raw arm strength but must sharpen his footwork and transfer to allow it to play. Runners succeeded on 87% of steal attempts against Hickey, a number that will have to change markedly for him to stick at catcher. Hickey does embrace the challenge of his position and plays with an edge to prove doubters wrong.

THE FUTURE: If Hickey emerges as a below-average defensive catcher, he'd have standout offensive potential at the position. If not, he might still bring enough as a hitter to play at DH or first base.

BA GRADE: 50/Very High	Hit: 50	Power: 55	Speed: 40	Fielding: 40	Arm: 50

Year	Age	Club (League)	Lvl	AVG	G	AB	R	H	2B	3B	HR	RBI	BB	SO	SB	OBP	SLG
2022	22	Salem (CAR)	LoA	.271	41	140	31	38	12	0	7	39	39	39	0	.429	.507
2022	22	Greenville (SAL)	HiA	.252	34	115	19	29	6	0	9	23	24	39	0	.397	.539
Minor League Totals				.258	86	283	55	73	20	0	16	64	72	88	0	.413	.498

16 BRAINER BONACI, SS/2B/3B

Born: July 9, 2002. **B-T:** B-R. **HT:** 5-10. **WT:** 175.
Signed: Venezuela, 2018. **Signed by:** Manny Padron/Junior Vizcaino/Eddie Romero.

TRACK RECORD: The Red Sox signed Bonaci for $290,000 on the basis of his good hands, strong arm and ability to switch hit. His middle infield defense and bat-to-ball skills stood out early in pro ball, but in 2022, his already solid plate discipline improved, leading to a .262/.397/.385 line with 28 steals and as many walks (89) as strikeouts.

SCOUTING REPORT: Bonaci showed excellent plate discipline but arguably lapsed into passivity while batting lefthanded, where he hit .257/.413/.357 with a 20.5% walk rate. He hit .279/.330/.523 righthanded, showing more thump and a more aggressive approach. He produces a lot of liners and ground balls to the opposite field, but Bonaci went from no homers through June (57 games) to six homers in the last three months (51 games). Though his speed is fringe-average, his feel for the game allows it to play up, and he took smart chances on the bases. Defensively, Bonaci proved capable at short and above-average with good range at second while also providing solid defense at third with a plus arm.

THE FUTURE: Bonaci's skill set of a disciplined switch-hitter with solid contact skills and the ability to handle three infield positions suggests a player with a utility profile. If the late-season power gains were a sign of double-digit home runs in his future, there's a chance for more upside.

BA GRADE: 50/Very High	Hit: 50		Power: 40		Speed: 45		Fielding: 55		Arm: 60			
Year	Age	Club (Leagu	Lvl	AVG	G	AB	R	H	2B	3B	HR	RBI	BB	SO	SB	OBP	SLG
2022	19	Salem (CAR)	LoA	.262	108	397	86	104	19	6	6	50	89	89	28	.397	.385
Minor League Totals				.263	218	814	152	214	49	10	11	112	136	174	58	.373	.388

17 LUIS PERALES, RHP

Born: April 14, 2003. **B-T:** R-R. **HT:** 6-1. **WT:** 160.
Signed: Venezuela, 2019. **Signing scout:** Lenin Rodriguez/Ernesto Gomez/Rollie Pino.
TRACK RECORD: After signing for $75,000 as a projectable righthander with a fast arm, Perales quickly emerged as a potentially electrifying pitcher who showed mid-90s velocity after a few months in the Red Sox academy in the Dominican Republic. The 2020 Covid shutdown and non-elbow arm injuries limited him to just two professional innings entering the 2022 season. Once on the mound, Perales overpowered hitters in the Rookie-level Florida Complex League, and earned a promotion for a season-ending stretch in Low-A Salem, where he struck out 31% of hitters.
SCOUTING REPORT: Perales overwhelmed FCL hitters even when throwing nothing but fastballs, sitting at 94-97 mph, topping out at 99 with ride from a low release height. Pushed to lean more frequently on his secondaries, Perales showed a power slider that flashed plus. It was especially effective against righties, but he couldn't control it consistently and he would sometimes slow his arm speed on it, allowing hitters to spit on pitches out of the zone. His changeup was fringy but showed promise as a third piece in a developing mix. Though capped at three innings per outing in 2022, Perales will continue to develop as a starter, learning to navigate lineups multiple times in 2023.
THE FUTURE: Perales has midrotation upside, but the variance of his potential outcomes is immense. If he doesn't start, his fastball makes it easy to see a future late-innings reliever if he can stay healthy.

BA GRADE: 50/Extreme	Fastball: 65		Slider: 50		Changeup: 45		Control: 50						
Year	Age	Club (League)	Lvl	W	L	ERA	G	GS	IP	H	HR	BB	SO	BB/9	SO/9	WHIP	AVG
2022	19	Red Sox (FCL)	R	0	1	1.08	9	7	25	10	0	9	34	3.2	12.2	0.76	.120
2022	19	Salem (CAR)	LoA	0	1	3.38	4	4	11	10	1	11	16	9.3	13.5	1.97	.250
Minor League Totals				0	2	1.91	14	12	38	21	1	21	53	5.0	12.7	1.12	.162

18 MATTHEW LUGO, SS/3B/2B

Born: May 9, 2001. **B-T:** R-R. **HT:** 6-1. **WT:** 185.
Drafted: HS—Florida, P.R., 2019 (2nd round). **Signed by:** Edgar Perez.
TRACK RECORD: When the Red Sox selected Lugo out of Puerto Rico and signed him to a $1.1 million bonus, they believed the nephew of Carlos Beltran would stick in the middle of the infield and grow into plus power. After he hit just four homers and slugged .364 in his first full pro season in 2021, a cleaned-up swing and a more hitter-friendly environment in High-A Greenville led to a .282/.338/.492 line with 18 homers and 54 extra-base hits in 2022.
SCOUTING REPORT: While Lugo showed solid bat-to-ball skills in 2021, a late trigger and some minor mechanical issues resulted in a ton of grounders and flat liners. In 2022, he changed his mindset to drive the ball in the air. That adjustment, complemented by a smoother setup, allowed Lugo to unload on pitches in front of the plate to the pull side with average power. His strikeout rate remained a modest 19.8%, but his lack of selectivity is likely to compromise his hit tool. With average speed and arm strength, Lugo showed fringy range at shortstop with 20 errors in 73 games and moved to second base and third base once Marcelo Mayer got to Greenville. Lugo will also get a look in center field in 2023 as he looks for a true defensive home.
THE FUTURE: Lugo's emerging power suggests a promising versatile righthanded bench player or a low-end regular. If he takes to the outfield or tightens his plate discipline, he could elevate that profile.

BA GRADE: 45/High	Hit: 45		Power: 50		Speed: 50		Fielding: 45		Arm: 50			
Year	Age	Club (League)	Lvl	AVG	G	AB	R	H	2B	3B	HR	RBI	BB	SO	SB	OBP	SLG
2022	21	Greenville (SAL)	HiA	.288	114	466	76	134	25	10	18	78	35	100	20	.344	.500
2022	21	Portland (EL)	AA	.083	3	12	1	1	1	0	0	1	0	4	0	.083	.167
Minor League Totals				.274	263	1040	157	285	52	14	23	142	88	236	38	.338	.417

19 ENMANUEL VALDEZ, 2B

Born: December 28, 1998. **B-T:** L-R. **HT:** 5-9. **WT:** 191.
Signed: Dominican Republic, 2015. **Signed by:** Oz Ocampo/Roman Ocumarez/Jose Lima (Astros).

TRACK RECORD: Signed by the Astros for $450,000 in 2015, Valdez's first four minor league seasons proved undistinguished. After working to stay back on the ball to help him better track pitches and drive the ball to the opposite field, Valdez in 2021 hit a career-high 26 homers, two more than he hit from 2016 to 2019. He followed that with a bonkers performance—.327/.410/.606 with 21 homers in 82 games—for Houston's Double-A and Triple-A teams in 2022 before becoming the lead piece in a deadline deal for catcher Christian Vazquez. Valdez saw his numbers fall with Triple-A Worcester, but the Red Sox added a near big league-ready bat to their 40-man roster in November.

SCOUTING REPORT: Valdez coils with a pronounced crouch and sizable leg kick before exploding into the ball, holding back little while driving balls in the air to all fields, especially against righthanders. Despite his pre-swing movement, Valdez doesn't have too much swing-and-miss to his game, though his strikeout rate did tick up after the trade. His strength and bat-to-ball skills create the potential for an average hitter with above-average power, though with major questions about his position. A below-average runner, Valdez has limited range at second base makes that him a below-average option there, and he doesn't look better at third base or left field.

THE FUTURE: Defensive development will determine if Valdez is an up-and-down bat or carves out a stable role as a bat-first platoon contributor off the bench, though there's a chance he could be more.

| BA GRADE: 45/High | | Hit: 45 | | Power: 55 | | Speed: 40 | | | Fielding: 40 | | Arm: 45 | |

Year	Age	Club (League)	Lvl	AVG	G	AB	R	H	2B	3B	HR	RBI	BB	SO	SB	OBP	SLG
2022	23	Corpus Christi (TL)	AA	.357	44	168	40	60	16	0	11	45	34	47	4	.463	.649
2022	23	Sugar Land (PCL)	AAA	.296	38	159	26	47	10	1	10	32	11	29	1	.347	.560
2022	23	Worcester (IL)	AAA	.237	44	173	26	41	9	1	7	30	19	48	3	.309	.422
Minor League Totals				.257	487	1800	301	462	121	11	79	320	204	419	41	.335	.468

20 CONNOR WONG, C

Born: May 19, 1996. **B-T:** R-R. **HT:** 6-1. **WT:** 181.
Drafted: Houston, 2017 (3rd round). **Signed by:** Clint Bowers (Dodgers).

TRACK RECORD: Wong spent three seasons in the Dodgers' system as a catcher with the athleticism to move around the infield, but after heading to the Red Sox as the third player in the Mookie Betts deal, he has stayed almost exclusively behind the plate. Wong has developed a solid reputation inside the organization for his work with pitchers. His offense took a step forward in 2022 with a more selective, contact-oriented approach with Triple-A Worcester, though he scuffled in 27 big league games.

SCOUTING REPORT: After struggling to control his strikeout rate in past years, Wong committed to a flat bat path with minimal pre-swing movement in 2022. That led to fewer swings-and-misses and more walks, but also a preponderance of liners and ground balls while rarely tapping into his wiry strength. Still, he has a chance to get on base enough to be a serviceable bottom-of-the-order hitter who runs extremely well for a catcher with average speed. Pitchers gave him solid reviews for his game-calling and his framing numbers in both Triple-A and the big leagues were solid. Wong has a plus arm and averaged 1.92 seconds on his pop times on throws to second base in the big leagues, though runners were successful on 15 of 18 stolen base attempts.

THE FUTURE: Wong should have a decent run as a big league backup catcher.

| BA GRADE: 40/Medium | | Hit: 40 | | Power: 40 | | Speed: 50 | | Fielding: 50 | | Arm: 60 | |

Year	Age	Club (League)	Lvl	AVG	G	AB	R	H	2B	3B	HR	RBI	BB	SO	SB	OBP	SLG
2022	26	Worcester (IL)	AAA	.288	81	323	47	93	20	0	15	44	27	80	7	.349	.489
2022	26	Boston (AL)	MLB	.188	27	48	8	9	3	0	1	7	5	16	0	.273	.313
Major League Totals				.213	33	61	11	13	4	1	1	8	6	23	0	.290	.361
Minor League Totals				.276	372	1426	208	393	83	9	71	230	113	446	32	.337	.496

21 CUTTER COFFEY, SS/3B/2B

Born: May 21, 2004. **B-T:** R-R. **HT:** 6-2. **WT:** 190.
Drafted: HS—Bakersfield, Calif., 2022 (2nd round). **Signed by:** Josh Labandeira.

TRACK RECORD: While Coffey garnered consideration as a pitcher in the 2022 draft thanks to a mid-90s fastball and quality slider, the Red Sox tabbed him with the No. 41 overall pick and signed him to a

slightly-below-slot bonus of $1.85 million based on his upside as a power-hitting infielder. Coffey played 11 games in the Florida Complex League, and hit .125 in 32 at-bats with seven walks and 11 strikeouts.
SCOUTING REPORT: Coffey's swing features power from the ground up, with a rhythmic leg kick, powerful torque and considerable bat speed. He possesses average pull power with the chance for more. There are small edges to his swing that will require cleaning up in order to develop his timing to the point where he can feature a fringy to average hit tool, but he showed good swing decisions and swings against breaking balls to suggest promise. Coffey played shortstop, second base and third base in his debut. He has the body control and athleticism to handle short, but some evaluators see him as better suited for third given his arm strength and limited speed. He's a fringy runner now who projects as below-average as he gains size.
THE FUTURE: Coffey has the size, strength and athleticism to become a power-hitting infielder who provides strong defense at third and fringy to average defense in the middle infield. He'll compete for a spot in full-season Class A in spring training but could open the year in extended spring training.

| BA GRADE: 50/Extreme | | Hit: 45 | | Power: 50 | | Speed: 40 | | Fielding: 55 | | Arm: 60 | |

Year	Age	Club (League)	Lvl	AVG	G	AB	R	H	2B	3B	HR	RBI	BB	SO	SB	OBP	SLG
2022	18	Red Sox (FCL)	R	.125	11	32	7	4	1	0	0	0	7	11	1	.300	.156
Minor League Totals				.125	11	32	7	4	1	0	0	0	7	11	1	.300	.156

22 WILYER ABREU, OF

Born: June 24, 1999. **B-T:** L-L. **HT:** 6-0. **WT:** 217.
Signed: Venezuela, 2017. **Signed by:** Oz Ocampo/Roman Ocumarez/Tom Shafer (Astros).
TRACK RECORD: Signed by the Astros for $300,000 as an 18-year-old in 2017, Abreu was unimpressive in his first three pro seasons. After he overhauled his approach to focus on selectivity with an eye towards damage, he blasted 16 homers in 82 games in High-A in 2021. He followed that in 2022 by drawing the second-most walks (114) in the minors while hitting a combined .247/.399/.435 in Double-A. The Red Sox acquired him from the Astros at the trade deadline deal for catcher Christian Vazquez.
SCOUTING REPORT: Though Abreu's selectivity can veer into passivity, he swings with bad intentions, creating three true outcomes potential. With Houston, Abreu closed off his front shoulder, then exploded with a rotational swing to generate average power. The Red Sox asked him to square up his stance, hoping that in doing so, it would become easier for Abreu to get to pitches in different parts of the zone. His basestealing instincts help his average speed play up as he went 31-for-34 on stolen base attempts in 2022. Despite a fire hydrant frame, Abreu moves well enough to be respectable in center field and good in the outfield corners with a solid-average arm.
THE FUTURE: The Red Sox added Abreu to the 40-man roster in November, seeing him as a potential fourth outfielder with a number of paths to contribute. He should open 2023 in Triple-A.

| BA GRADE: 45/High | | Hit: 40 | | Power: 50 | | Speed: 50 | | Fielding: 50 | | Arm: 55 | |

Year	Age	Club (League)	Lvl	AVG	G	AB	R	H	2B	3B	HR	RBI	BB	SO	SB	OBP	SLG
2022	23	Corpus Christi (TL)	AA	.249	89	329	81	82	24	0	15	54	78	108	23	.399	.459
2022	23	Portland (EL)	AA	.242	40	128	25	31	5	0	4	19	36	45	8	.399	.375
Minor League Totals				.255	345	1194	222	304	71	4	37	168	203	358	62	.367	.414

23 NIKO KAVADAS, 1B

Born: October 27, 1998. **B-T:** L-R. **HT:** 6-1. **WT:** 235.
Drafted: Notre Dame, 2021 (11th round). **Signed by:** Alonzo Wright.
TRACK RECORD: Despite a Bunyan-esque senior year at Notre Dame in which he hit .302/.473/.767 with 22 homers in 47 games, position questions and some uncertainty about his sought-after signing bonus left Kavadas on the board on day three of the 2021 draft. The Red Sox pounced in the 11th round and signed the slugger for $250,000. In his first full pro season, Kavadas hit .295/.460/.603 with 24 homers in 96 games between Low-A and High-A before tailing off in Double-A Portland. He finished second in the minors in on-base percentage (.443) and 12th in OPS (.990).
SCOUTING REPORT: Kavadas is unabashed about his desire to hit a homer every time he bats, but he's selective in his efforts to do so. Early in counts, he looks for a pitch either middle-in or middle-away to hammer in the air, something he did with exit velocities up to 110 mph. His power grades as at least plus, and Kavadas showed the ability to leave the yard to all fields while handling velocity in the lower levels. As command improved in Double-A, his quality and frequency of contact declined, suggesting a below-average to fringe-average future hit tool. A plodding runner, Kavadas can make routine plays at first but projects as a below-average defender with a below-average arm.

THE FUTURE: Kavadas' career will be defined by his bat, and more specifically by the development of his hit tool. He's an intelligent hitter, and if he finds ways to limit his holes, he could be a DH who sees some time at first. If not, he may see time as an up-and-down lefthanded bench bat.

BA GRADE: 45/High			Hit: 45		Power: 65			Speed: 20		Fielding: 40		Arm: 40	

Year	Age	Club (League)	Lvl	AVG	G	AB	R	H	2B	3B	HR	RBI	BB	SO	SB	OBP	SLG
2022	23	Salem (CAR)	LoA	.286	59	192	35	55	18	1	14	48	54	70	1	.453	.609
2022	23	Greenville (SAL)	HiA	.308	37	120	27	37	4	0	10	28	32	42	0	.472	.592
2022	23	Portland (EL)	AA	.222	24	81	9	18	3	0	2	10	16	40	0	.370	.333
Minor League Totals				.278	135	436	81	121	29	1	28	92	117	165	1	.443	.541

24 BROOKS BRANNON, C

Born: May 4, 2004. **B-T:** R-R. **HT:** 6-0. **WT:** 210.
Drafted: HS—Randleman, N.C., 2022 (9th round). **Signed by:** Kirk Fredriksson.
TRACK RECORD: Brannon mashed 20 homers as a high school senior, tying a North Carolina record that had previously been set by his father Paul, a Mariners draftee in 1990. The Red Sox signed him to an over-slot bonus of $712,500 as a ninth-round pick in 2022, then Brannon made his pro debut in the Rookie-level Florida Complex League.
SCOUTING REPORT: Brannon is a formidable physical presence, a broad-shouldered teenager with made-for-catching, tree-trunk legs. He funnels all of his strength into his swing, resulting in some tape-measure shots. It's an all-or-nothing approach that has allowed him to pulverize fastballs but has made him vulnerable to chasing secondaries out of the zone. Behind the plate, Brannon has good hands, a plus arm and excellent flexibility with a hunger to develop his defensive game.
THE FUTURE: Though mindful of the considerable risk attached to the high school catching demographic, the Red Sox viewed Brannon as having the tools and intangibles to be a worthwhile bet. He has a chance to emerge as an everyday big league catcher with offensive impact.

BA GRADE: 50/Extreme			Hit: 40		Power: 55			Speed: 30		Fielding: 45		Arm: 60.	

Year	Age	Club (League)	Lvl	AVG	G	AB	R	H	2B	3B	HR	RBI	BB	SO	SB	OBP	SLG
2022	18	Red Sox (FCL)	R	.462	5	13	6	6	1	2	0	5	2	5	0	.533	.846
Minor League Totals				.462	5	13	6	6	1	2	0	5	2	5	0	.533	.846

25 ELMER RODRIGUEZ-CRUZ, RHP

Born: August 18, 2003. **B-T:** L-R. **HT:** 6-3. **WT:** 160.
Drafted: HS—Guaynabo, P.R. 2021 (4th round). **Signed by:** Edgar Perez.
BACKGROUND: In high school, Rodriguez-Cruz was a reed-thin 17-year-old up to 94 mph with four pitches, showing the projectable physical traits and strike-throwing ability to suggest an attractive ceiling. The Red Sox took him in the fourth round—their highest selection of a high school righthander since Michael Kopech in 2014—and gave him a slightly below-slot bonus of $497,500. In his 2022 pro debut, Rodriguez-Cruz had a 1.88 ERA with a 26.1% strikeout rate and 9.3% walk rate in 38.1 innings, mostly in the Rookie-level Florida Complex League
SCOUTING REPORT: Even as he has room for considerable strength gains, Rodriguez-Cruz works with a fastball up to 95 mph and features good extension, and his fastball gets on hitters quickly. The athletic righthander isn't shy about attacking the strike zone with his fastball as the headliner of a mix that also includes a curveball that could be a tick above-average pitch, as well as a changeup and a fringy slider.
THE FUTURE: Rodriguez-Cruz has a mix that gives him a chance to emerge as a starter, most likely at the back of the rotation, so long as either his changeup or slider develops into a viable third big league pitch. He finished 2022 in Low-A Salem and likely will spend much of 2023 there.

BA GRADE: 50/Extreme		Fastball: 55		Curveball: 55		Slider: 45		Changeup: 45		Control: 50	

Year	Age	Club (League)	Lvl	W	L	ERA	G	GS	IP	H	HR	BB	SO	BB/9	SO/9	WHIP	AVG
2022	18	Red Sox (FCL)	R	0	3	1.95	11	8	32	28	0	12	36	3.3	10.0	1.24	.226
2022	18	Salem (CAR)	LoA	0	0	1.50	2	2	6	3	0	3	6	4.5	9.0	1.00	.143
Minor League Totals				0	3	1.88	13	10	38	31	0	15	42	3.5	9.9	1.20	.214

26 CHASE MEIDROTH, 2B

Born: July 23, 2001. **B-T:** R-R. **HT:** 5-10. **WT:** 170.
Drafted: San Diego, 2022 (4th round). **Signed by:** J.J. Altobelli.

TRACK RECORD: Largely unrecruited out of high school, Meidroth played just 19 games at San Diego before taking full advantage of regular playing time in 2022, hitting .329/.440/.544 with 10 homers. He improved his stock by holding his own in the Cape Cod League, leading the Red Sox to take him in the fourth round and sign him to a below-slot bonus of $272,500. Meidroth dominated in his pro debut, hitting .309/.424/.559 with four homers and more walks than strikeouts in 19 games with Low-A Salem.

SCOUTING REPORT: A stocky 5-foot-10 player whose raw tools are easily overlooked, Meidroth has excellent hand-eye coordination and gets his barrel to the ball with a flat bat path and a high contact rate. Once in pro ball, he embraced suggestions about small posture tweaks, with a more upright stance allowing him to more frequently pull the ball in the air. The results came so quickly that it created optimism about the possibility of 40- to 45-grade power along with an excellent hit tool. His limited arm makes his best fit second base, where his range grades as below-average, but his reliable hands and clock make him serviceable. He may also see time at third and short.

THE FUTURE: Meidroth may get pushed to High-A Greenville to start 2023, and has a chance to hit his way to a profile in the mold of a righthanded version of Tommy La Stella.

BA GRADE: 45/Very High		HIT: 55		Power: 40		Speed: 40		Fielding: 45		Arm: 40			
Year	Age	Club (League)	Lvl	AVG	G	AB	R	H	2B	3B	HR	RBI	BB	SO	SB	OBP	SLG
2022	20	Red Sox (FCL)	R	.375	3	8	4	3	0	0	0	3	2	0		.545	.375
2022	20	Salem (CAR)	LoA	.309	19	68	15	21	5	0	4	12	12	9	4	.424	.559
Minor League Totals				.316	22	76	19	24	5	0	4	15	14	11	4	.438	.539

27 ZACK KELLY, RHP

Born: March 3, 1995. **B-T:** R-R. **HT:** 6-3. **WT:** 205.
Signed: Newberry (S.C.), 2017 (NDFA). **Signed by:** Neil Avent (Athletics).

TRACK RECORD: Kelly has taken the road less traveled. Signed by the Athletics out of Division II Newberry College for $500, he was released twice—by the A's in 2018 and the Angels during the pandemic in 2020—and had non-Tommy John elbow surgery before the Red Sox signed him to a minor league deal in late 2020. Once with the Red Sox, Kelly cleaned up his mechanics to unlock more power on his fastball, making his changeup even more effective, and he excelled in the upper minors to earn a season-ending callup to Boston in 2022.

SCOUTING REPORT: Kelly, who posted a 36% strikeout rate in the minors in 2022, tunnels a mid-90s fastball that sits 93-96 mph and tops out at 97 with a low-80s changeup that features both depth and fade to avoid barrels. He also has a cutter/slider that he employs as a third offering, chiefly against righties, to open the plate. Kelly possesses good command within the strike zone, resulting in generally weak contact, including against big league hitters who posted an average 85.5 mph exit velocity against him.

THE FUTURE: Though he lacks wipeout stuff, Kelly's ability to throw strikes and limit hard contact suggests a ready-made middle-inning profile. He could be a frequent big league contributor in 2023.

BA GRADE: 40/Medium		Fastball: 50		Slider: 40		Changeup: 55		Control: 55					
Year	Age	Club (League)	Lvl	W	L	ERA	G	GS	IP	H	HR	BB	SO	BB/9	SO/9	WHIP	AVG
2022	27	Worcester (IL)	AAA	6	3	2.72	44	0	50	34	2	25	72	4.5	13.0	1.19	.191
2022	27	Boston (AL)	MLB	1	0	3.95	13	0	14	14	2	4	11	2.6	7.2	1.32	.259
Major League Totals				1	0	3.95	13	0	14	14	2	4	11	2.6	7.2	1.32	.259
Minor League Totals				19	14	3.07	132	13	246	214	13	94	290	3.4	10.6	1.25	.234

28 DALTON ROGERS, LHP

Born: January 18, 2001. **B-T:** R-L. **HT:** 5-11. **WT:** 172.
Drafted: Southern Mississippi, 2022 (3rd round). **Signed by:** Danny Watkins.

TRACK RECORD: Rogers enrolled at Southeast Louisiana as a freshman, but after the Covid year cut short his freshman campaign, he transferred to Jones (Miss.) JC, then transferred again as a sophomore to Southern Mississippi. As a multi-inning reliever, he struck out 37.7% of hitters while limiting opponents to a .128 batting average. Rogers then had a brief Cape Cod League stint as a starter, the role in which the Red Sox hope to develop him after signing him for a below-slot $447,500 as a third-round pick in 2022.

SCOUTING REPORT: Rogers is a diminutive lefty who hides the ball well while driving down the mound to create good extension and a low release height. That combination, along with the ride and armside run on his 93-94 mph fastball, which tops out at 96, has given hitters fits at the top of the zone. He's leaned heavily on his fastball to this point, though he has two secondaries—a low-80s changeup and low-80s slider—with the shape to develop into weapons if he can control them.

THE FUTURE: The Red Sox will develop Rogers as a starter, hoping that his control will improve to the point where his tantalizing mix can play to its fullest potential. If everything coalesces, he has the pitches to emerge as a No. 4 starter. If control remains elusive, Rogers could become a middle-innings lefty with high strikeout and walk rates.

BA GRADE: 45/Extreme	Fastball: 60 ,	Slider: 50	Changeup: 50	Control: 40										
Year	Age	Club (League)	Lvl	W	L	ERA	G	GS	IP	H	HR	BB	SO	BB/9	SO/9	WHIP	AVG
2022	21	Red Sox (FCL)	R	0	0	9.00	2	0	2	2	0	2	3	9.0	13.5	2.00	.286
Minor League Totals				0	0	9.00	2	0	2	2	0	2	3	9.0	13.5	2.00	.286

29 LUIS RAVELO, SS

Born: November 5, 2003. **B-T:** B-R. **HT:** 6-1. **WT:** 187.
Signed: Dominican Republic, 2021. **Signed by:** Manny Nanita/Eddie Romero.

TRACK RECORD: The Red Sox were drawn to Ravelo as a defensive magician whose lightning hands created a number of did-you-see-that double takes at shortstop. The team signed Ravelo for $525,000. After a respectable pro debut in the Dominican Summer League in 2021, he hit .197/.303/.265 in 2022, spending most of the season in the Rookie-level Florida Complex League before a promotion to Low-A Salem.

SCOUTING REPORT: Ravelo dazzles with his hands and flash, effortlessly executing between-the-legs or behind-the-back glove-to-hand transfers that would be unfathomable for most players. He has at least plus range and an above-average arm to profile as a true shortstop. The question is whether Ravelo will hit enough to be more than an up-and-down player. He's working to calm down his leg kick to improve timing, and at the end of the year, he drove some balls while hitting lefthanded in Salem to suggest a hint of power, but he will have to improve his swing decisions to make more regular contact. He doesn't have a single extra-base hit while batting righthanded, casting uncertainty over his future as a switch-hitter.

THE FUTURE: Ravelo is so good defensively that he doesn't need to hit much to forge a big league path, but he will need more strength and development as a hitter to get there.

BA GRADE: 45/Extreme	Hit: 30	Power: 30	Speed: 45	Fielding: 60	Arm: 55									
Year	Age	Club (League)	Lvl	AVG	G	AB	R	H	2B	3B	HR	RBI	BB	SO	SB	OBP	SLG
2022	18	Red Sox (FCL)	R	.187	31	107	19	20	1	2	0	6	17	31	6	.298	.234
2022	18	Salem (CAR)	LoA	.240	7	25	4	6	1	0	1	6	2	8	0	.321	.400
Minor League Totals				.221	81	276	43	61	6	4	2	25	38	61	6	.319	.293

30 DAVID HAMILTON, SS/2B

Born: September 29, 1997. **B-T:** L-R. **HT:** 5-10. **WT:** 175.
Drafted: Texas, 2019 (8th round). **Signed by:** K.J. Hendricks (Brewers).

TRACK RECORD: After a strong sophomore campaign at Texas, Hamilton ruptured his Achilles in a scooter accident, resulting in surgery that left him unable to play as a junior. In the 2019 draft, the Brewers took an eighth-round flier on his athleticism bouncing back and signed Hamilton for $400,000. After the 2021 season, the Red Sox acquired Hamilton and corner infielder Alex Binelas in a trade for Hunter Renfroe. Hamilton spent all of 2022 with Double-A Portland and tied an organizational record with 70 steals.

SCOUTING REPORT: Hamilton is at his best when he shoots liners from gap to gap and creates havoc with his legs. In 2022, he got away from that approach at times, forcing contact in the air with a resulting surge in pop outs. Down the stretch, he toned down that approach and took full advantage of his double-plus speed by running wild, hitting .267/.368/.408 with 39 steals in his last 54 games. He displayed solid defense at short and above-average defense at second while also showing considerable promise in a brief look in the outfield at the end of the season.

THE FUTURE: With speed and up-the-middle defense at a premium given MLB's 2023 rule changes, the Red Sox added Hamilton to the 40-man roster after 2022. He profiles as a season-opening depth option with a chance to emerge as a steady reserve by the end of 2023.

BA GRADE: 40/Medium	Hit: 40	Power: 40	Speed: 70	Fielding: 55	Arm: 50									
Year	Age	Club (League)	Lvl	AVG	G	AB	R	H	2B	3B	HR	RBI	BB	SO	SB	OBP	SLG
2022	24	Portland (EL)	AA	.251	119	463	81	116	16	9	12	42	56	119	70	.338	.402
Minor League Totals				.254	220	866	147	220	35	20	20	85	106	209	122	.340	.410

Chicago Cubs

BY KYLE GLASER

The first full season of the Cubs' rebuild went about as expected.

The Cubs went 74-88 in their first full year since trading Anthony Rizzo, Kris Bryant and Javier Baez, falling below .500 just 13 games into the season and staying there the rest of the year. Chicago's offense scored its fewest runs per game since 2014 and a young, untested pitching staff finished 20th in the majors in ERA.

The season, for all intents and purposes, served as an elongated tryout for Cubs young players to prove they belonged in the franchise's long-term plans. Chicago used 42 different pitchers during the season, tying an MLB record. They used 67 different players, two shy of the record.

Some 2022 newcomers, such as imported Japanese outfielder Seiya Suzuki, utility player Christopher Morel and lefthanded reliever Brandon Hughes, showed enough to solidify themselves as keepers. Others, like righthander Caleb Kilian and outfielder Nelson Velazquez, showed they still have work to do.

The Cubs' biggest challenge for more than a decade has been developing homegrown pitching. On that front, the organization made progress. Lefthander Justin Steele successfully seized a rotation spot and showed signs of being the club's first successful homegrown starter since Jeff Samardzija. Lefthander Jordan Wicks, the club's first-round pick in 2021, rose to Double-A in his first full season. The Cubs selected Oklahoma righthander Cade Horton and prep lefthander Jackson Ferris with their top two picks in the 2022 draft. At the trade deadline, they acquired talented pitching prospects Hayden Wesneski from the Yankees and Ben Brown from the Phillies.

The Cubs curiously held onto catcher Willson Contreras and outfielder Ian Happ at the trade deadline, but even without trading them, the organization now has its best group of pitching prospects in a decade.

Of course, collecting pitching prospects and developing them into successful starters are two different things. The club's pitcher outcomes have improved under assistant general manager and director of pitching Craig Breslow, and unexpected steps forward in 2022 from previously unheralded prospects such as righthanders Javier Assad, Luis Devers and Porter Hodge point to improvement in the Cubs' development processes.

Still, the Cubs' existing pitching prospects largely project to be midrotation starters at best, and whether the organization can unlock more to help them become frontline starters remains to be seen.

Japanese import Seiya Suzuki hit .262/.336/.433 with 14 homers in 111 games in his MLB debut.

PROJECTED 2026 LINEUP

Catcher	Miguel Amaya	27
First Base	Matt Mervis	28
Second Base	Nick Madrigal	29
Third Base	Christopher Morel	27
Shortstop	Nico Hoerner	29
Left Field	Kevin Alcantara	23
Center Field	Pete Crow-Armstrong	24
Right Field	Brennen Davis	26
Designated Hitter	Seiya Suzuki	31
No. 1 Starter	Jameson Taillon	34
No. 2 Starter	Cade Horton	24
No. 3 Starter	Justin Steele	30
No. 4 Starter	Ben Brown	26
No. 5 Starter	Hayden Wesneski	28
Closer	Keegan Thompson	31

Importantly, the Cubs appear to have hit on many of the trades they made during their 2021 trade deadline teardown. Outfielders Pete Crow-Armstrong (Baez), Kevin Alcantara (Rizzo) and Alexander Canario (Bryant) blossomed after joining the Cubs organization. Add in a breakout year from first baseman Matt Mervis, and the Cubs' position prospect group looks promising even with repeated injuries to talented outfielder Brennen Davis and catcher Miguel Amaya.

With a talented group of hitters and their deepest group of pitching prospects in years, the Cubs have the pieces of their next competitive team in place. Now, it's a matter of patience as they climb to the major leagues. ∎

CHICAGO CUBS

TOP 2023 MLB CONTRIBUTORS	RANK
Brennen Davis, OF	2
Matt Mervis, 1B	4
Hayden Wesneski, RHP	8
BREAKOUT PROSPECTS	**RANK**
Daniel Palencia, RHP	14
Porter Hodge, RHP	22
Pedro Ramirez, 2B	27

SOURCE OF TOP 30 TALENT

Homegrown	22	Acquired	8
College	7	Trade	8
Junior college	0	Rule 5 draft	0
High school	6	Independent league	0
Nondrafted free agent	0	Free agent/waivers	0
International	9		

LF
Yohendrick Pinango (19)
Jordan Nwogu
Cole Roederer

CF
Pete Crow-Armstrong (1)
Brennen Davis (2)
Darius Hill (23)
Ezequiel Pagan

RF
Kevin Alcantara (3)
Alexander Canario (12)
Owen Caissie (13)
Yonathan Perlaza

3B
James Triantos (18)
Chase Strumpf (24)
Jake Slaughter

SS
Cristian Hernandez (7)
Kevin Made (21)
Ed Howard
Andy Weber

2B
Pedro Ramirez (27)
Yeison Santana

1B
Matt Mervis (4)
Bryce Ball
B.J. Murray

C
Miguel Amaya (9)
Moises Ballesteros (16)
Pablo Aliendo (25)
Adan Sanchez

LHP

LHSP	LHRP
Jordan Wicks (11)	DJ Herz (17)
Jackson Ferris (15)	Luke Little
	Bailey Horn
	Brailyn Marquez
	Brendon Little
	Riley Martin
	Sheldon Reed

RHP

RHSP	RHRP
Cade Horton (6)	Daniel Palencia (14)
Ben Brown (7)	Cam Sanders (28)
Hayden Wesneski (8)	Kohl Franklin (29)
Caleb Kilian (10)	Riley Thompson (30)
Javier Assad (20)	Jeremiah Estrada
Porter Hodge (22)	Zac Leigh
Luis Devers (26)	Ryan Jensen
Matt Swarmer	Ethan Roberts
	Ben Leeper

1 PETE CROW-ARMSTRONG, OF

Born: March 25, 2002. **B-T:** L-L. **HT:** 6-0. **WT:** 184.
Drafted: HS—Los Angeles, 2020 (1st round).
Signed by: Rusty McNamara (Mets).

TRACK RECORD: Crow-Armstrong grew up in the shadow of Hollywood as the son of actors Ashley Crow and Matthew Armstrong. Rather than follow his parents into television and film, Crow-Armstrong found fame on the baseball diamond. He emerged as a budding star at a young age and was selected for USA Baseball's 12U, 15U and 18U national teams. He starred at Harvard-Westlake High, the same school that produced all-star pitchers Lucas Giolito, Max Fried and Jack Flaherty, and graduated as the program's all-time leader in hits and runs despite his senior season being cut short by the coronavirus pandemic. The Mets drafted him 19th overall and signed him for $3.359 million. Crow-Armstrong's pro debut in 2021 ended after just six games due to a torn labrum in his right shoulder, but the Cubs still acquired him at the trade deadline for Javier Baez and Trevor Williams. Crow-Armstrong rewarded the Cubs' faith in 2022, finishing among the organization's leaders in batting average (.312), hits (132), runs (89) and stolen bases (32) across the Class A levels and earning a selection to the Futures Game.

SCOUTING REPORT: Crow-Armstrong has long been known for his sensational defense in center field, but he's a threat at the plate, too. He has a discerning eye for the strike zone and makes frequent contact with a fast and fluid lefthanded swing. He stays balanced through his swing and has exceptional hand-eye coordination that allows him to hit pitches in any part of the zone. He occasionally gets jammed and is prone to weak contact, but he has the advanced instincts and self-awareness to adjust his setup and timing to close his holes. Crow-Armstrong is a contact hitter and primarily hits hard line drives all over the field, but he has begun showing average pull-side power and could add more as he physically matures. He is progressively getting stronger and posted the highest exit velocities of his career in 2022. Crow-Armstrong enhances his offense with his plus speed and a high-energy style of play. He is a threat to steal at any time and applies constant pressure to opposing defenses with his aggressive baserunning. He is occasionally overaggressive and runs into outs. Crow-Armstrong is an elite defender in center field whose graceful, fluid actions make the position look easy. His plus speed, elite anticipation and pristine routes give him exceptional range

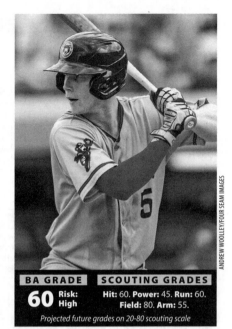

ANDREW WOOLLEY/FOUR SEAM IMAGES

BA GRADE	SCOUTING GRADES
60 Risk: High	Hit: 60. Power: 45. Run: 60. Field: 80. Arm: 55.

Projected future grades on 20-80 scouting scale

BEST TOOLS

BATTING
Best Hitter for Average	Pete Crow-Armstrong
Best Power Hitter	Alexander Canario
Best Strike-Zone Discipline	Matt Mervis
Fastest Baserunner	Pete Crow-Armstrong
Best Athlete	Kevin Alcantara

PITCHING
Best Fastball	Daniel Palencia
Best Curveball	Ben Brown
Best Slider	Hayden Wesneski
Best Changeup	Jordan Wicks
Best Control	Luis Devers

FIELDING
Best Defensive Catcher	Pablo Aliendo
Best Defensive Infielder	Ed Howard
Best Infield Arm	Kevin Made
Best Defensive Outfielder	Pete Crow-Armstrong
Best Outfield Arm	Brennen Davis

in all directions, particularly going into the gaps. He is fearless and aggressive going back to the wall and makes highlight-reel catches almost daily. His above-average, accurate throwing arm rounds out his premium defensive ability.

THE FUTURE: Crow-Armstrong projects to hit at the top of the Cubs' lineup and contend perennially for Gold Glove awards in center field. He will open 2023 at Double-A Tennessee and has a chance to reach Wrigley Field by the end of the season.

Year	Age	Club (League)	Lvl	AVG	G	AB	R	H	2B	3B	HR	RBI	BB	SO	SB	OBP	SLG
2022	20	Myrtle Beach (CAR)	LoA	.354	38	158	39	56	5	3	7	27	22	33	13	.443	.557
2022	20	South Bend (MWL)	HiA	.287	63	265	50	76	15	7	9	34	14	69	19	.333	.498
Minor League Totals				.318	107	447	95	142	22	10	16	65	43	108	34	.388	.519

2 BRENNEN DAVIS, OF

Born: November 2, 1999. **B-T:** R-R. **HT:** 6-4. **W T:** 210.
Drafted: HS—Chandler, AZ, 2018 (2nd round). **Signed by:** Steve McFarland.

TRACK RECORD: The son of former Chicago Bulls point guard Reggie Theus, Davis primarily played basketball growing up before choosing to focus on baseball his senior year of high school. The decision paid off when the Cubs drafted him in the second round and signed him for $1.1 million. Davis has excelled when healthy, but he's struggled with injuries throughout his career. He missed time with a hamstring injury, a broken finger, a broken nose and a concussion across his first three seasons. Expected to rise to the majors in 2022, he instead played just 43 games at Triple-A Iowa after having midseason surgery to repair a malformation of blood vessels in his back. He then made it through five games in the Arizona Fall League before being shut down with lower back tightness.

SCOUTING REPORT: Davis stands a long, lean 6-foot-4 and resembles a basketball player with his build and premium athleticism. He has plus raw power with his natural strength and leverage and does damage to all fields when he connects. He has good barrel control and covers the entire plate. Davis makes plenty of impact on contact, but he struggles to pick up spin and takes a lot of uncertain swings. He often gets caught in between and must improve his pitch recognition and swing decisions to make enough contact to be a fringe-average hitter. Davis is a serviceable defender in center field with his above-average speed and long strides, but he projects better in right field and has the above-average arm for the position. Davis' main challenge is to stay healthy.

THE FUTURE: Davis has the ability to be a solid everyday outfielder, but he has missed a lot of development time. He'll aim to make his big league debut in 2023.

SCOUTING GRADES		Hitting: 45		Power: 55		Speed: 55			Fielding: 50		Arm: 55	

Year	Age	Club (League)	Lvl	AVG	G	AB	R	H	2B	3B	HR	RBI	BB	SO	SB	OBP	SLG
2022	22	Cubs (ACL)	R	.143	5	14	2	2	0	0	1	2	2	5	0	.294	.357
2022	22	South Bend (MWL)	HiA	.130	5	23	0	3	0	0	0	2	0	8	0	.130	.130
2022	22	Iowa (IL)	AAA	.191	43	141	16	27	6	0	4	13	23	52	0	.322	.319
Minor League Totals				.255	220	762	126	194	42	3	32	103	103	233	18	.363	.444

3 KEVIN ALCANTARA, OF

Born: July 12, 2002. **B-T:** R-R. **HT:** 6-6. **WT:** 188.
Signed: Dominican Republic, 2018. **Signed by:** Edgar Mateo/Juan Piron (Yankees).

TRACK RECORD: Alcantara signed with the Yankees for $1 million during the 2018-19 international signing period and immediately stood out in the Rookie complex leagues. The Cubs acquired him along with righthander Alexander Vizcaino for Anthony Rizzo at the 2021 trade deadline. Alcantara made his full-season debut at Low-A Myrtle Beach in 2022 and continued to shine against better competition. He finished in the top 10 in the Carolina League in batting average, runs, hits, home runs, RBIs, slugging percentage and OPS despite playing his home games in the league's most pitcher-friendly park.

SCOUTING REPORT: Alcantara looks like a basketball player with a tall, lanky 6-foot-6 frame that has plenty of room to fill out. He is impressively coordinated for his size and is able to keep his swing short despite his long levers, giving him an advanced, repeatable swing with plenty of bat speed. His ability to recognize spin is inconsistent and he'll occasionally expand his strike zone, but he makes adjustments quickly and has a chance to be an average hitter with added strength and improved swing decisions. Alcantara already posts exit velocities above 110 mph and can hit balls out to all parts of the park. He has natural strength and leverage that give him plus power now, and he could grow into more power as he adds muscle to his lean frame. Alcantara is an above-average runner who has enough range to play center field for now, but he is likely to slow down as he matures and move to a corner. His average arm strength fits best in left field.

THE FUTURE: Alcantara has one of the highest ceilings in the Cubs' system as an athletic, power-hitting slugger, but he has lots of growth ahead. He'll move to High-A South Bend in 2023.

SCOUTING GRADES		Hitting: 45		Power: 60		Speed: 55			Fielding: 55		Arm: 50	

Year	Age	Club (League)	Lvl	AVG	G	AB	R	H	2B	3B	HR	RBI	BB	SO	SB	OBP	SLG
2022	19	Myrtle Beach (CAR)	LoA	.273	112	428	76	117	19	6	15	85	55	123	14	.360	.451
Minor League Totals				.281	187	708	134	199	31	14	21	128	80	195	24	.359	.453

4 MATT MERVIS, 1B

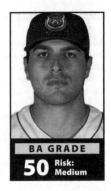

Born: April 16, 1998. **B-T:** L-R. **HT:** 6-4. **WT:** 225.
Signed: Duke, 2020 (NDFA). **Signed by:** Billy Swoope.

TRACK RECORD: Mervis played both ways at Duke as a first baseman/right-handed reliever and showed promising offensive potential in the Cape Cod League. He projected to be drafted between rounds six and 10 in 2020, but he went unpicked in the coronavirus-shortened, five-round draft. Mervis signed with the Cubs as an nondrafted free agent and broke out with one of the best seasons in the minors in 2022. He vaulted from High-A to Triple-A and led the minor leagues with 78 extra-base hits, 117 RBIs and 310 total bases and finished tied for third with 36 home runs.

BA GRADE

50 Risk: Medium

SCOUTING REPORT: Mervis is a hulking lefthanded hitter with plus raw power. He previously struggled to make enough contact to get to it, but he shortened his swing and honed his approach in 2022 to focus on pitches in the middle-third of the plate, leading to his breakout year. He has excellent bat speed and natural timing, and his improved swing path and selectivity give him a chance to be an average hitter. Mervis can be a touch aggressive on soft stuff below the zone and isn't as dangerous against lefthanders, but he demolishes fastballs, has good strike-zone recognition and keeps his strikeouts low for a power hitter. He mostly pulls the ball and will benefit from the new rules banning shifts in the majors. Mervis' value is tied almost exclusively to his bat. He is a well below-average runner and a below-average—but passable—defender at first base. He has retained the plus-plus arm strength that helped him reach 96 mph as a pitcher in college.
THE FUTURE: Mervis projects to be an everyday first baseman who hits for power, a case he amplified by tying for the Arizona Fall League lead with six home runs. His MLB debut should come in 2023.

SCOUTING GRADES	Hitting: 50	Power: 60	Speed: 30	Fielding: 40	Arm: 70

Year	Age	Club (League)	Lvl	AVG	G	AB	R	H	2B	3B	HR	RBI	BB	SO	SB	OBP	SLG
2022	24	South Bend (MWL)	HiA	.350	27	100	17	35	9	0	7	29	5	26	0	.389	.650
2022	24	Tennessee (SL)	AA	.300	53	203	34	61	16	1	14	51	20	46	2	.370	.596
2022	24	Iowa (IL)	AAA	.297	57	209	41	62	15	1	15	39	25	35	0	.383	.593
Minor League Totals				.275	209	771	132	212	52	3	45	163	87	177	8	.355	.525

5 CADE HORTON, RHP

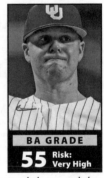

Born: August 20, 2001. **B-T:** R-R. **HT:** 6-2. **WT:** 190.
Drafted: Oklahoma, 2022 (1st round). **Signed by:** Ty Nichols.

TRACK RECORD: A standout quarterback and All-America pitcher in high school, Horton committed to Oklahoma to play both football and baseball but had Tommy John surgery as a freshman and dropped football. He began 2022 as the Sooners' starting third baseman while he eased his way back onto the mound and struggled early in his return to pitching, but he clicked at the end of the year to rocket up draft boards. Horton carried Oklahoma to the College World Series finals with a 2.81 ERA over four postseason starts and set a CWS finals record with 13 strikeouts against Mississippi. The Cubs drafted him seventh overall one month later and signed him for a below-slot $4.45 million.

BA GRADE

55 Risk: Very High

SCOUTING REPORT: Horton is a strong, athletic righthander with a power arsenal that overwhelms hitters. His fastball sits 94-96 mph and touches 98 with natural ride and cut that generates whiffs and weak popups at the top of the zone. His hard, vertical slider is a wipeout pitch at 87-90 mph and gives him a second plus offering that he can throw for strikes or use to get chases. Horton primarily throws his fastball and slider, but his low-80s curveball with downward bite is an average third offering he can land for strikes. His firm, upper-90s changeup is a usable, if fringy, fourth offering. Horton has a tick of effort to his delivery, but he maintains his stuff through his starts and throws everything for strikes with average control. He pitched only one partial season in college and still has to prove he can maintain his best stuff over a full season.
THE FUTURE: Horton has the ingredients to be a midrotation starter as long as he refines a third pitch and stays healthy. He'll make his pro debut in 2023.

SCOUTING GRADES:	Fastball: 70	Curveball: 50	Slider: 60	Changeup: 45	Control: 50

Year	Age	Club (League)	Level	W	L	ERA	G	GS	IP	H	HR	BB	SO	BB/9	SO/9	WHIP	AVG
2022	20	Did not play															

6 BEN BROWN, RHP

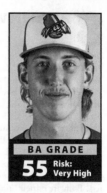

Born: September 9, 1999. **B-T:** R-R. **HT:** 6-6. **WT:** 210.
Drafted: HS—East Setauket, NY, 2017 (33rd round). **Signed by:** Alex Agostino (Phillies).
TRACK RECORD: A product of the same Long Island high school that produced Steven Matz and Anthony Kay, Brown signed with the Phillies for $60,000 as a 33rd-round pick in 2017 and would have been drafted higher if not for a burst appendix that caused him to miss the summer showcase circuit. He then had Tommy John surgery in 2019 and made just seven appearances in 2021 due to an elbow injury and a stint on the Covid-related injured list. Brown finally stayed healthy in 2022 and had a breakout season at High-A Jersey Shore, leading the Cubs to acquire him for closer David Robertson at the trade deadline. Brown rose to Double-A Tennessee after the trade and finished the year with 12.9 strikeouts per nine innings, the eighth best in the minors for pitchers with at least 100 innings.

BA GRADE
55 Risk: **Very High**

SCOUTING REPORT: Brown is an imposing 6-foot-6 righthander who keeps growing into more stuff. His fastball topped out at 92 mph in high school but now sits 94-97 with late ride and run to generate swings and misses in the strike zone. His primary secondary pitch is a plus mid-80s power curveball with biting downward action that he can land for strikes or bury for chase swings below the zone. Brown also has a short power slider in the 87-91 mph range that is an above-average offering. His rarely-used changeup is well below-average pitch and needs further development to help him better handle lefthanded hitters. Brown is an extremely confident pitcher who aggressively goes after hitters. He pounds the strike zone with average control and is efficient with his pitch counts.
THE FUTURE: Brown has a chance to be a hard-throwing No. 3 or 4 starter if he can stay healthy. If not, he has the stuff and mentality to be an impact reliever.

SCOUTING GRADES:	Fastball: 60		Curveball: 60		Slider: 55		Changeup: 30		Control: 50		

Year	Age	Club (League)	Lvl	W	L	ERA	G	GS	IP	H	HR	BB	SO	BB/9	SO/9	WHIP	AVG
2022	22	Jersey Shore (SAL)	HiA	3	5	3.08	16	15	73	53	7	23	105	2.8	12.9	1.04	.197
2022	22	Tennessee (SL)	AA	3	0	4.06	7	7	31	33	3	13	44	3.8	12.8	1.48	.273
Minor League Totals				11	9	3.39	56	37	204	177	15	73	261	3.2	11.5	1.22	.229

7 CRISTIAN HERNANDEZ, SS

Born: December 13, 2003. **B-T:** R-R. **HT:** 6-2. **WT:** 175.
Signed: Dominican Republic, 2021. **Signed by:** Gian Guzman/Louie Eljaua/Alex Suarez.
TRACK RECORD: Hernandez trained at the same program in the Dominican Republic that produced big league righthanders Cristian Javier and Deivi Garcia and emerged as arguably the top player in the 2020-21 international class. The Cubs signed him for a franchise-record $3 million bonus and assigned him the Dominican Summer League in 2021, where he had a solid pro debut. Hernandez made his U.S. debut in the Arizona Complex League in 2022 and continued to show promising tools and athleticism, but he slumped as the year progressed and struck out 30.2% of the time.

BA GRADE
55 Risk: **Extreme**

SCOUTING REPORT: Hernandez stands out with a lean, athletic 6-foot-2 frame that has plenty of room to fill out. He has excellent bat speed and generates plus power to all fields with remarkable ease. He consistently impacts the ball and could have plus-plus power once he reaches physical maturity. Hernandez hits balls hard when he connects, but his swing gets long and he chases too often, particularly against breaking balls. He has the physical ingredients to be an average hitter who gets to his power in games, but he has to tighten his swing and approach. Hernandez is a smooth defender at shortstop with the actions, hands and plus arm strength to stick at the position. He is a below-average runner with a tick below-average range, so he may move to third base as he gets bigger and loses a step. He would be at least an above-average defender at the hot corner.
THE FUTURE: Hernandez has the potential to be a power-hitting shortstop, but he has a lot of offensive adjustments to make before he can reach that ceiling. He'll make his full-season debut in 2023.

SCOUTING GRADES	Hitting: 50		Power: 60		Speed: 40		Fielding: 55		Arm: 60		

Year	Age	Club (Leag	Lvl	AVG	G	AB	R	H	2B	3B	HR	RBI	BB	SO	SB	OBP	SLG
2022	18	Cubs (ACL)	R	.261	44	157	21	41	4	1	3	21	13	53	6	.320	.357
Minor League Totals				.273	91	315	59	86	9	2	8	43	43	92	27	.361	.390

8 HAYDEN WESNESKI, RHP

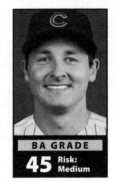

Born: December 5, 1997. **B-T:** R-R. **HT:** 6-3. **WT:** 210.
Drafted: Sam Houston State, 2019 (6th round). **Signed by:** Brian Rhees (Yankees).
TRACK RECORD: The Yankees drafted Wesneski in the sixth round in 2019 out of Sam Houston State and signed him for a below-slot $617,500. Wesneski rose three levels to Triple-A in his first full season in 2021 and delivered another strong showing in 2022. The Cubs acquired him for reliever Scott Effross at the trade deadline and called him up to the big leagues in September, when he posted a 2.18 ERA over 33 innings as a starter and long reliever in a tenure that also included an immaculate inning.

BA GRADE
45 Risk: **Medium**

SCOUTING REPORT: Wesneski succeeds by mixing and locating a deep, five-pitch mix. His four-seamer sits 93-94 mph and touches 97 with heavy sinking life, and his 92-95 mph two-seamer runs in hard and late on righthanded batters. Both are difficult pitches to elevate and result in a heavy dose of ground balls. Wesneski's low-80s slider with two-plane snap is a plus pitch that gets swings and misses both in and out of the strike zone, and he'll also mix in an 87-90 mph cutter to give batters a different look. He rounds out his arsenal with a below-average, upper-80s changeup he'll need to improve in order to better handle lefthanded batters. Wesneski's delivery is somewhat unconventional with his long arm action and low three-quarters arm slot, but he has a good feel for pitching and throws everything for strikes with above-average control. He is a tough competitor who earns the "bulldog" moniker from team officials.
THE FUTURE: Wesneski's deep pitch mix gives him a chance to be a back-of-the-rotation starter or bulk reliever. He'll compete for a spot in the Cubs' Opening Day rotation in spring training.

SCOUTING GRADES:	Fastball: 55	Slider: 60	Cutter: 50	Changeup: 40	Control: 55

Year	Age	Club (League)	Lvl	W	L	ERA	G	GS	IP	H	HR	BB	SO	BB/9	SO/9	WHIP	AVG
2022	24	Iowa (IL)	AAA	0	2	5.66	5	4	21	17	1	8	23	3.5	10.0	1.21	.227
2022	24	Scranton/WB (IL)	AAA	6	7	3.51	19	19	90	75	9	28	83	2.8	8.3	1.15	.227
2022	24	Chicago (NL)	MLB	3	2	2.18	6	4	33	24	3	7	33	1.9	9.0	0.94	.198
Major League Totals				3	2	2.18	6	4	33	24	3	7	33	1.9	9.0	0.94	.198
Minor League Totals				18	16	3.68	67	47	269	234	24	78	287	2.6	9.6	1.16	.233

9 MIGUEL AMAYA, C

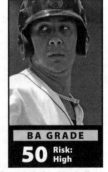

Born: March 9, 1999. **B-T:** R-R. **HT:** 6-2. **WT:** 200. **Signed:** Panama, 2015.
Signed by: Mario Encarnacion/Jose Serra/Alex Suarez/Louie Eljaua.
TRACK RECORD: Amaya signed with the Cubs for $1 million after a decorated amateur career in Panama and made the Futures Game in 2018 and 2019. His rise was halted by the coronavirus pandemic in 2020 and Tommy John surgery on his right elbow in 2021, but he returned midway through the 2022 season and picked up where he left off. Amaya posted an .864 OPS in 28 games for Double-A Tennessee while serving as a DH, but a Lisfranc fracture in his left foot abruptly cut his return short in mid September.

BA GRADE
50 Risk: **High**

SCOUTING REPORT: Amaya is a patient hitter who identifies pitches early out of the hand and rarely chases. He routinely gets ahead in counts and forces pitchers to throw the ball over the plate, earning him good pitches to hit. Amaya takes big, powerful cuts when he swings, but he struggles to elevate and frequently hits the ball on the ground. He has plus-plus raw power and can hit balls out to any part of the park, but he'll need to get the ball in the air more to reach his potential as a fringe-average hitter with above-average power. He crushes fastballs but struggles against breaking balls. Amaya used his rehab time to improve his conditioning and shed excess fat from his frame. Once an overly large backstop, he is now a sleeker, more explosive athlete. He was an average receiver and blocker with a plus arm before surgery, but it remains to be seen where he is now defensively with his new physique and surgically repaired elbow.
THE FUTURE: Amaya remains the Cubs' catcher of the future with Willson Contreras departed for the Cardinals. Amaya will move to Triple-A in 2023 and could make his MLB debut during the season.

SCOUTING GRADES	Hitting: 45	Power: 55	Speed: 30	Fielding: 50	Arm: 60

Year	Age	Club (League)	Lvl	AVG	G	AB	R	H	2B	3B	HR	RBI	BB	SO	SB	OBP	SLG
2022	23	Cubs (ACL)	R	.216	12	37	4	8	0	0	2	4	7	13	0	.341	.378
2022	23	Tennessee (SL)	AA	.278	28	97	15	27	6	1	4	19	14	28	0	.379	.485
Minor League Totals				.243	394	1404	184	341	81	4	34	193	178	299	15	.342	.379

10 CALEB KILIAN, RHP

Born: June 2, 1997. **B-T:** R-R. **HT:** 6-4. **WT:** 180.
Drafted: Texas Tech, 2019 (8th round). **Signed by:** Todd Thomas (Giants).

TRACK RECORD: Kilian led Texas Tech to consecutive College World Series as an anchor of its rotation and was drafted by the Giants in the eighth round in 2019. He emerged from the coronavirus shutdown stronger and throwing harder, leading to a breakout campaign in 2021. The Cubs acquired him with outfielder Alexander Canario for Kris Bryant at the trade deadline that year. Kilian started hot at Triple-A Iowa in 2022 and quickly rose to the majors for his big league debut, but his command evaporated in the majors and he got rocked for 13 earned runs in 11.1 innings. He continued to struggle throwing strikes after he returned to the minors and finished the year with a career-worst 4.22 ERA and 5.0 walks per nine innings.

BA GRADE
45 Risk: Medium

SCOUTING REPORT: Kilian is a physical, 6-foot-4 righthander with plenty of stuff. His above-average fastball sits 94-96 mph and he can manipulate it to give it cut, ride or sink. Kilian's 75-78 mph curveball with good depth is another above-average offering, and he'll mix in an average, upper-80s cutter that gets hitters to chase. His mid-80s changeup is below-average and rarely used. Kilian previously moved the ball around the strike zone with plus control, but he lost it in the majors and struggled to regain it in the minors. He no longer uses his lower half efficiently in his delivery and struggles to repeat his mechanics, leading to fringy control and a lack of quality strikes. Cubs officials identified the problem with his lower half and believe they can fix it.

THE FUTURE: Kilian has the stuff to be a No. 4 starter, but he has to rediscover his previous form. Doing so will be his main focus in 2023.

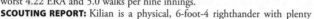

SCOUTING GRADES:	Fastball: 55		Curveball: 55		Cutter: 50		Changeup: 40		Control: 45			

Year	Age	Club (League	Lvl	W	L	ERA	G	GS	IP	H	HR	BB	SO	BB/9	SO/9	WHIP	AVG
2022	25	Iowa (IL)	AAA	5	4	4.22	26	26	107	108	7	59	125	5.0	10.5	1.57	.262
2022	25	Chicago (NL)	MLB	0	2	10.32	3	3	11	11	0	12	9	9.5	7.1	2.03	.262
Major League Totals				0	2	10.32	3	3	11	11	0	12	9	9.5	7.1	2.03	.262
Minor League Totals				12	8	3.11	52	51	223	190	12	74	254	3.0	10.3	1.18	.229

11 JORDAN WICKS, LHP

Born: Sept. 1, 1999. **B-T:** L-L. **HT:** 6-3. **WT:** 220.
Drafted: Kansas State, 2021 (1st round). **Signed by:** Ty Nichols.

TRACK RECORD: Wicks set Kansas State's single-season and career strikeout records and became the first Wildcats player drafted in the first round when the Cubs selected him 21st overall in 2021. He signed for $3.1 million and moved quickly to Double-A in his first full season in 2022. Wicks finished fifth in the Cubs system with 121 strikeouts and had only 28 walks in his full-season debut—the third-best strikeout-to-walk ratio among organization starters.

SCOUTING REPORT: Wicks keeps batters off balance with a deep, five-pitch mix. His four-seam fastball is an average pitch that ranges from 91-96 mph with cut and ride and his two-seamer sits at the same velocity with late run. He mixes in an average, low-80s slider that runs away from lefties, and he occasionally drops in a below-average, mid-70s curveball for strikes. All of them serve to set up Wicks' changeup, a plus pitch at 79-83 mph with late tumble and drop that he sells with his arm speed. He is comfortable throwing his changeup to both lefties and righties and gets awkward, off-balance swings and misses over the top in any count. His changeup particularly confounds righthanders, and he is a reverse-splits pitcher who is better against righties than lefties as a result. Wicks falls into deep counts and isn't very pitch efficient, but he makes pitches in big spots to avoid walking batters.

THE FUTURE: Wicks projects to settle in as a reliable, back-end starter. He has a chance to make his major league debut in 2023.

BA GRADE: 45/Medium		Fastball: 50		Slider: 50		Curveball: 40		Changeup: 60		Control: 50			

Year	Age	Club (League)	Lvl	W	L	ERA	G	GS	IP	H	HR	BB	SO	BB/9	SO/9	WHIP	AVG
2022	22	South Bend (MWL)	HiA	4	3	3.65	16	16	67	66	5	17	86	2.3	11.6	1.25	.256
2022	22	Tennessee (SL)	AA	0	3	4.18	8	8	28	24	5	11	35	3.5	11.2	1.25	.224
Minor League Totals				4	6	3.90	28	28	102	97	10	31	126	2.7	11.2	1.26	.247

12 ALEXANDER CANARIO, OF

Born: May 7, 2000. **B-T:** R-R. **HT:** 6-1. **WT:** 212.
Signed: Dominican Republic, 2016. **Signed by:** Ruddy Moreta (Giants).

TRACK RECORD: Canario signed with the Giants for $60,000 out of the Dominican Republic and didn't reach full-season ball until five years after he signed, but the Cubs were intrigued by his massive power potential and acquired him as part of the return for Kris Bryant at the 2021 trade deadline. Canario broke out in 2022 with 37 home runs, second-most in the minor leagues, and he rocketed from High-A to Triple-A, but his season ended on a down note when he suffered a fractured ankle and dislocated shoulder in the Dominican Winter League after he stepped awkwardly on first base and fell to the ground.

SCOUTING REPORT: Canario is a strong, physical hitter with the most power in the Cubs' system. His electric bat speed and impressive torque produce plus-plus power to all fields, including gargantuan home runs to his pull-side. He makes hard contact even when he's off-balance and is a constant threat to change games with one swing. Canario crushes balls when he connects, but he's an aggressive free swinger and frequently gets himself out by swinging at bad pitches. He is prone to chasing fastballs above the zone and breaking balls out of the zone and projects to be a well below-average hitter. Canario is a threat to steal bases with his above-average speed and is an above-average defender in right field with a plus arm. He is a good athlete and can play center field as needed.

THE FUTURE: Canario projects to be a low-average slugger who racks up homers and strikeouts. His big league debut may come in 2023 depending on how quickly he recovers from his rather significant offseason injuries.

BA GRADE: 50/High		Hit: 30		Power: 60		Speed: 55		Fielding: 55		Arm: 60			

Year	Age	Club (League)	Lvl	AVG	G	AB	R	H	2B	3B	HR	RBI	BB	SO	SB	OBP	SLG
2022	22	South Bend (MWL)	HiA	.281	24	89	17	25	6	0	7	22	10	35	3	.360	.584
2022	22	Tennessee (SL)	AA	.248	81	310	51	77	18	2	24	61	36	91	17	.329	.552
2022	22	Iowa (IL)	AAA	.231	20	65	16	15	2	0	6	14	13	21	3	.386	.538
Minor League Totals				.263	402	1519	275	399	88	14	82	272	182	443	74	.346	.501

13 OWEN CAISSIE, OF

Born: July 8, 2002. **B-T:** L-R. **HT:** 6-4. **WT:** 190.
Drafted: HS—Burlington, Ontario, 2020 (2nd round). **Signed by:** Chris Kemlo (Padres).

TRACK RECORD: Caissie showcased huge power for Canada's junior national team, including hitting a home run off the batter's eye in a spring training exhibition against minor leaguers, and was drafted 45th overall by the Padres in 2020. The Cubs acquired him as one of five players for Yu Darvish six months later, and he quickly emerged as the best prospect the Cubs received in the deal. Cassie made his full-season debut at High-A South Bend in 2022 and started slowly, but he rebounded to post an .811 OPS from May through the end of the season and helped South Bend win the Midwest League championship.

SCOUTING REPORT: Caissie stands a tall, projectable 6-foot-4 and has plenty of room to fill out his frame. His natural strength and leverage give him above-average power to all fields, and he gets to it with an easy, low-effort swing. Caissie's swing can get long and slow at times, but he puts together high-quality at-bats, swings at the right pitches and makes enough contact to project to be an average hitter. Caissie was previously raw in the outfield due to a lack of game experience, and it's notable that he's never played a pro game in center field. He has improved his routes and reads and now has a chance to be an average defender. His average speed and above-average arm profile best in right field.

THE FUTURE: Caissie projects to be an everyday, power-hitting corner outfielder as long as he continues to make strength gains. He'll head to Double-A Tennessee in 2023.

BA GRADE: 50/High		Hit: 50		Power: 55		Speed: 50		Fielding: 45		Arm: 55			

Year	Age	Club (League)	Lvl	AVG	G	AB	R	H	2B	3B	HR	RBI	BB	SO	SB	OBP	SLG
2022	19	South Bend (MWL)	HiA	.254	105	378	57	96	21	1	11	58	50	124	11	.349	.402
Minor League Totals				.270	159	560	92	151	32	2	18	87	92	191	12	.378	.430

14 DANIEL PALENCIA, RHP

Born: Feb. 5, 2000. **B-T:** R-R. **HT:** 5-11. **WT:** 195.
Signed: Venezuela, 2020. **Signed by:** Juan Carlos Villanueva/Argenis Paez (Athletics).

TRACK RECORD: Palencia signed with the Athletics for just $10,000 at age 20. That's quite old for international amateur to sign a first pro contract. He made only six appearances for 14 innings in Oakland's system before the A's traded him to the Cubs for reliever Andrew Chafin at the 2021 trade deadline.

Palencia struggled with his control early at High-A South Bend in 2022. He walked 12 in his first 12 innings. But he harnessed his stuff to become one of the system's breakthrough pitchers in the second half. He capped his season with five scoreless innings, no walks and eight strikeouts in the decisive game of the Midwest League semifinals.

SCOUTING REPORT: Palencia's arm strength is unmatched in the Cubs system. Though he's short, he has a strong, powerful build and generates triple-digit fastballs with ease. His fastball sits 98-99 mph and routinely reaches 101-102 with explosive late life up in the zone. He leans on his fastball heavily, but he also has a low-90s vertical, power slider that has become a plus pitch he can land for strikes or get chases. His firm, upper-80s changeup is an average third pitch. Palencia is a good athlete for his size, but he has struggled with a series of minor injuries—including foot and oblique injuries in 2022—and has below-average command and control, especially of his secondaries. He rarely completes five innings and is best in short bursts.

THE FUTURE: Palencia projects to be a high-leverage reliever in the majors, although the Cubs will continue starting him for now. He'll head to Double-A in 2023.

BA GRADE: 50/High		Fastball: 80		Slider: 60		Changeup: 50		Control: 40						

Year	Age	Club (League)	Lvl	W	L	ERA	G	GS	IP	H	HR	BB	SO	BB/9	SO/9	WHIP	AVG
2022	22	South Bend (MWL)	HiA	1	3	3.94	21	20	75	56	7	35	98	4.2	11.7	1.21	.204
Minor League Totals				2	5	4.24	34	33	117	90	12	59	150	4.6	11.6	1.28	.212

15 JACKSON FERRIS, LHP

Born: Jan. 15, 2004. **B-T:** L-L. **HT:** 6-4. **WT:** 195.
Drafted: HS—Bradenton, Florida, 2022 (2nd round). **Signed by:** Tom Clark

TRACK RECORD: Ferris starred as an underclassman at Mt. Airy (N.C.) High before transferring to national prep power IMG Academy to gain increased exposure. He took advantage by going 16-0, 0.80 over two seasons at the high-profile program and solidified himself as one of the top prep lefthanders in the 2022 draft class. The Cubs drafted him 47th overall and signed him for just over $3 million, nearly double the recommended slot amount, inducing him to forgo a commitment to Mississippi.

SCOUTING REPORT: Ferris is a tall, projectable lefthander with premium stuff for his age. His fastball comfortably sits at 93 mph, touches 96-97 and has room to tick up as he gets stronger. He complements his fastball with an above-average, high-spin curveball in the mid 70s with impressive depth and a mid-80s changeup he sells well with his arm speed. Ferris' stuff is loud, but his complicated, contorting delivery has a lot of moving parts that cause him difficulty throwing strikes. His posture and balance are inconsistent and his arm is often not where it needs to be at foot strike, leading to scattered command and control. He tends to stay around the plate but struggles to consistently locate his offerings in the zone.

THE FUTURE: Ferris has the stuff to be a midrotation starter, but he has to smooth out his delivery and improve his control and consistency. He is set to make his pro debut in 2023.

BA GRADE: 55/Extreme		Fastball: 60		Curveball: 55	Changeup: 55		Control: 40						

Year	Age	Club (League)	Lvl	W	L	ERA	G	GS	IP	H	HR	BB	SO	BB/9	SO/9	WHIP	AVG
2022	18	Did not play															

16 MOISES BALLESTEROS, C

Born: November 8, 2003. **B-T:** L-R. **HT:** 5-10. **WT:** 234.
Signed: Venezuela, 2021. **Signed by:** Louie Eljaua/Julio Figueroa/Hector Ortega.

TRACK RECORD: Ballesteros starred as Venezuela's cleanup hitter at the 2015 12U World Cup in Taiwan and maintained his status as a premium hitter throughout his amateur career. He signed with the Cubs for $1.5 million on the first day of the 2021 international signing period and showcased his offensive potential in his stateside debut in 2022. He rose from the Arizona Complex League to Low-A Myrtle Beach as an 18-year-old and hit 10 home runs in only 63 games.

SCOUTING REPORT: Ballesteros is a highly advanced hitter for his age. He manages at-bats well, has excellent plate discipline and boasts above-average bat speed and strength from the left side. He is a patient hitter who puts himself in good counts and punishes mistakes with above-average power to all fields. Ballesteros has the skills and approach to hit for average and power, but he's physically maxed out at a burly 234 pounds and will need to manage his conditioning closely. His thick lower half and chunky midsection sharply limit his mobility at catcher and his receiving is below-average. He has a plus arm that will buy him time to develop behind the plate, but he is likely to end up at first base or DH unless he loses weight.

THE FUTURE: Ballesteros' future depends on how well he manages his heavyset frame. Most observers project him to get bigger and become a DH similar to Daniel Vogelbach.

BA GRADE: 50/Very High	Hit: 50		Power: 55		Speed: 20		Fielding: 30		Arm: 60	

Year	Age	Club (League)	Lvl	AVG	G	AB	R	H	2B	3B	HR	RBI	BB	SO	SB	OBP	SLG
2022	18	Cubs (ACL)	R	.268	32	97	12	26	5	0	7	18	13	19	0	.355	.536
2022	18	Myrtle Beach (CAR)	LoA	.248	31	109	17	27	7	0	3	15	18	28	0	.349	.394
Minor League Totals				.261	111	360	51	94	22	0	13	58	62	71	6	.371	.431

17 D.J. HERZ, LHP

Born: Jan. 4, 2001. **B-T:** L-R. **HT:** 6-2. **WT:** 175.
Drafted: HS—Fayetteville, N.C., 2019 (8th round). **Signed by:** Billy Swoope.
TRACK RECORD: Herz starred in football and basketball as well as baseball in high school and signed with the Cubs for an above-slot $500,000 as an eighth-round pick. He led the organization in strikeouts in his first full season and again racked up whiffs with 134 strikeouts in 2022, second-most in the system, but he also had the most walks in the organization and struggled after a promotion to Double-A.
SCOUTING REPORT: Herz is an athletic lefthander with a potent combination of stuff and deception. His 91-94 mph fastball plays up with the deception and angle he generates from his crossfire delivery, which helps it jump on batters faster than they expect. He racks up swings and misses with his fastball and keeps hitters off-balance with a plus, 80-84 mph changeup he sells well with his arm speed. Herz leans heavily on his fastball and changeup, but he also has a tight, vertical curveball in the upper 70s that is an average third offering. Herz has plenty of stuff, but his extreme crossfire delivery and long arm action make it difficult for him to consistently throw strikes. His command and control are both well below-average and he relies on hitters chasing out of the zone, which they largely stopped doing once he reached Double-A.
THE FUTURE: Herz's control shortcomings will likely push him to the bullpen long-term. He has a chance to be a high-leverage, effectively wild lefty reliever similar to Jake Diekman.

BA GRADE: 45/High	Fastball: 55		Curveball: 50	Changeup: 60		Control: 30	

Year	Age	Club (League)	Lvl	W	L	ERA	G	GS	IP	H	HR	BB	SO	BB/9	SO/9	WHIP	AVG
2022	21	South Bend (MWL)	HiA	2	2	2.26	17	17	64	33	3	37	99	5.2	14.0	1.10	.150
2022	21	Tennessee (SL)	AA	1	4	8.24	9	9	32	24	5	33	42	9.4	11.9	1.80	.209
Minor League Totals				7	11	3.75	52	52	187	109	15	122	280	5.9	13.5	1.23	.169

18 JAMES TRIANTOS, 3B

Born: Jan. 29, 2003. **B-T:** R-T. **HT:** 6-1. **WT:** 195.
Drafted: HS—Vienna, Va., 2021 (2nd round). **Signed by:** Billy Swoope
TRACK RECORD: Triantos starred as both a pitcher and hitter in high school and was one of the top players in the 2022 draft class before he reclassified to be eligible for the 2021 draft. The Cubs drafted him in the second round and signed him for an above-slot $2.1 million to forgo a North Carolina commitment. Triantos made his full-season debut with Low-A Myrtle Beach in 2022 and led the Carolina League with 124 hits, but his lack of a clear position made him a divisive prospect.
SCOUTING REPORT: Triantos is one of the best pure hitters in the Cubs organization. He has a quick, compact righthanded swing with a heavy barrel that results in a lot of hard contact. He has a sharp eye for the strike zone and rarely strikes out, giving him the swing and approach to be an above-average hitter. Triantos primarily drives balls from gap to gap, but he projects to get stronger with age and grow into average power. A shortstop when he was drafted, Triantos gained weight and now has a pudgy build with limited athleticism. He is a well below-average defender at third base with a slow first step and poor balance, and he lacks the range or agility to play second base. Some Cubs officials want to move him to catcher, where his above-average arm strength will play.
THE FUTURE: Triantos has the bat to be an everyday player, but he needs to find a defensive home. That will be his main goal at High-A South Bend in 2023.

BA GRADE: 45/High	Hit: 55		Power: 50		Speed: 40		Fielding: 30		Arm: 55	

Year	Age	Club (League)	Lvl	AVG	G	AB	R	H	2B	3B	HR	RBI	BB	SO	SB	OBP	SLG
2022	19	Myrtle Beach (CAR)	LoA	.272	113	456	74	124	19	6	7	50	39	81	20	.335	.386
Minor League Totals				.282	138	557	101	157	26	7	13	69	46	99	23	.343	.424

19 YOHENDRICK PINANGO, OF

Born: May 7, 2002. **B-T:** L-L. **HT:** 5-11. **WT:** 170.
Signed: Venezuela, 2018. **Signed by:** Julio Figeuroa/Hector Ortega/Louie Eljaua.

TRACK RECORD: One of the top pure hitters in the 2018 international class, Pinango signed with the Cubs for $400,000 and quickly established himself as one of the best contact bats in the organization. He began trying to hit for power in 2022 at High-A South Bend, however, and sacrificed his patient approach and natural contact skills. He set new career-lows with a .250 batting average and .297 on-base percentage, overshadowing his career-high 13 home runs.

SCOUTING REPORT: At his best, Pinango is a natural hitter with a smooth, balanced swing from the left side that stays in the zone a long time. He sprays balls from line to line, makes hard contact and forces pitchers to throw strikes with a patient approach. Pinango's swing became more violent and his strike-zone discipline regressed sharply as he began chasing power in 2022. He became overly aggressive and expanded the zone too often, taking away from his potential to be an above-average hitter. Pinango has improved at lifting the ball in the air and flashes above-average raw power, especially to his pull side, but he has to find a better balance between hitting for average and power. Pinango is a below-average athlete with a short, stocky frame. He's a below-average defender who is limited to left field with his below-average speed and average arm strength.

THE FUTURE: Pinango needs to find a more balanced approach between average and power. He can be a solid everyday left fielder if he does.

BA GRADE: 45/High	Hit: 50	Power: 45	Speed: 40	Fielding: 40	Arm: 50

Year	Age	Club (League)	Lvl	AVG	G	AB	R	H	2B	3B	HR	RBI	BB	SO	SB	OBP	SLG
2022	20	South Bend (MWL)	HiA	.250	115	464	65	116	24	2	13	63	30	88	14	.297	.394
Minor League Totals				.283	285	1125	167	318	64	5	18	135	88	177	49	.337	.396

20 JAVIER ASSAD, RHP

Born: July 30, 1997. **B-T:** R-R. **HT:** 6-1. **WT:** 200.
Signed: Mexico, 2015. **Signed by:** Louie Eljaua/Sergio Hernandez.

TRACK RECORD: The Cubs scouted Mexico heavily last decade and signed Assad for $150,000 from the Yucatan franchise shortly before his 18th birthday. He spent his first five seasons as a steady, reliable innings-eater with pedestrian stuff, but he gained three mph on his fastball in 2022 and took off. Assad set new career-bests in ERA (2.99) and strikeouts (111) as he blitzed through Double-A Tennessee and Triple-A Iowa. He earned his first callup in late August and finished the year in the Cubs rotation.

SCOUTING REPORT: Assad goes right after hitters and fills up the strike zone with a five-pitch mix. His fastball ticked up from 88-91 mph to 92-95 mph and plays above its velocity with his ability to command it in the zone. His short, tight 85-88 mph cutter is an above-average offering with late tilt, and his above-average, low-80s slider with sharp break and movement gets chase swings at the bottom of the zone. He also has an average mid-80s changeup with solid fading action and a below-average mid-70s curveball he can ambush hitters with to steal a strike. Assad has an advanced feel for sequencing his pitches and impressive poise on the mound. He throws everything for strikes with above-average control and works efficiently.

THE FUTURE: Assad's command and feel for pitching should help him stick as a back-end starter or swingman. He could be more if his stuff continues to tick up.

BA GRADE: 40/Medium	Fastball: 50	Curveball: 40	Slider: 55	Cutter: 55	Changeup: 50	Control: 55

Year	Age	Club (League)	Lvl	W	L	ERA	G	GS	IP	H	HR	BB	SO	BB/9	SO/9	WHIP	AVG
2022	24	Tennessee (SL)	AA	4	1	2.51	15	14	72	68	6	28	74	3.5	9.3	1.34	.254
2022	24	Iowa (IL)	AAA	1	2	2.95	8	7	37	31	4	7	37	1.7	9.1	1.04	.223
2022	24	Chicago (NL)	MLB	2	2	3.11	9	8	38	35	4	20	30	4.8	7.2	1.46	.240
Major League Totals				2	2	3.11	9	8	38	35	4	20	30	4.8	7.2	1.46	.240
Minor League Totals				25	36	3.96	112	104	528	550	42	173	479	3.0	8.2	1.37	.271

21 KEVIN MADE, SS

Born: Sept. 10, 2002. **B-T:** R-R. **HT:** 6-1. **WT:** 180.
Signed: Dominican Republic, 2019. **Signed by:** Louis Eljaua/Jose Serra/Gian Guzman.

TRACK RECORD: Made signed with the Cubs for $1.5 million out of the Dominican Republic and quickly jumped on an accelerated track. He went straight to Low-A Myrtle Beach for his pro debut at 18 years old and returned to the Pelicans to begin 2022, when he showed improved power and patience and earned a midseason promotion to High-A South Bend. Made took over as South Bend's starting shortstop and helped lead the team to the Midwest League title, posting a .909 OPS in the championship series.

SCOUTING REPORT: Made has a promising foundation as a true shortstop who hits the ball hard. He has a mechanically sound swing and crushes fastballs in the strike zone. He recognizes breaking balls well for his age and has the hand-eye coordination and barrel accuracy to cover the entire plate. Made has the physical foundation to hit for average and power, but he is an extremely aggressive hitter prone to chasing fastballs. His approach limits him to a below-average hitter even with improvement. Made shines defensively at shortstop, where his soft hands, clean actions and advanced instincts make him a plus defender. He can make throws from anywhere on the field with his plus-plus arm.

THE FUTURE: Made's defense will buy him time to improve his plate discipline. He projects to be a glove-first shortstop even with offensive strides.

BA GRADE: 45/High	Hit: 40	Power: 40	Speed: 50	Fielding: 65	Arm: 70

Year	Age	Club (League)	Lvl	AVG	G	AB	R	H	2B	3B	HR	RBI	BB	SO	SB	OBP	SLG
2022	19	Myrtle Beach (CAR)	LoA	.266	57	222	41	59	14	0	9	30	27	49	0	.354	.450
2022	19	South Bend (MWL)	HiA	.162	37	130	14	21	6	1	1	14	19	31	3	.267	.246
Minor League Totals				.245	152	587	74	144	33	4	11	64	52	137	5	.312	.371

22 PORTER HODGE, RHP

Born: Feb. 21, 2001. **B-T:** R-R. **HT:** 6-4. **WT:** 230.
Drafted: HS—Salt Lake City, 2019 (13th round). **Signed by:** Steve McFarland.

TRACK RECORD: Hodge led Salt Lake City's Cottonwood High to two Utah 5A state championships in three years and was the winning pitcher in the 2019 championship game. The Cubs drafted him in the 13th round and signed him for $125,000 to forgo a Utah commitment. Hodge struggled with his conditioning early in his career, but he slimmed down in 2022 and had his best season. He tied for the organization lead with 141 strikeouts and finished second with a 2.36 ERA across the Class A levels.

SCOUTING REPORT: Hodge transformed from a chubby righthander to a lean, athletic 6-foot-4, which led to more explosive stuff and better body control. His fastball is now a plus pitch that sits 92-96 mph with natural cut and gets on batters quickly with the extension he generates in his delivery. He complements his heater with a plus, mid-80s Wiffle Ball slider that cuts across and under barrels for swings and misses. Hodge mostly dominates with those two pitches and has above-average control of both. His vertical, upper-70s curveball and firm, upper-80s changeup with late drop flash the ability to draw whiffs but have lots of development left. His long arm action does cause occasional bouts of wildness.

THE FUTURE: Hodge is trending up and frequently requested in trades. He has midrotation potential if he can refine a third pitch.

BA GRADE: 45/High	Fastball: 60	Curveball: 40	Slider: 60	Changeup: 40	Control: 50

Year	Age	Club (League)	Lvl	W	L	ERA	G	GS	IP	H	HR	BB	SO	BB/9	SO/9	WHIP	AVG
2022	21	Myrtle Beach (CAR)	LoA	4	2	3.00	17	17	69	54	1	39	90	5.1	11.7	1.35	.210
2022	21	South Bend (MWL)	HiA	3	3	2.01	8	7	40	26	3	16	51	3.6	11.4	1.04	.187
Minor League Totals				9	8	3.96	44	38	168	145	9	80	209	4.3	11.2	1.34	.229

23 DARIUS HILL, OF

Born: Aug. 17. 1997. **B-T:** L-L. **HT:** 6-1. **WT:** 170. **Drafted:** West Virginia, 2019 (20th round). **Signed by:** Jacob Williams.

TRACK RECORD: Hill started all four years at West Virginia and hit over .300 every season, but his unconventional swing, lack of power and perceived inability to play center field caused him to fall to the 20th round of the 2019 draft, where the Cubs took him and gave him a $5,000 signing bonus. Hill quickly proved those assessments wrong and conquered both Double-A and Triple-A in 2022, where he finished tied for the minor league lead with 166 hits.

SCOUTING REPORT: Hill is an undersized lefthanded hitter who knows his game and sticks to it. He has a short, quick swing from the left side and exceptional timing and barrel accuracy. He squares up pitches in all parts of the zone and drives them for singles and doubles. Hill's swing has minimal loft and leverage and he doesn't hit for much power, but he makes a ton of contact and should be an above-average hitter. He is also an excellent bunter. Hill is an average runner and gets good jumps and reads in center field, where he is an average defender. His well below-average arm makes him a better fit in left field than right when he plays the corners.

THE FUTURE: Hill's contact skills and ability to play center field has him in the Cubs outfield plans for 2023. His debut should come during the season.

BA GRADE: 40/Medium		Hit: 55			Power: 30			Speed: 50		Fielding: 50			Arm: 30	

Year	Age	Club (League)	Lvl	AVG	G	AB	R	H	2B	3B	HR	RBI	BB	SO	SB	OBP	SLG
2022	24	Tennessee (SL)	AA	.308	44	185	34	57	13	1	6	18	13	24	3	.360	.486
2022	24	Iowa (IL)	AAA	.318	89	343	48	109	23	4	3	35	21	53	4	.358	.434
Minor League Totals				.299	252	1015	148	303	52	7	16	108	71	152	13	.345	.411

24 CHASE STRUMPF, 2B/3B

Born: March 8, 1998. **B-T:** R-R. **HT:** 6-1. **WT:** 191.
Drafted: UCLA, 2019 (2nd round). **Signed by:** Tom Myers.
TRACK RECORD: Strumpf had a decorated amateur career as a member of USA Baseball's 15U national team and was a high-profile infielder at JSerra (Calif.) High and UCLA. The Cubs drafted him in the second round in 2019 and signed him for just over $1 million. Strumpf was known for his contact skills as an amateur, but he has morphed into a power hitter in pro ball. He hit 21 homers at Double-A Tennessee in 2022, tripling his previous career high, but also hit a team-low .234 and had a career-high 162 strikeouts.
SCOUTING REPORT: Strumpf is a strong righthanded hitter with a discerning eye for the strike zone. He draws plenty of walks and makes hard contact when he connects, sending balls out from left to right-center with above-average raw power. Strumpf has good rhythm and separation in the batter's box, but his swing has gotten too big as he's started chasing power. He swings and misses in the zone too often and has to shorten his swing to make more contact. A second baseman in college, Strumpf has taken well to third base as a pro. He is an above-average defender with a solid glove and average arm strength that plays up with a quick release.
THE FUTURE: Strumpf's power and infield versatility give him a path to the majors as a utilityman.

BA GRADE: 45/High		Hit: 30			Power: 50			Speed: 45		Fielding: 55			Arm: 50	

Year	Age	Club (League)	Lvl	AVG	G	AB	R	H	2B	3B	HR	RBI	BB	SO	SB	OBP	SLG
2022	24	Tennessee (SL)	AA	.234	116	393	73	92	22	2	21	57	73	162	2	.379	.461
Minor League Totals				.235	233	796	138	187	53	2	31	110	141	286	8	.369	.423

25 PABLO ALIENDO, C

Born: May 29, 2001. **B-T:** R-R. **HT:** 6-0. **WT:** 170.
Signed: Venezuela, 2018. **Signed by:** Hector Ortega/Julio Figueroa.
TRACK RECORD: Aliendo signed with the Cubs for $200,000 out of Venezuela shortly before his 17th birthday and quickly asserted himself as one of the best defensive catchers in the organization. His bat took longer to come around, but he steadily improved and had his best offensive season at High-A South Bend in 2022. He set new career highs in almost every category and led South Bend to the Midwest League championship.
SCOUTING REPORT: Aliendo is one of the best defensive catchers in the low minors. He is a plus receiver with soft, quiet hands and ably handles both premium velocity and quality secondary stuff. He is a superb athlete who moves well laterally, is a plus blocker and has a plus, accurate arm. Aliendo complements his physical gifts with elite makeup. He is an advanced game-caller for his age and is a natural leader behind the plate. He is bilingual and an excellent communicator. Aliendo has good hand-eye coordination in the batter's box, but he is overly aggressive and swings at too many pitches he can't drive. He'll need to refine his pitch selection to be a below-average hitter and better access his growing power.
THE FUTURE: Aliendo has a chance to be a second-division starter if his bat develops. If not, his defense and makeup give him a chance to have a long career as a backup catcher.

BA GRADE: 45/High		Hit: 40			Power: 30			Speed: 50		Fielding: 60			Arm: 60	

Year	Age	Club (League)	Lvl	AVG	G	AB	R	H	2B	3B	HR	RBI	BB	SO	SB	OBP	SLG
2022	21	South Bend (MWL)	HiA	.267	89	318	34	85	16	1	7	35	26	77	3	.336	.390
Minor League Totals				.235	244	765	117	180	33	3	13	82	78	221	21	.328	.337

26 LUIS DEVERS, RHP

Born: April 24, 2000. **B-T:** R-R. **HT:** 6-3. **WT:** 178.
Signed: Dominican Republic, 2017. **Signed by:** Alejandro Peña/Gian Guzman/Jose Serra
TRACK RECORD: Devers signed with the Cubs for just $30,000 and spent three unremarkable seasons in the complex leagues before breaking out in 2022. He added 3 mph to his fastball and breezed through Low-A and High-A, finishing second in the minor leagues with a 1.91 ERA and tied for third with 13

wins. He capped the year by allowing one run or fewer in each of his final 12 starts.

SCOUTING REPORT: Devers is a skinny righthander with extreme deception and an advanced feel for pitching. He frequently alters the tempo and mechanics of his delivery, similar to Johnny Cueto, and will quick-pitch opponents to catch them unprepared. Batters struggle to time him up and he rarely allows hard contact. Devers' stuff is unremarkable in a vacuum, but everything plays up with his deception and above-average control. He sets hitters up with his 90-94 mph fastball and finishes them with a plus, low-80s changeup he sells well with his arm speed. His slurvy breaking ball with 11-to-5 shape is a fringy third offering he can use to steal a strike. Devers only commands the ball to his glove side, but he throws strikes and limits mistakes. He is durable and consistent.

THE FUTURE: Devers has a chance to be a No. 5 starter with improvements to his command and velocity. He'll head to Double-A in 2022.

BA GRADE: 45/High		Fastball: 40		Curveball: 45		Changeup: 60		Control: 55				
Year	Age	Club (League)	Lvl	W	L	ERA	G	GS	IP	H	HR	BB	SO	BB/9	SO/9	WHIP	AVG
2022	22	Myrtle Beach (CAR)	LoA	9	3	2.58	15	14	66	57	3	14	75	1.9	10.2	1.07	.235
2022	22	South Bend (MWL)	HiA	4	0	1.05	11	8	51	29	1	12	47	2.1	8.2	0.80	.167
Minor League Totals				20	17	2.50	68	60	292	255	11	76	290	2.3	8.9	1.13	.236

27 PEDRO RAMIREZ, 2B

Born: April 1, 2004. **B-T:** B-R. **HT:** 5-10. **WT:** 180.
Signed: Venezuela, 2021. **Signed by:** Julio Figueroa/Carlos Figueroa/Cirilo Cumberbatch.

TRACK RECORD: Ramirez trained in the same program as fellow Cubs prospect Moises Ballesteros and signed with the Cubs for $75,000 on the first day of the 2021 international signing period. He made a loud first impression by leading the Dominican Summer League in hits in his pro debut and continued to impress stateside in 2022. Ramirez finished fifth in the Arizona Complex League with a .329 batting average and third with a .940 OPS, earning a late promotion to Low-A Myrtle Beach.

SCOUTING REPORT: Ramirez is a polished switch-hitter advanced beyond his years. He makes consistent contact with a short, fast swing and excellent barrel control. He covers the entire plate, has exceptional timing and puts together competitive at-bats. Ramirez mostly hits soft line drives and doesn't have much projection left, but his approach and feel for the barrel give him a chance to be an above-average hitter who runs into 10-12 home runs. Ramirez has good body control and is an average defender at second base. He is a plus runner and has the range for shortstop, but his fringy arm fits better at the keystone.

THE FUTURE: Opposing teams frequently ask about Ramirez in trade discussions. He has a chance to be a switch-hitting, everyday second baseman if he gets stronger.

BA GRADE: 50/Extreme		Hit: 55		Power: 40		Speed: 60		Fielding: 50		Arm: 45			
Year	Age	Club (League)	Lvl	AVG	G	AB	R	H	2B	3B	HR	RBI	BB	SO	SB	OBP	SLG
2022	18	Cubs (ACL)	R	.329	43	146	26	48	9	5	4	14	17	26	11	.399	.541
2022	18	Myrtle Beach (CAR)	LoA	.268	10	41	7	11	0	0	0	1	2	6	4	.348	.268
Minor League Totals				.338	103	382	70	129	20	12	5	45	32	52	24	.402	.492

28 CAM SANDERS, RHP

Born: Dec. 9, 1996. **B-T:** R-R. **HT:** 6-2. **WT:** 190.
Drafted: Louisiana State, 2018 (12th round). **Signed by:** Trey Forkerway

TRACK RECORD: The son of former Padres reliever Scott Sanders and All-American softball player Linda Lunceford Sanders, Cam began his college career at Northwest Florida State JC before spending one season as a swingman at Louisiana State. Sanders did little to distinguish himself in the low minors after the Cubs drafted him, but his stuff ticked up in 2022 to facilitate a rise to Triple-A. He moved to Iowa's bullpen in the second half and didn't allow an earned run in eight of his final nine appearances.

SCOUTING REPORT: Sanders is an athletic, 6-foot-2 righthander with five different pitches that miss bats. His 94-96 mph four-seam fastball and 92-94 mph two-seamer feature high spin rates and are both above-average, swing and miss pitches. His favored secondary is an above-average, mid-80s slider he has good feel to spin, and his average mid-80s changeup and average low-70s curveball get swings and misses in the zone, too. He creates different shapes and looks with all his weapons and keeps hitters guessing. Sanders repeats his delivery, but he has trouble commanding all of his offerings at the same time. He has struggled with walks throughout his career and is prone to hitting batters.

THE FUTURE: Sanders' good stuff and shoddy control have him on track to be a middle reliever like his dad. His major league debut should come in 2023.

Year	Age	Club (League)	Lvl	W	L	ERA	G	GS	IP	H	HR	BB	SO	BB/9	SO/9	WHIP	AVG
2022	25	Tennessee (SL)	AA	1	1	3.38	6	6	24	13	3	11	36	4.1	13.5	1.00	.151
2022	25	Iowa (IL)	AAA	1	8	5.45	29	11	74	56	9	49	75	5.9	9.1	1.41	.207
Minor League Totals				15	22	4.36	90	55	306	224	36	174	326	5.1	9.6	1.30	.204

29 KOHL FRANKLIN, RHP

Born: Sept. 9, 1999. **B-T:** R-R. **HT:** 6-4. **WT:** 195.
Drafted: HS—Broken Arrow, Oklahoma, 2018 (6th round). **Signed by:** Ty Nichols.

TRACK RECORD: A nephew of former all-star closer Ryan Franklin, Kohl signed with the Cubs for an overslot $540,000 bonus and showed promise at the short-season levels, but he missed 2020 due to the coronavirus pandemic and all of 2021 with a strained oblique. He returned to the mound for the first time in nearly three years in 2022 and showed enhanced stuff, but he struggled with his control and posted a 6.88 ERA in 23 starts at High-A South Bend.

SCOUTING REPORT: Franklin has filled out his frame and now possesses some of the best stuff in the Cubs organization. He powers his fastball 95-99 mph downhill and has added velocity and bite to his spike curveball to make it an above-average pitch at 79-83 mph. Franklin's changeup has also gotten firmer in the mid-80s, but it has lost movement with the added velocity and regressed to an average pitch. Franklin's stuff is loud, but his fastball command is extremely poor and his feel for pitching is raw. He frequently falls behind batters and throws the wrong pitch in the wrong counts, leading to short, ineffective outings.

THE FUTURE: The Cubs hope Franklin was just rusty after two missed seasons and that his command and feel will improve with experience. He'll try to prove them right in 2023.

BA GRADE: 50/Extreme   **Fastball:** 60   **Curveball:** 55   **Changeup:** 50   **Control:** 30

Year	Age	Club (League)	Lvl	W	L	ERA	G	GS	IP	H	HR	BB	SO	BB/9	SO/9	WHIP	AVG
2022	22	South Bend (MWL)	HiA	3	7	6.88	23	23	69	72	8	41	75	5.3	9.7	1.63	.264
Minor League Totals				4	11	5.25	39	37	120	108	10	66	135	5.0	10.1	1.45	.235

30 RILEY THOMPSON, RHP

Born: July 9, 1996. **B-T:** L-R. **HT:** 6-3. **WT:** 205.
Drafted: Louisville, 2018 (11th round). **Signed by:** Jacob Williams.

TRACK RECORD: Thompson has flashed big stuff since his days at Louisville, but he's pitched very little despite being 26. He had Tommy John surgery and shoulder injuries that limited him to just two seasons in college, didn't pitch in 2020 due to the coronavirus pandemic and missed all of 2021 with shoulder tightness. He returned to the mound for the first time in nearly three years in 2022 and improved as the year went on at Double-A Tennessee, providing optimism he can still be a part of the Cubs' future.

SCOUTING REPORT: Thompson has a strong, physical 6-foot-4 frame and has maintained his arm strength through his injuries. His fastball sits 94-98 mph and touches higher in relief. His 12-to-6 curveball in the low 80s has excellent spin and depth and is a plus pitch when he locates it, although his feel for it is inconsistent, and he has added a short, upper-80s slider that flashes average. He has also improved his feel for a fringy, mid-80s changeup. Thompson's stuff stands out, but his arm action allows batters to see the ball early out of his hand. His fastball plays down significantly, frequently getting crushed, and batters easily lay off his stuff out of the zone.

THE FUTURE: Thompson's arm strength gives him a chance to surface as a reliever despite his shortcomings. He'll head to Triple-A in 2023.

BA GRADE: 40/High   **Fastball:** 45   **Curveball:** 55   **Slider:** 50   **Changeup:** 45   **Control:** 40

Year	Age	Club (League)	Lvl	W	L	ERA	G	GS	IP	H	HR	BB	SO	BB/9	SO/9	WHIP	AVG
2022	25	Tennessee (SL)	AA	2	5	4.42	19	19	57	47	8	32	64	5.1	10.1	1.39	.230
Minor League Totals				10	13	3.47	49	48	176	156	18	72	176	3.7	9.0	1.29	.238

Chicago White Sox

BY BILL MITCHELL

The White Sox won 93 games and captured the American League Central title in 2021. With the nucleus of that team returning, it was expected that the 2022 club would contend for another postseason berth.

Instead, the White Sox finished 81-81, in part because of injuries but also a noticeable lack of effort among key performers. Controversial manager Tony La Russa had to step away in late August due to health issues and was replaced by bench coach Miguel Cairo. La Russa will not return, his Hall of Fame managerial career likely over, much to the relief of the White Sox faithful who often questioned his on-field decisions and his handling of the players during his two-year stint.

Shortly after the season ended, the White Sox chose Royals bench coach Pedro Grifol as their new manager. The decision was widely applauded around the game. Former Blue Jays manager Charlie Montoyo came aboard as bench coach. Pitching coach Ethan Katz and assistant pitching coach Curt Hasler were retained, while hitting coach Frank Menechino, third base coach Joe McEwing, and catching instructor Jerry Narron were let go.

While none of Chicago's U.S. affiliates posted a winning record, it was still a productive year for the White Sox's farm system, which ranked near the bottom of all organizations in terms of prospect talent coming into the year and now has bumped up at least a few positions into the mid 20s.

A strong draft crop, led by Chicago-area first-round high school lefthander Noah Schultz and college righthanders Peyton Pallette and Jonathan Cannon, all now rank in or near the top 10 in the organization.

Strong seasons by top prospects Colson Montgomery, a shortstop who hit .295/.408/.450 in a pair of Class A stops after being drafted in the first round in 2021, and Cuban outfielder Oscar Colas, as well as the rise of righthanders Sean Burke and Cristian Mena, have bolstered the system considerably.

A new wrinkle in player development, labeled "Project Birmingham," was added in 2022. The White Sox promoted many of the system's key prospects to Double-A Birmingham for extra work during the last few weeks of the Southern League season.

Players were moved on and off the roster to get extra playing time, and many of the minor league coordinators and coaches were there to provide daily hands-on instruction. Among those who benefit-

ted were a trio of righthanders in 2019 draft picks Matthew Thompson and Andrew Dalquist as well as 2020 pick Jared Kelley. All three finished strong thanks in part to the work they did in Birmingham.

International players such as third baseman Bryan Ramos and outfielder Luis Mieses also benefited from the exposure at a higher level of minor league competition.

Meanwhile, a number of Chicago's recent draft picks and key international prospects participated in instructional league in Arizona at roughly the same time as Project Birmingham. In particular, Schultz impressed talent evaluators with his multiple plus pitches coming from a deceptive lower-slot delivery. ∎

Rookie Jake Burger produced a 1.039 OPS versus lefthanders in a complementary role.

MARK BLINCH/GETTY IMAGES

PROJECTED 2026 LINEUP

Catcher	Seby Zavala	32
First Base	Andrew Vaughn	28
Second Base	Colson Montgomery	24
Third Base	Yoan Moncada	31
Shortstop	Tim Anderson	33
Left Field	Bryan Ramos	24
Center Field	Luis Robert	28
Right Field	Oscar Colas	27
Designated Hitter	Eloy Jimenez	29
No. 1 Starter	Dylan Cease	30
No. 2 Starter	Lucas Giolito	31
No. 3 Starter	Michael Kopech	30
No. 4 Starter	Noah Schultz	22
No. 5 Starter	Sean Burke	26
Closer	Norge Vera	26

CHICAGO WHITE SOX

TOP 2023 MLB CONTRIBUTORS	RANK
Oscar Colas, OF	2
Lenyn Sosa, SS/2B	10
BREAKOUT PROSPECTS	**RANK**
Tanner McDougal, RHP	15
Ryan Burrowes, SS	23
Loidel Chapelli, 2B	27

SOURCE OF TOP 30 TALENT			
Homegrown	**30**	**Acquired**	**0**
College	9	Trade	0
Junior college	0	Rule 5 draft	0
High school	7	Independent league	0
Nondrafted free agent	1	Free agent/waivers	0
International	13		

LF
Wilfred Veras (17)
Luis Mieses (20)
Godwin Bennett
Carlos Jimenez
Duke Ellis

CF
Yoelqui Cespedes (16)
Terrell Tatum (25)
Erick Hernandez (26)
Jacob Burke
Alvaro Aguero
James Beard
Cam Butler
Misael Gonzalez

RF
Oscar Colas (2)
Arnold Prado

3B
Bryan Ramos (3)
Wes Kath (18)
DJ Gladney
Arxy Hernandez
Brooks Baldwin

SS
Colson Montgomery (1)
Jose Rodriguez (9)
Lenyn Sosa (10)
Jordan Sprinkle (19)
Ryan Burrowes (23)
Layant Tapia
Wilber Sanchez
Moises Castillo

2B
Yolbert Sanchez (24)
Loidel Chapelli (27)
Javier Mora

1B
Dario Borrero
Tim Elko

C
Adam Hackenberg (30)
Carlos Perez
Ronny Hernandez
Colby Smelley
Luis Pineda
Troy Claunch

LHP

LHSP	LHRP
Noah Schultz (4)	Fraser Ellard
Tyler Schweitzer (28)	Caleb Freeman
Garrett Schoenle	Sammy Peralta
Shane Murphy	Gil Luna
Brooks Gosswein	

RHP

RHSP	RHRP
Sean Burke (5)	Eric Adler
Cristian Mena (6)	Lane Ramsey
Peyton Pallette (7)	Declan Cronin
Norge Vera (8)	Yoelvin Silven
Jonathan Cannon (11)	Zac Cable
Matthew Thompson (12)	Edgar Navarro
Kohl Simas (13)	
Jared Kelley (14)	
Tanner McDougal (15)	
Jonathan Stiever (21)	
Jason Bilous (22)	
Andrew Dalquist (29)	
Yohemy Nolasco	
Mark McLaughlin	
Johan Dominguez	
Drew McDaniel	
Chase Solesky	

1 COLSON MONTGOMERY, SS

Born: Feb. 27, 2002. **B-T:** L-R. **HT:** 6-4. **WT:** 221.
Drafted: HS—Huntingburg, IN, 2021 (1st round).
Signed by: Justin Wechsler.

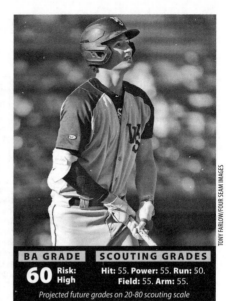

TONY FARLOW/FOUR SEAM IMAGES

TRACK RECORD: A three-sport athlete in high school, Montgomery was recruited for basketball by in-state powerhouse Indiana, with the Hoosiers baseball program also wanting his services. Montgomery broke the Southridge High basketball career scoring record and was also the quarterback for the football team. Baseball proved to be Montgomery's true love. After two professional seasons, it looks like he made the right choice. The White Sox drafted Montgomery 22nd overall in 2021 and signed him for just over $3 million. He began his pro career in the Arizona Complex League and hit .287/.396/.362 in 26 games. He played at three levels in 2022, reaching Double-A Birmingham for 14 games to conclude the year. Montgomery's combined batting line of .274/.381/.429 included 11 home runs, a figure which hinted at his developing power. His 54 walks contributed to a high on-base percentage and represented an impressive total for a young hitter in his first taste of full-season ball. Montgomery reached base in 50 straight games over one stretch that spanned time at Low-A Kannapolis and High-A Winston-Salem. He was especially impressive in the Low-A Carolina League, where he hit .324/.424/.477 in 45 games despite missing three weeks early in the season with a bone bruise in his hand.

SCOUTING REPORT: Montgomery has a polished approach at the plate, is the owner of the best strike-zone discipline in the system and doesn't often give away at-bats. His swing is simple and is geared toward driving the ball toward left-center field, while still showing enough barrel control to pull balls with authority. The 15 pounds of muscle he has added since turning pro and the torque generated by his long levers make evaluators believe he'll eventually hit for more power. Montgomery is an average runner, able to go first to third on a base hit, but so far has stolen only one base over two seasons. He's an instinctual, above-average defender, with solid footwork, hands and actions. His longer strides make up for the lack of pure speed. He ranges well to his left and is working at getting better on the backhand. Montgomery's above-average arm strength is enough for the position, especially considering he can throw before getting completely set up.

THE FUTURE: Montgomery played the entire 2022 season at age 20 and was a year older than other high school players in his draft class, but the fact that he's already made it to Double-A shows that he's ahead of the curve. At 6-foot-4, Montgomery consistently faces questions as to whether he can stay at shortstop, similar to doubts faced by Corey Seager a decade ago. If Montgomery doesn't grow too much, there's reason to believe he can stay at shortstop. If not, he has the tools to handle third base. Montgomery will return to Birmingham in 2023 but could reach Triple-A Charlotte before the end of the summer.

BA GRADE	SCOUTING GRADES
60 Risk: High	Hit: 55. Power: 55. Run: 50. Field: 55. Arm: 55.

Projected future grades on 20-80 scouting scale

BEST TOOLS

BATTING

Best Hitter for Average	Jose Rodriguez
Best Power Hitter	DJ Gladney
Best Strike-Zone Discipline	Colson Montgomery
Fastest Baserunner	Duke Ellis
Best Athlete	Colson Montgomery

PITCHING

Best Fastball	Sean Burke
Best Curveball	Peyton Pallette
Best Slider	Noah Schultz
Best Changeup	Jason Bilous
Best Control	Norge Vera

FIELDING

Best Defensive Catcher	Adam Hackenberg
Best Defensive Infielder	Jordan Sprinkle
Best Infield Arm	Wes Kath
Best Defensive Outfielder	Yoelqui Cespedes
Best Outfield Arm	Oscar Colas

Year	Age	Club (Legue)	Lvl	AVG	G	AB	R	H	2B	3B	HR	RBI	BB	SO	SB	OBP	SLG
2022	20	Kannapolis (CAR)	LoA	.324	45	170	31	55	12	1	4	26	26	42	0	.424	.476
2022	20	Winston-Salem (SAL)	HiA	.258	37	132	22	34	4	1	5	14	26	26	1	.387	.417
2022	20	Birmingham (SL)	AA	.146	14	48	5	7	1	0	2	7	2	15	0	.192	.292
Minor League Totals				.277	122	444	74	123	24	2	11	54	67	105	1	.384	.414

2 OSCAR COLAS, OF

Born: Sept. 17, 1998. **B-T:** L-L. **HT:** 6-1. **WT:** 226.
Signed: Cuba, 2022. **Signed by:** Marco Paddy/Ruddy Moreta.

TRACK RECORD: Colas was first eligible to sign in late 2020 but chose to wait until the next international signing period. He signed on Jan. 25, 2022, when the White Sox had replenished their international bonus pool. He signed for $2.7 million after being on the sidelines for two years. He previously played in his native Cuba and also spent three seasons in Nippon Professional Baseball, playing primarily in the Japanese minor leagues from ages 18 to 20. The White Sox started Colas at High-A Winston-Salem in 2022 before promoting him to Double-A Birmingham and eventually to Triple-A Charlotte. Colas finished his first affiliated season with 23 home runs and an .895 OPS despite missing time in May with a wrist injury.

BA GRADE
50 Risk: Medium

SCOUTING REPORT: Colas projects to be an above-average hitter with future plus power. He uses the whole field and shows the ability to get his barrel on tough pitches and take them the opposite way. He also is savvy enough to use his pull-side power early in counts before taking a more balanced approach as he gets deeper into at-bats. Colas has average power now but should develop into a more well-rounded hitter and could provide 25-30 home runs a year if he reaches his ceiling. To get there, he'll have to cure himself of a tendency to chase pitches down and away, which has led to strikeout rates around 20%. Colas is a below-average runner, especially down the line, but is better going first to third. He has the instincts and reads to play center field, but his plus arm and below-average speed will steer him toward a future in right field.

THE FUTURE: Colas will go to spring training aiming to earn the job as Chicago's starting right fielder but could return to Triple-A Charlotte for more seasoning.

SCOUTING GRADES	Hitting: 55	Power: 60	Speed: 40	Fielding: 50	Arm: 60

Year	Age	Club (League)	Lvl	AVG	G	AB	R	H	2B	3B	HR	RBI	BB	SO	SB	OBP	SLG
2022	23	Winston-Salem (SAL)	HiA	.311	59	244	37	76	13	3	7	42	22	54	1	.369	.475
2022	23	Birmingham (SL)	AA	.306	51	206	39	63	9	1	14	33	14	54	1	.364	.563
2022	23	Charlotte (IL)	AAA	.387	7	31	5	12	2	0	2	4	2	12	1	.424	.645
Minor League Totals				.314	117	481	81	151	24	4	23	79	38	120	3	.371	.524

3 BRYAN RAMOS, 3B

Born: March 12, 2002. **B-T:** R-R. **HT:** 6-3. **WT:** 225.
Signed: Cuba, 2018. **Signed by:** Ruddy Moreta/Doug Laumann/Marco Paddy.

TRACK RECORD: Ramos has been younger than his competition everywhere he's played since starting his pro career at age 17 in Rookie ball in 2019. He spent most of 2022 at High-A Winston-Salem, where he hit .272/.350/.471 with 19 home runs and showed impressive mastery of the strike zone with 40 walks and 71 strikeouts in 99 games. He finished the year with 21 games at Double-A Birmingham. Ramos' body has evolved over time as he has added 35 pounds to his 6-foot-3 frame while staying lean and athletic.

SCOUTING REPORT: Ramos' hit tool projects as above-average, but he still has plenty of development ahead. He gets overly aggressive and chases pitches, and he sometimes tries to pull pitches he should be driving to right-center field.

BA GRADE
50 Risk: High

Ramos makes loud enough contact to project above-average power and has proven he can handle high velocity. Ramos' biggest strides have come with his defense at third base. His improved body has been a contributing factor, and he has made strides with his hands, footwork and arm strength as well. He's adept at coming in on balls and making plays down the line, while his arm should reach above-average. Ramos is a capable defender at second base but fits best at third base. Ramos is a below-average runner but not a baseclogger. He's also shown excellent makeup and has worked diligently to learn English.

THE FUTURE: In 2023, Ramos will return to Double-A Birmingham, where he will again be young for the level. He projects as a solid-average regular in the big leagues.

SCOUTING GRADES	Hitting: 55	Power: 55	Speed: 40	Fielding: 50	Arm: 55

Year	Age	Club (League)	Lvl	AVG	G	AB	R	H	2B	3B	HR	RBI	BB	SO	SB	OBP	SLG
2022	20	Winston-Salem (SAL)	HiA	.275	99	382	64	105	16	1	19	74	40	71	1	.350	.471
2022	20	Birmingham (SL)	AA	.225	21	80	8	18	3	0	3	12	5	15	0	.279	.375
Minor League Totals				.259	286	1081	172	280	52	9	39	169	115	240	17	.344	.432

4 NOAH SCHULTZ, LHP

Born: Aug. 5, 2003. **B-T:** L-L. **HT:** 6-9. **WT:** 220.
Drafted: HS—Oswego, Ill., 2022 (1st round). **Signed by:** JJ Lally.

TRACK RECORD: It had been 21 years since the White Sox drafted a high school pitcher in the first round—suburban Chicago righthander Kris Honel in 2001—before another local product tempted them. The White Sox viewed the 6-foot-9 Schultz as too promising to pass up with the 26th overall pick in 2022. With a fastball that touches 98 mph, Schultz was Chicago's pick despite a limited senior season because of a bout with mononucleosis. Schultz signed for $2.8 million and saw his first action in a White Sox uniform at instructional league.

BA GRADE
55 Risk: Extreme

SCOUTING REPORT: The gem of Schultz's arsenal is a potentially plus-plus two-seam fastball that ranged from 93-97 mph in the fall. It's a pitch that explodes on hitters with run and sink to help get whiffs up in the zone. His 81-84 mph slider has a high spin rate and is a potentially plus pitch. It has devastating late life and hard sweeping action that plays against batters of either hand. He has enough feel for his slider to throw it in the zone consistently. Schultz's third pitch is an average, 86-87 mph changeup with hard fading action. He uses it to keep right-handed batters from sitting on his slider. Using a modified windup, Schultz starts from what looks like a stretch position before going into a small sidestep, which helps keep his long levers in sync. He throws from a lower arm slot that adds deception and allows his stuff to play up. He's shown surprisingly good feel to throw strikes, especially given his extreme height, and has impressive body control and great feel to land his breaking ball.

THE FUTURE: The White Sox will give Schultz plenty of time to develop at the lower levels. He might start 2023 in extended spring training to manage his innings before heading to Low-A.

SCOUTING GRADES	Fastball: 65	Slider: 60	Changeup: 50	Control: 50

Year	Age	Club (League)	Lvl	W	L	ERA	G	GS	IP	H	HR	BB	SO	BB/9	SO/9	WHIP	AVG
2022	19	Did not play															

5 SEAN BURKE, RHP

Born: Dec. 18, 1999. **B-T:** R-R. **HT:** 6-6. **WT:** 236.
Drafted: Maryland, 2021 (3rd round). **Signed by:** John Stott.

TRACK RECORD: After starring in both basketball and baseball in high school, Burke headed to Maryland to play baseball. He missed his freshman year after having Tommy John surgery, pitched just four games in 2020 because of the pandemic and then appeared in 14 games as a draft-eligible redshirt sophomore in 2021. Burke was drafted in the third round in 2021, signed for $900,000 and then pitched in seven games at two levels. Burke appeared in 27 games across three levels in 2022, finishing at Triple-A. His most eye-catching attribute was his strikeout rate of 11.4 per nine innings, which ranked inside the top 30 for minor leaguers with at least 100 innings.

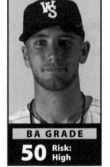

BA GRADE
50 Risk: High

SCOUTING REPORT: The key to Burke's breakout was him becoming more consistent and comfortable on the mound. His plus fastball ranges from 91-98 mph and sits 95-96. It has ride up in the zone, late tailing life and is effective in all quadrants of the zone. Burke improved his curveball enough in 2022 to bump it from average to a potentially plus offering. With 11-to-5 shape, it has tight downward break with depth. Burke added a couple ticks to it in 2022 to get it in the 77-80 mph range, and it's now a weapon against lefthanded hitters. Burke's slider is average and sits in the 84-88 mph range with two-plane break. His potentially average, fading changeup was used sparingly in 2022 but showed improvement and was delivered with good arm speed. Burke uses an abbreviated windup and drives the ball down in the zone.

THE FUTURE: The improvement that Burke showed in 2022 gives him a chance to be a back-end starter, adding to the wealth of pitching that the White Sox organization is building.

SCOUTING GRADES	Fastball: 60	Curveball: 60	Slider: 50	Changeup: 50	Control: 50

Year	Age	Club (League)	Lvl	W	L	ERA	G	GS	IP	H	HR	BB	SO	BB/9	SO/9	WHIP	AVG
2022	22	Winston-Salem (SAL)	HiA	2	1	2.89	6	5	28	24	3	12	31	3.9	10.0	1.29	.242
2022	22	Birmingham (SL)	AA	2	7	4.81	19	19	73	72	11	33	99	4.1	12.2	1.44	.259
2022	22	Charlotte (IL)	AAA	0	2	11.57	2	2	7	12	1	3	7	3.9	9.0	2.14	.375
Minor League Totals				4	11	4.46	34	33	125	118	15	59	162	4.2	11.7	1.42	.253

6 CRISTIAN MENA, RHP

Born: Dec. 21, 2002. **B-T:** R-R. **HT:** 6-2. **WT:** 214.
Signed: Dominican Republic, 2019. **Signed by:** Marino De Leon.

BA GRADE
50 Risk: High

TRACK RECORD: Mena signed with the White Sox for $250,000 during the 2019 international signing period, but his pro debut was delayed until 2021 by the pandemic. He impressed observers in the Arizona Complex League that season, paving the way for a breakthrough 2022. No other White Sox minor league pitcher has taken as big of a jump forward as Mena, who started the year at Low-A Kannapolis and finished in Double-A as part of the organization's "Project Birmingham" initiative to provide personalized instruction to its brightest prospects. Mena was one of five teenage pitchers to log at least 100 innings in 2022. His 3.80 ERA and strikeout rate of 29% were bettered only by the Phillies' Andrew Painter.

SCOUTING REPORT: Mena has added 40 pounds to his lanky 6-foot-2 frame since signing and increased the zip on his fastball. His heater ranges from 90-96 mph and sits 92-94 with good life. He has feel for the pitch and gets swings and misses up in the zone. His best offspeed pitch is a potentially plus curveball that he uses more than his fastball. His curve typically sits in the low 80s but can reach a few ticks higher. It shows 11-to-5 shape. During the 2022 season, Mena added a slider in the 83-86 mph range with sharpness and depth. It projects as at least a solid-average pitch and could trend up when he adds enough velocity to get more separation from his curveball. Mena is being encouraged to increase the usage of his average 87 mph changeup, which features splitter-type break. His high three-quarters delivery is clean and repeatable, but he overthrows at times and comes off the ball.

THE FUTURE: There is still a lot of growth ahead for Mena, but he has a complete package of pitches that he throws for strikes and a drive to improve. He'll head back to Double-A Birmingham to start 2023.

SCOUTING GRADES	Fastball: 55	Curveball: 60	Slider: 50	Changeup: 50	Control: 50

Year	Age	Club (League)	Lvl	W	L	ERA	G	GS	IP	H	HR	BB	SO	BB/9	SO/9	WHIP	AVG
2022	19	Kannapolis (CAR)	LoA	1	2	2.68	11	11	54	45	2	15	66	2.5	11.1	1.12	.227
2022	19	Winston-Salem (SAL)	HiA	1	3	4.65	10	10	41	39	4	22	47	4.9	10.4	1.50	.252
2022	19	Birmingham (SL)	AA	0	1	6.30	3	3	10	16	1	1	13	0.9	11.7	1.70	.364
Minor League Totals				3	10	5.07	37	36	153	169	15	59	188	3.5	11.1	1.49	.281

7 PEYTON PALLETTE, RHP

Born: May 9, 2001. **B-T:** R-R. **HT:** 6-1. **WT:** 180.
Drafted: Arkansas, 2022 (2nd round). **Signed by:** Torreon Woods.

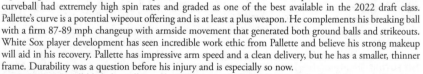

BA GRADE
55 Risk: Extreme

TRACK RECORD: Pallette had an abbreviated college career at Arkansas, where he pitched in just four games in relief in the shortened 2020 season and then appeared in 15 games in 2021 after moving to the rotation. His three-pitch mix and pitch data profile intrigued teams, but he didn't get to show his stuff in 2022 after he had Tommy John surgery before the start of the college season. The White Sox believe they got a bargain by selecting Pallette—who was a slam dunk first-rounder before his injury—in the second round. He began a throwing program shortly after signing for an over-slot $1.5 million and will return at some point in 2023.

SCOUTING REPORT: When healthy in 2021, Pallette's fastball sat in the 93-95 mph range and touched 99 with impressive vertical break. His 79-81 mph curveball had extremely high spin rates and graded as one of the best available in the 2022 draft class. Pallette's curve is a potential wipeout offering and is at least a plus weapon. He complements his breaking ball with a firm 87-89 mph changeup with armside movement that generated both ground balls and strikeouts. White Sox player development has seen incredible work ethic from Pallette and believe his strong makeup will aid in his recovery. Pallette has impressive arm speed and a clean delivery, but he has a smaller, thinner frame. Durability was a question before his injury and is especially so now.

THE FUTURE: It will likely be well into the 2023 season before Pallette gets back on the mound in game action. While he has plenty to prove, he will represent a draft bargain if he regains the crispness on his fastball and curveball that made him a first-round talent.

SCOUTING GRADES	Fastball: 60	Curveball: 60	Changeup: 50	Control: 50

Year	Age	Club (League)	Level	W	L	ERA	G	GS	IP	H	HR	BB	SO	BB/9	SO/9	WHIP	AVG
2022	21	Did not play—Injured															

8 NORGE VERA, RHP

Born: June 1, 2000. **B-T:** R-R. **HT:** 6-5. **WT:** 205.
Signed: Cuba, 2021. **Signed by:** Marco Paddy/Ruddy Moreta/Doug Laumann.
TRACK RECORD: The son of a Cuban baseball star by the same name, Vera signed with the White Sox in 2021 for $1.5 million. He began his career in the Dominican Summer League in 2021 and dominated much younger opponents but also missed time with arm fatigue. His 2022 season started late because of a lat injury, but he finally got on the mound in late May at extended spring training. Vera pitched in his first official game in the U.S. on June 9, and after seven more Low-A outings, he moved to High-A Winston-Salem before finishing with three starts for Double-A Birmingham.

BA GRADE
55 Risk: Extreme

SCOUTING REPORT: When healthy, Vera dominates with a plus-plus fastball with excellent life and extension. It sits 95-96 mph and peaks at 99. The ball explodes out of his hand, gets good carry and can seem invisible to hitters. Vera's velocity dropped to the low-to-mid 90s late in the season. The issue most likely stems from being out of action for so long, both before and after starting pro ball. His slider is a future above-average pitch that needs to be tightened and thrown with more conviction. It sits in the 82-86 mph range but needs to be harder. Vera rarely uses his mid-80s changeup, which is more of a downer pitch that lacks good action. With further refinement, the pitch could get to average. Vera pitches with a free and easy delivery which is inconsistent when he gets across his body and doesn't use his back side. At other times he gets high with his arm, but overall he has shown good feel for fixing issues.
THE FUTURE: Vera spent the offseason in Arizona working out at Chicago's complex. He projects as a starting pitcher but could also thrive in a late-inning relief role.

SCOUTING GRADES		Fastball: 70		Slider: 55			Changeup: 50			Control: 45		
Year	Age	Club (League)	Lvl	W	L	ERA	G	GS	IP	H	HR	BB	SO	BB/9	SO/9	WHIP	AVG
2022	22	Kannapolis (CAR)	LoA	0	2	1.88	8	8	24	12	1	15	35	5.6	13.1	1.12	.143
2022	22	Winston-Salem (SAL)	HiA	0	1	8.10	2	2	3	2	0	4	5	10.8	13.5	1.80	.182
2022	22	Birmingham (SL)	AA	0	0	5.62	3	3	8	5	0	12	12	13.5	13.5	2.12	.179
Minor League Totals				1	3	2.15	21	20	54	28	1	36	86	6.0	14.2	1.18	.150

9 JOSE RODRIGUEZ, SS/2B

Born: May 13, 2001. **B-T:** R-R. **HT:** 5-11. **WT:** 196.
Signed: Dominican Republic, 2018. **Signed by:** Ruddy Moreta.
TRACK RECORD: Rodriguez signed with the White Sox for $50,000 in 2018 and didn't reach full-season ball until 2021. He spent the entire season at Double-A Birmingham in 2022 but was still young for the level at age 21. Rodriguez started slowly, with an OPS under .700 for the first three months, until getting hot during July and August. A hamate injury ended his season a few weeks early. Rodriguez was particularly special in August, when he posted a 1.181 OPS with nine of his 11 home runs. He also showed much better plate discipline, walking nearly as often as he struck out during those last two months.

BA GRADE
45 Risk: Medium

SCOUTING REPORT: Rodriguez has a free-swinging, aggressive approach at the plate. His swing is simple and low maintenance, and he uses quick hands to drive the ball to all fields with gap-to-gap power. He also shows the ability to make adjustments during at-bats. Rodriguez should be able to stay in the middle infield, especially when he's locked in, but at times he's seen as too nonchalant on defense. While he is not a burner, he has a quick first step, a good internal clock and average arm strength and range. That lends optimism to the idea that he can develop into a more reliable defender at shortstop or second base as he matures. Rodriguez has been good for 30 to 40 stolen bases per year, supplementing his average speed with good baserunning instincts.
THE FUTURE: Rodriguez's late-season surge could indicate that he is ready to take a step forward in 2023. He projects now as a utility infielder, but continued improvements on both sides of the ball might steer him toward a starting role. He'll be just 22 for most of the 2023 season, so a return to Birmingham could be in the cards before he reaches Triple-A Charlotte.

SCOUTING GRADES		Hitting: 55		Power: 50		Speed: 50			Fielding: 50		Arm: 50		
Year	Age	Club (League)	Lvl	AVG	G	AB	R	H	2B	3B	HR	RBI	BB	SO	SB	OBP	SLG
2022	21	Birmingham (SL)	AA	.280	104	440	75	123	21	6	11	68	38	66	40	.340	.430
Minor League Totals				.291	319	1324	213	385	68	17	36	173	82	212	93	.334	.449

10 LENYN SOSA, SS/2B

Born: Jan. 25, 2000. **B-T:** R-R. **HT:** 6-0. **WT:** 208.
Signed: Venezuela, 2016. **Signed by:** Amador Arias.

TRACK RECORD: The White Sox signed Sosa for $350,000 on July 2, 2016. He was viewed as one of the best offensive shortstops from Venezuela in that international signing class. Sosa began his pro career at age 17 in the Rookie-level Arizona League in 2017 and made steady progress through the system until he broke out in 2022. With added strength came home run power, and he hit 23 longballs between Double-A Birmingham and Triple-A Charlotte. Sosa made his major league debut with 11 games over a 12-day span in August.

BA GRADE

45 Risk: Medium

SCOUTING REPORT: Sosa spent time prior to spring training working on his stance by getting into his load, using his back hip and having less movement in his load. Those changes led to improved bat speed and more consistent contact. Sosa now has power to all fields and drives balls with more loft. He also showed the ability to adjust to spin and handle fastballs up in the zone. He gets himself into trouble at times when his swing gets big. He gets better results when he stays within himself. Sosa is an above-average defender at both third base and second base, with fluid movements and good actions. He can also handle shortstop in a utility role. His average arm works wherever he's playing. Sosa is a below-average runner but is better underway. He's credited with having good makeup, with the work he put in during the offseason a testament to his work ethic.

THE FUTURE: Sosa profiles best as a utility infielder who sees lots of playing time at second base, third base and shortstop. He'll be just 23 in 2023 and will compete for a job on the major league team.

SCOUTING GRADES		Hitting: 50		Power: 50		Speed: 40			Fielding: 55		Arm: 50	

Year	Age	Club (League)	Lvl	AVG	G	AB	R	H	2B	3B	HR	RBI	BB	SO	SB	OBP	SLG
2022	22	Birmingham (SL)	AA	.331	62	257	47	85	10	2	14	48	21	40	0	.384	.549
2022	22	Charlotte (IL)	AAA	.296	57	226	30	67	12	0	9	31	18	43	3	.352	.469
2022	22	Chicago (AL)	MLB	.114	11	35	3	4	1	0	1	1	1	12	0	.139	.229
Major League Totals				.114	11	35	3	4	1	0	1	1	1	12	0	.139	.229
Minor League Totals				.280	463	1870	267	524	98	10	47	244	103	350	17	.322	.419

11 JONATHAN CANNON, RHP

Born: July 19, 2000. **B-T:** R-R. **HT:** 6-6. **WT:** 213.
Drafted: Georgia, 2022 (3rd round). **Signed by:** Kevin Burrell

TRACK RECORD: Cannon was available in the 2021 draft as an eligible sophomore at Georgia but went undrafted after announcing that he intended to return to school for his junior year. A regular weekend starter for the Bulldogs in 2022, Cannon led the staff with nine wins in 13 starts. The White Sox drafted Cannon in the third round and signed the righthander for $925,000. He made four brief appearances late in the regular season before taking the mound during fall instructional league.

SCOUTING REPORT: Cannon is a polished pitcher with a high floor and projects as a durable back-end starter. An effective strike-thrower, he pounds the zone with a 93-96 mph fastball that typically sits 94, and his sinking two-seamer is the better of his two fastball variants. He has the ability to work east to west but needs to improve the carry on his four-seamer in order to improve his vertical attack. His 83 mph slider is a slurvy breaking ball with plus spin. It could have more movement with depth in the future to improve its effectiveness versus lefthanded hitters. Cannon also mixes in a cutter at 89-91 mph against lefthanded batters and his 85 mph changeup has good run and downward action. Cannon has a repeatable delivery and consistent release point from a three-quarters slot, which allows him to pound the zone and attempt to induce weak contact.

THE FUTURE: A polished college pitcher with an SEC resume, Cannon could jump right to High-A Winston-Salem to start 2023. He has the look of a durable back-of-the rotation starter, with the stuff and pitchability to move quickly through the system.

BA GRADE: 50/High		Fastball: 55		Slider: 55		Changeup: 50		Cutter: 50			Control: 60	

Year	Age	Club (League)	Lvl	W	L	ERA	G	GS	IP	H	HR	BB	SO	BB/9	SO/9	WHIP	AVG
2022	21	White Sox (ACL)	R	0	0	0.00	1	0	1	0	0	1	1	9.0	9.0	1.00	.000
2022	21	Kannapolis (CAR)	LoA	0	0	1.42	3	3	6	4	0	2	3	2.8	4.3	0.95	.200
Minor League Totals				0	0	1.23	4	3	7	4	0	3	4	3.7	4.9	0.95	.174

12 MATTHEW THOMPSON, RHP

Born: Aug. 11, 2000. **B-T:** R-R. **HT:** 6-3. **WT:** 215.
Drafted: HS—Cypress, Texas, 2019 (2nd round). **Signed by:** Chris Walker

TRACK RECORD: The White Sox drafted Thompson in the second round after a notable high school career. After a rough first full season in 2021, Thompson flashed the potential that the baseball industry saw during his scholastic years, even with inconsistent results at times in 2022. He began the year with High-A Winston-Salem before finishing at Double-A Birmingham.

SCOUTING REPORT: The key to Thompson's improvement was in his maturation as a pitcher and his improved confidence in his stuff. While working at the bottom of the zone has been better for him, Thompson does have a 93-97 mph fastball with good carry that generates swings and misses up in the zone. The key to Thompson's arsenal is an above-average curveball with 11-to-5 shape that's thrown in the 76-80 mph range and flashes plus. His 82-83 mph slider with slurvy break is a newer pitch, added just a year ago, and needs consistency. His fourth pitch is an 86 mph changeup that has a chance to be an average pitch as he throws it more often and adds more feel. Thompson repeated his crossfire delivery more consistently in 2022 and his walk rate fell from 11.4% to 8.2%.

THE FUTURE: Thompson is athletic enough to continue the progression he showed in 2022. He'll be just 22 for most of next season and should return to Birmingham to start the year. He projects as a back-end starter but could be more with continued improvement.

BA GRADE: 45/High			**Fastball:** 55		**Curveball:** 55		**Slider:** 45		**Changeup:** 50		**Control:** 50				

Year	Age	Club (League)	Lvl	W	L	ERA	G	GS	IP	H	HR	BB	SO	BB/9	SO/9	WHIP	AVG
2022	21	Winston-Salem (SAL)	HiA	4	5	4.70	18	18	84	82	13	29	73	3.1	7.8	1.32	.258
2022	21	Birmingham (SL)	AA	0	2	5.33	7	7	25	26	3	11	31	3.9	11.0	1.46	.265
Minor League Totals				6	16	5.24	47	47	185	196	24	78	184	3.8	8.9	1.48	.275

13 KOHL SIMAS, RHP

Born: Dec. 22, 1999. **B-T:** R-R. **HT:** 6-1. **WT:** 220.
Signed: San Diego State, 2020 (NDFA). **Signed by:** Noah St. Urbain.

TRACK RECORD: The son of former White Sox six-year reliever Bill Simas, Kohl signed as a nondrafted free agent in 2020 after pitching for three different schools in college. After throwing just 21 innings in 2021, he broke out with a strong 2022 season at Low-A Kannapolis, where he posted a 3.65 ERA and struck out 76 batters in 61.2 innings before tiring late in the year after a promotion to Double-A.

SCOUTING REPORT: Simas thrives with an effortless fastball that averaged 92 mph and touched 97, with tail and run. His best breaking ball is a 12-to-6 curveball with tight break and average movement, used early in the count for strikes. It's a below-average pitch now but has the potential to be an average offering in time. He's still working on a short-breaking slider at 84-86 mph, but it sometimes gets flat and the velocity tapers. Simas throws an 85 mph, above-average changeup with good arm speed and arm action, with downward life off his fastball. He throws all of his pitches for strikes.

THE FUTURE: Simas profiles as a back-end starter but could also thrive as a multi-inning bullpen arm with weapons for both side hitters and increased velocity in shorter stints. His bulldog mentality and fiery demeanor also fit in a bullpen role, but for now the White Sox will continue his development as a starter.

BA GRADE: 45/High			**Fastball:** 55		**Curveball:** 50		**Slider:** 50		**Changeup:** 55		**Control:** 50				

Year	Age	Club (League)	Lvl	W	L	ERA	G	GS	IP	H	HR	BB	SO	BB/9	SO/9	WHIP	AVG
2022	22	Kannapolis (CAR)	LoA	2	2	3.65	16	15	62	51	7	25	76	3.6	11.1	1.23	.226
2022	22	Birmingham (SL)	AA	0	0	9.95	6	0	6	10	3	4	6	5.7	8.5	2.21	.385
Minor League Totals				4	3	3.64	35	15	89	73	11	34	107	3.4	10.8	1.20	.225

14 JARED KELLEY, RHP

Born: Oct. 3, 2001. **B-T:** R-R. **HT:** 6-3. **WT:** 234.
Drafted: HS—Refugio, Texas, 2020 (2nd round). **Signed by:** Tyler Wilt.

TRACK RECORD: The White Sox went for power arms with their top two picks in the abbreviated 2020 draft with Kelley and Matthew Thompson. They signed Kelley with a well over-slot $3 million bonus in the second round. After spending his first summer at the alternate training site, Kelley struggled with shoulder fatigue and forearm tightness in 2021. His stuff wasn't nearly as firm that year as it had been as an amateur. He battled back with a decent showing in 2022, mostly at Low-A Kannapolis. With an additional three starts at Double-A Birmingham in September, Kelley finished with 76.2 innings and a combined 3.52 ERA.

SCOUTING REPORT: The two keys to Kelley's improvement were using his two-seam fastball to get more ground balls and getting back to more regular use of his plus changeup. His plus fastball averages 95 mph and touches 98. The pitch is at its best when he pitches down in the zone to both sides of the plate and then elevates late in the count to get swings and misses with his four-seam fastball. An 80-83 mph changeup is his bread-and-butter pitch, thrown with good arm speed and deception. He has a short-breaking slider in the 82-84 mph range that is fringy, but improved later in the season when he started throwing it harder. Kelley needs to add more pitchability and repeat his delivery consistently to improve his below-average control.

THE FUTURE: Kelley will likely return to Birmingham to start in 2023. He needs to stay on top of his conditioning. That could play a role in determining if he's a starter for the long-term or eventually will move to the bullpen.

BA GRADE: 50/Extreme | **Fastball:** 55 | **Slider:** 50 | **Changeup:** 60 | **Control:** 40

Year	Age	Club (League)	Lvl	W	L	ERA	G	GS	IP	H	HR	BB	SO	BB/9	SO/9	WHIP	AVG
2022	20	Kannapolis (CAR)	LoA	1	4	3.34	18	18	65	52	6	40	59	5.6	8.2	1.42	.218
2022	20	Birmingham (SL)	AA	0	2	4.50	3	3	12	13	2	7	12	5.2	9.0	1.67	.317
Minor League Totals				1	13	4.49	33	33	100	89	11	73	98	6.5	8.8	1.61	.236

15 TANNER McDOUGAL, RHP

Born: April 3, 2003. **B-T:** R-R. **HT:** 6-5. **WT:** 229.
Drafted: HS—Las Vegas, 2021 (5th round). **Signed by:** Mike Baker

TRACK RECORD: The White Sox juggled bonus money early in the 2021 draft to grab McDougal in the fifth round for an over-slot bonus of $850,000. He got into six games in the Arizona Complex League in his first summer of pro ball before an elbow injury required Tommy John surgery in October 2021. He got back on the mound for bullpens and live batting practice sessions during the 2022 fall instructional league season. Getting back on the mound in 2022 was a key step in having him ready to break camp with a minor league team in 2023.

SCOUTING REPORT: McDougal has the potential for frontline quality pitches when healthy. His fastball was back up to 96 mph during the fall and an upper-70s curveball with tons of spin and depth looked like a future plus pitch. His 81-85 mph changeup is thrown with less arm speed than his fastball, which is an area for improvement once he's back on the mound regularly. McDougal's pre-injury crossfire delivery ended with a head whack, and White Sox coaches have been working with him during his rehab to smooth out the delivery.

THE FUTURE: McDougal should get to full-season ball in 2023 and will likely start the season in extended spring training to manage his innings. He has tantalizing stuff, and a better projection on his future will come after he's back on the mound in regular games.

BA GRADE: 50/Extreme | **Fastball:** 60 | **Curveball:** 60 | **Changeup:** 40 | **Control:** 45

Year	Age	Club (League)	Lvl	W	L	ERA	G	GS	IP	H	HR	BB	SO	BB/9	SO/9	WHIP	AVG
2022	19	Did not play—Injured															

16 YOELQUI CESPEDES, OF

Born: Sept. 24, 1997. **B-T:** R-R. **HT:** 5-9. **WT:** 197.
Signed: Cuba, 2021 **Signed by:** Marco Paddy

TRACK RECORD: Cespedes—the half-brother of Yoenis Cespedes—was already a known commodity when he signed with the White Sox in 2021 for $2.05 million. After finishing the 2021 regular season with Double-A Birmingham he returned there for all of 2022. He flashed plenty of tools but struggled to hit breaking balls and struck out 30.1% of the time, to go with a low walk rate of just 5.7%. His most challenging month was in May when he dealt with back spasms. After stealing eight bags in the first three months of the 2022 season, Cespedes stole 25 over the season's final three months.

SCOUTING REPORT: There's no doubt about Cespedes' plus raw power. He has good bat speed, but his aggressiveness at the plate and swing-and-miss against offspeed pitches limit his offensive upside. He can mash fastballs over the plate, but he needs to improve his contact against heaters up in the zone and breaking balls down and away. His above-average speed and instincts allow him to get good jumps in the outfield, where he should be an above-average defender. Like his brother, Cespedes has an above-average arm. His speed also plays on the basepaths, and he's stolen 51 bases in his two pro seasons.

THE FUTURE: Cespedes is ready for Triple-A Charlotte in 2023. Barring significant improvements in his approach at the plate, he profiles as a fourth outfielder. He has time to make the adjustments that could push him to more of an everyday role.

BA GRADE: 45/High			Hit: 40		Power: 55			Speed: 55		Fielding: 55			Arm: 55	
Year	Age	Club (League)	Lvl	AVG	G	AB	R	H	2B	3B	HR	RBI	BB	SO	SB	OBP	SLG
2022	24	Birmingham (SL)	AA	.258	119	458	65	118	29	1	17	59	29	154	33	.332	.437
Minor League Totals				.268	191	728	113	195	49	3	25	86	45	237	51	.339	.446

17 WILFRED VERAS, OF/3B

Born: Nov. 15, 2002. **B-T:** R-R. **HT:** 6-2. **WT:** 231.
Signed: Dominican Republic, 2019. **Signed by:** Ruddy Moreta
TRACK RECORD: Veras has baseball bloodlines, as the son of former big leaguer Wilton Veras and nephew of Fernando Tatis Sr. He forged his own path forward in 2022 by getting his body in better shape and moving to the outfield from the corner infield. His game power emerged with 20 home runs in a season split between Low-A Kannapolis and Double-A Birmingham.
SCOUTING REPORT: Veras takes big swings at the plate, and when he squares balls up they jump off his bat. His swing is built for damage, with a small load and short stride. He has the plus raw power to hit home runs to all fields, though at times he sells out for his power and sacrifices contact. Veras will always have a bat-first profile and is likely limited to left field. Scouts thought his arm looked worse in the outfield than it previously did at third base. At best it's an average arm that plays down because his throws are not always consistent or accurate. He's a below-average runner but isn't a base clogger.
THE FUTURE: Veras has middle-of-the-order power—which is a valuable commodity—but there are other parts of his game that need improvement. He'll get the chance to make the necessary adjustments at High-A Winston-Salem in 2023.

BA GRADE: 50/Extreme			Hit: 45		Power: 60			Speed: 40		Fielding: 45			Arm: 50	
Year	Age	Club (League)	Lvl	AVG	G	AB	R	H	2B	3B	HR	RBI	BB	SO	SB	OBP	SLG
2022	19	Kannapolis (CAR)	LoA	.266	101	394	58	105	19	2	17	67	27	118	5	.319	.454
2022	19	Birmingham (SL)	AA	.267	12	45	5	12	3	0	3	5	3	14	0	.313	.533
Minor League Totals				.281	159	591	88	166	38	4	24	98	51	174	8	.344	.481

18 WES KATH, 3B

Born: Aug. 3, 2002. **B-T:** L-R. **HT:** 6-3. **WT:** 217.
Drafted: HS—Scottsdale, Ariz., 2021 (2nd round). **Signed by:** John Kazanas.
TRACK RECORD: The White Sox stayed close to their Arizona complex when they selected Kath with their second-round pick in 2021 and signed the Scottsdale high school product for $1.8 million. After starting his career in the Rookie-level Arizona Complex League, Kath moved up to Low-A Kannapolis in 2022. He took some time getting acclimated to that level of baseball but finished his Low-A season with a strong month of August when he put up a .263/.382/.544 line and hit six of his 13 home runs.
SCOUTING REPORT: Kath has strength with a bit of loft and pull-side power, but his swing can get lengthy at times. He needs to improve his pitch recognition to cut down on the swing-and-miss, but a positive sign is that he reduced his strikeout rate slightly from 36.5% to 33.0% with the jump from rookie ball to Low-A . He also boosted his walk rate to 13.4%. Kath doesn't get good swings against lefthanded pitchers, with 12 of his 13 home runs coming off righties. Defensively, he makes the routine plays despite not having great footwork or a good first step—he needs to work on his body to get more quickness and lateral range. His plus arm is the best infield arm in the organization. Kath is a below-average runner but picks up speed underway thanks to long, strong strides.
THE FUTURE: Kath will need to proceed one level at a time, and likely will spend most or all of 2023 at High-A Winston-Salem.

BA GRADE: 50/Extreme			Hit: 45		Power: 55			Speed: 40		Fielding: 50			Arm: 60	
Year	Age	Club (League)	Lvl	AVG	G	AB	R	H	2B	3B	HR	RBI	BB	SO	SB	OBP	SLG
2022	19	Kannapolis (CAR)	LoA	.238	99	383	56	91	20	1	13	42	60	148	2	.343	.397
2022	19	Birmingham (SL)	AA	.170	13	47	1	8	1	0	0	3	4	23	0	.250	.191
Minor League Totals				.227	140	534	72	121	21	3	16	60	72	213	3	.325	.367

19 JORDAN SPRINKLE, SS

Born: March 6, 2001. **B-T:** R-R. **HT:** 5-11. **WT:** 180.
Drafted: UC Santa Barbara, 2022 (4th round). **Signed by:** Carlos Muniz.
TRACK RECORD: Regarded as a first-round talent coming into his junior year at UC Santa Barbara, Sprinkle underachieved at the plate with his approach, power and confidence all going backward. He posted an OPS of .797 after a much better .938 figure in 2021. He especially struggled to hit the ball with authority, which affected his defense that usually plays as plus. The White Sox picked him in the fourth round, and he signed for a $452,900 bonus. Sprinkle didn't show much more at Low-A Kannapolis, with a .237/.290/.301 batting line.
SCOUTING REPORT: Sprinkle has above-average bat speed with some power, with a leg kick that gets too aggressive and can create length in his swing. The power projects as below-average now but he showed more juice earlier in his college career. Swing adjustments may help him regain some of that pop. He has the hands, feet and range to be a plus defender with an above-average arm at shortstop. His defense and above-average speed should give him the tools to figure things out offensively as he progresses through the system. He was an effective basestealer in college, so he should be able to steal at least 20 bags a season if he gets on base enough.
THE FUTURE: Sprinkle will likely head back to Kannapolis after spring training, but a strong start could get him to High-A Winston-Salem. Sprinkle should have a future as a utility infielder. If he rediscovers the swing and approach he showed in his college career, there's a chance for a second-division starter.

BA GRADE: 45/High | **Hit:** 35 | **Power:** 40 | **Speed:** 55 | **Fielding:** 60 | **Arm:** 55

Year	Age	Club (League)	Lvl	AVG	G	AB	R	H	2B	3B	HR	RBI	BB	SO	SB	OBP	SLG
2022	21	White Sox (ACL)	R	.385	5	13	4	5	0	0	0	0	3	3	1	.556	.385
2022	21	Kannapolis (CAR)	LoA	.237	22	93	11	22	3	0	1	4	6	21	8	.290	.301
Minor League Totals				.255	27	106	15	27	3	0	1	4	9	24	9	.331	.311

20 LUIS MIESES, OF

Born: May 31, 2000. **B-T:** L-L. **HT:** 6-3. **WT:** 232.
Signed: Dominican Republic, 2016 **Signed by:** Marino De Leon
TRACK RECORD: Mieses has shown continual improvement as he's moved slowly through the White Sox system, after debuting in the Dominican Summer League in 2017. The lefthanded-hitting outfielder spent most of the season at High-A Winston-Salem before finishing the year at Double-A Birmingham, with solid numbers at both stops.
SCOUTING REPORT: Mieses flashes some of the best bat-to-ball skills and pure hitting ability in the organization. He showed improvement across the board in 2022, although he's still overly aggressive at the plate with a walk rate that consistently hovers between just 3-6%. He has loft in his swing and the ball comes off the bat hard, with below-average power now that could become solid-average in the future. One concern is that his groundball rate was up at both stops in 2022—particularly with High-A Winston-Salem, where he posted a 44.6% groundball rate. Mieses already has a major league body, having added around 50 pounds to his frame since the start of his career. A fringe-average defender with an average arm, he fits best in left field but also got some time at first base for the first time in his career. A below-average runner, speed is not part of his game but he's not a baseclogger.
THE FUTURE: Mieses has progressed one level at a time, and that pace is not likely to change much in 2023. He'll return to Birmingham but could see Triple-A before the end of the season. Mieses has not yet been added to the 40-man roster.

BA GRADE: 45/High | **Hit:** 50 | **Power:** 55 | **Speed:** 40 | **Fielding:** 45 | **Arm:** 50

Year	Age	Club (League)	Lvl	AVG	G	AB	R	H	2B	3B	HR	RBI	BB	SO	SB	OBP	SLG
2022	22	Winston-Salem (SAL)	HiA	.281	106	420	54	118	34	0	12	72	24	72	0	.324	.448
2022	22	Birmingham (SL)	AA	.299	23	97	12	29	5	0	3	16	4	20	1	.333	.443
Minor League Totals				.264	405	1602	194	423	102	8	36	241	73	296	7	.299	.405

21 JONATHAN STIEVER, RHP

Born: May, 12, 1997. **B-T:** R-R. **HT:** 6-2. **WT:** 221.
Drafted: Indiana, 2018 (5th round). **Signed by:** Adam Virchis.
TRACK RECORD: After making brief appearances with the White Sox in both 2020 and 2021 and despite an inconsistent 2021 season in Triple-A, Stiever would have been on target to contend for a rotation job

with the big league club. Instead, lat surgery in August 2021 and a long recovery period sidelined the righthander for most of the 2022 season. The 2018 fifth-round pick from Indiana finally got three short outings at Triple-A Charlotte near the end of September.

SCOUTING REPORT: Stiever's fastball's velocity was down upon his return, but when healthy it's his best pitch and sits in the mid 90s, touching 97-98 at peak. The pitch has easy velocity with run and average movement, thrown to both sides of the plate. His 82-84 mph slider was starting to show improvement in 2021. A mid-70s curveball had gone backward and needed to be thrown with a more consistent shape and feel to land it. He infrequently uses a changeup at 80-83 mph with heavy fade. Stiever's athleticism allows him to repeat a low-maintenance delivery which helps him project for average control.

THE FUTURE: Assuming he's fully recovered by the spring, Stiever will head to big league camp with a chance to earn a spot on the White Sox opening day roster. His ceiling is as a fourth starter, but his most likely role is as a middle reliever.

BA GRADE: 45/High   **Fastball:** 55   **Curveball:** 45   **Slider:** 55   **Changeup:** 45   **Control:** 50

Year	Age	Club (League)	Lvl	W	L	ERA	G	GS	IP	H	HR	BB	SO	BB/9	SO/9	WHIP	AVG
2022	25	Charlotte (IL)	AAA	0	0	0.00	3	2	3	0	0	0	1	0.0	3.0	0.00	.000
Major League Totals				0	1	14.21	3	2	6	11	4	4	3	5.7	4.3	2.37	.379
Minor League Totals				15	16	4.21	59	58	250	247	33	64	282	2.3	10.2	1.24	.254

22 JASON BILOUS, RHP

Born: Aug. 11, 1997. **B-T:** R-R. **HT:** 6-2. **WT:** 191.
Drafted: Coastal Carolina, 2018 (13th round). **Signed by:** Kevin Burrell.

TRACK RECORD: Bilous popped on the White Sox prospect list in 2022, ranking as high as No. 17 in the organization. He still possesses the best changeup in the organization, but his 2022 season, spent mostly at Double-A Birmingham, was extremely inconsistent. He finished the year with 12 games at Triple-A Charlotte and struggled to get batters out while walking more than one per inning.

SCOUTING REPORT: Bilous possesses an average fastball that sits around 93 mph and touches 96. He showed enough improvement in a mid-80s changeup with fade to grade as a potential plus pitch. His low-80s curveball, which features 12-to-6 shape, is his best breaking ball. It projects to be average. He also has a mid-80s slider that's more of a fringe-average offering. Bilous throws from a three-quarters arm slot but struggled to repeat his delivery in 2022, which led to control and command issues. He needs to be more consistent with his strikes moving forward.

THE FUTURE: Bilous finished strong at Charlotte, with a pair of 1-2-3 innings, and he struck out the side in his final appearance. He'll head back to either Birmingham or Charlotte in 2023. He'll have a whole laundry list of issues to fix in spring training, with the ongoing command and control issues pointing to a future in the bullpen rather than a starting role.

BA GRADE: 45/High   **Fastball:** 50   **Curveball:** 50   **Slider:** 45   **Changeup:** 60   **Control:** 40

Year	Age	Club (League)	Lvl	W	L	ERA	G	GS	IP	H	HR	BB	SO	BB/9	SO/9	WHIP	AVG
2022	24	Birmingham (SL)	AA	5	7	5.27	19	16	84	78	10	55	104	5.9	11.2	1.59	.241
2022	24	Charlotte (IL)	AAA	1	4	10.23	12	5	22	27	4	24	27	9.8	11.0	2.32	.300
Minor League Totals				15	33	5.51	96	72	327	318	36	196	381	5.4	10.5	1.57	.254

23 RYAN BURROWES, SS

Born: Aug. 17, 2004. **B-T:** R-R. **HT:** 6-3. **WT:** 170.
Signed: Panama, 2002 **Signed by:** Marco Paddy/Ricardo Ortiz/Ruddy Moreta

TRACK RECORD: One of the more interesting players from the White Sox 2022 international class, Burrowes signed for just $70,000. Based on his debut season in the Dominican Summer League, Burrowes could be a real bargain. He's athletic and plays with plenty of energy, and hit .266/.393/.392 in his pro debut with a 12.8% walk rate. He missed the fall instructional league as he returned home to Panama to complete his high school education.

SCOUTING REPORT: Burrowes stays upright at the plate with a very balanced swing and minimal movement. Using a little leg kick, he stays through the ball and avoids overswinging. He's expected to add power to his wiry frame as his body matures, but he lacks strength and power presently. Burrowes was not a true shortstop in Panama—he played all over the field—so he needs plenty of professional reps for his hands and footwork to get to the point where he can be an average defender. He has a strong arm, which should be above-average. A plus runner, Burrowes was successful on all 12 of his stolen base attempts in the DSL.

THE FUTURE: His pro career will continue with a 2023 assignment to the Arizona Complex League, and the fact that he's already bilingual will help him settle in quickly. There's a lot to dream on with a talent like Burrowes, but he's far away from solidifying what type of ballplayer he'll be.

BA GRADE: 50/Extreme	Hit: 50	Power: 50	Speed: 60	Fielding: 50	Arm: 55

Year	Age	Club (League)	Lvl	AVG	G	AB	R	H	2B	3B	HR	RBI	BB	SO	SB	OBP	SLG
2022	17	White Sox (DSL)	R	.266	47	158	38	42	9	1	3	18	25	34	12	.393	.392
Minor League Totals				.266	47	158	38	42	9	1	3	18	25	34	12	.393	.392

24 YOLBERT SANCHEZ, 2B

Born: March 3, 1997. **B-T:** R-R. **HT:** 5-11. **WT:** 200.
Signed: Cuba, 2019 **Signed by:** Marco Paddy

TRACK RECORD: Sanchez, who signed out of Cuba in 2019 for a $2.5 million bonus, intrigues with some elite tools but also frustrates scouts with his apparent lack of urgency and effort on the field. He got off to a hot start in 14 games at Double-A Birmingham before moving up to Triple-A Charlotte, where he slashed .280/.324/.341 in his age-25 season.

SCOUTING REPORT: Sanchez's strengths at the plate are his elite contact skills and plate discipline, though his walk rate dipped to 5.6% with Charlotte. A line drive, gap-to-gap hitter, Sanchez gets in trouble when he tries to pull the ball and his swing gets too big. Another concern is that he hit more than 50% of balls on the ground. Defensively, he's best at second base, where he's at least an average defender, and his average arm could help him handle shortstop in a utility role. The speed grade varies depending on when he's observed and ranges from 40 to 55 on the 20-to-80 scouting scale. Sanchez stole 11 bases with Charlotte but was thrown out nine times—a poor 55% success rate.

THE FUTURE: Sanchez will go to spring training with the major league team with a chance to make the major league roster as an extra infielder. No longer looked at as a potential regular, the ceiling for Sanchez now is as a utility infielder. He'll be 26 in the spring, so it's time for him to show that he's got what it takes to make it to Chicago.

BA GRADE: 40/Medium	Hit: 50	Power: 30	Speed: 45	Fielding: 50	Arm: 50

Year	Age	Club (League)	Lvl	AVG	G	AB	R	H	2B	3B	HR	RBI	BB	SO	SB	OBP	SLG
2022	25	Birmingham (SL)	AA	.353	14	51	7	18	1	0	0	6	13	7	0	.507	.373
2022	25	Charlotte (IL)	AAA	.280	113	443	44	124	16	1	3	40	27	71	11	.324	.341
Minor League Totals				.296	255	965	113	286	38	2	14	100	78	139	19	.353	.383

25 TERRELL TATUM, OF

Born: July 27, 1999. **B-T:** L-L. **HT:** 6-0. **WT:** 172.
Drafted: North Carolina State, 2021 (16th round). **Signed by:** John Stott

TRACK RECORD: An unheralded prospect who wasn't a regular until his senior season at North Carolina State, the White Sox saw potential in Tatum's tools and athleticism, grabbing the lefthanded-hitting outfielder in the 16th round in 2021. He split his first full-season assignment between Low-A Kannapolis and High-A Winston-Salem and was in the midst of a strong breakout season when he was suspended for 50 games for a positive test for amphetamines. He was assigned to the Arizona Fall League but got into just six games before an ankle injury put him on the sidelines.

SCOUTING REPORT: Tatum flashes high upside, with his speed and defense standing out the most. He projects as an average hitter with average raw power. He uses a short stroke with above-average bat speed and does a nice job hitting the ball back up the middle. Tatum has good awareness of the strike zone and walked at an 18.5% clip, but a 29% strikeout rate shows he needs to put more balls in play to take advantage of his plus speed. In addition to using his wheels on the bases, Tatum is an above-average outfielder with a fringe-average arm. He plays hard and has feel to play the game.

THE FUTURE: Already 23, Tatum should be ready for Double-A in 2023. It's tempting to slap a fourth outfielder label on him, but he could turn into more as a late-bloomer with some exciting tools and somewhat limited baseball experience for his age.

BA GRADE: 45/High	Hit: 45	Power: 45	Speed: 60	Fielding: 55	Arm: 45

Year	Age	Club (League)	Lvl	AVG	G	AB	R	H	2B	3B	HR	RBI	BB	SO	SB	OBP	SLG
2022	22	Kannapolis (CAR)	LoA	.320	10	25	6	8	2	0	0	1	11	11	6	.528	.400
2022	22	Winston-Salem (SAL)	HiA	.255	32	110	18	28	7	1	3	20	20	38	10	.371	.418
Minor League Totals				.263	68	213	43	56	17	1	4	33	56	83	23	.418	.408

26 ERICK HERNANDEZ, OF

Born: Jan. 15, 2005. **B-T:** L-L. **HT:** 6-0. **WT:** 170.
Signed: Dominican Republic, 2022. **Signed by:** Marco Paddy/Ruddy Moreta/Guillermo Peralta

TRACK RECORD: Hernandez was born in New York but grew up in the Dominican Republic. His $1 million bonus was the second highest in the White Sox 2022 international class, trailing only the $2.7 million for Oscar Colas. He began his career at home in the Dominican Summer League and started strong before struggling with a sore right knee.

SCOUTING REPORT: Hernandez's bat is his carrying tool. He has sound knowledge of the strike zone and the ability to put together good at-bats. With a good approach at the plate, he puts the barrel on the ball and has the ability to hit to all fields and also adjust nicely to offspeed pitches. He'll develop more home run pop with added strength and projects to have fringe-average in-game power. Hernandez is a natural center fielder now, with his impressive instincts and jumps compensating for just average speed. If he slows down with physical maturity, he may have to slide to an outfield corner, and his average arm strength could be a bit short for right field. A move to a corner would also put more pressure on his offense. Hernandez's consistently high energy on the field is impressive.

THE FUTURE: Hernandez spent time at the White Sox complex in Arizona during fall instructional league and will return in 2023 for his official stateside debut in the Arizona Complex League. As a hit-over-power prospect, he brings a different skill set from other international players signed by the organization.

| BA GRADE: 50/Extreme | | Hit: 55 | | Power: 45 | | Speed: 45 | | Fielding: 50 | | Arm: 50 | |

Year	Age	Club (League)	Lvl	AVG	G	AB	R	H	2B	3B	HR	RBI	BB	SO	SB	OBP	SLG
2022	17	White Sox (DSL)	R	.227	38	141	21	32	7	1	0	8	17	37	4	.333	.291
Minor League Totals				.227	38	141	21	32	7	1	0	8	17	37	4	.333	.291

27 LOIDEL CHAPELLI, 2B

Born: July 12, 2003 **B-T:** L-R. **HT:** 5-8. **WT:** 187.
Signed: Cuba, 2022. **Signed by:** Marco Paddy/Ruddy Moreta/Tomas Herrera.

TRACK RECORD: Chapelli was the MVP of the U15 World Cup in 2016 and was named Rookie of the Year in his native Cuba in 2019. He was a late acquisition during the 2022 international signing period and didn't sign until May for a bonus of $500,000. He began his White Sox career in the Dominican Summer League one month after signing and hit .344/.448/.636 as a 19-year-old who was old for the league. His father was a 14-year veteran for Camaguey of the Cuban National Series.

SCOUTING REPORT: Chapelli is more athletic than he looks at first glance considering his short, stocky frame and plays bigger than his size with a high-energy style of play. He can really swing the bat, with good bat-to-ball skills, advanced plate discipline and surprising power for his size. He has shown the ability to make adjustments at the plate. Chapelli has been strictly a second baseman with the White Sox after playing outfield in Cuba. He's an average defender with a solid-average arm. He gets out of the box quickly from the left side of the plate, with above-average speed overall.

THE FUTURE: Based on his age and previous experience in Cuba, Chapelli could break camp with one of the White Sox's two Class A teams. He's an intriguing prospect considering his size and the way he plays the game.

| BA GRADE: 50/Extreme | | Hit: 50 | | Power: 50 | | Speed: 55 | | Fielding: 50 | | Arm: 50 | |

Year	Age	Club (League)	Lvl	AVG	G	AB	R	H	2B	3B	HR	RBI	BB	SO	SB	OBP	SLG
2022	20	White Sox (DSL)	R	.344	46	154	41	53	7	7	8	29	27	22	10	.448	.636
Minor League Totals				.344	46	154	41	53	7	7	8	29	27	22	10	.448	.636

28 TYLER SCHWEITZER, LHP

Born: Sept. 19, 2000. **B-T:** L-L. **HT:** 6-0. **WT:** 185.
Drafted: Ball State, 2022 (5th round). **Signed by:** Justin Wechsler.

TRACK RECORD: The track record at Ball State for developing pitchers has been strong in recent years, and Schweitzer is one of the next in line after an outstanding junior season when he posted an 11-2 record with a 2.65 ERA in 17 games—with a 29.6% strikeout rate and 7.9% walk rate. That performance earned him MAC pitcher of the year honors in what was his first year as a starter. The White Sox drafted the southpaw in the fifth round and signed him for a $325,000 bonus. Because he didn't start a throwing program until reporting to the White Sox complex, Schweitzer didn't pitch in games until fall instructional league.

SCOUTING REPORT: Schweitzer's fastball ticked up a couple of miles per hour in the fall and sat 89-93 and touched 96, with good life up in the zone and plenty of spin. His breaking balls tend to blend, with a slider in the low 80s and a curveball in the mid-to-upper 70s. The focus for him moving forward is to get more separation between the pitches and create two distinct breaking balls—both of which have average potential. He rounds out his arsenal with an average changeup at 82 mph.

THE FUTURE: An undersized lefty, Schweitzer will begin his pro career at one of the White Sox Class A teams. His pitchability and feel for throwing strikes may result in Schweitzer's projection exceeding the sum of his mostly average parts.

BA GRADE: 45/Very High	Fastball: 50	Curveball: 50	Slider: 50	Changeup: 50	Control: 55

Year	Age	Club (League)	Lvl	W	L	ERA	G	GS	IP	H	HR	BB	SO	BB/9	SO/9	WHIP	AVG
2022	21	Did not play															

29 ANDREW DALQUIST, RHP

Born: Nov. 13, 2000. **B-T:** R-R. **HT:** 6-1. **WT:** 201.
Drafted: HS—Redondo Beach, Calif., 2019 (3rd round). **Signed by:** Mike Baker.

TRACK RECORD: Dalquist has become a tough prospect to project since being taken by the White Sox in the third round in 2019, when he signed for an over-slot $2 million bonus. He got just three innings on the mound in his draft year and then pitched at the alternate training site in 2020. With High-A Winston-Salem in 2022, he posted a 6.95 ERA and yielded 22 home runs in 90.2 innings.

SCOUTING REPORT: Evaluators have been both confused and frustrated when watching Dalquist, because he flashes the above-average stuff that got him drafted but gets tentative around the zone and is inconsistent. His fastball sits at 92 mph and has touched 97, but doesn't always get the carry it used to have. He's got two breaking balls, a slider at 83-84 mph and a curveball with 11-to-5 shape in the mid 70s. Rounding out his four-pitch mix is a changeup averaging 84 mph. Dalquist often doesn't stay on pitches long enough, which causes inconsistency with hand placement in his release and leads to control and command issues. He needs to trust his stuff better and get ahead in the count to avoid rough innings.

THE FUTURE: Dalquist's final start of the year at Double-A Birmingham was his best as a pro. He gave up just one hit and one unearned run while striking out six batters. He'll likely head back to that level in 2023. If it all comes together, he profiles as a back-of-the-rotation starter or a long man in the bullpen.

BA GRADE: 45/Very High	Fastball: 50	Curveball: 50	Slider: 50	Changeup: 50	Control: 40

Year	Age	Club (League)	Lvl	W	L	ERA	G	GS	IP	H	HR	BB	SO	BB/9	SO/9	WHIP	AVG
2022	21	Winston-Salem (SAL)	HiA	3	9	6.95	22	22	91	106	22	53	69	5.3	6.8	1.75	.304
2022	21	Birmingham (SL)	AA	0	2	3.38	4	4	13	11	1	11	11	7.4	7.4	1.65	.224
Minor League Totals				6	20	5.73	52	52	190	206	24	122	161	5.8	7.6	1.73	.281

30 ADAM HACKENBERG, C

Born: Sept. 8, 1999. **B-T:** R-R **HT:** 6-1. **WT:** 222.
Drafted: Clemson, 2021 (18th round). **Signed by:** Kevin Burrell.

TRACK RECORD: The Hackenberg family boasts a trifecta of pro athletes: Christian, who was a college football star drafted by the New York Jets; Brandon, who was a first-round pick in the Major League Soccer draft; and Adam, who played three years at Clemson before joining the White Sox organization as an 18th-round pick in 2021. His second pro year was spent primarily at High-A Winston-Salem, with late season action at Double-A Birmingham followed by an assignment to the Arizona Fall League.

SCOUTING REPORT: Hackenberg is a defense-first catcher. He needs to improve his approach to get more of a line drive stroke to go with his plus raw power. It's a slow bat and a stiffer swing with effort, which often causes him to mishit balls. He's consistently graded as the best defensive catcher in the system, and moves easily behind the plate. He's an aggressive framer with solid leadership skills who is an above-average defensive catcher now, and could become a plus defender in the future. Hackenberg has a plus arm and regularly records sub-2.00 pop times. He threw out 32% of runners at both levels in 2022.

THE FUTURE: He'll return to Double-A Birmingham in 2023. Hackenberg will continue to get plenty of time behind the plate as he advances through the system and profiles as a backup catcher.

BA GRADE: 45/Very High	Hit: 35	Power: 45	Speed: 40	Fielding: 55	Arm: 60

Year	Age	Club (League)	Lvl	AVG	G	AB	R	H	2B	3B	HR	RBI	BB	SO	SB	OBP	SLG
2022	22	Winston-Salem (SAL)	HiA	.231	78	277	32	64	10	0	7	28	32	70	1	.328	.343
2022	22	Birmingham (SL)	AA	.167	13	42	3	7	1	0	1	2	3	14	0	.239	.262
Minor League Totals				.246	118	419	46	103	18	1	9	43	43	100	1	.332	.358

Cincinnati Reds

BY JJ COOPER

Lost among a season that seemed almost designed to push Reds fans to renounce their allegiance, Cincinnati made steps toward potentially becoming competitive once again.

In the major leagues, it's easy to declare 2022 a season Reds fans would wisely wipe from memory. In April, on the heels of the owners' lengthy lockout of the players, team president Phil Castellini seemed to shrug his shoulders at complaints about the team's dwindling competitiveness by saying, "Where else are you going to go . . . be careful what you wish for."

The team went into the 2022 offseason largely giving away big league talent in an attempt to lower payroll.

Nick Castellanos departed in free agency. Catcher Tucker Barnhart and lefthander Wade Miley were given away in moves that brought back little other than payroll relief. Getting rid of Barnhart, a solid receiver, cost the Reds dearly when Tyler Stephenson was sidelined by a thumb injury. Without Stephenson or Barnhart, the Reds kept rolling out a rotating cast of catchers who should not have been on an MLB roster. The futility of the Reds' seven other MLB catchers was spelled out by the fact that they were all jettisoned when the season ended. As of December, only Stephenson was left on the 40-man roster.

The Reds also traded away Sonny Gray, Jesse Winker and Eugenio Suarez, which further cut the team's payroll. But at least in those trades, the Reds brought back solid prospects. Cincinnati's in-season trades saw righthanders Luis Castillo and Tyler Mahle and third baseman Brandon Drury dealt for more prospects.

The moves left the Reds with an inept lineup. Despite playing in hitter-friendly Great American Ballpark, Cincinnati finished 11th in the National League in runs scored. Other than Drury, who was traded, no Reds position player with 300 plate appearances produced even league-average offense as measured by OPS+.

The payroll dump meant Cincinnati lost 100 games for the first time since 1981. The good news for the Reds is it likely can't get any worse. Last year's trades have completely revitalized the Reds' farm system. Seven of the Reds' Top 10 Prospects are players who were acquired by trade. Cincinnati has an abundance of shortstop and middle infield prospects.

Even before the trades, Cincinnati had signs of a brighter future. The Reds saw lefthander Nick Lodolo and righthander Hunter Greene establish themselves as rotation fixtures as rookies. Having two young starters who should be there for years to

Nick Lodolo (pictured) and Hunter Greene give the Reds a foundation of a future rotation.

PROJECTED 2026 LINEUP

Catcher	Tyler Stephenson	29
First Base	Christian Encarnacion-Strand	26
Second Base	Jonathan India	29
Third Base	Noelvi Marte	25
Shortstop	Edwin Arroyo	23
Left Field	Jay Allen	23
Center Field	Elly De La Cruz	24
Right Field	Cam Collier	21
Designated Hitter	Sal Stewart	22
No. 1 Starter	Nick Lodolo	28
No. 2 Starter	Hunter Greene	26
No. 3 Starter	Chase Petty	23
No. 4 Starter	Brandon Williamson	28
No. 5 Starter	Graham Ashcraft	28
Closer	Connor Phillips	25

come is an excellent foundation. Graham Ashcraft had his moments as well. Alexis Diaz established himself as a reliable late-inning reliever.

And Elly De La Cruz gives the Reds a potential franchise cornerstone. The fast-moving shortstop has to lower his strikeout rate, but that's the only glaring concern for a player with speed, power, a strong arm, a quality glove and a history of hitting for average.

The Reds should start to get better in 2023, but the path to winning a playoff series still seems a long way in the future. For a team that hasn't won a playoff series since 1995, that's discouraging, even if Reds fans have no choice but to hope for improvements. ∎

DEPTH CHART

CINCINNATI REDS

TOP 2023 MLB CONTRIBUTORS — **RANK**

Player	Rank
Elly De La Cruz, SS	1
Brandon Williamson, LHP	10

BREAKOUT PROSPECTS — **RANK**

Player	Rank
Carlos Jorge, 2B	16
Hector Rodriguez, OF	24
Cade Hunter, C	26

SOURCE OF TOP 30 TALENT

Homegrown	19	Acquired	11
College	6	Trade	11
Junior college	2	Rule 5 draft	0
High school	5	Independent league	0
Nondrafted free agent	0	Free agent/waivers	0
International	6		

LF
- Hector Rodriguez (24)
- Justin Boyd (25)
- Allan Cerda
- Jack Rogers
- TJ Hopkins

CF
- Jay Allen (14)
- Michael Siani (18)
- Jacob Hurtubise
- JT Thompson

RF
- Ariel Almonte (21)
- Yerlin Confidan (28)
- Rece Hinds (30)
- Austin Hendrick

3B
- Noelvi Marte (2)
- Cam Collier (4)
- Nick Quintana

SS
- Elly De La Cruz (1)
- Edwin Arroyo (3)
- Ricardo Cabrera (13)
- Victor Acosta (17)
- Leonardo Balcazar (19)
- Trey Faltine

2B
- Spencer Steer (7)
- Matt McLain (12)
- Carlos Jorge (16)
- Tyler Callihan
- Ivan Johnson
- Jose Torres

1B
- Christian Encarnacion-Strand (5)
- Sal Stewart (8)
- Ruben Ibarra
- Alex McGarry

C
- Logan Tanner (23)
- Cade Hunter (26)
- Daniel Vellojin
- Matheu Nelson
- Chuckie Robinson

LHP

LHSP
- Brandon Williamson (10)
- Andrew Abbott (11)
- Steven Hajjar
- Bryce Hubbart

LHRP
- Evan Kravetz

RHP

RHSP
- Chase Petty (6)
- Levi Stoudt (15)
- Lyon Richardson (27)
- Javi Rivera
- Christian Roa
- Carson Spiers
- Ben Brutti
- Mason Pelio

RHRP
- Connor Phillips (9)
- Joe Boyle (20)
- Ricky Karcher (22)
- Casey Legumina (29)
- Fernando Cruz
- Andrew Moore
- Jared Solomon
- Connor Overton
- Bryce Bonnin
- Jose Acuña
- Luis Mey
- Zach Maxwell
- Vin Timpanelli
- Kenya Huggins
- Hunter Parks
- Thomas Farr

1 ELLY DE LA CRUZ, SS

Born: Jan. 11, 2002. **B-T:** B-R. **HT:** 6-5. **WT:** 200.
Signed: Dominican Republic, 2018.
Signed by: Richard Jimenez.

TRACK RECORD: In 2008, the Reds signed outfielder Juan Duran as one of their top targets on the international market. Duran was 6-foot-3 when he signed, but he quickly grew to 6-foot-7 in the next year. His body struggled to handle the sudden growth spurt, and he became a hulking, strikeout-prone slugger rather than the well-rounded outfielder the Reds thought they were signing. Like Duran, De La Cruz gained four inches soon after he signed. Unlike Duran, De La Cruz transformed from a skinny, overlooked Dominican teenager into a potential star following his growth spurt. As De La Cruz grew to 6-foot-5—or taller, as some officials suggest—he's gotten stronger and faster, thanks to his growth spurt and plenty of training. He went from a $65,000 signee in 2018 to a player who needed just 11 games in the Arizona Complex League in 2021 to prove he was too advanced for the level. Sent to High-A Dayton to start the 2022 season, De La Cruz finished second in the league with 20 home runs despite being promoted to Double-A Chattanooga in mid July.

SCOUTING REPORT: De La Cruz has the best raw power in the Reds' organization. He's also one of the fastest players. And he has the strongest arm. Add it all up and he's the best athlete the Reds have had since the days of Eric Davis and Deion Sanders. De La Cruz has long levers and a big strike zone. His strikeout rate of nearly 31% in 2022 ranked in the bottom 15% of all minor league hitters with at least 300 plate appearances. He was the only batting title qualifier to strike out at least 30% of the time while also hitting .300. While De La Cruz isn't just a hacker at the plate, his strikeout rate is the major hurdle standing in the way of potential stardom. De La Cruz's lefthanded swing is smoother and more powerful than his more contact-oriented righthanded one. His intelligence, focus and determination draw nearly as many raves as his tools. He has quickly picked up English, which has helped him become a team leader despite always being one of the youngest players on pretty much every team he plays on. De La Cruz has made it clear that he wants to be the Reds' shortstop of the future and has worked hard to stay there. His length and arm strength allow him to make highlight-reel plays, and he's comfortable making plays on the move. He could

MARK MEEKS AND TODD NORRIS/CHATTANOOGA LOOKOUTS

BA GRADE	SCOUTING GRADES
70 Risk: V High	Hit: 40. Power: 70. Run: 70. Field: 55. Arm: 70.

Projected future grades on 20-80 scouting scale

BEST TOOLS

BATTING

Best Hitter for Average	Cam Collier
Best Power Hitter	Elly De La Cruz
Best Strike-Zone Discipline	Spencer Steer
Fastest Baserunner	Elly De La Cruz
Best Athlete	Elly De La Cruz

PITCHING

Best Fastball	Connor Phillips
Best Curveball	Joe Boyle
Best Slider	Connor Phillips
Best Changeup	Levi Stoudt
Best Control	Javi Rivera

FIELDING

Best Defensive Catcher	Logan Tanner
Best Defensive Infielder	Edwin Arroyo
Best Infield Arm	Elly De La Cruz
Best Defensive Outfielder	Mike Siani
Best Outfield Arm	Rece Hinds

be an above-average shortstop, but evaluators see him as a potential plus-plus defender at third base with exceptional range to his left.

THE FUTURE: De La Cruz is the highest-ceiling prospect the Reds have had in years. His combination of athleticism, power and speed gives him a chance to be a big league star, but his strikeout rate could keep him from reaching that ceiling. Up through Double-A, his chase rates and swing-and-miss issues haven't slowed him down, but he will have to improve them to be a consistent hitter in the major leagues. He'll head to Triple-A Louisville to start the 2023 season. De La Cruz is typically a slow starter when it's cold, but by June or July he could be pushing for a callup to Cincinnati.

Year	Age	Club (League)	Lvl	AVG	G	AB	R	H	2B	3B	HR	RBI	BB	SO	SB	OBP	SLG
2022	20	Dayton (MWL)	HiA	.302	73	281	53	85	14	6	20	52	24	94	28	.359	.609
2022	20	Chattanooga (SL)	AA	.305	47	190	34	58	17	3	8	34	16	64	19	.357	.553
Minor League Totals				.298	224	883	146	263	60	19	37	154	68	283	60	.351	.535

2 NOELVI MARTE, SS

Born: Oct. 16, 2001. **B-T:** R-R. **HT:** 6-1. **WT:** 181.
Signed: Dominican Republic, 2018. **Signed by:** Eddy Toledo/Tim Kissner (Mariners).

BA GRADE
55 Risk: High

TRACK RECORD: Marte was considered one of the best prospects in the 2018 international class and signed with the Mariners for $1.55 million. He made a strong debut in the 2019 Dominican Summer League, but the pandemic in 2020 meant that his first U.S. action came at the alternate training site against mostly big leaguers. It was a tough transition, but it helped him when he went to Low-A in 2021. He struggled in the first half of the 2022 season and came into July hitting under .240. After being traded to the Reds in the Luis Castillo deal, Marte put together a strong second half. He went to the Arizona Fall League to work on playing third base.

SCOUTING REPORT: When Marte signed, he had a narrow base and a big leg kick. Now he hits from a much simpler, wider stance with a compact swing and toned-down mechanics. Marte combines big power potential with excellent bat-to-ball skills. When he's locked in, he's powerful enough to drive the ball up the middle for damage. He doesn't always make the best swing decisions, and pitchers in 2022 found they could frustrate him with a breaking ball-heavy approach. He also rolls over too many down-and-away breaking balls. Marte rarely misses hittable pitches in the strike zone. His top-end exit velocities are near the top of the scale, but he doesn't barrel the ball often enough. Defensively, Marte's move to third base in the Arizona Fall League likely foreshadows his future home. He has a thickening lower half and chest, and his short-range quickness is below-average. He has an average arm but needs to improve his throwing accuracy. Marte is an above-average runner now but projects to slow down.

THE FUTURE: Marte's combination of power and contact ability gives him a high ceiling, but he's going to have to stay on top of his conditioning to reach his potential. He's ready for Double-A Chattanooga.

SCOUTING GRADES	Hitting: 45	Power: 65	Speed: 50	Fielding: 45	Arm: 50

Year	Age	Club (League)	Lvl	AVG	G	AB	R	H	2B	3B	HR	RBI	BB	SO	SB	OBP	SLG
2022	20	Dayton (MWL)	HiA	.292	30	106	12	31	4	0	4	13	17	23	10	.397	.443
2022	20	Everett (NWL)	HiA	.275	85	342	62	94	19	0	15	55	42	84	13	.363	.462
Minor League Totals				.283	287	1154	221	327	69	6	45	193	148	279	64	.369	.471

3 EDWIN ARROYO, SS

Born: Aug. 25, 2003. **B-T:** B-R. **HT:** 6-0. **WT:** 175.
Drafted: HS—Arecibo, P.R., 2021 (2nd round). **Signed by:** Rob Mummau (Mariners).

BA GRADE
55 Risk: High

TRACK RECORD: Arroyo was considered one of the smoothest-fielding shortstops in a loaded 2021 high school shortstop class. Concerns about how much he would hit dropped him to the Mariners in the second round as the 11th prep shortstop picked. In 2022, Arroyo exceeded expectations at the plate while continuing to impress defensively. He showed surprising pop with Low-A Modesto and finished third in the California League in batting average (.316) and slugging percentage (.514). He struggled at Low-A Daytona after being traded to the Reds with Noelvi Marte for Luis Castillo.

SCOUTING REPORT: In an organization filled with shortstop prospects, Arroyo has the best glove. He has an excellent internal clock, soft hands and above-average range. He slows the game down, has a plus arm and makes accurate throws. He should stick at the position. Offensively, Arroyo cut his strikeout rate significantly in 2022 by making better swing decisions. The switch-hitter was remarkably consistent with his pair of swings. He had an .853 OPS hitting righthanded and an .854 OPS hitting lefthanded, and scouts think his lefty swing is a little more fluid. His emerging power was a surprise in 2022, but he profiles more as an above-average hitter with fringe-average power than as a slugger.

THE FUTURE: Arroyo was one of the youngest players in the 2021 draft class, and part of his improvement can be attributed to physical maturation. He's also shown a steadily improving approach and an advanced understanding of the game. He's ready for High-A Dayton to start 2023.

SCOUTING GRADES	Hitting: 55	Power: 45	Speed: 55	Fielding: 65	Arm: 60

Year	Age	Club (League)	Lvl	AVG	G	AB	R	H	2B	3B	HR	RBI	BB	SO	SB	OBP	SLG
2022	18	Reds (ACL)	R	.000	2	6	1	0	0	0	0	1	2	2	2	.222	.000
2022	18	Modesto (CAL)	LoA	.316	87	364	76	115	19	7	13	67	35	90	21	.385	.514
2022	18	Daytona (FSL)	LoA	.227	27	97	16	22	6	3	1	16	9	31	4	.303	.381
Minor League Totals				.283	137	538	109	152	27	10	16	94	56	149	31	.362	.459

4 CAM COLLIER, 3B

Born: Nov. 20, 2004. **B-T:** L-R. **HT:** 6-2. **WT:** 210.
Drafted: Chipola (Fla.) JC, 2022 (1st round). **Signed by:** Sean Buckley.

BA GRADE

60 Risk: Extreme

TRACK RECORD: Collier was set to be one of the best high school hitters in the 2023 draft class, but he sped up his timetable dramatically by passing the GED after his sophomore year at Mount Paran Christian School in Kennesaw, Ga. He jumped to junior college in 2022 during what would have been his junior year of high school. He hit .333/.419/.537 for juco power Chipola in Florida, then spent a couple of weeks in the Cape Cod League before the draft. Collier fell to the Reds at pick No. 18, but his $5 million bonus was 10th-largest in the draft class. He is the son of former big league shortstop Lou Collier.
SCOUTING REPORT: Collier has always been an advanced hitter, which explains how he handled the big jump to facing junior college pitchers as a 17-year-old. He has a smooth swing with plenty of adjustability thanks to excellent hands. He uses the whole field, with a hit-over-power approach, but he has above-average power potential as well. He knows how to work counts and draw walks. Collier showed improvement in his footwork and reactions at third base, but there remains some skepticism about whether he will have the range to remain there based on how his body is expected to fill out. He has an easy 65 arm on the 20-to-80 scouting scale, which fits at third.
THE FUTURE: Scouts who like Collier the most see a middle-of-the-order bat with enough athleticism to stick at third. More skeptical evaluators see a teenager who is already getting big. They fear he'll have to slide to first base eventually and don't know if his bat will be enough to handle the slide down the defensive spectrum. His 65-grade arm could also be an asset in right field.

SCOUTING GRADES	Hitting: 60	Power: 55	Speed: 40	Fielding: 50	Arm: 65

Year	Age	Club (League)	Lvl	AVG	G	AB	R	H	2B	3B	HR	RBI	BB	SO	SB	OBP	SLG
2022	17	Reds (ACL)	R	.370	9	27	7	10	1	0	2	4	7	6	0	.514	.630
Minor League Totals				.370	9	27	7	10	1	0	2	4	7	6	0	.514	.630

5 CHRISTIAN ENCARNACION-STRAND, 3B/1B

Born: Dec. 1, 1999. **B-T:** R-R. **HT:** 6-0. **WT:** 224.
Drafted: Oklahoma State, 2021 (4th round). **Signed by:** JR DiMercurio (Twins).

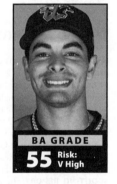

BA GRADE

55 Risk: V High

TRACK RECORD: Encarnacion-Strand was one of the hottest hitters in the minors in April, batting .410/.459/.679, but he slumped in May. He then returned to being one of the best bats in the minors in June and July, made the jump to Double-A and was traded to the Reds with Spencer Steer for righthander Tyler Mahle. Encarnacion-Strand finished second in the minors in RBIs (114) and top 10 in home runs (32), slugging (.587), extra-base hits (68) and total bases (284).
SCOUTING REPORT: Wherever Encarnacion-Strand has ever played, he's hit. Dating back to 2019, he has hit over .300 and slugged over .500 at every stop, including two seasons at Yavapai (Ariz.) JC, a season at Oklahoma State and his first two years of pro ball. He manages to do so despite an extremely aggressive approach that leads to plenty of swings and misses out of the zone. He's a streaky hitter, but if he's on time, he has the bat control to do damage. He also has plus-plus raw power that projects to be at least plus productive power, and he can drive the ball to the opposite field. Encarnacion-Strand's plus-plus arm gives him more time than the average third baseman to make plays on balls to his backhand or ones he knocks down. He has a quick first step despite below-average speed. The game often gets too fast for him at third, and he too often then rushes plays and commits errors.
THE FUTURE: Encarnacion-Strand's range of outcomes spans from that of an all-star third baseman to a first baseman with contact issues. With the Reds' surplus of shortstops and third base prospects, he is going to have to sharpen his defense quickly to avoid a move down the defensive spectrum.

SCOUTING GRADES	Hitting: 40	Power: 70	Speed: 40	Fielding: 45	Arm: 70

Year	Age	Club (League)	Lvl	AVG	G	AB	R	H	2B	3B	HR	RBI	BB	SO	SB	OBP	SLG
2022	22	Cedar Rapids (MWL)	HiA	.296	74	294	52	87	23	3	20	68	30	85	7	.370	.599
2022	22	Wichita (TL)	AA	.333	13	54	11	18	2	1	5	17	4	14	1	.400	.685
2022	22	Chattanooga (SL)	AA	.309	35	136	13	42	6	1	7	29	6	38	0	.351	.522
Minor League Totals				.317	144	571	93	181	33	7	36	132	45	163	10	.376	.588

6 CHASE PETTY, RHP

Born: April 4, 2003. **B-T:** R-R. **HT:** 6-1. **WT:** 190.
Drafted: HS—Linwood, N.J., 2021 (1st round). **Signed by:** John Wilson (Twins).
TRACK RECORD: Petty flashed 100 mph heat in his draft year, albeit with a high-effort, funky delivery. After the Twins selected him 26th overall, they helped him tone down his effort and focus on becoming a sinker/slider pitcher. Petty's velocity dipped, but his feel and control improved significantly. Traded to the Reds for righthander Sonny Gray in March 2022, Petty showed durability, consistency and feel to pitch.
SCOUTING REPORT: For all his gaudy fastball readings in high school, Petty is more of a pitcher than a thrower. He proved to be a much more polished pitcher in 2022 than he had appeared to be in high school. Petty has focused on working down in the zone with a two-seam fastball, a hard, potentially above-average slider and a quickly improving changeup. Petty topped at 95-97 mph in 2022 and generally sat in the 92-94 range, but he filled the zone with above-average control and command. Petty was limited to 50-70 pitches per outing, but he managed to still get through four to five innings on those limited pitch counts because he worked efficiently. The Reds have worked on helping him add a four-seamer that changes hitters' eye levels, but it's not as consistent as his two-seamer. His split-changeup helps keep lefthanded hitters from getting comfortable and could be above-average.
THE FUTURE: Petty handled a jump to High-A and got better as the season progressed. He projects as a solid No. 3 or No. 4 starter with multiple ways to attack hitters and above-average control.

BA GRADE

50 Risk: High

SCOUTING GRADES:	Fastball: 60	Slider: 55	Changeup: 55	Control: 55

Year	Age	Club (League)	Lvl	W	L	ERA	G	GS	IP	H	HR	BB	SO	BB/9	SO/9	WHIP	AVG
2022	19	Daytona (FSL)	LoA	0	4	3.06	18	13	68	57	5	24	63	3.2	8.4	1.20	.233
2022	19	Dayton (MWL)	HiA	1	2	4.40	7	7	31	27	2	7	33	2.1	9.7	1.11	.231
Minor League Totals				1	6	3.57	27	21	103	90	7	32	102	2.8	8.9	1.18	.236

7 SPENCER STEER, 3B/2B

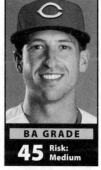

Born: Dec. 7, 1997. **B-T:** R-R. **HT:** 5-11. **WT:** 185.
Drafted: Oregon, 2019 (3rd round). **Signed by:** Kyle Blackwell (Twins).
TRACK RECORD: In his MLB debut on Sept. 2, Steer homered. In the penultimate game of the season, his walk-off RBI double staved off 100 losses until the next day. In between, there weren't many highlights in Steer's month in Cincinnati. Those moments were a fitting footnote on a season in which Steer made the Futures Game and was traded to the Reds along with Christian Encarnacion-Strand and Steven Hajjar for Tyler Mahle.
SCOUTING REPORT: Steer has long been equally praised and criticized for being a well-rounded player without any exceptional tools. Because Joey Votto was injured, Steer ended up playing nine games at first base with the Reds. For someone who has played second base, third base, shortstop and right field, it was just another position to pick up. Steer fits as a second or third baseman who can fill in at shortstop. He has excellent hands and a slow heartbeat. His average arm is just enough because of a quick release and accuracy. He's an average runner who isn't a basestealer but is a solid baserunner. Despite back-to-back seasons of 20-plus home runs, Steer is more of a solid hitter with sneaky pop, though Great American Ballpark should boost his home run numbers.
THE FUTURE: Steer will compete for the Reds' third base in 2023, but he'll likely end up playing there and everywhere as the need arises.

BA GRADE

45 Risk: Medium

SCOUTING GRADES	Hitting: 55	Power: 40	Speed: 50	Fielding: 55	Arm: 50

Year	Age	Club (League)	Lvl	AVG	G	AB	R	H	2B	3B	HR	RBI	BB	SO	SB	OBP	SLG
2022	24	Wichita (TL)	AA	.307	35	137	27	42	13	1	8	30	14	23	1	.385	.591
2022	24	Louisville (IL)	AAA	.293	23	92	14	27	7	0	3	13	9	23	1	.375	.467
2022	24	St. Paul (IL)	AAA	.242	48	198	39	48	10	1	12	32	28	43	2	.345	.485
2022	24	Cincinnati (NL)	MLB	.211	28	95	12	20	5	0	2	8	11	26	0	.306	.326
Major League Totals				.211	28	95	12	20	5	0	2	8	11	26	0	.306	.326
Minor League Totals				.268	280	1094	202	293	66	8	51	174	140	227	17	.363	.483

8 SAL STEWART, 3B

Born: Dec. 7, 2003. **B-T:** R-R. **HT:** 6-3. **WT:** 215.
Drafted: HS—Miami, 2022 (1st round). **Signed by:** Andrew Fabian.
TRACK RECORD: In recent drafts, the Reds selected Rece Hinds and Austin Hendrick. Both have massive power, but both have struck out more than 35% of the time as pros. In 2022, the Reds seemed to course-correct by going all-in on young hitters with advanced hit tools in the first round. They started with 17-year-old junior college third baseman Cam Collier at No. 18 overall, followed by Stewart, a polished high school hitter with below-average or worse defense and speed at No. 32. After signing for $2.1 million, Stewart showed his polished bat in an eight-game debut in the Arizona Complex League.
SCOUTING REPORT: Stewart hits both velocity and spin. Perhaps as importantly, he spits on pitches outside the zone while punishing hittable pitches in the zone. Amateur scouts loved his ability to consistently make loud contact. Stewart should hit for plus power and should be an above-average hitter as well. If he develops as expected, he could be a power hitter who avoids piling up strikeouts. Defensively, there are a lot more questions. Stewart made two throwing errors in just six games at third with the ACL Reds, but his range is the bigger long-term concern. He's a well-below average runner who will have to work to avoid slowing down even further. He has an above-average arm.
THE FUTURE: Stewart and Collier should both be ready for Low-A Daytona in 2023, which means they'll likely split time at third base. Collier is the better defender, so Stewart could end up getting experience at first base as well.

BA GRADE
55 Risk: Extreme

SCOUTING GRADES	Hitting: 55	Power: 60	Speed: 30	Fielding: 40	Arm: 55

Year	Age	Club (Leag	Lvl	AVG	G	AB	R	H	2B	3B	HR	RBI	BB	SO	SB	OBP	SLG
2022	18	Reds (ACL)	R	.292	8	24	5	7	4	0	0	5	4	5	0	.393	.458
Minor League Totals				.292	8	24	5	7	4	0	0	5	4	5	0	.393	.458

9 CONNOR PHILLIPS, RHP

Born: May 4, 2001. **B-T:** R-R. **HT:** 6-2. **WT:** 190.
Drafted: McLennan (Texas) JC, 2020 (2nd round supp). **Signed by:** Derek Miller (SEA).
TRACK RECORD: The Mariners organization has a "gas camp" each offseason to help its pitchers add velocity. Phillips didn't need to go camping. He arrived as a 2020 second-round pick already gassed up and ready to go. He featured a big fastball at McLennan (Texas) JC, but his heater has gotten more and more ferocious as a pro. He topped out at 99 mph as a starter in 2022, and could eventually reach triple-digits. He misses bats, too, and already has a pair of 13-strikeout starts on his pro résumé. The Reds picked up Phillips along with Brandon Williamson in the March 2022 deal in which they sent Eugenio Suarez and Jesse Winker to Seattle.
SCOUTING REPORT: Phillips' combination of top-end velocity, carry at the top of the zone and a flat plane on his fastball helps him generate a well above-average number of swings and misses with his heater. He will sit 95-97 mph pitch after pitch, with a little more available when necessary. His mid-80s slider gives him a second plus pitch, and it has plenty of sweep and some tilt. He can start it in the zone and leave hitters flailing at it after it ends up well out of the zone. He also throws a big-breaking, high-70s curveball that can lock up hitters who are geared up for his fastball. It has helped him survive against lefthanded hitters with only a below-average changeup. Phillips walks too many batters, but it's more of an approach and sequencing issue than an utter inability to throw strikes. He repeats his delivery relatively well and should eventually get to at least fringe-average control.
THE FUTURE: The easy projection is to look at Phillips' power stuff and walk rate and suggest a move to the bullpen, but the Reds have no reason to be so hasty. He has made strides as a starter and should be in the Double-A Chattanooga rotation for much of 2023.

BA GRADE
50 Risk: High

SCOUTING GRADES:	Fastball: 70	Curveball: 55	Slider: 60	Changeup: 40	Control: 45

Year	Age	Club (League)	Lvl	W	L	ERA	G	GS	IP	H	HR	BB	SO	BB/9	SO/9	WHIP	AVG
2022	21	Dayton (MWL)	HiA	4	3	2.95	12	12	64	39	5	32	90	4.5	12.7	1.11	.181
2022	21	Chattanooga (SL)	AA	1	5	4.93	12	12	46	48	3	34	60	6.7	11.8	1.80	.268
Minor League Totals				12	12	4.12	41	41	186	151	10	112	261	5.4	12.7	1.42	.222

10 BRANDON WILLIAMSON, LHP

Born: April 2, 1998. **B-T:** R-L. **HT:** 6-6. **WT:** 210.
Drafted: Texas Christian, 2019 (2nd round). **Signed by:** Jordan Bley (Mariners).

BA GRADE
50 Risk: High

TRACK RECORD: After two years at Northern Iowa JC, Williamson transferred to Texas Christian, where he joined Nick Lodolo in the Horned Frogs' weekend rotation. The Reds picked Lodolo as the first lefthander off the board in the 2019 draft, and the Mariners selected Williamson in the second round. After Williamson's standout 2021 season at Double-A Arkansas, the Reds reunited him with Lodolo by acquiring him in a trade that sent Jesse Winker and Eugenio Suarez to Seattle.
SCOUTING REPORT: Williamson's stuff and control all took a step backward in 2022. He nibbled more than he needed and saw his overall strike percentage drop from 64% in 2021 to 61% in 2022. After he was promoted to Triple-A, Williamson's strike percentage dipped to 59%. Behind in counts, his above-average curveball and fringe-average changeup didn't fool hitters as often. His above-average, big-breaking mid-70s curveball has been a weapon, but he didn't land it enough for it to be effective in his first year with the Reds. Similarly, his 82-84 mph changeup is better when he's ahead in counts. His average 82-85 mph slider showed improvement. It has gone from a barely-used pitch to one he showed the most feel for on many nights. Williamson's 90-93 mph fastball lost a tick in 2022, but it's effective even at a slightly reduced velocity thanks to its carry and precision.
THE FUTURE: Williamson looked more like a back-of-the-rotation arm in 2022 because of reduced stuff and more scattered control, but he's shown midrotation potential in the past. He was added to the Reds' 40-man roster in November. With a strong start at Triple-A Louisville, he could push for a spot in Cincinnati by midseason.

SCOUTING GRADES:	Fastball: 55	Curveball: 55	Slider: 50	Changeup: 45	Control: 45

Year	Age	Club (League)	Lvl	W	L	ERA	G	GS	IP	H	HR	BB	SO	BB/9	SO/9	WHIP	AVG
2022	24	Chattanooga (SL)	AA	5	2	4.14	14	14	67	61	5	40	74	5.3	9.9	1.50	.242
2022	24	Louisville (IL)	AAA	1	5	4.07	13	13	55	53	4	37	49	6.0	8.0	1.63	.251
Minor League Totals				10	13	3.69	56	55	236	206	20	115	301	4.4	11.5	1.36	.234

11 ANDREW ABBOTT, LHP

Born: June 1, 1999. **B-T:** L-L. **HT:** 6-0. **WT:** 190.
Drafted: Virginia, 2021 (2nd round). **Signed by:** Jeff Brookens.

TRACK RECORD: The Reds' plan with Abbott was to let him settle in and pitch at High-A Dayton for quite a while. Abbott blew up that plan by allowing just two runs in five starts while striking out 40 in 27 innings. He was promoted to Double-A Chattanooga in mid May and struck out 12 in five innings in his debut, but that level ended up proving to be a tougher test. He struggled until September, when he rattled off three straight scoreless starts to end the season.
SCOUTING REPORT: Abbott's fastball was good enough to dominate in Class A because of how well he located it, but once Double-A hitters saw Abbott a few times, they realized he didn't have confidence in his changeup and he would rarely come inside with his fastball. Abbott has an average 91-94 mph fastball and low-80s slider, and the slider is more effective now that he's made it a little sweepier. He will need to improve the feel for his below-average mid-80s changeup to give righthanded batters an additional look. Abbott is a consistent strike-thrower with plus control.
THE FUTURE: Abbott finished the season strong. He will likely return to Chattanooga to prove he's conquered the level. If he does, Triple-A Louisville should be calling before long. He's a back-of-the-rotation starter with a smart, cerebral and even-keeled approach.

BA GRADE: 45/Medium	Fastball: 50	Slider: 55	Changeup: 40	Control: 60

Year	Age	Club (League)	Lvl	W	L	ERA	G	GS	IP	H	HR	BB	SO	BB/9	SO/9	WHIP	AVG
2022	23	Dayton (MWL)	HiA	3	0	0.67	5	4	27	16	1	7	40	2.3	13.3	0.85	.168
2022	23	Chattanooga (SL)	AA	7	7	4.75	20	20	91	84	7	41	119	4.1	11.8	1.37	.248
Minor League Totals				10	7	3.85	31	29	131	112	10	52	181	3.6	12.4	1.25	.231

12 MATT McLAIN, 2B/SS

Born: Oct. 6, 1999. **B-T:** R-R. **HT:** 5-10. **WT:** 175.
Drafted: UCLA, 2021 (1st round). **Signed by:** Jimmy Moran.

TRACK RECORD: McLain was a two-time first-round pick. He turned down the D-backs as the 25th overall pick out of high school in 2018. After a productive career at UCLA he moved up to be picked 17th overall in 2021. After an excellent 2021 debut, the longer full pro season seemed to wear McLain down in 2022. He hit .248/.362/.544 in the first two months of the season, but only .221/.364/.392 from June 1 until the end of the season.

SCOUTING REPORT: McLain was Double-A Chattanooga's everyday shortstop in the first half of the season, but he played as much second base as shortstop once Elly De La Cruz arrived. That is likely a hint of his future role. He's fully capable of playing shortstop, with the feet and hands for the position. If he's asked to make those throws regularly, his average arm begins to wear down to fringe-average. He doesn't have the kind of arm strength to make difficult plays without setting his feet. Scouts loved McLain's competitiveness and all-out style of play, but that high-energy style also makes it harder for him to hold up, as he's a smaller-framed player without a lot of functional strength. He makes excellent swing decisions and has 10-15 home run power.

THE FUTURE: Even when he struggled at Chattanooga, McLain still strung together solid at-bats, drew walks and could punish pitchers who made mistakes. The offseason should give McLain a chance to work on gaining strength to help him hold up over the much longer pro season. He projects as a super-utility player who can play a variety of positions, including shortstop in a pinch.

BA GRADE: 45/Medium **Hitting:** 50 **Power:** 40 **Speed:** 55 **Fielding:** 50 **Arm:** 50

Year	Age	Club (League)	Lvl	AVG	G	AB	R	H	2B	3B	HR	RBI	BB	SO	SB	OBP	SLG
2022	22	Chattanooga (SL)	AA	.232	103	371	67	86	21	5	17	58	70	127	27	.363	.453
Minor League Totals				.243	134	477	84	116	29	6	20	77	87	151	37	.369	.455

13 RICARDO CABRERA, SS

Born: Oct. 31, 2004. **B-T:** R-R. **HT:** 5-11. **WT:** 178.
Signed: Venezuela, 2022. **Signed by:** Reds international scouting department.

TRACK RECORD: Back before the pandemic virtually shut down international scouting for a time, Cabrera was already gaining notice as a youngster who didn't look out of place in games and workouts against players one and two years older than him. That made Cabrera's initial pro struggles so surprising. In his first month in the Dominican Summer League, Cabrera didn't hit at all (.120/.274/.200) and he committed 13 errors in 16 games. But in the final two months he hit .320/.410/.420 with 10 errors in 28 games.

SCOUTING REPORT: Cabrera didn't show as much selectivity and contact skills as he had demonstrated on the amateur circuit. He was one of the younger players in the league and his short, direct swing should serve him well as he matures. He projects to have five average or better tools with a chance to stay at shortstop, depending on how he grows and fills out as he heads into his 20s. Cabrera's power is well below-average right now, but projects to get to average. He should be an above-average hitter with an all-fields approach. He has plus speed, a plus arm and the hands and feet to be an average defender at shortstop.

THE FUTURE: Cabrera is the most talented player the Reds have signed out of Venezuela in several years. As he comes to the U.S. he sits at the back of a log jam of shortstop prospects, but that shouldn't affect him in 2023, as the Reds' other shortstop prospects should all be in full-season ball.

BA GRADE: 55/Extreme **Hitting:** 55 **Power:** 50 **Speed:** 60 **Fielding:** 50 **Arm:** 60

Year	Age	Club (Leag	Lvl	AVG	G	AB	R	H	2B	3B	HR	RBI	BB	SO	SB	OBP	SLG
2022	17	Reds (DSL)	R	.253	45	150	30	38	6	5	1	19	13	40	5	.363	.380
Minor League Totals				.253	45	150	30	38	6	5	1	19	13	40	5	.363	.380

14 JAY ALLEN, OF

Born: Nov. 22, 2002. **B-T:** R-R. **HT:** 6-0. **WT:** 205.
Drafted: HS—Fort Pierce, Fla., 2021 (1st round). **Signed by:** Manuel Fabian.

TRACK RECORD: A three-sport star in high school who had scholarship offers as a quarterback, Allen was the Reds' second first-round pick in 2021. He had an excellent debut in the Arizona Complex League. His performance took a step back in 2022, but he still impressed with his high-intensity style of play.

SCOUTING REPORT: Everything hasn't clicked yet for Allen, but scouts see a path to a productive big leaguer. He's a plus center fielder with 65 speed on the 20-to-80 scouting scale. He can be a truly merciless basestealer when he finds a pitcher-catcher combination that can't control the running game. In one of his best games of the season, Allen had four hits and stole second all four times. He added a steal of third to finish the game with five stolen bases. Allen's swing is geared for line drives, not home runs. He has solid bat control, but his inability to lay off pitches out of the zone is hamstringing his ability to hit for average. He's a plus defender in center with an average arm.

THE FUTURE: Allen is going to have to make strides in his pitch recognition and selectivity, but he has the tools to be a well-rounded outfielder who can help a team in multiple ways.

| BA GRADE: 50/High | | Hitting: 45 | | Power: 40 | | Speed: 65 | | Fielding: 60 | | Arm: 50 | |

Year	Age	Club (League)	Lvl	AVG	G	AB	R	H	2B	3B	HR	RBI	BB	SO	SB	OBP	SLG
2022	19	Daytona (FSL)	LoA	.224	73	241	48	54	13	2	3	21	40	73	31	.359	.332
2022	19	Dayton (MWL)	HiA	.230	18	74	13	17	1	2	0	8	4	19	12	.301	.297
Minor League Totals				.242	110	376	81	91	17	5	6	40	52	104	57	.362	.362

15 LEVI STOUDT, RHP

Born: Dec. 4, 1997. **B-T:** R-R. **HT:** 6-1. **WT:** 195.
Drafted: Lehigh, 2019 (3rd round). **Signed by:** Patrick O'Grady (Mariners).

TRACK RECORD: Stoudt was a durable and effective starter at Lehigh, but wear and tear meant his right ulnar collateral ligament was torn when the Mariners picked him in the third round in 2019. He opted for Tommy John surgery and had to wait until 2021 to make his pro debut. A revelation in 2021, he struggled more in 2022. He improved after the Reds acquired him in the Luis Castillo trade and finished the season on a roll after a jump to Triple-A Louisville.

SCOUTING REPORT: Stoudt has plus control, a mid-90s above-average fastball that can touch 98 mph and a low-80s plus split-changeup that has been a diabolical weapon at its best. His changeup wasn't as consistent in 2022, but his now-average mid-80s slider has improved. He also flips over a mid-70s curveball. Neither the curve nor the changeup is an effective in-zone offering, but Stoudt controls his fastball well enough to get ahead in counts.

THE FUTURE: The Reds added Stoudt to their 40-man roster. He has a year or two more to help the Reds figure out if he's going to be a power reliever or back-of-the-rotation starter. He needs to gain consistency if he's going to avoid a future move to the pen, but his varied pitch mix and control seem to point to him being able to handle the challenge.

| BA GRADE: 50/High | | Fastball: 55 | | Curveball: 40 | | Slider: 50 | | Changeup: 60 | | Control: 60 | |

Year	Age	Club (League)	Lvl	W	L	ERA	G	GS	IP	H	HR	BB	SO	BB/9	SO/9	WHIP	AVG
2022	24	Arkansas (TL)	AA	6	6	5.28	18	18	87	92	13	22	82	2.3	8.5	1.31	.269
2022	24	Chattanooga (SL)	AA	1	0	0.00	1	1	5	2	0	0	6	0.0	10.8	0.40	.125
2022	24	Louisville (IL)	AAA	0	2	3.32	6	6	19	17	0	10	15	4.7	7.1	1.42	.243
Minor League Totals				14	11	4.11	40	40	193	172	21	69	189	3.2	8.8	1.25	.238

16 CARLOS JORGE, 2B

Born: Sept. 22, 2003. **B-T:** L-R. **HT:** 5-10. **WT:** 160.
Signed: Dominican Republic, 2021. **Signed by:** Edgard Melo/Enmanuel Cartagena/Richard Jimenez.

TRACK RECORD: It's easy to underestimate Jorge. He's somewhat undersized, and he doesn't have the twitchiness to be a big league shortstop. Despite that, Jorge has been among the best players at every stop in his career. He's posted a better than .400 on-base percentage and .500 slugging percentage twice.

SCOUTING REPORT: Jorge has a short and direct lefthanded stroke and the bat speed to give him excellent plate coverage. He has a tendency to roll over with his top hand on pitches inside, which limits his ability to drive those pitches. Even then, he still makes contact. If the pitch is in the middle or outer third of the strike zone, he punishes it. He combines contact ability with an advanced knowledge of the strike zone. Defensively, he's not going to beat out the Reds' bevy of shortstop prospects, but he's fine as an average defender at second with a fringe-average arm. He has a quick first step and is an excellent basestealer.

THE FUTURE: Jorge has a shot to be an offensive-oriented second baseman who hits for average, posts high on-base percentages and does damage when a pitcher makes mistakes. It's a nice, well-rounded package that should get a bigger test at Low-A Daytona.

| BA GRADE: 45/High | | Hitting: 60 | | Power: 40 | | Speed: 55 | | Fielding: 50 | | Arm: 45 | |

Year	Age	Club (League)	Lvl	AVG	G	AB	R	H	2B	3B	HR	RBI	BB	SO	SB	OBP	SLG
2022	18	Reds (ACL)	R	.261	42	119	32	31	7	2	7	21	25	41	27	.405	.529
Minor League Totals				.309	89	278	70	86	15	12	10	54	49	73	54	.422	.558

17 VICTOR ACOSTA, SS

Born: June 10, 2004. **B-T:** B-R. **HT:** 5-11. **WT:** 170.
Signed: Dominican Republic, 2021. **Signed by:** Alvin Duran/Trevor Schumm/Chris Kemp (Padres).

TRACK RECORD: As they traded away plenty of prospects in trades to build up the big league roster, the Padres signed Acosta for $1.8 million in 2021 to help restock the system. A year later, he was part of the next wave of prospects San Diego dealt, and he was sent to Cincinnati in the trade that brought Brandon Drury to the Padres. Acosta got into a few games with the Reds' Arizona Complex League squad before the season shut down.

SCOUTING REPORT: Acosta's first season in the U.S. wasn't as dominating as his exceptional Dominican Summer League debut in 2021, but his impressive extended spring bled into a solid season in the Arizona Complex League. Acosta's compact frame limits his projection, but he already has plenty of tools with plus speed, a plus arm and a potentially above-average bat. His lefthanded swing is a little ahead of his righthanded swing. He has the bat speed to hit for both average and power. Defensively, he has the feet and hands to stick at shortstop, but he could also be a plus defender at second base.

THE FUTURE: Acosta is yet another in the Reds' overflowing bevy of young shortstop prospects. Whether he sticks at shortstop is partly dependent on his development, but it also will be affected by the Reds' limited number of innings at shortstop available in Class A.

BA GRADE: 50/Extreme		Hitting: 55		Power: 45		Speed: 60		Fielding: 50		Arm: 60				
Year	Age	Club (League	Lvl	AVG	G	AB	R	H	2B	3B	HR	RBI	BB	SO	SB	OBP	SLG
2022	18	Padres (ACL)	R	.243	32	111	17	27	3	2	2	11	16	30	5	.346	.360
2022	18	Reds (ACL)	R	.214	10	28	5	6	4	0	0	1	5	7	0	.353	.357
Minor League Totals				.265	98	325	67	86	19	7	7	43	59	82	31	.397	.431

18 MICHAEL SIANI, OF

Born: July 16, 1999. **B-T:** L-L. **HT:** 6-1. **WT:** 188.
Drafted: HS—Philadelphia, 2018 (4th round). **Signed by:** Jeff Brookens.

TRACK RECORD: After a lost 2021 season that saw him miss time in the outfield because of an elbow injury and look lost at times at the plate, Siani had a much better 2022. He raised his batting average and on-base percentage and hit for more power as well. He hit a career-high 14 home runs, stole an organization-best 52 bases and made his MLB debut.

SCOUTING REPORT: Siani took a step forward in 2022 because he tried to do less. He toned down his swing, aiming less to lift the ball for home runs and focusing more on making contact. That helped him dramatically reduce his strikeout rate, but he found the gaps more as well, helping make his below-average power get into play more regularly. That's important because Siani is a truly exceptional defender in center. He's a plus-plus center fielder who flags down balls in the gap and is fearless going back to the wall. He also has a plus arm.

THE FUTURE: Siani's improved approach helped put him back into the Reds' long-term plans. He may not have the bat to be a regular, but his defense and speed make him a viable No. 4 outfielder.

BA GRADE: 45/Medium		Hitting: 45		Power: 30		Speed: 60		Fielding: 70		Arm: 60				
Year	Age	Club (League)	Lvl	AVG	G	AB	R	H	2B	3B	HR	RBI	BB	SO	SB	OBP	SLG
2022	22	Chattanooga (SL)	AA	.252	121	456	76	115	19	7	12	49	64	90	49	.351	.404
2022	22	Louisville (IL)	AAA	.250	8	36	6	9	0	0	2	6	1	5	3	.263	.417
2022	22	Cincinnati (NL)	MLB	.167	9	24	1	4	0	0	0	0	0	7	0	.167	.167
Major League Totals				.167	9	24	1	4	0	0	0	0	0	7	0	.167	.167
Minor League Totals				.248	393	1494	241	371	48	20	28	133	177	342	133	.336	.363

19 LEONARDO BALCAZAR, SS

Born: June 17, 2004. **B-T:** R-R. **HT:** 5-10. **WT:** 167.
Signed: Venezuela, 2021. **Signed by:** Aguido Gonzalez/Ricardo Quintero/Richard Castro.

TRACK RECORD: The Reds have gone from signing high-ceiling international amateurs with modest baseball skills but massive baseball tools to signing players with more skill overall. The new approach is best exemplified by players like Balcazar. He's not physically imposing, but he was one of the better players in the Dominican Summer League in 2021 and the Arizona Complex League in 2022. He finished in the top 10 in the ACL in batting average (.322), on-base percentage (.411) and stolen bases (13).

SCOUTING REPORT: Balcazar is more pesky than intimidating but he puts together quality at-bat after quality at-bat. He has enough power to yank an inside fastball over the wall, but he's most comfortable

covering most of the plate with a contact-oriented approach. He needs to continue to improve his pitch recognition, but he's showing steady development there. Defensively, he's an above-average shortstop as far as range and hands, but the accuracy of his plus arm needs work. He committed eight throwing errors in 31 games at shortstop. He's an average runner, but an opportunistic one who swiped 13 bags in 14 tries.
THE FUTURE: Balcazar may end up as an excellent utility infielder with contact skills, modest power and defensive versatility, but for now he should get plenty of opportunity to show he can be a regular. So far, he's earning plenty of playing time.

BA GRADE: 45/High	Hitting: 60	Power: 30	Speed: 50	Fielding: 55	Arm: 60

Year	Age	Club (Leag	Lvl	AVG	G	AB	R	H	2B	3B	HR	RBI	BB	SO	SB	OBP	SLG
2022	18	Reds (ACL)	R	.322	42	143	25	46	6	2	4	26	18	42	13	.411	.476
Minor League Totals				.294	71	255	51	75	11	6	10	41	31	71	21	.383	.502

20 JOE BOYLE, RHP

Born: Aug. 14, 1999. **B-T:** R-R. **HT:** 6-6. **WT:** 243.
Drafted: Notre Dame, 2020 (5th round). **Signed by:** Tyler Gibbons.
TRACK RECORD: Few pitchers have better stuff than Boyle, but even fewer have pitched as sparingly. He threw just 36 innings in three years at Notre Dame because he walked 48 batters and hit five more. The Reds' main focus was to get Boyle innings and get him comfortable finding the strike zone enough to let his exceptional stuff play. It worked in 2022. His 100 innings were more than he'd thrown in the previous four years combined. His .137 opponent batting average was easily the best in the minors among pitchers with 100 or more innings. He allowed 10 extra-base hits all year.
SCOUTING REPORT: Boyle "only" sat 95-97 mph and touched 99 after touching 102 in the past, which paid off in improved control. His fastball is a plus-plus pitch that can dominate, but it's his slider that should be his best pitch. Its success is dependent on its power. It has cutter-ish movement, but it sits in the high 80s and has been as hard as 92-93 mph. He also has a bigger, high-70s, fringe-average curve that he likes to flip over in early counts to steal a strike against hitters geared up for his fastball. Almost no one hit Boyle in Class A, but after his promotion to Double-A he learned he had to mix his pitches better.
THE FUTURE: Boyle's control currently is a 20 on the scouting scale, but it's taken massive strides. The trend is in the right direction, and it now seems feasible that he will eventually get to 30 or even 40 control. This would be enough for him to be a high-leverage reliever since he gives up so few hits.

BA GRADE: 50/Extreme	Fastball: 70	Slider: 70	Curveball: 45	Control: 30

Year	Age	Club (League)	Lvl	W	L	ERA	G	GS	IP	H	HR	BB	SO	BB/9	SO/9	WHIP	AVG
2022	22	Dayton (MWL)	HiA	3	4	2.17	17	17	75	25	3	59	122	7.1	14.7	1.13	.107
2022	22	Chattanooga (SL)	AA	0	2	4.85	6	5	26	21	3	25	31	8.7	10.7	1.77	.228
Minor League Totals				3	6	2.77	31	30	120	55	7	98	194	7.3	14.5	1.27	.141

21 ARIEL ALMONTE, OF

Born: Dec. 1, 2003. **B-T:** L-L. **HT:** 6-3. **WT:** 187.
Signed: Dominican Republic. **Signed by:** Reds international scouting department.
TRACK RECORD: Almonte was one of a pair of high-ceiling outfielders the Reds targeted in the 2021 international signing class. While the toolsier Malvin Valdez has struggled, Almonte has shown the polish the Reds anticipated when they signed him, and he has the best power among Reds lower-level hitters.
SCOUTING REPORT: Almonte needs a lot of refinement, but he fits the profile of a slugging right fielder who hits for enough average to make it work. His average exit velocities (90 mph) are already among the best in the Reds organization. He shows a mature, whole-field approach, but he needs to do a better job of recognizing breaking balls and he's going to need a lot more at-bats against lefties to get more comfortable against them. Almonte needs to improve his reads off the bat, as he sometimes takes false steps and then has to rush to make up for his misread. As he gets bigger, he'll slow down as well. He runs well underway but turns in below-average times from home to first. He has an above-average arm that fits in right.
THE FUTURE: Almonte's calm demeanor and grinder mentality help the Reds feel comfortable he will get the most out of his impressive tool set. He should make the jump to Low-A Daytona in 2023.

BA GRADE: 50/Extreme	Hitting: 40	Power: 60	Speed: 40	Fielding: 45	Arm: 55

Year	Age	Club (League)	Lvl	AVG	G	AB	R	H	2B	3B	HR	RBI	BB	SO	SB	OBP	SLG
2022	18	Reds (ACL)	R	.286	42	140	28	40	11	0	6	24	21	49	1	.390	.493
Minor League Totals				.281	90	302	63	85	20	1	11	57	47	101	16	.394	.464

22 RICKY KARCHER, RHP

Born: Sept. 18, 1997. **B-T:** R-R. **HT:** 6-4. **WT:** 215.
Drafted: Walters State (Tenn.) JC. **Signed by:** Jonathan Reynolds.
TRACK RECORD: In his third year as a pro, Karcher walked 30 batters in just 19 innings in Class A. Once again, his lack of control was derailing his promising career. His control is still far from even average, but he figured out how to stay around the zone in 2022. It resulted in him climbing to Triple-A to serve as Louisville's closer, and he earned a spot on the 40-man roster during the offseason.
SCOUTING REPORT: Karcher's a slider-first pitcher who just happens to also throw a 97-99 mph plus fastball. That's how he attacks hitters at his best. The fastball is a change-of-pace pitch after he's lulled them to sleep with a steady attack of 87-89 mph sliders in the strike zone. Karcher's delivery is that of a pure high-effort reliever, and his control is below-average. He's learned to control his slider better and has discovered that he can rely on it to get plenty of whiffs despite a shorter shape. Even then, he still piles up more walks than are ideal, but few hitters ever square him up. He didn't allow a home run in his final 24 outings.
THE FUTURE: Karcher has come a long way in a short amount of time. He'll most likely head back to Triple-A Louisville, but he should make his MLB debut in 2023. His stuff is as good as pretty much anyone in a major league bullpen, but only if he throws enough strikes to make it matter.

BA GRADE: 45/High	Fastball: 60	Slider: 70	Changeup: 50	Control: 30

Year	Age	Club (League)	Lvl	W	L	ERA	G	GS	IP	H	HR	BB	SO	BB/9	SO/9	WHIP	AVG
2022	24	Chattanooga (SL)	AA	3	2	3.24	20	0	25	20	1	21	42	7.6	15.1	1.64	.213
2022	24	Louisville (IL)	AAA	2	3	3.98	32	0	32	25	2	19	46	5.4	13.1	1.39	.219
Minor League Totals				6	12	5.53	100	18	143	128	12	128	189	8.0	11.9	1.79	.236

23 LOGAN TANNER, C

Born: Nov. 10, 2000. **B-T:** R-R. **HT:** 6-0. **WT:** 215.
Drafted: Mississippi State, 2022 (2nd round). **Signed by:** JR Reynolds.
TRACK RECORD: Tanner is already a star in Starkville, Miss., as he was the catcher for Mississippi State's first-ever national title team. He hit 15 home runs that year, but his offensive production tailed off in 2022, which led to him sliding to the second round.
SCOUTING REPORT: Tanner is the epitome of a glove-only catcher, but one whose glove is good enough to be worth carrying on a roster even if he hits under .200. His swing can get long and he struggles against top-notch velocity. He never hit .300 in three years at Mississippi State, and he projects as a nearly bottom-of-the-scale hitter with below-average power. For a player with that resume to get regular at-bats, the receiving has to be pretty special. Tanner's fits that bill. He's an above-average receiver with a plus-plus arm.
THE FUTURE: Tanner is the catcher his team's pitchers will love to throw to, but he needs to ensure he's not also the catcher other teams' pitchers love to face. If he can shorten his swing or tap more into his power, his glove will handle the rest.

BA GRADE: 40/Medium	Hitting: 30	Power: 40	Speed: 30	Fielding: 55	Arm: 70

Year	Age	Club (League)	Lvl	AVG	G	AB	R	H	2B	3B	HR	RBI	BB	SO	SB	OBP	SLG
2022	21	Reds (ACL)	R	.000	1	3	0	0	0	0	0	0	0	2	0	.000	.000
2022	21	Daytona (FSL)	LoA	.211	16	57	9	12	3	0	1	7	12	20	1	.343	.316
Minor League Totals				.200	17	60	9	12	3	0	1	7	12	22	1	.329	.300

24 HECTOR RODRIGUEZ, OF

Born: March 11, 2004. **B-T:** R-R. **HT:** 5-8. **WT:** 186.
Signed: Dominican Republic, 2021. **Signed by:** Moises De La Mota/Oliver Dominguez (Mets).
TRACK RECORD: With rules tweaks, MLB is trying to bring speed back into the game. The larger bases, limited number of pickoff throws and pitch clocks all combined to boost stolen bases around the minors in 2022, and those rules are coming to MLB in 2023. That's great news for speedsters like Rodriguez. The Reds acquired him and righthander Jose Acuña from the Mets for Tyler Naquin in July 2022.
SCOUTING REPORT: Rodriguez was battling for the Florida Complex League batting title before the trade. He is a pesky top-of-the-order hitter who sprays line drives but also can turn ground balls to shortstop or third base into infield hits. With a level swing from both sides of the plate, he feasts on high fastballs. He plays all-out seemingly all the time. There's very little home run power potential, but that's not Rodriguez's

game. He chases out of the zone too much, but he makes contact both in and out of the zone as well. Defensively, the Reds are going to give him every opportunity to acclimate to center field. He's quite raw out there right now, as he played second and third base in 2021. Some evaluators say he will most likely end up in left field.

THE FUTURE: Rodriguez has the makings of a fourth outfielder, but his extreme contact ability could help him exceed those expectations and give him a clear path to a role as a regular.

| BA GRADE: 45/High | | Hitting: 60 | | Power: 30 | | Speed: 70 | | Fielding: 50 | | Arm: 45 | |

Year	Age	Club (League)	Lvl	AVG	G	AB	R	H	2B	3B	HR	RBI	BB	SO	SB	OBP	SLG
2022	18	Reds (ACL)	R	.400	7	25	7	10	4	2	0	4	3	0	3	.464	.720
2022	18	Mets (FCL)	R	.349	27	106	19	37	4	4	3	16	6	10	12	.381	.547
2022	18	Daytona (FSL)	LoA	.289	13	45	7	13	4	2	0	6	2	10	1	.319	.467
2022	18	St. Lucie (FSL)	LoA	.143	2	7	1	1	0	0	0	0	1	0	0	.250	.143
Minor League Totals				.320	91	306	51	98	20	10	6	41	25	37	22	.374	.510

25 JUSTIN BOYD, OF

Born: March 30, 2001. **B-T:** R-R. **HT:** 6-0. **WT:** 201.
Drafted: Oregon State, 2022 (2nd round supplemental). **Signed by:** Brandon Marr.
TRACK RECORD: Boyd was an extremely productive player at Oregon State. He led the Beavers in batting average and on-base percentage and hit .373/.490/.577 in 2022. Despite that impressive season, many scouts were skeptical about Boyd's offensive impact with a wood bat because of his modest power, which is why he slid to the supplemental second round.
SCOUTING REPORT: Boyd has played second base in the past, and there are evaluators who believe his best long-term role will be as a multi-positional utilityman who can play second, all three outfield spots and maybe a little third base as well. For now, he's a center fielder with an above-average run tool. He looked comfortable in games in center with the Reds after primarily playing right field as a Beaver. He's an above-average hitter who looks to hit for average and get on base. He also can drop a bunt and is an adept basestealer.
THE FUTURE: Boyd is the type of low-ceiling, high-floor productive college player who sometimes exceeds expectations. His power potential seems modest, but he does everything else well.

| BA GRADE: 45/High | | Hitting: 55 | | Power: 30 | | Speed: 55 | | Fielding: 55 | | Arm: 55 | |

Year	Age	Club (League)	Lvl	AVG	G	AB	R	H	2B	3B	HR	RBI	BB	SO	SB	OBP	SLG
2022	21	Reds (ACL)	R	.667	1	3	2	2	1	0	0	0	0	0	1	.667	1.000
2022	21	Daytona (FSL)	LoA	.183	21	71	11	13	4	0	0	4	8	29	5	.263	.239
Minor League Totals				.203	22	74	13	15	5	0	0	4	8	29	6	.277	.270

26 CADE HUNTER, C

Born: Nov. 29, 2000. **B-T:** L-R. **HT:** 6-0. **WT:** 200.
Drafted: Virginia Tech, 2022 (5th round). **Signed by:** Kevin Buckley.
TRACK RECORD: The Reds' catching situation was a disaster in 2022. After Tyler Stephenson was sidelined with an injury, Cincinnati ran through catcher after catcher in the big leagues. None of the replacements stuck, and when the season ended the team dumped all of them off the 40-man roster. Not coincidentally, the Reds drafted two catchers, Logan Tanner and Hunter, in the top five rounds in 2022. Hunter is the son of Mariners amateur scouting director Scott Hunter.
SCOUTING REPORT: While Tanner is a glove-first catcher who faces questions about his bat, Hunter is a bat-first catcher who hears concerns about his glove. He mashed at Virginia Tech in 2022, hitting 17 home runs in 2022 before adding three in 14 games as a pro. Hunter will sacrifice some batting average to get to that above-average power, but it's a useful trade-off. He's improved as a receiver and has started to better handle pitches on the edge of the strike zone. He has a plus arm and quick transfer to help slow down basestealers. With average speed, Hunter runs very well for a catcher.
THE FUTURE: Lefthanded-hitting catchers who can hit for power are hard to find. Hunter's impressive debut raises hopes that he can develop into Tyler Stephenson's heir apparent in a few years.

| BA GRADE: 45/High | | Hitting: 40 | | Power: 55 | | Speed: 50 | | Fielding: 45 | | Arm: 60 | |

Year	Age	Club (League)	Lvl	AVG	G	AB	R	H	2B	3B	HR	RBI	BB	SO	SB	OBP	SLG
2022	21	Reds (ACL)	R	.400	6	15	5	6	2	1	1	5	5	4	0	.571	.867
2022	21	Daytona (FSL)	LoA	.308	8	26	5	8	1	0	2	8	2	7	3	.357	.577
Minor League Totals				.341	14	41	10	14	3	1	3	13	7	11	3	.449	.683

27 LYON RICHARDSON, RHP

Born: Jan. 18, 2000. **B-T:** B-R. **HT:** 6-1. **WT:** 200.
Drafted: HS—Jensen Beach, Fla., 2018 (2nd round). **Signed by:** Stephen Hunt.

TRACK RECORD: Richardson looked to be one of the Reds more promising and athletic young pitchers after a solid 2019 season. He didn't seem the same after the coronavirus pandemic, as he struggled at High-A Dayton before going down with an elbow injury that required Tommy John surgery. He missed the entire 2022 season but returned in time for instructional league, where he showed better stuff than he had demonstrated in 2021.

SCOUTING REPORT: Richardson touched 99 mph in high school, but he generally sat 91-95 as a pro. In his shorter stints in instructional league, he was once again showing the high-90s velocity that seemed to have disappeared. It's too soon to say for sure that he can carry that stuff into longer outings, but his improved arm speed will help his average slider and curveball and above-average changeup be more effective. Richardson's control backed up in 2021, but he showed average control before the pandemic.

THE FUTURE: The Reds were enamored enough with Richardson's impressive return that they added him to the 40-man roster rather than risk exposing him to the Rule 5 draft. That's a pretty significant vote of confidence in a pitcher who has yet to pitch above Class A. He should head to Chattanooga in 2023. With a strong season, he could vault back into the top-tier of Reds' starting pitching prospects.

BA GRADE: 50/Extreme	Fastball: 55	Curveball: 50	Slider: 50	Changeup: 55	Control: 50

Year	Age	Club (League)	Lvl	W	L	ERA	G	GS	IP	H	HR	BB	SO	BB/9	SO/9	WHIP	AVG
2022	22	Did not play—Injured															
Minor League Totals				5	19	4.88	56	55	218	237	22	87	221	3.6	9.1	1.49	.272

28 YERLIN CONFIDAN, OF

Born: Dec. 16, 2002. **B-T:** L-L. **HT:** 6-2. **WT:** 213.
Signed: Dominican Republic, 2019. **Signed by:** Edgard Melo/Emmanuel Catagena/Richard Jimenez.

TRACK RECORD: A $200,000 signee in 2019, Confidan was one of the stars of the Arizona Complex League in 2021, when he hit 11 home runs. A quad strain derailed his attempt at a follow-up in 2022. He injured the quad in early May, tried to come back in July, but then missed another month before finally returning in mid August for a rehab assignment. He made it back to Low-A Daytona on Aug. 30 but finished the year with just 103 plate appearances.

SCOUTING REPORT: Confidan is a prototypical power-hitting right fielder with all-fields power. He already can top 110 mph on his best drives, and his 90th-percentile exit velocity of 105.6 mph is among the best in the system. He is an average runner for now, but he will likely slow further as he gets bigger and stronger. The Reds moved him to left and right field in 2022. His plus arm would fit at either spot.

THE FUTURE: The Reds sped up Confidan's development in 2021 by having him skip the Dominican Summer League. He handled the jump, but it also means that he's on a reasonable developmental pace even with a lost 2022 season. He is still a high-risk, high-reward player, but he has the potential to be an everyday regular thanks to his power.

BA GRADE: 50/Extreme	Hitting: 45	Power: 60	Speed: 40	Fielding: 45	Arm: 60

Year	Age	Club (League)	Lvl	AVG	G	AB	R	H	2B	3B	HR	RBI	BB	SO	SB	OBP	SLG
2022	19	Reds (ACL)	R	.227	9	22	3	5	2	0	1	2	5	9	0	.370	.455
2022	19	Daytona (FSL)	LoA	.246	22	65	10	16	3	1	1	9	11	22	1	.355	.369
Minor League Totals				.291	81	265	46	77	14	3	13	45	28	79	8	.359	.513

29 CASEY LEGUMINA, RHP

Born: June 19, 1997. **B-T:** R-R. **HT:** 6-1. **WT:** 185.
Drafted: Gonzaga, 2019 (8th round). **Signed by:** Kyle Blackwell (Twins).

TRACK RECORD: Getting injured unfortunately seems to be part of being a pitcher, since the wear and tear of the pitching motion stresses the shoulder, elbow and arm muscles. A forearm injury somewhat derailed Legumina's draft year at Gonzaga, which led him to slide to the eighth round. As a pro, Legumina has handled staying healthy on the mound. He's had a bigger issue when he's been in the dugout. He was clipped by a line drive in 2021, which forced him to miss a month with a bruised pitching arm. He was traded to the Reds for shortstop Kyle Farmer in November 2022.

SCOUTING REPORT: Legumina has split time between starting and relieving as a pro, but he most likely will end up as a power reliever. He throws plenty of strikes with a fastball sits at 93-95 mph and touches 97 already. The pitch has the flat plane to be effective at the top of the zone, but it also has made him home run prone. It could get even better with a full-time move to shorter stints. His plus slider pairs well with it and his changeup is a fringe-average pitch as well. He needs to improve his below-average control of his slider and changeup or develop a secondary offering he can more consistently throw in the zone.

THE FUTURE: Legumina was added to the 40-man roster in advance of the 2023 season. That means he'll spend the year at Triple-A Louisville but could be on call to serve as a reinforcement for the big league team, where he should fit as a useful single- or multi-inning reliever.

| BA GRADE: 45/High | | Fastball: 60 | | Slider: 60 | | Changeup: 45 | | Control: 40 | | | | | |

Year	Age	Club (League)	Lvl	W	L	ERA	G	GS	IP	H	HR	BB	SO	BB/9	SO/9	WHIP	AVG
2022	25	Cedar Rapids (MWL)	HiA	0	1	4.05	3	3	13	10	0	4	16	2.7	10.8	1.05	.204
2022	25	Wichita (TL)	AA	2	5	4.93	30	13	73	78	11	32	76	3.9	9.4	1.51	.265
Minor League Totals				6	8	4.25	48	25	136	125	15	52	155	3.4	10.3	1.30	.238

30 RECE HINDS, OF

Born: Sept. 5, 2000. **B-T:** R-R. **HT:** 6-3. **WT:** 230.
Drafted: HS—Bradenton, Fla., 2019 (2nd round). **Signed by:** Sean Buckley.

TRACK RECORD: Hinds has great power but even greater strikeout concerns. Hinds hits the ball exceptionally hard, but his 39% strikeout rate ranks among the worst in the minors. A hamate injury cost him significant time in 2022, following a knee injury that sidelined him in 2021.

SCOUTING REPORT: Hinds has the power to clear batting eyes with ease and has true all-fields home run power. He has plenty of bat speed, but he doesn't make good swing decisions. He's too aggressive and can be beaten in the zone because he gets fooled too often. He could benefit from focusing more on making contact, since his power is so great that even a less than full-effort swing can clear the fence. The Reds moved him to the outfield in 2022 to try to reduce the wear and tear on his knees. He has taken to the outfield and his plus-plus arm shuts down running games. He had nine assists in 2022. He is an average runner who can swipe a bag against a pitcher who is slow to the plate.

THE FUTURE: Hinds' big league future is entirely dependent on making more contact. His power, arm, speed and defense are MLB caliber, but if he doesn't cut his strikeout rate by another 8-10% he won't hit enough to get to that power.

| BA GRADE: 45/Extreme | | Hitting: 30 | | Power: 60 | | Speed: 50 | | Fielding: 45 | | Arm: 70 | | | | | |

Year	Age	Club (League)	Lvl	AVG	G	AB	R	H	2B	3B	HR	RBI	BB	SO	SB	OBP	SLG
2022	21	Reds (ACL)	R	.063	6	16	2	1	0	0	0	0	2	6	2	.211	.063
2022	21	Dayton (MWL)	HiA	.235	67	247	33	58	9	4	10	26	23	107	13	.310	.425
2022	21	Chattanooga (SL)	AA	.310	6	29	3	9	2	1	2	4	0	12	0	.310	.655
Minor League Totals				.240	136	501	78	120	24	9	24	63	44	193	22	.314	.467

Cleveland Guardians

BY TEDDY CAHILL

The 2022 season had a fresh feel to it in Cleveland, and not just because the long process of changing the organization's name came to a conclusion. The club announced in 2020 that it would ditch its Indians nickname, with the follow-up announcement coming in July 2021 that the new name would be Guardians.

But 2022 marked the first time that Cleveland played under its new banner.

In addition to its new name, the team had a new look on the field. The Guardians had 17 players make their major league debuts, tying a franchise record. They were the youngest team in MLB and were younger than the average Triple-A team. That youth movement followed the Guardians' moves in November 2021 to turn over more than a quarter of the 40-man roster to protect their upper-level prospects from the Rule 5 draft. Those moves, coming off the organization's first losing season in 12 years and amid a quiet offseason, meant that expectations were low entering 2022.

But the Guardians far outpaced those expectations, and went 92-70 to win the American League Central going away. They swept the Rays in the Wild Card Series before falling to the Yankees in a taut, five-game Division Series. It was an impressive season on all fronts and one that proved the organization's belief in its young talent was well placed.

Of the debutants, outfielder Steven Kwan made the biggest impact. Drafted in the fifth round in 2018, he had never been a highly regarded prospect but broke out in 2021 and carried that performance into MLB. He finished third in AL Rookie of the Year voting and led the team with a .373 on-base percentage and won a Gold Glove. Fellow outfielder Oscar Gonzalez also proved impactful and delivered three game-winning hits in the playoffs, tying David Ortiz's record for a single postseason.

But it wasn't just the rookies who made good on their promise in 2022. Young players like right-hander Triston McKenzie, a former No. 1 prospect, and second baseman Andres Gimenez, part of the package the team acquired when it traded Francisco Lindor to the Mets, took big steps forward. Gimenez made the All-Star Game and won a Gold Glove in his third big league season. McKenzie, also in his third big league season, established himself as the team's No. 2 starter and threw 202 innings, including the postseason, displaying a level of durability some doubted he would ever reach.

With so many young players stepping up around stalwarts Jose Ramirez, who finished fourth

Steven Kwan made an immediate impact as a rookie who was impossible to strike out.

PROJECTED 2026 LINEUP

Catcher	Bo Naylor	26
First Base	Josh Naylor	29
Second Base	Andres Gimenez	27
Third Base	Jose Ramirez	33
Shortstop	Brayan Rocchio	25
Left Field	Steven Kwan	28
Center Field	Chase DeLauter	24
Right Field	Will Brennan	25
Designated Hitter	George Valera	25
No. 1 Starter	Shane Bieber	31
No. 2 Starter	Triston McKenzie	28
No. 3 Starter	Daniel Espino	25
No. 4 Starter	Gavin Williams	27
No. 5 Starter	Cal Quantrill	31
Closer	Emmanuel Clase	28

in MVP voting, and Shane Bieber, who finished seventh in Cy Young voting, the Guardians were able to not just outperform expectations for 2022, but also lay a promising foundation moving forward. No team has a more controllable long-term roster than Cleveland.

The youth movement is set to continue in 2023 and beyond. Cleveland's farm system continues to be among the sport's best.

Integrating those young players onto the big league roster while remaining competitive in the playoffs will be a challenge, but it is a familiar one for Cleveland's brain trust, from president Chris Antonetti to general manager Mike Chernoff and manager Terry Francona. ∎

DEPTH CHART

CLEVELAND GUARDIANS

TOP 2023 MLB CONTRIBUTORS	RANK
Logan Allen, LHP	6
Will Brennan, OF	10
Cody Morris, RHP	17
BREAKOUT PROSPECTS	**RANK**
Juan Brito, 2B	16
Angel Genao, SS	21

SOURCE OF TOP 30 TALENT			
Homegrown	**27**	**Acquired**	**3**
College	13	Trade	3
Junior college	1	Rule 5 draft	0
High school	6	Independent league	0
Nondrafted free agent	0	Free agent/waivers	0
International	7		

LF
Will Brennan (10)
Jhonkensy Noel (20)
Richie Palacios (24)

CF
Chase DeLauter (9)
Petey Halpin (25)
Will Benson (29)
Jaison Chourio

RF
George Valera (4)
Johnathan Rodriguez

3B
Gabriel Rodriguez (21)
Carson Tucker

SS
Brayan Rocchio (5)
Angel Martinez (8)
Gabriel Arias (12)
Jose Tena (14)
Angel Genao (23)
Milan Tolentino

2B
Tyler Freeman (11)
Jake Fox (15)
Juan Brito (16)
Nate Furman

1B
Joe Naranjo
Micah Pries

C
Bo Naylor (3)
Bryan Lavastida (30)
Victor Izturis

LHP

LHSP	LHRP
Logan Allen (6)	Tim Herrin
Joey Cantillo (18)	Will Dion
Parker Messick (19)	Ryan Webb
Doug Nikhazy (27)	
Jackson Humphries	
Rodney Boone	

RHP

RHSP	RHRP
Daniel Espino (1)	Cody Morris (17)
Gavin Williams (2)	Hunter Gaddis (26)
Tanner Bibee (7)	Jack Leftwich
Justin Campbell (13)	Andrew Misiaszek
Xzavion Curry (22)	Alaska Abney
Tanner Burns (28)	Nick Mikolajchak
Jacob Zibin	
Ross Carver	
Peyton Battenfield	
Tommy Mace	

1 DANIEL ESPINO, RHP

Born: Jan. 5, 2001. **B-T:** R-R. **HT:** 6-2. **WT:** 225.
Drafted: HS—Statesboro, GA, 2019 (1st round).
Signed by: Ethan Purser.

DAVID MONSEUR/ACCENT IMAGES PHOTOGRAPHY

TRACK RECORD: Espino was born in Panama and moved with his family to the U.S. when he was 15. He enrolled at Georgia Premier Academy, where he was able to continue his education while also adopting a near-professional mindset on the diamond. His performance and mentality carried over to pro ball and he put himself on the fast track. He impressed at the alternate training site in 2020, more than holding his own as a teenager against more experienced prospects, and then reached High-A in 2021, his first full professional season. He opened 2022 with Double-A Akron as one of the younger pitchers in the Eastern League. In just his third start he struck out 14 of the 18 batters he faced in five innings. He made just four starts in total before a knee injury at the end of April ultimately sidelined him for the season. He spent most of the remainder of the season rehabbing at the Guardians' complex in Arizona.

SCOUTING REPORT: Espino is on the shorter end of what teams look for in a righthanded starter, but his excellent athleticism and a rare combination of explosiveness and flexibility helps him access his lower half in a way most pitchers his size cannot. That helps him produce elite velocity, and his fastball can reach triple digits and sits 96 mph. Since entering pro ball, Espino has raised his arm slot and now generates significant ride on his fastball, adding to its effectiveness. He throws both a curveball and slider. His velocity helps his slider play up, and it's not uncommon for him to throw the pitch in the low 90s. It's a well above-average offering and creates swing-and-miss at an exceptional rate. His curveball is a big 12-to-6 breaker that works mostly as a chase pitch, but also creates groundball outs. His firm changeup is an effective fourth offering and has real promise but needs further refinement. He hasn't needed to use it often. Espino has a long arm action but typically pitches with average control. He has swing-and-miss stuff—in 2021 he ranked 15th in the minor leagues in strikeouts in just 91.2 innings—but he needs to continue to refine his command as he faces upper-level hitters with more mature approaches. While Espino made just four starts at Double-A before his injury, the early returns were impressive, and he was still getting plenty of swinging strikes against older hitters.

THE FUTURE: Espino's combination of premium stuff, control and makeup mark him one of the best pitching prospects in baseball. There's no tell-ing how far he would have advanced in 2022 if he had stayed healthy. As it is, he'll be 22 years old on Opening Day and ready to attack the upper levels. He'll likely return to Double-A Akron to begin the season. With a strong summer, a big league debut in 2023 isn't out of the question. The Guardians will likely be cautious with him, because he has never thrown more than 100 innings in a season. But ultimately he has the potential to one day lead the Cleveland rotation and he could provide a late-season boost in 2023.

BA GRADE	SCOUTING GRADES
70 Risk: Very High	Fastball: 80. Curve: 55. Slider: 70. Change: 50. Control: 55.

Projected future grades on 20-80 scouting scale

BEST TOOLS

BATTING

Best Hitter for Average	Tyler Freeman
Best Power Hitter	Jhonkensy Noel
Best Strike-Zone Discipline	Angel Martinez
Fastest Baserunner:	Isaiah Greene
Best Athlete	Will Benson

PITCHING

Best Fastball	Daniel Espino
Best Curveball	Gavin Williams
Best Slider	Daniel Espino
Best Changeup	Logan T. Allen
Best Control	Tanner Bibee

FIELDING

Best Defensive Catcher	Bo Naylor
Best Defensive Infielder	Brayan Rocchio
Best Infield Arm	Gabriel Arias
Best Defensive Outfielder	Will Brennan
Best Outfield Arm	Johnathan Rodriguez

Year	Age	Club (League)	Lvl	W	L	ERA	G	GS	IP	H	HR	BB	SO	BB/9	SO/9	WHIP	AVG
2022	21	Akron (EL)	AA	1	0	2.45	4	4	18	9	4	4	35	2.0	17.2	0.71	.141
Minor League Totals				4	11	3.57	33	33	134	89	15	53	221	3.6	14.9	1.06	.184

2 GAVIN WILLIAMS, RHP

Born: July 26, 1999. **B-T:** L-R. **HT:** 6-6. **WT:** 255.
Drafted: East Carolina, 2021 (1st round). **Signed by:** Pete Loizzo.

TRACK RECORD: Williams has long had a big arm and big potential, but it took him a full four years of college to truly realize it. After primarily pitching out of the East Carolina bullpen for his first three seasons on campus, he took over a spot in the rotation in 2021 and produced an All-America season, going 10-1, 1.88 with 130 strikeouts in 81.1 innings. That turned him into the 24th overall pick, and marked the first time the Guardians used a first-round pick on a college pitcher since taking Drew Pomeranz in 2010. Williams reached Double-A a year and a day after his last college start and ultimately was one of the best pitchers in the Eastern League. He made the BA Minor League All-Star Team after leading the minor leagues with a .173 opponent average and ranked third with a 1.96 ERA.

BA GRADE
65 Risk: High

SCOUTING REPORT: Williams stands out for his size and arm strength. His fastball sits around 95 mph, has touched 101 and can get swings and misses, especially up in the zone. He throws both a curveball and slider, with his 11-to-5 curveball being the better of the two, though the short slider is a solid pitch in its own right. He also has good feel for a firm changeup, though it's the least advanced of his offerings. Williams had control issues early in his college career and those can still crop up at times, but he should pitch with average command.

THE FUTURE: Williams showed all the characteristics of an above-average starter, and he has a tantalizing combination of upside and proximity to the big leagues, which he could reach in late 2023.

SCOUTING GRADES:	Fastball: 70	Curveball: 60	Slider: 55	Changeup: 50	Control: 50

Year	Age	Club (League)	Lvl	W	L	ERA	G	GS	IP	H	HR	BB	SO	BB/9	SO/9	WHIP	AVG
2022	22	Lake County (MWL)	HiA	2	1	1.40	9	9	45	25	0	14	67	2.8	13.4	0.87	.167
2022	22	Akron (EL)	AA	3	3	2.31	16	16	70	44	9	26	82	3.3	10.5	1.00	.176
Minor League Totals				5	4	1.96	25	25	115	69	9	40	149	3.1	11.7	0.95	.172

3 BO NAYLOR, C

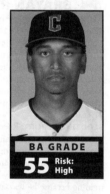

Born: February 21, 2000. **B-T:** L-R. **HT:** 6-0. **WT:** 205.
Drafted: HS—Mississauga, Ontario, 2018 (1st round). **Signed by:** Mike Kanen.

TRACK RECORD: After a trying 2021 season, Naylor bounced back in a big way in 2022. He started the year back with Double-A Akron, where he struggled a year prior, and eventually played his way to his MLB debut. Naylor joined his older brother Josh with the Guardians and even made Cleveland's postseason roster but did not appear in a game.

SCOUTING REPORT: Naylor got back on track at the plate in part because he overhauled his swing and got his strikeout rate back under control, lowering it from 31.5% in 2021 to 23.7% in 2022, while also raising his walk rate. His improved plate control was a return to his historical norms as a hitter, while he also showed off his above-average power potential and speed. Naylor hit

BA GRADE
55 Risk: High

21 home runs and stole 20 bases, an incredibly rare pairing for a catcher. His combination of power, speed and a disciplined plate approach makes for an impressive offensive profile. Defensively, Naylor has made some important strides over the last two years. His athleticism has always played well behind the plate, and he earns high grades for his blocking and framing ability. He's also worked hard to improve his throwing ability and has cut down the frequency with which opponents run on him, which was a concern early in his professional career. He has earned the respect of pitchers in the organization, who enjoy working with him.

THE FUTURE: After making the postseason roster, Naylor will have a chance to open the season with the Guardians. Naylor brings a rare profile to catching and can impact the game in multiple ways.

SCOUTING GRADES	Hitting: 50	Power: 50	Speed: 50	Fielding: 55	Arm: 55

Year	Age	Club (League)	Lvl	AVG	G	AB	R	H	2B	3B	HR	RBI	BB	SO	SB	OBP	SLG
2022	22	Akron (EL)	AA	.271	52	170	29	46	12	2	6	21	45	46	11	.427	.471
2022	22	Columbus (IL)	AAA	.257	66	245	44	63	14	2	15	47	37	75	9	.366	.514
2022	22	Cleveland (AL)	MLB	.000	5	8	0	0	0	0	0	0	0	5	0	.000	.000
Major League Totals				.000	5	8	0	0	0	0	0	0	0	5	0	.000	.000
Minor League Totals				.239	345	1244	191	297	60	18	44	194	183	365	42	.339	.422

4 GEORGE VALERA, OF

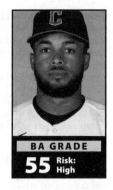

Born: November 13, 2000. **B-T:** L-L. **HT:** 6-0. **WT:** 195.
Signed: Dominican Republic, 2017. **Signed by:** Jhonathan Leyba/Domingo Toribio.
TRACK RECORD: The Guardians made a splash on the international market in 2017, signing Valera, the No. 5 prospect in his signing class, to a $1.3 million deal. He was born in New York and lived there until his family moved to the Dominican Republic when he was 13. Valera was added to the 40-man roster after the 2021 season. He spent most of 2022 at Double-A Akron before an August promotion to Triple-A Columbus, where he was one of the league's youngest everyday players.
SCOUTING REPORT: Valera has long stood out for his advanced setup at the plate, one that drew comparisons to Juan Soto as an amateur. He has quick hands and keeps the bat in the zone for a long time, traits that enable him to make a lot of hard contact. Despite that loose, easy swing, there is swing-and-miss to Valera's game, and he has struck out in about a quarter of his plate appearances in full-season ball. His patience and feel for the zone mean he also consistently works walks. He has above-average raw power and gets to it in games often. His 24 home runs ranked third among the organization's minor leaguers. Valera profiles as a corner outfielder with average speed and arm strength. He has mostly played right field as a professional.
THE FUTURE: Cleveland has been on the hunt for power bats for several years, and Valera could soon fill such a role in the middle of the order. He profiles as a traditional power-hitting corner outfielder.

BA GRADE 55 Risk: High

SCOUTING GRADES	Hitting: 50	Power: 55	Speed: 50	Fielding: 50	Arm: 50

Year	Age	Club (League)	Lvl	AVG	G	AB	R	H	2B	3B	HR	RBI	BB	SO	SB	OBP	SLG
2022	21	Akron (EL)	AA	.264	90	330	64	87	17	3	15	59	52	100	2	.367	.470
2022	21	Columbus (IL)	AAA	.221	42	154	25	34	8	0	9	23	22	45	0	.324	.448
Minor League Totals				.248	276	967	167	240	38	9	52	185	174	297	20	.367	.467

5 BRAYAN ROCCHIO, SS/2B

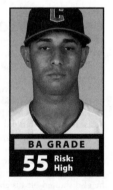

Born: January 13, 2001. **B-T:** B-R. **HT:** 5-10. **WT:** 170.
Signed: Venezuela, 2017. **Signed by:** Jhonathan Leyba.
TRACK RECORD: When the Guardians made a big splash on the 2017 international market with the heralded signings of Aaron Bracho and George Valera, their move to ink Rocchio flew more under the radar. The Venezuelan native has since made his own mark. Rocchio has been on an accelerated track throughout his career. In 2022 he reached Triple-A Columbus as a 21-year-old.
SCOUTING REPORT: Rocchio doesn't stand out physically but earned plaudits for his high baseball IQ and game awareness. A switch-hitter, he has a smooth, consistent swing from both sides of the plate and excellent pitch recognition. He's an aggressive hitter and consistently barrels balls. Following the pandemic layoff in 2020—a time when Rocchio was forced to focus more on strength training because he was stuck in Venezuela with few on-field options—he started showing above-average power potential. In both of the seasons that followed, he has had 46 extra-base hits. Rocchio has answered any questions about his ability to stick at shortstop. He's a plus runner, and his hands and arm are good enough for the position, especially because his instincts and baseball IQ help his tools play up. He's also seen time at second base and third base in the last two years to give him more versatility, which could come into play as he looks to break into a crowded Cleveland infield.
THE FUTURE: The Guardians have no shortage of middle infield prospects, and the strong play in 2022 of their major league double-play combination of Amed Rosario and Andres Gimenez only further adds to the logjam. Rosario has one year remaining before he reaches free agency, so Rocchio is in line to open 2023 back in Columbus and likely make his MLB debut later in the season.

BA GRADE 55 Risk: High

SCOUTING GRADES	Hitting: 50	Power: 50	Speed: 60	Fielding: 60	Arm: 50

Year	Age	Club (League)	Lvl	AVG	G	AB	R	H	2B	3B	HR	RBI	BB	SO	SB	OBP	SLG
2022	21	Akron (EL)	AA	.265	99	373	62	99	21	1	13	48	42	81	12	.349	.432
2022	21	Columbus (IL)	AAA	.234	33	137	21	32	6	0	5	16	12	21	2	.298	.387
Minor League Totals				.274	369	1461	235	401	77	13	40	183	122	279	71	.343	.427

6 LOGAN T. ALLEN, LHP

BA GRADE

55 Risk: High

Born: September 5, 1998. **B-T:** R-L. **HT:** 6-0. **WT:** 190.
Drafted: Florida International, 2020 (2nd round). **Signed by:** Jhonathan Leyba.

TRACK RECORD: Allen was one of the organization's breakout prospects in 2021. After a decorated amateur career, he wasted no time making his mark in pro ball, rocketing to Double-A in his first season. His 2022 wasn't quite as spectacular. He reached Triple-A but struggled with his command.

SCOUTING REPORT: Allen stands out for his feel and competitiveness on the mound, with the knocks on him being his size and lack of a big arm. His fastball velocity has ticked up in the last couple years, and he now works in the low 90s. The pitch plays up thanks to some deception in his delivery and his ability to locate it to all four quadrants of the strike zone. Allen's best pitch is his changeup, which is a plus offering and is a weapon he can use against hitters on either side of the plate. His slider has long lagged behind his other two pitches, though it does have the potential to be an average offering. Allen added a cutter in 2022, which benefited both his fastball and slider, giving hitters another hard offering to account for at the plate. His control was among the best in the 2020 draft, and that transferred to pro ball, where it showed plus. In Triple-A, Allen's walk rate increased as more mature hitters chased his stuff out of the zone less often. His control remains plus and he repeats his delivery well, but he'll have to learn to adjust against better opposition.

THE FUTURE: Allen's experience at Triple-A showed he still has some necessary refinements to make. Breaking into the Guardians' rotation isn't easy, but Allen should be ready to make his MLB debut in 2023. Without another tick up in stuff, his ceiling is that of a solid big league starter.

SCOUTING GRADES:	Fastball: 50	Slider: 50	Cutter: 55	Changeup: 60	Control: 60

Year	Age	Club (League)	Lvl	W	L	ERA	G	GS	IP	H	HR	BB	SO	BB/9	SO/9	WHIP	AVG
2022	23	Akron (EL)	AA	5	3	3.33	13	13	73	58	9	22	104	2.7	12.8	1.10	.216
2022	23	Columbus (IL)	AAA	4	4	6.49	14	14	60	64	8	29	73	4.4	11.0	1.56	.269
Minor League Totals				18	7	3.61	48	46	244	199	29	77	320	2.8	11.8	1.13	.220

7 TANNER BIBEE, RHP

BA GRADE

55 Risk: High

Born: March 5, 1999. **B-T:** R-R. **HT:** 6-2. **WT:** 205.
Drafted: Cal State Fullerton, 2021 (5th round). **Signed by:** Kyle Bamberger.

TRACK RECORD: The Guardians used 11 of their first 12 picks in the 2021 draft on college pitchers, a haul that included first-rounder Gavin Williams, now the organization's No. 2 prospect. Four rounds later, Cleveland selected Bibee, who had a solid but unheralded four years at Cal State Fullerton. His first professional season was anything but unheralded. He rocketed up the Guardians' depth chart, and reached Double-A by the start of July. Bibee finished sixth in the minor league ERA race at 2.17.

SCOUTING REPORT: Bibee's breakout was fueled by a strong uptick in stuff while still maintaining the underlying traits that had led to his success as an amateur. He fits a familiar profile for Cleveland, with above-average control, four pitches and solid pitchability. But as an average-sized righthander with a fastball that sat in the low 90s, he didn't appear to have significant upside. The Guardians were able to help him improve his velocity, and his fastball ticked into the mid 90s and touched as high as 99 mph. His improved velocity helped the rest of his arsenal, especially his slider, which separated more definitively from his curveball. His slider has the promise of a plus offering, while his curveball and changeup—which have made significant strides as well—project as average pitches. That repertoire helped him compile a strikeout-minus-walk percentage of 27.1, which ranked fourth among minor league pitchers with 100 innings. He did so without sacrificing control and threw strikes at an above-average rate.

THE FUTURE: Bibee's breakout 2022 season has raised his profile and expectations. He has put himself on an accelerated track and could make his MLB debut in 2023.

SCOUTING GRADES:	Fastball: 60	Curveball: 50	Slider: 60	Changeup: 50	Control: 55

Year	Age	Club (League)	Lvl	W	L	ERA	G	GS	IP	H	HR	BB	SO	BB/9	SO/9	WHIP	AVG
2022	23	Lake County (MWL)	HiA	2	1	2.59	12	12	59	50	8	13	86	2.0	13.1	1.07	.233
2022	23	Akron (EL)	AA	6	1	1.83	13	13	74	51	4	14	81	1.7	9.9	0.88	.194
Minor League Totals				8	2	2.17	25	25	133	101	12	27	167	1.8	11.3	0.96	.211

8 ANGEL MARTINEZ, SS/2B

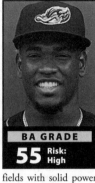

Born: January 27, 2002. **B-T:** B-R. **HT:** 6-0. **WT:** 186.
Signed: Dominican Republic, 2018. **Signed by:** Jhonathan Leyba.

TRACK RECORD: Martinez made the biggest jump of any Guardians' position prospect in 2021 and then built on that progress in 2022, reaching Double-A Akron as a 20-year-old. Martinez's rise has been meteoric for a player whose professional resume coming into 2021 was limited to the Dominican Summer League and instructional league. His experience around baseball likely eased his transition. His father is former big league catcher Sandy Martinez, now the Nationals' DSL manager, and his older brother is Sandy Martinez Jr., who also played professionally.

BA GRADE
55 Risk: High

SCOUTING REPORT: Martinez isn't the most tooled-up of Cleveland's middle infielders, but his baseball IQ and maturity make all his tools play up. The switch-hitter has a simple swing from both sides and can drive the ball to all fields with solid power potential, though it plays as doubles pop now. He's a disciplined hitter and makes a lot of contact. He prides himself in his ability to make quick adjustments at the plate. After struggling against lefthanders in 2021, he made significant strides with his righthanded swing in 2022, evening his splits. Martinez is an average runner but still covers a lot of ground thanks to his instincts, and he makes sound decisions defensively. He also has worked hard to improve his arm strength, which now grades out as plus. He can play anywhere on the infield and primarily played shortstop at High-A Lake County before playing mostly second base at Akron in deference to Jose Tena.

THE FUTURE: Martinez has consistently been one of the youngest players at his level, and the way Cleveland has challenged him is indicative of how advanced he is. He'll return to Akron to start 2023 and should find himself Cleveland's infield mix in the next couple years.

SCOUTING GRADES		Hitting: 50		Power: 50			Speed: 50			Fielding: 55			Arm: 60	
Year	Age	Club (League)	Lvl	AVG	G	AB	R	H	2B	3B	HR	RBI	BB	SO	SB	OBP	SLG
2022	20	Lake County (MWL)	HiA	.288	77	281	46	81	17	3	10	27	40	58	10	.384	.477
2022	20	Akron (EL)	AA	.244	24	82	10	20	6	1	3	17	12	18	2	.356	.451
Minor League Totals				.270	254	962	155	260	53	17	21	117	124	193	36	.361	.426

9 CHASE DeLAUTER, OF

Born: October 8, 2001. **B-T:** L-L. **HT:** 6-4. **WT:** 235.
Drafted: James Madison, 2022 (1st round). **Signed by:** Kyle Bamberger.

BACKGROUND: DeLauter was unheralded at Hedgesville (W.Va.) High and went to James Madison as a two-way player. While he played well at JMU over his first two seasons, the pandemic severely limited his game time, and he remained under the radar going into summer 2021. That's when he broke out in the Cape Cod League, where he tied for the league lead with nine home runs. DeLauter was off to a strong start in the spring of 2022, but a broken foot in April brought an end to his season. Despite the injury, he became the first player in program history to be drafted in the first round when Cleveland took him 16th overall.

BA GRADE
55 Risk: High

SCOUTING REPORT: DeLauter first stands out for his size at a listed 6-foot-4, 235 pounds and then for his powerful lefthanded swing. He is a disciplined hitter with good strike-zone awareness. He walked more than he struck out during his college career, rarely expanding his zone and showing good barrel control. He has plus raw power and gets to it well. He consistently makes hard contact. DeLauter looks like a prototypical corner outfielder, but he has plus speed, covers ground and has good instincts in the outfield. That has allowed him to play center field to this point, and he'll continue to develop there, though an eventual move to a corner would not be unexpected. He has a plus arm.

THE FUTURE: DeLauter is not as polished as a typical first-round college position player. He got just 323 plate appearances over three years at JMU—or about what an everyday player for a College World Series team gets in a season—and his experience against high-level competition is limited. He will likely need a bit more developmental time, but as less of a finished product there's room for more growth and plenty of upside. He'll look to start tapping into that as he makes his professional debut in 2023.

SCOUTING GRADES		Hitting: 50		Power: 60			Speed: 55			Fielding: 50			Arm: 60	
Year	Age	Club (League)	Level	AVG	G	AB	R	H	2B	3B	HR	RBI	BB	SO	SB	OBP	SLG
2022	20	Did not play															

10 WILL BRENNAN, OF

Born: February 2, 1998. **B-T:** L-L. **HT:** 6-0. **WT:** 195.
Drafted: Kansas State, 2019 (8th round). **Signed by:** Kyle Bamberger.

BACKGROUND: Brennan flew under the radar throughout his college and professional career until 2022, when he delivered a breakthrough season, made his MLB debut and earned a spot on the Guardians' postseason roster. While he has never been a famous player, Brennan has an impressive track record of hitting, going back to his Kansas State days. He tied for the minor league lead with 166 hits in 2022, and finished second with 42 doubles.

SCOUTING REPORT: Brennan has a simple, compact swing and a disciplined approach at the plate. That combination allows him to consistently put the bat on the ball, falling into the kind of barrel-control approach favored by the organization. Brennan put up a .909 OPS against righthanders in the minors and majors in 2022, but hit .252 with no impact in same-side matchups. His power mostly plays to the gaps because he consistently hits line drives. He offers some raw power, though his profile is likely always going to be hit-over-power. Brennan is an above-average runner and gets the most out of his speed on the bases, where he is a threat to run. His speed, above-average arm and actions give him the ability to play anywhere in the outfield. He has played mostly center field in the minors and has a chance to stay there, but his range profiles better in a corner.

THE FUTURE: Brennan heads to spring training looking to compete for a big league job—and after making the playoff roster, he stands a strong chance to break camp with the Guardians.

BA GRADE
50 Risk: Medium

SCOUTING GRADES	Hitting: 55	Power: 45	Speed: 55	Fielding: 50	Arm: 55

Year	Age	Club (League)	Lvl	AVG	G	AB	R	H	2B	3B	HR	RBI	BB	SO	SB	OBP	SLG
2022	24	Akron (EL)	AA	.311	36	135	16	42	12	1	4	39	17	16	5	.382	.504
2022	24	Columbus (IL)	AAA	.316	93	393	53	124	28	3	9	68	33	53	15	.367	.471
2022	24	Cleveland (AL)	MLB	.357	11	42	6	15	1	1	1	8	2	4	2	.400	.500
Major League Totals				.357	11	42	6	15	1	1	1	8	2	4	2	.400	.500
Minor League Totals				.296	288	1130	177	334	79	9	20	189	118	158	44	.367	.435

11 TYLER FREEMAN, 2B/SS

Born: May 21, 1999. **B-T:** R-R. **HT:** 6-0. **WT:** 190.
Drafted: HS—Rancho Cucamonga, Calif., 2017 (2nd round). **Signed by:** Mike Bradford.

TRACK RECORD: Freeman opened the 2022 season in Akron and played his way to the big leagues, debuting in August. He had a slow start in Cleveland, however, and did not make the playoff roster. Still, it was a solid year, as Freeman came back from a shoulder injury that cost him the second half of 2021.

SCOUTING REPORT: Freeman stands out most for his hitting ability and excellent feel for the barrel. He has a very aggressive approach at the plate and rarely walks as a result, but when he swings, he makes contact. While his pure hit tool is excellent, how much impact he'll provide offensively remains a question. His six home runs at Triple-A Columbus were a career high in just 72 games, but he otherwise struggled to produce power against upper-level pitchers. A return to his pre-surgery 2021 form, when a third of his hits went for extra bases would be a big boost. Freeman was drafted as a shortstop and has primarily played there as a professional, but his average speed and arm strength limit his range and many evaluators question whether he's a long-term fit at the position. He played shortstop, second and third base in the big leagues and he could still settle at any of the three positions. A move off shortstop, however, would put more pressure on his bat and, especially, his bottom-of-the-scale power.

THE FUTURE: Freeman will be 23 on Opening Day and will go to spring training competing for a spot on the roster. The Guardians have a very crowded middle infield, however, especially following strong 2022 seasons from Amed Rosario and Andres Gimenez. Freeman has perhaps the most hittability of the group, but his defense is not as advanced. To break the logjam, Cleveland will have to decide what it values more. His versatility could help him carve out a role in Cleveland in the immediate future, while in the long run it will be up to his bat to earn him a full-time role.

BA Grade: 45/Medium	Hit: 55	Power: 20	Speed: 50	Fielding: 45	Arm: 50

Year	Age	Club (League)	Lvl	AVG	G	AB	R	H	2B	3B	HR	RBI	BB	SO	SB	OBP	SLG
2022	23	Columbus (IL)	AAA	.279	72	297	51	83	7	0	6	44	25	32	6	.371	.364
2022	23	Cleveland (AL)	MLB	.247	24	77	9	19	3	0	0	3	4	11	1	.314	.286
Major League Totals				.247	24	77	9	19	3	0	0	3	4	11	1	.314	.286
Minor League Totals				.311	344	1352	234	420	91	11	15	159	74	140	48	.376	.428

12 GABRIEL ARIAS, SS

Born: Feb. 27, 2000. **B-T:** R-R. **HT:** 6-1. **WT:** 217.
Signed: Venezuela, 2016. **Signed by:** Luis Prieto/Yfrain Linares/Trevor Schumm (Padres).

TRACK RECORD: Arias was one of the top prospects in the 2016 international signing class and the Venezuelan native signed with the Padres. He initially stood out for his glove, but his profile rose after an offensive breakout in 2019. He was traded to Cleveland in 2020 as a part of the deal for Mike Clevinger and Greg Allen. He made his major league debut in 2022, but his season was sidetracked by a broken hand that required surgery in May, costing him several weeks on the injured list.

SCOUTING REPORT: Arias is a good athlete with a lot of raw ability. The righthanded hitter has a smooth swing and his wiry strength and bat speed give him average power. He has a very aggressive approach at the plate, but he's been able to keep his strikeout rate in check in the upper levels of the minor leagues. Arias is never going to be an on-base machine, but he's made important strides since coming to the organization. Defensively, there have never been many questions about Arias. He has advanced infield actions, clean hands and above-average arm strength. Despite his below-average speed, he has plenty of range for the position and can make all the plays necessary.

THE FUTURE: The play of Amed Rosario and Andres Gimenez, in addition to Arias' injury, meant he was unable to break into the lineup in 2022. Now, the organization is approaching a critical juncture with its current infield logjam. Rosario is only under contract for one more season and Arias and Tyler Freeman have already logged significant time at Triple-A, with Brayan Rocchio close behind them. Arias is ready to prove himself in the big leagues, though finding that opportunity in Cleveland may not be easy.

BA GRADE: 45/Medium	Hit: 45	Power: 50	Speed: 45	Fielding: 50	Arm: 55

Year	Age	Club (League)	Lvl	AVG	G	AB	R	H	2B	3B	HR	RBI	BB	SO	SB	OBP	SLG
2022	22	Guardians (ACL)	R	.231	5	13	2	3	1	0	0	0	3	7	1	.412	.308
2022	22	Columbus (IL)	AAA	.240	77	288	46	69	9	0	13	36	25	78	5	.310	.406
2022	22	Cleveland (AL)	MLB	.191	16	47	9	9	1	1	1	5	8	16	1	.321	.319
Major League Totals				.191	16	47	9	9	1	1	1	5	8	16	1	.321	.319
Minor League Totals				.269	494	1884	254	506	94	13	49	238	145	539	27	.325	.410

13 JUSTIN CAMPBELL, RHP

Born: Feb. 14, 2001. **B-T:** L-R. **HT:** 6-7. **WT:** 219.
Drafted: Oklahoma State, 2022 (1st round supplemental). **Signed by:** Ken Jarrett.

TRACK RECORD: Campbell arrived at Oklahoma State as a two-way player. While he made an immediate impact in both roles, he developed into the Cowboys' ace. He was an All-American in 2021 as a two-way player before focusing solely on pitching in 2022 and ranking seventh nationally with 141 strikeout.

SCOUTING REPORT: Listed at 6-foot-7, 219 pounds, Campbell has a long frame and has a loose, easy delivery. His fastball sits in the low 90s and reaches 95 mph with life up in the zone. He throws both a curveball and a slider. He can throw the curveball for a strike or as a chase pitch, while his slider works to keep righthanded hitters off balance. His changeup is perhaps his best pitch, earning plus grades thanks to its life and deception. He pitches with solid control and can throw strikes with all his offerings.

THE FUTURE: Campbell did not pitch after signing. He is advanced enough to make his professional debut in 2023 with High-A Lake County. He has the look of a back-of-the-rotation starter for now, but with the Guardians' developmental track record, a tick up in stuff and ceiling could be coming.

BA GRADE: 50/High	Fastball: 55	Curveball: 50	Slider: 50	Changeup: 60	Control: 55

Year	Age	Club (League)	Lvl	W	L	ERA	G	GS	IP	H	HR	BB	SO	BB/9	SO/9	WHIP	AVG
2022	21	Did not play															

14 JOSE TENA, SS

Born: March 20, 2001. **B-T:** L-R. **HT:** 5-10. **WT:** 190.
Signed: Dominican Republic, 2017. **Signed by:** Anthony Roa/Jhonathan Leyba.

TRACK RECORD: Cleveland's 2017 international class has developed into a blockbuster. Outfielder George Valera and shortstop Brayan Rocchio have been the headliners of this group, but Tena, a nephew of Juan Uribe, isn't far behind. He finished an impressive 2021 with the Arizona Fall League batting title (.387) and continued to hit in 2022, reaching Triple-A Columbus as a 21-year-old.

SCOUTING REPORT: Tena has a smaller frame that belies his ability. He has a loose, easy swing and good feel for the barrel, which allows him to consistently square up balls. He's an aggressive hitter who doesn't walk much and struck out in 25.1% of his plate appearances, a rate he'll have to manage while advancing toward the major leagues. He's an above-average runner and as he's physically matured has developed solid power potential. Tena has an above-average arm, good hands and solid range thanks to his speed and athleticism. He mostly has played shortstop as a professional, but also has seen time at second and third base. **THE FUTURE:** Tena is a part of the growing legion of talented middle infielders in the organization. His defensive versatility is an asset and could help him break through the crowd, but he'll likely start 2023 back in Columbus.

BA GRADE: 50/High		Hit: 55		Power: 45		Speed: 55			Fielding: 50		Arm: 55		

Year	Age	Club (League)	Lvl	AVG	G	AB	R	H	2B	3B	HR	RBI	BB	SO	SB	OBP	SLG
2022	21	Akron (EL)	AA	.264	127	516	74	136	25	6	13	66	25	138	8	.299	.411
2022	21	Columbus (IL)	AAA	.368	5	19	7	7	2	0	1	2	4	4	0	.478	.632
Minor League Totals				.286	334	1334	197	382	67	18	32	167	77	332	34	.329	.436

15 JAKE FOX, 2B/OF

Born: Feb. 12, 2003. **B-T:** L-R. **HT:** 6-0. **WT:** 180.
Drafted: HS—Lakeland, Fla., 2021 (3rd round). **Signed by:** Andrew Krause.
TRACK RECORD: Fox went strongly against the grain of the rest of the Guardians' 2021 draft class both as a position player and as a prep player. In both categories, he was one of just two players the club selected in their 21 picks. He's taken off in pro ball, first impressing in the Arizona Complex League after signing and then following that up with a solid season with low Class A Lynchburg as a 19-year-old.
SCOUTING REPORT: While Fox was an unusual pick for Cleveland in the context of the rest of its 2021 draft class, he has a familiar offensive profile for the organization. He has an unorthodox setup at the plate but has a loose, easy swing and a patient approach. He has a hit-over-power profile but has gotten stronger since getting into pro ball and he could grow into more. He's a plus runner and uses his speed well on the bases, where he is a threat to steal. Fox was drafted as a shortstop but was always unlikely to stay there because of his fringy arm strength. He primarily played second base in 2022 and his hands and infield actions are good enough to stay there, but he also played center field about a third of the time. His speed fits there and he will continue to develop at both positions.
THE FUTURE: Fox is off to a strong start to his professional career and his hittability and speed give him a pair of standout tools. He'll advance to high Class A Lake County for 2023.

BA GRADE: 50/High		Hit: 55		Power: 40		Speed: 60			Fielding: 50		Arm: 45		

Year	Age	Club (League)	Lvl	AVG	G	AB	R	H	2B	3B	HR	RBI	BB	SO	SB	OBP	SLG
2022	19	Lynchburg (CAR)	LoA	.247	104	380	74	94	25	4	5	44	74	90	21	.381	.374
Minor League Totals				.263	117	422	84	111	26	4	5	50	80	99	28	.389	.379

16 JUAN BRITO, 2B

Born: Sept. 24, 2001. **B-T:** B-R. **HT:** 5-11. **WT:** 162.
Signed: Dominican Republic, 2018. **Signed by:** Rolando Fernandez/Frank Roa (Rockies).
TRACK RECORD: Brito was an unheralded signing out of the Dominican Republic in 2018 by the Rockies. He's come on strong in the years since and made his full-season debut in 2022. He was traded to the Guardians in exchange for Nolan Jones and immediately was added to the 40-man roster.
SCOUTING REPORT: Brito fits in well with Cleveland's cadre of young middle infielders. He is a disciplined, patient hitter with good bat-to-ball skills. He has walked more than he's struck out over his professional career and in 2022 had just a 22% chase rate. While he has a contact-oriented approach, the switch-hitter has at least fringy power potential. He ranked fourth in the California League with 29 doubles. His swing has natural lift and as he gets stronger, he should grow into more pop. He's an average runner and is aggressive on the basepaths. Brito has primarily played second base as a professional and his average athleticism makes him a solid defender at the position. The Guardians believe he has the arm strength and range to see time on the left side of the infield as well.
THE FUTURE: Brito will make his organizational debut as a 21-year-old and he'll likely head to high Class A Lake County. His addition to the 40-man roster means that his developmental timeline is now facing a harder clock, but he gives the Guardians yet another high-upside middle infielder in their system.

BA GRADE: 50/High		Hit: 55		Power: 45		Speed: 50			Fielding: 55		Arm: 50		

Year	Age	Club (League)	Lvl	AVG	G	AB	R	H	2B	3B	HR	RBI	BB	SO	SB	OBP	SLG
2022	20	Fresno (CAL)	LoA	.286	107	402	91	115	29	6	11	72	78	71	17	.407	.470
Minor League Totals				.295	169	606	132	179	36	9	17	109	109	107	34	.406	.469

17 CODY MORRIS, RHP

Born: Nov. 4, 1996. **B-T:** R-R. **HT:** 6-4. **WT:** 205.
Drafted: South Carolina, 2018 (7th round). **Signed by:** Mike Bradford.

TRACK RECORD: Morris missed his freshman season at South Carolina due to Tommy John surgery before bouncing back to have a solid college career. Morris has continued to deal with injuries in pro ball, including a shoulder strain that cost him the first half of 2022, and has thrown just 171.1 innings in the minor leagues. However, when he's been healthy he's been impressive and he made his major league debut in September and was a part of the Guardians' playoff roster.

SCOUTING REPORT: Morris has a strong build and a powerful arm. His fastball reaches the upper 90s and sat at 95 mph in 2022. He mixes in a changeup, a sharp curveball and a cutter, which he added to his arsenal in 2021. His changeup is above-average, his cutter has quickly become a crucial pitch, and both account for about a third of his pitches. He pitches with average control, but when he's at his best, he shows even better command.

THE FUTURE: Injuries have been Morris' greatest obstacle as a professional and he hasn't had a full season since 2019. Despite that, he's gotten to the big leagues and shown he can have success at the level. He has the stuff to start, but as a 26-year-old who's never thrown more than 90 innings in a season (including college), a role in the bullpen may be where Morris fits best. He'll have a chance to start 2023 back with the Guardians.

BA GRADE: 50/High		Fastball: 60		Curveball: 45		Cutter: 50			Changeup: 55		Control: 50	

Year	Age	Club (League)	Lvl	W	L	ERA	G	GS	IP	H	HR	BB	SO	BB/9	SO/9	WHIP	AVG
2022	25	Guardians (ACL)	R	0	0	0.00	3	3	6	4	0	0	9	0.0	13.5	0.67	.190
2022	25	Columbus (IL)	AAA	0	0	2.35	6	3	15	5	2	6	30	3.5	17.6	0.72	.096
2022	25	Cleveland (AL)	MLB	1	2	2.28	7	5	24	21	3	12	23	4.6	8.7	1.39	.241
Major League Totals				1	2	2.28	7	5	24	21	3	12	23	4.6	8.7	1.39	.241
Minor League Totals				9	6	3.05	45	40	171	145	12	53	243	2.8	12.8	1.16	.226

18 JOEY CANTILLO, LHP

Born: Dec. 18, 1999. **B-T:** L-L. **HT:** 6-4. **WT:** 220.
Drafted: Kailua, Hawaii, 2017 (16th round). **Signed by:** Justin Baughman (Padres).

TRACK RECORD: Cantillo drew limited draft interest after his fastball sat in the mid 80s in high school, but the Padres were intrigued when he touched 91 mph in a pre-draft workout. They selected him in the 16th round and were able to sign him away from his Kentucky commitment. Cantillo rewarded that belief with a breakout 2019 season, when he led the organization with 144 strikeouts. He was traded to Cleveland at the 2020 trade deadline as a part of the return for Mike Clevinger. An oblique injury limited him to just 13 innings in 2021, but he made a strong impression with Double-A Akron in 2022 before a shoulder injury at the end of July ended his season.

SCOUTING REPORT: Cantillo long had a projectable look and his velocity had ticked up a bit while still with the Padres. He made a bigger move during the offseason and his fastball averaged 92 mph in 2022. Between the added velocity, the angle he throws from and the carry he gets on his fastball, the pitch has become an above-average offering capable of getting swings and misses. His changeup remains a plus pitch and generates swings and misses as well. He throws both a curveball and a slider, with the slider the more advanced of his breaking balls. He pitches with average control.

THE FUTURE: While injuries have slowed Cantillo in each of the last two seasons, the Guardians were still encouraged enough by his progress to add him to the 40-man roster in November. With a fully healthy 2023, he could pitch his way to Cleveland. Breaking into the Guardians' rotation is no easy task, but Cantillo has the tools to be a big league starter if he can maintain his velocity gains.

BA GRADE: 50/High		Fastball: 55		Curveball: 50		Slider: 50		Changeup: 60		Control: 50	

Year	Age	Club (League)	Lvl	W	L	ERA	G	GS	IP	H	HR	BB	SO	BB/9	SO/9	WHIP	AVG
2022	22	Akron (EL)	AA	4	3	1.93	14	13	61	38	2	28	87	4.2	12.9	1.09	.178
Minor League Totals				17	12	2.38	62	47	242	160	7	94	327	3.5	12.1	1.05	.186

19 PARKER MESSICK, LHP

Born: Oct. 26, 2000. **B-T:** L-L. **HT:** 6-0. **WT:** 225.
Drafted: Florida State, 2022 (2nd round). **Signed by:** Matt Linder.

TRACK RECORD: Messick starred at Florida State, where he was the Seminoles' ace for two seasons. He was named Atlantic Coast Conference pitcher of the year in 2021 and an All-American in 2022, piling up 270 strikeouts over 188.2 innings. The Guardians made him the 54th overall pick of the draft.

SCOUTING REPORT: Listed at 6-foot, 225 pounds, Messick has a short, stocky build. That belies his athleticism—he even showed some two-way ability in college—and he repeats his energetic delivery well, giving him above-average control. His pure stuff is not overpowering, as his fastball sits in the low 90s and touches 95 mph. He throws from a low release point, which helps him get swings and misses on his fastball at the top of the strike zone. His tumbling changeup is his best pitch and gives him a strong weapon against righthanded hitters. He throws two breaking balls, with his short slider roughly the equal of his curveball. He comes right after hitters and his feel for the game helps his entire arsenal play up.

THE FUTURE: Messick is advanced enough to make his professional debut in 2023 with high Class A Lake County and be a quick mover. His solid but unspectacular stuff makes him a potential back-of-the-rotation starter down the line, but with Cleveland's developmental track record, an eventual tick up for both his stuff and ceiling would be no surprise.

BA GRADE: 50/High	Fastball: 50	Curveball: 50	Slider: 50	Changeup: 55	Control: 55

Year	Age	Club (League)	Lvl	W	L	ERA	G	GS	IP	H	HR	BB	SO	BB/9	SO/9	WHIP	AVG
2022	21	Did not play															

20 JHONKENSY NOEL, OF/3B

Born: July 15, 2001. **B-T:** R-R. **HT:** 6-1. **WT:** 250.
Signed: Dominican Republic, 2017. **Signed by:** Domingo Toribio/Jhonathan Leyba.

TRACK RECORD: Another member of Cleveland's banner 2017 international class, Noel signed on his 16th birthday and debuted the following year in the Dominican Summer League. After a strong 2021 season that ended with High-A Lake County, he was added to the 40-man roster. He continued his aggressive progress in 2022 as he played at three different levels. He hit 32 home runs to lead all Guardians minor leaguers and reach Triple-A Columbus.

SCOUTING REPORT: Noel has a big, strong frame and produces tremendous bat speed and raw power. He regularly records elite exit velocities and doesn't have to sell out to get to his premium power. He's an aggressive hitter and struck out in 27% of his plate appearances in 2022, though that rate was actually better in Double-A Akron (22.7) than in Lake County (31.7). Noel primarily played the outfield in 2022 after previously being primarily a third baseman. His below-average range means third base is not his long-term future and he's still learning the outfield, where the hope is he can get to fringe-average with plenty of work.

THE FUTURE: Noel's raw power is tantalizing, and he could be a middle-of-the-order hitter. But as a right-right slugger who will play in a corner, there's a lot riding on his bat and he'll have to continue to develop as an overall hitter. He'll return to Columbus in 2023 and with the Guardians always looking for power, he could soon find his way to Cleveland.

BA GRADE: 50/Very High	Hit: 40	Power: 70	Speed: 45	Fielding: 45	Arm: 50

Year	Age	Club (League)	Lvl	AVG	G	AB	R	H	2B	3B	HR	RBI	BB	SO	SB	OBP	SLG
2022	20	Lake County (MWL)	HiA	.219	62	228	35	50	9	0	19	42	18	80	1	.286	.509
2022	20	Akron (EL)	AA	.242	67	240	43	58	16	2	13	42	30	63	2	.338	.488
2022	20	Columbus (IL)	AAA	.176	4	17	2	3	1	0	0	0	1	7	0	.222	.235
Minor League Totals				.266	314	1146	196	305	63	3	67	226	109	309	19	.343	.502

21 GABRIEL RODRIGUEZ, 3B

Born: Feb. 22, 2002. **B-T:** R-R. **HT:** 6-2. **WT:** 210.
Signed: Dominican Republic, 2018. **Signed by:** Hernan Albornoz.

TRACK RECORD: Rodriguez was the No. 8 prospect in the 2018 international class and headlined Cleveland's signing class that year. He has moved swiftly, reaching High-A Lake County as a 20-year-old in 2022, and has been among the youngest players at his level every step of the way.

SCOUTING REPORT: Rodriguez has a solid all-around skill set. He has a short, quick swing and can drive the ball to all fields. He projects for solid power as he physically matures and learns how to consistently employ the power-packed swing he demonstrates at times. He cut way down on his strikeouts in 2022, and struck out in just 19.9% of his plate appearances, while also increasing his walk rate to 9.4%, a positive sign for someone who has often been praised for his approach at the plate. Signed as a shortstop, Rodriguez has started to fill out his 6-foot-2 frame and primarily has played third base over the last two years. His strong arm and instinctive infield actions play well on the hot corner and he's likely to settle there over the long-term.

THE FUTURE: Rodriguez made encouraging progress in 2022, even while continuing to be one of the youngest players in his league. He'll look in 2023 to build on that momentum as he advances to Double-A Akron.

BA GRADE: 50/Very High		Hit: 45			Power: 55			Speed: 45			Fielding: 50			Arm: 55		

Year	Age	Club (League)	Lvl	AVG	G	AB	R	H	2B	3B	HR	RBI	BB	SO	SB	OBP	SLG
2022	20	Lake County (MWL)	HiA	.272	94	320	45	87	15	2	9	38	34	72	4	.343	.416
Minor League Totals				.248	247	901	121	223	43	7	15	111	78	232	11	.316	.361

22 XZAVION CURRY, RHP

Born: July 27, 1998. **B-T:** R-R. **HT:** 5-11. **WT:** 190.
Drafted: Georgia Tech, 2019 (7th round). **Signed by:** Ethan Purser.
TRACK RECORD: In 2017, Curry became the first true freshman to be Georgia Tech's Opening Day starter since 1995. He was a stalwart in the Yellow Jackets' rotation before being drafted by Cleveland. He broke out in 2021, and rose through three levels to reach Double-A. He continued that progress in 2022 and made his major league debut in August.
SCOUTING REPORT: Curry has an undersized frame and doesn't have overpowering stuff. His fastball sits around 93 mph and reaches the mid 90s, but it plays up thanks to its shape and spin rate. He locates the pitch well and can generate swings and misses with it. He relies heavily on his fastball, but also mixes in two breaking balls and a changeup. His slider has above-average potential and is his best secondary offering. Curry has always thrown a lot of strikes, but upper-level hitters tested his control more than previous opponents.
THE FUTURE: Curry's profile in Cleveland's pitching ranks has risen precipitously since the start of the 2021 season. His style meshes well with the Guardians' approach and his stuff fits a starter's profile. Breaking into Cleveland's rotation remains difficult, however, and Curry will have to continue to prove himself. He'll start 2023 with Triple-A Columbus.

BA GRADE: 45/High		Fastball: 55			Curveball: 50			Slider: 55			Changeup: 45		Control: 50		

Year	Age	Club (League)	Lvl	W	L	ERA	G	GS	IP	H	HR	BB	SO	BB/9	SO/9	WHIP	AVG
2022	23	Akron (EL)	AA	5	3	3.65	13	11	69	56	9	19	80	2.5	10.4	1.09	.218
2022	23	Columbus (IL)	AAA	4	1	4.58	12	10	53	50	9	23	54	3.9	9.2	1.38	.244
2022	23	Cleveland (AL)	MLB	0	1	5.79	2	2	9	13	1	6	3	5.8	2.9	2.04	.325
Major League Totals				0	1	5.79	2	2	9	13	1	6	3	5.8	2.9	2.04	.325
Minor League Totals				17	5	3.28	44	40	220	177	31	58	257	2.4	10.5	1.07	.215

23 ANGEL GENAO, SS

Born: May 19, 2003. **B-T:** B-R. **HT:** 6-0. **WT:** 165.
Signed: Dominican Republic, 2021. **Signed by:** Anthony Roa.
TRACK RECORD: Genao was Cleveland's top signing in the 2021 international market. He made his professional debut the following year in the Dominican Summer League and then made his U.S. debut in 2022. He followed an aggressive path, and earned a promotion to Low-A Lynchburg at the end of the season as a 19-year-old.
SCOUTING REPORT: Genao is a switch-hitter with an advanced, disciplined approach at the plate. He walked more than he struck out in the DSL (39 walks, 29 strikeouts) and while that ratio didn't carry over stateside, his barrel control and swing decisions still belie his age. His profile has always been hit over power and his 6-foot, 165-pound frame doesn't suggest much more power on the way, but he does have some pop, especially as a righthanded hitter. Genao is a savvy defender with all the tools to stay at shortstop. His infield actions, hands and plus arm strength all play well at the position.
THE FUTURE: Genao so far has lived up to his pre-signing billing and has put himself on an accelerated track. He joins the Guardians' burgeoning group of young shortstops and has significant promise, though he's still a long way from realizing it. He'll still be 19 on Opening Day as he returns to Lynchburg to begin the difficult task of his first year in full-season ball.

BA GRADE: 50/Extreme		Hit: 55			Power: 40			Speed: 50			Fielding: 55			Arm: 60		

Year	Age	Club (League)	Lvl	AVG	G	AB	R	H	2B	3B	HR	RBI	BB	SO	SB	OBP	SLG
2022	18	Guardians (ACL)	R	.322	38	149	22	48	6	1	2	18	16	40	6	.394	.416
2022	18	Lynchburg (CAR)	LoA	.179	8	28	3	5	1	0	0	3	4	5	0	.303	.214
Minor League Totals				.284	92	328	61	93	11	5	3	35	59	74	22	.400	.375

24 RICHIE PALACIOS, OF/2B

Born: May 16, 1997. **B-T:** L-R. **HT:** 5-10. **WT:** 180.
Drafted: Towson, 2018 (3rd round). **Signed by:** Aaron Etchison.

TRACK RECORD: Palacios had a decorated college career at Towson, where he became the fastest player in program history to reach 200 hits and set the program's single-season and career stolen base records. His professional career got off to a strong start in 2018 but he tore the labrum in his right shoulder that offseason and had season-ending surgery in March 2019. He's gotten back on track since getting healthy and made his major league debut in April 2022.

SCOUTING REPORT: Palacios has a good feel for the barrel and produces excellent bat speed. He has good plate discipline, knows how to work a walk and rarely strikes out. He has average power, which plays as doubles pop to this point. He's a good athlete with above-average speed. Where Palacios fits best defensively has long been a question. In Cleveland, he primarily played left field, which was a switch from the minor leagues, where he has mostly been a second baseman. His hands work on the infield, while his speed plays well in the outfield.

THE FUTURE: Having reached the major leagues, the challenge now for Palacios is to carve out a consistent role. It'll be up to his bat to make him a regular, but his speed, versatility and lefthanded swing all give him the tools to win a utility spot.

BA GRADE: 45/High		Hit: 50		Power: 45		Speed: 55		Fielding: 50		Arm: 45			
Year	Age	Club (League)	Lvl	AVG	G	AB	R	H	2B	3B	HR	RBI	BB	SO	SB	OBP	SLG
2022	25	Columbus (IL)	AAA	.279	45	179	34	50	10	5	4	36	24	43	12	.371	.458
2022	25	Cleveland (AL)	MLB	.232	54	112	7	26	6	0	0	10	9	20	2	.293	.286
Major League Totals				.232	54	112	7	26	6	0	0	10	9	20	2	.293	.286
Minor League Totals				.308	193	705	132	217	51	11	17	114	101	140	39	.400	.484

25 PETEY HALPIN, OF

Born: May 26, 2002. **B-T:** L-R. **HT:** 6-0. **WT:** 180.
Drafted: HS—Manhattan Beach, Calif., 2020 (3rd round). **Signed by:** Carlos Muniz.

TRACK RECORD: The Guardians have pushed Halpin aggressively since drafting him 95th overall in 2020. He was 19 years old on Opening Day 2022 and spent the season with High-A Lake County, where he was one of the youngest players in the Midwest League.

SCOUTING REPORT: Halpin has a top-of-the-order profile and a well-rounded skill set. He controls the strike zone well and makes adjustments quickly which helps him make a lot of contact. His swing is geared toward hitting line drives and he's not a slugger, but he drives the ball into gaps often. The combination of that hard contact and his above-average speed makes for a lot of extra-base hits. He's still learning to make the most of his speed on the bases, but he is a threat to run. Halpin has good outfield actions and an average arm. If he can stay in center field—where he's primarily played as a professional—he'd profile well. If he ends up in a corner, it would put more pressure on his bat.

THE FUTURE: Halpin has shown exciting offensive upside and has quickly found his stride in the professional ranks. He'll likely start 2023 with Double-A Akron.

BA GRADE: 45/High		Hit: 50		Power: 40		Speed: 55		Fielding: 50		Arm: 50			
Year	Age	Club (League)	Lvl	AVG	G	AB	R	H	2B	3B	HR	RBI	BB	SO	SB	OBP	SLG
2022	20	Lake County (MWL)	HiA	.262	105	382	68	100	21	4	6	36	45	92	16	.346	.385
Minor League Totals				.274	159	603	102	165	35	10	7	54	66	142	27	.353	.400

26 HUNTER GADDIS, RHP

Born: April 9, 1998. **B-T:** R-R. **HT:** 6-5. **WT:** 202.
Drafted: Georgia State, 2019 (5th round). **Signed by:** Ethan Purser.

TRACK RECORD: Gaddis became the highest drafted player out of Georgia State when Cleveland picked him in the fifth round in 2019. After a solid start to his professional career, he broke through in 2022 and made his major league debut in August.

SCOUTING REPORT: Gaddis first stands out for his size at 6-foot-5, 202 pounds and he also has solid stuff. His fastball averages about 94 mph with rising action. While it's ticked up as high as 97 mph in short stints, he hasn't shown that velocity as a starter. His changeup is his best pitch and earns plus grades. It is a very slow offering, about 15 mph slower than his fastball, and it is a swing-and-miss pitch. He also throws a slider, but it lags behind his other two pitches and doesn't miss many bats. He pitches with average control.

THE FUTURE: Gaddis struggled in two big league starts, in which he gave up seven home runs in 7.1 innings. That experience exposed some things he has to work on if he is to develop into a starter for the Guardians. Refining his breaking ball is a must, as he needs a third quality offering. His fastball/changeup combination would likely play up in the bullpen, however. Gaddis will likely open 2023 back at Triple-A Columbus to continue that development.

BA GRADE: 45/High		Fastball: 55		Slider: 45			Changeup: 60		Control: 50					
Year	Age	Club (League)	Lvl	W	L	ERA	G	GS	IP	H	HR	BB	SO	BB/9	SO/9	WHIP	AVG
2022	24	Akron (EL)	AA	4	3	4.24	15	14	76	63	12	26	102	3.1	12.0	1.17	.223
2022	24	Columbus (IL)	AAA	4	3	3.60	9	9	45	27	5	15	56	3.0	11.2	0.93	.171
2022	24	Cleveland (AL)	MLB	0	2	18.41	2	2	7	15	7	3	5	3.7	6.1	2.45	.405
Major League Totals				0	2	18.41	2	2	7	15	7	3	5	3.7	6.1	2.45	.405
Minor League Totals				13	20	3.90	57	53	252	197	39	76	338	2.7	12.1	1.08	.210

27 DOUG NIKHAZY, LHP

Born: Aug. 11, 1999. **B-T:** L-L. **HT:** 6-0. **WT:** 205.
Drafted: Mississippi, 2021 (2nd round). **Signed by:** C.T. Bradford.
TRACK RECORD: Nikhazy built a long track record of success at Mississippi. He earned Freshman All-America honors in 2019, pitched for USA Baseball's Collegiate National Team and was named a first-team All-American in 2021. His polish helped him hit the ground running in pro ball, as he debuted with high Class A Lake County and ended the season with Double-A Akron.
SCOUTING REPORT: Nikhazy has a slight frame and isn't overpowering but is an elite competitor. His fastball gets up to 94-95 mph, but typically sits around 90. It plays up thanks to his over-the-top arm slot and riding life on the pitch. He throws both a big, looping curveball and a slider that has late, biting action—both of which can be plus pitches. He also has a promising changeup. He pitched with above-average control in college only to struggle with strike-throwing in his professional debut. Shoring that up will be critical to his success.
THE FUTURE: Nikhazy had no trouble missing bats and his early success in the minor leagues is no surprise. An extended run in Double-A, which he'll get in 2023, will be more telling for his future. He'll have to show more consistency to succeed against better opposition.

BA GRADE: 45/High		Fastball: 45		Curveball: 60		Slider: 55		Changeup: 50		Control: 50				
Year	Age	Club (League)	Lvl	W	L	ERA	G	GS	IP	H	HR	BB	SO	BB/9	SO/9	WHIP	AVG
2022	22	Lake County (MWL)	HiA	4	4	3.19	21	21	93	59	8	68	118	6.6	11.4	1.37	.182
2022	22	Akron (EL)	AA	0	2	11.57	3	3	9	14	1	11	10	10.6	9.6	2.68	.359
Minor League Totals				4	6	3.96	24	24	102	73	9	79	128	6.9	11.3	1.49	.201

28 TANNER BURNS, RHP

Born: Dec. 28, 1998. **B-T:** R-R. **HT:** 6-0. **WT:** 210.
Drafted: Auburn, 2020 (1st round supplemental). **Signed by:** C.T. Bradford.
TRACK RECORD: A prominent player in high school who was the highest-rated player from the class of 2017 to make it to college, Burns stepped right into the rotation at Auburn. Cleveland in 2020 drafted him 36th overall, at the time the highest the organization had drafted a college pitcher since 2010. He spent 2022 at Double-A Akron, though he missed nearly all of May due to a shoulder strain.
SCOUTING REPORT: Burns has solid all-around stuff and a good understanding of pitching. His fastball sits 93-94 mph and reaches 97. It's a plus pitch that plays up thanks to his ability to consistently locate it. He throws both a big, 12-to-6 curveball and a slider/cutter hybrid that sits around 90 mph. His curveball has long been the better of his two breaking balls, but he has worked to reshape his slider and it is now a solid offering itself. He also mixes in a changeup with sinking action, but it lags behind his other pitches. He earns praise for his dedication to his craft and makeup.
THE FUTURE: Burns is a bit undersized, doesn't have the biggest pure stuff and has been banged up in each of the last two seasons. His aptitude and track record hint at further upside potential. He'll start 2023 with Triple-A Columbus.

BA GRADE: 45/High		Fastball: 60		Curveball: 55		Slider: 50		Changeup: 45		Control: 45				
Year	Age	Club (League)	Lvl	W	L	ERA	G	GS	IP	H	HR	BB	SO	BB/9	SO/9	WHIP	AVG
2022	23	Akron (EL)	AA	3	7	3.55	21	21	89	75	14	45	92	4.6	9.3	1.35	.227
Minor League Totals				5	12	3.56	39	39	164	139	24	74	183	4.1	10.0	1.30	.228

29 WILL BENSON, OF

Born: June 16, 1998. **B-T:** L-L. **HT:** 6-5. **WT:** 230.
Drafted: HS—Atlanta, 2016 (1st round). **Signed by:** CT Bradford.

TRACK RECORD: A heralded player coming out of the Atlanta prep ranks, Benson has long stood out for his athleticism and power. A first-round pick in 2016, he completed a long climb through the minor leagues in 2022 to make his major league debut as a 24-year-old.

SCOUTING REPORT: Benson produces exceptional bat speed thanks to his strength and quick hands. He turns that bat speed into big lefthanded raw power, and has consistently ranked among the organization's home run leaders. He significantly cut his strikeout rate in 2022, dropping it to 22.7% after it had been 30.8% in the three previous full seasons. That newfound discipline didn't come at the expense of his ability to take walks, as his patience has always been a defining part of his approach. He has solid speed and is a threat on the bases. Benson primarily has played right field in the minor leagues but is capable of playing all three outfield positions and did so in Cleveland. His arm strength and speed make him a solid defender.

THE FUTURE: Benson's combination of power and athleticism is exciting and he's worked hard to get to the major leagues. Whether he can turn that promise into a regular big league role will depend on his ability to make more consistent contact. Even if he ends up in a reserve role, he'll have value as a lefthanded hitter with power who can play all three outfield positions.

BA GRADE: 45/High		Hit: 45			Power: 60		Speed: 55			Fielding: 50			Arm: 50	
Year	Age	Club (League)	Lvl	AVG	G	AB	R	H	2B	3B	HR	RBI	BB	SO	SB	OBP	SLG
2022	24	Columbus (IL)	AAA	.278	89	316	75	88	20	3	17	45	75	91	16	.426	.522
2022	24	Cleveland (AL)	MLB	.182	28	55	8	10	1	0	0	3	3	19	0	.250	.200
Major League Totals				.182	28	55	8	10	1	0	0	3	3	19	0	.250	.200
Minor League Totals				.222	542	1881	332	417	88	23	94	295	352	680	86	.350	.443

30 BRYAN LAVASTIDA, C

Born: Nov. 27, 1998. **B-T:** R-R. **HT:** 6-0. **WT:** 200.
Drafted: Hillsborough (Fla.) JC, 2018 (15th round). **Signed by:** Steffan Segui.

TRACK RECORD: Lavastida was an infielder coming out of high school and converted to catching as a sophomore in junior college. Cleveland drafted him as a catcher in the 15th round in 2018 and continued to develop him behind the plate. He also impressed offensively, breaking out in 2021 to earn a spot on the 40-man roster. He made his major league debut in 2022, and started the year in Cleveland as the backup due to an injury to Luke Maile. He returned to Triple-A Columbus at the end of April and stayed there until late June when he suffered a hamstring injury, went on the injured list and then was sent to Double-A Akron for two months before returning to Columbus.

SCOUTING REPORT: Lavastida has a balanced swing and a good approach at the plate which allows him to control the strike zone well. He makes a lot of contact and has average raw power, though his line-drive oriented swing means he has more modest home run totals. Lavastida is a good athlete, moves well behind the plate and has average arm strength. He quickly picked up the mechanical aspects of catching and is continuing to progress with the finer points, like pitch-calling.

THE FUTURE: Lavastida had a clear arrow up following the 2021 season. Now, coming off a more challenging season, especially offensively, it appears his future as a backup catcher is clearer. The Guardians are ready to proceed with Bo Naylor as their future backstop, but the 24-year-old Lavastida still has potential as a big leaguer if he's able to get back on track at the plate.

BA GRADE: 45/High		Hit: 45			Power: 40		Speed: 50			Fielding: 50			Arm: 50	
Year	Age	Club (League)	Lvl	AVG	G	AB	R	H	2B	3B	HR	RBI	BB	SO	SB	OBP	SLG
2022	23	Akron (EL)	AA	.195	45	174	22	34	4	2	5	14	12	45	5	.257	.328
2022	23	Columbus (IL)	AAA	.224	39	147	24	33	6	2	4	16	16	35	2	.315	.374
2022	23	Cleveland (AL)	MLB	.083	6	12	0	1	0	0	0	0	3	4	0	.267	.083
Major League Totals				.083	6	12	0	1	0	0	0	0	3	4	0	.267	.083
Minor League Totals				.272	260	940	159	256	52	9	21	139	116	199	31	.360	.414

Colorado Rockies

BY GEOFF PONTES

The winds of change continued to howl throughout the Rockies organization in 2022 as alterations to personnel on the field and in the front office defined their season.

Interim general manager Bill Schmidt took over on a full-time basis, while team owner Dick Monfort's son Sterling took over as director of professional scouting.

Homegrown star shortstop Trevor Story left via free agency after 2021 for a lucrative long-term contract with the Red Sox. With Story's departure, Rockies fans bid adieu to a second homegrown star in as many years, leaving an ever-growing hole on the left side of the infield, following the trade of Nolan Arenado in early 2021.

While the last several seasons have been littered with departures, there were also arrivals of note. The Rockies splashed big in the post-lockout free agency frenzy, signing former Cubs star and National League MVP Kris Bryant to a seven-year, $182 million contract. Days later, they traded Raimel Tapia and prospect Adrian Pinto to the Blue Jays for slugging outfielder Randal Grichuk.

Despite the additions, the Rockies continued their downward spiral in 2022, when they finished in last place in the NL West with a record of 68-94. They finished the season as the fourth-worst team in the NL and tied for the eighth-worst record in the major leagues. They missed the playoffs for the fourth consecutive year and the 11th time over the past 13 seasons.

While times were tough in the major leagues in 2022, the Rockies' farm system was bursting at the seams with tantalizing talents who hint at a glimmer of promise.

Shortstop Ezequiel Tovar swung the bat well all spring, broke camp with Double-A Hartford and impressed over the early part of the season with a combination of contact and power at the plate and elite shortstop defense. By season's end, he was in the big leagues after a brief Triple-A stint following a lengthy stay on the injured list. Tovar looks like the Rockies' shortstop of the future and next homegrown star.

While Tovar's star shined brightest in 2022, there were plenty of other lights in the constellation. That group includes 2020 first-rounder Zac Veen, who cemented himself as one of the game's top prospects.

An exciting youth movement also began to take shape in Low-A Fresno and down through both of Colorado's Rookie complex league clubs, where a young crop of talented international signees emerged.

Players like shortstop Adael Amador, third

The Rockies' most notable rookie contributor was powerful 24-year-old Elehuris Montero.

PROJECTED 2026 LINEUP

Catcher	Drew Romo	24
First Base	Elehuris Montero	27
Second Base	Brendan Rodgers	29
Third Base	Ryan McMahon	31
Shortstop	Ezequiel Tovar	24
Left Field	Sterlin Thompson	24
Center Field	Benny Montgomery	23
Right Field	Zac Veen	24
Designated Hitter	Kris Bryant	34
No. 1 Starter	German Marquez	31
No. 2 Starter	Kyle Freeland	32
No. 3 Starter	Gabriel Hughes	24
No. 4 Starter	Antonio Senzatela	31
No. 5 Starter	Jordy Vargas	22
Closer	Tyler Kinley	35

baseman Warming Bernabel, outfielders Yanquiel Fernandez and Juan Guerrero as well as righthanders Jordy Vargas, Victor Juarez and Angel Chivilli all hinted at promising futures.

The Rockies continued to build their farm by adding a deep crop of reinforcements via the draft, selecting five players among the top 90 picks. That haul included Gonzaga righthander Gabriel Hughes with the No. 10 overall pick, as well as college stars Sterlin Thompson of Florida and Jordan Beck of Tennessee. All three rank among Colorado's top 10 prospects.

While the short-term forecast in Denver is cloudy, a deep farm system gives the Rockies hope for a sunny tomorrow. ∎

DEPTH CHART

COLORADO ROCKIES

TOP 2023 MLB CONTRIBUTORS	RANK
Ezequiel Tovar, SS	1
Michael Toglia, 1B	16
BREAKOUT PROSPECTS	**RANK**
Angel Chivilli, RHP	20
Bryant Betancourt, C	27
Ryan Ritter, SS	28

SOURCE OF TOP 30 TALENT

Homegrown	28	Acquired	2
College	12	Trade	2
Junior college	0	Rule 5 draft	0
High school	4	Independent league	0
Nondrafted free agent	0	Free agent/waivers	0
International	12		

LF
Yanquiel Fernandez (13)
Nolan Jones (19)
Juan Guerrero (22)
Zach Kokoska
Brad Cumbest

CF
Benny Montgomery (6)
Brenton Doyle (21)
Braiden Ward
Bladimir Restituyo

RF
Zac Veen (2)
Sterlin Thompson (8)
Jordan Beck (10)
Robby Martin Jr.

3B
Warming Bernabel (7)
Aaron Schunk

SS
Ezequiel Tovar (1)
Adael Amador (4)
Julio Carreras (18)
Dyan Jorge (23)
Ryan Ritter (28)

2B
Eddy Diaz
Hunter Stovall
Jack Blomgren

1B
Michael Toglia (16)
Grant Lavigne
Cuba Bess

C
Drew Romo (3)
Hunter Goodman (14)
Bryant Betancourt (27)
Ronaiker Palma
Willie MacIver

LHP

LHSP	LHRP
Carson Palmquist (24)	Alberto Pacheco (26)
Ryan Rolison	Michael Prosecky (30)
Nick Bush	Sam Weatherly
Evan Shawver	Evan Justice
Helcris Olivarez	
Mason Green	

RHP

RHSP	RHRP
Gabriel Hughes (5)	Angel Chivilli (20)
Jordy Vargas (9)	Gavin Hollowell (25)
Jackson Cox (11)	Blair Calvo
Victor Juarez (12)	Riley Pint
Jaden Hill (15)	Zach Agnos
Jeff Crsiwell (17)	
Connor Staine (29)	
Karl Kauffmann	

1 EZEQUIEL TOVAR, SS

Born: Aug. 1, 2001. **B-T:** R-R. **HT:** 6-0. **WT:** 162.
Signed: Venezuela, 2017.
Signed by: Rolando Fernandez/Orlando Medina.

TRACK RECORD: Since signing for $800,000 on his 16th birthday in 2017, Tovar has progressed each year on his way to ranking as one of the top prospects in baseball. He spent all of the 2020 pandemic working out at the Rockies' facility in Arizona because he was unable to return home to Venezuela. Over that time period, Tovar made substantial changes. He added strength and good weight and stopped switch-hitting in favor of batting righthanded only. The hard work paid off. Tovar broke out in his full-season debut in 2021, hitting .309/.346/.510 over 72 games with Low-A Fresno before being promoted to High-A Spokane for the final few months of the season. He was assigned to Double-A Hartford out of camp in 2022, making Tovar the third-youngest player to open the season in the Eastern League. Over the first few months of the season, Tovar impressed by hitting .318/.386/.545 with 13 home runs and 17 stolen bases in 66 games. Tovar went down in late June with a hip/groin injury that required a two-month stint on the injured list. Tovar returned in mid September, playing five games with Triple-A Albuquerque before he was called up to Colorado to make his MLB debut on Sept. 23 and he started nine of the Rockies' final 12 games of the season.
SCOUTING REPORT: Tovar is a talented all-around shortstop capable of impacting the game on both sides of the ball in a variety of ways. With a lanky build, Tovar lacks mass but has wiry strength and twitch that allow him to generate power at the plate and on his throws. His offensive profile is heavily driven by his above-average bat-to-ball skills and plus bat speed. An aggressive swinger, Tovar looks to put the ball in play and do damage. While his swing decisions are still less than ideal, he has an innate ability to adjust the barrel and make flush contact all over the zone. While his exit velocity data is below-average, Tovar's power plays up in games due to bat speed and the ability to strike his hardest hit balls at optimal launch angles. As Tovar adds strength to his frame and refinement to his approach in the coming years, he should blossom into an impact hitter. He's a plus runner and instinctual basestealer who is an asset as a baserunner, and his speed and quickness translates to the field. One of the best shortstop defenders in

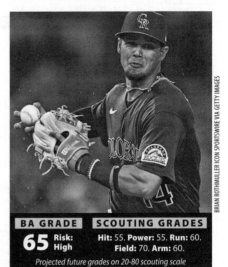

BRIAN ROTHMULLER/ICON SPORTSWIRE VIA GETTY IMAGES

BA GRADE	SCOUTING GRADES
65 Risk: High	Hit: 55. Power: 55. Run: 60. Field: 70. Arm: 60.
	Projected future grades on 20-80 scouting scale

BEST TOOLS

BATTING

Best Hitter for Average	Adael Amador
Best Power Hitter	Hunter Goodman
Best Strike-Zone Discipline	Zac Veen
Fastest Baserunner	Braiden Ward
Best Athlete	Juan Guerrero

PITCHING

Best Fastball	Gabriel Hughes
Best Curveball	Jordy Vargas
Best Slider	McCade Brown
Best Changeup	Jaden Hill
Best Control	Gabriel Barbosa

FIELDING

Best Defensive Catcher	Drew Romo
Best Defensive Infielder	Ezequiel Tovar
Best Infield Arm	Ezequiel Tovar
Best Defensive Outfielder	Benny Montgomery
Best Outfield Arm	Yanquiel Fernandez

the minors, Tovar is rangy and fluid at the position and moves to his right and left with ease. He showcases a plus arm and is capable of making all the necessary throws with an easy arm action. With an excellent internal clock, infield actions and soft hands, Tovar is capable of developing into one of the best defensive shortstops in the major leagues.
THE FUTURE: Tovar is a future everyday shortstop with above-average offensive potential. He is a cornerstone of the Rockies' lengthy rebuild. After making his MLB debut at the end of 2022, Tovar is poised to spend a majority of his 2023 season in Colorado and should be the team's shortstop for years to come.

Year	Age	Club (League)	Lvl	AVG	G	AB	R	H	2B	3B	HR	RBI	BB	SO	SB	OBP	SLG
2022	20	Hartford (EL)	AA	.318	66	264	39	84	15	3	13	47	25	64	17	.386	.545
2022	20	Albuquerque (PCL)	AAA	.333	5	21	3	7	0	0	1	2	2	2	0	.391	.476
2022	20	Colorado (NL)	MLB	.212	9	33	2	7	1	0	1	2	2	9	0	.257	.333
Major League Totals				.212	9	33	2	7	1	0	1	2	2	9	0	.257	.333
Minor League Totals				.283	283	1136	184	322	55	14	31	148	92	225	74	.343	.438

2 ZAC VEEN, OF

Born: Dec. 12, 2001. **B-T:** L-R. **HT:** 6-4. **WT:** 190.
Drafted: HS—Port Orange, Fla., 2020 (1st round). **Signed by:** John Cedarburg.
TRACK RECORD: Veen ranked as the top high school player in the 2020 draft, and the Rockies selected him with the ninth pick and signed him for an above-slot $5 million. He made his pro debut with Low-A Fresno in 2021 and hit .301/.399/.501 with 15 home runs and 36 stolen bases in 106 games. He was assigned to High-A Spokane out of camp in 2022 and once again produced a well above-average line. Veen was promoted to Double-A Hartford in early August but he struggled for 34 games before ending his campaign in the Arizona Fall League.

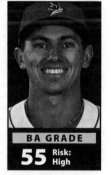

BA GRADE
55 Risk: High

SCOUTING REPORT: Veen is a lean 6-foot-4 with projectable strength and long levers. He has yet to add noticeable physical strength or mass early in his career. Veen's offensive profile is heavily based around his advanced plate discipline and average bat-to-ball skills. He prides himself on making pitchers grind and consistently works deep into at-bats. There's some swing-and-miss in Veen's game due to the length of his levers and mechanisms of his swing, but he manages to keep his strikeouts in check by rarely expanding the zone. Veen's power numbers and underlying exit velocity data is fringe-average, but added strength in the coming years and some tweaks to his swing could translate to above-average power at peak. While Veen may slow down over time, his advanced instincts and explosiveness should allow him to be a basestealing threat. He's an average outfielder capable of handling center field in a pinch but is best in a corner. He has an average, accurate arm and a quick release that would fit best in left field.
THE FUTURE: Veen should develop into an above-average offensive performer capable of hitting for average and producing some of the higher on-base percentages in baseball.

SCOUTING GRADES	Hitting: 60	Power: 50	Speed: 60	Fielding: 50	Arm: 50

Year	Age	Club (League)	Lvl	AVG	G	AB	R	H	2B	3B	HR	RBI	BB	SO	SB	OBP	SLG
2022	20	Spokane (NWL)	HiA	.269	92	342	72	92	19	3	11	60	50	90	50	.368	.439
2022	20	Hartford (EL)	AA	.177	34	124	12	22	4	0	1	7	14	42	5	.262	.234
Minor League Totals				.271	232	865	167	234	50	7	27	142	128	258	91	.368	.438

3 DREW ROMO, C

Born: Aug. 29, 2001. **B-T:** B-R. **HT:** 6-1. **WT:** 205.
Drafted: HS—The Woodlands, Texas, 2020 (1st round supp). **Signed by:** Jeff Edwards.
TRACK RECORD: Heralded as one of the top defensive catchers in recent memory during his time on the prep circuit, Romo was drafted by the Rockies with the 35th overall pick in 2020. He signed for slot value of $2,095,800 to forgo a Louisiana State commitment. Romo debuted with Low-A Fresno the following year and hit .314/.345/.439 in 79 games. He was assigned to High-A Spokane out of camp in 2022, made 56 starts at catcher and hit .254/.321/.372 in 101 games.

BA GRADE
55 Risk: High

SCOUTING REPORT: A switch-hitting high school catcher is a risky demographic, but Romo's game exudes polish and maturity. At the plate, Romo is a contact-over-power hitter with a swing-happy approach. His righthanded swing is more advanced than his lefthanded one, with a majority of Romo's best-struck balls coming from the right side. He generates more consistent contact quality while displaying better plate discipline as a righthanded hitter. Despite the gap in production, his two swings are similar mechanically. Romo's bat-to-ball skills are above-average and he uses a short, compact swing from both sides of the plate geared toward stinging line drives to the gaps. His raw power is below-average and is not a major part of his game. His speed is fringe-average, but he's a capable baserunner with good instincts. Behind the plate, Romo is a standout defender with a plus arm that consistently produces pop times in the range of 1.9 seconds on throws to second base. He's an athletic catcher who is comfortable in the crouch and moves well behind the plate. He's an average framer and earns rave reviews for his ability to handle a pitching staff.
THE FUTURE: Romo is a young, talented defensive catcher with above-average bat-to-ball skills who projects to be an everyday player capable of hitting for a high batting average in his peak seasons.

SCOUTING GRADES	Hitting: 55	Power: 40	Speed: 45	Fielding: 70	Arm: 60

Year	Age	Club (League)	Lvl	AVG	G	AB	R	H	2B	3B	HR	RBI	BB	SO	SB	OBP	SLG
2022	20	Spokane (NWL)	HiA	.254	101	374	52	95	19	5	5	58	35	81	18	.321	.372
Minor League Totals				.281	180	686	100	193	36	7	11	105	54	131	41	.332	.402

4 ADAEL AMADOR, SS

Born: April 11, 2003. **B-T:** B-R. **HT:** 6-0. **WT:** 160.
Signed: Dominican Republic, 2019. **Signed by:** Rolando Fernandez/Martin Cabrera.

TRACK RECORD: Signed during the 2019 international period for $1.5 million, Amador was a well-known talent as amateur who starred for the Dominican Republic's U-15 team. He debuted in the Arizona Complex League in the summer of 2021, hitting .299/.394/.445 in 47 games. Assigned to Low-A Fresno out of camp in 2022, Amador spent the entire season with the Grizzlies and hit .292/.415/.455 in 115 games.

BA GRADE
55 Risk: High

SCOUTING REPORT: Few hitters in the Rockies' system are as skilled and naturally gifted as Amador, who is potentially just scratching the surface of his upside. A switch-hitter with a contact-oriented but patient approach, he employs two distinctly different swings. His righthanded swing is closed with few moving parts, while his lefthanded setup is open with a leg kick timing mechanism. He's a slightly better contact hitter from the right side but projects as an easy plus hitter with high walk rates from either side of the plate. Amador's power is below-average, and with a slight build and level bat path, he's unlikely to project for more than mid-teens home run power at peak—though some evaluators haven't ruled out average power. Despite high stolen base totals in Low-A, Amador is a fringe-average runner who will likely see his steals dwindle as he ages. Defensively, Amador's actions and hands are average for a shortstop. He shows good game awareness but lacks quickness in his first step or a truly average infield arm. Amador projects best at second base, with the ability to be an above-average defender.

THE FUTURE: Amador at present is a hit-over-power second baseman with elite bat-to-ball and on-base skills for a teenager. With added power and improvements to his first step and arm, he could develop into an above-average everyday infielder.

SCOUTING GRADES	Hitting: 65	Power: 45	Speed: 45	Fielding: 50	Arm: 45

Year	Age	Club (League	Lvl	AVG	G	AB	R	H	2B	3B	HR	RBI	BB	SO	SB	OBP	SLG
2022	19	Fresno (CAL)	LoA	.292	115	449	100	131	24	0	15	57	87	67	26	.415	.445
Minor League Totals				.294	162	613	141	180	34	1	19	81	114	96	36	.409	.445

5 GABRIEL HUGHES, RHP

Born: Aug. 22, 2001. **B-T:** R-R. **HT:** 6-4. **WT:** 220.
Drafted: Gonzaga, 2022 (1st round). **Signed by:** Matt Pignataro.

TRACK RECORD: The grandson of former Tigers minor leaguer Don Hughes, Gabriel spent his first two seasons with Gonzaga as a two-way player. He was selected for the roster of USA Baseball's Collegiate National Team in summer of 2021 and converted to full-time pitching for the Zags the following spring. Hughes went 8-3, 3.21 in 15 starts with Gonzaga in 2022, earning second team All-America honors while compiling 138 strikeouts to 37 walks over 98 innings. The Rockies selected Hughes with the 10th overall pick and signed him to a below-slot bonus of $4 million. He made his pro debut on Sept. 10 with Low-A Fresno.

BA GRADE
50 Risk: High

SCOUTING REPORT: A big-bodied righthander with broad shoulders and natural strength throughout his frame, Hughes has little trouble generating power across his four-pitch mix. He works from a semi-windup with a large leg lift before he gives way to an uptempo move toward the plate and a long, extended arm action. His fastball sat 93-94 mph and touched 97 in the spring, but he was sitting 95-97 mph touching 98 in his three-inning pro debut. Hughes' fastball relies heavily on power with only average vertical break and some late cut. His fastball command took a significant jump as he cut his walk rate in the spring with Gonzaga and showed potential for average command. Hughes' primary secondary is a short slider with moderate spin rates that sits 83-85 mph. He used a cut fastball in his pro debut in the lower 90s that could be an added wrinkle to his arsenal. Hughes will also show a changeup in the low-to-mid 80s that will flash above-average, but he has not been able to consistently execute the pitch.

THE FUTURE: There's the makings of a potential midrotation starter if Hughes can improve his secondary offerings. If not, he has the potential to air it out as a two-pitch reliever.

SCOUTING GRADES	Fastball: 60	Slider: 55	Changeup: 45	Cutter: 50	Control: 50

Year	Age	Club (League	Lvl	W	L	ERA	G	GS	IP	H	HR	BB	SO	BB/9	SO/9	WHIP	AVG
2022	20	Fresno (CAL)	LoA	0	0	0.00	1	1	3	1	0	1	1	3.0	3.0	0.67	.100
Minor League Totals				0	0	0.00	1	1	3	1	0	1	1	3.0	3.0	0.67	.100

6 BENNY MONTGOMERY, OF

Born: Sept. 9, 2002. **B-T:** R-R. **HT:** 6-4. **WT:** 200.
Drafted: HS—Lewisberry, Pa.., 2021 (1st round). **Signed by:** Ed Santa.

BA GRADE

55 Risk: **Extreme**

TRACK RECORD: One of the top high school players in the 2021 draft, Montgomery flashed impressive tools and athleticism during his draft summer. He was selected by the Rockies eighth overall and signed for $5 million, the highest bonus in history for a Pennsylvania high school player. He debuted in the Arizona Complex League by hitting .340/.404/.383 in 14 games. Assigned to Low-A Fresno in 2022, Montgomery made 56 starts while dealing with two stints on the injured list for a quadriceps injury. He returned to the Fresno lineup on July 6 and hit .329/.420/.526 with 18 doubles, two triples and four home runs over his final 41 games.

SCOUTING REPORT: It's easy to dream on Montgomery's tantalizing tools, especially plus raw power and double-plus speed. While Montgomery has elite athleticism and twitch, his overall skills and swing are still raw. His setup at the plate has been a point of much debate dating back years. Montgomery has gone through multiple iterations of his swing with different levels of pre-pitch hand movement. His swing employs a high leg kick, a hand pump, a bat wrap and arm bar at the point of contact. Despite multiple mechanical red flags, Montgomery produced consistent hard contact in 2022. He faces questions about his approach and bat-to-ball skills due to a high whiff rate and high chase rate. Montgomery's raw power is plus, as evidenced by his standout 90th percentile exit velocity of 104.4 mph, and his speed should impact the game on both sides of the ball. Defensively, Montgomery has the speed, athleticism and skills to handle center field with a plus arm.

THE FUTURE: Few players in the game have the loud tools that Montgomery possesses, but it's a matter of him adding refinement and developing into an above-average regular center fielder.

SCOUTING GRADES	Hitting: 40		Power: 55		Speed: 70			Fielding: 60		Arm: 60	

Year	Age	Club (League)	Lvl	AVG	G	AB	R	H	2B	3B	HR	RBI	BB	SO	SB	OBP	SLG
2022	19	Rockies (ACL)	R	.273	6	22	3	6	1	1	0	2	0	6	0	.273	.409
2022	19	Fresno (CAL)	LoA	.313	56	233	48	73	20	3	6	42	21	71	9	.394	.502
Minor League Totals				.315	76	302	58	95	21	5	6	50	26	86	14	.388	.477

7 WARMING BERNABEL, 3B

Born: Aug. 6, 2002. **B-T:** R-R. **HT:** 6-0. **WT:** 180.
Signed: Dominican Republic, 2018. **Signed by:** Rolando Fernandez/Martin Cabrera.

BA GRADE

50 Risk: **High**

TRACK RECORD: The Rockies signed Bernabel out of the Dominican Republic for $900,000 in 2018. In the years since, he has developed into one of the best hitting prospects in their system. He had a strong 2021 campaign between the Arizona Complex League and Low-A Fresno, hitting .312/.367/.516 in 43 games. Bernabel was assigned to Low-A Fresno out of camp in 2022 and hit .317/.390/.504 with 10 home runs and just a 13% strikeout rate in 65 games. He was promoted to High-A Spokane in early July and hit .305/.315/.486 in 26 games before going down with an ankle injury in late August. Bernabel resurfaced in the Arizona Fall League, where he struggled over 15 games for Salt River.

SCOUTING REPORT: Bernabel offers a offensive-oriented profile with elite bat-to-ball skills, an aggressive approach and bat speed-driven power. His ability to make consistent contact is his standout tool. He has rarely struck out during his professional career, with just 13.4% of his professional plate appearances ending with a strikeout. Bernabel has projectable power, but he likely peaks with average home run totals. While he has above-average bat speed, Bernabel will have to make changes to his setup in order to tap into his full raw juice. Defensively, Bernabel is a fringe-average third baseman with an average arm. He faces questions around his ability to stick there long term due to a lack of elite arm strength and first-step quickness.

THE FUTURE: Bernabel has the offensive skill set that could fit as a big league corner infielder.

SCOUTING GRADES	Hitting: 55		Power: 45		Speed: 45			Fielding: 45		Arm: 50	

Year	Age	Club (League)	Lvl	AVG	G	AB	R	H	2B	3B	HR	RBI	BB	SO	SB	OBP	SLG
2022	20	Fresno (CAL)	LoA	.317	65	262	52	83	19	0	10	54	29	39	21	.390	.504
2022	20	Spokane (NWL)	HiA	.305	26	105	18	32	7	0	4	17	2	17	2	.315	.486
Minor League Totals				.295	189	736	134	217	50	2	25	140	59	111	35	.355	.470

8 STERLIN THOMPSON, OF

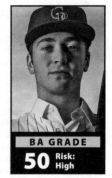

Born: June 26, 2001. **B-T:** L-R. **HT:** 6-4. **WT:** 200.
Drafted: Florida, 2022 (1st round). **Signed by:** John Cedarburg.

TRACK RECORD: A highly rated draft prospect as a prep, Thompson made it to campus at Florida and showed the advanced hitting skills he had been known for in high school. He hit .301/.396/.470 as a freshman and followed that up with a .351/.444/.559 line as draft-eligible sophomore in 2022. The Rockies selected Thompson with the 31st overall pick and signed him for the slot value of $2.41 million. He debuted in the Arizona Complex League in early August before a promotion to Low-A Fresno after 15 games.

SCOUTING REPORT: One of the best pure hitters in the 2022 college class, Thompson is a 6-foot-4, physical player who projects to add strength. At the plate, his game is heavily based around his well above-average bat-to-ball skills

BA GRADE

50 Risk: High

and balance of aggression and patience within his approach. His lefthanded swing is heavily geared toward opposite-field contact. It's a simple, hands-driven swing with a flatter bat path, making it most conducive to producing line-drive contact. While Thompson's raw power flashes above-average based on early exit velocity data in pro ball, his swing will be a hindrance in the pursuit of power development. For now, he projects to have average power without a concerted effort to hit more balls out in front. Defensively, Thompson has split time between third base and the corner outfield positions. He is unlikely to stick at third base due to subpar actions and footwork. His plus arm will allow him to make up for below-average speed in an outfield corner. His long-term home is likely left field.

THE FUTURE: Thompson offers a hit-over-power corner outfield profile, but he has enough power projection to dream on.

SCOUTING GRADES	Hitting: 55	Power: 50	Speed: 45	Fielding: 45	Arm: 60

Year	Age	Club (League)	Lvl	AVG	G	AB	R	H	2B	3B	HR	RBI	BB	SO	SB	OBP	SLG
2022	21	Rockies (ACL)	R	.273	15	55	9	15	3	0	1	6	2	16	1	.328	.382
2022	21	Fresno (CAL)	LoA	.348	11	46	9	16	4	0	1	4	3	12	2	.380	.500
Minor League Totals				.307	26	101	18	31	7	0	2	10	5	28	3	.351	.436

9 JORDY VARGAS, RHP

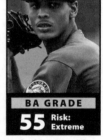

Born: Nov. 6, 2003. **B-T:** R-R. **HT:** 6-3. **WT:** 153.
Signed: Dominican Republic, 2021. **Signed by:** Rolando Fernandez/Manuel Cabrera.

TRACK RECORD: Vargas is the son of nine-year big league lefthander Yorkis Perez. The Rockies signed the highly-rated amateur out of the Dominican Republic for $500,000 in 2021. Vargas debuted in the Dominican Summer League in 2021 and pitched to an impressive 1.30 ERA with 46 strikeouts in 34.2 innings. Vargas made his U.S. debut in 2022 by making seven appearances in the Arizona Complex League, quickly earning a promotion to Low-A Fresno in early August and made six starts over the final month. He impressed at Low-A with a 3.65 ERA and 24 strikeouts over 24.2 innings.

SCOUTING REPORT: Vargas is a young, projectable righthander already flashing starter traits at 19 years old. His thin, wiry frame and slight build don't

BA GRADE

55 Risk: Extreme

project to add much physicality, but he should maintain a high level of fitness and athleticism. These traits translate to an easy, free-throwing motion. Vargas works from a tall-and-fall operation, delivering the ball from a high three-quarters arm slot. He mixes a trio of offerings led by his low-to-mid-90s four-seam fastball and a mid-70s two-plane curveball with depth and heavy horizontal break. He shows the makings of an average or better changeup in the mid 80s but is still inconsistent in executing it. Overall, Vargas shows the makings of three average or better pitches with potential for above-average command. While he manages to execute his fastball and curveball combination in a north-south manner effectively, he'll need to diversify his pitch usage as he advances up the minor league ladder.

THE FUTURE: A projectable and talented pitching prospect with hints of starter traits and feel for a three-pitch arsenal, Vargas has No. 3 starter upside.

SCOUTING GRADES	Fastball: 50	Curveball: 60	Changeup: 45	Control: 50

Year	Age	Club (League)	Lvl	W	L	ERA	G	GS	IP	H	HR	BB	SO	BB/9	SO/9	WHIP	AVG
2022	18	Rockies (ACL)	R	2	1	2.36	7	5	27	13	0	4	40	1.4	13.5	0.64	.141
2022	18	Fresno (CAL)	LoA	2	0	3.65	6	6	25	20	5	13	24	4.7	8.8	1.34	.225
Minor League Totals				6	1	2.30	24	20	86	51	5	33	110	3.5	11.5	0.98	.167

10 JORDAN BECK, OF

Born: April 19, 2001. **B-T:** R-R. **HT:** 6-3. **WT:** 225.
Drafted: Tennessee, 2022 (1st round supplemental). **Signed by:** Scott Corman.

TRACK RECORD: Beck developed into one of the better power hitters in college baseball during his three seasons with Tennessee. He entered 2022 as one of the highest-rated draft-eligible college position players and hit .298/.391/.595 with 18 home runs in 66 games. The Rockies selected Beck with the 38th overall pick and signed him for an above-slot $2.2 million. He made his pro debut in the Arizona Complex League before a promotion to Low-A Fresno over the final weeks of the 2022 season.

SCOUTING REPORT: A physically gifted player, Beck was one of the top athletes in the 2022 college draft class. He has a strong, physical frame with natural strength and explosiveness throughout his game. Beck's early professional returns have shown average bat-to-ball skills, but scouts have concerns around his ability to hit quality pitching. His swing and bat path drive these concerns because he has a tendency to impact the ball at too steep an angle, leading to popups and weakly hit fly balls. His swing is heavily hands-driven and lacks adjustability due to a long, extended hand load and a longer uppercut swing path that's too stiff to turn on pitches in on his hands. Beck struggled against spin as an amateur and that trend continued as a professional. Despite these concerns, Beck possesses some of the best game power in the Rockies' system with notable exit velocities. Defensively, Beck profiles as an above-average defender in an outfield corner, with above-average running ability and an above-average arm.

THE FUTURE: Beck offers a prototype power-hitting corner outfield profile. If he can make incremental improvements to his contact skills and approach, he should develop into an average corner outfielder.

SCOUTING GRADES		Hitting: 45		Power: 60		Speed: 55			Fielding: 55		Arm: 55	

Year	Age	Club (League)	Lvl	AVG	G	AB	R	H	2B	3B	HR	RBI	BB	SO	SB	OBP	SLG
2022	21	Rockies (ACL)	R	.306	15	49	9	15	5	0	1	10	8	11	0	.404	.469
2022	21	Fresno (CAL)	LoA	.282	11	39	11	11	2	0	2	9	13	9	0	.462	.487
Minor League Totals				.295	26	88	20	26	7	0	3	19	21	20	0	.431	.477

11 JACKSON COX, RHP

Born: Sept. 25, 2003. **B-T:** R-R. **HT:** 6-0. **WT:** 185.
Drafted: HS—Toutle, Wash., 2022 (2nd round) **Signed by:** Matt Pignataro.

TRACK RECORD: A high-upside prep talent out of the Pacific Northwest, Cox features a hellacious, high-spin breaking ball that kept prep hitters' knees buckling throughout his draft summer. Heading into his senior season, Cox added strength and cleaned up his operation and saw sizable stuff gains. The Rockies selected Cox in the second round with the No. 50 overall pick and signed him for $1.85 million. Cox was rested following the draft and will officially debut in 2023.

SCOUTING REPORT: Cox is capable of reaching elite spin rates on his fastball and had one of the best breaking balls in the 2022 prep class. He has a projectable, athletic build and should add size without sacrificing his athleticism. Cox needs to clean up some elements of his delivery, particularly when it comes to the consistency of his plant foot. His fastball sits between 92-95 mph and has peaked at 98 mph with heavy sink. His curveball is a potentially plus pitch that sits between 79-83 mph, averages 3,000 rpm of spin and displays two-plane break. His mid-80s changeup is fringy but could reach average with further development. Cox commands his entire arsenal well, hinting at potential above-average command at peak.

THE FUTURE: Cox is the type of high-upside prep arm the Rockies haven't targeted in years. He's a high-variance prospect with a midrotation ceiling and should debut at Low-A in 2023.

BA GRADE: 55/Extreme		Fastball: 55		Curveball: 60	Changeup: 45		Control: 50	

Year	Age	Club (League	Lvl	W	L	ERA	G	GS	IP	H	HR	BB	SO	BB/9	SO/9	WHIP	AVG
2022	18	Did not play															

12 VICTOR JUAREZ, RHP

Born: June 19, 2003. **B-T:** R-R. **HT:** 6-0. **WT:** 173.
Signed: Mexico, 2019. **Signed by:** Rolando Fernandez/Alving Mejias/Marc Russo.

TRACK RECORD: Juarez was a well-known amateur prospect in Mexico and represented the country in the 2016 Little League World Series. He signed with the Rockies in 2019 for $500,000. Juarez split his

2021 season between the Dominican Summer League and the Arizona Complex League before hitting full-season ball in 2022. He finished as one of two teenagers to pitch 100 innings and record 100 strikeouts in the Low-A California League.

SCOUTING REPORT: A slight righthander with an athletic frame, Juarez is a fluid mover who repeats his mechanics well. He deploys a simple, up-tempo operation with a high leg lift and a long but quick arm action before he slings the ball from a high three-quarters slot. Juarez's pitch mix consists of a low-90s four-seam fastball with pedestrian ride but above-average arm-side run, a curveball, slider and changeup. His curveball is a high-70s breaking ball with two-plane break and depth. His slider sits in the low 80s with classic shape. His changeup was his most-thrown secondary and sits in the low-to-mid 80s with tumble and fade. All of Juarez's secondaries tunnel well off of his fastball, driving high rates of chase swings against each pitch individually. Juarez shows average command of his arsenal and could improve to above-average in his peak seasons.

THE FUTURE: Juarez profiles as a No. 5 starter with a deep arsenal of pitches and command that plays above his pure stuff.

BA GRADE: 50/Very High	Fastball: 40	Curveball: 55	Slider: 50	Changeup: 55	Control: 50

Year	Age	Club (League	Lvl	W	L	ERA	G	GS	IP	H	HR	BB	SO	BB/9	SO/9	WHIP	AVG
2022	19	Fresno (CAL)	LoA	6	5	4.98	21	21	103	102	15	33	100	2.9	8.7	1.31	.263
Minor League Totals				8	6	4.25	31	29	140	126	17	40	147	2.6	9.5	1.19	.243

13 YANQUIEL FERNANDEZ, OF

Born: Jan. 1, 2003. **B-T:** L-L. **HT:** 6-2. **WT:** 207.
Signed: Cuba, 2019. **Signed by:** Rolando Fernandez/Marc Russo/Raul Gomez.

TRACK RECORD: Fernandez signed out of Cuba for $295,000 in 2019 and broke out in the Dominican Summer League during the summer of 2021, when he hit .333/.406/.531 with six home runs over 54 games. Fernandez moved to Low-A in 2022 and set the Fresno franchise record with 109 RBIs.

SCOUTING REPORT: Fernandez has a power-over-everything profile and looks to do damage on every swing. He swings quite often, partly because he can get his barrel to pitches in and out of the zone. Despite his swing-happy approach, Fernandez possesses above-average contact skills that allow him to put to bat to ball at a high rate on pitches in the zone. His contact ability, combined with his bat speed and strength, allows him to show plus power to all fields, with the high-end exit velocities to match. He's a below-average runner, and his speed limits him to an outfield corner, where he's a below-average defender. Fernandez keeps baserunners honest with a plus throwing arm that helped him rack up seven outfield assists at Fresno.

THE FUTURE: How Fernandez's approach develops will dictate his ultimate role. His ceiling is as a classic power-hitting corner outfielder.

BA GRADE: 50/Very High	Hit: 45	Power: 60	Run: 40	Field: 40	Arm: 60

Year	Age	Club (League	Lvl	AVG	G	AB	R	H	2B	3B	HR	RBI	BB	SO	SB	OBP	SLG
2022	19	Fresno (CAL)	LoA	.284	112	475	76	135	33	5	21	109	39	114	5	.340	.507
Minor League Totals				.298	166	652	105	194	50	5	27	143	61	140	5	.359	.514

14 HUNTER GOODMAN, C

Born: Oct. 8, 1999. **B-T:** R-R. **HT:** 6-1. **WT:** 210.
Drafted: Memphis, 2021 (4th round). **Signed by:** Zack Zulli

TRACK RECORD: After a standout freshman campaign with Memphis in 2019, Goodman put himself onto the national radar. He was the first Memphis player to earn Freshman All-American honors and continued to set off alarm bells in the industry over the next two seasons. He moved to catcher as a sophomore and hit 21 home runs, which tied him for third in all of Division I. The Rockies selected Goodman in the fourth round of the 2021 draft and signed him for an above-slot $600,000. He moved from Low-A to Double-A in 2022 while hitting 36 home runs, which tied him for third in the minors.

SCOUTING REPORT: Although he's a below-average hitter overall, Goodman has few peers when it comes to raw power. He has a simple swing with a big leg kick and an approach geared to hunt fastballs. He produces big-time bat speed with a violent, leveraged swing. His overall approach is tailored toward his pull side but he has plenty of power to all sectors. He's a fringe-average runner and won't clog the bases. Goodman is still gaining experience behind the plate but has plus arm strength that would play up further with improved mechanics and technique.

THE FUTURE: Goodman has a plus-plus carrying tool in his immense power but he lacks the approach typical of first base and DH-only types or supporting defensive skills to profile as an everyday regular at catcher.

BA GRADE: 45/High		Hit: 30		Power: 70			Run: 45			Field: 30			Arm: 60	
Year	Age	Club (League)	Lvl	AVG	G	AB	R	H	2B	3B	HR	RBI	BB	SO	SB	OBP	SLG
2022	22	Fresno (CAL)	LoA	.291	73	282	53	82	17	1	22	68	26	78	4	.368	.592
2022	22	Spokane (NWL)	HiA	.315	49	197	39	62	16	1	12	34	11	61	1	.351	.589
2022	22	Hartford (EL)	AA	.227	12	44	5	10	0	0	2	4	3	12	1	.277	.364
Minor League Totals				.295	156	583	113	172	40	2	38	118	49	165	7	.361	.566

15 JADEN HILL, RHP

Born: Dec. 22, 1999. **B-T:** R-R. **HT:** 6-4. **WT:** 235.
Drafted: Louisiana State, 2021 (2nd round) **Signed by:** Zack Zulli.
TRACK RECORD: Hill endured the coronavirus pandemic bookended by two injury plagued seasons at Louisiana State. Hill injured his elbow twice at LSU and had Tommy John surgery in his draft year. The Rockies took him in the second round and signed him for slot money. He made his debut in 2022 and split his year between the Rookie-level Arizona Complex League and Low-A Fresno.
SCOUTING REPORT: An athletic pitcher with a strong, muscular build, Hill has displayed upside and potential since high school. He has a fast arm with a long stroke and a low three-quarters slot. Hill throws his side-spinning four-seamer in the mid-90s and backs it up with a mid-90s cutter, a mid-80s gyro slider and a low-to-mid-80s changeup with tumble and fade. Hill's best offspeed is his changeup, which is effective to both lefties and righties. He's improved the shape on his slider and added more power to the version he showed at LSU. His command was fringy in 2022 but could tick up a bit the further removed he is from surgery. His mix is powerful and could fit in a variety of roles.
THE FUTURE: A strong return late in the season left little questions around Hill's big stuff returning to pre-injury form. Hill has No. 4 starter upside but with plenty of risk.

BA GRADE: 50/Extreme		Fastball: 55		Slider: 50			Changeup: 55		Cutter: 40			Control: 45	
Year	Age	Club (League)	Lvl	W	L	ERA	G	GS	IP	H	HR	BB	SO	BB/9	SO/9	WHIP	AVG
2022	22	Rockies (ACL)	R	0	0	3.48	7	7	10	11	0	4	11	3.5	9.6	1.45	.282
2022	22	Fresno (CAL)	LoA	0	0	2.45	3	3	7	7	0	2	14	2.5	17.2	1.23	.259
Minor League Totals				0	0	3.06	10	10	18	18	0	6	25	3.1	12.7	1.36	.273

16 MICHAEL TOGLIA, 1B

Born: Aug. 16, 1998. **B-T:** B-L. **HT:** 6-5. **WT:** 226.
Drafted: UCLA, 2019 (1st round) **Signed by:** Matt Hattabaugh.
TRACK RECORD: Toglia caught the eye of Rockies scouts first in high school. They liked him enough to draft him in the 39th round in 2016 but were unable to buy him out of his UCLA commitment. After three years with the Bruins, including a junior season in which Toglia hit .314/.392/.624 with 17 home runs, the Rockies got their man. Toglia made his big league debut on Aug. 30.
SCOUTING REPORT: Toglia has an unorthodox skill set but also has a few things working against him at the plate. He's both tall and a switch-hitter, both factors that usually lead to protracted developmental paths. His swings from both sides of the plate are fairly similar—slightly open and with a pull-heavy approach. Those factors, combined with his long levers, have led to a below-average hit tool. He has a discerning eye, though, and rarely expands the zone. Toglia's plus raw power plays from both sides of the plate thanks to above-average bat speed and strength. He has consistently gotten to power at each level and should be an above-average or plus power hitter in the major leagues. Toglia is a surprisingly good athlete from someone his size. He clocks fringe-average run times. Toglia has played in the outfield corner but will most likely stick at first base, where he's above-average.
THE FUTURE: Toglia has the makings of a three-true-outcome hitter whose contact rate will dictate his power output.

BA GRADE: 40/Medium		Hit: 40		Power: 60			Run: 45			Field: 55			Arm: 45	
Year	Age	Club (League)	Lvl	AVG	G	AB	R	H	2B	3B	HR	RBI	BB	SO	SB	OBP	SLG
2022	23	Hartford (EL)	AA	.234	97	363	63	85	13	1	23	66	51	127	7	.329	.466
2022	23	Albuquerque (PCL)	AAA	.333	17	66	11	22	7	0	7	17	9	22	0	.413	.758
2022	23	Colorado (NL)	MLB	.216	31	111	10	24	8	2	2	12	9	44	1	.275	.378
Major League Totals				.216	31	111	10	24	8	2	2	12	9	44	1	.275	.378
Minor League Totals				.240	270	999	165	240	47	4	61	193	153	336	18	.342	.478

17 JEFF CRISWELL, RHP

Born: March 10, 1999. **B-T:** R-R. **HT:** 6-4. **WT:** 203.
Drafted: Michigan, 2020 (2nd round). **Signed by:** Rich Sparks (Athletics).

TRACK RECORD: Criswell starred as a reliever in the 2019 College World Series and was Michigan's No. 1 starter during the pandemic-shortened 2020 season. The A's drafted him in the second round that year but a shoulder injury in 2021 limited him to just 12 innings through two years as a professional. He bounced back in 2022 and logged 130.1 innings with a 4.03 ERA among three levels. He was dealt to the Rockies in December for reliever Chad Smith.

SCOUTING REPORT: Criswell's frame and four-pitch mix provide foundational starter ingredients, although he continues to face questions about whether his delivery can hold up in that role. His four-seam fastball sits 93-94 mph and touches 97 with a bit of running life. Criswell's low-80s changeup may now be his best secondary and he's comfortable throwing it to righties and lefties. His tight, mid-80s slider is an above-average pitch with swing-and-miss potential, and his slower curveball is a pitch he can use early in counts. Criswell has focused on trying to add more fluidity to his delivery to help alleviate potential injury risk. It's still rather effortful and he can leave himself in compromising positions at foot strike. He repeats it fairly well, walking 3.4 batters per nine innings in 2022.

THE FUTURE: Criswell draws some comparisons to Chris Bassitt, another cold-weather arm who straddled the starter-reliever line as a prospect and had success in the A's system. With his new team he'll return to the upper levels in a starting role to open the 2023 season.

BA GRADE: 45/High	Fastball: 55	Curveball: 50	Slider: 55	Changeup: 55	Control: 50

Year	Age	Club (League)	Lvl	W	L	ERA	G	GS	IP	H	HR	BB	SO	BB/9	SO/9	WHIP	AVG
2022	23	Lansing (MWL)	HiA	2	3	3.78	10	10	50	37	7	18	58	3.2	10.4	1.10	.206
2022	23	Midland (TL)	AA	2	6	4.21	12	9	58	61	6	24	57	3.7	8.9	1.47	.274
2022	23	Las Vegas (PCL)	AAA	0	1	4.22	2	2	11	10	0	3	4	2.5	3.4	1.22	.263
Minor League Totals				4	10	4.07	29	26	130	117	14	49	131	3.4	9.0	1.27	.241

18 JULIO CARRERAS, SS

Born: Jan. 12, 2000. **B-T:** R-R. **HT:** 6-2. **WT:** 190.
Signed: Dominican Republic, 2018. **Signed by:** Rolando Fernandez/Frank Roa.

TRACK RECORD: Carreras was one of the Rockies' biggest breakout players in 2022. He signed for just $15,000 in 2018 and has blossomed into one of the system's best defenders. High-A Northwest League managers tabbed Carreras as the circuit's best defensive shortstop in BA's annual Best Tools survey, and his 42 doubles led the minor leagues.

SCOUTING REPORT: Carreras is a twitchy, athletic player who has begun to hint toward a ceiling as an everyday regular. While his defense is already polished and refined, his bat-to-ball skills and approach still need to improve. Carreras does the majority of his damage against heaters but struggles with offspeeds. His inability to pick up spin or differentiations in speed was accentuated during his time with Hartford, when he struggled against more advanced pitchers who consistently attacked him with spin off the plate. Carreras' present power is below-average but he projects to get to at least fringe-average as he grows into his 6-foot-2 frame. Carreras' speed translates to both sides of the ball. He's rangy and quick at short, where he displays clean actions, a good first step and internal clock and has the plus throwing arm to profile long-term at the position. He stole 19 bases in 24 chances.

THE FUTURE: Carreras is a standout defender who will need to improve his approach and refine his bat-to-ball skills to profile as anything more than a utility defender.

BA GRADE: 45/High	Hit: 40	Power: 45	Run: 55	Field: 65	Arm: 60

Year	Age	Club (League)	Lvl	AVG	G	AB	R	H	2B	3B	HR	RBI	BB	SO	SB	OBP	SLG
2022	22	Spokane (NWL)	HiA	.289	110	402	59	116	37	2	11	59	31	106	17	.352	.473
2022	22	Hartford (EL)	AA	.233	19	60	11	14	5	1	0	13	5	21	2	.303	.350
Minor League Totals				.278	358	1314	240	365	86	23	29	185	116	338	64	.349	.444

19 NOLAN JONES, 3B

Born: May 7 1998. **B-T:** L-R. **HT:** 6-2. **WT:** 185.
Drafted: HS—Bensalem, Pa.., 2016 (2nd round). **Signed by:** Mike Kanen (Guardians).

TRACK RECORD: The Rockies acquired Jones for infielder Juan Brito prior to the 40-man deadline in Nov. 2022. A 2016 second-round pick by the Guardians, Jones ranked as Cleveland's top prospect entering the 2020 season. Since then, his prospect status has collapsed as he struggled to hit for impact at

Triple-A. After spending the past two seasons at Triple-A Columbus, Jones made his major league debut in 2022, spending the majority of July and August with the big league club. He was demoted to Triple-A in late August and spent the rest of the season in the minor leagues.

SCOUTING REPORT: Not long ago, Jones was ranked as one of the top prospects in the game, with many evaluators liking his combination of on-base ability and projectable power. While Jones' ability to get on-base remains, the questions around his ability to get to his raw power persist. His underlying exit velocity data is above major league average, but too often his best-struck balls were hit on the ground. He made adjustments coming into 2022 and showed improved bat-to-ball skills and more consistent well-hit airborne contact to his pull side. Jones is an average runner but not a basestealer. Defensively, Jones has taken to a move to the corner outfield after spending a majority of his early career at third base. He's a fringe-average defender with an above-average throwing arm.

THE FUTURE: Jones' change of scenery and lack of major league depth in Colorado is a welcome change. He profiles best as a second-division regular with the ability to fill in at multiple positions.

BA GRADE: 45/High		Hit: 45		Power: 50		Run: 50		Field: 45			Arm: 55	
Year	Age	Club (League)	Lvl	AVG	G	AB	R	H	2B	3B	HR	RBI	BB	SO	SB	OBP	SLG
2022	24	Columbus (IL)	AAA	.276	55	214	44	59	11	1	9	43	31	64	4	.368	.463
2022	24	Cleveland (AL)	MLB	.244	28	86	10	21	5	0	2	13	8	31	0	.309	.372
Major League Totals				.244	28	86	10	21	5	0	2	13	8	31	0	.309	.372
Minor League Totals				.273	494	1739	305	475	102	10	60	262	341	574	27	.394	.447

20 ANGEL CHIVILLI, RHP

Born: July 28, 2002. **B-T:** R-R. **HT:** 6-2. **WT:** 162.
Signed: Dominican Republic, 2018. **Signed by:** Rolando Fernandez/Manuel Cabrera.

TRACK RECORD: After two seasons in the Dominican Summer League, Chivilli came stateside in 2022 and dominated over nine appearances in the Arizona Complex League. He was promoted to Low-A Fresno in early July and held down the Grizzlies' closer job for the remainder of the season. While Chivilli has impressed as a reliever, the Rockies plan to try him as a starter in 2023 at High-A Spokane.

SCOUTING REPORT: Chivilli announced his presence upon coming stateside with a three-pitch mix with exceptional power. Chivilli's four-seam fastball sits 94-97 mph and touches 98-99 mph with heavy arm-side run. While his fastball has plus power, his dead zone shape could limit the pitch's projection against advanced competition. His slider is a tight mid-80s breaker that generates whiffs and chases at elite rates and plays up due to his above-average command. Chivilli's changeup is used as often as his slider and shows splitter-type shape in the mid 80s. Chivilli misses bats and drives chase swings on all of his pitches due to his ability to tunnel his secondaries off of his mid-90s fastball.

THE FUTURE: Chivilli is one of the highest upside arms in the Rockies' system. He has the stuff of a high-leverage closer and the deep quality of pitches of a starter. If he is moved to a starting role next season, Chivilli could blossom.

BA GRADE: 50/Extreme		Fastball: 50		Slider: 60		Changeup: 55		Control: 50				
Year	Age	Club (League)	Lvl	W	L	ERA	G	GS	IP	H	HR	BB	SO	BB/9	SO/9	WHIP	AVG
2022	19	Rockies (ACL)	R	1	1	1.15	9	0	16	10	0	4	23	2.3	13.2	0.89	.182
2022	19	Fresno (CAL)	LoA	2	1	2.88	23	0	25	26	1	6	28	2.2	10.1	1.28	.257
Minor League Totals				3	10	3.26	55	20	124	120	5	28	141	2.0	10.2	1.19	.249

21 BRENTON DOYLE, OF

Born: May 14, 1998. **B-T:** R-R. **HT:** 6-3. **WT:** 200.
Drafted: Shepherd (W.Va.), 2019 (4th round). **Signed by:** Ed Santa.

TRACK RECORD: After initially committing to Virginia Military Academy out of high school, Doyle instead landed at Division II Shepherd where he hit .392 in his junior year. The Rockies selected Doyle in the fourth round of the 2019 draft and signed for an above-slot bonus of $500,000. He reached Double-A for the first time in 2022 and finished the year in Triple-A Albuquerque and played a scorching nine games. The Rockies added him to the 40-man roster in November.

SCOUTING REPORT: Doyle is a tooled-up athlete who has a variety of skills that buoy his profile. While he's a below-average hitter with a poor approach, Doyle displays above-average raw power and speed, making for an exciting, but far too often frustrating player. Doyle's bat-to-ball skills are below-average, with his overzealous approach further complicating matters. His inability to differentiate balls from strikes on the shadow of the zone was exploited by upper-level competition in 2022. While his raw power is above-average, his ability to consistently get to it is in question due to his poor swing decisions. He's an above-average runner and basestealing threat, and his speed translates to his defense in the outfield. Doyle is an above-average center fielder with a plus arm that would play in an outfield corner.

THE FUTURE: With strong tools but with major question marks around his ability to hit against upper-level pitching, Doyle profiles as a bench outfielder with the ability to create sparks on his best days.

BA GRADE: 45/High		Hit: 30			Power: 55		Run: 55			Field: 55			Arm: 60	
Year	Age	Club (League)	Lvl	AVG	G	AB	R	H	2B	3B	HR	RBI	BB	SO	SB	OBP	SLG
2022	24	Hartford (EL)	AA	.246	123	471	74	116	21	3	23	68	23	158	23	.287	.450
2022	24	Albuquerque (PCL)	AAA	.389	9	36	8	14	1	2	3	9	5	13	0	.463	.778
Minor League Totals				.286	280	1077	194	308	49	10	50	157	89	352	61	.345	.489

22 JUAN GUERRERO, OF

Born: Sept. 10, 2001. **B-T:** R-R. **HT:** 6-1. **WT:** 160.
Signed: Dominican Republic, 2018. **Signed by:** Rolando Fernandez/Frank Roa.
TRACK RECORD: Signed out of the Dominican Republic for $650,000 in 2018, Guerrero has blossomed alongside a group of young, talented hitters in the Rockies' lower levels over the last few seasons. He debuted in the Dominican Summer League in 2019, hitting .319 before coming stateside in 2021. He posted an .894 OPS in the Arizona Complex League, then followed with a strong year at Low-A Fresno.
SCOUTING REPORT: Guerrero is one of the best pure athletes in the Rockies system, with a tall, wiry build that portends strength gains. He's an aggressive swinger with a longer swing, but his ability to adjust the barrel allows him to make contact at a high rate. While Guerrero will chase, it's at a controlled level that doesn't limit his hitting. He's a fringe-average power hitter who could grow into average or better thump as he adds strength. He also shows steep enough launch angles to hit for power now on his best-struck balls. Guerrero is an above-average runner who picks up speed underway due to his long strides. After playing as an infielder as an amateur, Guerrero has since moved to the outfield and showed average defensive skills.
THE FUTURE: Guerrero is an athletic outfielder who is just beginning to scratch the surface of his upside. He is a potential everyday corner outfielder who should start the 2023 campaign with High-A Spokane.

BA GRADE: 45/High		Hit: 50			Power: 50		Run: 55			Field: 50			Arm: 45	
Year	Age	Club (League	Lvl	AVG	G	AB	R	H	2B	3B	HR	RBI	BB	SO	SB	OBP	SLG
2022	20	Fresno (CAL)	LoA	.274	113	453	89	124	24	4	14	89	39	85	18	.335	.437
Minor League Totals				.293	211	792	167	232	46	6	20	149	76	140	44	.359	.442

23 DYAN JORGE, SS

Born: March 18, 2003. **B-T:** R-R. **HT:** 6-3. **WT:** 170.
Signed: Cuba, 2022. **Signed by:** Rolando Fernandez/Raul Gomez/Marc Russo.
TRACK RECORD: A native of Cuba, Jorge left the country late in the 2020-21 international period at a point when most teams had already committed a majority of their bonus pools. Instead, Jorge opted to wait until the following signing period, when he landed with the Rockies for $2.8 million. He made his professional debut in the Dominican Summer League and posted an .853 OPS.
SCOUTING REPORT: An advanced hitter with a discerning eye and plate discipline unusual for a player his age, Jorge has a tall, svelte build with a high level of fitness and twitch. He's rail-thin at present but projects to add good weight as he ages because of broad shoulders and a lean, muscular shape. Jorge shows above-average hittability for his age with the ability to make a high rate of contact in-zone. Jorge limits his swings and misses out of the zone and stays inside his approach. At times, this is a hindrance because he rarely lets loose and instead opts to stay inside the ball and shoot it to the opposite field. He shows line-drive and gap power, which safely projects to fringe-average juice. Jorge is a plus runner who gets out of the blocks quickly and translates his speed to all areas of his game. Jorge projects to stick up the middle because of good infield actions, a quick first step and smooth transfers. He's an above-average infield defender with room to grow into plus.
THE FUTURE: A projectable player with advanced hitting acumen, Jorge could take off if he proves he can hit for power.

BA GRADE: 50/Extreme		Hit: 55			Power: 45		Run: 60			Field: 55			Arm: 55	
Year	Age	Club (League)	Lvl	AVG	G	AB	R	H	2B	3B	HR	RBI	BB	SO	SB	OBP	SLG
2022	19	Rockies (DSL)	R	.333	4	15	2	5	2	0	0	5	1	4	0	.375	.467
2022	19	Colorado (DSL)	R	.319	49	191	35	61	11	1	4	20	23	31	13	.404	.450
Minor League Totals				.320	53	206	37	66	13	1	4	25	24	35	13	.402	.451

24 CARSON PALMQUIST, LHP

Born: Oct. 17, 2000. **B-T:** L-L. **HT:** 6-3. **WT:** 185.
Draft: Miami, 2022 (3rd round) **Signed by:** Rafael Reyes

TRACK RECORD: A reliever for his first two seasons at Miami who dominated out of the pen for the Hurricanes, Palmquist struck out 75 batters over 44.2 innings in 2021. After a star turn with the Collegiate National Team over the summer, he jumped into the Hurricanes' rotation. He made 16 starts and compiled a 9-4, 2.89 mark with 118 strikeouts to 32 walks. The Rockies selected Palmquist in the third round and signed him for an above-slot bonus of $775,000. Palmquist made one appearance in the Arizona Complex League.

SCOUTING REPORT: With a lefthanded sidearm operation, Palmquist creates a difficult angle on all of his pitches, particularly to lefthanders. He mixes a fastball, changeup and slider. Palmquist's fastball sits in the low 90s as a starter but showed mid-90s velocity as a reliever his first two seasons at Miami. His changeup is a low-80s pitch that generated whiffs at a high rate in college. His breaking ball is a mid-70s sweeper with moderate horizontal break that plays up out of his hand due to his sidearm slot. He's shown average command across a variety of roles as an amateur, and how his fastball velocity progresses as a starter will ultimately define whether he can stick in the role.

THE FUTURE: Palmquist is a deceptive lefthander with a chance to start due to his average control, but a reliever role to fall back on if starting doesn't take.

BA GRADE: 45/High		Fastball: 50		Slider: 50		Changeup: 55		Control: 50				

Year	Age	Club (League)	Lvl	W	L	ERA	G	GS	IP	H	HR	BB	SO	BB/9	SO/9	WHIP	AVG
2022	21	Rockies (ACL)	R	0	0	0.00	1	0	1	0	0	2	1	18.0	9.0	2.00	.000
Minor League Totals				0	0	0.00	1	0	1	0	0	2	1	18.0	9.0	2.00	.000

25 GAVIN HOLLOWELL, RHP

Born: Nov. 4, 1997. **B-T:** R-R. **HT:** 6-7. **WT:** 215.
Drafted: St. John's, 2019 (6th round). **Signed by:** Mike Garlatti.

TRACK RECORD: Hollowell spent three seasons as a reliever at St. John's, showcasing big stuff from his 6-foot-7 frame. The Rockies selected Hollowell in the sixth round and he impressed with Rookie-level Grand Junction. He dealt with an elbow injury that delayed the start of his 2021 season but finished the campaign strong. He moved to Double-A in 2022, made 42 appearances and racked up 16 saves. He earned a late season callup to the major leagues and appeared in six games.

SCOUTING REPORT: Hollowell possesses above-average size and physicality that allows him to generate above-average extension. His ability to get down the mound amplifies his pitches, gives his fastball flat angle and makes it difficult for hitters to get on plane. Hollowell mixes three pitches but primarily works off of his fastball-slider combination. His fastball sits between 92-94 mph, touches 96 mph and features both a dead-zone four-seamer and a sinker. His slider is a low-80s sweeper with around 15 inches of horizontal break on average. He'll also flash a low-to-mid-80s changeup but it was a minor part of his repertoire in 2022. Hollowell has shown above-average command of his pitch mix.

THE FUTURE: Primarily a two-pitch reliever, Hollowell got his first big league exposure in 2022 and should be back as a factor in Colorado's 2023 bullpen.

BA GRADE: 40/High		Fastball: 50		Slider: 55		Changeup: 40		Control: 55				

Year	Age	Club (League)	Lvl	W	L	ERA	G	GS	IP	H	HR	BB	SO	BB/9	SO/9	WHIP	AVG
2022	24	Hartford (EL)	AA	4	2	3.14	42	0	49	30	3	14	64	2.6	11.8	0.90	.179
2022	24	Colorado (NL)	MLB	0	2	7.71	6	0	7	7	1	4	8	5.1	10.3	1.57	.259
Major League Totals				0	2	7.71	6	0	7	7	1	4	8	5.1	10.3	1.57	.259
Minor League Totals				10	2	2.86	83	0	91	61	6	26	127	2.6	12.5	0.95	.187

26 ALBERTO PACHECO, LHP

Born: Nov. 29, 2002. **B-T:** L-L. **HT:** 6-1. **WT:** 175.
Signed: Dominican Republic, 2019. **Signed by:** Rolando Fernandez/Manuel Cabrera.

TRACK RECORD: Pacheco signed for $400,000 when he became eligible on July 2, 2019. He made his debut in the Dominican Summer League in 2021, making 11 starts and pitching to a 4-1, 2.93 mark with 51 strikeouts to nine walks. He appeared in 11 Arizona Complex League games in 2022 and struck out 57 batters over 46 innings.

SCOUTING REPORT: A deceptive lefthander with a low slot and funky low-effort mechanics, Pacheco has a long arm stroke that swings behind his back as he begins his motion. His low, near-sidearm slot makes it difficult for lefthanded hitters to pick up the ball out of his hand and helps the shape on all of his pitches. He uses a fastball, slider and changeup. He'll show two fastball shapes but is likely to lean into a sinker as he progresses. His slider sits in the low-to-mid-80s with a cutter-hybrid shape driving grounders at a high rate. His changeup is a mid-80s pitch with Bugs Bunny shape that plays off of his fastball. He commands his entire arsenal at an average level and gets grounders against all of his pitches at a high rate.

THE FUTURE: A reliever long term, Pacheco shows feel for a trio of pitches with the ability to generate grounders.

BA GRADE: 45/Extreme		Fastball: 45		Slider: 50		Changeup: 50		Control: 50				

Year	Age	Club (League)	Lvl	W	L	ERA	G	GS	IP	H	HR	BB	SO	BB/9	SO/9	WHIP	AVG
2022	19	Rockies (ACL)	R	5	4	3.13	11	8	46	39	1	15	57	2.9	11.2	1.17	.222
Minor League Totals				9	5	3.03	22	19	92	76	4	24	108	2.3	10.6	1.09	.222

27 BRYANT BETANCOURT, C/1B

Born: Oct. 12, 2003. **B-T:** L-R. **HT:** 6-0. **WT:** 170.
Signed: Venezuela, 2021. **Signed by:** Rolando Fernandez/Orlando Medina.

TRACK RECORD: Betancourt signed out of Venezuela for $80,000 when his signing period opened on Jan. 15, 2021 as part of a class that also included Jordy Vargas. Over the past two seasons, Betancourt has made a name for himself with impressive hitting displays in the Dominican Summer League. In 2022, Betancourt hit .355/.462/.674 with 11 home runs that tied for third in the DSL.

SCOUTING REPORT: Betancourt is an advanced hitter at the plate who shows a balance of contact, approach and power to go with a strong, compact build that leads to explosiveness in his swing. He shows plus bat-to-ball skills for his level and makes contact in the zone at a high rate. He chased just 24.5% of the time in 2022. Betancourt walked more than he struck out during DSL play in 2022 and did so without sacrificing impact. His max exit velocity of 101 mph isn't eye-popping but solid for a teenager still growing into his strength. He makes his hardest contact at his steepest launch angles but doesn't sell out for loft. He's unlikely to stick behind the plate and has already seen a heavy dose of first base and DH.

THE FUTURE: Betancourt is a talented hitter with projectable power, but a lack of supporting skills leave his long term defensive role in doubt and put extra pressure on his bat.

BA GRADE: 45/Extreme		Hit: 55		Power: 50		Run: 30		Field: 30		Arm: 50	

Year	Age	Club (League)	Lvl	AVG	G	AB	R	H	2B	3B	HR	RBI	BB	SO	SB	OBP	SLG
2022	18	Colorado (DSL)	R	.355	44	138	34	49	11	0	11	36	27	21	0	.462	.674
Minor League Totals				.314	83	245	49	77	16	2	12	50	44	33	1	.417	.543

28 RYAN RITTER, SS

Born: Nov. 10, 2000. **B-T:** R-R. **HT:** 6-0. **WT:** 200.
Drafted: Kentucky, 2022 (4th round). **Signed by:** Scott Corman.

TRACK RECORD: Ritter spent his freshman season at Logan (Ill.) JC before transferring to Kentucky for his sophomore season. Ritter answered some of the questions surrounding his hitting the following summer by hitting .330/.431/.429 with Cotuit of the Cape Cod League. The following spring, Ritter showed improved power and on-base ability but saw his already poor strikeout rate rise to 25.9%. The Rockies selected Ritter in the fourth round and signed him for $530,000.

SCOUTING REPORT: While Ritter's strong defensive play carries his profile, his evolution as hitter over the past few seasons is an intriguing. He seemed to progress as a contact hitter throughout his first season at Kentucky and in the early part of his full summer on the Cape. As he made adjustments to his swing over that summer, Ritter tapped into above-average raw power, culminating in a power-happy display on the Cape. He made slight changes to his setup, but overall got more aggressive on pitches on the inner half as he looked to ambush fastballs early in counts. His combination of bat speed and leverage allows him to drive the ball to his pull side on his best contact, but this approach sacrifices his natural bat-to-ball abilities. Ritter is a strong defensive shortstop with above-average range, smooth hands and an above-average arm who should stick at the position.

THE FUTURE: Ritter is a polished and exciting defender at shortstop with a power-over-hit profile.

BA GRADE: 40/High		Hit: 30		Power: 55		Run: 55		Field: 60		Arm: 55	

Year	Age	Club (League)	Lvl	AVG	G	AB	R	H	2B	3B	HR	RBI	BB	SO	SB	OBP	SLG
2022	21	Rockies (ACL)	R	.320	8	25	9	8	4	1	1	4	2	3	2	.414	.680
Minor League Totals				.320	8	25	9	8	4	1	1	4	2	3	2	.414	.680

29 CONNOR STAINE, RHP

Born: Jan. 12, 2001. **B-T:** R-R. **HT:** 6-0. **WT:** 200.
Drafted: Central Florida, 2022 (5th round). **Signed by:** John Cedarburg.

TRACK RECORD: After a difficult 2021 campaign with Maryland, Staine entered the transfer portal and headed to Central Florida, where he joined the Knights' rotation. He made a dozen starts in the spring of 2022, going 4-1, 1.87 with 55 strikeouts to 22 walks over 43 innings. The Rockies selected Staine in the fourth round and signed the righthander for $400,000. Staine dealt with blister and back issues throughout the spring, the Rockies shut him down post-draft.

SCOUTING REPORT: A tall athletic righthander with a deceptive delivery, Staine is a fiery competitor with plenty of projection remaining. He features a long arm action with a plunge and fires from a high three-quarters slot. He mixes four pitches, but primarily works off of his fastball and pair of breaking balls. His four-seam fastball sits between 92-94 mph and touches 97 mph with ride and run. His low-80s slider with two-plane break is his primary secondary and plays well off of his fastball. He'll show a mid-70s curveball with more depth and loopy shape. His command has been fringe at times and leads to some questions around his strike-throwing due to his inability to repeat his operation.

THE FUTURE: Staine will be given every chance to prove he's a viable starter prospect, but his fastball and slider combination likely plays best in a relief role.

BA GRADE: 40/High	Fastball: 50	Slider: 55	Curveball: 40	Changeup: 30	Control: 45

Year	Age	Club (League)	Lvl	W	L	ERA	G	GS	IP	H	HR	BB	SO	BB/9	SO/9	WHIP	AVG
2022	21	Did not play															

30 MICHAEL PROSECKY, LHP

Born: Feb. 28, 2001. **B-T:** L-L. **HT:** 6-3. **WT:** 200.
Drafted: Louisville, 2022 (6th round). **Signed by:** Scott Corman.

TRACK RECORD: After an injury-riddled spring season in 2021, Prosecky resurfaced on the Cape Cod League pitching meaningful innings out of the pen for eventual-champion Brewster. The following spring he made 26 appearances for Louisville in a relief role, striking out 44 batters over 37.1 innings with below-average command. The Rockies liked the combination of fastball velocity from the left side and breaking ball shape and selected Prosecky in the sixth round. He signed for an above-slot bonus of $300,000 and made a single appearance in the Arizona Complex League.

SCOUTING REPORT: A tall athletic lefthander with a quick operation with few moving parts, Prosecky employs a short, fast arm action as he delivers the ball from a high three-quarters slot. He mixes a trio of pitches but primarily relies on his bread-and-butter fastball-curveball combination. His fastball sits between 93-95 mph on his best days but he's had bouts of dwindling velocity. Beyond just velocity from the left side, Prosecky features good shape with ride and bore, which allows him to live in the upper quadrants when he's commanding his heater. His best pitch is his upper-70s, hammer breaking ball with two-plane break and a near-impossible angle for opposing hitters in left-on-left matchups. He'll show a mid-80s changeup but it's not a major part of his arsenal and is a below-average pitch. Prosecky's command is below-average, and walks have been a problem throughout his amateur career.

THE FUTURE: Prosecky is a funky, two-pitch lefty reliever with an above-average breaking ball and above-average fastball shape and velocity. If things click, he could be a fast-moving reliever.

BA GRADE: 40/High	Fastball: 50	Curveball: 55	Changeup: 40	Control: 40

Year	Age	Club (League)	Lvl	W	L	ERA	G	GS	IP	H	HR	BB	SO	BB/9	SO/9	WHIP	AVG
2022	21	Rockies (ACL)	R	0	0	0.00	1	0	1	0	0	0	1	0.0	9.0	0.00	.000
Minor League Totals				0	0	0.00	1	0	1	0	0	0	1	0.0	9.0	0.00	.000

Detroit Tigers

BY EMILY WALDON

After a promising 2021 season that saw the Tigers begin to watch their young pitchers find their footing in the major leagues, the 2022 season was supposed to be the year the lineup caught up as well.

Additions of free agent shortstop Javier Baez and trade acquisitions outfielder Austin Meadows and catcher Tucker Barnhart as well as incoming rookies Spencer Torkelson and Riley Greene were expected to give Detroit a boost.

It didn't happen. Eric Haase was the only Tigers semi-regular to slug .400 or better, and Detroit had the American League's worst offense. The Tigers' earned their 66-96 record, for a sixth consecutive losing season.

General manager Al Avila was fired as a result, and Scott Harris was named president of baseball operations to replace him.

Harris, who had previously served as the Giants' general manager since 2019 was quick to promote his vision for a "culture of development," which the Tigers have struggled to maintain in the past.

Among his more notable moves, Harris did not retain assistant GM David Chadd and scouting director Scott Pleis. Standing assistant general managers Sam Menzin and Jay Sartori were retained.

Harris followed up those transactions with the announcement that the Tigers' domestic scouting effort would have a new look. Rays scouting director Rob Metzler would become the Tigers' new vice president and assistant general manager, while Padres scouting director Mark Conner would assume that same role in Detroit.

After the building prospect buzz that developed in 2021, the Tigers debuted 14 players in 2022, doubling the amount of debuts recorded the previous year.

These debuts included the long-awaited introductions of Greene and Torkelson, shortstop Ryan Krielder and lefthander Joey Wentz, who was not far removed from Tommy John surgery.

While Greene had a solid MLB debut, Torkelson had a much rockier transition. He did not hit, was demoted back to Triple-A Toledo and continued to struggle in the minors.

In the draft, the Tigers broke character from their usual early pursuit of pitching by selecting Texas Tech second baseman Jace Jung and Oklahoma third baseman Peyton Graham with their first two picks.

With Harris' focus on strengthening in-house development, the entire front office has worked to adapt their communication style to match that of the new figurehead.

DAVID BERDING/GETTY IMAGES

Riley Greene kept his head above water as a 21-year-old while grading well in center field.

PROJECTED 2026 LINEUP

Position	Player	Age
Catcher	Dillon Dingler	27
First Base	Spencer Torkelson	26
Second Base	Jace Jung	25
Third Base	Peyton Graham	25
Shortstop	Javier Baez	34
Left Field	Kerry Carpenter	28
Center Field	Riley Greene	25
Right Field	Parker Meadows	26
Designated Hitter	Colt Keith	24
No. 1 Starter	Eduardo Rodriguez	34
No. 2 Starter	Tarik Skubal	30
No. 3 Starter	Casey Mize	30
No. 4 Starter	Jackson Jobe	23
No. 5 Starter	Wilmer Flores	25
Closer	Reese Olson	26

That communication included continuing to build off of the work of director of performance science Georgia Giblin. Through Giblin's hire in 2021, the Tigers were—and continue to remain—vocal about their prioritization of modernizing their performance science study as a whole.

This study will allow the Tigers to individualize the development tracks for each prospect. By doing so, they hope to strength the homegrown talent for the future of the organization.

Fully aware of the raw talent accessible to them in the pipeline, the Tigers' front office has its sights set on slowing the pace, individualizing the development approach and ensuring a shared vision from the top down. ∎

DEPTH CHART

DETROIT TIGERS

TOP 2023 MLB CONTRIBUTORS	RANK
Wilmer Flores, RHP	3
BREAKOUT PROSPECTS	**RANK**
Parker Meadows, OF	12
Dylan Smith, RHP	17

SOURCE OF TOP 30 TALENT

Homegrown	26	Acquired	4
College	12	Trade	3
Junior college	1	Rule 5 draft	1
High school	4	Independent league	0
Nondrafted free agent	0	Free agent/waivers	0
International	9		

LF
Kerry Carpenter (8)
Bligh Madris
Dylan Rosa

CF
Parker Meadows (12)
Eric De La Rosa

RF
Roberto Campos (14)
Jose De La Cruz (29)
Daniel Cabrera
Austin Murr

3B
Colt Keith (5)
Peyton Graham (6)
Izaac Pacheco (15)
Gage Workman (27)

SS
Ryan Kreidler (9)
Cristian Santana (13)
Manuel Sequera (23)
Abel Bastidas (24)
Adinso Reyes (25)
Javier Osorio (28)

2B
Jace Jung (2)
Andre Lipcius (18)
Wencel Perez (19)

1B
Jake Holton

C
Dillon Dingler (7)
Josh Crouch (22)
Eliezer Alfonzo (30)
Chris Rabago

LHP

LHSP	LHRP
Joey Wentz (16)	Jack O'Loughlin
Brant Hurter (26)	Adam Wolf
Carlos Peña	Max Green

RHP

RHSP	RHRP
Jackson Jobe (1)	Brendan White
Wilmer Flores (3)	Angel De Jesus
Ty Madden (4)	Tyler Mattison
Reese Olson (11)	Keider Montero
Dylan Smith (17)	Gerson Moreno
Mason Englert (20)	Zack Hess
Troy Melton (21)	Chance Kirby
Austin Bergner	
Garrett Burhenn	
Elvin Rodriguez	

1 JACKSON JOBE, RHP

Born: July 30, 2002. **B-T:** R-R. **HT:** 6-2. **WT:** 190.
Drafted: HS—Oklahoma City, 2021 (1st round).
Signed by: Steve Taylor.

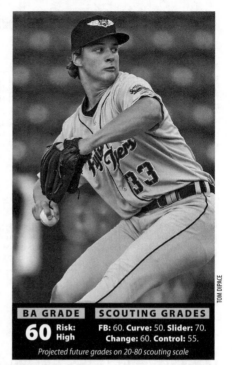

TOM DIPACE

TRACK RECORD: The son of professional golfer Brandt Jobe, Jackson carried Heritage Hall High to the Oklahoma 4A state championship as its star shortstop and top pitcher in 2021. His two-way exploits and pro promise helped him earn the BA High School Player of the Year award that season. Despite his natural ability as a position player, Jobe's top billing as the best high school pitcher in his class led the Tigers to select him third overall as a righthander. Detroit signed him for $6.9 million, about 96% of the slot value of $7.2 million. Jobe did not pitch after signing and made his pro debut with 18 starts for Low-A Lakeland in 2022. The Tigers promoted him to High-A West Michigan on Aug. 27, and in his final six starts of the season for Lakeland and West Michigan he recorded a 1.91 ERA while striking out 25, walking nine and allowing a .185 opponent average in 28.1 innings.
SCOUTING REPORT: Jobe stands at 6-foot-2, 190 pounds with a projectable, athletic frame and is expected to add a good deal of additional strength as his body continues to fill out. His most highly developed offering is a plus-plus, low-80s slider that combines depth and impressive spin, regularly surpassing 3,000 rpm. Despite his slider's tremendous horizontal break, Jobe has shown an ability to locate the pitch—though some scouts believed the consistency of his command could improve. His four-seam fastball averaged 94 mph in 2022 and has been up to 97, with around 17 inches of induced vertical break, though his results with the pitch weren't great and some scouts thought the pitch had just average life. Jobe's mid-80s changeup is a potential plus pitch that generated whiffs at a 42% rate, with impressive drop and solid feel. He also infrequently throws an upper-70s curveball that is less impressive than his slider, but gives him four legitimate pitches to round out his arsenal. Jobe generates downhill plane from his lanky frame. Jobe's clean mechanics and natural athleticism are traits that hint at above-average future control.
THE FUTURE: Over time, the Tigers have worked to perfect their ability to individualize a player's development track, as opposed to simply fast-tracking him through the pipeline. While Jobe's arsenal and mature understanding of his craft could help him rise faster than most high school pitchers, don't be surprised if the Tigers take their time with him to ensure both health and proper physical development. After beginning his professional career in 2022, Jobe spent three outings in the High-A Midwest League to end the regular season, so a return to the Whitecaps to start the 2023 season is likely. Depending on how his season develops, a midseason jump to Double-A Erie seems plausible.

BA GRADE	SCOUTING GRADES
60 Risk: High	**FB:** 60. **Curve:** 50. **Slider:** 70. **Change:** 60. **Control:** 55.

Projected future grades on 20-80 scouting scale

BEST TOOLS

BATTING

Best Hitter for Average	Wenceel Perez
Best Power Hitter	Kerry Carpenter
Best Strike-Zone Discipline	Cristian Santana
Fastest Baserunner	Seth Stephenson
Best Athlete	Parker Meadows

PITCHING

Best Fastball	Tyler Mattison
Best Curveball	Andrew Magno
Best Slider	Jackson Jobe
Best Changeup	Jackson Jobe
Best Control	Wilmer Flores

FIELDING

Best Defensive Catcher	Dillon Dingler
Best Defensive Infielder	Gage Workman
Best Infield Arm	Gage Workman
Best Defensive Outfielder	Parker Meadows
Best Outfield Arm	Jose De La Cruz

Year	Age	Club (League)	Lvl	W	L	ERA	G	GS	IP	H	HR	BB	SO	BB/9	SO/9	WHIP	AVG
2022	19	Lakeland (FSL)	LoA	2	5	4.52	18	18	62	59	12	25	71	3.6	10.4	1.36	.251
2022	19	West Michigan (MWL)	HiA	2	0	1.15	3	3	16	10	2	5	10	2.9	5.7	0.96	.175
Minor League Totals				4	5	3.84	21	21	77	69	14	30	81	3.5	9.4	1.28	.236

2 JACE JUNG, 2B

Born: Oct. 4, 2000. **B-T:** L-R. **HT:** 6-0. **WT:** 205.
Drafted: Texas Tech, 2022 (1st round). **Signed by:** Steve Taylor.

TRACK RECORD: Being a first-round pick is in the Jung family's bloodlines. Older brother Josh starred at Texas Tech and was drafted eighth overall in 2019 by the Rangers. Jace put together a strong spring campaign for the Red Raiders in 2022, leading the Tigers to draft him 12th overall and sign him for slot value of $4.59 million. The sturdy 6-foot, 205-pound lefthanded batter stood out among collegians for his hitting ability and strike-zone judgment. In 2022, he hit .335 with a .481 on-base percentage while ranking fifth in Division I with 59 walks. Jung made his pro debut with High-A West Michigan and continued to showcase his on-base skills.

BA GRADE
55 Risk: High

SCOUTING REPORT: Jung brings an old school approach to the plate in terms of hitting the ball where it's pitched, and has displayed power to all fields. He has an unorthodox setup at the plate, with his barrel dumped back toward the catcher, but the odd positioning has never been an issue. He consistently produced average, on-base ability and power in the Big 12 Conference. Jung has a chance for above-average hitting ability and above-average in-game power potential, but even if he doesn't reach those gaudy marks, his strong understanding of the strike zone should allow him to get on base consistently. He walked more frequently (20%) than he struck out (16%) in his college career and continued to show a good eye in his pro debut, with 25 walks and 28 strikeouts. Jung will need to hit because he's limited as a defender. He has below-average speed and range but adequate hands and arm strength to make routine plays.

THE FUTURE: With his combination of high baseball IQ, plate discipline and hitting ability, Jung is expected to be a fast-mover.

SCOUTING GRADES	Hitting: 55	Power: 55	Speed: 40	Fielding: 45	Arm: 50

Year	Age	Club (League)	Lvl	AVG	G	AB	R	H	2B	3B	HR	RBI	BB	SO	SB	OBP	SLG
2022	21	West Michigan (MWL)	HiA	.231	30	108	16	25	6	1	1	13	25	28	1	.373	.333
Minor League Totals				.231	30	108	16	25	6	1	1	13	25	28	1	.373	.333

3 WILMER FLORES, RHP

Born: Feb. 20, 2001. **B-T:** R-R. **HT:** 6-4. **WT:** 225.
Signed: Arizona Western JC, 2020 (NDFA). **Signed by:** Joey Lothrop.

TRACK RECORD: The younger brother of Giants infielder Wilmer Flores, the righthander of the same name signed as a nondrafted free agent in 2020 out of Arizona Western JC. Flores threw just 11.2 innings in his lone junior college season, and he ended up at Arizona Western because he enrolled there while visiting his brother in the U.S. from Venezuela. Flores began his professional career with four appearances in the Florida Complex League in 2021 before receiving a promotion to Low-A Lakeland. He represented Detroit in the Arizona Fall League, and the extended time on the mound prepared Flores for a strong campaign in 2022. Between High-A West Michigan and Double-A Erie, Flores posted a 2.79 ERA over 103.1 innings with 130 strikeouts and 23 walks.

BA GRADE
55 Risk: High

SCOUTING REPORT: Flores worked with a three-pitch mix in 2022, primarily throwing his four-seam fastball and mid-to-upper-80s cutter. His fastball sat in the 92-94 mph range and touched 99 with sinking life. He showed excellent feel to land the pitch and threw it for a strike 70% of the time. His go-to secondary was his cutter, which averaged around 9 mph slower than his fastball and was a slightly better whiff pitch and chase offering compared to his fastball. Scouts like Flores' curveball, which is an upper-70s to lower-80s breaking ball with 11-to-5 movement, solid two-plane break and depth. His curve shows spin rates in the 2,500-2,600 rpm range. Flores throws the pitch for strikes less frequently than his fastball or cutter, but it was also his best swing-and-miss offering in 2022, with a 41% whiff rate.

THE FUTURE: Two years after signing as an NDFA, Flores is looking like a steal, with considerably higher upside now and a path to a potential midrotation role.

SCOUTING GRADES:	Fastball: 55	Curveball: 55	Cutter: 50	Control: 60

Year	Age	Club (League)	Lvl	W	L	ERA	G	GS	IP	H	HR	BB	SO	BB/9	SO/9	WHIP	AVG
2022	21	West Michigan (MWL)	HiA	1	0	1.83	6	5	20	14	2	2	35	0.9	16.0	0.81	.192
2022	21	Erie (EL)	AA	6	4	3.01	19	19	84	67	8	21	95	2.3	10.2	1.05	.213
Minor League Totals				13	8	3.14	39	37	169	143	11	47	220	2.5	11.7	1.12	.225

4 TY MADDEN, RHP

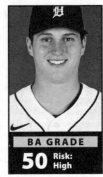

BA GRADE

50 Risk: High

Born: Feb. 21, 2000. **B-T:** R-R. **HT:** 6-3. **WT:** 215.
Drafted: Texas, 2021 (1st round supplemental). **Signed by:** George Schaefer.

TRACK RECORD: Madden spent three years in the Texas rotation and won Big 12 Conference pitcher of the year honors in 2021. Expected to be one of the top pitchers drafted that year, he instead slid to the Tigers with the 32nd overall pick. Detroit signed him for an above-slot $2.5 million. Madden made his pro debut in 2022 and excelled after tweaking his mechanics. In 122.2 innings between High-A West Michigan and Double-A Erie, Madden posted a 3.01 ERA and struck out 133 batters.

SCOUTING REPORT: As an amateur, Madden received criticism for a fastball shape that prevented the pitch from playing well up in the zone. In the off-season, Madden reworked his delivery to adopt a lower arm slot and release point—going from over the top to more of a three-quarters delivery. The change has helped Madden improve the spin efficiency and movement of his fastball. Now he is throwing the pitch with similar power—he sits 93-94 mph and touches 99—but with nearly 18 inches of induced vertical break. Using the pitch to attack at the top of the strike zone is now more of an option. The slider remains Madden's go-to swing-and-miss offering and generated a 45% whiff rate with mid-80s velocity, 2,400-2,500 rpm spin and occasional biting two-plane break down and away from righthanded hitters. Madden is still developing feel for his mid-to-upper-80s changeup that he needs to throw for strikes more frequently. He will also mix in a curveball with more top-down shape, and a newer cutter in the high 80s.

THE FUTURE: Madden made impressive adjustments in his first year in pro ball, and the results speak for themselves. He has No. 3 or 4 starter upside.

SCOUTING GRADES:	Fastball: 60	Curveball: 50	Slider: 60	Changeup: 40	Cutter: 50	Control: 55

Year	Age	Club (League)	Lvl	W	L	ERA	G	GS	IP	H	HR	BB	SO	BB/9	SO/9	WHIP	AVG
2022	22	West Michigan (MWL)	HiA	6	4	3.10	19	19	87	69	10	26	84	2.7	8.7	1.09	.212
2022	22	Erie (EL)	AA	2	2	2.78	7	7	36	28	6	12	49	3.0	12.4	1.12	.217
Minor League Totals				8	6	3.01	26	26	123	97	16	38	133	2.8	9.8	1.10	.214

5 COLT KEITH, 3B

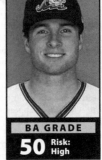

BA GRADE

50 Risk: High

Born: Aug. 14, 2001. **B-T:** L-R. **HT:** 6-3. **WT:** 211.
Drafted: HS—Biloxi, Miss., 2020 (5th round). **Signed by:** Mike Smith.

TRACK RECORD: The Tigers drafted Keith in the fifth round in 2020 and signed him for a slightly above-slot $500,000. The pandemic delayed his pro debut until 2021, when he slashed .286/.396/.393 at three levels and reached High-A West Michigan. Keith returned to the Midwest League in 2022 and showed newfound power by slugging .544 in 48 games. His season was cut short after sustaining an injury to his shoulder during a pickoff attempt. After completing a successful rehab, Keith headed to the Arizona Fall League in preparation for the upper levels of the minor leagues in 2023. He ranked fifth in the AFL with a .463 on-base percentage.

SCOUTING REPORT: Keith was a legitimate two-way prospect in high school as both a shortstop and righthanded pitcher. He showed impressive bat-to-ball skills amid a challenging assignment in 2022. After hitting just two home runs in 2021, Keith showcased a significant increase in his raw power in 2022 and finished with nine home runs despite not playing after June 9. Much of Keith's development hinges on both his health and the continued maturation of his approach, while also tapping into his power more consistently as his frame fills out. Detroit likes Keith's profile at third base—but he has steadily gotten bigger and stronger as he's matured. He shows a plus arm while continuing to develop feel for the position. Keith is a fringe-average runner.

THE FUTURE: Featuring the upside of an everyday big leaguer, Keith will be battling against 2022 draftee Peyton Graham if he hopes to hold the hot corner. Even if he moves off third base, Keith's natural athleticism and hitting upside should buy him a spot in Detroit's future lineup.

SCOUTING GRADES	Hitting: 55	Power: 50	Speed: 45	Fielding: 50	Arm: 60

Year	Age	Club (League)	Lvl	AVG	G	AB	R	H	2B	3B	HR	RBI	BB	SO	SB	OBP	SLG
2022	20	West Michigan (MWL)	HiA	.301	48	193	38	58	14	3	9	31	22	42	4	.370	.544
Minor League Totals				.293	113	417	79	122	22	8	11	63	63	108	8	.385	.463

6 PEYTON GRAHAM, SS

Born: Jan. 26, 2001. **B-T:** R-R. **HT:** 6-3. **WT:** 185.
Drafted: Oklahoma, 2022 (2nd round). **Signed by:** Steve Taylor.

TRACK RECORD: A lanky righthanded hitter with a long track record of hitting at a high level with Oklahoma, Graham showed improved in-game power in 2022 and hit a career-high 20 home runs while slashing .335/.417/.640. The Tigers liked what they saw and signed Graham for $1.8 million in the second round. He hit .270/.345/.370 in 27 games for Low-A Lakeland in his pro debut and went 7-for-8 in stolen base attempts.

BA GRADE

50 Risk: High

SCOUTING REPORT: Graham is an ultra-lean infielder listed at 6-foot-3, 185 pounds, and perhaps the biggest question he faces in pro ball is how his 20-homer season translates. His average exit velocities were modest in his 2022 pro debut, but his top-end numbers were encouraging. Graham has shown an ability to drive the ball to his pull side with bat speed and leverage. Graham has some swing-and-miss tendencies. He'll also expand the zone more often than he should and has a leg kick and long levers that could be detrimental to his pure bat-to-ball ability. He struck out at a near 26% rate in Low-A, where he was age-appropriate. Graham transitioned from third base to shortstop in college and played all over the infield in his pro debut. He has solid athleticism, a good first step and above-average arm strength that could allow him to stick at shortstop, depending on how his body develops. Graham is an above-average runner with excellent baserunning instincts. He stole 34 bags in 36 tries with Oklahoma during the spring.

THE FUTURE: If Graham can improve his swing decisions and cut down his swing-and-miss, he provides a well-rounded tool set with interesting defensive versatility. Whether he adds more strength and power could play a key role in his ultimate upside.

SCOUTING GRADES	Hitting: 50	Power: 50	Speed: 55	Fielding: 55	Arm: 55

Year	Age	Club (League)	Lvl	AVG	G	AB	R	H	2B	3B	HR	RBI	BB	SO	SB	OBP	SLG
2022	21	Lakeland (FSL)	LoA	.270	27	100	19	27	5	1	1	13	10	29	7	.345	.370
Minor League Totals				.270	27	100	19	27	5	1	1	13	10	29	7	.345	.370

7 DILLON DINGLER, C

Born: Sept. 17, 1998. **B-T:** R-R. **HT:** 6-3. **WT:** 210.
Drafted: Ohio State, 2020 (2nd round). **Signed by:** Austin Cousino.

TRACK RECORD: Dingler was viewed as arguably the best defensive catcher in the 2020 draft, and the Tigers took him in the second round and signed him for slightly over slot value at $1,952,300. Dingler reported to the Tigers' alternate training site shortly after and made his professional debut in 2021. His success with High-A West Michigan—he slashed .287/.376/.549—led to a promotion to Double-A Erie before he suffered a fractured finger. A return to Erie in 2022 presented Dingler the opportunity to represent the Tigers in the Futures Game. After the season he headed to the Arizona Fall League, but knee soreness forced the Tigers to shut him down for the year after just four games.

BA GRADE

45 Risk: Medium

SCOUTING REPORT: Dingler features a physical, well-proportioned frame, with advanced athleticism on both sides of the ball. Boasting plus speed, he has cat-like reflexes behind the plate. Despite still learning the nuances of his defensive position, Dingler has shown consistent improvement in both receiving and framing. His nearly pluB-plus arm holds opposing running games in check. With his defense-first profile, Dingler has worked to polish his offensive feel and more consistently tap into his raw power on contact. There is a still a great deal of swing-and-miss to his game, and he has a strikeout rate of nearly 30% over the last two seasons. Dingler projects as a well below-average hitter—his career minor league batting average is .238—but with average power.

THE FUTURE: With a mostly healthy 2022 in the rear-view, the 2023 season is going to be key as Dingler works to prove potential longevity. He should begin the year with Triple-A Toledo. His health will decide how quickly he'll see his MLB debut.

SCOUTING GRADES	Hitting: 30	Power: 50	Speed: 60	Fielding: 55	Arm: 65

Year	Age	Club (Lea	Lvl	AVG	G	AB	R	H	2B	3B	HR	RBI	BB	SO	SB	OBP	SLG
2022	23	Erie (EL)	AA	.238	107	387	56	92	22	3	14	58	45	143	1	.333	.419
Minor League Totals				.238	192	709	106	169	32	7	26	104	67	244	2	.323	.413

8 KERRY CARPENTER, OF

Born: Sept. 2, 1997. **B-T:** L-R. **HT:** 6-2. **WT:** 220.
Drafted: Virginia Tech, 2019 (19th round). **Signed by:** Matt Zmuda.
TRACK RECORD: Carpenter starred at Eustis (Fla.) High and then for two years at St. John's River (Fla.) JC before transferring to Virginia Tech for one season in 2019. The Tigers drafted him in the 19th round that year and signed him for $125,000. Carpenter made the jump to Double-A Erie in 2021 after riding out the pandemic year in 2020. He returned to Erie in 2022 and set about climbing to Triple-A Toledo and then to Detroit on Aug. 10. Carpenter popped 30 home runs on the farm and led the minor leagues with a .645 slugging percentage. In his time in Detroit, the lefthanded hitter put up an .851 OPS versus righthanders.

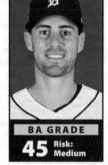

BA GRADE
45 Risk: Medium

SCOUTING REPORT: Carpenter is a sturdy 6-foot-2, 220 pounds and has a solid core and a lean lower half. His most noticeable achievement has been his ability to tap into plus raw power, the same power that had him leading the minors in home runs at the halfway point of the 2022 season. He has strong hands and good loft in his swing, but he is prone to chasing outside the zone. That contributed to his strikeout rate spiking to 28% in the big leagues and will be something to keep an eye on. With a clear bat-first profile, Carpenter is viewed as a below-average left fielder with average speed. His athleticism and instincts could benefit him as long as he can keep hitting.
THE FUTURE: Once viewed as an organizational player, Carpenter raised that evaluation to be a potential second-division strong-side platoon bat. He has nothing left to prove in the minors and is ready to take his swings against righthanders for a Tigers team that finished last in MLB in home runs in 2022.

SCOUTING GRADES	Hitting: 40	Power: 60	Speed: 50	Fielding: 40	Arm: 45

Year	Age	Club (League	Lvl	AVG	G	AB	R	H	2B	3B	HR	RBI	BB	SO	SB	OBP	SLG
2022	24	Erie (EL)	AA	.304	63	240	43	73	16	0	22	48	16	72	1	.359	.646
2022	24	Toledo (IL)	AAA	.331	35	118	17	39	11	1	8	27	17	17	2	.420	.644
2022	24	Detroit (AL)	MLB	.252	31	103	16	26	4	1	6	10	6	32	0	.310	.485
Major League Totals				.252	31	103	16	26	4	1	6	10	6	32	0	.310	.485
Minor League Totals				.289	257	952	151	275	67	5	54	184	84	204	15	.355	.540

9 RYAN KREIDLER, SS

Born: Nov. 12, 1997. **B-T:** R-R. **HT:** 6-4. **WT:** 208.
Drafted: UCLA, 2019 (4th round). **Signed by:** Tim McWilliam.
TRACK RECORD: The son of sportswriter and author Mark Kreidler, Ryan is a defensive standout who was drafted by the Tigers in the fourth round in 2019 and signed at slot value for $517,400. He emerged from the Tigers' alternate training site in 2020 as a vastly improved hitter. After hitting 15 home runs with Double-A Erie in 2021, Kreidler was promoted to Triple-A Toledo and continued to shine to end the regular season. Kreidler overcame a broken hand that put a damper on his 2022 campaign, and the Tigers rewarded him in September with his first big league callup.
SCOUTING REPORT: Standing at 6-foot-4, 208 pounds, Kreidler features a sturdy, daunting presence with eye-catching athleticism for his lanky build.

BA GRADE
45 Risk: Medium

Boasting excellent instincts and a quick first step, Kreidler has a natural ability to anticipate balls off the bat at shortstop and complements that feel with his plus arm strength and clean hands. Despite having a glove-first profile, Kreidler has worked very hard to bring more of a balance to his offensive skill set, with the fruits of his labor taking center stage in 2021. There is still a noticeable amount of swing-and-miss, as evidenced by his 25% or higher strikeout rate between Triple-A Toledo and Detroit. Kreidler moves extremely well for his size, has average speed and poses a threat on the basepaths.
THE FUTURE: Kreidler flashed natural feel on both sides of the ball in his MLB debut. To make his case as a starter, he will need to boost his offensive output.

SCOUTING GRADES	Hitting: 40	Power: 40	Speed: 50	Fielding: 55	Arm: 60

Year	Age	Club (League)	Lvl	AVG	G	AB	R	H	2B	3B	HR	RBI	BB	SO	SB	OBP	SLG
2022	24	West Michigan (MWL)	HiA	.231	4	13	3	3	2	0	0	4	4	3	2	.412	.385
2022	24	Toledo (IL)	AAA	.213	56	202	29	43	12	2	8	22	36	72	15	.352	.411
2022	24	Detroit (AL)	MLB	.178	26	73	8	13	1	0	1	6	6	22	0	.244	.233
Major League Totals				.178	26	73	8	13	1	0	1	6	6	22	0	.244	.233
Minor League Totals				.248	249	925	155	229	50	6	32	104	116	294	41	.341	.418

10 JUSTYN-HENRY MALLOY OF/3B

Born: Feb. **19,** 2000. **B-T:** R-R. **HT:** 6-3. **WT:** 212.
Drafted: Georgia Tech, 2021 (6th round). **Signed by:** Chris Lionetti (Braves).

BA GRADE

45 Risk: High

TRACK RECORD: Malloy ranked as the No. 214 prospect in the 2021 draft class out of Georgia Tech, where he showed impressive on-base skills and developing power. The Braves signed him for $300,000 in the sixth round, and he had a solid 2021 pro debut before breaking out in 2022 and pushing himself to Triple-A Gwinnett and then the Arizona Fall League. He was acquired by the Tigers in December for righthander Joe Jimenez.
SCOUTING REPORT: Malloy is a strong and physical righthanded hitter who homered 17 times between three minor league levels in 2022. He played in pitcher-friendly home parks, making the total more impressive. While Malloy might have above-average raw power, his strike-zone discipline and contact ability drive his value as a prospect. Malloy immediately becomes one of the most disciplined hitters in the Tigers' system. He chased just 18% of the time while also showing quick hands and good bat-to-ball skills. He has a chance to be an above-average hitter who walks at a high rate, though scouts are mixed on his true power potential. His exit velocity numbers are modest, but he has flashed impressive pop to his pull side. Of note, his power numbers trended down as he moved up levels. A well below-average runner, Malloy will be limited to a corner and his most likely defensive home is left field. He played third base at High-A Rome and flashed plus arm strength but had trouble with throwing accuracy and needs much more work on his hands and footwork at the position.
THE FUTURE: Malloy's defensive limitations could cap his upside as an everyday player, though his pure hitting ability and zone control could make him a quality platoon option.

SCOUTING GRADES	Hitting: 55		Power: 45		Speed: 30		Fielding: 40		Arm: 55					
Year	Age	Club (League)	Lvl	AVG	G	AB	R	H	2B	3B	HR	RBI	BB	SO	SB	OBP	SLG
2022	22	Rome (SAL)	HiA	.304	71	263	51	80	16	0	10	44	47	73	3	.409	.479
2022	22	Mississippi (SL)	AA	.268	54	190	35	51	11	0	6	31	43	60	0	.403	.421
2022	22	Gwinnett (IL)	AAA	.280	8	25	5	7	1	0	1	6	7	5	2	.424	.440
Minor League Totals				.285	170	600	114	171	33	0	22	102	121	168	9	.404	.450

11 REESE OLSON, RHP

Born: July 31, 1999. **B-T:** R-R. **HT:** 6-1. **WT:** 160.
Drafted: HS—Gainesville, Georgia, 2018 (13th round). **Signed by:** Steve Smith (Brewers).

TRACK RECORD: Olson was originally drafted as the Brewers' 13th-round pick in 2018 before being traded to the Tigers at the 2021 trade deadline for lefthander Daniel Norris. Prior to making the move to Detroit, Olson booked 14 starts with High-A Wisconsin, where he posted 10.3 strikeouts per nine innings over 69 frames. Following his acquisition, Olson was assigned to High-A West Michigan. He received a promotion to Double-A Erie after just 11 innings. The Tigers returned Olson to Erie in 2022, where he spent the entire season. He completed his Double-A campaign with 168 strikeouts—good for ninth-most in the minor leagues—over 119.2 innings with 2.9 walks per nine innings.
SCOUTING REPORT: Olson features a four-pitch mix that grades from fringy to above-average, with added room for development across the board. There is some concern surrounding Olson's history of inconsistent command, but the improvement he showed in 2022 led to optimism for his development track. Olson leads his arsenal with an above-average changeup with fade, one of his two very strong secondary offerings. The pitch has the ability to induce weak groundball contact and plenty of swing-and-miss. Next up is a sweeping low-80s slider that Olson shows the most confidence in because of its proven ability against righthanded hitters. His go-to offering against lefthanded hitters is a high-70s curveball. Olson is still developing deception with his mid-90s fastball, a pitch that could tick up as he fills out.
THE FUTURE: After Olson showcased his arsenal in 2022, there remains some debate as to whether he will stick in a rotation or face a move to the bullpen. But the proven quality of his pitch mix has established the righthander as a future multi-inning reliever at the very least.

BA GRADE: 45/High	Fastball: 55		Curveball: 45		Slider: 55		Changeup: 55		Control: 45						
Year	Age	Club (Lea	Lvl	W	L	ERA	G	GS	IP	H	HR	BB	SO	BB/9	SO/9	WHIP	AVG
2022	22	Erie (EL)	AA	8	6	4.14	26	25	120	109	15	38	168	2.9	12.6	1.23	.237
Minor League Totals				20	20	4.26	78	62	329	306	29	140	372	3.8	10.2	1.35	.245

12 PARKER MEADOWS, OF

Born: Nov. 2, 1999. **B-T:** L-R. **HT:** 6-5. **WT:** 205.
Drafted: HS—Loganville, Georgia, 2018 (2nd round). **Signed by:** Bryson Barber.

TRACK RECORD: In a year where the Tigers had a number of hitters struggle, Meadows was a development success story. The younger brother of current Tigers outfielder Austin Meadows, Parker's development seemed stuck heading into 2022. He was sent back to High-A West Michigan for a third year. This time, he quickly hit his way to Double-A Erie while showing improvement in nearly every facet at the plate. He was sent to the Arizona Fall League to wrap up the year.

SCOUTING REPORT: Meadows moves extremely well for a 6-foot-5 outfielder. He's a 65 runner on the 20-to-80 scouting scale and makes solid reads and takes direct routes in center field, where he is a plus defender with a plus arm. As a hitter, Meadows worked to shorten up his swing and it paid off in improved contact and better power when he did make contact. His 20 home runs easily doubled his previous career high. Meadows' defense and speed mean that if he's a fringe-average hitter with average power, he can be a productive regular.

THE FUTURE: If Meadows can further build on his impressive improvements in 2022, he could finish 2023 in line for a spot in the Tigers' outfield. His combination of speed, defense and improved power makes him one of the team's more intriguing position prospects. Meadows could begin the year back at Double-A, but he should get plenty of time at Triple-A Toledo later in the season.

BA GRADE: 45/High **Hit:** 45 **Power:** 50 **Speed:** 65 **Fielding:** 60 **Arm:** 60

Year	Age	Club (League)	Lvl	AVG	G	AB	R	H	2B	3B	HR	RBI	BB	SO	SB	OBP	SLG
2022	22	West Michigan (MWL)	HiA	.230	14	61	16	14	4	1	4	7	4	18	0	.288	.525
2022	22	Erie (EL)	AA	.275	113	425	64	117	21	6	16	51	52	90	17	.354	.466
Minor League Totals				.240	378	1388	204	333	59	12	39	153	150	354	43	.318	.384

13 CRISTIAN SANTANA, SS

Born: Nov. 25, 2003. **B-T:** R-R **HT:** 6-0. **WT:** 165.
Signed: Dominican Republic, 2021. **Signed by:** Aldo Perez/Carlos Santana.

TRACK RECORD: After making a push to increase their presence on the international market, the Tigers landed Santana for a team-record bonus of $2.95 million during the 2021 international signing period. After an impressive debut in the Dominican Summer League where he slashed .269/.421/.520 in 2021, he struggled after an aggressive promotion to Low-A Lakeland in 2022. He hit .215/.384/.374 while splitting time at second base and shortstop.

SCOUTING REPORT: Santana, who has a solid understanding of the strike zone and the developing power to potentially be an above-average hitter with above-average power, remains one of the Tigers' highest-ceiling position prospects. He has already proven to have an advanced approach at the plate, complemented by a pretty, Alfonso Soriano-ish swing and mature pitch recognition. After a brutal first two months when he was bothered by an oblique injury, Santana hit .244/.411/.429 from July 1 until the end of the season. Defensively, Santana projects as a future average infielder with advanced footwork and instincts beyond his years. Santana's arm is average, but has balanced it out with his quickness, light footwork and natural ability to navigate the infield with ease.

THE FUTURE: As with many of the young prospects within the Tigers' farm system, Santana's path is going to take time to navigate. Tigers are likely to start Santana back in Lakeland for the 2023 season, but he could see West Michigan later and will play the entire season at 19 years old.

BA GRADE: 50/Extreme **Hit:** 55 **Power:** 55 **Speed:** 50 **Fielding:** 50 **Arm:** 50

Year	Age	Club (League)	Lvl	AVG	G	AB	R	H	2B	3B	HR	RBI	BB	SO	SB	OBP	SLG
2022	18	Tigers (FCL)	R	.200	2	5	3	1	0	0	1	2	4	3	0	.556	.800
2022	18	Lakeland (FSL)	LoA	.215	80	265	52	57	13	0	9	30	54	88	10	.379	.366
Minor League Totals				.236	136	441	95	104	25	2	19	59	88	137	22	.398	.431

14 ROBERTO CAMPOS, OF

Born: June 14, 2003 **B-T:** R-R. **HT:** 6-3. **WT:** 200. **Drafted:** Cuba, 2019.
Signed by: Aldo Perez/Oliver Arias.

TRACK RECORD: After leaving Cuba at the age of 16 to train in the Dominican Republic, Campos signed for $2.85 million in 2019, the largest international signing bonus the Tigers handed out that year and the sixth-most in the class. Campos showed power in his debut in the Florida Complex League in 2021.

Promoted to Low-A Lakeland for 2022, Campos lowered his strikeout rate and strung together better at-bats but also saw his power production dip. His season was better than it appears. The Florida State League's average slugging percentage was .361.

SCOUTING REPORT: Campos has the physical and athletic build to be a future power hitter. Campos uses big-time bat speed and raw strength to drive the ball to all fields, but he didn't hit the ball in the air nearly as often in 2022, which explains the dip in his power production. Campos is currently a center fielder, but he's an average runner who will likely slow down further in the future. He has an above-average arm that should fit in right or left field.

THE FUTURE: Campos' power production may have dipped, but he has the potential to be a productive corner outfielder, especially if he gets more comfortable lofting the ball in hitters' counts. Campos should head to spring training competing for a spot at High-A West Michigan. Even if he doesn't start the season there, he should reach the Midwest League before too long.

| BA GRADE: 45/High | | Hit: 50 | | Power: 55 | | Speed: 45 | | Fielding: 50 | | Arm: 55 | |

Year	Age	Club (League)	Lvl	AVG	G	AB	R	H	2B	3B	HR	RBI	BB	SO	SB	OBP	SLG
2022	19	Lakeland (FSL)	LoA	.258	112	403	52	104	26	5	5	50	40	97	7	.326	.385
Minor League Totals				.250	151	539	72	135	31	5	13	69	57	138	10	.323	.399

15 IZAAC PACHECO, 3B

Born: Nov. 18, 2002. **B-T:** L-R. **HT:** 6-4. **WT:** 225.
Drafted: HS—Friendswood, Texas, 2021 (2nd round). **Signed by:** George Schaefer.

TRACK RECORD: The Tigers were enamored with Pacheco's power potential to the point that they were willing to accept some risk as far as his contact ability. Despite some swing-and-miss concerns, the appeal of natural, raw power has always been difficult to overlook. At 6-4, 225 pounds, Pacheco was selected 39th overall as the Tigers' 2021 second-round pick and signed for $2.75 million. The 18-year-old shortstop was in the mix about a month later, making his debut with the Florida Complex League Tigers in July. Entering the 2022 season at 20 years old, Pacheco split the year between Class A Lakeland and High-A West Michigan, slashing a combined .254/.331/.408 with 36 extra-base hits.

SCOUTING REPORT: Still just 20 years old, Pacheco has plenty of physical projection remaining. Like many young developing power hitters, Pacheco has some contact issues, but mainly because he expands the strike zone too much rather than missing hittable strikes. Pacheco's swing produces plus raw power with plenty of natural loft and solid bat speed. Defensively, the Tigers have moved Pacheco to third base. The speed of the game sometimes seemed too much for him at shortstop and his range was limited. He's more effective at third base, where he has a plus arm and a decent first step. His offensive profile should be fine at third base long-term.

THE FUTURE: With his first full-season campaign behind him, Pacheco's highly improved pitch recognition has him positioned for an impact season in 2023. Likely to begin the regular season with High-A West Michigan, Pacheco should move quickly as long as his offensive production and continuing maturation can keep up with the pace.

| BA GRADE: 45/High | | Hit: 50 | | Power: 55 | | Speed: 45 | | Fielding: 55 | | Arm: 60 | |

Year	Age	Club (League)	Lvl	AVG	G	AB	R	H	2B	3B	HR	RBI	BB	SO	SB	OBP	SLG
2022	19	Lakeland (FSL)	LoA	.267	88	330	54	88	21	2	8	39	38	80	12	.342	.415
2022	19	West Michigan (MWL)	HiA	.183	18	60	9	11	2	0	3	13	9	17	0	.274	.367
Minor League Totals				.248	136	496	79	123	27	4	12	59	65	140	13	.333	.391

16 JOEY WENTZ, LHP

Born: Oct. 6, 1997. **B-T:** L-L. **HT:** 6-5. **WT:** 220.
Drafted: HS—Prairie Village, Kan., 2016 (1st round supplemental). **Signed by:** Nate Dion (Braves).

TRACK RECORD: The Tigers dipped into the Braves' surplus of starting pitching prospects to acquire Wentz in 2019 at the trade deadline in exchange for Shane Greene. Soon thereafter he suffered an elbow injury that required Tommy John surgery. He returned to action in May 2021. He suffered a left shoulder strain in 2022, but threw 86 innings and made his MLB debut on May 11.

SCOUTING REPORT: Wentz has long been known as a soft-tossing lefty who tries to keep hitters off balance by mixing his pitches. He added an average, 81-84 mph cutter in 2022, which gives him a harder breaking ball that he can consistently throw for strikes. Wentz's fringe-average four-seam fastball touches 95-96, but he sits 91-93. He works up in the zone with his fastball, while the cutter works in on right-handed hitters and down and away from lefties. His fringe-average slow 73-77 mph curveball and average low-80s changeup are effective when he's used to them tickling the black. Wentz's control is-average, although he has excellent command. He doesn't have the stuff to sit in the zone, so he has to nibble.

THE FUTURE: After a successful return from Tommy John surgery, Wentz looks ready to handle a back-of-the-rotation role as a lefty with plenty of guile.

BA GRADE: 45/High	Fastball: 45		Cutter: 50		Curveball: 50		Changeup: 55		Control: 50	

Year	Age	Club (League)	Lvl	W	L	ERA	G	GS	IP	H	HR	BB	SO	BB/9	SO/9	WHIP	AVG
2022	24	West Michigan (MWL)	HiA	0	0	1.80	2	2	5	2	0	2	4	3.6	7.2	0.80	.125
2022	24	Toledo (IL)	AAA	2	2	3.17	12	11	48	37	6	20	53	3.7	9.9	1.18	.211
2022	24	Detroit (AL)	MLB	2	2	3.03	7	7	33	23	2	13	27	3.6	7.4	1.10	.195
Major League Totals				2	2	3.03	7	7	33	23	2	13	27	3.6	7.4	1.10	.195
Minor League Totals				21	28	3.39	111	110	497	395	41	207	534	3.8	9.7	1.21	.220

17 DYLAN SMITH, RHP

Born: May 28, 2000. **B-T:** R-R. **HT:** 6-2. **WT:** 180.
Drafted: Alabama, 2021 (3rd round). **Signed by:** Mike Smith.

TRACK RECORD: A Padres 18th-round pick out of high school, Smith raised his draft stock by going to Alabama, where he gained strength and earned a spot in the weekend rotation. After being picked in the third round in 2021, Smith made his pro debut in 2022, pitching effectively at High-A West Michigan.

SCOUTING REPORT: Smith arrived at Alabama weighing 160 pounds. He's worked at gaining weight and strength and now is considerably heavier than his listed 180 pounds. The extra strength and better use of his lower half has paid off in improved velocity to go with above-average control. He can touch 97 mph now and sits 92-94 with his average fastball. It doesn't have exceptional movement, but he has plus control of it. Smith's mid-to-high 80s slider that has split tilt and is a potential plus pitch. Smith's changeup is still a work in progress, although with more use, it projects as an average pitch. His slurvy, upper-70s curve is a fringe-average pitch as well.

THE FUTURE: Smith has steadily improved, but with a quick arm and a solid frame he could continue to add to his stuff. He projects as a useful back-end starter.

BA GRADE: 45/High	Fastball: 50		Curveball: 45	Slider: 60		Changeup: 50		Control: 55	

Year	Age	Club (League)	Lvl	W	L	ERA	G	GS	IP	H	HR	BB	SO	BB/9	SO/9	WHIP	AVG
2022	22	Lakeland (FSL)	LoA	0	0	0.00	2	2	5	3	0	0	3	0.0	5.4	0.60	.167
2022	22	West Michigan (MWL)	HiA	8	6	4.00	20	19	83	78	6	21	86	2.3	9.3	1.19	.244
Minor League Totals				8	6	3.77	22	21	88	81	6	21	89	2.1	9.1	1.15	.240

18 ANDRE LIPCIUS, 2B/3B

Born: May 22, 1998. **B-T:** R-R. **HT:** 6-1. **WT:** 190.
Drafted: Tennessee, 2019 (3rd round). **Signed by:** Harold Zonder.

TRACK RECORD: A shortstop earlier in his career at Tennessee, Lipcius moved to third base in his draft year and has shown versatility as a pro, adding second base to his array of positions. Detroit took the nuclear engineering major with its third-round pick in 2019. Lipcius has proven to be a productive infielder who knows how to pester pitchers and hit for average.

SCOUTING REPORT: Lipcius is a lean, athletic 6-1, 190 pounds with advanced hand-eye coordination. He's a polished contact hitter who knows how to spray the ball and get on base. He will show flashes of power, something that was a bigger part of his game in college. He does have enough pop to pile up doubles and should hit 10-15 home runs a year. Lipcius still plays third base more than second, but he's an average defender at either spot with an above-average arm. Lipcius has slow feet, but he has solid instincts, and good hands. He slows the game down and is reliable.

THE FUTURE: Players with Lipcius' hitting ability, upper-level success and versatility usually find a way to carve out major league careers. He may never be a regular, but his ability to get on base, hit for average and play solid defense at multiple infield spots could help him compete for playing time as soon as 2023. The Tigers added him to the 40-man roster to protect him from the Rule 5 draft.

BA GRADE: 40/Medium	Hit: 55		Power: 40		Speed: 40		Fielding: 50		Arm: 55	

Year	Age	Club (League)	Lvl	AVG	G	AB	R	H	2B	3B	HR	RBI	BB	SO	SB	OBP	SLG
2022	24	Erie (EL)	AA	.264	88	303	52	80	20	1	9	39	61	56	12	.392	.426
2022	24	Toledo (IL)	AAA	.302	46	159	18	48	13	1	3	24	25	33	1	.388	.453
Minor League Totals				.263	317	1139	167	300	71	6	26	151	164	244	23	.355	.405

19 WENCEEL PEREZ, 2B

Born: October 30, 1999. **B-T:** S-R. **HT:** 5-11. **WT:** 203.
Signed: Dominican Republic, 2016. **Signed by:** Ramon Perez/Carlos Santana.

TRACK RECORD: Signed out of the Dominican Republic in the 2016 international draft class for $550,000, Perez's progression has been a curious story to follow. After spending 2017 in the Dominican Summer League, he dazzled the following year with a jump across three affiliates, including slashing .309/.324/.441 with Low-A West Michigan. Between 2019 and 2021, Perez hit a snag at the plate and in the field, leading to some rough defense from a once-fluid infielder. Perez hit a new stride in 2022, earning a promotion to Double-A Erie where he slashed .307/.374/.540.

SCOUTING REPORT: One of the most confounding development stories within the Tigers' organization, Perez is once again proof that no prospect develops at the same pace. A confident, athletic infielder, Perez, at his strongest, is light of foot with polished hands and a mature first step. Although he spent the majority of his early years at shortstop, the Tigers have transitioned Perez to more work at second base, where he spent a good deal of his 2022 season. In addition to displaying more raw power in 2022, Perez showed better plate discipline by chasing fewer bad pitches.

THE FUTURE: With his successes at Double-A, in addition to added defensive versatility, Perez could stand to return to Erie to start the 2023 season. Perez was added to the 40-man roster in the offseason.

BA GRADE: 45/High		Hit: 45		Power: 45		Speed: 60		Fielding: 50		Arm: 55			

Year	Age	Club (League)	Lvl	AVG	G	AB	R	H	2B	3B	HR	RBI	BB	SO	SB	OBP	SLG
2022	22	West Michigan (MWL)	HiA	.286	55	206	35	59	13	5	9	38	27	38	13	.364	.529
2022	22	Erie (EL)	AA	.307	39	150	28	46	10	5	5	28	15	23	5	.374	.540
Minor League Totals				.273	449	1694	256	463	77	27	24	192	176	288	90	.342	.393

20 MASON ENGLERT, RHP

Born: Nov. 1, 1999. **B-T:** B-R. **Ht.:** 6-4. **Wt.:** 205.
Drafted: HS—Forney, Texas, 2018 (4th round). **Signed by:** Josh Simpson (Rangers).

TRACK RECORD: After signing for $1 million in 2018, Englert was part of the Rangers' ill-fated plan to shut down all of their 2018 top pitching signees. Englert quickly blew out his elbow. He had Tommy John surgery early in the 2019 season and didn't make his pro debut until 2021, nearly three years after he signed. Englert threw seven innings of a no-hitter in 2022, followed by six no-hit innings in his next start, but the no-hitter was broken up with two outs in the ninth. Englert was acquired by the Tigers as a Rule 5 pick.

SCOUTING REPORT: Englert has two and four-seam 91-93 mph fastballs, a low-80s slider, a mid-70s curveball and a low-80s changeup. He can attack hitters with a sinker/slider approach or four-seam fastballs up in the zone mixed with curveballs. None of his pitches is plus, and only his changeup grades as above-average, but every one of his pitches is fringe-average to above-average and he has above-average control.

THE FUTURE: As a Rule 5 pick, Englert will have to make a big leap from less than 200 innings of minor league experience and three starts of Double-A to the big leagues. His varied arsenal fits better as a No. 4 or No. 5 starter than it does as a reliever, but his short-term role more likely is as a long-man in the pen.

BA GRADE: 45/High		Fastball: 50		Curveball: 45		Slider: 50		Changeup: 55		Control: 55			

Year	Age	Club (League)	Lvl	W	L	ERA	G	GS	IP	H	HR	BB	SO	BB/9	SO/9	WHIP	AVG
2022	22	Hickory (SAL)	HiA	7	5	3.57	21	21	103	73	15	26	116	2.3	10.1	0.96	.193
2022	22	Frisco (TL)	AA	1	1	4.11	3	3	15	14	1	5	20	2.9	11.7	1.24	.237
Minor League Totals				14	9	3.93	43	43	199	160	20	57	226	2.6	10.2	1.09	.216

21 TROY MELTON, RHP

Born: Dec. 3, 2000. **B-T:** R-R. **HT:** 6-4. **WT:** 210.
Drafted: San Diego State, 2022 (4th round). **Signed by:** Steve Pack.

TRACK RECORD: Melton was a draft-eligible redshirt sophomore in 2021, but no team was going to meet his bonus demands at the end of a disappointing season that saw him go 4-5, 6.13 with a .291 opponents average. That proved to be a wise choice for Melton. He finished his marketing degree and blossomed after shortening his arm action. He went 5-2, 2.07 as the Aztecs ace. He barely pitched after signing, making two brief appearances in September.

SCOUTING REPORT: Melton sits 93-95 mph and will touch 98 with his above-average fastball. While he has started to fill out, there's still the potential for additional strength gains. Melton has added a low-90s sinker as well, which gives hitters another fastball to worry about. Melton mixes in a mid-80s, fringe-average slider with late break that could strengthen with more use. His final offering is an 87-88 mph changeup that projects as a future average offering. Melton's new, shorter arm action improved his ability to repeat his delivery, which has helped him improve his control. He slashed his walk rate from 8.8% of hitters in 2021 to 5.6% of hitters in 2022.

THE FUTURE: After taking a cautious approach to start his pro career, Melton should be ready for a full season of work in 2023. He could begin the season in the warmth of Low-A Lakeland, but should spend most of the year at High-A West Michigan.

BA GRADE: 45/High	**Fastball:** 55		**Slider:** 45		**Changeup:** 50		**Control:** 50			

Year	Age	Club (League)	Lvl	W	L	ERA	G	GS	IP	H	HR	BB	SO	BB/9	SO/9	WHIP	AVG
2022	21	Lakeland (FSL)	LoA	0	0	0.00	2	2	5	3	0	0	5	0.0	9.0	0.60	.188
Minor League Totals				0	0	0.00	2	2	5	3	0	0	5	0.0	9.0	0.60	.188

22 JOSH CROUCH, C

Born: Dec. 7, 1998. **B-T:** R-R. **HT:** 6-0. **WT:** 200.
Drafted: Central Florida, 2021 (11th round). **Signed by:** RJ Burgess.

TRACK RECORD: After navigating a pandemic just after transferring to Central Florida, Josh Crouch was able to find his stride with the Golden Knights the following year, slashing a team-best .311/.435/.574 and pushing him onto the Tigers' draft radar. The collegiate defensive standout was selected as Detroit's 11th-round pick that same year and signed for $125,000. Crouch received praise across the organization for his work behind the plate and climbed three levels in 2022.

SCOUTING REPORT: Crouch has quickly established himself as one of the best defensive catchers in the organization, with only Dillon Dingler rivaling him as a receiver. At the plate, Crouch has quickly come into his own and has used a sharpened batting eye to drop his strikeout percentage nearly 10 points between Low-A Lakeland and High-A West Michigan and has begun to string together good at-bats, although his power is still hit or miss. He has also worked to develop behind the plate. Crouch boasts a plus arm, which helps him shut down running games. He's thrown out 31% of basestealers for his career.

THE FUTURE: Crouch has looked like a steal so far as a late-round pick. His initial assignment in 2022 may depend in part on him and in part on where Dingler begins the season, but he should spend a good part of the season at Double-A Erie.

BA GRADE: 45/High	**Hit:** 50		**Power:** 40		**Speed:** 35		**Fielding:** 55		**Arm:** 55	

Year	Age	Club (League)	Lvl	AVG	G	AB	R	H	2B	3B	HR	RBI	BB	SO	SB	OBP	SLG
2022	23	Lakeland (FSL)	LoA	.333	11	36	7	12	3	0	0	5	5	10	0	.419	.417
2022	23	West Michigan (MWL)	HiA	.290	90	335	43	97	22	0	10	61	38	56	1	.366	.445
2022	23	Erie (EL)	AA	.167	6	24	1	4	0	0	1	4	0	6	0	.167	.292
Minor League Totals				.276	131	482	63	133	26	1	13	86	48	103	1	.343	.415

23 MANUEL SEQUERA, SS/3B

Born: Sept. 28, 2002. **B-T:** R-R. **HT:** 6-1. **WT:** 170.
Signed: Venezuela, 2019. **Signed by:** Jesus Mendoza.

TRACK RECORD: One of Detroit's top signings during the 2019 international signing period, Sequera didn't get to make his pro debut until 2021 because of the coronavirus pandemic, but he used the layoff to get bigger and stronger. Sequera's 11 home runs led the Florida Complex League in 2021. This year, he fell one short of going back-to-back on home run titles, as his 19 home runs were second best in the Florida State League, one behind the Mets' Carlos Dominguez.

SCOUTING REPORT: A physical player with a broad-shouldered power hitter's build, Sequera has a swing geared to consistently get to that power. He has a significant leg kick and excellent rotational speed paired with a fluid swing. Sequera's top end exit velocities (106 mph) aren't all that spectacular, but he should continue to get stronger. Sequera has one glaring flaw at the plate that he has to improve. He currently swings at most anything and chases out of the zone way too often. If he gets a pitch in the zone, his above-average bat-to-ball skills are apparent, but he's too often swinging at unhittable pitches. His 22% strikeout rate is an impressive testament to those bat-to-ball skills considering his incredibly aggressive approach. Defensively, Sequera has limited range and below-average speed. He started playing second and third base regularly, which are better fits than shortstop. His average arm should be able to handle either spot.

THE FUTURE: Sequera's 2022 season was better than the slash line may indicate. As a multi-position infielder with power potential, he has everyday regular potential. High-A West Michigan beckons.

BA GRADE: 50/Extreme		Hit: 40		Power: 55		Speed: 40		Fielding: 50		Arm: 50	

Year	Age	Club (League)	Lvl	AVG	G	AB	R	H	2B	3B	HR	RBI	BB	SO	SB	OBP	SLG
2022	19	Lakeland (FSL)	LoA	.232	116	457	59	106	28	1	19	64	20	110	4	.279	.422
Minor League Totals				.236	162	628	90	148	40	1	30	104	35	167	5	.289	.446

24 ABEL BASTIDAS, SS

Born: Nov. 24, 2003. **B-T:** B-R. **HT:** 6-2. **WT:** 165.
Signed: Venezuela, 2021. **Signed by:** Jesus Mendoza.
TRACK RECORD: One of the more prominent signings in the Tigers' 2021 international class, Bastidas seemed overmatched at times in his pro debut. To his credit, he bounced back to produce a solid season in the Florida Complex League in 2022. The Venezuelan native had drawn high praise for his defensive profile, polished from his work with Cesar and Maicer Izturis.
SCOUTING REPORT: Bastidas is a tall, lanky shortstop. He's skinny and fluid, so he may be able to be a taller-than-average shortstop, but he also has the potential to thicken up and turn into a more powerful third baseman. Currently, his lack of functional strength is apparent. He makes excellent swing decisions, but pitchers do not need to fear him as he barely has gap power at this point. Bastidas has a fluid swing from both sides of the plate with fringe-average power that is expected to develop as his physique fills out. Defensively, Bastidas has quick feet, a good first step, an accurate, above-average arm and instincts well beyond his years for reading the ball off the bat. He's an above-average runner
THE FUTURE: Still 19 years old, there is no cause for Detroit to rush Bastidas. Based on his success, he'll likely begin 2023 with Low-A Lakeland. He remains one of the Tigers' most promising young position prospects.

BA GRADE: 50/Extreme		Hit: 55		Power: 45		Speed: 55		Fielding: 55		Arm: 55	

Year	Age	Club (League	Lvl	AVG	G	AB	R	H	2B	3B	HR	RBI	BB	SO	SB	OBP	SLG
2022	18	Tigers (FCL)	R	.260	44	154	18	40	10	2	3	26	24	33	4	.361	.409
Minor League Totals				.221	98	335	42	74	14	5	5	53	59	79	16	.341	.337

25 ADINSO REYES, SS

Born: Oct. 22, 2001. **B-T:** R-R. **HT:** 6-1. **WT:** 195.
Signed: Dominican Republic, 2018. **Signed by:** Aldo Perez.
TRACK RECORD: The Tigers liked Reyes' projectable frame and natural strength enough to sign him for $1.45 million in 2018. Reyes torched the Dominican Summer League in 2019, hitting .331/.379/.508 with seven home runs and 48 RBIs. Reyes was overmatched in the Florida Complex League in 2021, but bounced back in a return to the FCL before struggling after a late-season promotion to Low-A Lakeland.
SCOUTING REPORT: When you watch Reyes in action, it's easy to see why much the Tigers had to dream on. In addition to his pure strength, Reyes has an advanced approach that has helped him drive the ball to all fields. His swing is often too long, but there is apparent power potential. Reyes improved his chase rate significantly in 2022, but it remains an issue. The Tigers moved Reyes to third base nearly full-time in August. There were some adjustment issues as he posted an .887 fielding percentage in 36 games there, but that is his likely long-term home, as his feet and average arm play better there.
THE FUTURE: Reyes has shown himself to be a player who needs to be promoted slowly, as he often requires some time at a level to acclimate himself before getting comfortable. His late-season stint at Lakeland should help prep him for a return there in 2023.

BA GRADE: 50/Extreme		Hit: 40		Power: 50		Speed: 50		Fielding: 50		Arm: 50	

Year	Age	Club (League)	Lvl	AVG	G	AB	R	H	2B	3B	HR	RBI	BB	SO	SB	OBP	SLG
2022	20	Tigers (FCL)	R	.333	32	117	19	39	6	0	5	21	12	32	1	.394	.513
2022	20	Lakeland (FSL)	LoA	.187	22	75	11	14	1	0	4	4	8	35	0	.265	.360
Minor League Totals				.273	164	597	95	163	34	1	23	91	46	191	5	.338	.449

26 BRANT HURTER, LHP

Born: Sept. 6, 1998. **B-T:** L-L. **HT:** 6-6. **WT:** 250.
Drafted: Georgia Tech, 2021 (7th round). **Signed by:** Bryson Barber.
TRACK RECORD: Hurter first grabbed attention as a sophomore with Georgia Tech in 2019 before suffer-

ing an elbow injury that led to Tommy John surgery. After missing the entirety of the 2020 season, Hurter worked his way back to commanding attention and landed as the Tigers' seventh-round selection in 2021. He didn't look fully recovered in 2021, but his stuff ticked back up in 2022. He climbed through three levels in a season that ended at Double-A Erie.

SCOUTING REPORT: Hurter is a massive presence on the mound as a 6-foot-6, 250-pound southpaw. At his best, he pounds the zone with a 91-94 mph two-seam fastball and an above-average slider. His fastball was up 2-3 mph compared to where he was sitting in 2021. His low-80s slider produces swings and misses from hitters on both sides of the plate. Hurter finishes his mix with a mid-80s, tumbling changeup that he mostly uses against righthanders. It's primarily a chase pitch. Hurter is a strike-thrower who spots his fastball and slider around the zone.

THE FUTURE: With just four outings with Erie in 2022, Hurter will likely begin the 2023 season back with the SeaWolves for more exposure against upper-level hitters. His impressive 2022 season hints at his potential as a back-of-the-rotation starter.

| BA GRADE: 40/High | | Fastball: 45 | | Slider: 55 | | Changeup: 50 | | Control: 55 | | | |

Year	Age	Club (League)	Lvl	W	L	ERA	G	GS	IP	H	HR	BB	SO	BB/9	SO/9	WHIP	AVG
2022	23	Lakeland (FSL)	LoA	3	3	2.98	10	6	42	34	4	6	57	1.3	12.1	0.94	.212
2022	23	West Michigan (MWL)	HiA	4	1	3.20	11	10	51	44	2	11	62	2.0	11.0	1.09	.234
2022	23	Erie (EL)	AA	0	2	7.90	4	2	14	21	1	4	17	2.6	11.2	1.83	.350
Minor League Totals				7	6	3.71	25	18	107	99	7	21	136	1.8	11.5	1.13	.243

27 GAGE WORKMAN, 3B

Born: Oct. 24, 1999. **B-T:** B-R. **HT:** 6-3. **WT:** 202.
Drafted: Arizona State, 2020 (4th round). **Signed by:** Joey Lothrop.

TRACK RECORD: The Tigers doubled down on Arizona State products in the 2020 draft. Spencer Torkelson was the team's first-round pick and Workman, his Sun Devils' teammate, was the team's fourth-round pick. The son of Padres' 1996 third-round pick Widd Workman, Gage struck out in 40% of plate appearances in 2022 and his 206 strikeouts were fourth-most in the minors. Workman was sent to the Arizona Fall League to try to help finish the season on a high note, but he hit .193/.230/.386 with a 39% strikeout rate.

SCOUTING REPORT: Workman is a switch-hitter whose lefthanded swing has been better and more consistent than his righthanded swing. He has above-average power from both sides of the plate. Workman's ability to hit to all fields, combined with his base-running savvy is praised, but unless he makes more contact, his otherwise well-rounded skill set won't get him to the majors. Workman struggles with chasing pitches out of the zone, but he also misses hittable pitches in the zone as well. He is extremely fluid defensively with soft hands, average range and an above-average arm that make him an average defender at third base. He's an average runner but is aggressive on the basepaths

THE FUTURE: Workman likely needs to return to Erie after struggling at the plate. He is going to need to make much more contact to have a shot at an MLB role, as MiLB players with his current strikeout rates almost always end up falling short.

| BA GRADE: 45/Extreme | | Hit: 30 | | Power: 55 | | Speed: 50 | | Fielding: 50 | | Arm: 55 | | | |

Year	Age	Club (League)	Lvl	AVG	G	AB	R	H	2B	3B	HR	RBI	BB	SO	SB	OBP	SLG
2022	22	Erie (EL)	AA	.225	128	475	61	107	30	9	14	68	34	206	30	.276	.415
Minor League Totals				.235	246	927	129	218	67	15	26	126	87	363	61	.301	.424

28 JAVIER OSORIO, SS

Born: March 29, 2005. **B-T:** R-R. **HT:** 6-0. **WT:** 165.
Signed: Venezuela, 2022. **Signed by:** Jesus Mendoza/Oscar Garcia.

TRACK RECORD: Osorio was the Tigers' top target in the 2022 international class. Just five months later he made his pro debut in the Dominican Summer League, but the speed of the game seemed a little too fast. He hit .175/.281/.227 with just six extra-base hits, 12 RBIs and a 38% strikeout rate in 46 games. On back-to-back days Osorio went 0-for-5 with five strikeouts.

SCOUTING REPORT: As rough as his debut may have been, Osorio has an interesting blend of natural athleticism and abundant projection remaining in his lanky teenage frame. He just needs to get a lot stronger, which will help his bat speed and power continue to improve. He has a very whippy bat already, and should add more power as his frame fills out. When he was an amateur, some scouts projected him to eventually have 20-home run potential. He has a shot to stay at shortstop with quick hands, solid athleticism and a plus arm. He's an above-average runner.

THE FUTURE: Osorio won't turn 18 until the end of 2023's spring training. His struggles in 2022 show he may benefit from a return to the Dominican Summer League to start 2023, although a strong first half could earn him a stateside debut later in the season.

BA GRADE: 45/Extreme		Hit: 50			Power: 50		Speed: 55			Fielding: 50		Arm: 60	
Year	Age	Club (League)	Lvl	AVG	G	AB	R	H	2B	3B	HR	RBI	BB	SO	SB	OBP	SLG
2022	17	Tigers 1 (DSL)	R	.175	46	154	17	27	5	0	1	12	16	68	15	.281	.227
Minor League Totals				.175	46	154	17	27	5	0	1	12	16	68	15	.281	.227

29 JOSE DE LA CRUZ, OF

Born: Jan. 3, 2002. **B-T:** R-R. **HT:** 6-0. **WT:** 216.
Signed: Dominican Republic, 2018. **Signed by:** Aldo Perez/Carlos Santana.
TRACK RECORD: De La Cruz was a $1.8 million signing in 2018. He dazzled in his Dominican Summer League debut, slashing .307/.375/.556 with 11 home runs. In each of the past two seasons he has struggled and failed to hit .210 or post a .300 on-base percentage. He did hit 11 home runs in 2022.
SCOUTING REPORT: De La Cruz has drawn praise for his all-out style of play. Despite his rough stat lines, there's still plenty of power potential. De La Cruz produces hard contact thanks to his plus bat speed, but his 38% strikeout rate in the past two seasons has so far kept him from utilizing that plus power as much as he and the Tigers desire. He struggles against righthanders. Defensively, De La Cruz boasts plus speed and a plus arm, which profiles well across the outfield. His power potential probably fits best in right field ,where he can continue to get bigger and stronger.
THE FUTURE: De La Cruz did show improvements in 2022, even if he still has a long ways to go at the plate. He should reach High-A West Michigan in 2023.

BA GRADE: 45/Extreme		Hit: 40			Power: 55		Speed: 60			Fielding: 55		Arm: 60	
Year	Age	Club (League)	Lvl	AVG	G	AB	R	H	2B	3B	HR	RBI	BB	SO	SB	OBP	SLG
2022	20	Tigers (FCL)	R	.238	6	21	5	5	2	0	1	3	1	11	1	.304	.476
2022	20	Lakeland (FSL)	LoA	.202	92	307	31	62	10	1	10	42	29	132	3	.287	.339
Minor League Totals				.231	237	854	126	197	37	8	27	109	75	350	33	.312	.388

30 ELIEZER ALFONZO JR., C

Born: Sept. 23, 1999. **B-T:** B-R. **HT:** 5-10. **WT:** 155.
Signed: Venezuela, 2016. **Signed by:** Alejandro Rodriguez/Raul Leiva.
TRACK RECORD: The son of big league catcher Eliezer Alfonzo, the younger Alfonzo has always been moved slowly by the Tigers, but he's generally hit while drawing raves for his defense. A 2016 signee out of Venezuela, Alfonso has hit over .300 in four out of five pro seasons, but he's generally been asked to repeat levels. He missed significant time in 2022 because of a thigh strain, a back injury and an elbow fracture.
SCOUTING REPORT: Drawing comparisons to former Tigers backstop Brayan Peña—now a Tigers MiLB manager—Alfonzo shows advanced maturity and impressive defensive chops. Defensively, Alfonzo moves more quickly than his solid frame would suggest and should continue to polish that as he loses weight. His fringe-average arm plays up because of a quick release. Alfonzo's offensive profile has always been more of a concern. His swing can be a little choppy, but he has consistently performed. He's often been old for the levels where he's played, but he's a career .304/.370/.392 hitter. He makes good swing decisions and has solid bat-to-ball skills but below-average power.
THE FUTURE: The Tigers did not protect Alfonzo from the Rule 5 draft, figuring correctly that a Class A catcher would not merit much attention.

BA GRADE: 40/High		Hit: 55			Power: 40		Speed: 45			Fielding: 55		Arm: 45	
Year	Age	Club (League)	Lvl	AVG	G	AB	R	H	2B	3B	HR	RBI	BB	SO	SB	OBP	SLG
2022	22	Tigers (FCL)	R	.500	2	6	3	3	0	0	0	0	2	0	0	.625	.500
2022	22	Lakeland (FSL)	LoA	.185	7	27	3	5	1	0	0	0	1	6	0	.214	.222
2022	22	West Michigan (MWL)	HiA	.354	12	48	11	17	1	0	2	10	6	6	0	.421	.500
Minor League Totals				.304	274	959	132	292	42	3	12	136	100	99	16	.370	.392

Houston Astros

BY GEOFF PONTES

The Astros' dominance of the American League continued in 2022, when they won the pennant and reached the World Series for the sixth straight year and captured their third title since 2017.

Success has become a habit in Houston. Unfortunately, so have dramatic offseasons.

While nowhere near the magnitude of the sign-stealing scandal of 2017, the departures of general manager James Click and assistant general manager Scott Powers shook the team while it was basking in its post-championship glow.

Click rejected a one-year contract after his previous deal expired in November. In the aftermath, Powers was relieved of his duties and left many wondering who would take over control of the team. Owner Jim Crane became more involved in front office decisions in the offseason as the team searched for Click's replacement.

The Astros also lost a pair of executives to other clubs. International cross-checker Oz Ocampo left to become an assistant general manager with the Marlins and assistant general manager Pete Putila left to take the GM job in San Francisco.

Despite the front office shakeup, the Astros remain one of the strongest organizations in the game and boast a talented major league roster built predominantly on homegrown talents.

The Astros were aggressive early in the offseason. Soon after free agency began they signed former White Sox first baseman Jose Abreu to add to an already formidable lineup. They also re-signed reliever Rafael Montero to a three-year, $34.5 million contract.

Houston lost ace Justin Verlander to the Mets as a free agent, but boasts five returning starters from last year's team plus top prospect Hunter Brown.

Despite being viewed as one of the worst farm systems in baseball the last several seasons, the Astros have continued to supplement their roster with homegrown big league regulars.

With the departure of all-star shortstop Carlos Correa before the season, the Astros plugged top prospect Jeremy Peña into an everyday role. Peña went through ups and downs over the course of the season but ultimately proved a worthy replacement. He hit his stride at the right time and starred in a postseason run by winning MVP honors in both the ALCS and World Series.

Brown also made his debut late in the season and was included on the Astros' playoff roster. Catchers Korey Lee and Yainer Diaz each made their major league debuts as well, as did infielders David Hensley and J.J. Matijevic.

With their penalties for the sign-stealing scandal

Rookie Jeremy Peña hit .345 with four homers, eight RBIs and 12 runs in 13 postseason games.

PROJECTED 2026 LINEUP

Catcher	Korey Lee	27
First Base	Yainer Diaz	27
Second Base	Jose Altuve	36
Third Base	Alex Bregman	32
Shortstop	Jeremy Peña	28
Left Field	Chas McCormick	31
Center Field	Drew Gilbert	25
Right Field	Kyle Tucker	29
Designated Hitter	Yordan Alvarez	28
No. 1 Starter	Framber Valdez	32
No. 2 Starter	Lance McCullers Jr.	32
No. 3 Starter	Cristian Javier	29
No. 4 Starter	Luis Garcia	29
No. 5 Starter	Hunter Brown	27
Closer	Rafael Montero	35

in the books, the Astros had a first-round pick once more and used it to land Tennesee outfielder Drew Gilbert. The Astros drafted 11 college players over the first 10 rounds of the draft and didn't dip into the high school ranks until their selection of outfielder Ryan Clifford in the 11th round.

On the heels of another World Series win, the Astros look like a machine built to contend for the title for years to come.

Their farm system certainly isn't the deepest, but the team has proved time and time again that it's adept at uncovering hidden talent and polishing that into players who star on the game's biggest stage.

Now, the only question is: Who's next? ∎

HOUSTON ASTROS

TOP 2023 MLB CONTRIBUTORS	RANK
Hunter Brown, RHP	1
Yainer Diaz, C	2
David Hensley, 3B	5
Pedro Leon, OF	6
Korey Lee, C	7
BREAKOUT PROSPECTS	**RANK**
Andrew Taylor, RHP	12
Kenedy Corona, OF	14
Jose Fleury, RHP	24

SOURCE OF TOP 30 TALENT

Homegrown	28	Acquired	2
College	18	Trade	2
Junior college	0	Rule 5 draft	0
High school	4	Independent league	0
Nondrafted free agent	1	Free agent/waivers	0
International	5		

LF
Ryan Clifford (20)
Corey Julks (29)
Marty Costes
Ross Adolph

CF
Drew Gilbert (3)
Jacob Melton (4)
Pedro Leon (6)
Colin Barber (11)
Kenedy Corona (14)
Michael Sandle
Logan Cerny

RF
Justin Dirden (9)
Quincy Hamilton (16)
Alex McKenna
Zach Daniels
Tyler Whitaker
Luis Baez

3B
David Hensley (5)
Joe Perez (13)
Waner Luciano

SS
Dauri Lorenzo
Cristian Gonzalez
Grae Kessinger
Freudis Nova
Alejandro Nuñez
Yamal Encarnacion

2B
Will Wagner (18)
Shay Whitcomb
Luis Santana

1B
Joey Loperfido (17)
J.J. Matijevic (23)
Scott Schreiber

C
Yainer Diaz (2)
Korey Lee (7)
J.C. Correa
Ryan Wrobleski

LHP

LHSP	LHRP
Trey Dombroski (19)	Parker Mushinski (26)
Colton Gordon (28)	Max Roberts
Julio Robiana	Bryan King

RHP

RHSP	RHRP
Hunter Brown (1)	Miguel Ullola (10)
Spencer Arrighetti (8)	J.P. France (21)
Andrew Taylor (12)	Jose Fleury (24)
Misael Tamarez (15)	Shawn Dubin (27)
Jaime Melendez (22)	
Michael Knorr (25)	
Forrest Whitley (30)	
Jayden Murray	
Jimmy Endersby	
Edinson Batista	
Brett Conine	
Nolan Devos	
A.J. Blubaugh	
Alimber Santa	

1 HUNTER BROWN, RHP

Born: Aug. 29, 1998. **B-T:** R-R. **HT:** 6-2. **WT:** 212.
Drafted: Wayne State (Mich.), 2019 (5th round).
Signed by: Scott Oberhelman.

EDDIE KELLY

TRACK RECORD: The Astros drafted Brown in the fifth round in 2019 and signed him for an above-slot $325,000 bonus following a breakout season at Division II Wayne State in Detroit. Brown debuted that summer in the short-season New York-Penn League, then missed 2020 because of the pandemic. He jumped straight to Double-A Corpus Christi when play resumed in 2021 and reached Triple-A Sugar Land in early August. Brown made 11 Triple-A appearances over the final two months of the season and struck out 55 batters in 51 innings. He returned to Sugar Land to begin 2022 and made 23 appearances, alternating time as a traditional starter and a bulk pitcher behind an opener. Brown showed improved command of his powerful arsenal as he posted a career-best strikeout-to-walk ratio and was selected to pitch in the Futures Game. The Astros called up Brown in early September and he joined his childhood hero Justin Verlander as a member of the Astros staff. He pitched effectively in September, was selected for the Astros' postseason roster and made three scoreless appearances between the Division Series and the Championship Series. Brown was included on Houston's World Series roster but did not appear in a game.

SCOUTING REPORT: Few define the modern pitcher archetype like Brown, who is a tall right-hander with a muscular build and above-average athleticism. He works from a semi-windup with a longer arm action and delivers pitches from an over-the-top release. Brown in many ways mimics the operation of former Astros teammate Justin Verlander, whom he grew up watching in Detroit. In this way, Brown, like Verlander, is able to fluidly generate power across his pitch mix. Brown's arsenal consists of four pitches, with his four-seam fastball and two breaking ball shapes working as his primary repertoire. His fastball sits 95-97 mph and touches 100. It plays up even further because of efficient back spin and an unusually flat plane from his high arm slot. Brown uses two breaking balls with distinctively different shapes in a low-90s slider/cutter hybrid and a low-to-mid-80s curveball with significant depth. Each of Brown's breaking pitches succeeds for different reasons. His ability to command his slider in and out of the zone drives mishits and chase swings, while his curveball depth plays perfectly off of his four-

seam shape. This allows Brown to dominate with a north-south plan of attack. He'll mix in an upper-80s changeup, but it was rarely used. Brown's command bumped to average in 2022.

THE FUTURE: A power pitcher capable of succeeding in a variety of roles, Brown is poised to claim a rotation spot for the reigning World Series-champion Astros in 2023.

BA GRADE	SCOUTING GRADES
65 Risk: High	FB: 70. SL: 55. CB: 55. CHG: 45. CTL: 50.

Projected future grades on 20-80 scouting scale

BEST TOOLS

BATTING

Best Hitter for Average	Yainer Diaz
Best Power Hitter	Yainer Diaz
Best Strike-Zone Discipline	David Hensley
Fastest Baserunner	Logan Cerny
Best Athlete	Zach Daniels

PITCHING

Best Fastball	Hunter Brown
Best Curveball	Hunter Brown
Best Slider	Spencer Arrighetti
Best Changeup	Shawn Dubin
Best Control	Colton Gordon

FIELDING

Best Defensive Catcher	Korey Lee
Best Defensive Infielder	Cristian Gonzalez
Best Infield Arm	Drew Gilbert
Best Defensive Outfielder	Joe Perez
Best Outfield Arm	Pedro Leon

Year	Age	Club (League)	Lvl	W	L	ERA	G	GS	IP	H	HR	BB	SO	BB/9	SO/9	WHIP	AVG
2022	23	Sugar Land (PCL)	AAA	9	4	2.55	23	14	106	70	5	45	134	3.8	11.4	1.08	.186
2022	23	Houston (AL)	MLB	2	0	0.89	7	2	20	15	0	7	22	3.1	9.7	1.08	.205
Major League Totals				2	0	0.89	7	2	20	15	0	7	22	3.1	9.7	1.08	.205
Minor League Totals				17	11	3.40	59	39	230	175	17	113	298	4.4	11.7	1.25	.210

2 YAINER DIAZ, C

Born: Sept. 21, 1998. **B-T:** R-R. **HT:** 6-0. **WT:** 195. **Signed:** Dominican Republic, 2016. **Signed by:** Rigo De Los Santos/Jhonathan Leyba/Koby Perez (Guardians).

TRACK RECORD: Originally signed by the Guardians out of the Dominican Republic for $25,000, Diaz hit .331/.358/.470 over his first three pro seasons, all in short-season leagues. He continued hitting with Low-A Lynchburg in 2021 to catch the attention of the Astros, who acquired him and Phil Maton at the 2021 trade deadline for Myles Straw. Diaz split the 2022 season between Double-A and Triple-A, and hit .306/.356/.542 with 25 home runs to earn his first MLB callup in early September.

SCOUTING REPORT: A strong combination of bat-to-ball skills and power drives Diaz's aggressive plate profile. Stockily built with a strong, barrel-chested frame, Diaz shows the ability to drive stinging liners and hard-struck fly balls to all fields. His simple swing is heavily hands-driven, but his strong

BA GRADE

50 Risk: Medium

wrists and loose adjustability within his hands allow him to attack a variety of pitch shapes. He's a free-swinger who will get himself into trouble on the outer parts of the plate. Diaz's power plays to all fields, and he slugged nine of his 25 home runs in 2022 to right field. His average exit velocity of 92.3 mph in the minors is well above the major league average. He is most likely to hit for a higher average with home run totals in the mid 20s but lower on-base percentages because of his aggressive nature. Defensively, Diaz is a good thrower and average framer, but his blocking skills are fringy. He has faced questions around his game-calling, leading to a heavy dose of starts at first base.

THE FUTURE: One of the best hitting catchers in the minor leagues, Diaz will likely slide into a part-time catching role, seeing time at first base and DH to keep his powerful bat in the lineup.

SCOUTING GRADES	Hitting: 50	Power: 60	Speed: 30	Fielding: 50	Arm: 60

Year	Age	Club (League)	Lvl	AVG	G	AB	R	H	2B	3B	HR	RBI	BB	SO	SB	OBP	SLG
2022	23	Corpus Christi (TL)	AA	.316	57	244	37	77	13	3	9	48	21	40	1	.367	.504
2022	23	Sugar Land (PCL)	AAA	.294	48	201	38	59	9	1	16	48	13	39	1	.342	.587
2022	23	Houston (AL)	MLB	.125	6	8	0	1	1	0	0	1	1	2	0	.222	.250
Major League Totals				.125	6	8	0	1	1	0	0	1	1	2	0	.222	.250
Minor League Totals				.321	340	1353	203	434	76	12	52	275	75	208	7	.358	.510

3 DREW GILBERT, OF

Born: Sept. 27, 2000. **B-T:** L-L. **HT:** 5-9. **WT:** 185.
Drafted: Tennessee, 2022 (1st round). **Signed by:** Freddy Perez.

TRACK RECORD: Gilbert stood out as the heart and soul of the Tennessee team that ranked No. 1 all through 2022. He hit .362/.455/.673 with 11 home runs in 58 games. He went viral when he was ejected from Tennessee's super regional showdown with Notre Dame for arguing a called strike in a bizarre moment. The Astros selected Gilbert with the 28th overall pick and signed him for $2,497,500. He debuted with Low-A Fayetteville in August, but his season ended abruptly after a collision with an outfield wall.

SCOUTING REPORT: A high-energy player with an all-gas-no-brakes approach to the game, Gilbert plays with an edge, but his tooled-up skill set is well-rounded on both sides of the ball. At the plate, Gilbert's game is predicated

BA GRADE

50 Risk: High

on his ability to manage the strike zone and make high rates of barrel contact, particularly to right field. His maxed-out and muscular frame doesn't portend future power gains, but he's an average power hitter adept at ambushing pitches on the inner half to drive the ball to his pull side. While he's not an aggressive basestealer, Gilbert will flash plus run times, though he's more consistently an above-average runner. His speed translates to center field, where he's an above-average defender. Gilbert gets good jumps and has a plus arm that will play in any spot in the outfield. His all-around game and skill set should translate to an everyday role in the outfield, with little debate around Gilbert's medley of tools.

THE FUTURE: A strong all-around talent with average or better tools across the board, Gilbert likely settles in as an average everyday center fielder.

SCOUTING GRADES	Hitting: 55	Power: 50	Speed: 55	Fielding: 55	Arm: 60

Year	Age	Club (League)	Lvl	AVG	G	AB	R	H	2B	3B	HR	RBI	BB	SO	SB	OBP	SLG
2022	21	Astros Orange (FCL)	R	.455	4	11	5	5	1	0	1	4	3	2	3	.600	.818
2022	21	Fayetteville (CAR)	LoA	.238	6	21	4	5	0	0	1	2	1	0	3	.273	.381
Minor League Totals				.312	10	32	9	10	1	0	2	6	4	2	6	.405	.531

4 JACOB MELTON, OF

Born: Sept. 7, 2000. **B-T:** L-L. **HT:** 6-3. **WT:** 208.
Drafted: Oregon State, 2022 (2nd round). **Signed by:** Tim Costic.
TRACK RECORD: Melton split time between first base and right field for Oregon State in 2021 but took over in center field in 2022 and hit .360/.424/.671 with 17 home runs. He was a first-team All-American and the Pacific-12 Conference player of the year. The Astros selected Melton with the 64th overall pick in the second round and signed him for an under-slot bonus of $1 million. He reached Low-A Fayetteville in his debut.
SCOUTING REPORT: A tooled-up and athletic player, Melton's advanced hitting abilities are deceptive because of his unusual setup and move at the plate. He has a tall, strong frame that is fairly close to maxed out, but he should maintain a high level of fitness and twitch deep into his 20s. At the

BA GRADE	
50	Risk: High

plate, he sets up open with a wide-based stance. He begins his move with a high leg kick and a dip in his hand positioning before his load. His swing has a clean, whippy path that is adept at catching balls in the middle of the zone and balls in the lower quadrants. While Melton's pure bat-to-ball skills are fringe-average, he shows the ability to work deep into counts. His power plays to all fields. Melton's exit velocities highlight his above-average power, with a 105.4 mph 90th percentile exit velocity in his pro debut. His plus straight-line speed allows him to leg out infield hits and turn singles into doubles. In the outfield, Melton covers ground and gets good jumps in center field. He has an average arm that fits in any of the three outfield spots.
THE FUTURE: As a toolsy player with an above-average offensive game capable of handling center field, Melton projects as an average everyday regular.

SCOUTING GRADES	Hitting: 45	Power: 55	Speed: 60	Fielding: 50	Arm: 50

Year	Age	Club (League)	Lvl	AVG	G	AB	R	H	2B	3B	HR	RBI	BB	SO	SB	OBP	SLG
2022	21	Astros Blue (FCL)	R	.000	4	17	0	0	0	0	0	0	0	6	1	.000	.000
2022	21	Fayetteville (CAR)	LoA	.324	19	71	11	23	6	0	4	13	11	20	4	.424	.577
Minor League Totals				.261	23	88	11	23	6	0	4	13	11	26	5	.353	.466

5 DAVID HENSLEY, SS/3B

Born: March 28, 1996. **B-T:** R-R. **HT:** 6-6. **WT:** 190.
Drafted: San Diego State, 2018 (26th round). **Signed by:** Ryan Leake.
TRACK RECORD: Drafted in the 26th round in 2018 as a senior sign out of San Diego State, Hensley played all over the diamond for the Aztecs and converted from right fielder to shortstop his senior season. Noted for his athleticism, Hensley was primarily a contact-driven player in college. As a professional, he has slowly tapped into more raw power. After a full season at Double-A Corpus Christi in 2021, Hensley was assigned to Triple-A Sugar Land to start 2022. There, he hit .298/.420/.478 with 30 doubles, 10 home runs and 20 stolen bases in 104 games. Called up to Houston in late August, Hensley hit .345/.441/.586 in 16 games and made the Astros' postseason roster. He made two starts in the World Series, collecting a hit in each game.

BA GRADE	
45	Risk: Medium

SCOUTING REPORT: Hensley is a well-rounded player but with an unusual profile as a 6-foot-6 middle infielder. He's also a late-bloomer who will play the 2023 season at age 27. At the plate, his hitting identity is centered on his above-average bat-to-ball skills and advanced approach. Hensley rarely expands his zone, and his 17% chase rate was among the lowest for qualified Triple-A hitters. While his raw power and exit velocity data is plus, Hensley's power mostly manifests in the form of hard-struck, stinging liners. His swing is fairly level and produces lots of ground balls. Hensley is an average runner and instinctive basestealer capable of reading opposing pitchers' timing. Defensively, Hensley is a tweener. While he can fill in at shortstop when needed, his best position is second base or third base.
THE FUTURE: Hensley fits the profile of a super-utility player for a competitive team and is most capable on the infield but also playable at any position but catcher in a pinch.

SCOUTING GRADES	Hitting: 55	Power: 50	Speed: 50	Fielding: 45	Arm: 45

Year	Age	Club (League)	Lvl	AVG	G	AB	R	H	2B	3B	HR	RBI	BB	SO	SB	OBP	SLG
2022	26	Sugar Land (PCL)	AAA	.298	104	379	80	113	30	4	10	57	80	103	20	.420	.478
2022	26	Houston (AL)	MLB	.345	16	29	7	10	2	1	1	5	5	6	0	.441	.586
Major League Totals				.345	16	29	7	10	2	1	1	5	5	6	0	.441	.586
Minor League Totals				.271	380	1397	208	379	88	12	29	174	193	381	44	.359	.414

6 PEDRO LEON, OF

Born: May 28, 1998. **B-T:** R-R. **HT:** 5-10. **WT:** 170.
Signed: Cuba, 2020. **Signed by:** Charlie Gonzalez.

TRACK RECORD: Signed out of Cuba for $4 million in 2020, Leon was a decorated professional in Serie Nacional. His U.S. debut was delayed in 2021 by visa issues, so he got a late start to spring training. Still, Leon headed straight to Double-A Corpus Christi and hit .249/.349/.443 in 52 games. He was promoted to Triple-A in late July but missed all of August with an injury. In 2022, the Astros assigned Leon to Triple-A Sugar Land, where he hit .228/.365/.431 in 115 games. Despite being billed as a fast-mover when he signed at age 22, Leon has yet to make his MLB debut.

BA GRADE
45 Risk: Medium

SCOUTING REPORT: An explosive and tooled-up outfielder with elite on-base skills, Leon is both an exciting and frustrating player. While he has produced high walk rates as a professional, his bat-to-ball skills are well below-average, leading to low batting averages and a fair amount of swing-and-miss, but Leon's plate discipline is strong enough to offset his poor contact skills. His raw power is heavily bat speed-driven and he looks to put the ball in the air consistently to his pull side. Leon is likely capable of home run totals in the mid 20s in his peak seasons because of his ability to ambush middle-in fastballs. He is a basestealing threat who has 56 stolen bases across two pro seasons, though he can often get overly aggressive on the bases. His double-plus speed makes up for a lack of good reads. Defensively, Leon has primarily played center field, which is his best position. His speed and plus throwing arm are assets, despite the fact he often runs inefficient routes. Leon has seen time at shortstop and second base over the last two seasons but lacks the instincts and actions for the infield.
THE FUTURE: Leon might fit best on a good team as more of a part-time or platoon outfielder.

SCOUTING GRADES	Hitting: 40	Power: 55	Speed: 70	Fielding: 45	Arm: 60

Year	Age	Club (League)	Lvl	AVG	G	AB	R	H	2B	3B	HR	RBI	BB	SO	SB	OBP	SLG
2022	24	Sugar Land (PCL)	AAA	.228	115	413	71	94	27	3	17	63	71	145	38	.365	.431
Minor League Totals				.225	187	668	111	150	36	4	26	99	110	237	56	.355	.407

7 KOREY LEE, C

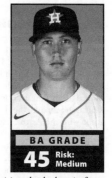

Born: July 25, 1998. **B-T:** R-R. **HT:** 6-2. **WT:** 210.
Drafted: California, 2019 (1st round). **Signed by:** Tim Costic.

TRACK RECORD: Lee was a surprise first-rounder when the Astros drafted him out of California with the 32nd overall pick in 2019. He debuted in the short-season New York-Penn League out of the draft and then missed 2020 due to the coronavirus pandemic. Lee emerged as a better player after making adjustments to both his swing and catching setup during the time off. When he reached full-season ball in 2021, he hit .277/.340/.438 across three levels. Lee reached Triple-A Sugar Land in 2022 but hit just .238/.307/.483 in 104 games. Called up in late June, he spent July with the major league club.

BA GRADE
45 Risk: Medium

SCOUTING REPORT: Lee's profile and prospect status have been heavily boosted by his defensive skills behind the plate. After flashing an average combination of contact and approach in 2021, Lee's bat-to-ball skills and swing decisions backed up in favor of a more power-centric approach. The change resulted in inconsistent production from Lee. His total of 25 home runs was a nice step up in slugging, but his overall line was below-average for the Pacific Coast League. Once a hit-over-power profile, Lee now hunts power at the plate with a lofted swing. His power plays average. Behind the plate, Lee is far more of a sure thing, with a variety of average-to-plus skills. He is an average framer based on the team's internal metrics, an above-average blocker and a true 80-grade thrower. Lee's arm is a real weapon against the running game. He is able to nab basestealers at a high rate with powerful and accurate throws, consistently clocking elite pop times on throws to second base.
THE FUTURE: Lee is a defense-first catcher with the ability to contribute about 15-20 home runs.

SCOUTING GRADES	Hitting: 40	Power: 50	Speed: 40	Fielding: 55	Arm: 80

Year	Age	Club (League)	Lvl	AVG	G	AB	R	H	2B	3B	HR	RBI	BB	SO	SB	OBP	SLG
2022	23	Sugar Land (PCL)	AAA	.238	104	404	74	96	20	2	25	76	36	127	12	.307	.483
2022	23	Houston (AL)	MLB	.160	12	25	1	4	2	0	0	4	1	9	0	.192	.240
Major League Totals				.160	12	25	1	4	2	0	0	4	1	9	0	.192	.240
Minor League Totals				.258	256	957	156	247	44	7	39	149	95	244	24	.331	.441

8 SPENCER ARRIGHETTI, RHP

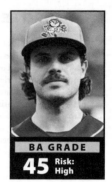

Born: Jan. 2, 2001. **B-T:** R-R. **HT:** 6-2. **WT:** 186.
Drafted: Louisiana-Lafayette, 2021 (6th round). **Signed by:** Landon Townsley.
TRACK RECORD: Arrighetti spent three seasons at three different colleges. He started at Texas Christian in 2019, moved to Navarro (Texas) JC in 2020 and spent his junior season in 2021 as Louisiana-Lafayette's Friday night starter. The Astros drafted him in the sixth round in 2021 and signed him for $147,800. Assigned to High-A Asheville out of spring training in 2022, Arrighetti struck out 124 batters in 85.2 innings but struggled with his command. He was promoted to Double-A Corpus Christi in late August.

BA GRADE
45 Risk: High

SCOUTING REPORT: Arrighetti is a high-effort and athletic pitcher who moves rapidly on the mound. He gets downhill in his extreme drop-and-drive delivery at a frenetic pace. His operation features a late, deceptive hand break, a long arm action that gives way to whippy arm speed and delivered the ball from a true three-quarters slot. Arrighetti's deception and ability to get downhill allow his four-pitch mix to play up. His arsenal is led by a mid-90s four-seam fastball that sits 93-94 mph and touches 96-97 with a flat vertical approach angle and hoppy shape. He pairs that primarily with a sweepy, low-to-mid-80s slider that is his best bat-missing pitch. He blends in a curveball in the high 70s as his third pitch. It shows two-plane break and more depth than his slider. Arrighetti throws a changeup to lefthanded batters that will flash good tumble and fade, but he struggles to command it consistently. His strike-throwing is below-average, but he showed improvements in that area throughout 2022.
THE FUTURE: Arrighetti has the deep arsenal of a starter, but his fringy command may push him to the bullpen, where his fastball/slider combination should play up.

SCOUTING GRADES	Fastball: 55	Slider: 60	Curveball: 50	Changeup: 40	Control: 45

Year	Age	Club (League)	Lvl	W	L	ERA	G	GS	IP	H	HR	BB	SO	BB/9	SO/9	WHIP	AVG
2022	22	Asheville (SAL)	HiA	6	5	5.04	22	13	86	88	6	46	124	4.8	13.0	1.56	.259
2022	22	Corpus Christi (TL)	AA	1	1	3.43	5	4	21	13	3	9	28	3.9	12.0	1.05	.181
Minor League Totals				10	8	4.49	33	19	120	111	10	57	174	4.3	13.0	1.40	.239

9 JUSTIN DIRDEN, OF

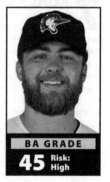

Born: July 16, 1997. **B-T:** L-R. **HT:** 6-3. **WT:** 209.
Signed: Southeast Missouri State, 2020 (NDFA). **Signed by:** Jim Stevenson.
TRACK RECORD: Dirden followed an unusual path to pro ball after spending five seasons in college. He began at East Carolina in 2016 but missed the 2017 campaign after he transferred to Southeastern Missouri State. After Dirden went unselected in the five-round 2020 draft, he signed as a nondrafted free agent with the Astros. He made his pro debut with Low-A Fayetteville out of camp in 2021 and hit his way to High-A Asheville. In 2022, Dirden was assigned to Double-A Corpus Christi and hit his way to Triple-A Sugar Land, where he struggled for 32 games.

BA GRADE
45 Risk: High

SCOUTING REPORT: The Astros believe not even Dirden knew how athletic he was when he entered the organization. As the lefthanded hitter began to believe more in the player he could become, the Astros began to see signs of a potential everyday regular. His offensive game is centered on his ability to consistently hit the ball hard in the air. He shows average bat-to-ball skills, though he is prone to expanding his zone and getting out of his approach. Dirden's ability to hit the ball hard consistently plays into his slightly aggressive tendencies. He lets his plus raw power drive the ball deep to all parts of the park. An above-average runner, Dirden's speed plays less in the form of basestealing and more in his ability to get out of the box and stretch singles to doubles. His running ability allows him to play center field at an average level, but he's best in an outfield corner where his above-average arm will be an asset.
THE FUTURE: Dirden is a late-bloomer—he turns 26 late in the 2023 season—with an unusual background who has developed into a potential everyday regular.

SCOUTING GRADES	Hitting: 45	Power: 55	Speed: 55	Fielding: 50	Arm: 55

Year	Age	Club (League)	Lvl	AVG	G	AB	R	H	2B	3B	HR	RBI	BB	SO	SB	OBP	SLG
2022	24	Corpus Christi (TL)	AA	.324	92	349	64	113	32	5	20	73	41	94	7	.411	.616
2022	24	Sugar Land (PCL)	AAA	.242	32	128	18	31	8	0	4	28	10	40	5	.305	.398
Minor League Totals				.291	207	762	141	222	58	11	39	159	103	234	22	.389	.550

10 MIGUEL ULLOLA, RHP

Born: June 19, 2002. **B-T:** R-R. **HT:** 6-1. **WT:** 184.
Signed: Dominican Republic, 2021. **Signed by:** Alfredo Ulloa/Hassan Wessin.

TRACK RECORD: Signed out of the Dominican Republic during the 2021 international signing period, Ullola first popped during that year's Dominican Summer League season. He struck out 34 batters in 21 innings before coming to the Florida Complex League for two appearances. In 2022, Ullola made his full-season debut for Low-A Fayetteville on May 1. He made 22 appearances and recorded a 3.25 ERA, while allowing a .155 average and striking out 38% of batters. At 19 years old on Opening Day, Ullola was one of the youngest pitchers in a full-season league.

BA GRADE

50 Risk: Extreme

SCOUTING REPORT: A fire-breathing dragon in the making, Ullola's current form is heavily centered on his easy plus fastball. He sits 93-95 mph and touches 98 at peak. Ullola's fastball creates both heavy riding life and a flat plane of approach to the plate. The combination of velocity, movement and release traits translated to eye-popping whiff numbers against the pitch. Among pitchers who threw 700 or more fastballs in 2022, Ullola's 48% whiff rate was the highest in the minor leagues by nearly eight full percentage points. While Ullola's fastball is plus, his trio of secondaries is still fairly raw. He uses a mid-80s slider, low-80s curveball and high-80s changeup but struggles to command all of his secondary offerings for long stretches. His command overall is below-average, but it's reasonable to expect improved strike-throwing as Ullola moves up the minor league ladder.

THE FUTURE: A tantalizing talent who has drawn comparisons with Cristian Javier from some within the Astros' organization, Ullola has the look of a high-leverage power reliever in the long term.

SCOUTING GRADES	Fastball: 60	Slider: 50	Curveball: 50	Changeup: 40	Control: 45

Year	Age	Club (League)	Lvl	W	L	ERA	G	GS	IP	H	HR	BB	SO	BB/9	SO/9	WHIP	AVG
2022	20	Fayetteville (CAR)	LoA	2	2	3.25	22	11	72	39	3	55	120	6.9	15.0	1.31	.157
Minor League Totals				3	3	3.46	32	16	96	51	4	76	158	7.1	14.8	1.32	.154

11 COLIN BARBER, OF

Born: Dec. 4, 2000. **B-T:** L-L. **HT:** 6-0. **WT:** 200.
Drafted: HS—Chico, Calif., 2019, (4th round). **Signed By:** Tim Costic.

TRACK RECORD: After a shoulder injury cut his season short in 2021, Barber needed a resurgent year. Signed for $1 million as a fourth-round pick in 2019, Barber had just 44 games of affiliated ball under his belt entering 2022. He returned to High-A Asheville, where he had played just 16 games the year before. Barber missed a month with a right shoulder strain but hit .298/.408/.450 otherwise, albeit with a stark home-road split.

SCOUTING REPORT: Barber's profile is centered on his combination of above-average bat-to-ball skills, above-average approach and projectable power. Despite a well-synced leg lift trigger, Barber's swing is mostly based around his upper body and the way his hands work. He shows an above-average ability to discern balls from strikes and rarely expands the zone. His contact quality leaves something to be desired, and he struggles to drive the ball in the air to his pull side. A majority of Barber's best contact comes in the form of hard-struck liners to the opposite field and fly balls to center. Barber's present power is below-average but he shows flashes of above-average potential and has traits that could still be further optimized. An above-average runner, Barber has seen time in all three outfield spots and has a chance to stick in center field. He has an average throwing arm.

THE FUTURE: The 2022 season was the first in which Barber has put together a lengthy stretch when he was both productive and healthy. He profiles as a second-division regular but his shoulder issues in recent seasons are concerning. Barber should begin the 2023 season with Double-A Corpus Christi.

BA GRADE: 50/Extreme	Hit: 55	Power: 45	Run: 55	Field: 50	Arm: 50

Year	Age	Club (League)	Lvl	AVG	G	AB	R	H	2B	3B	HR	RBI	BB	SO	SB	OBP	SLG
2022	21	Astros Blue (FCL)	R	.000	1	3	0	0	0	0	0	0	0	0	0	.000	.000
2022	21	Astros Orange (FCL)	R	.286	2	7	0	2	0	0	0	0	0	1	0	.286	.286
2022	21	Asheville (SAL)	HiA	.298	63	218	35	65	10	1	7	33	30	57	7	.408	.450
Minor League Totals				.276	110	369	64	102	16	2	12	46	58	109	10	.392	.428

12 ANDREW TAYLOR, RHP

Born: Sept. 23, 2001. **B-T:** R-R. **HT:** 6-5. **WT:** 190.
Drafted: Central Michigan, 2022 (2nd round supplemental). **Signed By:** Scott Oberhelman.

TRACK RECORD: Taylor enjoyed a standout sophomore season with Central Michigan, where he went 11-4, 1.81 with 125 strikeouts and 24 walks over 94.1 innings. He ended his breakout campaign in the Cape Cod League, where he made another seven appearances with Bourne. In 2022, Taylor failed to replicate his sophomore season, though his underlying numbers looked identical. The Astros selected Taylor with the 80th overall pick in the supplemental second round. He did not pitch post draft.

SCOUTING REPORT: Blessed with plus ride on his fastball, Taylor lived and died by his hop-heavy four-seamer during his collegiate career. The low-90s fastball averaged 20 inches of induced vertical break—an elite number—with late, arm-side run. His ability to command the pitch at the top of the zone allows his trio of secondaries to waterfall off of it. His low-80s slider has a cutter-hybrid type shape and could improve with added power. His mid-70s curveball features heavy two-plane break and is his most-used secondary. He also utilizes a mid-80s changeup with tumble and fade. Taylor has average command of his arsenal and could project for above-average control at peak.

THE FUTURE: With excellent pitch shapes across his arsenal and a track record of success as a starter, Taylor is the type of pitcher the Astros have had success developing into a rotation option. Taylor has the look of a potential No. 4 starter.

BA GRADE: 45/High	Fastball: 55	Curveball: 50	Slider: 45	Changeup: 50	Control: 50

Year	Age	Club (League)	Lvl	W	L	ERA	G	GS	IP	H	HR	BB	SO	BB/9	SO/9	WHIP	AVG
2022	20	Did not play															

13 JOE PEREZ, 3B

Born: Aug. 12, 1999. **B-T:** R-R. **HT:** 6-2. **WT:** 198.
Drafted: HS—Southwest Ranches, Fla., 2017 (2nd round). **Signed By:** Charlie Gonzalez.

TRACK RECORD: After an injury-plagued start to Perez's professional career, he found health in 2021, rose through three levels of the minors and hit .262/.326/.454 with 18 home runs. He broke camp with the major league team but was reassigned to Double-A within a week. He went down with an oblique injury in late April and missed two months of the season, returning to Corpus Christi in mid-July. Perez was promoted to Triple-A Sugar Land in late September.

SCOUTING REPORT: Over his five-year professional career Perez has improved his physique and conditioning to the point where he now has a more toned build. While health continues to be a concern, Perez has a high-skill profile with projectable power in his frame. He's an above-average contact hitter with an average approach and rarely gets himself into trouble by expanding the zone. He has a clean, level righthanded swing with a quiet load. While his exit velocity data is above-average, he makes his hardest contact at flatter launch angles, which leads to hard-stuck liners to the gap. Perez's power currently plays best for doubles. He's a below-average runner with limited range at third base. Whether he sticks at third base is an open question, though he's made improvements in the field over the last two seasons. A former two-way star in high school, Perez has a plus throwing arm.

THE FUTURE: Perez has a bat-first profile with defensive questions, and his most likely role is as a strong-side platoon bat with the ability to fill in on the infield corners.

BA GRADE: 40/Medium	Hit: 50	Power: 50	Run: 40	Field: 45	Arm: 60

Year	Age	Club (League)	Lvl	AVG	G	AB	R	H	2B	3B	HR	RBI	BB	SO	SB	OBP	SLG
2022	22	Astros Blue (FCL)	R	.333	4	12	1	4	2	0	0	1	2	2	1	.429	.500
2022	22	Astros Orange (FCL)	R	.308	7	26	2	8	1	0	0	2	0	7	0	.308	.346
2022	22	Corpus Christi (TL)	AA	.265	64	257	30	68	16	0	6	28	26	70	3	.335	.397
2022	22	Sugar Land (PCL)	AAA	.483	8	29	6	14	1	0	1	6	6	6	0	.571	.621
2022	22	Houston (AL)	MLB	.000	1	1	0	0	0	0	0	0	0	1	0	.000	.000
Major League Totals				.000	1	1	0	0	0	0	0	0	0	1	0	.000	.000
Minor League Totals				.272	243	946	128	257	61	2	32	125	91	254	11	.337	.442

14 KENEDY CORONA, OF

Born: March 21, 2000. **B-T:** R-R. **HT:** 5-11. **WT:** 184.
Signed: Venezuela, 2019. **Signed By:** Wilson Peralta (Mets).

TRACK RECORD: Corona was signed by the Mets out of Venezuela and acquired by the Astros alongside Blake Taylor in the deal that made Jake Marisnick a Met. After an underwhelming season at Low-A

Fayetteville in 2021, Corona reworked his swing and approach at the plate, optimized his bat path to add launch and cut down on his swing-happy tendencies. The changes worked. Corona had a breakout 2022, and hit .278/.362/.495 with 24 doubles, 19 home runs and 28 stolen bases split between Low-A Fayetteville and High-A Asheville.

SCOUTING REPORT: Corona is a well-rounded center fielder with an exciting power and speed mix. The changes to Corona's swing allowed him to tap into more of his raw power while sacrificing a minimal amount of contact. A fringe-average contact hitter with an above-average approach, Corona manages his swing-and-miss by rarely chasing and aggressively attacking pitches in the zone. His tweaked approach resulted in a 10-degree uptick in his average launch angle on batted balls hit harder than 95 mph. His 90th percentile exit velocity also increased two mph in 2022. A plus runner and aggressive basestealer, Corona's speed translates to all parts of his game. He's a rangy defender in center field capable of covering ground in a hurry, and his average throwing arm allows him to handle an outfield corner when needed.

THE FUTURE: Corona is a sneaky breakout candidate with a realistic platoon outfield role in his future.

| BA GRADE: 50/Extreme | Hit: 45 | | Power: 50 | Run: 60 | | Field: 55 | | Arm: 50 |

Year	Age	Club (League)	Lvl	AVG	G	AB	R	H	2B	3B	HR	RBI	BB	SO	SB	OBP	SLG
2022	22	Fayetteville (CAR)	LoA	.261	45	165	32	43	9	1	9	30	21	43	8	.346	.491
2022	22	Asheville (SAL)	HiA	.290	62	245	56	71	15	3	10	37	28	63	20	.373	.498
Minor League Totals				.276	227	830	163	229	50	9	26	118	92	195	66	.359	.452

15 MISAEL TAMAREZ, RHP

Born: Jan. 16, 2000. **B-T:** R-R. **HT:** 6-1. **WT:** 206.
Signed: Dominican Republic, 2019. **Signed By:** Roman Ocumarez.

TRACK RECORD: Tamarez was nearly 20 years old when he signed out of the Dominican Republic. He debuted in the summer of 2019, pitching in both the Dominican Summer League and the Gulf Coast League. He made his full-season debut in 2021 and performed well across two Class A levels. He was assigned to Double-A Corpus Christi to begin 2022 and struck out 122 batters to 55 walks across 103.1 innings before a late-season promotion to Triple-A.

SCOUTING REPORT: A lean, long-limbed righthander with an athletic, repeatable operation, Tamarez works exclusively from the stretch. He has a longer arm action and a high, three-quarters arm slot with a crossfire finish that hinders his command. It's a deep pitch mix of quality pitches with above-average pitch shapes. His four-seam fastball sits 93-95 mph and touches 99 mph at peak with above-average ride and late cut. His primary secondary is a tight, mid-80s slider that topped out at 90 mph in 2022. The slider is his best bat-missing pitch, as it generated whiffs on 48% of swings against it. His curveball is a slurvy, low-80s offering that offers a different look. His changeup is his go-to secondary against lefthanded hitters, as lefties whiffed at a rate north of 40% against the pitch. Despite excellent stuff, walks have been an issue for Tamarez due to his below-average control.

THE FUTURE: Tamarez has potential back-of-the-rotation upside with a likely up-and-down starter role approaching in 2023.

| BA GRADE: 45/High | Fastball: 55 | Curveball: 40 | Slider: 60 | Changeup: 55 | Control: 40 |

Year	Age	Club (League)	Lvl	W	L	ERA	G	GS	IP	H	HR	BB	SO	BB/9	SO/9	WHIP	AVG
2022	22	Corpus Christi (TL)	AA	3	6	4.62	24	19	103	76	18	55	122	4.8	10.6	1.27	.204
2022	22	Sugar Land (PCL)	AAA	1	1	2.50	4	4	18	6	2	15	20	7.5	10.0	1.17	.105
Minor League Totals				13	14	3.84	61	40	237	174	28	132	289	5.0	11.0	1.29	.203

16 QUINCY HAMILTON, OF

Born: June 12, 1998. **B-T:** L-L. **HT:** 5-10. **WT:** 190.
Drafted: Wright State, 2021 (5th round). **Signed By:** Scott Oberhelman.

TRACK RECORD: Hamilton spent four seasons at Wright State, with a breakout season in his junior campaign in 2021. He hit .374/.535/.771 that year with 15 home runs and 20 stolen bases and was named the Horizon League player of the year and a second team All-American. The Astros selected Hamilton in the fifth round and signed him for $47,500. He played 33 games with Low-A Fayetteville after the draft. Hamilton ascended from Low-A to Double-A in 2022.

SCOUTING REPORT: Hamilton is an advanced, experienced college hitter with refined bat-to-ball skills, a discerning eye and average power. His lefthanded swing is driven by his loose hands and strong wrists. His swing can get long, but he has enough bat speed and bat-to-ball ability to keep his swing-and-miss in check. Hamilton shows average game power but is unlikely to see substantial gains because he's nearly maxed out physically. He's a plus runner who has been a highly successful basestealer. Hamilton primarily played center field, where he's average and shows good closing speed and instincts. His below-average arm might be stretched every day in a corner outfield spot.

THE FUTURE: Hamilton is a well-rounded player with a strong combination of plate skills and supporting tools. He has a realistic ceiling as a fourth outfielder on a competitive team. Hamilton will be challenged by a return to Double-A Corpus Christi in 2023.

BA GRADE: 40/High			Hit: 50			Power: 50		Run: 60			Field: 50			Arm: 40	
Year	Age	Club (League)	Lvl	AVG	G	AB	R	H	2B	3B	HR	RBI	BB	SO	SB	OBP	SLG
2022	24	Fayetteville (CAR)	LoA	.291	36	134	22	39	8	0	6	19	20	27	8	.400	.485
2022	24	Asheville (SAL)	HiA	.321	49	187	44	60	15	1	7	30	37	39	12	.442	.524
2022	24	Corpus Christi (TL)	AA	.206	34	126	15	26	5	0	4	19	19	34	7	.320	.341
Minor League Totals				.276	152	562	99	155	33	1	19	88	94	128	36	.390	.440

17 JOEY LOPERFIDO, 1B/OF

Born: May 11, 1999. **B-T:** L-R. **HT:** 6-4. **WT:** 195.
Drafted: Duke, 2021 (7th round). **Signed By:** Andrew Johnson.

TRACK RECORD: Loperfido went unselected in the 2020 draft and returned to Duke for a fourth season. It proved a wise decision when he had a standout campaign in 2021, and hit .374/.474/.612. He won MVP honors at the Atlantic Coast Conference tournament and entered the draft on a high note. He was selected by the Astros in the seventh round, signed for $72,500 and got his feet wet at Low-A Fayetteville. He split his 2022 season between both Class A levels.

SCOUTING REPORT: Loperfido has a tall, athletic build and is an above-average athlete and runner for someone with a 6-foot-4 frame. He's best defined as a tweener with a variety of abilities but no stand-out tool. His lefthanded swing is driven by his rapid-fire hands that generate good bat speed despite a somewhat stiff upper half. He's a fringe-average contact hitter but limits his strikeouts because of strong pitch-recognition skills. His move at the plate and bat path project more for line drive contact, but he's shown an ability to turn on pitches on the inner half of the plate and drive them to his pull side. He's an above-average runner who's less of a true burner than a player who uses long, powerful strides to reach top speed underway. Loperfido is a fringe-average center fielder and projects best at first base. He has the ability to play all three outfield positions, second and first base.

THE FUTURE: Loperfido has the look of a super-utility player who beat up on younger competition in 2022. His balance of plate skills and pull-side power could make him a useful bench bat.

BA GRADE: 40/High			Hit: 50			Power: 50		Run: 55			Field: 45			Arm: 45	
Year	Age	Club (League)	Lvl	AVG	G	AB	R	H	2B	3B	HR	RBI	BB	SO	SB	OBP	SLG
2022	23	Fayetteville (CAR)	LoA	.304	82	296	51	90	17	3	9	45	40	76	30	.399	.473
2022	23	Asheville (SAL)	HiA	.354	26	96	19	34	8	1	3	24	13	25	2	.434	.552
Minor League Totals				.286	127	461	80	132	29	4	14	75	61	132	33	.387	.458

18 WILL WAGNER, 2B/3B

Born: July 29, 1998. **B-T:** L-R. **HT:** 6-0. **WT:** 210.
Drafted: Liberty, 2021 (18th Round). **Signed By:** Andrew Johnson.

TRACK RECORD: The son of former all-star closer Billy Wagner, the younger Wagner hit .305/.377/.462 over three seasons with Liberty. The Astros drafted Wagner in the 18th round of the 2021 draft and signed him for $50,000. He got his first pro experience at Low-A Fayetteville and split his 2022 season between High-A and Double-A. Wagner starred in the Arizona Fall League after the season, and hit .346/.433/.712 with three home runs over 14 games.

SCOUTING REPORT: Wagner has a hit-over-power profile but started to show more thump in the season and into the fall. He makes contact at an above-average rate and manages the zone well, making him a difficult player to strike out. He shows above-average on-base abilities and works deep into counts. He's a highly skilled hitter who consistently takes professional at-bats. The questions around Wagner's bat center on his lack of power projection. He's fairly close to physically maxed out with a setup that isn't conducive for much juice. The Astros have had success coaxing more power out of their prospects, however, so Wagner's progress in that department is worth watching. Wagner is a below-average runner who lacks range in the infield. He is a smart defender with good actions who profiles best at second base, where his average arm won't be as taxed as it is at third.

FUTURE: Wagner is a bat-first utility type with the upside to grow into second-division regular status if he discovers average game power.

| BA GRADE: 40/High | | Hit: 55 | | Power: 40 | | Run: 40 | | Field: 45 | | Arm: 45 | |

Year	Age	Club (League)	Lvl	AVG	G	AB	R	H	2B	3B	HR	RBI	BB	SO	SB	OBP	SLG
2022	23	Asheville (SAL)	HiA	.276	45	163	22	45	7	1	4	25	32	41	3	.392	.405
2022	23	Corpus Christi (TL)	AA	.251	72	251	40	63	12	2	6	28	35	57	5	.361	.386
Minor League Totals				.269	148	531	84	143	27	4	12	67	83	131	13	.377	.403

19 TREY DOMBROSKI, LHP

Born: March 13, 2001. **B-T:** R-L. **HT:** 6-5. **WT:** 235.
Drafted: Monmouth, 2022 (4th Round). **Signed By:** Steve Payne.
TRACK RECORD: Dombroski broke out in the Cape Cod League over the summer of 2021, when he posted a 0.85 ERA with 45 strikeouts to two walks over 31.2 innings while winning the Most Outstanding Pitcher award. He returned to Monmouth and struck out 120 batters against just 14 walks across 95 innings. The Astros selected Dombroski in the fourh round and signed him for slot value. He did not pitch after the draft.
SCOUTING REPORT: Dombroski attacks hitters with a four-pitch mix that lacks power but plays up due to his elite execution. His four-seam fastball sits 88-91 mph with ride and late run and is effective for setting up his trio of secondaries. His slider is his primary offspeed pitch and is used equally as often as his fastball. Dombroski commands his slider—which shows two-plane break—well to both lefties and righties. He'll also show a slower, deep-breaking curveball that's an effective early-count strike-stealer as well as a below-average changeup. Dombroski's ability to sequence and locate all of his pitches allows his entire arsenal to play up and gives him a chance to make it as a viable starter.
THE FUTURE: Adding power over the next year could help Dombroski's profile take a step forward and give him a viable ceiling as a back-end starter. For now, he has the look of an up-and-down depth starter.

| BA GRADE: 40/High | | Fastball: 45 | | Curveball: 40 | | Slider: 55 | | Changeup: 40 | | Control: 70 | |

Year	Age	Club (League)	Lvl	W	L	ERA	G	GS	IP	H	HR	BB	SO	BB/9	SO/9	WHIP	AVG
2022	21	Did not play															

20 RYAN CLIFFORD, OF

Born: July 20, 2003. **B-T:** L-L. **HT:** 6-3. **WT:** 200.
Drafted: HS—Apex, N.C., 2022 (11th round). **Signed By:** Andrew Johnson.
TRACK RECORD: A decorated amateur who played on Team USA's 12U and 15U squads, Clifford played high-level travel ball and became known for his uncommon strength at a young age. While many evaluators questioned Clifford's bat speed and how his power would translate to the next level, the Astros liked his combination of plus power and hitterish traits enough to select him in the 11th round and award him their second-largest bonus of the class behind first-round pick Drew Gilbert.
SCOUTING REPORT: A bat-first prospect who's already close to his physical max, Clifford's standout tool is his light-tower power. He has the below-average bat-to-ball skills typical of all-or-nothing power hitters, but his discerning eye showed well in his brief professional sample, when he showed the ability to identify balls and strikes and work deep into at-bats. His power translates in-game with a 90th percentile exit velocity over 105 mph. Clifford hits the ball hard consistently, but the question is if he'll hit the ball enough or have the bat speed to continue to do so against upper-level competition. He's a below-average runner who's limited to an outfield corner with just fringe-average arm strength.
THE FUTURE: Clifford's profile will go as far as his bat-to-ball skills and approach will take him. Those factors will determine how much of his power he gets to ultimately. Clifford will return to Low-A Fayetteville to begin 2023.

| BA GRADE: 45/Extreme | | Hit: 40 | | Power: 60 | | Run: 40 | | Field: 40 | | Arm: 50 | |

Year	Age	Club (League)	Lvl	AVG	G	AB	R	H	2B	3B	HR	RBI	BB	SO	SB	OBP	SLG
2022	18	Astros Orange (FCL)	R	.222	13	36	8	8	3	0	1	5	12	16	2	.440	.389
2022	18	Fayetteville (CAR)	LoA	.268	12	41	5	11	2	0	1	5	10	15	0	.412	.390
Minor League Totals				.247	25	77	13	19	5	0	2	10	22	31	2	.426	.390

21 J.P. FRANCE, RHP

Born: April 4, 1995. **B-T:** R-R. **HT:** 6-0. **WT:** 216.
Drafted: Mississippi State, 2018 (14th round). **Signed By:** Travis Coleman.

TRACK RECORD: After three seasons at Tulane, France transferred to Mississippi State and spent his final collegiate season working out of the Bulldogs' pen. The Astros took a shot on France in the 14th round of the 2018 draft and signed him for just $1,000. He debuted that summer in short-season Tri-City and reached Low-A by season's end. He spent 2019 at High-A Fayetteville and split 2021 between Double-A and Triple-A. France returned to Triple-A Sugar Land to begin 2022 and made 34 appearances while striking out 136 batters over 110.2 innings.

SCOUTING REPORT: France's game centers around his mastery of the art of deception. By throwing all five of his pitches in near-equal measure, France does an excellent job of keeping hitters off-balance. France's fastball sits 91-94 mph with riding cut and a flat vertical approach angle. He mixes in a quartet of secondaries in a mid-80s cutter, a low-80s sweeping slider, a mid-70s curveball with depth and a low-80s changeup with Bugs Bunny shape. France keeps hitters guessing by throwing any of his pitches in any count. Despite his advanced feel for his arsenal, France's control is below-average and he'll often rely too heavily on his breaking balls and lose the zone with his fastball.

THE FUTURE: France's likely role is as a depth starter who can eat innings in a variety of roles. He will likely shuttle between Houston and Sugar Land in 2023.

BA GRADE: 35/Medium		Fastball: 45	Curveball: 50	Slider: 55	Cutter: 50	Changeup: 50	Control: 40

Year	Age	Club (League)	Lvl	W	L	ERA	G	GS	IP	H	HR	BB	SO	BB/9	SO/9	WHIP	AVG
2022	27	Sugar Land (PCL)	AAA	3	4	3.90	34	15	111	99	15	51	136	4.1	11.1	1.36	.233
Minor League Totals				18	16	3.80	94	53	343	292	41	161	421	4.2	11.0	1.32	.227

22 JAIME MELENDEZ, RHP

Born: Sept. 26, 2001. **B-T:** L-R. **HT:** 5-8. **WT:** 190.
Signed: Mexico, 2019. **Signed By:** Miguel Pintor.

TRACK RECORD: Melendez moved rapidly after signing in 2019 and reached Double-A by the end of his first full professional season in 2021. He returned to Double-A Corpus Christi to begin his 2022 campaign as the second-youngest pitcher—behind the Marlins' Eury Perez—to break camp in Double-A. The assignment proved to be too aggressive as Melendez fell flat, and went 2-8, 5.01 and walked 15.6% of the batters he faced.

SCOUTING REPORT: Melendez is a smaller righthander with a fairly filled-out frame. He throws from a choppy but clean operation, with a quick, fast arm action that slingshots the ball from an overhand slot. Melendez's tempo and "inverted W" motion in his arm action cause him to fall out of rhythm. His stuff is above-average across his arsenal but his lack of command is a problem. His fastball is an above-average pitch, sitting 93-95 mph and touching 98 mph with plus induced vertical break and cut. Despite his struggles overall, Melendez got good results against his fastball, which could play up in a relief role. Melendez mixes in a tight, mid-80s slider, an upper-70s curveball with depth and a changeup with tumble and fade. On paper, Melendez has a deep mix of plus pitch shapes, but he lacks the control and command to help them play to their potential.

THE FUTURE: After being fast-tracked to the upper minors, Melendez will likely return to starting. If he fails to throw enough strikes he could be moved to the bullpen, where his fastball will likely play up.

BA GRADE: 40/High		Fastball: 55		Slider: 40	Curveball: 40		Changeup: 55	Control: 40

Year	Age	Club (League)	Lvl	W	L	ERA	G	GS	IP	H	HR	BB	SO	BB/9	SO/9	WHIP	AVG
2022	20	Corpus Christi (TL)	AA	2	8	5.01	23	16	74	59	7	51	106	6.2	13.0	1.49	.219
Minor League Totals				7	17	4.11	54	32	160	128	10	100	235	5.6	13.2	1.43	.217

23 J.J. MATIJEVIC, 1B/ OF

Born: Nov. 14, 1995. **B-T:** L-R. **HT:** 6-0. **WT:** 206.
Drafted: Arizona, 2017 (2nd round supplemental). **Signed By:** Mark Ross.

TRACK RECORD: Matijevic ranked as a top 200 draft prospect twice, first as a Pennsylvania prep and again out of Arizona. The Astros selected Matijevic in the supplemental second round and watched him take a tumultuous path to the big leagues. He missed 50 games in 2019 after failing two drug tests for drugs of abuse. After spending the 2021 season at Double-A and Triple-A, Matijevic returned to Triple-A to begin 2022. He made his major league debut in April and had three stints on the major league roster.

SCOUTING REPORT: Matijevic has had a few different forms at the plate over the years, altering his swing from power-focused to more contact-oriented. He saw a sharp increase in groundball contact this season. He's carried average or better walk rates throughout his career but was exposed against major league-quality pitching and chased at a high rate. He has a below-average hit tool with a fringy approach. Matijevic has above-average power—it flashes plus as raw power—and consistently makes hard contact. He's a below-average runner whose best defensive position is first base.

THE FUTURE: Matijevic has an up-and-down profile with a chance to earn platoon player status.

| BA GRADE: 35/Medium | | Hit: 40 | | Power: 55 | | Run: 40 | | Field: 30 | | Arm: 45 |

Year	Age	Club (League)	Lvl	AVG	G	AB	R	H	2B	3B	HR	RBI	BB	SO	SB	OBP	SLG
2022	26	Sugar Land (PCL)	AAA	.285	64	246	46	70	16	2	16	54	33	68	10	.372	.561
2022	26	Houston (AL)	MLB	.209	32	67	7	14	2	0	2	5	2	25	1	.254	.328
Major League Totals				.209	32	67	7	14	2	0	2	5	2	25	1	.254	.328
Minor League Totals				.260	411	1554	259	404	101	10	81	259	178	486	48	.337	.494

24 JOSE FLEURY, RHP

Born: March 8, 2002. **B-T:** R-R. **HT:** 6-0. **WT:** 185.
Signed: Dominican Republic, 2021. **Signed By:** Roman Ocumarez/Alfredo Ulloa/Jose Torres.

TRACK RECORD: Fleury was an unheralded signing during the 2021 international signing period but made waves in his professional debut. He led the Dominican Summer League in K-BB% with a 38.4% rate. His 41.1% strikeout percentage ranked second for pitchers with 30 or more innings in the DSL while his walk rate of 2.7% was 13th-lowest. He has breakout potential in 2023.

SCOUTING REPORT: Fleury uses an athletic operation and explosive motion downhill. He has a short, quick arm action and delivers the ball from a true three-quarters slot. He moves well on the mound and shows balance and fluidity throughout his mechanics as well as the ability to repeat them consistently. He uses a fastball, slider, curveball and changeup. His low-90s four-seam fastball has plus vertical movement with heavy ride that explodes as it hits the zone. The pitch touches 93-94 at times. Fleury's changeup is his primary secondary and was a true plus pitch for him. He sold it with arm speed and landed it consistently in the zone. Fleury's high-70s curveball has slurvy shape and at times blends with his lower-80s slider, which has a tighter gyro shape. Overall, his pitch mix is strong and played up due to above-average command.

THE FUTURE: Fleury should make his U.S. debut in 2023, with the potential to break out with a starter's pitch mix and command. Adding power to his pitch mix would likely pay dividends long term.

| BA GRADE: 45/Extreme | | Fastball: 50 | | Curveball: 55 | | Slider: 50 | | Changeup: 60 | | Control: 50 |

Year	Age	Club (League)	Lvl	W	L	ERA	G	GS	IP	H	HR	BB	SO	BB/9	SO/9	WHIP	AVG
2022	20	Astros Orange (DSL)	R	2	0	1.42	10	4	38	27	1	4	60	0.9	14.2	0.82	.193
Minor League Totals				2	0	1.42	10	4	38	27	1	4	60	0.9	14.2	0.82	.193

25 MICHAEL KNORR, RHP

Born: May 12, 2000. **B-T:** R-R. **HT:** 6-5. **WT:** 245.
Drafted: Coastal Carolina, 2022 (3rd round). **Signed by:** Andrew Johnson.

TRACK RECORD: After three difficult seasons at Cal State-Fullerton, Knorr transferred to Coastal Carolina and saw a significant velocity bump and success. He made 13 starts during the spring of 2022, going 5-0, 3.39 with 86 strikeouts to 13 walks across 69 innings. The year served as a nice departure from his previous collegiate seasons and led the Astros to select him in the third round and sign him for a bonus of $487,500. He was shut down following the draft and will make his professional debut in 2023.

SCOUTING REPORT: Knorr made adjustments to his arm action and slot upon moving to Coastal Carolina and discovered more velocity and better shape on his pitches. His pitch mix consists of four pitches, led by a four-seam fastball that sits between 93-95 mph and touches 98 mph with heavy ride and bore. He mixes in a trio of secondaries in a low-80s slider with classic slider shape, a mid-70s curveball with depth and heavy two-plane break and a changeup in the low-to-mid 80s. After moving to a stretch-only delivery Knorr found average control.

THE FUTURE: After a sizable step forward in stuff, Knorr has the pitch mix and control of a starter. If that fails, he has a fastball-slider combination to fall back on in a relief role.

| BA GRADE: 40/High | | Fastball: 55 | | Curveball: 50 | | Slider: 50 | | Changeup: 45 | | Control: 50 |

Year	Age	Club (League)	Lvl	W	L	ERA	G	GS	IP	H	HR	BB	SO	BB/9	SO/9	WHIP	AVG
2022	22	Did not play															

26 PARKER MUSHINSKI, LHP

Born: Nov. 22, 1995. **B-T:** L-L. **HT:** 6-0. **WT:** 218.
Drafted: Texas Tech, 2017 (7th round). **Signed By:** Noel Gonzalez-Luna.
TRACK RECORD: After three seasons of pitching in relief for Texas Tech, the Astros selected Mushinski in the seventh round of the 2017 draft. He toiled in the lower minors for two seasons before he reached Triple-A Sugar Land in 2021. He added a sweeping slider heading into the 2022 season, which proved to be the perfect complement to his arsenal. He pitched well out of the bullpen for Sugar Land and earned a promotion to the major league roster, where he made seven appearances for the Astros.
SCOUTING REPORT: A relief-only prospect who is a major league-ready finished product, Mushinski lacks power across his arsenal but mixes a variety of pitch shapes that play well off each other. He creates excellent extension and averages 6.5 feet on his fastball. His delivery is full of arms and legs, which adds plenty of deception. Mushinski uses a low-90s four-seam fastball with ride and cut, a mid-80s traditional cutter, a sweepy low-80s slider, a curveball with depth and heavy two-plane break and a rarely-used mid-80s changeup. While Mushinski gets by on advanced sequencing, he lacks average control.
THE FUTURE: Mushinski is a relief-only prospect who can handle lower-leverage situations and creates a unique look that could have value against lefthanded-heavy lineups.

BA GRADE: 35/Medium		Fastball: 40	Curveball: 50	Slider: 50	Cutter: 50	Changeup: 30	Control: 40

Year	Age	Club (League)	Lvl	W	L	ERA	G	GS	IP	H	HR	BB	SO	BB/9	SO/9	WHIP	AVG
2022	26	Sugar Land (PCL)	AAA	2	2	2.66	38	0	41	28	3	19	41	4.2	9.1	1.16	.193
2022	26	Houston (AL)	MLB	0	0	3.68	7	0	7	5	0	3	8	3.7	9.8	1.09	.192
Major League Totals				0	0	3.68	7	0	7	5	0	3	8	3.7	9.8	1.09	.192
Minor League Totals				9	11	3.23	117	38	287	239	18	127	353	4.0	11.1	1.28	.222

27 SHAWN DUBIN, RHP

Born: Sept. 6, 1995. **B-T:** R-R. **HT:** 6-1. **WT:** 171.
Drafted: Georgetown (Ky.), 2018 (13th round). **Signed By:** Travis Coleman.
TRACK RECORD: Dubin signed for a bonus of $1,000 out of NAIA Georgetown (Ky.). He's dealt with injuries and command issues throughout his professional career but has shown enough bat-missing ability to earn a spot on the Astros' 40-man roster. He spent the majority of his 2022 season with Triple-A Sugar Land, where he struck out 80 batters across 58.1 innings. Dubin missed time in 2022 with a forearm strain.
SCOUTING REPORT: Dubin's fastball velocity took a significant jump upon entering pro ball. After sitting in the low 90s in college, Dubin grew into mid-90s velocity. That velocity spike has also come with arm troubles. When he's on, Dubin's fastball sits between 96-98 mph and touches 101 mph with ride and cut. He mixes in four secondary pitches in a high-80s cutter, a mid-80s slider, a low-80s curveball and a low-90s changeup. His primary secondary is his cutter but he plays his two breaking ball shapes off of his fastball-cutter combination in two-strike counts. Dubin has below-average control and is prone to bouts of losing the zone.
THE FUTURE: Dubin profiles as a hybrid reliever capable of going multiple innings without losing his powerful stuff. He should serve as reliever depth for the Astros in 2023.

BA GRADE: 35/Medium	Fastball: 60	Curveball: 45	Slider: 50	Changeup: 30	Cutter: 45	Control: 40

Year	Age	Club (League)	Lvl	W	L	ERA	G	GS	IP	H	HR	BB	SO	BB/9	SO/9	WHIP	AVG
2022	26	Astros Orange (FCL)	R	0	0	0.00	2	2	2	2	0	0	2	0.0	9.0	1.00	.250
2022	26	Sugar Land (PCL)	AAA	3	5	4.78	23	12	58	52	3	32	80	4.9	12.3	1.44	.243
Minor League Totals				16	14	3.92	80	46	250	190	14	108	333	3.9	12.0	1.19	.209

28 COLTON GORDON, LHP

Born: Dec. 20, 1998. **B-T:** L-L. **HT:** 6-4. **WT:** 225.
Drafted: Central Florida, 2021 (8th Round). **Signed By:** Charlie Gonzalez.
TRACK RECORD: After transferring to Central Florida before the 2020 season, Gordon earned a spot in the Knights' rotation and went 5-2, 2.77 over nine starts in 2021 before succumbing to a torn ulnar collateral ligament and having Tommy John surgery. The Astros saw enough to select Gordon in the eighth round of the 2021 draft. He returned to the mound in the summer of 2022 and made nine appearances across Low-A and High-A. Following the season, Gordon participated in the Arizona Fall League.
SCOUTING REPORT: A pitchability lefty who found success in 2022 with his four-pitch mix of average offerings, Gordon uses a low-90s four-seam fastball, an upper-70s sweeping slider, a mid-80s curveball

with more depth than his slider and a lower-80s changeup. While all of his pitches drove whiffs at high rates in 2022, none of his pitches stood out individually. Instead, Gordon's ability to locate his arsenal and deliver a variety of shapes from a similar release point amplified the deception of his entire mix.

THE FUTURE: Gordon projects as an up-and-down starter with the ability to eat innings when needed.

BA GRADE: 40/High		Fastball: 40		Curveball: 50		Slider: 50		Changeup: 45		Control: 55			
Year	Age	Club (League)	Lvl	W	L	ERA	G	GS	IP	H	HR	BB	SO	BB/9	SO/9	WHIP	AVG
2022	23	Astros Blue (FCL)	R	0	1	0.00	4	4	7	3	0	1	11	1.3	14.1	0.57	.120
2022	23	Astros Orange (FCL)	R	0	0	4.50	2	1	6	6	1	1	11	1.5	16.5	1.17	.261
2022	23	Fayetteville (CAR)	LoA	0	0	2.21	5	3	20	13	1	3	27	1.3	12.0	0.79	.183
2022	23	Asheville (SAL)	HiA	2	0	2.66	4	3	20	13	2	3	29	1.3	12.8	0.79	.178
Minor League Totals				2	1	2.35	15	11	54	35	4	8	78	1.3	13.1	0.80	.182

29 COREY JULKS, OF

Born: Feb. 27, 1996. **B-T:** R-R. **HT:** 6-1. **WT:** 185.
Drafted: Houston, 2017 (8th round). **Signed By:** Noel Gonzales-Luna.

TRACK RECORD: A swing change made in-season during 2021 catapulted Julks to the cusp of the major leagues in 2022 and changed the trajectory not only of his swing but of his career. On June 29, 2021, Julks was placed on the Astros' developmental list. After two weeks of work in Florida to try to unlock his power, he returned to Corpus Christi. Before that work in the cage, Julks had averaged a home run every 73 plate appearances. Since his developmental list stint, Julks has averaged a home run every 19 plate appearances.

SCOUTING REPORT: After a swing change revitalized his profile, Julks has been one of the more well-rounded players in the Astros' system. He's an above-average contact hitter with an average approach who shows the ability to limit strikeouts and get on base at a fringe-average rate. His power now plays above-average and it's backed by exit velocity data above the major league average. He has above-average speed and baserunning ability and can handle any of the outfield positions but is best fit for a corner.

THE FUTURE: Julks is a ready-made fourth outfielder who can fill in situationally off of the bench.

BA GRADE: 40/High		Hit: 45		Power: 55		Run: 55		Field: 45		Arm: 45				
Year	Age	Club (League)	Lvl	AVG	G	AB	R	H	2B	3B	HR	RBI	BB	SO	SB	OBP	SLG
2022	26	Sugar Land (PCL)	AAA	.270	130	523	100	141	21	4	31	89	56	128	22	.351	.503
Minor League Totals				.265	479	1809	304	479	102	13	60	235	217	431	86	.350	.435

30 FORREST WHITLEY, RHP

Born: Sept. 15, 1997. **B-T:** R-R. **HT:** 6-7. **WT:** 238.
Drafted: HS—San Antonio, Texas, 2016 (1st round) **Signed by:** Noel Gonzales-Luna.

TRACK RECORD: In the not too distant past, Whitley ranked among the top pitching prospects in the game, with many believing the tall righthander was a potential ace in the making. After a breakout 2017 season when he reached Double-A as a 19-year-old, Whitley has dealt with suspensions, injuries and ineffectiveness. With only one minor league option remaining unless he is granted a fourth option, Whitley's time on the 40-man roster is a running clock.

SCOUTING REPORT: It's difficult to discern whether or not Whitley's best stuff will ever return. His once hop-heavy fastball has lost its bite. The current version sits between 94-95 mph and touches 99 mph with dead zone shape. Whitley missed a below-average amount of bats with the pitch in 2022. He throws a trio of secondaries in a mid-to-high-80s slider, an upper-70s curveball with depth and two-plane break and a mid-to-upper-80s changeup. In his 2022 sample, Whitley showed limited command of his arsenal.

THE FUTURE: The hopes of Whitley returning to his previous form are gone. He should begin his season with Triple-A Sugar Land, where he could be fast tracked with a full-time move to the bullpen.

BA GRADE: 45/Extreme		Fastball: 50		Curveball: 50		Slider: 50		Changeup: 50		Control: 40			
Year	Age	Club (League)	Lvl	W	L	ERA	G	GS	IP	H	HR	BB	SO	BB/9	SO/9	WHIP	AVG
2022	24	Astros Blue (FCL)	R	0	0	13.50	1	1	2	3	0	2	2	9.0	9.0	2.50	.333
2022	24	Fayetteville (CAR)	LoA	0	0	0.00	2	2	5	1	0	0	7	0.0	12.6	0.20	.059
2022	24	Sugar Land (PCL)	AAA	0	2	7.09	10	8	33	32	2	25	36	6.8	9.8	1.73	.250
Minor League Totals				9	17	5.01	70	58	237	207	20	122	334	4.6	12.7	1.39	.233

Kansas City Royals

BY BILL MITCHELL

With a sixth straight losing season, the Royals rebuilding process hit a substantial speed bump in 2022 as the major league team sputtered to a 65-97 record.

The underwhelming season cost Dayton Moore his job as president of baseball operations. Moore was the architect of the previous rebuild that resulted in an American League championship in 2014 and World Series championship in 2015. He was replaced by long-time lieutenant J.J. Picollo, who already held the title general manager and now hold the keys to baseball operations.

Picollo didn't waste time after the conclusion of the season, firing manager Mike Matheny and major league pitching coach Cal Eldred. Matheny was replaced by Rays bench coach Matt Quatraro, who gets his first chance to manage a major league team. Paul Hoover followed Quatraro from Tampa Bay and will take over as bench coach.

Former Guardians bench coach Brian Sweeney—who was hired as the team's major league pitching coach—will be tasked with starting a much-needed overhaul of the system-wide pitching development program. Multiple pitchers at all levels, starting with the major league staff and running through the entire farm system, took steps backward in 2022.

It's not like the minor league system failed to contribute. In fact, there's quite a seismic shift in the organization's Top 30 Prospects in only one year. Ten players who were on the list in 2022—headlined by future face of the franchise Bobby Witt Jr.—earned enough major league playing time in 2022 to graduate from prospect eligibility, and three more players from that list saw time with the Royals. New talent was added to the system from trade deadline deals, with major league regulars Andrew Benintendi and Whit Merrifield finding new homes. Three additional prospects were acquired from the Braves for a supplemental first-round pick in the 2022 draft.

The farm system's success also tailed off noticeably in 2022. After two affiliates captured league championships in 2021, none of the Royals' five domestic affiliates had winning records. As an organization, the Royals' minor league teams posted a .426 winning percentage that ranked 29th among the 30 MLB teams.

The recently revamped hitting development program under Alec Zumwalt continued to pay dividends, even after Zumwalt was promoted to major league hitting coach at midseason. Vinnie Pasquantino, Nick Pratto, MJ Melendez, and Michael Massey all continued their rise through

Bobby Witt Jr. is expected to be the Royals' shortstop for the rest of the decade.

PROJECTED 2026 LINEUP

Catcher	MJ Melendez	27
First Base	Nick Pratto	27
Second Base	Michael Massey	28
Third Base	Cayden Wallace	25
Shortstop	Bobby Witt Jr.	26
Left Field	Drew Waters	27
Center Field	Kyle Isbel	29
Right Field	Gavin Cross	25
Designated Hitter	Vinnie Pasquantino	28
No. 1 Starter	Brady Singer	29
No. 2 Starter	Daniel Lynch	29
No. 3 Starter	Kris Bubic	28
No. 4 Starter	Ben Kudrna	23
No. 5 Starter	Jon Heasley	29
Closer	Dylan Coleman	29

the system before making it to Kansas City for the second half of the season. It was the pitching development that suffered considerably in 2022, though effective strike-throwers Angel Zerpa and Noah Cameron took steps forward, and 2021 top draft picks Ben Kudrna and Frank Mozzicato turned in nice seasons at Low-A in their first taste of pro ball.

After going heavy for high school pitching early in the 2021 draft, the focus in 2022 shifted to college hitters, with Virginia Tech outfielder Gavin Cross and Arkansas third baseman Cayden Wallace taken with the top two picks. Cross and Wallace immediately jump to the top of the Royals' prospect list—which is currently one of the worst in baseball. ∎

KANSAS CITY ROYALS

TOP 2023 MLB CONTRIBUTORS	RANK
Drew Waters, OF	3
Maikel Garcia, SS	6
Angel Zerpa, LHP	9
BREAKOUT PROSPECTS	**RANK**
Noah Cameron, LHP	21
Lizandro Rodriguez, 2B	29

SOURCE OF TOP 30 TALENT

Homegrown	23	Acquired	7
College	13	Trade	7
Junior college	0	Rule 5 draft	0
High school	5	Independent league	0
Nondrafted free agent	0	Free agent/waivers	0
International	5		

LF
Brewer Hicklen
Tucker Bradley

CF
Gavin Cross (1)
Drew Waters (3)
Nick Loftin (8)
Diego Hernandez (19)
Erick Peña

RF
Tyler Gentry (7)
Nate Eaton
Levi Usher
River Town

3B
Cayden Wallace (2)
Brennon McNair

SS
Maikel Garcia (6)
Austin Charles (22)
Daniel Vazquez (30)
Tyler Tolbert
Omar Florentino

2B
Samad Taylor (24)
Peyton Wilson (25)
Lizandro Rodriguez (29)

1B
Robbie Glendinning
Dillon Shrum

C
Carter Jensen (10)
Luca Tresh (23)
Hayden Dunhurst

LHP

LHSP	LHRP
Frank Mozzicato (5)	Christian Chamberlain
Angel Zerpa (9)	Cooper McKeehan
Asa Lacy (13)	Chazz Martinez
T.J. Sikkema (17)	
Noah Cameron (21)	
Drew Parrish	

RHP

RHSP	RHRP
Ben Kudrna (4)	Will Klein (31)
Jonathan Bowlan (11)	Yefri Del Rosario
Jackson Kowar (12)	Andres Nuñez
Alec Marsh (14)	Ben Sears
Beck Way (15)	Wesley Scott
Andrew Hoffmann (16)	Brandon Johnson
Max Castillo (18)	Marcus Olivarez
Mason Barnett (20)	
Chandler Champlain (26)	
Ben Hernandez (27)	
Steven Zobac (28)	
Shane Panzini	
William Fleming	

1 GAVIN CROSS, OF

Born: February 13, 2001. **B-T:** L-L. **HT:** 6-3. **WT:** 210.
Drafted: Virginia Tech, 2022 (1st round).
Signed by: Tim Bittner.

TRACK RECORD: Cross broke out in his second year at Virginia Tech in 2021 to establish himself as a likely first-round pick in 2022. He was also one of the top hitters for USA Baseball's Collegiate National Team during the summer of 2021. Cross' draft stock was boosted further in 2022 when he showed that he could handle center field defensively. He also improved at the plate by cutting his strikeout rate from 20% in 2021 to 14% in 2022 and boosting his walk rate from 7% to 11%. Cross finished his Hokies career with a trophy case full of awards, including All-Atlantic Coast Conference first team honors in both 2021 and 2022. The Royals drafted him ninth overall in 2022 and signed him for $5,200,400. Cross began his pro career with three games in the Rookie-level Arizona Complex League before reporting to Low-A Columbia, where he appeared in 26 games and posted an outstanding 1.019 OPS. He wrapped up his first season by getting some additional playing time in instructional league.

SCOUTING REPORT: Cross stands out for his above-average hit tool, knowledge of the strike zone and above-average power to all fields. He also has the ability to slow the game down at the plate. Cross hits with good balance and has the ability to let the ball travel into the hitting zone, which allows him to consistently barrel balls and pepper line drives from gap to gap. There's enough lift in his lefthanded swing and easy pop to put balls over the fence, too. A 25% strikeout rate in Low-A shows there's still work to be done with his approach, but the improvements he made in college and a willingness to learn demonstrate that he can continue to develop. An average runner, Cross reads balls well in the outfield and is athletic enough to potentially handle center field, but his more likely home will be in right field, where his above-average to plus arm will be plenty for the position. Speed is not a separating tool for Cross, but he can steal the occasional base and go first to third on a single. Royals officials noted his solid demeanor and how quickly he fit in with his new teammates, indicating that he can be a leader both on the field and in the clubhouse.

THE FUTURE: After getting enough time at Low-A to show his advanced ability at the plate and on the field, Cross is ready for the next level. He likely heads to High-A Quad Cities to start the 2023 season. If he can handle the Midwest League,

BRIAN WESTERHOLT/FOUR SEAM

BA GRADE	SCOUTING GRADES
55 Risk: High	Hit: 55. Power: 55. Run: 50. Field: 50. Arm: 55.

Projected future grades on 20-80 scouting scale

BEST TOOLS

BATTING

Best Hitter for Average	Tyler Gentry
Best Power Hitter	Gavin Cross
Best Strike-Zone Discipline	Carter Jensen
Fastest Baserunner	Tyler Tolbert
Best Athlete	Drew Waters

PITCHING

Best Fastball	Will Klein
Best Curveball	Frank Mozzicato
Best Slider	Beck Way
Best Changeup	Ben Kudrna
Best Control	Noah Cameron

FIELDING

Best Defensive Catcher	Luca Tresh
Best Defensive Infielder	Maikel Garcia
Best Infield Arm	Cayden Wallace
Best Defensive Outfielder	Diego Hernandez
Best Outfield Arm	Peyton Wilson

he should get to Double-A Northwest Arkansas before too long. Evaluators see him as a player who can move quickly through the system and in a best case scenario develop into an above-average regular. He's on track to be the Royals' right fielder by the middle of the decade.

Year	Age	Club (League)	Lvl	AVG	G	AB	R	H	2B	3B	HR	RBI	BB	SO	SB	OBP	SLG
2022	21	Royals (ACL)	R	.500	3	10	4	5	2	0	1	3	2	2	0	.583	1.000
2022	21	Columbia (CAR)	LoA	.293	26	99	20	29	5	2	7	22	22	31	4	.423	.596
Minor League Totals				.312	29	109	24	34	7	2	8	25	24	33	4	.437	.633

2 CAYDEN WALLACE, 3B

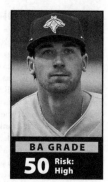

Born: August 7, 2001. **B-T:** R-R. **HT:** 6-1. **WT:** 205.
Drafted: Arkansas, 2022 (2nd round). **Signed by:** Matt Price.

TRACK RECORD: Wallace had a strong two-year career at Arkansas, where he hit for both average and power. He comes from a sports-minded family. His father was a college quarterback and a brother played in the Angels organization and independent ball. The Royals drafted the righthanded-hitting Wallace in the second round in 2022 as an eligible sophomore. He began his pro career with three games in the Arizona Complex League before moving up to Low-A Columbia for 27 games and hitting a combined .293/.379/.466. He participated in the Royals' instructional league program in the fall.

BA GRADE

50 Risk: High

SCOUTING REPORT: Wallace has strong wrists and a compact stroke at the plate, with good torque in his swing. Those qualities help him project to be an above-average hitter with average power. Wallace uses a traditional stance with a lower hand set just below his shoulder line, which helps him create plenty of power from an easy, efficient swing. Wallace's double-plus arm should help him stick at third base, where he is a potentially above-average defender. His arm strength is big enough that he can get plenty of zip on his throws even when he doesn't have time to set his feet. Wallace is no more than an average runner but steals bases on instincts.

THE FUTURE: Wallace may be the regular third baseman the Royals have sought for much of the past decade, where he should team with shortstop Bobby Witt Jr.

SCOUTING GRADES	Hitting: 55	Power: 50	Speed: 50	Fielding: 55	Arm: 70

Year	Age	Club (League)	Lvl	AVG	G	AB	R	H	2B	3B	HR	RBI	BB	SO	SB	OBP	SLG
2022	20	Royals (ACL)	R	.286	3	7	3	2	1	0	0	1	3	1	0	.500	.429
2022	20	Columbia (CAR)	LoA	.294	27	109	15	32	7	3	2	16	12	22	8	.369	.468
Minor League Totals				.293	30	116	18	34	8	3	2	17	15	23	8	.379	.466

3 DREW WATERS, OF

Born: December 30, 1998. **B-T:** B-R. **HT:** 6-2. **WT:** 185.
Drafted: HS—Woodstock, GA, 2017 (2nd round). **Signed by:** Dustin Evans (Braves).

TRACK RECORD: The Braves drafted Waters out of their backyard in the second round in 2017. The Woodstock, Ga., native signed for $1.5 million. He was the MVP of the Double-A Southern League in 2019, but the jump to Triple-A in 2021 gave Waters his first real speed bump. Waters again struggled in 49 games at Triple-A Gwinnett in 2022 before being one of three players traded to the Royals in July 2022 for a supplemental first-round pick in that year's draft. The change of scenery suited Waters, who hit .295/.399/.541 with Triple-A Omaha before being called up to Kansas City on Aug. 22.

BA GRADE

45 Risk: Medium

SCOUTING REPORT: Waters didn't make any big mechanical swing changes when he joined the Royals organization. Instead, he became more confident and consistent with his decisions at the plate. A switch-hitter, Waters has a narrow setup with a high leg kick and a hand position right around shoulder level. He uses the setup from both sides of the plate, giving him a quick and powerful swing. Waters especially excels in center field, with potential Gold Glove-caliber defense earning him plus grades in both fielding and throwing. A plus runner, Waters stole 18 bases at Triple-A in 2022.

THE FUTURE: Waters showed enough in his late-season time with Kansas City that he heads to spring training with a chance to earn a big league roster spot and perhaps a starting outfield job. His speed, defense and ability to play all three outfield positions will be valuable in spacious Kauffman Stadium.

SCOUTING GRADES	Hitting: 40	Power: 45	Speed: 60	Fielding: 60	Arm: 60

Year	Age	Club (League)	Lvl	AVG	G	AB	R	H	2B	3B	HR	RBI	BB	SO	SB	OBP	SLG
2022	23	Rome (SAL)	HiA	.364	3	11	5	4	1	0	1	2	1	3	0	.417	.727
2022	23	Gwinnett (IL)	AAA	.246	49	191	26	47	7	3	5	16	16	57	5	.305	.393
2022	23	Omaha (IL)	AAA	.295	31	122	29	36	5	2	7	17	20	41	13	.399	.541
2022	23	Kansas City (AL)	MLB	.240	32	96	14	23	6	1	5	18	12	40	0	.324	.479
Major League Totals				.240	32	96	14	23	6	1	5	18	12	40	0	.324	.479
Minor League Totals				.281	484	1913	315	537	128	26	44	187	175	582	91	.347	.444

4 BEN KUDRNA, RHP

Born: January 30, 2003. **B-T:** R-R. **HT:** 6-3. **WT:** 215.
Drafted: HS—Overland Park, KS, 2021 (2nd round). **Signed by:** Matt Price.

TRACK RECORD: Kudrna was a known commodity to the Royals given that his high school career was spent just 30 miles south in the Kansas City suburb of Overland Park. The Royals drafted him in the second round in 2021 and signed him for just shy of $3 million, going more than $1.25 million over slot and handing out the largest bonus of the second round. Both Kudrna and fellow top pick Frank Mozzicato were brought along slowly, and didn't make their official pro debuts until May 2022. Kudrna pitched his first game at Low-A Columbia on May 21 to begin a promising first season in which he posted a 3.48 ERA with a .239 opponent average.

BA GRADE

50 Risk: High

SCOUTING REPORT: Kudrna has a big, 6-foot-3 frame that has added strength since he turned pro, and he projects to continue to get stronger as he grows into his body. He attacks hitters with a fastball that has generally been in the range of 92-95 mph but can touch a couple of ticks higher. The pitch has good vertical break and plays up in the zone. Kudrna's velocity dipped later in the season, which was unsurprising for a pitcher in his first full season. A developmental goal coming into the 2022 season was to improve his mid-80s changeup, and he used it so much that it was a better pitch for him than his slider. His changeup plays well off his fastball but needs more deception. Kudrna's gyro slider at 82-84 mph has late bite and depth but needs to get firmer to reach its ceiling as an above-average pitch. His delivery is clean and repeatable, which leads evaluators to project Kudrna to have average control, though at times he'll work across his body and spin open.

THE FUTURE: Kudrna projects as a hard-throwing back-end starter, especially if his slider develops into more of a swing-and-miss pitch. The next step will be an assignment to High-A Quad Cities.

SCOUTING GRADES:	Fastball: 55		Slider: 50				Changeup: 50			Control: 50		

Year	Age	Club (League)	Lvl	W	L	ERA	G	GS	IP	H	HR	BB	SO	BB/9	SO/9	WHIP	AVG
2022	19	Columbia (CAR)	LoA	2	5	3.48	17	17	72	66	4	32	61	4.0	7.6	1.35	.239
Minor League Totals				2	5	3.48	17	17	72	66	4	32	61	4.0	7.6	1.35	.239

5 FRANK MOZZICATO, LHP

Born: June 10, 2003. **B-T:** L-L. **HT:** 6-3. **WT:** 190.
Drafted: HS—Manchester, CT, 2021 (1st round). **Signed by:** Casey Fahy.

TRACK RECORD: Mozzicato was best known at his Manchester, Conn., high school for throwing four straight no-hitters, fueled by one of the best curveballs in the prep ranks. The Royals surprised the industry by taking Mozzicato with the seventh overall pick in the 2021 draft and signing him for $3,547,500, nearly $2 million under slot. Like fellow Royals 2021 draftee Ben Kudrna, Mozzicato's game action was confined to extended spring training until he finally made his debut at Low-A Columbia in May. Mozzicato made 19 starts for the Fireflies, and struck out 11.6 batters per nine innings but with a high walk rate of 6.7 per nine. In addition to having one of the highest strikeout rates in the Carolina League, he also generated a high groundball rate of 54%.

BA GRADE

50 Risk: High

SCOUTING REPORT: While he still has a lot of development ahead, Mozzicato has a promising repertoire. His average fastball sat between 89-92 mph with rise that allowed it to play up in the zone and get whiffs. His plus curveball at 78-80 mph is a downer with good glove-side break and 16 inches of vertical movement. Mozzicato's changeup is still in the developmental stage because he didn't need to use it much in high school. Even so, it projects as an above-average offering at 84-85 mph. His changeup plays well off his fastball because it has 11 inches of vertical break, and he sells it with solid arm speed. Mozzicato's high walk rate is fueled in part by inconsistency in the way he lands with his lead leg. If he can correct that issue, he could have average control. He also needs to get stronger.

THE FUTURE: Mozzicato has the attributes of a major league starter, though some observers see a future bullpen arm. He'll head to High-A Quad Cities in 2023, likely moving one level per year as he matures physically.

SCOUTING GRADES:	Fastball: 50		Curveball: 60				Changeup: 55			Control: 45		

Year	Age	Club (League)	Lvl	W	L	ERA	G	GS	IP	H	HR	BB	SO	BB/9	SO/9	WHIP	AVG
2022	19	Columbia (CAR)	LoA	2	6	4.30	19	19	69	55	6	51	89	6.7	11.6	1.54	.219
Minor League Totals				2	6	4.30	19	19	69	55	6	51	89	6.7	11.6	1.54	.219

6 MAIKEL GARCIA, SS

Born: March 3, 2000. **B-T:** R-R. **HT:** 6-0. **WT:** 180.
Signed: Venezuela, 2016. **Signed by:** Richard Castro.

TRACK RECORD: It's been a slow, steady progression through the Royals system for Garcia, who signed out of Venezuela in 2016 and is a cousin of Ronald and Luisangel Acuña. Garcia's prospect stock continued to rise during the 2022 season as he got stronger and developed a better approach at the plate. Those changes helped him make his big league debut on July 15. He appeared in nine games and finished the year with Triple-A Omaha. Garcia's plate discipline has consistently improved as he has tackled every level of the full-season minors in 2021 and 2022. While he still needs to add strength, Garcia's 11 home runs in 2022 were more than double his combined amount from the previous four pro seasons.

BA GRADE
45 Risk: Medium

SCOUTING REPORT: Garcia is an instinctual player both at the plate and on the field. He is regarded as a throwback type of hitter who steps open at the plate and uses the entire field. He has very good hand-eye coordination and solid barrel control, with gap-to-gap power that helped him produce 34 doubles between Double-A and Triple-A. His above-average hit tool has jumped a full grade from last year. As impressive as Garcia's development has been at the plate, he's still better known for his defense at shortstop, where he shows quick hands, solid range and an above-average arm.
THE FUTURE: Garcia will continue building strength, which observers regard as the difference between him being a good utility player or a starting middle infielder. He may get the chance to earn a bench role out of spring training, but it's more likely he returns to Triple-A.

SCOUTING GRADES		Hitting: 55		Power: 30		Speed: 50			Fielding: 60			Arm: 55			
Year	Age	Club (League)	Lvl	AVG	G	AB	R	H	2B	3B	HR	RBI	BB	SO	SB	OBP	SLG
2022	22	NW Arkansas (TL)	AA	.291	78	323	63	94	24	1	4	33	41	60	27	.369	.409
2022	22	Omaha (IL)	AAA	.274	40	164	41	45	10	0	7	28	17	42	12	.341	.463
2022	22	Kansas City (AL)	MLB	.318	9	22	1	7	1	0	0	2	1	5	0	.348	.364
Major League Totals				.318	9	22	1	7	1	0	0	2	1	5	0	.348	.364
Minor League Totals				.272	379	1470	261	400	69	14	16	164	180	273	122	.349	.371

7 TYLER GENTRY, OF

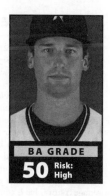

Born: February 1, 1999. **B-T:** R-R. **HT:** 6-2. **WT:** 210.
Drafted: Alabama, 2020 (3rd round). **Signed by:** Travis Ezi.

TRACK RECORD: Gentry started his collegiate career at junior college powerhouse Walters State in Tennessee, leading the team with 18 home runs as a freshman, and continued to hit during two seasons at Alabama. The Royals drafted Gentry in the third round in 2020, signed him for $750,000, then got him on the field for instructional league. No Royals prospect took as big of a jump forward in 2022 as Gentry. Hampered by a knee injury that limited him to 44 games in his first pro season at High-A Quad Cities in 2021, Gentry returned to the level and hit .336/.434/.516. Promoted to Double-A Northwest Arkansas on June 14, he took no time at all adjusting to Texas League pitchers and compiled a .972 OPS with 16 home runs in 73 games. Key to Gentry's breakout at Double-A were improvements to his strikeout rate—26% at High-A to 20% at Double-A—and a spike in power production.

BA GRADE
50 Risk: High

SCOUTING REPORT: Gentry shows plenty of pop from the right side with a low-maintenance swing that keeps him consistent at the plate. He's patient in the box with a good knowledge of the strike zone. Gentry bought into the Royals' revamped hitting program, and became a patient hitter with the ability to pick the part of the zone in which to be aggressive. He's a capable defender at both corner outfield spots, with an above-average arm that is suited for right field. He stole 10 bases in 2022, but as an average runner who may slow down as he matures, speed isn't expected to be a big part of his game.
THE FUTURE: Gentry has a chance to be a corner outfield regular with more experience, and he should be ready for Triple-A in 2023.

SCOUTING GRADES		Hitting: 55		Power: 50		Speed: 45			Fielding: 50			Arm: 55			
Year	Age	Club (League)	Lvl	AVG	G	AB	R	H	2B	3B	HR	RBI	BB	SO	SB	OBP	SLG
2022	23	Quad Cities (MWL)	HiA	.336	35	128	22	43	6	1	5	23	20	39	2	.434	.516
2022	23	NW Arkansas (TL)	AA	.321	73	274	57	88	16	0	16	63	40	66	8	.417	.555
Minor League Totals				.308	152	549	108	169	32	1	27	114	89	160	14	.415	.517

8 NICK LOFTIN, 3B/OF

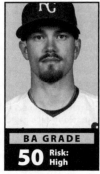

Born: September 25, 1998. **B-T:** R-R. **HT:** 6-1. **WT:** 180.
Drafted: Baylor, 2020 (1st round supplemental). **Signed by:** Josh Hallgren.

TRACK RECORD: Loftin was regarded as a solid all-around performer during his career at Baylor and was one of the top college shortstops in the 2020 draft class. The Royals selected him in the supplemental first round and signed him for $3 million. Since launching his pro career at High-A Quad Cities in 2021, Loftin has played all three infield positions and also center field and left field. He spent most of his time in center field in 2022 between Double-A Northwest Arkansas and Triple-A Omaha.

BA GRADE

50 Risk: High

SCOUTING REPORT: Loftin isn't regarded as a pure hitter, but rather as a quality ballplayer who provides good value. He's a gap-to-gap contact hitter with a cerebral approach at the plate. His potentially average hit tool is not a separator, but he's the type of player who will consistently find ways to get it done. His strikeout rates jumped from 13% in Double-A to 24% after moving to Triple-A, and his walk rates dropped from 10.6% to 6%, indicating there's improvement needed at the higher level. Loftin's athleticism will allow him to handle the super-utility role that the Royals envision. Now that he's proven to be an average outfielder in only one season, he will get back to playing the infield a little more regularly. Loftin is an above-average runner with an above-average arm, and in his time as a regular shortstop he showed good first-step quickness, good hands and solid range. The first-step quickness that helps him in the field also helped him steal 39 bases in 2022.

THE FUTURE: Loftin will return to Triple-A looking to improve at the plate and get more experience around the field.

SCOUTING GRADES		Hitting: 45		Power: 40		Speed: 55			Fielding: 55		Arm: 55	

Year	Age	Club (League)	Lvl	AVG	G	AB	R	H	2B	3B	HR	RBI	BB	SO	SB	OBP	SLG
2022	23	NW Arkansas (TL)	AA	.270	90	363	78	98	17	1	12	47	45	57	24	.354	.421
2022	23	Omaha (IL)	AAA	.216	38	153	26	33	7	0	5	19	10	41	5	.280	.359
Minor League Totals				.268	218	872	171	234	46	6	27	123	97	158	40	.349	.428

9 ANGEL ZERPA, LHP

Born: September 27, 1999. **B-T:** L-L. **HT:** 6-0. **WT:** 225.
Signed: Venezuela, 2016. **Signed by:** Richard Castro/Joelvis Gonzalez/Orlando Estevez.

TRACK RECORD: Zerpa signed with the Royals in July 2016 and spent three seasons working in various Rookie leagues, ranging from the Dominican Summer, Arizona and Pioneer leagues. Then the pandemic wiped out the 2020 minor league season. So it was a bit surprising when Zerpa, a fifth-year pro with no full-season experience, was added to the Royals' 40-man roster in November 2020 to make him ineligible for the Rule 5 draft. The Royals were on to something. Zerpa has climbed steadily since then and has pitched for Kansas City in 2021 and 2022.

BA GRADE

45 Risk: Medium

SCOUTING REPORT: Long regarded as someone who relies more on pitchability than stuff, Zerpa now has a complete package of pitches and above-average control. He is competitive on the mound and does all the little things to be successful. Zerpa uses four- and two-seam fastballs—both of which average 94 mph. His four-seamer is thrown mostly to his glove side and shows sinking action to combat righthanded hitters. He throws both fastballs with good arm speed and sneaky life. Zerpa shows solid command of his 84 mph slider. The pitch is short and tight with downward bite and at times resembles a cutter. His changeup is a hard pitch at 87 mph, used mostly down and away to righthanded batters and is delivered with conviction.

THE FUTURE: In the past, Zerpa has straddled the line between bulk reliever and back-end starter. Now, evaluators see him as more of a No. 4 or No. 5 starter.

SCOUTING GRADES:		Fastball: 55		Slider: 55			Changeup: 50		Control: 55		

Year	Age	Club (League)	Lvl	W	L	ERA	G	GS	IP	H	HR	BB	SO	BB/9	SO/9	WHIP	AVG
2022	22	NW Arkansas (TL)	AA	2	5	4.36	13	13	64	70	7	21	69	3.0	9.7	1.42	.276
2022	22	Omaha (IL)	AAA	0	0	1.17	6	6	8	2	0	4	0	4.7	0.0	0.78	.083
2022	22	Kansas City (AL)	MLB	2	1	1.64	3	2	11	9	2	3	3	2.5	2.5	1.09	.220
Major League Totals				2	2	1.12	4	3	16	12	2	4	7	2.2	3.9	1.00	.207
Minor League Totals				18	22	3.62	79	72	328	302	28	90	305	2.5	8.4	1.20	.244

10 CARTER JENSEN, C

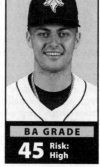

Born: July 3, 2003. **B-T:** L-R. **HT:** 6-1. **WT:** 215.
Drafted: HS—Kansas City, MO, 2021 (3rd round). **Signed by:** Matt Price.

TRACK RECORD: Jensen and fellow Kansas City-area high school product Ben Kudrna were both set to head off to Louisiana State in 2021. Instead, they began their pro careers with the Royals. After being drafted in the third round in 2021 and signing for an over-slot $1,097,500, Jensen got into 19 games in the Arizona Complex League. The Royals challenged him with an assignment to Low-A Columbia out of spring training in 2022. He struggled in the first half before heating up in the second half. From July 1 onward, he hit .286/.440/.429 with 51 walks and 38 strikeouts in 52 games.

BA GRADE **45** Risk: High

SCOUTING REPORT: Jensen has feel for the barrel, with quick hands and a compact swing. He uses an upright stance, with his swing getting some carry forward as he tries to get to a position to fire. He gets loft from his swing and uses a path that produces gap-to-gap line drives. If Jensen adds strength, those line drives could start going over the fence. He was passive at times early in 2022 but stuck with the process and stayed committed to pitches he could drive. He also improved his two-strike approach, which should correlate with a lower whiff rate. Jensen has only been catching for about five years, and his relative inexperience shows at times. He needs to continue to improve his blocking and receiving. Projected as an average defender or better, he has the athleticism and strong hands to stay behind the plate along with an above-average arm.

THE FUTURE: Lefthanded-hitting catchers with power are a valuable commodity, so Jensen will be given every opportunity to stay behind the plate. He'll move to High-A in 2023.

SCOUTING GRADES	Hitting: 40	Power: 55	Speed: 40	Fielding: 50	Arm: 55

Year	Age	Club (League)	Lvl	AVG	G	AB	R	H	2B	3B	HR	RBI	BB	SO	SB	OBP	SLG
2022	18	Columbia (CAR)	LoA	.226	113	393	66	89	24	2	11	50	83	103	8	.363	.382
Minor League Totals				.233	132	450	75	105	26	3	12	57	93	123	12	.366	.384

11 JONATHAN BOWLAN, RHP

Born: Dec. 1, 1996. **B-T:** R-R. **HT:** 6-6. **WT:** 240.
Drafted: Memphis, 2018 (2nd round) **Signed by:** Travis Ezi

TRACK RECORD: Kansas City's second round pick in 2018, Bowlan was on target to make his major league debut during the 2021 season until he suffered an elbow injury requiring Tommy John surgery. With a successful rehab period behind him Bowlan was back on the mound just a little more than a year after surgery. He did struggle to replicate his pre-injury success. Bowlan was dominating Double-A Northwest Arkansas at the time of his injury. In a return there, he gave up a .317 opponents batting average and a .330 average overall in 2022.

SCOUTING REPORT: Bowlan's four-seam fastball has averaged 93 mph since his return, just a tick lower than before surgery, and was a bit more cutter-ish. There is hope he may regain a bit more velocity as he gets further from his Tommy John surgery. His gyro slider at 85 mph got swings-and-misses at Double-A, and an 87-mph changeup is a little too firm but has action to it. Bowlan's low-80s curveball with downward break was his newest pitch pre-surgery, and he needs to get to the front of it and rebuild his trust in the pitch. The biggest issue is that the fastball command wasn't completely back yet. Bowlan's 9.3% walk rate in Double-A is high for him, another issue that should clear up in time.

THE FUTURE: His most likely landing spot to start 2023 is Triple-A Omaha. While inconsistent in his first partial year back from surgery, Bowlan has a strong history and had enough good outings to be placed on the 40-man in October.

BA GRADE: 45/High	Fastball: 60	Curveball: 55	Slider: 55	Changeup: 50	Control: 60

Year	Age	Club (League)	Lvl	W	L	ERA	G	GS	IP	H	HR	BB	SO	BB/9	SO/9	WHIP	AVG
2022	25	Royals (ACL)	R	0	1	5.12	7	7	19	29	1	4	26	1.9	12.1	1.71	.354
2022	25	Quad Cities (MWL)	HiA	0	0	0.00	1	1	4	6	0	1	6	2.2	13.5	1.75	.333
2022	25	NW Arkansas (TL)	AA	1	3	6.92	9	9	39	51	7	17	30	3.9	6.9	1.74	.317
Minor League Totals				15	13	4.22	56	53	260	271	23	57	260	2.0	9.0	1.26	.268

12 ASA LACY, LHP

Born: June 2, 1999. **B-T:** L-L. **HT:** 6-4. **WT:** 215.
Drafted: Texas A&M, 2020 (1st round). **Signed by:** Josh Hallgren.

TRACK RECORD: Lacy exploded on the scene at Texas A&M where he starred for three years, posting a combined 2.07 ERA and striking out 224 hitters in 152 innings. Drafted with the fourth overall pick in 2020 and signing for a $6.67 million bonus, the Royals keep waiting for the pitcher with exhilarating pure stuff who was expected to move quickly through the system. Lacy's progress has been impeded by delivery issues caused by shoulder problems in 2021 and ongoing back spasms in 2022, resulting in another lost season despite the presence of elite level stuff.

SCOUTING REPORT: When he's right, Lacy delivers his plus-plus fastball in the upper 90s with sharp downward angle and a wipeout slider that gets swings and misses in the strike zone. At times in 2022 Lacy experimented with a cutter to get more horizontal movement and shape to the pitch instead of just simplifying his mechanics and using what has worked for him in the past. His changeup has late life, projecting as a plus pitch when he commands it, and his curveball has late bite as well. Lacy's biggest issue is the recurring back issue that caused problems in getting extension and release of the ball, affecting how he was landing and thus causing erratic pitches.

THE FUTURE: Lacy will head to spring training hopefully fresh and with no health issues and will look for another shot at Double-A to prove that he's back to being the pitcher the Royals drafted. He not only needs to stay healthy but also become more consistent with his mechanics. If the pitcher that everyone saw at Texas A&M returns, it's top-of-the-rotation potential—but that's a big if.

BA GRADE: 50/Extreme	Fastball: 70	Curveball: 50	Slider: 55	Changeup: 60	Control: 30

Year	Age	Club (League)	Lvl	W	L	ERA	G	GS	IP	H	HR	BB	SO	BB/9	SO/9	WHIP	AVG
2022	23	Royals (ACL)	R	1	0	9.00	4	2	8	4	1	14	10	15.8	11.2	2.25	.143
2022	23	NW Arkansas (TL)	AA	1	2	11.25	11	3	20	9	2	28	25	12.6	11.2	1.85	.132
Minor League Totals				4	7	7.09	29	19	80	54	8	83	114	9.3	12.8	1.71	.192

13 BECK WAY, RHP

Born: Aug. 6, 1999. B-T: R-R. **HT:** 6-4. **WT:** 185.
Drafted: Northwest Florida State JC, 2020 (4th round). **Signed by:** Chuck Bartlett (Yankees).

TRACK RECORD: Way began his college career with one season at Division II Belmont-Abbey (N.C.) before transferring to Northwest Florida State JC for his draft year. He ranked nationally in several categories in the abbreviated 2020 junior college season, including an impressive 13.05 strikeouts per nine innings, after which he was picked by the Yankees in the fourth round. Way was included in a trade that sent outfielder Andrew Benintendi to the Yankees. He finished the season at High-A Quad Cities where he posted a 30.7% strikeout rate and held opposing hitters to a .185 average in seven starts.

SCOUTING REPORT: Way's fastball is a two-seamer that sits 93-95 mph with heavy sink and good life. He pairs that pitch with an 83-mph sweepy slider with potential elite horizontal break that he used more than 50 percent of the time. Way rounds out his repertoire with an 87-mph changeup that he uses infrequently. That pitch will be more effective when he gets more separation from the fastball. Way has added strength since being drafted, which has led to the quality of his pitches ticking up, and he shows a competitive edge on the mound.

THE FUTURE: Way will head to Double-A in 2023. With the fastball and slider both above-average pitches, he may be suited for a bullpen role as he gets closer to the big leagues. If the changeup develops and he improves the command of his pitches, he's got the frame to be a durable back-end starter.

BA GRADE: 45/High	Fastball: 55	Slider: 55	Changeup: 40	Control: 50

Year	Age	Club (League)	Lvl	W	L	ERA	G	GS	IP	H	HR	BB	SO	BB/9	SO/9	WHIP	AVG
2022	22	Hudson Valley (SAL)	HiA	5	5	3.73	15	15	72	55	9	26	80	3.2	10.0	1.12	.212
2022	22	Quad Cities (MWL)	HiA	3	3	3.79	7	7	36	24	1	17	47	4.3	11.9	1.15	.189
Minor League Totals				12	11	3.83	41	40	171	120	15	81	210	4.3	11.0	1.17	.197

14 ALEC MARSH, RHP

Born: May 14, 1998. **B-T:** R-R. **HT:** 6-2. **WT:** 225.
Drafted: Arizona State, 2019 (2nd round supplemental). **Signed by:** Kenny Munoz.

TRACK RECORD: The 2022 season was a strange trip for Marsh, one of Kansas City's second round picks in 2019 after a career at Arizona State. At times he flashed some of the best stuff in the system, but inconsistency and the inability to command the ball in the zone led to a season of ugly stats (6.88 ERA, 28 home runs in 124 innings) albeit with 11.3 strikeouts per 9 innings.

SCOUTING REPORT: Marsh's issues primarily stem from lack of fastball command. The pitch sits around 94 mph and ticks up a bit more in shorter outings, but he missed with it too much in the middle of the plate and it also cut on him. Essentially, he was throwing too many strikes instead of not enough and not self-correcting problems. He gets swings-and-misses from both the 85-mph slider and 87-mph changeup, although scouts noted that his breaking balls were sharper in previous years. The 79-mph curveball is his fourth pitch, used as a change-of-pace breaking ball he mixes in occasionally. Improving the repeatability of his delivery is another area for improvement.

THE FUTURE: Marsh was added to the 40-man roster and will head to big league camp looking for a spot on the opening day roster. He will most likely return to Triple-A Omaha for more refinement of his repertoire. He finished 2022 with his two best outings of the year—something to build on if he can continue to improve his consistency and pitch mix. Overall, it was a good learning year coming off the 2021 season when he got only six starts due to biceps soreness and arm fatigue.

BA GRADE: 45/High	Fastball: 50	Curveball: 40	Slider: 55	Changeup: 55	Control: 45

Year	Age	Club (League)	Lvl	W	L	ERA	G	GS	IP	H	HR	BB	SO	BB/9	SO/9	WHIP	AVG
2022	24	NW Arkansas (TL)	AA	1	15	7.32	25	25	114	137	27	54	147	4.3	11.6	1.67	.290
2022	24	Omaha (IL)	AAA	1	1	1.80	2	2	10	5	1	5	9	4.5	8.1	1.00	.135
Minor League Totals				3	20	6.10	46	46	183	192	37	76	236	3.7	11.6	1.46	.264

15 ANDREW HOFFMANN, RHP

Born: Feb. 2, 2000. **B-T:** R-R. **HT:** 6-5. **WT:** 210.
Drafted: Illinois, 2021 (12th round). **Signed by:** Terry Tripp (Braves).

TRACK RECORD: Hoffmann was a somewhat unheralded pick by The Braves in 2021. He was selected in the 12th round in 2021 and signed for $125,000 after pitching at Illinois—his third school in as many years. He was the Illini team leader in ERA and WHIP, with a 64-to-15 strikeout-to-walk rate. He jumped onto the radar with strong showings in the Atlanta system at Low-A in 2021 and High-A in 2022. Hoffmann was one of three players sent to the Royals in exchange for a 2022 supplemental first round draft pick and he finished the year with nine starts at Double-A Northwest Arkansas.

SCOUTING REPORT: Hoffman delivers a four-seamer into lefthanded batters and a two-seamer into righties. Both fastballs sit around 91 mph and touch the mid-90s and he has shown command of both variants to both sides of the plate. His money pitch is a plus, sweeping slider around 82 mph that has rather unique pitch shape with plenty of horizontal movement. He's got good feel for the pitch and used it 44% of the time in Double-A. He rounds out his arsenal with a fading changeup that averages 84 mph. Hoffmann's pitches play up from the deception he gets from a funky delivery that starts with a leg pump and a pause before releasing the ball.

THE FUTURE: Hoffmann will head back to Double-A in 2023. The key to his future is how well his fastball will play at higher levels and whether he'll fit better as a starter or reliever. He has a tall, lean starter's frame but with the stuff to potentially excel out of the bullpen.

BA GRADE: 45/High	Fastball: 45	Slider: 60	Changeup: 50	Control: 50

Year	Age	Club (League)	Lvl	W	L	ERA	G	GS	IP	H	HR	BB	SO	BB/9	SO/9	WHIP	AVG
2022	22	Rome (SAL)	HiA	7	2	2.36	15	15	80	63	9	21	90	2.4	10.1	1.05	.217
2022	22	NW Arkansas (TL)	AA	2	4	6.64	9	9	39	50	5	20	30	4.6	6.9	1.78	.312
Minor League Totals				11	8	3.56	31	31	149	134	16	49	157	3.0	9.5	1.23	.241

16 T.J. SIKKEMA, LHP

Born: July 25, 1998. **B-T:** L-L. **HT:** 6-0. **WT:** 210.
Drafted: Missouri, 2019 (1st round supplemental). **Signed by:** Steve Lemke (Yankees).

TRACK RECORD: Sikkema made a name for himself early in his college career at Missouri, where he led the staff in wins in both his freshman and junior seasons. That pedigree got him drafted by the Yankees with the 38th overall pick, starting his pro career with four effective starts at short-season Staten Island. Sikkema went two years without pitching in an official game due to the canceled season in 2020 and lat and shoulder issues in 2021. He returned in 2022 with a productive year at High-A Hudson Valley. He was swapped to Kansas City at the trade deadline and finished the year at Double-A Northwest Arkansas, followed by an assignment to the Arizona Fall League.

SCOUTING REPORT: Primarily a two-seam/slider lefty, Sikkema delivers an average fastball in the 88-91 mph range, which plays up thanks to the deception he gets from the various arm angles he uses in his delivery. He drops his arm down to the side and then later climbs to create a different angle and create a different break from his slider and fastball. His above-average slider averages 79 mph with plenty of spin and comes from behind his back—which makes it tough for lefthanded hitters to pick up. His 83-mph changeup with sink is an effective pitch against righthanders. Sikkema is athletic and throws strikes but needs to improve his command.

THE FUTURE: Sikkema was left off the 40-man roster, but went unpicked in the Rule 5 draft. He will likely get an invitation to big league camp. It's unclear whether he will be a starter or reliever long-term.

BA GRADE: 45/High		Fastball: 50		Slider: 55		Changeup: 50		Control: 55						

Year	Age	Club (League)	Lvl	W	L	ERA	G	GS	IP	H	HR	BB	SO	BB/9	SO/9	WHIP	AVG
2022	23	Hudson Valley (SAL)	HiA	1	1	2.48	11	10	36	21	3	9	54	2.2	13.4	0.83	.165
2022	23	NW Arkansas (TL)	AA	0	5	7.44	8	8	33	42	6	15	29	4.1	8.0	1.74	.313
Minor League Totals				1	6	4.29	23	22	80	69	9	25	96	2.8	10.8	1.18	.231

17 JACKSON KOWAR, RHP

Born: October 4, 1996. **B-T:** R-R. **HT:** 6-5. **WT:** 210.
Drafted: Florida, 2018 (1st round). **Signed by:** Jim Buckley.

TRACK RECORD: The 2022 season was one of ups and downs—but more downs—for Kowar, one of two Royals first round picks in 2018 after a stellar career for the Florida Gators. He got another chance in major league games, but just like in 2021 he was pummeled by big league hitters. While he had flashes of his old stuff in Triple-A, Kowar wasn't the same pitcher that he's been in the past.

SCOUTING REPORT: Kowar's problems stem from the command and life of his mid-90s fastball, which was a tick or two down from the past. The pitch is hittable when he tries to stay behind the pitch and get armside run, and later in games the tilt and vertical break would drop. He still gets swings-and-misses when the fastball is true with carry. The 86-mph changeup is a double-plus pitch that dives down in the zone and can get ugly swings-and-misses, but at times he didn't command the pitch and left it up and out over the plate. Compounding his issues, he also struggled to throw his breaking balls for strikes. The 78-mph curveball was developing nicely prior to this year and has potential to be an above-average pitch, but he's been using an 83-mph slider more often and needs to find more consistency with it.

THE FUTURE: Past versions of Kowar profiled as a No. 3 starter, but talent evaluators believe he'd be best suited to a bullpen role where he can work with his fastball/changeup combo. Getting Kowar back on track in 2023 will be one of many challenges for the new Royals pitching development team.

BA GRADE: 45/High		Fastball: 40		Curveball: 55		Slider: 45		Changeup: 70		Control: 40					

Year	Age	Club (League)	Lvl	W	L	ERA	G	GS	IP	H	HR	BB	SO	BB/9	SO/9	WHIP	AVG
2022	25	Omaha (IL)	AAA	4	10	6.16	20	20	83	95	14	43	88	4.6	9.5	1.66	.287
2022	25	Kansas City (AL)	MLB	0	0	9.77	7	0	16	27	4	11	17	6.3	9.8	2.43	.380
Major League Totals				0	6	10.76	16	8	46	70	11	31	46	6.1	9.0	2.20	.352
Minor League Totals				20	25	4.15	72	71	339	321	35	132	369	3.5	9.8	1.34	.249

18 MAX CASTILLO, RHP

Born: May 4, 1999. **B-T:** R-R. **HT:** 6-2. **WT:** 260.
Signed: Venezuela, 2015 **Signed by:** Ismael Cruz/Luis Marquez/Jose Contreras (Blue Jays)

TRACK RECORD: It was a long, slow trek through the Blue Jays farm system for Castillo. His career started as a 17-year-old in 2016 and he finally made it to Toronto for nine games in 2022, making his MLB debut on June 19, 2022. The Venezuelan native was included along with second baseman Samad Taylor to acquire Whit Merrifield at the trade deadline, and he split the rest of the season with five games in Kansas City and seven games at Triple-A Omaha.

SCOUTING REPORT: Castillo isn't flashy. He's more of a yeoman capable of fulfilling various roles on a pitching staff. His 93-mph fastball plays up because of how well he locates it, and induces weak contact with armside run. A key to his development in 2022 was switching from a two-seamer to a four-seamer— which helped the rest of his pitches play up thanks to the different shape. Castillo's best secondary offering is an above-average, 87-88 mph changeup that he commands well. It is firm and lacks a lot of separation from the fastball, but the above-average vertical separation allows it to play solidly. Castillo's best bat-missing pitch is an 83-mph slider with short shape that has paired well with his fastball and changeup. While there's nothing plus in his repertoire, Castillo succeeds with his pitching smarts.

THE FUTURE: Castillo will head to spring training with his versatility giving him a leg up on a roster spot. Starting pitcher? Long reliever? Swingman? Castillo could fill any or all of these roles.

AUSTIN CHARLES, SS

	BA GRADE: 40/Medium		Fastball: 55		Slider: 50		Changeup: 55		Control: 50						
Year	Age	Club (League)	Lvl	W	L	ERA	G	GS	IP	H	HR	BB	SO	BB/9	SO/9	WHIP	AVG
2022	23	New Hampshire (EL)	AA	3	1	3.10	6	6	29	21	3	14	35	4.3	10.9	1.21	.198
2022	23	Buffalo (IL)	AAA	2	0	0.66	5	3	27	10	2	10	29	3.3	9.5	0.73	.112
2022	23	Omaha (IL)	AAA	1	1	8.44	7	6	21	35	3	9	22	3.8	9.3	2.06	.354
2022	23	Kansas City (AL)	MLB	0	2	9.16	5	4	19	23	4	10	17	4.8	8.2	1.77	.307
2022	23	Toronto (AL)	MLB	0	0	3.05	9	2	21	15	4	5	20	2.2	8.7	0.97	.197
Major League Totals				0	2	5.95	14	6	39	38	8	15	37	3.4	8.5	1.35	.252
Minor League Totals				46	19	3.93	114	103	539	528	46	161	496	2.7	8.3	1.28	.255

19 DIEGO HERNANDEZ, OF

Born: Nov. 21. 2000. **B-T:** L-L. **HT:** 6-0. **WT:** 185.
Signed: Dominican Republic, 2017. **Signed by:** Fabio Herrera/Felix Francisco.
TRACK RECORD: It's been a slow, steady climb through the Royals system for Hernandez, with his most recent season—split between High-A Quad Cities and Double-A Northwest Arkansas—being his biggest step forward yet. He was remarkably consistent between the two levels and finished with a combined .284/.347/.408 batting line. His 40 stolen bases ranked third among all Royals minor leaguers and he's now swiped more than 30 bags for two years in a row.
SCOUTING REPORT: Prior to the 2022 season Hernandez made changes to his swing mechanics. He developed more of a line drive stroke in order to make more contact. While he's added nearly 40 pounds since originally joining the organization in 2017, he'll need to continue adding strength to his still-lanky frame in order to be able to handle major league pitching. A gap-to-gap hitter with plus speed, he projects to have more doubles power than over-the-fence pop, but a positive sign in 2022 was the nine home runs he hit—surpassing his combined total of two from his previous three seasons. Hernandez is a plus defender who can stay in center field, with an average arm that would allow him to play all three positions in a fourth outfielder role. He's aggressive on the field and a hard worker who has adapted well to new hitting philosophies introduced by the Royals hitting development team.
THE FUTURE: Hernandez's development is not going to be rushed, with a return to Double-A in 2023 his most likely destination. He's been added to the 40-man roster.

	BA GRADE: 45/High		Hit: 50		Power: 40		Speed: 60		Fielding: 60		Arm: 50				
Year	Age	Club (League)	Lvl	AVG	G	AB	R	H	2B	3B	HR	RBI	BB	SO	SB	OBP	SLG
2022	21	Quad Cities (MWL)	HiA	.279	83	330	55	92	17	4	7	29	27	72	27	.343	.418
2022	21	NW Arkansas (TL)	AA	.298	32	124	23	37	4	0	2	11	12	28	13	.357	.379
Minor League Totals				.278	246	948	154	264	34	8	11	83	87	209	88	.344	.366

20 MASON BARNETT, RHP

Born: Nov. 7, 2000. **B-T:** R-R. **HT:** 6-0. **WT:** 218.
Drafted: Auburn, 2022 (3rd round). **Signed by:** Will Howard.
TRACK RECORD: Barnett pitched three seasons at Auburn, but it wasn't until his junior year that he saw significant action when he pitched in 19 games and struck out 83 in 63.2 innings. Part of his improvement came from working with former big league ace Tim Hudson—a volunteer assistant pitching coach at his alma mater. Barnett saved one of his best college outings for the NCAA regional tournament, when he pitched 5.1 scoreless innings with 10 strikeouts to beat a tough UCLA team.
SCOUTING REPORT: Barnett delivers an above-average fastball that sits 95 mph and is up to 98 from a flat approach angle. His best secondary pitch is an average or better mid-80s slider with bite that he locates well. Barnett has feel for an average changeup at 85 mph that is best against lefthanded hitters. He could use the changeup more often, and also has a fringy 76-mph curveball with depth that needs more refinement. He projects to have average command and control, which will be the determining factor as to whether he's a starter or a reliever long-term.
THE FUTURE: After rarely throwing more than 80 pitches per game in college, he'll need to be built up for a starter role, though his fastball/slider combo could also be effective in a bullpen.

	BA GRADE: 45/High		Fastball: 55		Curveball: 45		Slider: 50		Changeup: 50		Control: 50				
Year	Age	Club (League)	Lvl	W	L	ERA	G	GS	IP	H	HR	BB	SO	BB/9	SO/9	WHIP	AVG
2022	21	Royals (ACL)	R	0	0	0.00	1	1	1	0	0	0	1	0.0	9.0	0.00	.000
2022	21	Columbia (CAR)	LoA	1	0	0.00	3	0	7	0	0	1	11	1.3	14.1	0.14	.000
Minor League Totals				1	0	0.00	4	1	8	0	0	1	12	1.1	13.5	0.12	.000

21 AUSTIN CHARLES, SS

Born: Nov. 13, 2003. **B-T:** R-R. **HT:** 6-6. **WT:** 215.
Drafted: HS—Bakersfield, Calif., 2022 (20th round). **Signed by:** Todd Guggiana.
TRACK RECORD: One of the top two-way players in the 2022 draft, Charles popped onto the radar with a promising showing during the 2021 wood bat championships in Jupiter. Just before the signing deadline, Charles agreed to a well above-slot $429,500.
SCOUTING REPORT: Charles will move slowly through the system to fully develop his impressive set of tools. Because of the long levers from his 6-foot-6 frame, Charles is susceptible to breaking balls away from the plate, but he has the strength to hit balls far when he connects. Right now, his best swings come in batting practice, but he's a hard worker and shows the ability to take instruction to turn that into in-game production. Charles will continually face questions whether he can stay at shortstop, but for now he has the athleticism, the feel, the instincts and the internal clock for the position. He gets good first step reads and creates good angles to the ball. Charles sports a plus arm and is an average runner.
THE FUTURE: With a return to rookie ball likely, there's a lot to dream on with this kind of size and athleticism, but it will take time to see just what kind of ballplayer Charles turns into.

| BA GRADE: 50/Extreme | | Hit: 45 | | Power: 60 | | Speed: 50 | | Fielding: 55 | | Arm: 60 | |

Year	Age	Club (League	Lvl	AVG	G	AB	R	H	2B	3B	HR	RBI	BB	SO	SB	OBP	SLG
2022	18	Royals (ACL)	R	.273	3	11	1	3	0	0	0	0	0	4	0	.273	.273
Minor League Totals				.273	3	11	1	3	0	0	0	0	0	4	0	.273	.273

22 LUCA TRESH, C

Born: Jan. 11, 2000. **B-T:** R-R. **HT:** 6-0. **WT:** 190.
Drafted: North Carolina State, 2021 (17th round). **Signed by:** Tim Bittner.
TRACK RECORD: Tresh was on target in his junior year at North Carolina State to be the second straight Wolfpack catcher to be drafted in the first round until a second half slump raised questions as to just how much he'd hit as a pro. The Royals signed him to an overslot $423,000 bonus.
SCOUTING REPORT: Tresh handled the demands of catching in 72 games without that workload affecting his bat. He stayed efficient with his swing, made good swing decisions, and adapted to velocity and high-usage spin. He's cut his strikeout rate at each level since turning pro and projects more as a high contact, line drive gap-to-gap hitter. His power is mostly to the pull side and will result more in extra-base hits than balls over the fence. A solid defender, Tresh has shown the ability to lead a staff, and is athletic behind the plate with at least an average arm.
THE FUTURE: Tresh will likely return to Double-A. It's still to be determined whether he will profile as a frontline regular or a backup catcher, but he's showing that he can be at least a solid major leaguer.

| BA GRADE: 45/High | | Hit: 45 | | Power: 40 | | Speed: 30 | | Fielding: 50 | | Arm: 55 | |

Year	Age	Club (League)	Lvl	AVG	G	AB	R	H	2B	3B	HR	RBI	BB	SO	SB	OBP	SLG
2022	22	Quad Cities (MWL)	HiA	.273	80	300	48	82	15	1	14	54	41	85	3	.360	.470
2022	22	NW Arkansas (TL)	AA	.253	24	91	16	23	4	0	5	14	13	25	1	.358	.462
Minor League Totals				.264	120	444	66	117	23	1	20	76	59	125	4	.352	.455

23 NOAH CAMERON, LHP

Born: July 19, 1999. **B-T:** L-L. **HT:** 6-3. **WT:** 225.
Drafted: Central Arkansas, 2021 (7th round). **Signed by:** Matt Price.
TRACK RECORD: Cameron got only 18 starts during his college career at Central Arkansas after losing his junior year to Tommy John surgery. The Royals grabbed him in the seventh round in 2021 and signed him to a below-slot $197,500 bonus. Cameron got back on the mound in 2022 with 19 starts split between three levels—with excellent results at each stop. Most notable was an eye-popping 13.6 strikeouts per nine innings while walking just 2.2 per nine.
SCOUTING REPORT: A touch-and-feel southpaw, Cameron commands all three of his pitches. His tick below-average fastball sits 88-91 mph and touches 94, with good carry and movement. His best secondary pitch is a plus changeup at 79-81 mph with tumbling action and deception thanks to the lower speed—which also helps his fastball play up. Cameron has good feel for a 77-80 mph above-average curveball with 11-to-5 shape and tight break that he throws for strikes and tunnels well with the fastball. He also mixes in a cutter that flashes plus. Cameron's arm action and repeatable delivery work and he's recognized as having the best control in the organization.

THE FUTURE: Cameron is ready for a full season of work and will get that chance in 2023 with a move to Double-A. He's an intriguing pop-up prospect because he throws strikes and knows how to pitch.

BA GRADE: 45/High		Fastball: 45		Curveball: 50		Changeup: 60		Cutter: 55		Control: 55				

Year	Age	Club (League)	Lvl	W	L	ERA	G	GS	IP	H	HR	BB	SO	BB/9	SO/9	WHIP	AVG
2022	22	Royals (ACL)	R	0	1	3.18	3	3	6	9	1	0	7	0.0	11.1	1.59	.346
2022	22	Columbia (CAR)	LoA	0	1	3.72	7	7	29	22	3	9	39	2.8	12.1	1.07	.208
2022	22	Quad Cities (MWL)	HiA	2	1	3.48	9	9	31	27	2	7	53	2.0	15.4	1.10	.229
Minor League Totals				2	3	3.56	19	19	66	58	6	16	99	2.2	13.6	1.13	.232

24 SAMAD TAYLOR, 2B/OF

Born: July 11, 1998. **B-T:** R-R. **HT:** 5-10. **WT:** 170.
Drafted: HS—Corona, Calif., 2016 (10th round). **Signed by:** Mike Bradford (Guardians).
TRACK RECORD: Taylor is now with his third organization after being drafted in the 10th round by Cleveland in 2016, traded a year later to Toronto, and finally received by Kansas City as part of the trade for Whit Merrifield. He was sidelined after mid-July due to an oblique injury, and didn't make his Royals debut until the Arizona Fall League. Despite playing just 70 games with Triple-A Buffalo, he was named both the best baserunner and the fastest baserunner in the International League in 2022.
SCOUTING REPORT: Taylor is aggressive at the plate—a free swinger who likes to hit to his pull side. He has the bat-to-ball skills to get to the power that he does have, and homered nine times in his half-season in Buffalo, but that power has also come with holes in his swing—resulting in a 22% strikeout rate. He needs to change his approach to put more balls in play so that he can take advantage of his plus speed. Taylor has the tools to be a better defender at second base and has also seen time in the outfield but is more fringe-average wherever he plays. He'll be an adequate defender in a utility role.
THE FUTURE: The Royals added Taylor to the 40-man roster to keep him out of the Rule 5 draft, and he'll likely spend most of 2023 with Triple-A Omaha.

BA GRADE: 40/	Medium		Hit: 45		Power: 45		Speed: 70		Fielding: 45		Arm: 45					

Year	Age	Club (League	Lvl	AVG	G	AB	R	H	2B	3B	HR	RBI	BB	SO	SB	OBP	SLG
2022	23	Buffalo (IL)	AAA	.258	70	244	41	63	10	2	9	45	28	62	23	.337	.426
Minor League Totals				.256	470	1663	276	426	93	16	48	232	200	450	136	.341	.418

25 PEYTON WILSON, 2B

Born: November 1, 1999. **B-T:** B-R. **HT:** 5-9. **WT:** 180.
Drafted: Alabama, 2021 (2nd round supplemental). **Signed by:** Cody Clark.
TRACK RECORD: The Wilson family has Crimson Tide blood running through it, with one of Peyton's brothers playing football at Alabama and another on the baseball team. He played two years at Alabama, and was selected in 2021 in the supplemental second round as a draft-eligible sophomore—signing for a bonus just over $1 million. Wilson broke out in 2022. He came on especially strong in the second half after a hamstring issue delayed the start of his season.
SCOUTING REPORT: Wilson just oozes twitchy athleticism and is a fundamentally sound player. He has good bat speed from both sides of the plate, and even when struggling he stayed consistent with his routine and the process. Wilson is slight of build and needs to continue gaining strength, but his 14 home runs show there's close to average power in the tank. An average defender with an above-average arm, he saw time at both second base and center field in 2022 and could handle the left side of the infield in a utility role. A plus runner, Wilson stole 23 bases in 25 attempts at Quad Cities.
THE FUTURE: With Double-A being his next step, Wilson has the tools for a super utility role and just needs to gain strength and continue to develop the hit tool.

BA GRADE: 40/High		Hit: 45		Power: 45		Speed: 60		Fielding: 50		Arm: 55					

Year	Age	Club (League)	Lvl	AVG	G	AB	R	H	2B	3B	HR	RBI	BB	SO	SB	OBP	SLG
2022	22	Quad Cities (MWL)	HiA	.268	88	340	60	91	16	3	14	44	41	97	23	.359	.456
Minor League Totals				.258	111	414	73	107	22	5	15	52	51	118	30	.356	.444

26 CHANDER CHAMPLAIN, RHP

Born: July 23, 1999. **B-T:** R-R. **HT:** 6-5. **WT:** 240.
Drafted: Southern California, 2021 (9th round). **Signed by:** David Keith (Yankees).

TRACK RECORD: Champlain was one of the top high school pitching prospects in California in his senior year but stuck to his strong commitment to Southern California. His three-year career there didn't go as expected but he was still drafted by the Yankees in the ninth round in 2021. Champlain didn't pitch that summer, with the Yankees instead working with him to improve his selection of pitches. He got into 16 games at Low-A Tampa, with an impressive 11.5 strikeouts per nine innings and just 2.3 walks per nine. Champlain was part of the package of prospects acquired by the Royals for outfielder Andrew Benintendi.

SCOUTING REPORT: Champlain has a tall, sturdy pitcher's frame. The extra work that the Yankees did with him after being drafted resulted in a more dynamic fastball, which now averages 93 mph and touches as high as 99 with added riding life through the zone. He's known for the quality of his breaking balls. Both a curveball and slider have above-average spin: the curve is a 79-mph breaker with 12-to-6 shape and the slider checks in a few ticks higher at 82. He also tinkered with a changeup with some sink as an occasional weapon against lefthanded batters, but it's mostly the fastball and breaking balls coming out of his quick-paced, smooth delivery.

THE FUTURE: He'll head to Double-A to start 2023. Unless he develops a more useful changeup, Champlain will probably wind up in the bullpen, but with a nice three-pitch mix to thrive in that role.

BA GRADE: 40/High		Fastball: 55		Curveball: 55		Slider: 55		Changeup: 40		Control: 50				
Year	Age	Club (League)	Lvl	W	L	ERA	G	GS	IP	H	HR	BB	SO	BB/9	SO/9	WHIP	AVG
2022	22	Tampa (FSL)	LoA	2	5	4.30	16	15	73	72	11	19	94	2.3	11.5	1.24	.251
2022	22	Quad Cities (MWL)	HiA	1	3	9.84	8	7	32	58	3	11	22	3.1	6.2	2.16	.414
Minor League Totals				3	8	5.98	24	22	105	130	14	30	116	2.6	9.9	1.52	.304

27 BEN HERNANDEZ, RHP

Born: July 1, 2001. **B-T:** R-R. **HT:** 6-2. **WT:** 215.
Drafted: HS—Chicago, 2020 (2nd round). **Signed by:** Scott Melvin

TRACK RECORD: Hernandez was known for having the best changeup among 2020 high school pitchers, and the Royals signed him for a $1.45 million bonus. He got only nine starts at Low-A Columbia in 2021 due to arm fatigue, and returned there for the entire 2022 season with subpar results.

SCOUTING REPORT: Hernandez pounds the zone with his 92 mph fringe-average fastball. He was sitting 94-96 mph before a late-season drop in velocity. The fastball plays up because of the sink he gets on it, but he uses it too much thanks to a lack of confidence in his offspeed pitches. He needs to be more aggressive with his fringy, 76-mph curveball and throw it harder. The 83-mph plus changeup is better when he stays through it and gets shorter movement down over the plate, but it also needs to be a harder pitch. The issue with both off-speed pitches is that he struggles to throw them for strikes, so batters wait for the fringy fastball and punish it for hard contact. Hernandez gets deception in his delivery from a lower arm slot.

THE FUTURE: He'll get the chance to regain his previous form at High-A in 2023. With his step back in 2022, Hernandez faces questions as to whether he would be better pitching out of the bullpen where his stuff could potentially tick up in shorter outings.

BA GRADE: 45/Extreme		Fastball: 45		Curveball: 45		Changeup: 60		Control: 40						
Year	Age	Club (League)	Lvl	W	L	ERA	G	GS	IP	H	HR	BB	SO	BB/9	SO/9	WHIP	AVG
2022	20	Columbia (CAR)	LoA	1	7	5.38	23	23	77	83	7	40	71	4.7	8.3	1.60	.280
Minor League Totals				2	9	5.05	35	35	112	120	9	57	104	4.6	8.3	1.58	.279

28 STEVEN ZOBAC, RHP

Born: October 14, 2000. **B-T:** L-R. **HT:** 6-3. **WT:** 185.
Drafted: California, 2022 (4th round). **Signed by:** Buddy Goldsmith.

TRACK RECORD: The Zobac family had their version of double trouble at California the last three years, as Steven pitched for the baseball team while twin sister Casey played on the Golden Bears softball team. After moving between the mound and the outfield for his first two college seasons, Zobac focused strictly on pitching in 2022. He saw his first Royals mound action during the fall instructional league.

SCOUTING REPORT: Zobac has an exciting arm with a lot of upside, especially now that he's no longer a two-way player and will get more pitching experience. The fastball is a potential plus pitch, sitting 95 mph and touching 97. It doesn't have much side-to-side movement but has solid carry. It's easy velocity as the ball comes out clean without a lot of effort in his high, three-quarters delivery, which he repeats well thanks to his athleticism. His best secondary pitch is an above-average slider, delivered in the mid-80s with bite at the strike zone. His 83-84 mph changeup is still very much a work-in-progress, but he shows some feel for it.

THE FUTURE:. He'll start his Royals career in 2023 with an assignment to one of the Class A teams. There's still plenty of development needed to improve his repertoire.

BA GRADE: 45/Extreme		Fastball: 55		Slider: 55		Changeup: 30		Control: 50					

Year	Age	Club (League)	Lvl	W	L	ERA	G	GS	IP	H	HR	BB	SO	BB/9	SO/9	WHIP	AVG
2022	21	Did not play															

29 LIZANDRO RODRIGUEZ, 2B

Born: Nov. 16, 2022. **B-T:** B-R. **HT:** 5-11. **WT:** 180.
Signed: Dominican Republic, 2019. **Signed by:** Fausto Morel

TRACK RECORD: Perhaps the least-known but most-notable prospect in the Royals system is Rodriguez, a switch-hitting infielder who started the season in the Arizona Complex League before moving up to Low-A Columbia, where he showed advanced baseball instincts and high energy playstyle at both levels. After posting a .317/.400/.573 line in the ACL, the 19-year-old Dominican Republic native had no trouble adjusting to full season ball, with a .290/.389/.436 line at Columbia. He has an innate ability to make contact and draws a fair share of walks, with a 10.2% walk rate.

SCOUTING REPORT: Rodriguez takes high-aptitude at-bats, with quick hands and an efficient swing. A gap-to-gap hitter, he's better from the left side but should improve from the right side with more reps. His power is currently a tick below average but should increase as he gets stronger. He's an above-average defender in the infield, but his average arm likely makes him a better fit for second base. His arm might be stretched at third base and he could be able to handle shortstop in a pinch. He's an above-average runner.

THE FUTURE: Considering how productive Rodriguez was in his late-season trial at Low-A, it wouldn't be a push to get him to High-A Quad Cities to start the 2023 season. He's most likely is a utility infielder, perhaps with the chance to also play some outfield.

BA GRADE: 45/Extreme		Hit: 55		Power: 45		Speed: 55		Fielding: 55		Arm: 50	

Year	Age	Club (League)	Lvl	AVG	G	AB	R	H	2B	3B	HR	RBI	BB	SO	SB	OBP	SLG
2022	19	Royals (ACL)	R	.317	25	82	17	26	4	1	5	12	9	16	5	.400	.573
2022	19	Columbia (CAR)	LoA	.290	18	62	13	18	4	1	1	5	8	11	1	.389	.435
Minor League Totals				.307	77	241	57	74	13	3	12	40	38	45	20	.417	.535

30 DANIEL VAZQUEZ, SS

Born: Dec. 15, 2003. **B-T:** R-R. **HT:** 6-0. **WT:** 185.
Signed: Dominican Republic, 2021 Signed by: Edis Perez.

TRACK RECORD: Vazquez signed for a bonus of $1.5 million at the start of the 2020-2021 international signing period and began his career later that summer in the Dominican Summer League. He first came to the states for instructional league that fall and impressed talent evaluators with his raw tools and ability to play shortstop. Instead of the expected assignment to the Arizona Complex League for 2022, the Royals challenged the 18-year-old with a trip to Low-A Columbia where he struggled.

SCOUTING REPORT: Vazquez has grown taller and stronger since he signed, which should help his offensive profile. He currently has a glove-over-hit profile but the added strength and above-average bat speed show his offensive potential. He uses a narrow, open stance, and lacks bat control with too many balls driven on the ground—he had a 52% ground ball rate in Columbia. Vazquez has good actions at shortstop but is erratic both on ground balls and throws to first base. He has the potential to become a plus defender, and flashes a plus arm, but needs more reps and polish to get to that projection. An above-average runner, Vazquez takes big strides and is a better runner underway than on his first burst.

THE FUTURE: Still just 19, Vazquez may go back to Columbia for another year of seasoning. His defense could make him a utility infielder. If the bat comes along, he'll profile as a regular shortstop.

BA GRADE: 45/Extreme		Hit: 40		Power: 40		Speed: 55		Fielding: 60		Arm: 60	

Year	Age	Club (League)	Lvl	AVG	G	AB	R	H	2B	3B	HR	RBI	BB	SO	SB	OBP	SLG
2022	18	Columbia (CAR)	LoA	.195	77	293	25	57	10	0	0	31	28	86	10	.262	.229
Minor League Totals				.192	109	395	42	76	13	1	1	41	42	117	14	.266	.238

Los Angeles Angels

Reid Detmers posted a 3.77 ERA as a starter.

RONALD MARTINEZ/GETTY IMAGES

BY TAYLOR BLAKE WARD

It has become a tiresome comment, but the fact remains the same that the Angels have not been able to win with two generational players in their lineup.

Shohei Ohtani is entering the final year of his contract in 2023, while Mike Trout is entering his age-32 season and playing for his third general manager since 2015. Running through three different regimes in a short time tends to result in a lack of consistency, but the one constant over the span of seven consecutive losing seasons and an eight-year playoff drought—tied for longest in the majors—is the Angels' lack of impact players or depth from homegrown talent.

It has been 13 years since the Angels found incredible success in the 2009 draft when they selected Randal Grichuk, Trout, Tyler Skaggs, Garrett Richards and Patrick Corbin in succession. Since then, the Angels have produced a total of three drafted or internationally signed players who have produced five or more wins above replacement—outfielder Kole Calhoun (14.3), Ohtani (13.6) and second baseman David Fletcher (10.5).

The Angels' struggles in the draft altered with each general manager. Jerry Dipoto didn't have a first-round pick each of the first two years due to the signings of Albert Pujols, C.J. Wilson and Josh Hamilton. Billy Eppler went for high-risk, high-reward athletes such as Jo Adell, Jordyn Adams, Jeremiah Jackson and Kyren Paris, hoping they could translate their athleticism to baseball. To date, it hasn't happened.

For Dipoto and Eppler—and now current GM Perry Minasian—a common theme was losing a high draft pick as an exchange for owner Arte Moreno's affinity for signing free agents.

Moreno has attempted to put a winning team on the field every year since he bought the team in 2003, which can be commended, but the constant pursuit of upper-tier free agents and lack of spend-

PROJECTED 2026 LINEUP

Catcher	Logan O'Hoppe	26
First Base	Jared Walsh	32
Second Base	David Fletcher	32
Third Base	Luis Rengifo	29
Shortstop	Zach Neto	25
Left Field	Jo Adell	27
Center Field	Mike Trout	34
Right Field	Taylor Ward	31
Designated Hitter	Anthony Rendon	36
No. 1 Starter	Patrick Sandoval	29
No. 2 Starter	Reid Detmers	26
No. 3 Starter	Jose Suarez	28
No. 4 Starter	Chase Silseth	26
No. 5 Starter	Ky Bush	26
Closer	Sam Bachman	26

ing on the international front has greatly impacted the depth of the Angels' system, leading to struggles in producing impact or even role players.

After years of failure, there is new optimism for the Angels' farm system under Minasian. The organization has placed an emphasis on contact skills and has begun spending again on the international market.

Minasian's focus on building the organization's pitching depth has already reaped benefits. The Angels drafted pitchers with all 20 of their picks in Minasian's first draft in 2021 and have already seen righthander Chase Silseth reach the majors, with many others from the class, including lefthanders Ky Bush and Eric Torres, standing out in the upper levels.

Though most evaluators see the Angels' farm system filled with future relievers, there is a constant mention of how much more upside and improved control there is among the organization's pitching prospects compared to years past.

To be clear, the Angels' farm system is still years away from having the quantity of talent necessary to turn around the franchise's fortunes. But with noticeably more contact being made amongst the organization's young hitters, and improved stuff and control all around from their pitching prospects, there is optimism that the Angels farm system is finally getting on the right track. ∎

DEPTH CHART

LOS ANGELES ANGELS

TOP 2023 MLB CONTRIBUTORS — RANK
Logan O'Hoppe, C — 1
Chase Silseth, RHP — 3
Ben Joyce, RHP — 10
BREAKOUT PROSPECTS — RANK
Ryan Costeiu, RHP — 20
Victor Mederos, RHP — 29

SOURCE OF TOP 30 TALENT

Homegrown	29	Acquired	1
College	11	Trade	1
Junior college	1	Rule 5 draft	0
High school	8	Independent league	0
Nondrafted free agent	0	Free agent/waivers	0
International	9		

LF
Randy de Jesus (19)
Anthony Scull
D'Shawn Knowles

CF
Nelson Rada (9)
David Calabrese (17)
Jordyn Adams (24)

RF
Jadiel Sanchez
Alexander Ramirez
Orlando Martinez
Ryan Aguilar

3B
Werner Blakely (8)
Capri Ortiz

SS
Zach Neto (2)
Denzer Guzman (6)
Jeremiah Jackson (18)
Arol Vera (25)
Luis Rodriguez

2B
Adrian Placencia (11)
Kyren Paris (16)
Livan Soto (26)

1B
Sonny DiChiara
Trey Cabbage

C
Logan O'Hoppe (1)
Edgar Quero (4)
Dario Laverde (30)

LHP

LHSP
Ky Bush (5)
Mason Albright
Kenny Rosenberg
Sadiel Baro

LHRP
Eric Torres (27)
Kolton Ingram
Mo Hanley

RHP

RHSP
Chase Silseth (3)
Sam Bachman (7)
Jake Madden (12)
Caden Dana (13)
Ryan Costeiu (20)
Coleman Crow (21)
Landon Marceaux (22)
Mason Erla (23)
Victor Mederos (29)
Nixon Encarnacion

RHRP
Ben Joyce (10)
Walbert Urena (14)
Chris Rodriguez (15)
Luke Murphy (28)
Brandon Dufault
Kelvin Caceras
Jose Marte
Max Gieg

BaseballAmerica.com

Baseball America 2023 Prospect Handbook · **211**

1 LOGAN O'HOPPE, C

Born: February 9, 2000. **B-T:** R-R. **HT:** 6-2. **WT:** 185.
Drafted: HS—West Islip, N.Y., 2018 (23rd round).
Signed by: Alex Agostino (Phillies).

TRACK RECORD: O'Hoppe largely fell under the radar as a high school catcher on Long Island, but the Phillies scouted the region heavily and were one of the few teams to identify him as a promising potential draft prospect. The Phillies selected him in the 23rd round in 2018 and signed him for an over-slot $215,000 to sway him from an East Carolina commitment. O'Hoppe quickly emerged as a potential late-round steal in the lower levels and was invited to the Phillies' alternate training site during the canceled 2020 minor league season. He spent the following offseason at Driveline Baseball in Seattle to improve his hitting and broke out in 2021, slashing his strikeout rate nearly in half and climbing from High-A to Triple-A on the strength of a banner offensive campaign. O'Hoppe picked up where he left off in 2022, and hit .275 with a .889 OPS and 15 home runs with Double-A Reading. He earned an invitation to the Futures Game. The Angels acquired him at the trade deadline in exchange for center fielder Brandon Marsh, hoping to address their long-term organizational hole at catcher. O'Hoppe carried his offensive success over to his new organization at Double-A Rocket City and earned his first big league callup in the final week of the season, when he had four hits in five games for the Angels.
SCOUTING REPORT: O'Hoppe is a physical, 6-foot-2 catcher who has the offensive and defensive tools to be a two-way threat at a premium position. He has progressively improved his bat-to-ball skills while finding a flatter bat path from the right side and now makes consistently hard contact, especially against pitches low in the zone. He is a pull-heavy hitter who has a tendency to open up at times, but he has solid pitch recognition and rarely swings and misses. O'Hoppe should be at least an average hitter and has been able to tap into his power more with his refined swing and approach. He has plenty of natural strength in his swing and makes enough quality contact to produce average power. As solid as O'Hoppe is now offensively, he's even better defensively. He's an above-average catcher who receives well with soft hands and is an able blocker with good agility and flexibility. He has a plus, accurate arm with a quick release and frequently records sub-1.9 second pop times on throws to second base. Beyond his physi-

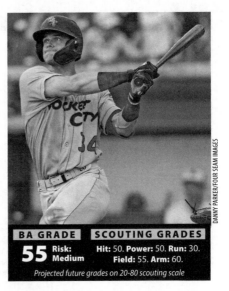

DANNY PARKER/FOUR SEAM IMAGES

BA GRADE	SCOUTING GRADES
55 Risk: Medium	**Hit:** 50. **Power:** 50. **Run:** 30. **Field:** 55. **Arm:** 60.

Projected future grades on 20-80 scouting scale

BEST TOOLS

BATTING

Best Hitter for Average	Zach Neto
Best Power Hitter	Jeremiah Jackson
Best Strike-Zone Discipline	Michael Stefanic
Fastest Baserunner	Jordyn Adams
Best Athlete	Jordyn Adams

PITCHING

Best Fastball	Ben Joyce
Best Curveball	Chris Rodriguez
Best Slider	Sam Bachman
Best Changeup	Ryan Costeiu
Best Control	Landon Marceaux

FIELDING

Best Defensive Catcher	Logan O'Hoppe
Best Defensive Infielder	Zach Neto
Best Infield Arm	Zach Neto
Best Defensive Outfielder	Bryce Teodosio
Best Outfield Arm	Jadiel Sanchez

cal skills, O'Hoppe expertly retains information, is a natural leader and is extremely popular with his pitchers. He calls a good game and has the toughness teams look for behind the plate.
THE FUTURE: O'Hoppe has all the tools to be the Angels' long-term backstop and projects to be an above-average regular in the near future. The Angels haven't had a regular at catcher who can contribute offensively in years, but O'Hoppe should end that drought. He has an opportunity to break camp with the Angels out of spring training and split time with Max Stassi during the regular season.

Year	Age	Club (League)	Lvl	AVG	G	AB	R	H	2B	3B	HR	RBI	BB	SO	SB	OBP	SLG
2022	22	Rocket City (SL)	AA	.306	29	98	24	30	3	0	11	33	29	22	1	.473	.673
2022	22	Reading (EL)	AA	.275	75	262	48	72	11	1	15	45	41	52	6	.392	.496
2022	22	Los Angeles (AL)	MLB	.286	5	14	1	4	0	0	0	2	2	3	0	.375	.286
Major League Totals				.286	5	14	1	4	0	0	0	2	2	3	0	.375	.286
Minor League Totals				.276	287	1024	162	283	55	6	50	183	125	227	18	.362	.488

2 ZACH NETO, SS

Born: January 31, 2001. **B-T:** R-R. **HT:** 6-0. **WT:** 185.
Drafted: Campbell, 2022 (1st round). **Signed by:** Nick Gorneault.
TRACK RECORD: Neto's freshman season at Campbell was limited by the coronavirus pandemic, but he broke out as a sophomore, and hit .405 with a 1.234 OPS while logging a 3.43 ERA in 21 innings as a reliever. He carried that performance into the Cape Cod League. He continued hitting his junior year, and hit .407/.514/.769 to win his second consecutive Big South Conference player of the year award. The Angels made Neto the first first-rounder in Campbell history when they took him 13th overall in 2022 and signed him for an under-slot $3.5 million. Neto was aggressively assigned to High-A after signing and quickly hit his way to Double-A.

BA GRADE
55 Risk: High

SCOUTING REPORT: Neto has an unorthodox setup at the plate, beginning with a massive inward leg kick and his hands moving toward his lower half, but he makes it work. Neto is regularly on time and makes consistent contact from the right side with an uphill swing that allows him to drive the ball in the air with authority. Neto is an aggressive hitter focused on making contact, but he will draw the occasional walk and limits his strikeouts. A potentially plus hitter, Neto has just average raw power and modest exit velocities, but his ability to backspin the ball and solid bat speed give him a chance to approach 20 home runs at maturity. Neto is a good athlete with a plus, accurate arm in the infield. He has good footwork, hands, and instincts at shortstop, but he'll have to improve his focus and learn when to hold onto the ball rather than force ill-advised throws. He is an above-average runner who is aggressive on the basepaths.
THE FUTURE: Neto has a chance to be the Angels' long-term solution at shortstop and has the bat to be an above-average regular even if he moves positions. He could reach Anaheim as soon as 2023.

| SCOUTING GRADES | Hitting: 60 | | Power: 50 | | Speed: 55 | | Fielding: 55 | | Arm: 60 | |

Year	Age	Club (League)	Lvl	AVG	G	AB	R	H	2B	3B	HR	RBI	BB	SO	SB	OBP	SLG
2022	21	Tri-City (NWL)	HiA	.200	7	25	2	5	0	1	1	4	4	4	1	.355	.400
2022	21	Rocket City (SL)	AA	.320	30	122	22	39	9	0	4	23	8	29	4	.382	.492
Minor League Totals				.299	37	147	24	44	9	1	5	27	12	33	5	.377	.476

3 CHASE SILSETH, RHP

Born: May 18, 2000. **B-T:** R-R. **HT:** 6-0. **WT:** 217.
Drafted: Arizona, 2021 (11th round). **Signed by:** Jayson Durocher.
TRACK RECORD: Silseth began his college career as a reliever at Tennessee, transferred to the JC of Southern Nevada as a sophomore and transferred again to Arizona as a junior, where he took over as the Wildcats' Friday night starter. Silseth delivered a lackluster performance on paper, but his loud stuff intrigued the Angels enough to draft him in the 11th round in 2021 and sign him overslot for $485,000. Silseth flourished immediately after the Angels reworked his pitch design and became the first player from the 2021 draft to reach the majors when the Angels called him up last May. He returned to Double-A Rocket City and spent most of the 2022 there.

BA GRADE
50 Risk: Medium

SCOUTING REPORT: Silseth is a short but strong righthander who has steadily improved his four-pitch mix. Silseth reshaped his fastball to make it a livelier pitch that now sits 95-96 mph and touches 99. Both his tight, mid-80s slider and low-80s, curveball with 12-to-6 action flash plus and collect swings and misses after he revamped their shapes. He rounds out his arsenal with a upper-80s splitter with good depth that flashes average and gets swings and misses, though it is inconsistent. Silseth works around the zone, but his control comes and goes the deeper he goes into outings. His size and durability questions lead some to projections that he will be a multi-inning power reliever, but with strength and conditioning gains and a full arsenal of weapons, he will get every chance to remain a starter.
THE FUTURE: Silseth has the arsenal to reach an upside of No. 3 or 4 starter, but he has to prove he can hold up late into outings. He should return to the majors again at some point in 2023.

| SCOUTING GRADES: | Fastball: 60 | | Curveball: 55 | | Slider: 50 | | Splitter: 45 | | Control: 45 | |

Year	Age	Club (League)	Lvl	W	L	ERA	G	GS	IP	H	HR	BB	SO	BB/9	SO/9	WHIP	AVG
2022	22	Rocket City (SL)	AA	7	0	2.28	15	15	83	52	11	27	110	2.9	11.9	0.95	.182
2022	22	Los Angeles (AL)	MLB	1	3	6.59	7	7	29	33	7	12	24	3.8	7.5	1.57	.287
Major League Totals				1	3	6.59	7	7	29	33	7	12	24	3.8	7.5	1.57	.287
Minor League Totals				7	2	2.75	18	17	88	59	12	28	117	2.9	11.9	0.98	.191

4 EDGAR QUERO, C

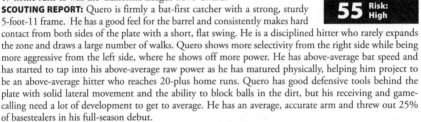

Born: April 6, 2003. **B-T:** B-R. **HT:** 5-11. **WT:** 170.
Signed: Cuba, 2021. **Signed by:** Brian Parker.

TRACK RECORD: Quero emerged as a player to watch after shining with Cuba's national team at the U-15 World Cup in Panama in 2018. The switch-hitting catcher signed with the Angels three years later in February 2021 for $200,000, five weeks before his 18th birthday. Quero made his pro debut in the Arizona Complex League that summer and quickly emerged as one of the league's most intriguing prospects. He took that to another level in his full-season debut at Low-A Inland Empire in 2022, and hit .312/.435/.530 with 17 home runs to win the California League MVP award.

BA GRADE

55 Risk: High

SCOUTING REPORT: Quero is firmly a bat-first catcher with a strong, sturdy 5-foot-11 frame. He has a good feel for the barrel and consistently makes hard contact from both sides of the plate with a short, flat swing. He is a disciplined hitter who rarely expands the zone and draws a large number of walks. Quero shows more selectivity from the right side while being more aggressive from the left side, where he shows off more power. He has above-average bat speed and has started to tap into his above-average raw power as he has matured physically, helping him project to be an above-average hitter who reaches 20-plus home runs. Quero has good defensive tools behind the plate with solid lateral movement and the ability to block balls in the dirt, but his receiving and game-calling need a lot of development to get to average. He has an average, accurate arm and threw out 25% of basestealers in his full-season debut.

THE FUTURE: Quero's bat makes him promising, but he'll need to refine his catching technique to become an everyday backstop in the major leagues. He'll be just 20 years old on Opening Day and has time to make the necessary improvements.

SCOUTING GRADES	Hitting: 55	Power: 50	Speed: 40	Fielding: 45	Arm: 50

Year	Age	Club (League)	Lvl	AVG	G	AB	R	H	2B	3B	HR	RBI	BB	SO	SB	OBP	SLG
2022	19	Inland Empire (CAL)	LoA	.312	111	413	86	129	35	2	17	75	73	91	12	.435	.530
Minor League Totals				.296	150	534	109	158	45	3	22	105	101	135	14	.428	.515

5 KY BUSH, LHP

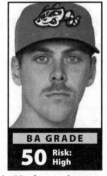

Born: November 12, 1999. **B-T:** L-L. **HT:** 6-6. **WT:** 240.
Drafted: Saint Mary's, 2021 (2nd round). **Signed by:** Scott Richardson.

TRACK RECORD: An unsigned 40th-round pick by the Royals out of high school, Bush began his college career at Washington State but transferred out after a poor freshman season and turnover on the Cougars' coaching staff. He spent the shortened 2020 season at Central Arizona JC and returned to Division I with Saint Mary's as a junior in 2021. Bush saw his velocity spike and control improve with the Gaels to fly up draft boards and was selected by the Angels in the second round, No. 45 overall, in the 2021 draft. He signed for an over-slot $1,747,500 and rose quickly to Double-A for his full-season debut in 2022, where he anchored a dominant Rocket City rotation and was selected to represent the Angels at the Futures Game.

BA GRADE

50 Risk: High

SCOUTING REPORT: Bush is a big, hulking lefthander at 6-foot-6, 240 pounds. His four-pitch mix is headlined by an above-average fastball that sits 93-94 mph and touches 96 with sinking action out of his high, three-quarters arm slot. His best secondary offering is a sharp, plus slider in the mid 80s with a late vertical break that gets swings and misses. Bush manipulates the speed and break of his slider and uses it best going down and away from lefthanded hitters and to the back foot of righthanders. Bush can generate swings and misses with his fringy, slow curveball and he has a feel for an average, fading changeup, but both remain inconsistent. He is a sneaky-good athlete given his large frame and throws strikes with average control out of repeatable delivery.

THE FUTURE: Bush's four-pitch mix and ability to throw strikes give him a chance to settle in as a quality back-of-the-rotation starter. He is in position to make his major league debut with the Angels in mid-to-late 2023.

SCOUTING GRADES:	Fastball: 55	Curveball: 45	Slider: 60	Changeup: 50	Control: 50

Year	Age	Club (League)	Lvl	W	L	ERA	G	GS	IP	H	HR	BB	SO	BB/9	SO/9	WHIP	AVG
2022	22	Rocket City (SL)	AA	7	4	3.67	21	21	103	93	14	29	101	2.5	8.8	1.18	.237
Minor League Totals				7	6	3.76	26	26	115	107	14	34	121	2.7	9.5	1.23	.243

6 DENZER GUZMAN, SS

Born: February 8, 2004. **B-T:** R-R. **HT:** 6-1. **WT:** 180.
Signed: Dominican Republic, 2021. **Signed by:** Domingo Garcia.

TRACK RECORD: Guzman signed with the Angels out of the Dominican Republic for $2 million as one of the top prospects in the 2020-21 international class that was delayed by the coronavirus pandemic. He showed positive traits despite mediocre numbers in his pro debut in the Dominican Summer League and flourished with a move to the U.S. in 2022. Guzman showed some of the best physical tools of any infielder in the Arizona Complex League and earned a promotion to Low-A Inland Empire for the final week of the season. He wrapped up his year with a standout performance in instructional league that had team officials buzzing.

BA GRADE
55 Risk: Extreme

SCOUTING REPORT: Guzman is a rhythmic hitter with excellent plate coverage who regularly finds the barrel with a fast, loose swing. He consistently makes hard contact and drives the ball back up the middle with an advanced approach. Guzman has solid raw power and explosive bat speed, but he'll have to continue growing and adding strength to his frame to tap into his potentially average power. He is a disciplined hitter with good strike-zone awareness who draws plenty of walks and rarely strikes out. On top of his offensive promise, Guzman has great instincts, sound footwork, soft hands and above-average arm strength at shortstop, but he's a fringe-average runner and could slow down and outgrow the position as he gets bigger. He would be an above-average defender at third base. Guzman receives high praise for his aptitude and work ethic and is a high-energy player who is fun to watch on the field.

THE FUTURE: Guzman has many years of physical development left, but he has a chance to grow into an above-average everyday player who makes an impact on both sides of the ball.

SCOUTING GRADES	Hitting: 55	Power: 45	Speed: 45	Fielding: 50	Arm: 55

Year	Age	Club (League)	Lvl	AVG	G	AB	R	H	2B	3B	HR	RBI	BB	SO	SB	OBP	SLG
2022	18	Angels (ACL)	R	.286	52	192	38	55	11	3	3	33	15	44	3	.341	.422
2022	18	Inland Empire (CAL)	LoA	.176	5	17	2	3	0	0	0	2	6	10	1	.391	.176
Minor League Totals				.251	101	350	61	88	21	4	6	62	41	78	15	.332	.386

7 SAM BACHMAN, RHP

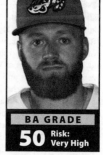

Born: September 30, 1999. **B-T:** R-R. **HT:** 6-1. **WT:** 235.
Drafted: Miami (Ohio), 2021 (1st round). **Signed by:** John Burden.

TRACK RECORD: Bachman started three years in the Miami (Ohio) rotation and saw his velocity spike from the low 90s to 96-101 mph his junior year. Angels general manager Perry Minasian attended Bachman's final collegiate start and saw enough for the club to select him ninth overall and sign him for an under-slot $3,847,500. Bachman jumped straight to Double-A for his full-season debut in 2022, but he missed the first month with back spasms and another two months with biceps inflammation. His velocity and command regressed throughout the year as he battled injuries, but his stuff ticked back up late and he touched 97 mph in instructional league.

BA GRADE
50 Risk: Very High

SCOUTING REPORT: Bachman is a physical 6-foot-1 righthander with a powerful, high-effort delivery and arm action. His fastball sits 95-97 mph at its best with immense armside run and sink that induces a heavy dose of weak ground balls. Bachman complements his fastball with a plus 86-89 mph vertical slider with late dive that is his go-to swing-and-miss pitch. When he doesn't finish his slider, it has cutter traits in the upper-80s and is more of an above-average offering. Bachman mostly attacks hitters with his fastball and slider. He has to learn to throw his fringe-average mid-80s changeup for strikes more often to make it a competitive pitch and remain a starter. Bachman is a pure power pitcher who tries to blow the ball by hitters and has below-average control. He has a long injury history and his velocity tends falls off sharply around the third inning.

THE FUTURE: Bachman's delivery, arsenal and injury history point strongly to a relief future. The Angels believe he can start and will continue developing him in the rotation.

SCOUTING GRADES:	Fastball: 60	Slider: 60	Changeup: 45	Control: 40

Year	Age	Club (League)	Lvl	W	L	ERA	G	GS	IP	H	HR	BB	SO	BB/9	SO/9	WHIP	AVG
2022	22	Rocket City (SL)	AA	1	1	3.92	12	12	44	41	4	25	30	5.2	6.2	1.51	.248
Minor League Totals				1	3	3.88	17	17	58	54	5	29	45	4.5	7.0	1.43	.248

8 WERNER BLAKELY, 3B

Born: February 21, 2002. **B-T:** L-R. **HT:** 6-3. **WT:** 185.
Drafted: HS—Detroit, 2020 (4th round). **Signed by:** Drew Dominguez.

TRACK RECORD: Blakely was an athletic but raw prep shortstop who missed his senior year due to the coronavirus pandemic when the Angels selected him in the fourth round of the 2020 draft. Blakely hit just .182 in the Arizona Complex League in his pro debut, but he returned vastly improved in 2022 and was one of the California League's best hitters at Low-A Inland Empire before injuries sidetracked his season. Blakely missed five weeks with a hamstring injury and missed another seven weeks after he was hit by a pitch that bruised his hand. He made up for the lost reps as one of the youngest players in the Arizona Fall League after the season.

BA GRADE
50 Risk: Very High

SCOUTING REPORT: Blakely has loads of projection in his long, lean and athletic 6-foot-3 frame. He has a loose swing from the left side with plus bat speed that allows him to consistently be on time despite a heavy bat wrap. Blakely mostly drives hard liners the other way, but he has above-average raw power he is starting to tap into and has the potential to add more as he continues to grow into his body. Blakely is a disciplined hitter with a good eye who improved his pitch recognition, which has led to fewer swings and misses in the zone and allows him to project as an average hitter with average power. Signed as a shortstop, Blakely has moved to third base and has a lot of work to do. He's athletic enough to stay in the infield and has average arm strength, but his upper and lower body are often disconnected and he boots a lot of routine ground balls. He may need to move to the outfield, where his above-average speed and long strides will allow him to cover enough ground at all three positions.

THE FUTURE: Blakely needs to stay healthy and get regular reps to continue his growth on both sides of the ball. He'll move to High-A in 2023.

SCOUTING GRADES	Hitting: 50	Power: 50	Speed: 55	Fielding: 45	Arm: 50

Year	Age	Club (League)	Lvl	AVG	G	AB	R	H	2B	3B	HR	RBI	BB	SO	SB	OBP	SLG
2022	20	Inland Empire (CAL)	LoA	.295	55	183	36	54	13	2	5	40	45	70	24	.447	.470
Minor League Totals				.245	99	331	58	81	19	2	8	59	78	139	39	.399	.387

9 NELSON RADA, OF

Born: August 24, 2005. **B-T:** L-L. **HT:** 5-10. **WT:** 160.
Signed: Venezuela, 2022. **Signed by:** Marlon Urdaneta/Joel Chicarelli.

TRACK RECORD: Rada was one of the youngest players in the 2022 international signing class and signed with the Angels for $1.85 million as a 16-year-old. The son of a former Venezuelan professional basketball player, Rada stood out for his instincts and pro-ready mentality despite his youth. He excelled in his pro debut in the Dominican Summer League as one of the youngest players in professional baseball. Rada hit .311/.446/.439 with as many walks (26) as strikeouts (26) and 27 stolen bases in the DSL. He followed that with a strong showing in instructional league after the season.

BA GRADE
50 Risk: Extreme

SCOUTING REPORT: Rada is a slim but projectable 5-foot-10 outfielder with exciting instincts and athleticism. He is a selective hitter with a short, line-drive swing and excellent natural bat-to-ball skills that lead to consistent hard contact from the left side. He manages at-bats well beyond his years and is not fazed by facing older, more physically advanced competition. Rada is firmly a contact-first hitter, but he has shown the ability to pull the ball in the air with authority. He has enough raw power to project double-digit home runs as he matures physically and hits the ball in the air more consistently. A slightly above-average runner and solid athlete, Rada has improved his speed with physical gains to increase his chances of staying in center field. He gets good reads off the bat and closes on balls quickly in all directions. He has average arm strength that could increase as he gets stronger.

THE FUTURE: Rada has the potential to be a leadoff-hitting center fielder, but he is many years away from that ceiling. He will make his U.S. debut in 2023 as a 17-year-old.

SCOUTING GRADES	Hitting: 55	Power: 40	Speed: 55	Fielding: 50	Arm: 50

Year	Age	Club (League	Lvl	AVG	G	AB	R	H	2B	3B	HR	RBI	BB	SO	SB	OBP	SLG
2022	16	Angels (DSL)	R	.311	50	164	50	51	12	3	1	26	26	26	27	.446	.439
Minor League Totals				.311	50	164	50	51	12	3	1	26	26	26	27	.446	.439

10 BEN JOYCE, RHP

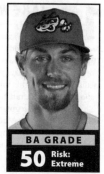

Born: September 17, 2000. **B-T:** R-R. **HT:** 6-5. **WT:** 225.
Drafted: Tennessee, 2022 (3rd round). **Signed by:** Joel Murrie.
TRACK RECORD: No college pitcher has had a cult following quite like Joyce in 2022. He grew eight inches after high school and attended Walters State (Tenn.) JC to start his college career before transferring to Tennessee. He missed the 2021 season after having Tommy John surgery but returned in 2022 and set modern records for fastball velocity out of the bullpen. Joyce averaged 101 mph and touched 105.5 to become a staple of Pitching Ninja GIFs on Twitter. The Angels drafted him in the third round and signed him for $997,500. Joyce jumped straight to Double-A after signing.
SCOUTING REPORT: Joyce has a top-of-the-scale fastball with elite velocity. His fastball sits 98-102 mph and has repeatedly reached 104-105, though not always for strikes. His fastball features armside run out of his low three-quarters arm slot and will occasionally sail on him. It also flattens out sometimes. Joyce dominates with his fastball when he's on and leans on it heavily, throwing it more than 80% of the time. He complements it with a hard, sweeping slider that flashes plus in the mid 80s, but it's a chase pitch he struggles to command or land in the strike zone. Joyce has worked with different slider grips to try to improve his feel and comfortability. He also has a fringy changeup that is not a significant part of his arsenal. Tall and strong at 6-foot-5, Joyce has little track record prior to 2022 and will have to prove he can maintain his premium stuff pitching regularly over a full professional season.
THE FUTURE: Joyce's velocity could play in the majors immediately, but the Angels will continue developing his offspeed pitches and command to make him a more impactful reliever.

BA GRADE
50 Risk: Extreme

SCOUTING GRADES:	Fastball: 80	Slider: 55	Changeup: 45	Control: 40

Year	Age	Club (League)	Lvl	W	L	ERA	G	GS	IP	H	HR	BB	SO	BB/9	SO/9	WHIP	AVG
2022	21	Rocket City (SL)	AA	1	0	2.08	13	0	13	11	0	4	20	2.8	13.8	1.15	.220
Minor League Totals				1	0	2.08	13	0	13	11	0	4	20	2.8	13.8	1.15	.220

11 ADRIAN PLACENCIA, 2B

Born: June 2, 2003. **B-T:** B-R. **HT:** 5-11. **WT:** 155.
Signed: Dominican Republic, 2019. **Signed by:** Jochy Cabrera/Rusbell Cabrera.
TRACK RECORD: One of the youngest players in the 2019-20 international class, Placencia signed with the Angels for $1.1 million as a hit-first, switch-hitting middle infielder. He hit well at instructional league in 2020 but struggled to make contact in his pro debut in the Arizona Complex League in 2021, hitting .175 with a 28.0% strikeout rate. Placencia's knee bothered him for most of his full season debut at Low-A Inland Empire in 2022, but he still performed well with an .813 OPS as one of the youngest players in the California League.
SCOUTING REPORT: Placencia has a slender, 5-foot-11 build but has sneaky impact in his bat. He shows a feel for hitting from both sides of the plate with quick hands and good barrel control to project as an average hitter. He struggles with pitch recognition and high-end velocity at times, but he sees a lot of pitches to draw walks and should improve with experience and physical maturity. Placencia has good strength for his size and plus bat speed, but his diminutive frame limits him to below-average power. Signed as a shortstop, Placencia has clean defensive actions but lacks the arm strength and quickness to stay at the position. He already plays second base primarily and projects to be an above-average defender with average arm strength. He has below-average speed but shows good instincts on the basepaths.
THE FUTURE: Placencia will still be a teenager on 2023 Opening Day and will aim to improve his physicality and pitch recognition. If he does, he has a chance to be a utility middle infielder or second-division second baseman.

BA GRADE: 45/High	Hit: 50	Power: 40	Speed: 40	Fielding: 55	Arm: 50

Year	Age	Club (League)	Lvl	AVG	G	AB	R	H	2B	3B	HR	RBI	BB	SO	SB	OBP	SLG
2022	19	Inland Empire (CAL)	LoA	.254	104	382	83	97	23	2	13	64	76	142	21	.387	.427
Minor League Totals				.232	147	525	112	122	26	5	18	83	104	191	25	.370	.404

12 JAKE MADDEN, RHP

Born: December 26, 2001. **B-T:** R-R. **HT:** 6-6. **WT:** 185.
Drafted: Northwest Florida State JC, 2022 (4th round). **Signed by:** Chris McAlpin.

TRACK RECORD: Madden had Tommy John surgery after his senior season of high school and re-routed to Northwest Florida State JC rather than stick with his commitment to South Carolina. Madden delivered mediocre results in his long season with the Raiders, but the Angels liked his pure stuff and physical projection enough to draft him in the fourth round and sign him for an overslot $997,500 bonus. Madden didn't pitch in the regular season after signing, but he stood out in instructional league in the fall.

SCOUTING REPORT: Madden looks the part with a lanky 6-foot-6 frame and a powerful, loose right arm. His fastball sits 93-96 mph and touches 98 with heavy armside bore and overwhelms hitters at its best. Madden's power slider flashes above-average with sweep across the zone with late vertical break, while his firm changeup is an average pitch with good diving action, although it is less consistent than the slider. Madden's stuff is explosive, but his control is fringe-average and he needs to refine his command to be more consistent. He has physical projection remaining and spent the winter in an offseason strength and conditioning program. Madden needs to refine the command of his full arsenal but the explosiveness–mixed with a projectable frame and athleticism–give him immense rotation upside.

THE FUTURE: Madden has the stuff to start but needs to refine his command to reach his rotation upside. He'll make his pro debut in 2023.

BA GRADE: 45/High	Fastball: 60	Slider: 55	Changeup: 50	Control: 45

Year	Age	Club (League)	Lvl	W	L	ERA	G	GS	IP	H	HR	BB	SO	BB/9	SO/9	WHIP	AVG
2022	20	Did not play															

13 CADEN DANA, RHP

Born: December 17, 2003. **B-T:** L-R. **HT:** 6-4. **WT:** 215.
Drafted: HS—Ramsey, N.J., 2022 (11th round). **Signed by:** Drew Dominguez.

TRACK RECORD: Dana stood out on the summer showcase circuit for his size and arm strength and was drafted by the Angels in the 11th round of the 2022 draft. He signed for $1,497,500—a record for a player selected after the 10th round—to forgo a Kentucky commitment. Dana pitched well in the Arizona Complex League in his pro debut.

SCOUTING REPORT: Dana has a strong, 6-foot-4 frame and power stuff. He throws his high-spin fastball at 91-95 mph and holds his velocity and command deep into starts. His best secondary is a high-spin, downer curveball in the mid 70s with a high arc and late vertical drop. The pitch flashes plus potential, but he'll need to locate it and stay on top of it better to make it more consistent. Dana rounds out his arsenal with a firm, mid-80s changeup with late fade that is fringy but improving and a developing slider that is below-average. Dana has a clean and repeatable delivery, but his control is inconsistent.

THE FUTURE: Dana needs to refine his general command and arsenal, but already has polish and the present frame of a potential back-of-the-rotation starter. He'll open back at Inland Empire in 2023.

BA GRADE: 50/Extreme	Fastball: 50	Curveball: 55	Slider: 40	Changeup: 45	Control: 45

Year	Age	Club (League)	Lvl	W	L	ERA	G	GS	IP	H	HR	BB	SO	BB/9	SO/9	WHIP	AVG
2022	18	Angels (ACL)	R	0	0	1.35	3	3	7	6	0	0	6	0.0	8.1	0.90	.240
2022	18	Inland Empire (CAL)	LoA	0	0	27.00	1	1	2	6	0	1	2	5.4	10.8	4.20	.545
Minor League Totals				0	0	6.48	4	4	8	12	0	1	8	1.1	8.6	1.56	.333

14 WALBERT UREÑA, RHP

Born: January 25, 2004. **B-T:** R-R. **HT:** 6-0. **WT:** 170.
Signed: Dominican Republic, 2021. **Signed by:** Jochy Cabrera.

TRACK RECORD: Ureña received a $140,000 bonus out of the Dominican Republic late in the 2021 international signing period and made his presence known with a fastball that regularly hit 100 mph in the Arizona Complex League in his 2022 pro debut. Ureña regularly missed bats but also struggled to throw strikes and finished the year working on his command and breaking ball at instructional league.

SCOUTING REPORT: Ureña is a slight, 6-foot righthander but possesses premium velocity and arm strength. His fastball sits 95-97 mph and frequently touches 100. His best secondary pitch is an above-average, mid-80s changeup with late fade. Ureña lacks a real breaking ball and constantly tinkers with multiple grips and hand positions to try and find one. He flashes a true, mid-80s slider in side sessions but has yet to find it in games. Ureña has well below-average control, although he does work around the zone. He is a good athlete and has a clean, compact arm strike, providing hope his control will improve with experience and maturity.

THE FUTURE: The Angels will let Ureña pitch as a starter for as long as he can in the hopes he'll find a third pitch and better control, but he is most likely to end up a hard-throwing reliever. He has a chance to pitch in high-leverage situations at his peak and will make his full-season debut at Low-A Inland Empire in 2023.

BA GRADE: 50/Extreme	Fastball: 70	Slider: 40	Changeup: 55	Control: 30

Year	Age	Club (League	Lvl	W	L	ERA	G	GS	IP	H	HR	BB	SO	BB/9	SO/9	WHIP	AVG
2022	18	Angels (ACL)	R	3	4	3.86	12	10	37	25	2	32	45	7.7	10.8	1.53	.187
Minor League Totals				3	4	3.86	12	10	37	25	2	32	45	7.7	10.8	1.53	.187

15 CHRIS RODRIGUEZ, RHP

Born: July 20, 1998. **B-T:** R-R. **HT:** 6-2. **WT:** 185.
Drafted: HS—Miami Gardens, Fla., 2016 (4th round). **Signed by:** Ralph Reyes.
TRACK RECORD: Rodriguez had plenty of helium as a Miami-based prep arm in 2016, and the Angels were ecstatic to take him in the fourth round and sign him for an over-slot $850,000 bonus. Rodriguez missed all of 2018 and most of 2019 with a stress reaction in his back, but he broke camp with the Angels after a strong spring training in 2021 and pitched in high-leverage relief before going down with shoulder inflammation. He had capsule repair surgery and missed the entire 2022 season.
SCOUTING REPORT: Rodriguez has an exceptional four-pitch mix when healthy. His four-seam fastball and sinker both sit 95-96 mph and touch 98-99 with heavy run that puts batters away. Rodriguez's best secondary is a swing-and-miss, mid-80's curveball with extreme vertical break and his upper-80's, wipeout slider and diving changeup regularly flash above-average. Rodriguez has shown the ability to command all four of his pitches and throw strikes with average control, but his violent herky-jerky delivery puts a lot of stress on his body and has led to injuries and durability issues.
THE FUTURE: Still just 24, Rodriguez is young enough to reach his potential but has to stay on the mound. He has a chance to emerge as a high-leverage reliever and should be healthy for spring training.

BA GRADE: 50/Extreme	Fastball: 60	Curveball: 60	Slider: 55	Changeup: 55	Control: 50

Year	Age	Club (League	Lvl	W	L	ERA	G	GS	IP	H	HR	BB	SO	BB/9	SO/9	WHIP	AVG
2022	23	Did not play—Injured															

16 KYREN PARIS, SS

Born: November 11, 2001. **B-T:** R-R. **HT:** 6-0. **WT:** 180.
Drafted: HS—Oakley, Calif., 2019 (2nd round). **Signed by:** Brian Tripp
TRACK RECORD: The Angels drafted Paris with the 55th overall pick in the 2019 draft as one of the youngest players in the class and signed him for $1.4 million to pass up a California commitment. He played just 50 games in his first three seasons due to a broken hamate, broken tibia and the coronavirus pandemic but finally got on the field for a full season in 2022. He struggled early at High-A Tri-Cities but heated up in July and August and earned a late-season promotion to Double-A Rocket City.
SCOUTING REPORT: Paris has a natural feel for hitting with a compact swing and quick hands from the right side. He sprays the ball to all fields and has added strength to begin hitting the ball harder, although he mostly hits liners to the gaps and still projects for below-average power. Paris' swing gets too big at times and he has a 30% career strikeout rate, but he reaches base at a high-clip (.373 career on-base percentage) and should sustain his high walk rates with regular reps and a more contact-driven approach. He is a plus runner who is aggressive on the base paths and a consistent threat to steal bases. Paris has quick actions and good hands at shortstop, but his average arm strength may limit him to second base. He has a strong work ethic that allows him to maximize his tools.
THE FUTURE: Paris has the potential to be a contact and speed-driven, everyday second baseman, but he'll need to stay healthy and cut down his strikeouts. He'll open 2023 back at Double-A.

BA GRADE: 45/High	Hit: 50	Power: 40	Speed: 60	Fielding: 50	Arm: 50

Year	Age	Club (League)	Lvl	AVG	G	AB	R	H	2B	3B	HR	RBI	BB	SO	SB	OBP	SLG
2022	20	Angels (ACL)	R	.143	2	7	1	1	0	0	1	2	2	3	0	.333	.571
2022	20	Tri-City (NWL)	HiA	.229	89	328	58	75	18	5	8	32	49	117	28	.345	.387
2022	20	Rocket City (SL)	AA	.359	14	39	11	14	2	0	3	8	10	14	5	.510	.641
Minor League Totals				.250	155	556	112	139	28	12	16	69	94	202	55	.373	.430

17 DAVID CALABRESE, OF

Born: September 26, 2002. **B-T:** L-R. **HT:** 5-11. **WT:** 160.
Drafted: HS—Thornhill, Ontario, 2020 (3rd round). **Signed by:** Chris Cruz.

TRACK RECORD: Reclassifying to be draft-eligible in 2020, Calabrese was seen sparsely over the spring due to the coronavirus pandemic, including not being seen with Team Canada when their annual trip to Spring Training was canceled. The Angels liked Calabrese's contact and speed combination, selecting him in the third round of the 2020 draft, signing him for full slot at $744,200 keeping him from his Arkansas commitment. Injuries and missed reps from Covid hindered Calabrese's pro debut, and it looked to be much of the same in his full season debut in Low-A where he struggled in the first half. He was dubbed a "different player" in the second half where he had an .843 OPS in his final 57 games and carried that performance to a standout showing at instructional league.

SCOUTING REPORT: Calabrese is a rhythmic hitter with a loose swing from the left side. Growing an inch while adding strength to his compact five-foot-11 frame, Calabrese changed his setup, lowering his hands and getting into a more upright stance and started making harder contact and had emerging power that still projects to be below-average. Calabrese's best tool is his 70-grade speed which he uses well on the base paths and outfield. He is a plus defender who covers a lot of ground and has the athleticism to make challenging plays that should allow him to stick in center field.

THE FUTURE: Calabrese has the speed and defense to be a serviceable bench option, but the Angels feel he is a sleeper that has everyday upside with physical gains.

| BA GRADE: 45/Very High | | Hit: 50 | | Power: 40 | | Speed: 70 | | Fielding: 60 | | Arm: 50 | |

Year	Age	Club (League)	Lvl	AVG	G	AB	R	H	2B	3B	HR	RBI	BB	SO	SB	OBP	SLG
2022	19	Inland Empire (CAL)	LoA	.250	112	424	68	106	23	7	7	64	50	116	26	.326	.387
Minor League Totals				.238	154	568	93	135	31	9	8	81	70	170	31	.320	.366

18 JEREMIAH JACKSON, SS/2B

Born: March 26, 2000. **B-T:** R-R. **HT:** 6-0. **WT:** 165.
Drafted: HS—Mobile, Ala., 2018 (2nd round). **Signed by:** J.T. Zink.

TRACK RECORD: The Angels selected Jackson 57th overall in the 2018 draft as an athletic prep shortstop from Alabama and signed him for an underslot $1.194 million to lure him away from a Mississippi State commitment. He set a Pioneer League record with 23 home runs in his first full year and spent part of 2020 at the alternate training site facing older players. Jackson was limited to 45 games in 2021 by a quad strain, but the Angels still aggressively pushed him to Double-A to begin the 2022 season. He struggled with the assignment and hit just .215 while missing six weeks with an oblique strain.

SCOUTING REPORT: Jackson has some of the biggest power in the Angels system but struggles to get to it in games. He has a loose, uphill swing with plenty of bat speed and punishes mistakes in the strike zone, hitting towering drives to left field and showing enough strength to make hard contact on pitches away. Jackson simplified his setup and shortened his swing to improve his problematic strikeout and chase rates in 2022, but he still lacks a consistent plan and approach at the plate and is a well below-average hitter. He is an above-average runner with the range and athleticism to stay at shortstop, but the Angels have moved him around the infield and also gave him time in left field to increase his versatility. He has above-average arm strength.

THE FUTURE: Jackson's power and athleticism give him a chance to be a bench player who moves around the diamond. He'll aim to find an approach in 2023.

| BA GRADE: 45/Very High | | Hit: 30 | | Power: 60 | | Speed: 55 | | Fielding: 50 | | Arm: 55 | |

Year	Age	Club (League)	Lvl	AVG	G	AB	R	H	2B	3B	HR	RBI	BB	SO	SB	OBP	SLG
2022	22	Rocket City (SL)	AA	.215	87	307	44	66	16	0	14	44	38	77	7	.308	.404
Minor League Totals				.249	246	924	151	230	55	10	54	177	102	304	35	.326	.505

19 RANDY DE JESUS, OF

Born: February 13, 2005. **B-T:** R-R. **HT:** 6-4. **WT:** 210.
Signed: Dominican Republic, 2022. **Signed by:** Jochy Cabrera.

TRACK RECORD: The Angels signed De Jesus for $1.2 million out of the Dominican Republic during the 2022 international signing period, and paired him with fellow outfielder Nelson Rada as the headliners of their international class. De Jesus made his pro debut in the Dominican Summer League and stood out as one of the league's most alluring prospects with his lean, strong build. He won MVP of the DSL

All-Star Game and hit seven home runs before missing the final five games of the DSL Angels' season with a minor hamstring tweak.

SCOUTING REPORT: De Jesus is a big-bodied, righthanded hitter with immense power potential. He consistently makes hard contact and drives the ball with authority with good extension in his swing. He is working to get his hands in a better position to hit and find better timing as he adjusts to his growing body, but he already has above-average power potential and could grow into more. De Jesus is an aggressive hitter who will swing and miss and doesn't project to ever hit for a high average, but he should improve enough with experience to be a below-average hitter. De Jesus has slimmed down since he's signed and is now an average runner with explosive strides. He is an average defender with enough arm strength and athleticism to profile in a corner outfield spot.

THE FUTURE: De Jesus still has room to add strength to his large frame and has a chance to grow into a low-average slugger. He'll make his stateside debut in the Arizona Complex League in 2023.

| BA GRADE: 45/Extreme | Hit: 40 | | Power: 55 | | Speed: 50 | | Fielding: 50 | | Arm: 50 | |

Year	Age	Club (League	Lvl	AVG	G	AB	R	H	2B	3B	HR	RBI	BB	SO	SB	OBP	SLG
2022	17	Angels (DSL)	R	.272	52	184	33	50	13	1	7	43	20	45	5	.362	.467
Minor League Totals				.272	52	184	33	50	13	1	7	43	20	45	5	.362	.467

20 RYAN COSTEIU, RHP

Born: November 28, 2000. **B-T:** R-R. **HT:** 6-0. **WT:** 200.
Drafted: Arkansas, 2021 (7th round). **Signed by:** Joel Murrie.
TRACK RECORD: Costeiu began his college career as a starter at Sacramento (Calif.) City JC before transferring to Arkansas and becoming a go-to reliever for the Razorbacks bullpen. The Angels were intrigued by Costeiu's pitch data and drafted him in the seventh round in 2021, signing him for $222,500. Costeiu immediately impressed with a 41.9% strikeout rate in his pro debut and forced his way from a piggyback role into the starting rotation at High-A Tri-City in 2022. He was having success when an oblique injury ended his season in July.
SCOUTING REPORT: Costeiu is a 6-foot righthander with two plus pitches and a good feel for using them. He works mostly off a 92-95 mph fastball that he elevates for a strikeout pitch. Despite its average velocity, Costeiu's fastball receives high marks for its high-spin efficiency and late movement with 19-20 inches of carry. Costeiu's best secondary is a low-80's changeup that regularly flashes plus and gets swings and misses. An emphasis in Costeiu's development is his fringe-average curveball, which he throws as a setup pitch and has adjusted the shape of. He has thrown it more in pro ball than he did in college and could see continued gains with more use. Costeiu works around the strike zone but has fringe-average control.
THE FUTURE: Costeiu's arsenal is best suited for middle relief, but the Angels view him as a potential back-end starter as he gets stronger and develops his curveball. He'll move to Double-A in 2023.

| BA GRADE: 40/High | Fastball: 60 | | Curveball: 45 | Changeup: 60 | | Control: 45 | |

Year	Age	Club (League)	Lvl	W	L	ERA	G	GS	IP	H	HR	BB	SO	BB/9	SO/9	WHIP	AVG
2022	21	Tri-City (NWL)	HiA	3	5	3.42	16	10	68	60	7	19	81	2.5	10.7	1.16	.239
Minor League Totals				4	5	3.45	27	10	86	75	10	25	112	2.6	11.7	1.16	.237

21 COLEMAN CROW, RHP

Born: December 30, 2000. **B-T:** R-R. **HT:** 6-0. **WT:** 175.
Drafted: HS—Zebulon, Ga., 2019 (28th round). **Signed by:** Todd Hogan.
TRACK RECORD: The Angels selected Crow in the 28th round of the 2019 draft and signed him over slot for $317,500—equivalent to fifth-round money—to lure him from a Kennesaw State commitment. Crow didn't pitch after signing or during the coronavirus pandemic, but he impressed in his delayed pro debut at Low-A Inland Empire in 2021 and shined as one of the youngest players in the Arizona Fall League. The Angels challenged Crow with an aggressive assignment to Double-A Rocket City in 2022, where he pitched well early but tired down the stretch. He had a 2.82 ERA in his first 12 starts and a 7.08 ERA in his final 12 appearances.
SCOUTING REPORT: Crow is a slight, 6-foot righthander who is an excellent athlete and intense competitor. His fastball sits 91-93 mph and touches 95 with solid sinking action out of his low, three-quarters arm slot. He still has room to get stronger and add velocity as he matures. Crow's high-spin, low-80's slider is an above-average pitch he can vary the shape of and morph into a power curve as needed. He rounds out his arsenal with an above-average changeup that flashes plus with split action. Crow throws plenty of strikes but has fringe-average command.

THE FUTURE: Crow's size and control may limit him to a multi-inning reliever, but the Angels are banking on his athleticism to help him remain a starter. He could see Triple-A in 2023.

BA GRADE: 40/High		Fastball: 50		Curveball: 45		Slider: 55		Changeup: 55		Control: 45			

Year	Age	Club (League)	Lvl	W	L	ERA	G	GS	IP	H	HR	BB	SO	BB/9	SO/9	WHIP	AVG
2022	21	Rocket City (SL)	AA	9	3	4.85	24	23	128	133	20	35	128	2.5	9.0	1.31	.263
Minor League Totals				13	6	4.63	37	33	190	201	27	64	190	3.0	9.0	1.39	.266

22 LANDON MARCEAUX, RHP

Born: October 8, 1999. **B-T:** R-R. **HT:** 6-0. **WT:** 199.
Drafted: Louisiana State, 2021 (3rd round). **Signed by:** Brandon McArthur.
TRACK RECORD: Following two years on USA Baseball's 18U national team, Marceaux skipped signing with the Yankees as a 37th-round pick in 2018 and became a three-year starter at Louisiana State. He ended his junior season with a 2.54 ERA and 116 strikeouts over 102.2 innings and was drafted in the third round by the Angels, who signed him for $765,000. Marceaux made his full-season debut at High-A Tri-Cities in 2022 and posted a 2.65 ERA in 16 starts to earn a promotion to Double-A, but he made only two starts for Rocket City before his season ended due to oblique and back injuries.
SCOUTING REPORT: Marceaux is a righthanded command specialist who changes speeds with a four-pitch mix to keep hitters off balance. His fastball sits 89-94 mph with late sink that makes it hard to lift and plays up with his ability to locate it. His low-80's, fading changeup and slider are above-average pitches and his curveball has improved to near average. His ability to manipulate his offspeed pitches and locate them on the corners makes for soft contact and occasional swings and misses. Marceaux has a repeatable, low-effort delivery that allows him to pound the strike zone and locate everything with plus control.
THE FUTURE: Marceaux's stuff is pedestrian, but his ability to command a four-pitch mix gives him a chance to be a depth starter or swingman. He'll return to Double-A in 2023.

BA GRADE: 40/High		Fastball: 45		Curveball: 45		Slider: 55		Changeup: 55		Control: 60			

Year	Age	Club (League)	Lvl	W	L	ERA	G	GS	IP	H	HR	BB	SO	BB/9	SO/9	WHIP	AVG
2022	22	Tri-City (NWL)	HiA	4	5	2.65	16	16	85	64	5	14	69	1.5	7.3	0.92	.204
2022	22	Rocket City (SL)	AA	0	1	7.94	2	2	6	6	1	2	4	3.2	6.4	1.41	.273
Minor League Totals				4	7	3.43	20	20	94	77	6	16	79	1.5	7.5	0.99	.218

23 MASON ERLA, RHP

Born: August 19, 1997. **B-T:** R-R. **HT:** 6-4. **WT:** 200.
Drafted: Michigan State, 2021 (17th round). **Signed by:** Drew Dominguez.
TRACK RECORD: Passed over in the 2019 draft and pandemic-shortened 2020 draft, Erla returned to Michigan State as a fifth-year senior in 2021. The Angels liked his arm strength and took him in the 17th round of their all-pitcher draft, and signed him for $125,000. Erla impressed in his brief pro debut and was a standout during instructional league. He suffered a minor injury that kept him out for two months in 2022 but returned to pitch well in Double-A Rocket City's rotation the rest of the year.
SCOUTING REPORT: Erla is older at 25, but he has excellent arm strength and a good feel for throwing strikes. His fastball has jumped from 90-94 mph in college to 93-97 mph in pro ball and he commands it well to make it a plus pitch. The Angels believe even more velocity is coming as he gets completely healthy. Erla shows good feel for an average, mid-80s changeup that induces chase swings below the zone. He has improved his slider over the year, tightening the break, but it can still be overly sweepy due to his violent delivery and low three-quarters arm slot. Erla throws strikes with above-average control despite his delivery and locates his pitches in the zone.
THE FUTURE: The Angels will continue to develop Erla as a starter, but he'll need to develop his offspeed pitchers to avoid a move to the bullpen. He is likely to end up a useful middle reliever.

BA GRADE: 40/High		Fastball: 60		Slider: 45		Changeup: 50		Control: 55			

Year	Age	Club (League)	Lvl	W	L	ERA	G	GS	IP	H	HR	BB	SO	BB/9	SO/9	WHIP	AVG
2022	24	Rocket City (SL)	AA	5	6	4.28	16	16	82	88	9	19	64	2.1	7.0	1.30	.274
Minor League Totals				6	7	4.03	19	18	89	92	9	19	75	1.9	7.6	1.24	.265

24 JORDYN ADAMS, OF

Born: October 18, 1999. **B-T:** R-R. **HT:** 6-2. **WT:** 180.
Drafted: HS—Cary, N.C., 2018 (1st round). **Signed by:** Chris McAlpin.
TRACK RECORD: A three-sport athlete committed to play baseball and football at North Carolina, Adams stood out at the 2018 National High School Invitational rocketing up boards to become the first-round pick by the Angels, who signed him for $4.1 million. Adams held his own in his first full seasons and spent 2020 at the alternate training site, but he suffered a hamstring injury three games into the 2021 season and has floundered since. He failed to hit .250 or hit more than five home runs at either High-A or Double-A and went unprotected and unpicked in the 2022 Rule 5 draft.
SCOUTING REPORT: The best athlete in the Angels system, Adams has enticing tools but is still raw from a baseball perspective. He has tinkered with multiple swing alterations to try and get into proper hitting position, resulting in inconsistent at-bats and different swings. He struggles to be on time against velocity and mostly makes weak contact off the barrel. Adams has solid bat speed and natural strength to give him above-average raw power, although he can't tap into it. He'll have to find a swing and improve his breaking ball recognition to tap into any offensive upside. An 80-grade runner, Adams steals bases at will and covers lots of ground in center field, where he is a plus defender with an average, accurate arm.
THE FUTURE: Adams has to prove he can hit to be even a backup outfielder. He'll try to find his swing at Double-A in 2023.

BA GRADE: 40/High		Hit: 30		Power: 40		Speed: 80			Fielding: 60		Arm: 50	
Year	Age	Club (League)	Lvl	AVG	G	AB	R	H	2B	3B	HR	RBI	BB	SO	SB	OBP	SLG
2022	22	Tri-City (NWL)	HiA	.228	58	219	31	50	11	3	0	22	21	54	18	.308	.306
2022	22	Rocket City (SL)	AA	.249	62	209	33	52	7	2	4	20	21	70	15	.326	.359
Minor League Totals				.242	329	1230	177	298	48	13	17	118	140	381	72	.326	.344

25 AROL VERA, SS

Born: September 12, 2002. **B-T:** B-R. **HT:** 6-2. **WT:** 170.
Signed: Venezuela, 2019. **Signed by:** Andres Garcia/Joel Chicharelli.
TRACK RECORD: Vera signed with the Angels for $2 million as one of the top prospects in the 2019 international class but had his pro debut delayed by the coronavirus pandemic. He impressed with his athleticism and contact skills when he finally got onto the field for his pro debut in the Rookie-level Arizona League, but his lack of strength was exposed in his full-season debut at Low-A Inland Empire in 2022. Vera hit .207/.291/.281 with the 66ers, the lowest batting average, slugging percentage and OPS of any qualified hitter in the California League.
SCOUTING REPORT: Vera is an athletic, switch-hitting infielder whose potential rests on how much stronger he gets. He has good instincts in the batters box, but he struggles to make hard contact from either side of the plate even when he finds the barrel. He's an aggressive hitter who chases out of the zone and allowed his swing to get too long in 2022, leading to 149 strikeouts, fourth-most in the league. Vera has above-average bat speed and average raw power from the left side, but he still has to get significantly stronger in his upper half to be a playable hitter. Vera is an impactful defender with smooth actions, soft hands, and an above-average arm that should keep him at shortstop even as he gets bigger. He is an average runner with solid instincts on the basepaths.
THE FUTURE: Vera's defense will buy him time to get stronger at the plate. He may need to repeat Low-A in 2022.

BA GRADE: 40/High		Hit: 30		Power: 30		Speed: 50			Fielding: 55		Arm: 55	
Year	Age	Club (League)	Lvl	AVG	G	AB	R	H	2B	3B	HR	RBI	BB	SO	SB	OBP	SLG
2022	19	Inland Empire (CAL)	LoA	.207	120	487	71	101	16	4	4	59	53	149	19	.291	.281
Minor League Totals				.238	177	714	105	170	32	7	4	81	71	208	30	.316	.319

26 LIVAN SOTO, SS

Born: June 22, 2000. **B-T:** L-R. **HT:** 6-0. **WT:** 160.
Signed: Venezuela, 2017. **Signed by:** Rolando Petit (Braves).
TRACK RECORD: Soto was one of 12 international amateurs who signed with the Braves but were later declared free agents by MLB due to the Braves' violations of international signing rules. Soto signed with Angels for $850,000 shortly after and progressively worked his way up the system, leading up to a break-out 2022. Soto hit a career-high .281 at Double-A in 2022 and earned a September callup to the Angels,

where he hit .400 (22-for-55) in 18 games.

SCOUTING REPORT: Soto is a defense-first middle infielder whose hitting ability is slowly improving. He has solid pure contact skills and finds the barrel with ease from the left side. He rarely swings and misses and should hit for contact, but it's often soft contact. He rarely impacts the ball and his power is below-average due to his small frame. The Angels tweaked Soto's hand position to allow for more separation and an inclined swing path, but the results have only changed slightly. He has solid plate discipline and gives competitive at-bats, leading to high walk and low strikeout rates. Soto is one of the best defensive infielders in the Angels system with twitchy actions, soft hands, and advanced instincts at shortstop. He has an average arm strength that plays up with a quick release and good internal clock.

THE FUTURE: Soto may be a bench option for the Angels in 2023. He will have to impact the ball more to garner attention as a utility option.

BA GRADE: 40/High		Hit: 50			Power: 30		Speed: 50			Fielding: 55		Arm: 50	

Year	Age	Club (League)	Lvl	AVG	G	AB	R	H	2B	3B	HR	RBI	BB	SO	SB	OBP	SLG
2022	22	Rocket City (SL)	AA	.281	119	456	69	128	17	1	6	57	71	102	18	.379	.362
2022	22	Los Angeles (AL)	MLB	.400	18	55	9	22	5	1	1	9	2	13	1	.414	.582
Major League Totals				.400	18	55	9	22	5	1	1	9	2	13	1	.414	.582
Minor League Totals				.247	384	1474	204	364	54	9	14	143	197	306	54	.338	.324

27 ERIC TORRES, LHP

Born: September 22, 1999. **B-T:** L-L. **HT:** 6-0. **WT:** 195.
Drafted: Kansas State, 2021 (14th round). **Signed by:** Jayson Durocher.

TRACK RECORD: Torres spent three years as a reliever at Kansas State and was drafted by the Angels in the 14th round of their all-pitcher 2021 draft, signing for $125,000. Torres jumped to Double-A to start his first full season in 2022 and broke out as one of the most dominant relievers in the minor leagues with Rocket City. He posted a 1.59 ERA, struck out nearly 40% of the batters he faced and led the Southern League with 22 saves en route to being named the league's reliever of the year.

SCOUTING REPORT: An undersized lefthanded reliever, Torres finds most of his success from his low three-quarters arm slot that makes it hard for hitters to pick the ball up, especially lefties. Torres' fastball sits 91-95 with late life in the zone and plays up with his deceptive delivery. He added velocity to his sweepy slider to make it an above-average pitch that now sits in the low 80s with tough angle. Torres' changeup remains a work in progress and is below-average, but his fastball and slider combo make him still effective against righthanded hitters. Torres works around the zone but has just fringe-average control. He is comfortable in high-leverage situations and has the mentality to succeed under pressure.

THE FUTURE: Torres is moving quickly and could be part of the Angels bullpen by the middle of the 2023 season. He projects to be a deceptive middle reliever who annihilates lefties.

BA GRADE: 40/High		Fastball: 50		Slider: 50		Changeup: 40		Control: 45	

Year	Age	Club (League)	Lvl	W	L	ERA	G	GS	IP	H	HR	BB	SO	BB/9	SO/9	WHIP	AVG
2022	22	Rocket City (SL)	AA	2	2	1.59	42	0	51	25	3	23	81	4.1	14.3	0.94	.143
Minor League Totals				2	3	2.12	50	0	59	32	4	27	94	4.1	14.3	0.99	.155

28 LUKE MURPHY, RHP

Born: November 5, 1999. **B-T:** R-R. **HT:** 6-5. **WT:** 190.
Drafted: Vanderbilt, 2021 (4th round). **Signed by:** Joel Murrie.

TRACK RECORD: Murphy redshirted his freshman year at Vanderbilt after having Tommy John surgery and pitched just two innings the following year, but he finally got extended mound time in 2021 and recorded nine saves as the Commodores closer. The Angels drafted him in the fourth round and signed him for an over slot $747,500 bonus. Murphy jumped straight to Double-A to begin his full-season debut in 2022 and dominated with a 2.62 ERA and 10.5 strikeouts per nine as Rocket City's top setup man.

SCOUTING REPORT: Murphy is a tall, lanky righthander who dominates with two pitches. He heavily uses his 94-97 mph fastball that plays well up in the zone and complements it with a sweepy 83-87 mph slider that misses bats but is inconsistent because he struggles to locate it. Murphy has a cross-body delivery that limits him to well below-average control, but he has cleaned it up somewhat to keep his body more on line to the plate and prevent him from yanking his slider. Murphy's deceptive delivery and high three-quarters arm slot allow him to create good plane on his pitches and make him difficult to square up when he's in the strike zone.

THE FUTURE: Murphy has moved quickly through the system and is developing quickly. He could be a middle reliever in the Angels bullpen by mid-2023 if he improves his control.

BA GRADE: 40/High		Fastball: 60		Slider: 55		Control: 30										
Year	Age	Club (League)	Lvl	W	L	ERA	G	GS	IP	H	HR	BB	SO	BB/9	SO/9	WHIP	AVG
2022	22	Rocket City (SL)	AA	7	2	2.62	37	0	45	25	0	26	52	5.2	10.5	1.14	.164
Minor League Totals				7	3	2.68	44	0	54	32	0	27	67	4.5	11.2	1.10	.172

29 VICTOR MEDEROS, RHP

Born: June 8, 2001. **B-T:** R-R. **HT:** 6-2. **WT:** 227.
Drafted: Oklahoma State, 2022 (6th round). **Signed by:** K.J. Hendricks.
TRACK RECORD: Mederos won Most Valuable Player of the 2019 Under Armour High School All-America Game and arrived at Miami as a heralded recruit, but he struggled to throw strikes with the Hurricanes and transferred to Oklahoma State. He got hit hard in the Cowboys rotation, but the Angels looked past his lackluster performance and selected him in the sixth round as a draft-eligible sophomore in 2022, signing him for a below-slot $227,750. Mederos pitched briefly at High-A Tri-Cities and regained his previous buzz in instructional league, where he impressed as one of the top standouts in Angels camp.
SCOUTING REPORT: Mederos is a tall, strong righthander with a competitive four-pitch mix. His four-seam fastball sits 94-97 mph as a starter and ticks up to 98-99 in short bursts. He also has a mid-90s two-seamer with powerful armside run. Mederos' fastball command has long been below-average, limiting his effectiveness, but it has improved as he's learned to throw his four-seamer up in the zone more. Mederos' primary out pitch is a plus, mid-80's slider that is effective against both righties and lefties. His low-80's downer curveball and mid-80's fading changeup are inconsistent but flash above average. Despite his spotty track record, Mederos is eager to learn and a natural leader.
THE FUTURE: Mederos' plus fastball and slider project well in a bullpen, but the Angels will continue to let him start for now. How much his fastball command improves will determine if he can remain a starter long-term.

BA GRADE: 40/Very		High Fastball: 60		Curveball: 45		Slider: 60		Changeup: 45		Control: 45						
Year	Age	Club (League)	Lvl	W	L	ERA	G	GS	IP	H	HR	BB	SO	BB/9	SO/9	WHIP	AVG
2022	21	Tri-City (NWL)	HiA	0	1	5.62	6	6	16	15	1	9	15	5.1	8.4	1.50	.242
Minor League Totals				0	1	5.62	6	6	16	15	1	9	15	5.1	8.4	1.50	.242

30 DARIO LAVERDE, C

Born: February 26, 2005. **B-T:** L-R. **HT:** 5-10. **WT:** 160.
Signed: Venezuela, 2022. **Signed by:** Marlon Urdaneta.
TRACK RECORD: Laverde primarily played the outfield before converting to catching in 2020 and signed with the Angels out of Venezuela for $350,000 on the first day of the 2022 international signing period. He immediately stood out in his pro debut in the Dominican Summer League, batting .298/.403/.404 and showing advanced skills behind the plate for someone with so little experience.
SCOUTING REPORT: Laverde is a solid athlete who has a good foundation behind the plate with his advanced receiving skills and impressive lateral mobility. He has the strong, athletic build to hold up under the rigors of catching and a plus, accurate arm that frequently records 1.95-2.00 second pop times. Laverde is still fine-tuning his setup and blocking, but he has all the raw ingredients to be an average receiver. At the plate, Laverde drives balls from gap to gap with a flat, line-drive swing and rarely chases out of the strike zone. His contact skills and plate discipline are promising, but his power is well below-average and he struggles to get the ball in the air. He is an average runner who uses his advanced instincts to take an extra base.
THE FUTURE: Laverde's defensive traits and advanced instincts indicate a future backup role. He'll have to add more offensive impact to be an everyday catcher.

BA GRADE: 40/Extreme		Hit: 45		Power: 30		Speed: 50		Fielding: 50		Arm: 60						
Year	Age	Club (League	Lvl	AVG	G	AB	R	H	2B	3B	HR	RBI	BB	SO	SB	OBP	SLG
2022	17	Angels (DSL)	R	.298	45	151	35	45	4	6	0	28	21	19	9	.403	.404
Minor League Totals				.298	45	151	35	45	4	6	0	28	21	19	9	.403	.404

Los Angeles Dodgers

BY KYLE GLASER

The Dodgers face an unusual amount of uncertainty heading into the 2023 season. If the recent past is any indication, it's unlikely to slow them down.

The Dodgers won a franchise-record 111 games in 2022 despite setbacks that would have sunk almost any other team. Max Scherzer, Corey Seager and Kenley Jansen left in free agency before the season, Walker Buehler was lost to an elbow injury that eventually required Tommy John surgery, sluggers Max Muncy and Cody Bellinger suffered through miserable years and closer Craig Kimbrel pitched so poorly he was left off the playoff roster.

Yet, due to their combination of unparalleled financial resources and remarkable organizational depth, the Dodgers steamrolled all comers to win their ninth National League West division title in 10 years before being upset by the Padres in the NL Division Series.

The Dodgers again face a similar predicament in 2023. Shortstop Trea Turner (Phillies), center fielder Cody Bellinger (Cubs) and lefthander Tyler Anderson (Angels) all signed with new teams in the offseason and leave the Dodgers with holes to fill. Longtime clubhouse leader Justin Turner was expected to depart in free agency, and Buehler will miss all of 2023 rehabbing from surgery.

In short, the Dodgers stand to look very different than they have for the last half-decade. The departures of longtime franchise cornerstones Seager, Bellinger and Jansen over the past two years have already altered the franchise's identity, and that will be even more the case when Clayton Kershaw, who re-signed with the Dodgers on a one-year deal, decides to call it quits.

But just as the Dodgers have absorbed all their previous personnel losses with a stream of homegrown talent, they are positioned to keep winning with a new wave of players from the minors ready to break through.

The Dodgers boast not only one of the best farm systems in baseball, but one of the most major league-ready.

Hard-throwing righthander Ryan Pepiot and precocious hitter Miguel Vargas made their major league debuts last year and are ready to assume larger roles in 2023. Righthanders Bobby Miller and Gavin Stone and second baseman Michael Busch finished last season at Triple-A and are on the verge of their big league debuts.

Outfielder James Outman shined in his brief debut last year and has a chance to replace Bellinger in center field. Even somewhat lesser prospects like Andy Pages, Jacob Amaya and Nick

Tony Gonsolin had a standout 2022, going 16-1 with a 2.14 ERA and 0.76 WHIP in 24 starts.

PROJECTED 2026 LINEUP

Catcher	Will Smith	31
First Base	Freddie Freeman	36
Second Base	Michael Busch	28
Third Base	Miguel Vargas	26
Shortstop	Gavin Lux	28
Left Field	Andy Pages	25
Center Field	James Outman	29
Right Field	Mookie Betts	34
Designated Hitter	Diego Cartaya	24
No. 1 Starter	Walker Buehler	31
No. 2 Starter	Julio Urias	29
No. 3 Starter	Tony Gonsolin	32
No. 4 Starter	Bobby Miller	27
No. 5 Starter	Dustin May	28
Closer	Brusdar Graterol	27

Nastrini finished last season in the upper levels and have a chance to help the big league club in 2023.

With such a collection of talent ready to ascend to the majors, the Dodgers are in position to plug almost all of their holes and continue their winning ways. Combined with remaining homegrown talents Julio Urias, Will Smith, Tony Gonsolin, Gavin Lux and Dustin May all entering their peak seasons and MLB superstars Mookie Betts and Freddie Freeman continuing to perform at peak levels, there is little reason to expect the Dodgers to fall off any time soon.

The faces may be changing, but just as has been the case with the Dodgers for years, the winning ways should continue unabated. ∎

DEPTH CHART

LOS ANGELES DODGERS

TOP 2023 MLB CONTRIBUTORS	RANK
Bobby Miller, RHP	2
Miguel Vargas, 3B	3
Ryan Pepiot, RHP	5
BREAKOUT PROSPECTS	**RANK**
Nick Frasso, RHP	12
Josue De Paula, OF	13
River Ryan, RHP	17

SOURCE OF TOP 30 TALENT

Homegrown	27	Acquired	3
College	14	Trade	3
Junior college	1	Rule 5 draft	0
High school	3	Independent league	0
Nondrafted free agent	0	Free agent/waivers	0
International	9		

LF
Josue De Paula (13)
Ryan Ward
Luis Rodriguez

CF
James Outman (10)
Jonny DeLuca (18)
Drew Avans

RF
Andy Pages (7)
Jose Ramos (24)
Damon Keith (27)
Juan Alonso

3B
Miguel Vargas (3)
Logan Wagner
Luis Yanel Diaz

SS
Jacob Amaya (11)
Rayne Doncon
Alex Freeland

2B
Michael Busch (4)
Eddys Leonard (15)
Jorbit Vivas (21)
Devin Mann (22)

1B
Yunior Garcia
Justin Yurchak
Brandon Lewis

C
Diego Cartaya (1)
Dalton Rushing (8)
Yeiner Fernandez (25)
Thayron Liranzo
Hunter Feduccia

LHP

LHSP	LHRP
Maddux Bruns (20)	Ronan Kopp (16)
Justin Wrobleski (30)	Jeff Belge
Lael Lockhart	

RHP

RHSP	RHRP
Bobby Miller (2)	Emmet Sheehan (14)
Ryan Pepiot (5)	River Ryan (17)
Gavin Stone (6)	Kyle Hurt (28)
Nick Nastrini (9)	Carlos Duran (29)
Nick Frasso (12)	Edgardo Henriquez
Michael Grove (19)	Nick Robertson
Landon Knack (23)	Maximo Martinez
Peter Heubeck (26)	
Hyun-il Choi	
Kendall Williams	
Payton Martin	

1 DIEGO CARTAYA, C

Born: Sept. 7, 2001. **B-T:** R-R. **HT:** 6-3. **WT:** 219.
Signed: Venezuela, 2018.
Signed by: Luis Marquez/Roman Barinas/Cliff Nuiter/
Jean Castro.

TRACK RECORD: Cartaya played for Venezuela in international tournaments from the time he was 10 years old and progressively emerged as the country's best player in his class. The Dodgers made him their top target during the 2018-19 international period and signed him for $2.5 million. Cartaya played just 80 games in his first three years after signing due to the canceled 2020 minor league season and an assortment of injuries, including a pair of back flareups and a hamstring strain. He made staying on the field a top priority in 2022 and played a career-high 95 games as he rose from Low-A to High-A. He finished in the top 10 in the Dodgers' system in doubles (22), home runs (22) and OPS (.892), earned a selection to the Futures Game at Dodger Stadium and was named the Dodgers' minor league player of the year.

SCOUTING REPORT: A large, physical masher at 6-foot-3, 219 pounds, Cartaya has grown into plus-plus power and has become one baseball's most promising young power hitters. He demolishes baseballs from left-center to right-center field with a fast, powerful swing and drives balls over the wall even when he mishits them. He crushes both high-end velocity and good breaking stuff and has a knack for playing up to his competition, including when he homered off Padres lefthander Blake Snell during a rehab start last May. Cartaya's swing gets a tad long at times, leading to bouts of strikeouts, but he has the instincts and awareness to self-correct and make adjustments. Cartaya recognizes pitches, stays in the strike zone and draws plenty of walks to post high on-base percentages on top of his power. He projects to be an average hitter with plus-plus power and still has room to improve as he becomes more consistent with his swing mechanics. Cartaya's defense has further to go. Once considered a potential plus defender, he has gotten tighter in his hips and upper body. He's gotten bigger and as a result has started to lose quickness and mobility. He has yet to find an optimal setup with his new physique and receives pitches too deeply, resulting in drops and framing issues at the top of the zone. He is frequently late on blocks and allowed 93 wild pitches and 11 passed balls in just 64 games in 2022. The Dodgers ascribe Cartaya's struggles to rust at the beginning of the year and fatigue at the end of it, but his setup, receiving technique and blocking all need

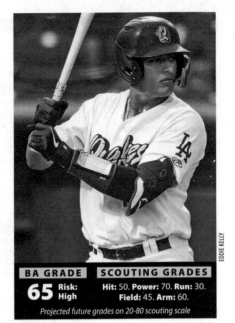

EDDIE KELLY

BA GRADE	SCOUTING GRADES
65 Risk: High	Hit: 50. Power: 70. Run: 30. Field: 45. Arm: 60.

Projected future grades on 20-80 scouting scale

BEST TOOLS

BATTING

Best Hitter for Average	Miguel Vargas
Best Power Hitter	Andy Pages
Best Strike-Zone Discipline	Michael Busch
Fastest Baserunner	Jeren Kendall
Best Athlete	James Outman

PITCHING

Best Fastball	Nick Frasso
Best Curveball	Maddux Bruns
Best Slider	Carlos Duran
Best Changeup	Ryan Pepiot
Best Control	Gavin Stone

FIELDING

Best Defensive Catcher	Diego Cartaya
Best Defensive Infielder	Jacob Amaya
Best Infield Arm	Logan Wagner
Best Defensive Outfielder	Jeren Kendall
Best Outfield Arm	Andy Pages

significant improvement for him to be an average defender. Cartaya does have the intangible components for catching. He is an advanced game-caller who communicates well with his pitchers and is bilingual. He has above-average arm strength that plays up with a quick release.

THE FUTURE: With Will Smith entrenched as the Dodgers' catcher, Cartaya has plenty of time to improve his defense without being rushed. He projects to be a middle-of-the-order force in the Dodgers' lineup no matter where he ends up defensively.

Year	Age	Club (League)	Lvl	AVG	G	AB	R	H	2B	3B	HR	RBI	BB	SO	SB	OBP	SLG
2022	20	R. Cucamonga (CAL)	LoA	.260	33	131	31	34	9	1	9	31	23	44	0	.405	.550
2022	20	Great Lakes (MWL)	HiA	.251	62	231	43	58	13	0	13	41	40	75	1	.379	.476
Minor League Totals				.269	175	661	141	178	40	3	36	125	97	198	2	.380	.502

2 BOBBY MILLER, RHP

Born: April 5, 1999. **B-T:** R-R. **HT:** 6-5. **WT:** 220.
Drafted: Louisville, 2020 (1st round). **Signed by:** Marty Lamb.
TRACK RECORD: Miller flashed explosive stuff at Louisville but didn't get a consistent chance to start until his junior year, when he made four starts before the pandemic canceled the 2020 season. The Dodgers saw enough to draft him 29th overall and sign him for $2,197,500. A right oblique strain limited Miller in his pro debut, but he took off with full health in 2022. He recorded 145 strikeouts against just 37 walks and rose from Double-A to Triple-A. He started the Futures Game at Dodger Stadium and struck out the side as the only pitcher in the game to top 100 mph.

BA GRADE
65 Risk: High

SCOUTING REPORT: Miller is an intimidating physical presence at 6-foot-5, 220 pounds and has the stuff to match. His high-octane fastball explodes out of his hand at 97-99 mph and routinely touches 100-101. His fastball doesn't have overwhelming movement, but he has improved his command of it to make it a plus-plus pitch and can blow it by hitters with his pure power. Miller also has a two-seam fastball that sits 97-100 mph with hard tail and sink that gives batters another hard offering to consider. Miller's tight upper-80s slider with late bite is another plus-plus pitch that overwhelms hitters, and his sinking 87-90 mph changeup has become a plus pitch as he's learned to reach out and finish it. He rounds out his arsenal with a sweeping, 11-to-4 curveball in the low 80s that is an average pitch. Previously wild, Miller has streamlined his delivery and now pounds the strike zone with average control. He is still learning how to properly sequence his pitches and can be too intense at times.
THE FUTURE: Miller has the stuff, physicality and control to be a frontline starter similar to Brandon Woodruff if he can polish his mental approach. His big league debut should come in 2023.

SCOUTING GRADES:	Fastball: 70	Curveball: 50	Slider: 70	Changeup: 60	Control: 50

Year	Age	Club (League)	Lvl	W	L	ERA	G	GS	IP	H	HR	BB	SO	BB/9	SO/9	WHIP	AVG
2022	23	Tulsa (TL)	AA	6	6	4.45	20	19	91	78	8	31	117	3.1	11.6	1.20	.223
2022	23	Oklahoma City (PCL)	AAA	1	1	3.38	4	4	21	17	4	6	28	2.5	11.8	1.08	.218
Minor League Totals				9	9	3.63	41	37	169	135	14	50	215	2.7	11.5	1.10	.212

3 MIGUEL VARGAS, 3B

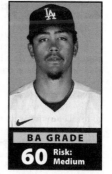

Born: Nov. 17, 1999. **B-T:** R-R. **HT:** 6-3. **WT:** 205.
Signed: Cuba, 2017. **Signed by:** Roman Barinas/Mike Tosar.
TRACK RECORD: Lazaro Vargas was one of Cuba's best hitters throughout the 1980s and '90s. His son Miguel inherited his father's gifts and emerged as one of Cuba's top amateur hitters before he left the country in 2015. He signed with the Dodgers two years later for $300,000. Vargas continued to hit at every level and owns a career .313 average. He earned a selection to the Futures Game in July and received his first big league callup on Aug. 3.
SCOUTING REPORT: Vargas is as complete a hitter as any player his age. He has outstanding control of the strike zone, an innate sense for which pitches to attack and an elite feel for the barrel. He squares up all types of pitches with a direct, inside-out swing that stays in the zone for a long time and covers the

BA GRADE
60 Risk: Medium

entire plate, giving pitchers few holes to attack. He naturally drives the ball the opposite way to right-center field and has begun turning on pitches on the inner half. Vargas doesn't have huge raw power, but he's a borderline plus-plus hitter who makes so much quality contact that he should reach 20-plus home runs as he gets stronger. Vargas has remade his body to become sleeker and faster and is now a plus runner who posted the second-fastest sprint speed on the Dodgers in 2022. The improved agility has helped his range at third base, but he's still a below-average defender whose actions, footwork, throwing accuracy and focus need improvement. He is raw and inexperienced at first base, second base and left field.
THE FUTURE: Vargas earns comparisons to countryman Yuli Gurriel and has similar potential to be a premier hitter. The Dodgers will try to find Vargas' best position to get him in the lineup every day.

SCOUTING GRADES	Hitting: 65	Power: 50	Speed: 60	Fielding: 40	Arm: 55

Year	Age	Club (League)	Lvl	AVG	G	AB	R	H	2B	3B	HR	RBI	BB	SO	SB	OBP	SLG
2022	22	Oklahoma City (PCL)	AAA	.304	113	438	100	133	32	4	17	82	71	76	16	.404	.511
2022	22	Los Angeles (NL)	MLB	.170	18	47	4	8	1	0	1	8	2	13	1	.200	.255
Major League Totals				.170	18	47	4	8	1	0	1	8	2	13	1	.200	.255
Minor League Totals				.313	410	1612	309	504	112	12	49	265	194	284	47	.390	.488

4 MICHAEL BUSCH, 2B

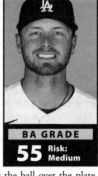

Born: Nov. 9, 1997. **B-T:** L-R. **HT:** 6-1. **WT:** 210.
Drafted: North Carolina, 2019 (1st round). **Signed by:** Jonah Rosenthal.
TRACK RECORD: Growing up in Minnesota as one of eight brothers and sisters in his family, Busch starred in football, hockey and baseball in high school and blossomed into one of college baseball's top hitters at North Carolina. The Dodgers drafted him 31st overall in 2019 and signed him for $2.312 million. Injuries to his right hand after he was hit by pitches limited Busch in both his pro debut and first full season, but he excelled with full health in 2022. Busch led the minor leagues with 118 runs scored and ranked third with 70 extra-base hits and 285 total bases.

BA GRADE

55 Risk: Medium

SCOUTING REPORT: Busch's exceptional plate discipline is the foundation of his success. He exudes calm in the batter's box and rarely chases outside the strike zone, putting together high-quality at-bats and forcing pitchers to throw the ball over the plate. Busch unloads on balls with a short, balanced swing from the left side and drives them hard in the air from left-center to right-center field. He occasionally gets underneath fastballs at the top of the zone, but he has the strength, hand-eye coordination and feel for the barrel to do damage against all types of pitches. Busch can be too passive at times, leading to too many strikeouts looking, but he has improved his aggressiveness and projects to be an average hitter with plus power as he further refines his approach. A first baseman in college, Busch transitioned to second base as a pro and remains a work in progress defensively. He's a fringe-average runner with limited mobility and isn't particularly smooth, but he tends to make the plays even if it isn't always pretty.
THE FUTURE: Busch earns frequent comparisons with Max Muncy as a middle-of-the-order masher and functional, albeit limited, defender. He'll open 2023 at Triple-A and is poised to make his MLB debut.

SCOUTING GRADES		Hitting: 50		Power: 60			Speed: 45			Fielding: 40		Arm: 40	

Year	Age	Club (League)	Lvl	AVG	G	AB	R	H	2B	3B	HR	RBI	BB	SO	SB	OBP	SLG
2022	24	Tulsa (TL)	AA	.306	31	108	31	33	6	0	11	29	24	36	1	.445	.667
2022	24	Oklahoma City (PCL)	AAA	.266	111	444	87	118	32	0	21	79	50	131	3	.343	.480
Minor League Totals				.267	259	985	207	263	65	1	52	177	151	301	6	.374	.493

5 RYAN PEPIOT, RHP

Born: Aug. 21, 1997. **B-T:** R-R. **HT:** 6-3. **WT:** 215.
Drafted: Butler, 2019 (3rd round). **Signed by:** Stephen Head.
TRACK RECORD: Pepiot became Butler's highest-drafted player ever when the Dodgers selected him in the third round in 2019. After a star turn at the alternate training site in 2020, Pepiot reached Triple-A in his first full season in 2021 and took another leap in 2022. He finished second in the Pacific Coast League in ERA (2.56) with Triple-A Oklahoma City while becoming the Dodgers' go-to callup option when they needed a starter. He made his MLB debut in May and made nine appearances with the Dodgers across the season.

BA GRADE

55 Risk: Medium

SCOUTING REPORT: Pepiot is a physical, 6-foot-3 righthander with premium stuff. His high-spin fastball sits 94 mph and touches 98 with hard armside run out of his strong, powerful delivery. His slider has been a point of emphasis in his development and now sits 84-87 mph with added sweep to make it an average pitch he can locate down in the zone. Pepiot's formerly elite changeup has regressed with his focus on his slider, but it's still a plus offering in the upper 80s with late dive that gets empty swings and weak contact from experienced hitters. Pepiot's below-average control has long been a work in progress and remains so. He struggles to command his fastball and his changeup is more of a chase pitch, which hitters laid off of in the majors. Pepiot doesn't miss the zone by much and generally throws enough strikes to get through just four or five innings.
THE FUTURE: Pepiot projects to be a hard-throwing starter who goes five innings before handing it off to his bullpen. He has the stuff to be an elite setup man or potential closer.

SCOUTING GRADES:		Fastball: 70		Slider: 50			Changeup: 60			Control: 40		

Year	Age	Club (League)	Lvl	W	L	ERA	G	GS	IP	H	HR	BB	SO	BB/9	SO/9	WHIP	AVG
2022	24	Oklahoma City (PCL)	AAA	9	1	2.56	19	17	91	62	10	36	114	3.5	11.2	1.07	.193
2022	24	Los Angeles (NL)	MLB	3	0	3.47	9	7	36	26	6	27	42	6.7	10.4	1.46	.200
Major League Totals				3	0	3.47	9	7	36	26	6	27	42	6.7	10.4	1.46	.200
Minor League Totals				14	10	3.46	58	49	216	161	29	96	272	4.0	11.3	1.19	.206

6 GAVIN STONE, RHP

Born: Oct. 15, 1998. **B-T:** R-R. **HT:** 6-1. **WT:** 175.
Drafted: Central Arkansas, 2020 (5th round). **Signed by:** Brian Kraft.

BA GRADE
55 Risk: Medium

TRACK RECORD: Stone spent most of his first two seasons at Central Arkansas pitching in relief before moving to the rotation as a junior. He pitched a no-hitter with 13 strikeouts in his final start before the coronavirus pandemic ended the 2020 season. Drafted by the Dodgers in the fifth round, he signed for a below-slot $97,500. Stone immediately showed himself to be a potential steal when he led the Dodgers' system in strikeouts in his pro debut. He solidi-fied that status in 2022 by leading the minor leagues with a 1.48 ERA as he rocketed from High-A to Triple-A.

SCOUTING REPORT: Stone is undersized with a small frame, but he's an elite athlete who keeps getting stronger and adding velocity. His fastball has grown from 90-92 mph in college to 93-96 in his pro debut to now 94-98 to make it a plus pitch he com-mands well. His fastball doesn't have exceptional movement characteristics, but he moves it around the zone effectively and mixes it well with his secondary pitches. Stone's best pitch is a plus-plus 84-87 mph changeup with late run and dive he will throw in any count. He can land it for strikes or get chase swings with it and almost never allows hard contact. Stone's tight, vertical slider in the mid 80s tunnels well off his fastball and is a potentially average pitch that gives him a quality third offering. He rarely throws his fringy 79-82 mph curveball, but he can land it for a strike. Stone has improved his command in unison with his velocity and throws crisp strikes with plus control.

THE FUTURE: Stone's enhanced stuff gives him a chance to be a midrotation starter, though his slight frame still gives some evaluators pause. His major league debut should come in 2023.

SCOUTING GRADES:	Fastball: 60	Curveball: 45	Slider: 50	Changeup: 70	Control: 60

Year	Age	Club (League)	Lvl	W	L	ERA	G	GS	IP	H	HR	BB	SO	BB/9	SO/9	WHIP	AVG
2022	23	Great Lakes (MWL)	HiA	1	1	1.44	6	6	25	19	1	6	28	2.2	10.1	1.00	.204
2022	23	Tulsa (TL)	AA	6	4	1.60	14	13	73	59	1	30	107	3.7	13.1	1.21	.219
2022	23	Oklahoma City (PCL)	AAA	2	1	1.16	6	6	23	14	1	8	33	3.1	12.7	0.94	.169
Minor League Totals				**11**	**8**	**2.45**	**49**	**47**	**213**	**179**	**10**	**69**	**306**	**2.9**	**12.9**	**1.17**	**.225**

7 ANDY PAGES, OF

Born: Dec. 8, 2000. **B-T:** R-R. **HT:** 6-1. **WT:** 212.
Signed: Cuba, 2018. **Signed by:** Luis Marquez/Roman Barinas/Manelik Pimentel.

BA GRADE
50 Risk: High

TRACK RECORD: Pages starred as one of the top hitters in Cuba's junior leagues and signed with the Dodgers for $300,000 after he left the country. He promptly finished among the league leaders in home runs in the Dominican Summer League and Rookie-level Pioneer League in his first two seasons and led the Midwest League with 31 homers in 2021, earning the league's MVP award. Pages moved to Double-A Tulsa in 2022 and continued his power binge with 26 home runs, third-most in the Texas League, but he also hit a career-low .236. He earned a measure of redemption by tying for second in the Arizona Fall League with five home runs.

SCOUTING REPORT: Pages possesses enormous power that is the best in the Dodgers' system. His fast bat speed, immense strength and uphill swing path combine to produce tower-ing home runs that leave all parts of the stadium and clear scoreboards. Pages has a knack for delivering big home runs in clutch situations and gets to his power enough to project 30 homers annually. Pages is a cerebral hitter, but his uphill swing path leaves him vulnerable to elevated fastballs and he is prone to chasing sliders off the plate. He is learning to lay off pitches he can't drive but has holes that will limit him to a below-average hitter. Pages has gotten heavier as he's aged and is now a well below-average runner with a thick lower half. He gets good jumps in right field and has improved his focus to be an average defender, but he'll have to monitor his conditioning to make sure he doesn't get much bigger and lose mobility. He has plus-plus arm strength and has improved his throwing accuracy to make his arm a game-changing weapon.

THE FUTURE: Pages' youth and power give him a chance to be a low-average slugger who hits just enough to play every day. He'll head to Triple-A in 2023 and could make his MLB debut later in the year.

SCOUTING GRADES	Hitting: 40	Power: 70	Speed: 30	Fielding: 50	Arm: 70

Year	Age	Club (Leag	Lvl	AVG	G	AB	R	H	2B	3B	HR	RBI	BB	SO	SB	OBP	SLG
2022	21	Tulsa (TL)	AA	.236	132	487	69	115	29	3	26	80	62	140	6	.336	.468
Minor League Totals				**.256**	**367**	**1326**	**261**	**339**	**85**	**6**	**86**	**259**	**194**	**386**	**29**	**.374**	**.523**

8 DALTON RUSHING, C

Born: Feb. 21, 2001. **B-T:** L-R. **HT:** 6-1. **WT:** 220.
Drafted: Louisville, 2022 (2nd round). **Signed by:** Marty Lamb.

TRACK RECORD: Rushing spent his first two seasons at Louisville backing up future No. 1 overall pick Henry Davis at catcher and didn't get a chance to start until his junior year. He impressed with a standout showing in the Cape Cod League before the season and followed with a team-high 23 home runs in the spring. The Dodgers drafted Rushing with the 40th overall pick in 2022 after he wowed them during interviews at the draft combine and signed him for $1,956,800. Rushing continued to mash after signing, hitting .424 with eight home runs in 30 games for Low-A Rancho Cucamonga and solidifying the Dodgers' belief he was a first-round talent who fell.

BA GRADE
50 Risk: High

SCOUTING REPORT: A standout linebacker in high school, Rushing is a muscular, physical slugger who squats 700 pounds and does immense damage with his raw strength. He unloads on balls with a compact, violent swing and crushes them to all fields, frequently clearing 400 feet. He has exceptional plate discipline and an advanced feel for picking out pitches he can drive, helping him project to be an average hitter with plus power. Rushing has holes in his swing, primarily against fastballs up and in, but the Dodgers believe adjustments to his posture will rectify the issue. Rushing is a good athlete despite his bulk and is an average runner underway. He maintains that athleticism behind the plate, but he is very raw as a receiver and is a below-average defender overall. Rushing's glove frequently gets beat by the ball to the spot, and he has timing issues in his framing and blocking. His plus arm strength is hindered by below-average throwing accuracy. Rushing has the elite work ethic and competitive makeup to improve.
THE FUTURE: Rushing projects to be a slugger who hits in the middle of the order regardless of position. He'll focus on improving his defense to stay behind the plate in 2023.

SCOUTING GRADES	Hitting: 50	Power: 60	Speed: 45	Fielding: 40	Arm: 55

Year	Age	Club (League)	Lvl	AVG	G	AB	R	H	2B	3B	HR	RBI	BB	SO	SB	OBP	SLG
2022	21	Dodgers (ACL)	R	.000	2	5	0	0	0	0	0	0	1	1	0	.167	.000
2022	21	R. Cucamonga (CAL)	LoA	.424	28	99	27	42	11	0	8	30	21	21	1	.539	.778
Minor League Totals				.404	30	104	27	42	11	0	8	30	22	22	1	.522	.740

9 NICK NASTRINI, RHP

Born: Feb. 18, 2000. **B-T:** R-R. **HT:** 6-3. **WT:** 215.
Drafted: UCLA, 2021 (4th round). **Signed by:** Dennis Moeller.

TRACK RECORD: Nastrini arrived at UCLA as a top recruit out of San Diego's Cathedral Catholic High and grew into premium stuff. He entered his junior year with the Bruins considered a potential first-rounder, but he suffered a horrendous case of the yips and was dropped from the rotation by April. The Dodgers decided to take a shot on Nastrini's raw stuff and drafted him in the fourth round in 2021, signing him for $497,500. He rediscovered his control and composure under the Dodgers' instruction and flew up to Double-A in his first full season in 2022.

BA GRADE
50 Risk: High

SCOUTING REPORT: Nastrini is a physical, 6-foot-3 righthander with power stuff. His fastball sits 94-95 mph and touches 98 with above-average ride and extension that helps it play as a borderline plus-plus pitch, especially at the top of the strike zone. His short, vertical slider in the mid 80s flashes above-average with late drop below barrels, and his fading mid-80s changeup is an average pitch that is more consistent than his slider. He added an 80-83 mph power curveball late in the year that is fringy now but has a chance to improve with more development. Nastrini has a polished, repeatable delivery, but he tends to be too methodical in his tempo and mechanics, leading to below-average control. He is best when he works quickly and lets his natural athleticism take over on the mound.
THE FUTURE: Nastrini's loud stuff and improved control give him a chance to be a No. 4 starter if he can maintain his strides. He has an outside chance to reach the majors during the season.

SCOUTING GRADES:	Fastball: 65	Curveball: 45	Slider: 55	Changeup: 50	Control: 40

Year	Age	Club (League)	Lvl	W	L	ERA	G	GS	IP	H	HR	BB	SO	BB/9	SO/9	WHIP	AVG
2022	22	Great Lakes (MWL)	HiA	5	3	3.86	21	21	86	61	12	39	127	4.1	13.2	1.16	.192
2022	22	Tulsa (TL)	AA	1	1	4.15	6	6	30	14	5	16	42	4.7	12.5	0.99	.140
Minor League Totals				6	4	3.72	34	34	131	82	19	62	201	4.3	13.8	1.10	.176

10 JAMES OUTMAN, OF

Born: May 14, 1997. **B-T:** L-R. **HT:** 6-3. **WT:** 215.
Drafted: Sacramento State, 2018 (7th round). **Signed by:** Tom Kunis.

TRACK RECORD: Outman starred as a middle linebacker in high school, but he chose to pursue baseball and became a three-year stater at Sacramento State. The Dodgers drafted him in the seventh round in 2018 after he led the Western Athletic Conference in home runs as a junior and signed him for $157,500. Outman rebuilt his swing under the Dodgers' instruction and broke out offensively in 2022. He rose from Double-A to the majors and homered in his first MLB at-bat on July 31. He returned to Triple-A and hit for the cycle twice in four games, headlining a season in which he finished second among Dodgers prospects with 69 extra-base hits.

BA GRADE

45 Risk: Medium

SCOUTING REPORT: Outman is a strong, physical athlete at 6-foot-3, 215 pounds. He previously struggled to make contact against pitches on the inner half, but after controlling his leg lift and lowering his hands in 2022, he became more athletic in his swing and began clearing his hips to eliminate the hole. Outman hits balls hard with his raw strength and now covers enough of the plate to reach average power and be the strong side of a platoon. He still has some length to his swing and holes against breaking balls that will prevent him from hitting for a high average. Outman is a powerful, plus runner who accelerates well to chase down balls in the outfield. He has the athleticism and timing to scale walls and rob home runs and projects to be an above-average defender at all three outfield positions. He has a plus, accurate arm that produced six outfield assists last season.

THE FUTURE: Outman is frequently requested in trades by teams who believe he can be an everyday center fielder with his swing improvements. He fits best in a platoon and is ready to fill that role.

SCOUTING GRADES		Hitting: 40		Power: 50		Speed: 60		Fielding: 55		Arm: 60			
Year	**Age**	**Club (League)**	**Lvl**	**AVG**	**G**	**AB**	**R**	**H**	**2B**	**3B**	**HR**	**RBI**	**BB**	**SO**	**SB**	**OBP**	**SLG**
2022	25	Tulsa (TL)	AA	.295	68	261	59	77	17	1	16	45	38	89	7	.394	.552
2022	25	Oklahoma City (PCL)	AAA	.292	57	212	42	62	14	6	15	61	32	63	6	.390	.627
2022	25	Los Angeles (NL)	MLB	.462	4	13	6	6	2	0	1	3	2	7	0	.563	.846
Major League Totals				.462	4	13	6	6	2	0	1	3	2	7	0	.563	.846
Minor League Totals				.263	403	1537	300	404	75	23	79	249	213	475	68	.363	.496

11 JACOB AMAYA, SS

Born: Sept. 3, 1998. **B-T:** R-R. **HT:** 6-0. **WT:** 180.
Drafted: HS—West Covina, Calif., 2017 (11th round). **Signed by:** Dennis Moeller.

TRACK RECORD: The grandson of former Brooklyn Dodgers prospect Frank Amaya, Jacob grew up 25 miles east of Dodger Stadium and was drafted by his hometown team in the 11th round in 2017. He quickly asserted himself as the best defensive shortstop in the Dodgers system, but his offense declined each level he rose and cratered with a disastrous showing at Double-A in 2021. Amaya reined in his approach to emphasize strike-zone discipline and bounced back in 2022. He set new career highs in hits (124), home runs (17) and total bases (203) and climbed to Triple-A.

SCOUTING REPORT: Amaya's greatest strength is his defense. He is a consistent, reliable shortstop who makes every play and has few weaknesses. He positions himself well with his elite instincts, gets excellent reads off the bat, expertly assesses hops and calmly handles every ball with his smooth, fluid hands. He completes every throw with his plus, accurate arm and has an advanced internal clock. Amaya's defense is at least plus, but his well below-average hitting ability will likely prevent him from being an everyday player. He flashes good strike-zone discipline, but he lacks a natural feel for contact and constantly tinkers with his swing mechanics. Amaya gets in trouble when he starts chasing power and gets overly frustrated and down on himself offensively, although he has a knack for coming through with runners in scoring position.

THE FUTURE: Amaya projects to be a light-hitting utilityman whose ability to play shortstop will keep him on a roster. He has a chance to make his major league debut in 2023.

BA GRADE: 45/Medium		Hit: 30		Power: 40		Speed: 50		Fielding: 60		Arm: 60			
Year	**Age**	**Club (League)**	**Lvl**	**AVG**	**G**	**AB**	**R**	**H**	**2B**	**3B**	**HR**	**RBI**	**BB**	**SO**	**SB**	**OBP**	**SLG**
2022	23	Tulsa (TL)	AA	.264	49	182	39	48	10	3	9	26	32	29	3	.370	.500
2022	23	Oklahoma City (PCL)	AAA	.259	84	294	46	76	10	1	8	45	49	83	3	.368	.381
Minor League Totals				.256	463	1702	298	435	77	15	42	232	280	385	34	.361	.392

12 NICK FRASSO, RHP

Born: Oct. 18, 1998. **B-T:** R-R. **HT:** 6-5. **WT:** 200.
Drafted: Loyola Marymount, 2020 (4th round). **Signed by:** Bud Smith (Blue Jays).

TRACK RECORD: Frasso impressed as a starter on USA Baseball's Collegiate National team and was drafted by the Blue Jays in the fourth round in 2020 despite having forearm tightness that required Tommy John surgery. Frasso returned to the mound for his first extended work in 2022 and starred at the Class A levels, leading the Dodgers to acquire him at the trade deadline in a four-player swap that sent Mitch White to Toronto. He continued to shine in six starts in the Dodgers system and finished the year in Double-A.
SCOUTING REPORT: Frasso is built like a basketball player with a tall, lean 6-foot-5 frame and has a potent mix of stuff and funk. His high-spin fastball explodes out of his hand at 95-100 mph and jumps on hitters quickly with his nearly seven feet of extension in his delivery. His fastball plays up further with late run and the deception he generates from his long limbs, making it a plus-plus pitch that hitters consistently swing through. Frasso's fastball is an impact pitch, but his secondaries are raw. He alternates between a hard, short slider and sweepier one with depth and is still figuring out which to use. His fading changeup plays well off his fastball and flashes plus, but he needs to improve his command of it. Frasso is a good athlete who throws strikes with average control and keeps his walks to a minimum.
THE FUTURE: Frasso's arm strength and athleticism excite, but his secondary development will determine whether he becomes a starter or reliever. He'll begin 2023 back at Double-A.

| BA GRADE: 50/High | · | Fastball: 70 | | Slider: 50 | | Changeup: 55 | | Control: 50 | | | | |

Year	Age	Club (League)	Lvl	W	L	ERA	G	GS	IP	H	HR	BB	SO	BB/9	SO/9	WHIP	AVG
2022	23	Dunedin (FSL)	LoA	0	0	0.70	7	7	26	13	0	8	42	2.8	14.7	0.82	.146
2022	23	Great Lakes (MWL)	HiA	0	0	1.59	2	2	6	5	0	0	9	0.0	14.3	0.88	.238
2022	23	Vancouver (NWL)	HiA	0	0	0.82	3	3	11	3	1	2	15	1.6	12.3	0.45	.081
2022	23	Tulsa (TL)	AA	0	0	5.40	4	4	12	12	1	7	10	5.4	7.7	1.63	.261
Minor League Totals				0	0	1.68	19	18	59	36	2	19	84	2.9	12.8	0.93	.170

13 JOSUE DE PAULA, OF

Born: May 24, 2005. **B-T:** L-L. **HT:** 6-3. **WT:** 185.
Signed: Dominican Republic, 2022. **Signed by:** Laiky Uribe.

TRACK RECORD: De Paula was born and raised in New York and moved to the Dominican Republic when he was 15 to sign as an international free agent. He signed with the Dodgers for $397,500 on the first day of the 2022 international signing period and quickly emerged as one of the organization's most exciting hitters in the lower levels. De Paula tore through the Dominican Summer League with a .350 batting average and 20 extra-base hits in only 53 games while posting more walks (32) than strikeouts (31) in his pro debut. He followed with an eye-opening performance in instructional league.
SCOUTING REPORT: De Paula is a tall, projectable teenager with a gorgeous lefthanded swing. He is a calm, composed hitter who squares balls up with an efficient, balanced stroke that stays on plane through the hitting zone and hits balls hard no matter where they are pitched. He has an advanced knowledge of the strike zone and consistently conducts high-quality at-bats. De Paula is still growing into his wiry body, but he has the frame to pack on muscle and grow into plus power at maturity on top of potential plus hitting ability. De Paula is coordinated in the batter's box but less so in the field. He's a below-average runner and middling athlete who relies on getting good reads to make plays in the outfield. He projects to be a corner outfielder and may have to move to first base as he gets bigger.
THE FUTURE: De Paula has a chance to be an impactful offensive force but is many years away from that ceiling. He'll make his stateside debut in the Arizona Complex League in 2023.

| BA GRADE: 55/Extreme | | Hit: 60 | | Power: 60 | | Speed: 40 | | Fielding: 30 | | Arm: 55 | | |

Year	Age	Club (League)	Lvl	AVG	G	AB	R	H	2B	3B	HR	RBI	BB	SO	SB	OBP	SLG
2022	17	Dodgers Bautista (DSL)	R	.349	53	186	42	65	13	2	5	30	32	31	16	.448	.522
Minor League Totals				.349	53	186	42	65	13	2	5	30	32	31	16	.448	.522

14 EMMET SHEEHAN, RHP

Born: Nov. 15, 1999. **B-T:** R-R. **HT:** 6-5. **WT:** 215.
Drafted: Boston College, 2021 (6th round). **Signed by:** John Pyle.

TRACK RECORD: Sheehan pitched sparingly his first two seasons at Boston College but stepped into the Friday night starter's role as a junior and had a banner season, highlighted by a school-record 15 strikeouts in a game against Pittsburgh. The Dodgers drafted Sheehan in the sixth round and signed him for

$244,500. Sheehan impressed in his pro debut and blossomed in his first full season in 2022. He struck out 106 batters in only 68 innings while rising from High-A to Double-A and finished the year with a strong showing in the Arizona Fall League.

SCOUTING REPORT: Sheehan is a big righthander who overwhelms hitters with his fastball. He hides his 94-98 mph fastball well behind his big frame and throws it with extreme rise and run out of a low arm slot, generating repeated swings and misses up in the zone. His fastball is a plus pitch he throws liberally, but he also has a low-80s changeup with downward action that projects to be an average pitch. His fringe, upper-70s curveball shows promising characteristics but lacks finish and he struggles to maintain feel for his hard, bullet slider. His control is below-average and prevents him from lasting deep into starts.

THE FUTURE: Sheehan projects to be a late-inning reliever who dominates with his fastball. He'll keep developing as a starter for now and will open 2023 back at Double-A.

BA GRADE: 50/High	Fastball: 60	Curveball: 45	Slider: 40	Changeup: 50	Control: 40

Year	Age	Club (League)	Lvl	W	L	ERA	G	GS	IP	H	HR	BB	SO	BB/9	SO/9	WHIP	AVG
2022	22	Great Lakes (MWL)	HiA	7	2	2.83	18	12	64	41	2	28	101	4.0	14.3	1.08	.180
2022	22	Tulsa (TL)	AA	0	0	4.15	2	2	4	2	1	3	5	6.2	10.4	1.15	.133
Minor League Totals				10	2	3.33	27	16	84	53	5	39	140	4.2	15.1	1.10	.176

15 EDDYS LEONARD, SS/2B

Born: Nov. 10, 2000. **B-T:** R-R. **HT:** 6-0. **WT:** 195.
Signed: Dominican Republic, 2017. **Signed by:** Roman Barinas/Luis Marquez/Manelik Pimentel

TRACK RECORD: Leonard moved slowly through the complex leagues before delivering a breakout season at the Class A levels in 2021. The Dodgers added him to the 40-man roster after the season, but that became an issue when Leonard wasn't allowed to work with organizational coaches or use team facilities in the offseason due to the lockout. He returned noticeably rusty to start the 2022 season and never found any consistency, alternating good months with bad months throughout the year at High-A Great Lakes.

SCOUTING REPORT: Leonard is a compact righthanded hitter with electric hands and bat speed. He swings hard and is consistently on time to drill hard line drives from gap to gap. Leonard smokes fastballs and has improved against breaking balls, but he is an aggressive, free-swinger with below-average plate discipline. He chases pitches he can't drive and will have to tighten his pitch selection to be an average hitter. Leonard's pure bat speed gives him average power as he's learned to elevate balls to his pull side, and he could grow into more with maturity. Leonard is a threat offensively, but he lacks a defensive home. Though he's a good athlete, he is an erratic middle infielder at both shortstop and second base and is still learning to play third base and center field. He's a fringy to below-average defender at every position and will have to move around to avoid being overexposed. He is an average runner with average arm strength.

THE FUTURE: Leonard projects to be an offensively-driven utilityman if he can refine his pitch selection. He'll open 2023 at Double-A Tulsa.

BA GRADE: 45/High	Hit: 40	Power: 50	Speed: 50	Fielding: 40	Arm: 50

Year	Age	Club (League)	Lvl	AVG	G	AB	R	H	2B	3B	HR	RBI	BB	SO	SB	OBP	SLG
2022	21	Great Lakes (MWL)	HiA	.264	127	496	80	131	32	4	15	61	45	119	4	.348	.435
Minor League Totals				.276	334	1263	235	349	78	12	45	179	152	328	28	.372	.464

16 RONAN KOPP, LHP

Born: July 29, 2002. **B-T:** L-L. **HT:** 6-7. **WT:** 250.
Drafted: South Mountain (Ariz.) JC, 2021 (12th round). **Signed by:** Brian Compton.

TRACK RECORD: Kopp looked like a potential first-rounder in high school before velocity fluctuations his senior year led him to go unpicked in the shortened 2020 draft. Rather than head to Arizona State, Kopp went to South Mountain (Ariz.) JC and showed enough for the Dodgers to draft him in the 12th round and sign him for $250,000. Kopp began the 2022 season at Low-A in the bullpen but forced his way into the rotation and was voted the California League's best pitching prospect by opposing managers.

SCOUTING REPORT: Kopp is an enormous pitcher and overpowers hitters with his pure stuff. His fastball sits between 96-98 mph with late life in short bursts and plays up with the funky angles he generates from his long limbs. He complements his fastball with a mid-80s slider that has added lateral movement to become an average pitch. Kopp dominates lefties with his stuff and angle, but he hasn't settled on a splitter or changeup as his third pitch and will have to develop one to handle righties. Kopp is a lumbering giant and below-average athlete who struggles to keep his long limbs in sync, leading to well below-average control. He dominates when he's synced up but sometimes struggles to get through an inning or two.

THE FUTURE: Kopp projects to be a big, hard-throwing reliever who neutralizes lefthanders. He'll head to High-A Great Lakes in 2023.

BA GRADE: 45/High		Fastball: 65		Slider: 50		Changeup: 30		Control: 30					

Year	Age	Club (League)	Lvl	W	L	ERA	G	GS	IP	H	HR	BB	SO	BB/9	SO/9	WHIP	AVG
2022	19	R. Cucamonga (CAL)	LoA	5	2	2.81	24	9	58	36	3	37	102	5.8	15.9	1.27	.170
2022	19	Great Lakes (MWL)	HiA	0	1	1.93	3	2	5	3	0	6	6	11.6	11.6	1.93	.167
Minor League Totals				5	3	2.66	30	11	64	41	3	44	113	6.2	15.8	1.32	.172

17 RIVER RYAN, RHP

Born: Aug. 17, 1998. **B-T:** R-R. **HT:** 6-2. **WT:** 195.
Drafted: UNC Pembroke, 2021 (11th round). **Signed by:** Jake Koenig/Nick Brannon (Padres).
TRACK RECORD: Ryan played both ways as a middle infielder and pitcher at North Carolina-Pembroke and hit exclusively as a DH in his pro debut after the Padres drafted him in the 11th round and signed him for $100,000. He shined on the mound at instructs after the season, leading the Dodgers to acquire him for utilityman Matt Beaty during 2022 spring training. Ryan's stuff ticked up with his focus solely on pitching in his first full season, fueling a breakout season across the Class A levels.
SCOUTING REPORT: Ryan is an elite athlete with a quick arm who is steadily gaining velocity with his focus on pitching. His fastball has ticked up to sit 95-97 mph with rising action and his cutter has become a plus pitch that sits 90-92 mph with tight spin. His firm, upper-80s changeup with late run is an above-average pitch and he has feel to spin an above-average mid-80s curveball. Ryan's control comes and goes, but it should sharpen with more experience on the mound. He has the arsenal to start but has to put on weight and strength and improve his durability. He experienced general soreness after throwing only 47.2 innings during the season and will need multiple years to build up to a starter's workload.
THE FUTURE: Ryan has a chance to take off if he proves he can log enough innings to remain a starter. Otherwise, his stuff will play in late relief.

BA GRADE: 45/High		Fastball: 60		Curveball: 55		Cutter: 60		Changeup: 55		Control: 45					

Year	Age	Club (League)	Lvl	W	L	ERA	G	GS	IP	H	HR	BB	SO	BB/9	SO/9	WHIP	AVG
2022	23	R. Cucamonga (CAL)	LoA	1	3	2.67	10	10	34	29	2	13	48	3.5	12.8	1.25	.228
2022	23	Great Lakes (MWL)	HiA	1	1	1.93	5	3	14	9	2	8	22	5.1	14.1	1.21	.176
Minor League Totals				2	4	2.45	15	13	48	38	4	21	70	4.0	13.2	1.24	.213

18 JONNY DELUCA, OF

Born: July 10, 1998. **B-T:** R-R. **HT:** 5-11. **WT:** 196.
Drafted: Oregon, 2019 (25th round). **Signed by:** Jeff Stevens.
TRACK RECORD: DeLuca participated in both baseball and track in high school and was one of the top prep long jumpers in the state of California. The Twins drafted him in the 39th round out of high school, but he instead went to Oregon and spent two seasons as the Ducks starting center fielder. The Dodgers drafted him in the 25th round as a draft-eligible sophomore in 2019 and signed him for $300,000—equivalent to sixth-round money. DeLuca's athleticism and tools stood out in his first full season and he jumped offensively in 2022. He set new career highs with 25 home runs and an .888 OPS across High-A and Double-A and was added to the 40-man roster after the season.
SCOUTING REPORT: DeLuca struggled as a switch-hitter at Oregon but has flourished offensively after the Dodgers made him hit righthanded only. He crushes lefthanded pitching with a strong, powerful swing and generates above-average power with his bulging, muscular forearms. He catches up to velocity, has above-average plate discipline and battles through at-bats. DeLuca is still getting used to seeing the ball from the right side against righthanded pitchers, but he crushes mistakes when they leave them over the plate. DeLuca is a plus runner and athlete in the outfield who can play all three positions. He has above-average arm strength that yielded seven outfield assists in 2022.
THE FUTURE: DeLuca projects to be a platoon or reserve outfielder who bashes lefties and plays all three outfield spots. He'll begin 2023 back at Double-A Tulsa.

BA GRADE: 45/High		Hit: 40		Power: 50		Speed: 60		Fielding: 55		Arm: 55					

Year	Age	Club (League)	Lvl	AVG	G	AB	R	H	2B	3B	HR	RBI	BB	SO	SB	OBP	SLG
2022	23	Great Lakes (MWL)	HiA	.245	73	277	51	68	17	2	18	51	37	56	12	.343	.516
2022	23	Tulsa (TL)	AA	.298	25	104	22	31	5	3	7	20	8	17	5	.359	.606
Minor League Totals				.263	225	867	167	228	49	12	48	148	99	163	46	.347	.513

19 MICHAEL GROVE, RHP

Born: Dec. 18, 1996. **B-T:** R-R. **HT:** 6-3. **WT:** 200.
Drafted: West Virginia, 2018 (2nd round). **Signed by:** Jonah Rosenthal

TRACK RECORD: Grove looked like a future first-round pick as an underclassman at West Virginia but had Tommy John surgery midway through his sophomore year and missed all of his junior year as well. The Dodgers bet on his pre-injury stuff and drafted him in the second round in 2018, signing him for $1,229,500. Grove's velocity and command took four years to fully come back, but he finally clicked in 2022 at Double-A and Triple-A and earned his first big league callup in May. He went 1-0, 4.60 in seven appearances for the Dodgers and took regular rotation turns at the end of the season.

SCOUTING REPORT: Grove is a strong, athletic righthander who flashes big stuff. His fastball has plus velocity at 94-97 mph, but it plays down because it's straight and he lacks consistent command of it. He shows feel to spin an average mid-80s slider with decent depth, and his upper-70s curveball flashes above-average. Grove has feel to manipulate the length and shape of his breaking balls, giving them bigger shape early in counts before shortening them to get swings and misses to put hitters away. Grove doesn't throw a changeup, leaving him vulnerable against lefties, and his control is fringy. His fastball command is particularly inconsistent and leads to widely varied quality of his outings.

THE FUTURE: Grove projects to be a spot starter and long reliever who can handle righthanded-heavy lineups. He is ready to assume that role now and will try to win an Opening Day roster spot.

BA GRADE: 40/Medium		Fastball: 55		Curveball: 55		Slider: 50		Control: 45						

Year	Age	Club (League)	Lvl	W	L	ERA	G	GS	IP	H	HR	BB	SO	BB/9	SO/9	WHIP	AVG
2022	25	Tulsa (TL)	AA	0	1	2.76	5	5	16	11	1	5	22	2.8	12.1	0.98	.180
2022	25	Oklahoma City (PCL)	AAA	1	4	4.07	14	12	60	56	10	21	68	3.2	10.3	1.29	.247
2022	25	Los Angeles (NL)	MLB	1	0	4.60	7	6	29	32	6	10	24	3.1	7.4	1.43	.260
Major League Totals				1	0	4.60	7	6	29	32	6	10	24	3.1	7.4	1.43	.260
Minor League Totals				2	14	5.84	61	57	199	213	37	87	251	3.9	11.4	1.51	.270

20 MADDUX BRUNS, LHP

Born: June 20, 2002. **B-T:** L-L. **HT:** 6-2. **WT:** 205.
Drafted: HS—Mobile, Ala., 2021 (1st round). **Signed by:** Benny Latino

TRACK RECORD: Bruns showed some of the best stuff of any high school pitcher in the 2021 draft class but also the shakiest control. The Dodgers bet on his raw talent and drafted him 29th overall, signing him for $2,197,500 to forgo an Alabama commitment. Bruns made his full-season debut at Low-A Rancho Cucamonga in 2022 and showed moderate control improvements early, but after missing a month with a lat strain he struggled to rediscover his release point and unraveled. He finished the year with 45 walks, nine wild pitches and eight hit batters in only 44.1 innings and averaged barely two innings per start.

SCOUTING REPORT: Bruns looks the part with a strong, projectable frame, an athletic delivery and a gifted left arm. His fastball sits 94-96 mph and touches 98 with armside life and late jump through the strike zone. His 74-77 mph curveball is a plus pitch with hard snap and big depth and his 82-85 mph slider with tough angle and late bite is another plus offering. He also has a fading changeup with average potential, but rarely throws it. Bruns flashes a fluid delivery and arm action, but he struggles to maintain his mechanics or release point and needs to improve his mental approach. He often focuses on chasing big velocity numbers or spin metrics rather than executing pitches to get hitters out. He's poor at holding runners and often displays his frustration publicly, throwing his arms up or kicking the dirt when his defense makes an error or umpires miss a call.

THE FUTURE: Bruns has rotation upside but has to mature to reach it. He projects to be a slow mover and will take time.

BA GRADE: 50/Extreme		Fastball: 60		Curveball: 60		Slider: 60		Changeup: 50		Control: 30					

Year	Age	Club (League)	Lvl	W	L	ERA	G	GS	IP	H	HR	BB	SO	BB/9	SO/9	WHIP	AVG
2022	20	R. Cucamonga (CAL)	LoA	0	3	5.68	21	21	44	36	1	45	67	9.1	13.6	1.83	.226
Minor League Totals				0	5	6.75	25	25	49	44	3	52	72	9.5	13.1	1.95	.243

21 JORBIT VIVAS, 2B

Born: March 9, 2001. **B-T:** L-R. **HT:** 5-10. **WT:** 171.
Signed: Venezuela, 2017. **Signed by:** Luis Marquez/Roman Barinas/Andres Simancas.

TRACK RECORD: Vivas put together a long track record of hitting as an amateur and signed with the Dodgers for $300,000 out of Venezuela in 2017. He continued that trend in his stateside debut and fol-

lowed by hitting .312 in his full-season debut in 2021 at the Class A levels. The Dodgers added Vivas to the 40-man roster after the season, though the lockout meant he couldn't work with organizational coaches or use team facilities during the offseason. Vivas got off to a slow start at High-A Great Lakes in 2022 after those restrictions, but he found his stroke and hit .285 from mid May through the rest of the season.
SCOUTING REPORT: Vivas is a small lefthanded hitter with a short, compact swing and an excellent feel for the barrel. He shoots balls from line to line and puts the ball in play on a regular basis. He controls the strike zone, works counts and battles through long at-bats. Vivas has the approach and contact skills to hit for average, but he's undersized and lacks the strength to impact the ball consistently. He'll occasionally get into a ball and drive it over the fence, but his power is below-average and he doesn't have room to add much more. Vivas is a below-average runner who is limited defensively to second base, where he is an average defender who makes the routine plays. His arm strength is fringy but enough to make the throws.
THE FUTURE: Vivas has pure contact skills but will need to hit the ball harder to be a major leaguer. He'll head to Double-A in 2023.

BA GRADE: 45/High		Hit: 50		Power: 30		Speed: 40		Fielding: 50		Arm: 45	

Year	Age	Club (League)	Lvl	AVG	G	AB	R	H	2B	3B	HR	RBI	BB	SO	SB	OBP	SLG
2022	21	Great Lakes (MWL)	HiA	.269	128	479	73	129	19	7	10	66	63	58	2	.374	.401
Minor League Totals				.286	339	1267	222	362	73	15	26	196	148	179	36	:383	.429

22 DEVIN MANN, 2B/OF

Born: Feb. 11, 1997. **B-T:** R-R. **HT:** 6-3. **WT:** 180.
Drafted: Louisville, 2018 (5th round). **Signed by:** Marty Lamb.
TRACK RECORD: Mann primarily hit for contact at Louisville but got stronger and made swing changes to hit for power after the Dodgers drafted him in 2018. He made his way up the minors with solid production at every level and reached Triple-A for the first time in 2022. Traditionally a slow starter, Mann heated up after the first six weeks and finished with an .844 OPS, 10th-highest among Dodgers prospects.
SCOUTING REPORT: Mann is a well-rounded player who does a little bit of everything. He is a persistent on-base threat with strong strike-zone discipline and good pitch recognition and has the contact skills and power to do damage when he gets a pitch to hit. Mann generates average raw power with a short, controlled swing and drives balls from gap to gap. He crushes lefties in particular and has a chance to be an average hitter who hits 10-15 home runs, although he has a hole on the outer half that can be exploited. Mann is a stiff defender at second base, but he loosens up in the outfield and covers enough ground in the corners with his long strides. His fringy arm fits best at second base or left field.
THE FUTURE: Mann's bat and defensive versatility give him a chance to carve out a career as a lefty-mashing reserve. He'll aim to make his big league debut in 2023.

BA GRADE: 40/Medium		Hit: 50		Power: 45		Speed: 40		Fielding: 45		Arm: 45	

Year	Age	Club (League)	Lvl	AVG	G	AB	R	H	2B	3B	HR	RBI	BB	SO	SB	OBP	SLG
2022	25	Tulsa (TL)	AA	.267	74	243	45	65	16	0	11	35	43	50	1	.384	.469
2022	25	Oklahoma City (PCL)	AAA	.258	44	132	25	34	5	3	5	26	21	36	0	.372	.455
Minor League Totals				.261	396	1354	212	353	82	7	51	217	195	333	19	.362	.445

23 LANDON KNACK, RHP

Born: July 15, 1997. **B-T:** R-R. **HT:** 6-2. **WT:** 220.
Drafted: East Tennessee State, 2020 (2nd round). **Signed by:** Marty Lamb.
TRACK RECORD: Knack began his college career at Walters State (Tenn.) JC before transferring to East Tennessee State, where his velocity jumped as a senior to send him rising up draft boards. The Dodgers drafted him in the second round, No. 60 overall, and signed him for an underslot $712,500 in the shortened 2020 draft. Knack impressed in his pro debut, but his stuff and control regressed in 2022 as he battled injuries and conditioning issues. He missed the first month of the season with a hamstring strain and never got on track as he struggled to a 2-10, 5.01 mark at Double-A Tulsa.
SCOUTING REPORT: Knack is a thick, burly righthander who flashes power stuff. His fastball sits 93-94 and touches 96 with above-average rise at the top of the zone to generate swings and misses. He ditched his sweepy, loose slider for a short, vertical one with hard break in the mid 80s that he can land for strikes or use to get chases and is a potentially above-average pitch. Knack's changeup has regressed as his slider has improved, but it's still an average offering in the low-to-mid 80s with solid fade. He also has a below-average 77-80 mph curveball he'll mix in. Knack previously flashed pinpoint control, but he's lost it as his conditioning has worsened. He has poor nutrition and sleep habits that affect his weight and make it

difficult for him to maintain his delivery. His poor conditioning is also the root of frequent muscle pulls and strains he suffers every year.

THE FUTURE: The Dodgers have challenged Knack to improve his fitness in 2023. Whether he does will determine if he has a major league future.

BA GRADE: 45/High		Fastball: 55		Curveball: 40		Slider: 55		Changeup: 50		Control: 50		

Year	Age	Club (League)	Lvl	W	L	ERA	G	GS	IP	H	HR	BB	SO	BB/9	SO/9	WHIP	AVG
2022	24	Tulsa (TL)	AA	2	10	5.01	17	17	65	64	8	27	80	3.8	11.1	1.41	.257
Minor League Totals				9	11	4.11	33	28	127	114	16	35	162	2.5	11.5	1.17	.238

24 JOSE RAMOS, OF

Born: Jan. 1, 2001. **B-T:** R-R. **HT:** 6-1. **WT:** 200.
Signed: Panama, 2018. **Signed by:** Luis Marquez/Cliff Nuitter.

TRACK RECORD: Ramos signed with the Dodgers for $30,000 out of Panama and broke out with a big season across the Rookie and Low-A levels in 2021. He entered 2022 looking to build on that momentum, but instead struggled to make contact against higher-level pitching. He struck out 169 times across Low-A and High-A and was left unprotected in the Rule 5 draft.

SCOUTING REPORT: Ramos is an athletic outfielder who has the raw ingredients to hit. He has elite bat speed, a smooth, rhythmic swing and plus raw power to all fields. He crushes fastballs and isn't fazed by velocity in any part of the zone. Ramos struggles to recognize or lay off breaking balls, resulting in bad plate discipline and poor at-bats. He's overly aggressive in his approach and swings and misses at almost any breaking pitch, limiting him to a future as a well below-average hitter. Ramos is an average runner who gets good reads and runs clean routes in the outfield. He is an above-average defender in right field and a playable one in center with a plus-plus, accurate arm that produces jaw-dropping throws.

THE FUTURE: Ramos' power and defense give him a chance to be a bench bat. He'll have to learn to recognize spin to be more.

BA GRADE: 45/High		Hit: 30		Power: 50		Speed: 50		Fielding: 55		Arm: 70		

Year	Age	Club (League)	Lvl	AVG	G	AB	R	H	2B	3B	HR	RBI	BB	SO	SB	OBP	SLG
2022	21	R. Cucamonga (CAL)	LoA	.277	28	112	20	31	3	3	6	23	18	36	2	.391	.518
2022	21	Great Lakes (MWL)	HiA	.240	95	362	63	87	19	3	19	74	39	133	2	.322	.467
Minor League Totals				.277	242	936	160	259	61	9	38	183	100	286	15	.360	.483

25 YEINER FERNANDEZ, C/2B

Born: Sept. 19, 2002. **B-T:** R-R. **HT:** 5-9. **WT:** 170.
Signed: Venezuela, 2019. **Signed by:** Roman Barinas/Jean Castro/Cristian Guzman.

TRACK RECORD: Fernandez played for Venezuela in the 2015 Little League World Series and hit a game-winning, three-run homer against Australia in the tournament opener. He signed with the Dodgers for $717,5000 in 2019 and quickly stood out as one of the top pure hitters in the system. Fernandez struggled early at Low-A Rancho Cucamonga in 2022 with inconsistent playing time as Diego Cartaya's backup, but he flourished after Cartaya was promoted to High-A. Fernandez hit .322/.422/.502 after becoming the starting catcher in June and had two separate hitting streaks of at least 10 games.

SCOUTING REPORT: Fernandez is a short, stocky hitter who uses his frame to his advantage. He has a small strike zone for pitchers to attack and uses his short arms to make quick, direct contact with pitches over the plate. He has elite hand-eye coordination and barrel control and sprays the ball all over the field. Fernandez doesn't hit the ball overly hard because his bat speed is just average and he's not particularly strong, but he should add muscle and make harder contact as he matures. Fernandez is a good athlete with soft hands and above-average arm strength at second base, but he recently converted to catching and hasn't translated those attributes behind the plate. He allowed 100 wild pitches and 15 passed balls in only 62 games behind the plate and allowed a minor-league worst 131 stolen bases in 158 attempts. He's a bottom-of-the-scale defensive catcher who needs years to become playable.

THE FUTURE: Opposing teams frequently request Fernandez in trades because of his contact skills, but he needs to get stronger and improve defensively. He'll head to High-A in 2023.

BA GRADE: 45/High		Hit: 50		Power: 30		Speed: 45		Fielding: 30		Arm: 55		

Year	Age	Club (League)	Lvl	AVG	G	AB	R	H	2B	3B	HR	RBI	BB	SO	SB	OBP	SLG
2022	19	R. Cucamonga (CAL)	LoA	.292	89	363	76	106	16	2	10	68	46	55	3	.383	.430
Minor League Totals				.312	131	535	104	167	28	3	13	93	58	85	4	.393	.449

26 PETER HEUBECK, RHP

Born: July 22, 2002. **B-T:** R-R. **HT:** 6-3. **WT:** 170.
Drafted: HS—Baltimore, 2021 (3rd round). **Signed by:** Paul Murphy
TRACK RECORD: Heubeck emerged early as the top pitcher in a banner 2021 Maryland prep class that included Padres first-rounder Jackson Merrill. He struck out 15 batters in the state semifinals to help lead Baltimore's Gilman High to a championship and was drafted by the Dodgers in the third round, signing for $1,269,500 to forgo a Wake Forest commitment. Heubeck impressed in extended spring training to start the 2022 season, but his control disappeared when he moved to Low-A Rancho Cucamonga in June. He posted a 7.39 ERA in 15 games with the Quakes and failed to last more than three innings in any start.
SCOUTING REPORT: Heubeck is a tall, lean righthander who has lots of room to add weight and strength. He's a good athlete with a quick arm and already sits 92-95 mph with late life on his fastball. His best pitch is a plus overhand curveball that sits 77-80 mph with depth and bite at the bottom of the zone. He also has a changeup that is still developing and flashes average with slight fade and dive. Heubeck has intriguing stuff, but his lack of strength results in an effortful delivery and well below-average control. He struggles to maintain his velocity and tires quickly.
THE FUTURE: Heubeck has to get stronger to fulfill his back-of-the-rotation starter potential. Adding strength will be his primary goal in 2023.

BA GRADE: 45/Extreme   **Fastball:** 55   **Curveball:** 60   **Changeup:** 45   **Control:** 30

Year	Age	Club (League)	Lvl	W	L	ERA	G	GS	IP	H	HR	BB	SO	BB/9	SO/9	WHIP	AVG
2022	19	R. Cucamonga (CAL)	LoA	0	1	7.39	15	13	32	22	7	25	42	7.1	11.9	1.48	.196
Minor League Totals				0	1	6.56	17	14	36	23	7	27	51	6.8	12.9	1.40	.184

27 DAMON KEITH, OF

Born: May 28, 2000. **B-T:** R-R. **HT:** 6-3. **WT:** 195.
Drafted: California Baptist, 2021 (18th round). **Signed by:** Brent Mayne
TRACK RECORD: Keith emerged as a draft prospect at California Baptist, where he won Western Athletic Conference player of the year honors as a junior. The Dodgers drafted him in the 18th round and signed him for $125,000. Keith posted some of the top exit velocities in the Dodgers system across the Class A levels in his full-season debut and became a favorite of big league hitting coach Robert Van Scoyoc. He finished in the top 10 in the organization in hits, runs, doubles, RBIs, total bases and OPS.
SCOUTING REPORT: Keith is a powerful slugger with plus bat speed, plus raw power and good leverage in his swing. He gets to his power easily with a quick flick of his wrists and hits towering drives down the left-field line. Keith has holes at the top of the zone and will strike out, but he battles with two strikes and has enough plate discipline to be a below-average hitter who gets to his power. Keith is an average runner with good instincts on the bases and is athletic enough to play all three outfield positions, although he still has to work on his reads off the bat. His plus arm strength profiles in right field.
THE FUTURE: Keith's power, athleticism and defense have made him a popular trade target of other teams. He projects to be a reserve outfielder but could grow into more.

BA GRADE: 40/High   **Hit:** 40   **Power:** 60   **Speed:** 50   **Fielding:** 45   **Arm:** 60

Year	Age	Club (League)	Lvl	AVG	G	AB	R	H	2B	3B	HR	RBI	BB	SO	SB	OBP	SLG
2022	22	R. Cucamonga (CAL)	LoA	.299	88	334	75	100	23	4	12	65	69	95	5	.433	.500
2022	22	Great Lakes (MWL)	HiA	.204	31	103	16	21	4	1	5	14	21	33	0	.339	.408
Minor League Totals				.285	142	506	104	144	33	8	18	92	103	152	7	.417	.488

28 KYLE HURT, RHP

Born: May 30, 1998. **B-T:** R-R. **HT:** 6-3. **WT:** 220.
Drafted: Southern California, 2020 (5th round). **Signed by:** Eric Brock (Marlins).
TRACK RECORD: The Marlins drafted Hurt in the fifth round in 2020 and traded him with Alex Vesia to the Dodgers for Dylan Floro before the 2021 season. Hurt broke out in 2022 with a dominant showing at High-A Great Lakes before struggling after a promotion to Double-A. He struck out 32.7% of the batters he faced, third-highest in the organization among starters, but also had a system-worst 17.7% walk rate.
SCOUTING REPORT: Hurt is a burly 6-foot-3 righthander with big stuff he is still learning to harness. His fastball sits 95-97 mph with extreme ride and run out of a low slot and generates lots of swings and misses. He holds his velocity through his outings and dominates with his fastball alone when he throws it for strikes. Hurt has long had advanced feel for a plus 87-89 mph changeup he locates well and his short,

upper-80s slider has improved to flash average. Hurt's stuff is loud, but he has well below-average control and struggles to command his fastball. He'll walk batters en masse and has long struggled to maintain his poise for more than a few innings at a time, although he is slowly moving in the right direction.

THE FUTURE: Hurt has the stuff to be an effective reliever if he can polish his control. He'll open 2023 back at Double-A.

BA GRADE: 40/High | **Fastball:** 60 | **Slider:** 45 | **Changeup:** 60 | **Control:** 30

Year	Age	Club (League)	Lvl	W	L	ERA	G	GS	IP	H	HR	BB	SO	BB/9	SO/9	WHIP	AVG
2022	24	Great Lakes (MWL)	HiA	4	2	2.21	13	11	41	21	1	22	64	4.9	14.2	1.06	.151
2022	24	Tulsa (TL)	AA	1	5	9.29	12	8	31	35	3	37	45	10.7	13.1	2.32	.280
Minor League Totals				7	9	5.34	37	23	93	74	6	69	145	6.7	14.1	1.54	.215

29 CARLOS DURAN, RHP

Born: July 30, 2001. **B-T:** R-R. **HT:** 6-7. **WT:** 230.
Signed: Dominican Republic, 2018. **Signed by:** Luis Marquez/Maneleik Pimentel.
TRACK RECORD: Duran sprouted to 6-foot-7 as a teenager and signed with the Dodgers for $300,000 out of the Dominican Republic in 2018. He progressively grew into more stuff as he filled out his frame and began to harness it at High-A Great Lakes in 2022. Duran's season had opposing teams targeting him heavily in trades, but he suffered an elbow injury and had Tommy John surgery after the season.
SCOUTING REPORT: Duran is physically huge and has power stuff befitting his frame. His two-seam fastball sits 93-96 mph and touches 98 with huge run to stay off barrels and get weak contact from right-handed hitters. His four-seam fastball sits in the same velocity band, but he lacks extension or movement on the pitch and it gets crushed. Duran's primary weapon is a plus-plus, mid-80s slider that may be the best individual pitch in the Dodgers system. Duran hides the ball well behind his big body and the pitch turns hard with power sweep and dive to get consistent swings and misses off the plate. Duran's firm, 87-90 mph changeup is a below-average pitch, but he has improved his command of it to become more competitive against lefties. He is a power pitcher with fringy control and is best in short bursts.
THE FUTURE: Duran will miss the entire 2023 season recovering from surgery. He has a chance to be a slider-heavy, power reliever if his stuff returns intact.

BA GRADE: 45/Extreme | **Fastball:** 55 | **Slider:** 70 | **Changeup:** 40 | **Control:** 40

Year	Age	Club (League)	Lvl	W	L	ERA	G	GS	IP	H	HR	BB	SO	BB/9	SO/9	WHIP	AVG
2022	20	Dodgers (ACL)	R	0	0	0.00	1	1	1	0	0	0	1	0.0	9.0	0.00	.000
2022	20	Great Lakes (MWL)	HiA	1	3	4.25	14	13	49	43	6	24	68	4.4	12.6	1.38	.235
Minor League Totals				4	14	4.18	62	59	213	209	19	77	253	3.3	10.7	1.34	.252

30 JUSTIN WROBLESKI, LHP

Born: July 14, 2000. **B-T:** L-L. **HT:** 6-1. **WT:** 194.
Drafted: Oklahoma State, 2021 (11th round). **Signed by:** Heath Holliday.
TRACK RECORD: Wrobleski bounced from Clemson as a freshman to State JC of Florida as a sophomore and finally to Oklahoma State as a junior. He had Tommy John surgery after just nine appearances for the Cowboys, but he showed enough pre-surgery for the Dodgers to draft him in the 11th round and sign him for an above-slot $197,500. Wrobleski returned midway through the 2022 season and flashed some of the best lefthanded stuff in the Dodgers organization. He dominated over two months in the Arizona Complex League and finished with a late promotion to Low-A Rancho Cucamonga.
SCOUTING REPORT: Wrobleski is an athletic lefthander with growing arm strength. He came back throwing harder after surgery and now sits 93-96 mph on his fastball with room to keep ticking up as he gets stronger. He has a natural feel to spin the ball and gets swings and misses on his above-average, vertical, mid-80s slider and average low-90s cutter. His mid-80s changeup is a well below-average pitch he rarely throws. Wrobleski stands on the far third base side of the rubber and has some funk in his arm stroke that adds to his angle and deception. He throws strikes with average control and works quickly and efficiently.
THE FUTURE: Wrobleski has a chance to take off as he moves further from surgery. The Dodgers expect him to have a breakout year in 2023 at High-A Great Lakes.

BA GRADE: 45/Extreme | **Fastball:** 55 | **Slider:** 55 | **Cutter:** 50 | **Changeup:** 30 | **Control:** 50

Year	Age	Club (League)	Lvl	W	L	ERA	G	GS	IP	H	HR	BB	SO	BB/9	SO/9	WHIP	AVG
2022	21	Dodgers (ACL)	R	0	1	1.80	10	8	15	12	0	0	21	0.0	12.6	0.80	.211
2022	21	R. Cucamonga (CAL)	LoA	1	2	5.40	3	2	7	8	1	5	5	6.8	6.8	1.95	.364
Minor League Totals				1	3	2.91	13	10	22	20	1	5	26	2.1	10.8	1.15	.253

Miami Marlins

BY JOSH NORRIS

It is a tough time to be a Marlins fan.

The Braves are two years removed from winning the World Series and have a glut of young talent locked up for the next several years. The Phillies won the National League pennant in 2022 with a hobbled Bryce Harper and then went out and added Trea Turner and Taijuan Walker to their collection of all-stars. The Mets are rejuvenated under Steve Cohen's ownership and fortified their rotation by adding Justin Verlander and Kodai Senga to a rotation that already included Max Scherzer.

Even the Nationals, who continued to languish at the bottom of the NL East, pulled off a blockbuster trade by sending Juan Soto to the Padres.

The move replenished their moribund farm system with a cornucopia of high-end talent, led by big league-ready shortstop CJ Abrams and skyscraper-upside outfielder James Wood. And they are just a few years removed from the 2019 World Series title.

That is a lot of words to paint a very bleak picture, but it gets worse.

The Marlins are in a time of transition. Gary Denbo, who oversaw the farm system, was fired in the middle of the season. Manager Don Mattingly stepped down at season's end and was replaced by Skip Schumaker. Farm director Geoff DeGroot and professional scouting director Hadi Raad were also let go, as were several scouts on the amateur and professional sides.

The team's top five overall draft picks from 2019 and 2020—outfielder JJ Bleday from Vanderbilt and Max Meyer from Minnesota—both reached the big leagues, but Bleday underwhelmed and Meyer suffered a torn ulnar collateral ligament and had Tommy John surgery.

There is a glimmer of hope at the top of the farm system in righthander Eury Perez, who dominated Double-A at 19 years old and achieved his stated goal of pitching in the Futures Game. Perez, a towering figure who has the potential to join all-world righthander Sandy Alcantara—who was the NL's unanimous Cy Young Award winner—at the top of the rotation in the coming years.

The farm system also saw big gains from young middle infielders Yiddi Cappe and Jose Salas, and lefthander Dax Fulton shook off all the rust from Tommy John surgery, got into better shape and showed glimmers of the potential he showed as an amateur in Oklahoma.

But the news on the farm was a mixed bag at best.

The Marlins' 2021 first-rounder, shortstop Kahlil Watson, dealt with failure for the first time and was demoted from Low-A after an on-field

In his final 11 starts, Edward Cabrera put up a 2.89 ERA with 60 strikeouts in 56 innings.

PROJECTED 2026 LINEUP

Catcher	Nick Fortes	28
First Base	Jacob Berry	25
Second Base	Jose Salas	23
Third Base	Jordan Groshans	25
Shortstop	Jazz Chisholm	28
Left Field	Peyton Burdick	29
Center Field	Bryan De La Cruz	29
Right Field	JJ Bleday	27
Designated Hitter	Jesus Sanchez	28
No. 1 Starter	Sandy Alcantara	30
No. 2 Starter	Eury Perez	22
No. 3 Starter	Edward Cabrera	27
No. 4 Starter	Max Meyer	27
No. 5 Starter	Trevor Rogers	27
Closer	Sixto Sanchez	27

incident with an umpire. He also struck out at an alarming rate, even for a player who came into pro ball with questions surrounding his two-strike approach.

Miami went with a relatively safe pick at No. 6 overall in the 2022 draft, and chose Louisiana State slugger Jacob Berry. The current system and big league roster are bereft of bats, so Berry's success or failure in the minor leagues could go a long way toward determining whether the team finds a better long-term trajectory.

The Marlins could also get big boosts if pitchers Sixto Sanchez and Jake Eder return from injury and to their healthy forms. That's especially true for Sanchez—the main piece in the trade that sent J.T. Realmuto to Philadelphia—who was electric in 2020 before a litany of injuries derailed his next two seasons. ∎

DEPTH CHART

MIAMI MARLINS

TOP 2023 MLB CONTRIBUTORS	RANK
Peyton Burdick, OF	9
Jordan Groshans, SS/3B	10
Xavier Edwards, SS/2B	11
BREAKOUT PROSPECTS	**RANK**
Joe Mack, C	12
Marco Vargas, 2B	20

SOURCE OF TOP 30 TALENT

Homegrown	25	Acquired	5
College	7	Trade	4
Junior college	0	Rule 5 draft	1
High school	7	Independent league	0
Nondrafted free agent	1	Free agent/waivers	0
International	10		

LF
Peyton Burdick (9)

CF
Jose Gerardo (21)
Byron Chourio (29)
Victor Mesa Jr.

RF
Antony Peguero (19)
Jerar Encarnacion (23)
Griffin Conine

3B
Jordan Groshans (10)
Ynmanol Mariñez

SS
Jose Salas (4)
Yiddi Cappe (5)
Nasim Nuñez (14)
Jordan McCants

2B
Xavier Edwards (11)
Kahlil Watson (15)
Ian Lewis (18)
Marco Vargas (20)
Javier Sanoja
Cody Morissette

1B
Jacob Berry (3)
Torin Montgomery

C
Joe Mack (12)
Paul McIntosh (30)
Ronald Hernandez
Will Banfield

LHP

LHSP	LHRP
Jake Eder (7)	Josh Simpson (24)
Dax Fulton (8)	Luis Palacios
Luifer Romero	Patrick Monteverde
	Jefry Yan
	Zach King

RHP

RHSP	RHRP
Eury Perez (1)	Nic Enright (17)
Max Meyer (2)	George Soriano (25)
Sixto Sanchez (6)	Sean Reynolds (26)
Jacob Miller (13)	Zach McCambley (27)
Karson Milbrandt (16)	Franklin Sanchez (28)
Bryan Hoeing (22)	Aneurys Zabala
Evan Fitterer	Jorge Mercedes
MD Johnson	Jeff Lindgren
Walin Castillo	
Juan De La Cruz	
Jhon Cabral	
Lester Nin	

1 EURY PEREZ, RHP

Born: April 15, 2003. **B-T:** R-R. **HT:** 6-8. **WT:** 220.
Signed: Dominican Republic, 2019.
Signed by: Angel Izquiero/Fernando Seguignol.

TRACK RECORD: Perez has grown by leaps and bounds since the Marlins signed him in 2019. That's true physically and regarding his status in the sport. He's gone from a wiry 6-foot-5 to a thicker, more sturdy build at 6-foot-8 and 220 pounds and has used the extra strength to amplify his arsenal and blossom into one of the game's top pitching prospects. Perez's official debut was delayed a year by the pandemic, but the Marlins were so confident in his abilities that they jumped him straight to Low-A Jupiter for his 2021 professional debut. Not only did he pitch in Low-A at 17, but he also pitched in a league where the Automated Ball-Strike system was being tested, meaning that there was no leeway in terms of control—either hit the strike zone or it's a ball. Under those conditions and with no professional experience, Perez thrived. He used an exemplary pitch mix to pound the zone with consistent, quality strikes until the Marlins moved him to High-A Beloit, where he faced slightly more resistance but was still quite impressive. Miami continued its aggressive tact with Perez when they assigned him to Double-A to open the 2022 season. His first start of the year came as an 18-year-old, which made him the youngest pitcher at the level. After a couple of inconsistent turns, Perez found his groove on April 29, when he fired five one-hit innings with 12 strikeouts. The next two months were marked by pure dominance. He posted sub-2.50 ERAs in May and June before a strained lat muscle derailed his progress. He returned in time to help Double-A Pensacola win the Southern League championship and punctuated the win by striking out the first eight hitters he faced in the decisive Game 3 against Tennessee.

SCOUTING REPORT: Perez's allure is simple: He combines a powerful four-pitch mix with athleticism and command that ranks as exceptional for anyone but jumps off the page for someone of his size. His added strength has amplified his repertoire, which begins with a fastball that sits in the mid 90s and touches triple digits. Perez's excellent body control helps him command his fastball better than would be expected for someone his size. He worked hard to command the top of the strike zone in 2022 and elevate his fastball for swings and misses. In 2021, Perez employed a curveball and a changeup. His changeup is his best offspeed pitch and grades as the best in the system, with outstanding fade and sink away from lefthanded hitters. In

BEST TOOLS

BATTING

Best Hitter for Average	Yiddi Cappe
Best Power Hitter	Griffin Conine
Best Strike-Zone Discipline	Nasim Nuñez
Fastest Baserunner	Nasim Nuñez
Best Athlete	Kahlil Watson

PITCHING

Best Fastball	Eury Perez
Best Curveball	Zach McCambley
Best Slider	Max Meyer
Best Changeup	Eury Perez
Best Control	Luis Palacios

FIELDING

Best Defensive Catcher	Will Banfield
Best Defensive Infielder	Nasim Nuñez
Best Infield Arm	Nasim Nuñez
Best Defensive Outfielder	Victor Mesa Jr
Best Outfield Arm	Jerar Encarnacion

2022, he added a slider to give his arsenal a more powerful breaking pitch that also would serve as an effective weapon against righthanders. The mid-80s pitch grades as a potential plus offering. Perez's spike curveball is a two-plane breaker that serves as an effective strike-stealer early in counts and grades as at least above-average, though some evaluators have it a tick higher.

THE FUTURE: Perez has the ceiling of a true ace. He's the clear-cut best prospect in Miami's system and a candidate for the sport's best pitching prospect. After a full season at Double-A, Perez should be ready for Triple-A in 2023 and could make his MLB debut before his 21st birthday.

Year	Age	Club (League)	Lvl	W	L	ERA	G	GS	IP	H	HR	BB	SO	BB/9	SO/9	WHIP	AVG
2022	19	Jupiter (FSL)	LoA	0	0	0.00	1	1	2	1	0	0	4	0.0	18.0	0.50	.143
2022	19	Pensacola (SL)	AA	3	3	4.08	17	17	75	62	9	25	106	3.0	12.7	1.16	.223
Minor League Totals				6	8	2.96	38	38	155	106	16	51	218	3.0	12.7	1.01	.190

2 MAX MEYER, RHP

Born: March 12, 1999. **B-T:** L-R. **HT:** 6-0. **WT:** 196.
Drafted: Minnesota, 2020 (1st round). **Signed by:** Shaeffer Hall.

TRACK RECORD: The 2020 season was supposed to be Meyer's time to transition from Minnesota's bullpen to the rotation. Instead, the pandemic happened, and the season was cut short. Still, the Marlins saw enough to draft him No. 3 overall and send him directly to Double-A to start his first season as a pro in 2021. Most questions surrounding Meyer out of the draft involved his ability to hold up as a starter. Those concerns surfaced in 2022, first with a nerve issue in his elbow and eventually Tommy John surgery that ended his season a few starts after his MLB debut.

BA GRADE

55 Risk: High

SCOUTING REPORT: In 2021, Meyer thrived despite an arsenal that was vanilla to open the year but got better as the Double-A Pensacola season wore on. A year later, he emerged with a changeup that had taken a dramatic jump as a perfect third pitch to go with his dynamic fastball/slider combination. Scouts who saw Meyer in the minors were wowed by the power in his arsenal. His fastball sat in the mid 90s and set up a dastardly slider that grades as a legitimate double-plus pitch capable of getting silly swings from talented hitters. The emergence of the changeup came in part because Meyer started to use it more as a third potentially above-average pitch to complete his arsenal rather than the show-me offering when he was in the bullpen. The second component was that Meyer improved his arm speed on his changeup to match what he showed on his other two pitches.

THE FUTURE: Meyer likely will miss all of 2023, leaving Miami in a holding pattern until he, Jake Eder and Sixto Sanchez are healthy again.

SCOUTING GRADES		Fastball: 60		Slider: 70			Changeup: 55			Control: 55				
Year	Age	Club (League)	Lvl	W	L	ERA	G	GS	IP	H	HR	BB	SO	BB/9	SO/9	WHIP	AVG
2022	23	Jupiter (FSL)	LoA	0	0	3.00	1	1	3	1	0	0	4	0.0	12.0	0.33	.091
2022	23	Jacksonville (IL)	AAA	3	4	3.72	12	12	58	39	5	19	65	2.9	10.1	1.00	.188
2022	23	Miami (NL)	MLB	0	1	7.50	2	2	6	7	2	2	6	3.0	9.0	1.50	.292
Major League Totals				0	1	7.50	2	2	6	7	2	2	6	3.0	9.0	1.50	.292
Minor League Totals				9	8	2.77	35	35	172	130	13	61	199	3.2	10.4	1.11	.207

3 JACOB BERRY, 3B

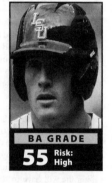

Born: May 5, 2001. **B-T:** B-R. **HT:** 6-0. **WT:** 212.
Drafted: Louisiana State, 2022 (1st round). **Signed by:** Chris Joblin.

TRACK RECORD: After a standout freshman campaign at Arizona, Berry followed his head coach Jay Johnson and transferred to Louisiana State. In the higher-profile Southeastern Conference, Berry continued to mash. He finished with a .370 average and a 1.094 OPS to go with 15 home runs, 27 walks and just 22 strikeouts. His offensive potential was enough for the Marlins to draft him sixth overall and sign him for an even $6 million. He reached Low-A Jupiter in his pro debut.

BA GRADE

55 Risk: High

SCOUTING REPORT: Nearly all of Berry's value lies with his combination of hitting ability, power and plate discipline. The switch-hitter historically makes more impact from the left side, though he had far more success against southpaws in his brief pro debut. In fact, his two home runs against lefties as a pro were one more than he had during the entirety of his draft year at LSU. Berry was also lauded as an amateur for his ability to vary his approach, specifically when it came to going gap-to-gap against elevated fastballs. As a pro, there was some concern about the length of his swing and how it would translate as he rose through the ranks. Defensively, his lack of twitch will likely require a move to first base, though he didn't get any reps at the position at either of his two minor league stops. He's a below-average runner with a throwing arm that grades as a tick below-average as well. Neither of those traits suggests a player who can stick at third base.

THE FUTURE: Berry should start 2022 at High-A Beloit, where he'll be challenged both by the colder climate early in the season and the advanced pitching. His ceiling is a slugger either at first base or DH.

SCOUTING GRADES		Hitting: 55		Power: 60		Speed: 40			Fielding: 30			Arm: 45		
Year	Age	Club (League)	Lvl	AVG	G	AB	R	H	2B	3B	HR	RBI	BB	SO	SB	OBP	SLG
2022	21	Marlins (FCL)	R	.125	4	16	1	2	0	0	0	2	1	6	0	.222	.125
2022	21	Jupiter (FSL)	LoA	.264	33	125	19	33	7	0	3	24	13	23	1	.358	.392
Minor League Totals				.248	37	141	20	35	7	0	3	26	14	29	1	.343	.362

4 JOSE SALAS, SS/3B

Born: April 26, 2003. **B-T:** B-R. **HT:** 6-2. **WT:** 191.
Signed: Venezuela, 2019. **Signed by:** Angel Izquierdo.

TRACK RECORD: Salas split his youth between Orlando and Venezuela, where the Marlins signed him out of in 2019 as part of an international signing class that also includes top prospect Eury Perez. Salas began the 2022 season as part of a well-stocked group of talented middle infielders clustered at the Marlins' lower levels. His balanced skill set helped him emerge as the best of those players and earn a midseason promotion to High-A Beloit. His numbers took a bit of a dip in the Midwest League, but scouts still came away impressed with his broad skill set.

BA GRADE

50 Risk: High

SCOUTING REPORT: Salas is a steady player who won't wow or disappoint in any area. He worked hard with Beloit hitting coach Ty Hawkins to improve the consistency of the movement in his lower half and put himself in better positions to drive the ball with authority. His swings are low-effort and feature minimal moving parts, qualities that should allow him to hit for a high average and sneaky power. His power could be further unlocked by learning how to hit the ball more toward the front of the strike zone. Where Salas lands defensively will depend on the way his body develops as he matures. He's already gotten a little sturdier, which has cost him a bit of foot speed and leads scouts to believe he'll eventually wind up at third base. If that's the case, he has the above-average arm strength to allow him to hold down the position adequately. Salas also catches evaluators' eyes as a player with the strong work ethic to help improve as he ages.

THE FUTURE: A great deal of Salas' defensive future relies on the way his body grows. No matter where he winds up on the diamond, his offensive skills should make him a valuable player.

SCOUTING GRADES		Hitting: 55		Power: 50		Speed: 45		Fielding: 50		Arm: 55			
Year	Age	Club (League)	Lvl	AVG	G	AB	R	H	2B	3B	HR	RBI	BB
2022	19	Jupiter (FSL)	LoA	.267	61	221	40	59	13	3	5	24	23
2022	19	Beloit (MWL)	HiA	.230	48	191	29	44	7	1	4	17	20
Minor League Totals				.268	164	612	95	164	34	4	11	60	65

SO	SB	OBP	SLG
54	15	.355	.421
41	18	.319	.340
146	47	.356	.391

5 YIDDI CAPPE, SS/3B

Born: September 17, 2002. **B-T:** R-R. **HT:** 6-3. **WT:** 175.
Signed: Cuba, 2021. **Signed by:** Marlins international scouting department.

TRACK RECORD: Instead of signing out of Cuba in 2019 when he was first eligible, Cappe waited until teams' bonus pools reset. Then the pandemic happened, and he had to wait a little longer while baseball was in the midst of a shutdown. Once the restrictions were lifted, the 18-year-old Cappe signed with Miami for a bonus of nearly $3 million in January 2021. He opened his career in the Dominican Summer League for tax purposes, then had an excellent U.S. debut in 2022 split between the Florida Complex League and Low-A Jupiter. He hit .305/.364/.517 with six home runs and six stolen bases in 30 games in Rookie ball.

BA GRADE

50 Risk: High

SCOUTING REPORT: Cappe is among the purest hitters in the system and was selected by internal evaluators as the prospect who projects to hit for the highest average. To reach that ceiling, he will have to reduce the rate at which he chases pitches. Scouts note that Cappe has no issue recognizing pitches. Rather, he simply needs to become less eager to swing. He's already got sneaky power and could grow into even more as he packs more muscle onto his lanky frame. He also needs to do a better job using the whole field because his current approach is strongly geared to pull. Cappe is a good athlete with a plus throwing arm that will fit nicely at third base if he has to move as he gets bigger and stronger.

THE FUTURE: If he can iron out his rough edges, Cappe has one of the most intriguing ceilings in the system. Even if he doesn't stick at shortstop, his power potential could allow him to fit nicely as a classic masher at third base.

SCOUTING GRADES		Hitting: 55		Power: 55		Speed: 55		Fielding: 50		Arm: 60			
Year	Age	Club (League)	Lvl	AVG	G	AB	R	H	2B	3B	HR	RBI	BB
2022	19	Marlins (FCL)	R	.305	30	118	23	36	7	0	6	25	9
2022	19	Jupiter (FSL)	LoA	.278	37	158	18	44	5	1	3	15	6
Minor League Totals				.282	121	465	72	131	29	2	11	67	34

SO	SB	OBP	SLG
19	6	.364	.517
22	7	.299	.380
76	22	.328	.424

6 SIXTO SANCHEZ, RHP

Born: July 29, 1998. **B-T:** R-R. **HT:** 6-0. **WT:** 234.
Signed: Dominican Republic, 2015. **Signed by:** Carlos Salas (Phillies).

TRACK RECORD: Sanchez was signed by the Phillies in 2015 and was their top prospect before being traded to the Marlins in February 2019 as the centerpiece of the deal that brought catcher JT Realmuto to Philadelphia. Sanchez dazzled in his MLB debut during the pandemic-shortened 2020 season, showing the stuff to potentially fill a huge hole at the top of Miami's rotation. He took the ball in Game 3 of that year's Division Series, which turned out to be the final game of the Marlins' season. He allowed four runs in three innings in that outing, which proved to be the last time he pitched in an official game. He had surgery in July 2021 to repair a tear in his right shoulder, then spent all of 2022 rehabbing. He had a second surgery on his shoulder in October 2022, this time an arthroscopic bursectomy, and was expected to be ready for 2023 spring training.
SCOUTING REPORT: When he is healthy, Sanchez is absolutely filthy. He slices and dices hitters with a powerful arsenal that features two double-plus pitches in his fastball and changeup as well as a pair of above-average breaking balls. The mix gave him weapons against batters of either hand. Even more impressively, Sanchez showed excellent control and command of his arsenal. Sanchez is rarely healthy, however, and there has been plenty of concern in the past about his overall level of conditioning and fitness. Given Sanchez's lengthy absence, there will be plenty of questions to answer once he returns.
THE FUTURE: If Sanchez makes it to the mound this spring in Jupiter, all eyes will be on him. If his stuff returns intact, he could begin a long climb back to his ceiling as a high-end rotation piece, though the calculus behind his workload will be tricky given his two-year hiatus.

BA GRADE: 55 Risk: Extreme

SCOUTING GRADES:	Fastball: 70	Curveball: 55	Slider: 55	Changeup: 70	Control: 60

Year	Age	Club (League)	Lvl	W	L	ERA	G	GS	IP	H	HR	BB	SO	BB/9	SO/9	WHIP	AVG
2022	23	Did not play—Injured															
Minor League Totals				23	18	2.58	68	59	335	278	9	64	294	1.7	7.9	1.02	.223
Major League Totals				3	2	3.46	7	7	39	36	3	11	33	2.5	7.6	1.21	.250

7 JAKE EDER, LHP

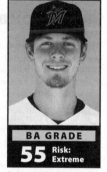

Born: October 9, 1998. **B-T:** L-L. **HT:** 6-4. **WT:** 2015.
Drafted: Vanderbilt, 2020 (4th round). **Signed by:** J.T. Zink.

TRACK RECORD: In 2020, Eder was ready to make his move from the bullpen to the rotation at Vanderbilt. The pandemic prevented that move, but the Marlins were convinced enough to draft him with the fourth of their five picks of the shortened draft that year. The next spring, the Marlins pushed Eder and his fellow draftee Max Meyer to Double-A Pensacola to officially begin their professional careers. Eder rewarded their faith by being one of the biggest breakout stories in the minor leagues before having Tommy John surgery in August 2021.
SCOUTING REPORT: Before the surgery, Eder showed a dynamic two-pitch mix fronted by a one-two punch of a low-to-mid-90s fastball and slider which each project as plus. His fastball had the type of riding life at the top of the strike zone that is coveted today. Eder also showed a strong feel to lengthen and shorten the break on his slider, with the former version looking like a harder curveball. Eder's third pitch, a low-80s changeup, had a ceiling as an average offering with further refinement. A small tweak in the way Eder removed the ball from his glove at the beginning of his delivery helped improve his command and control, which projected as plus before the operation. He is a dedicated student of the game who keeps a journal of what worked and didn't work during each of his starts.
THE FUTURE: Eder missed the entire 2022 season but should be ready in time for spring training in 2023. If his stuff comes back intact, he has the ceiling of a midrotation starter. If he shows the same form, he'll add an element of clarity to the Marlins' long-term rotation picture, which is currently clouded by injuries to Eder, Meyer and righthander Sixto Sanchez.

BA GRADE: 55 Risk: Extreme

SCOUTING GRADES	Fastball: 60	Slider: 60	Changeup: 50	Control: 60

Year	Age	Club (League)	Lvl	W	L	ERA	G	GS	IP	H	HR	BB	SO	BB/9	SO/9	WHIP	AVG
2022	23	Did not play—Injured															
Minor League Totals				3	5	1.77	15	15	71	43	3	27	99	3.4	12.5	0.98	.169

8 DAX FULTON, LHP

Born: October 16, 2001. **B-T:** L-L. **HT:** 6-7. **WT:** 225.
Drafted: HS—Mustang, Okla. (2nd round). **Signed by:** James Vilade.

TRACK RECORD: Fulton was selected in the second round of the pandemic-shortened 2020 draft even though the Marlins knew his development would be a slow burn. He was recovering from Tommy John surgery he had as a high school senior but was healthy enough to pitch during instructional league. He debuted in 2021 and split the season between both Class A levels. Fulton returned to High-A Beloit to begin 2022 and was inconsistent. He turned it on once he was promoted to Double-A Pensacola, where he was magnificent in the season's final month and during the team's run to the Southern League crown. In his only playoff start, versus Montgomery in the semifinals, Fulton went six shutout innings and allowed just a hit and a walk while fanning 13 hitters.

BA GRADE
50 Risk: High

SCOUTING REPORT: Two years removed from Tommy John surgery, Fulton is starting to resemble the pitcher the Marlins believed they were drafting. He worked hard to get back into better shape, which helped improve his stamina and keep his stuff crisp deep into starts. Now, instead of his four-seam fastball sitting in the low 90s and tickling 94-95 mph, it sits in the mid 90s and scrapes 96-97. The Marlins also gave Fulton a two-seamer, which sits in the same range as his four-seamer. His signature offspeed pitch is a powerful 1-to-7 curveball in the high 70s that he's done a better job landing for strikes as well as burying for chases. After tinkering with a changeup grip in 2021, Fulton settled for one that gave him the movement he desired. Now, that pitch, a key to him remaining a starter, projects as a fringe-average offering and could be the key to him sticking in the rotation.

THE FUTURE: The Marlins were pleased with Fulton's late-season breakout and will look for an encore in 2023, when he will likely reach Triple-A. He's got a ceiling as a back-end starter.

SCOUTING GRADES	Fastball: 55	Curveball: 60	Changeup: 45	Control: 50

Year	Age	Club (League)	Lvl	W	L	ERA	G	GS	IP	H	HR	BB	SO	BB/9	SO/9	WHIP	AVG
2022	20	Beloit (MWL)	HiA	5	6	4.07	20	20	97	104	6	35	120	3.2	11.1	1.43	.276
2022	20	Pensacola (SL)	AA	1	1	2.57	4	3	21	9	2	7	30	3.0	12.9	0.76	.125
Minor League Totals				8	12	4.12	44	42	197	184	14	80	234	3.7	10.7	1.34	.248

9 PEYTON BURDICK, OF

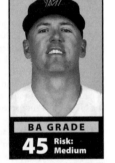

Born: February 26, 1997. **B-T:** R-R. **HT:** 6-0. **WT:** 205.
Drafted: Wright State, 2019 (3rd round). **Signed by:** Nate Adcock.

TRACK RECORD: Burdick's strong junior campaign at Wright State resulted in both the Horizon League's player of the year award and a third-round selection in the 2019 draft. The pandemic's shutdown of the 2020 season meant that Burdick had to wait until 2021 for his full-season debut, which came at Double-A Pensacola in the pitcher-friendly Southern League. Despite the unfriendly atmosphere, Burdick slammed 23 home runs—which tied for the SL lead—before earning a late-season promotion. He returned to Triple-A in 2022 and made his major league debut on Aug. 5.

BA GRADE
45 Risk: Medium

SCOUTING REPORT: Burdick's calling card is his power, which showed up in an average exit velocity of 90 mph during his short stint in the big leagues. To get to that power more often, he'll need to improve his approach. If he tries to use the whole field, he'll likely see big improvements in all aspects of his offensive game. If he continues to focus on trying to hit balls out to the pull side, he'll likely fit more into a power-over-hit profile. He also showed an extreme platoon split in the minors, where he hit just .186 against righthanders over 242 at-bats. Defensively, scouts are split on where he'll wind up. He played all three spots during his time in Miami, with a heavy emphasis on both center and left field. His speed should give him a chance in center field, but scouts differ on whether he can stick at that position.

THE FUTURE: Burdick will have a good shot to make the big league roster out of spring training. If not, he'll head back to Triple-A Jacksonville for more seasoning. He likely fits as a second-division regular.

SCOUTING GRADES	Hitting: 40	Power: 55	Speed: 50	Fielding: 50	Arm: 55

Year	Age	Club (League)	Lvl	AVG	G	AB	R	H	2B	3B	HR	RBI	BB	SO	SB	OBP	SLG
2022	25	Jacksonville (IL)	AAA	.214	99	364	74	78	16	5	15	58	53	120	13	.326	.409
2022	25	Miami (NL)	MLB	.207	32	92	8	19	4	0	4	11	8	35	1	.284	.380
Major League Totals				.207	32	92	8	19	4	0	4	11	8	35	1	.284	.380
Minor League Totals				.242	282	1025	210	248	56	11	49	175	166	338	29	.363	.461

10 JORDAN GROSHANS, SS/3B

Born: November 10, 1999. **B-T:** R-R. **HT:** 6-3. **WT:** 200.
Drafted: HS—Magnolia, Texas, 2018 (1st round). **Signed by:** Brian Johnston (Blue Jays).
TRACK RECORD: Groshans was the Blue Jays' first-round selection in 2018. His pro debut was a smashing success, punctuated by a long home run off Shane McClanahan in the Appalachian League playoffs. A broken foot and the coronavirus pandemic limited him to just 23 games over the next two seasons. When he returned, he showed the same hit-driven offensive profile as he did in his debut. Groshans was dealt to Miami in 2022 for relievers Zach Pop and Anthony Bass. He made his big league debut on Sept. 13.
SCOUTING REPORT: Groshans' big league future will be determined by whether he can unlock his power in games. Scouts believe in his ability to hit because he has short arms that help him get to pitches on the inner half and the timing in his swing to make plenty of contact. He doesn't show much raw power during batting practice, so scouts have had a difficult time figuring out his profile. Groshans is not likely to stick at shortstop, and all his time in the big leagues came at third base. If that's his future home, he needs to make more impact on contact. He has a plus arm and enough quickness and range for third, but some scouts have questioned his mobility and believe he will wind up in left field.
THE FUTURE: Groshans will likely get time at both Triple-A and in the big leagues in 2023. He will be 23 on Opening Day and his professional reps have been limited, so there might be more to unlock.

BA GRADE

50 Risk: High

SCOUTING GRADES		Hitting: 50		Power: 40		Speed: 40		Fielding: 45		Arm: 60	
Year	Age	Club (League)	Lvl	AVG	G	AB	R	H	2B	3B	HR	RBI	BB	SO	SB	OBP	SLG
2022	22	Dunedin (FSL)	LoA	.211	5	19	2	4	1	0	0	0	1	5	0	.250	.263
2022	22	Buffalo (IL)	AAA	.250	67	240	30	60	8	0	1	24	35	46	2	.348	.296
2022	22	Jacksonville (IL)	AAA	.301	31	113	14	34	7	0	2	10	19	19	1	.398	.416
2022	22	Miami (NL)	MLB	.262	17	61	9	16	0	0	1	2	4	13	0	.308	.311
Major League Totals				.262	17	61	9	16	0	0	1	2	4	13	0	.308	.311
Minor League Totals				.285	249	919	125	262	58	0	17	130	117	189	4	.366	.404

11 XAVIER EDWARDS, 2B/SS

Born: August 9, 1999. **B-T:** B-R. **HT:** 5-10. **WT:** 175.
Drafted: HS—Coconut Creek, Fla, 2018 (1st round supplemental). **Signed by:** Brian Cruz (Padres).
TRACK RECORD: Edwards was drafted by the Padres out of high school in 2018 and has been traded twice. First, he was dealt in 2019 to the Rays as part of the Hunter Renfroe swap that also sent Jake Cronenworth to San Diego. In November, after a year bouncing around the infield at Triple-A Durham, Edwards was traded by Tampa Bay to Miami for prospects Marcus Johnson and Santiago Suarez.
SCOUTING REPORT: Edwards doesn't have a particular standout tool, but the Marlins don't have any standout infielders. He competes well in at-bats, makes sound swing decisions and did a good job making plenty of contact, but still projects to have bottom-end power. He's improved defensively at all three non-first base infield positions but fits best at second base because of fringy arm strength and naturally lower arm slot that is better suited for the right side of the infield. The new shift rules should also mitigate some of his lack of standout arm strength. He can hack it on the left side, too, because of a quicker release. Edwards has a solid internal clock but got in trouble when he laid back too often on balls. He is a plus runner who can play average defense at all three infield spots.
THE FUTURE: In Edwards and Jordan Groshans, the Marlins have bought low on two former Top 100 Prospects. Edwards should see the big leagues in 2023 and could be a super-utility player.

BA GRADE: 45/Medium		Hit: 50		Power: 20		Speed: 60		Fielding: 50		Arm: 45	
Year	Age	Club (Leagu	Lvl	AVG	G	AB	R	H	2B	3B	HR	RBI	BB	SO	SB	OBP	SLG
2022	22	Durham (IL)	AAA	.246	93	349	48	86	19	1	5	33	43	75	7	.328	.350
Minor League Totals				.300	340	1302	204	391	58	13	6	119	154	196	82	.373	.379

12 JOE MACK, C

Born: December 27, 2002. **B-T:** L-R. **HT:** 6-1. **WT:** 210.
Drafted: HS—East Amherst, N.Y., 2021 (1st round supplemental). **Signed by:** Alex Smith.
TRACK RECORD: Mack was Miami's second pick in the 2021 draft, following first-rounder Kahlil Watson. He was also the No. 22 player on BA's annual top 500 draft rankings, and the Marlins paid him $2.5

million to forgo a commitment to Clemson. His 2022 regular season was limited to just 35 non-rehab games after a hamstring injury that cropped up toward the end of spring training that cropped up again in the regular season. He made up for the lost time during the Arizona Fall League.

SCOUTING REPORT: Mack profiles as an offensive-minded backup with a strong throwing arm. He hits the ball quite hard—his average exit velocity was 88.2 mph and peaked at 107.6—but needs to shore up his in-zone miss rates a bit. He was a favorite of the Marlins' player-development staff for his ability and desire to learn and immediately process his lessons. Specifically, they wanted to work with him to tweak his approach to help him access his pull-side power more often. Mack is a work in progress defensively and needs to stay more focused from pitch to pitch. His attention sometimes wanders and will lead to clanking catchable balls. He worked from the one-knee setup this year but will likely go back to the traditional crouch in 2023 to allow him to move more fluidly. He's got plus arm strength but caught just 23.2% of runners between the minor leagues and the AFL.

THE FUTURE: Mack will likely move to High-A Beloit in 2023, when he'll look to be more consistent in both his receiving and his offensive approach.

| BA GRADE: 50/High | Hit: 45 | | Power: 55 | | Speed: 30 | | Fielding: 40 | | Arm: 60 | |

Year	Age	Club (League)	Lvl	AVG	G	AB	R	H	2B	3B	HR	RBI	BB	SO	SB	OBP	SLG
2022	19	Marlins (FCL)	R	.296	9	27	2	8	0	0	2	3	4	7	0	.387	.519
2022	19	Jupiter (FSL)	LoA	.231	35	121	18	28	4	1	3	12	29	40	0	.382	.355
Minor League Totals				.214	63	201	29	43	5	1	6	17	53	69	0	.380	.338

13 JACOB MILLER, RHP

Born: August 10, 2003. **B-T:** R-R. **HT:** 6-2. **WT:** 180.
Drafted: HS—Baltimore, Ohio (2nd round). **Signed by:** JT Zink.

TRACK RECORD: Miller first started to gain helium during the 2021 showcase circuit, when his fastball jumped into the low-90s with hints of 94-95 mph. The upward trend continued during his draft year, when he topped out at 97 mph with his fastball. The growing fastball, combined with an excellent ability to spin the ball—his breaking pitches spun between 2,300-2,400 rpm as an amateur—pushed him up draft boards and convinced the Marlins to select him in the second round. He received a signing bonus of $1,697,900 to pry him from his commitment to Louisville.

SCOUTING REPORT: Miller's newfound fastball velocity showed up in his four minor league starts as well. He topped at 95 mph in his lone turn in the Florida State League, where he made his final start of the year. He pairs his fastball with a slider and a curveball, with the latter grading a tick better than the former. As an amateur, both pitches tended to blend with one another. Professional coaches will work to separate them into two distinct pitches. Miller's fourth pitch is a changeup in the mid 80s, and the Marlins are impressed with how much feel he's shown for it despite its seldom use in high school. Miller is not particularly projectable, but he's already shown the ability to repeat his delivery and pound the zone with plenty of strikes. There are some delivery kinks to iron out—specifically a stabbing arm action and a tendency to spin out of his delivery—that could affect his command and consistency. Those will be addressed as he moves up the ladder.

THE FUTURE: Miller made his final start of the season at Low-A Jupiter. He is likely to return there to begin 2022 and has the ceiling of a mid-rotation starter if everything clicks.

| BA GRADE: 55/Extreme | Fastball: 60 | | Curveball: 60 | Slider: 55 | | Changeup: 45 | | Control: 50 | |

Year	Age	Club (League)	Lvl	W	L	ERA	G	GS	IP	H	HR	BB	SO	BB/9	SO/9	WHIP	AVG
2022	18	Marlins (FCL)	R	0	1	7.36	3	3	4	4	1	2	3	4.9	7.4	1.64	.250
2022	18	Jupiter (FSL)	LoA	0	1	0.00	1	1	2	1	0	0	3	0.0	13.5	0.50	.125
Minor League Totals				0	2	4.76	4	4	6	5	1	2	6	3.2	9.5	1.24	.208

14 NASIM NUÑEZ, SS

Born: August 18, 2000. **B-T:** B-R. **HT:** 5-9. **WT:** 158.
Drafted: HS—Suwanee, Ga., 2019 (2nd round). **Signed by:** Christian Castorri.

TRACK RECORD: Nuñez was the Marlins' second-round pick in 2019, when he was one of the best available prep infielders on the board. The Marlins spent $2.2 million to buy him out of his commitment to Clemson but had to wait until 2021 to see him in full-season ball because of the pandemic. He split 2022 between High-A Beloit and Double-A Pensacola and hit his first two career home runs.

SCOUTING REPORT: Nuñez is laden with superlatives. He's the system's best infield defender, has the strongest knowledge of the strike zone and is its fastest runner. He used those skills to draw 95 walks and steal 70 bases—which placed him in a three-way tie for third in the minors. The Marlins worked with Nuñez to be less passive on hittable pitches, and it showed up in the summer months, when he hit .278

from May 1 through July 31 before a promotion to Double-A. The Marlins' player development staff also worked with Nuñez to get him to hit the ball out in front more often. In Nuñez, scouts see a player who can make contact and cause havoc on the bases while playing excellent defense up the middle. He's a smooth defender with excellent first-step quickness and a strong throwing arm that needs a touch more in the way of accuracy.

THE FUTURE: Nuñez will likely reach Triple-A at some point in 2023 and his speed and defense should help him find a way to reach the big leagues as a bottom-of-the-order hitter or defensive replacement.

| BA GRADE: 50/High | | Hit: 40 | | Power: 20 | | Speed: 70 | | Fielding: 55 | | Arm: 60 | |

Year	Age	Club (League)	Lvl	AVG	G	AB	R	H	2B	3B	HR	RBI	BB	SO	SB	OBP	SLG
2022	21	Beloit (MWL)	HiA	.247	85	300	53	74	11	3	2	27	71	103	49	.390	.323
2022	21	Pensacola (SL)	AA	.261	38	142	22	37	6	0	0	14	24	36	21	.371	.303
Minor League Totals				.238	226	816	146	194	24	5	2	63	165	233	131	.367	.287

15 KAHLIL WATSON, SS

Born: April 16, 2003. **B-T:** L-R. **HT:** 5-9. **WT:** 178.
Drafted: HS—Wake Forest, N.C., 2021 (1st round). **Signed by:** Blake Newsome.

TRACK RECORD: There was plenty of surprise around the industry when Watson, who entered the year as one of the top-ranked players available, tumbled all the way to the Marlins at the 16th overall pick. He was as tooled-up as any player on the board and had performed well, so Miami was happy to snatch him up and sign him for $4,540,790. His first full season as a pro was rough and was plagued by both high amounts of swing and miss and an incident that led to a month-long demotion from Low-A.

SCOUTING REPORT: Watson is still as talented as anyone in the system, but he needs a lot of work to turn those skills into production. His bat speed is electric and he makes plenty of impact on contact—his average exit velocity was 87.5 mph—but he still struck out 35% of the time at Low-A. Evaluators will see bright spots in spurts and the Marlins' player-development staff believes he's done a good job taking the lessons from his coaching staff but he sometimes gets too impatient when they don't provide immediate results and starts trying to do too much too soon. More than anything, he needs to be more selective to let his natural fits shine. He chased at a 36% rate and swung and missed in the zone at a 26% rate. He will likely move off of shortstop, though not immediately. Watson has the quick feet and strong arm to play an excellent second base, but he has to clean up his consistency and stay more focused. He's an above-average runner now but might slow down a tick as he ages.

THE FUTURE: Watson will move to High-A Beloit in 2023. He needs a huge rebound to achieve anything close to his original ceiling but the tools are there to be a big leaguer of some stripe one day.

| BA GRADE: 50/Very High | | Hit: 40 | | Power: 55 | | Speed: 50 | | Fielding: 55 | | Arm: 60 | |

Year	Age	Club (League)	Lvl	AVG	G	AB	R	H	2B	3B	HR	RBI	BB	SO	SB	OBP	SLG
2022	19	Marlins (FCL)	R	.273	5	11	4	3	2	0	1	3	5	5	0	.500	.727
2022	19	Jupiter (FSL)	LoA	.231	83	324	50	75	16	5	9	44	27	127	16	.296	.395
Minor League Totals				.247	97	368	67	91	21	7	10	52	40	139	20	.328	.424

16 KARSON MILBRANDT, RHP

Born: April 21, 2004. **B-T:** R-R. **HT:** 6-2. **WT:** 190.
Drafted: HS—Liberty, Mo., 2022 (3rd round). **Signed by:** Ryan Cisterna.

TRACK RECORD: Milbrandt's draft stock started rising at the 2021 Area Code Games, where his mix of present stuff and projectability caught the eyes of scouts. He carried that momentum into his senior season at Liberty (Mo.) High and impressed the Marlins enough for them to select him with their third-round selection, the second in Miami's run of 12 consecutive pitchers drafted after first-rounder Jacob Berry. The former Vanderbilt commit signed for $1,497,500 and made one start in the Low-A Florida State League to get his feet wet as a professional.

SCOUTING REPORT: Milbrandt works from a full windup and delivers from a three-quarters slot. From there, he typically delivers fastballs in the 90-94 mph range, though he began touching a few ticks higher toward season's end and peaked at 96 in his only pro start. He backs the fastball with a full complement of offspeed pitches, including a pair of potentially above-average breaking balls. Both pitches have 11-to-5 shape, with the biggest difference coming via velocity. The slider is thrown in the low 80s and the curveball checks in a few ticks lower, typically around 75-78 mph, though it was a touch hotter in the Florida State League. He rounds out his arsenal with a potentially average, fading changeup that he sells well through a consistent, repeatable arm action. The Marlins are particularly intrigued by Milbrandt's size and project-ability. Once he gets bigger and stronger, they expect his stuff to tick up in kind. The cleanliness and

repeatability in Milbrandt's delivery leads evaluators to believe he could develop above-average control.
THE FUTURE: Milbrandt's only official start came with Low-A Jupiter, where he's likely to return in 2023. His present stuff and projectability give him a high ceiling that could land him in a big league rotation.

BA GRADE: 50/Extreme		Fastball: 60		Curveball: 55		Slider: 55			Changeup: 50		Control: 55	
Year	Age	Club (League)	Lvl	W	L	ERA	G	GS	IP	H	HR	BB	SO	BB/9	SO/9	WHIP	AVG

Year	Age	Club (League)	Lvl	W	L	ERA	G	GS	IP	H	HR	BB	SO	BB/9	SO/9	WHIP	AVG
2022	18	Jupiter (FSL)	LoA	0	0	9.00	1	1	2	2	0	1	1	4.5	4.5	1.50	.250
Minor League Totals				0	0	9.00	1	1	2	2	0	1	1	4.5	4.5	1.50	.250

17 NIC ENRIGHT, RHP

Born: January 8, 1997. **B-T:** R-R. **HT:** 6-3. **WT:** 205.
Drafted: Virginia Tech, 2019 (20th round). **Signed by:** Pete Loizzo (Guardians).
TRACK RECORD: Enright was drafted out of high school in 2015 by the Mets but opted to head to Virginia Tech. He pitched three years with the Hokies in a predominantly reliever's role before Cleveland called his name in the 20th round of the 2019 draft. Enright advanced quickly through the minors and spent all of 2022 at the upper levels, where he racked up 11.9 strikeouts and just 1.9 walks per nine innings. He was taken by Miami in the 2022 Rule 5 draft.
SCOUTING REPORT: Enright was attractive to the Marlins as a plug-and-play reliever with a high amount of success at every stop. He mixes a low-90s fastball that peaks at 94 and shows outstanding carry through the zone. The life on his fastball, coupled with Enright's ability to command it in the zone, helps it play well beyond its radar gun readings. He backs the fastball primarily with a low-80s slider that functions as an excellent out pitch and got whiffs 52% of the time. He also sprinkles in a mid-80s changeup and a mid-70s curve. Enright ties the arsenal together with plus control.
THE FUTURE: Enright was taken in the Rule 5, so he'll get plenty of chances to succeed in the big league bullpen. He has a ceiling of a middle-innings reliever.

BA GRADE: 40/Medium		Fastball: 55		Curveball: 30		Slider: 60			Changeup: 30		Control: 60	

Year	Age	Club (League)	Lvl	W	L	ERA	G	GS	IP	H	HR	BB	SO	BB/9	SO/9	WHIP	AVG
2022	25	Akron (EL)	AA	1	1	3.14	19	0	29	19	2	8	37	2.5	11.6	0.94	.186
2022	25	Columbus (IL)	AAA	4	0	2.68	29	1	37	30	5	6	50	1.5	12.2	0.97	.216
Minor League Totals				9	8	2.80	97	1	142	100	13	35	201	2.2	12.8	0.95	.193

18 IAN LEWIS, 2B

Born: February 4, 2003. **B-T:** B-R. **HT:** 5-10. **WT:** 177.
Signed: Bahamas, 2019. **Signed by:** Adrian Lorenzo.
TRACK RECORD: Lewis is part of a growing cadre of players from the Bahamas, including current Marlins second baseman Jazz Chisholm. He is also enmeshed amid a pack of talented middle infielders at the lower levels of Miami's system. After a strong 2021 season in the Rookie-level Florida Complex League, Lewis put together a solid but not spectacular first turn at full-season ball in the Florida State League, which ended early because of an injury to his hamate bone that required season-ending surgery.
SCOUTING REPORT: Lewis' move to the FSL didn't begin until May 10, but he showed flashes of his potential the rest of the way. He's far too aggressive at the plate, swinging nearly 56% of the time and chasing at a 39% rate. That approach was somewhat mitigated by strong hand-eye coordination and bat-to-ball skills that allowed him to strike out just 45 times in 213 plate appearances. He's wiry strong as well, as shown by average and max exit velocities of 86.4 mph and 109.6, respectively. If he tones down his approach and stops hunting home runs, that raw strength will play better. Lewis needs plenty of refinement in the field, where he bounced mainly between second and third base. Scouts believe all the movement led to some inconsistencies, including taking bad angles to the ball. His arm isn't strong enough to play third base so he'll likely settle in at second, where his offensive skills would profile just fine. He's an above-average runner.
THE FUTURE: Lewis might return to Low-A in 2023 because of the numbers game at High-A Beloit and the small sample he got in 2022 before his injury. No matter the level, he needs to tone down his aggressiveness and become more consistent in the field.

BA GRADE: 45/High		Hit: 40		Power: 55		Speed: 55		Fielding: 40		Arm: 40	

Year	Age	Club (League)	Lvl	AVG	G	AB	R	H	2B	3B	HR	RBI	BB	SO	SB	OBP	SLG
2022	19	Jupiter (FSL)	LoA	.265	51	185	21	49	7	3	2	21	22	45	16	.347	.368
Minor League Totals				.281	94	334	45	94	17	8	5	48	33	69	25	.350	.425

19 ANTONY PEGUERO, OF

Born: June 14, 2005. **B-T:** R-R. **HT:** 6-0. **WT:** 175.
Signed: Dominican Republic, 2022. **Signed by:** Domingo Ortega/Fernando Seguignol.

TRACK RECORD: Peguero was one of the gems of Miami's most recent international class, joining Jose Gerardo in that group. As an amateur, Peguero was lauded for a simple swing, excellent bat speed and outstanding raw power. He also did well against live pitching. Peguero started his career in the Dominican Summer League, where he showed a power-based skill set with plenty of contact.

SCOUTING REPORT: Peguero is the most well-rounded of all the players in Miami's most recent international class. He's got big-time bat speed with excellent bat-to-ball skills and power that projects a fringe-average now but could get a tick higher as he fills out and gets stronger. Peguero needs to tone down his swing-happy approach and greatly improve his rates of chase and in-zone miss. He moves around well in center field but is likely to head a corner spot as his body thickens up. If that happens, his above-average speed and potentially plus arm will fit nicely in right field, though that will make the further development of his power even more pressing.

THE FUTURE: Peguero will head stateside in 2023, with a trip to the Florida Complex League on the docket. He has a chance to be an everyday corner outfielder with further improvement of his hittability.

BA GRADE: 50/Extreme	Hit: 50	Power: 45	Speed: 55	Fielding: 50	Arm: 60

Year	Age	Club (Leagu	Lvl	AVG	G	AB	R	H	2B	3B	HR	RBI	BB	SO	SB	OBP	SLG
2022	17	Miami (DSL)	R	.286	50	196	24	56	10	1	5	33	13	35	7	.355	.423
Minor League Totals				.286	50	196	24	56	10	1	5	33	13	35	7	.355	.423

20 MARCO VARGAS, 2B

Born: May 14, 2005. **B-T:** L-R. **HT:** 6-0. **WT:** 170.
Signed: Mexico, 2022. **Signed by:** Andres Guzman/Adrian Puig.

TRACK RECORD: Vargas signed later in the process than most of his peers, inking his deal with the Marlins on May 25, more than four months after the opening of the most recent international period. It all came together when the Marlins realized their talent pool was outfielder-heavy and they needed infielders for their second DSL club. Vargas was attempting to get noticed as a catcher but had enough infield chops to garner a contract. He put together an outstanding first season as a pro in the DSL.

SCOUTING REPORT: The first thing that stands out about Vargas is his excellent bat-to-ball skills. He whiffed just 13.8% of the time in the DSL, including a scintillating rate of just 9% miss within the strike zone. There's a pinch of impact there, too, with 18 extra-base hits and a 90th percentile exit velocity of 97.8 mph. Internal evaluators also note excellent barrel accuracy that helps him hold his own against both fastballs and secondaries in all quadrants of the strike zone. He bounced around the infield in 2022, with most of his reps at third base and then a near-equal split between shortstop and second base. He's likely to wind up at second, where his average speed and arm strength will play. He's a fair athlete with solid actions on the infield.

THE FUTURE: Vargas will move to the Florida Complex League in 2023. He has the ceiling of an everyday second baseman with above-average hittability and a bit of impact.

BA GRADE: 50/Extreme	Hit: 55	Power: 45	Speed: 50	Fielding: 40	Arm: 50

Year	Age	Club (Leagu	Lvl	AVG	G	AB	R	H	2B	3B	HR	RBI	BB	SO	SB	OBP	SLG
2022	17	Miami (DSL)	R	.319	53	182	30	58	13	3	2	38	35	32	14	.421	.456
Minor League Totals				.319	53	182	30	58	13	3	2	38	35	32	14	.421	.456

21 JOSE GERARDO, OF

Born: June 12, 2005. **B-T:** R-R. **HT:** 6-1. **WT:** 179.
Signed: Dominican Republic, 2022. **Signed by:** Sahir Fersobe/Adrian Lorenzo.

TRACK RECORD: The Marlins' most recent international signing class was headed by Gerardo and fellow outfielder Antony Peguero. Gerardo was initially identified as part of the weekly tryouts the Marlins hold at their Dominican Academy. He stuck out for his loose, athletic actions, and the team's pitching staff liked the cleanliness of his arm stroke so much that they wanted to see what he could do on the mound. His offensive gifts were too great, however, and he put together a fine debut season in the DSL.

SCOUTING REPORT: Despite an average frame, Gerardo has excellent hip and shoulder mobility and generates plenty of torque that helps him impact the baseball. His 11 home runs were tied for third in the DSL, and his 91 total bases and 24 extra-base hits each also placed among the league's top 10. The impact is there, but now he needs to shore up his swing decisions. He struck out at a roughly 30% rate in the DSL, with a vulnerability to breaking balls. He's got fringe-average speed, which should allow him to stay in center field for a while, but he ultimately fits in in right field with a double-plus arm. His footwork and route-running need to improve for his defense to get to even fringe-average.

THE FUTURE: Gerardo's next stop is the Florida Complex League, where he'll work to clean up his swing decisions and outfield defense in the hopes of becoming bat-first right fielder for a second-division club.

| BA GRADE: 50/Extreme | | Hit: 30 | | Power: 55 | | Speed: 45 | | Fielding: 40 | | Arm: 70 | |

Year	Age	Club (League)	Lvl	AVG	G	AB	R	H	2B	3B	HR	RBI	BB	SO	SB	OBP	SLG
2022	17	Marlins (DSL)	R	.284	50	176	44	50	12	1	11	31	33	66	18	.417	.551
Minor League Totals				.284	50	176	44	50	12	1	11	31	33	66	18	.417	.551

22 BRYAN HOEING, RHP

Born: October 19, 1996. **B-T:** R-R. **HT:** 6-6. **WT:** 210.
Drafted: Louisville, 2019 (7th round). **Signed by:** Nate Adcock.

TRACK RECORD: Hoeing was drafted out of high school by the D-backs in 2015 but opted to head to Louisville. He was drafted again in 2018, this time by the Giants, but returned to school. He finally turned pro a year later, when Miami called his name in the seventh round and signed him for $227,200. The tall, athletic righthander made his big league debut on Aug. 20 and made eight appearances.

SCOUTING REPORT: Hoeing cuts an intimidating presence on the mound from his 6-foot-6 frame but does not possess the kind of blowaway velocity one would expect from a man his size. Instead, he relies on command and control of a mix built around a sinker-slider combination. The former pitch sits around 92 and touches 94 while the latter comes in about 10 mph slower. He altered the grip on his slider before the 2022 season and now puts more pressure on his middle finger during the pitch. He rounds out his arsenal with a mid-80s changeup and a four-seam fastball in roughly the same velocity range as his sinker.

THE FUTURE: Hoeing is largely a finished product and fits best as a spot starter or bulk reliever. He'll likely bounce between Triple-A and the big leagues.

| BA GRADE: 40/Medium | | Fastball: 45 | | Slider: 50 | | Changeup: 40 | | Control: 45 | |

Year	Age	Club (League)	Lvl	W	L	ERA	G	GS	IP	H	HR	BB	SO	BB/9	SO/9	WHIP	AVG
2022	25	Pensacola (SL)	AA	2	1	0.35	4	4	26	20	0	4	26	1.4	9.1	0.94	.211
2022	25	Jacksonville (IL)	AAA	7	5	5.07	18	17	94	100	14	35	49	3.4	4.7	1.44	.280
2022	25	Miami (NL)	MLB	1	1	12.08	8	1	13	19	5	5	6	3.6	4.3	1.89	.352
Major League Totals				1	1	12.08	8	1	13	19	5	5	6	3.6	4.3	1.89	.352
Minor League Totals				16	14	4.45	53	43	263	276	28	68	188	2.3	6.4	1.31	.269

23 JERAR ENCARNACION, OF

Born: October 22, 1997. **B-T:** R-R. **HT:** 6-4. **WT:** 250.
Signed: Dominican Republic, 2015. **Signed by:** Alberto Encarnacion/Sandy Nin.

TRACK RECORD: Encarnacion signed in 2015 and slowly wound his way through the system before a breakout in 2019. He missed a chance for an encore in 2020 because of the pandemic and had his 2021 season severely curtailed by injuries. He made his MLB debut on June 19 and homered in his first game.

SCOUTING REPORT: Encarnacion is a big man with big power and a big throwing arm who reminds some evaluators of the Reds Aristides Aquino. His raw power is elite but he is unlikely to tap into it particularly often in games because of an extremely aggressive approach and long arms that leave him vulnerable to pitches both in and out of the zone. Encarnacion mashed lefties in Triple-A but was severely neutralized by righthanders, against whom he produced an OPS of just .678. He's a decent enough athlete but not a particularly nimble defender who evaluators noted tended to let a lot of balls drop. His arm is an equalizer and grades out to easily double-plus if not a true 80. He also began getting reps at first base at Triple-A.

THE FUTURE: Encarnacion is a finished product and likely fits best as a platoon outfielder who needs a caddy on defense. He should bounce back and forth between Triple-A and Miami in 2023.

| BA GRADE: 40/Medium | | Hit: 30 | | Power: 60 | | Speed: 40 | | Fielding: 30 | | Arm: 70 | |

Year	Age	Club (League)	Lvl	AVG	G	AB	R	H	2B	3B	HR	RBI	BB	SO	SB	OBP	SLG
2022	24	Pensacola (SL)	AA	.358	31	120	26	43	3	0	8	18	13	35	4	.426	.583
2022	24	Jacksonville (IL)	AAA	.265	68	264	43	70	12	0	14	40	29	87	0	.333	.470
2022	24	Miami (NL)	MLB	.182	23	77	7	14	3	0	3	14	3	32	2	.210	.338
Major League Totals				.182	23	77	7	14	3	0	3	14	3	32	2	.210	.338
Minor League Totals				.263	414	1573	219	414	76	8	57	217	127	506	19	.323	.430

24 JOSH SIMPSON, LHP

Born: August 19, 1997. **B-T:** L-L. **HT:** 6-2. **WT:** 190.
Drafted: Columbia, 2019 (32nd round). **Signed by:** Dana Duquette.

TRACK RECORD: Simpson pitched three seasons at Columbia and was signed for $25,000 in the 32nd round of the 2019 draft. He missed the 2018 season with Tommy John surgery but rebounded the following spring to go 4-3, 3.06 with the Lions in 10 starts. He's made a handful of starts as a pro but the bulk of his work has been out of the bullpen. The Marlins added him to the 40-man roster after the 2022 season.

SCOUTING REPORT: Simpson works predominantly with two pitches: a four-seam fastball that sits around 95 mph and touches a few ticks higher and a nasty sweeper curveball in the low 80s. He works with a curveball-heavy approach and threw the breaker 56% of the time. Considering the curveball garnered a whiff rate of 50%, the philosophy seems sound. He also very sparingly sprinkled in a low-90s cutter as an extra weapon against righthanders, who hit him hard in a small sample at Triple-A. He needs to iron out his control and command—specifically of his fastball—to have success in the big leagues. He issued fewer walks but allowed more hits after a promotion from Double-A Pensacola to Triple-A Jacksonville.

THE FUTURE: Simpson is likely to return to Jacksonville for more seasoning but could fit as a middle-innings reliever—especially against lefties—if he makes gains with his control and command.

| **BA GRADE:** 40/Medium | **Fastball:** 55 | | **Curveball:** 60 | **Cutter:** 30 | | **Control:** 40 | | | |

Year	Age	Club (League)	Lvl	W	L	ERA	G	GS	IP	H	HR	BB	SO	BB/9	SO/9	WHIP	AVG
2022	24	Pensacola (SL)	AA	5	2	3.88	40	0	56	31	5	29	89	4.7	14.4	1.08	.164
2022	24	Jacksonville (IL)	AAA	2	0	4.38	10	0	12	10	0	5	23	3.6	16.8	1.22	.233
Minor League Totals				8	4	4.31	85	5	138	101	11	59	200	3.9	13.1	1.16	.203

25 GEORGE SORIANO, RHP

Born: March 24, 1999. **B-T:** R-R. **HT:** 6-2. **WT:** 210.
Signed: Dominican Republic, 2015. **Signed by:** Albert Gonzalez/Sandy Nin.

TRACK RECORD: Soriano was signed out of the Dominican Republic in 2015 for $55,000 and has slowly made his way through the minor leagues. He broke out in 2022, starting with Double-A Pensacola, where he saw a boost in fastball velocity. From there, he took off and finished the year with eight appearances (six starts) at Triple-A. He was added to the Marlins' 40-man roster to keep him from becoming a minor league free agent.

SCOUTING REPORT: Soriano's fastball jump was key to his breakout at Pensacola. By season's end, the pitch averaged 96 mph and touched triple-digits with excellent life at the top of the zone. Soriano backed it up with a high-spin, mid-80s slider that garnered plenty of whiffs and chases. He has a high-80s changeup but needs it to improve to give him a better chance against lefthanders. He needs to tighten his fastball command and overall control, as shown by his 4.7 walks per nine innings between both stops. Soriano also worked throughout the year to keep his front side firm. When it got too loose, his arm slot would drop and the life on his pitches would suffer.

THE FUTURE: Soriano's addition to the 40-man roster means he'll likely get his first big league look in 2023. He fits best as a middle-innings reliever but will need to improve his control to reach that ceiling.

| **BA GRADE:** 40/Medium | **Fastball:** 60 | | **Slider:** 55 | | **Changeup:** 30 | **Control:** 30 | | | |

Year	Age	Club (League)	Lvl	W	L	ERA	G	GS	IP	H	HR	BB	SO	BB/9	SO/9	WHIP	AVG
2022	23	Pensacola (SL)	AA	0	2	3.10	8	6	29	25	2	17	36	5.3	11.2	1.45	.227
2022	23	Jacksonville (IL)	AAA	4	2	2.49	32	0	47	31	2	23	49	4.4	9.4	1.15	.194
Minor League Totals				18	19	3.29	109	56	383	325	23	164	390	3.9	9.2	1.28	.227

26 SEAN REYNOLDS, RHP

Born: April 19, 1998. **B-T:** L-R. **HT:** 6-8. **WT:** 240.
Drafted: HS—Redondo Beach, CA, 2016 (4th round). **Signed by:** Tim McDonnell.

TRACK RECORD: In high school, Reynolds intrigued evaluators as a two-way prospect. He touched 92 mph with his fastball by his senior year and showed raw power at the plate, albeit with a swing with length and holes that would be exploited as a pro. He was drafted as a hitter but converted to pitching in 2021 and proved himself valuable enough on the mound to earn a spot on the 40-man roster to avoid minor league free agency.

SCOUTING REPORT: Reynolds is a big man with a big arm. His four-seamer averaged 96 mph and touched 100 mph with excellent life at the top of the zone. Some scouts were willing to go as high as a true 80 on the pitch. He backs it up with a curveball and a changeup, both of which have their moments. Reynolds has a decent enough feel for spin but often will cast the curveball, which parks in the low 80s and has a spin rate around 2,400 rpm. His changeup averages around 88 mph and is the third pitch in his mix. He has fringe-average control.

THE FUTURE: Reynolds is still kicking the rust off as a pitcher, but his stuff is plenty intriguing, especially his fastball. He likely fits as an extra arm out of the pen who can blow away hitters.

BA GRADE: 40/Medium   **Fastball:** 70   **Curveball:** 40   **Changeup:** 40   **Control:** 45

Year	Age	Club (League)	Lvl	W	L	ERA	G	GS	IP	H	HR	BB	SO	BB/9	SO/9	WHIP	AVG
2022	24	Beloit (MWL)	HiA	0	1	3.25	26	0	28	17	2	14	39	4.6	12.7	1.12	.170
2022	24	Pensacola (SL)	AA	2	0	5.11	24	0	25	22	3	10	27	3.6	9.9	1.30	.234
Minor League Totals				4	2	3.74	69	0	84	65	5	47	103	5.0	11.0	1.33	.206

27 ZACH McCAMBLEY, RHP

Born: May 4, 1999. **B-T:** L-R. **HT:** 6-2. **WT:** 220.
Drafted: Coastal Carolina, 2020 (3rd round). **Signed by:** Blake Newsome.

TRACK RECORD: McCambley was one of the better college arms available in the 2020 class but always came with significant risk of moving to the pen. He spent two seasons with Coastal Carolina and a summer on the Cape before the pandemic cut short his junior year with the Chanticleers. The Marlins popped him in the third round and signed him for $775,000. He reached the upper levels for the first time in 2022.

SCOUTING REPORT: McCambley is the owner of a low-to-mid-90s four-seam fastball and a high-80s curveball that internal evaluators rank as the organization's best. The curve is a true 12-to-6 breaker with average spin rates around 2,600 rpm and a whiff rate better than 50%. McCambley also has a changeup, but scouts were not impressed by it overall. The Marlins want to see the pitch take a step forward. If not, McCambley likely heads to the pen. He also walked five hitters per nine innings, which equates to well below-average control. The issue might stem from an uptempo, high-effort delivery that is not often found in big league starters.

THE FUTURE: McCambley will move to Triple-A in 2023 and likely has a future as a middle-innings reliever. A bullpen move might give him a velocity boost and could mask some of his control issues.

BA GRADE: 40/High   **Fastball:** 50   **Curveball:** 55   **Changeup:** 30   **Control:** 30

Year	Age	Club (League)	Lvl	W	L	ERA	G	GS	IP	H	HR	BB	SO	BB/9	SO/9	WHIP	AVG
2022	23	Pensacola (SL)	AA	6	8	5.65	19	19	94	83	12	52	101	5.0	9.7	1.44	.237
Minor League Totals				9	18	4.99	39	39	191	176	33	78	221	3.7	10.4	1.33	.243

28 FRANKLIN SANCHEZ, RHP

Born: September 12, 2000. **B-T:** R-R. **HT:** 6-6. **WT:** 183.
Signed: Dominican Republic, 2019. **Signed by:** Gerardo Cabrera (Mets).

TRACK RECORD: Cabrera was inked by the Mets out of the Dominican Republic in 2019, the same class as Alexander Ramirez. Sanchez signed late in the period, on Halloween, more than three months after it opened. He made stops on the development list and injured list in 2022 and ultimately pitched just 35.2 innings in the regular season. He made up for those lost innings in the Arizona Fall League and then was traded to the Marlins in the deal that sent Elieser Hernandez and Jeff Brigham to the Mets.

SCOUTING REPORT: Sanchez is primarily a two-pitch reliever prospect who pairs a hard, sinking fastball in the high 90s with a hard-darting slider in the low 90s. His fastball touched 100 mph in the AFL. He also added a four-seamer in the upper 90s. He has a tough time finding the zone—his strike rate at High-A Brooklyn was just 57%—because of a frenetic delivery with lots of moving parts and a head whack. Still, all of his pitches show late life, giving him the upside of a late-inning option if he can throw more strikes as he moves up the ladder. If his control doesn't improve, he could be a lower-leverage option.

THE FUTURE: Sanchez should reach the upper levels for the first time at some point in 2023. He'll need to smooth out his delivery to harness his enviable mix and reach his ceiling.

BA GRADE: 40/High   **Fastball:** 60   **Slider:** 60   **Control:** 30

Year	Age	Club (League)	Lvl	W	L	ERA	G	GS	IP	H	HR	BB	SO	BB/9	SO/9	WHIP	AVG
2022	21	St. Lucie (FSL)	LoA	1	1	3.90	13	7	30	22	1	17	37	5.1	11.1	1.30	.204
2022	21	Brooklyn (SAL)	HiA	1	1	3.18	4	0	6	6	0	4	5	6.4	7.9	1.76	.286
Minor League Totals				4	5	4.97	34	8	63	49	1	42	77	6.0	10.9	1.44	.215

29 BYRON CHOURIO, OF

Born: May 20, 2005. **B-T:** B-R. **HT:** 6-2. **WT:** 171.
Signed: Venezuela, 2022. **Signed by:** Fernando Seguignol/Nestor Moreno.
TRACK RECORD: Chourio was a part of the Marlins' most recent international signing class and was lauded as an amateur for his remaining physical projection and balanced set of swings from both sides of the plate. He signed in June, then put together an excellent debut in the Dominican Summer League, where his .344 average, 63 hits and 47 runs each placed among the circuit's top 10.
SCOUTING REPORT: Chourio has a long way to go but showed some intriguing signs for a player his age. First, his swing decisions were sound and finished with nearly as many walks (25) as strikeouts (27) while producing an in-zone miss rate of just 12%. Chourio didn't hit the ball particularly hard, but the Marlins expect that to improve as he gains strength. They are also heartened by the natural loft in his swing as well as his strong, quick hands. Chourio's above-average speed and above-average arm should help him stick in center field as he moves up the ladder, which would be a great help to his profile and put less pressure on his ability to develop power.
THE FUTURE: Chourio should come to the U.S. in 2023, when he'll continue to work toward adding strength and power to his game in an effort to enhance his overall profile and give himself a spot in the big leagues.

BA GRADE: 45/Extreme	Hit: 45	Power: 40	Speed: 55	Fielding: 50	Arm: 55

Year	Age	Club (League)	Lvl	AVG	G	AB	R	H	2B	3B	HR	RBI	BB	SO	SB	OBP	SLG
2022	17	Marlins (DSL)	R	.344	51	183	47	63	9	0	1	23	25	27	19	.429	.410
Minor League Totals				.344	51	183	47	63	9	0	1	23	25	27	19	.429	.410

30 PAUL McINTOSH, C

Born: November 20, 1997. **B-T:** R-R. **HT:** 6-1. **WT:** 220.
Signed: West Virginia , 2021 (NDFA). **Signed by:** Alex Smith.
TRACK RECORD: McIntosh is the king of Morgantown. The catcher spent three seasons behind the plate for the University of West Virginia, then spent time after graduating with West Virginia of the MLB Draft League. The Marlins signed him out of the Draft League and sent him to Low-A for his first taste of pro ball. He spent all of 2022 with Double-A Pensacola, where he put up excellent numbers for a player in a pitcher's league.
SCOUTING REPORT: McIntosh is a fringy prospect to be sure, but coaches and player-development staff inside the Marlins rave about his makeup and believe there might just be enough bat to get him to the big leagues. He makes plenty of contact—he struck out just 19.6% of the time in the Southern League—and hits the ball plenty hard, with average and 90th percentile exit velocities of 87 mph and 107 mph, respectively. He makes sound decisions as well and walked at 14% clip. He's got plenty of strength and a good bat path, but internal evaluators acknowledge he has a hole at the top of the strike zone. McIntosh has plenty of work to do defensively as well. He has well below-average arm strength and accuracy and the team has worked with him to get better grips on balls for throws to second base, where he caught just 15% of attempted base stealers. He also saw time at first base and DH but puts in plenty of work behind the plate.
THE FUTURE: If McIntosh gets to the big leagues, it will be because of his offense. He'll move to Triple-A in 2023 in the hopes he can keep it rolling with the bat and improve his defense enough to make himself an option.

BA GRADE: 40/High	Hit: 40	Power: 50	Speed: 30	Fielding: 30	Arm: 30

Year	Age	Club (League)	Lvl	AVG	G	AB	R	H	2B	3B	HR	RBI	BB	SO	SB	OBP	SLG
2022	24	Pensacola (SL)	AA	.258	90	318	66	82	25	1	13	51	55	75	10	.379	.465
Minor League Totals				.256	114	394	80	101	31	3	19	71	70	95	10	.382	.495

Milwaukee Brewers

BY BEN BADLER

While the Brewers have churned out quality major league pitchers from their farm system, the organization has struggled to develop homegrown hitters.

Their pitching pipeline has yielded Brandon Woodruff, Corbin Burnes, Devin Williams and Aaron Ashby—all Brewers draft picks—plus Freddy Peralta, whom they acquired from the Mariners in a trade when he was a teenager in Rookie ball.

On the hitting side, it's been quiet. Some of their draft picks, like outfielders Mitch Haniger and Trent Grisham—have found success in other organizations, but homegrown hitters have delivered minimal value to the lineup.

As the Brewers went 29-31 from August on to finish 86-76 and one game out of a National League wild card, the team received little help from rookie contributors, particularly on the hitting side.

All of that is about to change in 2023. Today, the Brewers farm system leans heavily on hitters, with several who should factor into the major league picture this season. Center fielder Sal Frelick, the 15th overall pick in the 2021 draft and No. 2 prospect in the system, flew through three levels to reach Triple-A in 2022 and showed outstanding contact skills and speed.

Joey Wiemer, their No. 3 prospect, is an athletic 6-foot-5 outfielder with well above-average raw power who runs well enough where he could be another option in center field, though right field is more likely. He has more swing-and-miss risk, but he hit .287/.368/.520 in 43 games in Triple-A and should factor into the 2023 picture. Center fielder Garrett Mitchell, No. 5 in the system, saw brief time in Milwaukee last season and gives them another rookie outfielder in the 2023 mix.

Perhaps the most polished of their likely 2023 rookies is shortstop Brice Turang, who has 779 plate appearances at Triple-A. His skill set is emblematic of a focus the Brewers have put at the amateur level on high-contact hitters who make good swing decisions. While he doesn't project to be a big power hitter, his 13 home runs in 2022 were a career high.

That's all before getting to the crown jewel of the farm system, Jackson Chourio, a potential superstar. The Brewers have put a heavy emphasis on scouting Venezuela and may have hit the jackpot with Chourio, a $1.8 million signing in Jan. 2021.

As an 18-year-old in his first full season, Chourio dazzled with his combination of power, speed and maturity at the plate and reached Double-A at the end of the season. He might not figure into the

Lefthander Aaron Ashby could be the next Brewers pitching development success story.

PROJECTED 2026 LINEUP

Catcher	Jeferson Quero	23
First Base	Rowdy Tellez	31
Second Base	Brice Turang	26
Third Base	Luis Urias	29
Shortstop	Willy Adames	30
Left Field	Sal Frelick	26
Center Field	Jackson Chourio	22
Right Field	Joey Wiemer	27
Designated Hitter	Christian Yelich	34
No. 1 Starter	Corbin Burnes	31
No. 2 Starter	Brandon Woodruff	33
No. 3 Starter	Freddy Peralta	30
No. 4 Starter	Aaron Ashby	28
No. 5 Starter	Jacob Misiorowski	24
Closer	Devin Williams	31

major league picture until 2024, though the rare players with his talent level have a way of bulldozing typical timetables.

Milwaukee's Top 10 Prospects are almost entirely hitters, with the pitching in the minors now fairly light.

Righthander Jacob Misiorowski, a second-round pick in 2022, has high-octane stuff that comes with wild control. Acquiring lefthander Robert Gasser from the Padres in the 2022 trade deadline deal for Josh Hader gives the Brewers a solid rotation option at the upper levels. Beyond them, their best pitching prospects are relievers or pitchers who otherwise project to move to the bullpen. ∎

DEPTH CHART

MILWAUKEE BREWERS

TOP 2023 MLB CONTRIBUTORS   **RANK**
Sal Frelick, OF — 2
Joey Wiemer, OF — 3
Brice Turang, SS — 4

BREAKOUT PROSPECTS   **RANK**
Robert Moore, 2B — 12
Luis Lara, OF — 13
Daniel Guilarte, SS — 21

SOURCE OF TOP 30 TALENT

Homegrown	27	Acquired	3
College	9	Trade	3
Junior college	2	Rule 5 draft	0
High school	4	Independent league	0
Nondrafted free agent	0	Free agent/waivers	0
International	12		

LF
Hedbert Perez (20)
Luke Adams (26)
Luis Castillo
Carlos Rodriguez

CF
Jackson Chourio (1)
Sal Frelick (2)
Garrett Mitchell (5)
Esteury Ruiz (8)
Luis Lara (13)
Jace Avina

RF
Joey Wiemer (3)
Hendry Mendez (19)
Tristen Lutz

3B
Johan Barrios
Jhonny Severino
Zavier Warren
Jheremy Vargas

SS
Brice Turang (4)
Eric Brown (10)
Daniel Guilarte (21)
Gregory Barrios (22)
Eduardo Garcia (29)
Freddy Zamora (30)

2B
Tyler Black (9)
Robert Moore (12)
Felix Valerio (18)
Dylan O'Rae (25)
Jadher Areinamo (28)

1B
Ernesto Martinez

C
Jeferson Quero (6)
Matt Wood (23)
Mario Feliciano
Darien Miller

LHP

LHSP	LHRP
Robert Gasser (11)	Ethan Small (17)
Russell Smith	

RHP

RHSP	RHRP
Carlos Rodriguez (15)	Abner Uribe (14)
Logan Henderson (16)	Cam Robinson (24)
Victor Castaneda (27)	Gus Varland
Patricio Aquino	Lucas Erceg
Yujanyer Herrera	
Stiven Cruz	
Justin Jarvis	
Edwin Jimenez	

1 JACKSON CHOURIO, OF

Born: March 11, 2004. **B-T:** R-R. **HT:** 6-1. **WT:** 170.
Signed: Venezuela, 2021.
Signed by: Fernando Veracierto/Luis Perez.

TRACK RECORD: Chourio was one of the elite international prospects for his year when the Brewers made him the centerpiece of their class, signing him out of Venezuela for $1.8 million on Jan. 15, 2021. He put together a solid pro debut in the Dominican Summer League in 2021 before skyrocketing through the system in 2022. After starting the season in extended spring training, Chourio joined Low-A Carolina in May and crushed the level. He drew a promotion to High-A Wisconsin at the end of July before reaching Double-A Biloxi in September as an 18-year-old. He then played winter ball in the Venezuelan League. His younger brother Jaison is a promising outfield prospect in the Guardians' system who spent 2022 in the Dominican Summer League.

SCOUTING REPORT: Chourio has a dazzling array of tools and skills as a power-speed threat at a premium position. He's an explosive player whose quick-twitch athleticism is evident at the plate and in the field. Chourio snaps the barrel through the zone with outstanding bat speed, enabling him to drive the ball with impact to all fields. For a teenager who still has considerable strength gains to realize on his lean, athletic frame, the ball flies off his bat with surprising carry, especially to right-center field. He's flashing plus raw power now with a chance to hit 30-plus home runs in a season. Chourio is an advanced pure hitter for his age, too. He manipulates the bat head well, enabling him to consistently find the sweet spot, square up different types of pitches and smoke balls the opposite way. His strike-zone judgment is solid for his age, particularly given the caliber of pitching he faced in 2022 as an 18-year-old, though he will need to tighten up some of the chase tendencies he showed. Chourio is a plus-plus runner who goes home to first in 4.1 seconds, and his body type suggests he should be able to hold that speed into his prime years. As an amateur, Chourio split time between shortstop and center field, with a lot of time at shortstop. He had an issue with his right elbow, though, and that played into the Brewers' decision to move him to center field during his pro debut in 2021, with a handful of games at second base. He's a full-time center fielder now who looks natural at the position. He plays shallow at times and goes back well on balls. He takes good routes in every direction and proj-

DAN VENN/PENSACOLA BLUE WAHOOS

BA GRADE	SCOUTING GRADES
70 Risk: High	Hit: 60. Power: 70. Run: 70. Field: 55. Arm: 50.

Projected future grades on 20-80 scouting scale

BEST TOOLS

BATTING
Best Hitter for Average	Sal Frelick
Best Power Hitter	Joey Wiemer
Best Strike-Zone Discipline	Tyler Black
Fastest Baserunner	Garrett Mitchell
Best Athlete	Sal Frelick

PITCHING
Best Fastball	Jacob Misiorowski
Best Curveball	Cam Robinson
Best Slider	Jacob Misiorowski
Best Changeup	Ethan Small
Best Control	Carlos Rodriguez

FIELDING
Best Defensive Catcher	Jeferson Quero
Best Defensive Infielder	Brice Turang
Best Infield Arm	Eduardo Garcia
Best Defensive Outfielder	Garrett Mitchell

ects to be an average to plus defender. Chourio at his best will flash an average arm, though given the history with his elbow, the Brewers have cautioned him to be judicious with his throws and just hit the cutoff man, so it often plays below-average in games.

THE FUTURE: Chourio is the type of prospect who doesn't come through an organization often. He looks like a franchise cornerstone with a chance to be Milwaukee's version of Ronald Acuña Jr. After he made it to Double-A as an 18-year-old, even a conservative timetable would put him in the big leagues when he's 20 in 2024, and he could get there as a 19-year-old in 2023.

Year	Age	Club (League)	Lvl	AVG	G	AB	R	H	2B	3B	HR	RBI	BB	SO	SB	OBP	SLG
2022	18	Carolina (CAR)	LoA	.324	62	250	51	81	23	5	12	47	19	76	10	.373	.600
2022	18	Wisconsin (MWL)	HiA	.252	31	127	24	32	6	0	8	24	11	31	4	.317	.488
2022	18	Biloxi (SL)	AA	.087	6	23	0	2	1	0	0	4	2	11	2	.154	.130
Minor League Totals				.290	144	559	106	162	37	6	25	100	55	146	24	.355	.512

2 SAL FRELICK, OF

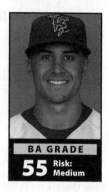

Born: April 19, 2000. **B-T:** L-R. **HT:** 5-9. **WT:** 180.
Drafted: Boston College, 2021 (1st round). **Signed by:** Ty Blankmeyer.

TRACK RECORD: Frelick developed from an undrafted Massachusetts high school infielder into one of college baseball's most exciting and polished center fielders when the Brewers drafted him 15th overall out of Boston College in 2021 and signed him for $4 million. He raced through the system in his first full season, playing at three levels to reach Triple-A Nashville.

SCOUTING REPORT: Frelick is an elite athlete with a smaller 5-foot-9 frame and outstanding hand-eye coordination. He drew nearly as many walks as strikeouts in 2022 and posted an 11% strikeout rate, including a microscopic 7% in Triple-A. He goes with pitches, spraying balls on the outer third to the opposite field and turning on pitches inside with his quick, compact swing geared for line drives. While he's an aggressive hitter, he doesn't chase too much and has the bat-to-ball skills to square up balls even when he does expand. Frelick isn't a power threat but isn't an empty singles hitter either, with a chance for 10-15 home runs, especially as he learns which pitches to try to turn on for damage. A 70 runner on the 20-80 scale with a fringe-average arm, Frelick has good range and instincts in center field, especially for a player who hasn't been a full-time outfielder for long. He projects as an average to plus defender in center field.

THE FUTURE: As a potential plus-plus hitter who can play up the middle but lacks big power, Frelick has a chance to develop into a tick above-average to plus regular in center field. Frelick should open 2023 in Triple-A, though If he keeps hitting he could make his major league debut early in the season.

BA GRADE: 55 Risk: Medium

SCOUTING GRADES	Hitting: 70	Power: 40	Speed: 70	Fielding: 50	Arm: 45

Year	Age	Club (League)	Lvl	AVG	G	AB	R	H	2B	3B	HR	RBI	BB	SO	SB	OBP	SLG
2022	22	Wisconsin (MWL)	HiA	.291	21	79	12	23	5	1	2	9	13	14	6	.391	.456
2022	22	Biloxi (SL)	AA	.317	52	224	40	71	12	3	5	25	20	33	9	.380	.464
2022	22	Nashville (IL)	AAA	.365	46	189	38	69	11	2	4	25	19	16	9	.435	.508
Minor League Totals				.331	154	638	118	211	36	9	13	80	73	88	36	.406	.476

3 JOEY WIEMER, OF

Born: Feb. 11, 1999. **B-T:** R-R. **HT:** 6-5. **WT:** 215.
Drafted: Cincinnati, 2020 (4th round). **Signed by:** Jeff Bianchi.

TRACK RECORD: During his college years at Cincinnati, Wiemer stood out for his size, athleticism and tools, but he hit just .264/.379/.408 in three seasons with an unorthodox swing. The Brewers drafted Wiemer in the fourth round in 2020, signed him for $150,000 and watched as he quickly proved to be a bargain. After an outstanding pro debut at the Class A levels in 2021, Wiemer again posted big numbers in 2022, slumping in June and July with Double-A Biloxi before an August promotion to Triple-A Nashville, where he flourished.

SCOUTING REPORT: Wiemer is a big, strong, outlier athlete, especially for his size at 6-foot-5. He has 70 raw power on the 20-80 scale and has been able to get to his power more frequently in pro ball than he did in college. Wiemer could develop into a 30-home run hitter in the big leagues, though he will have to keep his strikeouts in check. He has toned down some of the moving parts in his swing from college, but he's still prone to overswinging and has to better adjust to offspeed stuff and become a more selective hitter. He posted a 27% strikeout rate in 2022, though he cut it down to 20% in Triple-A. Wiemer has surprising wheels for his size with plus speed, which is why he has spent time in center field and could be a physical defender in center field along the lines of Jason Heyward. More likely—especially given the other prospects in the system—Wiemer will play more in right field, with an 80 arm and a chance to be a plus defender at the position.

THE FUTURE: There's still a wide range of outcomes for Wiemer, but after Jackson Chourio, he has arguably the highest upside in the Brewers' farm system. He likely opens 2023 back in Triple-A but should make his major league debut during the season.

BA GRADE: 55 Risk: High

SCOUTING GRADES	Hitting: 30	Power: 70	Speed: 60	Fielding: 55	Arm: 80

Year	Age	Club (League)	Lvl	AVG	G	AB	R	H	2B	3B	HR	RBI	BB	SO	SB	OBP	SLG
2022	23	Biloxi (SL)	AA	.243	84	334	57	81	19	1	15	47	34	113	25	.321	.440
2022	23	Nashville (IL)	AAA	.287	43	150	24	43	15	1	6	30	21	34	6	.368	.520
Minor League Totals				.274	236	880	167	241	52	4	48	154	118	252	61	.367	.506

4 BRICE TURANG, SS/OF

Born: Nov. 21, 1999. **B-T:** L-R. **HT:** 6-0. **WT:** 175.
Drafted: HS—Corona, Calif., 2018 (1st round). **Signed by:** Wynn Pelzer.

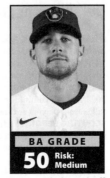

BA GRADE

50 Risk: Medium

TRACK RECORD: Turang was a celebrated high school star who fell to the Brewers at No. 21 overall in the 2018 draft. He has touched every level of Milwaukee's system and spent 2022 in the Triple-A International League, where he was one of five players 22 or younger to qualify for the batting title. Turang ranked top 10 in the IL in hits, runs, stolen bases and walks.

SCOUTING REPORT: There's nothing flashy about Turang, who doesn't have one spectacular tool but is an athletic middle infielder and steady offensive performer. He recognizes pitches well, controls the strike zone and has good bat-to-ball skills with a flat swing geared to hit line drives around the park and also a low swing-and-miss rate in the zone. His Triple-A strikeout rate jumped from 15% in 2021 to 20% in 2022 as he focused on trying to do more damage in the air, with the tradeoff resulting in 13 home runs that more than doubled his previous high of six from 2021. Turang's offensive game will always center around his on-base skills more than his below-average power. Still, his max exit velocity has peaked at 110 mph, and he could one day hit 10-15 home runs. A plus runner, Turang's defense has improved to the point that he is at least an average defender at shortstop, where he has good body control, instincts, hands and footwork to go with an average arm. With the composition of their major league roster, the Brewers also gave Turang some time in center field and second base, where he has a chance to develop into a plus defender.

THE FUTURE: The Brewers traded second baseman Kolten Wong in December, creating a potential opening for Turang, who has played 175 games at Triple-A, at some point in 2023.

SCOUTING GRADES	Hitting: 55		Power: 40		Speed: 60			Fielding: 50		Arm: 50	

Year	Age	Club (League)	Lvl	AVG	G	AB	R	H	2B	3B	HR	RBI	BB	SO	SB	OBP	SLG
2022	22	Nashville (IL)	AAA	.286	131	532	89	152	24	2	13	78	65	118	34	.360	.412
Minor League Totals				.269	419	1595	267	429	70	12	23	186	239	336	98	.362	.371

5 GARRETT MITCHELL, OF

Born: Sept. 4, 1998. **B-T:** L-R. **HT:** 6-3. **WT:** 215.
Drafted: UCLA, 2020 (1st round). **Signed by:** Daniel Cho/Corey Rodriguez.

BA GRADE

50 Risk: High

TRACK RECORD: The coronavirus pandemic cut short Mitchell's junior year in 2020 after he hit .349/.418/.566 the previous season for UCLA. The Brewers drafted him 20th overall in 2020, and while injuries have limited his playing time as a pro, he made his MLB debut in August 2022.

SCOUTING REPORT: Mitchell has unusual size, athleticism and tools. He's a powerful, explosive 6-foot-3, 215 pounds and catches infielders off guard with elite speed. If everything clicks, Mitchell could be a power-speed threat, with raw power in batting practice that grades out at least plus and the ability to make some of the hardest contact in the organization. The question is whether Mitchell will be able to evolve his swing and approach to ever tap into that power. He uses a choppy, downhill swing geared to slap the ball and use his wheels rather than driving the ball in the air for damage. Mitchell has made some tweaks to his setup, but his swing path and attack angle prevent him from hitting for power. He has solid patience, but his 26% strikeout rate in the minors in 2022 is high for a player without accompanying game power. Mitchell's speed translates to elite range in center field to go with his plus arm, giving him the attributes to be an at least plus defender. A leg injury limited Mitchell in 2021 and an oblique injury caused him to miss time in 2022, so he will have to prove his durability.

THE FUTURE: If Mitchell is able to unlock his power in games, he has the upside to significantly outperform expectations. If not, his defensive ability in center field and speed offer a nice safety net.

SCOUTING GRADES	Hitting: 45		Power: 50		Speed: 80			Fielding: 60		Arm: 60	

Year	Age	Club (League)	Lvl	AVG	G	AB	R	H	2B	3B	HR	RBI	BB	SO	SB	OBP	SLG
2022	23	Brewers Blue (ACL)	R	.083	4	12	5	1	1	0	0	0	4	4	1	.353	.167
2022	23	Biloxi (SL)	AA	.277	44	166	29	46	9	2	4	25	16	52	7	.353	.428
2022	23	Nashville (IL)	AAA	.342	20	73	15	25	6	0	1	9	10	18	9	.435	.466
2022	23	Milwaukee (NL)	MLB	.311	28	61	9	19	3	0	2	9	6	28	8	.373	.459
Major League Totals				.311	28	61	9	19	3	0	2	9	6	28	8	.373	.459
Minor League Totals				.273	132	472	98	129	22	4	13	64	76	145	34	.382	.419

6 JEFERSON QUERO, C

Born: Oct. 8, 2002. **B-T:** R-R. **HT:** 5-10. **WT:** 180.
Signed: Venezuela, 2019. **Signed by:** Reinaldo Hidalgo.

TRACK RECORD: Signed out of Venezuela for $200,000 in 2019, Quero quickly proved to be one of the top international catchers any team signed that year. The pandemic prevented him from playing in 2020, but he had a strong pro debut in the Rookie-level Arizona Complex League in 2021, though he separated his left shoulder and had surgery after the season. In 2022 he took another step forward, reaching High-A Wisconsin as a 19-year-old at the end of the season. Quero was one of just six teenage catchers to bat at least 300 times in full-season ball and was then one of the youngest players in the Arizona Fall League.

BA GRADE

50 Risk: High

SCOUTING REPORT: Quero earns glowing reviews for his defense. He has soft hands, receives the ball well and is adept at blocking with his quick, athletic and agile movements. He has a plus arm and a quick release, recording occasional pop times under 1.9 seconds on throws to second base to erase 29% of basestealers during the regular season and 11 of 24 (46%) in the AFL. Quero has the high baseball IQ, attention to detail and energetic leadership style that managers and pitchers appreciate. He projects to be a plus defender, but he's not an empty bat either. Quero has good bat control and contact skills when he's swinging at pitches in the strike zone, though he will need to develop a more selective hitting approach. He has average bat speed with an aggressive, slasher approach geared for line drives, but he has a chance for average power, though it might play below that level because of his approach.

THE FUTURE: Quero has the potential to be a league-average regular behind the plate, with a chance for more depending on his offensive growth. He's likely to return to High-A Wisconsin to open 2023.

SCOUTING GRADES	Hitting: 55	Power: 45	Speed: 40	Fielding: 60	Arm: 60

Year	Age	Club (League)	Lvl	AVG	G	AB	R	H	2B	3B	HR	RBI	BB	SO	SB	OBP	SLG
2022	19	Carolina (CAR)	LoA	.278	75	284	44	79	18	1	6	43	28	61	10	.345	.412
2022	19	Wisconsin (MWL)	HiA	.313	20	83	10	26	4	1	4	14	2	15	0	.329	.530
Minor League Totals				.290	118	435	69	126	27	3	12	65	42	86	14	.357	.448

7 JACOB MISIOROWSKI, RHP

Born: April 3, 2002. **B-T:** R-R. **HT:** 6-7. **WT:** 190.
Drafted: Crowder (Mo.) JC, 2022 (2nd round). **Signed by:** Riley Bandelow.

TRACK RECORD: The Brewers drafted Aaron Ashby out of Crowder (Mo.) JC in the fourth round in 2018 and he became their No. 1 prospect entering the 2022 season. They drafted Misiorowski from the same school with their second-round pick in 2022, and his $2.35 million bonus topped that of first-rounder Eric Brown Jr. for the highest in the Brewers' draft class.

SCOUTING REPORT: Misiorowski is an extremely tall, gangly pitcher with outstanding raw stuff. He sits in the mid 90s, touches 101 mph and might end up consistently living in the upper 90s once he packs on more strength to his 6-foot-7 frame. In one short-burst outing during instructional league, Misiorowski didn't throw a fastball under 99 mph. It's a power pitch that

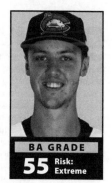

BA GRADE

55 Risk: Extreme

plays up even more because of his extension. The carry on his fastball helps him miss bats when he attacks hitters up in the zone. Misiorowski's slider is a wipeout pitch, flashing as a 70 on the 20-80 scale. Misiorowski was primarily a two-pitch guy before signing, but he has a good curveball that he shelved in college and some evaluators think can be plus. He rarely uses his changeup but that pitch shows promise as well, though it's often misidentified as a two-seamer in the low 90s. The major risk Misiorowski presents is his well below-average control. In his draft year at Crowder he walked 45 batters and hit 11 others in 76 innings. After signing, Misiorowski walked seven and hit another one of the 14 batters he faced in 1.2 innings for Low-A Carolina. His control was better during instructs, but his high-effort delivery makes it difficult for him to throw strikes.

THE FUTURE: Misiorowski's premium stuff gives him the upside to be a front-end starter, but his control troubles make him an enormous wild card, with a chance he ends up in the bullpen.

SCOUTING GRADES:	Fastball: 70	Curveball: 60	Slider: 70	Changeup: 45	Control: 40

Year	Age	Club (League)	Lvl	W	L	ERA	G	GS	IP	H	HR	BB	SO	BB/9	SO/9	WHIP	AVG
2022	20	Carolina (CAR)	LoA	0	0	5.40	2	2	2	1	0	7	3	37.8	16.2	4.80	.167
Minor League Totals				0	0	5.40	2	2	2	1	0	7	3	37.8	16.2	4.80	.167

8 ESTEURY RUIZ, OF

Born: Feb. 15, 1999. **B-T:** R-R. **HT:** 6-0. **WT:** 170.
Signed: Dominican Republic, 2015. **Signed by:** Edys De Oleo (Royals).

TRACK RECORD: Ruiz generated buzz by winning MVP of the Rookie-level Arizona League in 2017. His performance slowed the next few seasons until 2022, when he hit well in the upper minors and made his MLB debut before the Padres sent him to Milwaukee at the trade deadline as part of the return for Josh Hader.

SCOUTING REPORT: Ruiz posted huge numbers in several categories in 2022. He has a wiry build, loads with a simple toe tap and—despite a long swing—has good contact skills. Ruiz showed more patience in 2022, with 66 walks in 114 minor league games after drawing 54 in 182 games combined the previous two seasons. Despite an impressive slash line, Ruiz faces skepticism about how his bat will translate to the major leagues. His swing has leverage and generates loft, but his average exit velocity of 85 mph in the minor leagues in 2022 would rank among the worst in the majors, with all of his home runs coming pull side. Ruiz is a plus-plus runner who likes to bunt and steal. He swiped a minor league-best 85 bases in 99 attempts and should be a prolific basestealer in the majors. Ruiz mostly played second base until 2019 when he moved to the outfield, and after a learning curve the first few years, he has developed into at least an average center fielder.

THE FUTURE: If Ruiz can show enough power to translate against MLB pitchers, he could become an everyday player. If not, he could end up a righthanded-hitting reserve with speed and defense.

BA GRADE
45 Risk: Medium

SCOUTING GRADES		Hitting: 50		Power: 40		Speed: 70		Fielding: 50		Arm: 40					
Year	Age	Club (League)	Lvl	AVG	G	AB	R	H	2B	3B	HR	RBI	BB	SO	SB	OBP	SLG
2022	23	San Antonio (TL)	AA	.344	49	180	54	62	17	2	9	37	32	40	37	.474	.611
2022	23	El Paso (PCL)	AAA	.315	28	111	30	35	6	0	4	9	20	25	23	.457	.477
2022	23	Nashville (IL)	AAA	.329	37	146	30	48	10	0	3	19	14	29	25	.402	.459
2022	23	San Diego (NL)	MLB	.222	14	27	1	6	1	1	0	2	0	5	1	.222	.333
2022	23	Milwaukee (NL)	MLB	.000	3	8	2	0	0	0	0	0	1	2	0	.000	.000
Major League Totals				.171	17	35	3	6	1	1	0	2	1	7	1	.194	.257
Minor League Totals				.285	521	1947	363	554	125	26	53	261	190	498	243	.363	.457

9 TYLER BLACK, 2B/OF

Born: July 26, 2000. **B-T:** L-R. **HT:** 6-2. **WT:** 190.
Drafted: Wright State, 2021 (1st round supplemental). **Signed by:** Pete Vukovich Jr.

TRACK RECORD: At Wright State in 2021, Black hit .383/.496/.683 with 39 walks and 25 strikeouts and became the 33rd overall pick in the draft. He showed off his on-base skills in his first full season with High-A Wisconsin in 2022 until July, when he made a diving catch in center field and fractured his scapula, ending his regular season. He went to the Arizona Fall League but that too ended prematurely when he broke his thumb.

SCOUTING REPORT: Black is the most disciplined hitter in the Brewers' farm system. He's extremely patient, works deep counts and rarely chases outside the strike zone. With a setup at the plate reminiscent of fellow Canadian Joey Votto, Black makes frequent contact with a quick swing. He keeps his hands inside the

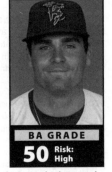

BA GRADE
50 Risk: High

ball well and maintains an all-fields approach, enabling him to turn on balls on the inner third or use the opposite field when pitchers attack him away. Black's swing path is geared for low-trajectory line drives and there are times when he could more aggressively swing for extra-base damage, but his power ultimately grades as below-average. Black is an offensive-oriented player in search of a defensive home. He's a good athlete and a slightly above-average runner whose footwork, range and below-average arm make him below-average at second base. He also plays center field and should continue to see time in the outfield, but he's probably always going to be below-average at any position. Black also had surgery to repair a torn labrum in his right shoulder in 2020, so his durability bears monitoring.

THE FUTURE: If Black can squeeze out more extra-base juice and become an adequate defender somewhere—or possibly a bat-first utility player—he has the components to be an everyday player with high on-base percentages. He should move up to Double-A Biloxi in 2023.

SCOUTING GRADES		Hitting: 55		Power: 40		Speed: 55		Fielding: 40		Arm: 40					
Year	Age	Club (League)	Lvl	AVG	G	AB	R	H	2B	3B	HR	RBI	BB	SO	SB	OBP	SLG
2022	21	Wisconsin (MWL)	HiA	.281	64	231	45	65	13	4	4	35	45	44	13	.406	.424
Minor League Totals				.270	90	318	60	86	17	4	5	43	71	75	18	.412	.396

10 ERIC BROWN JR., SS

Born: Dec. 19, 2000. **B-T:** R-R. **HT:** 5-10. **WT:** 190.
Drafted: Coastal Carolina, 2022 (1st round). **Signed by:** Taylor Frederick.
TRACK RECORD: Brown had a big summer in the Cape Cod League in 2021, hitting .282/.375/.476 with five home runs as a rising junior. The following spring with Coastal Carolina, he hit .330/.460/.544 with seven homers, 39 walks and 28 strikeouts in 57 games. The Brewers drafted him in the first round at pick No. 27 overall and signed him for $2.05 million.
SCOUTING REPORT: Brown has a tool set that projects to grade out around average across the board. Scouts highest on Brown are drawn to him for his advanced feel for hitting and consistent offensive track record. He does it with an unorthodox swing, starting his hands above his head and away from his body, then using a long, swinging leg kick to load his swing. On his own, he tweaked his setup after signing, moving his hands back behind his head and dropping them down a bit to create a simpler move into his hitting position. Even with the more exaggerated setup, Brown showed a knack for being on time and barreling balls in games, with a high contact rate and solid sense of the strike zone. If Brown can drive the ball in the air more often, he could end up with average power. A tick above-average runner, Brown should continue to develop at shortstop. He has good actions to stick in the dirt, but his arm is average at best. He has a chance to stick at shortstop but second base or third base are equally possible landing spots.
THE FUTURE: Some scouts see Brown as a utility player, but his contact skills and solid tool set could be good enough for him to develop into a regular somewhere in the infield. He's advanced enough to open 2023 in High-A Wisconsin.

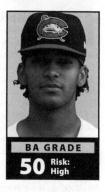

BA GRADE
50 Risk: High

SCOUTING GRADES	Hitting: 50	Power: 50	Speed: 55	Fielding: 50	Arm: 50

Year	Age	Club (League)	Lvl	AVG	G	AB	R	H	2B	3B	HR	RBI	BB	SO	SB	OBP	SLG
2022	21	Brewers Gold (ACL)	R	.308	4	13	7	4	3	0	0	1	4	4	4	.471	.538
2022	21	Carolina (CAR)	LoA	.262	23	84	16	22	4	1	3	7	11	17	15	.370	.440
Minor League Totals				.268	27	97	23	26	7	1	3	8	15	21	19	.385	.454

11 ROBERT GASSER, LHP

Born: May 31, 1999. **B-T:** L-L. **HT:** 6-1. **WT:** 190.
Drafted: Houston, 2021 (2nd round). **Signed by:** Kevin Ham (Padres).
TRACK RECORD: Gasser pitched for New Mexico in 2018 and transferred to pitch at Houston in 2020, but the pandemic ended that season early. His stock soared in 2022 as he showed more velocity and significantly improved performance, prompting the Padres to draft him in the second round and sign him for $884,200. In the midst of Gasser's first full season of pro ball, the Brewers acquired him in the trade deadline deal that sent Josh Hader to San Diego.
SCOUTING REPORT: Gasser throws a 50/50 mix of fastballs and offspeed stuff, mainly relying on his fastball and slider. Pitching from the third base side of the rubber, Gasser isn't overpowering, sitting at 89-93 mph with the ability to reach back for 95. His low-80s slider is his most effective pitch, a tick above-average offering around 2,600 rpm that sweeps across the zone with 15 inches of horizontal break to miss bats against lefties or righties. He'll mix in a shorter cutter as well to try to get soft contact against righthanded hitters. Gasser's average changeup comes in firm off his fastball in the mid 80s, but it has good movement with 18 inches of horizontal break, giving him another weapon against righties. Gasser has generally shown good control, though his walk rate spiked when he got to Triple-A.
THE FUTURE: Gasser has the stuff and control to project as a back-end starter. He likely opens 2023 back in Triple-A, but he could be an early callup option if a big league opportunity opens.

BA GRADE: 45/Medium	Fastball: 50	Slider: 55	Cutter: 50	Changeup: 50	Control: 50

Year	Age	Club (League)	Lvl	W	L	ERA	G	GS	IP	H	HR	BB	SO	BB/9	SO/9	WHIP	AVG
2022	23	Fort Wayne (MWL)	HiA	4	9	4.18	18	18	90	86	8	28	115	2.8	11.5	1.26	.252
2022	23	Biloxi (SL)	AA	1	1	2.21	4	4	20	14	2	8	26	3.5	11.5	1.08	.194
2022	23	Nashville (IL)	AAA	2	2	4.44	5	5	26	26	1	16	31	5.5	10.6	1.59	.255
Minor League Totals				7	12	3.67	33	33	152	137	12	54	186	3.2	11.0	1.26	.242

12 ROBERT MOORE, 2B

Born: March 31, 2002. **B-T:** B-R. **HT:** 5-9. **WT:** 170.
Drafted: Arkansas, 2022 (2nd round). **Signed by:** Mark Muzzi.

TRACK RECORD: Moore bypassed the draft out of high school and enrolled early at Arkansas for the 2020 spring and was off to a strong start as a 17-year-old before the pandemic ended the season early. After an outstanding 2021 season, Moore looked positioned to be a first-round pick in 2022, but instead he hit .232/.374/.427 in 65 games. The Brewers drafted him in the supplemental second round with the 72nd overall pick and signed him for $800,000.

SCOUTING REPORT: Moore is small but has an outstanding baseball IQ, which is no surprise as the son of former Royals president Dayton Moore. A switch-hitter with an aggressive swing, Moore's performance dipped in 2022 but he didn't have a high strikeout rate, lending optimism for him to bounce back. Moore had no trouble catching up to good velocity, but several scouts thought he got too pull-oriented in an attempt to show he can hit for power, rather than maintaining an all-fields approach. His offensive game should center more around his OBP skills, with power for 10-15 home runs. An above-average runner, Moore's defensive game didn't slump. He's an instinctive second baseman who has a chance to be an above-average defender with an average arm. He should see time at shortstopl, but his future is at second base.

THE FUTURE: The underlying skills are there for Moore's offensive game to rebound from his 2022 performance. If that happens, he could develop into an everyday second baseman who offers value on both sides of the ball.

BA GRADE: 45/High		Hitting: 50		Power: 40		Speed: 55		Fielding: 55		Arm: 50			

Year	Age	Club (League)	Lvl	AVG	G	AB	R	H	2B	3B	HR	RBI	BB	SO	SB	OBP	SLG
2022	20	Brewers Gold (ACL)	R	.250	1	4	2	1	0	0	0	1	1	1	1	.400	.250
2022	20	Brewers Blue (ACL)	R	.091	3	11	1	1	1	0	0	1	1	1	0	.231	.182
2022	20	Carolina (CAR)	LoA	.264	27	110	14	29	8	0	3	14	13	28	6	.352	.418
Minor League Totals				.248	31	125	17	31	9	0	3	16	15	30	7	.343	.392

13 LUIS LARA, OF

Born: Nov. 17, 2004. **B-T:** B-R. **HT:** 5-9. **WT:** 160.
Signed: Venezuela, 2022. **Signed by:** Jose Rodriguez.

TRACK RECORD: As an amateur in Venezuela, Lara didn't much attention early in the scouting process as a slender 5-foot-6 outfielder. The Brewers have been as aggressive as any team in Venezuela, and they watched him develop into an explosive athlete with impressive game skills, and signed him for $1.1 million when the international signing period opened on Jan. 15, 2022. He drew more excitement after making his pro debut in the Dominican Summer League.

SCOUTING REPORT: Lara is a quick-burst athlete with a sweet swing from both sides of the plate. It's a short, quick swing with good rhythm and timing. He has strong bat-to-ball skills with a 12% strikeout rate in the DSL and a solid grasp of the strike zone for his age. Lara is small but he isn't a slap hitter, and takes aggressive swings with good bat speed from both sides of the plate with exit velocities up to 108 mph. Some scouts question his future power because of his size, while others think he could hit 20 homers in the big leagues. He's a 70 runner on the 20-80 scale with a quick first step and good range in center field, where he has a solid-average arm.

THE FUTURE: A potential table-setter at the top of a lineup who can play a premium position, Lara has been an arrow-up player and the most exciting Latin American signing in the system beneath the full-season level. He should make his U.S. debut in the Rookie-level Arizona Complex League, though time at Low-A Carolina by the end of the year is possible.

BA GRADE: 50/Extreme		Hitting: 55		Power: 45		Speed: 70		Fielding: 50		Arm: 55			

Year	Age	Club (League)	Lvl	AVG	G	AB	R	H	2B	3B	HR	RBI	BB	SO	SB	OBP	SLG
2022	17	Brewers 1 (DSL)	R	.260	58	200	39	52	11	4	2	21	21	28	7	.341	.385
Minor League Totals				.260	58	200	39	52	11	4	2	21	21	28	7	.341	.385

14 ABNER URIBE, RHP

Born: June 20, 2000. **B-T:** R-R. **HT:** 6-2. **WT:** 200.
Signed: Dominican Republic, 2018. **Signed by:** Elvis Cruz.

TRACK RECORD: Uribe was 18 and touching the low 90s when the Brewers signed him for $85,000 out of the Dominican Republic in 2018. By the next year, Uribe reached the mid 90s, and by the end of 2020 he was reaching 101 mph. Uribe made two appearances in 2022 before missing the rest of the regular season to have left knee surgery for a torn meniscus, though he returned for the Arizona Fall League and the Brewers added him to their 40-man roster after the season.

SCOUTING REPORT: Few pitchers in the world can match Uribe's raw velocity. The relief prospect regularly operates in the upper 90s, consistently touches triple digits and has hit 103 mph, though some scouts have said Uribe's fastball is more hittable than the radar gun readings might suggest. Some of that might stem from poor fastball command. Uribe is a high-energy pitcher with an aggressive, up-tempo delivery he's still learning to corral, which leads to poor control. He throws a slider with power in the upper 80s which has shown enough to improvement to flash as an above-average pitch. Uribe has a changeup but it's rare for him to throw one.

THE FUTURE: If Uribe can tame his wildness and throw a more consistent slider, he has the stuff to pitch high-leverage innings. If not, he will join a long list of flamethrowers who were never able to translate their velocity into big league success.

| BA GRADE: 45/High | | Fastball: 70 | | Slider: 55 | | Changeup: 30 | | Control: 30 | | |

Year	Age	Club (Leagu	Lvl	W	L	ERA	G	GS	IP	H	HR	BB	SO	BB/9	SO/9	WHIP	AVG
2022	22	Biloxi (SL)	AA	0	0	0.00	2	0	3	2	0	4	4	12.0	12.0	2.00	.182
Minor League Totals				6	2	4.57	38	6	65	51	3	50	84	6.9	11.6	1.55	.222

15 CARLOS RODRIGUEZ, RHP

Born: Nov 27, 2001. **B-T:** R-R. **HT:** 6-0. **WT:** 190.
Drafted: Florida Southwestern State JC, 2021 (6th round). **Signed by:** Mike Burns.

TRACK RECORD: Rodriguez was pitching in junior college at Florida Southwestern State when the Brewers drafted him in the sixth round in 2021 and signed him for $250,000. He has been a pleasant surprise in the system since then, winning the organization's minor league pitcher of the year award in 2022 following a strong season split between Low-A Carolina and High-A Wisconsin.

SCOUTING REPORT: In a system that's lighter on pitchers, Rodriguez sticks out for his success and his feel for pitching. He pitches at 89-93 mph and touches 95 with good control of his fastball. His best pitch is an above-average changeup at 83-86 mph with a lot of fading action and 17 inches of horizontal break to keep hitters off balance. Rodriguez also throws a fringe-average slider in the low-80s that spins around 2,400 rpm and is an effective pitch at the lower levels but will get tested against more advanced hitters. He dabbles with a low-70s curveball to give hitters another look as well. Rodriguez doesn't have knockout stuff, but his feel for mixing his pitches, changing speeds and moving the ball around the zone has yielded good results.

THE FUTURE: Rodriguez will get his first test at the upper levels in 2023 when he gets to Double-A. There's a split camp among scouts about whether his future will be in a rotation or a relief role, but the upside is there for a back-end starter.

| BA GRADE: 45/High | | Fastball: 45 | | Curveball: 40 | | Slider: 45 | | Changeup: 55 | | Control: 50 | |

Year	Age	Club (League)	Lvl	W	L	ERA	G	GS	IP	H	HR	BB	SO	BB/9	SO/9	WHIP	AVG
2022	20	Carolina (CAR)	LoA	3	4	3.53	19	13	71	53	7	27	84	3.4	10.6	1.12	.213
2022	20	Wisconsin (MWL)	HiA	3	1	1.98	7	7	36	21	0	13	45	3.2	11.1	0.94	.168
Minor League Totals				6	5	3.01	26	20	108	74	7	40	129	3.3	10.8	1.06	.198

16 LOGAN HENDERSON, RHP

Born: March 2, 2002. **B-T:** R-R. **HT:** 5-11. **WT:** 194.
Drafted: McLennan (Texas) JC, 2021 (4th round). **Signed by:** K.J. Hendrick.

TRACK RECORD: Henderson was the NJCAA Division I pitcher of the year as a true freshman in 2021, when he led McLennan (Texas) JC to a national title. His 169 strikeouts led the country and he walked 23 in 97.2 innings with a 1.66 ERA that ranked third in the nation. The Brewers signed him that year for $495,000 as a fourth-round pick. Henderson suffered an avulsion fracture of his throwing elbow during spring training 2022, which required surgery and kept him out of action until August. Henderson ramped up during instructional league to pitch in the Arizona Fall League, but he felt arm soreness there and the Brewers scrapped those plans and shut him down.

SCOUTING REPORT: Henderson has a compact, 5-foot-11 frame and pitches off a low-90s fastball that can hit 94 mph. The velocity doesn't stand out, but it's a lively pitch with good carry up in the zone. His changeup is a plus pitch with more than 10 mph of separation off his fastball at 78-80 mph. It's a deceptive pitch with late tumble and fade, a swing-and-miss weapon he's comfortable throwing to both lefties and righties. Henderson didn't throw his breaking ball much when he returned in 2022, but he shows some feel for a slider with slurvy action. Henderson's ability to control his three-pitch mix and use his fastball in all quadrants of the strike zone helps everything play up.

THE FUTURE: Henderson's 2022 campaign raised red flags about his durability. If he's able to answer those questions, he has the stuff and pitchability to project as a back-end starter with a chance for more.

BA GRADE: 45/Very High		Fastball: 50			Slider: 50			Changeup: 60		Control: 50			
Year	Age	Club (League)	Lvl	W	L	ERA	G	GS	IP	H	HR	BB	SO	BB/9	SO/9	WHIP	AVG
2022	20	Brewers Blue (ACL)	R	0	0	0.00	2	2	2	1	0	0	5	0.0	22.5	0.50	.125
2022	20	Carolina (CAR)	LoA	0	1	4.63	5	5	12	14	0	6	18	4.6	13.9	1.71	.286
Minor League Totals				0	1	3.95	7	7	14	15	0	6	23	4.0	15.1	1.54	.263

17 ETHAN SMALL, LHP

Born: Feb. 14, 1997. **B-T:** L-L. **HT:** 6-4. **WT:** 215.
Drafted: Mississippi State, 2019 (1st round). **Signed by:** Scott Nichols

TRACK RECORD: After having Tommy John surgery in college, Small returned to Mississippi State as a redshirt junior in 2019 and led the Southeastern Conference in strikeouts and ranked second in ERA. The Brewers' first-round pick at No. 28 overall that year, Small reached Triple-A in 2021, but his stock dropped afterward. He started 2022 with an ERA of 0.77 through five April starts and made a pair of major league appearances in May and July, but from June on he had a 6.82 ERA as he struggled with walks and moved to the bullpen at the end of the year.

SCOUTING REPORT: Small pitches at 89-92 mph and can reach back for 95. It's not big velocity, but when Small is at his best, he's able to keep hitters off balance by liberally mixing his plus changeup. He sells his changeup like a fastball out of his hand, then it tumbles underneath bats to rack up whiffs with lots of separation off his fastball at 78-81 mph. Finding a reliable breaking ball has been a focal point for Small, who has made some progress with a slider, though it's still a below-average pitch. Small drew praise for his pitchability coming out of college, but he got into trouble last year because his control escaped him. He walked 13% of hitters in Triple-A and especially struggled to land his offspeed stuff in the zone. That allowed opponents to get ahead in the count and tee off on a hittable fastball.

THE FUTURE: Entering his age-26 season, Small will need to improve his control to carve out a big league role, which is looking more likely to be in relief. He probably opens 2023 back in Triple-A.

BA GRADE: 40/High		Fastball: 40			Slider: 40			Changeup: 60		Control: 40			
Year	Age	Club (League)	Lvl	W	L	ERA	G	GS	IP	H	HR	BB	SO	BB/9	SO/9	WHIP	AVG
2022	25	Nashville (IL)	AAA	7	6	4.46	27	21	103	82	8	58	114	5.1	10.0	1.36	.217
2022	25	Milwaukee (NL)	MLB	0	0	7.11	2	2	6	8	1	8	7	11.4	9.9	2.53	.320
Major League Totals				0	0	7.11	2	2	6	8	1	8	7	11.4	9.9	2.53	.320
Minor League Totals				11	10	3.13	52	46	201	148	12	104	242	4.6	10.8	1.25	.205

18 FELIX VALERIO, 2B/OF

Born: Dec. 26, 2000. **B-T:** R-R. **HT:** 5-7. **WT:** 165.
Signed: Dominican Republic, 2018. **Signed by:** Anderson Taveras/Gerardo Cabrera (Mets).

TRACK RECORD: When the Mets signed Valerio for $10,000 out of the Dominican Republic in 2018, he was a 5-foot-7 infielder who didn't have any great tools, but the Mets liked his instincts and feel for hitting. Traded to the Brewers in January 2019 in a deal for outfielder Keon Broxton, Valerio reached Double-A as a 21-year-old in 2022. After a torrid April, Valerio was hitting .260/.331/.450 by the end of June, but his performance tumbled in the second half, dropping to .228/.313/.357 for the year.

SCOUTING REPORT: When he's at his best, Valerio shows good bat control, makes frequent contact and maintains a disciplined offensive approach that helped him produce a 10% walk rate and 17% strikeout rate in 2022. Valerio has well below-average raw power but added loft to his swing in 2021, which resulted in a surprising 11 home runs, but his power numbers cratered in the second half of the 2022 season. After June, he had just four extra-base hits with two home runs in 52 games, and his exit velocity numbers declined as well. Valerio's offensive game will have to carry him because he's a below-average defender with a below-average arm at second base. He's an average runner who also spent time in left field, but he doesn't have the offensive impact to project there.

THE FUTURE: Getting stronger to withstand the rigors of a full season will be critical for Valerio. Given his second-half struggles, he could return to Double-A Biloxi to start 2023.

BA GRADE: 40/High	Hitting: 45	Power: 30	Speed: 50	Fielding: 40	Arm: 40

Year	Age	Club (League)	Lvl	AVG	G	AB	R	H	2B	3B	HR	RBI	BB	SO	SB	OBP	SLG
2022	21	Biloxi (SL)	AA	.228	113	417	60	95	14	2	12	51	48	80	30	.313	.357
Minor League Totals				.278	335	1264	220	351	81	7	26	170	168	193	93	.371	.415

19 HENDRY MENDEZ, OF

Born: Nov. 7, 2003. **B-T:** L-L. **HT:** 6-3. **WT:** 180.
Signed: Dominican Republic, 2021. **Signed by:** Gary Peralta.

TRACK RECORD: Throughout the scouting process as a teenager in the Dominican Republic, Mendez grew taller and started to show more consistent contact skills as his Jan. 15, 2021 signing date approached. He signed with the Brewers for $800,000. After a strong debut that year, Mendez was one of the youngest players in the Low-A Carolina league in 2022 as an 18-year-old who showed a high-contact bat, albeit with limited damage.

SCOUTING REPORT: Mendez stands out for his patience and hand-eye coordination. He drew nearly as many walks as strikeouts in 2022 with a 14% walk rate and a 16% strikeout rate. He's a selective hitter with an accurate barrel and seldomly misses when he swings at a pitch in the strike zone. Mendez will need to find a way to tap into more power, a process that will involve both getting stronger and likely changing his swing. There is bat speed and more physical projection in his frame to project him to get to average or better raw power, but his slashing, downhill swing path lends itself to a high groundball rate, so Mendez will have to figure out a way to generate more loft to ever hit for power. He's a right fielder with an average arm and at least average speed that will likely slow down as he fills out.

THE FUTURE: Whether Mendez will provide enough offensive impact to be a big leaguer hinges on the development of his game power. High-A Wisconsin will be his next step in 2023.

BA GRADE: 45/Very High	Hitting: 50	Power: 40	Speed: 50	Fielding: 45	Arm: 50

Year	Age	Club (League)	Lvl	AVG	G	AB	R	H	2B	3B	HR	RBI	BB	SO	SB	OBP	SLG
2022	18	Carolina (CAR)	LoA	.244	105	377	47	92	11	1	5	39	62	70	7	.357	.318
Minor League Totals				.261	145	494	63	129	20	4	6	58	79	82	10	.369	.354

20 HEDBERT PEREZ, OF

Born: April 4, 2003. **B-T:** L-L. **HT:** 5-11. **WT:** 190.
Signed: Venezuela, 2019. **Signed by:** Reinaldo Hidalgo.

TRACK RECORD: Perez generated buzz soon after signing with the Brewers for $700,000 and was so advanced that the Brewers sent him to their alternate training site in 2020 during the canceled minor league season. He showed a power stroke with free-swinging tendencies in his pro debut in the Rookie-level Arizona Complex League in 2021, but pitchers effectively exploited holes in his game in 2022 in the Low-A Carolina League.

SCOUTING REPORT: Perez has a lefthanded swing that works well and stays smooth and usually compact with a good path through the zone. When Perez gets the sweet spot on the ball, especially down and in, he's able to drive it for damage, with exit velocities up to 113 mph. There's above-average raw power, but he will need to become a more selective hitter. He expands the zone too often and struggles to recognize offspeed pitches, so he doesn't walk much and he struck out at a 30% clip. Perez has gained significant power since signing as he's bulked up, but that added weight has caused his speed to regress. He's now a below-average runner who moved from center to left field. His defensive instincts are solid, though his throwing arm has backed up to below-average.

THE FUTURE: The 2022 season was difficult for Perez, but there are still promising traits intact for him to build upon. The 2023 season will be a critical rebound year.

BA GRADE: 40/High	Hitting: 30	Power: 55	Speed: 40	Fielding: 50	Arm: 40

Year	Age	Club (League)	Lvl	AVG	G	AB	R	H	2B	3B	HR	RBI	BB	SO	SB	OBP	SLG
2022	19	Carolina (CAR)	LoA	.216	105	407	53	88	23	2	15	57	30	132	9	.272	.393
Minor League Totals				.235	153	592	77	139	36	2	22	85	39	191	11	.290	.414

21 DANIEL GUILARTE, SS

Born: Oct. 29, 2003. **B-T:** R-R. **HT:** 6-1. **WT:** 170.
Signed: Venezuela, 2021. **Signed by:** Trino Aguilar.

TRACK RECORD: When the international signing period opened on Jan. 15, 2021, the Brewers awarded seven-figure bonuses to three Venezuelan prospects: Jackson Chourio, Gregory Barrios and Guilarte.

While Chourio has catapulted himself into the conversation for the top prospect in baseball already, Guilarte—a $1 million signing—has impressed at the lower levels. He missed the 2021 season due to a left shoulder injury but was one of the top hitters in the Rookie-level Arizona Complex League in 2022 during his pro debut.

SCOUTING REPORT: A wiry athlete, Guilarte has the tools and athleticism to handle shortstop. A plus runner, Guilarte has good quickness at the position and finishes plays with a plus arm. At the plate, Guilarte performed well and showed a good sense of the strike zone for his age as well as the bat control to make frequent contact. He had little swing-and-miss in the zone, though he will need to get stronger and might need to tweak his swing if he is ever going to hit for power. His lack of strength means his power is limited to occasional doubles right now, while his bat path lends itself more to low line drives and ground balls rather than loft.

THE FUTURE: Guilarte's 2022 season had a lot of positives, but layering on more strength to be able to handle more advanced pitchers will be critical for his future. He should make the jump to Low-A Carolina in 2023.

| BA GRADE: 45/Extreme | | Hitting: 45 | | Power: 30 | | Speed: 60 | | Fielding: 50 | | Arm: 60 | |

Year	Age	Club (League)	Lvl	AVG	G	AB	R	H	2B	3B	HR	RBI	BB	SO	SB	OBP	SLG
2022	18	Brewers Blue (ACL)	R	.306	36	124	17	38	8	0	0	20	19	31	8	.403	.371
Minor League Totals				.306	36	124	17	38	8	0	0	20	19	31	8	.403	.371

22 GREGORY BARRIOS, SS

Born: April 8, 2004. **B-T:** R-R. **HT:** 6-0. **WT:** 180.
Signed: Venezuela, 2021. **Signed by:** Jose Rodriguez/Fernando Veracierto.

TRACK RECORD: Barrios was one of the top shortstops in Venezuela when the Brewers signed him for $1 million in Jan. 2021. A switch-hitter when he signed, Barrios made his pro debut in the Dominican Summer League in 2021 and took some of his at-bats from the right side against righthanders, then in 2022 hit exclusively righthanded in the Rookie-level Arizona Complex League.

SCOUTING REPORT: From the time he signed, Barrios has always stood out for his defensive acumen. He has smooth, easy actions at shortstop, where he's light on his feet with soft hands and good body control. He's not especially tooled up—it's average speed with a solid-average arm—but his instincts and internal clock help everything play up in the field. At the plate, Barrios has a good eye for the strike zone, makes good swing decisions and makes frequent contact, albeit with limited power. Dropping his weaker lefthanded swing helped his numbers tick up in 2022 and should benefit him long-term, though he will need to get stronger to do more damage on contact.

THE FUTURE: Barrios should get his first test of full-season ball in Low-A Carolina in 2023. He has a good mix of OBP skills and defense at a premium position, but becoming more than primarily a singles hitter will be critical as he faces more advanced pitchers.

| BA GRADE: 45/Extreme | | Hitting: 50 | | Power: 30 | | Speed: 50 | | Fielding: 55 | | Arm: 55 | |

Year	Age	Club (League)	Lvl	AVG	G	AB	R	H	2B	3B	HR	RBI	BB	SO	SB	OBP	SLG
2022	18	Brewers Gold (ACL)	R	.291	48	175	33	51	5	2	0	26	17	30	13	.360	.343
Minor League Totals				.261	78	276	52	72	9	2	0	32	31	44	22	.339	.308

23 MATT WOOD, C

Born: March 2, 2001. **B-T:** L-R. **HT:** 5-10. **WT:** 190.
Drafted: Penn State, 2022 (4th round). **Signed by:** James Fisher.

TRACK RECORD: At Penn State in 2022, Wood's 1.147 OPS ranked second in the Big Ten Conference and he hit .379/.480/.667 with more walks (36) than strikeouts (26). He finished top five in the conference in batting average, on-base percentage and slugging. The Brewers drafted him that year with their fourth-round pick and signed him for $347,500.

SCOUTING REPORT: There isn't one standout tool with Wood. He's a steady prospect on both sides of the ball and offers a consistent mix of 40s and 50s on his scouting card. He's a disciplined hitter who recognizes pitches well and makes frequent contact against both fastballs and breaking balls. Wood has a high-contact bat, isn't particularly physical, so his offensive value comes more on his on-base skills, but the uptick in power he showed in 2022 points to a chance for 15-20 home runs. Wood is a good athlete for a catcher and moves around well behind the plate. His arm strength is average but plays up because of his quick exchange and allows him to record pop times around 2.0 seconds and at times in the low 1.9-second range, though he will need to improve his accuracy and avoid a tendency to rush his throws.

THE FUTURE: Jeferson Quero is the best catching prospect in the organization and has more upside, but Wood is another young catcher who projects to stick at the position and has intriguing offensive potential. He could start his first full season in Low-A Carolina.

| BA GRADE: 40/High | | Hitting: 45 | | Power: 45 | | Speed: 40 | | Fielding: 50 | | Arm: 50 | |

Year	Age	Club (League)	Lvl	AVG	G	AB	R	H	2B	3B	HR	RBI	BB	SO	SB	OBP	SLG
2022	21	Brewers Blue (ACL)	R	.200	2	5	0	1	0	0	0	1	0	0	0	.200	.200
Minor League Totals				.200	2	5	0	1	0	0	0	1	0	0	0	.200	.200

24 CAM ROBINSON, RHP

Born: Sept. 6, 1999. **B-T:** R-R. **HT:** 6-1. **WT:** 194.
Drafted: HS—Orlando, Fla., 2017 (23rd round). **Signed by:** Mike Burns.
TRACK RECORD: Young for his high school class, Robinson signed at 17 as a 23rd-round pick in 2017. He spent his first few seasons mostly in Rookie ball with swollen ERAs and walk rates that made him a candidate to get released. Instead, Robinson turned around his career and returned after the canceled 2020 minor league season with an uptick in stuff in 2021 and moved through three levels up to Triple-A in 2022.
SCOUTING REPORT: Robinson is a relief prospect whose fastball operates at 92-95 mph and can touch 97 from his high three-quarters slot. He has a cutter-heavy approach and moves the ball around to all quadrants of the strike zone, though he will have to continue to improve his control after walking 11% of batters in 2022 with 14 wild pitches in 65 innings. When he's able to keep it down, Robinson flashes a plus curveball that has power in the low 80s with good depth and rotation at 2,600-2,700 rpm. He mixes in a mid-80s slider as well to give hitters another look.
THE FUTURE: Robinson doesn't have the elite stuff or good enough control to project as a closer in the majors, but his repertoire should allow him to carve out a middle relief role. Added to the 40-man roster after the 2022 season, Robinson will likely return to Triple-A Nashville but could make his major league debut at some point in 2023.

| BA GRADE: 40/High | | Fastball: 50 | | Curveball: 60 | | Slider: 45 | | Cutter: 50 | | Control: 40 | |

Year	Age	Club (League)	Lvl	W	L	ERA	G	GS	IP	H	HR	BB	SO	BB/9	SO/9	WHIP	AVG
2022	22	Wisconsin (MWL)	HiA	3	1	1.45	28	0	37	21	0	17	52	4.1	12.5	1.02	.163
2022	22	Biloxi (SL)	AA	0	0	1.23	13	0	15	8	0	5	16	3.1	9.8	0.89	.167
2022	22	Nashville (IL)	AAA	0	0	6.92	11	0	13	16	1	8	16	5.5	11.1	1.85	.314
Minor League Totals				7	13	4.87	126	13	198	204	9	119	237	5.4	10.8	1.63	.265

25 DYLAN O'RAE, SS

Born: Feb. 14, 2004. **B-T:** L-R. **HT:** 5-7. **WT:** 160.
Drafted: HS—Sarnia, Ontario, 2022 (3rd round). **Signed by:** Pete Orr.
TRACK RECORD: The Brewers made one of the surprise picks toward the top of the draft when they picked O'Rae in the third round (No. 102 overall) in 2022 and signed him for $597,500. Despite O'Rae's smaller stature, the Brewers loved what they saw from him as an amateur, including his time on the Canadian junior national team, and he made his pro debut in the Rookie-level Arizona Complex League.
SCOUTING REPORT: O'Rae is a small, savvy, high-energy player. He uses his smaller strike zone to his advantage and maintains a selective approach to not chase much off the plate and has the hand-eye coordination to put the ball in play at a high clip when he swings. A plus-plus runner underway, O'Rae's speed gives him another tool that plays on both sides of the ball. The biggest risk factor with O'Rae is how much power he will develop. He's mostly a singles hitter now with little impact, so he will have to get stronger and prove he can be more than a slap hitter. O'Rae has the hands and actions to play in the middle infield and is comfortable throwing from different angles, but his arm strength is fringy at best. Second base is his most likely defensive home, though his speed could help make center field another option.
THE FUTURE: O'Rae's athleticism, on-base skills and ability to play up the middle make for an intriguing prospect if he's able to do more damage on contact. He should play in Low-A Carolina in 2023.

| BA GRADE: 45/Extreme | | Hitting: 45 | | Power: 20 | | Speed: 70 | | Fielding: 45 | | Arm: 45 | |

Year	Age	Club (League)	Lvl	AVG	G	AB	R	H	2B	3B	HR	RBI	BB	SO	SB	OBP	SLG
2022	18	Brewers Gold (ACL)	R	.308	8	26	6	8	0	0	0	3	6	7	4	.424	.308
Minor League Totals				.308	8	26	6	8	0	0	0	3	6	7	4	.424	.308

26 LUKE ADAMS, 3B

Born: April 4, 2004. **B-T:** R-R. **HT:** 6-4. **WT:** 210.

Drafted: HS—Hinsdale, Ill., 2022 (12th round). **Signed by:** Ginger Poulson.

TRACK RECORD: Adams wasn't a high-profile amateur prospect in Illinois, but the Michigan State commit helped himself after his high school season by playing for Illinois Valley in the summer collegiate Prospect League, where he hit .404/.478/.737 in 68 plate appearances. The Brewers drafted him in the 12th round, and his success carried over into the Rookie-level Arizona Complex League.

SCOUTING REPORT: Adams is a physical 6-foot-4, 210 pounds and he finds a way to make a lot of contact despite an unorthodox swing. He starts his swing with a big hitch, at times bringing his hands from his back shoulder to below his belt and then up to his shoulder again, all while taking a leg kick into a big stride out front. He has an accurate barrel, a good sense of the strike zone and the strength to drive the ball with impact and projects for above-average power. Adams signed as a third baseman, though his time there might be limited. A below-average runner, he more likely ends up in an outfield corner, with a chance he could be a first baseman.

THE FUTURE: The Brewers found good value in a college hitter with a funky swing in 2020 when they drafted Joey Wiemer. Adams isn't that level of athlete, but he could prove to be another undervalued hitter. Low-A Carolina is up next.

| BA GRADE: 45/Extreme | | Hitting: 40 | | Power: 55 | | Speed: 40 | | Fielding: 40 | | Arm: 50 | |

Year	Age	Club (League)	Lvl	AVG	G	AB	R	H	2B	3B	HR	RBI	BB	SO	SB	OBP	SLG
2022	18	Brewers Gold (ACL)	R	.375	11	32	9	12	3	0	1	7	7	8	9	.512	.563
Minor League Totals				.375	11	32	9	12	3	0	1	7	7	8	9	.512	.562

27 VICTOR CASTANEDA, RHP

Born: Aug. 27, 1998. **B-T:** R-R. **HT:** 6-1. **WT:** 190.

Signed: Mexico, 2017. **Signed by:** Taylor Green.

TRACK RECORD: Signed out of Mexico in 2017, Castaneda's pitchability and atypical repertoire have allowed him to steadily progress through the system. He spent most of 2022 in Double-A Biloxi before a September promotion to Triple-A Nashville.

SCOUTING REPORT: Castaneda delivers the ball with a long arm swing in the back that moves into a three-quarters slot, and he throws a fastball in the low 90s that touches 94 mph. He keeps hitters off balance by throwing his offspeed stuff more than his fastball. The pitch that draws the most praise is his low-80s splitter, which kills spin and misses bats with its late tumble, though it's the pitch he has most trouble commanding. Castaneda also throws an average changeup, primarily against lefties. His slider improved in 2022 and he has feel to spin it, typically in the 2,600-2,700 rpm range, with enough movement to get empty swings against righties. Castaneda isn't wild, but has a hittable fastball and will need to tighten his command after walking 10% of batters in 2022.

THE FUTURE: Castaneda has developed as a starter, though there's a chance he ends up in the bullpen, where he could find a role pitching backward and giving hitters a different look in low-leverage situations. He'll return to Triple-A and could make his debut by the end of 2023.

| BA GRADE: 40/High | | Fastball: 40 | | Slider: 50 | | Changeup: 50 | | Splitter: 55 | | Control: 45 | |

Year	Age	Club (League)	Lvl	W	L	ERA	G	GS	IP	H	HR	BB	SO	BB/9	SO/9	WHIP	AVG
2022	23	Biloxi (SL)	AA	4	6	3.97	23	22	107	97	16	47	110	4.0	9.3	1.35	.240
2022	23	Nashville (IL)	AAA	2	0	5.14	3	3	14	14	1	5	8	3.2	5.1	1.36	.246
Minor League Totals				21	23	4.46	104	60	345	337	49	134	359	3.5	9.4	1.37	.253

28 JADHER AREINAMO, 2B/3B/SS

Born: Nov. 28, 2003. **B-T:** R-R. **HT:** 5-10. **WT:** 160.

Signed: Venezuela, 2021. **Signed by:** Jose Rodriguez/Javier Castillo.

TRACK RECORD: During showcases in Venezuela, Areinamo was a smaller player who didn't have big tools that would stand out during a workout, but his game savvy and ability to hit in games helped him land a $150,000 deal with the Brewers on Jan. 15, 2021. After debuting in the Dominican Summer League that year, Areinamo made an impressive jump to the United States in 2022 in the Rookie-level Arizona Complex League and drew a promotion to Low-A Carolina in August.

SCOUTING REPORT: Areinamo isn't tooled up, but he's a skillful player with a high baseball IQ. He's small and has minimal power, but he has a good grasp of the strike zone and excellent bat control. That leads to a high contact rate—he struck out in just 14% of plate appearances in 2022—as he sprayed line drives around the field. As he moves up the ladder, he will need to get stronger to have more than occasional gap power. A below-average runner, Areinamo is a high-energy player who has moved around between shortstop, second base and third base. He's an instinctive defender with a good internal clock who should continue to serve a utility role in the field, with second base probably his best defensive fit.

THE FUTURE: Areinamo likely returns to Low-A Carolina to begin 2023. If he gets stronger and increases his power, he could go from a sleeper to a more prominent prospect in the organization.

BA GRADE: 40/High | **Hitting:** 50 | **Power:** 30 | **Speed:** 40 | **Fielding:** 50 | **Arm:** 50

Year	Age	Club (League)	Lvl	AVG	G	AB	R	H	2B	3B	HR	RBI	BB	SO	SB	OBP	SLG
2022	18	Brewers Gold (ACL)	R	.323	34	127	31	41	10	3	1	21	19	19	4	.416	.472
2022	18	Carolina (CAR)	LoA	.299	28	97	16	29	2	0	0	11	9	14	2	.373	.320
2022	18	Wisconsin (MWL)	HiA	.077	7	26	0	2	1	0	0	1	0	8	0	.077	.115
Minor League Totals				.284	113	402	79	114	20	5	1	43	45	63	11	.367	.366

29 EDUARDO GARCIA, SS

Born: July 10, 2002. **B-T:** R-R. **HT:** 6-2. **WT:** 188.
Signed: Venezuela, 2018. **Signed by:** Reinaldo Hidalgo.

TRACK RECORD: Garcia signed with the Brewers for $1.1 million when he turned 16 in 2018. He didn't play much the next two years and was limited to just 10 games in 2019 because of an ankle injury before the pandemic wiped out the 2020 season. Garcia spent most of 2022 in Low-A Carolina before an August promotion to High-A Wisconsin, where his free-swinging tendencies were magnified as he struck out 40 times and didn't draw a walk in 108 plate appearances.

SCOUTING REPORT: Garcia's defense stands out the most. While he's a fringe-average runner, his instincts at the position help him cover ground well in the dirt, where he moves his feet well and has good body control, soft hands and a plus arm. Garcia surprised with 15 home runs in 2022 and can sting the ball up to 110 mph, so while he's not a big slugger, he has a chance to be a 15-20 home run hitter. His most glaring holes are in his approach and breaking ball recognition. Garcia swings at nearly everything and is vulnerable to whiffing through breaking stuff, which led to a 4% walk rate and 34% strikeout rate.

THE FUTURE: Garcia still has promising physical tools and the ability to play a premium position, but he will need to figure out a way to become a more selective hitter and make more contact. He's likely to return to Wisconsin for 2023.

BA GRADE: 40/High | **Hitting:** 20 | **Power:** 40 | **Speed:** 45 | **Fielding:** 55 | **Arm:** 60

Year	Age	Club (League)	Lvl	AVG	G	AB	R	H	2B	3B	HR	RBI	BB	SO	SB	OBP	SLG
2022	19	Carolina (CAR)	LoA	.262	85	347	43	91	13	3	10	48	19	122	14	.309	.403
2022	19	Wisconsin (MWL)	HiA	.248	26	105	11	26	3	0	5	17	0	40	1	.269	.419
Minor League Totals				.264	167	652	95	172	34	6	20	102	41	226	19	.323	.426

30 FREDDY ZAMORA, SS

Born: Nov. 1, 1998. **B-T:** R-R. **HT:** 6-1. **WT:** 190.
Drafted: Miami, 2020 (2nd round). **Signed by:** Lazaro Llanes.

TRACK RECORD: Injuries have continued to plague Zamora, who tore an anterior cruciate ligament in his left knee during a 2020 preseason practice at Miami but still became a second-round pick that year. After making his pro debut in 2021, Zamora played 24 games for Double-A Biloxi in 2022, then had season-ending surgery to repair a dislocated left shoulder suffered in May.

SCOUTING REPORT: Zamora got off to a slow start before his 2022 season ended abruptly, but at his best he has shown the ability to handle shortstop with solid bat-to-ball skills. Those injuries create more concern about his ability to handle shortstop. When healthy, he has shown good lateral range and quickness at the position and a solid-average arm, but he needs to be more reliable after committing 11 errors in just 24 games. A tick above-average runner, Zamora doesn't swing and miss excessively, but he's also entering his age-24 season and hasn't shown much power, with a chance for 8-12 home runs.

THE FUTURE: The 2023 season will be critical for Zamora, both in terms of staying on the field and proving himself against upper-level competition, with a likely return to Double-A.

BA GRADE: 40/High | **Hitting:** 40 | **Power:** 30 | **Speed:** 55 | **Fielding:** 50 | **Arm:** 55

Year	Age	Club (Leagu	Lvl	AVG	G	AB	R	H	2B	3B	HR	RBI	BB	SO	SB	OBP	SLG
2022	23	Biloxi (SL)	AA	.209	24	91	10	19	4	0	1	5	5	22	4	.270	.286
Minor League Totals				.281	116	438	80	123	26	1	7	54	62	98	14	.378	.393

Minnesota Twins

BY JJ COOPER

Failure has found a new level in the Twin Cities. Minnesota finished 78-84 and in third place in the American League Central in 2022. Crushed by injuries that saw the team use 13 different outfielders, the Twins found they could not keep up with the Guardians or White Sox as September wore on.

For a team with playoff hopes, it was a failure. And it was an understandably frustrating season for fans, but also a sign of the health of the organization. The Twins managed to lock up homegrown center fielder Byron Buxton and sign shortstop Carlos Correa to a $35 million contract to make a playoff push.

The narrative has changed. A team that 20 years ago was slated for contraction now can be disappointed by seasons in which it carried payrolls that make AL Central rivals in Cleveland and Kansas City blanch.

Minnesota was in the division race until September, and that meant the team went big on trades—for Tyler Mahle and Jorge Lopez—to try to help acquire needed reinforcements when the deficiencies in the bullpen and rotation became apparent.

Those moves should help the pitching staff in 2023. With Kenta Maeda, Sonny Gray, Joe Ryan and Mahle, the Twins have a solid core of starting pitchers to build around. Jhoan Duran and Lopez should give the team a solid back of the bullpen.

But with Correa opting out of his contract and Buxton reminding everyone that he's both extremely talented and not very durable, the Twins' lineup has a lot more questions. Unlike 2022, if the club wants to bolster the big league team with trades, it's going to offer prospects from a thinner farm system, largely because of the trades it has already made.

Minnesota has traded away its first-, second-, third- and fourth-round picks in the 2021 draft. The Twins also dealt the team's third-, sixth- and eighth-round picks from the 2019 draft. The deal to bring in Lopez from the Orioles cost Juan Rojas and Juan Nuñez, two of the organization's best young arms in the Florida Complex League.

Add it up, and the depth of the Twins' farm system is not nearly what it was a few years ago. A couple of apparently missed first-round picks in Keoni Cavaco (2019) and Aaron Sabato (2020) have hurt, but the Twins have largely made up for those misses by drafting well after the first round.

The 2021 draft saw numerous day two picks turn into solid trade chips, and 14th-rounder David Festa is now one of the team's better pitching prospects. The Twins' supplemental first-

The Twins' bullpen was shaky for much of 2022, but rookie Jhoan Duran was one constant.

PROJECTED 2026 LINEUP

Catcher	Ryan Jeffers	26
First Base	Jose Miranda	28
Second Base	Luis Arraez	29
Third Base	Brooks Lee	25
Shortstop	Royce Lewis	27
Left Field	Emmanuel Rodriguez	23
Center Field	Byron Buxton	32
Right Field	Matt Wallner	28
Designated Hitter	Edouard Julien	27
No. 1 Starter	Connor Prielipp	25
No. 2 Starter	Joe Ryan	30
No. 3 Starter	Louie Varland	28
No. 4 Starter	Marco Raya	24
No. 5 Starter	David Festa	26
Closer	Jhoan Duran	28

rounder in 2019, outfielder Matt Wallner, should play in the majors in 2023. Righthander Matt Canterino, the 2019 second-rounder, remains a potential power arm, and that same draft also brought in righthander Louie Varland and second baseman Edouard Julien in the late rounds.

A wave of international signings, led by outfielders Emmanuel Rodriguez and Yasser Mercedes, could help ease some of those concerns.

There is still risk that the Twins will find themselves in purgatory in 2023. They are good enough to potentially contend for a playoff spot if they get better health from their regulars, but they still seem far from able to compete for an American League pennant. ∎

MINNESOTA TWINS

TOP 2023 MLB CONTRIBUTORS	RANK
Royce Lewis, SS	1
Edouard Julien, 2B/1B	4
Louie Varland, RHP	8
BREAKOUT PROSPECTS	**RANK**
Yasser Mercedes, OF	12
Jose Rodriguez, OF	14
Bryan Acuña, SS	21

SOURCE OF TOP 30 TALENT

Homegrown	26	Acquired	4
College	13	Trade	0
Junior college	1	Rule 5 draft	0
High school	5	Independent league	0
Nondrafted free agent	0	Free agent/waivers	0
International	7		

LF
Misael Urbina (21)
Kala'i Rosaio
Alerick Soularie

CF
Emmanuel Rodriguez (3)
Yasser Mercedes (12)
Mark Contreras
DaShawn Keirsey
Fredy Michel

RF
Matt Wallner (6)
Jose Rodriguez (14)

3B
Brooks Lee (2)
Dalton Shuffield
Jake Rucker
Rafael Cruz

SS
Royce Lewis (1)
Noah Miller (15)
Danny De Andrade (17)

2B
Austin Martin (13)
Tanner Schobel (25)
Bryan Acuña (21)
Michael Helman (27)

1B
Edouard Julien (4)
Aaron Sabato (30)

C
Noah Cardenas
Ricardo Peña

LHP

LHSP	LHRP
Connor Prielipp (5)	Jaylen Nowlin (29)
Brent Headrick (18)	

RHP

RHSP	RHRP
Marco Raya (7)	Matt Canterino (11)
Louie Varland (8)	Ronny Henriquez (24)
David Festa (9)	Steven Cruz (28)
Simeon Woods-Richardson (10)	Andrew Morris
Jordan Balazovic (16)	Brayan Medina
Cole Sands (19)	Cory Lewis
Blayne Enlow (20)	
Alejandro Hidalgo (22)	
Sean Mooney (23)	
Miguel Olivares	
Travis Adams	

1 ROYCE LEWIS, SS

Born: June 5, 1999. **B-T:** R-R. **HT:** 6-2. **WT:** 200.
Drafted: HS—San Juan Capistrano, Calif., 2017 (1st round).
Signed by: John Leavitt.

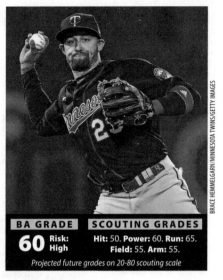

BRACE HEMMELGARN/MINNESOTA TWINS/GETTY IMAGES

BA GRADE	SCOUTING GRADES
60 Risk: High	Hit: 50. Power: 60. Run: 65. Field: 55. Arm: 55.

Projected future grades on 20-80 scouting scale

TRACK RECORD: The No. 1 pick in the 2017 draft, Lewis has already endured numerous peaks and valleys in his career before he has even graduated from prospect status. After establishing himself as a promising hitter with an excellent 2018 season at Class A, Lewis looked lost at the plate in 2019. His batting average, on-base percentage and slugging percentage all dipped by 60-70 points while his strikeout rate soared. The coronavirus pandemic meant he didn't get to play in any real games in 2020, and his 2021 season never got going because he was diagnosed in spring training with a completely torn anterior cruciate ligament in his right knee that required surgery. He returned to action in 2022 and earned a pair of callups to Minnesota. In his first game in center field with the Twins, he re-tore his right ACL while making a catch at the wall. He had surgery to repair this partial tear in June. While multiple ACL tears are rare in baseball, they are more common in football. A study in the Orthopaedic Journal of Sports Medicine showed that NFL players with two ACL injuries in the same knee returned to play with similar recovery rates as players who had one ACL injury, but it did often take them a little longer to return to action.

SCOUTING REPORT: For all his injuries and struggles, Lewis should still turn out to be a middle-of-the-lineup force who can hit for average and power while being an asset defensively and on the basepaths. Before his second knee injury, Lewis was looking like everything the Twins had hoped for when they drafted him first overall. He has cleaned up his setup at the plate, which closed some holes in his swing. Most significantly, Lewis turned a big leg lift into a much smaller toe tap. That has allowed him to reduce a tendency to bail out with his lower half, which has improved his ability to stay on breaking pitches on the outer third of the plate. Lewis has excellent trunk rotation speed, which allows him to generate bat speed and power to all fields when he keeps his lower half in sync. His power proved to be a revelation in 2022. His 114 mph max exit velocity ranked in the top 6% of all MLB hitters. With better plate coverage, he has a shot to be an average hitter with plus power. Defensively, Lewis has above-average range at shortstop with a plus arm. He has the tools to be a plus defender at second or third base,

BEST TOOLS

BATTING

Best Hitter for Average	Brooks Lee
Best Power Hitter	Matt Wallner
Best Strike-Zone Discipline	Edouard Julien
Fastest Baserunner	Royce Lewis
Best Athlete	Royce Lewis

PITCHING

Best Fastball	Matt Canterino
Best Curveball	Marco Raya
Best Slider	Connor Prielipp
Best Changeup	David Festa
Best Control	Louie Varland

FIELDING

Best Defensive Catcher	Noah Cardenas
Best Defensive Infielder	Noah Miller
Best Infield Arm	Royce Lewis
Best Defensive Outfielder	Yasser Mercedes
Best Outfield Arm	Matt Wallner

above-average in center field and plus in either outfield corner. Lewis was a plus-plus runner before his knee injuries. It's possible he may be a little slower when he returns, but his speed should still be an asset.

THE FUTURE: Lewis will likely miss the first few months of 2023 as he rehabs his right knee. When he is ready to go, he should fit onto the Twins' MLB roster as a righthanded hitter with power. In addition to his impressive tools, Lewis' makeup is lauded, and he quickly made a positive impression on his big league teammates. His versatility means that when he's ready he could play wherever the Twins need him.

Year	Age	Club (League)	Lvl	AVG	G	AB	R	H	2B	3B	HR	RBI	BB	SO	SB	OBP	SLG
2022	23	St. Paul (IL)	AAA	.313	34	131	30	41	12	1	5	14	18	32	12	.405	.534
2022	23	Minnesota (AL)	MLB	.300	12	40	5	12	4	0	2	5	1	5	0	.317	.550
Major League Totals				.300	12	40	5	12	4	0	2	5	1	5	0	.317	.550
Minor League Totals				.270	336	1335	240	361	75	11	35	164	124	272	80	.338	.422

2 BROOKS LEE, SS

Born: Feb. 14, 2001. **B-T:** B-R. **HT:** 6-2. **WT:** 205.
Drafted: Cal Poly, 2022 (1st round). **Signed by:** Brian Tripp.

TRACK RECORD: Lee ranked No. 38 on the Baseball America ranking of draft prospects in 2019, but everyone knew he was headed to Cal Poly to play for his father, hitting guru Larry Lee, so he went unpicked. After a hamstring injury sidelined him for the shortened 2020 season, Lee put up a 1.010 OPS in 2021 and then hit .357/.462/.664 with 46 walks and just 28 strikeouts in 2022. He also hit with wood in the Cape Cod League and was a star for USA Baseball's Collegiate National Team. Heading into the 2022 daft, Lee ranked as the No. 2 prospect in the class but slid to the Twins at No. 8 overall. His $5.675 million signing bonus was the sixth-largest in the class and second only to Jacob Berry's $6 million among collegians.

BA GRADE

60 Risk: High

SCOUTING REPORT: Lee is a switch-hitter who has hit everywhere he has played. His lefthanded swing is a work of art. He is short and direct to the ball with the balance to provide adjustability if he gets a little fooled. His righthanded swing is not as smooth and is more pull-heavy. He projects as a plus-plus hitter with average power. Lee has the hands to play shortstop and the internal clock, but he doesn't move fluidly, and his range is fringe-average at best. His body is somewhat maxed out already, and he's not expected to add agility. He has the hands and accurate, above-average arm to be a plus defender at third base, which is where he most likely ends up.
THE FUTURE: Lee was viewed as arguably the safest pick in the 2022 draft because of his bat. He'll have to show he can stay healthy after battling back and hamstring injuries. If he does, he should be a fast mover as a potential .300 hitter with the ability to stay on the infield.

SCOUTING GRADES	Hitting: 70	Power: 50	Speed: 40	Fielding: 50	Arm: 55

Year	Age	Club (League)	Lvl	AVG	G	AB	R	H	2B	3B	HR	RBI	BB	SO	SB	OBP	SLG
2022	21	Twins (FCL)	R	.353	4	17	2	6	2	0	0	3	0	0	0	.353	.471
2022	21	Cedar Rapids (MWL)	HiA	.289	25	97	14	28	4	0	4	12	16	18	0	.395	.454
2022	21	Wichita (TL)	AA	.375	2	8	1	3	0	0	0	0	0	2	0	.375	.375
Minor League Totals				.303	31	122	17	37	6	0	4	15	16	20	0	.388	.451

3 EMMANUEL RODRIGUEZ, OF

Born: Feb. 28, 2003. **B-T:** L-L. **HT:** 5-10. **WT:** 210.
Signed: Dominican Republic, 2019. **Signed by:** Manuel Luciano.

TRACK RECORD: When Rodriguez signed for $2.5 million in 2019 as Minnesota's top signee, his combination of power and athleticism was intriguing. Thanks to an excellent work ethic, he has turned into one of the best young hitters in the minor leagues. After struggling to hit breaking balls in his 2021 pro debut, Rodriguez turned a weakness into a strength. He hit .272/.492/.551 in 47 games with Low-A Fort Myers in 2022 before his season ended in early June when he suffered a knee injury that required surgery. Rodriguez's walk rate (28.6%) and on-base percentage (.492) were both best among full-season players to bat at least 150 times.

BA GRADE

60 Risk: Very High

SCOUTING REPORT: Rodriguez's combination of power and an elite batting eye gives him a high ceiling as a middle-of-the-order bat. His chase rate ranked among the best in the minors in 2022. At an age when many hitters' approaches are rudimentary, Rodriguez knows the strike zone better than some umpires. He has to learn how to better handle pitchers who can change speeds, which led to some swing-and-miss in the zone in 2022. In addition to having a highly advanced understanding of the strike zone, Rodriguez hits the ball very hard, with average exit velocities above 90 mph. Rodriguez will stay in center field for now, but as an average runner who will likely continue to get bigger, he projects as an above-average defender in a corner outfield spot. He has a plus arm.
THE FUTURE: Rodriguez's 2022 season was both revelatory and frustrating. In his two months of action, he showed signs of immense upside that teams dream of developing, but his season ended early and prevented the Twins from testing him at High-A. With a strong 2023 season, Rodriguez could establish himself as one of the top prospects in baseball as an on-base machine with 25-plus home run potential.

SCOUTING GRADES	Hitting: 60	Power: 60	Speed: 50	Fielding: 50	Arm: 60

Year	Age	Club (League)	Lvl	AVG	G	AB	R	H	2B	3B	HR	RBI	BB	SO	SB	OBP	SLG
2022	19	Fort Myers (FSL)	LoA	.272	47	136	35	37	5	3	9	25	57	52	11	.492	.551
Minor League Totals				.244	84	262	66	64	10	5	19	48	80	108	20	.429	.538

4 EDOUARD JULIEN, 2B/1B

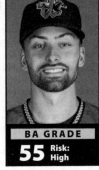

BA GRADE

55 Risk: High

Born: April 30, 1999. **B-T:** L-R. **HT:** 6-2. **WT:** 195.
Drafted: Auburn, 2019 (18th round). **Signed by:** Jack Powell.
TRACK RECORD: When the Twins drafted Julien in 2019, the Quebec native was one of the youngest eligible college players in the class. He had been a consistent power threat at Auburn, and his 429-foot home run in the 2019 College World Series was at the time tied for the longest in TD Ameritrade Park history. As a pro, Julien has been an on-base machine. His 208 walks during the 2021-22 seasons are 30 more than any other minor leaguer, and his .437 on-base percentage is best at the 700-plate appearance cutoff. Julien boosted his stock in the Arizona Fall League, which he led with a .400 average, .563 OBP and 1.249 OPS while popping five homers in 21 games.
SCOUTING REPORT: Julien's combination of strengths and weaknesses makes him an intriguing but somewhat limited prospect. He knows how to work counts and get on base, and his above-average power will make a pitcher pay for a mistake. But going back to his college days at Auburn, he has struggled to find a position to play. The Twins have worked extensively with Julien on his defense, but he still lacks a clear position. His hands have improved, but his limited range makes him well below-average at second base. He also played third base at Auburn and then in 2021 as a Twins minor leaguer, but left field or first base are his most likely landing spots. Even at those positions, the hope is he can be playable defensively. Before 2022, Julien had never hit even .275 in a season, either as a pro or at Auburn, but he raised that to .300 at Double-A Wichita. As a hitter, Julien works counts, hits line drives and has average power to punish a pitcher who falls behind in the count. He's not nearly as effective against lefthanders.
THE FUTURE: Julien's ability to get on base and hit righthanders will earn him a big league job, possibly as early as 2023. Improving on defense and at the plate against lefties could help him earn a larger role.

SCOUTING GRADES .	Hitting: 60	Power: 50	Speed: 45	Fielding: 30	Arm: 50

Year	Age	Club (League)	Lvl	AVG	G	AB	R	H	2B	3B	HR	RBI	BB	SO	SB	OBP	SLG
2022	23	Wichita (TL)	AA	.300	113	400	77	120	19	3	17	67	98	125	19	.441	.490
Minor League Totals				.283	225	794	170	225	47	4	35	139	208	269	53	.437	.485

5 CONNOR PRIELIPP, LHP

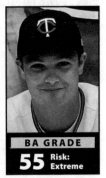

BA GRADE

55 Risk: Extreme

Born: Jan. 10, 2001. **B-T:** L-L. **HT:** 6-2. **WT:** 210.
Drafted: Alabama, 2022 (2nd round). **Signed by:** Matt Williams.
TRACK RECORD: Because of the coronavirus pandemic and a 2021 elbow injury that required Tommy John surgery, Prielipp threw just 28 innings for Alabama in three years. He was so impressive when he arrived at Alabama that he earned the Opening Day start as a freshman in the rugged Southeastern Conference. He didn't allow a run in his four starts in 2020 before the pandemic ended the season. He made an effective Opening Day start to begin 2021 but threw just two other innings in two starts before being shut down. Prielipp's recovery from Tommy John surgery allowed him to get back on the mound throwing bullpens before the 2022 draft. The Twins selected him in the second round.
SCOUTING REPORT: Before his injury, Prielipp was viewed as one of the best arms in the 2022 draft. His slider has earned plus-plus grades at its best. It's a nearly 3,000 rpm snapdragon that left college hitters baffled. Prielipp's fastball has touched 95-96 mph but generally sits more in the 92-93 range. The pitch is amplified by Prielipp's arm slot, release point and angle. The lefthander also throws an above-average changeup in the low 80s that has potential to become a weapon against righthanded hitters, but he barely used it in college. Prielipp looked rusty in his predraft bullpens, but his velocity was fine.
THE FUTURE: If Prielipp returns to his pre-injury form, something he hinted at in instructional league, the Twins may have landed a top-of-the-draft pitching prospect with a second-round pick. By Opening Day 2023, he'll be nearly two years removed from Tommy John surgery and should be ready for an assignment to High-A Cedar Rapids. As impressive as Prielipp has been when healthy, he's a Wisconsin prep product with very few innings of experience, which may influence how quickly he moves.

SCOUTING GRADES	Fastball: 60	Slider: 70	Changeup: 55	Control: 55

Year	Age	Club (League)	Lvl	W	L	ERA	G	GS	IP	H	HR	BB	SO	BB/9	SO/9	WHIP	AVG
2022	21	Did not play—Injured															

6 MATT WALLNER, OF

Born: Dec. 12, 1997. **B-T:** L-R. **HT:** 6-5. **WT:** 220.
Drafted: Southern Mississippi, 2019 (1st round supp). **Signed by:** Derrick Dunbar.

TRACK RECORD: A Minnesota native and Twins draftee out of high school, Wallner committed to North Dakota, where he would have likely been the team's best hitter and pitcher as a true freshman. The school dropped its baseball program and Wallner ended up at Southern Mississippi, where he became the Baseball America Freshman of the Year in 2017. The Twins drafted him again in 2019. After a solid 2021 season, Wallner broke out in 2022 as he climbed three levels and made his MLB debut. He totaled 30 home runs between the minors and majors.

SCOUTING REPORT: Wallner's plus-plus arm is the bane of third base coaches. He can turn what seem like easy send decisions into outs where the baserunner

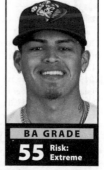

BA GRADE
50 Risk: High

never even got a chance to slide. He had 13 assists in 2022, and he topped out at 100.3 mph on throws in his brief MLB stint. Wallner's plus-plus power is nearly as impressive. He hits screaming line drives and mammoth home runs. His nearly 94 mph average exit velocity was among the best in the minors in 2022. Among MLB hitters with 25 or more balls in play, his 53% hard-hit percentage ranked 10th out of 565 batters. The catch? Wallner has significant swing-and-miss issues. His selectivity isn't an issue as much as his swing. Wallner's lofted, lengthy bat path translates to swings and misses in the strike zone. That's the trade-off he has made to get to his big power. He's a well below-average hitter, but one who could hit 35 home runs in a full season.

THE FUTURE: Wallner's power and arm are top tier, but he faces questions about whether he will make enough contact to get to his power. He heads to spring training with a shot at a big league role.

SCOUTING GRADES	Hitting: 30	Power: 70	Speed: 55	Fielding: 45	Arm: 70

Year	Age	Club (League)	Lvl	AVG	G	AB	R	H	2B	3B	HR	RBI	BB	SO	SB	OBP	SLG
2022	24	Wichita (TL)	AA	.299	78	268	61	80	15	1	21	64	62	107	8	.436	.597
2022	24	St. Paul (IL)	AAA	.247	50	190	29	47	17	3	6	31	35	63	1	.376	.463
2022	24	Minnesota (AL)	MLB	.228	18	57	4	13	3	0	2	10	6	25	1	.323	.386
Major League Totals				.228	18	57	4	13	3	0	2	10	6	25	1	.323	.386
Minor League Totals				.269	261	974	173	262	67	8	50	176	149	350	10	.382	.508

7 MARCO RAYA, RHP

Born: Aug. 7, 2002. **B-T:** R-R. **HT:** 6-1. **WT:** 170.
Drafted: HS—Laredo, Texas, 2020 (4th round). **Signed by:** Trevor Brown.

TRACK RECORD: Raya was a pitcher trending in the right direction when the coronavirus pandemic shutdown ended the 2020 high school season in mid-March. The Twins nabbed him in the fourth round with the 128th overall pick and signed him for $410,000. So far, Raya has looked like a steal. He has shown feel for four pitches, throws strikes and is an excellent competitor on the mound. He missed the entire 2021 season with shoulder fatigue and made his pro debut with Low-A Fort Myers in 2022.

SCOUTING REPORT: Raya has some of the best stuff in the Twins' organization, with a 93-95 mph four-seam fastball with riding life that comes in on a flat plane thanks to his short stature. He already has two quality breaking

BA GRADE
55 Risk: Extreme

pitches, and his changeup made strides in 2022. Raya's average changeup has more deception and depth than it had coming into 2022 thanks to a new split-change grip he learned from fellow Twins prospect Matt Canterino. Raya's plus slider has both depth and sweep, and he already has feel for locating it in the zone or down and out for chases as needed. His bigger, slower, high-70s curveball is above-average with plenty of depth. It can be a bat-misser, like his slider. He has average control.

THE FUTURE: With four major league-caliber pitches, Raya has the ingredients to be an MLB starter. He's got a lot of development ahead to get to that point, and his biggest focus will be on adding strength and durability. His legs are skinny and could use some more mass. Raya topped 65 pitches in just six of his 19 outings in 2022, which explains why he threw just 65 innings. He needs to add weight and show he can more consistently get through five or six innings. He should be bound for High-A Cedar Rapids in 2023.

SCOUTING GRADES	Fastball: 65	Curveball: 55	Slider: 60	Changeup: 50	Control: 50

Year	Age	Club (League)	Lvl	W	L	ERA	G	GS	IP	H	HR	BB	SO	BB/9	SO/9	WHIP	AVG
2022	19	Fort Myers (FSL)	LoA	3	2	3.05	19	17	65	47	8	23	76	3.2	10.5	1.08	.199
Minor League Totals				3	2	3.05	19	17	65	47	8	23	76	3.2	10.5	1.08	.199

8 LOUIE VARLAND, RHP

Born: Dec. 9, 1997. **B-T:** L-R. **HT:** 6-1. **WT:** 205.
Drafted: Concordia (Minn.), 2019 (15th round). **Signed by:** Joe Bisenius.

TRACK RECORD: When he made his MLB debut against the Yankees on Sept. 7, Varland became the first player in Division II Concordia (Minn.) history to reach the big leagues. His biggest competition for that honor was his older brother. Gus Varland, a fellow alum of the St. Paul school, pitched in Double-A in 2022. Louie Varland is a scouting and development success story as a 15th-round pick in 2019 who has steadily gotten better each year.

BA GRADE

45 Risk: Medium

SCOUTING REPORT: Varland draws raves for his willingness to work and his ability to absorb and process instruction. When he arrived at Concordia, he generally sat in the mid 80s. These days he throws nearly 10 mph harder, with a fastball that sits 93-95 mph and touches 98 thanks to plenty of time in the weight room. He's also steadily developed his secondary offerings. Early in his pro career, Varland developed an average changeup. Now his slider has improved from well below-average to average. He has added sweep to it, making it more of a swing-and-miss pitch. He has started to throw a fringe-average 88-90 mph cutter. That's important, because while his slider is a chase pitch, his cutter is something he consistently throws for strikes. The cutter enhances his slider's effectiveness because now he can steal a strike if hitters read spin and lay off. Varland doesn't have a true plus offspeed pitch, but he generates deception from a slightly closed delivery and has plus control.

THE FUTURE: Varland is the next in what has been a long line of Twins' crafty righthanders. He projects as a back-of-the-rotation starter who should compete for a big league job in spring training.

SCOUTING GRADES	Fastball: 60	Slider: 50	Changeup: 50	Cutter: 45	Control: 60

Year	Age	Club (League)	Lvl	W	L	ERA	G	GS	IP	H	HR	BB	SO	BB/9	SO/9	WHIP	AVG
2022	24	Wichita (TL)	AA	7	4	3.34	20	19	105	102	14	39	119	3.3	10.2	1.34	.251
2022	24	St. Paul (IL)	AAA	1	1	1.69	4	4	21	15	1	3	27	1.3	11.4	0.84	.192
2022	24	Minnesota (AL)	MLB	1	2	3.81	5	5	26	26	4	6	21	2.1	7.3	1.23	.263
Major League Totals				1	2	3.81	5	5	26	26	4	6	21	2.1	7.3	1.23	.263
Minor League Totals				18	10	2.61	47	42	238	208	22	76	298	2.9	11.3	1.19	.231

9 DAVID FESTA, RHP

Born: March 8, 2000. **B-T:** R-R. **HT:** 6-6. **WT:** 185.
Drafted: Seton Hall, 2021 (13th round). **Signed by:** John Wilson.

TRACK RECORD: In recent years, the Twins have done an excellent job of finding and developing pitchers in the draft's later rounds. Between Bailey Ober (12th round, 2017), Josh Winder (seventh, 2018) and Louie Varland (15th, 2019), the Twins are averaging about one sleeper per draft. It looks likely that Festa, a 13th-rounder in 2021, will join that group. When the Twins drafted Festa out of Seton Hall in 2021, he was a college pitcher who had the projectability of a prep pitcher. A tall and skinny 6-foot-6, 185 pounds, Festa has gone from throwing 86-88 mph early in his college career to touching 98 in 2022. He earned a quick promotion to High-A Cedar Rapids after he held Florida State League opponents to a .148 average.

BA GRADE

50 Risk: High

SCOUTING REPORT: Festa's once below-average fastball is now a plus-plus 94-96 mph pitch that generates swings-and-misses in and above the strike zone thanks to its carry and velocity. His lanky build and somewhat funky delivery seems to make it harder for hitters to take comfortable swings. Festa has long had a plus mid-80s changeup, a pitch he perfected before he added velocity. Newfound power has improved Festa's high-80s power slider, which now flashes above-average. It's not consistent yet. When he's on, Festa has three swing-and-miss pitches to go with average control. Festa may need to add a slower curve to give him something to mess with hitters' timing.

THE FUTURE: The strides Festa has taken in the past two years are a strong indicator of what he could become. There's still room for the lanky righty to fill out. He should head to Double-A Wichita in 2023 and is a potential midrotation starter who would also fit as a higher-leverage reliever.

SCOUTING GRADES	Fastball: 70	Slider: 55	Changeup: 60	Control: 50

Year	Age	Club (League)	Lvl	W	L	ERA	G	GS	IP	H	HR	BB	SO	BB/9	SO/9	WHIP	AVG
2022	22	Fort Myers (FSL)	LoA	2	1	1.50	5	5	24	12	1	6	33	2.2	12.4	0.75	.148
2022	22	Cedar Rapids (MWL)	HiA	7	3	2.71	16	13	80	67	5	28	75	3.2	8.5	1.19	.233
Minor League Totals				10	4	2.57	25	18	112	82	6	38	120	3.1	9.6	1.07	.207

10 SIMEON WOODS RICHARDSON, RHP

Born: Sept. 27, 2000. **B-T:** R-R. **HT:** 6-3. **WT:** 210.
Drafted: HS—Sugar Land, Texas, 2018 (2nd round). **Signed by:** Ray Corbett (Mets).

TRACK RECORD: Before he ever made it out of Double-A, Woods Richardson had twice been traded for a big league starting pitcher. The Mets drafted him in the second round in 2018, then traded him to the Blue Jays for Marcus Stroman in 2019. The Twins picked him up in 2021, along with Austin Martin, for Jose Berrios. Woods Richardson missed roughly a month of the 2022 season on the Covid injured list, but he returned in mid July and made his MLB debut for the Twins in the final week of the regular season.

BA GRADE

45 Risk: Medium

SCOUTING REPORT: Woods Richardson's stuff and success varies from outing to outing. Seen on the right day, he'll locate a fringe-average 92-94 mph fastball that can touch 95-96, and he'll mix in three solid secondaries consisting of a slider, curveball and changeup. On other days, Woods Richardson sits 90-92 mph with less consistent offspeed pitches and scattershot control. The tricky part is separating how much of his success is based around the same delivery issues that lead to his inconsistency. He isn't direct to the plate with his delivery, but that helps add deception to an assortment of pitches that otherwise are fairly generic. Woods Richardson has a high over-the-top release point, so he generally works up and down in the strike zone, which also helps his average curveball play. His fringe-average low-80s slider gives hitters something different to worry about. His above-average changeup is more consistent.

THE FUTURE: Woods Richardson is not a finished product, and if he can improve his velocity as well as the movement on his slider and his control, he has the ability to be a No. 4 starter.

SCOUTING GRADES   **Fastball:** 45   **Curveball:** 50   **Slider:** 45   **Changeup:** 55   **Control:** 50

Year	Age	Club (League)	Lvl	W	L	ERA	G	GS	IP	H	HR	BB	SO	BB/9	SO/9	WHIP	AVG
2022	21	Wichita (TL)	AA	3	3	3.06	16	15	71	56	4	26	77	3.3	9.8	1.16	.217
2022	21	St. Paul (IL)	AAA	2	0	2.21	7	7	37	21	2	10	38	2.5	9.3	0.85	.165
2022	21	Minnesota (AL)	MLB	0	1	3.60	1	1	5	3	1	2	3	3.6	5.4	1.00	.167
Major League Totals				0	1	3.60	1	1	5	3	1	2	3	3.6	5.4	1.00	.167
Minor League Totals				15	18	3.67	71	66	285	236	18	98	344	3.1	10.9	1.17	.223

11 MATT CANTERINO, RHP

Born: Dec. 14, 1997. **B-T:** R-R. **HT:** 6-2. **WT:** 222.
Drafted: Rice, 2019 (2nd round). **Signed by:** Greg Runser.

TRACK RECORD: Canterino demonstrated flashes of dominance at Rice, although his fastball/slider approach and funky and deceptive but unorthodox delivery led many to see a future in the bullpen. A new grip helped transform his changeup into his best pitch. When healthy, Festa has dominated, but a balky elbow has bothered him since 2021. He was shut down again in 2022 and eventually had Tommy John surgery in August.

SCOUTING REPORT: Elbow reconstruction surgery requires a difficult, taxing rehabilitation process, but Canterino's surgery also hopefully puts a nagging problem in his rear-view mirror. Elbow issues limited him to 23 innings in 2021 and he never topped 70 pitches in a start in 2022. When healthy, Canterino has the best stuff of any Twins minor leaguer. His mid-90s, plus fastball has life and arm-side run, but it's sometimes his third best pitch. Canterino can carve up lineups with his low-80s, plus-plus changeup and high-80s, plus power slider. Both are able to generate plenty of whiffs and are deadly with two strikes. His control faltered in 2022, but he's generally been a fringe-average strike thrower.

THE FUTURE: Canterino will likely miss all of 2023 recovering, but once healthy, he has the stuff to make an immediate impact. He has the weapons to close if the Twins want to speed up his path by moving him to the pen, but he also has enough control to be a funky, somewhat dominating five-inning starter.

BA GRADE: 50/High   **Fastball:** 60   **Slider:** 60   **Changeup:** 70   **Control:** 45

Year	Age	Club (League)	Lvl	W	L	ERA	G	GS	IP	H	HR	BB	SO	BB/9	SO/9	WHIP	AVG
2022	24	Twins (FCL)	R	0	0	3.38	2	2	3	3	1	1	4	3.4	13.5	1.50	.300
2022	24	Wichita (TL)	AA	0	1	1.83	11	10	34	17	1	22	50	5.8	13.1	1.14	.142
Minor League Totals				2	2	1.48	26	25	85	38	3	35	130	3.7	13.8	0.86	.130

12 YASSER MERCEDES, OF

Born: Nov. 16, 2004. **B-T:** R-R. **HT:** 6-2. **WT:** 175.
Signed: Dominican Republic, 2021. **Signed by:** Fred Guerrero.

TRACK RECORD: Mercedes was born in Puerto Rico but grew up in the Dominican Republic. He was a longtime target of the Twins and signed for $1.7 million. He immediately demonstrated the kind of power and speed that Minnesota had seen as an amateur, but combined with a more advanced understanding of the strike zone than could have been expected. He finished fifth in the Dominican Summer League in batting average (.355), 10th in slugging (.555) and third in stolen bases (30).

SCOUTING REPORT: Mercedes has a chance to be a center fielder who can hit for power and average. Mercedes' 87 mph average exit velocity in 2022 was significantly higher than the average DSL player. He consistently barrels the ball. He will chase breaking balls away and sometimes gets a little pull happy, but the building blocks are there to be an above-average hitter. When he wants to, Mercedes can also be a very contact-oriented pest of a hitter. He's an above-average athlete with plus speed and shows the routes and reads to stick in center field. His arm is at least average as well, and he's shown an above-average arm in the past as an amateur.

THE FUTURE: Mercedes will come to the U.S. to play in the Florida Complex League in 2023. He's far from Minnesota, but it would not be surprising to see him leap up into the Twins top 10 before long. He has one of the more well-rounded tool sets in the organization and seems to be quickly adding baseball skills as well.

| BA GRADE: 55/Extreme | | Hitting: 55 | | Power: 55 | | Run: 60 | | Field: 55 | | Arm: 50 | |

Year	Age	Club (League)	Lvl	AVG	G	AB	R	H	2B	3B	HR	RBI	BB	SO	SB	OBP	SLG
2022	17	Twins (DSL)	R	.355	41	155	34	55	13	3	4	20	18	35	30	.420	.555
Minor League Totals				.355	41	155	34	55	13	3	4	20	18	35	30	.420	.555

13 AUSTIN MARTIN, 2B/OF

Born: March 23, 1999. **B-T:** R-R. **HT:** 6-0. **WT:** 185.
Drafted: Vanderbilt, 2020 (1st round). **Signed by:** Nate Murrie (Blue Jays).

TRACK RECORD: Martin was considered one of the best hitters in his college class, and he also showcased his versatility by playing six different positions at Vanderbilt. After being a productive singles hitter as a freshman, he slugged over .600 in 2019 and in the pandemic-shortened 2020 season in his draft year. The Blue Jays quickly traded him to the Twins in 2021's Jose Berrios deal. His disappointing 2022 season was interrupted by a wrist injury, but he did finish strong by hitting .373 in the Arizona Fall League.

SCOUTING REPORT: Two different teams have now tried to get Martin to drive the ball more, but he almost always reverts to focusing on getting his front foot down early and taking a direct, contact-oriented bat path. That approach should let him hit for average and get on base, but with zero impact at the plate. He has a .094 isolated slugging percentage for his pro career so far. He is a heady baserunner with plus speed. Martin is a confounding defender in the infield. Give him time, and he will revert to a tendency to get mechanical and double pump before throwing. He's much more fluid and his arm action is better when he is forced to rush himself, or when he's playing in the outfield. Because of that, his average arm plays better in the outfield than in the infield. At this point, it's unlikely he can stick at shortstop, but he could be a rangy second baseman and he's shown he can be an above-average defender in center or left.

THE FUTURE: Martin's 2022 season was a clear step backward in his development, both as far as his production and his potential. He can still be a useful big leaguer, but one who will likely be limited offensively and defensively as a rangy second baseman or center fielder with limited power.

| BA GRADE: 45/High | | Hitting: 55 | | Power: 30 | | Run: 60 | | Field: 55 | | Arm: 50 | |

Year	Age	Club (League)	Lvl	AVG	G	AB	R	H	2B	3B	HR	RBI	BB	SO	SB	OBP	SLG
2022	23	Twins (FCL)	R	.250	2	8	1	2	1	0	0	3	2	1	1	.400	.375
2022	23	Wichita (TL)	AA	.241	90	336	59	81	13	3	2	32	47	54	34	.367	.315
Minor League Totals				.255	185	674	127	172	32	5	7	70	109	138	49	.391	.349

14 JOSE RODRIGUEZ, OF

Born: June 10, 2005. **B-T:** R-R. **HT:** 6-2. **WT:** 196.
Signed: Dominican Republic, 2022. **Signed by:** Daniel Sanchez.

TRACK RECORD: Signed in January 2022, Rodriguez had an extremely impressive pro debut. He led the Dominican Summer League with 13 home runs, 49 RBIs and 31 extra-base hits while also ranking among the league leaders with a .605 slugging percentage and 115 total bases. He was named a Dominican League all-star.

SCOUTING REPORT: Rodriguez was viewed as the best slugger in the Twins' 2022 international signing class, but he's shown already as a pro that he can also handle velocity, a key benchmark for young sluggers to clear. Like many young power hitters, Rodriguez is overaggressive and is currently an easy mark for a pitcher with confidence in a changeup. He has bat speed and all-fields power, but with a pull-heavy approach. He's already big and thick, so depending on how he matures, he could end up sliding to first base, although his above-average arm fits in right field.

THE FUTURE: Rodriguez has yet to play in the U.S., but he passed his first pro test in impressive fashion. He's one of the team's best young power prospects in years, but he'll need to stay on top of his conditioning to remain in the outfield.

BA GRADE: 50/Extreme		Hit: 40		Power: 60		Run: 40			Field: 45			Arm: 60		

Year	Age	Club (League)	Lvl	AVG	G	AB	R	H	2B	3B	HR	RBI	BB	SO	SB	OBP	SLG
2022	17	Twins (DSL)	R	.289	55	190	39	55	15	3	13	49	21	52	5	.361	.605
Minor League Totals				.289	55	190	39	55	15	3	13	49	21	52	5	.361	.605

15 NOAH MILLER, SS

Born: Nov. 12, 2002. **B-T:** B-R. **HT:** 6-0. **WT:** 185.
Drafted: HS—Fredonia, Wis., 2021 (1st round supplemental). **Signed by:** Joe Bisenius.

TRACK RECORD: Miller is part of a family of slick-fielding infielders. He's the younger brother of Guardians infielder Owen Miller. Before he'd ever played a full-season MiLB game, Noah had already given the Twins MLB coaching staff a hint of what's to come. Given a few innings during early-March spring training games, Miller made difficult backhand plays look routine. He carried that same knack of making the hard play look easy to Low-A Fort Myers.

SCOUTING REPORT: Miller is the Twins' best MiLB defender at shortstop, with the actions, hands, range and internal clock to stay at the position for years to come. He's a potential Gold Glover with a plus arm. Defensively, he just needs to keep doing what he's doing. Offensively, he's got a lot more work ahead of him if he's to become a big leaguer. Miller has always had a contact-oriented approach, but he has to generate more pop to hit effectively with a wood bat. The switch-hitter doesn't use his legs effectively yet in his swing and he doesn't generate enough separation to get significant torque. He wore down over the course of his first full season. Over his final 46 games, he had just six extra-base hits and slugged under .200 in two different months.

THE FUTURE: Miller's future is extremely dependent on his development at the plate. He was overmatched in 2022, but with the caveat that he's a Wisconsin prep product who was adjusting to a faster game. He will need to spend a lot of work in the cage, but his exceptional glove should give him plenty of time to develop.

BA GRADE: 45/High		Hit: 40		Power: 20		Run: 50			Field: 65			Arm: 60		

Year	Age	Club (League)	Lvl	AVG	G	AB	R	H	2B	3B	HR	RBI	BB	SO	SB	OBP	SLG
2022	19	Fort Myers (FSL)	LoA	.211	108	383	62	81	12	4	2	24	76	110	23	.348	.279
Minor League Totals				.216	130	467	73	101	15	5	4	38	85	136	24	.342	.296

16 JORDAN BALAZOVIC, RHP

Born: Sept. 17, 1998. **B-T:** R-R. **HT:** 6-5. **WT:** 215.
Drafted: HS—Mississauga, Ont., 2016 (5th round). **Signed by:** Walt Burrows.

TRACK RECORD: After an impressive 2021 season with Double-A Wichita, Balazovic seemed poised to help the Twins' rotation at some point in 2022. Instead, he took a massive step backward. His stuff backed up and hitters feasted on him for much of the season with Triple-A St. Paul. He had the ninth-worst ERA and 12th-worst FIP among all MiLB pitchers with 70 or more innings.

SCOUTING REPORT: Balazovic's 2022 season was almost a disaster from start to finish, though he did show improved stuff and success in September, which sent him into the offseason on a high note. Balazovic came into the season without the same strength he showed in 2021. He also seemed to be stiffer and less athletic in his delivery all season. That played a part in his fastball losing 2-3 mph. He sat 94-96 mph in 2021 and touched 99. He topped out at 96 and sat 92-94 in 2022. Balazovic added a somewhat promising hard, high-80s slider. If he can regain his previous arm speed, it could become a plus pitch, but right now both it and his changeup are fringe-average. Grading Balazovic's pitches right now requires blending what he's shown in the past versus what he showed in 2022.

THE FUTURE: Balazovic has used two options already. The 2023 season should determine whether his 2022 season was a one-year setback or a new and troubling trend.

BA GRADE: 45/High			Fastball: 55		Slider: 50		Changeup: 45		Control: 40				
Year	Age	Club (League)	Lvl	W	L	ERA	G	GS	IP	H	HR	BB	SO	BB/9	SO/9	WHIP	AVG
2022	23	Fort Myers (FSL)	LoA	0	0	18.00	1	0	2	4	1	2	1	9.0	4.5	3.00	.400
2022	23	St. Paul (IL)	AAA	0	7	7.39	22	21	71	102	20	35	76	4.5	9.7	1.94	.336
Minor League Totals				23	23	4.19	92	79	397	398	44	143	431	3.2	9.8	1.36	.256

17 DANNY DE ANDRADE, SS

Born: April 10, 2004. **B-T:** R-R. **HT:** 5-11. **WT:** 173.
Signed: Venezuela, 2021. **Signed by:** Fred Guerrero/Luis Lajara.
TRACK RECORD: One of the Twins top targets in the 2021 international amateur class, De Andrade had long impressed scouts with a short, direct swing, a track record of performance in games and an advanced understanding of the game.
SCOUTING REPORT: When he signed, De Andrade swung at most anything, but he's developing a solid approach to get to pitches in the zone he can punish. He's developing into an above-average hitter with excellent contact skills and in 2022 demonstrated solid bat-to-ball skills. The only disappointment with De Andrade's development so far is something that's not really all that controllable. As he's matured, it's becoming clear he's not particularly twitchy. He's athletic with good body control, but without the quick first step that teams look for in a rangy shortstop. He does have a good head on his shoulders and feel for the game teams want in a shortstop. He has a plus arm and can throw from multiple arm angles. His actions and controlled approach can make him an average defender at shortstop, but he might be better as an above-average second or third baseman.
THE FUTURE: De Andrade is ready for full-season ball. He'll have to keep working hard to maintain his foot speed as he fills out, but his ability to slow the game down and process instruction should serve him well.

BA GRADE: 45/High		Hitting: 55		Power: 50		Run: 50			Field: 50			Arm: 60		
Year	Age	Club (League)	Lvl	AVG	G	AB	R	H	2B	3B	HR	RBI	BB	SO	SB	OBP	SLG
2022	18	Twins (FCL)	R	.242	48	178	27	43	9	1	4	23	19	34	4	.333	.371
Minor League Totals				.253	98	356	43	90	22	2	4	39	34	61	10	.337	.360

18 BRENT HEADRICK, LHP

Born: Dec. 17, 1997. **B-T:** L-L. **HT:** 6-6. **WT:** 227.
Drafted: Illinois State, 2019 (9th round). **Signed by:** Jeff Pohl.
TRACK RECORD: When the Twins drafted Headrick in the ninth round in 2019, they were taking a gamble that a pitcher with modest stuff but loads of competitiveness could embrace and improve in a pro pitching development program. It's worked. Headrick was the Missouri Valley Conference pitcher of the year in 2019, but his stuff was modest, as he often topped out in the high 80s. Now he touches 94 mph and still competes. He struck out 19 and walked no one in 12 innings while not allowing an earned run in two postseason starts for Double-A Wichita.
SCOUTING REPORT: Headrick is still a soft-tosser by the standards of 2022, but he's gained two ticks of velocity since he became a pro. He now sits 90-92 and can touch 95 mph. As importantly, he's embraced the Twins' work with him on his control and command. He threw just 45% strikes in his brief pro debut in 2019. Now, he's one of the best control artists in the Twins' organization. He threw his fringe-average fastball for strikes a remarkable 75% of the time. His average slider is especially effective against right-handers, while his changeup is above-average and keeps righthanders honest.
THE FUTURE: Headrick was rewarded for his breakout season by being added to the Twins' 40-man roster. He's got a shot to be a back-end starter or multi-inning reliever who can carve up lefties but survive against righties.

BA GRADE: 45/High			Fastball: 45		Slider: 50		Changeup: 55		Control: 60				
Year	Age	Club (League)	Lvl	W	L	ERA	G	GS	IP	H	HR	BB	SO	BB/9	SO/9	WHIP	AVG
2022	24	Cedar Rapids (MWL)	HiA	8	2	2.34	15	15	65	45	7	13	77	1.8	10.6	0.89	.188
2022	24	Wichita (TL)	AA	2	3	4.81	10	8	43	47	11	12	59	2.5	12.3	1.37	.273
Minor League Totals				13	10	3.39	44	40	175	159	23	65	226	3.3	11.6	1.28	.237

19 MISAEL URBINA, OF

Born: April 26, 2002. **B-T:** R-R. **HT:** 6-0. **WT:** 175.
Signed: Venezuela, 2018. **Signed by:** Fred Guerrero.

TRACK RECORD: Urbina's 2022 season got off to a late start as he was delayed in arriving in the U.S. because of visa issues, which likely ended any hope he had of making it to High-A Cedar Rapids before the end of the season. Instead, his season didn't get going until late July. In a second season with Low-A Fort Myers, he showed an improved approach and a modest improvement in power. He was hitting .300 at the end of August, but a 1-for-39 finish to the season carved 57 points off his batting average and more than 100 points off his season-ending slugging percentage.

SCOUTING REPORT: Urbina has gotten significantly bigger, stronger and slower since he signed, but the increased size and decreased speed has yet to pay off in increased power. He's a contact hitter who is a tough out for pitchers thanks to his ability to sneer at pitches off the plate and a stroke that doesn't miss often when he swings at hittable pitches. His two-strike approach is especially impressive. Defensively, he's now stretched in center field and will likely start playing more in the corners as he moves up the ladder.

THE FUTURE: Urbina remains a promising hitter, but one who will need to find more power to go with his steadily improving approach at the plate. He's ready for Cedar Rapids.

BA GRADE: 50/Extreme	Hitting: 55	Power: 40	Run: 50	Field: 45	Arm: 50

Year	Age	Club (League)	Lvl	AVG	G	AB	R	H	2B	3B	HR	RBI	BB	SO	SB	OBP	SLG
2022	20	Twins (FCL)	R	.250	10	40	3	10	4	0	0	5	2	9	1	.326	.350
2022	20	Fort Myers (FSL)	LoA	.246	50	191	28	47	16	1	5	22	23	51	9	.323	.419
Minor League Totals				.228	211	781	115	178	46	10	12	105	102	156	45	.326	.359

20 ALEJANDRO HIDALGO, RHP

Born: May 22, 2003. **B-T:** R-R. **HT:** 6-1. **WT:** 160.
Signed: Venezuela, 2019. **Signed by:** Andres Garcia/Joel Chicarelli/Aneudi Mercado/Rusbell Cabrera (Angels).

TRACK RECORD: Coming out of Venezuela, Hidalgo impressed with his stuff and feel for pitching, but an elbow injury as an amateur that required a screw in his elbow left some teams wary. Hidalgo was firmly establishing himself in 2022 as one of the better pitching prospects in the Angels system when shoulder soreness ended his season in early June. He worked on strengthening and rehabbing his shoulder in the second half, and the Twins were happy enough with his recovery to acquire him in the November trade that sent Gio Urshela to the Angels.

SCOUTING REPORT: Hidalgo's 88-93 mph average fastball has the flat plane and excellent life to be effective up in the zone. The pitch has around 20 inches of induced vertical break and he also gets plenty of arm-side run. He has plenty of confidence in his plus, low-80s changeup, as he can get hitters to swing over it. Sometimes it will show late fade as well. He is comfortable using it to righthanders and lefties. His high-70s curveball is a clear third pitch. It is a bigger breaker he struggles to command. He has above-average control and command.

THE FUTURE: Hidalgo was one of the youngest players in the California League in 2022. Even if the Twins start him back at Low-A, he still is on a relatively speedy track. He's a crafty back-end starter who will eventually need a better breaking ball, but can retire Class A hitters with the quality of his fastball and changeup.

BA GRADE: 45/High	Fastball: 50	Curveball: 40	Changeup: 60	Control: 55

Year	Age	Club (League)	Lvl	W	L	ERA	G	GS	IP	H	HR	BB	SO	BB/9	SO/9	WHIP	AVG
2022	19	Inland Empire (CAL)	LoA	0	3	4.62	10	10	39	34	3	19	58	4.4	13.4	1.36	.225
Minor League Totals				3	5	4.64	17	16	66	60	9	28	89	3.8	12.1	1.33	.232

21 BRYAN ACUÑA, SS

Born: Aug. 11, 2005. **B-T:** R-R. **HT:** 6-1. **WT:** 176.
Signed: Venezuela, 2022. **Signed by:** Jose Leon.

TRACK RECORD: Any diligent observer can tell Bryan Acuña was the younger brother of Ronald Acuña Jr., even if he didn't wear his name on his jersey, because he has a very similar swing clearly modeled after his brother. He has impressed with his hard-nosed approach and advanced understanding of the game.

SCOUTING REPORT: When he started making the rounds of the amateur showcase circuit, Acuña's short stature was a concern. He's kept growing. He was 5-foot-11 when he signed and he's now 6-foot-1. Acuña is a middle infielder who can play shortstop but may end up more effective as a plus defender at second base. He has good hands, a steady heartbeat and a quick transfer with a plus arm, although his range is a little limited. He's a fringe-average runner. Offensively, he makes good swing decisions and has above-average bat-to-ball skills. His power is quite modest for now, but likely will develop into below-average power or better as he matures.

THE FUTURE: Acuña's development so far has been encouraging. He's one of a number of very interesting young international prospects who could quickly climb the ladder in the next couple of years.

| BA GRADE: 50/Extreme | | Hit: 55 | | Power: 40 | | Run: 45 | | Field: 50 | | Arm: 60 | |

Year	Age	Club (League)	Lvl	AVG	G	AB	R	H	2B	3B	HR	RBI	BB	SO	SB	OBP	SLG
2022	16	Twins (DSL)	R	.310	43	145	33	45	12	0	0	16	20	36	9	.409	.393
Minor League Totals				.310	43	145	33	45	12	0	0	16	20	36	9	.409	.393

22 RONNY HENRIQUEZ, RHP

Born: June 20, 2000. **B-T:** R-R. **HT:** 5-10. **WT:** 155.
Signed: Dominican Republic, 2017. **Signed by:** Willy Espinal (Rangers).

TRACK RECORD: When Matt Wisler became a Twin, they looked at his ability to command his plus slider and asked him to start thinking about using it as his primary pitch. Henriquez is the next generation of this, as he's a short reliever who throws a slider and changeup, but rarely mixes in a fastball. Acquired along with Isiah Kiner-Falefa for Mitch Garver, Henriquez made his MLB debut late in the 2022 season with three brief appearances after a somewhat rocky Triple-A season.

SCOUTING REPORT: Henriquez may touch 97 mph and sit 94 with a relatively flat and lively average fastball, but batters can go an entire at-bat without ever seeing it. In his MLB debut, he threw three straight sliders to start off his first batter. Two batters later, he did the same thing again. He will double or triple-up on his above-average slider or above-average changeup, pop an average fastball at the top of the strike zone, then go back to working away from hitters with his best pitches with average control overall.

THE FUTURE: Henriquez had a rough 2022 season, but the pieces are there to be a useful MLB reliever, although he is somewhat prone to giving up big hits if he misses his spots. He'll compete for a spot in the Twins bullpen in 2023 as a pitcher with two remaining options.

| BA GRADE: 40/Medium | | Fastball: 50 | | Slider: 55 | | Changeup: 55 | | Control: 50 | |

Year	Age	Club (League)	Lvl	W	L	ERA	G	GS	IP	H	HR	BB	SO	BB/9	SO/9	WHIP	AVG
2022	22	St. Paul (IL)	AAA	3	4	5.66	24	14	95	99	19	33	106	3.1	10.0	1.38	.266
2022	22	Minnesota (AL)	MLB	0	1	2.31	3	0	12	8	1	3	9	2.3	6.9	0.94	.178
Major League Totals				0	1	2.31	3	0	12	8	1	3	9	2.3	6.9	0.94	.178
Minor League Totals				19	17	4.38	77	60	329	305	44	93	389	2.5	10.6	1.21	.243

23 BLAYNE ENLOW, RHP

Born: March 21, 1999. **B-T:** R-R. **HT:** 6-3. **WT:** 170.
Drafted: HS—St. Amant, La., 2017 (3rd round). **Signed by:** Greg Runser.

TRACK RECORD: When the Twins bought Enlow out of his Louisiana State commitment with a well above-slot $2 million bonus as a third-round pick in 2018, the hope was he would steadily gain velocity as he filled out to go with his already impressive feel for pitching. Tommy John surgery in 2021 derailed that to some extent, but he came back and pitched reasonably effectively in 2022.

SCOUTING REPORT: Enlow sits between 91-93 mph with his fastball, with flashes of 94-96, and doesn't have the stuff to rear back and blow hitters away. Instead, he has developed into a crafty pitcher with an array of average-ish pitches that play because he'll pitch backward. His cutter might be his best pitch, and it generates weak contact from same-side hitters and he has shown he can consistently command it. His curveball will flash above-average as well and his average changeup is enough to give lefties something to worry about. His normally average control took a step back in 2022, but that may be post-surgery rust.

THE FUTURE: Enlow is yet another in a seemingly long line of crafty pitchers the Twins have developed. He still has to get stretched out further if he's going to handle a starter's role long-term, but his most likely future is as a useful Triple-A arm who can fill in where needed in Minnesota as injuries arise.

| BA GRADE: 40/Medium | | Fastball: 45 | | Curveball: 50 | | Changeup: 50 | | Cutter: 55 | | Control: 45 | |

Year	Age	Club (League)	Lvl	W	L	ERA	G	GS	IP	H	HR	BB	SO	BB/9	SO/9	WHIP	AVG
2022	23	Fort Myers (FSL)	LoA	0	0	16.20	1	1	2	5	1	1	1	5.4	5.4	3.60	.417
2022	23	Wichita (TL)	AA	1	3	4.40	24	10	57	60	4	30	64	4.7	10.0	1.57	.270
Minor League Totals				16	16	3.56	75	52	299	285	19	114	273	3.4	8.2	1.34	.250

24 COLE SANDS, RHP

Born: July 17, 1997. **B-T:** R-R. **HT:** 6-3. **WT:** 215.
Drafted: Florida State, 2018 (5th round). **Signed by:** Brett Dowdy.
TRACK RECORD: The younger brother of Cubs minor league lefthander Carson Sands, Cole was a durable starter for three years at Florida State. Sands made his MLB debut as a reliever on May 1, 2022. He struggled through three starts in the Twins rotation a month later and was sent back to Triple-A. He was hit pretty hard, both at St. Paul and in return trips to Minnesota, but finished the year with four effective innings of relief to help fellow rookie Louie Varland get his first MLB win.
SCOUTING REPORT: Sands has to change hitters' eye levels and keep them off balance because he doesn't have a pitch that can dominate a hitter. His below-average four-seam fastball sits 90-93 mph and lacks life, but it does give hitters something they have to look for up in the zone, which helps set up the rest of his arsenal. Everything else—his fringe-average changeup and splitter, and his below-average slider and fringe-average curveball—are trying to get below hitters' bats at the bottom of the zone or generate weak contact. Sands relies heavily on getting ahead in the count. His command is better than his control because he needs to nibble and avoid the heart of the strike zone.
FUTURE: Sands' best role is likely as an on-call starter who pitches in Triple-A. There's enough variety of pitches and moxie to make successful spot starts or serve as a low-leverage reliever, but his lack of a plus pitch will make it hard for him to stick in a big league rotation.

BA GRADE: 40/Medium	Fastball: 40	Curveball: 45	Slider: 40	Changeup: 45	Split: 45	Control: 45

Year	Age	Club (League)	Lvl	W	L	ERA	G	GS	IP	H	HR	BB	SO	BB/9	SO/9	WHIP	AVG
2022	24	St. Paul (IL)	AAA	3	6	5.55	19	13	62	78	9	24	72	3.5	10.5	1.65	.310
2022	24	Minnesota (AL)	MLB	0	3	5.87	11	3	31	35	4	13	28	3.8	8.2	1.57	.276
Major League Totals				0	3	5.87	11	3	31	35	4	13	28	3.8	8.2	1.57	.276
Minor League Totals				14	11	3.35	56	49	239	218	19	78	276	2.9	10.4	1.24	.243

25 TANNER SCHOBEL, SS/2B

Born: June 4, 2001. **B-T:** R-R. **HT:** 5-10. **WT:** 170.
Drafted: Virginia Tech, 2022. **Signed by:** John Wilson.
TRACK RECORD: Schobel was an immediate contributor as a freshman at Virginia Tech, but in his draft-eligible sophomore year he raised his game another notch. He moved from second base to shortstop while developing newfound power, going from seven to 18 home runs.
SCOUTING REPORT: Schobel's 18 home runs as a sophomore at Virginia Tech are unlikely to be replicated with a wood bat, but he does have the power to hit plenty of doubles while sneaking a ball over the fence to his pull side on occasion. He's best as a top- or bottom-of-the-lineup hitter who makes plenty of contact and is tough to strike out. The Twins had Schobel focus on second and third base in his pro debut, and those are the spots he projects best at moving forward. Most likely, he's a multi-positional infielder who can play shortstop in an emergency, while providing average defense at second and third. He has reliable hands and an average arm. He's an average runner as well.
THE FUTURE: Schobel does a lot of things well, which makes him the kind of productive college middle infielder who finds a path to the majors. It's hard to see him as a regular, but he has enough hitting ability and defensive value to potentially fit as a versatile backup.

BA GRADE: 45/High	Hitting: 55	Power: 30	Run: 50	Field: 50	Arm: 50

Year	Age	Club (League)	Lvl	AVG	G	AB	R	H	2B	3B	HR	RBI	BB	SO	SB	OBP	SLG
2022	21	Twins (FCL)	R	.200	4	15	3	3	1	0	0	1	1	3	1	.250	.267
2022	21	Fort Myers (FSL)	LoA	.242	28	99	11	24	3	0	1	10	18	23	6	.367	.303
Minor League Totals				.237	32	114	14	27	4	0	1	11	19	26	7	.353	.298

26 MICHAEL HELMAN, 2B/OF

Born: May 23, 1996. **B-T:** R-R. **HT:** 6-1. **WT:** 195.
Drafted: Texas A&M, 2018 (11th round). **Signed by:** Greg Runser.
TRACK RECORD: When Helman was in college, he was a grinding second baseman who starred at Hutchinson (Kan.) JC and Texas A&M. As a pro, he quickly learned to carry a lot more gloves in his bag. He's demonstrated the ability to plausibly play most everywhere while also showing a knack for making contact with some thump in his bat.
SCOUTING REPORT: Helman's speed is arguably his best tool. He's a plus runner who is judiciously aggressive on the basepaths. The new pickoff and pitch clock rules have further boosted his basestealing

value and he is a useful pinch runner. Defensively he's best in center field and at second base, but even at those spots, he's fringe-average at best. He played everywhere but catcher and right field in 2022, and he's playable in the big leagues at everywhere but those positions and shortstop.

THE FUTURE: Helman is the kind of jack-of-all-trades who can find a way to carve out a useful role on a big league bench, especially now that teams are mandated to carry more position players. He's not good enough anywhere to be a regular, but he's competent at enough positions to fill-in most anywhere.

BA GRADE: 40/Medium   **Hitting:** 45   **Power:** 45   **Run:** 60   **Field:** 40   **Arm:** 45

Year	Age	Club (League)	Lvl	AVG	G	AB	R	H	2B	3B	HR	RBI	BB	SO	SB	OBP	SLG
2022	26	Wichita (TL)	AA	.278	39	144	34	40	6	2	6	20	21	32	10	.367	.472
2022	26	St. Paul (IL)	AAA	.250	96	368	67	92	17	1	14	40	40	80	30	.325	.416
Minor League Totals				.253	367	1341	226	339	63	10	46	164	138	257	74	.325	.418

27 SEAN MOONEY, RHP

Born: Jan. 11, 1998. **B-T:** R-R. **HT:** 6-1. **WT:** 185.
Drafted: St. John's, 2019 (12th round). **Signed by:** John Wilson.

TRACK RECORD: The coronavirus pandemic affected a lot of baseball careers, but Mooney is one case where it didn't cause him to miss much. He had Tommy John surgery in 2019 late in his season at St. John's and was already ticketed to miss some of the 2020 season. He had recovered from that injury in 2021 but a shoulder strain and neck strain derailed that season as well. He missed time again in 2022 with a neck injury but was generally effective at High-A Cedar Rapids.

SCOUTING REPORT: As a shorter but well-built righthander with a lower three-quarters arm slot, Mooney's low-90s fastball is extremely flat and can get above bats in the top of the strike zone. He locates it well. Mooney tightened up his 81-85 mph average slider, which has made it a more effective pitch. It is a sweeper without much depth. He shows conviction and feel to locate his fringe-average changeup. There is sometimes recoil in his delivery, but the delivery itself is simple. He pitches exclusively from the stretch, going from hand break to release point with a direct and simple arm action.

THE FUTURE: Mooney projects as a swingman type who is a spot starter or multi-inning reliever in the big leagues. Nothing about his arsenal is flashy, but he could move quickly in 2023 as a pitcher with feel and an ability to throw strikes.

BA GRADE: 40/High   **Fastball:** 50   **Slider:** 50   **Changeup:** 45   **Control:** 50

Year	Age	Club (League)	Lvl	W	L	ERA	G	GS	IP	H	HR	BB	SO	BB/9	SO/9	WHIP	AVG
2022	24	Cedar Rapids (MWL)	HiA	2	3	3.30	18	12	60	45	7	30	82	4.5	12.3	1.25	.205
Minor League Totals				2	5	3.09	31	24	102	67	9	53	153	4.7	13.5	1.18	.183

28 STEVEN CRUZ, RHP

Born: June 15, 1999. **B-T:** R-R. **HT:** 6-2. **WT:** 185.
Signed: Dominican Republic, 2017. **Signed by:** Fred Guerrero.

TRACK RECORD: Cruz was a low-cost signing in 2017 and one the Twins knew they'd have to be patient to develop. He spent three years in rookie ball and didn't make his full-season debut until five years after he signed. He spent all of 2022 in Double-A, but the control troubles that have long bedeviled him remain. His results have struggled to match his considerable potential.

SCOUTING REPORT: Sometimes watching Cruz, it's hard to explain why he isn't more effective. His plus fastball is hard enough to force every hitter to respect it. He sits between 96-99 mph and has touched 101. It has the potential to be a plus-plus pitch if he locates it better. His plus slider is even harder to hit. It's an 89-91 mph power pitch that has just enough movement to miss bats. The 6-foot-7 Cruz struggles to be consistent with his mechanics. His bottom-of-the-scale control keeps him from dominating hitters the way he would if he could get to strike two before he gets to ball three. He also throws a below-average changeup that can surprise hitters.

THE FUTURE: An effective stint in winter ball with Escogido should help Cruz head into 2023 with some momentum. He was Rule 5 eligible and went unpicked. His top-tier velocity and slider will ensure he keeps getting plenty of chances to figure things out, whether it ever clicks in Minnesota or not.

BA GRADE: 40/High   **Fastball:** 60   **Slider:** 60   **Changeup:** 40   **Control:** 20

Year	Age	Club (League)	Lvl	W	L	ERA	G	GS	IP	H	HR	BB	SO	BB/9	SO/9	WHIP	AVG
2022	23	Wichita (TL)	AA	1	4	5.14	46	0	56	54	4	35	72	5.6	11.6	1.59	.252
Minor League Totals				11	9	4.07	120	7	192	151	8	129	259	6.0	12.1	1.46	.213

29 JAYLEN NOWLIN, LHP

Born: Jan. 29, 2001. **B-T:** L-L. **HT:** 6-1. **WT:** 180.
Drafted: Chipola (Fla.) JC, 2021 (19th round). **Signed by:** Jack Powell.

TRACK RECORD: Nowlin pitched effectively out of the Chipola (Fla.) JC bullpen as a freshman in 2021. He signed with Alabama-Birmingham, but the Twins picked him in the 19th round and swayed him to pro ball. In his final start with Low-A Fort Myers, he struck out eight in six scoreless innings. Then he set a career high by striking out 11 and carrying a no-hitter into the sixth inning in his High-A debut with Cedar Rapids.

SCOUTING REPORT: Nowlin has the feel and intelligence to potentially be a back-end starter, but his most likely role will be as a lefty reliever with a fastball and slider that will both play up in that role. As a starter, Nowlin's fastball sits in the low 90s and his slider sits in the low 80s. He will also mix in a mid-80s changeup. None of the trio is plus, but his ability to mix three pitches with a quality changeup is enough to stymie Class A hitters.

THE FUTURE: Nowlin should return to Cedar Rapids to start 2023. In a system that traded away many of its best young arms, the opportunity is there for Nowlin to carve out a spot in the Twins' future.

BA GRADE: 40/High   **Fastball:** 55   **Slider:** 50   **Changeup:** 50   **Control:** 45

Year	Age	Club (League)	Lvl	W	L	ERA	G	GS	IP	H	HR	BB	SO	BB/9	SO/9	WHIP	AVG
2022	21	Fort Myers (FSL)	LoA	4	3	3.65	19	11	57	47	2	29	89	4.6	14.1	1.34	.221
2022	21	Cedar Rapids (MWL)	HiA	1	1	4.40	3	3	14	13	2	7	22	4.4	13.8	1.40	.241
Minor League Totals				5	5	4.16	23	14	71	62	4	38	112	4.8	14.1	1.40	.230

30 AARON SABATO, 1B

Born: June 4, 1999. **B-T:** R-R. **HT:** 6-2. **WT:** 230.
Drafted: North Carolina, 2020 (1st round). **Signed by:** Ty Dawson.

TRACK RECORD: A massively framed prep shortstop, Sabato moved to first base/DH immediately in college and settled in to do what he did best—hit. Sabato was a dominating slugger at North Carolina, but the Twins' 2020 first-round pick has not carried that success to pro ball. He's a career .209 hitter, albeit with solid on-base percentages and slugging numbers.

SCOUTING REPORT: Sabato hits the ball quite hard when he connects and he also draws walks, but that's pretty much all he can do right now to help a team, which makes him a relatively limited player as a right-right first baseman. The problem is he's struggled to make contact more than was expected. Sabato can be beaten by quality stuff in the zone, especially on the inner third. He has power but his selective approach makes him vulnerable to velocity. When he tries to catch up to fastballs, he ends up starting his swing early and then becomes vulnerable to offspeed. When he tries to be patient, he finds himself hamstrung by velocity. He does have a solid feel for the strike zone. When he does walk, Sabato is a baseclogger as a 20 runner. He's below-average at first base defensively.

THE FUTURE: Sabato is a righthanded-hitting first base/DH who is eaten up by velocity and righthanders. He's going to have to improve his approach and timing to become a platoon big league bat who feasts on lefthanders. That's admittedly a limited profile for a first-round pick.

BA GRADE: 40/High   **Hitting:** 30   **Power:** 55   **Run:** 20   **Field:** 30   **Arm:** 40

Year	Age	Club (League)	Lvl	AVG	G	AB	R	H	2B	3B	HR	RBI	BB	SO	SB	OBP	SLG
2022	23	Cedar Rapids (MWL)	HiA	.226	80	288	50	65	13	0	17	57	49	111	2	.351	.448
2022	23	Wichita (TL)	AA	.179	23	84	13	15	4	0	5	18	10	31	2	.283	.405
Minor League Totals				.209	210	733	132	153	35	0	41	132	151	291	5	.355	.424

New York Mets

BY MATT EDDY

The Mets made a lot of progress in 2022, even as the season ended on a disappointing note with a Wild Card Series loss to the lower-seeded Padres.

To keep the ball rolling, the organization needs to continue playing to its strengths, which includes flexing its financial muscle in free agency, after winning 101 games.

On the player development front, the Mets saw their top two prospects—catcher Francisco Alvarez and third baseman Brett Baty—make their major league debuts. The duo heads into 2023 ranked as upper-tier prospects and is ready to contribute in New York when called upon.

The Mets' farm system ranked as the eighth most talented in MLB at the end of the season, buoyed by the additions of 2022 first-rounders Kevin Parada and Jett Williams and the emergence of 19-year-old center fielder Alex Ramirez.

That's a positive step because the Mets' system simply hasn't produced enough new big league contributors since delivering Jeff McNeil in 2018 and Pete Alonso in 2019. Righthander Tylor Megill and lefthander David Peterson graduated from prospects status in 2021 and took steps forward in 2022, but neither has a lock on a 2023 rotation spot.

The Mets' farm system has been more productive than it appears because many top talents have been traded away. Andres Gimenez debuted in 2020 and was key to the Francisco Lindor deal with the Guardians made after that season.

Gimenez blossomed into an all-star in 2022, while two other prospects traded by the Mets—Pirates catcher Endy Rodriguez and Cubs center fielder Pete Crow-Armstrong—rank as No. 1 prospects for their new organizations.

A 2022 deadline deal also sacrificed organizational depth that could come back to haunt the Mets. Desperate for righthanded power, the Mets traded four players to the Giants for Darin Ruf, who flopped in New York. Righthander Carson Seymour went back the other way and would have ranked top 15 for the Mets had he been retained.

Even with those regrettable recent trades, the Mets have steadily reinforced their prospect core in recent years, primarily through the draft. They will have to keep up that pace, because building needed organizational depth requires several incoming classes of domestic and international talent.

The Mets front office, headed by general manager Billy Eppler since November 2021, has shined in free agency. In the past two offseasons, the club has signed top-tier free agents, including Max Scherzer, Justin Verlander and Starling Marte, to short-term deals without sacrificing draft capital.

Opening Day starter Tylor Megill had a 2.43 ERA through six starts before succumbing to injury.

PROJECTED 2026 LINEUP

Catcher	Francisco Alvarez	24
First Base	Pete Alonso	31
Second Base	Jett Williams	22
Third Base	Brett Baty	26
Shortstop	Francisco Lindor	32
Left Field	Jeff McNeil	34
Center Field	Brandon Nimmo	33
Right Field	Alex Ramirez	23
Designated Hitter	Kevin Parada	24
No. 1 Starter	Kodai Senga	33
No. 2 Starter	Tylor Megill	30
No. 3 Starter	David Peterson	30
No. 4 Starter	Blade Tidwell	25
No. 5 Starter	Calvin Ziegler	23
Closer	Edwin Diaz	32

New York has lost key pitchers, including Jacob deGrom, Chris Bassitt and Noah Syndergaard, but netted compensatory draft picks for all three.

Under owner Steve Cohen, the Mets are the first club ever to push its payroll past $300 million. After the 2022 season, the Mets committed $81 million in average annual value to free agents Verlander, Jose Quintana, David Robertson and 30-year-old Japanese ace Kodai Senga, while re-signing Edwin Diaz and Brandon Nimmo at an AAV rate of nearly $41 million.

As a result, New York incurs the highest luxury tax penalty—named in honor of Cohen—and will have its top 2023 pick pushed back 10 spots. ∎

DEPTH CHART

NEW YORK METS

TOP 2023 MLB CONTRIBUTORS	RANK
Francisco Alvarez, C	1
Kodai Senga, RHP	2
Brett Baty, 3B	3
BREAKOUT PROSPECTS	**RANK**
Jesus Baez, SS	14
Jordany Ventura, RHP	16
Layonel Ovalles, RHP	17

SOURCE OF TOP 30 TALENT

Homegrown	28	Acquired	2
College	6	Trade	0
Junior college	0	Rule 5 draft	1
High school	7	Independent league	0
Nondrafted free agent	1	Free agent/waivers	1
International	14		

LF
Carlos Cortes

CF
Alex Ramirez (5)
Nick Morabito (21)
Omar De Los Santos
Jaylen Palmer

RF
Stanley Consuegra
Khalil Lee
Carlos Dominguez

3B
Brett Baty (3)
Jesus Baez (14)
Jacob Reimer (23)
William Lugo (29)
Luke Ritter

SS
Ronny Mauricio (8)
Dangelo Sarmiento (22)
Wilmer Reyes

2B
Jett Williams (6)
Kevin Kendall
Wyatt Young
D'Andre Smith
Junior Tilien
Jose Peroza

1B
Mark Vientos (7)
JT Schwartz

C
Francisco Alvarez (1)
Kevin Parada (4)
Vincent Perozo
Hayden Senger

LHP

LHSP	LHRP
Luis Rodriguez (19)	Tayler Saucedo
Javier Atencio (25)	
Josh Walker	

RHP

RHSP	RHRP
Kodai Senga (2)	Junior Santos (20)
Blade Tidwell (9)	Zach Greene (26)
Calvin Ziegler (10)	Christian Scott (27)
Matt Allan (11)	Eric Ozre (28)
Dominic Hamel (12)	Grant Hartwig (30)
Mike Vasil (13)	William Woods
Joel Diaz (15)	Bryce Montes de Oca
Jordany Ventura (16)	Stephen Ridings
Layonel Ovalles (17)	Daison Acosta
Jose Butto (18)	Robert Dominguez
Luis Moreno (24)	
Jeffery Colon	
Tyler Stuart	
Jonah Tong	
Dylan Tebrake	

1 FRANCISCO ALVAREZ, C

Born: Nov. 19, 2001. **B-T:** R-R. **HT:** 5-10. **WT:** 233.
Signed: Venezuela, 2018.
Signed by: Andres Nuñez/Ismael Perez.

RICH SCHULTZ/GETTY IMAGES

BA GRADE	SCOUTING GRADES
65 Risk: Medium	Hit: 50. Power: 70. Run: 30. Field: 45. Arm: 50.

Projected future grades on 20-80 scouting scale

TRACK RECORD: Alvarez grew up working for his father's construction company in Venezuela. After signing with the Mets for $2.7 million in 2018, he quickly constructed a case as one of the top prospects in baseball. Alvarez hit his way to the Rookie-advanced Appalachian League as a 17-year-old in his 2019 pro debut. The lost 2020 minor league season did nothing to slow him. Alvarez shined at the Mets' alternate training site that summer and emerged as the organization's clear-cut No.1 prospect. When minor league baseball returned in 2021, he was ready. Alvarez popped 24 home runs—only one teenager hit more—in a season spent primarily at High-A. Along the way he also played in the Futures Game. He made further offensive gains in 2022, hitting .260/.374/.511 in 112 games and tallying career highs with 27 homers and 70 walks. Alvarez spent July, August and September with Triple-A Syracuse, but he missed nearly three weeks with a right ankle injury late in the season. He returned from the injured list to hit .362 with three homers and a 1.079 OPS in 13 games to earn his first big league callup on Sept. 30. With New York, a 20-year-old Alvarez popped his first big league homer, caught his first game and made the Mets' postseason roster. He was the youngest player in MLB in 2022.

SCOUTING REPORT: Few prospects can match Alvarez's raw power. Built like a fire hydrant at a listed 5-foot-10, 233 pounds, he unleashes a compact, powerful swing that inflicts damage and earns double-plus power grades. Alvarez's average exit velocity in the minors in 2022 was 90 mph and his 90th percentile EV checked in at nearly 108 mph, an elite reading. He was one of just 20 minor leaguers to top 50 home runs combined in 2021 and 2022. Alvarez has a good feel for the strike zone, but like many young hitters will expand his zone and chase. He should be an average hitter in MLB but can improve that grade slightly with better swing decisions and more zone contact. While he clears the offensive bar at catcher, Alvarez has work to do behind the plate. He receives well and has an average arm he used to throw out 29% of 108 minor league basestealers. He emphasized learning English and conducted meetings in his second language in 2022, underscoring his leadership initiative. Alvarez has a large frame and must remain flexible and strong in his ankles to weather a long season. Game-calling and understanding situations is the final hurdle in his development. With time, he has the potential to develop into a near-average defensive catcher.

THE FUTURE: The Mets have long been enamored with Alvarez's work ethic, composure and competitive makeup. He has that "it" factor to become a star on baseball's biggest stage. Alvarez has already reached the summit of his climb in pro ball, and he is poised to hit in the middle of the Mets' order for a long time. It just might require a bit more Triple-A time to shore up his hitting approach and gain more reps behind the plate. After the season, Alvarez had surgery on his right ankle to remove a loose body and repair damaged cartilage. He is expected to be ready for spring training and will spend most of 2023 with the big club.

BEST TOOLS

BATTING

Best Hitter for Average	Jett Williams
Best Power Hitter	Francisco Alvarez
Best Strike-Zone Discipline	Kevin Parada
Fastest Baserunner	Omar De Los Santos
Best Athlete	Alex Ramirez

PITCHING

Best Fastball	Blade Tidwell
Best Curveball	Calvin Ziegler
Best Slider	Blade Tidwell
Best Changeup (Splitter)	Kodai Senga
Best Control	Kodai Senga

FIELDING

Best Defensive Catcher	Nick Meyer
Best Defensive Infielder	Jose Peroza
Best Infield Arm	Ronny Mauricio
Best Defensive Outfielder	Alex Ramirez
Best Outfield Arm	Stanley Consuegra

Year	Age	Club (League)	Lvl	AVG	G	AB	R	H	2B	3B	HR	RBI	BB	SO	SB	OBP	SLG
2022	20	Binghamton (EL)	AA	.277	67	253	43	70	16	0	18	47	36	71	0	.368	.553
2022	20	Syracuse (IL)	AAA	.234	45	158	31	37	6	0	9	31	34	52	0	.382	.443
2022	20	New York (NL)	MLB	.167	5	12	3	2	1	0	1	1	2	4	0	.286	.500
Major League Totals				.167	5	12	3	2	1	0	1	1	2	4	0	.286	.500
Minor League Totals				.274	253	895	173	245	50	1	58	174	146	249	9	.384	.526

2 KODAI SENGA, RHP

Born: January 30, 1993. **B-T:** R-R. **HT:** 6-1. **WT:** 203.
Signed: Japan, 2022. **Signed by:** Jeff Kusumoto.

TRACK RECORD: Senga blossomed into one of Japan's top pitchers and broke out on an international stage at the 2017 World Baseball Classic. He became one of Japan's most highly-desired pitchers following that showing. Senga led the Pacific League in wins, ERA and strikeouts in 2020, led Japan to a gold medal at the Tokyo Olympics in 2021 and posted a 1.94 ERA in 2022. He exercised an opt out in his contract after the 2022 season and signed a five-year, $75 million deal with the Mets in early December.

SCOUTING REPORT: Senga is a power pitcher with a ready-made big league arsenal. His fastball sits 94-97 mph as a starter and touches 100-101 in short bursts with high spin rates and late explosion. He holds his velocity through

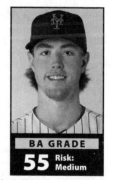

his starts and has a good feel for manipulating his fastball, alternately giving it ride, sink or armside bore. Senga's best pitch is a plus-plus, mid-80s forkball nicknamed the "ghost fork" for how it disappears on hitters. It jumps out of his hand like a fastball before falling off the table with late fade and dive to get wild, off-balance swings and misses over the top. Senga mostly dominates with his fastball and forkball, but he has a deep arsenal like many Japanese pitchers. His 86-89 mph cutter is a darting pitch he uses to jam lefthanded hitters. His vertical 83-85 mph slider has a chance to be an average pitch if he improves its shape. He gets around his 77-80 mph curveball to make it slurvy at times. Senga modifies his tempo and delivery to add deception but sacrifices control when he does. He shows average control when he keeps his delivery simple and straightforward.

THE FUTURE: Senga has the stuff to be a No. 3 starter and can reach that potential if he refines his breaking balls and control. Even if he doesn't, he should be a quality No. 4 who occasionally dominates.

SCOUTING GRADES:	Fastball: 60	Curveball: 50	Slider: 45	Cutter: 50	Splitter: 70	Control: 50

Year	Age	Club (League)	Lvl	W	L	ERA	G	GS	IP	H	HR	BB	SO	BB/9	SO/9	WHIP	AVG
2022	29	Softbank (PL)	NPB	11	6	1.94	22	—	144	103	7	49	156	3.1	9.8	1.06	—
Japanese League Totals				87	44	2.59	224	—	1089	800	85	414	1252	3.4	10.3	1.12	—

3 BRETT BATY, 3B/OF

Born: November 13, 1999. **B-T:** L-R. **HT:** 6-3. **WT:** 210.
Drafted: HS—Austin, Texas, 2019 (1st round). **Signed by:** Harry Shelton.

TRACK RECORD: Baty stood out for his feel to hit, power and discipline as a high school senior in a loaded 2019 draft class. But his age—he turned 20 in November of his draft year—turned off many teams. The Mets drafted Baty 12th overall and watched him hit his way to MLB as a 22-year-old in 2022. He earned his first callup on Aug. 17 after a dominating minor league season that included a Double-A Eastern League-leading .950 OPS. His season ended on Aug. 28 with a torn thumb ligament that required surgery.

SCOUTING TREPORT: Baty homered in his first big league at-bat, a validation of the work he had put in to hit the ball in the air more often in 2022. He lowered his groundball rate from 56% in 2021 to 44% a year later even as he

climbed to the upper levels. Baty hit all batting benchmarks in 2022. He hit the ball hard with regularity—near 92 mph average exit velocity with a 90th percentile reading of 107 mph—he didn't chase out of the zone often and he made contact when he swung at pitches in the zone. Baty takes his walks and should be a high on-base hitter with above-average power. Baty has improved his defensive play at third base, where his plus arm plays but his range and release grade as more capable than outstanding. He started 11 games in left field in the minors and is athletic enough to play there to get his bat in the lineup.

THE FUTURE: Baty is a good hitter with power and will bat toward the middle of the Mets' lineup at his peak. He projects to be playable at third base, but a stronger defender could push him to left field.

SCOUTING GRADES	Hitting: 60	Power: 55	Speed: 45	Fielding: 45	Arm: 60

Year	Age	Club (League)	Lvl	AVG	G	AB	R	H	2B	3B	HR	RBI	BB	SO	SB	OBP	SLG
2022	22	Binghamton (EL)	AA	.312	89	340	73	106	22	0	19	59	46	98	2	.406	.544
2022	22	Syracuse (IL)	AAA	.364	6	22	3	8	0	0	0	1	3	6	0	.462	.364
2022	22	New York (NL)	MLB	.184	11	38	4	7	0	0	2	5	2	8	0	.244	.342
Major League Totals				.184	11	38	4	7	0	0	2	5	2	8	0	.244	.342
Minor League Totals				.289	237	882	156	255	60	3	38	149	130	267	8	.390	.493

4 KEVIN PARADA, C

BA GRADE

60 Risk: High

Born: August 3, 2001. **B-T:** R-R. **HT:** 6-1. **WT:** 197.
Drafted: Georgia Tech, 2022 (1st round). **Signed by:** Marlin McPhail.
TRACK RECORD: Parada ably continued Georgia Tech's rich catcher tradition that includes first-round picks Jason Varitek, Matt Wieters and Joey Bart. Parada took his game to a new level as a sophomore after offseason strength gains. He hit .361/.453/.709 with 26 home runs, 30 walks and 32 strikeouts in 60 games. Ranked as the No. 6 draft prospect, Parada slipped to the Mets at No. 11 and signed for $5,019,735, or 5% over slot value. He joined Low-A St. Lucie for 10 games and helped the club win the Florida State League title by going 6-for-15 with two walks in four playoff games.
SCOUTING REPORT: Parada is a disciplined hitter who makes steady, hard contact to all fields. His swing features some pre-pitch movement, but he gets into launch position consistently. When Parada swings, he tends to make contact, and his 10.5% strikeout rate in college was easily the lowest among Division I hitters with at least 25 homers. He struck out just twice in four FSL playoff games. Parada did not show crazy exit velocities in his pro debut but has demonstrated power that is at least above-average. Parada is regarded as a fringe-average defensive catcher with a fringe arm, but he is committed to improving. He bought a house in Port St. Lucie, Fla., in order to spend his offseason around Mets instructors. He also spent time at Cressey Sports Performance to work on lateral movement and flexibility. Like most young catchers, he must improve his game-calling and situational awareness.
THE FUTURE: The Mets were thrilled to land Parada, a potential first-division catcher, when he fell to the 11th pick. He will begin challenging for MLB at-bats in 2024.

SCOUTING GRADES		Hitting: 60		Power: 55		Speed: 45		Fielding: 45		Arm: 45				
Year	Age	Club (League)	Lvl	AVG	G	AB	R	H	2B	3B	HR	RBI	BB	SO	SB	OBP	SLG
2022	20	Mets (FCL)	R	.273	3	11	1	3	2	0	0	3	2	1	0	.429	.455
2022	20	St. Lucie (FSL)	LoA	.276	10	29	5	8	1	0	1	5	10	12	0	.463	.414
Minor League Totals				.275	13	40	6	11	3	0	1	8	12	13	0	.455	.425

5 ALEX RAMIREZ, OF

BA GRADE

55 Risk: High

Born: January 13, 2003. **B-T:** R-R. **HT:** 6-3. **WT:** 170.
Signed: Dominican Republic, 2019. **Signed by:** Gerardo Cabrera/Fernando Encarnacion.
TRACK RECORD: International amateurs who signed in July 2019 were deprived of a 2020 minor league season by the pandemic, effectively pushing their pro debuts to 2021. That list includes Ramirez, who made his pro debut for Low-A St. Lucie in June 2021, nearly two years after signing. He gained valuable reps in the pitcher-friendly Florida State League that summer and returned there to begin 2022. Ramirez earned a July 4 bump to High-A Brooklyn after he cut his chase rate nearly in half from May to June.
SCOUTING REPORT: Ramirez is the top athlete in the system and has raw tools few Mets prospects can approach. It's going to come down to how much he hits. Ramirez has an exaggerated load to his swing that includes a bat wrap, but up through High-A he has been able to get into launch position on time. From that point, his swing mechanics are fluid and his bat speed exceptional. Ramirez's overall numbers in 2022 were strong for a teenager, and he backed up that production by working deeper counts and hunting his pitch more often as the season progressed. Further growth in his chase rate and in terms of swinging less often could key a breakout. A key offseason goal for Ramirez will be adding strength to his 6-foot-3 frame. The Mets want to begin to turn his doubles—just four teenagers had more than his 30 two-baggers—into home runs as he embarks on his age-20 season. Ramirez is an above-average runner and graceful defender in center field. His plus arm would play in right field if he outgrows center. Ramirez tends to play on cruise control and could show more urgency.
THE FUTURE: Ramirez scuffled at times at High-A, and the Mets believe he will be better for the challenge. He is on track to reach Double-A as a 20-year-old at some point in 2023.

SCOUTING GRADES		Hitting: 50		Power: 55		Speed: 55		Fielding: 55		Arm: 60				
Year	Age	Club (League)	Lvl	AVG	G	AB	R	H	2B	3B	HR	RBI	BB	SO	SB	OBP	SLG
2022	19	St. Lucie (FSL)	LoA	.284	67	271	40	77	13	6	6	37	28	68	17	.359	.443
2022	19	Brooklyn (SAL)	HiA	.278	54	227	22	63	17	1	5	34	16	54	4	.329	.427
Minor League Totals				.273	197	800	103	218	45	11	16	106	67	226	37	.339	.416

6 JETT WILLIAMS, SS

Born: November 3, 2003. **B-T:** R-R. **HT:** 5-8. **WT:** 175.
Drafted: HS—Heath, Texas (1st round). **Signed by:** Gary Brown.

TRACK RECORD: The Mets were linked to Williams throughout the 2022 draft season. The club had been dialed in on him since the 2021 Area Code Games and viewed drafting the Dallas-Fort Worth metroplex product with the 14th overall pick as an ideal outcome. Williams signed for $3.9 million, which was about 8% under slot value. He reported to the Florida Complex League after signing and was not fazed by the assignment. He continued to make quality contact while exercising good swing decisions and going 6-for-6 on stolen base attempts in 10 games.

BA GRADE
55 Risk: Extreme

SCOUTING REPORT: "Unafraid" may be the best adjective to describe the 5-foot-8 Williams. He plays with a chip on his shoulder similar to short middle infielders like Dustin Pedroia or Alex Bregman. Time will tell if Williams' skills measure up to those all-stars, but he was a scout's favorite on the high school showcase circuit for his bat-to-ball skill, plus speed and overall exciting style of play. The Mets have little doubt Williams will develop into a plus hitter with on-base ability that would fit at the top of the lineup. Because he does such a good job hitting his pitch, he could approach average power in his peak seasons, but below-average is the more likely outcome. He is a skilled basestealer who also runs well enough to have played center field as an amateur. The Mets like Williams on the middle infield, most likely at second base in the big leagues because his range and overall efficiency at shortstop are light. His average arm will fit at the keystone.

THE FUTURE: Williams projects to be the Mets' second baseman of the future and potential leadoff hitter. He is a strong bet to open 2023 as the shortstop for Low-A St. Lucie.

SCOUTING GRADES		Hitting: 60		Power: 40		Speed: 60		Fielding: 50		Arm: 50	

Year	Age	Club (League)	Lvl	AVG	G	AB	R	H	2B	3B	HR	RBI	BB	SO	SB	OBP	SLG
2022	18	Mets (FCL)	R	.250	10	32	7	8	1	1	1	6	4	6	6	.366	.438
Minor League Totals				.250	10	32	7	8	1	1	1	6	4	6	6	.366	.438

7 MARK VIENTOS, 3B

Born: December 11, 1999. **B-T:** R-R. **HT:** 6-4. **WT:** 185.
Drafted: HS—Plantation, FL, 2017 (2nd round). **Signed by:** Cesar Aranguren.

TRACK RECORD: The youngest player drafted in 2017, Vientos took a few seasons to find his footing in pro ball before breaking out at the upper levels in 2021. He hit 25 home runs that season and then hit 24 more for Syracuse in 2022 as one of just 10 qualified 22-year-olds at Triple-A. He ranked fifth in the International League with an .877 OPS. That performance earned Vientos his first big league callup on Sept. 11. He picked up a handful of starts at DH versus lefthanded starters down the stretch but did not make the Mets' postseason roster.

BA GRADE
45 Risk: Medium

SCOUTING REPORT: Vientos' game is predicated on power. He shows plus raw power to all fields and even hit his first MLB home run the other way, but he doesn't get to that power as much as he could because of his approach. Vientos chases too much and misses in the zone too much to hit for a high average, though he showed a healthy walk rate at Triple-A and in MLB. He struggled to impact righthanded pitchers in 2022, giving up nearly 375 OPS points at Triple-A. If it persists it could point to more of a platoon or part-time role. Drafted as a shortstop, Vientos moved to third base early in his pro career but will struggle to stick there in the big leagues. He throws well but has a thick lower half, below-average speed and substandard range. First base is his most likely position.

THE FUTURE: The Mets struggled to get production at DH versus lefthanders in 2022, as J.D. Davis and then Darin Ruf floundered. If that trend continues, a door opens for Vientos to earn MLB playing time. Given his youth and the Mets' competitive window, he will likely enter the season as plan B as he sees more time at Triple-A.

SCOUTING GRADES		Hitting: 40		Power: 55		Speed: 40		Fielding: 40		Arm: 60	

Year	Age	Club (League)	Lvl	AVG	G	AB	R	H	2B	3B	HR	RBI	BB	SO	SB	OBP	SLG
2022	22	Syracuse (IL)	AAA	.280	101	378	66	106	16	1	24	72	44	122	0	.358	.519
2022	22	New York (NL)	MLB	.167	16	36	3	6	1	0	1	3	5	12	0	.268	.278
Major League Totals				.167	16	36	3	6	1	0	1	3	5	12	0	.268	.278
Minor League Totals				.272	406	1518	221	413	87	2	76	275	151	421	2	.341	.482

8 RONNY MAURICIO, SS

Born: April 4, 2001. **B-T:** B-R. **HT:** 6-3. **WT:** 166.
Signed: Dominican Republic, 2017. **Signed by:** Marciano Alvarez/Gerardo Cabrera.

TRACK RECORD: Mauricio headlined the Mets' 2017 international signing class and was playing full-season ball as an 18-year-old in 2019. He hit just four home runs in 116 Low-A games that season, but his fast hands and developing body suggested more power was in the tank. That turned out to be the case. When Mauricio emerged from the lost 2020 season, he hit 19 home runs for High-A Brooklyn in 2021 and 26 more for Double-A Binghamton in 2022. He also stole 20 bases in 2022, making him one of just 27 minor leaguers to go 20-20.

SCOUTING REPORT: With easy plus raw power and an average exit velocity north of 90 mph, Mauricio impacts the ball about as well as organization-mates Francisco Alvarez or Brett Baty. He just doesn't do it as frequently because of poor swing decisions. Mauricio swings too often to work favorable counts and chases too much off the plate. He has compiled a combined .296 on-base percentage in 2021 and 2022, making him one of just 12 minor leaguers with a sub-.300 mark and at least 800 plate appearances in that span. Mauricio is a reliable fielder at shortstop who made a large number of his 25 errors for Binghamton on throws. His glove could play as average at shortstop and perhaps plus at third base. His plus arm would also fit on an outfield corner as needed, though he has not appeared at a position other than shortstop as a pro.

THE FUTURE: Mauricio will be a 22-year-old at Triple-A in 2023, with a chance to earn MLB time if he makes better swing decisions. With a low-on-base, high-slugging profile, he would fit as a bottom-third-of-the-order hitter whose position value helps keep him in the lineup.

BA GRADE
50 Risk: High

SCOUTING GRADES	Hitting: 40	Power: 60	Speed: 40	Fielding: 50	Arm: 60

Year	Age	Club (League)	Lvl	AVG	G	AB	R	H	2B	3B	HR	RBI	BB	SO	SB	OBP	SLG
2022	21	Binghamton (EL)	AA	.259	123	509	71	132	26	2	26	89	24	125	20	.296	.472
Minor League Totals				.261	404	1629	223	425	77	15	53	225	86	376	39	.300	.424

9 BLADE TIDWELL, RHP

Born: June 8, 2001. **B-T:** R-R. **HT:** 6-4. **WT:** 207.
Drafted: Tennessee, 2022 (2nd round). **Signed by:** Nathan Beuster.

TRACK RECORD: Tidwell shined as a Tennessee freshman in 2021, going 10-3 with a 3.74 ERA in 18 starts. His 90 strikeouts ranked top 20 in the Southeastern Conference and set him up as one of the top college pitching prospects for the 2022 draft. Tidwell fell out of the first-round conversation when he missed the first two months of the season with shoulder soreness, but his stuff looked firm when he returned in late March. The Mets drafted him at No. 52 overall in the second round and signed him for $1.85 million, or 25% over slot value.

SCOUTING REPORT: Tidwell made just five regular-season appearances after signing, but he made enough of an impression to rank as the organization's top pitching prospect. He helped Low-A St. Lucie win the Florida State League championship by pitching 9.2 scoreless innings over two playoff starts with 13 strikeouts and two walks. Tidwell delivers mid-90s fastballs that peak at 99 mph from a high arm slot. The pitch showed more a efficient spin axis in his pro debut as Tidwell focused on working up in the zone and inside to batters, as contrasted with his college game plan of working low and away. Tidwell throws the best slider in the Mets' system. It's a mid-80s breaker with high spin and plus potential. Tidwell's fastball command wavers, and he needs to throw his changeup more often after it got good results in college. Refining command and developing a third pitch will be developmental focal points in 2023.

THE FUTURE: Tidwell has the 6-foot-4 build of a big league starter and the type of competitive edge, electric stuff and confidence that top starters have. He should see Double-A at some point in 2023, and how he fares there will help determine his MLB timeline.

BA GRADE
50 Risk: High

SCOUTING GRADES:	Fastball: 60	Slider: 60	Changeup: 45	Control: 50

Year	Age	Club (League)	Lvl	W	L	ERA	G	GS	IP	H	HR	BB	SO	BB/9	SO/9	WHIP	AVG
2022	21	Mets (FCL)	R	0	0	0.00	1	1	1	0	0	1	2	9.0	18.0	1.00	.000
2022	21	St. Lucie (FSL)	LoA	0	1	2.16	4	4	8	4	0	6	9	6.5	9.7	1.20	.143
Minor League Totals				0	1	1.93	5	5	9	4	0	7	11	6.8	10.6	1.18	.129

10 CALVIN ZIEGLER, RHP

Born: October 3, 2002. **B-T:** R-R. **HT:** 6-0. **WT:** 205.
Drafted: HS—Ocoee, Fla., 2021 (2nd round). **Signed by:** Jon Updike/John Kosciak.

TRACK RECORD: The pandemic made it difficult for Canadian high school prospects to be scouted. Ziegler went undrafted in 2020 and had to play tournaments for a Florida charter school and pitch for an Ohio travel team in 2021 to be seen for the draft. The Mets liked Ziegler's power arsenal and signed him for $910,000 as a second-round pick, expecting to apply the bonus pool savings to first-rounder Kumar Rocker, who did not sign. Because of Ziegler's long layoff, the Mets deployed him cautiously at Low-A St. Lucie, keeping him on tight pitch counts and having him sit out roughly six weeks at midseason with general soreness.

BA GRADE

50 Risk: High

SCOUTING REPORT: Ziegler missed bats at a rate few teenage pitchers could match in 2022. The issue for him will be not missing the strike zone as much after he walked 35 in 46.2 innings. Ziegler's 35.2% strikeout rate ranked sixth among teens with more than 12 starts. His fastball averages 94 mph touches 96 with plus ride up in the zone. Ziegler's curveball has top-to-bottom shape at 78-84 mph and can be a plus pitch for him if he learns to command it for strikes. Ziegler didn't throw a changeup as an amateur, so he added a splitter to give him a usable third pitch. His north-south attack is highly effective on young, inexperienced hitters. Improving his overall command will help the strategy play as he advances. Ziegler has a long arm stroke and tends to catapult toward the hitter. Adding strength to help him repeat his mechanics will help him throw more strikes and stay in the rotation. Ziegler has a fiery, competitive demeanor and always seems to be in motion.

THE FUTURE: Ziegler has velocity and feel to spin, if not much physical projection. A midrotation outcome is possible in three or four years, but first he moves to High-A Brooklyn is 2023.

SCOUTING GRADES:	Fastball: 60	Curveball: 60	Splitter: 40	Control: 45

Year	Age	Club (League)	Lvl	W	L	ERA	G	GS	IP	H	HR	BB	SO	BB/9	SO/9	WHIP	AVG
2022	19	St. Lucie (FSL)	LoA	0	6	4.44	16	16	47	26	3	35	70	6.8	13.5	1.31	.166
Minor League Totals				0	6	4.44	16	16	47	26	3	35	70	6.8	13.5	1.31	.166

11 MATT ALLAN, RHP

Born: April 17, 2001. **B-T:** R-R. **HT:** 6-3. **WT:** 225.
Drafted: HS—Sanford, Fla., 2019 (3rd round). **Signed by:** Jon Updike.

TRACK RECORD: The top high school righthander in the 2019 draft, Allan slipped to the Mets in the third round and signed for $2.5 million, the equivalent of late first-round money. He made six pro appearances that summer in preparation for a full-season assignment that had not yet materialized. Allan shined at the Mets' alternate training site in 2020 when the pandemic wiped out the minor league season and then looked sharp at 2021 spring training. He had Tommy John surgery that May and then ulnar transposition surgery in January 2022 that kept him off a mound for both seasons. Allan was throwing side sessions for most of the 2022 season. By the fall he was throwing all pitch types off flat ground, with a goal to get on a mound in the winter.

SCOUTING REPORT: Allan flashed top-shelf stuff when healthy. The Mets are hopeful he can recover his mid-90s fastball with vertical life and his high-70s curveball with tight spin and plus potential. He made big strides with his changeup at the alternate site in 2020, but the pitch is largely untested in game situations. Allan has worked to overcome the mental block associated with pitching through scar tissue in his elbow and getting used to normal ligament soreness. The followup elbow surgery he had in 2022 is not uncommon for Tommy John patients. Jacob deGrom, Steven Matz and Zack Wheeler all had it when they pitched for the Mets. Like Allan, Matz and Wheeler also missed the equivalent of multiple seasons while rehabbing.

THE FUTURE: In four short years, Allan has experienced the ups and downs of pro ball. But what he hasn't experienced is a full season. That should change in 2023. Health permitting, he has the type of repertoire and cerebral approach to occupy a spot in the middle of a big league rotation.

BA Grade: 55/Extreme	Fastball: 60	Curveball: 60	Changeup: 50	Control: 50

Year	Age	Club (League)	Lge	W	L	ERA	G	GS	IP	H	HR	BB	SO	BB9	SO9	WHIP	AVG
2022	21	Did not play—Injured															
Minor League Totals				1	0	2.61	6	5	10	10	0	5	14	4.4	12.2	1.45	.250

12 DOMINIC HAMEL, RHP

Born: March 2, 1999. **B-T:** R-R. **HT:** 6-2. **WT:** 206.
Drafted: Dallas Baptist, 2021 (3rd round). **Signed by:** Gary Brown.
TRACK RECORD: Hamel returned to Dallas Baptist for a fourth collegiate season after he went undrafted in the five-round 2020 draft. His fortune improved in 2021 after he ranked ninth in Division I with 136 strikeouts and was drafted 81st overall. Hamel earned Mets organization pitcher of the year honors in 2022, when he pitched his way to High-A Brooklyn and led the system with 10 wins, 145 strikeouts and a 1.15 WHIP.
SCOUTING REPORT: Hamel pitches with a modern fastball. His ability to backspin the baseball with efficient shape translates to a flatter plane of approach and makes it difficult for opposing hitters to barrel. He throws a high rate of strikes with his low-90s four-seamer that topped at 95 mph and drew a high rate of swinging strikes from Class A hitters. He holds his velocity deep into starts and is mindful of baserunners, who attempted just eight stolen bases in 2022. Hamel's low-80s slider grades as above-average based on its tight spin, and he commands the pitch to both sides of the plate. He also throws a curveball that has shape but lacks power. Hamel has developed his changeup into a usable third pitch, which helped him push his strikeout rate from 26% in the first half to 33% in the second.
THE FUTURE: Hamel will be 24 as he embarks on his first season in the upper minors. With continued health and performance, he is an MLB debut candidate in 2023 or 2024. Unless he finds more velocity, he probably fits best as a No. 5 starter or quality reliever.

BA Grade: 50/High			Fastball: 55		Curveball: 40		Slider: 55		Changeup: 45		Control: 50			

Year	Age	Club (League)	Lvl	W	L	ERA	G	GS	IP	H	HR	BB	SO	BB/9	SO/9	WHIP	AVG
2022	23	St. Lucie (FSL)	LoA	5	2	3.84	14	13	63	48	5	29	71	4.1	10.1	1.22	.209
2022	23	Brooklyn (SAL)	HiA	5	1	2.59	11	11	56	35	0	25	74	4.0	12.0	1.08	.180
Minor League Totals				10	3	3.17	27	26	122	83	5	54	152	4.0	11.2	1.12	.192

13 MIKE VASIL, RHP

Born: March 19, 2000. **B-T:** L-R. **HT:** 6-5. **WT:** 225.
Drafted: Virginia, 2021 (8th round). **Signed by:** Daniel Coles.
TRACK RECORD: An arm injury shut down Vasil as a Boston high school senior in 2018, so he withdrew from the draft and headed to Virginia. He never really launched in three collegiate seasons but attracted the Mets' interest in the eighth round in 2021. Vasil logged just 71 innings in 2022 as he dealt with bone spurs in his elbow, though he returned for the Arizona Fall League and looked sharp in 15.1 innings.
SCOUTING REPORT: Vasil throws four pitches for strikes and used them to stymie Class A hitters in 2022, drawing whiff rates of 25% or better with all four. No individual pitch type grades as plus, but he mixes and matches to good effect. Vasil sat 94 mph and topped out at 98, using his four-seamer up in the zone and his secondary pitches down. His low-80s curveball is his best pitch and features 12-to-6 bite and good depth. His slider has average potential and is thrown in the high 80s with more break, and he throws a variation at 92 mph that is more of a cutter. He made strides commanding his mid-80s changeup that flashes average when located low in the zone. Vasil is a fierce competitor who relies on control more than true command, leading some scouts to project him to high-leverage relief.
THE FUTURE: The Mets are excited that prospects like Vasil plus Dominic Hamel, Junior Santos and Luis Moreno will give them upper-levels pitching depth in 2023 that had been lacking in recent seasons. Ultimately, Vasil probably fits as a No. 5 starter or quality reliever.

BA Grade: 50/High			Fastball: 55		Curveball: 55		Slider: 50		Changeup: 50		Control: 50			

Year	Age	Club (League)	Lvl	W	L	ERA	G	GS	IP	H	HR	BB	SO	BB/9	SO/9	WHIP	AVG
2022	22	Mets (FCL)	R	0	0	0.00	1	1	1	1	0	0	2	0.0	18.0	1.00	.250
2022	22	St. Lucie (FSL)	LoA	3	1	2.19	9	8	37	26	1	11	39	2.7	9.5	1.00	.193
2022	22	Brooklyn (SAL)	HiA	1	1	5.13	8	8	33	24	3	15	44	4.1	11.9	1.17	.197
Minor League Totals				4	2	3.33	21	20	78	54	4	26	95	3.0	10.9	1.02	.189

14 JESUS BAEZ, SS/3B

Born: February 26, 2005. **B-T:** R-R. **HT:** 5-10. **WT:** 180.
Signed: Dominican Republic, 2022. **Signed by:** Oliver Dominguez/Moises De La Mota.
TRACK RECORD: Baez's plus raw power enticed the Mets to sign the 17-year-old for $275,000 out of the Dominican Republic in 2022. He made a memorable pro debut in the Dominican Summer League,

hitting five home runs and slugging .648 in his first 14 games. While Baez's pace slowed after that, he finished with seven homers, a total topped by just five 17-or-younger hitters in the 49-team DSL. The Mets rewarded him with the organization's DSL player of the year award.

SCOUTING REPORT: Baez has plus-plus bat speed and hits the ball hard for his age. His average exit velocity in the DSL bordered on 88 mph and his 90th percentile reading of 104 mph puts him in good company. Baez's swing has some adjustability and he draws his share of walks, but his 27% chase rate will need to improve against more advanced pitchers. His 5-foot-10 frame is filled out but not totally mature. In the field, Baez has a plus-plus arm that gives him greater margin for error and allows him to play deep at shortstop. His range, hands and actions may be light for the position, especially as he physically matures, and he faces a likely move to third base. He is an average runner who figures to slow a tick or two.

THE FUTURE: Baez plays with swagger and has a chance to back it up with impact power. A big spring could propel him to Low-A at some point early in 2023.

BA Grade: 50/Extreme		Hit: 40		Power: 55		Speed: 45		Fielding: 40		Arm: 70		

Year	Age	Club (League)	Lvl	AVG	G	AB	R	H	2B	3B	HR	RBI	BB	SO	SB	OBP	SLG
2022	17	Mets 1 (DSL)	R	.255	30	98	23	25	6	0	2	12	17	24	3	.373	.378
2022	17	Mets 2 (DSL)	R	.227	24	88	13	20	3	0	5	22	9	22	5	.303	.432
Minor League Totals				.242	54	186	36	45	9	0	7	34	26	46	8	.341	.403

15 JOEL DIAZ, RHP

Born: February 26, 2004. **B-T:** R-R. **HT:** 6-2. **WT:** 200.
Signed: Dominican Republic, 2021. **Signed by:** Moises de Mota/Oliver Dominguez.

TRACK RECORD: Diaz's velocity jumped in the period leading up to the opening of the international signing period in January 2021. He signed with the Mets and quickly asserted his prospect status in the Dominican Summer League by allowing three earned runs in 50.1 innings while striking out 63. Diaz recorded an 0.54 ERA that was the lowest for a qualified 17-year-old DSL pitcher since at least 2006. The Mets assigned Diaz to Low-A St.Lucie in late May 2022 and he took his lumps in the Florida State League as the only 18-year-old starting pitcher to toss 50 innings.

SCOUTING REPORT: Diaz is an athletic 6-foot-2 righthander who pitches at 93 mph and tops out at 97. He throws strikes at a high rate with his fastball and generates a good rate of swing-and-miss due to a low vertical approach angle and riding life. His secondary pitches proved to be less advanced in a full-season setting. Low-A hitters were less tempted to swing at Diaz's 75-77 mph curveball, though he added power to the pitch as the season progressed. It is his favorite pitch and could become average or better. His changeup is a third pitch that requires better command and more conviction to reach average. The automated ball-strike system in the FSL did Diaz no favors in terms of getting borderline calls.

THE FUTURE: Diaz finished on a strong note in the FSL, recording a 3.33 ERA and allowing a .212 opponent average in his final six starts, and still has upside he can reach as his secondary pitches develop. He has starter upside but a long way to go to reach it.

BA Grade: 50/Extreme		Fastball: 60		Curveball: 50		Changeup: 45		Control: 50			

Year	Age	Club (League)	Lvl	W	L	ERA	G	GS	IP	H	HR	BB	SO	BB/9	SO/9	WHIP	AVG
2022	18	St. Lucie (FSL)	LoA	3	2	5.86	16	10	55	62	7	25	51	4.1	8.3	1.57	.284
Minor League Totals				3	4	3.32	31	25	106	91	7	34	114	2.9	9.7	1.18	.230

16 JORDANY VENTURA, RHP

Born: July 6, 2000. **B-T:** R-R. **HT:** 6-0. **WT:** 162.
Signed: Dominican Republic, 2018. **Signed by:** Andres Nuñez.

TRACK RECORD: Ventura signed as a 17-year-old out of the Dominican Republic in 2018 and began to vault up the Mets' organizational depth chart with a strong showing at the alternate training site in 2020. He continued to look good at spring training in 2021 but had Tommy John surgery that spring and missed all of that season plus the first half of 2022. Ventura got on the mound for Low-A St. Lucie on June 12 and made three brief starts before he injured his pectoral muscle and missed the rest of the season.

SCOUTING REPORT: Ventura has a sleeper vibe and could break out and assert himself as part of the organization's future in 2023. He is an athletic, 6-foot righthander who is lauded for his competitiveness and for how he attacked his rehab. Ventura's velocity returned intact from Tommy John surgery—he ranged from 92-97 mph and sat about 94—and showed encouraging feel for his secondary pitches. He focused on throwing his mid-80s changeup in his 2022 return, executing it with arm speed and late diving action frequently enough to project as at least above-average. He gets swings and misses with his power 79-80 mph curveball, though command of the pitch proved fleeting in 2022. Ventura throws enough strikes to stay in the rotation.

THE FUTURE: With the potential for three average-or-better major league pitches, a strong work ethic and an athletic build, Ventura has an upside of future No. 4 or 5 starter.

BA Grade: 50/Extreme		Fastball: 55		Curveball: 50			Changeup: 60		Control: 50				
Year	**Age**	**Club (League)**	**Lvl**	**W**	**L**	**ERA**	**G**	**GS**	**IP**	**H**	**HR**	**BB**	**SO**	**BB/9**	**SO/9**	**WHIP**	**AVG**
2022	21	Mets (FCL)	R	0	0	0.00	1	1	2	0	0	0	3	0.0	13.5	0.00	.000
2022	21	St. Lucie (FSL)	LoA	0	0	5.40	3	3	7	7	0	2	10	2.7	13.5	1.35	.259
Minor League Totals				2	3	3.46	22	18	68	52	3	28	70	3.7	9.3	1.18	.215

17 LAYONEL OVALLES, RHP

Born: June 16, 2003. **B-T:** R-R. **HT:** 6-3. **WT:** 175.
Signed: Dominican Republic, 2019. **Signed by:** Felix Romero.

TRACK RECORD: The Mets signed Ovalles out of the Dominican Republic when he was 16 in 2019. Because of the pandemic, nearly two years passed before he made his pro debut in the Dominican Summer League in 2021. Ovalles opened the 2022 season as a reliever in the Florida Complex League but quickly opened eyes—striking out 16 of 17 batters during one stretch—to become a priority prospect. In August he moved to Low-A St. Lucie, where three of his five Florida State League appearances were starts.

SCOUTING REPORT: Ovalles opened the season pitching at 89-90 mph, but his velocity climbed steadily over the summer. By the end, he was sitting 94 mph and had touched 97. Ovalles unleashes three pitches from a physically mature 6-foot-3 frame and a high three-quarters arm slot. He pours in four-seam fastball strikes at an above-average rate and gets his share of swing-and-miss thanks to the cutting action on the pitch. Ovalles' 81-84 mph slider is his best whiff pitch with about a foot of sweep and late drop. He developed a greater feel for his low-80s changeup the more he threw it. The 10 mph separation alone marks the pitch as having big league potential.

THE FUTURE: Ovalles has a promising pitch mix and control. If he can hold his velocity deep into starts and succeed against more advanced competition, he has breakout potential.

BA Grade: 50/Extreme		Fastball: 60		Slider: 55			Changeup: 50		Control: 50				
Year	**Age**	**Club (League)**	**Lvl**	**W**	**L**	**ERA**	**G**	**GS**	**IP**	**H**	**HR**	**BB**	**SO**	**BB/9**	**SO/9**	**WHIP**	**AVG**
2022	19	Mets (FCL)	R	1	2	2.76	11	1	29	26	0	5	44	1.5	13.5	1.06	.230
2022	19	St. Lucie (FSL)	LoA	0	1	6.23	5	3	17	15	3	12	22	6.2	11.4	1.56	.227
Minor League Totals				1	5	3.53	28	10	82	57	3	25	100	2.8	11.0	1.00	.190

18 JOSE BUTTO, RHP

Born: March 19, 1998. **B-T:** R-R. **HT:** 6-1. **WT:** 205. **Signed:** Venezuela, 2017.
Signed by: Hector Rincones.

TRACK RECORD: Butto signed at age 19 in 2017 and surged forward during the canceled 2020 season. He was one of the most impressive pitching prospects at the Mets' alternate training site. Butto reached Double-A in 2021 and then Triple-A in 2022 before making his big league debut with an Aug. 21 spot start. He led the Mets' system with 129 innings and ranked among the leaders with 138 strikeouts, a 17.5 K-BB% and a 3.56 ERA.

SCOUTING REPORT: Butto has worked almost exclusively as a starter in the minors, but his repertoire would probably be best suited to a big league bullpen. His four-seam fastball tops out at 96 mph and sits closer to 93. The pitch rides to the top of the strike zone and has good shape. Butto throws an outstanding changeup with armside fade and separation of 10 mph or more off his fastball. The pitch enhances his effectiveness against lefthanded hitters. Butto doesn't have the same type of differentiating weapon against righthanded hitters. His high-70s curveball and low-80s slider lack the type of power and late bite associated with dominant breaking pitches. He is a flyball pitcher susceptible to the longball when he misses his spots, which makes facing hitters multiple times more perilous.

THE FUTURE: Based on the strength of his two primary pitches and solid-average control, Butto has a chance to fill a swingman role for a contending team.

BA Grade: 40/Medium		Fastball: 50		Curveball: 40		Slider: 40			Changeup: 60		Control: 50	

Year	Age	Club (League)	Lvl	W	L	ERA	G	GS	IP	H	HR	BB	SO	BB/9	SO/9	WHIP	AVG
2022	24	Binghamton (EL)	AA	6	5	4.00	20	18	92	86	14	35	108	3.4	10.5	1.31	.244
2022	24	Syracuse (IL)	AAA	1	1	2.45	8	7	37	26	3	9	30	2.2	7.4	0.95	.198
2022	24	New York (NL)	MLB	0	0	15.75	1	1	4	9	2	2	5	4.5	11.2	2.75	.429
Major League Totals				0	0	15.75	1	1	4	9	2	2	5	4.5	11.2	2.75	.429
Minor League Totals				20	25	3.44	102	89	450	402	51	130	453	2.6	9.1	1.18	.237

19 LUIS RODRIGUEZ, LHP

Born: December 3, 2002. **B-T:** L-L. **HT:** 6-3. **WT:** 190.
Signed: Dominican Republic, 2019. **Signed by:** Kelvin Dominguez.

TRACK RECORD: Rodriguez burst on the scene in 2021 when he pitched his way to Low-A St. Lucie as an 18-year-old after dominating Florida Complex League competition. He had signed for little fanfare in 2019 and had his debut delayed by the pandemic in 2020. Rodriguez didn't get a chance for an encore in 2022 because he had Tommy John surgery in March and missed the entire season.

SCOUTING REPORT: As Rodriguez has filled out his 6-foot-3 frame, he has added velocity and was pitching in the mid 90s from a low three-quarters arm slot when healthy in 2021. He topped out at 97 mph. Rodriguez's low-80s slider has peaked at 86 mph and has wipeout potential thanks to impressive horizontal break to his glove side. He was throwing a changeup in side sessions in 2021 and had encouraging arm speed, but he lacks feel for the pitch overall and didn't throw it much in games. The tall lefthander stood out for his athletic ability and physicality.

THE FUTURE: Barring a setback, Rodriguez is on target to return to action around midseason 2023. Given his raw stuff and throwing hand, he has major league potential and plenty of time to realize it.

BA Grade: 50/Extreme		Fastball: 60		Slider: 55		Changeup: 45		Control: 45	

Year	Age	Club (League)	Lvl	W	L	ERA	G	GS	IP	H	HR	BB	SO	BB/9	SO/9	WHIP	AVG
2022	19	Did not play—Injured															

20 JUNIOR SANTOS, RHP

Born: August 16, 2001. **B-T:** R-R. **HT:** 6-7. **WT:** 244.
Signed: Dominican Republic, 2018. **Signed by:** Anderson Taveras/Gerardo Cabrera.

TRACK RECORD: The Mets don't typically splurge on international amateur pictures, but they made an exception for the 6-foot-7 Santos and signed him for $275,000 out of the Dominican Republic when he was 16 in 2018. He eased into a pro workload in his initial pro seasons and missed the alternate training site in 2020 with a broken foot. But in the past two seasons, only Jose Butto has thrown more innings in the Mets' system. Santos spent 2022 in the High-A Brooklyn rotation, where his fielding-independent numbers look much better than his 4.47 ERA.

SCOUTING REPORT: Santos uses his height to his advantage to drive his 93-95 mph sinker—up to 98—down in the strike zone with tailing life to his arm side. Just two minor league pitchers with at least 100 innings had a higher groundball rate than Santos' 59% mark. He allowed 0.3 home runs per nine innings, which was the fourth-best rate in the minors in that same sample. He throws a mid-80s slider that flashes plus and accounts for a majority of his swings and misses. He has less conviction in a high-80s straight changeup that has some sinking life. Santos has a loose arm but below-average athleticism and control.

THE FUTURE: If Santos moves to the bullpen, it's possible his velocity could spike to triple digits. Many see relief as his future role as he approaches the big leagues.

BA Grade: 45/High		Fastball: 65		Slider: 55		Changeup: 40		Control: 45	

Year	Age	Club (League)	Lvl	W	L	ERA	G	GS	IP	H	HR	BB	SO	BB/9	SO/9	WHIP	AVG
2022	20	Brooklyn (SAL)	HiA	8	13	4.47	26	23	117	126	4	44	105	3.4	8.1	1.46	.272
Minor League Totals				15	25	4.27	75	63	303	319	17	113	259	3.4	7.7	1.42	.269

21 NICK MORABITO, OF

Born: May 7, 2003. **B-T:** R-R. **HT:** 5-11. **WT:** 185.
Drafted: HS—Washington, D.C., 2022 (2nd round supplemental). **Signed by:** Joe Raccuia.

TRACK RECORD: Morabito did not play at the major high school showcases as a rising senior but popped onto radars in 2022 with a big spring at Gonzaga High in downtown Washington, D.C. Mets area scout

Joe Raccuia pegged Morabito as a second-round talent early in the spring, and New York ultimately drafted him 75th overall, using the compensatory pick after the second round it gained when Noah Syndergaard signed with the Angels. The Mets signed Morabito for an over-slot $1 million to steer him away from a Virginia Tech commitment. He looked overmatched—going 2-for-22 with 14 strikeouts—in his pro debut in the Florida Complex League.

SCOUTING REPORT: Morabito has a short, compact build and explosive raw power and speed, but his pro debut demonstrates that work is required to realize his potential. Morabito has premium bat speed and is quick to the ball with short levers, but he simply swings and misses in the zone too much. His swing tends to be a bit one-piece and rotational, so the Mets will work to correct his lower-half hitting mechanics. If the development takes, then he could hit about .250 with above-average power output. Morabito's best tool is his speed, with double-plus being the most common grade. He played shortstop in high school and second base at the draft combine, but the Mets are developing him as a center fielder. His high-end speed gives him upside in the outfield, while his quick first step makes him a basestealing threat. His arm is below-average.

THE FUTURE: Morabito's promising power-speed combination gives him upside to unlock if he can adjust his swing. His development will take time.

BA Grade: 50/Extreme		Hit: 45		Power: 55		Speed: 70		Fielding: 55		Arm: 40	

Year	Age	Club (League)	Lvl	AVG	G	AB	R	H	2B	3B	HR	RBI	BB	SO	SB	OBP	SLG
2022	19	Mets (FCL)	R	.091	6	22	1	2	1	0	0	2	2	14	1	.167	.136
Minor League Totals				.091	6	22	1	2	1	0	0	2	2	14	1	.167	.136

22 DANGELO SARMIENTO, SS

Born: January 4, 2005. **B-T:** R-R. **HT:** 6-2. **WT:** 160.
Signed: Venezuela, 2022. **Signed by:** Andres Nuñez/Ismael Perez.

TRACK RECORD: The Mets made Sarmiento one of their bigger-ticket international amateur acquisitions in 2022 and signed him for $700,000 out of Venezuela about a week after he turned 17. He made a successful pro debut in the Dominican Summer League in which he hit .295, got on base and used his speed to rack up nine stolen bases.

SCOUTING REPORT: Sarmiento has a lean, 6-foot-2 frame that is twitchy but underdeveloped at this stage. He has a contact-oriented righthanded swing and a good eye for the strike zone. His power is almost nonexistent but should improve as he adds strength to his frame. Sarmiento's well above-average speed, overall athleticism and strong defensive ability at shortstop are his headlining attributes. He is energetic in the field, with sure hands, a quick first step and a plus arm capable of throwing out runners from the shortstop hole.

THE FUTURE: As a glove-first shortstop with bat-to-ball skill and command of the strike zone, Sarmiento has a strong foundation to build on. If his hitting ability can come up to par with his glove, he has intriguing upside.

BA Grade: 50/Extreme		Hit: 50		Power: 40		Speed: 70		Fielding: 60		Arm: 60	

Year	Age	Club (League)	Lvl	AVG	G	AB	R	H	2B	3B	HR	RBI	BB	SO	SB	OBP	SLG
2022	17	Mets 1 (DSL)	R	.296	32	108	21	32	5	1	1	16	13	21	9	.373	.389
2022	17	Mets 2 (DSL)	R	.250	2	4	0	1	1	0	0	0	0	1	0	.400	.500
Minor League Totals				.295	34	112	21	33	6	1	1	16	13	22	9	.374	.393

23 JACOB REIMER, 3B

Born: February 22, 2004. **B-T:** R-R. **HT:** 6-2. **WT:** 205.
Drafted: HS—Yucaipa, Calif., 2022 (4th round). **Signed by:** Glenn Walker.

TRACK RECORD: Reimer hails from rural California power Yucaipa High and starred on the showcase circuit as a rising senior. He caught the attention of decision-makers with his hitting ability and swing decisions at the 2022 National High School Invitational. Still, questions about his maxed-out physique and performance against velocity pushed Reimer to the fourth round, where the Mets drafted him and went over-slot to sign him for $775,000. He got into seven Florida Complex League games and showed bat-to-ball skill, discipline and encouraging power.

SCOUTING REPORT: The Mets stayed on Reimer all spring, even as many other teams lost interest, and came away convinced that improvements he made were real. Reimer has a physical 6-foot-2 frame, large hands and present strength. He puts on a show in batting practice and did not look fazed in his brief pro debut. Area scouts dinged him for a stiff, uphill swing that goes in and out of the hitting zone quickly, but he counteracts that with a discerning eye and raw power that grades at least plus. A shortstop in high school, Reimer will develop as a third baseman and to stick there will have to improve his range, mobility and ability to throw on the run. He is a below-average runner who is not a factor on the bases.

THE FUTURE: It all comes down to the bat for Reimer. He faces the potential for further moves down the defensive spectrum but has a chance to stand out in the batter's box.

BA Grade: 45/High		Hit: 45		Power: 50		Speed: 40		Fielding: 45		Arm: 50				
Year	Age	Club (League)	Lvl	AVG	G	AB	R	H	2B	3B	HR	RBI	BB	SO	SB	OBP	SLG
2022	18	Mets (FCL)	R	.261	7	23	5	6	0	1	1	7	6	3	0	.414	.478
Minor League Totals				.261	7	23	5	6	0	1	1	7	6	3	0	.414	.478

24 LUIS MORENO, RHP

Born: May 29, 1999. **B-T:** R-R. **HT:** 6-2. **WT:** 170.
Signed: Dominican Republic, 2019. **Signed by:** Carlos Perez.

TRACK RECORD: The Mets signed Moreno out of the Dominican Republic when he was 20 in 2019. He got in one season in the Dominican Summer League before the pandemic wiped out the 2020 minor league season. When play resumed in 2021, Moreno made the jump to Low-A St. Lucie. He started 2022 back in the Florida State League but quickly pitched his way to High-A Brooklyn in early June.

SCOUTING REPORT: Moreno has added velocity to a two-seam fastball that now sits 92-94 mph and touches 96. He gets fair sink and good armside run on his two-seamer he used to generate a 57% ground-ball rate that ranked fifth in the minors among pitchers with at least 100 innings in 2022. Moreno has always had feel to spin the baseball and throws a slurvy 79-81 mph slider as his money pitch. The pitch has sweeping 10-to-4 action and average depth. He throws a curveball that often blends with his slider. Moreno wears out righthanded hitters with his above-average breaking stuff, which he throws for strikes frequently. He throws a fringy changeup to lefthanded hitters that is not a featured pitch.

THE FUTURE: Moreno's control took a big step forward in 2022, giving him a chance to continue starting. He has No. 5 starter or swingman upside.

BA Grade: 45/High		Fastball: 50		Curveball: 45		Slider: 55			Changeup: 45		Control: 45			
Year	Age	Club (League)	Lvl	W	L	ERA	G	GS	IP	H	HR	BB	SO	BB/9	SO/9	WHIP	AVG
2022	23	St. Lucie (FSL)	LoA	4	0	2.68	9	3	40	36	1	20	37	4.5	8.3	1.39	.245
2022	23	Brooklyn (SAL)	HiA	4	7	2.92	16	14	77	61	7	23	70	2.7	8.2	1.09	.216
Minor League Totals				15	13	3.94	59	39	233	205	17	123	216	4.8	8.3	1.41	.239

25 JAVIER ATENCIO, LHP

Born: November 26, 2001. **B-T:** L-L. **HT:** 6-0. **WT:** 160.
Signed: Venezuela, 2018. **Signed by:** Andres Nuñez.

TRACK RECORD: Atencio's development has been a slow burn since he signed out of Venezuela at age 16 in 2018. He spent 2019 and 2021 in the Dominican Summer League, sandwiched around the canceled 2020 minor league season. Atencio flashed promise in his second DSL summer, when he ranked second with 76 strikeouts. He made his U.S. debut in 2022 when he joined Low-A St. Lucie on May 24, but his season was limited to 43.2 innings by a bout with Covid.

SCOUTING REPORT: Atencio is an athletic lefthander with solid velocity, feel for spin and a developing changeup. He pitches in the low 90s and tops at 95 mph with his four-seam fastball, using it to set up effective secondary weapons. His high-70s slider has slurvy shape and is his most reliable bat-missing pitch. Atencio used his changeup more often in 2022 and gained more confidence in the pitch.

THE FUTURE: Evaluating Atencio was a difficult task because of all the missed time. Most see him as a future reliever or, if everything breaks right, a No. 5 starter.

BA Grade: 45/High		Fastball: 55		Slider: 50			Changeup: 40		Control: 40			
Year	Age	Club (League)	Lvl	W	L	ERA	G	GS	IP	H	HR	BB	SO	BB/9	SO/9	WHIP	AVG
2022	20	Mets (FCL)	R	0	0	0.00	3	3	4	4	0	2	8	4.5	18.0	1.50	.250
2022	20	St. Lucie (FSL)	LoA	2	0	2.27	10	8	40	30	1	23	48	5.2	10.9	1.34	.208
Minor League Totals				3	4	2.96	40	33	128	104	4	60	157	4.2	11.1	1.28	.222

26 ZACH GREENE, RHP

Born: August 29, 1996. **B-T:** R-R. **HT:** 6-1. **WT:** 215.
Drafted: South Alabama, 2019 (8th round). **Signed by:** Chuck Bartlett (Yankees).

TRACK RECORD: The Yankees drafted Greene out of South Alabama in the eighth round in 2019 after he spent his junior and senior seasons there. He spent the entirety of his fourth pro season in 2022 at Triple-A, working as a reliever and opener. Greene was squeezed out of the Yankees' crowded 40-man roster picture and left exposed to the major league Rule 5 draft. The Mets selected him and must keep him on their active 26-man roster all season to retain his rights.
SCOUTING REPORT: Greene throws four pitches but leans on his four-seam fastball and slider. His low-90s four-seamer has riding life and heavy cut from a low release angle. He pairs his unique four-seam shape with a sweeping slider at 78-80 mph. The majority of his whiffs come from those two pitches. Greene will mix in a changeup and cutter as well, but his success is heavily driven from his ability to generate whiffs against his cut four-seam fastball. He misses bats but his control wavers, so he is not a candidate for late-inning, high-leverage work.
THE FUTURE: Greene could be a serviceable low-leverage reliever for the Mets in 2023. If he doesn't make the Opening Day roster, he will be waived and offered back to the Yankees for $50,000 if not claimed.

BA Grade: 40/Medium	Fastball: 55	Slider: 50	Changeup: 40	Cutter: 40	Control: 40

Year	Age	Club (League)	Lvl	W	L	ERA	G	GS	IP	H	HR	BB	SO	BB/9	SO/9	WHIP	AVG
2022	25	Scranton/WB (IL)	AAA	9	0	3.42	48	4	68	51	11	32	96	4.2	12.6	1.21	.201
Minor League Totals				14	8	3.08	96	4	146	101	17	57	211	3.5	13.0	1.08	.191

27 CHRISTIAN SCOTT, RHP

Born: June 15, 1999. **B-T:** R-R. **HT:** 6-4. **WT:** 215.
Drafted: Florida, 2021 (5th round). **Signed by:** Jon Updike.

TRACK RECORD: Scott pitched mostly in relief in three years at Florida. He went undrafted as an eligible sophomore in the five-round 2020 draft but made the cut in 2021, when the Mets drafted him in the fifth round. Scott pitched at two levels of Class A in his 2022 full-season debut, working as a starter and bulk pitcher while averaging nearly 15 batters per appearance with a high of 23 in one start.
SCOUTING REPORT: Scott is a 6-foot-4 righthander who stands out for his fastball/slider combo, good extension toward home plate and a lot of confidence on the mound. His fastball sits 92-94 mph and tops at 97 with running life to his arm side. Scott's slider is above-average with a chance to get to plus. He throws a changeup that he can use as a chase pitch against lefthanded hitters but is below-average. Scott throws a lot of strikes with his fastball and slider but lacks the type of feel typically associated with major league starters.
THE FUTURE: Scott has the goods to become a quality big league reliever with a fastball/slider mix that could grade plus overall. If he moves to the bullpen, he could pop on the MLB radar by 2024.

BA Grade: 45/High	Fastball: 55	Slider: 55	Changeup: 40	Control: 45

Year	Age	Club (League)	Lvl	W	L	ERA	G	GS	IP	H	HR	BB	SO	BB/9	SO/9	WHIP	AVG
2022	23	St. Lucie (FSL)	LoA	3	3	4.82	12	4	37	40	2	12	52	2.9	12.5	1.39	.272
2022	23	Brooklyn (SAL)	HiA	0	0	3.80	6	5	21	21	0	10	25	4.2	10.5	1.45	.247
Minor League Totals				3	3	4.38	21	9	62	64	2	23	78	3.4	11.4	1.41	.264

28 ERIC ORZE, RHP

Born: August 21, 1997. **B-T:** R-R. **HT:** 6-4. **WT:** 195.
Drafted: New Orleans, 2020 (5th round). **Signed by:** Jet Butler.

TRACK RECORD: Orze had one of the more inspirational stories in the 2020 draft. He beat cancer twice as an amateur, first testicular cancer in 2018 and then skin cancer later that summer. He missed all of 2019 recovering and returned in 2020 to make four appearances before the pandemic scuttled the season. The Mets drafted him in the fifth and final round of the truncated 2020 draft.
SCOUTING REPORT: Orze touched Triple-A in his pro debut season in 2021 and returned there in 2022. He is the rare pitcher to throw his splitter more than any other pitch type. Orze's low-80s splitter has tumbling action and draws swings-and-misses about half the time it is thrown. His low-90s fastball tops out at 96 mph but tends to get hit hard. He struck out 33% of batters and walked 7%—for one of the best K-BB% ratios in Triple-A—yet he surrendered 2.1 home runs per nine innings. Orze's mid-80s slider has average depth and is effective in keeping hitters off his fastball.

THE FUTURE: Orze throws a lot of strikes and misses bats with a rare pitch type. He has low-leverage relief upside and could see big league innings in 2023.

BA Grade: 40/Medium		Fastball: 45		Slider: 45		Splitter: 55		Control: 50				
Year	Age	Club (League)	Lvl	W	L	ERA	G	GS	IP	H	HR	BB	SO	BB/9	SO/9	WHIP	AVG
2022	24	St. Lucie (FSL)	LoA	0	0	0.00	2	0	3	2	0	0	5	0.0	15.0	0.67	.182
2022	24	Syracuse (IL)	AAA	4	3	5.13	32	0	47	42	11	14	64	2.7	12.2	1.18	.232
Minor League Totals				8	5	3.96	68	0	100	82	16	28	136	2.5	12.2	1.10	.219

29 WILLIAM LUGO, 3B/SS

Born: January 2, 2002. **B-T:** R-R. **HT:** 6-3. **WT:** 230.
Signed: Dominican Republic, 2018. **Signed by:** Fernando Encarnacion/Gerardo Cabrera.
TRACK RECORD: When the 2018 international signing period opened in July, the Mets prioritized Francisco Alvarez—now the system's top prospect—and Freddy Valdez. They had bonus pool money left over to sign Lugo for $475,000 on Aug. 23 in what turned out to be former international director Chris Becerra's last major signing before leaving for the Red Sox when Brodie Van Wagenen took over as general manager. Sandwiched around the lost 2020, Lugo stumbled through the Rookie complex levels in 2019 and 2021 before emerging in 2022 with a solid hitting performance as a 20-year-old at two Class A levels.
SCOUTING REPORT: Lugo is a bat-first prospect who is powerfully built at 6-foot-3, 230 pounds. What he lacks in future projection, he makes up for with impressive raw power and frequent quality contact. Lugo needs to do a better job staying in his strike zone after chasing too much in 2022, and he could unlock further power with experience by hunting pitches he can drive in the air. Lugo signed as a shortstop and has become more of a third baseman, where his above-average arm plays. He's a below-average athlete and a well below-average runner who will have to work to stay at the hot corner.
THE FUTURE: With a maxed-out physique and questions surrounding his ultimate position, Lugo is not the type of prospect who is valued highly in the industry. But he has interesting power attributes with some hitting upside still to reach.

BA Grade: 45/High		Hit: 45		Power: 45		Speed: 30		Fielding: 40		Arm: 55		
Year	Age	Club (League)	Lvl	AVG	G	AB	R	H	2B	3B	HR	RBI	BB	SO	SB	OBP	SLG
2022	20	St. Lucie (FSL)	LoA	.261	84	314	47	82	18	2	10	45	37	90	0	.347	.427
2022	20	Brooklyn (SAL)	HiA	.267	28	105	18	28	7	0	4	18	13	27	0	.347	.448
Minor League Totals				.232	201	721	107	167	37	2	21	99	94	215	6	.329	.376

30 GRANT HARTWIG, RHP

Born: December 18, 1997. **B-T:** R-R. **HT:** 6-5. **WT:** 235.
Signed: Miami (Ohio), 2021 (NDFA). **Signed by:** Chris Heidt/Moises De La Mota
TRACK RECORD: The Mets signed Hartwig as an nondrafted fifth-year senior out of Miami (Ohio) in 2021. Latin America scouting supervisor Moises De La Mota, who was on assignment watching American amateurs, and area scout Chris Heidt saw Hartwig in the Northwoods League and recommended him. Hartwig made eight appearances the summer he signed and then touched all four full-season levels of the Mets' system in 2022, reaching Triple-A for two games and notching a system-best 13 saves overall.
SCOUTING REPORT: The 6-foot-5 Hartwig came to camp in better shape in 2022 and upped his fastball velocity from an average of 91 mph to 94 with a peak of 97. He finds the zone frequently with a fastball that has heavy sink. Hartwig's best pitch is his low-80s slider that draws a high rate of swinging strikes, often when batters chase out of the zone. He throws an occasional changeup to give him a different look.
THE FUTURE: Hartwig struck out 34% of batters and had a 1.01 ERA in the second half of 2022, which he spent entirely at Double-A and Triple-A. If he keeps up that pace, his MLB debut could be on tap in 2023.

BA Grade: 40/Medium		Fastball: 50		Slider: 55		Changeup: 40		Control: 45				
Year	Age	Club (League)	Lvl	W	L	ERA	G	GS	IP	H	HR	BB	SO	BB/9	SO/9	WHIP	AVG
2022	24	St. Lucie (FSL)	LoA	3	0	4.30	10	0	15	15	0	5	21	3.1	12.9	1.36	.259
2022	24	Brooklyn (SAL)	HiA	1	0	0.59	11	0	15	9	1	6	24	3.5	14.1	0.98	.173
2022	24	Binghamton (EL)	AA	0	2	1.14	16	0	24	14	0	11	34	4.2	12.9	1.06	.167
2022	24	Syracuse (IL)	AAA	2	0	0.00	2	0	3	0	0	2	4	6.0	12.0	0.67	.000
Minor League Totals				6	3	1.98	47	3	68	48	2	28	95	3.7	12.5	1.11	.194

New York Yankees

BY JOSH NORRIS

The 2022 Yankees season was all about Aaron Judge. The massive slugger hit an American League-record 62 home runs, won the AL MVP in a runaway and signed a nine-year, $360 million contract to stay with the Yankees after testing the free agent waters. Judge fueled his team to the AL East crown and an eventual berth in the AL Championship Series, where it was swept by the eventual-champion Astros.

With Judge back in tow, the next phase is figuring out how to build around him and get over the hump for their first World Series win since 2009. If that is to happen, the architects will be the same as ever, with general manager Brian Cashman and manager Aaron Boone signing new contracts after the year.

Cashman dug into the Yankees' system to supplement the big league roster, shelling out three pitchers to the Royals for outfielder Andrew Benintendi, then sending four more prospects to the Athletics—headlined by lefthander Ken Waldichuk—for righthander Frankie Montas and reliever Lou Trivino. One of Cashman's moves went awry when the Yankees sent promising righty Hayden Wesneski to the Cubs for reliever Scott Effross, who got hurt shortly thereafter and had Tommy John surgery.

Of those traded, only Waldichuk and Wesneski likely would have impacted the 2023 Yankees.

New York got a taste of its next wave down the stretch, when touted prospects Oswaldo Cabrera and Oswald Peraza made their big league debuts. The former acted as a Swiss Army knife, seeing time all over the diamond and providing a boost of youth for a team mostly comprised of veterans.

The gem of the Yankees' system is Anthony Volpe, who continued to light up the diamond in a season spent primarily with Double-A Somerset. The 2019 first-rounder shook off a slow April to finish with a .249/.342/.460 slash line with 35 doubles, 21 home runs and 50 stolen bases, including the last month at Triple-A. His walk-off home run to end the first half of the minor league season clinched a playoff berth for eventual Eastern League-champion Somerset.

Jasson Dominguez, the system's No. 3 prospect, put together an excellent season that started at Low-A and finished in Double-A, where his two home runs—one from each side of the plate—punctuated a championship-sealing no-hitter from Randy Vasquez and Carson Coleman.

Below the system's most famous prospects, Mexican righthander Luis Serna made a name for himself. The 17-year-old showed a four-pitch mix in the Florida Complex League headed by a double-plus changeup and uncommon pitchability

Rookie Oswaldo Cabrera started games at five positions and made the postseason roster.

PROJECTED 2026 LINEUP

Catcher	Austin Wells	26
First Base	DJ LeMahieu	37
Second Base	Gleyber Torres	29
Third Base	Anthony Volpe	25
Shortstop	Oswald Peraza	26
Left Field	Jasson Dominguez	23
Center Field	Spencer Jones	25
Right Field	Aaron Judge	34
Designated Hitter	Giancarlo Stanton	36
No. 1 Starter	Gerrit Cole	35
No. 2 Starter	Luis Severino	32
No. 3 Starter	Nestor Cortes	31
No. 4 Starter	Drew Thorpe	25
No. 5 Starter	Will Warren	27
Closer	Jonathan Loaisiga	31

for someone his age and bull-rushed his way onto the team's radar.

In the draft, New York added toolsy Vanderbilt outfielder Spencer Jones, who brings standout athleticism with the lefthanded power that would fit perfectly at Yankee Stadium. They followed Jones' selection with a pair of West Coast righthanders—Cal Poly's Drew Thorpe and Gonzaga's Trystan Vrieling—before adding even more lefthanded thump with Oregon's Anthony Hall in the fourth round.

Mets owner Steve Cohen has thrown down his wallet—and with it the gauntlet—in his early days in charge of Queens. Now, it's on Hal Steinbrenner and company to answer, break the franchise's championship drought and show the world that they still have it in them to be the best team in the Empire State. ∎

DEPTH CHART

NEW YORK YANKEES

TOP 2023 MLB CONTRIBUTORS	RANK
Anthony Volpe, SS	1
Oswald Peraza, SS	2
BREAKOUT PROSPECTS	**RANK**
Engelth Ureña, C	16
Anthony Hall, OF	19

SOURCE OF TOP 30 TALENT

Homegrown	28	Acquired	2
College	11	Trade	2
Junior college	0	Rule 5 draft	0
High school	1	Independent league	0
Nondrafted free agent	1	Free agent/waivers	0
International	15		

LF
Elijah Dunham (15)

CF
Jasson Dominguez (3)
Everson Pereira (4)
Estevan Florial (10)

RF
Spencer Jones (6)
Anthony Hall (19)

3B
Tyler Hardman (17)

SS
Anthony Volpe (1)
Oswald Peraza (2)
Roderick Arias (13)

2B
Trey Sweeney (14)
Jared Serna (29)
Keiner Delgado

1B
TJ Rumfield
Agustin Ramirez
Andres Chaparro

C
Austin Wells (5)
Engelth Ureña (16)
Antonio Gomez (25)

LHP

LHSP
Brock Selvidge
Joel Valdez
Henry Lalane

LHRP
Matt Krook
Matt Minnick
Edgar Barclay
Will Brian

RHP

RHSP
Will Warren (7)
Drew Thorpe (8)
Randy Vasquez (9)
Luis Gil (11)
Luis Serna (12)
Richard Fitts (18)
Trystan Vrieling (20)
Omar Gonzalez (22)
Angel Benitez (23)
Yoendrys Gomez (26)
Juan Carela (30)
Kris Bow
Jordarlin Mendoza
Sean Hermann
Brendan Beck

RHRP
Clayton Beeter (21)
Greg Weissert (24)
Carson Coleman (27)
Jhony Brito (28)
Josue Panacual
Eric Reyzelman
Chase Hampton
Ryan Harvey
Jackson Fristoe

1 ANTHONY VOLPE, SS

Born: April 28, 2001. **B-T:** R-R. **HT:** 5-11. **WT:** 180.
Drafted: HS—Morristown, N.J., 2019 (1st round).
Signed by: Matt Hyde.

TRACK RECORD: Volpe had a standout senior season in 2019 at Delbarton High, the New Jersey program where he was teammates with fellow future first-rounder Jack Leiter. The Yankees believed enough in both Volpe's performance and makeup that they spent their first-round pick and a bonus of $2,740,300 to keep him from a commitment to Vanderbilt. His pro debut was hampered by a case of mononucleosis that muted his performance at Rookie-level Pulaski. Then the pandemic happened, and Volpe spent the season working remotely to improve his game. When he re-emerged in 2021, he looked like a player with the potential to be the team's shortstop of the future. When the Yankees passed on signing free agents Carlos Correa or Trevor Story following the 2021 season, those thoughts were reinforced. Now, it was on Volpe to produce an encore. After a winter of training that included a stop at Wake Forest's pitching lab to help strengthen his throwing arm, Volpe got his first upper-level test when he was assigned to Double-A Somerset. Volpe stumbled out of the blocks in April but turned it on thereafter. From May 1 until the close of the season, the 21-year-old hit .268/.356/.493 in a tenure split between Double-A and Triple-A. He closed the first half of the season with a walk-off home run that sent Somerset to the Eastern League playoffs, where they would eventually win the championship.

SCOUTING REPORT: Volpe is the purest hitter in the Yankees' system, a title he comes by through an extremely mature approach that allows him to pick through pitches he doesn't want until he gets something he can impact. Then he unleashes a powerful yet compact swing that produces hard line drives thanks to a swing path that keeps the barrel in the zone for a long time. Scouts noticed a few early tweaks that might have gotten him a little off-kilter in the early going. Notably, they saw a bigger stride and a higher hand-set than in years past. The former was causing unwanted head movement and the latter upset his timing and was causing him to work around pitches instead of through them. Once Volpe corrected those issues, he started looking like the 2021 version of himself. Multiple scouts brought up a weakness against spin from righthanders, which is among the final holes he'll have to close before he's ready to take over in the Bronx. Scouts are split about whether

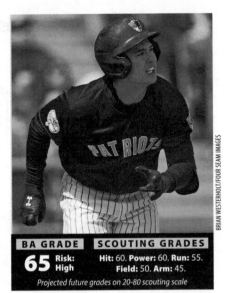

BRIAN WESTERHOLT/FOUR SEAM IMAGES

BA GRADE	SCOUTING GRADES
65 Risk: High	Hit: 60. Power: 60. Run: 55. Field: 50. Arm: 45.

Projected future grades on 20-80 scouting scale

BEST TOOLS

BATTING

Best Hitter for Average	Anthony Volpe
Best Power Hitter	Austin Wells
Best Strike-Zone Discipline	Anthony Volpe
Fastest Baserunner	Estevan Florial
Best Athlete	Spencer Jones

PITCHING

Best Fastball	Luis Gil
Best Curveball	Randy Vasquez
Best Slider	Will Warren
Best Changeup	Luis Serna
Best Control	Jhony Brito

FIELDING

Best Defensive Catcher	Antonio Gomez
Best Defensive Infielder	Oswald Peraza
Best Infield Arm	Oswald Peraza
Best Defensive Outfielder	Estevan Florial
Best Outfield Arm	Estevan Florial

Volpe can remain at shortstop. Nobody believes he will be an elite defender at the position, but there are some who think he can be average and that his lack of standout arm strength can be mitigated by excellent instincts and a quick release. He has quick feet but his range at shortstop is average at best. He's an above-average runner whose strong instincts helped him swipe 50 bases.

THE FUTURE: Volpe might return to Triple-A to begin 2023, but it's clear the Yankees view him as a key part of their long-term future and possibly part of the shorter-term future. Whether that's at shortstop or elsewhere on the infield is the biggest remaining question.

Year	Age	Club (League)	Lvl	AVG	G	AB	R	H	2B	3B	HR	RBI	BB	SO	SB	OBP	SLG
2022	21	Somerset (EL)	AA	.251	110	422	71	106	31	4	18	60	57	88	44	.348	.472
2022	21	Scranton/WB (IL)	AAA	.236	22	89	15	21	4	1	3	5	8	30	6	.313	.404
Minor League Totals				.262	275	1044	218	274	77	13	50	162	166	257	89	.376	.505

2 OSWALD PERAZA, SS

Born: June 15, 2000. **B-T:** R-R. **HT:** 6-0. **WT:** 200.
Signed: Venezuela, 2016. **Signed by:** Roney Calderon/Jose Gavidia.

TRACK RECORD: Peraza was signed out of Venezuela in 2016 as a player with gifts on both sides of the ball. He showed hints of that potential before the pandemic, but he truly broke out in 2021, when he reached new offensive heights. He opened the 2022 season as the youngest player in the International League and the second-youngest in Triple-A. He struggled initially before getting hot in the summer months. Through April and May, he produced an OPS of .621. In June and July, that figure jumped to .913. He made his big league debut on Sept. 2 and was included on the Yankees' roster for the American League Championship Series.

BA GRADE
50 Risk: Medium

SCOUTING REPORT: Part of Peraza's struggles in the early portion of the season revolved around the cold weather in the Northeast. Another part was that he was facing advanced arms at Triple-A who relentlessly exploited his weakness against sliders that broke down and away. Peraza and Scranton hitting coach Trevor Amicone worked hard behind the scenes to improve that part of his game, and the results started showing up during the summer months. Peraza's power is fringe-average and geared more toward doubles than home runs and is presently mostly to his pull side. He's a cinch to stick at shortstop and grades as the best infielder in the system, with the quickness, range and plus arm strength to handle most everything hit his way. His above-average speed helped both on defense and on the bases, where he stole 33 bags in 38 tries.

THE FUTURE: Peraza has the defensive chops to be the Yankees' long-term shortstop, especially if they choose to push Anthony Volpe to second base.

| SCOUTING GRADES | Hitting: 55 | | Power: 45 | | Speed: 55 | | Fielding: 60 | | Arm: 55 | |

Year	Age	Club (League)	Lvl	AVG	G	AB	R	H	2B	3B	HR	RBI	BB	SO	SB	OBP	SLG
2022	22	Scranton/WB (IL)	AAA	.259	99	386	57	100	16	0	19	50	34	100	33	.329	.448
2022	22	New York (AL)	MLB	.306	18	49	8	15	3	0	1	2	6	9	2	.404	.429
Major League Totals				.306	18	49	8	15	3	0	1	2	6	9	2	.404	.429
Minor League Totals				.274	373	1473	240	404	64	8	42	173	129	327	115	.347	.414

3 JASSON DOMINGUEZ, OF

Born: Feb. 7, 2003. **B-T:** B-R. **HT:** 5-10. **WT:** 190. **Signed:** Dominican Republic, 2019. **Signed by:** Juan Rosario/Lorenzo Piron/Edgar Mateo.

TRACK RECORD: Dominguez signed for $5.1 million in 2019 but had his pro debut delayed a year by the pandemic. He had spurts of success as one of the youngest players in the Low-A Florida State League in 2021. He returned to Tampa in 2022 but finished the year in Double-A, where he helped Somerset win the Eastern League crown. Dominguez made the 2021 and 2022 Futures Games and hit a long homer at Dodger Stadium in the latter.

SCOUTING REPORT: Dominguez's season got better as the year went on, in terms of both public and private evaluation methods. From June 1 forward, he hit .273/.389/.464. That period also included 11 of his 16 home runs, which speaks to the Yankees' efforts to get him to hit the ball in the air more often.

BA GRADE
55 Risk: High

He also worked hard to improve his swing decisions. Even during Dominguez's early struggles with Low-A Tampa, scouts believed he was recognizing pitches well but still swinging at ones he couldn't impact. Now, he's got the potential to be at least an above-average hitter with plus power. He has a chance to stick as an average center fielder. A lot will depend on how his body develops as he matures. Dominguez is strong and compact rather than the lithe athletes who typically hold down center. Still, scouts see a player whose above-average speed, as well as excellent reads and jumps, could allow him to stay in center field even if he's unlikely to be a standout. His arm strength is above-average and would play in right field if necessary.

THE FUTURE: After a cameo at Double-A and a stint in the Arizona Fall League, Dominguez will spend all of 2023 as a 20-year-old at the upper levels.

| SCOUTING GRADES | Hitting: 55 | | Power: 60 | | Speed: 55 | | Fielding: 50 | | Arm: 55 | |

Year	Age	Club (League)	Lvl	AVG	G	AB	R	H	2B	3B	HR	RBI	BB	SO	SB	OBP	SLG
2022	19	Tampa (FSL)	LoA	.265	75	275	54	73	17	2	9	36	46	89	19	.373	.440
2022	19	Hudson Valley (SAL)	HiA	.306	40	157	33	48	6	4	6	22	23	34	17	.397	.510
2022	19	Somerset (EL)	AA	.105	5	19	5	2	0	1	1	1	3	5	1	.227	.368
Minor League Totals				.266	176	657	123	175	32	8	21	78	99	201	46	.368	.435

4 EVERSON PEREIRA, OF

Born: April 10, 2001. **B-T:** R-R. **HT:** 6-0. **WT:** 191.
Signed: Venezuela, 2017. **Signed by:** Roney Calderon.

TRACK RECORD: Pereira signed in 2017 but has had his career severely limited by injuries and the pandemic, and the 102 games he played in 2022 are just shy of half of his career total. Pereira launched 20 home runs in just 49 games in 2021 and continued to show flashes of his ceiling throughout the 2022 season, which included a late promotion to Double-A Somerset for his first upper-level test.

SCOUTING REPORT: Evaluators love Pereira's raw power, with some even going as high as a 70 on the 20-80 scale for his ability to lose balls to the deepest recesses of parks during batting practice. His swing-and-miss tendencies caused that power to play down in games, as did his propensity for hitting the ball on the ground early in the season. The Yankees tweaked Pereira's bat path to make his swing more flyball-oriented. Still, scouts point to Pereira's chase rate and timing issues that could limit his ceiling to no more than an average hitter. Defensively, Pereira has a chance to stick in center field but could also move to a corner, and his above-average arm strength would fit nicely in right field. Some scouts would like to see Pereira become more accurate on his throws. He's an above-average runner who gets excellent jumps in the outfield.

THE FUTURE: Pereira's season was once again stunted by injuries, though not as severely as in the past. He'll get another test at the upper levels in 2023 and has the ceiling of an above-average regular outfielder with a profile leaning slightly toward power over hit.

BA GRADE: 55 Risk: High

SCOUTING GRADES	Hitting: 50	Power: 55	Speed: 55	Fielding: 50	Arm: 55

Year	Age	Club (League)	Lvl	AVG	G	AB	R	H	2B	3B	HR	RBI	BB	SO	SB	OBP	SLG
2022	21	Hudson Valley (SAL)	HiA	.274	73	288	55	79	13	6	9	43	34	87	19	.354	.455
2022	21	Somerset (EL)	AA	.283	29	113	21	32	4	3	5	13	9	37	2	.341	.504
Minor League Totals				.271	210	826	153	224	38	12	38	141	90	271	36	.346	.484

5 AUSTIN WELLS, C

Born: July 12, 1999. **B-T:** L-R. **HT:** 6-2. **WT:** 220.
Drafted: Arizona, 2020 (1st round). **Signed by:** Troy Afenir.

TRACK RECORD: The Yankees were on Wells for much of his amateur career, having drafted him out of high school in 2018 and then again in 2020, when he was an eligible sophomore at Arizona. Since turning pro, Wells has done nothing but hit as he's climbed from Low-A to Double-A. He was limited to just 92 games in 2022 because of a ruptured testicle that cost him a chunk of time at midseason. He moved to Double-A upon return from the injury and showed an excellent combination of power and on-base skills.

SCOUTING REPORT: Wells' profile is almost entirely driven by his bat, which has proved potent at every level. He combines excellent knowledge of the strike zone with brute strength and a lofted swing path designed to hit balls

BA GRADE: 55 Risk: High

hard and in the air, which raised his fly ball plus line drive rate to nearly 50%. Wells also worked with the Yankees to adjust his bat path to reduce in his in-zone whiff rate, which was around 20% in 2022, an improvement of 11% from 2021. Wells' hands aren't the most mobile, but scouts still saw the ability to punish line drives to all sectors. One scout noted that he was strong enough to turn a 100 mph fastball into a home run the opposite way off the left-field foul pole. Defensively, Wells is not likely to be an average defender, but he's worked diligently and has improved his catching by quite a bit. He's improved his overall arm strength but could make further improvements by cleaning up his footwork and shortening his release. His pop times are usually between 2.00 and 2.15 seconds.

THE FUTURE: Wells' next step is likely Triple-A, and he could make his big league debut at some point in 2023. He has the look of a masher who is passable behind the plate.

SCOUTING GRADES	Hitting: 50	Power: 55	Speed: 45	Fielding: 40	Arm: 45

Year	Age	Club (League)	Lvl	AVG	G	AB	R	H	2B	3B	HR	RBI	BB	SO	SB	OBP	SLG
2022	22	Tampa (FSL)	LoA	.231	9	26	5	6	2	0	2	6	8	5	0	.412	.538
2022	22	Hudson Valley (SAL)	HiA	.323	28	99	21	32	7	0	6	16	19	27	9	.429	.576
2022	22	Somerset (EL)	AA	.261	55	211	34	55	8	1	12	43	29	58	7	.360	.479
Minor League Totals				.270	195	718	142	194	40	6	36	141	127	207	32	.388	.493

6 SPENCER JONES, OF

Born: May 14, 2001. **B-T:** L-L. **HT:** 6-7. **WT:** 225.
Drafted: Vanderbilt, 2022 (1st round). **Signed By:** Chuck Bartlett.
TRACK RECORD: As a high schooler, Jones had enough athleticism to excel as a two-way player. A broken elbow ended his senior season and stifled his draft stock enough that he made it to campus at Vanderbilt as a position player only. Jones was a standout in the Cape Cod League in 2021 and backed it up with an excellent junior season in Nashville, where he produced an 1.104 OPS with 12 home runs. The Yankees liked his combination of athleticism, lefthanded power and bat-to-ball skills enough to draft him 25th overall. He signed for $2,880,800 and split his pro debut between the Florida Complex League and Low-A Tampa.

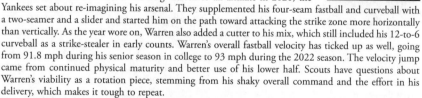

BA GRADE
55 Risk: Very High

SCOUTING REPORT: Much like the Yankees' other towering sluggers, Jones uses his massive frame to produce corresponding power and the exit velocities to match. He hit three home runs in the Florida State League, including one which produced an exit velocity of 111.3 mph. As expected with a hitter his size, Jones has holes to close at the plate, though scouts who saw him as a pro noted he'd done a good job learning how to manipulate the barrel and slowly minimize areas where he can be exploited. He had also done well to go the other way against lefthanders. Defensively, Jones has the speed to stick in center field but might be more natural on an outfield corner. His big-time power and average arm strength would help him profile as a classic masher who hits toward the middle of an order. He's a plus runner now who is likely to tick down a half-grade as he ages.
THE FUTURE: Jones and his Vanderbilt pedigree are likely to head to High-A Hudson Valley to begin 2023. He'll work to continue maintaining his hitting ability against higher-caliber pitchers.

SCOUTING GRADES	Hitting: 45	Power: 60	Speed: 55	Fielding: 55	Arm: 50

Year	Age	Club (League)	Lvl	AVG	G	AB	R	H	2B	3B	HR	RBI	BB	SO	SB	OBP	SLG
2022	21	Yankees (FCL)	R	.500	3	10	3	5	1	0	1	4	1	2	2	.545	.900
2022	21	Tampa (FSL)	LoA	.325	22	83	18	27	5	0	3	8	10	18	10	.411	.494
Minor League Totals				.344	25	93	21	32	6	0	4	12	11	20	12	.425	.538

7 WILL WARREN, RHP

Born: June 16, 1999. **B-T:** R-R. **HT:** 6-2. **WT:** 175.
Drafted: Southeastern Louisiana, 2021 (8th round). **Signed by:** Mike Leuzinger.
TRACK RECORD: Warren is the latest in the line of gems the Yankees' pitching department has polished into intriguing prospects. He was selected in the eighth round of the 2021 draft out of Southeastern Louisiana but did not pitch professionally after signing. He opened the 2022 season at High-A Hudson Valley and was one of the organization's biggest pop-up arms as he ascended to Double-A Somerset in early June, making him one of the first handful of 2021 draft picks to advance past Class A. Warren racked up a 53% groundball rate that ranked 18th in the minors for pitchers with at least 100 innings and second in the Yankees' system behind Matt Krook.

BA GRADE
50 Risk: High

SCOUTING REPORT: Instead of sending Warren to an affiliate in 2021, the Yankees set about re-imagining his arsenal. They supplemented his four-seam fastball and curveball with a two-seamer and a slider and started him on the path toward attacking the strike zone more horizontally than vertically. As the year wore on, Warren also added a cutter to his mix, which still included his 12-to-6 curveball as a strike-stealer in early counts. Warren's overall fastball velocity has ticked up as well, going from 91.8 mph during his senior season in college to 93 mph during the 2022 season. The velocity jump came from continued physical maturity and better use of his lower half. Scouts have questions about Warren's viability as a rotation piece, stemming from his shaky overall command and the effort in his delivery, which makes it tough to repeat.
THE FUTURE: Optimistic evaluators see Warren as a back-end starter, while more bearish scouts see him as a middle reliever who can eat innings and get ground balls.

SCOUTING GRADES:	Fastball: 60	Curveball: 40	Slider: 60	Cutter: 40	Control: 50

Year	Age	Club (League)	Lvl	W	L	ERA	G	GS	IP	H	HR	BB	SO	BB/9	SO/9	WHIP	AVG
2022	23	Hudson Valley (SAL)	HiA	2	3	3.60	8	8	35	30	2	9	42	2.3	10.8	1.11	.234
2022	23	Somerset (EL)	AA	7	6	4.02	18	18	94	89	8	33	83	3.2	7.9	1.30	.251
Minor League Totals				9	9	3.91	26	26	129	119	10	42	125	2.9	8.7	1.25	.246

8 DREW THORPE, RHP

Born: Oct. 1, 2000. **B-T:** L-R. **HT:** 6-4. **WT:** 190.
Drafted: Cal Poly, 2022 (2nd round). **Signed by:** Tyler Robertson.

TRACK RECORD: Thorpe had two-way potential when he arrived in college, but Cal Poly believed there was more potential as a pitcher. They were right. Part of the decision was because of Thorpe's outstanding changeup, which continued to be his signature pitch throughout three seasons with the Mustangs, where was teammates with shortstop and No. 8 overall pick Brooks Lee. He also pitched in the Cape Cod League and was a member of USA Baseball's Collegiate National Team in 2021. Thorpe's outstanding junior campaign saw him strike out 149 hitters in 103.2 innings, which earned him not only a spot as a BA first-team All-American but led the Yankees to draft him in the second round and sign him for $1,187,600.

BA GRADE
50 Risk: High

SCOUTING REPORT: In Thorpe, the Yankees saw untapped potential, thanks to a more physical pitcher than would be expected from someone whose fastball only averaged 90.5 mph during his draft season at Cal Poly. They also like what they saw in Thorpe's natural movement patterns, which suggest a pitcher who with further development and strength will see an uptick in fastball velocity and amplified offspeed pitches. Instead of sending him to an affiliate after signing, the Yankees brought Thorpe in and rested him before inviting him to their fall instructional program, which is typically divided into groups focusing on specific skill development. This is the same tact they took with Will Warren after the 2021 season, when he emerged as a different pitcher.

THE FUTURE: After an offseason of rest and instruction, Thorpe's college pedigree means he's likely to head to High-A Hudson Valley to officially begin his pro career. He has a shot at becoming a back-end rotation piece, with a chance for more.

SCOUTING GRADES:	Fastball: 45	Slider: 55	Changeup: 65	Control: 60

Year	Age	Club (League)	Lvl	W	L	ERA	G	GS	IP	H	HR	BB	SO	BB/9	SO/9	WHIP	AVG
2022	21	Did not play—Injured															

9 RANDY VASQUEZ, RHP

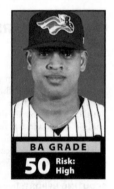

Born: Nov. 3, 1998. **B-T:** R-R. **HT:** 6-0. **WT:** 165.
Signed: Dominican Republic, 2018. **Signed by:** Arturo Peña.

TRACK RECORD: Vasquez was signed out of the Dominican Republic in 2018 and earned enough of a rep in 2021, when he pitched in full-season ball for the first time, that he was originally part of the deal that brought Joey Gallo from the Rangers to New York in exchange for four prospects. A few last-minute alterations to the trade kept him and outfielder Everson Pereira with the Yankees. Vasquez pitched exclusively at Double-A Somerset in 2022 and finished his season with a flourish when he spun the first eight innings of a no-hitter that helped the Patriots win the Eastern League championship.

BA GRADE
50 Risk: High

SCOUTING REPORT: Vasquez works primarily with a combination of four- and two-seam fastballs, each of which average roughly 92-93 mph, and a sweeping curveball that he uses to get swings and misses. He also added a cutter this season. His curveball, which ranks as the best in the system, is sharp enough that it helped him earned the nickname "El Cuchillo," or "The Knife" in Spanish. In 2021, Vasquez lowered his arm slot in an effort to add more velocity. The goal worked, but in 2022 he didn't show the same command of his arsenal. His strike percentage and walk rates were nearly identical year over year, but his strikeout rate dipped from nearly 29% in 2021 to 24% a year later. He'll need to improve the quality of his strikes in order to get more whiffs. Vasquez's overall numbers are somewhat stunted by a horrid July in which he allowed five home runs in just 14.2 innings. By contrast, he allowed just six home runs during the rest of the season.

THE FUTURE: Vasquez will move to Triple-A in 2023. If he can improve his command, he has a chance to stick as a back-end starter. If not, he fits as a middle-innings reliever.

SCOUTING GRADES:	Fastball: 55	Curveball: 60	Changeup: 50	Control: 50

Year	Age	Club (League)	Lvl	W	L	ERA	G	GS	IP	H	HR	BB	SO	BB/9	SO/9	WHIP	AVG
2022	23	Somerset (EL)	AA	2	7	3.90	25	25	115	106	11	41	120	3.2	9.4	1.27	.239
Minor League Totals				15	13	3.10	68	64	308	249	22	119	331	3.5	9.7	1.20	.217

10 ESTEVAN FLORIAL, OF

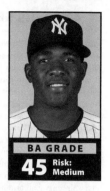

BA GRADE

45 Risk:
Medium

Born: Nov. 25, 1997. **B-T:** L-R. **HT:** 6-1. **WT:** 195.
Signed: Haiti, 2015. **Signed by:** Esteban Castillo.

TRACK RECORD: From an identification issue that complicated his initial signing, to his rise through the system and ascent to its No. 1 prospect in 2019, to two years marred by injuries before his MLB debut during the pandemic season of 2020, Florial's career has gone through numerous peaks and valleys. He's been healthy the last two seasons and has made up for lost development while getting sporadic callups in the past three seasons. He appeared in 17 big league games in 2022, just nine of them starts.

SCOUTING REPORT: The biggest problem in Florial's game has long revolved around the frequency at which he swings and misses at pitches in the strike zone. He reduced that total to 25% in 2022, while similarly dropping his chase rate to 21%. The result is more contact—often hard contact. More than half of the balls Florial hit in 2022 resulted in exit velocities of 95 mph or better, and his 90th percentile exit velocity of 107.2 mph was among the best in the entire system. While the Yankees are encouraged by Florial's improvement, they believe there is still more to come. He also needs to improve his output against lefthanders, against whom he hit just .222 in the minors. He sharpened his left-on-left skills by taking rounds of batting practice against Scranton coach Raul Dominguez, who is lefthanded. Florial is arguably the best defender in the system, earning plus grades in center field and for his throwing arm. He's an above-average runner.

THE FUTURE: Despite his long career in the minor leagues, Florial is still relatively young in terms of on-field reps. The 2022 season was the first time since 2017 that he played more than 100 games.

SCOUTING GRADES	Hitting: 40	Power: 55	Speed: 55	Fielding: 60	Arm: 60

Year	Age	Club (League)	Lvl	AVG	G	AB	R	H	2B	3B	HR	RBI	BB	SO	SB	OBP	SLG
2022	24	Scranton/WB (IL)	AAA	.283	101	403	66	114	31	2	15	46	54	140	39	.368	.481
2022	24	New York (AL)	MLB	.097	17	31	4	3	0	0	0	1	3	13	2	.200	.097
Major League Totals				.185	29	54	7	10	2	0	1	3	8	21	3	.302	.278
Minor League Totals				.267	580	2257	397	602	123	27	74	306	282	745	125	.350	.444

11 LUIS GIL, RHP

Born: June 3, 1998. **B-T:** R-R. **HT:** 6-2. **WT:** 185.
Signed: Dominican Republic, 2015. **Signed by:** Luis Lajara (Twins).

TRACK RECORD: Gil was signed out of the Dominican Republic in 2015 by the Twins for $50,000, then dealt to the Yankees in 2018 for outfielder Jake Cave. Gil began his Yankees career in Low-A Charleston, where he was part of a stacked rotation that also included the since-traded Luis Medina, Roansy Contreras and Alexander Vizcaino. Gil cut his way through the minor leagues before making his big league debut on Aug. 8, 2021. Gil spent the bulk of his 2022 season in Triple-A, save for one big league start, after which he was sent down. He made one more start with Triple-A before a torn ulnar collateral ligament required Tommy John surgery.

SCOUTING REPORT: Gil works with a three-pitch mix fronted by a fastball that averages around 96 mph and can touch a few ticks higher. The pitch has plenty of spin and riding life through the zone, placing it among the organization's best fastballs. He backs the fastball with a potentially plus slider in the mid 80s. This past season was the first time since before the pandemic that baseball was played in the northeast in April, and Gil had early struggles finding a good feel for the slider in the cold weather. He rounds out his mix with a potentially fringe-average changeup in the low 90s. He has near-average control and command of his mix.

THE FUTURE: For now, Gil will play the waiting game while he rehabs. Once he returns, the long layoff might make it tough to build him back into a starter's workload. If that's the case, his fastball-slider combo should play out of the bullpen.

BA GRADE: 45/Medium	Fastball: 60	Slider: 60	Changeup: 45	Control: 45

Year	Age	Club (League)	Lvl	W	L	ERA	G	GS	IP	H	HR	BB	SO	BB/9	SO/9	WHIP	AVG
2022	24	Scranton/WB (IL)	AAA	0	3	7.89	6	6	22	21	6	15	31	6.2	12.9	1.66	.244
2022	24	New York (AL)	MLB	0	0	9.00	1	1	4	5	0	2	5	4.5	11.2	1.75	.294
Major League Totals				1	1	3.78	7	7	33	25	4	21	43	5.7	11.6	1.38	.198
Minor League Totals				13	16	3.42	88	69	308	229	22	184	412	5.4	12.0	1.34	.204

12 LUIS SERNA, RHP

Born: July 20, 2004. **B-T:** R-R. **HT:** 5-11. **WT:** 162.
Signed: Mexico, 2021. **Signed by:** Lee Sigman.

TRACK RECORD: When he was an amateur, Serna piqued the Yankees' interest with his combination of outstanding feel to pitch, a quick arm and gumption on the mound. He signed in May of 2021 for $50,000 and spent his first pro campaign in the Dominican Summer League. He moved to the states in 2022 and opened eyes with his pitchability and dynamic changeup while helping lead his team to the Florida Complex League championship. Serna ranked as the third-best prospect in the FCL.

SCOUTING REPORT: Serna works with a four-pitch mix headlined by an excellent changeup that could get to a true double-plus grade and was pegged by internal evaluators as the system's best. Serna's strength gains have led to corresponding velocity boosts on his fastball. The pitch, which sat in the mid 80s when he signed, averaged around 91 mph and scraped 94 last season. Scouts also noticed that he did a good job driving the pitch in the lower parts of the strike zone. He finishes the mix with a pair of breaking balls—a high-spin curveball and a high-70s slider—that each flash average. He commands the mix exceptionally well, especially for someone his age, and projects to have plus control. The only thing that gives scouts pause is a longer, hooking arm action, but it has not presented an impediment thus far.

THE FUTURE: Serna will move to Low-A next year. If he can continue adding strength, his combination of stuff and pitchability could lead to a midrotation future.

BA GRADE: 55/Very High	Fastball: 55	Curveball: 50	Slider: 50	Changeup: 70	Control: 60

Year	Age	Club (League)	Lvl	W	L	ERA	G	GS	IP	H	HR	BB	SO	BB/9	SO/9	WHIP	AVG
2022	17	Yankees (FCL)	R	0	0	1.96	11	10	41	33	0	17	56	3.7	12.2	1.21	.221
Minor League Totals				1	5	2.10	23	21	81	58	0	34	102	3.8	11.3	1.13	.199

13 RODERICK ARIAS, SS

Born: Sept. 9, 2004. **B-T:** B-R. **HT:** 6-2. **WT:** 178.
Signed: Dominican Republic, 2022. **Signed by:** Esdras Abreu.

TRACK RECORD: Arias was the jewel of the Yankees' 2021-22 international class and signed for $4 million, the second-highest bonus in the class behind only the Nationals' Cristhian Vaquero. As an amateur, he was lauded for an enviable blend of tools and projectablity. Arias' pro debut was delayed by a minor thumb injury, but he showed hints of his talent throughout his time in the Dominican Summer League.

SCOUTING REPORT: Arias' swings from both sides of the plate are quick and compact and he's shown solid ability to identify spin in both showcases and against pro pitching. The rust showed a bit when Arias returned from the injured list on July 4, roughly a month into the DSL season, which some evaluators believe might have been a hair too early. The Yankees tailor their hitting department around the development of exit velocity, and he showed early signs of being able to hit the ball very hard. His average EV in a limited sample was 88.7 mph, which is outstanding for someone so young. Defensively, he's got the skills and actions to be an everyday shortstop but his rail gun of an arm stands out. His elite arm strength allows him to make every throw both strong and accurate from every angle.

THE FUTURE: After spending his first season in the DSL, Arias will move to the Florida Complex League in 2023. He has one of the highest ceilings in the system and will hope for better luck with health.

BA GRADE: 55/Extreme	Hit: 50	Power: 60	Speed: 55	Fielding: 50	Arm: 80

Year	Age	Club (League)	Lvl	AVG	G	AB	R	H	2B	3B	HR	RBI	BB	SO	SB	OBP	SLG
2022	17	Yankees (DSL)	R	.194	31	108	25	21	6	2	3	11	28	46	10	.379	.370
Minor League Totals				.194	31	108	25	21	6	2	3	11	28	46	10	.379	.370

14 TREY SWEENEY, SS

Born: April 24, 2000. **B-T:** L-R. **HT:** 6-4. **WT:** 2000.
Drafted: Eastern Illinois, 2021 (1st round). **Signed by:** Steve Lemke.

TRACK RECORD: In 2021, Sweeney was the Yankees' first-rounder out of Eastern Illinois, the same school that has produced big leaguers Tim Bogar, Kevin Seitzer, Randy Myers and Nick Maton. Sweeney spent his entire first season at Low-A Tampa, then moved to High-A Hudson Valley for most of the 2022 season. He reached Double-A for Somerset's run to the Eastern League championship.

SCOUTING REPORT: Sweeney doesn't wow with any one tool, but he's decent enough across the board to carve out a big league career. He improved his command of the strike zone in the second half of the season and has begun hitting balls higher and with more authority. He posted solid exit velocity data as well, with an average of 86.2 mph and a whiff rate of just 24%. Scouts see a player who will eventually be power over hit because of excellent bat speed, solid hand speed and contact skills but with a lofted path geared toward trying to take balls out of the yard. Though the swing itself is fine, some evaluators worry about Sweeney's overall adjustability because of stiff hands and actions. Defensively, he's should move around among shortstop, second and third and handle just about any routine play, though he is unlikely to stand out at any spot. He's a fringe-average runner.

THE FUTURE: After finishing the year in Double-A, Sweeney will return to the level in 2023. He's got a ceiling as an offensive-minded utilityman who sees a lot of playing time.

| BA GRADE: 45/High | | Hit: 45 | | Power: 50 | | Speed: 45 | | Fielding: 45 | | Arm: 50 | |

Year	Age	Club (League)	Lvl	AVG	G	AB	R	H	2B	3B	HR	RBI	BB	SO	SB	OBP	SLG
2022	22	Hudson Valley (SAL)	HiA	.241	100	390	70	94	18	4	14	51	59	108	29	.350	.415
2022	22	Somerset (EL)	AA	.233	11	43	6	10	1	0	2	5	7	10	2	.340	.395
Minor League Totals				.245	143	548	106	134	23	8	23	70	88	149	35	.357	.442

15 ELIJAH DUNHAM, OF

Born: May 29, 1998. **B-T:** L-L. **HT:** 6-0. **WT:** 213.
Signed: Indiana, 2020 (NDFA). **Signed by:** Mike Gibbons/Mitch Colahan.
TRACK RECORD: If not for the pandemic, Dunham might have gotten drafted in the first 10 rounds. Instead, the draft was shortened to five rounds and Dunham signed with the Yankees as a free agent after a standout career at Indiana. He split his first pro season between both Class A levels before spending all of 2022 helping Double-A Somerset to the Eastern League championship. After the season, Dunham played winter ball in the Venezuelan Winter League.

SCOUTING REPORT: Dunham was lauded for his combination of power and speed. That blend showed up in 2022, when he was one of just four Yankees minor leaguers to hit at least 15 home runs and steal 35+ bases. Internal evaluators were pleased by improvements in Dunham's swing decisions and launch angle. He doesn't chase particularly often but his rate of in-zone swing and miss is a bit high at 20%. Because he is limited to a corner-outfield spot—he split 2022 between both right and left field—Dunham's power needs to at least maintain its current level or take a step forward in order to profile at either spot. To that end, evaluators noticed that Dunham appeared stronger than a season ago, and he moved to a toe tap instead of a leg lift. He's an average defender with an average arm that would fit in either corner. He's a below-average runner who gets stolen bases because of his instincts.

THE FUTURE: Dunham will move to Triple-A in 2023 and has a future as a role player on a championship club or a regular on a second-division team.

| BA GRADE: 45/High | | Hit: 40 | | Power: 50 | | Speed: 40 | | Fielding: 50 | | Arm: 50 | |

Year	Age	Club (League)	Lvl	AVG	G	AB	R	H	2B	3B	HR	RBI	BB	SO	SB	OBP	SLG
2022	24	Somerset (EL)	AA	.248	110	415	67	103	26	3	17	63	59	103	37	.348	.448
Minor League Totals				.255	203	754	139	192	51	5	30	120	106	188	65	.355	.455

16 ENGELTH UREÑA, C

Born: Aug. 17, 2004. **B-T:** R-R. **HT:** 6-0. **WT:** 196.
Signed: Dominican Republic, 2022 **Signed by:** Jose Ravelo/Edgar Mateo.
TRACK RECORD: When the 2022 international signing period opened, most of the ink around the Yankees' class went to shortstop Roderick Arias, but the club is also excited by Ureña, their second-highest signing of the class at $275,000. A broken hand limited Ureña's season to just 11 games, but he still homered three times in 31 at-bats.

SCOUTING REPORT: Ureña showed his combination of power and strength immediately upon commencing his pro career by homering to the opposite field in his first official at-bat. The feat became more impressive after the game, when x-rays revealed he'd broken his hand on a foul ball behind the plate in the top of the first inning. The injury cost Ureña two months, but he returned in time for 10 more games and two more home runs. The Yankees value Ureña as one of the best potential hitters in their lower minors and believe he has a chance to hit for a combination of average and power. Ureña is new to catching, having converted from the outfield roughly two years before signing. He's an excellent athlete with an above-average arm but understandably has some catching up to do when it comes to receiving, blocking and the finer points of the positon.

THE FUTURE: Ureña's next step will likely be stateside in the Florida Complex League, where he'll work to achieve his ceiling as an offensive-minded everyday catcher.

BA GRADE: 50/Extreme		Hit: 55		Power: 55		Speed: 40		Fielding: 40		Arm: 55				

Year	Age	Club (League)	Lvl	AVG	G	AB	R	H	2B	3B	HR	RBI	BB	SO	SB	OBP	SLG
2022	17	Yankees Bombers (DSL)	R	.226	11	31	8	7	2	0	3	12	5	6	0	.351	.581
Minor League Totals				.226	11	31	8	7	2	0	3	12	5	6	0	.351	.581

17 TYLER HARDMAN, 3B

Born: Jan. 27, 1999. **B-T:** R-R. **HT:** 6-3. **WT:** 204.
Drafted: Oklahoma, 2021 (4th round). **Signed by:** Matt Ranson.

TRACK RECORD: Hardman proved himself for four years at Oklahoma, where he hit 24 home runs over four years, including a dozen in his senior year. He bolstered his reputation as a power broker with eight more homers in the Cape Cod League with Brewster—where he was teammates with fellow Yankees prospect Carson Coleman. He's spent most of his first two pro seasons at Class A levels but reached Double-A Somerset late in 2022, in time for the team's run to the Eastern League championship.

SCOUTING REPORT: Hardman's game is built around his power potential. He swatted a system-best 22 home runs in 2022 and is one of the best ball-strikers in the organization, with an average exit velocity of 91.4 mph and raw power that is nearly double-plus. His power would be amplified further by cutting down on his swing and miss rate, which showed up in a 30.6% strikeout rate. His 27% miss rate on pitches in the zone is also worrisome, and scouts have noticed he's particularly vulnerable to sliders. Hardman was a first baseman in college but the Yankees drafted him as a third baseman, and he's proved to be an average defender with an average arm.

THE FUTURE: After a successful stint in the Arizona Fall League, Hardman will return to Double-A to begin 2023. If he fixes his swing-and-miss issues, he'll have a chance at being a second-division regular at third base.

BA GRADE: 45/High		Hit: 40		Power: 55		Speed: 40		Fielding: 50		Arm: 50				

Year	Age	Club (League)	Lvl	AVG	G	AB	R	H	2B	3B	HR	RBI	BB	SO	SB	OBP	SLG
2022	23	Hudson Valley (SAL)	HiA	.262	107	397	53	104	16	2	22	79	40	136	14	.329	.479
2022	23	Somerset (EL)	AA	.067	4	15	0	1	0	0	0	2	0	6	0	.063	.067
Minor League Totals				.252	144	519	73	131	23	2	26	100	50	187	18	.318	.455

18 RICHARD FITTS, RHP

Born: Dec. 17, 1999. **B-T:** R-R. **HT:** 6-3. **WT:** 215.
Drafted: Auburn, 2021 (6th round). **Signed by:** Chuck Bartlett/Mike Wagner

TRACK RECORD: In the early portion of his draft year, Fitts looked spectacular. His fastball had jumped from the low 90s to the mid 90s and was peaking at 97. His slider was razor sharp, too, giving him the look of a future first-rounder. He dealt with a foot injury later in the year and his stuff took a bit of a tumble. The Yankees were encouraged by Fitts' highs to draft him in the sixth round. After resting post draft, he split his first pro year between both Class A levels.

SCOUTING REPORT: Fitts' first foray into pro ball was a bit of a Jekyll and Hyde act. He struggled at Low-A, where a pitcher with a Southeastern Conference pedigree should thrive. He let up a 5.01 ERA and 13 home runs in 79 innings. The script flipped after a promotion to High-A Hudson Valley, where he went 4-0, 0.55 with 38 strikeouts against just three walks. The improvement was due in large part to a delivery alteration that allowed him to keep his front side firm so he could better drive the ball down in the zone. The change also helped his velocity increase and made his slider sharper. His four-seamer sat around 93 mph, touched 96 and posted an average spin rate of 2,439 rpm. Fitts backed the four-seamer with his typical nasty slider, which sat in the low 80s and peaked at 88 while flashing plus potential. He rounds out his arsenal with a high-80s changeup that could get to average with increased usage.

THE FUTURE: Fitts could advance to Double-A in 2023, when he'll have to prove that the gains he made in Hudson Valley were sticky. If so, he could fit in the back of a rotation. If not, his fastball and slider would help in relief.

BA GRADE: 45/High		Fastball: 55		Slider: 60		Changeup: 45		Control: 45				

Year	Age	Club (League)	Lvl	W	L	ERA	G	GS	IP	H	HR	BB	SO	BB/9	SO/9	WHIP	AVG
2022	22	Tampa (FSL)	LoA	3	8	5.01	17	17	79	73	13	17	93	1.9	10.6	1.14	.239
2022	22	Hudson Valley (SAL)	HiA	4	0	0.55	5	5	33	17	1	3	38	0.8	10.4	0.61	.152
Minor League Totals				7	8	3.70	22	22	112	90	14	20	131	1.6	10.5	0.98	.216

19 ANTHONY HALL, OF

Born: Feb. 9, 2001. **B-T:** L-L. **HT:** 6-2. **WT:** 200.
Drafted: Oregon, 2022 (4th round). **Signed by:** Mike Thurman.

TRACK RECORD: Hall was drafted by the Braves in the 35th round of the 2019 draft but chose to honor his commitment to Oregon. In three years with the Ducks, he showed a combination of power and contact—his strikeout rate was just 19%—as well as the athleticism to hold down center field while moving around to either corner spot and first base. Hall was set to transfer from Oregon after his junior season, but the Yankees called his name in the fourth round and signed him for $456,500. He doubled in his first and only professional at-bat before a wrist injury ended his season. He returned for the Yankees' fall mini camp.

SCOUTING REPORT: After two uneven seasons with Oregon, Hall's approach was noticeably better in a stint on the Cape Cod League, and then again for his junior season with the Ducks. The changes translated into 1.042 OPS and 17 home runs in 60 games to go with a strikeout rate of just 16.6%. He does plenty of damage against fastballs, even at higher velocities, but needs to be better against breaking stuff. Hall is athletic enough to hold down center field, but his combination of average speed and an average arm would likely be better served in right field, where his power potential would allow him to profile nicely.

THE FUTURE: Hall's pro debut was cut short, but he's got the pedigree to easily fit at High-A in 2023. He has the look of a solid but not spectacular everyday player.

BA GRADE: 45/High	Hit: 45	Power: 50	Speed: 50	Fielding: 50	Arm: 50

Year	Age	Club (League)	Lvl	AVG	G	AB	R	H	2B	3B	HR	RBI	BB	SO	SB	OBP	SLG
2022	21	Yankees (FCL)	R	.000	1	1	0	0	0	0	0	0	0	0	0	.000	.000
Minor League Totals				.000	1	1	0	0	0	0	0	0	0	0	0	.000	.000

20 TRYSTAN VRIELING, RHP

Born: Oct. 2, 2000. **B-T:** R-R. **HT:** 6-4. **WT:** 200.
Drafted: Gonzaga, 2022 (3rd round). **Signed by:** Mike Thurman.

TRACK RECORD: Gonzaga was a wellspring of draft talent in the summer of 2022. The Bulldogs had three players taken in the first 100 picks, including righthander Gabriel Hughes in the first round, outfielder Nick Morabito in the second supplemental round and Vrieling in the third round. Vrieling moved to the rotation full-time in 2022 and started strong before sputtering a bit in the second half. Yankees pitching guru Scott Lovekamp in particular was intrigued about what Vrieling could do under the guidance of the team's player development group, which believed the righthander's fastball was underutilized in college.

SCOUTING REPORT: Vrieling works with a full, four-pitch complement headed by a fastball and curveball that could each be above-average. The former sat in the low 90s and touched 96, while the latter averaged around 80 mph. He backs that combo up with two potentially averages—a slider in the mid 80s and a changeup that comes in a few ticks hotter, around 87 mph. His control was a little scattershot in college and projects to be fringe-average as a pro. The Yankees believe some of Vrieling's season-ending downturn was due to fatigue, so they shut him down for the rest of the season after signing and had him do foundational work before an offseason of remote training.

THE FUTURE: The Yankees have done an excellent job in recent years of getting the most out of their pitching prospects, and they hope Vrieling can extract a bit more ceiling under their tutelage.

BA Grade: 45/High	Fastball: 55	Curveball: 55	Slider: 50	Changeup: 50	Control: 45

Year	Age	Club (League)	Lvl	W	L	ERA	G	GS	IP	H	HR	BB	SO	BB/9	SO/9	WHIP	AVG
2022	21	Did not play															

21 CLAYTON BEETER, RHP

Born: Oct. 9, 1998. **B-T:** R-R. **HT:** 6-2. **WT:** 220.
Drafted: Texas Tech, 2020 (2nd round supplemental). **Signed by:** Clint Bowers (Dodgers).

TRACK RECORD: After having Tommy John surgery in high school, Beeter honored his commitment to Texas Tech and spent his first season as the Red Raiders' closer. He moved into a starting role in 2020 before the season was cancelled by the pandemic. The Dodgers selected him in the supplemental second round and signed him for $1,196,500. He spent his first pro season between High-A and Double-A. He returned to Double-A in 2022 before being traded to the Yankees for outfielder Joey Gallo.

SCOUTING REPORT: Beeter's pitch mix centers around the kind of fastball-slider combination the Yankees covet. His fastball, which sat in the mid 90s and touched 98 mph, features excellent riding life and above-average spin rates. His mid-80s slider got a whiff rate of around 56% and played well to both righties and lefties. He also has a changeup, but it is sparingly used and typically sits in the same velocity range as his slider and serves as another weapon for lefties. Scouts also note his delivery creates some deception while also sapping a bit of command and control, which is below-average.

THE FUTURE: Though he's been a starter as a pro, he's likely to land in a reliever's role unless his changeup takes significant steps forward. He'll head to Triple-A in 2023.

BA GRADE: 45/High	Fastball: 60	Slider: 60	Changeup: 40	Control: 40										
Year	Age	Club (League)	Lvl	W	L	ERA	G	GS	IP	H	HR	BB	SO	BB/9	SO/9	WHIP	AVG
2022	23	Tulsa (TL)	AA	0	3	5.75	18	16	52	48	10	35	88	6.1	15.3	1.61	.235
2022	23	Somerset (EL)	AA	0	0	2.13	7	7	25	16	1	11	41	3.9	14.6	1.07	.176
Minor League Totals				0	9	4.11	53	50	129	102	16	68	207	4.7	14.4	1.31	.212

22 OMAR GONZALEZ, RHP

Born: July 25, 2005. **B-T:** R-R. **HT:** 6-4. **WT:** 175.
Signed: Panama, 2022. **Signed by:** Carlos Levy.

TRACK RECORD: Gonzalez was signed out of Panama on Jan. 15, 2022 after an excellent amateur career in Panama, and scout Carlos Levy tracked him throughout the process before the Yankees inked him for $135,000. He was 16 years old for each of his six appearances in the DSL, and he still dominated with 36 strikeouts against just nine walks in 20.1 innings. He was shut down with a bit of a dead arm in July.

SCOUTING REPORT: Gonzalez has an excellent mix of size, projection and present stuff. His fastball sits in the low 90s and touched 93 with high spin rates and excellent spin efficiency. When he signed, Gonzalez featured a curveball but was in the process of switching to the Yankees' preferred, sweepier slider shape in the DSL. To do so, he dropped his arm slot a touch. He rounds out his mix with a high-70s changeup that internal evaluators believe could be above-average. He should have at least fringe-average control, but that forecast could improve with further strength gains and more time with his newer arm slots.

THE FUTURE: After a short but sweet turn in the DSL, Gonzalez will likely move stateside in 2023 and pitch in the Florida Complex League. He has one of the higher upsides among the Yankees' lower level arms and could fit in the middle of a rotation if everything clicks.

BA GRADE: 50/Extreme	Fastball: 60	Slider: 55	Changeup: 50	Control: 45										
Year	Age	Club (League)	Lvl	W	L	ERA	G	GS	IP	H	HR	BB	SO	BB/9	SO/9	WHIP	AVG
2022	16	Yankees Bombers (DSL)	R	1	0	0.44	6	5	20	6	0	9	36	4.0	15.9	0.74	.091
Minor League Totals				1	0	0.44	6	5	20	6	0	9	36	4.0	15.9	0.74	.091

23 ANGEL BENITEZ, RHP

Born: Sept. 10, 2003. **B-T:** R-R. **HT:** 6-7. **WT:** 204.
Signed: Dominican Republic, 2021. **Signed by:** Esdras Abreu/Edgar Mateo.

TRACK RECORD: Benitez was signed on the strength of a tall, projectable frame that the Yankees believed had plenty of room for more strength and velocity. Those gains began happening as he got older, and New York signed him on July 16, 2021 for $120,000. He made his pro debut in 2022 in the Dominican Summer League but had Tommy John surgery after the season and will miss all of 2023.

SCOUTING REPORT: At his best, Benitez shows a tantalizing mix of size and stuff. His fastball sat around 94 mph and bumped 97 with excellent cut and ride through the zone. He backed the fastball with a potentially plus changeup that averaged around 89 mph and a sweeper slider in the mid 80s that flashed above-average. Benitez's pitch package was accentuated by a lower slot that created tricky angles and big-time extension from his long levers. He'd whiffed 24 in 17 innings before his elbow flared up in early July.

THE FUTURE: In the winter of 2021, Yankees officials pointed out Benitez as a pitcher to watch. He showed hints of his upside in 2022 but will have to wait a year before getting back on the mound. If it all clicks, he might be worth the wait.

BA GRADE: 50/Extrême	Fastball: 60	Slider: 55	Changeup: 60	Control: 50										
Year	Age	Club (League)	Lvl	W	L	ERA	G	GS	IP	H	HR	BB	SO	BB/9	SO/9	WHIP	AVG
2022	18	Yankees Bombers (DSL)	R	0	0	1.06	5	5	17	9	0	7	24	3.7	12.7	0.94	.150
Minor League Totals				0	0	1.06	5	5	17	9	0	7	24	3.7	12.7	0.94	.150

24 GREG WEISSERT, RHP

Born: Feb. 4, 1995. **B-T:** R-R. **HT:** 6-2. **WT:** 215.
Drafted: Fordham, 2016 (18th round). **Signed by:** Scott Lovekamp/Cesar Presbott.
TRACK RECORD: After being drafted out of Fordham in 2016, Weissert moved deliberately through the system and didn't reach the upper levels until his fourth season as a pro. He took a leap forward in 2021 and built on it in 2022, when he won the Triple-A International League's pitcher of the year and made his MLB debut. He made the American League Championship Series roster but did not get into a game.
SCOUTING REPORT: Weissert's game is built predominantly around two pitches: a mid-90s sinker and a filthy sweeper slider in the low 80s that rates as the best in the system. The pitch mix fits the horizontal style of attack the Yankees prefer from their pitchers. He'll also mix in a four-seamer in the same velo band as his two-seamer, as well as a low-90s cutter and mid-80s changeup, but the two-seamer and slider accounted for nearly three quarters of his pitches in the minor leagues. Both pitches could get to plus with upgraded control and command, which was needed after five walks in 11 big league innings.
THE FUTURE: Weissert will get a long look at the big league bullpen come spring training. If he can throw more strikes, he can be a middle-innings reliever who sinks and slides his way into outs.

BA GRADE: 40/Low	Fastball: 60	Slider: 60	Cutter: 40	Changeup: 30	Control: 40

Year	Age	Club (League)	Lvl	W	L	ERA	G	GS	IP	H	HR	BB	SO	BB/9	SO/9	WHIP	AVG
2022	27	Scranton/WB (IL)	AAA	2	1	1.69	42	0	48	24	3	19	70	3.6	13.1	0.90	.149
2022	27	New York (AL)	MLB	3	0	5.56	12	0	11	6	1	5	11	4.0	8.7	0.97	.146
Major League Totals				3	0	5.56	12	0	11	6	1	5	11	4.0	8.7	0.97	.146
Minor League Totals				15	15	2.90	193	0	270	186	14	129	352	4.3	11.7	1.17	.192

25 ANTONIO GOMEZ, C

Born: Nov. 13, 2001. **B-T:** R-R. **HT:** 6-2. **WT:** 212.
Signed: Venezuela, 2018. **Signed by:** Edgar Mateo/Raul Gonzalez
TRACK RECORD: Gomez was signed in 2018, when he ranked as one of the top players in the class and yet other talented catcher who hailed from Venezuela. He ranked among the top players in the Florida Complex League in both 2019 and 2021. He spent most of the 2022 season with Low-A Tampa, where he showed flashes of his upside on both offense and defense.
SCOUTING REPORT: Gomez's two calling cards revolve around his power, both in his bat and his throwing arm. Despite a middling line, scouts who saw Gomez this year in the Florida State League graded him as with potentially double-plus grades for his raw power and his throwing arm. The former translated into an excellent average exit velocity of 87 mph while the former led to a caught-stealing rate just north of 30% and pop times regularly below 1.9 seconds. He has plenty to improve with his overall hittability, and his in-zone miss rate of 27% is particularly concerning. Gomez is extremely athletic and shows good footwork behind the plate, but the quality of his framing and blocking varies between average and well below-average. He's a 30-grade runner on the 20-80 scouting scale.
THE FUTURE: Gomez will move to High-A in 2023, when he'll try to continue to polish his rough edges and reach his ceiling of a well-rounded backup.

BA GRADE: 45/High	Hit: 40	Power: 50	Speed: 30	Fielding: 45	Arm: 70

Year	Age	Club (Leagu	Lvl	AVG	G	AB	R	H	2B	3B	HR	RBI	BB	SO	SB	OBP	SLG
2022	20	Tampa (FSL)	LoA	.252	89	325	36	82	10	2	8	48	35	100	1	.332	.369
Minor League Totals				.259	150	533	75	138	25	3	13	79	65	158	6	.347	.390

26 YOENDRYS GOMEZ, RHP

Born: Oct. 15, 1999. **B-T:** R-R. **HT:** 6-3. **WT:** 175.
Signed: Venezuela, 2016. **Signed by:** Alan Atacho
TRACK RECORD: Gomez signed in 2016 and looked every bit of a projectable, high-upside pitcher. Things got off track in 2021, when a combination of Covid and Tommy John surgery limited him to just 23.2 innings. He re-emerged in June 2022 and, after a couple of tuneups in the Florida Complex League, split his year between High-A and Double-A.
SCOUTING REPORT: In 2022, Gomez looked a bit different than pre-surgery. His fastball backed up and now sits in the low 90s, and his slider wasn't as tight as its previous iteration. The Yankees believe Gomez's backsliding is rust-based and note that his delivery got longer and out of sync. As a result, he has been getting around his pitches instead of driving through them in his delivery. Once he tightens his mechanics, the velocity and life should bump a tick or two. In service of that goal, Gomez was invited to New York's

instructional league camp after the season. Gomez's changeup, which sat around 89 mph, could stand to gain a bit of separation from his fastball. He has average control of his mix, and his strike percentage got better upon a move from Hudson Valley to Somerset.

THE FUTURE: Gomez, who has a place on the 40-man roster, is likely to return to Double-A in 2023. If he can knock off some of the rust, he has a ceiling as a No. 5 starter or a bulk reliever.

BA GRADE: 45/High		Fastball: 50		Slider: 55			Changeup: 40		Control: 50				
Year	Age	Club (League)	Lvl	W	L	ERA	G	GS	IP	H	HR	BB	SO

Year	Age	Club (League)	Lvl	W	L	ERA	G	GS	IP	H	HR	BB	SO	BB/9	SO/9	WHIP	AVG
2022	22	Yankees (FCL)	R	0	0	0.00	1	1	3	3	0	0	3	0.0	10.1	1.13	.300
2022	22	Hudson Valley (SAL)	HiA	0	0	1.93	10	10	28	20	0	12	27	3.9	8.7	1.14	.204
2022	22	Somerset (EL)	AA	1	0	3.86	4	4	16	14	1	6	19	3.3	10.5	1.22	.230
Minor League Totals				9	9	3.39	59	56	210	175	10	86	214	3.7	9.2	1.24	.228

27 CARSON COLEMAN, RHP

Born: April 7, 1998. **B-T:** R-R. **HT:** 6-2. **WT:** 190.
Drafted: Kentucky, 2019 (33rd round). **Signed by:** Mike Gibbons.

TRACK RECORD: Coleman was a late-round flier who pitched three years at Kentucky in a strictly relief role. He also pitched three seasons of summer ball, once in the Ripken League and twice for Brewster in the Cape Cod League, where he was teammates with fellow Yankees prospect Tyler Hardman for a season. Amateur scouting analyst Scott Benecke in particular was intrigued by Coleman's fastball. That analysis has proved prescient as Coleman has dominated his way up the ladder. In his last outing of the season, Coleman spun a scoreless ninth inning to finish a championship-sealing no-hitter for Double-A Somerset.

SCOUTING REPORT: As was the case in college, Coleman is a relief-only prospect. His fastball is the key to his arsenal. The pitch sat in the mid 90s and touched 97 with tremendous movement and spin rates that allowed it to get whiffs at a 35% clip and strikes at a rate of nearly 70%. Coleman backed the fastball with a shorter slider in the low 80s that could get to average with further improvement. He has a changeup in the high 80s as well, but it was a clear third pitch in the arsenal and was thrown very rarely. He throws strikes at a high rate as well, and did even better in that regard when he moved from High-A to Double-A.

THE FUTURE: Coleman should move to Triple-A in 2023 and has a chance to make his big league debut at some point in the year. He's got a future as a middle-innings reliever.

BA GRADE: 40/High		Fastball: 60		Slider: 50			Changeup: 30		Control: 60				

Year	Age	Club (League)	Lvl	W	L	ERA	G	GS	IP	H	HR	BB	SO	BB/9	SO/9	WHIP	AVG
2022	24	Hudson Valley (SAL)	HiA	0	0	0.47	9	0	19	7	1	9	26	4.2	12.1	0.83	.115
2022	24	Somerset (EL)	AA	2	3	2.86	35	0	44	30	2	10	69	2.0	14.1	0.91	.191
Minor League Totals				4	6	3.56	75	0	99	72	5	45	144	4.1	13.1	1.19	.203

28 JHONY BRITO, RHP

Born: Feb. 17, 1998. **B-T:** R-R. **HT:** 6-2. **WT:** 160.
Signed: Dominican Republic, 2015. **Signed by:** Raymi Dicent/Victor Mata.

TRACK RECORD: Brito was signed out of the Dominican Republic in 2015 but didn't reach the upper levels of the minor leagues until 2021, when he finished the year with eight starts at Double-A Somerset. He split his 2022 season between Double-A and Triple-A sandwiched around a bout of dead arm that landed him on the injured list for about a month.

SCOUTING REPORT: Brito is considered the organization's most adept strike-thrower, and his pitch package has gotten deeper and better in recent years as well. He throws his changeup most often of his five pitches. It sits around 87 mph, peaks in the low 90s and scouts see it as a potential plus. The changeup serves as an effective complement to his array of mid-90s two- and four-seam fastballs and his low-90s cutter, which was introduced as another option for lefthanders. Brito's biggest wart is his need for a consistent breaking ball. The version this year was a gyro slider added during the season that sits around 80-82 mph and fits better with a delivery that was tweaked to help him drive through the ball more often.

THE FUTURE: Brito was added to the Yankees' 40-man roster after the season and fits best as bulk reliever. He should make his big league debut at some point in 2023.

BA GRADE: 40/High		Fastball: 50		Cutter: 45		Slider: 40		Changeup: 60		Control: 60			

Year	Age	Club (League)	Lvl	W	L	ERA	G	GS	IP	H	HR	BB	SO	BB/9	SO/9	WHIP	AVG
2022	24	Somerset (EL)	AA	5	2	2.36	8	8	42	36	4	11	38	2.4	8.1	1.12	.232
2022	24	Scranton/WB (IL)	AAA	6	2	3.31	18	15	71	59	5	24	53	3.1	6.8	1.17	.229
Minor League Totals				26	21	3.71	86	70	393	375	28	81	344	1.9	7.9	1.16	.250

29 JARED SERNA, 2B

Born: June 1, 2002. **B-T:** R-R. **HT:** 5-8. **WT:** 168.
Signed: Mexico, 2019. **Signed by:** Lee Sigman.

TRACK RECORD: Serna was signed out of Mexico in 2019, but had to wait to make his official Yankees debut because of the pandemic. He accumulated more walks (34) than strikeouts (27) in the DSL in 2021, then opened eyes in the Florida Complex League by repeating the feat, with 25 walks against 24 strikeouts in 160 plate appearances. He struggled mightily in a brief bump to Low-A. He is the cousin of fellow Yankees prospect Luis Serna.

SCOUTING REPORT: Virtually all of Serna's value is tied to his bat and strong knowledge of the strike zone. He makes excellent impact for contact for someone his age, having produced average and maximum exit velocities of 88 and 106 mph, respectively, in 2022. He also showed strong swing decisions, with rate of just 23% and 17% for chase and in-zone swings and misses. Scouts see a player with solid barrel accuracy but will need to keep honing his skills when he faces better pitching full-time in 2023. He's a below-average runner who plays a solid but not spectacular second base with arm strength befitting the position.

THE FUTURE: Serna will head back to Low-A full time in 2023, when he'll try to show the same combination of barrel accuracy and strike zone discipline he utilized in the lower levels.

BA GRADE: 40/High		Hit: 50			Power: 45		Speed: 40			Fielding: 45		Arm: 40	
Year	Age	Club (League)	Lvl	AVG	G	AB	R	H	2B	3B	HR	RBI	BB	SO	SB	OBP	SLG
2022	20	Yankees (FCL)	R	.302	37	129	40	39	9	1	6	28	25	24	16	.438	.527
2022	20	Tampa (FSL)	LoA	.179	12	39	6	7	2	0	0	2	3	15	1	.250	.231
Minor League Totals				.257	99	319	80	82	20	3	9	46	62	66	41	.401	.423

30 JUAN CARELA, RHP

Born: Dec. 15, 2001. **B-T:** R-R. **HT:** 6-3. **WT:** 186.
Signed: Dominican Republic, 2018. **Signed by:** Jose Sabino.

TRACK RECORD: Carela was part of the Yankees' 2018 international class, which also included Kevin Alcantara (since traded to the Cubs) and Antonio Gomez. Carela stood out as an amateur for his projectable frame and fastball when he signed for $335,000.. He's intrigued but not overwhelmed evaluators as he's worked his way through the low minors and has shown a trend of taking a little while to adjust to a new level.

SCOUTING REPORT: Carela's mix centers around a combination of two-seam fastballs, sliders and cutters, with hints of a four-seam and changeup scattered in as well. The two-seamer averaged around 91 mph and touched 94, while the slider sat in the low 80s and touched 86. The cutter, which was introduced toward the end of his time in Low-A, showed a wide velo band, ranging anywhere from 85-93 mph. External scouts see potential that might take a while to extract as he figures out how to better harness his command and control, which internal evaluators feel might have been affected by learning the two-seamer as well as a tendency to rush through his delivery when he got out of whack. Scouts also saw a frame with projection as well as a clean delivery. Just as it did in 2021 when he moved from Rookie-ball to Low-A, Carela's control took a dip upon his move to High-A, and he produced a strike rate of just 60%.

THE FUTURE: Carela has some upside remaining, but there's work to be done to make it a reality. He has a future as a middle reliever who lives off his sinker and slider with a chance for a little more if he can show gains in his control and command.

BA GRADE: 40/High		Fastball: 50		Cutter: 40		Slider: 55		Changeup: 30		Control: 40		
Year	Age	Club (League)	Lvl	W	L	ERA	G	GS	IP	H	HR	BB	SO	BB/9	SO/9	WHIP	AVG
2022	20	Tampa (FSL)	LoA	7	2	2.96	16	14	79	49	5	35	110	4.0	12.5	1.06	.175
2022	20	Hudson Valley (SAL)	HiA	1	4	7.71	7	7	28	25	4	17	21	5.5	6.8	1.50	.238
Minor League Totals				10	16	5.31	47	40	181	155	13	104	210	5.2	10.4	1.43	.231

Oakland Athletics

BY MARK CHIARELLI

By the end of the 2021 season, it was clear Oakland's window of contention had slammed shut as the Athletics fell out of playoff contention.

Shortly after the 2022 lockout was lifted, the A's wasted little time accelerating the clock on a rebuild and shedding payroll.

Within three weeks, Oakland had traded first baseman Matt Olson, third baseman Matt Chapman, righthander Chris Bassitt and lefthander Sean Manaea, dismantling the core of a team that annually pushed for contention at the back half of the previous decade. The A's weren't done. They shipped righty Frankie Montas to the Yankees in exchange for four more players at the 2022 trade deadline.

The A's acquired 16 players in total from the five trades, a much-needed boost to a system that ranked 27th in baseball entering 2022.

Unsurprisingly, the A's were not competitive and finished 60-102 and 46 games out of first place in the American League West. Oakland's .370 winning percentage was the club's worst since 1979.

Ongoing speculation of potential relocation provided the backdrop to Oakland's disastrous season, with MLB commissioner Rob Manfred saying on Sirius XM radio in late October that a new ballpark in Oakland "just doesn't look like it's going to happen."

The A's are now tasked with developing the next core that will carry them back toward contention, whether in Oakland or not.

They'll do so without two key faces who helped oversee the prior rebuild. Oakland allowed manager Bob Melvin to leave prior to the season to pursue a multi-year contract with the Padres. Billy Beane, who first became Oakland's general manager in 1997, stepped away from his role as executive vice president of baseball operations after the season. He transitioned to a senior advisor role to A's owner Josh Fisher and ceded day-to-day operations to longtime A's GM David Forst.

Oakland's player development department otherwise remains largely intact and has been together for the better part of the last decade.

The A's made a conscious effort during their fire sale to inject their system with pitching. That included lefthander Ken Waldichuk, who made his MLB debut with Oakland, a pair of first-rounders in righthanders Gunnar Hoglund and Ryan Cusick, as well as righty J.T. Ginn, who was once selected 30th overall by the Dodgers in 2018. The latter three all dealt with injuries in 2022.

The Olson deal with the Braves also netted center fielder Cristian Pache, who once ranked as

Catcher Shea Langeliers is going to need to be a fixture in a lengthy Athletics rebuilding effort.

PROJECTED 2026 LINEUP

Catcher	Shea Langeliers	28
First Base	Tyler Soderstrom	24
Second Base	Zack Gelof	26
Third Base	Max Muncy	23
Shortstop	Nick Allen	27
Left Field	Lawrence Butler	25
Center Field	Cristian Pache	27
Right Field	Denzel Clarke	25
Designated Hitter	Daniel Susac	25
No. 1 Starter	Cole Irvin	32
No. 2 Starter	Mason Miller	27
No. 3 Starter	Ken Waldichuk	27
No. 4 Starter	Gunnar Hoglund	26
No. 5 Starter	J.T. Ginn	26
Closer	Luis Medina	26

baseball's No. 7 prospect before his bat stalled over the last two seasons, and catcher Shea Langeliers, who was a Top 100 Prospect prior to his graduation in late September.

It's unclear whether the bevy of trades netted an abundance of impact talent. Only catcher Tyler Soderstrom, Oakland's 2020 first-round pick, ranked among baseball's Top 100 Prospects at the end of the 2022 season, and its top three prospects entering 2023 are all homegrown.

Still, Oakland is early in the process of an arduous rebuild. The A's will have their chances to stockpile more talent, notably by trading prized catcher Sean Murphy and via the No. 6 overall pick in the 2023 draft. ∎

MITCHELL LAYTON/GETTY IMAGES

DEPTH CHART

OAKLAND ATHLETICS

TOP 2023 MLB CONTRIBUTORS	RANK
Zack Gelof, 2B	2
Ken Waldichuk, LHP	4
Jordan Diaz, 2B/1B	9
BREAKOUT PROSPECTS	**RANK**
Hogan Harris, LHP	14
Clark Elliott, OF	19
Jefferson Jean, RHP	24

SOURCE OF TOP 30 TALENT

Homegrown	20	Acquired	10
College	10	Trade	9
Junior college	0	Rule 5 draft	1
High school	4	Independent league	0
Nondrafted free agent	1	Free agent/waivers	0
International	5		

LF
Lawrence Butler (7)
Luis Barrera
Cody Thomas

CF
Denzel Clarke (8)
Henry Bolte (11)
Brayan Buelvas (23)
Pedro Pineda (26)
Carlos Pacheco
Cal Stevenson

RF
Clark Elliott (18)
Junior Perez (28)

3B
Brett Harris (15)
T.J. Schofield-Sam

SS
Max Muncy (5)
Logan Davidson (27)
Drew Swift

2B
Zack Gelof (2)
Jordan Diaz (9)
Euribiel Angeles (19)
Cooper Bowman (30)

1B
Tyler Soderstrom (1)
Ryan Noda (20)

C
Daniel Susac (6)
Kyle McCann

LHP

LHSP
Ken Waldichuk (4)
Hogan Harris (14)
Eduardo Rivera

LHRP
Brady Basso

RHP

RHSP
Mason Miller (3)
Gunnar Hoglund (12)
J.T. Ginn (13)
Joey Estes (16)
Ryan Cusick (17)
Jefferson Jean (24)
Kyle Virbitsky (29)
Blake Beers

RHRP
Luis Medina (10)
Garrett Acton (21)
Colin Peluse (22)
Jorge Juan (25)
Jacob Watters
Dheygler Gimenez
Jack Weisenburger
Hunter Breault
Grant Judkins

1 TYLER SODERSTROM, C/1B

Born: Nov. 24, 2001. **B-T:** L-R. **HT:** 6-2. **WT:** 200.
Drafted: HS—Turlock, Calif., 2020 (1st round).
Signed by: Kevin Mello.

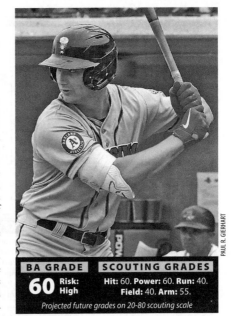

PAUL R. GIERHART

BA GRADE	SCOUTING GRADES
60 Risk: High	Hit: 60. Power: 60. Run: 40. Field: 40. Arm: 55.

Projected future grades on 20-80 scouting scale

TRACK RECORD: The Athletics' decision to go above-slot in the 2020 draft to lure Soderstrom away from a UCLA commitment with a $3.3 million signing bonus continues to look like a major coup. Oakland was plenty familiar with Soderstrom, a Northern California product who is the son of Giants 1993 first-rounder Steve Soderstrom. Oakland believed Tyler's bat rivaled some of the best prep hitters to come through its system over the last 30 years, including the likes of Eric Chavez and Ben Grieve. Those parallels seem apt. Soderstrom hit a system-best 29 homers across three levels and he finished with a .267/.324/.501 line. That slash line is even more impressive considering his dreadful April with High-A Lansing where he hit just .159 and struck out 33% of the time as he dealt with a hand injury. He eventually turned it around, earning a promotion to Double-A Midland in early August, then ending his season with nine games at Triple-A Las Vegas.

SCOUTING REPORT: Evaluators are hard-pressed to find holes in Soderstrom's beautiful lefthanded swing. It's geared for damage to all fields, and he accesses his plus raw power as frequently as any hitter in Oakland's system. He posted average exit velocities north of 91 mph in 2022, the second-best mark among all A's minor leaguers, and he has continued to add strength to his frame since turning pro. He also has above-average contact ability and an advanced feel for the barrel. Soderstrom is hard to beat within the strike zone and shows solid pitch-recognition skills. He needs to tighten his plate discipline after more advanced pitchers exploited his aggressive nature. Soderstrom's early-season struggles may have impacted his approach both at the plate and defensively, but the A's believe he displayed a marked improvement in maturity as the season progressed. Soderstrom's bat remains far ahead of his catching. He didn't have much exposure to high-level pitching as an amateur. Evaluators note that he's athletic enough to handle the position and has made strides, especially with his blocking and receiving, but fringe-average catching ability remains a best-case scenario. Soderstrom essentially split time between catcher and first base in 2022. The A's believe he became more comfortable at first base with the additional reps throughout the season. Evaluators have long wondered whether Soderstrom, who has above-

BEST TOOLS

BATTING
Best Hitter for Average	Jordan Diaz
Best Power Hitter	Tyler Soderstrom
Best Strike-Zone Discipline	Cal Stevenson
Fastest Baserunner	Denzel Clarke
Best Athlete	Denzel Clarke

PITCHING
Best Fastball	Mason Miller
Best Curveball	Sheygler Gimenez
Best Slider	Blake Beers
Best Changeup	Hogan Harris
Best Control	Kyle Virbitsky

FIELDING
Best Defensive Catcher	Shane McGuire
Best Defensive Infielder	Drew Swift
Best Infield Arm	Jeremy Eierman
Best Defensive Outfielder	Denzel Clarke
Best Outfield Arm	Henry Bolte

average arm strength, could handle third base, or perhaps even a corner outfield spot, but Oakland hasn't tried him at any of those spots as of yet.

THE FUTURE: Soderstrom possesses the ingredients teams seek in a potential middle-of-the-order hitter. A return to Triple-A Las Vegas appears in order, where the A's hope he'll show a more discerning approach. If he does, his bat could force his way to Oakland at some point in 2023, although his eventual defensive position remains less certain.

Year	Age	Club (League)	Lvl	AVG	G	AB	R	H	2B	3B	HR	RBI	BB	SO	SB	OBP	SLG
2022	20	Lansing (MWL)	HiA	.260	89	335	47	87	19	3	20	71	29	99	0	.323	.513
2022	20	Midland (TL)	AA	.278	36	133	17	37	1	2	8	28	10	33	0	.327	.496
2022	20	Las Vegas (PCL)	AAA	.297	9	37	2	11	1	0	1	6	1	13	0	.316	.405
Minor League Totals				.279	191	727	105	203	41	6	41	154	67	206	2	.344	.521

2 ZACK GELOF, 2B/3B

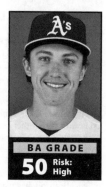

BA GRADE
50 Risk: High

Born: Oct. 19, 1999. **B-T:** R-R. **HT:** 6-3. **WT:** 205.
Drafted: Virginia, 2021 (2nd round). **Signed by:** Tripp Faulk.

TRACK RECORD: Gelof was a stalwart at Virginia and performed well at the 2021 College World Series. He carried that momentum into his professional career after the Athletics drafted him No. 60 overall and in the second round that summer. Gelof hit so well in his pro debut that Oakland felt comfortable sending him to Triple-A Las Vegas in late September for a brief stint. He performed again in 2022, hitting .270/.352/.463 with 18 homers between Double-A Midland and Las Vegas, though he missed roughly six weeks with a left shoulder injury sustained while diving for a ball.

SCOUTING REPORT: Gelof's simple, strength-based swing allows for an abundance of hard contact, and he averaged nearly 90 mph in average exit velocity for the second consecutive season. His power continues to play best to the pull side, though he's capable of shooting balls to right field as well. Gelof is physically strong and has raw power, but his swing is fairly flat and will likely lead to above-average power potential. He has a solid approach but will chase at times and fights a tendency to offer at the first pitch of at-bats. Gelof was a third baseman in college, but he battled arm issues and throwing inconsistency during his draft year. The A's transitioned him more to second base in 2022, where they believe his arm slot is better suited. They also aren't ruling out a potential role in the outfield. Gelof is one of the better runners underway in Oakland's system and he appeared in one game in center field with Midland.

THE FUTURE: Gelof needs to fine-tune his approach and aggressiveness, but he is nearly ready for the big leagues. He has a chance to develop into a solid-average regular for the rebuilding A's.

SCOUTING GRADES	Hitting: 50	Power: 55	Speed: 55	Fielding: 50	Arm: 50

Year	Age	Club (League)	Lvl	AVG	G	AB	R	H	2B	3B	HR	RBI	BB	SO	SB	OBP	SLG
2022	22	Midland (TL)	AA	.271	87	354	54	96	16	2	13	61	47	110	9	.356	.438
2022	22	Las Vegas (PCL)	AAA	.257	9	35	7	9	1	0	5	5	3	11	1	.316	.714
Minor League Totals				.287	132	527	91	151	26	3	25	96	70	159	23	.371	.490

3 MASON MILLER, RHP

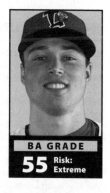

BA GRADE
55 Risk: Extreme

Born: Aug. 24, 1998. **B-T:** R-R. **HT:** 6-5. **WT:** 220.
Drafted: Gardner-Webb, 2021 (3rd round). **Signed by:** Neil Avent.

TRACK RECORD: Miller dealt with confounding weight loss early in his college career until a doctor diagnosed him with Type I diabetes at 20 years old. His strength returned following the discovery and his velocity has steadily risen since. Oakland drafted Miller in the third round in 2021. He missed nearly all of the 2022 season with a right shoulder strain, returning in late August to pitch 16 innings, including a brief stint with Triple-A Las Vegas. Miller then dazzled scouts in an extended look at the Arizona Fall League, where he touched 102 mph.

SCOUTING REPORT: Miller has two premium pitches—his fastball and slider—and another intriguing offering could be on the way in 2023. His four-seamer sits 97-99 mph with solid carry and a bit of arm-side run. He pairs it with a sweeping mid-80s slider that profiles as a plus swing-and-miss offering that he throws to both sides of the plate. Miller has also flashed a firm low-90s changeup, but it's more of a developmental pitch. Miller is expected to reintroduce his upper-90s cutter in 2023. He didn't throw the pitch in 2022 as the A's approached his return from injury cautiously, but it's been a weapon for him in the past. Miller has a starter's frame and his delivery is fairly simple despite a bit of effort, but he'll need to demonstrate he can withstand the rigors of regular rotation turns and maintain his fiery arsenal throughout a full season.

THE FUTURE: Some evaluators believe Miller's arsenal could play in an MLB bullpen now. But if the A's are patient, Miller has the ceiling of at least a No. 3 starter based on his pitch mix—if he stays healthy.

SCOUTING GRADES	Fastball: 70	Slider: 60	Changeup: 50	Control: 55

Year	Age	Club (League)	Lvl	W	L	ERA	G	GS	IP	H	HR	BB	SO	BB/9	SO/9	WHIP	AVG
2022	23	Athletics (ACL)	R	0	0	0.00	1	1	2	0	0	0	5	0.0	22.5	0.00	.000
2022	23	Lansing (MWL)	HiA	0	1	3.86	3	3	7	3	1	2	13	2.6	16.7	0.71	.125
2022	23	Las Vegas (PCL)	AAA	0	1	5.40	2	2	5	5	2	1	7	1.8	12.6	1.20	.294
Minor League Totals				0	3	3.15	9	8	20	12	3	6	34	2.7	15.3	0.90	.176

4 KEN WALDICHUK, LHP

Born: Jan. 8, 1998. **B-T:** L-L. **HT:** 6-4. **WT:** 220.
Drafted: Saint Mary's, 2019 (5th round). **Signed by:** Tyler Robertson (Yankees).

TRACK RECORD: The Yankees signed Waldichuk for $307,000 as a fifth-rounder in 2019. He added strength to his 6-foot-4 frame and worked with New York's pitching development program to enhance his slider during the shutdown in 2020. He returned a different pitcher, striking out 163 over 110 innings in 2021 while reaching Double-A. Oakland acquired Waldichuk along with three other players in a 2022 deadline deal for Frankie Montas.

SCOUTING REPORT: Waldichuk's fastball velocity now sits in the mid 90s and his four-seamer carries well to the upper half of the strike zone. The low-80s slider he developed with the Yankees is a true sweeper that dives at the back foot of righthanded batters and is one of the better breaking balls in Oakland's system. Both pitches play up because of the deception in his funky delivery. Waldichuk also throws a solid-average low-80s changeup almost exclusively to righthanded hitters, and some evaluators believe it has a chance to keep improving. He rounds out his four-pitch mix with a mid-70s curveball that he'll occasionally flash early in counts. While Waldichuk's lefthanded arsenal is potent, he's more control—he has a fair walk rate of 3.6 per nine innings in the minors—than command at this point, sometimes missing his spots within the strike zone. The lower half of his delivery can fall out of sync at times. Still, his ability to miss bats given his stuff allows for a bit more margin of error.

THE FUTURE: Waldichuk has the ceiling of a midrotation starter as he continues to tighten his delivery. He'll compete for a spot in Oakland's Opening Day rotation in spring training.

BA GRADE
50 Risk: High

SCOUTING GRADES	Fastball: 55	Curveball: 45	Slider: 60	Changeup: 55	Control: 50

Year	Age	Club (League)	Lvl	W	L	ERA	G	GS	IP	H	HR	BB	SO	BB/9	SO/9	WHIP	AVG
2022	24	Somerset (EL)	AA	4	0	1.26	6	6	29	16	2	10	46	3.1	14.4	0.91	.158
2022	24	Las Vegas (PCL)	AAA	0	1	3.38	4	4	19	20	3	3	21	1.4	10.1	1.23	.267
2022	24	Scranton/WB (IL)	AAA	2	3	3.59	11	11	48	38	5	23	70	4.3	13.2	1.28	.218
2022	24	Oakland (AL)	MLB	2	2	4.93	7	7	35	32	5	10	33	2.6	8.6	1.21	.244
Major League Totals				2	2	4.93	7	7	35	32	5	10	33	2.6	8.6	1.21	.244
Minor League Totals				12	9	3.03	54	52	234	169	25	94	349	3.6	13.4	1.12	.199

5 MAX MUNCY, SS

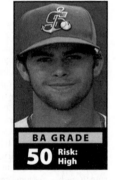

Born: Aug. 25, 2002. **B-T:** R-R. **HT:** 6-1. **WT:** 180.
Drafted: HS—Thousand Oaks, Calif., 2021 (1st round). **Signed by:** Dillon Tung.

TRACK RECORD: The Athletics followed their 2020 first-round selection of Tyler Soderstrom by again drafting a California prep prospect with their first-round pick in 2021, taking Muncy 25th overall and signing him for $2.85 million. They sent Muncy to Low-A Stockton to begin his age-19 season in 2022, where he hit 16 homers through 81 games before a promotion to High-A Lansing in late July. Overall, Muncy hit .229/.336/.422 with 19 home runs while also leading Oakland's system with 169 strikeouts.

SCOUTING REPORT: Muncy tested out as one of the system's better overall athletes prior to the season and continues to add strength to his frame. He uses his strong hands and wrists to generate ample bat speed and began to consistently flash plus raw power potential in 2022. The power gains came with more swing-and-miss than expected. Muncy's strikeout rate hovered around 30% in 2022 and he tends to overswing at times, even with two strikes. Opposing evaluators noted his setup at the plate can get inconsistent, though he made a subtle change that helped him use the opposite field more later in the season. The A's were also encouraged by Muncy's walk rate and pitch recognition. Muncy made 32 errors at shortstop. He has solid hands, but needs to continue to clean up his actions and become more comfortable throwing from various arm slots. Some evaluators wonder whether his range and arm would be better suited for second base as he continues to grow into his frame.

THE FUTURE: Muncy projects as an offensive-minded infielder who could hit 20-25 homers a year, though he'll need to harness his approach to define the quality of his hit tool.

BA GRADE
50 Risk: High

SCOUTING GRADES	Hitting: 50	Power: 55	Speed: 50	Fielding: 50	Arm: 50

Year	Age	Club (League)	Lvl	AVG	G	AB	R	H	2B	3B	HR	RBI	BB	SO	SB	OBP	SLG
2022	19	Stockton (CAL)	LoA	.230	81	304	50	70	16	1	16	51	51	109	6	.352	.447
2022	19	Lansing (MWL)	HiA	.226	42	168	19	38	12	2	3	19	18	60	13	.305	.375
Minor League Totals				.223	134	503	72	112	28	3	19	74	72	181	20	.328	.404

6 DANIEL SUSAC, C

Born: May 14, 2001. **B-T:** R-R. **HT:** 6-4. **WT:** 218.
Drafted: Arizona, 2022 (1st round). **Signed by:** Jeff Urlaub.

BA GRADE
50 Risk: High

TRACK RECORD: Susac is the younger brother of former big league catcher Andrew Susac. Daniel was a prominent amateur prospect, landing at No. 118 on Baseball America's draft ranking in 2020. Susac instead opted to attend Arizona, where he hit .352 with 24 homers over 125 games. He played for Chip Hale, a former Athletics bench coach, in 2022 and was the top player remaining on Oakland's draft board when it selected him 19th overall and signed him for $3,531,200.

SCOUTING REPORT: Teams were split on Susac in the pre-draft process, but those highest projected he will have a chance for above-average hitting ability and power. He is physically strong with plus raw power. That translates to plenty of hard contact when he connects, and Susac shows solid feel for contact despite his long levers. He'll need to add a bit more polish to his offensive approach to unlock his contact ability more consistently. Susac showed a surprising amount of chase in a small sample with Low-A Stockton. The A's also believe Susac could stand to improve his balance and stride, as he can get caught out over his front foot at times. His calling card defensively is his above-average throwing arm. Susac is capable of throwing runners out from his knees with ease. He also has soft hands and solid receiving skills. Like other tall catchers—he is 6-foot-4—he will need to continue to monitor his footwork and mobility behind the plate, and he sometimes struggles to get out of his crouch.

THE FUTURE: Susac has the ceiling of an everyday big league catcher with more refinement to his approach and defense.

SCOUTING GRADES	Hitting: 50	Power: 55	Speed: 40	Fielding: 45	Arm: 55

Year	Age	Club (League)	Lvl	AVG	G	AB	R	H	2B	3B	HR	RBI	BB	SO	SB	OBP	SLG
2022	21	Athletics (ACL)	R	.500	2	6	1	3	1	0	0	2	0	0	0	.500	.667
2022	21	Stockton (CAL)	LoA	.286	25	98	14	28	7	0	1	13	7	25	0	.346	.388
Minor League Totals				.298	27	104	15	31	8	0	1	15	7	25	0	.354	.404

7 LAWRENCE BUTLER, OF/1B

Born: July 10, 2000. **B-T:** L-R. **HT:** 6-2. **WT:** 215.
Drafted: HS—Atlanta, 2018 (6th round). **Signed by:** Jemel Spearman.

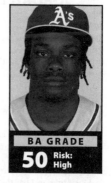

BA GRADE
50 Risk: High

TRACK RECORD: Oakland drafted Butler out of the Atlanta high school ranks in the sixth round in 2018, drawn to his plus raw power, loose swing and youth. He didn't turn 18 until about a month after the draft. Butler didn't do much damage in short-season leagues in 2018 or 2019 but emerged from the pandemic as one of Oakland's most-improved players, reaching High-A Lansing by the end of 2021. Butler returned to Lansing in 2022 and slashed .270/.357/.468 with 11 homers despite a slow start in April. He also missed six weeks with an arm injury.

SCOUTING REPORT: Butler's raw power rivals anyone in Oakland's system and his hard-hit rate in games was above-average in 2022. He has made a considerable effort over the last two seasons to shorten his lofted swing and tighten his strike-zone recognition in an effort to let his power play more consistently in games. He's a selective hitter, sometimes overly passive, but he upped his swing rate in 2022. He still struck out 31.5% of the time with Lansing and will always have to manage his swing-and-miss, especially in the zone, but again paired it with a high walk rate, this time at 12%. Butler is a plus athlete and runner. He transitioned to primarily playing right field in 2022 after playing more first base early in his career, and he has experience at all three outfield positions. He covers plenty of ground at either corner outfield position, but his routes to the ball remain inconsistent.

THE FUTURE: Butler's patience and power provide a ceiling as an everyday regular in a corner if he can make enough contact. He's ready for the upper levels of the minors in 2023.

SCOUTING GRADES	Hitting: 45	Power: 60	Speed: 60	Fielding: 50	Arm: 50

Year	Age	Club (League)	Lvl	AVG	G	AB	R	H	2B	3B	HR	RBI	BB	SO	SB	OBP	SLG
2022	21	Athletics (ACL)	R	.111	3	9	0	1	0	0	0	0	0	4	0	.111	.111
2022	21	Lansing (MWL)	HiA	.270	81	293	52	79	19	3	11	41	40	105	13	.357	.468
Minor League Totals				.247	287	985	168	243	52	11	35	153	143	388	46	.341	.428

8 DENZEL CLARKE, OF

Born: May 1, 2000. **B-T:** R-R. **HT:** 6-5. **WT:** 225.

Drafted: Cal State Northridge, 2021 (4th round). **Signed by:** Dillon Tung.

TRACK RECORD: Clarke grew up in Ontario and is cousins with Josh and Bo Naylor of the Guardians. His mother is Donna Clarke, who represented Canada in the 1984 Summer Olympics as a heptathlete. Clarke burnished a reputation as a dynamic outfielder at Cal State Northridge and carried that into the pro ranks after the Athletics made him their fourth-round selection in 2021. He hit .248 with 15 homers and 30 steals across Low-A Stockton and High-A Lansing in 2022. He also appeared in the Futures Game.

SCOUTING REPORT: Simply put, Clarke is a tool shed. He has arguably the best raw power of any player in Oakland's system and pairs it with easy 70-grade speed in center field, where he routinely makes spectacular defensive

BA GRADE

55 Risk: Extreme

plays. Clarke's offensive game is still quite raw. He has tinkered with several iterations of his setup and stance going back to college in an effort to help simplify his swing, unlock more consistent contact and cut down on the swing-and-miss in the strike zone. He settled on a short stride in 2022, though his hands can drift higher in his setup than the A's prefer. Clarke has a solid understanding of the strike zone, but also has a tendency to chase offspeed pitches and posted a 36% strikeout rate in his first taste of High-A. Breaking ball recognition was a point of emphasis throughout the season. Already a prolific runner, Clarke's basestealing could continue to improve as he learns the nuances of baserunning.

THE FUTURE: Clarke is commended by the organization for his makeup and work ethic. He has one of the highest ceilings in the Oakland organization as a potential impact center fielder—if his hit tool improves.

SCOUTING GRADES	Hitting: 40	Power: 60	Speed: 70	Fielding: 70	Arm: 50

Year	Age	Club (League)	Lvl	AVG	G	AB	R	H	2B	3B	HR	RBI	BB	SO	SB	OBP	SLG
2022	22	Stockton (CAL)	LoA	.295	42	156	37	46	14	2	7	26	28	56	14	.420	.545
2022	22	Lansing (MWL)	HiA	.209	51	187	30	39	9	2	8	21	28	79	16	.317	.406
Minor League Totals				.251	100	362	69	91	25	4	16	48	59	141	31	.367	.475

9 JORDAN DIAZ, 2B/1B

Born: Aug. 13, 2000. **B-T:** R-R. **HT:** 5-9. **WT:** 190.

Signed: Colombia, 2016. **Signed by:** Jose Quintero.

TRACK RECORD: Diaz turned in his most impressive professional season in 2022, six years after the Colombia native signed for $275,000. It culminated in his MLB debut. Diaz hit .319 in 94 games with Double-A Midland to finish third in the Texas League batting race despite being one of the league's youngest hitters at 21 years old. He continued to rake upon promotion to Triple-A Las Vegas and was called up to Oakland in late September.

SCOUTING REPORT: The book on Diaz hasn't changed much over the years. His exceptional feel for contact, short swing and flat bat path lead to ample loud contact. His power continues to tick up as well—his 19 homers in 2022 were a career high. Diaz has extreme confidence in his barrel ability. He's one

BA GRADE

45 Risk: Medium

of the most aggressive hitters in Oakland's system, saw the fewest number of pitches of any qualified Texas League hitter and has never posted a walk rate above 6.8% in full-season ball. More skeptical evaluators keep waiting for more advanced pitchers to exploit Diaz's ultra-aggressive approach. He still doesn't have a clear defensive home. Diaz has a strong arm and good hands, but he's compromised at third base because of his lack of range. He played more first base in 2022, but he's undersized for the position. The A's have tried him in left field, though his lack of speed is an issue in the outfield. Oakland deployed him mostly at second base in the big leagues and was encouraged by the results.

THE FUTURE: Diaz's pure hitting ability continues to stand out despite his obvious defensive limitations. He'll compete for playing time with the rebuilding A's in 2023.

SCOUTING GRADES	Hitting: 60	Power: 50	Speed: 30	Fielding: 40	Arm: 55

Year	Age	Club (League)	Lvl	AVG	G	AB	R	H	2B	3B	HR	RBI	BB	SO	SB	OBP	SLG
2022	21	Midland (TL)	AA	.319	94	379	48	121	26	0	15	58	22	61	0	.361	.507
2022	21	Las Vegas (PCL)	AAA	.348	26	112	19	39	8	1	4	25	6	15	0	.383	.545
2022	21	Oakland (AL)	MLB	.265	15	49	3	13	3	0	0	1	2	7	0	.294	.327
Major League Totals				.265	15	49	3	13	3	0	0	1	2	7	0	.294	.327
Minor League Totals				.290	378	1424	183	413	93	5	42	231	96	228	7	.338	.451

10 LUIS MEDINA, RHP

Born: May 3, 1999. **B-T:** R-R. **HT:** 6-3. **WT:** 195.
Signed: Dominican Republic, 2015. **Signed by:** Juan Rosario (Yankees).

TRACK RECORD: Medina was a flame-throwing righthander who needed to find the strike zone more often when the Yankees signed him for $280,000 in 2015. That reputation has stuck with him as a pro. Medina reached Double-A for the first time in 2021. He returned to Somerset to start 2022 and posted a 3.38 ERA through 17 starts. Medina was one of four players Oakland acquired from the Yankees for Frankie Montas at the deadline. Medina was erratic upon arriving in Midland, walking 22 batters in 20.2 innings.

SCOUTING REPORT: While Medina has yet to consistently command his high-powered arsenal, no one doubts his ability to miss bats. His upper-90s four-seam fastball routinely touches triple digits and he has shown the ability to manipulate the pitch. Scouts have long been impressed with the potential of Medina's low-80s curveball. The pitch has considerable break and flashes great shape, but he struggles to land it within the strike zone. His solid-average upper-80s changeup also continues to improve and he throws it for strikes more consistently than his breaking ball. Hitters whiffed on both pitches north of 40% of the time in 2022. Medina has never quite synced up his delivery. He's fairly athletic but has long levers and struggles with timing, especially from the stretch, and can cut himself off at the end of his delivery. Medina needs to trust his stuff to avoid compounding mistakes.

THE FUTURE: The clock is ticking on Medina, who is out of minor league options, to throw enough strikes to stick in a rotation. A future as a nasty, high-leverage reliever seems more likely.

BA GRADE
50 Risk: High

SCOUTING GRADES	Fastball: 70	Curveball: 60	Changeup: 55	Control: 40

Year	Age	Club (League)	Lvl	W	L	ERA	G	GS	IP	H	HR	BB	SO	BB/9	SO/9	WHIP	AVG
2022	23	Midland (TL)	AA	1	4	11.76	7	7	21	35	3	22	26	9.6	11.3	2.76	.389
2022	23	Somerset (EL)	AA	4	3	3.38	17	17	72	46	4	40	81	5.0	10.1	1.19	.179
Minor League Totals				15	24	4.85	93	91	382	322	31	266	457	6.3	10.8	1.54	.228

11 HENRY BOLTE, OF

Born: Aug. 4, 2003. **B-T:** R-R. **HT:** 6-0. **WT:** 195.
Drafted: HS—Palo Alto, Calif., 2022 (2nd round). **Signed by:** Troy Stewart.

TRACK RECORD: Bolte grew up an A's fan and starred in the Bay Area at Palo Alto High School. The A's selected him 56th overall in the 2022 draft and signed him to a $2 million bonus, buying him out of a Texas commitment and continuing a trend of prioritizing local products at the top of their draft. Bolte debuted at the Rookie-level Arizona Complex League, hitting .212 with 19 strikeouts in 11 games.

SCOUTING REPORT: Bolte draws some comparisons to fellow A's prospect Denzel Clarke in the sense both are extremely tooled-up with a clear need to develop their hitting ability. Bolte is already one of the most dynamic athletes in Oakland's system and has a chance for double-plus raw power as he gets stronger. Bolte's contact ability will be tested without improvements to his swing, approach and pitch recognition. His swing gets long at times, leading to plenty of swing and miss in the strike zone. The A's focused on reworking parts of his swing during instructs, toning down his leg kick and stride to help improve his balance and setup. The rest of Bolte's skill set is eye-opening. He's a plus runner with a strong throwing arm and a chance to be an elite defender in center field.

THE FUTURE: While his development will likely be a slow burn, Bolte has immense upside, especially if his swing changes stick. He should reach Low-A Stockton at some point in 2023.

BA GRADE: 55/Extreme	Hit: 40	Power: 60	Run: 60	Field: 60	Arm: 60

Year	Age	Club (League)	Lvl	AVG	G	AB	R	H	2B	3B	HR	RBI	BB	SO	SB	OBP	SLG
2022	18	Athletics (ACL)	R	.212	11	33	5	7	0	0	0	2	5	19	0	.333	.212
Minor League Totals				.212	11	33	5	7	0	0	0	2	5	19	0	.333	.212

12 GUNNAR HOGLUND, RHP

Born: Dec. 17, 1999. **B-T:** L-R. **HT:** 6-4. **WT:** 220.
Drafted: Mississippi, 2021 (1st round). **Signed by:** Don Norris (Blue Jays).

TRACK RECORD: The Pirates drafted Hoglund 36th overall in 2018 but failed to sign the righthander. He instead made it to Ole Miss and was one of the best pitchers in the Southeastern Conference until an elbow injury ended his 2021 season and required Tommy John surgery. The Blue Jays still drafted Hoglund 19th overall that year. They traded the rehabbing Hoglund to Oakland along with three others in exchange for 3B Matt Chapman. Hoglund made his pro debut in late July, including one start with Low-A Stockton, but an arm issue ended his season after just eight innings.

SCOUTING REPORT: The A's hope a normal offseason of rest and recovery will help Hoglund's stuff return to pre-injury levels. Plenty of evaluators viewed Hoglund as a safe bet to reach the big leagues because of his polished three-pitch mix and strike-throwing acumen. At Ole Miss, his fastball sat 92-94 and touched 96 mph at his peak with good shape. It wasn't as firm in his brief 2022 cameo, when it sat 89-92 mph. Hoglund also throws an above-average, low-80s slider that is more of a downer breaking ball and a low-80s changeup with arm-side fade that gives lefthanded hitters fits. Hoglund could throw all three pitches for strikes in any count as an amateur and has a chance for plus command.

SCOUTING REPORT: Getting Hoglund healthy is the top priority for the A's. The injury issues cloud his outlook, but his pitch mix, command and experience provided the ingredients for a quick-moving starter with a midrotation ceiling.

BA GRADE: 50/High		Fastball: 55		Slider: 55		Changeup: 55		Control: 60					
Year	Age	Club (League)	Lvl	W	L	ERA	G	GS	IP	H	HR	BB	SO	BB/9	SO/9	WHIP	AVG
2022	22	Athletics (ACL)	R	0	1	0.00	2	2	5	4	0	0	7	0.0	12.6	0.80	.200
2022	22	Stockton (CAL)	LoA	0	0	0.00	1	1	3	3	0	1	1	3.0	3.0	1.33	.250
Minor League Totals				0	1	0.00	3	3	8	7	0	1	8	1.1	9.0	1.00	.219

13 J.T. GINN, RHP

Born: May 20, 1999. **B-T:** R-R. **HT:** 6-2. **WT:** 200.
Drafted: Mississippi State, 2020 (2nd round). **Signed by:** Jet Butler (Mets).

TRACK RECORD: The A's explored the signability of Ginn in the 2020 draft, but the Mets landed the Mississippi State product at 52nd overall for a $2.9 million bonus as he rehabbed from Tommy John surgery. Oakland ultimately acquired the righty less than two years later in a trade for righthander Chris Bassitt. A forearm injury limited Ginn to just 42.1 innings in 2022 and he struggled in his first taste of the upper minors at Double-A Midland, but he pitched well in the Arizona Fall League after the season.

SCOUTING REPORT: Ginn operated with a mid-90s fastball that touched 99 mph at his peak, but his fastball settled into the low 90s and touched 95-96 as he returned from surgery. The pitch has nasty sinking action and leads to elevated groundball rates. Ginn can manipulate his fastball, sometimes tinkering with his approach from start-to-start, and experimented with a cutter in the fall league. His most effective secondary is a tight, low-80s gyro slider that flashes plus. His mid-80s changeup tunnels well with his sinker. Ginn attacks hitters from the extreme first-base side of the rubber. He doesn't have the most fluid delivery, but he repeats it well and his athleticism allows for slightly above-average command potential.

THE FUTURE: Ginn has thrown just 89.1 innings as a professional and his track record of arm injuries is a concern. He has a fairly high floor and the ceiling of a No. 4 starter with a usable three-pitch mix if he can remain healthy.

BA GRADE: 50/High		Fastball: 55		Slider: 55		Changeup: 50		Control: 50					
Year	Age	Club (League)	Lvl	W	L	ERA	G	GS	IP	H	HR	BB	SO	BB/9	SO/9	WHIP	AVG
2022	23	Athletics (ACL)	R	0	0	0.00	2	2	7	4	0	0	5	0.0	6.4	0.57	.167
2022	23	Midland (TL)	AA	1	4	6.11	10	10	35	38	3	14	41	3.6	10.4	1.47	.264
Minor League Totals				6	9	3.68	30	30	134	117	6	36	127	2.4	8.5	1.14	.232

14 HOGAN HARRIS, LHP

Born: Dec. 26, 1996. **B-T:** R-L. **HT:** 6-2. **WT:** 208.
Drafted: Louisiana-Lafayette, 2018 (3rd round). **Signed by:** Kelcey Mucker.

TRACK RECORD: Oblique and elbow injuries delayed the start of Harris' professional career after the A's drafted him 85th overall in 2018, and he missed all of 2021 after having Tommy John surgery. Harris pitched a career-high 73.2 innings in 2022 despite being built up slowly, striking out 105 batters and ending the season with Triple-A Las Vegas. Oakland added him to the 40-man roster after the season.

SCOUTING REPORT: Harris has swing-and-miss stuff but has walked 4.3 batters per nine innings as a professional. His fastball was a touch firmer a year removed from surgery, averaging 93 mph and touching 97. He runs into trouble when he tries to overthrow his four-seamer. Harris' upper-70s changeup is quite good and his best swing-and-miss secondary. He also throws a slow, arcing curveball that has roughly 20 mph separation from his fastball and may be more of a strike-stealer than a swing-and-miss offering. At the end of the season, Harris added an upper-80s slider/cutter hybrid into his repertoire, which the A's believe will be the key to Harris turning over more advanced lineups. Harris used his rehab to improve his body. His delivery is still a bit rigid and he struggles at times staying on line to the plate. He has fringe-average command potential that is mitigated by the quality of his stuff.

THE FUTURE: Harris' arsenal returned following his surgery. He's expected to head back to Triple-A Las Vegas to open the 2023 season, where the A's hope his strike-throwing improves.

BA GRADE: 45/High		Fastball: 55		Curveball: 50		Slider: 50		Changeup: 60		Control: 45		

Year	Age	Club (League)	Lvl	W	L	ERA	G	GS	IP	H	HR	BB	SO	BB/9	SO/9	WHIP	AVG
2022	25	Lansing (MWL)	HiA	0	1	1.38	7	7	13	5	0	7	18	4.8	12.5	0.92	.114
2022	25	Midland (TL)	AA	1	0	1.67	8	7	32	15	0	19	48	5.3	13.4	1.05	.136
2022	25	Las Vegas (PCL)	AAA	1	3	6.35	8	8	28	31	6	17	39	5.4	12.4	1.69	.277
Minor League Totals				3	9	3.16	38	35	128	83	10	62	170	4.3	11.9	1.13	.182

15 BRETT HARRIS, 3B

Born: June 24, 1998. **B-T:** R-R. **HT:** 6-3. **WT:** 210.
Drafted: Gonzaga, 2021 (7th round). **Signed by:** James Coffman.

TRACK RECORD: Oakland's player development group believes the club found a steal in Harris, who was a steady all-around performer at Gonzaga that they drafted in the seventh round in 2021 and signed to a $120,000 bonus. He continued to perform well between High-A Lansing and Double-A Midland in 2022, hitting .290/.375/.475 with 17 homers in his age-24 season.

SCOUTING REPORT: While Harris doesn't have an obvious carrying tool, he also doesn't have a glaring weakness. He greets pitchers with a wide, slightly open stance and his simple righthanded swing makes plenty of contact. Harris is a selective hitter who makes good swing decisions and rarely whiffs on pitches in the zone. He wasn't much of a home run hitter in college, although amateur scouts noted Harris had some raw power potential, and he showed more thump in his first year as a professional despite middling exit velocities. A ceiling of 15 homers a year in the majors is not out of the question. Harris is a solid defender at third base with good instincts and an accurate throwing arm. Those skills translate to second base as well, where the A's deployed him more frequently in 2022. He also stole 11 bases, but he's a fringe-average runner.

THE FUTURE: Harris endears himself to coaches because of his well-rounded skills and instincts. His power may be stretched thin in an everyday role at third base, but he has the ceiling of a superutility type.

BA GRADE: 45/High		Hit: 55		Power: 50		Run: 45		Field: 55		Arm: 5		

Year	Age	Club (League)	Lvl	AVG	G	AB	R	H	2B	3B	HR	RBI	BB	SO	SB	OBP	SLG
2022	24	Lansing (MWL)	HiA	.304	29	102	22	31	7	0	7	18	19	21	0	.415	.578
2022	24	Midland (TL)	AA	.286	84	315	51	90	15	2	10	45	31	62	11	.361	.441
Minor League Totals				.281	140	501	89	141	25	2	20	77	60	103	14	.370	.459

16 JOEY ESTES, RHP

Born: Oct. 8, 2001. **B-T:** R-R. **HT:** 6-2. **WT:** 190.
Drafted: HS—Lancaster, Calif., 2019 (16th round). **Signed by:** Kevin Martin (Braves).

TRACK RECORD: The Braves bought Estes out of a Long Beach State commitment in 2019 for $497,500. He experienced a breakout season two years later, striking out 32.1% of batters over 99 innings with Low-A Augusta. The A's acquired Estes as part of the Matt Olson trade and sent him to High-A Lansing for his age-20 season in 2022, when he posted a 4.55 ERA and struck out 92 batters in 91 innings as one of the youngest pitchers at the level.

SCOUTING REPORT: Estes attacks hitters with athleticism, arm speed and a competitive mentality. He has three solid pitches, albeit without an elite swing-and-miss offering. His 92-94 mph fastball has nearly equal amounts of carry and run, boring in on righthanded batters but with enough vertical break to play at the top of the strike zone. His mid-80s slider has late bite, but he sometimes struggles to stay on top of it. Estes also throws a mid-80s changeup with good hand speed that tunnels well with the fastball but is still inconsistent. Estes is generally around the strike zone, but can rush his delivery at times and his command wavers as a result. The A's worked with Estes in instructs to move down the mound a bit more efficiently.

THE FUTURE: There's some reliever risk because of the delivery, but Estes is still quite young and has thrown enough strikes to continue to move up the ladder in the rotation. He has the ceiling of a back-end starter.

BA GRADE: 45/High			Fastball: 55		Slider: 55		Changeup: 50		Control: 50				
Year	Age	Club (League)	Lvl	W	L	ERA	G	GS	IP	H	HR	BB	SO	BB/9	SO/9	WHIP	AVG
2022	20	Lansing (MWL)	HiA	3	7	4.55	20	20	91	86	17	30	92	3.0	9.1	1.27	.250
Minor League Totals				6	14	3.92	45	45	200	162	24	66	227	3.0	10.2	1.14	.218

17 RYAN CUSICK, RHP

Born: Nov. 12, 1999. **B-T:** R-R. **HT:** 6-6. **WT:** 235.
Drafted: Wake Forest, 2021 (1st round). **Signed by:** Billy Best (Braves).
TRACK RECORD: The 6-foot-6 Cusick touched triple-digits at Wake Forest and the Braves drafted him 24th overall in 2021, signing him for $2.7 million. He dominated Low-A hitters in six subsequent starts that year. Cusick was one of four players the A's acquired in exchange for Matt Olson in March of 2022. A rib injury limited Cusick to just 41 innings with Double-A Midland, where he never got on track and walked 6.6 batters per nine innings.
SCOUTING REPORT: Scouts loved Cusick's power potential in college but harbored concerns about his inconsistent command. That assessment has held true so far as a pro. His plus fastball sat more in the 95-97 mph range in 2022 and the metric-savvy righthander worked with the A's to tweak the grip on his fastball to restore some induced vertical break. He's still working to find a consistent feel for his breaking ball. The Braves worked with Cusick to throw a harder, vertically-breaking slider. The pitch sat 85-86 and has above-average potential, but was inconsistent in both shape and command. He rarely turns to his firm, low-90s changeup that needs considerable refinement. There's some reliever risk in Cusick's delivery, although his injury may have contributed to his strike-throwing woes in 2022.
THE FUTURE: Cusick needs to develop his changeup and throw more strikes to remain a starter. Otherwise, he profiles as a potential high-leverage reliever. He could return to Double-A Midland to start 2023, when the A's hope he regains the form he showed that made him a first-round pick.

BA GRADE: 45/High			Fastball: 70		Slider: 55		Changeup: 40		Control: 40				
Year	Age	Club (League)	Lvl	W	L	ERA	G	GS	IP	H	HR	BB	SO	BB/9	SO/9	WHIP	AVG
2022	22	Athletics (ACL)	R	0	0	9.00	1	1	2	3	0	0	3	0.0	13.5	1.50	.333
2022	22	Midland (TL)	AA	1	6	7.02	12	9	41	53	4	30	43	6.6	9.4	2.02	.319
Minor League Totals				1	7	5.92	19	16	59	71	5	34	80	5.2	12.1	1.77	.300

18 CLARK ELLIOTT, OF

Born: Sept. 29, 2000 **B-T:** L-R. **HT:** 6-0. **WT:** 183.
Drafted: Michigan, 2022 (2nd round). **Signed by:** Rich Sparks.
TRACK RECORD: Elliott surged up draft boards when he hit .344 to win the Cape Cod League batting title after his sophomore season. He returned to Michigan and kept on hitting as a junior, hitting .337/.460/.630 while slugging 16 homers after previously hitting just five in his first two college seasons. The A's drafted him 69th overall and signed him to a $900,000 bonus, feeling as if they landed one of the best pure hitters in college baseball. He appeared in just one game in the Rookie-level Arizona Complex League.
SCOUTING REPORT: Elliott has great feel for the barrel. He punishes fastballs in the strike zone, especially in the lower half, utilizing his flat bat path to turn pitches around. He struggled at times in college with pitches on the outer third of the strike zone and also ran into some swing-and-miss issues with breaking balls. He'll have to prove the power gains he made in his final college season are real, but he has a chance for average power potential as he better learns which pitches he can damage. Elliott played mostly right field in college, although the A's think he has the athleticism to handle center. He's an above-average runner right now with a solid-average throwing arm. Elliott, a cognitive science major at Michigan, also draws rave reviews for his makeup.
THE FUTURE: Elliott is ready for Low-A Stockton. He has the ceiling of a top-of-the-order everyday outfielder if the power develops.

BA GRADE: 45/High			Hit: 55		Power: 50		Run: 55		Field: 55		Arm: 50		
Year	Age	Club (League)	Lvl	AVG	G	AB	R	H	2B	3B	HR	RBI	BB	SO	SB	OBP	SLG
2022	21	Athletics (ACL)	R	.000	1	1	1	0	0	0	0	0	1	0	0	.500	.000
Minor League Totals				.000	1	1	1	0	0	0	0	0	1	0	0	.500	.000

19 EURIBIEL ANGELES, 2B/SS

Born: May 11, 2022. **B-T:** R-R. **HT:** 5-11. **WT:** 175.
Signed: Dominican Republic, 2018. **Signed by:** Alvin Duran/Jake Koenig/Chris Kemp (Padres).

TRACK RECORD: Angeles signed with the Padres for $300,000 in 2018 and emerged as a breakout prospect three years later, hitting .343 to win the California League batting title as a 19-year-old with Lake Elsinore in 2021. The A's acquired Angeles alongside righthander Adrian Martinez from the Padres in exchange for Sean Manaea just before the start of the 2022 season. Angeles spent all of 2022 with High-A Lansing, hitting a nondescript .278/.316/.353.

SCOUTING REPORT: Angeles' game is built around his elite hand-eye coordination and bat-to-ball skills. He has an unorthodox setup at the plate, standing fairly straight up before employing a sizable leg kick as he gets into his swing, but there also isn't a lot of excess movement in his swing. His swing path is geared for gap-to-gap contact with marginal power potential. He's a very aggressive hitter who trusts his contact ability. That can work against him at times, as he rarely misses pitches in the zone and keeps his strikeouts in check, but also owned a 4.4% walk rate and chased pitches more than a third of the time, leading to weak contact overall. Angeles is an instinctual player, both defensively and on the basepaths, but he's just a fair athlete who is more likely to move around the infield as opposed to sticking at shortstop moving forward.

THE FUTURE: He needs to become more selective, but Angeles' contact ability is exceptional. His lack of power or standout supplemental tool likely limits him to a ceiling of a utilityman.

| BA GRADE: 45/High | | Hit: 60 | | Power: 30 | | Run: 50 | | Field: 50 | | Arm: 50 | |

Year	Age	Club (League)	Lvl	AVG	G	AB	R	H	2B	3B	HR	RBI	BB	SO	SB	OBP	SLG
2022	20	Lansing (MWL)	HiA	.278	97	363	29	101	19	1	2	32	17	58	8	.316	.353
Minor League Totals				.305	246	970	134	296	54	9	6	122	72	154	44	.359	.398

20 RYAN NODA, 1B

Born: March 30, 1996. **B-T:** L-L. **HT:** 6-3. **WT:** 217.
Drafted: Cincinnati, 2017 (15th round). **Signed by:** Coulson Barbiche (Blue Jays).

TRACK RECORD: A powerful but strikeout-prone slugger at Cincinnati, Noda was drafted by the Blue Jays in the 15th round in 2017 and traded to the Dodgers as the player to be named later for Ross Stripling before the 2021 season. He took a leap in the Dodgers' system and delivered a strong showing at Triple-A Oklahoma City in 2022, finishing in the top 10 in the organization in runs (86), doubles (23), home runs (25), RBIs (90), stolen bases (20), walks (92) and on-base percentage (.395). The A's selected him with the second pick of the Rule 5 draft after the season.

SCOUTING REPORT: Noda stands a physical 6-foot-3, 217 pounds from the left side and is one of the most patient hitters in the minors. He owns a career .407 on-base percentage and walks in nearly one out of every five plate appearances. Noda works long at-bats and has above-average raw power when he connects, but his swing is a bit stiff and leaves him prone to swinging and missing in the zone. He's mostly a three true outcomes hitter reliant on walking. Noda is a good athlete for his size and a plus defensive first baseman. He moves around the bag fluidly and is excellent at picking balls out of the dirt to prevent errors. He has good range and is a reliable, consistent defender.

THE FUTURE: Noda's power, on-base skills and defense give him a chance to stick as a reserve. He'll aim to make his big league debut in 2023.

| BA GRADE: 40/Medium | | Hit: 30 | | Power: 50 | | Run: 40 | | Field: 60 | | Arm: 50 | |

Year	Age	Club (League)	Lvl	AVG	G	AB	R	H	2B	3B	HR	RBI	BB	SO	SB	OBP	SLG
2022	26	Oklahoma City (PCL)	AAA	.259	135	464	86	120	23	1	25	90	92	162	20	.395	.474
Minor League Totals				.264	555	1843	361	487	107	10	94	361	408	622	58	.407	.486

21 GARRETT ACTON, RHP

Born: June 15, 1998. **B-T:** R-R. **HT:** 6-2. **WT:** 215.
Signed: Illinois, 2020 (NDFA). **Signed by:** Derek Lee.

TRACK RECORD: Acton transferred from Saint Louis to Illinois and was a standout closer for two seasons for the Illini before the A's signed him as a nondrafted free agent in 2020 after the shortened draft. Acton overpowered hitters in 2021, striking out more than 40% of batters at the lower levels. He didn't quite replicate those gaudy strikeout numbers in the upper minors in 2022, but he still posted a strikeout rate near 30% in relief and reached Triple-A Las Vegas.

SCOUTING REPORT: Acton attacks hitters with brute force. He has added velocity since turning pro and parks his fastball in the upper 90s. The pitch has good shape, generating whiffs at the top of the strike zone. Acton pitches from the stretch and his shorter arm action creates some deception against right-handed hitters. Lefthanders fared much better against Acton in 2022. Acton's favorite secondary is a mid-80s slider that has sharp vertical break and flashes above-average. He turned to his upper-80s changeup less than 10% of the time, but the pitch showed above-average potential and could become more of a factor against lefties. Acton has smoothed out his delivery since turning pro, but his fair command is best suited for shorter outings.

THE FUTURE: Acton could settle in as a seventh- or eighth-inning option in a bullpen one day. He should reach Oakland at some point in 2023.

BA GRADE: 45/High		Fastball: 60		Slider: 55			Changeup: 55		Control: 45				

Year	Age	Club (League)	Lvl	W	L	ERA	G	GS	IP	H	HR	BB	SO	BB/9	SO/9	WHIP	AVG
2022	24	Midland (TL)	AA	1	3	4.23	19	0	28	29	3	14	42	4.6	13.7	1.55	.269
2022	24	Las Vegas (PCL)	AAA	2	6	5.53	32	2	42	46	12	15	50	3.2	10.6	1.44	.279
Minor League Totals				6	9	4.44	85	2	124	116	24	47	179	3.4	13.0	1.32	.248

22 COLIN PELUSE, RHP

Born: June 11, 1998. **B-T:** R-R. **HT:** 6-3. **WT:** 230.
Drafted: Wake Forest, 2019 (9th round). **Signed by:** Neil Avent.

TRACK RECORD: Peluse reworked his body during the shutdown in 2020 and returned with a fastball touching 98 mph in shorter outings at the A's instructional league that fall. He carried that momentum into the 2021 season, where his fastball settled into the mid 90s and he reached Double-A Midland, ultimately winning Oakland's minor league pitcher of the year award. Peluse's stuff backed up a bit in 2022 and he pitched to a 5.38 ERA as a starter with Midland. The A's left him unprotected ahead of the Rule 5 draft.

SCOUTING REPORT: Peluse's aggressive mentality and lack of a clear third pitch led some evaluators to wonder whether he's better suited for a relief role. That chorus grew louder in 2022. His fastball averaged 92 mph and topped out around 95 mph. The pitch still has good shape and he threw it for a strike 70% of the time for the second consecutive season. Peluse continues to seek a consistent breaking ball. He worked with an average mid-80s slider in 2022 that didn't miss a ton of bats. Neither did his upper-80s changeup, although Peluse showed he could land it in the strike zone consistently. He experimented with a curveball and a cutter in the Arizona Fall League.

THE FUTURE: With his secondaries stalling out, a multi-inning relief role in the big leagues now seems more likely for Peluse, where his fastball-slider combination could play up.

BA GRADE: 45/High		Fastball: 55		Slider: 50			Changeup: 45		Control: 55				

Year	Age	Club (League)	Lvl	W	L	ERA	G	GS	IP	H	HR	BB	SO	BB/9	SO/9	WHIP	AVG
2022	24	Midland (TL)	AA	10	6	5.38	23	21	119	133	17	28	92	2.1	7.0	1.36	.278
2022	24	Las Vegas (PCL)	AAA	0	1	37.80	1	1	2	7	2	1	1	5.4	5.4	4.80	.538
Minor League Totals				21	11	4.48	53	45	245	252	31	61	228	2.2	8.4	1.28	.262

23 BRAYAN BUELVAS, OF

Born: June 8, 2022. **B-T:** R-R. **HT:** 5-10. **WT:** 183.
Signed: Colombia, 2018. **Signed by:** Jose Quintero.

TRACK RECORD: Buelvas was a breakout performer in the Arizona League in 2019 and was one of the youngest players invited to Oakland's alternate site in 2020. He has struggled to replicate that success in full-season ball. Buelvas experienced mixed results with Low-A Stockton in 2021, hitting .221 with 16 homers, then hit just .195 with High-A Lansing as a 20-year-old in 2022 while missing nearly two months with a hamstring injury. Buelvas played winter ball each of the last two winters, competing for Colombia's U-23 World Cup team in 2022.

SCOUTING REPORT: The A's wonder if Buelvas simply ran out of energy in 2022. He also needs to determine what type of hitter he wants to be. Buelvas has average power potential and is still growing into his frame, but he chases that power too frequently and loses his approach. The A's believe he's better off sticking to a more contact-oriented, line-to-line approach to maximize his feel for the barrel. Buelvas is a solid-average runner. He has just enough foot speed and arm strength to handle center field now. Some evaluators aren't convinced he can stick there as he matures, and a move to a corner would put even more strain on his bat.

THE FUTURE: Buelvas doesn't turn 21 until June. He still has the ceiling of a second-division regular in the outfield, but he needs to make more consistent contact.

BA GRADE: 45/High		Hit: 55		Power: 45		Run: 50		Field: 55		Arm: 55				
Year	Age	Club (League)	Lvl	AVG	G	AB	R	H	2B	3B	HR	RBI	BB	SO	SB	OBP	SLG
2022	20	Athletics (ACL)	R	.261	7	23	4	6	1	1	1	4	4	6	4	.400	.522
2022	20	Lansing (MWL)	HiA	.195	69	236	28	46	14	1	7	26	17	57	7	.265	.352
Minor League Totals				.231	231	844	116	195	41	14	27	121	88	218	44	.317	.409

24 JEFFERSON JEAN, RHP

Born: Jan. 29, 2005. **B-T:** R-R. **HT:** 6-3. **WT:** 170.
Signed: Dominican Republic, 2022. **Signed by:** Wilfredo Magallanes.
TRACK RECORD: Jean was a late riser in the international scouting process as a projectable 6-foot-3 arm who touched 96 mph at 16 years old despite being more of a thrower than a pitcher at the time. The A's signed him for $600,000 and he threw 7.1 innings over six games in the Dominican Summer League. He was the youngest player at Oakland's instructional league, where he turned heads by touching 100 mph.
SCOUTING REPORT: Jean is quite raw, but he pairs considerable arm strength with an athletic, projectable frame. His upper-90s fastball has plus potential and he relies upon it heavily. The A's also experimented with a two-seamer at their fall instructional league. Jean's offspeed pitches and command are still a work in progress as he learns to harness his long levers. He throws a sweeping 80-82 mph slider and also possesses a firm, upper-80s changeup that he didn't utilize in the DSL. Jean's primary focus upon turning pro was fastball command. He has a lengthy arm stroke that raises reliever concerns, but the rest of his delivery is fairly clean.
THE FUTURE: Jean's arm talent and age make it easy to dream on a ceiling of a midrotation starter one day, but a long road of refinement awaits. He has a chance to open his age-18 season at the Rookie-level Arizona Complex League in 2023.

BA GRADE: 50/Extreme		Fastball: 70		Slider: 55		Changeup: 50		Control: 45					
Year	Age	Club (League)	Lvl	W	L	ERA	G	GS	IP	H	HR	BB	SO	BB/9	SO/9	WHIP	AVG
2022	17	Athletics (DSL)	R	0	0	4.91	6	6	7	5	0	4	9	4.9	11.0	1.23	.185
Minor League Totals				0	0	4.91	6	6	7	5	0	4	9	4.9	11.0	1.23	.185

25 JORGE JUAN, RHP

Born: March 6, 1999. **B-T:** R-R. **HT:** 6-8. **WT:** 200.
Signed: Dominican Republic, 2017. **Signed by:** Juan Carlos de la Cruz.
TRACK RECORD: Juan's experienced an unusual odyssey through the A's system since signing in 2017 as an under-the-radar arm. The 6-foot-8 righthander broke out with Low-A Stockton in 2021, striking out 37.8% of hitters. An elbow injury ended his season early, but the A's still added him to their 40-man roster to protect him from the Rule 5 draft. More arm troubles delayed the start to his 2022 season. Oakland designated him for assignment in early May, then signed him to a minor league deal. He returned in late July and threw 16.2 innings for High-A Lansing.
SCOUTING REPORT: Juan's breakout 2021 season was rooted in a velocity bump that he sustained in 2022 as well. Juan attacks hitters with a plus, mid-90s fastball that touches 97-98 mph. He pairs it with a hammer of a low-to-mid-80s breaking ball that changes eye levels of hitters, appearing as if it drops out of the clouds thanks to his long levers. His firm changeup still lags behind his other two offerings and can sometimes be mistaken for a fastball. His strike-throwing remains inconsistent, although he has made improvements over the last two seasons.
THE FUTURE: Juan is less experienced than one might expect given his age and roster status, so a future as a starter isn't out of the question. A role as a multi-inning reliever where his stuff could play up seems far more likely given his command and injury history.

BA GRADE: 45/High		Fastball: 60		Slider: 60		Changeup: 40		Control: 45					
Year	Age	Club (League)	Lvl	W	L	ERA	G	GS	IP	H	HR	BB	SO	BB/9	SO/9	WHIP	AVG
2022	23	Athletics (ACL)	R	1	0	0.00	2	0	4	1	0	1	8	2.2	18.0	0.50	.077
2022	23	Lansing (MWL)	HiA	0	0	4.86	6	4	17	10	3	8	20	4.3	10.8	1.08	.169
Minor League Totals				3	13	4.72	44	22	124	97	8	77	152	5.6	11.0	1.40	.214

26 PEDRO PINEDA, OF

Born: Sept. 6, 2003. **B-T:** R-R. **HT:** 6-2. **WT:** 185.
Signed: Dominican Republic, 2021. **Signed by:** Juan Carlos de la Cruz.

TRACK RECORD: Pineda was the centerpiece of Oakland's 2021 international signing class and he reached the Rookie-level Arizona Complex League by the end of the season. The A's aggressively sent Pineda to Low-A Stockton to open his age-18 season in 2022. Pineda was overmatched, hitting .188 with 77 strikeouts in 42 games before being sent back to the complex, where he also dealt with a shoulder injury. **SCOUTING REPORT:** Scouts were so alarmed by Pineda's swing-and-miss issues that they struggled to evaluate him. Pineda's difficulties stemmed from shaky pitch recognition, especially on breaking balls. He also had trouble identifying which pitches in the strike zone he should try to punish. Those issues were surprising considering Pineda's track record of performance against high-level pitching as an amateur. He still flashes high-level bat speed that suggests plus power potential if he can make enough contact. Pineda fared better defensively. He's an above-average runner with a chance to stick in center, although his arm could handle a move to right field if his body fills out as he matures. **THE FUTURE:** Pineda is still a dynamic athlete with a loud tool set and a high ceiling, but the glaring contact issues were a red flag. He'll get a mulligan and a chance to redeem himself at Low-A Stockton in 2023.

BA GRADE: 50/Extreme		Hit: 40		Power: 60		Run: 55		Field: 55		Arm: 50	
Year	Age	Club (League)	Lvl	AVG	G	AB	R	H	2B	3B	HR	RBI	BB	SO	SB	OBP	SLG
2022	18	Athletics (ACL)	R	.000	1	3	0	0	0	0	0	0	0	3	0	.000	.000
2022	18	Stockton (CAL)	LoA	.188	42	144	22	27	3	3	4	13	17	77	5	.306	.333
Minor League Totals				.205	76	244	41	50	6	6	5	22	35	121	11	.328	.340

27 LOGAN DAVIDSON, SS/3B

Born: Dec. 26, 1997. **B-T:** B-R. **HT:** 6-3. **WT:** 210.
Drafted: Clemson, 2019 (1st round). **Signed by:** Neil Avent.

TRACK RECORD: Davidson's father, Mark, was a standout at Clemson before spending six years in the big leagues. Logan followed in his footsteps and was a solid all-around performer in the Atlantic Coast Conference despite skepticism around the strength of his hit tool. The A's drafted him 29th overall in 2019 and concerns about his hitting ability have persisted. Davidson repeated at Double-A Midland in 2022, hitting .252/.337/.406 with 14 homers and a 27.7% strikeout rate in his age-24 season. **SCOUTING REPORT:** While Davidson doubled his home run output in his second year at Midland, he was still a below-average performer at the plate. Davidson is a fairly selective hitter, but he swings through too many pitches at the bottom of the strike zone, especially breaking balls. The swing-and-miss keeps Davidson from consistently tapping into his above-average raw power potential. A switch-hitter, Davidson did make strides from the right side of the plate after struggling mightily in 2021. Defensively, Davidson can play anywhere in the dirt. He has solid hands and an accurate, above-average throwing arm at shortstop, although his range is likely best suited for third base. **THE FUTURE:** Davidson should reach the big leagues in some capacity on the strength of his approach, power potential and versatility, although his contact ability likely limits him to a bench role.

BA GRADE: 40/High		Hit: 40		Power: 55		Run: 50		Field: 55		Arm: 55	
Year	Age	Club (League)	Lvl	AVG	G	AB	R	H	2B	3B	HR	RBI	BB	SO	SB	OBP	SLG
2022	24	Midland (TL)	AA	.252	111	424	72	107	21	1	14	56	53	134	4	.337	.406
Minor League Totals				.233	284	1077	167	251	50	2	25	116	146	344	13	.326	.353

28 JUNIOR PEREZ, OF

Born: July 4, 2001. **B-T:** R-R. **HT:** 6-1. **WT:** 200.
Signed: Dominican Republic, 2017. **Signed by:** Felix Perez/Trevor Schumm (Padres).

TRACK RECORD: Perez broke out after hitting 11 homers for the Padres' Rookie-level Arizona League team in 2019. The A's acquired him as the player to be named later in a trade for Jorge Mateo, but strikeout issues plagued him in his first taste of full-season ball in 2021. He repeated Low-A Stockton and fared much better, hitting .249/.363/.425 with 15 homers. **SCOUTING REPORT:** Swing-and-miss will always be part of Perez's game, but he made enough improvements with his swing mechanics, pitch recognition and preparation to more consistently tap into his considerable raw power. Perez produces high-end exit velocity and has a decent understanding of the strike zone, leading to impressive walk rates. He improved at recognizing spin throughout the season. Still, Perez struck out 30.7% of the time against Low-A pitching and needs to work on getting his hands in better positions to hit more consistently, especially against velocity. Perez looked more explosive in 2022 and stole 32 bases. He can handle all three outfield positions, though he takes the best routes and looks most comfortable in right field. He has an above-average throwing arm.

THE FUTURE: Perez has an intriguing blend of power and patience, but he'll need to tighten his hit tool to keep moving up the ladder. He'll get a chance to prove his improvements will stick against High-A pitching in 2023.

BA GRADE: 40/High		Hit: 40		Power: 55		Run: 55		Field: 50		Arm: 55				
Year	Age	Club (League)	Lvl	AVG	G	AB	R	H	2B	3B	HR	RBI	BB	SO	SB	OBP	SLG
2022	20	Stockton (CAL)	LoA	.249	116	398	74	99	21	2	15	62	70	148	32	.363	.425
Minor League Totals				.227	323	1140	198	259	57	11	37	161	198	432	79	.346	.394

29 KYLE VIRBITSKY, RHP

Born: Oct. 8, 1998. **B-T:** R-R. **HT:** 6-7. **WT:** 230.
Drafted: Penn State, 2021 (17th round). **Signed by:** Matthew Higginson.
TRACK RECORD: Virbitsky was a steady yet unspectacular performer at Penn State, leading the Nittany Lions in strikeouts in 2021. The A's drafted him in the 17th round and signed him to a $50,000 bonus, deploying him in short bursts with High-A Lansing the rest of the year. They sent him to Low-A Stockton to open 2022 and develop his changeup as a starter. He pitched his way back to Lansing by the end of the season, leading all A's minor leaguers with 140 strikeouts.
SCOUTING REPORT: The 6-foot-7 Virbitsky repeats his delivery quite well despite his long levers, filling up the strike zone from an over-the-top arm slot. He works with a solid four-pitch mix. He's comfortable locating his low-90s four-seam fastball to all four quadrants of the strike zone. Virbitsky has two distinct breaking balls that both have average upside. His mid-80s slider is a vertical breaker while his upper-70s curve functions as more of a sweeper. Virbitsky's mid-80s changeup remains a work in progress. Virbitsky's height already creates uncomfortable at-bats for hitters, and he loves to disrupt timing with his delivery as well. The A's think he has a chance to add slightly more velocity as he gets stronger.
THE FUTURE: Virbitsky lacks an obvious plus offering, but his strike-throwing and polish provide a potential ceiling as a back-of-the-rotation arm, especially if his stuff ticks up.

BA GRADE: 40/High		Fastball: 50		Curveball: 50		Slider: 50		Changeup: 45		Control: 55						
Year	Age	Club (League)	Lvl	W	L	ERA	G	GS	IP	H	HR	BB	SO	BB/9	SO/9	WHIP	AVG
2022	23	Stockton (CAL)	LoA	5	4	4.78	16	15	87	101	9	20	99	2.1	10.3	1.40	.285
2022	23	Lansing (MWL)	HiA	2	3	4.31	7	7	40	35	9	10	41	2.3	9.3	1.13	.236
Minor League Totals				8	9	4.49	30	25	142	157	19	34	162	2.1	10.2	1.34	.277

30 COOPER BOWMAN, 2B

Born: Jan. 25, 2000. **B-T:** R-R. **HT:** 6-0. **WT:** 205.
Drafted: Louisville, 2021 (4th round) **Signed by:** Mike Gibbons (Yankees).
TRACK RECORD: Bowman transferred to Louisville prior to the 2021 season after two years in junior college and performed well, hitting .293 with eight homers and 20 steals. The Yankees drafted him in the fourth round and signed him to a $353,000 bonus. They traded him to Oakland a year later as part of the Frankie Montas deal. Bowman's contact skills have yet to translate fully to the pros and he hit .209 with a 29.5% strikeout rate in 33 games with High-A Lansing upon arrival.
SCOUTING REPORT: Bowman is a dynamic athlete with speed and strength. The Yankees tried to unlock more of his power potential, adding a leg kick and working with him to optimize his batted ball trajectory. Bowman's contact ability has suffered as a result and he's dealt with a bit of bad luck. Putting more balls in play will allow Bowman's plus speed to play more frequently. Bowman has sufficient range at second base, and evaluators have wondered whether he'll eventually try the outfield because of his speed.
THE FUTURE: Whether Bowman makes enough contact remains to be seen, but his supplemental skill set provides the ceiling of an intriguing utility type.

BA GRADE: 40/High .		Hit: 50		Power: 45		Run: 60		Field: 55		Arm: 50				
Year	Age	Club (League)	Lvl	AVG	G	AB	R	H	2B	3B	HR	RBI	BB	SO	SB	OBP	SLG
2022	22	Hudson Valley (SAL)	HiA	.217	80	299	54	65	15	1	8	35	55	97	35	.343	.355
2022	22	Lansing (MWL)	HiA	.209	33	115	12	24	2	0	3	12	9	38	12	.287	.304
Minor League Totals				.223	143	516	86	115	26	2	15	70	75	165	60	.334	.368

Philadelphia Phillies

BY CHRIS HILBURN-TRENKLE

Despite bringing in big-money free agent signings in Nick Castellanos (5 years, $100 million) and Kyle Schwarber (4 years, $79 million) to give them one of the most dangerous lineups in baseball, the Phillies struggled out of the gate in 2022 and looked to be in danger of missing the postseason for an 11th consecutive season.

But after starting the year 22-29, Philadelphia fired manager Joe Girardi and replaced him with bench coach Rob Thomson.

From there a switch was flipped. The Phillies finished the season with a 65-46 mark to narrowly grab the third and final National League wild card. They did so despite star right fielder Bryce Harper being relegated to DH duties after tearing the UCL in his right elbow and later missing time with a fractured thumb, and Castellanos putting up his worst offensive season since 2015.

Schwarber paced the lineup with an NL-leading 46 home runs, righthanders Zack Wheeler and Aaron Nola led the way at the top of the rotation, and the Phillies got some much-needed help from a pair of prospects in Bryson Stott, who became the team's everyday shortstop, and lefthander Bailey Falter, who provided valuable innings as a starter.

Once they got to the postseason, the Phillies made easy work of the Cardinals, sweeping them in the best-of-three Wild Card Series to set up a showdown with the Braves in the NL Division Series. After splitting the first two games in Atlanta, the Braves outscored the Braves 17-4 in Philadelphia to advance to the NL Championship Series.

Philadelphia dispatched the Padres in five games in the NLCS, with Harper taking home MVP honors, to advance to the World Series. The Phillies took a 2-1 series lead over the juggernaut Astros, but Houston's pitching staff prevailed by wearing down the Phillies' bats, and allowed just three runs over the final three games.

It was undoubtedly a successful season for the Phillies, and it also saw encouraging signs of optimism down on the farm. Andrew Painter, the 2021 first-round pick, emerged as one of the top pitching prospects in the game and was named BA's inaugural Minor League Pitcher of the Year. Fellow righthanders Mick Abel and Griff McGarry gave the organization three Top 100 Prospects, all of whom are on a similar timeline.

After missing on three consecutive first-round picks from 2015 to 2017—Cornelius Randolph, Mickey Moniak and Adam Haseley—the Phillies appear to have hit on their last four: Alec Bohm, Stott, Abel and Painter.

Bryson Stott took over as everyday shortstop in August for the pennant-winning Phillies.

PROJECTED 2026 LINEUP

Catcher	JT Realmuto	35
First Base	Rhys Hoskins	33
Second Base	Bryson Stott	28
Shortstop	Trea Turner	33
Third Base	Alec Bohm	29
Left Field	Justin Crawford	22
Center Field	Brandon Marsh	28
Right Field	Bryce Harper	33
Designated Hitter	Nick Castellanos	34
No. 1 Starter	Aaron Nola	33
No. 2 Starter	Andrew Painter	23
No. 3 Starter	Mick Abel	24
No. 4 Starter	Ranger Suarez	30
No. 5 Starter	Griff McGarry	27
Closer	Seranthony Dominguez	31

They added another intriguing talent in 2022 in Justin Crawford, the son of all-star Carl Crawford. Justin immediately became the top position prospect in the system and provides a blend of above-average hitting ability, speed and plus defense in center field. The team further reloaded in the draft with the additions of outfielder Gabriel Rincones and righthander Alex McFarlane, two prospects who rank among the top half in the system.

The Phillies' pitching development plan appears to be a success, but now the club will look to see the same growth among its hitting prospects, a group that is without Top 100 Prospect Logan O'Hoppe, who was traded to the Angels at the 2022 trade deadline.

But with a World Series appearance in 2022 and three exciting young arms at the top of the system, it's looking sunny in Philadelphia. ∎

DEPTH CHART

PHILADELPHIA PHILLIES

TOP 2023 MLB CONTRIBUTORS	RANK
Griff McGarry, RHP	3
Andrew Baker, RHP	12

BREAKOUT PROSPECTS	RANK
Alex McFarlane, RHP	11
Jordan Viars, OF	15
Christian McGowan, RHP	18

SOURCE OF TOP 30 TALENT

Homegrown	28	Acquired	2
College	7	Trades	2
Junior college	2	Rule 5 draft	0
High school	6	Independent leagues	0
Nondrafted free agents	2	Free agents/waivers	0
International	11		

LF
Jordan Viars (15)

CF
Justin Crawford (4)
Johan Rojas (5)
Simon Muzziotti (9)
Emaarion Boyd (24)
Yhoswar Garcia (25)

RF
Ethan Wilson (10)
Carlos De La Cruz (20)
Jhailyn Ortiz (22)

3B
Kendall Simmons

SS
William Bergolla Jr. (14)
Casey Martin
Erick Brito

2B
Hao Yu Lee (6)
Alexeis Azuaje
Nikau Pouaka-Grego

1B
Gabriel Rincones (8)

C
Rickardo Perez (17)
Donny Sands (23)
Rafael Marchan (27)
Caleb Ricketts

LHP

LHSP	LHRP
Jordi Martinez	Erubiel Armenta
Ethan Lindow	Tristan Garnett
Mavis Graves	Taylor Lehman
Matt Osterberg	Jared Wetherbee

RHP

RHSP	RHRP
Andrew Painter (1)	Andrew Baker (12)
Mick Abel (2)	Francisco Morales (13)
Griff McGarry (3)	Hans Crouse (16)
Alex McFarlane (11)	Orion Kerkering (26)
Christian McGowan (18)	Alex Rao (28)
Micah Ottenbreit (19)	Tommy McCollum (30)
Jaydenn Estanista (21)	McKinley Moore
Enrique Segura (29)	Cristian Hernandez
Noah Song	Estibenzon Jimenez

1 ANDREW PAINTER, RHP

Born: April 10, 2003. **B-T:** R-R. **HT:** 6-7. **WT:** 215.
Drafted: HS—Fort Lauderdale, Fla., 2021 (1st round).
Signed by: Victor Gomez.

TRACK RECORD: Painter was a unanimous choice for the 2021 Preseason High School All-America team, voted on by scouting directors. He continued to shine during his senior season at Calvary Christian Academy in Fort Lauderdale, Fla. and the Phillies drafted him 13th overall and signed him to an under-slot $3.9 million. Painter made four appearances in the Florida Complex League after signing, striking out 12 batters in six scoreless innings before finishing the season in instructional league. In 2022 he emerged as one of the top pitching prospects in the sport, rising three levels to Double-A Reading while showcasing a combination of mound maturity beyond his years and an explosive four-pitch arsenal filled with average to double-plus offerings. Painter didn't give up an earned run over his first 32 innings as a pro and finished 2022 with a 1.56 ERA and 155 strikeouts and 25 walks over 103.2 innings. He was named the inaugural BA Minor League Pitcher of the Year.

SCOUTING REPORT: The 6-foot-7, 215-pound righthander stands out for his imposing body on the mound and an electric arsenal that stacks up against any prospect in the minor leagues. Painter's fastball averages just over 96 mph and tops out at 101 with plus-plus induced vertical break and spin rates around 2,400 rpm, and he has excellent command of the pitch. His primary secondary offering is a low-80s slider that averages close to a foot of horizontal break and with spin rates that exceed 2,500 rpm. He rounds out his arsenal with a high-80s changeup and high-70s curveball. While those two pitches don't grade out as his fastball and slider, he showed more confidence throwing his changeup as he got further into the 2022 season, adding a different spin axis to the pitch to attack hitters on both sides of the plate. His changeup was his most devastating pitch, with a whiff rate over 55% and a chase rate over 38%. His curveball has a tendency to blend with his slider at times, but it still shows enough to profile as an average offering. While Painter's pitch mix is excellent, he also shows remarkable poise and maturity on the mound, especially for a 19-year-old. Despite his length he has a repeatable delivery with good body control, excellent hand feel out front and a strong ability to control the running game. He has plus-plus control and walked just two batters

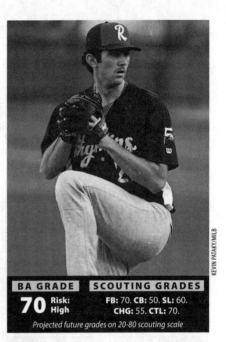

KEVIN PATAKY/MiLB

BA GRADE	SCOUTING GRADES
70 Risk: High	**FB:** 70. **CB:** 50. **SL:** 60. **CHG:** 55. **CTL:** 70.

Projected future grades on 20-80 scouting scale

BEST TOOLS

BATTING
Best Hitter for Average	Hao Yu Lee
Best Power Hitter	Baron Radcliff
Best Strike-Zone Discipline	Rafael Marchan
Fastest Baserunner	Yhoswar Garcia
Best Athlete	Yhoswar Garcia

PITCHING
Best Fastball	Griff McGarry
Best Curveball	Andrew Baker
Best Slider	Andrew Painter
Best Changeup	Griff McGarry
Best Control	Andrew Painter

FIELDING
Best Defensive Catcher	Rafael Marchan
Best Defensive Infielder	Erick Brito
Best Infield Arm	Kendall Simmons
Best Defensive Outfielder	Johan Rojas
Best Outfield Arm	Jhailyn Ortiz

in 28.1 Double-A innings. Painter has the traits to profile as a top-of-the-rotation starter in the major leagues.

THE FUTURE: Painter bulldozed through the Class A levels on his way to finishing the season with five starts at Double-A. He will start the 2023 season back at Reading, but he's on track to make his MLB debut at some point during the season. He could quickly make his presence felt near the top of the rotation.

Year	Age	Club (League)	Lvl	W	L	ERA	G	GS	IP	H	HR	BB	SO	BB/9	SO/9	WHIP	AVG
2022	19	Clearwater (FSL)	LoA	1	1	1.40	9	9	39	17	0	16	69	3.7	16.1	0.85	.130
2022	19	Jersey Shore (SAL)	HiA	3	0	0.98	8	8	37	25	2	7	49	1.7	12.0	0.87	.185
2022	19	Reading (EL)	AA	2	1	2.54	5	5	28	25	3	2	37	0.6	11.8	0.95	.238
Minor League Totals				6	2	1.48	26	26	110	71	6	25	167	2.1	13.7	0.88	.181

2 MICK ABEL, RHP

Born: August 18, 2001. **B-T:** R-R. **HT:** 6-5. **WT:** 190.
Drafted: HS—Portland, Ore., 2020 (1st round). **Signed By:** Zach Friedman.

TRACK RECORD: Abel was a decorated high school arm out of Oregon considered the top prep pitching prospect in the 2020 draft. He never got to pitch as a senior because the coronavirus pandemic canceled the season. The Phillies drafted Abel 15th overall in 2020 and signed him for an over-slot $4.08 million. He only pitched 44.2 innings in 2021 for Low-A Clearwater due to a shoulder injury that shelved him for two months. Abel impressed in 2022 at High-A Jersey Shore and Double-A Reading, posting 130 strikeouts in 108.1 innings as the organization gradually increased his workload over the season.

SCOUTING REPORT: The lanky 6-foot-5, 190-pound righthander has a powerful four-pitch mix, with a plus fastball that averages over 95 mph and tops out at 99. It's a swing-and-miss offering with huge vertical break and spin rates approaching 2,500 rpm. While Abel relied on his fastball over 60% of the time in 2022, his slider was his most-used secondary. It's a hard, mid-80s offering with late diving life that was his best pitch at getting hitters to chase. It induced whiffs over 33% of the time in 2022. Though Abel's slider projects as plus, he struggled to land it at times during the season. Abel focused on incorporating his changeup more in 2022. It's a high-80s offering that topped out around 90 mph with tumble and late fading life. The pitch flashes plus, but lacks consistency. His curveball, a low-80s offering, was a distant fourth pitch. Abel has trouble repeating his delivery at times because he struggles to sync his long levers, which led to command issues.

THE FUTURE: Abel will start 2023 back at Double-A Reading. He projects as a quality midrotation starter with a powerful arsenal who should make his MLB debut early in 2024.

BA GRADE
60 Risk: High

SCOUTING GRADES:	Fastball: 60	Curveball: 50	Slider: 60	Changeup: 55	Control: 50

Year	Age	Club (League)	Lvl	W	L	ERA	G	GS	IP	H	HR	BB	SO	BB/9	SO/9	WHIP	AVG
2022	20	Jersey Shore (SAL)	HiA	7	8	4.01	18	18	85	75	6	38	103	4.0	10.9	1.32	.230
2022	20	Reading (EL)	AA	1	3	3.52	5	5	23	19	5	12	27	4.7	10.6	1.35	.224
Minor League Totals				9	14	4.06	37	37	153	121	16	77	196	4.5	11.5	1.29	.214

3 GRIFF MCGARRY, RHP

Born: June 8, 1999. **B-T:** R-R. **HT:** 6-2. **WT:** 190.
Drafted: Virginia, 2021 (5th round). **Signed by:** Kellan McKeon.

TRACK RECORD: McGarry has always featured electric stuff, dating back to his collegiate days. But he struggled mightily to throw strikes at Virginia. The Phillies took a chance on his upside in the fifth round in 2021, and he immediately impressed in his debut following the draft, striking out 43 batters in 24.1 innings between Low-A Clearwater and High-A Jersey Shore. McGarry spent the 2022 season as a starter between High-A and Double-A Reading before he was pushed to the bullpen in late August due to a blister issue. He finished the season with seven appearances at Triple-A Lehigh Valley.

SCOUTING GRADES: McGarry's arsenal stacks up well against any pitcher in pro baseball. His plus-plus four-seamer averages over 95 mph and tops out at

BA GRADE
55 Risk: Very High

99 from a low slot with a flat vertical approach angle and plus spin. He added a cutter to his arsenal this season. It's a mid-80s offering that tops out at 89 mph with elite spin rates that had a 49% whiff rate and a chase rate over 34%. His slider is a swing-and-miss pitch with two-plane break and plus spin that sits in the mid 80s. He rounds out his arsenal with a low-80s curveball and high-80s changeup. The organization worked on making McGarry more direct toward home plate to improve his control and repeat his delivery, but there are still timing issues in his delivery that cause strike-throwing problems.

THE FUTURE: McGarry's stuff fits at the top of a rotation, but his struggles with strike throwing and execution could limit him to a back-end starter or lockdown closer role. The Phillies are confident in his ability to start.

SCOUTING GRADES:	Fastball: 70	Curveball: 50	Cutter: 60	Slider: 60	Changeup: 55	Control: 40

Year	Age	Club (League)	Lvl	W	L	ERA	G	GS	IP	H	HR	BB	SO	BB/9	SO/9	WHIP	AVG
2022	23	Jersey Shore (SAL)	HiA	3	3	3.86	12	12	47	33	6	24	82	4.6	15.8	1.22	.199
2022	23	Reading (EL)	AA	1	3	2.20	8	7	33	13	1	20	39	5.5	10.7	1.01	.123
2022	23	Lehigh Valley (IL)	AAA	0	2	9.00	7	0	8	7	2	9	9	10.1	10.1	2.00	.250
Minor League Totals				5	8	3.55	35	23	112	66	9	67	173	5.4	13.9	1.19	.171

4 JUSTIN CRAWFORD, OF

Born: January 13, 2004. **B-T:** L-R. **HT:** 6-3. **WT:** 175.
Drafted: HS—Las Vegas, 2022 (1st round). **Signed by:** Zach Friedman.

TRACK RECORD: The son of Carl Crawford, Justin was one of the best athletes in the 2022 draft. He impressed over the 2021 summer showcase circuit and had an excellent senior season at Las Vegas' Bishop Gorman High. The Phillies drafted him 17th overall and signed him for an over-slot $3.89 million. Crawford started his pro career in the Florida Complex League before finishing the season with a five-game stint at Low-A Clearwater.

SCOUTING REPORT: Crawford has a long and lanky, 6-foot-3, 175-pound frame with room to add strength. He began putting on muscle during the fall of his senior year, and it was a continued area of emphasis for him during 2022 instructional league. He has a contact-oriented offensive approach with

BA GRADE
55 Risk: Extreme

good bat-to-ball skills, and does a lot of his damage on the ground and to the gaps, with a swing that can get lengthy at times. He has plus-plus speed underway that should allow him to turn singles into doubles and doubles into triples. He shows occasional power, but he struggles at times to get his barrel out and use leverage in his swing. He has solid raw power with the potential to reach solid-average power with the necessary tweaks and strength gains. Crawford's 70-grade speed allows him to cover a lot of ground in center field, and he's a plus defender there with an average arm.

THE FUTURE: Crawford is still raw and is years away from the big leagues, but his exciting blend of tools profiles well as a top-of-the-order bat who provides plus defense in center field. After getting his first taste of full-season ball in 2022, he'll head back to Low-A Clearwater in 2023.

SCOUTING GRADES	Hitting: 55	Power: 40	Speed: 70	Fielding: 60	Arm: 50

Year	Age	Club (League)	Lvl	AVG	G	AB	R	H	2B	3B	HR	RBI	BB	SO	SB	OBP	SLG
2022	18	Phillies (FCL)	R	.297	11	37	6	11	0	1	0	5	5	6	8	.395	.351
2022	18	Clearwater (FSL)	LoA	.143	5	21	2	3	0	0	0	0	2	9	2	.217	.143
Minor League Totals				.241	16	58	8	14	0	1	0	5	7	15	10	.333	.276

5 JOHAN ROJAS, OF

Born: August 14, 2000. **B-T:** R-R. **HT:** 6-0. **WT:** 175.
Signed: Dominican Republic, 2018. **Signed by:** Carlos Salas

TRACK RECORD: After scuffling for much of the 2021 season, Rojas ended the season on a tear at High-A Jersey Shore, posting his highest OPS in the month of September. The same held true in 2022, when Rojas scuffled for the first two months of the season but seemed to reach another gear once he was promoted to Double-A Reading. In his final 25 games in the Eastern League, he hit .305/.389/.463 with 12 stolen bases, 11 walks and 19 strikeouts. He headed to the Arizona Fall League after the season.

SCOUTING GRADES: Rojas stands out for his plus-plus speed and plus defense in center field to go with an above-average arm. Most of the questions surrounding Rojas involve his bat and the amount of impact he'll make. With an 87 mph average exit velocity and 103 mph 90th percentile exit velocity in

BA GRADE
50 Risk: High

2022, Rojas projects to get to average power, but he'll do his biggest damage in finding the gaps in the outfield that will allow his speed to play on the basepaths. He worked in 2021 on cutting down his groundball rate and improving his recognition against offspeed pitches, and that continued to be an area of emphasis for him in 2022. He has a tendency to pull the ball, but he showed improvement with his chase rate and managed to do a better job of lifting the ball in the air as the season progressed. Rojas has good bat speed and good bat-to-ball skills, but still struggles to understand what pitches to do damage on and needs to improve his plate decisions and bat path.

THE FUTURE: Rojas should start the 2022 season back at Double-A Reading. He has a chance to be a bottom-of-the-order table setter who provides plus defense in center field.

SCOUTING GRADES	Hitting: 45	Power: 50	Speed: 70	Fielding: 65	Arm: 55

Year	Age	Club (League)	Lvl	AVG	G	AB	R	H	2B	3B	HR	RBI	BB	SO	SB	OBP	SLG
2022	21	Jersey Shore (SAL)	HiA	.230	70	265	40	61	12	2	3	22	21	55	33	.287	.325
2022	21	Reading (EL)	AA	.260	60	235	42	61	8	5	4	16	21	44	29	.333	.387
Minor League Totals				.267	354	1378	223	368	61	26	22	136	107	254	129	.328	.397

6 HAO YU LEE, SS/2B

Born: February 3, 2003. **B-T:** R-R. **HT:** 5-10. **WT:** 190.
Signed: Taiwan, 2021. **Signed by:** Youngster Wang.

TRACK RECORD: Lee signed out of Taiwan for $500,000 in June 2021 and immediately made his pro debut in the Florida Complex League that summer. He impressed team officials with his play in instructional league and became one of the organization's most highly regarded position prospects in 2022 in his full-season debut. Lee, who missed two months with a broken hand, spent the majority of his season at Low-A Clearwater before ending the season with a nine-game stint at High-A Jersey Shore.

SCOUTING REPORT: Lee has a hit-first approach at the plate, and shows above-average barrel awareness and impressive bat-to-ball skills. He uses a quick, simple, line-drive swing to all fields with good extension, and he has surprising pop. Lee recognizes breaking balls and hits well even when off time, but he still needs to develop quicker bat speed to access more power. He has below-average power now, but Lee still has room to add some strength to his frame. The Phillies tested Lee at shortstop, third base and second base in 2022, but his future home is likely at second. He's a good athlete with average speed and showed solid actions on the infield with a below-average arm, but improving his defense will be a continued area of focus for Lee.

THE FUTURE: Lee has the above-average hit tool and instincts at the plate to profile as a bat-first second baseman, but he'll need to add a tick more power. He'll head back to High-A Jersey Shore in 2023 and could make his upper-minors debut later in the summer.

BA GRADE
50 Risk: High

SCOUTING GRADES		Hitting: 60		Power: 40		Speed: 50		Fielding: 45		Arm: 40						
Year	Age	Club (League)	Lvl	AVG	G	AB	R	H	2B	3B	HR	RBI	BB	SO	SB	OBP	SLG
2022	19	Phillies (FCL)	R	.500	2	6	4	3	1	0	1	1	2	1	1	.625	1.167
2022	19	Clearwater (FSL)	LoA	.283	68	258	37	73	11	1	7	50	36	57	10	.384	.415
2022	19	Jersey Shore (SAL)	HiA	.257	9	35	5	9	3	1	1	2	5	9	3	.350	.486
Minor League Totals				.290	88	321	55	93	17	4	10	58	46	72	14	.389	.461

7 ERIK MILLER, LHP

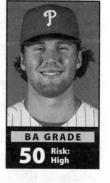

Born: February 13, 1998. **B-T:** L-L. **HT:** 6-5. **WT:** 240.
Drafted: Stanford, 2019 (4th round). **Signed by:** Joey Davis.

TRACK RECORD: The 2019 fourth-rounder from Stanford had just 36 professional innings under his belt before the coronavirus pandemic canceled the 2020 minor league season. He impressed that fall in instructional league, then missed most of 2021 with an injury. After splitting time between the rotation and bullpen to start 2022, Miller moved to the bullpen full time in June. He put up a 2.23 ERA with Double-A Reading, then struggled in 10 appearances with Triple-A Lehigh Valley to end the season.

SCOUTING REPORT: The imposing 6-foot-5, 240-pound Miller has swing-and-miss stuff from the left side, but he's had trouble accessing it due to command issues that have plagued him throughout his career. Miller has a herky-jerky, deceptive delivery without a clean arm action, and he struggles to repeat his delivery consistently—which leads to injury concerns—but there's no questioning the quality of his pitch mix. He aggressively attacks hitters with his above-average four-seamer, which averages 94 mph and tops out above 98, and the pitch features big running life and carry up in the zone. He throws a hard, high-80s slider that reaches the low 90s with three-quarters tilt and cross-breaking action. The pitch earns plus grades. Miller's changeup is his best swing-and-miss offering. It's a mid-80s pitch that induced whiffs more than 58% of the time in 2022. The organization has worked with Miller to have a more consistent delivery, but with his below-average command and control, he's likely destined for a bullpen role.

THE FUTURE: Miller should begin the season back at Triple-A, but could earn a callup to the big leagues by midseason. His powerful pitch mix could fit at the back of the bullpen, with the team considering the possibility of deploying him as an opener as well.

BA GRADE
50 Risk: High

SCOUTING GRADES:		Fastball: 55		Slider: 60			Changeup: 60		Control: 40					
Year	Age	Club (League)	Lvl	W	L	ERA	G	GS	IP	H	HR	BB	SO	BB/9	SO/9	WHIP	AVG
2022	24	Reading (EL)	AA	1	0	2.23	22	7	36	25	0	17	44	4.2	10.9	1.16	.198
2022	24	Lehigh Valley (IL)	AAA	0	1	7.50	10	0	12	14	4	14	18	10.5	13.5	2.33	.280
Minor League Totals				2	1	2.51	48	19	97	72	4	57	130	5.3	12.1	1.33	.203

8 GABRIEL RINCONES, OF

Born: March 3, 2001. **B-T:** L-R. **HT:** 6-4. **WT:** 225.
Drafted: Florida Atlantic, 2022 (3rd round). **Signed by:** Victor Gomez

TRACK RECORD: Rincones turned in a stellar season at St. Petersburg (Fla.) JC in 2021 and was drafted by the Padres in the 19th round that year. Instead of signing, he headed to Florida Atlantic in 2022 and hit .346/.451/.658 with 19 home runs in 58 games. The Phillies drafted him in the third round in 2022 and signed him to an under-slot $627,500 bonus. Rincones didn't make his official pro debut because of a minor shoulder injury, but he returned to the field during instructional league and showed well there.

BA GRADE

45 Risk: High

SCOUTING REPORT: Rincones showcased some of the best power of any college player during the 2022 season, ranking among the leaders in average exit velocity and 90th percentile exit velocity. At 6-foot-4, 225 pounds, Rincones has plus to plus-plus raw power from the left side that plays as a plus tool in games. He showed the ability to hit 93-plus mph velocity and power to all fields. Rincones is a below-average hitter. He does a good job of controlling the zone, but he struggles against secondaries and can sell out at times to access his power. Though he played right field at Florida Atlantic and was drafted as an outfielder, he is likely bound for first base. He spent his time in instructional league working on his defense, footwork and route-running in the outfield, but he's a below-average defender with a below-average arm. Rincones will need to hit, but he immediately has one of the best combinations of hit tools and power in the system.

THE FUTURE: Rincones should make his pro debut at High-A Jersey Shore in 2023. His 60-grade power should allow him to profile as a first baseman.

SCOUTING GRADES	Hitting: 40	Power: 60	Speed: 30	Fielding: 40	Arm: 40

Year	Age	Club (League)	Level	AVG	G	AB	R	H	2B	3B	HR	RBI	BB	SO	SB	OBP	SLG
2022	21	Did not play—Injured															

9 SIMON MUZZIOTTI, OF

Born: December 27, 1998. **B-T:** L-L. **HT:** 6-1. **WT:** 198.
Signed: Venezuela, 2016. **Signed by:** Claudio Scerrato.

TRACK RECORD: Muzziotti's tool set is impressive, but he's had trouble staying on the field for a variety of reasons. He had an encouraging performance at 2020 instructional league but then missed the majority of 2021 due to a visa issue that kept him in Venezuela. He made his MLB debut in April 2022 before heading to the injured list with a hamstring injury. After returning from injury, Muzziotti spent time with Double-A Reading and Triple-A Lehigh Valley before landing on the injured list again in late August with a partial tear of the patellar tendon in his right knee.

BA GRADE

45 Risk: High

SCOUTING REPORT: Power was never a big part of Muzziotti's game, but he turned in encouraging numbers in 2022, with an 89.2 mph average exit velocity. It didn't translate to home runs, but he's shown gap-to-gap power with some pull-side juice. He has some looseness to his bat, with good bat-to-ball skills, a line-drive stroke and the ability to hit the ball to all fields. Muzziotti has worked on his approach and expanding his strike zone early in counts, but he still needs improvement in those areas, as well as lowering his chase rate and learning to hit the ball in the air more frequently. Muzziotti is a plus defender in center field, with above-average speed, good instincts, strong route-running ability and an average arm.

THE FUTURE: It will be crucial for Muzziotti's development that he stays on the field for the majority of the 2023 season. He'll likely start the year back at Triple-A Lehigh Valley, with the potential to join the MLB team later in the summer. With improvements to his approach at the plate he could turn into a bottom-of-the-order table-setter who provides good baserunning and plus defense in the outfield.

SCOUTING GRADES	Hitting: 50	Power: 40	Speed: 55	Fielding: 60	Arm: 50

Year	Age	Club (League)	Lvl	AVG	G	AB	R	H	2B	3B	HR	RBI	BB	SO	SB	OBP	SLG
2022	23	Phillies (FCL)	R	.000	1	2	0	0	0	0	0	0	0	0	0	.000	.000
2022	23	Clearwater (FSL)	LoA	.000	2	8	0	0	0	0	0	0	1	4	0	.111	.000
2022	23	Reading (EL)	AA	.259	38	143	23	37	5	4	5	20	19	31	7	.339	.455
2022	23	Lehigh Valley (IL)	AAA	.313	5	16	2	5	0	0	0	0	2	3	1	.389	.313
2022	23	Philadelphia (NL)	MLB	.143	9	7	0	1	0	0	0	0	0	2	0	.250	.143
Major League Totals				.143	9	7	0	1	0	0	0	0	0	2	0	.250	.143
Minor League Totals				.267	339	1309	164	350	52	18	9	118	101	176	67	.319	.355

10 ETHAN WILSON, OF

Born: November 7, 1999. **B-T:** L-L. **HT:** 6-1. **WT:** 210.
Drafted: South Alabama, 2021 (2nd round). **Signed By:** Mike Stauffer.

BA GRADE
45 Risk: High

TRACK RECORD: Wilson had an impressive collegiate career at South Alabama, earning freshman All-America honors in 2019 and posting a .947 OPS in 2021. He was considered one of the top collegiate hitters in 2021, and the Phillies nabbed him in the second round with the 49th overall pick. He struggled in his pro debut with Low-A Clearwater following the draft and turned in a disappointing 2022 season between High-A Jersey Shore and Double-A Reading, posting a .626 OPS.

SCOUTING REPORT: Wilson was drafted as a bat-first outfielder with a strong ability to control the zone and an above-average hit tool, but his tools took a step back during his first full season. He was plagued by poor swing decisions and chased too much to go with a high groundball rate. The organization worked with him to understand the zone better, find the right pitches to swing at and drive the ball more, and those are areas he'll need to continue to work on in 2023. Wilson has good bat-to-ball skills, but his tendency to swing at bad pitches causes him to make weak contact. He has plus raw power, with impressive max exit velocities, but struggles to access it due to his flat bat path and compact swing, leading to an average exit velocity near 86 mph. If Wilson is able to get better timing at the plate and more load in his setup, it should lead to better power production. Wilson is a solid athlete and an average runner underway, and his strong baserunning skills led to 26 stolen bases in 2022. He's an average defender in right field with an average arm.

THE FUTURE: The 2023 season could very well be a make-or-break year for Wilson. If he's able to make adjustments to his approach and bat path to access his power, he profiles as a second-division regular. He'll likely start the season back at Double-A Reading.

SCOUTING GRADES		Hitting: 45		Power: 55		Speed: 50		Fielding: 50		Arm: 50		

Year	Age	Club (League)	Lvl	AVG	G	AB	R	H	2B	3B	HR	RBI	BB	SO	SB	OBP	SLG
2022	22	Jersey Shore (SAL)	HiA	.238	112	424	39	101	20	2	7	45	28	93	25	.290	.344
2022	22	Reading (EL)	AA	.214	18	70	7	15	2	0	1	3	5	21	1	.286	.286
Minor League Totals				.231	160	601	61	139	26	4	11	65	43	139	28	.288	.343

11 ALEX McFARLANE, RHP

Born: June 9, 2001. **B-T:** R-R. **HT:** 6-4. **WT:** 205.
Drafted: Miami, 2022 (4th round). **Signed by:** Victor Gomez.

TRACK RECORD: McFarlane was mainly used as a reliever in his first two seasons at Miami, but the Hurricanes moved him to the rotation in 2022. The move proved to be short lived, as McFarlane made just four starts, with 23 appearances coming out of the bullpen. The Phillies believed in his ability to start, and drafted him in the fourth round. He made three starts with Low-A Clearwater after signing.

SCOUTING REPORT: McFarlane has an electric, three-pitch mix, with a high-spin fastball that averaged 96 mph and topped out at 97.7 mph in his pro debut. The organization is having McFarlane work on the pitch's shape and efficiency, as it doesn't have much movement. Although his command of the pitch can waver, it still projects as an above-average offering. He has no trouble commanding his secondaries—a pair of above-average or better pitches led by his plus slider. The pitch averages over 2,700 rpm of spin, and projects as a legitimate swing-and-miss offering. It sat at 84.7 mph in his pro debut and produced a whiff rate greater than 44%. His mid-80s split-changeup gives him another bat-missing weapon with fading life, but he didn't use it in his brief debut. McFarlane has below-average control, and will need to throw more strikes to profile as a starter.

THE FUTURE: McFarlane should start the 2023 season at High-A Jersey Shore. With his explosive arsenal he has the ceiling of a mid-rotation starter, but he'll need to become a more consistent strike-thrower.

BA GRADE: 45/High		Fastball: 55		Slider: 60		Changeup: 55		Control: 40			

Year	Age	Club (League)	Lvl	W	L	ERA	G	GS	IP	H	HR	BB	SO	BB/9	SO/9	WHIP	AVG
2022	21	Clearwater (FSL)	LoA	0	3	9.00	3	3	8	12	1	3	12	3.4	13.5	1.88	.364
Minor League Totals				0	3	9.00	3	3	8	12	1	3	12	3.4	13.5	1.88	.364

12 ANDREW BAKER, RHP

Born: March 24, 2000. **B-T:** R-R. **HT:** 6-3. **WT:** 190.
Drafted: Chipola (Fla.) JC, 2021 (11th round). **Signed by:** Mike Stauffer

TRACK RECORD: Baker was a catcher in high school who converted to pitching as a freshman at Chipola (Fla.) JC, and after striking out 92 batters in 57.1 innings in 2021 the Phillies drafted him in the 11th round. He struggled in a 2021 pro debut mostly spent at Low-A Clearwater, but showed an electric arsenal at High-A Jersey Shore in 2022 en route to receiving a promotion to Double-A Reading, where he closed the season with six appearances.

SCOUTING REPORT: Baker has a dominant two-pitch mix, and after maxing out at around 96 mph in 2021, he now averages 98 mph on his fastball and tops out at 101 mph, with above-average spin. Although his fastball is an impressive offering, his curveball is his best pitch, and generated whiffs over 62% of the time during the 2022 season. It's a true swing-and-miss offering that sat just under 84 mph and topped out at 87.4 mph, with heavy, two-plane break. He struggled to command both pitches to begin the 2022 season, but members of the organization felt he improved his command, as well as his strike-throwing and mound presence, as the year progressed.

THE FUTURE: Some opposing evaluators are skeptical of Baker's ability to throw enough strikes long term to be anything more than an up/down emergency reliever, but he made improvements this season and has the stuff to profile as a lockdown closer. He'll likely begin the 2023 season back at Double-A Reading.

| BA GRADE: 45/High | | Fastball: 65 | | Curveball: 70 | | Control: 30 | | | | | | | | |

Year	Age	Club (League)	Lvl	W	L	ERA	G	GS	IP	H	HR	BB	SO	BB/9	SO/9	WHIP	AVG
2022	22	Jersey Shore (SAL)	HiA	3	1	4.74	40	0	44	41	5	24	61	4.9	12.6	1.49	.237
2022	22	Reading (EL)	AA	1	0	0.84	6	0	11	3	0	5	11	4.2	9.3	0.75	.094
Minor League Totals				5	3	5.02	55	1	66	49	6	46	92	6.2	12.5	1.43	.199

13 FRANCISCO MORALES, RHP

Born: Oct. 27, 1999. **B-T:** R-R. **HT:** 6-5. **WT:** 260.
Signed: Venezuela, 2016. **Signed by:** Jesus Mendez.

TRACK RECORD: Morales entered the 2021 season as the Phillies No. 4 prospect but struggled mightily in his first stint in the upper minors, posting a 6.94 ERA in 22 appearances (20 starts) at Double-A Reading. He moved to the bullpen full-time in 2022 and dominated Reading over the first month before receiving his first promotion to the big leagues. After making two appearances in the big leagues, Morales spent the rest of the season mostly split between Reading and Triple-A Lehigh Valley, where he showcased swing-and-miss stuff but lacked consistency.

SCOUTING REPORT: Morales has long struggled to throw consistent strikes, as was the case once again in 2022. The 6-foot-5 righthander had a tendency to get behind in the count, which made it more difficult for him to use his wipeout offering, a hard mid-80s slider that induced whiffs over 57% of the time in 2022. Morales pairs the plus offering with a fastball that averaged 94.9 mph and topped out at 98.7 mph in 2022. Morales struggles to command the pitch well, often throwing it over the middle of the plate. He ditched his below-average changeup after moving to the bullpen, relying entirely on his fastball and slider. His pitches play up thanks to the deception generated from his crossfire delivery, but he needs to establish a consistent release point to throw more strikes moving forward.

THE FUTURE: Morales will likely start the 2023 season back at Lehigh Valley, but could quickly join the Phillies bullpen as a high-leverage weapon to complement Seranthony Dominguez.

| BA GRADE: 45/High | | Fastball: 55 | | Slider: 60 | | Control: 40 | | | | | | | | |

Year	Age	Club (League)	Lvl	W	L	ERA	G	GS	IP	H	HR	BB	SO	BB/9	SO/9	WHIP	AVG
2022	22	Reading (EL)	AA	2	0	1.48	23	0	30	9	0	17	54	5.0	16.0	0.86	.092
2022	22	Lehigh Valley (IL)	AAA	3	3	9.58	22	0	21	24	1	28	16	12.2	7.0	2.52	.289
2022	22	Philadelphia (NL)	MLB	0	0	7.20	3	0	5	2	1	6	3	10.8	5.4	1.60	.143
Major League Totals				0	0	7.20	3	0	5	2	1	6	3	10.8	5.4	1.60	.143
Minor League Totals				17	32	4.78	119	59	337	285	27	211	428	5.6	11.4	1.47	.225

14 WILLIAM BERGOLLA JR., SS

Born: October 20, 2004. **B-T:** L-R. **HT:** 5-10. **WT:** 155.
Signed: Venezuela, 2022. **Signed by:** Rafael Alvarez/William Mota.

TRACK RECORD: Bergolla Jr. was one of the top international signings in the 2021-2022 class. He received a $2.05 million signing bonus, and started his minor league career in the Dominican Summer League, where he posted a .380/.470/.423 slash line and walked more times (11) than he struck out (three).

SCOUTING REPORT: Bergolla stands out for his above-average hitting ability and smooth defense at shortstop, where he has the instincts and speed to stick long term. Bergolla has a compact, quick swing with strong bat-to-ball skills and the ability to hit to all fields. He does a good job recognizing pitches and makes a high rate of contact, with good bat control. At 5-foot-10, 155 pounds, he doesn't hit for much power—just 5% of his balls in play were hit 95 mph or higher—but he should add more strength in the future and get to near below-average power. It's likely going to be more gap-to-gap power than over-the-fence juice in the future, and Bergolla has the skill set that fits as a table setter at the top or bottom of the lineup. He's an effective basestealer with plus speed and good baserunning skills, which led to eight stolen bases in nine tries in his debut. The organization was pleased with his work at shortstop in 2022, citing his impressive actions, and he profiles as an above-average defender with an above-average arm.
THE FUTURE: Bergolla should make his stateside debut in the Florida Complex League in 2023. He's years away from making an impact in the big leagues, but he profiles as a high-contact table setter who provides above-average defense at shortstop.

| BA GRADE: 50/Extreme | | Hitting: 55 | | Power: 35 | | Speed: 60 | | Fielding: 55 | | Arm: 55 | |

Year	Age	Club (League)	Lvl	AVG	G	AB	R	H	2B	3B	HR	RBI	BB	SO	SB	OBP	SLG
2022	17	Phillies White (DSL)	R	.380	24	71	18	27	3	0	0	14	11	3	2	.470	.423
Minor League Totals				.380	24	71	18	27	3	0	0	14	11	3	2	.470	.423

15 JORDAN VIARS, OF

Born: July 18, 2003. **B-T:** L-L. **HT:** 6-4. **WT:** 215.
Drafted: HS—Frisco, Texas, 2021 (3rd round). **Signed by:** Tommy Field.
TRACK RECORD: Viars was an under-the-radar talent coming into the 2021 draft, but the Phillies were intrigued with his offensive upside and signed him to an over-slot $747,500 bonus in the third round. Viars missed time during the 2022 season after fracturing his wrist and later spraining his ankle, and he accumulated just eight games at the full-season level with Low-A Clearwater.
SCOUTING REPORT: Viars has an advanced approach at the plate with solid bat speed. He sees the ball well and doing a good job of putting balls in play, but he struggles against spin and some opposing scouts were concerned with the quality of his at-bats. At 6-foot-4, 215 pounds, Viars has the potential to be an average to above-average power hitter, and he's put on impressive displays in batting practice, but he struggled to make consistent hard contact in 2022, with an average exit velocity under 86 mph. He has some length in his swing, and he needs to do a better job of working longer counts and finding the right pitches to hit—aspects that should improve with more at-bats. Viars is a good athlete with solid speed now, although he's likely to slow down as he puts on muscle. He's raw defensively, and there's a split camp as to whether he will be more than a below-average defender in an outfield corner.
THE FUTURE: After missing the majority of the season due to injuries, Viars will look to get a full season under his belt at the Class A levels in 2023. He shows potential as a bat-first, power-hitting corner outfielder.

| BA GRADE: 50/Extreme | | Hitting: 45 | | Power: 55 | | Speed: 40 | | Fielding: 40 | | Arm: 45 | |

Year	Age	Club (League)	Lvl	AVG	G	AB	R	H	2B	3B	HR	RBI	BB	SO	SB	OBP	SLG
2022	18	Phillies (FCL)	R	.240	44	154	28	37	6	1	2	20	17	40	5	.330	.331
2022	18	Clearwater (FSL)	LoA	.208	8	24	2	5	0	0	0	3	2	9	0	.286	.208
Minor League Totals				.240	74	225	43	54	7	1	5	41	30	61	7	.343	.347

16 HANS CROUSE, RHP

Born: Sept. 15, 1998. **B-T:** R-R. **HT:** 6-5. **WT:** 208.
Drafted: HS—Dana Point, Calif., 2017 (2nd round). **Signed by:** Steve Flores (Rangers).
TRACK RECORD: Crouse has struggled with injuries since being selected by the Rangers in the second round in 2017, but he posted a 5-4, 3.28 record with 98 strikeouts in 85 innings in 2021 and was acquired by the Phillies as part of the trade that netted the club righthanders Kyle Gibson and Ian Kennedy at the 2021 trade deadline. Crouse, who made his MLB debut in September of 2021, missed the majority of the 2022 season with tendinitis in his right biceps and made just five starts for Triple-A Lehigh Valley.
SCOUTING REPORT: Crouse has flashed a pair of plus pitches in the past, but his fastball velocity regressed in 2021, topping out around 94 mph after previously sitting in the mid 90s and touching 97 mph. The pitch has quality sinking action, but averaged just 91.5 mph in 2022 in five starts, and with the velocity regression profiles more as an average pitch. Crouse's hard upper-80s slider with late diving action is his best swing-and-miss offering, and gives him a plus pitch. He developed a changeup during the 2019 season, and it's a potentially above-average weapon. Crouse is a solid strike-thrower with average control, but his violent delivery has led to significant injury concerns. With only 259.2 innings logged in five minor

league seasons, it seems increasingly likely that Crouse is best suited for the bullpen.

THE FUTURE: Crouse should be ready to help the Phillies bullpen early in the 2023 season, and he could be used in a piggyback relief role.

BA GRADE: 45/High		Fastball: 50		Slider: 60		Changeup: 55		Control: 50		

Year	Age	Club (League)	Lvl	W	L	ERA	G	GS	IP	H	HR	BB	SO	BB/9	SO/9	WHIP	AVG
2022	23	Lehigh Valley (IL)	AAA	0	3	13.14	5	5	12	21	2	6	13	4.4	9.5	2.19	.375
Major League Totals				0	2	5.14	2	2	7	4	2	7	2	9.0	2.6	1.57	.167
Minor League Totals				16	11	3.74	67	63	260	213	27	85	279	2.9	9.7	1.15	.222

17 RICKARDO PEREZ, C

Born: Dec. 4, 2003. **B-T:** L-R. **HT:** 5-10. **WT:** 172.

Signed: Venezuela, 2021. **Signed by:** Ebert Velasquez.

TRACK RECORD: Perez was the centerpiece of the Phillies 2020-2021 international signing class and agreed to a $1.2 million deal. He posted solid numbers as a 17-year-old in the Dominican Summer League in 2021, then had an impressive stateside debut in the Florida Complex League in 2022, where he slashed .349/.387/.398 in 30 games, despite missing time with a knee injury suffered in April.

SCOUTING REPORT: Perez is a bat-first catcher with a smooth swing from the left side, with quick bat speed, feel for the barrel and good bat-to-ball skills. He has an aggressive approach at the plate, with a high chase rate and well below-average power currently. The Phillies believe he will add more power as he matures, thanks in part to his bat control, but some opposing scouts are skeptical that he will ever hit for much impact. He struggled to make hard contact and had an 83.8 mph average exit velocity in 2022. Perez has solid catch-and-throw skills and an average arm, but he isn't a standout athlete, with bottom-of-the-scale speed, and will need to improve his conditioning to prevent injuries moving forward.

THE FUTURE: With power gains Perez could profile as a second-division regular, although some opposing scouts feel he's more likely to be an emergency up/down catcher. He will make his full-season debut at Low-A Clearwater in 2023 as a 19-year-old.

BA GRADE: 45/Extreme		Hitting: 50		Power: 30		Speed: 20		Fielding: 45		Arm: 50	

Year	Age	Club (League)	Lvl	AVG	G	AB	R	H	2B	3B	HR	RBI	BB	SO	SB	OBP	SLG
2022	18	Phillies (FCL)	R	.349	30	83	5	29	1	0	1	14	7	13	0	.387	.398
Minor League Totals				.294	73	204	20	60	4	0	1	23	29	28	3	.377	.328

18 CHRISTIAN MCGOWAN, RHP

Born: March 7, 2000. **B-T:** R-R. **HT:** 6-3. **WT:** 205.

Drafted: Eastern Oklahoma State JC, 2021 (7th round). **Signed by:** Tommy Field

TRACK RECORD: McGowan had an impressive 2021 season at Eastern Oklahoma JC, where he struck out 109 batters in 74 innings, and the Phillies selected him in the seventh round and gave him an over-slot $577,000 bonus. He pitched just five innings in his pro debut in 2021 due to minor injuries, and only made two starts in 2022 for High-A Jersey Shore—after an impressive showing in spring training—before having Tommy John surgery.

SCOUTING REPORT: McGowan has an effective three-pitch mix, with a four-seam fastball with sinking action that sat 94-97 mph during 2021 instructs and averaged 93.3 mph in his two starts in 2022. The pitch projects as above-average thanks to its hard movement in the zone, and should be a weapon that gives hitters headaches. He pairs it with a hard, mid-80s slider with above-average spin that induced whiffs at a 42.9% rate in his two starts and projects as an above-average or better offering. He didn't use his changeup in his two starts in 2022, but in the past it was a weapon for attacking lefties in the upper 80s with good deception that flashed above-average. McGowan has a repeatable delivery with three intriguing pitches, but his strike-throwing issues in the past likely make him a better option out of the bullpen, where his mix should play up.

THE FUTURE: McGowan will likely spend most of the 2023 season back at High-A Jersey Shore. Assuming he stays healthy, he could emerge as a high-leverage option out of the bullpen for later in the 2024 season.

BA GRADE: 45/Extreme		Fastball: 55		Slider: 60		Changeup: 50		Control: 40		

Year	Age	Club (League)	Lvl	W	L	ERA	G	GS	IP	H	HR	BB	SO	BB/9	SO/9	WHIP	AVG
2022	22	Jersey Shore (SAL)	HiA	0	1	4.91	2	2	7	8	1	2	7	2.5	8.6	1.36	.320
Minor League Totals				0	1	2.92	6	3	12	10	1	3	15	2.2	10.9	1.05	.238

19 MICAH OTTENBREIT, RHP

Born: May 7, 2003. **B-T:** R-R. **HT:** 6-4. **WT:** 190.
Drafted: HS—Trenton, Mich., 2021 (4th round). **Signed by:** Derrick Ross
TRACK RECORD: Ottenbreit was one of the top prep arms in Michigan in the 2021 draft class, and the Phillies nabbed him with a fourth-round pick. He made five appearances in the Florida Complex League in 2021 before impressing with his performance in instructional league. After making a pair of starts for Low-A Clearwater in 2022, Ottenbreit was shut down and had Tommy John surgery.
SCOUTING REPORT: Ottenbreit has a three-pitch mix from the right side, with a fastball that sits in the low 90s and tops out at 95 mph, with more velocity possible as he fills out his 6-foot-4, 190-pound frame. His mid-70s curveball has the potential to be a plus pitch, with spin rates that registered over 3,000 rpm at instructional league. He struggles to command it at times, but it has the potential to be a swing-and-miss weapon as he gets more innings under his belt. Ottenbreit rounds out his arsenal with a low-80s changeup that he's shown feel to throw, with solid velocity separation off his fastball. He has a repeatable delivery, but struggled to throw strikes during his brief pro tenure and needs to work on his pitch sequencing.
THE FUTURE: Ottenbreit should head back to Low-A Clearwater for the 2023 season. With three average or better offerings and the potential for average control he projects as a back-end starter.

BA GRADE: 45/Extreme		Fastball: 50		Curveball: 60		Changeup: 50		Control: 45		

Year	Age	Club (League)	Lvl	W	L	ERA	G	GS	IP	H	HR	BB	SO	BB/9	SO/9	WHIP	AVG
2022	19	Clearwater (FSL)	LoA	0	1	7.94	2	2	6	6	1	5	4	7.9	6.4	1.94	.273
Minor League Totals				1	1	6.17	7	2	12	12	1	8	8	6.2	6.2	1.71	.273

20 CARLOS DE LA CRUZ, OF

Born: Oct. 6, 1999. **B-T:** R-R. **HT:** 6-8. **WT:** 210.
Signed: HS—New York, 2017 (NDFA). **Signed by:** Alex Agostino
TRACK RECORD: De La Cruz went under the radar as a high school senior in 2017 and wasn't selected in the 40-round draft, but an impressive showing during the travel ball circuit that summer led the Phillies to sign him as a nondrafted free agent. After struggling in full-season ball in 2019 and 2021, De La Cruz took a huge step forward in 2022 with High-A Jersey Shore. He slashed .266/.344/.463 with 10 homers before posting an .825 OPS in 38 games with Double-A Reading. He ended the season with a 17-game stint in the Arizona Fall League. De La Cruz was left unprotected for the 2022 Rule 5 draft.
SCOUTING REPORT: De La Cruz stands out for his massive 6-foot-8 frame and plus-plus raw power, as evidenced by his 108.6 mph 90th percentile exit velocity, which led to a career-high 17 home runs in 2022. De La Cruz does struggle to consistently get to his power, however, due to his long levers and tendency to chase out of the zone. While he was at Jersey Shore he worked to sync up all parts of his body, shortening his movements and swing while concentrating on staying on pitches to hit. He needs to improve his approach and cut down on his swing-and-miss and chase rates moving forward, and due to his long levers and aggressive approach he's unlikely to be more than a 40-grade hitter. The organization believes he can stick in an outfield corner moving forward, but opposing scouts view him as a below-average defender who's more suited for first base, with below-average speed.
THE FUTURE: Few players within the organization improved as much in 2022 as De La Cruz. He has the potential to be a 30-home run, 175-strikeout player in the major leagues, but he'll need to cut down on his swing-and-miss to get to that point. He'll start 2023 back at Double-A Reading.

BA GRADE: 40/High		Hitting: 40		Power: 60		Speed: 40		Fielding: 40		Arm: 40	

Year	Age	Club (League)	Lvl	AVG	G	AB	R	H	2B	3B	HR	RBI	BB	SO	SB	OBP	SLG
2022	22	Jersey Shore (SAL)	HiA	.266	64	214	29	57	10	1	10	24	19	75	5	.344	.463
2022	22	Reading (EL)	AA	.278	38	151	21	42	12	1	7	23	8	45	1	.315	.510
Minor League Totals				.238	325	1145	131	272	56	6	35	144	91	422	20	.304	.389

21 JAYDENN ESTANISTA, RHP

Born: Oct. 3, 2001. **B-T:** R-R. **HT:** 6-3. **WT:** 180.
Signed: Curacao, 2019. **Signed by:** Carlos Salas/Dargello Lodowica
TRACK RECORD: Estanista, signed by the Phillies in 2019 from Curacao, had his development stunted due to the coronavirus pandemic and didn't make his pro debut until 2021, when he posted a 3.23 ERA in 30.2 innings in the Dominican Summer League. He made his stateside debut in 2022, and boasted a 3-0, 2.01 mark with 14 hits allowed and 35 strikeouts in 31.1 innings in the Florida Complex League.
SCOUTING REPORT: Estanista has an easy delivery out of his athletic frame, and routinely gets his fastball into the mid 90s and tops out at 98.3 mph, with room for more velocity gains in the future. His fastball

has the potential to be a near plus-plus offering, with heavy riding life, above-average spin and good deception. He mixes in a high-80s changeup with huge velocity separation off his fastball. The pitch is average, with the potential to improve to above-average thanks to his ability to sell the pitch, although it lacks much movement. He rounds out his arsenal with a big breaking ball in the low 80s that showed improvement in 2022 and served as a swing-and-miss pitch, but he needs to improve his feel for spin. He struggles with his command at times and lacks repeatability, but impressed with his ability to adjust and improve in 2022. Estanista could move quickly in a bullpen role, but if he can improve his control and sharpen his curveball the Phillies could continue to use him as a starter.

THE FUTURE: Estanista should make his full-season debut at Low-A Clearwater in 2023, with a high-octane fastball capable of giving hitters headaches at the back of a bullpen.

BA GRADE: 45/Extreme	Fastball: 65	Curveball: 45	Changeup: 50	Control: 40

Year	Age	Club (League)	Lvl	W	L	ERA	G	GS	IP	H	HR	BB	SO	BB/9	SO/9	WHIP	AVG
2022	20	Phillies (FCL)	R	3	0	2.01	12	5	31	14	3	16	35	4.6	10.1	0.96	.139
Minor League Totals				4	1	2.61	22	11	62	33	4	35	68	5.1	9.9	1.10	.163

22 JHAILYN ORTIZ, OF

Born: Nov. 18, 1998. **B-T:** R-R. **HT:** 6-3. **WT:** 264.
Signed: Dominican Republic, 2015. **Signed by:** Sal Agostinelli.

TRACK RECORD: Ortiz was a big-money signing out of the Dominican Republic in 2015, but he struggled through his first four minor league seasons before having a breakout campaign in 2021 split between High-A Jersey Shore and Double-A Reading. He crushed 23 home runs and cut down on his strikeout rate, but regressed in 2022 back at Reading, posting a career-worst 32.7% strikeout rate while struggling to access his plus-plus raw power.

SCOUTING REPORT: Ortiz stood out to members of the organization coming into the 2022 season thanks to a refocused approach that included a healthier diet, and he showed up to spring training in better shape and with a shorter swing to help him catch up to mid-90s velocity. Those gains didn't translate to the 2022 season, as Ortiz continued to struggle to make contact. He had trouble figuring out pitches to swing at, and had a high swing-and-miss rate while chasing a high amount of sliders out of the zone. Ortiz has plus bat speed and plus-plus raw power, but his inability to make consistent contact makes it more of an above-average tool in games. He posted an impressive 106.3 mph 90th percentile exit velocity, and over 39% of his balls in play were hit 95 mph or harder, but he managed just 17 home runs due to his contact issues. Ortiz struggled with his timing and starting his stride earlier in his swing, and those will be areas of emphasis in 2023. He's a solid athlete for his size, but is a below-average runner and defender in right field who could end up at first base. He has a plus arm.

THE FUTURE: Time is running out for Ortiz to make the necessary adjustments to unlock more of his power in games and prove himself as more than an emergency up/down player. He'll likely head to Triple-A Lehigh Valley in 2023.

BA GRADE: 40/High	Hitting: 30	Power: 55	Running: 40	Fielding: 40	Arm: 60

Year	Age	Club (League	Lvl	AVG	G	AB	R	H	2B	3B	HR	RBI	BB	SO	SB	OBP	SLG
2022	23	Reading (EL)	AA	.237	119	448	67	106	25	2	17	61	43	165	9	.319	.415
Minor League Totals				.233	533	1955	290	456	94	9	88	284	187	675	30	.317	.426

23 DONNY SANDS, C

Born: May 16, 1996. **B-T:** R-R. **HT:** 6-2. **WT:** 190.
Drafted: HS—Tucson, Ariz. 2015 (8th round). **Signed by:** Steve Kmetko (Yankees).

TRACK RECORD: Acquired from the Yankees in November 2021, Sands had an impressive first season in the Phillies organization, hitting .308/.413/.428 in 57 games at Triple-A Lehigh Valley. He made his major league debut on Sept. 2 and finished the season with three at-bats in the big leagues.

SCOUTING REPORT: Sands has a good approach at the plate, with good swing decisions and bat-to-ball skills that have improved in the last few years. He works counts well, controls the zone and uses the whole field, but will likely never hit for power. He consistently shows more gap-to-gap juice than over-the-fence pop. He had an average exit velocity of 85.7 mph in 2022, with a 90th percentile exit velocity of 104.1 mph. Sands draws rave reviews for his leadership skills and framing ability, and he handles the pitching staff well. He has a below-average arm, which holds him back from being more than an average defender in the big leagues.

THE FUTURE: Sands has leapfrogged Rafael Marchan on the organization's depth chart, and he has an opportunity to make the big league team out of camp as the third catcher behind JT Realmuto and Garrett Stubbs. Sands will likely never be a starter in the big leagues, but he could have a solid career as a backup thanks to his hit tool and defensive skills.

BA GRADE: 35/Medium		Hitting: 50		Power: 40		Speed: 30		Fielding: 50		Arm: 40				

Year	Age	Club (League)	Lvl	AVG	G	AB	R	H	2B	3B	HR	RBI	BB	SO	SB	OBP	SLG
2022	26	Clearwater (FSL)	LoA	.300	3	10	1	3	1	0	1	2	1	2	0	.364	.700
2022	26	Lehigh Valley (IL)	AAA	.308	57	201	41	62	9	0	5	34	38	44	1	.413	.428
2022	26	Philadelphia (NL)	MLB	.000	3	3	0	0	0	0	0	0	1	1	0	.250	.000
Major League Totals				.000	3	3	0	0	0	0	0	0	1	1	0	.250	.000
Minor League Totals				.274	428	1521	198	416	79	1	32	219	154	272	13	.343	.390

24 EMAARION BOYD, OF

Born: Aug. 22, 2003. **B-T:** R-R. **HT:** 6-1. **WT:** 177.
Drafted: HS—Batesville, Miss., 2022 (11th round). **Signed by:** Mike Stauffer.
TRACK RECORD: Boyd has a pair of clear carrying tools that allowed him to separate himself in the 2022 draft class, with plus-plus speed and at least plus defense in center field. There were questions around his offensive impact, but the Phillies were confident enough in his potential that they drafted him in the 11th round and signed him to a well over-slot $647,500 bonus. Boyd had an encouraging 2022 pro debut, hitting .361/.477/.389 across 11 games between the Florida Complex League and Low-A.
SCOUTING REPORT: Boyd was one of the top athletes in the 2022 draft class, and his plus-plus speed allowed him to steal eight bases in 10 tries in his pro debut. In the outfield he has great instincts and the speed to cover a lot of ground in center field, with a solid arm to go with it. He has strong bat-to-ball skills, with the ability to hit to all fields, but he lacks present power in his 6-foot-1, 177-pound frame. There's a belief that he could add power in the future, but it's likely to be below-average, gap-to-gap power at best.
THE FUTURE: After a brief full-season debut in 2022, Boyd should spend the 2023 season at Low-A.

BA GRADE: 45/Extreme		Hitting: 50		Power: 30		Running: 70		Fielding: 65		Arm: 50				

Year	Age	Club (League)	Lvl	AVG	G	AB	R	H	2B	3B	HR	RBI	BB	SO	SB	OBP	SLG
2022	18	Phillies (FCL)	R	.345	9	29	6	10	1	0	0	2	5	5	7	.472	.379
2022	18	Clearwater (FSL)	LoA	.429	2	7	1	3	0	0	0	0	0	0	1	.500	.429
Minor League Totals				.361	11	36	7	13	1	0	0	2	5	5	8	.477	.389

25 YHOSWAR GARCIA, OF

Born: Sept. 13, 2001. **B-T:** R-R. **HT:** 6-1. **WT:** 155.
Signed: Venezuela, 2020. **Signed by:** Ebert Velasquez.
TRACK RECORD: Originally expected to sign in 2019, Garcia's signing was delayed due to a discrepancy with his age. He eventually signed in March of 2020 as one of the top players in the international class. Garcia has played in just 55 minor league games over two seasons due to a myriad of injuries. He played in 18 games in his pro debut in 2021, but missed a significant amount of time after fouling a ball off his leg, then missed the majority of the 2022 season with a broken leg.
SCOUTING REPORT: Garcia has plus-plus speed, plus defense in center field and an above-average arm, but he's had little time to show those skills on the field. Garcia makes solid contact at the plate, but he's prone to chasing pitches out of the zone and hits too many balls on the ground. He has an uppercut swing, and the organization has worked with him to flatten his swing path and develop a more patient approach, as he rarely walks and has an overaggressive approach that leads to soft contact. Garcia has added muscle to his frame, but will need to continue making strength gains to project for even below-average power—he had an 82 mph average exit velocity in 2022. He is a smooth defender in center field with plus-plus speed that allows him to cover a lot of ground, with good instincts to go with an above-average arm.
THE FUTURE: Garcia is still an extremely raw talent and needs a full year of experience under his belt in 2023. He'll likely spend the 2023 season at the Class A levels.

BA GRADE: 45/Extreme		Hitting: 40		Power: 30		Running: 70		Fielding: 60		Arm: 55				

Year	Age	Club (League)	Lvl	AVG	G	AB	R	H	2B	3B	HR	RBI	BB	SO	SB	OBP	SLG
2022	20	Phillies (FCL)	R	.333	2	6	0	2	0	0	0	1	1	1	3	.429	.333
2022	20	Clearwater (FSL)	LoA	.206	35	126	26	26	4	3	1	16	14	35	29	.303	.310
Minor League Totals				.218	55	202	33	44	5	4	1	25	21	59	43	.306	.297

26 ORION KERKERING, RHP

Born: April 4, 2001. **B-T:** R-R. **HT:** 6-2. **WT:** 204.
Drafted: South Florida, 2022 (fifth round). **Signed by:** Bryce Harman.
TRACK RECORD: Kerkering pitched primarily out of the bullpen for South Florida in 2020 and 2021, but split his time between starting and relief in 2022. He struck out 12.1 batters per nine and walked just 2.5 per nine, but gave up 75 hits in 67.2 innings. The Phillies drafted him in the fifth round in 2022 on the strength of his fastball/slider combination. He made six appearances in 2022 between the Florida Complex League and Low-A Clearwater.
SCOUTING REPORT: The Phillies plan to use Kerkering as a reliever and believe he can move quickly in that role. His fastball sits in the mid 90s and tops out at 97 mph, and he used it more than 50% of the time in 2022. His slider sits in the mid 80s with plenty of spin and on average exceeded 2,700 rpm in 2022. It's a plus pitch that gives him a swing-and-miss offering. He also has an infrequently-used changeup that's a below-average pitch and could end up being ditched as he progresses through the minor leagues. Kerkering throws quality strikes with average control.
THE FUTURE: The Phillies believe Kerkering should move quickly in a relief role, and he'll likely start the 2023 season at High-A Jersey Shore.

BA GRADE: 40/High	Fastball: 55	Slider: 60	Changeup: 40	Control: 50

Year	Age	Club (League)	Lvl	W	L	ERA	G	GS	IP	H	HR	BB	SO	BB/9	SO/9	WHIP	AVG
2022	21	Phillies (FCL)	R	0	0	0.00	1	0	1	0	0	1	1	9.0	9.0	1.00	.000
2022	21	Clearwater (FSL)	LoA	1	0	4.50	5	0	6	7	0	0	6	0.0	9.0	1.17	.292
Minor League Totals				1	0	3.86	6	0	7	7	0	1	7	1.3	9.0	1.14	.269

27 RAFAEL MARCHAN, C

Born: Feb. 25, 1999. **B-T:** B-R. **HT:** 5-9. **WT:** 196.
Signed: Venezuela, 2015. **Signed by:** Jesus Mendez.
TRACK RECORD: Marchan, who appeared in 20 games for the Phillies in 2021, had several stints on the injured list in 2022, first missing time with a left hamstring strain to start the year and then missing time in August. The slick-fielding backstop received two call ups to the major leagues in 2022, but did not see any game action, and spent the majority of the season with Triple-A Lehigh Valley.
SCOUTING REPORT: Marchan is one of the best defensive catchers in the minor leagues, with above-average blocking skills, good leadership skills and excellent catch-and-throw ability, with pop times in the 1.8-second range. Despite strong strike-zone awareness skills and low whiff and chase rates, he's a below-average hitter, with below-average bat speed and a high groundball rate. He has well below-average power, as evidenced by his 84.2 mph average exit velocity in 2022, and the organization has worked with him on adding some loft in his swing to hit the ball in the air more frequently. He's a solid runner for a catcher.
THE FUTURE: Marchan's excellent defense should translate to a solid big league career as a second-division backup, but he's currently blocked in Philadelphia by backup Garrett Stubbs and Donny Sands.

BA GRADE: 35/Medium	Hitting: 40	Power: 30	Speed: 40	Fielding: 70	Arm: 60

Year	Age	Club (League)	Lvl	AVG	G	AB	R	H	2B	3B	HR	RBI	BB	SO	SB	OBP	SLG
2022	23	Jersey Shore (SAL)	HiA	.231	4	13	1	3	2	0	0	0	2	2	0	.333	.385
2022	23	Lehigh Valley (IL)	AAA	.233	66	232	26	54	17	0	4	29	20	24	1	.316	.358
Major League Totals				.267	23	60	10	16	1	1	2	7	5	12	0	.323	.417
Minor League Totals				.259	348	1252	144	324	67	3	4	127	106	151	20	.325	.327

28 ALEX RAO, RHP

Born: Oct. 25, 1999. **B-T:** R-R. **HT:** 6-4. **WT:** 230.
Drafted: Notre Dame, 2022 (8th round). **Signed by:** Derrick Ross.
TRACK RECORD: Rao was an effective piece out of the bullpen for Notre Dame in 2022, and he finished the season with a 3-1, 3.83 mark with 57 strikeouts and 28 walks in 47 innings. The Phillies selected him in the eighth round of the 2022 draft, and Rao made three scoreless appearances after signing between the Florida Complex League and Low-A Clearwater.
SCOUTING REPORT: Rao has an effective three-pitch mix, with a plus fastball that sat in the mid 90s in 2022 and topped out above 98 mph. It's a high-spin offering with good riding life up in the zone that proved to be an effective bat-misser. His best pitch is a mid-80s split-changeup that the organization believes can be a wipeout offering. It's at its best when Rao uses it down in the zone. He rounds out his mix with an infrequently used mid-80s slider that is a below-average offering. Rao has below-average control that likely led to him falling to the eighth round in the draft.

THE FUTURE: With two plus pitches, Rao has a chance to move quickly through the system, but he'll have to throw more consistent strikes. He should start the 2023 season at High-A Jersey Shore, and could prove to be an effective middle reliever.

BA GRADE: 40/High		Fastball: 60		Changeup: 60		Slider: 40		Control: 40			

Year	Age	Club (League)	Lvl	W	L	ERA	G	GS	IP	H	HR	BB	SO	BB/9	SO/9	WHIP	AVG
2022	22	Phillies (FCL)	R	0	0	0.00	1	0	1	0	0	1	0	9.0	0.0	1.00	.000
2022	22	Clearwater (FSL)	LoA	0	0	0.00	2	0	2	0	0	0	1	0.0	4.5	0.00	.000
Minor League Totals				0	0	0.00	3	0	3	0	0	1	1	3.0	3.0	0.33	.000

29 ENRIQUE SEGURA, RHP

Born: Dec. 19, 2004. **B-T:** R-R. **HT:** 6-3. **WT:** 175.
Signed: Dominican Republic, 2022. **Signed by:** Carlos Salas/Bernardo Perez.
TRACK RECORD: Segura was part of the Phillies 2021-2022 international signing class. He signed out of the Dominican Republic, then spent the 2022 season in the Dominican Summer League and posted a 5-1, 2.32 mark with 39 strikeouts and 22 walks in 42.2 innings split between the rotation and relief.
SCOUTING REPORT: Segura has a projectable frame with a long, loose arm action. His fastball averaged 91.6 mph in 2022 and got up to 95.5 mph, and he should add velocity to the pitch as he gains strength and matures. He shows feel to throw his breaking ball, an upper-70s slider that induced a 50% whiff rate in 2022. Some evaluators have graded it as an above-average offering now, with the potential to become plus in the future. He rounds out his arsenal with an average, mid-80s changeup. Segura struggled to throw strikes at times in 2022, but the organization believes he can get to average control in the future.
THE FUTURE: Segura will continue to move forward as a starter, and he should make his stateside debut as an 18-year-old in the Florida Complex League in 2023.

BA GRADE: 45/Extreme		Fastball: 60		Slider: 55		Changeup: 50		Control: 50			

Year	Age	Club (League)	Lvl	W	L	ERA	G	GS	IP	H	HR	BB	SO	BB/9	SO/9	WHIP	AVG
2022	17	Phillies Red (DSL)	R	5	1	2.32	13	8	43	36	1	22	39	4.6	8.2	1.36	.234
Minor League Totals				5	1	2.32	13	8	43	36	1	22	39	4.6	8.2	1.36	.234

30 TOMMY McCOLLUM, RHP

Born: June 8, 1999. **B-T:** R-R. **HT:** 6-5. **WT:** 260.
Signed: Wingate, 2021 (NDFA). **Signed by:** Kellan McKeon.
TRACK RECORD: McCollum pitched mainly out of the bullpen for Wingate in each of his three seasons with the program, but he struggled mightily in 2021 and went unselected in the 20-round draft. The Phillies signed him as a nondrafted free agent, and he had an impressive 2022 campaign at Low-A Clearwater, striking out 52 batters in 31 innings to go with a 1.45 ERA.
SCOUTING REPORT: McCollum has a powerful, three-pitch mix out of the bullpen, with a four-seam fastball that averaged over 94 mph in 2022 and topped out above 97 mph. The pitch has riding life at the top of the zone with good extension, and it induced a whiff rate just below 42% in 2022. He pairs the pitch with a hard, mid-80s slider that has cutter-like shape, and rounds out his arsenal with a split-changeup that could prove to be his best swing-and-miss weapon. The pitch sits in the mid 80s and induced a 50% whiff rate in 2022 in a limited sample. McCollum was plagued by command issues in college, but he took a step forward in that department with Clearwater. McCollum's delivery and arm action have led to injury concerns, but he has the weapons to succeed in a big league bullpen if he can stay healthy.
THE FUTURE: McCollum could be a quick mover in 2023 and will likely start the season at High-A Jersey Shore. He has the potential to be a power arm at the back of an MLB bullpen.

BA GRADE: 40/High		Fastball: 60		Slider: 55		Changeup: 55		Control: 30			

Year	Age	Club (League)	Lvl	W	L	ERA	G	GS	IP	H	HR	BB	SO	BB/9	SO/9	WHIP	AVG
2022	23	Clearwater (FSL)	LoA	1	0	1.45	23	0	31	11	3	16	52	4.6	15.1	0.87	.111
Minor League Totals				1	0	2.89	32	0	44	20	4	32	67	6.6	13.8	1.19	.138

Pittsburgh Pirates

BY MARK CHIARELLI

When owner Bob Nutting embarked on the Pirates' latest rebuild in the fall of 2019, his newly hired president Travis Williams warned of a full teardown.

"This is not going to be where we flip the switch and the next day, all of a sudden, we're in the World Series," Williams said at the time. "We're going to have to get a general manager in place, put a plan in place that charts a path forward within the framework that we're operating so that we can get back to being a very successful team."

Pirates fans will likely settle for just contending for a playoff spot again, let alone a World Series. Pittsburgh finished 30-plus games out of first place in the National League Central in 2022 for the second consecutive season. The Pirates have finished above .500 only once since 2015—an 82-79 season in 2018 that did not result in a postseason appearance.

The Pirates chose Ben Cherington to preside over the rebuild. And while Pittsburgh hasn't flipped the switch toward contention, the organization is inching closer.

One potential cornerstone is shortstop Oneil Cruz, who reached Pittsburgh for good in 2022, and showed prodigious power potential (17 home runs) and an inconsistent hit tool (34.9% strikeout rate). Rookie righthander Roansy Contreras pitched to a 3.79 ERA in 95 innings, while fellow righthander Mitch Keller, once a top Pirates prospect before well-documented struggles, turned his career around, as he went 3.91 ERA over 159 innings.

Cherington, meanwhile, has methodically added to Pittsburgh's farm system over his first three seasons, and the Pirates now boast one of baseball's deepest talent pools.

Three consecutive years of high draft picks and a slew of trades helped restock the system. But it remains an open question whether there's enough impact talent to turn the tide. For example, Pittsburgh didn't have a top 40 talent in the final Top 100 Prospects update of 2022.

The 2022 season was a mixed bag. The Pirates were encouraged by breakout seasons from catcher Endy Rodriguez and righthander Luis Ortiz. Rodriguez slugged 25 homers and reached Triple-A Indianapolis. He now looks like Pittsburgh's catcher of the future and represents a major coup for the organization, who quietly acquired him from the Mets in a three-team deal that sent Joe Musgrove to the Padres after the 2020 season.

Ortiz, meanwhile, reached Pittsburgh by the end of 2022 and hit triple digits as a starter for the pitching-needy Pirates. Pittsburgh also selected middle infielder Termarr Johnson, one of the top

NUCCIO DINUZZO/GETTY IMAGES

Oneil Cruz's elite power, speed and arm could make him an asset with a better plate approach.

PROJECTED 2026 LINEUP

Position	Player	Age
Catcher	Endy Rodriguez	25
First Base	Henry Davis	26
Second Base	Termarr Johnson	21
Third Base	Ke'Bryan Hayes	29
Shortstop	Liover Peguero	25
Left Field	Ji-Hwan Bae	26
Center Field	Bryan Reynolds	31
Right Field	Oneil Cruz	27
Designated Hitter	Nick Gonzales	26
No. 1 Starter	Mitch Keller	29
No. 2 Starter	Roansy Contreras	26
No. 3 Starter	Luis Ortiz	27
No. 4 Starter	Quinn Priester	25
No. 5 Starter	Mike Burrows	26
Closer	Kyle Nicolas	27

high school hitters in recent years, with the No. 4 pick in the 2022 draft.

The system's outlook will brighten if catcher Henry Davis and second baseman Nick Gonzales can remain healthy in 2023 and rebuild some of their stock after inconsistent starts to their careers. The Pirates would also benefit from another pitcher taking a step forward—they've amassed a glut of arms that mostly profile as midrotation starters at best.

Seven of Pittsburgh's Top 10 Prospects have either reached Triple-A or are expected to do so at some point in 2023, meaning the next wave of talent is closing in on Pittsburgh and brighter days may soon be coming. ■

DEPTH CHART

PITTSBURGH PIRATES

TOP 2023 MLB CONTRIBUTORS	RANK
Endy Rodriguez, C	1
Luis Ortiz, RHP	4
Ji-Hwan Bae, 2B/CF	12
BREAKOUT PROSPECTS	**RANK**
Anthony Solometo, LHP	13
Dariel Lopez, 3B	23
Axiel Plaz, C	27

SOURCE OF TOP 30 TALENT

Homegrown	25	Acquired	5
College	10	Trade	5
Junior college	0	Rule 5 draft	0
High school	9	Independent league	0
Nondrafted free agent	0	Free agent/waivers	0
International	6		

LF
Canaan Smith-Njigba (19)
Miguel Sosa
Braylon Bishop

CF
Lonnie White (28)
Travis Swaggerty
Matthew Fraizer
Hudson Head
Connor Scott
Shalin Polanco
Jase Bowen
Sammy Siani

RF
Matt Gorski (16)
Rodolfo Nolasco (26)
Ryan Vilade
Bligh Madris
Lolo Sanchez

3B
Jared Triolo (15)
Dariel Lopez (23)
Andres Alvarez (29)
Jack Brannigan
Juan Jerez

SS
Liover Peguero (7)
Tsung-Che Cheng (24)
Maikol Escotto
Yordany De Los Santos

2B
Termarr Johnson (2)
Nick Gonzales (8)
Ji-Hwan Bae (12)

1B
Malcom Nuñez (20)
Mason Martin
Aaron Shackelford
Alexander Mojica

C
Endy Rodriguez (1)
Henry Davis (3)
Axiel Plaz (27)
Abrahan Gutierrez
Carter Bins
Wyatt Hendrie

LHP

LHSP	LHRP
Anthony Solometo (13)	Tyler Samaniego (30)
Hunter Barco (17)	Jose Hernandez
Michael Kennedy (18)	Nick Dombkowski
Luis Peralta	

RHP

RHSP	RHRP
Luis Ortiz (4)	Cody Bolton (22)
Quinn Priester (5)	Colin Selby (25)
Bubba Chandler (6)	Tahnaj Thomas
Mike Burrows (9)	Colin Holderman
Thomas Harrington (10)	J.C. Flowers
Jared Jones (11)	
Kyle Nicolas (14)	
Carmen Mlodzinski (21)	
Carlos Jimenez	
Ricky DeVito	
Nick Garcia	
Max Kranick	
Po-Yu Chen	
Miguel Yajure	
Braxton Ashcraft	

1 ENDY RODRIGUEZ, C

Born: May 26, 2000. **B-T:** B-R. **HT:** 6-0. **WT:** 195.
Signed: Dominican Republic, 2018.
Signed by: Anderson Taveras (Mets).

TRACK RECORD: The Mets didn't spend much to sign Rodriguez, inking him for $10,000 as an 18-year-old out of the Dominican Republic in 2018, but they're paying the price now for letting him go. New York shipped Rodriguez to the Pirates in January 2021 in a three-team deal that sent Joe Musgrove to the Padres and netted the Mets Joey Lucchesi. Rodriguez has raked ever since. He won the batting title in the Low-A Florida State League in 2021, and hit .294 with 15 homers. He then took another leap forward in 2022, where he hit 25 homers and posted a .996 OPS across three levels and ending the year with Triple-A Indianapolis. Rodriguez was especially impactful from July 1 to the end of the season, and ranked first among qualified minor league hitters in average (.377), slugging (.723), OPS (1.181) and extra-base hits (43).

SCOUTING REPORT: The switch-hitting Rodriguez turned in one of 2022's biggest breakout performances on the strength of his exceptional bat-to-ball skills and contact quality. Scouts covet Rodriguez's pure hitting ability—he has hit .310 in full-season ball the past two seasons—and his power emerged more consistently from both sides of the plate in 2022. Rodriguez always seems to have a plan at the plate and controls the strike zone well. His proclivity for strong swing decisions allows him to maximize his above-average power potential despite middle-of-the-road exit velocities. Rodriguez has steadily added strength to his wiry frame, too, and is athletic. Those in the Pirates organization rave about his aptitude, leadership and baseball IQ. Rodriguez made strides defensively in 2022. He improved his blocking and receiving, especially after he settled into a more consistent defensive stance and got consistent reps once Henry Davis was promoted to Double-A Altoona in May. Before Davis' promotion, Rodriguez was playing left and first base as often as he played catcher and was handling second base as well. Rodriguez made a conscious effort to improve his throwing accuracy to second base and his transfer after struggling with inconsistency in 2021, when he threw out just 17% of basestealers. He nearly doubled that figure in 2022 and threw out 45% of baserunners once he arrived in Altoona. Opposing evaluators were impressed with Rodriguez's game management, and Pirates

MIKE JANES/FOUR SEAM IMAGES

BA GRADE	SCOUTING GRADES
65 Risk: High	Hit: 60. Power: 60. Run: 45. Field: 50. Arm: 55.

Projected future grades on 20-80 scouting scale

BEST TOOLS

BATTING
Best Hitter for Average	Jared Triolo
Best Power Hitter	Matt Gorski
Best Strike-Zone Discipline	Lolo Sanchez
Fastest Baserunner	Ji-Hwan Bae
Best Athlete	Bubba Chandler

PITCHING
Best Fastball	Bubba Chandler
Best Curveball	Quinn Priester
Best Slider	Colin Selby
Best Changeup	Ricky DeVito
Best Control	Nick Dombkowski

FIELDING
Best Defensive Catcher	Wyatt Hendrie
Best Defensive Infielder	Jared Triolo
Best Infield Arm	Jack Brannigan
Best Defensive Outfielder	Travis Swaggerty

minor league pitchers liked throwing to him. He still needs to refine his framing. Rodriguez also spent time at first base, second base and left field in 2022, and he's athletic enough to handle any of those positions.

THE FUTURE: Rodriguez emerged as one of baseball's best catching prospects in 2022 and profiles as an impact big leaguer with plus hitting and power potential. He could ultimately become one half of an enviable catching duo with Davis in Pittsburgh. It's easy to dream on Rodriguez becoming a foundational piece who helps usher the Pirates out of their lengthy rebuild.

Year	Age	Club (League)	Lvl	AVG	G	AB	R	H	2B	3B	HR	RBI	BB	SO	SB	OBP	SLG
2022	22	Greensboro (SAL)	HiA	.302	88	318	63	96	23	3	16	55	42	77	3	.392	.544
2022	22	Altoona (EL)	AA	.356	31	118	27	42	14	0	8	32	18	21	1	.442	.678
2022	22	Indianapolis (IL)	AAA	.455	6	22	2	10	2	1	1	8	0	3	0	.435	.773
Minor League Totals				.303	289	1052	206	319	84	13	44	205	145	222	12	.393	.533

2 TERMARR JOHNSON, 2B

Born: June 11, 2004. **B-T:** L-R. **HT:** 5-7. **WT:** 175.
Drafted: HS—Atlanta, 2022 (1st round). **Signed by:** Cam Murphy.

TRACK RECORD: Amateur evaluators have long marveled at Johnson's preternatural feel for hitting and magnetic personality. He's one of the purest high
school hitters in recent memory, possessed the best hit tool and strike-zone
judgment of any prep hitter in the 2022 draft. The Pirates selected him No.
4 overall and signed him to a $7,219,000 bonus to forgo an Arizona State
commitment. He debuted in the Florida Complex League and finished the
year with Low-A Bradenton.

SCOUTING REPORT: Johnson is a lefthanded hitter who greets pitchers with
a sizable leg kick before lashing at pitches with remarkable bat speed, which
suggests potential for plus power along with a future as a 70-grade hitter. He
pairs bat control and the ability to manipulate the barrel with a discerning eye.

BA GRADE

60 Risk: High

He also showed the ability to identify strikes and punish them. Like many young hitters, Johnson will
need to adapt to premium velocity and offspeed pitches in pro ball, especially considering he faced weak
competition in high school. There's pressure on Johnson's bat to perform because of marginal supplemental tools. His body is already close to maxed out. The Pirates will give him a shot to stick at shortstop
and he's sure-handed defensively, but his average arm and limited range are better suited for second base.
Johnson draws rave reviews as a teammate and plays with notable passion.

THE FUTURE: Johnson is a long way away—he will still be 18 years old on Opening Day—but his brief
pro debut teased his potential as an impact big league hitter for both average and power.

| SCOUTING GRADES | Hitting: 70 | | Power: 60 | | Speed: 50 | | Fielding: 50 | | Arm: 50 | |

Year	Age	Club (League)	Lvl	AVG	G	AB	R	H	2B	3B	HR	RBI	BB	SO	SB	OBP	SLG
2022	18	Pirates (FCL)	R	.130	9	23	0	3	2	0	0	0	6	8	2	.310	.217
2022	18	Bradenton (FSL)	LoA	.275	14	40	7	11	4	0	1	6	10	13	4	.396	.450
Minor League Totals				.222	23	63	7	14	6	0	1	6	16	21	6	.366	.365

3 HENRY DAVIS, C

Born: Sept. 21, 1999. **B-T:** R-R. **HT:** 6-0. **WT:** 210.
Drafted: Louisville, 2021 (1st round). **Signed by:** Adam Bourassa.

TRACK RECORD: Injuries have beset Davis' professional development since the
Pirates made him the No. 1 pick in a 2021 draft that lacked an obvious top
prospect. Pittsburgh signed him to a $6.5 million bonus that was $2 million
under slot value. Davis appeared in just eight games in 2021 before an oblique
injury ended his season. A pair of left wrist injuries limited him to just 53
non-rehab games in 2022.

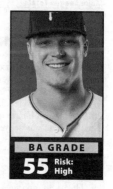

SCOUTING REPORT: Davis has reaffirmed the hitting traits that made him the
top college bat in his class. He packs considerable strength into his brawny
6-foot-2 frame, and it translates to easy plus power. Davis' barrel control and
flat bat path allow him to hit all types of pitch shapes. He cuts an unorthodox
presence in the batter's box. Davis sinks into a wide stance, lifting the bat

BA GRADE

55 Risk: High

just above his shoulder, sans batting gloves, and then bends forward at the waist, unwilling to cede any
ground on the inside part of the plate. Therein lies the problem. Davis was hit by nearly as many pitches
(20) as he had extra-base hits (23) in 2022. The Pirates have tried to convince him to move off the plate
to maintain his health. Davis' catching lags behind his bat. He's a stiff mover who needs to continue to
clean up his footwork and pitch framing. His arm strength is his calling card, but evaluators note he has
struggled with accuracy. Some wonder whether a corner outfield position may be a better long-term fit,
though he's only a fringe-average runner.

THE FUTURE: Davis needs to stay on the field. His ceiling remains that of a middle-of-the-order hitter,
though his defensive position remains a question mark.

| SCOUTING GRADES | Hitting: 55 | | Power: 60 | | Speed: 45 | | Fielding: 40 | | Arm: 60 | |

Year	Age	Club (League)	Lvl	AVG	G	AB	R	H	2B	3B	HR	RBI	BB	SO	SB	OBP	SLG
2022	22	Pirates (FCL)	R	.000	1	3	0	0	0	0	0	0	0	1	0	.250	.000
2022	22	Bradenton (FSL)	LoA	.364	5	11	2	4	1	0	1	2	1	2	1	.467	.727
2022	22	Greensboro (SAL)	HiA	.341	22	82	18	28	3	1	5	22	8	18	5	.450	.585
2022	22	Altoona (EL)	AA	.207	31	116	19	24	8	0	4	18	12	30	3	.324	.379
Minor League Totals				.269	67	238	46	64	14	2	13	49	25	61	10	.381	.508

4 LUIS ORTIZ, RHP

Born: Jan. 27, 1999. **B-T:** R-R. **HT:** 6-2. **WT:** 240.
Signed: Dominican Republic, 2018. **Signed by:** Junior Vizcaino.

TRACK RECORD: Ortiz was one of the Pirates' best player development success stories in 2022. They initially signed him for just $25,000 as a 19-year-old out of the Dominican Republic in October 2018. Even in 2021, Ortiz operated in relative obscurity while striking out 30% of hitters for Low-A Bradenton. Pittsburgh jumped him to Double-A Altoona to begin 2022. From there, Ortiz zoomed through the upper levels before making his MLB debut on Sept. 13, when he became the first Pirates starter to throw 100 mph since Gerrit Cole in 2015.

SCOUTING REPORT: Power oozes from Ortiz's operation. He has a starter's build at 6-foot-2, 240 pounds and is one of the hardest throwers in Pittsburgh's system, and he does it without overwhelming effort in his delivery. He averages 96.5 mph on his four-seamer. He also throws a two-seamer that touches 99 mph and befuddles righthanded hitters. The Pirates worked with Ortiz to create more distinction between the two fastballs and he became more comfortable deploying both in the second half of 2022. Ortiz also enhanced his upper-80s slider, and threw it harder with more vertical break. It's now easily a plus offering and his best swing-and-miss pitch. Ortiz trusted his solid-average changeup more, though it performs better against righthanded batters. He repeats his delivery well enough to suggest playable future command. The next step is adding polish, specifically around game-planning and sequencing.

THE FUTURE: Ortiz owns one of the system's most tantalizing pitch mixes and has a shot to win a spot in the big league rotation in 2023. He has midrotation potential.

BA GRADE
55 Risk: High

SCOUTING GRADES	Fastball: 70	Slider: 60	Changeup: 50	Control: 45

Year	Age	Club (League)	Lvl	W	L	ERA	G	GS	IP	H	HR	BB	SO	BB/9	SO/9	WHIP	AVG
2022	23	Altoona (EL)	AA	5	9	4.64	24	23	114	100	19	34	126	2.7	9.9	1.17	.238
2022	23	Indianapolis (IL)	AAA	0	0	3.60	2	2	10	4	1	4	12	3.6	10.8	0.80	.108
2022	23	Pittsburgh (NL)	MLB	0	2	4.50	4	4	16	8	1	10	17	5.6	9.6	1.12	.136
Major League Totals				0	2	4.50	4	4	16	8	1	10	17	5.6	9.6	1.12	.136
Minor League Totals				12	14	3.98	59	55	262	234	29	90	288	3.1	9.9	1.24	.236

5 QUINN PRIESTER, RHP

Born: Sept. 15, 2000. **B-T:** R-R. **HT:** 6-3. **WT:** 210.
Drafted: HS—Cary, Ill., 2019 (1st round). **Signed by:** Anthony Wycklendt.

TRACK RECORD: The Pirates have challenged Priester with aggressive assignments every year since they drafted him 18th overall out of high school in 2019 and signed him to a $3.4 million bonus. That trend continued in 2022. Priester's debut was delayed two months by an oblique injury, but he spent the majority of his age-21 season with Double-A Altoona, and posted a 2.87 ERA in 75 innings as one of the youngest pitchers at that level.

SCOUTING REPORT: Priester relies on a deep repertoire of pitches he can throw for strikes at any time to help mitigate the lack of an elite swing-and-miss offering. His 94-96 mph four-seam fastball has decent velocity but ordinary shape, resulting in one of the lowest four-seam whiff percentages in Pittsburgh's system. Priester instead turned to a sinker midway through 2021 that has better angle.

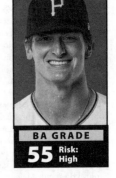

BA GRADE
55 Risk: High

He now throws it nearly as much as his four-seamer, and he generated a 51% groundball rate with Altoona in 2022. Priester's best secondary pitch continues to be his 78-82 mph curveball, a plus offering with good shape that batters chase as it dives out of the strike zone. He added an upper-80s slider during the pandemic in 2020 that is still inconsistent but has above-average potential. He also throws a firm upper-80s changeup with decent arm speed and fade.

THE FUTURE: Priester has the ceiling of a midrotation starter as he embarks on his age-22 season.

SCOUTING GRADES	Fastball: 50	Curveball: 60	Slider: 50	Changeup: 50	Control: 55

Year	Age	Club (League)	Lvl	W	L	ERA	G	GS	IP	H	HR	BB	SO	BB/9	SO/9	WHIP	AVG
2022	21	Bradenton (FSL)	LoA	0	0	0.00	1	1	3	0	0	0	1	0.0	3.0	0.00	.000
2022	21	Greensboro (SAL)	HiA	0	0	16.88	1	1	3	6	1	1	3	3.4	10.1	2.63	.429
2022	21	Altoona (EL)	AA	4	4	2.87	15	15	75	68	4	22	75	2.6	9.0	1.19	.241
2022	21	Indianapolis (IL)	AAA	1	1	3.86	2	2	9	5	1	7	10	6.8	9.6	1.29	.156
Minor League Totals				13	10	3.16	48	47	225	193	15	83	228	3.3	9.1	1.23	.230

6 BUBBA CHANDLER, RHP

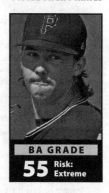

Born: Sept. 14, 2022. **B-T:** B-R. **HT:** 6-3. **WT:** 200.
Drafted: HS—Bogart, Ga., 2021 (3rd round). **Signed by:** Cam Murphy.

TRACK RECORD: Chandler excelled as a three-sport star at North Oconee High in Georgia and committed to Clemson to play both baseball and football. The Pirates made sure Chandler never reached campus, and signed the 2021 third-rounder to an above-slot $3 million. He debuted that summer as a hitter in the Florida Complex League and returned to the FCL in 2022 as a two-way player before ultimately reaching Low-A Bradenton.

SCOUTING REPORT: Chandler is dynamic enough to warrant a shot at both pitching and hitting, but most evaluators believe he ends up exclusively on the mound. His athleticism allows him to naturally create tension in his delivery, which leads to premium velocity that he already holds deep into starts as a

BA GRADE

55 Risk: Extreme

19-year-old. His 95-97 mph four-seamer is one of the best in Pittsburgh's system. Hitters whiffed on it 40% of the time in 2022, and it has great carry at the top of the zone. The rest of his operation is still quite raw. Chandler's best secondary pitch is an 86-88 mph changeup that flashes plus. His mid-80s slider is a work in progress—sometimes appearing as two distinct pitches—but projects as plus with more reps. Chandler has little issue repeating his delivery but still posted a 16% walk rate. The Pirates attribute some of the command issues to youth and inexperience as he learns to pitch and not simply rely on his stuff. At the plate, the switch-hitting Chandler has legitimate power potential—his average exit velocity was nearly 90 mph—but he also struck out nearly 40% of the time against low-level pitchers.
THE FUTURE: Chandler has immense upside—and also a long way to go to reach it. He is expected to return to Low-A Bradenton to begin 2023.

SCOUTING GRADES	Fastball: 70	Slider: 60	Changeup: 55	Control: 50

Year	Age	Club (League)	Lvl	W	L	ERA	G	GS	IP	H	HR	BB	SO	BB/9	SO/9	WHIP	AVG
2022	19	Pirates (FCL)	R	0	0	0.00	6	5	15	3	0	10	27	15.8	0.85	.061	
2022	19	Bradenton (FSL)	LoA	1	1	4.15	8	6	26	20	3	18	33	6.2	11.4	1.46	.215
Minor League Totals				1	1	2.61	14	11	41	23	3	28	60	6.1	13.1	1.23	.162

7 LIOVER PEGUERO, SS

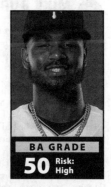

Born: Dec. 31, 2000. **B-T:** R-R. **HT:** 6-0. **WT:** 200.
Signed: Dominican Republic, 2017. **Signed by:** Cesar Geronimo Jr. (D-backs).

TRACK RECORD: Peguero made his unlikely MLB debut in 2022, three years after the Pirates acquired him in a deal for Starling Marte. He raced to a .784 OPS in his first 54 games with Double-A Altoona in 2022 and was just a two-hour drive away from Pittsburgh when the club needed a last-minute replacement after Tucupita Marcano tested positive for Covid on June 17. The Pirates called up Peguero and he debuted a day later.

SCOUTING REPORT: Peguero bundles an array of intriguing traits but doesn't always blend them together. He has a chance to become an above-average hitter thanks to impressive bat-to-ball skills and lightning-quick hands. His penchant for hard-hit balls allows for average power potential, though his swing isn't necessarily geared for lift. Peguero continues to work on optimizing his

BA GRADE

50 Risk: High

bat path to keep his barrel in the zone longer. More advanced pitchers exploited his aggressive approach at times in 2022 by peppering him with breaking balls, and his 5.6% walk rate was one of the lowest in the system. In the field, Peguero is prone to bouts of wildness and struggled with his throwing mechanics, making the most throwing errors of any infielder in the system. Still, the ingredients remain for a future plus defender. Peguero turns in his share of dazzling plays, thanks to a plus throwing arm, soft hands and sizable range. He is a plus runner who stole 28 bases in 2022.
THE FUTURE: Peguero will be just 22 years old on Opening Day. He has the ceiling of a first-division shortstop if everything comes together.

SCOUTING GRADES	Hitting: 55	Power: 50	Speed: 55	Fielding: 55	Arm: 50

Year	Age	Club (League)	Lvl	AVG	G	AB	R	H	2B	3B	HR	RBI	BB	SO	SB	OBP	SLG
2022	21	Altoona (EL)	AA	.259	121	483	65	125	22	5	10	58	29	111	28	.305	.387
2022	21	Pittsburgh (NL)	MLB	.333	1	3	0	1	0	0	0	0	1	2	0	.500	.333
Major League Totals				.333	1	3	0	1	0	0	0	0	1	2	0	.500	.333
Minor League Totals				.275	312	1231	201	338	55	15	30	162	93	296	74	.328	.417

8 NICK GONZALES, 2B

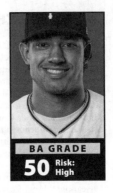

Born: May 27, 1999. **B-T:** R-R. **HT:** 5-9. **WT:** 190.
Drafted: New Mexico State, 2020 (1st round). **Signed by:** Derrick Van Dusen.

TRACK RECORD: Some wondered whether Gonzales could jump on a fast track because of his advanced hitting ability when the Pirates drafted him No. 7 overall in 2020 out of New Mexico State. But injuries have slowed his ascent. A broken finger sidelined him for a month in 2021. He missed two months in 2022 after tearing the plantar fascia in the heel of his foot, which limited him to just 74 games. Gonzales struggled prior to the injury, and struck out nearly 33% of the time in his first taste of Double-A. Upon returning, he cut his strikeouts by 10% and posted a .913 OPS in his final 28 games.

BA GRADE

50 Risk: High

SCOUTING REPORT: Gonzales continues to show more swing-and-miss than expected for a player who built his game around elite bat-to-ball skills. Scouts still believe he can hit for high averages on the basis of his short levers and punchy swing. He has strong hands and transfers considerable energy through his lower half, which, combined with his barrel ability, suggests average power potential despite his 5-foot-9 frame. Now, Gonzales needs to optimize when to chase that power. He gets over-aggressive in his approach, especially against breaking pitches, and it hurts him. He's a limited defender, which puts pressure on his bat. Gonzales occasionally played shortstop in 2022, and the Pirates tried him at third base in the AFL for the first time. His fringe-average arm and range still work best at second base.

THE FUTURE: There's hope that more consistent at-bats will help Gonzales find his rhythm and chase his ceiling as a solid first-division second baseman.

SCOUTING GRADES	Hitting: 55	Power: 50	Speed: 55	Fielding: 45	Arm: 50

Year	Age	Club (League)	Lvl	AVG	G	AB	R	H	2B	3B	HR	RBI	BB	SO	SB	OBP	SLG
2022	23	Pirates (FCL)	R	.429	2	7	1	3	1	1	0	3	0	1	1	.429	.857
2022	23	Bradenton (FSL)	LoA	.000	1	3	0	0	0	0	0	1	1	2	0	.250	.000
2022	23	Altoona (EL)	AA	.263	71	259	47	68	20	1	7	33	43	90	5	.383	.429
Minor League Totals				.285	154	593	101	169	44	6	25	91	84	194	13	.384	.506

9 MIKE BURROWS, RHP

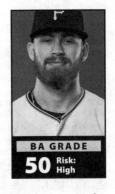

Born: Nov. 8, 1999. **B-T:** R-R. **HT:** 6-1. **WT:** 190.
Drafted: HS—Waterford, Conn., 2018 (11th round). **Signed by:** Eddie Charles.

TRACK RECORD: Burrows, a Connecticut high school product, was expected to honor his commitment to Connecticut in 2018 until the Pirates swooped in and signed him to an above-slot $500,000 deal in the 11th round. The 22-year-old reached the upper levels for the first time in 2022, and pitched 94.1 innings across Double-A and Triple-A, and also appeared in the Futures Game. Burrows spent a month on the injured list with a shoulder injury late in the season after he had missed two months in 2021 with an oblique injury.

BA GRADE

50 Risk: High

SCOUTING REPORT: Burrows has built a reputation as a two-pitch data darling. His plus 93-95 mph fastball has some of the best carry of any four-seamer in Pittsburgh's system. He pairs it with a 77-81 mph hammer of a curveball that routinely surpasses spin rates of 2,900 rpm. Burrows' one inning at the Futures Game showed a glimpse of how the two pitches work in tandem in short bursts by generating five total whiffs and earning the distinction of best fastball and breaking pitch at the game. Burrows needs a third pitch to take a step forward to remain on a starter's track. The Pirates are bullish on Burrows' mid-80s changeup, and he finally threw it more in 2022. As a result, he flashed solid-average potential and more feel for the pitch. Pittsburgh may also explore adding a second, shorter breaking ball to his arsenal to help turn over lineups more efficiently. Burrows throws plenty of strikes via a repeatable delivery that uses a short arm path and over-the-top release, though some evaluators see more control than command.

THE FUTURE: Burrows has the potential to become a No. 4 starter, though the allure of deploying him as a multi-inning power reliever remains strong. He should arrive in Pittsburgh at some point in 2023.

SCOUTING GRADES	Fastball: 60	Curveball: 60	Changeup: 50	Control: 50

Year	Age	Club (League)	Lvl	W	L	ERA	G	GS	IP	H	HR	BB	SO	BB/9	SO/9	WHIP	AVG
2022	22	Altoona (EL)	AA	4	2	2.94	12	12	52	38	3	19	69	3.3	11.9	1.10	.199
2022	22	Indianapolis (IL)	AAA	1	4	5.31	12	10	42	45	5	12	42	2.6	8.9	1.35	.271
Minor League Totals				9	11	3.36	52	49	201	157	13	75	229	3.4	10.3	1.15	.213

10 THOMAS HARRINGTON, RHP

Born: July 12, 2001. **B-T:** R-R. **HT:** 6-2. **WT:** 185.
Drafted: Campbell, 2022 (1st round supplemental). **Signed by:** Mike Bradford.

BA GRADE

50 Risk: High

TRACK RECORD: The rare projectable college pitcher with limited innings, Harrington was a two-sport star at Southern Lee High in Sanford, N.C., who only became a full-time pitcher as a junior and made only one start as a senior in 2020 before the pandemic ended his season. Harrington received minimal Division I interest and opted to walk on at Campbell. He quickly won the Camels' Sunday starter role entering the spring. He was even better as a sophomore in 2022, as he posted a 2.53 ERA to go with 111 strikeouts, 18 walks and only one home run allowed in 92.2 innings. The Pirates drafted him 36th overall and signed him for $2.047 million.
SCOUTING REPORT: Harrington provides an intriguing foundation for the Pirates to mold. When he signed, his deep arsenal was fronted by a low-90s two-seam fastball. He also experimented with a four-seam fastball at Campbell that touched 96 mph. Both his sweeping low-80s slider and tailing mid-80s changeup have intriguing shape, but neither showed plus potential as an amateur. Harrington flashes a slower upper-70s curveball as a change-of-pace look for hitters. Scouts like his arm action, while his athleticism allows him to repeat his delivery, and suggests plus command potential. Harrington could enhance his entire profile if he finds a way to unlock a bit more power in his arsenal. There's reason to believe more could be in the tank, because Harrington added nearly 20 pounds of muscle in two years at Campbell and has room on his frame to continue adding strength.
THE FUTURE: Harrington is a polished strike-thrower who could move quickly through the lower levels. He will make his professional debut in 2023.

SCOUTING GRADES	Fastball: 50	Curveball: 40	Slider: 55	Changeup: 55	Control: 60

Year	Age	Club (Lge)	Level	W	L	ERA	G	GS	IP	H	HR	BB	SO	BB/9	SO/9	WHIP	AVG
2022	21	Did not play															

11 JARED JONES, RHP

Born: Aug. 6, 2001. **B-T:** L-R. **HT:** 6-1. **WT:** 190.
Drafted: HS—La Mirada, Calif., 2020 (2nd round). **Signed by:** Brian Tracy.

TRACK RECORD: Jones was a two-way star as an amateur and scouts voted him the second-best athlete in the 2020 high school class in Baseball America's best tools series. The Pirates drafted him No. 44 overall that year and signed him to a $2.2 million bonus to buy him out of a commitment to Texas. He made his pro debut with Low-A Bradenton in 2021, then spent all of 2022 with High-A Greensboro in his age-20 season, where he threw the most innings (124.1) of any pitcher in Pittsburgh's minor league system.
SCOUTING REPORT: Jones' 6-foot frame belies the horsepower in his four-pitch mix. He's a dynamic athlete and his upper-90s fastball can touch 100 mph while being boring in on righthanded hitters. Both his breaking balls have plus potential. The slider, in particular, tunnels well with his fastball and gives hitters fits. Jones also throws a firm, upper-80s changeup that lags behind his other pitches. A combination of bad luck (.310 BABIP) and wavering command led to Jones battling high pitch counts and inefficiency, especially early in the season. The Pirates believe he made command improvements, especially with his secondaries, as the season progressed. A demonstrative and fiery competitor, Jones is still learning the finer points of pitching and the Pirates believe he dealt with adversity more effectively in 2022.
THE FUTURE: There's some skepticism Jones' size and command hold up over an entire season as a starting pitcher. His electric bat-missing arsenal is suited for a high-leverage relief role if it doesn't.

BA GRADE: 50/High	Fastball: 70	Curveball: 55	Slider: 60	Changeup: 45	Control: 45

Year	Age	Club (League)	Lvl	W	L	ERA	G	GS	IP	H	HR	BB	SO	BB/9	SO/9	WHIP	AVG
2022	20	Greensboro (SAL)	HiA	5	7	4.62	26	26	123	115	19	51	142	3.7	10.4	1.35	.246
Minor League Totals				8	13	4.63	44	41	189	178	25	85	245	4.1	11.7	1.39	.246

12 JI-HWAN BAE, 2B/OF

Born: July 26, 1999. **B-T:** L-R. **HT:** 5-11. **WT:** 180.
Signed: South Korea, 2018. **Signed by:** Fu-Chun Chiang/Tony Harris.

TRACK RECORD: Bae's reputation is forever impacted by the 30-game suspension he served in 2019 for violating Minor League Baseball's domestic violence policy after a South Korean court convicted him of assaulting his then-girlfriend at a New Year's Eve party in 2017. The Pirates chose not to release Bae and he has steadily risen through Pittsburgh's system since, culminating in his big league debut in 2022, when he hit .333 over 33 at-bats.

SCOUTING REPORT: The industry has long viewed Bae as a burner with impressive bat control and those foundational elements remained intact in 2022. He did, however, make two notable adjustments. Bae cut his strikeout rate (16.9%) by nearly 6%. He also added a bit more strength to his 185-pound frame, with evaluators seeing more hard contact than in years past. Still, it's low power potential, and his swing is geared to keep the ball low and accentuate his plus hitting ability. Bae times pitches with a sizable leg kick, recoiling as he waits, then jumps at the ball, sometimes dropping to one knee as he makes contact. Bae's groundball rate annually hovers around 50%. It allows his 70-grade speed to flourish as he dashes to first base and then steals bases in bunches. Bae doesn't necessarily stand out at any one position defensively, but can capably play almost anywhere, including all three up-the-middle spots, although his arm is stretched at shortstop.

THE FUTURE: Bae could be a plug-and-play option for the Pirates in 2023 as a contact-oriented super-utility type.

BA GRADE: 45/Medium	Hit: 60	Power: 30	Speed: 70	Fielding: 50	Arm: 50

Year	Age	Club (League)	Lvl	AVG	G	AB	R	H	2B	3B	HR	RBI	BB	SO	SB	OBP	SLG
2022	22	Indianapolis (IL)	AAA	.289	108	419	81	121	23	6	8	53	48	80	30	.362	.430
2022	22	Pittsburgh (NL)	MLB	.333	10	33	5	11	3	0	0	6	2	6	3	.405	.424
Major League Totals				.333	10	33	5	11	3	0	0	6	2	6	3	.405	.424
Minor League Totals				.294	314	1203	240	354	66	18	16	137	144	256	91	.373	.419

13 ANTHONY SOLOMETO, LHP

Born: Dec. 2, 2002. **B-T:** L-L. **HT:** 6-2. **WT:** 208.
Drafted: HS—Pennsauken, N.J., 2021 (2nd round). **Signed by:** Dan Radcliff.
TRACK RECORD: Solometo vaulted to No. 28 on Baseball America's draft board in 2021 and the Pirates nabbed him at No. 37 overall, and signed him to an above-slot $2.8 million bonus. Pittsburgh built him up slowly at extended spring training in Florida, but Solometo finally debuted a year later with Low-A Bradenton in late May. He proved worth the wait, and pitched to a 2.64 ERA over 47.2 innings.
SCOUTING REPORT: The 6-foot-5 lefthander is mesmerizing to watch. His long levers seemingly fly in all directions as he drives down the mound toward hitters. His delivery and arm stroke consistently draw comparisons to Madison Bumgarner. Unsurprisingly, he's a nightmare at-bat for lefthanded hitters. He creates considerable deception, which helps his arsenal play up despite no clear plus pitch. He attacks hitters with a sinking low-90s fastball and tunnels it well with his mid-80s changeup. He also throws a sweeping 82-84 mph slider that flashes plus, but fluctuates in velocity and command. The Pirates hope to help optimize the shape and design of his breaking ball so it's more effective against experienced hitters. Solometo throws plenty of strikes and repeats his intricate delivery well. He's also a meticulous learner capable of making quick adjustments—the Pirates note he essentially learned how to hold runners over the span of one week—and he draws rave reviews for his maturity and commitment to his routine.
THE FUTURE: His arsenal isn't flashy, but Solometo impresses with his aptitude and pitchability. He has a ceiling of a midrotation starter.

BA GRADE: 50/High ·	Fastball: 55	Slider: 55	Changeup: 50	Control: 55

Year	Age	Club (League)	Lvl	W	L	ERA	G	GS	IP	H	HR	BB	SO	BB/9	SO/9	WHIP	AVG
2022	19	Bradenton (FSL)	LoA	5	1	2.64	13	8	48	31	0	19	51	3.6	9.6	1.05	.188
Minor League Totals				5	1	2.64	13	8	48	31	0	19	51	3.6	9.6	1.05	.188

14 KYLE NICOLAS, RHP

Born: Feb. 22, 1999. **B-T:** R-R. **HT:** 6-4. **WT:** 220.
Drafted: Ball State, 2020 (2nd round). **Signed by:** Joe Dunigan (Marlins).
TRACK RECORD: Nicolas pitched his way up draft boards in 2020 by substantially cutting his walk rate while maintaining premium stuff in a small sample size at Ball State. The Marlins drafted him No. 61 overall that summer, then traded him to the Pirates for catcher Jacob Stallings just over a year later. Nicolas spent all of 2022 at Double-A Altoona, where he struck out 25.9% of batters but also walked 12.1% in 90.2 innings.
SCOUTING REPORT: Nicolas has plenty of firepower, but he needs to harness it more consistently to remain a starter. His 93-95 mph fastball touches 97 and is his best pitch. The heater has elite carry, averaging nearly 20 inches of induced vertical break, and he shows the ability to add and subtract velocity as needed. Nicolas' mid-80s slider dives out of the zone and has become a plus pitch. Nicolas' low-80s

curveball is a bit softer, thrown with 11-to-5 break, and he also dabbles with a firm upper-80s changeup that lags behind his other three offerings. Internal and external evaluators alike note there are mechanical inconsistencies in Nicolas' delivery that require attention and currently hinder his strike-throwing. He showed marginal improvements early in 2022, but walked 28 batters over his final 44.1 innings.

THE FUTURE: The Pirates believe Nicolas is on the verge of a breakout if they can clean up his delivery. His powerful pitch mix could play up in a big league bullpen if he can't find more strikes.

BA GRADE: 50/High	Fastball: 70	Curveball: 50	Slider: 60	Changeup: 40	Control: 40

Year	Age	Club (League	Lvl	W	L	ERA	G	GS	IP	H	HR	BB	SO	BB/9	SO/9	WHIP	AVG
2022	23	Altoona (EL)	AA	2	4	3.97	24	22	91	71	9	47	101	4.7	10.0	1.30	.216
Minor League Totals				8	8	4.08	45	42	190	151	25	96	237	4.6	11.2	1.30	.216

15 JARED TRIOLO, 3B

Born: Feb. 8, 1998. **B-T:** R-R. **HT:** 6-3. **WT:** 210.
Drafted: Houston, 2019 (2nd round supplemental). **Signed by:** Wayne Mathis.

TRACK RECORD: Triolo performed well over three seasons at Houston, as well as a pair of summers on the Cape, and the Pirates signed him to a $868,200 bonus after drafting him No. 72 overall in 2019. His debut was nondescript and he lost all of 2020 due to the pandemic. He returned a far more consistent hitter. Triolo hit .282 with nine homers at Double-A Altoona in 2022, and managers voted him the best defensive third baseman in the Eastern League. He missed the final month of the season with a knee injury, but the Pirates added him to their 40-man roster in November.

SCOUTING REPORT: While Triolo's defensive chops are well-known, his improvement in several offensive categories helped elevate his profile. Triolo has premier barrel skills despite an unorthodox swing and stance. His bat path works well, though, and he makes excellent swing decisions, which led to an 80% contact rate and a 14% swing-and-miss rate in the zone that are among the better marks in Pittsburgh's system. His average power plays best to right-center but he worked on pulling the ball more in 2022. Triolo has won the Pirates' minor league defender of the year award two years in a row. He plays a premium third base, and shows a desirable combination of arm strength, accuracy and agility. Triolo is athletic enough to handle shortstop as well, and appeared in center field for the first time as a professional while with Altoona.

THE FUTURE: Triolo's contact ability and defensive versatility provide a ceiling as a super utility option in the big leagues.

BA GRADE: 45/High	Hit: 55	Power: 50	Speed: 50	Fielding: 60	Arm: 55

Year	Age	Club (League	Lvl	AVG	G	AB	R	H	2B	3B	HR	RBI	BB	SO	SB	OBP	SLG
2022	24	Altoona (EL)	AA	.282	112	425	66	120	21	5	9	39	63	87	24	.376	.419
Minor League Totals				.281	280	1080	170	304	69	10	26	151	132	230	52	.360	.436

16 MATT GORSKI, OF

Born: Dec. 22, 1997 **B-T:** R-R. **HT:** 6-2. **WT:** 215.
Drafted: Indiana, 2019 (2nd round). **Signed by:** Anthony Wycklendt.

TRACK RECORD: Gorski was a second-round pick by the Pirates in 2019 who entered pro ball with immense power and concerns about his hit tool. Those concerns persisted throughout much of his pro career, and he hit just .223 with a 31.2% strikeout rate as a 23-year-old with High-A Greensboro in 2021. But Gorski rebuilt his swing in the offseason and altered the trajectory of his career, posting a .956 OPS with 23 homers through 81 games, although he missed two months with a quad injury. He was unprotected and unselected in the Rule 5 draft.

SCOUTING REPORT: Gorski made a myriad of changes to his swing. He slightly opened his stance and altered his stride, better engaging his lower half to become more rotational toward the ball. He also worked to flatten his bat path. The changes unlocked just enough contact ability to allow his plus-plus power to play. Gorski's 91.4 mph average exit velocity trailed only Oneil Cruz among Pirates minor leaguers with more than 100 plate appearances. There's still considerable swing-and-miss—he whiffed on 32% of pitches in the strike zone—and High-A Greensboro is a hitter's haven. Gorski is a plus runner who impacts every aspect of the game. He's a plus defender in the corners with a railgun of an arm and could steal 30-plus bases over a full season. The Pirates may try Gorski at first base as well to find him even more reps.

THE FUTURE: There's reason for skepticism considering Gorski will be 25 on Opening Day with 161 career plate appearances in the upper levels. If the swing changes stick, he has a shot at a three true outcome-type big league role with considerable supplemental tools.

BA GRADE: 45/High		Hit: 35			Power: 70			Speed: 60		Fielding: 60		Arm: 80		

Year	Age	Club (League)	Lvl	AVG	G	AB	R	H	2B	3B	HR	RBI	BB	SO	SB	OBP	SLG
2022	24	Bradenton (FSL)	LoA	.176	5	17	1	3	0	0	1	1	1	6	1	.222	.353
2022	24	Greensboro (SAL)	HiA	.294	37	126	34	37	3	2	17	37	17	39	9	.377	.754
2022	24	Altoona (EL)	AA	.277	38	141	27	39	8	2	6	28	15	47	10	.354	.489
2022	24	Indianapolis (IL)	AAA	.500	1	2	0	1	0	0	0	0	0	1	1	.500	.500
Minor League Totals				.243	225	823	156	200	38	6	44	144	86	266	50	.317	.464

17 HUNTER BARCO, LHP

Born: Dec. 15, 2000. **B-T:** L-L. **HT:** 6-4. **WT:** 210.
Drafted: Florida, 2022 (2nd round). **Signed by:** Cam Murphy.
TRACK RECORD: Scouts viewed Barco as a potential first-rounder as a high schooler in 2019, but the lefthander instead made it to Florida, where he quickly won a spot in the Gators' rotation and was a solid performer over three seasons. He pitched to a 2.50 ERA and struck out 69 batters in 50.1 innings during his draft year until an elbow injury that required Tommy John surgery ended his season in May. The Pirates nabbed Barco No. 44 overall and signed him to a $1,520,000 bonus.
SCOUTING REPORT: The 6-foot-4 lefthander was trending upward prior to his injury. He's built like a prototypical starting pitcher and attacks hitters from a low three-quarters arm slot. Barco presently lacks a true plus offering. His fastball has touched 95 mph in the past but mostly sat in the low 90s in 2022 with ordinary sink and run. His sweeping, low-80s slider darts at the back foot of righthanded hitters and is his best swing-and-miss offering, although some scouts wonder whether Barco will struggle to command the pitch because of his arm slot. His mid-80s changeup was popular as a high schooler and remains a solid-average offering. Barco's crossfire delivery and arm slot add deceptive tilt and he was a consistent strike-thrower against Southeastern Conference hitters in college.
THE FUTURE: Barco's injury will delay his debut, but his polish, pitch mix and competitiveness provide a relatively high floor. He has back-of-the-rotation starter upside with a chance for more if he adds velocity.

BA GRADE: 50/Extreme		Fastball: 50		Slider: 55		Changeup: 50		Control: 55		

Year	Age	Club (Lge)	Level	W	L	ERA	G	GS	IP	H	HR	BB	SO	BB/9	SO/9	WHIP	AVG
2022	21	Did not play															

18 MICHAEL KENNEDY, LHP

Born: Nov 30, 2004. **B-T:** L-L. **HT:** 6-1. **WT:** 205.
Drafted: HS—Troy, N.Y., 2022 (4th round). **Signed by:** Eddie Charles.
TRACK RECORD: Kennedy joined Pirates first-rounder Termarr Johnson on Team USA's 18U National Team roster in 2021 and was the top-ranked draft prospect in New York entering the 2022 draft. He was expected to be a tough sign considering his commitment to Louisiana State until the Pirates drafted him in the fourth round and signed him to a $1 million bonus, nearly double the expected slot value. A knee injury kept Kennedy from making his pro debut.
SCOUTING REPORT: Kennedy pairs a cerebral, competitive approach with a surprisingly refined three-pitch mix for a cold-weather prep arm. The Pirates are excited by the characteristics of Kennedy's 88-92 mph fastball, which carries well from his low arm slot. He pairs it with a sweeping upper-70s slider and has shown aptitude to quickly learn and enhance his low-80s changeup. His delivery is controlled and he repeats it well. He shows good feel for his entire arsenal and his shorter arm path provides a bit of deception against lefties. Kennedy would benefit from a bit more power across his arsenal, but some scouts worry there isn't a ton of room for projection on his frame.
THE FUTURE: One of the youngest prospects in the draft, Kennedy will be just 18 years old throughout all of 2023. He's in line to make his professional debut and begin his ascent through Pittsburgh's system as a strike-throwing lefty with a useful three-pitch mix.

BA GRADE: 50/Extreme		Fastball: 55		Slider: 55		Changeup: 50		Control: 55		

Year	Age	Club (Lge)	Level	W	L	ERA	G	GS	IP	H	HR	BB	SO	BB/9	SO/9	WHIP	AVG
2022	17	Did not play—Injured															

19 CANAAN SMITH-NJIGBA, OF

Born: April 30, 1999. **B-T:** L-R. **HT:** 6-0. **WT:** 240.
Drafted: HS—Heath, Texas, 2017 (4th round). **Signed by:** Mike Leuzinger (Yankees).
TRACK RECORD: Smith-Njigba has been known for posting high walk rates all the way back to his days as a high school star in Texas when teams mostly pitched around him. The Yankees drafted him in 2017 and traded him along with three others to the Pirates in 2021 in exchange for Jameson Taillon. He made his big league debut in mid-June, but suffered a season-ending fractured right wrist in an outfield collision just three games into his stint in Pittsburgh. His brother, Jaxon, stars at wide receiver for Ohio State and is a potential first-round NFL draft pick in 2023.
SCOUTING REPORT: Smith-Njigba parses balls and strikes as well as any hitter in Pittsburgh's system, walking 15.1% of the time with Triple-A Indianapolis in 2022. He pairs that plate discipline with considerable strength-based power, exceeding 90 mph average exit velocity. His natural swing plane, though, is not geared for lift and curbs his in-game power. The good news is Smith-Njigba slashed his groundball rate by roughly 13% in the minors in 2022, but it still clocked in at 52.8%. Defensively, he's likely ticketed for left field because of his fringe-average running ability, throwing arm and range, although he can handle right field in a pinch.
THE FUTURE: Smith-Njigba has a chance to reach a platoon-type role in the big leagues. He should vie for opportunities in Pittsburgh's wide-open corner outfield competition in 2023.

BA GRADE: 45/High | **Hit:** 45 | **Power:** 50 | **Speed:** 45 | **Fielding:** 45 | **Arm:** 45

Year	Age	Club (League)	Lvl	AVG	G	AB	R	H	2B	3B	HR	RBI	BB	SO	SB	OBP	SLG
2022	23	Indianapolis (IL)	AAA	.277	52	184	31	51	15	3	1	19	33	52	8	.387	.408
2022	23	Pittsburgh (NL)	MLB	.200	3	5	1	1	1	0	0	0	1	0	0	.429	.400
Major League Totals				.200	3	5	1	1	1	0	0	0	1	0	0	.429	.400
Minor League Totals				.276	351	1212	176	334	76	7	26	179	219	331	42	.387	.414

20 MALCOM NUÑEZ, 1B

Born: March 9, 2001. **B-T:** R-R. **HT:** 6-2. **WT:** 232.
Signed: Cuba, 2018. **Signed by:** Alix Martinez/Angel Ovalles (Cardinals).
TRACK RECORD: Nuñez starred as an amateur in Cuba and carried that momentum into his 2018 pro debut upon signing with the Cardinals, winning the Dominican Summer League triple crown with a .415/.497/.774 slash line. He struggled mightily the following year, but has shown far more consistency over the last two seasons. The Pirates acquired Nuñez at the 2022 deadline in the Jose Quintana trade. He hit 23 homers between the two systems, and briefly reached Triple-A as a 21-year-old. The Pirates left him unprotected ahead of the 2022 Rule 5 Draft.
SCOUTING REPORT: Nuñez is capable of cranking out some majestic pull-side homers via his violent, strength-based swing. He has a relatively simple move to the ball, although scouts point out he still has a minor hitch in his load, and posts exit velocities in excess of 110 mph. He became more selective in 2022, and swung at just under 40% of pitches. His breaking ball recognition improved out of necessity as older pitchers found it unwise to challenge him with too many fastballs. Nuñez doesn't always maximize his power potential, though, as his groundball rate traditionally hovers around 50%. Almost all of Nuñez's value is tied to his hitting ability. Despite a strong arm, he has outgrown third base and his range is tested even at first base.
THE FUTURE: There isn't much margin for error in Nuñez's bat-only profile, but he shows intriguing hitting traits and will be just 22 years old on Opening Day. He should open 2023 with Triple-A Indianapolis.

BA GRADE: 45/High | **Hit:** 45 | **Power:** 60 | **Speed:** 30 | **Fielding:** 40 | **Arm:** 55

Year	Age	Club (League)	Lvl	AVG	G	AB	R	H	2B	3B	HR	RBI	BB	SO	SB	OBP	SLG
2022	21	Springfield (TL)	AA	.255	85	298	51	76	11	0	17	66	48	71	4	.360	.463
2022	21	Altoona (EL)	AA	.286	29	105	20	30	5	0	5	21	17	27	1	.381	.476
2022	21	Indianapolis (IL)	AAA	.231	5	13	1	3	0	0	1	1	4	5	0	.412	.462
Minor League Totals				.280	310	1120	181	314	59	4	47	204	145	250	18	.368	.466

21 CARMEN MLODZINSKI, RHP

Born: Feb. 19, 1999. **B-T:** R-R. **HT:** 6-2. **WT:** 225.
Drafted: South Carolina, 2020 (1st round supplemental). **Signed by:** Cam Murphy.

TRACK RECORD: Mlodzinski generated first-round buzz on the strength of a dominant Cape Cod League showing in 2019 despite never putting it all together at South Carolina. Pittsburgh drafted him No. 31 overall in 2020. Mlodzinski turned heads in his pro debut with High-A Greensboro the following year, where he struck out 54 batters in his first 41 innings, but right shoulder stiffness sidelined him for more than a month. He hasn't regained that form since. He spent all of 2022 with Double-A Altoona, and posted a 4.78 ERA in 105.1 innings.

SCOUTING REPORT: The metric-savvy Mlodzinski has a bevy of offerings but is still seeking the optimal pitch mix. He has experimented with both a sinker and four-seamer as his predominant fastball, opting to stick with his preferred 93-95 mph four-seamer. Mlodzinski also re-introduced a two-seamer and can occasionally cut his fastball as well, but it doesn't generate many whiffs. His two offspeed pitches are above-average. Mlodzinski altered the movement profile of his mid-80s slider to add more depth in 2022, and he rounds out his arsenal with an upper-80s changeup. There's some deception in his effortful delivery, but his command wavers and he battles inefficiency.

THE FUTURE: Erraticism has defined Mlodzinski's pro career. Clean health and improved command in 2023 would help him stay on track to his ceiling as a back-of-the-rotation starter.

BA GRADE: 45/High   **Fastball:** 50   **Slider:** 55   **Changeup:** 50   **Control:** 50

Year	Age	Club (League	Lvl	W	L	ERA	G	GS	IP	H	HR	BB	SOBB/9	SO/9	WHIP	AVG
2022	23	Altoona (EL)	AA	6	8	4.78	27	22	105	109	10	40	111	3.4	9.5	1.41	.267
Minor League Totals				8	12	4.51	42	36	158	157	17	62	177	3.5	10.1	1.39	.258

22 CODY BOLTON, RHP

Born: June 19, 1998. **B-T:** R-R. **HT:** 6-2. **WT:** 230.
Drafted: HS—Tracy, Calif., 2017 (6th round). **Signed by:** Mike Sansoe.

TRACK RECORD: Simply pitching on a consistent basis represented a massive step forward for Bolton, who once ranked as one of Pittsburgh's top prospects but hadn't appeared in a game since 2019. A knee injury wiped out Bolton's 2021 season, and he also missed time with forearm and groin injuries in 2018 and 2019, respectively. Pittsburgh was cautious when deploying Bolton in 2022 given his history, and used him in short outings or as an opener over 30 games with Triple-A Indianapolis.

SCOUTING REPORT: Bolton worked hard in the offseason to improve his conditioning after the lost 2021 season. His fastball is still a tick below where it was prior to his layoff, but his four-seamer sat 92-94 mph and touched 96. He occasionally mixes in a two-seamer. His best pitch may now be a low-80s slider. Bolton worked to turn the pitch into more of a true sweeper with two-plane break, and it has some of the higher horizontal break and spin rates of any slider in Pittsburgh's system. He also features a firm upper-80s changeup. Bolton struggles with pitch efficiency, and walked 12.4% of hitters in 2022. There's skepticism he can throw considerably more strikes because of his lengthy arm action.

THE FUTURE: Given Bolton's durability and command concerns, a bullpen role seems likely. He should reach the majors at some point 2023, and could pitch his way into middle- to high-leverage relief situations in relatively short order.

BA GRADE: 45/High   **Fastball:** 55   **Slider:** 60   **Changeup:** 55   **Control:** 45

Year	Age	Club (League)	Lvl	W	L	ERA	G	GS	IP	H	HR	BB	SOBB/9	SO/9	WHIP	AVG
2022	24	Indianapolis (IL)	AAA	4	2	3.09	30	14	76	57	4	40	82	4.8	9.8	1.28	.207
Minor League Totals				15	13	3.27	69	53	247	199	18	85	251	3.1	9.1	1.15	.218

23 DARIEL LOPEZ, 3B

Born: Feb. 7, 2002. **B-T:** R-R. **HT:** 6-1. **WT:** 213.
Signed: Dominican Republic, 2018. **Signed by:** Esteban Alvarez.

TRACK RECORD: Lopez was one of the high-profile names in Pittsburgh's 2018 international class, signing for $400,000. He has acquitted himself well at the plate since debuting at the lower levels in 2021. He spent all of 2022 with High-A Greensboro, and hit .286 with 19 homers in his age-20 season.

SCOUTING REPORT: Evaluators take note of Lopez's intriguing blend of tools while also acknowledging he needs to refine his game, especially defensively. Lopez's swing is surprisingly compact given his large frame and he has notable raw strength. He also has plenty of faith in his above-average contact ability. Lopez was one of the most aggressive hitters in Pittsburgh's system in 2022. His aggressiveness outside the strike zone results in too much weak contact and ground balls, something older pitchers will exploit.

His power is presently geared toward right-center field, which was rewarded at Greensboro—15 of his 19 homers came at home. It's unclear where Lopez best fits defensively. He has smooth actions, solid hands and a plus throwing arm, but he's mistake-prone (25 errors) and will likely be too big to play shortstop. He played more third base and second base in 2022.

THE FUTURE: Lopez's hitting ability combined with his versatility is intriguing. He's still young, but he needs to clean up the mistakes to ensure he sticks in the dirt.

BA GRADE: 45/High	Hit: 50	Power: 55	Speed: 45	Fielding: 45	Arm: 60

Year	Age	Club (League)	Lvl	AVG	G	AB	R	H	2B	3B	HR	RBI	BB	SO	SB	OBP	SLG
2022	20	Greensboro (SAL)	HiA	.286	102	391	58	112	15	1	19	58	21	107	6	.329	.476
Minor League Totals				.285	247	919	151	262	42	6	31	155	76	240	12	.348	.445

24 TSUNG-CHE CHENG, SS

Born: July 26, 2001. **B-T:** L-R. **HT:** 5-7. **WT:** 174.
Signed: Taiwan, 2019. **Signed by:** Fu-Chan Chiang.

TRACK RECORD: Cheng enjoyed a breakout 2022 campaign with Low-A Bradenton, three years after Pittsburgh signed him as a 17-year-old via Taiwan for $380,000. Cheng, who goes by the nickname "Z," led all Pirates minor leaguers with 33 steals and was among qualified Florida State League leaders in batting average (.270) and doubles (25). He was named to the league's all-star team and also named the Pirates' minor league baserunner of the year.

SCOUTING REPORT: Cheng marries a line-drive approach with a simple lefthanded swing that accentuates his bat-to-ball skills and results in plenty of contact. There's a bit more power than some might expect considering his 5-foot-7 frame, but it will never be a focal point of his game. The Pirates lauded his pre-pitch preparation. His 20.7% strikeout rate was a bit higher than anticipated, but Cheng made subtle improvements to his plate discipline as the season progressed and his in-zone contact ability was strong. He also graded out as one of the Pirates' best infield defenders. He checks all the boxes at shortstop, and shows good hands, range and an above-average throwing arm. Cheng's baseball IQ and meticulous preparation help enhance his skill set, even if he's not the most toolsy player.

THE FUTURE: The type of player coaches adore, Cheng has the makings of a super-utility type thanks to his defensive acumen and contact ability.

BA GRADE: 45/High	Hit: 55	Power: 30	Speed: 60	Fielding: 60	Arm: 55

Year	Age	Club (League)	Lvl	AVG	G	AB	R	H	2B	3B	HR	RBI	BB	SO	SB	OBP	SLG
2022	20	Bradenton (FSL)	LoA	.270	104	385	79	104	25	7	6	52	63	95	33	.376	.418
Minor League Totals				.280	142	507	111	142	33	8	10	83	93	109	49	.395	.436

25 COLIN SELBY, RHP

Born: Oct. 24, 1997. **B-T:** R-R. **HT:** 6-1. **WT:** 220.
Drafted: Randolph-Macon (Va.), 2018 (16th round). **Signed by:** Dan Radcliff.

TRACK RECORD: Selby was a three-year starter at Division III Randolph-Macon (Va.) and became the seventh draft pick in program history when the Pirates selected him in the 16th round in 2018, and signed him to a $125,000 bonus. Pittsburgh initially deployed him as a starter, but Selby had Tommy John surgery during the shutdown in 2020 and returned as a reliever. He spent most of 2022 with Double-A Altoona, where he struck out nearly 30% of batters faced, although he missed two months due to injury.

SCOUTING REPORT: From the fastball touching 99 mph to the wipeout slider and even the big, bushy beard, Selby's entire operation screams power reliever. He has steadily added velocity since turning pro and his fastball now sits in the upper 90s. Both his offspeed pitches are nasty. He snaps off an upper-80s slider with considerable depth that rates as one of the best sliders in Pittsburgh's system and batters whiffed on it more than 70% of the time. Selby also mixes in a sweeping low-80s curve. Command isn't a strength. Selby attacks hitters with brute force, falling toward the first base line as he finishes his delivery.

THE FUTURE: Selby has the ceiling of a hard-throwing late-inning reliever if he can throw enough strikes.

BA GRADE: 45/High	Fastball: 60	Curveball: 60	Slider: 60	Control: 40

Year	Age	Club (League)	Lvl	W	L	ERA	G	GS	IP	H	HR	BB	SO	BB/9	SO/9	WHIP	AVG
2022	24	Altoona (EL)	AA	2	2	2.20	26	1	33	27	1	14	41	3.9	11.3	1.26	.225
2022	24	Indianapolis (IL)	AAA	0	1	3.00	3	0	3	2	1	0	2	0.0	6.0	0.67	.182
Minor League Totals				12	10	3.47	88	29	231	182	21	92	237	3.6	9.2	1.19	.213

26 RODOLFO NOLASCO, OF

Born: Sept. 23, 2001. **B-T:** R-R. **HT:** 5-10. **WT:** 207.
Signed: Dominican Republic, 2018. **Signed by:** Victor Santana.

TRACK RECORD: Nolasco was part of a Pirates 2018 international signing class that included players like Dariel Lopez, Alexander Mojica and Luis Ortiz, but injuries slowed his development compared to his peers. He made his full-season debut in 2022, and hit 11 homers in 77 games for Low-A Bradenton sandwiched around two trips to the injured list.

SCOUTING REPORT: Nolasco's physicality and raw strength have always separated him from other players his age. It results in wicked bat speed, top-end exit velocities and gargantuan home runs. There still are questions about whether he'll make enough contact to consistently utilize his plus power. Nolasco struck out 34% of the time in Bradenton. Like plenty of inexperienced hitters, he needs to improve his pitch recognition and can stray from his approach, although he has a solid understanding of the strike zone. Nolasco showed signs of improvement in July—he hit five homers with nearly as many walks as strikeouts over 13 games—until an injury essentially ended his season. Nolasco isn't the most fleet of foot defensively and is most comfortable playing right field, where he has average potential and can utilize his plus throwing arm.

THE FUTURE: His hit tool remains unrefined, but it's easy to dream on Nolasco's power. He needs more seasoning in the low minors in 2023.

| BA GRADE: 50/Extreme | Hit: 35 | | Power: 60 | | Speed: 45 | | Fielding: 50 | | Arm: 60 | | |

Year	Age	Club (League)	Lvl	AVG	G	AB	R	H	2B	3B	HR	RBI	BB	SO	SB	OBP	SLG
2022	20	Bradenton (FSL)	LoA	.239	77	280	40	67	15	2	11	48	37	109	7	.330	.425
Minor League Totals				.269	173	613	110	165	36	7	24	114	79	178	10	.362	.468

27 AXIEL PLAZ, C

Born: Aug. 12, 2005. **B-T:** R-R. **HT:** 5-11. **WT:** 165.
Signed: Dominican Republic, 2022. **Signed by:** Jesus Morelli.

TRACK RECORD: Pittsburgh signed the Venezuelan native in January 2022 on the strength of his intriguing combination of defensive ability and power potential. Plaz then hit .382/.500/.706 with three homers over 32 games as a 16-year-old in the Dominican Summer League, earned an all-star nod, and was one of the Pirates' most impressive hitters at their fall instructional camp.

SCOUTING REPORT: Plaz flashed power potential as an amateur and has already added more strength, especially to his lower half, with room to add more to his frame. He times up pitchers with a toe tap and is capable of driving the ball to center field when he connects, already showing feel for the barrel, pitch recognition and strike-zone awareness. Amateur evaluators noted Plaz may battle some swing-and-miss as he grows into his power, but he kept his strikeouts in check in his first taste of the DSL (18.6% strikeout rate). He also has a chance to stick behind the plate due to solid receiving skills for his age and an above-average arm, although his footwork remains a work in progress.

THE FUTURE: Plaz will be just 17 years old on Opening Day and has a myriad of potential outcomes, but he caught the Pirates' attention. There are indicators that suggest a potential for both impact defense and power at a premium position.

| BA GRADE: 50/Extreme | Hit: 55 | | Power: 55 | | Speed: 45 | | Fielding: 55 | | Arm: 55 | | |

Year	Age	Club (League)	Lvl	AVG	G	AB	R	H	2B	3B	HR	RBI	BB	SO	SB	OBP	SLG
2022	16	Pirates Gold (DSL)	R	.382	32	68	16	26	11	1	3	21	13	16	2	.500	.706
Minor League Totals				.382	32	68	16	26	11	1	3	21	13	16	2	.500	.706

28 LONNIE WHITE JR., OF

Born: Dec. 31, 2002. **B-T:** R-R. **HT:** 6-2. **WT:** 214.
Drafted: HS—Malvern, Pa., 2021 (2nd round supplemental). **Signed by:** Dan Radcliff.

TRACK RECORD: White is a dynamic athlete who planned to play both baseball and football at Penn State until the Pirates drafted him No. 64 overall in 2021 and went $500,000 over slot to sign him to a $1.5 million bonus. His professional career has yet to come into focus. White has played just 11 games at the rookie-level Florida Complex League since turning pro, and he missed essentially all of the 2022 season because of elbow and hamstring injuries.

SCOUTING REPORT: The injury woes hit particularly hard for White, who was already in need of consistent reps to catch up as a cold-weather prep bat who never focused on baseball full-time. While it's tough to draw anything conclusive from 40 career plate appearances, he still appears to be the same strong, explosive athlete with plus raw power potential who battles swing-and-miss issues (42% strikeout rate).

White is already physically mature. He's a plus runner now who could slow down a tick as he gets older, which could force him to a corner outfield spot.

THE FUTURE: The Pirates expect White will be healthy for spring training and he'll be just 20 years old on Opening Day. There's a bundle of intriguing traits to work with, but he needs to remain healthy and make up for lost time.

BA GRADE: 50/Extreme		Hit: 40		Power: 55			Speed: 55		Fielding: 55		Arm: 50			

Year	Age	Club (League)	Lvl	AVG	G	AB	R	H	2B	3B	HR	RBI	BB	SO	SB	OBP	SLG
2022	19	Pirates (FCL)	R	.286	2	7	1	2	1	0	1	3	0	3	0	.286	.857
Minor League Totals				.263	11	38	7	10	3	0	3	8	2	17	0	.300	.579

29 ANDRES ALVAREZ, 3B/2B/SS

Born: March 29, 1997. **B-T:** R-R. **HT:** 5-10. **WT:** 175.
Drafted: Washington State, 2019 (22nd round). **Signed by:** Junior Vizcaino.
TRACK RECORD: The Pirates signed Alvarez for just $2,000 as a 22nd-round pick out of Washington State in 2019 and he was still in extended spring training until an opening emerged with High-A Greensboro in July 2021. Alvarez made an impression, and hit .288 with seven homers, but his true breakout came in 2022 after reworking his swing. Alvarez hit .220 with 20 homers and 21 steals for Double-A Altoona in his age-25 season.
SCOUTING REPORT: Alvarez credits his work with Pirates minor league hitting coach Jon Nunnally for unlocking his power potential. They worked on two things: Identifying better pitches to hit and back-spinning the baseball to maximize Alvarez's average power when he lifts the ball. The results led to the first 20-20 season in Altoona history. Previously a contact-oriented hitter, Alvarez's strikeout rate climbed and his production dipped throughout the season as he tried to find the right balance in his approach. Defensively, Alvarez is sure-handed and capable of playing anywhere in the dirt. He also expanded his versatility to left field for the first time in 2022. The Pirates admire Alvarez's work ethic, and note he's played winter ball each of the last two seasons.
THE FUTURE: He'll have to prove his swing changes stick, but Alvarez's improved power potential, speed and defensive versatility have put him on the Pirates' prospect radar.

BA GRADE: 40/High		Hit: 50		Power: 50			Speed: 55		Fielding: 55		Arm: 50			

Year	Age	Club (League	Lvl	AVG	G	AB	R	H	2B	3B	HR	RBI	BB	SO	SB	OBP	SLG
2022	25	Altoona (EL)	AA	.220	110	368	53	81	13	2	20	50	64	123	21	.339	.429
Minor League Totals				.236	193	653	99	154	27	4	27	91	98	194	34	.342	.413

30 TYLER SAMANIEGO, LHP

Born: Jan. 30, 1999. **B-T:** R-L. **HT:** 6-2. **WT:** 211.
Drafted: South Alabama, 2021 (15th round). **Signed by:** Darren Mazeroski.
TRACK RECORD: Samaniego's college career began at Mississippi JC, where he was a two-way standout before ultimately transferring to South Alabama and exclusively pitching out of the bullpen. The Pirates signed him to a $75,000 bonus in 2021. Samaniego burst onto the scene a year later, and posted a 2.45 ERA between High-A Greensboro and Double-A Altoona and earning Pirates minor league reliever of the year honors.
SCOUTING REPORT: Samaniego bum-rushed High-A hitters early in 2022 on the strength of his fastball-slider combination, and struck out 35.3% of batters, although his strikeout rate dropped to just 19.8% once he reached the upper levels. His mid-90s heater touches 97 with some arm-side run. He pairs it with a tight, high-spin mid-80s slider, which he's still working to command more consistently. He rarely utilized his mid-80s changeup. Hitters—especially lefthanders—have a hard time picking up Samaniego's deceptive delivery, which he repeats well.
THE FUTURE: The Pirates asked Samaniego to close out games for Altoona and believe he has both the mentality and aptitude to one day slot into a leverage role in a big league bullpen. He'll get another crack at hitters in the upper levels of the minors in 2023.

BA GRADE: 40/High		Fastball: 55		Slider: 55			Changeup: 45		Control: 50			

Year	Age	Club (League)	Lvl	W	L	ERA	G	GS	IP	H	HR	BB	SO	BB/9	SO/9	WHIP	AVG
2022	23	Greensboro (SAL)	HiA	1	1	0.53	14	0	17	3	0	11	24	5.8	12.7	0.82	.054
2022	23	Altoona (EL)	AA	3	3	3.52	24	0	31	15	2	9	23	2.6	6.8	0.78	.147
Minor League Totals				5	4	2.30	43	0	55	22	3	22	62	3.6	10.2	0.80	.120

St. Louis Cardinals

BY GEOFF PONTES

It was a season of goodbyes in St. Louis.

The Cardinals bid farewell to two legends in future Hall of Fame slugger Albert Pujols and franchise icon Yadier Molina after the duo retired. Pujols surged throughout the summer, and led a red-hot Cardinals team down the stretch as he surpassed historic milestones, including slugging his 700th career home run in September. Molina enjoyed his farewell tour, too, and the Cardinals won the National League Central by seven games with a 93-69 record.

Despite the regular season success, the Cardinals' season, and the farewell for Pujols and Molina, ended with a loss to the eventual NL champion Phillies in the Wild Card Series.

While Pujols and Molina stole the headlines, the heart and soul of the Cardinals' lineup consisted of the dynamic duo of third baseman Nolan Arenado and first baseman Paul Goldschmidt, both acquired in lopsided trades that have been the Cardinals' hallmark for years. Arenado worked on adding bat speed during the offseason and hit .298/.358/.533 with 30 home runs en route to finishing third in NL MVP voting. Goldschmidt enjoyed the best season of his career, and hit .317/.404/.578 with 35 home runs on the way to taking home the NL MVP award, his first time winning it after twice finishing as the runner-up.

While the star power was bright in St. Louis, a young group of role players matriculated to the major leagues and provided critical support. Rookie utilityman Brendan Donovan won a Gold Glove award at second base and finished third in NL Rookie of the Year voting. First baseman/outfielder Juan Yepez, outfielder Lars Nootbaar, second baseman Nolan Gorman and righthander Andre Pallante all contributed throughout the season and could take on larger roles in 2023.

Things blossomed in the St. Louis farm system as well. Third baseman Jordan Walker continued to mash at Double-A and then the Arizona Fall League and emerged as one of the top positional prospects in the game.

Shortstop Masyn Winn made strides offensively and showed an improved swing with added power. He made headlines during the summer after he ripped off a 100-mph throw from shortstop in the Futures Game at Dodger Stadium. Righthanders Gordon Graceffo and Michael McGreevy, both 2021 draftees, flew up the system to Double-A in their first full professional seasons.

Perhaps no player announced his presence quite like righthander Tink Hence, who dominated the Low-A Florida State League in his first full-season

Nolan Gorman got called up in late May and hit .226/.300/.420 with 14 home runs in 89 games.

PROJECTED 2026 LINEUP

Catcher	Willson Contreras	34
First Base	Juan Yepez	28
Second Base	Brendan Donovan	29
Third Base	Nolan Arenado	35
Shortstop	Masyn Winn	24
Left Field	Lars Nootbaar	28
Center Field	Dylan Carlson	27
Right Field	Jordan Walker	24
Designated Hitter	Alec Burleson	27
No. 1 Starter	Tink Hence	23
No. 2 Starter	Matthew Liberatore	26
No. 3 Starter	Cooper Hjerpe	25
No. 4 Starter	Gordon Graceffo	26
No. 5 Starter	Michael McGreevy	26
Closer	Ryan Helsley	32

assignment, albeit in pitch-limited outings.

The Cardinals once again went back to the starting pitching well in the 2022 draft, and selected three college lefthanders with their first three picks, topped by Oregon State ace Cooper Hjerpe.

It was a shrewd move for an organization with a lengthy track record of developing college starters into quality major league rotation options.

With a competitive veteran team in the majors, a farm system with premium talent at the top and a plethora of role players throughout the minor leagues, the Cardinals remain one of the healthiest organizations in the game. They show no signs of slowing down, but the pressure is building for postseason success. ∎

ST. LOUIS CARDINALS

TOP 2023 MLB CONTRIBUTORS	RANK
Matthew Liberatore, LHP	4
Alec Burleson, OF	6
Zack Thompson, LHP	11
BREAKOUT PROSPECTS	**RANK**
Leonardo Bernal, C	12
Alec Willis, RHP	17
Jimmy Crooks, C	22

SOURCE OF TOP 30 TALENT

Homegrown	27	Acquired	3
College	16	Trade	1
Junior college	0	Rule 5 draft	0
High school	5	Independent league	0
Nondrafted free agent	1	Free agent/waivers	2
International	5		

LF
Moises Gomez (18)
Matt Koperniak
Chase Pinder
Won Bin-Cho

CF
Mike Antico (25)
Victor Scott
Scott Hurst
Justin Toerner

RF
Jordan Walker (1)
Alec Burleson (6)
Joshua Baez (13)

3B
Jose Fermin
Jacob Buchburger
R.J. Yeager

SS
Masyn Winn (3)
Jonathan Mejia (10)
Jeremy Rivas
Kramer Robertson

2B
Nick Dunn
Samil De La Rosa
Lisandro Espinoza

1B
Luken Baker
Chandler Redmond

C
Ivan Herrera (8)
Leonardo Bernal (12)
Jimmy Crooks (22)
Pedro Pages

LHP

LHSP	LHRP
Matthew Liberatore (4)	Zack Thompson (11)
Cooper Hjerpe (5)	Chris Gerard
Brycen Mautz (14)	Nathanael Heredia
Pete Hansen (15)	John Beller
Connor Thomas (19)	Levi Prater
Alexander Beltre	Alex Cornwell

RHP

RHSP	RHRP
Tink Hence (2)	Freddy Pacheco (23)
Gordon Graceffo (7)	Jake Walsh (24)
Michael McGreevy (9)	Ryan Loutos (29)
Inohan Paniagua (16)	Guillermo Zuniga (30)
Alec Willis (17)	Andrew Marrero
Austin Love (20)	Andre Granillo
Max Rajcic (21)	Gustavo J. Rodriguez
Ian Bedell (26)	Edwin Nuñez
Zane Mills (27)	
Trent Baker (28)	
Dionys Rodriguez	
Leonel Sequera	
Dalton Roach	

1 JORDAN WALKER, 3B

Born: May 22, 2002. **B-T:** R-R. **HT:** 6-5. **WT:** 220.
Drafted: HS—Decatur, Ga., 2020 (1st round).
Signed by: Charles Peterson.

BILL MITCHELL

TRACK RECORD: As a rising high school senior, Walker was viewed as one of the best power hitters in the 2020 prep class, but he struggled with swing-and-miss on the summer showcase circuit. He rectified the issue and showed improved bat-to-ball skills and plate discipline for Decatur (Ga.) High prior to the 2020 coronavirus shutdown. The Cardinals selected Walker with the 21st overall pick that June and signed him for $2.9 million, enough for Walker to forgo a Duke commitment. Walker debuted with Low-A Palm Beach in 2021 and moved quickly to High-A Peoria after he put up a 1.162 OPS in 27 games. He spent 55 games in the Midwest League and hit .292/.344/.487 as one of the youngest players at the level. In 2022, Walker moved to Double-A Springfield, where he was the youngest position player at the classification to start the season. Walker responded with another standout campaign and hit .306/.388/.510 with 31 doubles and 19 home runs. Late in the season, the Cardinals moved Walker from third base to right field, where he projects to settle.

SCOUTING REPORT: Walker has a tall, well-conditioned frame that projects strength and athleticism. He balances both power and contact at the plate. His longer levers lead to swing-and-miss, but he balances it with a simple, powerful swing and good tracking skills. Despite a longer swing path, Walker shows the ability to hit a variety of pitch shapes and locations. His best contact comes on the outer half of the plate, where he can extend his arms and drive balls to all fields. He's an aggressive hitter who likes to swing. While this approach can often lead to strikeouts, Walker's innate bat-to-ball skills and strength allows him to overcome his aggressive tendencies. The length of his levers and bat path help him cover the whole plate, while also allowing him to barrel pitches in the outside shadow zone. Walker's double-plus raw power flashes in games and is backed by standout exit velocity numbers. During the 2022 season, 45% of Walker's balls in play were hit at 95 mph or harder, and his 114.6 mph max exit velocity was in the 99th percentile among players 21 years or younger. Walker is an above-average runner and capable basestealer who has had a high success rate on stolen base attempts in the minor leagues. His speed comes from long, powerful strides that allow him to run the bases and roam the outfield at an above-average rate. In this way, Walker is equipped

BA GRADE	SCOUTING GRADES
70 Risk: High	Hit: 50. Power: 70. Run: 55. Field: 50. Arm: 60.
Projected future grades on 20-80 scouting scale	

BEST TOOLS

BATTING

Best Hitter for Average	Alec Burleson
Best Power Hitter	Moises Gomez
Best Strike-Zone Discipline	Ivan Herrera
Fastest Baserunner	Mike Antico
Best Athlete	Masyn Winn

PITCHING

Best Fastball	Tink Hence
Best Curveball	Zack Thompson
Best Slider	Andrew Marrero
Best Changeup	Logan Gragg
Best Control	Michael McGreevy

FIELDING

Best Defensive Catcher	Pedro Pages
Best Defensive Infielder	Jeremy Rivas
Best Infield Arm	Mike Antico
Best Defensive Outfielder	Masyn Winn
Best Outfield Arm	Jordan Walker

for his move to the outfield. He possesses a plus arm capable of making all the throws from a corner outfield position. He profiles best in right field, but has seen some time in center field as well.

THE FUTURE: Few players flash upside as immense as Walker's. He should see a majority of his time in 2023 in the major leagues. Equipped with plus power and average or better plate skills, Walker could develop into a perennial all-star.

Year	Age	Club (League)	Lvl	AVG	G	AB	R	H	2B	3B	HR	RBI	BB	SO	SB	OBP	SLG
2022	20	Springfield (TL)	AA	.306	119	461	100	141	31	3	19	68	58	116	22	.388	.510
Minor League Totals				.310	201	786	163	244	56	7	33	116	91	203	36	.388	.525

2 TINK HENCE, RHP

Born: Aug. 6, 2002. **B-T:** R-R. **HT:** 6-1. **WT:** 175.
Drafted: HS—Pine Bluff, Ark., 2020 (2nd round supplemental). **Signed by:** Dirk Kinney.

TRACK RECORD: The Cardinals drafted Hence in the supplemental second round in 2020 and signed him for an over-slot $1.15 million. He was eased into his first pro season in 2021 and made eight appearances in the Florida Complex League. Hence was held back to start the 2022 season before being assigned to Low-A Palm Beach, where he dominated. Over 16 starts spanning 52.1 innings, he posted a 1.38 ERA with 81 strikeouts and just 15 walks. He worked as a reliever in the Arizona Fall League after the season.

SCOUTING REPORT: An undersized righthander with a slight but athletic frame, Hence displays explosive arm speed that allows him to generate more power than his build would suggest. His operation is smooth and athletic from the windup, but there's added effort from the stretch. Hence's pitch mix consists of a four-seam fastball, curveball, slider and changeup. His primary mix relies heavily on a four-seam fastball with mid-90s velocity and above-average hop. He primarily pairs it with his high-70s curveball with sweepy, two-plane break. He uses the depth of his curveball to play off his fastball's flatter plane. His slider is a low-80s sweeper that looks like a flattened variation of his curveball. Hence's changeup showed well in limited usage, with good separation off his fastball. His strike-throwing is solidly average, with bouts of command issues from the stretch. While Hence is undersized for a starter, he has a deep arsenal of above-average to plus pitches and a rare level of athleticism.

THE FUTURE: One of the most exciting pitchers in the minor leagues, Hence will look to take on a bigger workload in the coming seasons. If he can hold his stuff deep into starts, he could one day rank as the top pitching prospect in the game.

SCOUTING GRADES	Fastball: 60	Curveball: 60	Slider: 50	Changeup: 55	Control: 50

Year	Age	Club (League)	Lvl	W	L	ERA	G	GS	IP	H	HR	BB	SO	BB/9	SO/9	WHIP	AVG
2022	19	Palm Beach (FSL)	LoA	0	1	1.38	16	16	52	31	1	15	81	2.6	13.9	0.88	.174
Minor League Totals				0	2	2.39	24	17	60	42	2	18	95	2.7	14.2	0.99	.196

3 MASYN WINN, SS

Born: March 21, 2002. **B-T:** R-R. **HT:** 5-11. **WT:** 180.
Drafted: HS—Kingwood, Texas, 2020 (2nd round). **Signed by:** Jabari Bennett.

TRACK RECORD: Winn was known for his two-way ability on the showcase circuit and for Kingwood (Texas) High. The Cardinals drafted him in the second round in 2020 and signed him for an above-slot $2.1 million. After making one appearance as a pitcher in 2021, Winn moved to shortstop in 2022. He responded with a breakout season and hit .283/.364/.468 in 119 games between High-A and Double-A. Winn played in the 2022 Futures Game and made headlines by hitting 100.5 mph on a throw from shortstop.

SCOUTING REPORT: Winn transformed from an average contact hitter with below-average power to an above-average hitter with zone awareness and developing power. Early in minor league spring training, Winn showed improved swing mechanics with better synchronization between his upper and lower halves. His performance and metrics improved across the board as he made more contact, chased less and hit for more power. He added loft to his swing path and improved as a contact hitter in the process. His 86% zone contact rate was among the highest in the Cardinals' system in 2022, and it was reflected in his low strikeout rate of just under 21%. Winn has plus speed and instincts on the basepaths, which led to 43 stolen bases in 48 attempts. Defensively, Winn stands out for his top-of-the-scale arm. It's one of the best throwing arms in baseball at any level. While his footwork and infield actions are average, his arm allows him to make up ground and throw out runners on anything he can knock down in front of him. Winn's arm is accurate, allowing it to play as a true 80-grade tool.

THE FUTURE: Winn fully committed to a future at shortstop in 2022 and has positioned himself as a serious candidate to be the Cardinals' future everyday regular there.

SCOUTING GRADES	Hitting: 55	Power: 45	Speed: 60	Fielding: 55	Arm: 80

Year	Age	Club (League)	Lvl	AVG	G	AB	R	H	2B	3B	HR	RBI	BB	SO	SB	OBP	SLG
2022	20	Peoria (MWL)	HiA	.349	33	129	22	45	11	7	1	15	13	29	15	.404	.566
2022	20	Springfield (TL)	AA	.258	86	345	69	89	25	1	11	48	50	86	28	.349	.432
Minor League Totals				.264	217	859	167	227	55	13	17	107	109	215	75	.346	.418

4 MATTHEW LIBERATORE, LHP

BA GRADE

50 Risk: Medium

Born: Nov. 6, 1999. **B-T:** L-L. **HT:** 6-5. **WT:** 200.
Drafted: HS—Glendale, Ariz., 2018 (1st round). **Signed by:** David Hamlett (Rays).
TRACK RECORD: Liberatore ranked as the No. 2 prospect in the 2018 draft but fell down the board to No. 16, where the Rays selected him and signed him to an under-slot $3.5 million deal. The lefthander enjoyed a strong debut in 2019, and made 16 appearances for Low-A Bowling Green. In January 2020, Liberatore was traded to the Cardinals as a part of the deal that sent Randy Arozarena to the Rays. St. Louis aggressively assigned Liberatore to Triple-A in 2021 despite him having no experience above Low-A. He returned to Triple-A Memphis in 2022 and made 22 starts. Liberatore made his MLB debut on May 21 and appeared in eight games for the Cardinals.
SCOUTING REPORT: Liberatore is a tall lefthander with an athletic, slender build that should hold up to the rigors of starting. He has a simple and smooth operation, with some length to his arm action as he delivers the ball from a high three-quarters slot. He throws five different pitches, including two variations of his fastball. His four-seamer sits 93-95 mph with ride and cut. His two-seamer doesn't sink but has less ride than his fastball, with a heavy amount of late, arm-side run. His high-spin, mid-70s curveball is a 1-to-7 bender with over 16 inches of drop and a foot of horizontal break and is his best whiff-inducing option. His gyro slider sits 85-86 mph and gives Liberatore a chase pitch versus lefthanded hitters. His changeup is a mid-to-high-80s offering that mimics his two-seam shape, performing at a fringe-average level. Liberatore displays average control of his pitch mix but battles his command at times.
THE FUTURE: An improvement in command and execution could see Liberatore make the jump from experienced prospect to big league No. 4 starter with midrotation upside.

SCOUTING GRADES		Fastball: 50	Curveball: 60	Slider: 50	Changeup: 45	Control: 50

Year	Age	Club (League)	Lvl	W	L	ERA	G	GS	IP	H	HR	BB	SO	BB/9	SO/9	WHIP	AVG
2022	22	Memphis (IL)	AAA	7	9	5.17	22	22	115	118	16	41	116	3.2	9.1	1.38	.269
2022	22	St. Louis (NL)	MLB	2	2	5.97	9	7	35	42	5	18	28	4.7	7.3	1.73	.304
Major League Totals				2	2	5.97	9	7	35	42	5	18	28	4.7	7.3	1.73	.304
Minor League Totals				24	22	3.95	69	64	351	332	37	118	352	3.0	9.0	1.28	.251

5 COOPER HJERPE, LHP

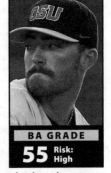

BA GRADE

55 Risk: High

Born: March 16, 2001. **B-T:** L-L. **HT:** 6-3. **WT:** 200.
Drafted: Oregon State, 2022 (1st round). **Signed by:** Chris Rodriguez/Donnie Marbut.
TRACK RECORD: Hjerpe made six appearances out of the bullpen as an Oregon State freshman in 2020. He made the jump to the rotation as a sophomore in 2021 and made 16 starts with a respectable 4.21 ERA. Hjerpe used that summer to focus on improving his secondary offerings. What followed was a dominant junior season with Oregon State in 2022. He went 11-2, 2.53 and led the nation with 161 strikeouts. The Cardinals drafted Hjerpe 22nd overall and signed him for a bonus of $3.18 million.
SCOUTING REPORT: On the surface, Hjerpe has the look of an unusual lefty who gets by on his deceptive sidearm slot. While this is true in part, he projects for more power than a typical sidearmer. His four-pitch mix is heavily fastball-driven due to the unique characteristics generated by his 4.5-foot release height and—on average—6.5 feet of extension. This creates an outlier approach angle and plays up his average vertical break. While Hjerpe sits 90-92 mph and touches 94, his ability to command his fastball works in harmony with his deception to generate whiffs at the top of the zone. His primary secondaries are a sweepy slider at 77-79 mph and changeup at 79-82 with heavy tumble and fade. Both pitches generated whiffs last spring at a rate of 49% or better. Hjerpe will also mix in a curveball, which is a slower version of his slider with more depth. Hjerpe shows command for the entirety of his pitch mix and could continue to excel in a starting role should he add power to his fastball without compromising its shape.
THE FUTURE: While Hjerpe's profile is unusual, his combination of stuff, pitchability and projection gives him a chance to develop into a solid midrotation option who should move quickly.

SCOUTING GRADES		Fastball: 60	Curveball: 40	Slider: 55	Changeup: 55	Control: 55

Year	Age	Club (League)	Lvl	W	L	ERA	G	GS	IP	H	HR	BB	SO	BB/9	SO/9	WHIP	AVG
2022	21	Did not play															

6 ALEC BURLESON, OF

Born: Nov. 25, 1998. **B-T:** L-L. **HT:** 6-2. **WT:** 212.
Drafted: East Carolina, 2020 (2nd round supplemental). **Signed by:** T.C. Calhoun.

TRACK RECORD: At East Carolina, Burleson was a two-way player who earned a Collegiate National Team nod in 2019. He was drafted by the Cardinals in the supplemental second round in 2020 and has excelled as a position player in his two pro seasons. Burleson played 109 games with Triple-A Memphis in 2022 and hit .331/.372/.532 with 20 home runs, winning the International League batting title. He made his MLB debut on Sept. 8 and played in 16 games.

BA GRADE
50 Risk: Medium

SCOUTING REPORT: Burleson's profile is heavily driven by his ability to hit for both average and power. He's a career .300 hitter in the minors, and while he hit just .188 for St. Louis, he also struck out just 17% of the time. Burleson's swing is geared for contact, with a flatter bat path that is adept at spraying a high rate of line drives to all fields. He's a plus bat-to-ball hitter who runs high in-zone contact rates. Burleson's approach borders on aggressive, and he's prone to expanding the zone. His stout, 6-foot-2, 212-pound build has natural strength. His ability to muscle the ball manifests in his batted-ball data, with an average Triple-A exit velocity of 89.7 mph in 2022. While Burleson gets to average power in games, he never gets out of his line-drive focused approach and swing. Defensively, Burleson is limited to a corner, where his range and route-running are fringy. His arm is average but is strong enough to project to left or right field.

THE FUTURE: Hit-over-power corner outfield prospects aren't the most attractive profiles, but Burleson has performed dating back to his amateur days and is a potential everyday corner outfielder.

SCOUTING GRADES	Hitting: 60	Power: 50	Speed: 40	Fielding: 45	Arm: 50

Year	Age	Club (League)	Lvl	AVG	G	AB	R	H	2B	3B	HR	RBI	BB	SO	SB	OBP	SLG
2022	23	Memphis (IL)	AAA	.331	109	432	68	143	25	1	20	87	29	67	4	.372	.532
2022	23	St. Louis (NL)	MLB	.188	16	48	4	9	1	0	1	3	5	9	1	.264	.271
Major League Totals				.188	16	48	4	9	1	0	1	3	5	9	1	.264	.271
Minor League Totals				.300	228	888	129	266	43	1	42	163	71	168	7	.350	.492

7 GORDON GRACEFFO, RHP

Born: March 17, 2000. **B-T:** R-R. **HT:** 6-4. **WT:** 210.
Drafted: Villanova, 2021 (5th round). **Signed by:** Jim Negrych.

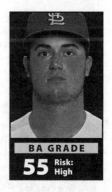

TRACK RECORD: Graceffo made three predraft starts in the Cape Cod League in 2021 and flashed increased velocity, which had been climbing throughout the spring. The Cardinals drafted Graceffo in the fifth round and signed him for an above-slot $500,000. He debuted with Low-A Palm Beach after signing and made 11 appearances out of the bullpen. In spring training 2022, Graceffo showed even more power in his pitch mix and hit 100 mph. He held his velocity throughout the season and earned a promotion to Double-A by late May after eight dominant starts with High-A Peoria.

BA GRADE
55 Risk: High

SCOUTING REPORT: A strong-bodied righthander with a prototypical pitcher's build, Graceffo lacks eye-popping athleticism but repeats his unusual mechanics. He steps back with his left foot to begin his windup as he sets square to the hitter. He has a longer arm action and high three-quarters slot with crossfire finish at release. Graceffo's operation creates deception that amplifies his four-pitch mix. His four-seam fastball sits 93-95 mph and touches 99. While his fastball has above-average velocity, it lacks life and ride. It plays due to his combination of velocity and plus command. His best secondary is his 85-88 mph slider, which has tight, cement-mixer shape that plays off his fastball. His low-80s changeup with tumble and fade generates whiffs and chases from lefthanded hitters. Graceffo's fourth pitch is a 12-to-6 curveball with moderate depth. He shows an advanced understanding of sequencing and mixes all four of his pitches effectively. His command across his entire arsenal is plus.

THE FUTURE: With power across his arsenal, a deep pitch mix and plus strike-throwing ability, Graceffo projects as a reliable No. 4 starter.

SCOUTING GRADES	Fastball: 55	Curveball: 50	Slider: 60	Changeup: 55	Control: 65

Year	Age	Club (League)	Lvl	W	L	ERA	G	GS	IP	H	HR	BB	SO	BB/9	SO/9	WHIP	AVG
2022	22	Peoria (MWL)	HiA	3	2	0.99	8	8	46	27	1	4	56	0.8	11.0	0.68	.170
2022	22	Springfield (TL)	AA	7	4	3.94	18	18	94	76	16	24	83	2.3	8.0	1.07	.217
Minor League Totals				11	6	2.78	37	27	165	131	18	37	176	2.0	9.6	1.02	.213

8 IVAN HERRERA, C

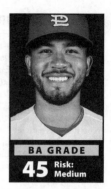

Born: June 1, 2000. **B-T:** R-R. **HT:** 5-11. **WT:** 220.
Drafted: Panama, 2016. **Signed by:** Damaso Espino.

TRACK RECORD: Herrera signed out of Panama for $200,000 days after the July 2 signing period opened in 2016. In his first few pro seasons, Herrera proved to be one of the better contact and on-base hitters in the Cardinals' system. He spent the 2020 season at the alternate training site and was assigned to Double-A Springfield out of camp in 2021, reaching Triple-A for a game by year's end. After a down season offensively in 2021, Herrera returned to Triple-A Memphis out of camp in 2022. He responded with a solid season and spent a month in St. Louis as Yadier Molina's understudy.

BA GRADE

45 Risk: Medium

SCOUTING REPORT: A stout, stocky player with plenty of physical strength, Herrera has limited athleticism and twitch. Despite his stiff physical nature, his game is predicated on his above-average contact skills and on-base ability. Herrera deploys a level swing that leads to lots of grounders. He runs high contact rates and rarely expands the zone. While his exit velocity data is fringy, Herrera showed improvements to his 90th percentile exit velocity, hinting at average raw power. In games, his average power rarely flashes, and Herrera projects to hit 10-14 home runs over a full season. His low-end speed limits his numbers because he is unlikely to beat out any infield grounders. Behind the plate, Herrera has regressed as both a receiver and thrower, and he caught just 18% of basestealers in 2022. He is likely to stick at catcher, but as the offensively-slanted side of a platoon.

THE FUTURE: After being pushed aggressively over the past two seasons, Herrera has a year to adjust and catch up in 2023, when he likely will split time once again between Triple-A Memphis and St. Louis.

SCOUTING GRADES	Hitting: 55	Power: 40	Speed: 20	Fielding: 45	Arm: 45

Year	Age	Club (League)	Lvl	AVG	G	AB	R	H	2B	3B	HR	RBI	BB	SO	SB	OBP	SLG
2022	22	Memphis (IL)	AAA	.268	65	235	41	63	10	1	6	34	38	52	5	.374	.396
2022	22	St. Louis (NL)	MLB	.111	11	18	0	2	0	0	0	1	2	8	0	.190	.111
Major League Totals				.111	11	18	0	2	0	0	0	1	2	8	0	.190	.111
Minor League Totals				.276	330	1194	183	330	54	5	34	196	167	278	11	.375	.415

9 MICHAEL McGREEVY, RHP

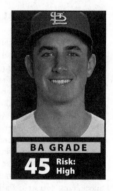

Born: July 8, 2000. **B-T:** R-R. **HT:** 6-4. **WT:** 215.
Drafted: UC Santa Barbara, 2021 (1st round). **Signed by:** Michael Garciaparra.

TRACK RECORD: A three-year standout at UC Santa Barbara, McGreevy moved to the rotation in 2020 after earning freshman All-America honors as a reliever. He made just four starts prior to the pandemic shutdown, but returned in 2021 to lead the Gauchos' rotation with a 2.92 ERA and 115 strikeouts to just 11 walks in 101.2 innings. The Cardinals drafted McGreevy 18th overall in 2021 and signed him for $2.75 million. He reached Double-A Springfield in late May 2022 but struggled across 20 starts in the Texas League as he allowed more hard contact and missed fewer bats.

BA GRADE

45 Risk: High

SCOUTING REPORT: An athletic righthander with a rapid-fire move to the plate from both the windup and stretch, McGreevy has a longer arm action and delivers the ball from a three-quarters arm slot. He mixes four pitches, but his primary plan of attack revolves around his fastball/slider combination. His fastball sits 90-92 mph and tops out at 95, with below-average ride and heavy arm-side run. He commands his fastball, which works primarily as a setup for his above-average slider. McGreevy threw his slider—which shows classic shape at 82-84 mph—more than his curveball and changeup combined. His slider drives more whiffs and chase swings than any pitch in his arsenal. His mid-80s changeup flashes average, but he commanded it poorly in 2022. His curveball is a high-70s breaker with average spin and more depth than his slider. With above-average command and some deception due to his high-effort throwing motion, McGreevy has more of a swingman's profile.

THE FUTURE: McGreevy is likely to return to Double-A Springfield to begin 2023 before reaching Triple-A. He projects best as a No. 5 starter with a chance his stuff would play up in a relief role.

SCOUTING GRADES	Fastball: 45	Curveball: 50	Slider: 55	Changeup: 40	Control: 60

Year	Age	Club (League)	Lvl	W	L	ERA	G	GS	IP	H	HR	BB	SO	BB/9	SO/9	WHIP	AVG
2022	21	Peoria (MWL)	HiA	3	1	2.58	8	8	45	41	1	4	41	0.8	8.1	0.99	.238
2022	21	Springfield (TL)	AA	6	4	4.64	20	20	99	109	14	26	76	2.4	6.9	1.36	.284
Minor League Totals				9	7	4.26	35	35	152	164	16	32	124	1.9	7.3	1.29	.277

10 JONATHAN MEJIA, SS

Born: April 12, 2005. **B-T:** B-R. **HT:** 6-0. **WT:** 185.
Signed: Dominican Republic, 2022. **Signed by:** Alix Martinez/Angel Ovalles.

TRACK RECORD: Mejia was one of the early standouts in the 2021-22 international class and ranked as one of its top prospects. The Cardinals signed him for $2 million out of the Dominican Republic on Jan. 15, 2022. Mejia made his pro debut in the Dominican Summer League, and hit .267/.418/.479 with 22 extra-base hits in 45 games. Among 17-year-olds in the DSL, he had the 15th-best OPS (.897) among qualified hitters and the 10th-best isolated slugging percentage (.212).

SCOUTING REPORT: Mejia is a switch-hitter who flashes good bat speed and loft from both sides of the plate and has ample offensive projection. His setup features lots of pre-swing movement—with his hands and body rocking, and a moderate leg kick. Mejia's stance is square to the pitcher, but his body and front foot are rotated closed. Mejia's swing is aesthetically pleasing and helps him elevate the ball and do damage. He flashed above-average power for a 17-year-old, including a max exit velocity of 107 mph. Mejia shows above-average bat-to-ball skills and an average approach, and he displayed more maturity than expected in his pro debut. He's not a twitchy infielder but has made progress over the last few years to improve his actions and footwork. His profile revolves around his offense, and he likely projects best at second or third base, with an average throwing arm.

THE FUTURE: After a strong debut campaign as a 17-year-old, Mejia looks like one of the top players who will come from the DSL to the United States in 2023.

BA GRADE
50 Risk: Extreme

SCOUTING GRADES	Hitting: 55	Power: 55	Speed: 45	Fielding: 40	Arm: 50

Year	Age	Club (League)	Lvl	AVG	G	AB	R	H	2B	3B	HR	RBI	BB	SO	SB	OBP	SLG
2022	17	Cardinals (DSL)	R	.267	45	165	33	44	14	3	5	34	33	48	3	.418	.479
Minor League Totals				.267	45	165	33	44	14	3	5	34	33	48	3	.418	.479

11 ZACK THOMPSON, LHP

Born: Oct. 28, 1997. **B-T:** L-L. **HT:** 6-2. **WT:** 225.
Drafted: Kentucky, 2019 (1st round). **Signed by:** Jason Bryans.

TRACK RECORD: Thompson was a highly-touted and decorated college starter at Kentucky and one of the top pitchers available in the 2019 draft. The Cardinals selected him 19th overall despite a history of elbow injuries and signed him for an under-slot $3 million bonus. Thompson quickly ascended the minors but got rocked at Triple-A Memphis in the first year back from the pandemic. He repeated Triple-A in 2022 and had much greater success, pitching well as a starter to earn his first callup to the big leagues. He settled in as a reliever for the Cardinals down the stretch and logged a 2.08 ERA in 22 appearances.

SCOUTING REPORT: Thompson utilized a four-pitch mix as a starter, but he leans on his fastball and curveball as a reliever. His fastball sits 94-96 mph with average ride and life out of the bullpen and touches 100 mph at peak. His slow, high-spin curveball with plus depth plays well off his fastball and induces a heavy dose of ground balls. Thompson will mix in a fringy upper-80s cutter and below-average, upper-80s changeup to give batters a different look. He throws strikes with average control.

THE FUTURE: Thompson's primary two-pitch combination and average command make the bullpen his long-term destination. He should take on a bigger role as one of the Cardinals' primary relievers in 2023.

BA GRADE: 45/ High	Fastball: 50	Curveball: 60	Changeup: 40	Cutter: 45	Control: 50

Year	Age	Club (League)	Lvl	W	L	ERA	G	GS	IP	H	HR	BB	SO	BB/9	SO/9	WHIP	AVG
2022	24	Memphis (IL)	AAA	2	3	4.73	19	10	53	44	6	21	67	3.5	11.3	1.22	.219
2022	24	St. Louis (NL)	MLB	1	1	2.08	22	1	35	20	3	14	27	3.6	7.0	0.98	.164
Major League Totals				1	1	2.08	22	1	35	20	3	14	27	3.6	7.0	0.98	.164
Minor League Totals				4	13	5.96	54	31	162	177	24	82	172	4.6	9.6	1.60	.276

12 LEONARDO BERNAL, C

Born: Feb. 13, 2004. **B-T:** B-R. **HT:** 6-0. **WT:** 200.
Signed: Panama, 2021. **Signed by:** Damaso Espino.

TRACK RECORD: The Cardinals signed Bernal out of Panama for $680,000 during the 2020-2021 international signing period, the second time in recent years they've signed a top amateur catcher from Panama after Ivan Herrera in 2016. Bernal struggled to hit for average but showed power in his pro debut in the

Dominican Summer League and jumped stateside for the 2022 season. He began the year in extended spring training but rose to Low-A Palm Beach in June, where he hit .256/.316/.455 as the youngest hitter to receive 100 or more at-bats in the Florida State League.

SCOUTING REPORT: Bernal is a switch-hitting catcher with projectable abilities on both sides of the ball. He's an average contact hitter with a solid approach, although he can be a little passive batting right-handed. His main offensive calling card is his power. He already shows above-average power as a teenager and showcased it when he hit a ball 423 feet at 110 mph for a pull-side home run in late August. Bernal makes his best contact at his steepest launch angles and projects to keep hitting for power long-term. Behind the plate, Bernal showcases advanced receiving skills and plus arm strength. He is comfortable in the crouch and has the athleticism to move fluidly behind the plate.

THE FUTURE: Bernal is a long way off, but has the traits of a potential everyday catcher who contributes on both sides of the ball. He may see High-A as a 19-year-old in 2023.

BA GRADE: 50/Extreme		Hit: 50		Power: 55		Run: 30			Field: 55			Arm: 60	

Year	Age	Club (League)	Lvl	AVG	G	AB	R	H	2B	3B	HR	RBI	BB	SO	SB	OBP	SLG
2022	18	Palm Beach (FSL)	LoA	.256	45	156	22	40	8	1	7	29	12	32	1	.316	.455
Minor League Totals				.232	89	314	45	73	17	2	12	58	29	60	4	.307	.414

13 JOSHUA BAEZ, OF

Born: June 28, 2003. **B-T:** R-R. **HT:** 6-4. **WT:** 220.
Drafted: HS—Brookline, Mass., 2021 (2nd round). **Signed by:** Jim Negrych

TRACK RECORD: Baez looked like one of the top high school players to come out of Massachusetts in years after he dominated the summer showcase circuit, but he struggled to make consistent contact against lesser high school pitching in the spring and fell out of first-round consideration. The Cardinals believed enough in Baez's plus-plus raw power and supporting skills to draft the muscular slugger in the second round, No. 54 overall, and sign him for $2,250,000, nearly a million above slot value. Baez's contact struggles continued in the Florida Complex League in his debut and he played just 32 games in 2022 due to a wrist injury.

SCOUTING REPORT: Baez stands out from his teenage peers for his extreme physicality. He has a muscular, well-proportioned build that exudes natural strength and allows him to pulverize baseballs. Baez's offensive game is centered around his excellent game power, showcasing exit velocities already well above the major league average. Baez makes loud contact when he connects, but he rarely gets to his power due to poor contact skills and a somewhat aggressive approach. Baez swings and misses at a high rate against both high fastballs and spin and generally shows an aversion to both pitches, limiting him to a well below-average hitter, at best. Baez is a fringe-average runner who ticks up to average underway. He is a good athlete who was a two-way player in high school and is an average defender with a plus-plus arm that allowed him to touch 97 mph on the mound.

THE FUTURE: Baez's huge power is easy to dream on, but his poor contact skills will need to improve for him to be a low-average, power-hitting outfielder.

BA GRADE: 50/Extreme		Hit: 30		Power: 65		Run: 45		Field: 50			Arm: 70	

Year	Age	Club (League)	Lvl	AVG	G	AB	R	H	2B	3B	HR	RBI	BB	SO	SB	OBP	SLG
2022	19	Cardinals (FCL)	R	.237	12	38	4	9	3	0	1	5	5	14	6	.326	.395
2022	19	Palm Beach (FSL)	LoA	.286	20	63	11	18	5	1	3	16	11	30	4	.418	.540
Minor League Totals				.220	55	177	33	39	11	2	6	29	30	72	15	.350	.407

14 BRYCEN MAUTZ, LHP

Born: July 17, 2001. **B-T:** L-L. **HT:** 6-3. **WT:** 190.
Drafted: San Diego, 2022 (2nd round). **Signed by:** Chris Rodriguez

TRACK RECORD: Mautz spent his first two seasons alternating between starting and relieving at San Diego before moving into the rotation full-time in 2022. He broke out and led the West Coast Conference in wins, finished second in strikeouts and had his signature moment when he dominated Vanderbilt over seven innings in the NCAA Tournament to lead the Toreros to an upset victory. The Cardinals drafted him in the second round, No. 59 overall, and signed him for a below-slot $1.1 million bonus. The Cardinals held Mautz out of games after signing after he pitched a full college workload.

SCOUTING REPORT: A deceptive lefthander who works exclusively from the stretch, Mautz mixes three pitches with a heavy focus on his fastball and slider. He hides the ball well to help his 90-93 mph four-seamer play up and get on hitters faster than they expect. His primary weapon is his above-average, sweepy slider in the low 80s. It silences lefthanded batters and is an effective weapon against righthanded hitters as well. Mautz will mix in a mid-80s changeup, but it's poorly executed and not a major part of his arsenal. Mautz's control is fringy and his success varies widely from outing to outing depending on if he has command of his fastball that day.

THE FUTURE: Mautz will get a chance to start, but his fastball and slider combination, stretch-only setup and fringy control project best in the bullpen long-term. He'll make his pro debut at the Class A levels in 2023.

BA GRADE: 45/High		Fastball: 45		Slider: 55		Changeup: 30		Control: 45				
Year	**Age**	**Club (League)**	**Lvl**	**W**	**L**	**ERA**	**G**	**GS**	**IP**	**H**	**HR**	**BB**	**SO**	**BB/9**	**SO/9**	**WHIP**	**AVG**
2022	20	Did not play											

15   PETE HANSEN, LHP

Born: July 28, 2000. **B-T:** R-L. **HT:** 6-2. **WT:** 205.
Drafted: Texas, 2022 (3rd round). **Signed by:** Joseph Quezada.

TRACK RECORD: Hansen was one of baseball's most reliable college starters at Texas, going 22-4 over two-plus seasons in the Longhorns rotation and emerging as their de facto ace. The Cardinals selected him in the third round, No. 97 overall, and signed him for $629,800, making him the third of three college lefthanders the clubs selected with its top three picks. The Cardinals chose to rest Hansen due to his heavy college workload and did not send him out to an affiliate after signing.

SCOUTING REPORT: Hansen is a soft-tossing lefthander whose sum is greater than his parts. His fastball sits 88-91 mph and scrapes 94 with only average life. His secondaries consist of an above-average low-80s slider with two-plane break, an average changeup and a low-70s curveball that acts as an early-count strike-stealer. Hansen's arsenal lacks velocity across the board, but everything plays up with his plus-plus control and advanced feel for sequencing. He executes at a high level consistently and keeps hitters guessing and off-balance, yielding results on par with a pitcher who has much louder stuff.

THE FUTURE: College pitchers historically add a few ticks of velocity upon entering professional ball. If Hansen can do that to add power to his deep arsenal of pitches, he has a chance to be a back-of-the-rotation starter.

BA GRADE: 45/High		Fastball: 40		Curveball: 40		Slider 55		Changeup 50		Control: 70		
Year	**Age**	**Club (League)**	**Lvl**	**W**	**L**	**ERA**	**G**	**GS**	**IP**	**H**	**HR**	**BB**	**SO**	**BB/9**	**SO/9**	**WHIP**	**AVG**
2022	21	Did not play											

16   INOHAN PANIAGUA, RHP

Born: Feb. 6, 2000. **B-T:** R-R. **HT:** 6-1. **WT:** 148.
Signed: Dominican Republic, 2017. **Signed by:** Raymi Dicent.

TRACK RECORD: Paniagua signed with the Cardinals for $160,000 out of the Dominican Republic in 2017 and moved slowly through their system. After splitting the previous season between starting and relieving, Paniagua became a full-time starter in 2022 and had a breakout season at Low-A Palm Beach. He led the Florida State League in ERA for most of the season and earned a promotion to High-A Peoria, where he made eight starts to finish his season.

SCOUTING REPORT: Paniagua slings a quartet of pitches from his low three-quarters slot with a smooth and effortless delivery. He has both a four-seamer and sinker that sit in the low 90s, and he alternates which one he throws depending on the situation. Paniagua pairs his fastballs with an above-average, low-to-mid-80s changeup and an average curveball in the mid 70s with two-plane break. His changeup and curveball act as his primary swing-and-miss weapons and had above-average whiff and chase rates in 2022. Paniagua shows advanced feel for sequencing, mixing in all four pitches regardless of the handedness of the opposing batter. He has average control of his entire arsenal and could tap into more velocity as he matures physically.

THE FUTURE: Paniagua projects to be a back-of-the-rotation starter who shows batters a variety of looks. He has a chance to grow into more if he adds velocity.

BA GRADE: 45/High		Fastball: 45		Curveball: 50		Changeup 55		Control: 50				
Year	**Age**	**Club (League)**	**Lvl**	**W**	**L**	**ERA**	**G**	**GS**	**IP**	**H**	**HR**	**BB**	**SO**	**BB/9**	**SO/9**	**WHIP**	**AVG**
2022	22	Palm Beach (FSL)	LoA	6	4	2.18	17	17	99	72	4	23	107	2.1	9.7	0.96	.202
2022	22	Peoria (MWL)	HiA	2	2	4.42	8	8	39	34	8	16	38	3.7	8.8	1.29	.236
Minor League Totals				17	15	3.83	68	55	296	262	21	96	306	2.9	9.3	1.21	.237

17 ALEC WILLIS, RHP

Born: March 30, 2003. **B-T:** R-R. **HT:** 6-5. **WT:** 220.
Drafted: HS—Aurora, Colo., 2021 (7th round). **Signed by:** Mauricio Rubio

TRACK RECORD: Willis missed most of the high school showcase circuit after having ulnar nerve decompression surgery before his senior year, but he returned healthy in the spring and showed premium stuff and physicality to become one of the 2021 draft's biggest risers. The Cardinals drafted him in the seventh round and signed him for an above-slot $1 million bonus to forgo a Minnesota commitment. Willis has struggled to stay on the mound since signing. He pitched only one inning in his pro debut and missed most of 2022 with an unspecified arm issue.
SCOUTING REPORT: Standing 6-foot-5 with a broad physical frame, Willis has the build of a rotation workhorse at just 19 years old. While his pure strength is yet to surface as a professional there's hope he can make significant velocity gains once healthy for a long stretch. Willis' fastball sits 89-91 mph and tops out at 92, but it plays up with moderate ride and cut and the more than seven feet of extension he generates in his delivery. His slurvy curveball sits in the upper 70s and tunnels well off his fastball. His fringy, low-80s changeup features splitter-like action, but he rarely throws it. Willis has flashed average control of his stuff, but he's rarely been on the mound long enough to show whether he can sustain it.
THE FUTURE: Willis has to get healthy. If he does, he shows the raw ingredients of a projectable, righthanded starter capable of eating innings.

BA GRADE: 50/Extreme		Fastball: 50		Curveball: 50		Changeup 45			Control: 50			
Year	Age	Club (League)	Lvl	W	L	ERA	G	GS	IP	H	HR	BB	SO	BB/9	SO/9	WHIP	AVG
2022	19	Cardinals (FCL)	R	0	1	1.59	6	4	11	6	1	2	16	1.6	12.7	0.71	.140
Minor League Totals				0	1	1.46	7	5	12	6	1	2	17	1.5	12.4	0.65	.130

18 MOISES GOMEZ, OF

Born: Aug. 27, 1998. **B-T:** R-R. **HT:** 5-11. **WT:** 200.
Signed: Venezuela, 2015. **Signed by:** Juan Castillo/Ronnie Blanco (Rays).

TRACK RECORD: Gomez was once an up-and-coming power prospect in the Rays system, but after consecutive poor seasons, the Rays allowed him to leave as a minor league free agent. The Cardinals signed Gomez before the 2022 season and reaped the benefits of his long-awaited breakout. The powerful slugger led all of minor league baseball with 39 home runs as he climbed from Double-A to Triple-A and hit a career-best .294. The Cardinals added him to the 40-man roster after the season, keeping him from reaching minor league free agency a second time.
SCOUTING REPORT: Gomez's calling card is his plus-plus raw power. He swings hard and looks to do damage every time he swings, leading to long home runs when he connects but also a lot of strikeouts. Gomez's approach teeters on the edge of being over-aggressive and he is prone to chase swings against righthanded breaking balls, but he makes enough contact against lefties to be a potential platoon option. He is a below-average hitter overall. Gomez is a below-average runner and defender who lacks range in the outfield. He does show the ability to keep the ball in front of him and uses his plus arm to keep runners honest.
THE FUTURE: Gomez has a chance to be a backup or platoon option who plays against lefties. He could make his major league debut in 2023.

BA Grade: 40/Medium		Hit: 40		Power: 70		Run: 40			Field: 40		Arm: 60		
Year	Age	Club (League)	Lvl	AVG	G	AB	R	H	2B	3B	HR	RBI	BB	SO	SB	OBP	SLG
2022	23	Springfield (TL)	AA	.321	60	224	53	72	17	0	23	54	27	90	7	.401	.705
2022	23	Memphis (IL)	AAA	.266	60	218	36	58	8	2	16	40	25	84	3	.340	.541
Minor League Totals				.255	584	2169	340	554	128	16	94	337	209	707	45	.323	.459

19 CONNOR THOMAS, LHP

Born: May 29, 1998. **B-T:** L-L. **HT:** 5-11. **WT:** 173.
Drafted: Georgia Tech, 2019 (5th round). **Signed by:** Charles Peterson.

TRACK RECORD: Thomas pitched three years at Georgia Tech and emerged as its top starter as a junior, leading the Cardinals to draft him in the fifth round in 2019 and sign him for $340,000. After briefly appearing in the short-season leagues in his debut, Thomas jumped straight to Double-A after the pandemic and quickly moved to Triple-A. Thomas returned to Memphis in 2022 and spent the entire year in the Redbirds rotation, then led the Arizona Fall League in strikeouts after the season.

SCOUTING REPORT: Thomas is a pitchability lefty almost to an extreme. His fastball sat 85-87 mph as an amateur and has ticked up marginally to now sit 88-91 mph and touch 93. He shows two different fastballs shapes with a four-seamer and a sinker, using his sinker especially against lefties. Thomas' secondaries consist of an average, low-to-mid-80s slider, a fringy mid-80s changeup and a below-average cutter. He has above-average control of his entire arsenal and effectively locates all of his pitches to help them play up. He has a good feel for sequencing and lasts deep into his starts.

THE FUTURE: Thomas' varied arsenal, control and feel for pitching give him a chance to emerge as a No. 5 starter. He has a chance to settle in as a swingman or depth starter even if he doesn't reach that ceiling.

BA Grade: 40/Medium		Fastball: 40	Slider 50	Changeup 45	Cutter: 40	Control: 55

Year	Age	Club (League)	Lvl	W	L	ERA	G	GS	IP	H	HR	BB	SO	BB/9	SO/9	WHIP	AVG
2022	24	Memphis (IL)	AAA	6	12	5.47	28	25	135	172	16	40	110	2.7	7.3	1.57	.307
Minor League Totals				16	19	4.38	69	47	300	348	34	83	262	2.5	7.9	1.44	.288

20 AUSTIN LOVE, RHP

Born: Jan. 26, 1999. **B-T:** R-R. **HT:** 6-3. **WT:** 232.
Drafted: North Carolina, 2021 (3rd round). **Signed by:** T.C. Calhoun

TRACK RECORD: Love spent two seasons in North Carolina's bullpen before breaking out as a starter in 2021. The Cardinals drafted him in the third round after that season and signed him for a below-slot $600,000. Love began his first full season at High-A Peoria in 2022 and struggled to a 5.73 ERA, but he showed the underlying stuff to miss bats and was often victimized by bad luck.

SCOUTING REPORT: While Love's maiden voyage was rough, he showcased several promising traits. He has a large, physical starter's frame at 6-foot-3, 232 pounds and a potent four-pitch mix. His fastball sits 92-94 mph and touches 97 at its peak and his mid-80s, gyro-slider is an above-average pitch that regularly misses bats. Love can get outs with those two pitches, but the rest of his arsenal is further behind. He struggles to land his fringy changeup and his low-80s curveball is a below-average pitch, although it shows solid depth. He throws strikes with average control but has room to improve his command.

THE FUTURE: Love has a chance to remain a starter if he can command his changeup better. If not, his fastball and slider combination should play up out of the bullpen.

BA GRADE: 45/High		Fastball: 50	Curveball: 40	Slider 55	Changeup 45	Control: 50

Year	Age	Club (League)	Lvl	W	L	ERA	G	GS	IP	H	HR	BB	SO	BB/9	SO/9	WHIP	AVG
2022	23	Peoria (MWL)	HiA	7	12	5.73	26	25	126	139	15	52	151	3.7	10.8	1.52	.277
Minor League Totals				7	12	5.45	33	30	134	142	16	53	164	3.6	11.0	1.46	.269

21 MAX RAJCIC, RHP

Born: Aug. 3, 2001. **B-T:** R-R. **HT:** 6-1. **WT:** 205.
Drafted: UCLA, 2022 (6th round). **Signed by:** Michael Garciaparra.

TRACK RECORD: Rajcic starred as the ace of national prep power Orange (Calif.) Lutheran High and arrived at UCLA as a top recruit in the 2020 class. He served as the Bruins' closer as a freshman and transitioned to starting in the Cape Cod League. Rajcic took over as UCLA's top starter as a draft-eligible sophomore in 2022 and wore down at the end of the season, but he showed enough for the Cardinals to draft him in the sixth round and sign him for an above-slot $600,000 bonus.

SCOUTING REPORT: Rajcic is a stocky, undersized righthander with an above-average breaking ball. With a long track record of success as an amateur, Rajcic has shown an ability to command and sequence his arsenal in such a way that it plays above his raw stuff. Rajcic mixes three pitches in his fastball, curveball and changeup. His fastball sits 90-93 mph with heavy ride but is easy to track due to his very visible release point. His fastball is primarily a setup weapon for his two secondaries. His primary secondary is his low-80s, above-average curveball with heavy two-plane break. His changeup is a low-to-mid-80s pitch that shows hellacious arm-side run. He throws all of his pitches for strikes, showing average command across his arsenal.

THE FUTURE: Rajcic will have to make it as a starter because he doesn't have enough power to profile in relief. He projects to be an up-and-down starter who possibly sneaks into a No. 5 starter's role.

BA GRADE: 45/High		Fastball: 45	Curveball: 55	Changeup 50	Control: 50

Year	Age	Club (League)	Lvl	AVG	G	AB	R	H	2B	3B	HR	RBI	BB	SO	SB	OBP	SLG
2022	20	Did not play															

22 JIMMY CROOKS III, C

Born: July 19, 2001. **B-T:** L-R. **HT:** 6-1. **WT:** 210.
Drafted: Oklahoma, 2022 (4th round). **Signed by:** Pete Parise.

TRACK RECORD: Crooks spent one season at McLennan (Texas) JC before transferring to Oklahoma where he started 100 games behind the plate with the Sooners. He hit for average and power to emerge as one of the top catchers in the draft class and was selected by the Cardinals in the fourth round, signing for $470,300. Crooks debuted with Low-A Palm Beach after signing and hit .266/.396/.468 with eight extra-base hits in 23 games, continuing to show ability on both sides of the ball.

SCOUTING REPORT: Crooks has the typical strong, stout catcher's build and is muscled throughout his frame. He employs a large leg kick to start his swing and has explosive bat speed through the zone with a level bat path. Crooks' noisy swing mechanics may limit him against higher-level pitching, but he should make enough contact to be a fringe-average hitter who taps into his average power in games. He shows a solid approach and is best when he attacks pitches in the inner half and drives them to his pull side. Crooks is an average defender behind the plate who is comfortable in the crouch. His average arm strength plays up with a quick transfer and release.

THE FUTURE: Crooks is a well-rounded player who keeps trending up as a hitter. He projects to be a backup catcher and could be more if his hitting continues to improve.

BA GRADE: 45/High	Hit: 45	Power: 50	Run: 30	Field: 50	Arm: 50

Year	Age	Club (League)	Lvl	AVG	G	AB	R	H	2B	3B	HR	RBI	BB	SO	SB	OBP	SLG
2022	20	Palm Beach (FSL)	LoA	.266	23	79	12	21	3	2	3	7	12	22	0	.396	.468
Minor League Totals				.266	23	79	12	21	3	2	3	7	12	22	0	.396	.468

23 FREDDY PACHECO, RHP

Born: April 17, 1998. **B-T:** R-R. **HT:** 5-11. **WT:** 203.
Signed: Venezuela, 2017. **Signed by:** Jose Gonzalez.

TRACK RECORD: Pacheco signed with the Cardinals out of Venezuela in 2017 and steadily rose up the minor league ladder with little fanfare. He opened the 2022 season at Double-A Springfield and continued to perform, earning a promotion to Triple-A Memphis by late June. Pacheco emerged as one of the Redbirds' top relievers and recorded four saves while averaging well over a strikeout per inning, leading the Cardinals to add him to the 40-man roster after the season.

SCOUTING REPORT: Pacheco is undersized at 5-foot-11 but has a big right arm. His fastball sits 95-97 mph and touches 99 with above-average vertical break, resulting in swings and misses at a high rate. Pacheco throws his fastball nearly 60% of the time and commands it well, making it a swing-and-miss offering even when hitters know it's coming. Pacheco's primary secondary pitch is a tight mid-80s slider that gets whiffs both in and out of the zone to be a second plus pitch he can turn to at any time. Pacheco hardly ever throws his well below-average changeup but rarely needs it. He throws plenty of strikes with his fastball and has a fiery mentality on the mound that fits the archetype of a hard-throwing reliever. But he struggles to locate his secondary offerings, which he will need to improve.

THE FUTURE: Pacheco will likely join the Cardinals bullpen at some point during the 2023 season. He should settle in as a middle reliever and could pitch his way into a leverage role.

BA GRADE: 40/High	Fastball: 60	Slider: 60	Changeup: 30	Control: 45	

Year	Age	Club (League)	Lvl	W	L	ERA	G	GS	IP	H	HR	BB	SO	BB/9	SO/9	WHIP	AVG
2022	24	Springfield (TL)	AA	1	5	3.81	24	0	28	20	4	16	41	5.1	13.0	1.27	.208
2022	24	Memphis (IL)	AAA	2	2	2.41	26	0	34	17	2	12	43	3.2	11.5	0.86	.145
Minor League Totals				9	13	3.16	152	1	205	119	12	131	325	5.8	14.3	1.22	.167

24 JAKE WALSH, RHP

Born: July 20, 1995. **B-T:** R-R. **HT:** 6-1. **WT:** 192.
Drafted: Florida Southern, 2017 (16th round). **Signed by:** Mike DiBiase.

TRACK RECORD: A 16th-round pick out of Florida Southern in 2017, Walsh began his pro career as a starter but moved to the bullpen after having Tommy John surgery. He returned to the mound in 2021 as a hard-throwing short reliever and was added to the 40-man roster after the season. Walsh opened 2022 at Triple-A Memphis and pitched well enough over 13 appearances to earn his first big league callup, but he went down with elbow soreness in early June and had a platelet-rich plasma injection that ended his season.

SCOUTING REPORT: When healthy, Walsh flashes big stuff capable of getting outs in the major leagues.

His fastball sits 94-96 mph and touches 99 mph with heavy ride and bore. He pairs his above-average fastball with an above-average curveball that sits in the low 80s with big depth and plays perfectly off his fastball shape. Walsh's pitch mix is primarily built around the vertical attack of his fastball and curveball, locating his four-seam fastball at the top of the zone and tunneling his downer curveball off of it to drive chase swings. Walsh also throws a hard, below-average slider with less depth in the upper 80s and a below-average, mid-80s changeup. His control is fringy but usable.

THE FUTURE: Walsh projects to be a solid middle reliever, but only if he can stay healthy. He'll have a chance to win a spot in the Cardinals bullpen in 2023.

BA GRADE: 40/High		Fastball: 55		Curveball: 55		Slider: 40		Changeup: 40		Control: 45		

Year	Age	Club (League)	Lvl	W	L	ERA	G	GS	IP	H	HR	BB	SO	BB/9	SO/9	WHIP	AVG
2022	26	Memphis (IL)	AAA	1	0	1.17	13	0	15	11	1	7	22	4.1	12.9	1.17	.196
2022	26	St. Louis (NL)	MLB	0	1	13.50	3	0	3	3	0	2	5	6.8	16.9	1.88	.250
Major League Totals				0	1	13.50	3	0	3	3	0	2	5	6.8	16.9	1.88	.250
Minor League Totals				17	7	2.30	73	25	207	149	15	62	215	2.7	9.3	1.02	.199

25 MIKE ANTICO, OF

Born: Feb. 16, 1998. **B-T:** L-R. **HT:** 5-10. **WT:** 200.
Drafted: Texas, 2021 (8th round). **Signed by:** Jabari Barnnett.

TRACK RECORD: Antico played four seasons with St. John's before transferring to Texas for his final season of eligibility. He broke out in his lone season with the Longhorns, and hit .273/.437/.489 with 10 home runs, 41 stolen bases and more walks than strikeouts. The Cardinals selected Antico as a senior sign in the eighth round and signed him for $20,000. Antico made his full-season debut in 2022 and he quickly hit his way up to Double-A Springfield while showing the best speed in the organization. He finished the year with a system-high 67 stolen bases and was assigned to the Arizona Fall League after the season.

SCOUTING REPORT: Antico's game is centered around his explosiveness as a runner and at the plate. He is a fringe-average contact hitter with a discerning eye who rarely expands the zone, allowing him to draw walks and get on base to use his plus speed. Unlike most speedsters, Antico looks to elevate the ball to his pull side and hits a lot of fly balls. He hits the ball at steep launch angles but doesn't have the strength to punish balls, leading to fringy power. Antico's speed translates to the outfield, where he covers a lot of ground in center to be an above-average defender. He has fringy arm strength.

THE FUTURE: While Antico will already be 25 on Opening Day, he shows the traits to be a reserve outfielder who provides speed and occasional pop off the bench. He'll see Triple-A in 2023.

BA GRADE: 40/High		Hit: 45		Power: 45		Run: 60		Field: 55		Arm: 45	

Year	Age	Club (League)	Lvl	AVG	G	AB	R	H	2B	3B	HR	RBI	BB	SO	SB	OBP	SLG
2022	24	Peoria (MWL)	HiA	.255	71	274	41	70	19	2	6	32	41	76	37	.358	.405
2022	24	Springfield (TL)	AA	.233	60	240	44	56	12	0	8	31	30	67	30	.327	.383
Minor League Totals				.250	170	657	106	164	39	5	20	82	84	176	75	.343	.416

26 IAN BEDELL, RHP

Born: Sept. 5, 1999. **B-T:** R-R. **HT:** 6-2. **WT:** 198.
Drafted: Missouri, 2020 (4th round). **Signed by:** Dirk Kinney.

TRACK RECORD: Bedell skipped his senior year of high school to enroll at Missouri, where he worked primarily out of the bullpen as an underclassman. He broke out as a starter for Wareham in the Cape Cod League in 2019 and moved into Missouri's rotation the following spring, but made only four starts before the coronavirus pandemic shut down the season. The Cardinals saw enough in that limited time to draft Bedell in the fourth round and sign him for an above-slot bonus of $800,000. Bedell's pro debut lasted just one month before he had Tommy John surgery, but he returned midway through the 2022 season and made six appearances.

SCOUTING REPORT: Bedell looks the part as a 6-foot-2 righthander with a lean, athletic frame. His stuff doesn't jump out on the radar gun, but he delivers the ball from a low three-quarters arm slot that allows his stuff to play above its velocity. Bedell's fastball sits 91-93 mph and touches 96 mph with ride and heavy arm-side run, making it difficult for hitters to get on plane with. His primary secondary is a fringy, high-70s curveball with two-plane break and solid depth. He'll also mix in a fringy changeup in the mid 80s with heavy arm-side run that plays off his fastball. Bedell had above-average control before surgery, but it remains unknown whether it is still intact due to his limited innings.

THE FUTURE: Bedell has a chance to be a back-of-the-rotation starter if his stuff and control return to pre-injury form. If not, he'll likely be limited to an up-and-down starter.

BA GRADE: 45/Extreme		Fastball: 55		Curveball: 45		Changeup: 45		Control: 50				

Year	Age	Club (League)	Lvl	W	L	ERA	G	GS	IP	H	HR	BB	SO	BB/9	SO/9	WHIP	AVG
2022	22	Cardinals (FCL)	R	0	0	0.00	3	2	3	3	0	2	6	6.0	18.0	1.67	.250
2022	22	Palm Beach (FSL)	LoA	0	0	6.75	3	0	3	6	0	1	4	3.4	13.5	2.63	.429
Minor League Totals				0	1	5.40	8	3	8	16	0	5	14	5.4	15.1	2.52	.400

27 ZANE MILLS, RHP

Born: July 4, 2000. **B-T:** R-R. **HT:** 6-4. **WT:** 220.
Drafted: Washington State, 2021 (4th round). **Signed by:** Chris Rodriguez.

TRACK RECORD: A Portland native, Mills went undrafted out of high school and was little-known until he broke out in the summertime West Coast League between his freshman and sophomore years at Washington State. He spent the next two seasons in the Cougars' rotation and was drafted by the Cardinals in the fourth round in 2021, signing for a below-slot $375,000. Mills made his full-season debut in 2022 and rose from Low-A to High-A, compiling a 4-6, 4.03 mark with a 51% groundball rate.

SCOUTING REPORT: Mills lacks premium stuff but uses his pitch mix effectively to limit hard contact. A tall righthander with an easy, effortless operation, Mills has a short arm action as he delivers the ball from a high three-quarters slot. Due to his size and release height, he creates downhill plane on his low-90s sinker and induces an extreme amount of ground balls with it. He pairs his sinker with an above-average, low-80s slider with tight gyro spin and a fringy, mid-80s changeup he uses against lefties but has inconsistent command of. Mills is an efficient strike-thrower with above-average control and effectively uses his sinking fastball to control contact.

THE FUTURE: Mills' stuff is a tick short to be a No. 5 starter, but he could be an up-and-down starter or an effective middle reliever with his sinker and slider playing up out of the bullpen.

BA GRADE: 40/High		Fastball: 45		Slider: 55		Changeup: 45		Control: 55				

Year	Age	Club (League)	Lvl	W	L	ERA	G	GS	IP	H	HR	BB	SO	BB/9	SO/9	WHIP	AVG
2022	21	Palm Beach (FSL)	LoA	1	2	3.48	7	7	41	44	3	7	35	1.5	7.6	1.23	.272
2022	21	Peoria (MWL)	HiA	4	6	4.03	19	19	103	112	10	28	69	2.5	6.0	1.36	.277
Minor League Totals				5	8	3.74	33	26	152	160	13	35	113	2.1	6.7	1.29	.270

28 TRENT BAKER, RHP

Born: Dec. 28, 1998. **B-T:** R-R. **HT:** 6-3. **WT:** 240.
Drafted: Angelo State (Texas), 2021 (9th round). **Signed by:** Jabari Barnett.

TRACK RECORD: A decorated pitcher at Division II Angelo State (Texas), Baker set school records in strikeouts and wins as he led the Rams to the Division II World Series in 2021 and won Lone Star Conference pitcher of the year honors. The Cardinals selected Baker in the ninth round that year and signed him for $75,000. Baker made his full-season debut in 2022 with Low-A Palm Beach and continued his track record of success. He led the Florida State League in strikeouts, wins and innings pitched.

SCOUTING REPORT: Baker is a large-bodied righthander at 6-foot-3, 240 pounds with a big, round build. His two-seam fastball sits 92-94 mph with downhill plane out of his high three-quarters arm slot and touches 95. He pairs his fastball with a fringy, mid-80s slider with cutter shape and an above-average, low-to-mid-80s changeup that is the best pitch in his arsenal. Baker throws his changeup liberally and is comfortable throwing it against hitters on both sides of the plate. He shows average control of his three-pitch mix and is particularly proficient at landing his changeup.

THE FUTURE: Baker's success came as an older pitcher at Low-A, so he'll have to prove his stuff plays against age-appropriate competition. He projects to be a depth starter and will move to High-A in 2023.

BA GRADE: 40/High		Fastball: 45		Slider: 45		Changeup: 55		Control: 50				

Year	Age	Club (League)	Lvl	W	L	ERA	G	GS	IP	H	HR	BB	SO	BB/9	SO/9	WHIP	AVG
2022	23	Palm Beach (FSL)	LoA	9	7	3.14	25	25	123	114	8	48	138	3.5	10.1	1.31	.241
Minor League Totals				9	7	3.30	33	25	131	123	10	50	148	3.4	10.2	1.32	.243

29 RYAN LOUTOS, RHP

Born: Jan. 29, 1999. **B-T:** R-R. **HT:** 6-5. **WT:** 215.
Signed: Washington (Mo.), 2021 (NDFA). **Signed by:** Julia Prusaczyk.
TRACK RECORD: When Loutos committed to Division III powerhouse Washington University in St. Louis, he expected to play baseball while majoring in computer science and training for a technical career. The Cardinals instead signed Loutos as a nondrafted free agent following his senior season and used him as both a pitcher and a member of the front office, where he helped build analytical models. Loutos arrived at his first spring training throwing 4-5 mph harder and rocketed up the minors from High-A to Triple-A in his first full season in 2022 to establish himself as a prospect independent of his front office work. He finished the year with nine solid appearances in the Arizona Fall League.
SCOUTING REPORT: Loutos is a big, physical 6-foot-5 righthander and has grown into power stuff. After sitting 91-93 mph and touching 94 in college, Loutos' fastball now sits 95-96 and touches 99 with riding life and heavy bore. He not only added velocity to his fastball, but added six inches of sweep to his slider with the added power. His slider now averages almost a foot of sweep and sits 81-83 mph as his de facto out pitch. Loutos' low-80s curveball sits in a similar velocity band to his slider but with a distinctly different movement pattern featuring depth and two-plane break. He relies on overpowering hitters and has just fringe-average control.
THE FUTURE: With substantial gains in his first full professional season and a high level of intelligence, Loutos could blossom into a viable middle relief option. He is in position to make his major league debut in 2023.

BA GRADE: 40/High | **Fastball:** 55 | **Slider:** 50 | **Curveball:** 45 | **Control:** 45

Year	Age	Club (League)	Lvl	W	L	ERA	G	GS	IP	H	HR	BB	SO	BB/9	SO/9	WHIP	AVG
2022	23	Peoria (MWL)	HiA	2	2	3.14	9	0	14	11	1	3	17	1.9	10.7	0.98	.224
2022	23	Springfield (TL)	AA	1	1	1.61	15	0	22	14	0	10	26	4.0	10.5	1.07	.175
2022	23	Memphis (IL)	AAA	0	3	6.33	22	2	27	44	4	12	29	4.0	9.7	2.07	.373
Minor League Totals				4	8	4.38	58	3	86	97	5	31	98	3.2	10.2	1.48	.283

30 GUILLERMO ZUNIGA, RHP

Born: Oct. 10, 1998. **B-T:** R-R. **HT:** 6-5. **WT:** 230.
Signed: Colombia, 2016. **Signed by:** Carlos Garcia (Braves).
TRACK RECORD: Originally signed by the Braves out of Colombia back in 2016, Zuniga signed with the Dodgers as a minor league free agent and spent the last four seasons in their system, including the last two at Double-A Tulsa. The Cardinals signed him as a minor league free agent after the 2022 season and immediately added him to their 40-man roster.
SCOUTING REPORT: A true power reliever, Zuniga stands an imposing 6-foot-5, 230 pounds and mixes a trio of pitches with well above-average velocity. His fastball sits 97-98 mph and touches 102 mph at its peak with heavy arm-side run. He pairs his heater with a tight, plus slider in the mid 80s with two-plane movement that is his go-to swing-and-miss pitch. Zuniga's changeup is his third offering but is still part of his arsenal, sitting 89-91 mph with heavy tumble and fade. Like many hard-throwing relievers, Zuniga has plenty of stuff but is hindered by below-average control.
THE FUTURE: A pure power reliever with elite velocity and a prime bat-missing secondary in his slider, Zuniga should see time in the Cardinals bullpen in 2023.

BA GRADE: 40/High | **Fastball:** 60 | **Slider:** 60 | **Changeup:** 45 | **Control:** 40

Year	Age	Club (League)	Lvl	W	L	ERA	G	GS	IP	H	HR	BB	SO	BB/9	SO/9	WHIP	AVG
2022	23	Tulsa (TL)	AA	4	4	4.77	48	0	55	47	12	30	66	4.9	10.9	1.41	.227
Minor League Totals				19	13	4.11	131	13	225	208	26	99	258	4.0	10.3	1.36	.246

San Diego Padres

BY JEFF SANDERS

Apparently, not all farm systems are meant to supplement the big league roster. At least, not directly.

Two years after making a barrage of trades to prop up the organization's first postseason run in 14 years, Padres president of baseball operations A.J. Preller again dipped into his farm system at the 2022 trade deadline to sustain a playoff run that ended with the Padres reaching the National League Championship Series for just the third time in franchise history.

The minor league stolen bases leader (Esteury Ruiz) and a second-round draft pick (Robert Gasser) helped reel in closer Josh Hader from the Brewers. A teenage shortstop (Victor Acosta) brought in Brandon Drury from the Reds as a rental. Two more recent draftees (Max Ferguson and Corey Rosier) helped Preller finally unload Eric Hosmer on the Red Sox—but not his contract.

And then there was the big one: For two and a half years of generational talent Juan Soto, the Padres sent five present or former top prospects to the Nationals in shortstop CJ Abrams, lefthander MacKenzie Gore, outfielders Robert Hassell III and James Wood and fast-rising righthander Jarlin Susana.

"It's a huge part of our organization," Preller said a day after the Padres were eliminated in Game 5 of the NLCS. "You have to draft well. You have to sign well . . . We've had a really strong system, and sometimes that's reflected in the rankings. A lot of times, it's reflected in other clubs' interest in your players and our own evaluations."

The Padres delivered their deepest playoff run in more than two decades despite the absence of star shortstop Fernando Tatis Jr. for the entire season after his offseason wrist surgery and an 80-game PED suspension.

Provided Tatis returns to his previous levels of production, the big league product in San Diego is as healthy as it's ever been heading into 2023. Tatis, Soto and Manny Machado give the Padres a 1-2-3 punch few teams can rival. The rotation is deep with Yu Darvish and Blake Snell under contract for one more season and Joe Musgrove starting his five-year, $100 million extension. The back of the bullpen—with NPB import Robert Suarez emerging as a lights-out setup man to Hader—is again a weapon.

In the meantime, a hollowed-out farm system is filled with players looking to prove themselves.

Shortstop Jackson Merrill, the Padres' first-round pick in 2021, emerged as a burgeoning talent but played just 55 games due to injuries. The Padres remain high on catcher Luis Campusano,

Shortstop Ha-Seong Kim showed he could play every day in the absence of Fernando Tatis Jr.

PROJECTED 2026 LINEUP

Catcher	Luis Campusano	27
First Base	Jake Cronenworth	32
Second Base	Jackson Merrill	23
Third Base	Manny Machado	33
Shortstop	Xander Bogaerts	33
Left Field	Samuel Zavala	21
Center Field	Trent Grisham	29
Right Field	Fernando Tatis Jr.	27
Designated Hitter	Juan Soto	27
No. 1 Starter	Blake Snell	33
No. 2 Starter	Joe Musgrove	33
No. 3 Starter	Adrian Morejon	27
No. 4 Starter	Dylan Lesko	22
No. 5 Starter	Robby Snelling	22
Closer	Josh Hader	32

but he stagnated in a repeat stint at Triple-A El Paso and didn't do enough to convince the big league coaching staff to use him much.

Much deeper in the system, the aggressive Padres, led now by director Chris Kemp in both international and amateur scouting, are gambling on the upside of 2022 first-rounder Dylan Lesko, who might have been a top-five pick if he didn't have Tommy John surgery in the spring.

Lesko, as well as intriguing 2022 draftees Robby Snelling, Adam Mazur and Henry Williams could all play themselves onto the radar in the coming years, whether they debut in San Diego or help Preller put together his next blockbuster trade package. ■

SAN DIEGO PADRES

TOP 2023 MLB CONTRIBUTORS	RANK
Luis Campusano, C	2
Jay Groome, LHP	8

BREAKOUT PROSPECTS	RANK
Rosman Verdugo, SS	11
Korry Howell, OF	13
Jakob Marsee, OF	20

SOURCE OF TOP 30 TALENT

Homegrown	27	Acquired	3
College	9	Trade	2
Junior college	1	Rule 5 draft	0
High school	8	Independent league	0
Nondrafted free agent	0	Free agent/waivers	1
International	9		

LF
Tirso Ornelas (30)
Albert Fabian

CF
Samuel Zavala (4)
Korry Howell (13)
Jakob Marsee (19)

RF
Joshua Mears (16)
Oliver Carrillo

3B
Eguy Rosario (9)
Marcos Castanon

SS
Jackson Merrill (1)
Yendry Rojas (28)
Jarryd Dale
Charlis Aquino

2B
Nerwilian Cedeno (10)
Rosman Verdugo (11)
Matt Batten

1B
Nathan Martorella (20)
Taylor Kohlwey

C
Luis Campusano (2)
Lamar King Jr. (15)
Juan Zabala
Brandon Valenzuela

LHP

LHSP	LHRP
Robby Snelling (5)	Tom Cosgrove (29)
Jay Groome (8)	Ray Kerr
Noel Vela (18)	Jose Castillo
Zack Qin (24)	Aaron Leasher
Jackson Wolf	Gabe Morales
	Fred Schlichtholz
	Osvaldo Hernandez

RHP

RHSP	RHRP
Dylan Lesko (3)	Jairo Iriarte (12)
Victor Lizarraga (6)	Alek Jacob (22)
Adam Mazur (7)	Angel Felipe (28)
Henry Williams (14)	Kevin Kopps
Reiss Knehr (17)	Michel Báez
Garrett Hawkins (21)	Moises Lugo
Isaiah Lowe (23)	Justin Lopez
Ryan Bergert (25)	Lake Bachar
Kobe Robinson (27)	
Pedro Avila	
Matt Waldron	

1 JACKSON MERRILL, SS

Born: April 19, 2003. **B-T:** L-R. **HT:** 6-3. **WT:** 195.
Drafted: HS—Severna Park, Md., 2021 (1st round).
Signed by: Danny Sader.

TRACK RECORD: Merrill didn't attend many of the top high school showcase events during the summer of 2020 and was subsequently viewed as a pop-up prospect when he began to emerge in 2021 in the Baltimore-Washington metro area. The Padres were on Merrill well before he tied the Severna Park High record with 13 homers and were happy to select him 27th overall. He signed for a below-slot $1.8 million to forgo a Kentucky commitment and held his own during his pro debut in the Arizona Complex League until a minor hip flexor injury ended his season. In 2022 he was limited to 55 games in his full-season debut because of a fractured left wrist and a hamstring injury. Even in that limited time, Merrill stood out. He hit .339/.385/.511 in the regular season and went 11-for-17 with four doubles and three steals in four postseason games to help Low-A Lake Elsinore win the California League title. The Padres sent Merrill to the Arizona Fall League after the season, where he held his own.
SCOUTING REPORT: Merrill had a huge growth spurt and added nearly 30 pounds leading up to the draft. The added strength gave him plus raw power, which continues to be the main selling point even as he learns to leverage it in games. Merrill's solid bat speed and feel for hitting intrigued the Padres over multiple pre-draft workouts, where they tested him against the type of high-velocity pitching he did not see regularly on Maryland's prep circuit. Likewise, he was rather raw against spin during his professional debut. A year later, Merrill has developed advanced offspeed coverage for his age, not to mention an impressive left-on-left approach. He handles all types of pitches and is rarely fazed in the batter's box. His sweet swing and advanced pitch recognition and approach give him a chance to be a plus hitter with above-average power at maturity, though he is still learning to pull the ball in the air. Just as Merrill rapidly improved as a hitter, he upped his range, mobility, first-step reads and arm strength in his first full year to silence concerns about him moving off shortstop. He is a fundamentally sound defender with polished hands and footwork that is the result of his dedication to his pregame work. Just an average runner, Merrill makes every play as a result of his excellent pre-pitch positioning and anticipation and completes every throw with his above-average, accurate arm. Club officials rave

CHRIS BERNACCHI/DIAMOND IMAGES VIA GETTY IMAGES

BA GRADE	SCOUTING GRADES
60 Risk: High	Hit: 60. Power: 55. Run: 50. Field: 55. Arm: 55.

Projected future grades on 20-80 scouting scale

BEST TOOLS

BATTING

Best Hitter for Average	Jackson Merrill
Best Power Hitter	Joshua Mears
Best Strike-Zone Discipline	Jakob Marsee
Fastest Baserunner	Korry Howell
Best Athlete	Robby Snelling

PITCHING

Best Fastball	Angel Felipe
Best Curveball	Robby Snelling
Best Slider	Adam Mazur
Best Changeup	Dylan Lesko
Best Control	Victor Lizarraga

FIELDING

Best Defensive Catcher	Luis Campusano
Best Defensive Infielder	Jackson Merrill
Best Infield Arm	Eguy Rosario
Best Defensive Outfielder	Jakob Marsee

about his culture-changing makeup that will help him overcome any challenges.
THE FUTURE: Merrill has the ability to play shortstop, but the Padres' enviable depth at that position could ultimately push him to second or third base, where he would be an athletic defender with a bat that could produce in the middle of the order. He projects to move quickly for a high school player and could jump straight to Double-A San Antonio to begin 2023, which would put him on a pace to reach the major leagues before his 22nd birthday.

Year	Age	Club (League)	Lvl	AVG	G	AB	R	H	2B	3B	HR	RBI	BB	SO	SB	OBP	SLG
2022	19	Padres (ACL)	R	.433	10	30	5	13	3	1	1	6	1	2	3	.452	.700
2022	19	Lake Elsinore (CAL)	LoA	.325	45	197	33	64	10	3	5	34	19	42	8	.387	.482
Minor League Totals				.320	86	334	57	107	20	6	6	50	30	71	16	.377	.470

2 DYLAN LESKO, RHP

Born: Sept. 7, 2003. **B-T:** R-R. **HT:** 6-2. **WT:** 195.
Drafted: HS—Buford, Ga., 2022 (1st round). **Signed by:** Tyler Stubblefield.

BA GRADE
65 Risk: Extreme

TRACK RECORD: Lesko appeared headed for a top five overall selection in the 2022 draft after he struck out 112 batters over 60 innings and had a 0.35 ERA as a high school junior. He even won Gatorade national player of the year honors as a junior in 2021. That trajectory was altered after Lesko had Tommy John surgery as a senior, but that did little to scare off the Padres. The club did its due diligence and didn't hesitate when Lesko slipped to the 15th overall pick. San Diego signed him for a below-slot $3.9 million to lure him away from a Vanderbilt commitment.

SCOUTING REPORT: With an athletic 6-foot-2 frame that draws comparisons to a more physical Zack Greinke, a healthy Lesko boasts a four-seam fastball that sits 93-95 mph and touches 98 with carry at the top of the strike zone. His fading low-80s changeup earns plus-plus grades with its "Bugs Bunny" action and is one of the best seen in recent years from a high school pitcher. Lesko has power in his 12-to-6 curveball that can push 3,000 rpm, but it's a pitch that lacks consistency, mainly because he didn't need anything more than his fastball and changeup to dominate high school hitters. He doesn't currently throw a slider, but Padres staffers believe he can add one down the road given his aptitude on the mound. As much as Lesko's pure stuff impresses, his polished delivery and clean arm action stand out even more for a pitcher his age. Before the surgery, Lesko threw strikes with plus control and showed an advanced feel for pitching.

THE FUTURE: Lesko should return to the mound by summer and make his professional debut in the Rookie-level Arizona Complex League. He has the talent to be a No. 2 or 3 starter as long as he returns healthy.

SCOUTING GRADES	Fastball: 70	Curveball: 55	Changeup: 70	Control: 60

Year	Age	Club (League)	Lvl	W	L	ERA	G	GS	IP	H	HR	BB	SO	BB/9	SO/9	WHIP	AVG
2022	18	Did not play—Injured															

3 LUIS CAMPUSANO, C

Born: Sept. 29, 1998. **B-T:** R-R. **HT:** 5-11. **WT:** 232.
Drafted: HS—Augusta, Ga., 2017 (2nd round). **Signed by:** Tyler Stubblefield.

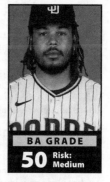

BA GRADE
50 Risk: Medium

TRACK RECORD: The first catcher selected in the 2017 draft, Campusano overcame a pair of early concussions to win co-MVP honors in the High-A California League in 2019. A year later, he hit his way from the alternate training site to the majors and homered in his debut, but a wrist injury quickly ended that stint and he has been blocked in San Diego the past two seasons by veteran catchers. Campusano spent most of 2022 at Triple-A El Paso but finished the season in the majors and made the Padres' postseason roster. He spent his offseason playing in the Dominican League and swung the bat well in eight games as Estrellas' starting catcher.

SCOUTING REPORT: Campusano projects as a middle-of-the-order threat who will hit for both average and power. He has demonstrated excellent strike-zone control at his best, though he has been too aggressive during spot duty in the majors. Defensively, Campusano is an athletic backstop who has improved his blocking significantly in pro ball. Improving his framing has long been a point of emphasis, while above-average arm strength remains his best asset behind the plate. Something of an introvert, Campusano has worked to assert himself in game-planning with pitchers, but his focus and effort level over the course of an entire game have long been flagged as areas that need improvement.

THE FUTURE: With nothing left to prove in the minors, Campusano must earn the trust of a big league coaching staff helmed by former catcher Bob Melvin if he's going to fulfill his potential as the Padres' long-term backstop. He'll report to camp looking for a share of the catching job with Austin Nola.

SCOUTING GRADES	Hitting: 50	Power: 55	Speed: 30	Fielding: 50	Arm: 55

Year	Age	Club (League)	Lvl	AVG	G	AB	R	H	2B	3B	HR	RBI	BB	SO	SB	OBP	SLG
2022	23	El Paso (PCL)	AAA	.298	81	319	62	95	15	1	14	60	33	62	0	.363	.483
2022	23	San Diego (NL)	MLB	.250	16	48	4	12	1	0	1	5	1	11	0	.260	.333
Major League Totals				.188	28	85	6	16	1	0	2	7	5	24	0	.239	.271
Minor League Totals				.301	379	1427	206	429	82	5	51	251	146	253	1	.369	.472

4 SAMUEL ZAVALA, OF

Born: July 15, 2004. **B-T:** L-L. **HT:** 6-1. **WT:** 175.
Signed: Venezuela, 2021. **Signed by:** Luis Prieto/Trevor Schumm/Chris Kemp.

TRACK RECORD: Zavala was regarded as one of the best pure hitters in the 2021 international signing class and signed with the Padres for $1.2 million out of Venezuela. He made his pro debut in the Dominican Summer League that year and did not disappoint, hitting for both average and power while showing remarkable plate discipline for his age. The Padres thought about starting Zavala at Low-A to begin 2022 but held him back in extended spring training to work on his speed. A hamstring strain slowed him initially, but he moved to Low-A Lake Elsinore after the trade deadline and homered seven times in 33 games before a broken hamate bone ended his season.

BA GRADE

55 Risk: Very High

SCOUTING REPORT: Zavala possesses a knack for finding the barrel with a smooth, whip-like swing from the left side. He doesn't have the brute strength of other teenagers, but he has added more power and loft to his swing as he's matured physically and could wind up with average power. His swing, patience and plate discipline give him a chance to be at least an above-average hitter as he adds strength. An above-average runner, Zavala also shows good reads, a quick first step and fluid movements. He'll have to prove he can continue to handle center field as he climbs the system and gets bigger. If not, arm strength that could get to above-average would help him in either corner. Zavala is bilingual and a heady player, leading the Padres to push him as they do with many of the younger prospects they believe in.

THE FUTURE: Zavala participated in instructional league last fall following his hamate surgery and should be ready for Opening Day in 2023.

SCOUTING GRADES	Hitting: 55	Power: 50	Speed: 55	Fielding: 55	Arm: 55

Year	Age	Club (League)	Lvl	AVG	G	AB	R	H	2B	3B	HR	RBI	BB	SO	SB	OBP	SLG
2022	17	Padres (ACL)	R	.345	10	29	6	10	3	1	1	6	4	11	0	.412	.621
2022	17	Lake Elsinore (CAL)	LoA	.254	33	122	24	31	6	2	7	26	19	37	5	.355	.508
Minor League Totals				.286	98	346	74	99	25	9	11	72	55	84	16	.385	.506

5 ROBBY SNELLING, LHP

Born: Dec. 19, 2003. **B-T:** R-L. **HT:** 6-3. **WT:** 210.
Drafted: HS—Reno, 2022 (1st round supplemental). **Signed by:** Tim Reynolds.

TRACK RECORD: A physical quarterback and four-star recruit as a linebacker, Snelling originally had aspirations of playing both football and baseball in college before a breakout senior spring made him one of the fastest risers in the 2022 draft class. Snelling struck out a Nevada state record 146 batters while showing premium arm strength from the left side and was drafted 39th overall by the Padres. The Padres signed him away from a Louisiana State commitment with a $3 million signing bonus, nearly $1 million above slot, and unveiled him in fall instructional league.

BA GRADE

55 Risk: Extreme

SCOUTING REPORT: Snelling is a physical lefthander who is built like a football player with broad, tapered shoulders and a thick and muscular lower half. His fastball jumped from 90-94 mph to 92-96 as a senior and he maintained that increased velocity when the Padres finally pushed him to the mound at instructional league. Snelling possesses a natural ability to spin the baseball and throws a spike-grip curveball with excellent rotation that was one of the best secondary pitches in the draft. He can manipulate its velocity anywhere from the mid 70s to mid 80s and can alter the shape to give it more sweeping action across the zone or two-plane break with sharp and late vertical bite. Snelling also has a low-80s changeup that he did not throw much in high school but is a focal point of his development. A physical pitcher with a football player's mentality, Snelling pounds the strike zone aggressively and is athletic enough to repeat his delivery. Padres officials rave about Snelling's competitive makeup as the son of a high school football coach.

THE FUTURE: Snelling will make his pro debut in 2023 and could see Low-A Lake Elsinore by the end of the year. He has a chance to be a midrotation starter as long as he develops his changeup.

SCOUTING GRADES	Fastball: 55	Curveball: 60	Changeup: 40	Control: 55

Year	Age	Club (League)	Lvl	W	L	ERA	G	GS	IP	H	HR	BB	SO	BB/9	SO/9	WHIP	AVG
2022	18	Did not pitch															

6 VICTOR LIZARRAGA, RHP

Born: Nov. 30, 2003. **B-T:** R-R. **HT:** 6-3. **WT:** 180. **Signed:** Mexico, 2021.
Signed by: Bill McLaughlin/Emmanuel Rangel/Trevor Schumm/Chris Kemp.
TRACK RECORD: Lizarraga was Mexico's best pitching prospect in the 2021 international class and signed with the Padres for $1 million shortly after the signing period began. The Padres challenged him with an assignment to the Arizona Complex League as a 17-year-old after he signed and pushed him to Low-A Lake Elsinore to begin his first full season at age 18 in 2022. Lizarraga rose to the task by finishing fourth in the California League with a 3.43 ERA and started two playoff games on the road, winning both to help the Storm claim the league title.

BA GRADE
50 Risk: High

SCOUTING REPORT: Lizarraga is a long, lean and athletic righthander who is easy to dream on. His fastball sits 90-94 mph and should tick up as he adds weight and strength to his projectable, 6-foot-3 frame. His firm, fading changeup in the mid 80s could reach plus, though to do so it would need more separation from his fastball. His vertical, upper-70s curveball is a developing pitch that is fringy but has potential to improve. Lizarraga mixes his three pitches effectively and has the aptitude to develop a slider, though the Padres prefer he focus on improving his curveball. Beyond his pure stuff, Lizarraga demonstrates impressive moxie and competitiveness in between the lines and has an advanced ability to read swings. He stays calm and poised in tough situations and pounds the strike zone with average control. As is the case with most young pitchers, his fastball command still needs refinement. Lizarraga is still learning the importance of putting in the work between starts, including in the weight room and bullpen sessions, but should improve with experience and maturity.
THE FUTURE: Lizarraga has a solid foundation to be a back-of-the-rotation starter and could be more depending on how much his velocity jumps. He'll be 19 in 2023 and has plenty of time to add strength.

SCOUTING GRADES	Fastball: 55		Curveball: 45		Changeup: 60			Control: 50			

Year	Age	Club (League)	Lvl	W	L	ERA	G	GS	IP	H	HR	BB	SO	BB/9	SO/9	WHIP	AVG
2022	18	Lake Elsinore (CAL)	LoA	8	3	3.43	20	19	94	87	5	34	95	3.2	9.1	1.28	.244
Minor League Totals				8	7	3.84	31	30	124	112	10	49	130	3.5	9.4	1.29	.239

7 ADAM MAZUR, RHP

Born: April 20, 2001. **B-T:** R-R. **HT:** 6-2. **WT:** 180.
Drafted: Iowa, 2022 (2nd round). **Signed by:** Troy Hoerner.
TRACK RECORD: Mazur logged a 5.50 ERA over two years at South Dakota State, but he began to turn things around with a standout showing in the Cape Cod League after his sophomore year. He transferred to Iowa for his junior season in 2022 and went 7-3, 3.08 with a .178 opponent average, seventh in the nation, en route to winning Big Ten Conference pitcher of the year honors. The Padres drafted Mazur in the second round, No. 53 overall, and signed him for an under-slot $1.25 million. He did not appear in a regular season game after signing but pitched in instructional league.

BA GRADE
50 Risk: High

SCOUTING REPORT: The rare college pitcher who still had physical projection left, Mazur has already added 10 pounds of muscle since signing and has seen his stuff tick up. His fastball sat between 92-94 mph and topped out at 97 during the college season but now touches 99 out of a loose, easy delivery. His slider has jumped to 87-90 mph with added power to become a plus pitch, and his changeup has ticked up to 84-86 mph with enhanced two-seam action and arm-side life to become an average pitch. He also has an average 12-to-6 curveball he will throw to keep hitters off-balance. Mazur repeats his delivery and three-quarters arm slot well and has made progressive strides with his control. He cut his walk rate from 5.3 per nine innings as a freshman to 4.1 as a sophomore to 2.9 as a junior and projects to have average control.
THE FUTURE: Mazur is advanced enough to make his pro debut at High-A Fort Wayne in 2023. He has to prove he can maintain his enhanced stuff over a full season, but he has a chance to be a No. 3 or 4 starter. His plus slider could play in the bullpen if his other secondaries stall.

SCOUTING GRADES	Fastball: 55		Slider: 60		Curveball: 50		Changeup: 50		Control: 50			

Year	Age	Club (League)	Lvl	W	L	ERA	G	GS	IP	H	HR	BB	SO	BB/9	SO/9	WHIP	AVG
2022	21	Did not pitch															

8 JAY GROOME, LHP

Born: Aug. 23, 1998. **B-T:** L-L. **HT:** 6-6. **WT:** 262.
Drafted: HS—Barnegat, N.J., 2016 (1st round). **Signed by:** Ray Fagnant (Red Sox).

TRACK RECORD: Groome was arguably the top high school pitcher in the country when the Red Sox drafted him 12th overall in 2016, but his career has been sidetracked by injuries. He missed all of 2018 and most of 2019 after having Tommy John surgery and lost the 2020 season due to the coronavirus pandemic but threw at the alternate training site. He returned to the mound with diminished stuff and athleticism but still made his way from Double-A to Triple-A in 2022. That's the point at which the Padres acquired him in the deal that sent Eric Hosmer to the Red Sox. Groome stepped into the rotation at Triple-A El Paso and finished the year strong.

BA GRADE
45 Risk: Medium

SCOUTING REPORT: Because his stuff never fully bounced back after surgery, Groome is more of a pitchability lefthander than someone who overwhelms hitters. His fastball sits 90-94 mph and can touch 95-96. He commands the pitch to all quadrants of the zone and has added a two-seamer and an average cutter. His formerly elite curveball is more horizontal these days than a true north-south biter, but it is still average. Groome has ballooned from 220 to 262 pounds, so his conditioning and stamina are issues the Padres would like addressed. He often dominated early only to fall apart after a few innings, so it was a step in the right direction for him to complete eight innings for the first time after arriving in El Paso. He has reverse platoon splits and dominates righthanded hitters while struggling against lefties.

THE FUTURE: Groome may no longer have a top-end ceiling, but he can still help the Padres in the back of the rotation or in the bullpen. He'll head to spring training with an eye on winning a roster spot.

SCOUTING GRADES	Fastball: 55	Curveball: 50	Slider: 50	Changeup: 50	Control: 50

Year	Age	Club (League)	Lvl	W	L	ERA	G	GS	IP	H	HR	BB	SO	BB/9	SO/9	WHIP	AVG
2022	23	Portland (EL)	AA	3	4	3.52	16	14	77	58	11	38	81	4.5	9.5	1.25	.207
2022	23	El Paso (PCL)	AAA	3	2	3.16	10	10	51	52	4	19	44	3.3	7.7	1.38	.267
2022	23	Worcester (IL)	AAA	1	1	3.94	3	3	16	17	2	7	15	3.9	8.4	1.50	.274
Minor League Totals				15	24	4.25	70	68	307	272	35	135	362	4.0	10.6	1.32	.235

9 EGUY ROSARIO, 2B/3B

Born: Aug. 25, 1999. **B-T:** R-R. **HT:** 5-9. **WT:** 204.
Signed: Dominican Republic, 2015. **Signed by:** Felix Felix/Trevor Schumm/Chris Kemp.

TRACK RECORD: Rosario signed with the Padres for $300,000 on his 16th birthday and has annually been among the youngest players in his league. He was overmatched in his early years, but he showed signs of life in High-A in 2019 and led the Double-A Texas League with 31 doubles and finished fifth with 30 stolen bases in 2021. Like many hitters, Rosario set a career high in homers in his first year in the hitter-friendly Pacific Coast League in 2022 and received his first big league callup in late August, though he was used sparingly before returning to El Paso.

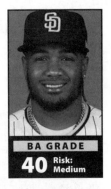

BA GRADE
40 Risk: Medium

SCOUTING REPORT: Surprisingly twitchy and athletic despite a stocky build, Rosario has a short, quick righthanded swing. He is at his best when his approach is aimed at shooting balls from gap to gap. Like a lot of hitters, he fares better against fastballs than offspeed pitches and is susceptible to chasing below the strike zone. Rosario showed off his strength gains with his first double-digit homer campaign in 2021, then moved to Triple-A El Paso in 2022 and got off to a slow start while trying to pull balls in a hitter's haven. Rosario is an above-average runner who has improved his ability to put that speed to use on the bases. He is playable at shortstop, but his range and actions fit better at second or even third base. His plus arm rates as the best in the system, even if it has regressed a tick. Though Rosario has the physical skills to be an average defender, he'll have to cut down on mistakes on routine plays.

THE FUTURE: Rosario got his first taste of the big leagues in 2022 and projects as a utility infielder. He'll be in position to battle for a spot on the bench this spring.

SCOUTING GRADES	Hitting: 45	Power: 45	Speed: 55	Fielding: 50	Arm: 60

Year	Age	Club (League)	Lvl	AVG	G	AB	R	H	2B	3B	HR	RBI	BB	SO	SB	OBP	SLG
2022	22	El Paso (PCL)	AAA	.288	124	490	98	141	34	4	22	81	59	109	21	.368	.508
2022	22	San Diego (NL)	MLB	.200	7	5	0	1	0	0	0	0	1	2	0	.333	.200
Major League Totals				.200	7	5	0	1	0	0	0	0	1	2	0	.333	.200
Minor League Totals				.274	644	2442	381	668	161	26	52	332	254	577	137	.348	.425

10 NERWILIAN CEDEÑO, 2B

Born: March 16, 2002. **B-T:** B-R. **HT:** 5-11. **WT:** 175.
Drafted: Venezuela, 2018. **Signed by:** Trevor Schumm/Luis Prieto.

TRACK RECORD: Cedeño signed with the Padres for $300,000 out of Venezuela in 2018 and quickly emerged as a favored low-level sleeper candidate. Club officials believed he was primed for a breakout season in 2021, but he suffered a meniscus tear before spring training and didn't get on the field in the Rookie-level Arizona Complex League until late August. Arm trouble then delayed Cedeño by nearly two months in 2022, but he finally made it to Low-A Lake Elsinore on May 31 for his full-season debut.
SCOUTING REPORT: A developing switch-hitter, Cedeño boasts a mature, line-drive approach, solid bat-to-ball skills and good strike-zone discipline. He's been a better hitter from the left side of the plate, but he closed the gap on his splits drastically in 2022. Cedeño's swing can get too rotational, but he uses gaps well when he's locked in and flashes solid bat speed. He has strong forearms and could develop double-digit home run power as his body matures and he learns to use his lower half to drive the ball. He is an average runner with average arm strength and has the potential to be an average defender across the infield, though he profiles best at third base or as an offensive-minded second baseman. Cedeño is a hard worker and a leader in the clubhouse among players.
THE FUTURE: Cedeño needs reps more than anything after two injury-shortened seasons. He's still young and has time to make the improvements to fulfill his potential as an everyday infielder.

BA GRADE
45 Risk: High

SCOUTING GRADES	Hitting: 50	Power: 45	Speed: 50	Fielding: 50	Arm: 50

Year	Age	Club (League)	Lvl	AVG	G	AB	R	H	2B	3B	HR	RBI	BB	SO	SB	OBP	SLG
2022	20	Lake Elsinore (CAL)	LoA	.256	71	270	60	69	13	4	6	54	42	79	18	.362	.400
Minor League Totals				.233	136	490	94	114	27	6	8	82	91	142	24	.358	.361

11 ROSMAN VERDUGO, 2B/3B

Born: Feb. 2, 2005. **B-T:** R-R. **HT:** 6-0. **WT:** 180.
Drafted: Mexico, 2022. **Signed by:** Emmanuel Rangel/Bill McLaughlin

TRACK RECORD: A product of the Diablos Rojos academy in Mexico City, Verdugo signed for $700,000 as Mexico's top amateur in the 2022 international class. While most international amateurs head to the Dominican Summer League, Verdugo's advanced feel to hit led the Padres to start his professional career in the Arizona Complex League. There, his seven homers were off the league lead as a 17-year-old. He finished his first year in pro ball playing in the Mexican Pacific League, where the average age is 29.
SCOUTING REPORT: Verdugo's smooth feel to hit and contact skills draw comparisons to the Brewers' Luis Urias, whom the Padres originally signed from the same academy. Verdugo keeps his hands inside the ball and, while he will swing and miss, shows the early traits of being at least an average hitter. He also has good raw power for his age, which he demonstrated in the ACL. The Padres will play Verdugo all over the infield in the early going, but he will most likely land at third base unless he can speed up his lower half.
THE FUTURE: Verdugo held his own as the youngest player in a domestic league, warranting a push to Low-A Lake Elsinore in 2023. He has a chance to hit for average and power while staying in the dirt.

BA GRADE: 50/Extreme	Hit: 50	Power: 45	Run: 40	Field: 50	Arm: 50

Year	Age	Club (League)	Lvl	AVG	G	AB	R	H	2B	3B	HR	RBI	BB	SO	SB	OBP	SLG
2022	17	Padres (ACL)	R	.251	52	167	26	42	7	4	7	35	22	69	3	.338	.467
Minor League Totals				.251	52	167	26	42	7	4	7	35	22	69	3	.338	.467

12 JAIRO IRIARTE, RHP

Born: Dec. 15, 2001. **B-T:** R-R. **HT:** 6-5. **WT:** 200.
Drafted: Venezuela, 2018. **Signed by:** Luis Prieto/Chris Kemp.

TRACK RECORD: Iriarte stood 6-foot-2 and 160 pounds when he signed out of Venezuela for $75,000 in 2018 and has since matured into an imposing figure at 6-foot-5 and 200 pounds. He showed well in the Dominican Summer League after signing (3.31 ERA), started the following year in Arizona and was hit hard when Covid protocols forced an early promotion to Low-A Lake Elsinore. Iriarte returned to the California League in 2022 and showed intriguing arm strength that made him a frequent target of opposing teams in trade discussions.

SCOUTING REPORT: Iriarte is a long, lean, athletic righthander whose growth spurt has pushed his fastball up to 95-97 mph. His fastball plays up beyond its velocity with good carry through the top of the zone and is a plus pitch, although he can be scattershot with it. Iriarte's best secondary offering is an 86-87 mph changeup with late fade that could be a future above-average pitch. His mid-80s slider has been inconsistent in the early going in pro ball but shows average potential. Iriarte is athletic on the mound, but struggles with timing in his delivery that has led to fringy control.

THE FUTURE: Iriarte will head to High-A Fort Wayne in 2023. His flashes of three average or better pitches will keep him as a starter for now, but his stuff will play up in the bullpen if he has to move to relief.

BA GRADE: 45/High	Fastball: 60	Slider: 50	Changeup: 55	Control: 45

Year	Age	Club (League)	Lvl	W	L	ERA	G	GS	IP	H	HR	BB	SO	BB/9	SO/9	WHIP	AVG
2022	20	Lake Elsinore (CAL)	LoA	4	7	5.12	21	18	91	83	13	42	109	4.1	10.7	1.37	.236
Minor League Totals				5	14	5.92	45	29	157	161	23	69	164	4.0	9.4	1.47	.263

13 KORRY HOWELL, OF

Born: Sept. 1, 1998. **B-T:** R-R. **HT:** 6-3. **WT:** 180.
Drafted: Kirkwood (Iowa) JC, 2018 (12th round). **Signed by:** Drew Anderson (Brewers)

TRACK RECORD: Lightly recruited out of high school, Howell blossomed over two seasons at Kirkwood (Iowa) JC and signed with the Brewers for an above-slot $210,000 bonus as a 12th-round pick in 2018. That made him the second-highest draftee in Kirkwood history. He used the coronavirus shutdown to add muscle to his frame and improve his plate approach and was rewarded with a breakout season across High-A and Double-A in 2021. The Padres acquired Howell before the start of the 2022 season as part of the deal that sent Victor Caratini to Milwaukee, and Howell was in the midst of an excellent first season as a Padres prospect through 48 games at Double-A before having season-ending wrist surgery.

SCOUTING REPORT: Howell is a high-end athlete whose best asset is his versatility. He spent time at shortstop, second base and all three outfield positions at San Antonio and is a plus runner with twitchy actions and excellent range in the field. An above-average defender everywhere, Howell remains a work in progress at the plate. He has an enticing combination of bat speed, pull-side power and a discerning eye at the plate. He will have to iron out a hand-pump in his swing and improve his ability to hit spin in order to develop into an everyday regular.

THE FUTURE: Howell will head to Triple-A El Paso in 2023. He projects to be a versatile bench piece and could grow into more if his offensive gains hold.

BA GRADE: 45/High	Hit: 40	Power: 45	Run: 60	Field: 55	Arm: 50

Year	Age	Club (League)	Lvl	AVG	G	AB	R	H	2B	3B	HR	RBI	BB	SO	SB	OBP	SLG
2022	23	San Antonio (TL)	AA	.253	48	146	37	37	8	4	6	20	25	52	12	.390	.486
Minor League Totals				.251	264	898	170	225	41	12	24	99	122	302	67	.356	.403

14 HENRY WILLIAMS, RHP

Born: Sept. 18, 2001. **B-T:** R-R. **HT:** 6-5. **WT:** 200.
Drafted: Duke, 2022 (3rd round). **Signed by:** Jake Koenig.

TRACK RECORD: The Padres scouted Williams at Darien (Conn.) High and kept tabs on him as he made his way to Duke. He pitched just 37.2 innings in his college career before having Tommy John surgery, but the Padres saw enough in that limited stint to draft him in the third round, No. 91 overall, and sign him for an above-slot $800,000 signing bonus. Williams continued rehabbing after being selected and did not pitch in live games, but he flew out to the Padres' complex in Arizona every other weekend to throw bullpens while continuing to work toward his degree at Duke.

SCOUTING REPORT: Before his elbow reconstruction, Williams sat 94-98 mph with a high-spin fastball that played up with carry at the top of the strike zone. His three-pitch mix also includes a wipeout slider that projects as an above-average pitch and a fading, mid-80s changeup. Athletic on the mound, Williams still has room on his lean frame to get stronger and add more velocity as he moves further away from surgery. He throws strikes with above-average control and has solid command of all of his pitches. Williams' build, arsenal and control are that of a no-doubt starter, but if something stalls in his rehab, his stuff would also be rather loud in a relief role.

THE FUTURE: Williams is expected to be ready for spring training and could push for a spot in Low-A Lake Elsinore's rotation to start the year. He could move quickly up the organizational depth chart if he regains his pre-injury form.

BA GRADE: 50/Extreme		Fastball: 55		Slider: 55		Changeup: 55		Control: 55			

Year	Age	Club (League)	Lvl	W	L	ERA	G	GS	IP	H	HR	BB	SO	BB/9	SO/9	WHIP	AVG
2022	20	Did not play															

15 LAMAR KING JR., C

Born: Dec. 7, 2003. **B-T:** R-R. **HT:** 6-3. **WT:** 215.
Drafted: HS—Towson, Md., 2022 (4th round). **Signed by:** Danny Sader.
TRACK RECORD: King is the son of Lamar King, an NFL first-round pick who played defensive end for five years for the Seattle Seahawks. The younger King emerged as one of the top prep catchers in his class during national travel ball tournaments and was committed to Georgia Tech before the Padres drafted him in the fifth round and signed him for $502,800. He played just four games in the Rookie-level Arizona Complex League in his pro debut while focusing on development away from live games.
SCOUTING REPORT: Built like a defensive end similarly to his father, King's loud, pull power from the right side is his carrying tool. He has above-average power and could grow into more, but his swing is long and a bit stiff and will need to be ironed out in pro ball. While size typically works against catchers, King is an average runner, is quick in small spaces and sits well behind the plate. Like most catchers he will likely slow down because of the wear and tear of catching. He has above-average arm strength, but his hands and receiving need work as evidenced by some of his defensive struggles in instructional league.
THE FUTURE: King is raw and has a lot of development ahead, but he has enough projectable tools to potentially click as an offensive-minded catcher with an impact bat. He'll likely open 2023 back in the ACL.

BA GRADE: 50/Extreme		Hit: 40		Power: 55		Run: 40		Field: 45		Arm: 55			

Year	Age	Club (League)	Lvl	AVG	G	AB	R	H	2B	3B	HR	RBI	BB	SO	SB	OBP	SLG
2022	18	Padres (ACL)	R	.111	4	9	1	1	0	0	0	1	1	2	0	.273	.111
Minor League Totals				.111	4	9	1	1	0	0	0	1	1	2	0	.273	.111

16 JOSHUA MEARS, OF

Born: Feb. 21, 2001. **B-T:** R-R **HT:** 6-3. **WT:** 242.
Drafted: HS—Federal Way, Wash., 2019 (2nd round). **Signed by:** Justin Baughman.
TRACK RECORD: Mears went viral during 2021 spring training with a 117 mph home run off Rockies reliever Carlos Estevez in a Cactus League game. His power continued to play at Low-A Lake Elsinore for his first full season, at least when he was in the lineup. Mears missed time to a shoulder injury, a concussion, the Covid list and a broken nose on a bunt he fouled off his face in the fall. He returned to hit 22 home runs while rising to Double-A in 2022, including 11 in 47 games after spending several weeks in the middle of the season at the Padres' complex to attempt to retool his swing.
SCOUTING REPORT: Mears stands a chiseled 6-foot-3, 242 pounds and destroys baseballs with his plus-plus raw power. He doesn't chase much and draws walks with a good eye for the zone, but he misses too many pitches in the heart of the plate and struggles with high-carry fastballs and breaking balls below the zone. He has a career 39% strikeout rate and will have to make major strides with his swing to be even a well-below average hitter. Mears has surprising speed for a big man and is playable in center field. His long-term landing spot is likely right field, where he projects to be an average defender with an average arm.
THE FUTURE: No one in the Padres system has as much raw power as Mears, but there are real questions if he'll ever make enough contact to showcase it. He'll return to Double-A San Antonio to start 2023.

BA GRADE: 50/Extreme		Hit: 30		Power: 50		Run: 45		Field: 50		Arm: 50			

Year	Age	Club (League)	Lvl	AVG	G	AB	R	H	2B	3B	HR	RBI	BB	SO	SB	OBP	SLG
2022	21	Padres (ACL)	R	.268	17	56	10	15	6	1	3	10	8	26	2	.364	.571
2022	21	Fort Wayne (MWL)	HiA	.223	52	184	29	41	11	0	14	34	16	90	1	.304	.511
2022	21	San Antonio (TL)	AA	.169	24	83	9	14	2	0	5	15	10	45	1	.266	.373
Minor League Totals				.234	207	731	123	171	33	8	46	131	93	334	23	.338	.490

17 REISS KNEHR, RHP

Born: Nov. 3, 1996. **B-T:** L-R. **HT:** 6-3. **WT:** 231.
Drafted: Fordham, 2018 (20th round). **Signed by:** Jake Koenig.

TRACK RECORD: A two-way player at Fordham, Knehr intrigued the Padres as a pitcher and signed for $80,000 after they selected him in the 20th round in 2018. Knehr was the darling of the Padres' 2020 instructional league and pitched his way to the majors in 2021, appearing both out of the rotation and out of the bullpen for the Padres' injury-ravaged staff. He was an up-and-down arm again in 2022, faring far better in the majors (3.95 ERA in 13.2 innings) than he did at hitter-friendly Triple-A El Paso (6.88 ERA in 87.2 innings).

SCOUTING REPORT: Knehr packs a dangerous 1-2 punch with a high-spin, 93-95 mph fastball and an upper-80s changeup with horizontal break that has improved to become a plus pitch. He is still figuring out his mound presence and pitch usage, however. Lauded in the minors for an aggressive, bulldog mentality, Knehr spent much of his initial big league time nibbling around the strike zone and was too reliant on his upper-80s cutter. His changeup gets hit when he overthrows it, so he continues to work to choke off velocity. Knehr added an average curveball in 2022 to add a bit more variance in his pitch speeds and he threw that pitch 20% of the time in the majors. His control took a step back in 2022 and is firmly below-average.

THE FUTURE: Knehr will again be in big league spring training with a chance to win a job. He projects to be a swingman and is ready to fill that role now.

BA GRADE: 40/Medium **Fastball:** 55 **Curveball:** 50 **Cutter:** 50 **Changeup:** 60 **Control:** 45

Year	Age	Club (League)	Lvl	W	L	ERA	G	GS	IP	H	HR	BB	SO	BB/9	SO/9	WHIP	AVG
2022	25	El Paso (PCL)	AAA	4	4	6.88	32	15	88	89	18	55	92	5.6	9.4	1.64	.259
2022	25	San Diego (NL)	MLB	0	0	3.95	5	1	14	11	1	4	10	2.6	6.6	1.10	.216
Major League Totals				1	2	4.64	17	6	43	34	3	24	30	5.1	6.3	1.36	.219
Minor League Totals				16	13	5.11	88	44	264	242	39	129	286	4.4	9.7	1.40	.240

18 NOEL VELA, LHP

Born: Dec. 21, 1998. **B-T:** L-L. **HT:** 6-1. **WT:** 175.
Drafted: HS—Mission, Texas, 2017 (28th round). **Signed by:** Kevin Ham.

TRACK RECORD: Vela drew little attention in high school and was committed to Texas-Rio Grande Valley, but the Padres took a chance on him and signed him for $125,000 as a 28th-rounder in 2017. The late-blooming Vela spent his first two full professional seasons in the rookie levels, came back from the coronavirus shutdown in top shape and finally ventured into full-season ball in 2021. He impressed as one of the breakout pitchers in the Padres system and continued his ascent in 2022, rising to Double-A while pitching a career-high 109.2 innings.

SCOUTING REPORT: Vela's fastball has ticked up from the added strength gains as a pro to become an above-average weapon. His four-seamer now sits 91-95 mph and plays up with carry at the top of the strike zone. His fastball command remains raw, but he gets swings and misses when he locates his heater. Vela's curveball with 1-to-7 break flashes plus and has been among the best curves in the system, but some evaluators prefer his deceptive, side-spinning changeup that shows above-average potential. Vela has below-average control because he tends to rush his delivery, but his stuff plays against hitters on both sides of the plate.

THE FUTURE: Vela appeared out of the bullpen in roughly half his appearances after his promotion to San Antonio. Without improvement of his command and control, Vela might have to settle for a middle relief role.

BA GRADE: 45/High **Fastball:** 55 **Curveball:** 55 **Changeup:** 55 **Control:** 40

Year	Age	Club (League)	Lvl	W	L	ERA	G	GS	IP	H	HR	BB	SO	BB/9	SO/9	WHIP	AVG
2022	23	Fort Wayne (MWL)	HiA	6	7	3.83	20	20	87	74	6	47	101	4.9	10.4	1.39	.228
2022	23	San Antonio (TL)	AA	1	3	6.35	9	4	23	25	1	20	24	7.9	9.5	1.99	.284
Minor League Totals				11	28	4.38	75	56	255	239	18	161	303	5.7	10.7	1.57	.244

19 JAKOB MARSEE, OF

Born: June 28, 2001. **B-T:** L-L. **HT:** 6-0. **WT:** 200.
Drafted: Central Michigan, 2022 (6th round). **Signed by:** Matt Maloney.

TRACK RECORD: Marsee lettered in baseball, football and basketball at Allen Park (Mich.) High and became a two-year starter at Central Michigan, where he hit .345/.467/.550 as a redshirt sophomore while showing elite contact skills. The Padres drafted him in the sixth round and signed him for an under-slot $250,000 bonus. Marsee quickly rose to Low-A Lake Elsinore after signing and hit .254/.419/.463 as the leadoff hitter on a Storm team that went on to win the California League title.

SCOUTING REPORT: A blue-collar, baseball rat, Marsee wears out pitchers with a discerning eye at the plate, plus contact skills and the ability to handle velocity. He presently has below average power and needs to learn to drive and lift the ball. More power could come with some weight gain—he was up from 180 pounds to nearly 200 late in the year—but the Padres will press upon the need for Marsee to remain athletic. He's an average runner with an average arm, but his knack for good reads and quick first steps gives him a chance to stay in center field. He has plus makeup and has shown the ability to outperform his tools.

THE FUTURE: Marsee's advanced approach at the plate could help him move quickly up the Padres system. He'll head to High-A Fort Wayne in 2023.

| BA GRADE: 45/High | | Hit: 55 | | Power: 40 | | Run: 50 | | Field: 55 | | Arm: 50 | |

Year	Age	Club (League)	Lvl	AVG	G	AB	R	H	2B	3B	HR	RBI	BB	SO	SB	OBP	SLG
2022	21	Padres (ACL)	R	.212	13	33	13	7	1	1	0	3	14	10	3	.447	.303
2022	21	Lake Elsinore (CAL)	LoA	.254	18	67	18	17	6	1	2	8	16	15	12	.419	.463
Minor League Totals				.240	31	100	31	24	7	2	2	11	30	25	15	.429	.410

20 NATHAN MARTORELLA, 1B

Born: Feb. 18, 2001. **B-T:** L-L. **HT:** 6-1. **WT:** 224.
Drafted: California, 2022 (5th round). **Signed by:** Tim Reynolds.

TRACK RECORD: An unsigned 30th-round pick of the Red Sox out of high school, Martorella started all three years at California and hit .388 during conference play in 2022, best in the Pac-12. The Padres drafted him in the fifth round and signed him for an under-slot $325,000. Martorella rose quickly to Low-A Lake Elsinore after signing and finished his pro debut batting in the middle of the Storm lineup as they went on to win the California League title.

SCOUTING REPORT: A strong, physical lefthanded hitter who gets into a low crouch similar to former Padres slugger Phil Plantier, Martorella manages the strike zone well but hasn't yet developed a ton of feel to hit. His swing is fueled by brute strength rather than true bat speed or barrel accuracy, and he still hits the ball on the ground too often to showcase his average power consistently. Limited defensively to first base, Martorella is an average defender who has good footwork around the bag and soft hands. He is a bottom-of-the-scale runner.

THE FUTURE: Without positional flexibility or a ton of athleticism, Martorella will go as far as his bat takes him. He'll open 2023 at High-A Fort Wayne.

| BA GRADE: 45/High | | Hit: 45 | | Power: 50 | | Run: 20 | | Field: 50 | | Arm: 50 | |

Year	Age	Club (League)	Lvl	AVG	G	AB	R	H	2B	3B	HR	RBI	BB	SO	SB	OBP	SLG
2022	21	Padres (ACL)	R	.387	11	31	4	12	4	0	1	10	4	6	0	.457	.613
2022	21	Lake Elsinore (CAL)	LoA	.288	17	59	10	17	4	0	2	11	12	15	0	.403	.458
Minor League Totals				.322	28	90	14	29	8	0	3	21	16	21	0	.421	.511

21 GARRETT HAWKINS, RHP

Born: Feb. 10, 2000. **B-T:** R-R. **HT:** 6-5. **WT:** 230.
Drafted: British Columbia, 2021 (9th round). **Signed by:** Chris Kemlo.

TRACK RECORD: A native of Biggar, Saskatchewan, Hawkins didn't get to pitch much at the University of British Columbia due to Canada's coronavirus protocols, but he impressed in the MLB Draft League in 2021 to become a late riser. The Padres drafted him in the ninth round and signed him for $75,000, about half of slot value. Hawkins made his full-season debut at Low-A Lake Elsinore and stood out as one of the California League's top pitchers before getting hit hard after an early August promotion to High-A Fort Wayne.

SCOUTING REPORT: Hawkins cuts an imposing figure at 6-foot-5, 230 pounds. His big frame and incredibly long arms generate significant extension down the mound, allowing his 93-96 mph fastball to get tons of swings and misses in the strike zone. It has carry and finish from an over-the-top slot. Hawkins is heavily reliant on his plus fastball that is far and away his best pitch. His split changeup flashes above-average but is inconsistent and his slurvy, downward breaking ball is a fringier offering. Hawkins has good control of his long limbs and has a long track record of throwing strikes, but his walk rate spiked after his promotion to Fort Wayne.

THE FUTURE: Hawkins' fastball plays now, but how well he develops his secondaries will determine whether he ends up a starter or reliever. He'll begin 2023 back at Fort Wayne.

BA GRADE: 45/High		Fastball: 60		Slider: 45		Changeup: 55		Control: 55				
Year	**Age**	**Club (League)**	**Lvl**	**W**	**L**	**ERA**	**G**	**GS**	**IP**	**H**	**HR**	**BB**	**SO**	**BB/9**	**SO/9**	**WHIP**	**AVG**
2022	22	Lake Elsinore (CAL)	LoA	5	5	3.94	17	17	78	73	9	20	108	2.3	12.5	1.20	.245
2022	22	Fort Wayne (MWL)	HiA	0	3	8.80	4	4	15	22	6	10	12	5.9	7.0	2.09	.328
Minor League Totals				8	9	4.40	28	21	108	110	16	32	147	2.7	12.2	1.31	.259

22 ALEK JACOB, RHP

Born: June 16, 1998. **B-T:** L-R. **HT:** 6-3. **WT:** 190.
Drafted: Gonzaga, 2021 (16th round). **Signed by:** Justin Baughman.
TRACK RECORD: Jacob's fastball sat just 85-89 mph as a starter at Gonzaga, but the Padres scouted him closely because their analytics team identified his changeup as a potential outlier. He struck out 323 batters in 288.1 collegiate innings and won West Coast Conference pitcher of the year honors as a senior, leading the Padres to draft him in the 16th round and sign him for $75,000. Jacob immediately moved to the bullpen after being drafted and didn't allow a run in 13 appearances in his pro debut. He climbed three levels up to Triple-A in his first full season in 2022 and finished the year in the Arizona Fall League.
SCOUTING REPORT: Jacob's two-seam fastball remains well below-average at 85-89 mph, but it plays well off his plus-plus 70-74 mph changeup with heavy fade and sink. He hides the ball well in his delivery and pounds the strike zone with a whip-like stroke out of a sidearm slot. Jacob's sweepy, low-70s slider is a solid offering that he commands well, as he does with all of his pitches. He varies his delivery to disrupt hitters' timing and attacks the zone with plus control and the confidence of someone who throws much harder.
THE FUTURE: The Padres have had success developing soft-throwing relievers such as Adam Cimber and Eric Yardley into big leaguers. Jacob could be the next to make the leap in 2023.

BA GRADE: 40/Medium		Fastball: 30		Slider: 50		Changeup: 70		Control: 60				
Year	**Age**	**Club (League)**	**Lvl**	**W**	**L**	**ERA**	**G**	**GS**	**IP**	**H**	**HR**	**BB**	**SO**	**BB/9**	**SO/9**	**WHIP**	**AVG**
2022	24	Fort Wayne (MWL)	HiA	3	0	0.00	4	0	9	4	0	0	16	0.0	16.0	0.44	.129
2022	24	San Antonio (TL)	AA	1	0	1.83	23	1	34	27	1	10	43	2.6	11.3	1.08	.214
2022	24	El Paso (PCL)	AAA	1	1	6.59	16	0	14	18	4	5	18	3.3	11.9	1.68	.305
Minor League Totals				7	1	2.00	56	1	77	63	5	17	106	2.0	12.4	1.04	.221

23 ISAIAH LOWE, RHP

Born: May 7, 2003. **B-T:** R-R. **HT:** 6-1. **WT:** 220.
Drafted: HS—Lincolnton, N.C., 2022 (11th round). **Signed by:** Jake Koenig.
TRACK RECORD: Lowe attended little-known Combine Academy in remote Lincolnton, N.C., but Padres scouts found him and considered him one of the better prep pitchers in the draft class. They considered him a fourth- or fifth-round talent and ultimately took him in the 11th round and signed him for an above-slot $400,000 bonus to forgo a Wake Forest commitment. The Padres opted to work with Lowe on the backfields after signing him and did not have him pitch in the Arizona Complex League.
SCOUTING REPORT: Lowe is exceptionally strong with a sturdy lower half in his 6-foot-1, 220-pound frame. His four-seam fastball has been up to 97 mph with good carry at the top of the zone out of his three-quarters slot. He generates good extension in his delivery that allows his fastball to further jump on hitters. Lowe's primary secondary offering is a sweeping slider with horizontal break that projects to be an above-average pitch with more development. His changeup is a work in progress, but he has demonstrated feel for it to be an average pitch. Lowe throws strikes with average control, although he has yet to face high-level hitters on a consistent basis.
THE FUTURE: Lowe is raw and will need time, but his physicality and three-pitch mix give him a good foundation to work from. He'll make his pro debut in 2023.

BA GRADE: 50/Extreme		Fastball: 60		Slider: 55		Changeup: 50		Control: 50				
Year	**Age**	**Club (League)**	**Lvl**	**W**	**L**	**ERA**	**G**	**GS**	**IP**	**H**	**HR**	**BB**	**SO**	**BB/9**	**SO/9**	**WHIP**	**AVG**
2022	19	Did not play															

24 ZACK QIN, LHP

Born: July 3, 2005. **B-T:** L-L. **HT:** 6-1. **WT:** 198.
Signed: China, 2022. **Signed by:** Jake Koenig.
TRACK RECORD: The first ever Chinese international amateur signed by the Padres, Qin hails from Major League Baseball's China Academy. He landed on the Padres' radar while pitching in the United States for the West team at Perfect Game's national showcase after the draft. The Padres pegged Qin as a top-five round talent, signed him for $90,000 on July 30 and got him on the mound in fall instructional league.
SCOUTING REPORT: Qin has added a considerable amount of velocity as he's matured, improving from 78-80 mph early in his days at the academy to 87-88 mph while pitching in the United States and up to 92 mph once the Padres' development staff got their hands on him. He rounds out his four-pitch mix with a big-bending curveball that sits 72-74 mph, a slider that sits in the upper 70s and a changeup in the low 80s. He has a classic, overhand delivery with a Clayton Kershaw look to it and wide enough shoulders to project more mass and velocity as he continues to fill out his 6-foot-1 frame.
THE FUTURE: Raw and projectable, Qin will still be just 17 on Opening Day in 2023. He has the early traits of a potential back-of-the-rotation starter but has a long way to go.

BA GRADE: 50/Extreme	Fastball: 55	Curveball: 55	Changeup: 50	Control: 50

Year	Age	Club (League)	Lvl	W	L	ERA	G	GS	IP	H	HR	BB	SO	BB/9	SO/9	WHIP	AVG
2022	16	Did not play															

25 RYAN BERGERT, RHP

Born: March 8, 2000. **B-T:** R-R. **HT:** 6-1. **WT:** 210.
Drafted: West Virginia, 2021 (6th round). **Signed by:** Danny Sader.
TRACK RECORD: Bergert pitched mostly in the bullpen as a freshman at West Virginia and saw his move to the rotation as a sophomore cut short after four starts due to the coronavirus pandemic. He continued to trend upward in the Northwoods League but had Tommy John surgery after the summer, wiping out his junior season. The Padres had second-round grades on Bergert before his surgery and remained a believer, drafting him in the sixth round and signing him for $500,000, nearly double the slot value. Bergert got back on the mound for his first full season in three years in 2022 and struggled statistically at High-A Fort Wayne but flashed promising stuff.
SCOUTING REPORT: Bergert has a well-rounded four-pitch mix he is progressively regaining feel for. His fastball sits 92-93 mph and touches 96 mph with east-west movement, although it stays true at times and gets hammered when he doesn't locate it up in the zone. His mid-80s slider, upper-70s curveball and mid-80s changeup all flash above-average and were more effective pitches than his fastball in his return. Bergert's arm slot and delivery were inconsistent in his first full year back from surgery, leading to fringe-average control. The Padres hope his control will improve the further he moves away from surgery.
THE FUTURE: The Padres believe Bergert is ready to take a significant step forward in his second year back from surgery in 2023. He should start the year at Double-A San Antonio and will look to accumulate innings.

BA GRADE: 45/High	Fastball: 50	Curveball: 50	Slider: 55	Changeup: 55	Control: 45

Year	Age	Club (League)	Lvl	W	L	ERA	G	GS	IP	H	HR	BB	SO	BB/9	SO/9	WHIP	AVG
2022	22	Fort Wayne (MWL)	HiA	4	10	5.84	24	24	103	124	18	42	129	3.7	11.2	1.61	.290
Minor League Totals				5	10	5.27	31	27	114	127	18	42	143	3.3	11.3	1.48	.274

26 YENDRY ROJAS, SS

Born: Jan. 27, 2005. **B-T:** L-R. **HT:** 6-0. **WT:** 185.
Signed: Cuba, 2022. **Signed by:** Trevor Schumm.
TRACK RECORD: While his older brother Kendry signed with the Blue Jays in 2020 as a pitcher, Rojas made a name for himself in the 2022 international class as one of its best pure hitters. The Padres signed the younger Rojas for $1.3 million just before his 17th birthday and sent him to the Dominican Summer League, where he demonstrated advanced plate discipline with more walks (26) than strikeouts (23) while hitting .279/.373/.357.
SCOUTING REPORT: Rojas hasn't yet shown in-game power, but the Padres believe he has a chance to be a five-tool player. He has a quiet, balanced swing that's quick and compact and complements his ability to track and recognize pitches. His feel for the barrel produces a high contact rate and extra-base power that could result in more balls over the walls as he physically matures. An average runner with a plus arm,

Rojas saw time in the outfield as an amateur but is exclusively an infielder now. He has a chance to be a shortstop, but second base and third base could be future destinations.

THE FUTURE: Rojas is far from the big leagues, but his offensive aptitude could convince the Padres to push him aggressively. He'll make his stateside debut in 2023 and has a chance to be a bat-first infielder.

BA GRADE: 50/Extreme	Hit: 50	Power: 50	Run: 50	Field: 50	Arm: 60

Year	Age	Club (League)	Lvl	AVG	G	AB	R	H	2B	3B	HR	RBI	BB	SO	SB	OBP	SLG
2022	17	Padres (DSL)	R	.279	46	154	29	43	4	4	0	18	26	23	14	.373	.357
Minor League Totals				.279	46	154	29	43	4	4	0	18	26	23	14	.373	.357

27 KOBE ROBINSON, RHP

Born: March 3, 2001. **B-T:** R-R. **HT:** 6-2. **WT:** 160.
Drafted: Chattanooga State (Tenn.) JC, 2021 (13th round). **Signed by:** Tyler Stubblefield.
TRACK RECORD: The Padres first got eyes on Robinson when he was a raw high school senior with an 86-88 mph fastball and a skinny, projectable frame. They followed him closely as he moved on to Chattanooga State (Tenn.) JC and decided to draft him in the 13th round in 2021 after he touched 99 mph in the MLB Draft League. Robinson was limited to just 22.2 innings at Low-A Lake Elsinore by minor injuries in 2022, but he got back on the mound in the Arizona Fall League and spent the offseason training in Atlanta.
SCOUTING REPORT: Robinson is raw as a pitcher but has a lot of intriguing traits. His fastball sits 92-96 mph with plus life and explodes out of his loose arm. His hard, mid-80s slider is developing but flashes above-average and he has flashed a promising changeup with fading life, although he rarely throws it. Robinson's control is below average and both his command and quality of his offspeed pitches are inconsistent. He should improve with more reps on the mound.
THE FUTURE: With under 30 innings on his pro resume so far, Robinson will look to build innings as a starting pitcher in the lower levels in 2023. Long-term, he profiles as a reliever with his fastball and slider combination.

BA GRADE: 45/Extreme	Fastball: 60	Slider: 55	Changeup: 45	Control: 40

Year	Age	Club (League)	Lvl	W	L	ERA	G	GS	IP	H	HR	BB	SO	BB/9	SO/9	WHIP	AVG
2022	21	Lake Elsinore (CAL)	LoA	1	0	3.57	7	3	23	18	2	12	31	4.8	12.3	1.32	.220
Minor League Totals				1	0	3.86	10	3	26	24	2	14	34	4.9	11.9	1.48	.250

28 ANGEL FELIPE, RHP

Born: Aug. 30, 1997. **B-T:** R-R. **HT:** 6-5. **WT:** 190.
Signed: Dominican Republic, 2015. **Signed by:** Miguel Richardson/Daniel Santana (Rays).
TRACK RECORD: Felipe signed with the Rays on the last day of the 2014-15 international signing period for $115,000 but struggled with his control and never advanced past the Class A levels in six seasons in Tampa's system. The Padres liked Felipe's tall frame and big fastball and signed him as a minor league free agent in 2022. Felipe took off with a fresh start and dominated as the closer at Double-A San Antonio before receiving a late promotion to Triple-A El Paso. He allowed just one home run in 62 innings all year and was added to the 40-man roster after the season.
SCOUTING REPORT: A former shortstop as an amateur who simply outgrew the position, Felipe has been working to repeat a whip-like delivery since moving to the mound. His four-seam and two-seam fastballs both sit 97-98 mph and touch 101, with his two-seam the better and more frequently used of the two offerings. His mid-80s slider is a potential above-average pitch with tilt and bite when he stays on top of it and his upper-80s changeup with sink and fade is a potential above-average offering, although he needs to continue to refine his command and consistency of both pitches. Felipe has long had well below-average control, but he improved his strike-throwing as the season progressed last year.
THE FUTURE: Armed with the best fastball in the system, Felipe will be in big league spring training and has a chance to break camp with the Padres. His command will have to continue to improve if he's going to be more than an up-and-down reliever in the bullpen.

BA GRADE: 40/High	Fastball: 65	Slider: 55	Changeup: 55	Control: 30

Year	Age	Club (League)	Lvl	W	L	ERA	G	GS	IP	H	HR	BB	SO	BB/9	SO/9	WHIP	AVG
2022	24	San Antonio (TL)	AA	3	5	3.18	32	0	40	36	1	25	49	5.7	11.1	1.54	.240
2022	24	El Paso (PCL)	AAA	2	1	4.43	19	0	22	13	0	11	35	4.4	14.1	1.07	.167
Minor League Totals				14	18	4.55	144	6	226	199	6	160	262	6.4	10.4	1.59	.236

29 TOM COSGROVE, LHP

Born: June 14, 1996. **B-T:** L-L. **HT:** 6-2. **WT:** 190.
Drafted: Manhattan, 2017 (12th round). **Signed by:** John Stewart.
TRACK RECORD: Cosgrove led the Metro Atlantic Athletic Conference in strikeouts as a junior at Manhattan and was drafted in the 12th round by the Padres. He was infamously arrested alongside Jacob Nix in the fall of 2019 in a home break-in near the Padres' spring training complex while he was rehabbing from Tommy John surgery but was never charged. Cosgrove moved to the bullpen after returning from surgery and thrived after a mechanical change in 2022, rising to Triple-A and earning a spot on the Padres 40-man roster after the season.
SCOUTING REPORT: A 6-foot-2 lefthander, Cosgrove's stuff was largely vanilla until he dropped his arm slot to three-quarters at the suggestion of Padres pitching development director Rob Marcello in 2022. The change added angle to his 92-95 mph fastball to make it an average pitch and altered his breaking ball from a 12-to-6, hammer curve to a sweeping, 79-82 mph slider. The changes made him particularly tough on lefties, who he held to a .136/.240/.273 line in 2022. Cosgrove also has a seldom-used changeup that is not a major part of his arsenal. He has fringy control but puts the ball over the plate enough to be effective.
THE FUTURE: Cosgrove will compete for an Opening Day bullpen spot in spring training. He projects to be a low-leverage reliever who handles lefties.

BA GRADE: 40/High		Fastball: 50		Slider: 55		Changeup: 30		Control: 45								
Year	Age	Club (League)	Lvl	W	L	ERA	G	GS	IP	H	HR	BB	SO	BB/9	SO/9	WHIP	AVG
2022	26	San Antonio (TL)	AA	6	1	2.45	20	0	26	12	3	13	39	4.6	13.7	0.97	.140
2022	26	El Paso (PCL)	AAA	2	1	4.80	28	0	30	22	6	15	43	4.5	12.9	1.23	.200
Minor League Totals				14	16	3.71	116	36	276	266	22	98	310	3.2	10.1	1.32	.248

30 TIRSO ORNELAS, OF

Born: March 11, 2000. **B-T:** L-R. **HT:** 6-3. **WT:** 200.
Signed: Mexico, 2016. **Signed by:** Chris Kemp/Bill McLaughlin.
TRACK RECORD: The Padres purchased Ornelas' rights from the Mexican League for $1.5 million in 2016 and pushed him quickly up their system, but he stalled at High-A and went through multiple swing changes to try and rediscover his previous success. Ornelas finally advanced to Double-A in 2022 and set new career highs in nearly every offensive category to earn a late promotion to Triple-A, but he continued to struggle to hit for power with only seven home runs.
SCOUTING REPORT: Ornelas is a strong, physical hitter with exceptional strike-zone recognition. He flashes above-average raw power in batting practice, but he lacks bat speed and he struggles to create contact out front, preventing him from accessing his power in games. He has adjusted his hand position to get quicker to the ball but still has a long way to go with his swing to be more than a fringy hitter with below-average power. Ornelas has slowed down as he's filled out and is a below-average runner with fringy defense in the corner outfield spots. His arm strength has regressed to fringe-average and makes him a left fielder only.
THE FUTURE: Ornelas will open 2023 at Triple-A El Paso. He'll still be only 23 on Opening Day, giving hope he can begin to access the power necessary to be a big leaguer.

BA GRADE: 40/High		Hit: 45		Power: 40		Run: 40			Field: 45			Arm: 45			
Year	Age	Club (League)	Lvl	AVG	G	AB	R	H	2B	3B	HR	RBI	BB	SO	SB	OBP	SLG
2022	22	San Antonio (TL)	AA	.288	112	441	62	127	28	2	7	51	43	85	7	.355	.408
2022	22	El Paso (PCL)	AAA	.214	3	14	2	3	1	0	0	2	1	2	0	.267	.286
Minor League Totals				.254	471	1763	259	448	97	14	26	215	229	427	22	.342	.369

San Francisco Giants

BY JOSH NORRIS

After leading the majors with 107 wins in 2021, the Giants took a step backward in 2022. The team went 81-81, finished third in the National League West and missed the playoffs.

That led to a bit of transition in the offseason. General manager Scott Harris left to become the Tigers' president of baseball operations, and former Astros farm director Pete Putila was hired to replace him.

The Giants' pitching staff faced a transition of its own. Lefthander Carlos Rodon, who went 14-8, 2.88 and led the majors with 12.0 strikeouts per nine innings, became a free agent after the season, and left an ace-sized hole at the front of San Francisco's rotation.

Though the Giants have a decent farm system, a vast majority of their best prospects are not in position to help the big league club to start 2023.

The system's best hitter, shortstop Marco Luciano, missed a chunk of 2022 with a back injury but generally showed improvement when healthy. The best pitcher, lefthander Kyle Harrison, finished second in the minor leagues with 186 strikeouts across High-A and Double-A, but he is just 21 years old and still working through command issues.

The Giants' recent draft picks have produced uneven results as the team has struggled at the top of the draft.

Their top two picks from 2021, righthander Will Bednar and lefty Matt Mikulski, were ineffective and injured at Low-A San Jose. Their 2020 first-rounder, catcher Patrick Bailey, struggled to hit in a repeat year at High-A Eugene. Outfielder Hunter Bishop, the 10th overall pick in 2019, has struggled to hit or stay on the field.

Those downturns were counterbalanced by breakout years from outfielders Grant McCray and Vaun Brown. McCray, who has big league bloodlines, showed an impressive set of tools including standout defense in center field, though he still needs more polish as a hitter. Brown led the minors with a .346 batting average and showed explosive tools from one of the most enviably sculpted bodies in the sport.

Righthander Mason Black, whom the Giants selected after Bednar and Mikulski in 2021, represented a breakout on the pitching side. The Lehigh product was excellent at both Class A stops, where he showed a dynamic pitch mix to go with a fiercely competitive demeanor on the mound.

The Giants added little certainty by taking two of the riskiest players available with their top two picks in the 2022 draft. Lefthander Reggie Crawford, who doubled as Connecticut's first

Joey Bart had an up-and-down first season as Buster Posey's replacement at catcher.

PROJECTED 2026 LINEUP

Catcher	Joey Bart	29
First Base	David Villar	29
Second Base	Thairo Estrada	30
Third Base	Casey Schmitt	27
Shortstop	Marco Luciano	24
Left Field	Luis Matos	24
Center Field	Grant McCray	25
Right Field	Vaun Brown	28
Designated Hitter	Mike Yastrzemski	35
No. 1 Starter	Logan Webb	29
No. 2 Starter	Kyle Harrison	25
No. 3 Starter	Carson Whisenhunt	25
No. 4 Starter	Mason Black	25
No. 5 Starter	Eric Silva	23
Closer	Camilo Doval	28

baseman, had Tommy John surgery and missed the season but recovered enough to hit in the Arizona Complex League.

The team's second pick, lefty Carson Whisenhunt, tested positive for performance-enhancing substances and was suspended for the entire season at East Carolina before pitching briefly in the Cape Cod League.

The end result is a big league team that needs immediate help but whose best prospects are still a year or more away. As such, free agency remains the team's best option to quickly achieve another 100-win season in a division with two teams—the Dodgers and Padres—who are acting aggressively to win now. ∎

SAN FRANCISCO GIANTS

TOP 2023 MLB CONTRIBUTORS	RANK
Heliot Ramos, OF	15
Cole Waites, RHP	17
BREAKOUT PROSPECTS	**RANK**
Carson Seymour, RHP	12
Adrian Sugastey, C	18

SOURCE OF TOP 30 TALENT

Homegrown	28	Acquired	2
College	16	Trade	2
Junior college	1	Rule 5 draft	0
High school	4	Independent league	0
Nondrafted free agent	0	Free agent/waivers	0
International	7		

LF
Jairo Pomares (16)
Wade Meckler (21)

CF
Grant McCray (4)
Luis Matos (5)
Bryce Johnson

RF
Vaun Brown (6)
Heliot Ramos (15)

3B
Casey Schmitt (3)
Carter Aldrete

SS
Marco Luciano (1)
Aeverson Arteaga (7)
Anthony Rodriguez
Diego Velasquez
Ryan Reckley

2B
Will Wilson
Brett Wisely

1B
Logan Wyatt
Luis Toribio

C
Adrian Sugastey (18)
Blake Sabol (23)
Patrick Bailey (25)
Ford Proctor
Brett Auerbach

LHP

LHSP
Kyle Harrison (2)
Carson Whisenhunt (8)
Reggie Crawford (11)
Nick Swiney (22)
Matt Mikulski (26)

LHRP
Thomas Szapucki

RHP

RHSP
Mason Black (9)
Eric Silva (10)
Carson Seymour (12)
Landen Roupp (13)
Keaton Winn (14)
Ryan Murphy (19)
Will Bednar (20)
Sean Hjelle
Tristan Beck
Carson Ragsdale
Mikell Manzano

RHRP
Cole Waites (17)
William Kempner (24)
RJ Dabovich (27)
Randy Rodriguez (28)
Jose Cruz (29)
Hayden Birdsong (30)
Tyler Myrick
Mat Olsen
Liam Simon
Ryan Walker
Kai-Wei Teng

1 MARCO LUCIANO, SS

Born: Sept. 10, 2001. **B-T:** R-R. **HT:** 6-2. **WT:** 178.
Signed: Dominican Republic, 2018.
Signed by: Jonathan Bautista.

TRACK RECORD: Luciano has been the Giants' top prospect for four consecutive seasons, yet he might just be beginning to scratch the surface of his talent. He was lauded as an amateur for his offensive gifts, which included the potential to hit for both average and power while sticking on the left side of the infield. The Giants paid $2.6 million to sign Luciano and he smashed the Rookie-level Arizona League in his 2019 pro debut, then earned a quick cameo at short-season Salem-Keizer before a hamstring tweak ended his season. After spending the 2020 season as one of the youngest players at an alternate training site, Luciano put together a standout 2021 campaign at Low-A San Jose before running into some resistance at High-A Eugene. Luciano's 2022 season was interrupted by a back injury that limited him to just 57 non-rehab games, but he showed offensive and defensive skills.

SCOUTING REPORT: First and foremost, Luciano's value will be in the batter's box. After running roughshod through the California League in 2021, he got into trouble against older pitchers who were better equipped to execute a game plan. Luciano countered in 2022 by learning how pitchers were going to attack him and making better swing decisions. He still could stand to be a bit more selective, but a 90th percentile exit velocity of 106.2 mph shows that his impact potential is among the upper echelon of minor leaguers. Scouts say Luciano doesn't have to over-swing to get to that power, either. Instead, he can take a controlled swing and let his natural strength shoot balls over the fence with surprising ease for someone his age. Instead of trying to hit every ball out of the park, he's content to shorten up and settle for singles when appropriate. The next improvements for Luciano involve becoming more adept at handling pitches in on his hands or in the upper part of the strike zone. If upper-level pitchers can execute there, scouts expect Luciano's rate of swing-and-miss to get a tick higher. Defensively, Luciano is looking more like a player who can play an average shortstop instead of having to move to third base—an ideal development considering the Giants have standout third baseman Casey Schmitt already in the pipeline. He's become more sure-handed at shortstop, looks more confident playing the position and is a good bet to cleanly field balls he can reach. His range isn't standout,

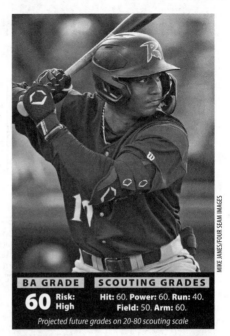

MIKE JANES/FOUR SEAM IMAGES

BA GRADE	SCOUTING GRADES
60 Risk: High	Hit: 60. Power: 60. Run: 40. Field: 50. Arm: 60.

Projected future grades on 20-80 scouting scale

BEST TOOLS

BATTING

Best Hitter for Average	Vaun Brown
Best Power Hitter	Marco Luciano
Best Strike-Zone Discipline	Wade Meckler
Fastest Baserunner	Grant McCray
Best Athlete	Vaun Brown

PITCHING

Best Fastball	Cole Waites
Best Curveball	Landen Roupp
Best Slider	Kyle Harrison
Best Changeup	Jose Cruz
Best Control	Nick Sinacola

FIELDING

Best Defensive Catcher	Patrick Bailey
Best Defensive Infielder	Casey Schmitt
Best Infield Arm	Casey Schmitt
Best Defensive Outfielder	Grant McCray
Best Outfield Arm	PJ Hilson

and there is still the possibility that his body will get big enough to force him off the position. He has the plus arm strength to handle either position on the left side of the infield. He is a below-average runner.

THE FUTURE: Luciano was promoted to Double-A Richmond for the Eastern League playoffs and will return to the level in 2023. If he continues making strides against advanced pitching, he could be a centerpiece in the middle of future San Francisco lineups.

Year	Age	Club (League)	Lvl	AVG	G	AB	R	H	2B	3B	HR	RBI	BB	SO	SB	OBP	SLG
2022	20	Giants Black (ACL)	R	.318	8	22	6	7	2	0	1	6	4	7	0	.444	.545
2022	20	Eugene (NWL)	HiA	.263	57	205	27	54	10	0	10	30	22	51	0	.339	.459
Minor League Totals				.271	218	801	153	217	42	7	40	149	106	225	15	.363	.491

2 KYLE HARRISON, LHP

Born: Aug. 12, 2001. **B-T:** L-L. **HT:** 6-2. **WT:** 200.
Drafted: HS—Concord, CA, 2020 (3rd round). **Signed by:** Keith Snider.

TRACK RECORD: The Giants went over slot to sign Harrison for $2,497,500 in the third round in 2020 to sway him from his commitment to UCLA. The athletic lefthander immediately rewarded the Giants' faith, first by dominating at instructional league, then by taking the Low-A California League by storm in his pro debut in 2021. His 157 strikeouts tied him for eighth most in the minor leagues. He upped the ante in 2022, when his 186 strikeouts ranked second in the minors. He split the year between High-A Eugene and Double-A Richmond, with a stop at the Futures Game as well.

SCOUTING REPORT: Harrison's three-pitch mix is one of the nastiest in the minor leagues. He starts with a mid-90s four-seam fastball that peaked at 97 mph and got swings and misses at an absurd rate of 40.5%, the highest among any minor leaguer who threw 1,000 or more four-seamers. The pitch, along with the rest of his arsenal, is amplified by the deception created in his delivery and an extremely low release point. Harrison's slider was equally nasty. The low-80s sweeper was the better of his two offspeed pitches and was thrown for a strike more often than either his fastball or changeup. Harrison rounds out his mix with a still-developing changeup with plenty of upside. Part of his development in 2022 was centered around improving his changeup, and ideally the Giants would like him throw it between 10 and 20% of the time. Harrison's delivery is a double-edged sword. The elasticity of his body allows him to create funky angles for hitters but also gives him below-average command.

THE FUTURE: Harrison will likely head to Triple-A to begin 2023, and he has a ceiling of a starter who can dominate at the top of a rotation.

BA GRADE
60 Risk: High

SCOUTING GRADES:	Fastball: 70	Slider: 60	Changeup: 50	Control: 45

Year	Age	Club (League)	Lvl	W	L	ERA	G	GS	IP	H	HR	BB	SO	BB/9	SO/9	WHIP	AVG
2022	20	Eugene (NWL)	HiA	0	1	1.55	7	7	29	19	2	10	59	3.1	18.3	1.00	.179
2022	20	Richmond (EL)	AA	4	2	3.11	18	18	84	60	11	39	127	4.2	13.6	1.18	.201
Minor League Totals				8	6	2.93	48	48	212	165	16	101	343	4.3	14.6	1.26	.213

3 CASEY SCHMITT, 3B

Born: March 1, 1999. **B-T:** R-R. **HT:** 6-2. **WT:** 215.
Drafted: San Diego State, 2020 (2nd round). **Signed by:** Brad Cameron.

TRACK RECORD: A two-way standout at San Diego State, where he also worked as a closer, Schmitt was the Giants' second pick in the shortened 2020 draft, which also yielded No. 2 prospect Kyle Harrison. Schmitt's first month at Low-A San Jose in 2021 was rough, but he rebounded with a strong summer. In 2022, Schmitt hit his way from High-A to Triple-A while playing stellar defense at third base, even spending an extended stretch at shortstop in High-A Eugene while Marco Luciano was on the injured list.

SCOUTING REPORT: Schmitt's swing has never been considered the most orthodox, but he shows the balance to get his body and barrel in the right positions to provide consistent production. The Giants worked with Schmitt to clean up his bat path and increase his hip mobility in order to unlock more power, and the results were clear. His .897 OPS ranked third in the organization, behind rising outfielders Vaun Brown and Grant McCray. His 90th percentile exit velocity was 101.5 mph, which was the same figure produced by Top 100 Prospects Anthony Volpe, Ezequiel Tovar and Alex Ramirez. Defensively, Schmitt was electric. He's a potential Gold Glove winner at third base, with a double-plus arm and an exhaustive pregame ritual that permits him to make plays to all directions. Moreover, once he gets to the big leagues, Schmitt's range could allow the Giants to play a less rangy shortstop.

THE FUTURE: Schmitt is likely to return to Triple-A Sacramento in 2023. If he reaches his ceiling, he can be a lockdown third baseman with the bat to profile at the position.

BA GRADE
55 Risk: High

SCOUTING GRADES	Hitting: 55	Power: 50	Speed: 50	Fielding: 65	Arm: 70

Year	Age	Club (League)	Lvl	AVG	G	AB	R	H	2B	3B	HR	RBI	BB	SO	SB	OBP	SLG
2022	23	Eugene (NWL)	HiA	.273	93	333	58	91	14	1	17	59	42	86	1	.363	.474
2022	23	Richmond (EL)	AA	.342	29	120	13	41	10	1	3	16	6	29	2	.378	.517
2022	23	Sacramento (PCL)	AAA	.333	4	15	1	5	1	0	1	3	0	5	0	.313	.600
Minor League Totals				.277	190	719	108	199	39	3	29	107	70	164	5	.349	.465

4 GRANT McCRAY, OF

Born: Dec. 7, 2000. **B-T:** L-R. **HT:** 6-2. **WT:** 190.
Drafted: HS—Bradenton, FL, 2019 (3rd round). **Signed by:** Jim Gabella.

TRACK RECORD: The Giants have done a fantastic job unearthing hidden gems in Florida in recent years. The first find came in 2019, when they selected McCray—the son of former big leaguer Rodney McCray—out of high school in Bradenton, Fla. The younger McCray played football and ran track in high school, but the Giants thought enough of his abilities on the diamond to give him $697,500 to keep him from a commitment to Florida State. McCray spent most of his first two seasons—sandwiched around the pandemic—at the lowest levels of the minor leagues. His tools began to translate in 2022, when he was among the system's biggest breakouts.

BA GRADE

55 Risk: Very High

SCOUTING REPORT: A series of mechanical adjustments helped unlock some of McCray's offensive potential. Opposing scouts noticed a shorter swing, a shorter load and a stance that was more open and upright than what they'd seen in 2021. The next step will be better swing decisions and a slightly less steep bat path to help him improve 26% rates of swing-and-miss both in and out of the zone. If those changes happen, McCray has the potential to be an average hitter with above-average power. McCray's average exit velocity (88.9 mph) and rate of hard contact are already excellent but would play even better if he could get the ball in the air more often. McCray is regarded internally as the system's best defensive outfielder. Opposing scouts see it similarly, universally grading him as at least a plus defender with double-plus speed and an above-average arm. California League managers voted him the league's best defensive outfielder.

THE FUTURE: McCray ended 2022 in High-A Eugene and will likely return there in 2023. If everything clicks, he could be an everyday center fielder with standout defense and some offensive impact.

SCOUTING GRADES		Hitting: 50		Power: 55		Speed: 70			Fielding: 60		Arm: 55			
Year	Age	Club (League)	Lvl	AVG	G	AB	R	H	2B	3B	HR	RBI	BB	SO	SB	OBP	SLG
2022	21	San Jose (CAL)	LoA	.291	106	436	92	127	21	9	21	69	58	148	35	.383	.525
2022	21	Eugene (NWL)	HiA	.269	14	52	12	14	2	0	2	10	9	22	8	.387	.423
Minor League Totals				.282	213	808	171	228	33	14	27	108	112	274	67	.376	.458

5 LUIS MATOS, OF

Born: Jan. 28, 2002. **B-T:** R-R. **HT:** 5-11. **WT:** 160.
Signed: Venezuela, 2018. **Signed by:** Edgar Fernandez.

TRACK RECORD: Matos was signed out of Venezuela in 2018, then was impressive in his pro debut in 2019, mostly in the Dominican Summer League. Strict lockdowns in Venezuela in 2020 meant he was stranded in the U.S. during the pandemic, when his only on-field action came during instructional league. That is where he first showed hints of what was to come. He broke out in 2021, when his name was splashed all over the Low-A California League leaderboards. Matos struggled in 2022, both with performance and a nagging quad strain that limited him to 91 games at High-A Eugene before a stint in the Arizona Fall League.

BA GRADE

50 Risk: High

SCOUTING REPORT: Matos' numbers in 2021 masked a swing-first mentality, which he tried to correct in 2022. In doing so, internal evaluators believe he became too passive and got himself into bad counts. He also struggled to maintain an effective bat path, which got too choppy and wasn't in the zone for very long, and he also had a difficult time keeping his upper and lower halves connected. He chased a bit too much but balanced it somewhat with a solid in-zone miss rate of 18%. At his best, Matos shows electric bat speed and good hand-eye coordination that could make him a fringe-average hitter with above-average power potential. Matos' average speed and excellent instincts give him a chance to be an average everyday center fielder with an above-average arm that could play in right field if he has to move to a corner.

THE FUTURE: After a season of inconsistency, Matos will work hard to re-establish himself in 2023. If he finds his way, he has the upside to become an everyday outfielder in San Francisco.

SCOUTING GRADES		Hitting: 45		Power: 55		Speed: 50			Fielding: 50		Arm: 55			
Year	Age	Club (League)	Lvl	AVG	G	AB	R	H	2B	3B	HR	RBI	BB	SO	SB	OBP	SLG
2022	20	Giants Black (ACL)	R	.429	2	7	3	3	1	0	1	4	1	1	0	.500	1.000
2022	20	Eugene (NWL)	HiA	.211	91	369	55	78	14	1	11	43	27	65	11	.275	.344
Minor League Totals				.291	262	1078	207	314	75	4	34	181	76	158	53	.350	.463

6 VAUN BROWN, OF

Born: June 23, 1998. **B-T:** R-R. **HT:** 6-1. **WT:** 215.
Drafted: Florida Southern, 2021 (10th round). **Signed by:** Jim Gabella.

BA GRADE
50 Risk: High

TRACK RECORD: Brown's fifth-year senior season at Division II Florida Southern was largely played under wraps when the team's home park was closed to the public because of Covid-related restrictions. Giants area scout Jim Gabella improvised by viewing the games from a hole in the fence. After more scouts got their eyes on Brown, the Giants were convinced to draft him in the 10th round in 2021 and sign him for $7,500. He clobbered the Arizona Complex League after turning pro to set the stage for a 2022 breakthrough, when he hit .346 to lead all full-season minor leaguers.

SCOUTING REPORT: Brown is as chiseled a player as you'll see in the sport, with a body some scouts compared to that of an NFL linebacker, with sinewy muscle packed up and down his 6-foot-2 frame. The age gap between Brown—who opened the year as a 23-year-old—and his competition at the lower levels certainly contributed to his gaudy numbers, but scouts still see a potential for an everyday player. Brown cut some of the moving parts from his swing, but it's still a bit unorthodox. Opposing scouts believe his swing path is a bit grooved and suspect Brown might have trouble with elevated fastballs and potentially with soft stuff on the outer part of the plate. Ultimately, Brown might wind up a fringe-average hitter with plus power. Defensively, he's got the double-plus speed to play any of the three outfield spots with ease and the average arm to fit in right field.

THE FUTURE: Brown should return to Double-A in 2023 and will have a chance to prove himself against the type of advanced pitching he only tasted toward the end of 2022. He has the ceiling of an average everyday outfielder who provides value on both sides of the ball.

SCOUTING GRADES	Hitting: 45	Power: 55	Speed: 70	Fielding: 55	Arm: 50

Year	Age	Club (League)	Lvl	AVG	G	AB	R	H	2B	3B	HR	RBI	BB	SO	SB	OBP	SLG
2022	24	San Jose (CAL)	LoA	.346	59	228	50	79	14	5	14	41	25	67	23	.427	.636
2022	24	Eugene (NWL)	HiA	.350	43	157	50	55	10	2	9	34	22	52	21	.454	.611
2022	24	Richmond (EL)	AA	.000	1	2	0	0	0	0	0	0	0	0	0	.000	.000
Minor League Totals				.348	128	466	124	162	31	11	25	89	54	148	52	.444	.622

7 AEVERSON ARTEAGA, SS

Born: March 16, 2003. **B-T:** R-R. **HT:** 6-1. **WT:** 170.
Signed: Venezuela, 2019. **Signed by:** Edgar Fernandez.

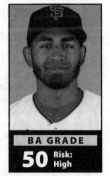

BA GRADE
50 Risk: High

TRACK RECORD: Arteaga received a $1 million bonus in 2019, when he was the highest-paid member of San Francisco's international signing class. His official debut was pushed forward a year by the lost pandemic season in 2020. A year later, he spent most of the season in the Arizona Complex League before joining Low-A San Jose for its championship run. He returned to the California League in 2022, where he led the league with 136 hits and 35 doubles) and finished in the top five with 51 extra-base hits. His 155 strikeouts were also third in the league.

SCOUTING REPORT: Arteaga is one of the best defenders in the system, second only to Casey Schmitt among infielders. He's got slick hands and feet, plays under control and has the plus arm to stick on the left side of the infield and the internal clock to understand when he has to unleash a throw from shortstop without getting his feet set. Arteaga's swing-and-miss numbers—especially his 23% rate on pitches in the zone—is something to monitor, as is his willingness to chase pitches down and away. When he makes contact, he has a sound feel for the barrel and enough strength to impact the ball. Early in the season, internal evaluators believed Arteaga was hunting power rather than letting his natural strength and excellent bat speed produce line drives into the alleys. He might show even more power by more consistently hitting the ball out front. He's a fringe-average runner who can get to a tick better underway.

THE FUTURE: If Arteaga can swing and miss less, he has a chance to be an everyday shortstop with offensive impact. If not, he could settle as a second-division player with excellent defense.

SCOUTING GRADES	Hitting: 40	Power: 55	Speed: 45	Fielding: 60	Arm: 60

Year	Age	Club (League)	Lvl	AVG	G	AB	R	H	2B	3B	HR	RBI	BB	SO	SB	OBP	SLG
2022	19	San Jose (CAL)	LoA	.270	122	503	87	136	35	2	14	84	49	155	11	.345	.431
Minor League Totals				.276	179	703	129	194	47	3	23	127	72	225	19	.350	.450

8 CARSON WHISENHUNT, LHP

Born: Oct. 20, 2000. **B-T:** L-L. **HT:** 6-3. **WT:** 209.
Drafted: East Carolina, 2022 (2nd round). **Signed by:** DJ Jauss.

TRACK RECORD: Under normal circumstances, Whisenhunt might have used his junior season at East Carolina to cement himself as one of the top pitchers for the 2022 draft. However, he tested positive for a performance-enhancing substance before the season and was banned for the year. He didn't get back on the mound until the Cape Cod League, where he added enough to his previous body of work. The Giants selected him in the second round, signed him for $1,866,220 and then sent him to the Arizona Complex League and Low-A San Jose. After recovering from a bout of Covid, Whisenhunt made three short starts in the Arizona Fall League.

BA GRADE
50 Risk: High

SCOUTING REPORT: In his stints on the Cape and as a pro, Whisenhunt showed off a largely intact arsenal of three average or better pitches. He starts with a low-90s fastball that peaked at 94 mph both on the Cape and during the minor league season. The pitch also features riding action. The gem of Whisenhunt's arsenal is a dastardly changeup with nearly 10 mph of separation from his fastball and the trapdoor action to flummox hitters. The pitch got whiffs at a 35% rate on the Cape and an eye-popping 74% rate in the low minors. The changeup, thrown in the low 80s, is a true double-plus weapon that should get plenty of whiffs as he moves up the ladder. Whisenhunt rounds out his mix with an average, high-70s curveball with two-plane break. The Giants have worked with Whisenhunt to tinker with the grip on the curveball to help him get a better feel for spin. He should have above-average control.

THE FUTURE: Whisenhunt threw 38.1 innings between the Cape, the minor leagues and the AFL, so he'll have to be managed carefully in 2023. He has the ceiling of a solid No. 4 starter.

SCOUTING GRADES:	Fastball: 50	Curveball: 50	Changeup: 70	Control: 55

Year	Age	Club (League)	Lvl	W	L	ERA	G	GS	IP	H	HR	BB	SO	BB/9	SO/9	WHIP	AVG
2022	21	Giants Orange (ACL)	R	0	0	0.00	2	1	3	1	0	0	7	0.0	21.0	0.33	.100
2022	21	San Jose (CAL)	LoA	0	0	0.00	2	2	5	5	0	1	7	1.9	13.5	1.29	.263
Minor League Totals				0	0	0.00	4	3	8	6	0	1	14	1.2	16.4	0.91	.207

9 MASON BLACK, RHP

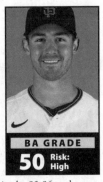

Born: Dec. 10, 1999. **B-T:** R-R. **HT:** 6-3. **WT:** 230.
Drafted: Lehigh, 2021 (3rd round). **Signed by:** John DiCarlo.

TRACK RECORD: In 2021, the Giants stocked up on pitchers from the Northeast. In addition to nabbing Black in the third round, San Francisco also chose lefties Matt Mikulski (Fordham) and Rohan Handa (Yale) in the second and fifth rounds and righthander Nick Sinacola (Maine) in the seventh round. Before the season, Black looked like a lock to go in the first two rounds, but he sputtered late and the Giants decided to buy low. In his first official pro action, Black looked like a steal. He split his 2022 season between Low-A San Jose and High-A Eugene and was one of four pitchers in the system who threw 100 or more innings and averaged more than 10 strikeouts and fewer than three walks per nine innings.

BA GRADE
50 Risk: High

SCOUTING REPORT: Black heads his arsenal with two- and four-seam fastballs in the 93-96 mph range and backs them up with a mid-80s sweeper slider that ranks as one of the best in the system. The sweeping shape is a change from the more traditional movement on the slider he threw in college. The new version worked splendidly, getting whiffs at rate of nearly 39% while generating a little more than a foot of sweep and about 2,650 rpm of spin. Black has a high-80s changeup, but it's a bit of a work in progress and was thrown just 9% of the time during the regular season. He has above-average control and produced a 63% strike rate. Scouts like Black's loose, easy delivery, his competitive demeanor on the mound and the chance to add strength.

THE FUTURE: If Black can bring his changeup forward, he has a chance to be an innings-eater at the back of the rotation. If not, his fastball and slider could make him a high-leverage reliever.

SCOUTING GRADES:	Fastball: 60	Slider: 60	Changeup: 40	Control: 55

Year	Age	Club (League)	Lvl	W	L	ERA	G	GS	IP	H	HR	BB	SO	BB/9	SO/9	WHIP	AVG
2022	22	San Jose (CAL)	LoA	1	1	1.57	8	8	34	25	1	8	44	2.1	11.5	0.96	.198
2022	22	Eugene (NWL)	HiA	5	3	3.94	16	16	78	70	11	28	92	3.2	10.7	1.26	.240
Minor League Totals				6	4	3.21	24	24	112	95	12	36	136	2.9	10.9	1.17	.227

10 ERIC SILVA, RHP

Born: Oct. 3, 2002. **B-T:** R-R. **HT:** 6-1. **WT:** 185.
Drafted: HS—San Juan Capistrano, CA, 2021 (4th round). **Signed by:** Brad Cameron.

TRACK RECORD: When they drafted Silva, the Giants followed their Kyle Harrison playbook. Find a high-end high school arm committed to UCLA, pay him nearly double slot value to sign, then watch as he develops. The Giants signed Silva for $1,497,500, which stood as the record a for a fourth-round pick until the Rangers took Michigan prep righthander Brock Porter in 2022. Silva spent all of 2022 at Low-A San Jose, where scouts were more optimistic than the numbers might suggest.

BA GRADE
50 Risk: High

SCOUTING REPORT: Despite Silva's smaller frame, scouts are encouraged by his combination of an explosive four-pitch arsenal and an athletic delivery. Silva leads his mix with four- and two-seam fastball that each average around 93 mph and peak at 96. His best offspeed is a sweeper slider in the 83-86 mph range and a peak of 87. Silva threw the slider roughly a quarter of the time and got whiffs at a nearly 40% clip. His curveball, a true downer pitch in the high 70s, offers a stark comparison in shape and velocity to his slider and has spin rates of nearly 3,000 rpm. It flashes average. He rounds out his repertoire with a mid-80s changeup he throws with good feel and no fear when behind counts. The pitch could get to average, and some scouts see it a little better. Silva was more control than command in 2022, in part because of a delivery with enough moving parts to create deception but sometimes sap the quality from his strikes.

THE FUTURE: Silva will graduate to High-A Eugene in 2023. There, he'll be challenged to improve his command without downgrading his deception. He has the ceiling of a back-end starter.

SCOUTING GRADES:	Fastball: 55	Curveball: 50	Slider: 55	Changeup: 50	Control: 45

Year	Age	Club (League)	Lvl	W	L	ERA	G	GS	IP	H	HR	BB	SO	BB/9	SO/9	WHIP	AVG
2022	19	San Jose (CAL)	LoA	3	7	5.88	22	22	86	77	11	39	99	4.1	10.4	1.35	.244
Minor League Totals				3	8	6.23	24	22	87	81	11	42	101	4.4	10.5	1.42	.251

11 REGGIE CRAWFORD, LHP/1B

Born: Dec. 4, 2000. **B-T:** L-L. **HT:** 6-4. **WT:** 235.
Drafted: Connecticut, 2022 (1st round). **Signed by:** Ray Callari.

TRACK RECORD: Crawford's limited track record made him one of the biggest wild cards in the 2022 draft. A two-way player at Connecticut who doubled as a first baseman, Crawford pitched just eight innings in two seasons for the Huskies and had Tommy John surgery that wiped out his entire junior year. But his athletic background and a strong stint for USA Baseball's Collegiate National Team convinced the Giants to draft him in the first round, No. 30 overall, and sign him for $2,297,500. Crawford made his pro debut in the Arizona Complex League and hit in 10 games while his arm recovered from surgery.

SCOUTING REPORT: Between his time at UConn, Team USA and the Cape Cod League, Crawford flashed a three-pitch mix topped by a fastball that averaged 95 mph and touched 99 from the left side. He backed it up with a low-to-mid 80s slider that flashed plus and was beginning to develop a changeup before he tore his ulnar collateral ligament. In addition to his stuff, Crawford intrigued the Giants with his physical frame and strong makeup. He has big raw power at the plate but could stand to improve his swing decisions and shows soft hands and a strong arm when he plays first base.

THE FUTURE: Crawford began throwing bullpens in the fall and should be ready for spring training. His surgery and lack of innings will lead to a limited workload in 2023, which will come in the Class A levels.

BA GRADE: 55/Extreme	Fastball: 70	Slider: 60	Changeup: 40	Control: 45

Year	Age	Club (League)	Lvl	AVG	G	AB	R	H	2B	3B	HR	RBI	BB	SO	SB	OBP	SLG
2022	21	Giants Black (ACL)	R	.158	6	19	2	3	0	0	0	0	2	9	0	.238	.158
Minor League Totals				.158	6	19	2	3	0	0	0	0	2	9	0	.238	.158

12 CARSON SEYMOUR, RHP

Born: Dec. 16, 1998. **B-T:** R-R. **HT:** 6-6. **WT:** 260.
Drafted: Kansas State, 2021 (6th round). **Signed by:** Scott Thomas (Mets).

TRACK RECORD: Seymour began his college career at Dartmouth and transferred to Kansas State, which forced him to sit out the 2019 season. The redshirt year plus the lost pandemic season added up to a severely stunted college career, which ended with just 84.2 innings in three seasons. The Mets drafted

Seymour in the sixth round in 2021 and traded him to the Giants a year later as part of the four-player package that sent Darin Ruf to New York.

SCOUTING REPORT: Seymour is a big, 6-foot-6 righthander with twitchy athleticism and the potential for a four-pitch mix. He gets a great deal of his outs with his high-octane fastball and a short, sharp, cutter-slider hybrid. His fastball sits in the mid 90s and peaks at 97 while his slider hovers in the upper 80s and scrapes 91. His fastball is not especially effective at getting whiffs or chases, but his slider is an above-average swing-and-miss pitch. Seymour also has a true downer curveball in the low 80s that gives him an excellent weapon against lefthanded hitters. He has a seldom-used changeup, but the Giants have considered switching it to a split-fingered fastball that better fits his massive hands. Seymour has some reliever risk because of a long arm action and below-average command, but he limits his walks and throws strikes at a solid clip.

THE FUTURE: Seymour will get his first upper-level test in 2023 at Double-A Richmond. If he can improve his command, he could be a No. 4 starter.

BA GRADE: 50/High   **Fastball:** 50   **Slider:** 55   **Curveball:** 50   **Changeup:** 40   **Control:** 45

Year	Age	Club (League)	Lvl	W	L	ERA	G	GS	IP	H	HR	BB	SO	BB/9	SO/9	WHIP	AVG
2022	23	St. Lucie (FSL)	LoA	4	0	1.19	7	4	30	23	0	9	27	2.7	8.0	1.05	.209
2022	23	Brooklyn (SAL)	HiA	1	5	3.68	11	9	51	45	8	12	65	2.1	11.4	1.11	.228
2022	23	Eugene (NWL)	HiA	2	3	3.99	6	6	29	25	1	10	43	3.1	13.2	1.19	.229
Minor League Totals				7	8	3.04	28	19	115	96	9	37	139	2.9	10.8	1.15	.223

13 LANDEN ROUPP, RHP

Born: Sept. 10, 1998. **B-T:** R-R. **HT:** 6-2. **WT:** 205.
Drafted: UNC Wilmington, 2021 (12th round). **Signed by:** Mark O'Sullivan.

TRACK RECORD: Roupp was a standout starter in four seasons with UNC Wilmington and showed he could handle better competition with a strong stint with Wareham of the Cape Cod League. The Giants drafted him in the 12th round in 2021 and signed him for a below-slot $75,000. Roupp made his full-season debut in 2022 and zoomed three levels from Low-A to Double-A, and finished third in the organization with 152 strikeouts.

SCOUTING REPORT: Roupp throws his curveball more often than any other pitcher in the minors, and with good reason. The pitch is a potentially plus weapon with more than 3,000 rpm of spin and vicious two-plane break and depth. He gets frequent chases and swings and misses on the pitch and can dominate with it alone. Roupp backs up his curveball with a two-seam fastball that averages 93 mph with excellent sinking and tailing life. He rounds out his mix with a low-80s slider and an infrequently used mid-80s changeup that are both fringy to below-average. Roupp's lower release height accentuates his arsenal and adds deception. He gets ground balls by the bunch and throws strikes with above-average control.

THE FUTURE: Roupp is likely to return to Double-A to begin 2023. He has a chance to be a back-end starter if his slider or changeup develop. If not, his sinker and curveball combination will fit in the bullpen.

BA GRADE: 50/High   **Fastball:** 55   **Curveball:** 60   **Slider:** 45   **Changeup:** 40   **Control:** 55

Year	Age	Club (League)	Lvl	W	L	ERA	G	GS	IP	H	HR	BB	SO	BB/9	SO/9	WHIP	AVG
2022	23	San Jose (CAL)	LoA	5	2	2.59	14	2	49	33	2	17	69	3.1	12.8	1.03	.188
2022	23	Eugene (NWL)	HiA	3	0	1.67	7	7	32	19	1	9	52	2.5	14.5	0.87	.165
2022	23	Richmond (EL)	AA	2	1	3.76	5	5	26	19	3	11	31	3.8	10.6	1.14	.194
Minor League Totals				10	3	2.58	31	14	115	77	6	38	166	3.0	13.0	1.00	.184

14 KEATON WINN, RHP

Born: Feb. 20, 1998. **B-T:** R-R. **HT:** 6-4. **WT:** 238.
Drafted: Iowa Western JC, 2018 (5th round). **Signed by:** Todd Coryell.

TRACK RECORD: Winn was committed to Texas Christian before the Giants selected him in 2018 with their fifth-round pick and signed him for $500,000. After spending his first two seasons in the low minors, Winn had Tommy John surgery and missed the 2021 season. He returned with a refreshed arsenal in 2022 and cut his way from Low-A to Double-A while racking up 125 strikeouts in 108 innings.

SCOUTING REPORT: Winn's fastball averaged 93 mph and touched 95 before surgery, but he came back throwing harder. His fastball now sits 95 mph and touches 100 to be a plus pitch, although it unintentionally behaves like a two-seamer at times. Winn also replaced his traditional changeup with a splitter—which the Giants suggested because of his large hands—and the new offering flashes plus in the upper-80s while getting frequent swings and misses. Winn rounds his mix with a mid-80s slider that projects to be an average pitch. If he can get it there, his mix will pair with his above-average control to form the makings of a back-end starter.

THE FUTURE: Winn ran into some fatigue toward the end of last season. He'll likely return to Double-A Richmond in 2023 to continue building up his stamina.

BA GRADE: 50/High		Fastball: 60		Slider: 50		Splitter: 60		Control: 55				

Year	Age	Club (League)	Lvl	W	L	ERA	G	GS	IP	H	HR	BB	SO	BB/9	SO/9	WHIP	AVG
2022	24	San Jose (CAL)	LoA	1	1	4.87	13	11	41	38	3	16	55	3.5	12.2	1.33	.247
2022	24	Eugene (NWL)	HiA	3	2	3.16	8	8	37	38	2	10	46	2.4	11.2	1.30	.264
2022	24	Richmond (EL)	AA	2	3	4.15	6	6	30	35	4	6	24	1.8	7.1	1.35	.294
Minor League Totals				16	14	3.85	68	50	278	283	22	71	260	2.3	8.4	1.27	.264

15 HELIOT RAMOS, OF

Born: Sept. 7, 1999. **B-T:** R-R. **HT:** 5-9. **WT:** 233.
Drafted: HS—Guaynabo, P.R., 2017 (1st round). **Signed by:** Junior Roman.

TRACK RECORD: The Giants' first-round pick in 2017, Ramos has been one of the youngest players at every stop in the minor leagues and has appeared in three Futures Games. After a solid but unspectacular season at the upper levels in 2021, he scuffled at Triple-A in 2022 but made his major league debut on April 22. Ramos got into nine games with the Giants and struggled mightily, going 2-for-20.

SCOUTING REPORT: A thickly-built righthanded hitter, Ramos hits balls hard when he connects. His 90.7 mph average exit velocity puts him in the upper tier of minor leaguers, but that hard contact is often on the ground. He's an aggressive swinger who frequently mishits balls and needs to improve his launch angle to get the ball in the air more. His strength and pure contact skills give him a chance to be a below-average hitter with average power if he can rein in his swing and approach, but it won't be easy. Defensively, Ramos has slowed to a below-average runner and will have to play a corner in the major leagues. His above-average arm fits best in right field.

THE FUTURE: Ramos needs to retool his swing and approach to get more impact out of his hard contact. If he can, he has a chance to be an everyday right fielder. He'll likely shuttle between the majors and minors again in 2023.

BA GRADE: 45/Medium		Hit: 40		Power: 50		Speed: 40		Fielding: 45		Arm: 55			

Year	Age	Club (League)	Lvl	AVG	G	AB	R	H	2B	3B	HR	RBI	BB	SO	SB	OBP	SLG
2022	22	Sacramento (PCL)	AAA	.227	108	427	61	97	17	1	11	45	41	112	6	.305	.349
2022	22	San Francisco (NL)	MLB	.100	9	20	4	2	0	0	0	0	2	6	0	.182	.100
Major League Totals				.100	9	20	4	2	0	0	0	0	2	6	0	.182	.100
Minor League Totals				.260	485	1888	285	491	101	19	58	235	170	552	47	.332	.426

16 JAIRO POMARES, OF

Born: Aug. 4, 2000. **B-T:** L-R. **HT:** 6-1. **WT:** 185.
Signed: Cuba, 2018. **Signed by:** Jonathan Bautista/Gabriel Elias.

TRACK RECORD: The Giants signed Pomares for $1.1 million out of Cuba as part of a loaded 2018 international signing class. He played only briefly in his pro debut the following year and wasn't able to enter the U.S. in 2020 due to visa issues, but he broke out in 2021 by tying for the system lead with 20 home runs in only 77 games across the Class A levels. Pomeras began 2022 back at High-A Eugene expecting to move up quickly, but his aggressive approach got him into trouble and his performance regressed.

SCOUTING REPORT: Pomares' calling card is his massive, plus-plus raw power from the left side. He destroys mistakes and posts loud exit velocities when he connects, sending balls upwards of 450 feet. Pomares has the power to make an impact, but he short-circuits it with his approach. He's an extraordinarily aggressive hitter who swings nearly 50% of the time and takes huge cuts aimed at trying to hit balls out of the park, leading to gobs of strikeouts. He'll have to control his approach substantially better to be even a below-average hitter and get to his power enough against higher-level pitching. Pomares is a fringy but adequate defender in either outfield corner, but he's played left field almost exclusively when he's not the DH. He is a fringe-average runner with an average arm.

THE FUTURE: Pomares will head to the upper levels for the first time in 2023 at Double-A Richmond. His aggressive approach will face a make-or-break moment against advanced pitching.

BA GRADE: 45/High		Hit: 40		Power: 55		Speed: 45		Fielding: 40		Arm: 50			

Year	Age	Club (League)	Lvl	AVG	G	AB	R	H	2B	3B	HR	RBI	BB	SO	SB	OBP	SLG
2022	21	Giants Orange (ACL)	R	.533	4	15	5	8	3	0	3	7	1	2	0	.563	1.333
2022	21	Eugene (NWL)	HiA	.254	95	338	49	86	20	0	14	59	36	127	0	.330	.438
Minor League Totals				.304	227	868	136	264	63	5	40	162	64	259	6	.358	.526

17 COLE WAITES, RHP

Born: June 10, 1998. **B-T:** R-R. **HT:** 6-3. **WT:** 180.
Drafted: West Alabama, 2019 (18th round). **Signed by:** Jeff Wood.

TRACK RECORD: Waites was a hidden gem at Division II West Alabama uncovered by Giants area scout Jeff Wood, who was intrigued enough by the fireballing righthander to push for his selection. The Giants drafted Waites in the 18th round and signed him for $100,000. Waites' first full season was delayed by the coronavirus pandemic and he was limited to 13.1 innings in 2021 after having knee surgery, but he finally got a full season in 2022 and cruised up three levels of the minors before earning his first big league callup on Sept. 13.

SCOUTING REPORT: Waites' hallmark is his fastball, which is not only the best in the Giants' system but one of the best in the minor leagues. The pitch averages 96 mph and touches 100 with high spin rates and excellent life through the zone. He pounds the strike zone with his heater and gets swings and misses against it by the bunch, making it an 80-grade pitch. Waites complements his fastball with a high-spin, mid-80s slider that is adept at getting whiffs both in and out of the zone. His previous shortcoming was scattershot command and control, but he improved both a tick in 2022 to below-average.

THE FUTURE: Waites is a straight reliever and could pitch in high leverage if he further improves his command and control. He'll likely bounce back and forth between Triple-A and San Francisco in 2023.

BA GRADE: 40/Medium   **Fastball:** 80   **Slider:** 60   **Control:** 40

Year	Age	Club (League)	Lvl	W	L	ERA	G	GS	IP	H	HR	BB	SO	BB/9	SO/9	WHIP	AVG
2022	24	Eugene (NWL)	HiA	1	1	3.55	13	0	13	10	1	4	27	2.8	19.2	1.11	.208
2022	24	Richmond (EL)	AA	2	2	1.71	18	0	21	12	0	15	38	6.4	16.3	1.29	.162
2022	24	Sacramento (PCL)	AAA	1	0	0.00	7	0	8	3	0	3	11	3.4	12.4	0.75	.120
2022	24	San Francisco (NL)	MLB	0	0	3.18	7	0	6	6	1	4	4	6.4	6.4	1.76	.286
Major League Totals				0	0	3.18	7	0	6	6	1	4	4	6.4	6.4	1.76	.286
Minor League Totals				7	4	2.74	60	7	72	43	2	41	135	5.1	16.8	1.16	.169

18 ADRIAN SUGASTEY, C

Born: Oct. 23, 2002. **B-T:** R-R. **HT:** 6-1. **WT:** 210.
Signed: Panama, 2019. **Signed by:** Rogelio Castillo.

TRACK RECORD: Sugastey starred for Panama's junior national team as an amateur and signed with the Giants for $525,000 as part of their 2019 international signing class. His pro debut was delayed by the coronavirus pandemic, but he emerged in 2021 with an excellent season in the Rookie-level Arizona Complex League and made the jump to Low-A San Jose in 2022. His season was limited to 84 games by a hamstring injury and his performance suffered, but he got additional reps in the Arizona Fall League at the end of the year and showed well.

SCOUTING REPORT: Sugastey has excellent bat-to-ball skills and a knack for contact. He chases out of the zone a fair amount but is able to still make contact off the plate and rarely strikes out. Sugastey has yet to grow into power, but he should get stronger in his big frame, particularly in his upper half, and start making more impact on contact. He will need to be more selective and shorten his swing in order to reach his potential as an average hitter with 10-15 home run power. Sugastey isn't the best athlete and he needs to clean up his receiving, but he capably handles advanced arms and has a chance to grow into an average defender behind the plate. He has plus arm strength and a quick release that helped him throw out 28% of attempted basestealers in 2022.

THE FUTURE: Sugastey will head to High-A Eugene in 2023 and focus on adding power.. He projects to be a second-division regular or a backup on a championship contender.

BA GRADE: 45/High   **Hit:** 50   **Power:** 45   **Speed:** 30   **Fielding:** 50   **Arm:** 60

Year	Age	Club (League)	Lvl	AVG	G	AB	R	H	2B	3B	HR	RBI	BB	SO	SB	OBP	SLG
2022	19	Giants Orange (ACL)	R	.231	9	26	4	6	1	1	0	2	4	5	0	.323	.346
2022	19	San Jose (CAL)	LoA	.240	75	300	41	72	11	1	5	32	30	53	1	.329	.333
Minor League Totals				.276	127	474	68	131	18	2	7	59	46	84	2	.352	.367

19 RYAN MURPHY, RHP

Born: Oct. 8, 1999. **B-T:** R-R. **HT:** 6-1. **WT:** 190.
Drafted: Le Moyne (N.Y.), 2020 (5th round). **Signed by:** Ray Callari.

TRACK RECORD: Murphy followed current Nationals righthander Josiah Gray as the ace at Division II Le Moyne and was drafted by the Giants in the fifth and final round of the shortened 2020 draft. He signed

for just $22,500 and immediately made the Giants look astute by striking out 164 hitters across the Class A levels in his pro debut, third-most in the minor leagues. Murphy's encore in 2022 was disrupted by back spasms and elbow inflammation that limited him to just 43.2 innings, but he did reach Double-A.
SCOUTING REPORT: None of Murphy's pitches stand out in a vacuum, but he does an excellent job of mixing and matching four pitches to keep hitters off balance. Murphy's fastball sits 91-92 mph, peaks at 94 and plays up because he locates it well. His upper-70s curveball and low-80s slider are both average pitches and his changeup is a fringy but usable fourth offering. While none are overwhelming, Murphy does a good job tunneling his pitches off one another to keep hitters guessing and get swings and misses. He ran into control issues prior to going on the IL but has plus control when he's healthy. Murphy has a slighter build and has pitched more than 100 innings in a season only once, but he stuck around the Giants' spring training complex over the winter to learn how to better manage a full-season's workload.
THE FUTURE: Murphy has a chance to be a No. 5 starter and should at least be a usable swingman or bulk reliever. He'll open 2023 back at Double-A.

BA GRADE: 45/High		Fastball: 50		Curveball: 50		Slider: 50		Changeup: 45		Control: 60	

Year	Age	Club (League)	Lvl	W	L	ERA	G	GS	IP	H	HR	BB	SO	BB/9	SO/9	WHIP	AVG
2022	22	Giants Black (ACL)	R	0	0	9.00	1	0	1	2	1	0	0	0.0	0.0	2.00	.400
2022	22	San Jose (CAL)	LoA	0	0	10.80	1	0	2	3	1	1	3	5.4	16.2	2.40	.375
2022	22	Eugene (NWL)	HiA	1	0	2.90	7	7	31	20	1	12	47	3.5	13.6	1.03	.180
2022	22	Richmond (EL)	AA	1	1	9.35	2	2	9	9	2	10	7	10.4	7.3	2.19	.265
Minor League Totals				8	5	3.13	32	30	150	106	17	49	221	2.9	13.3	1.04	.197

20 WILL BEDNAR, RHP

Born: June 13, 2000. **B-T:** R-R. **HT:** 6-2. **WT:** 230.
Drafted: Mississippi State, 2021 (1st round). **Signed by:** Jeff Wood.
TRACK RECORD: The younger brother of Pirates closer David Bednar, Will won Most Outstanding Player of the 2021 College World Series as the ace of Mississippi State's championship team. The Giants drafted him 14th overall and signed him for $3,647,500. Bednar began his first full season at Low-A San Jose in 2022 with high expectations, but he instead delivered a middling performance over 12 starts before going on the injured list with a season-ending lower back strain. He returned in the Arizona Fall League but made only two starts before his back strain recurred and shut him down.
SCOUTING REPORT: Bednar's fastball and slider combination made him a top pitcher in college, but his fastball regressed since signing. His velocity has dropped from 92-96 mph in college to 90-94 as a pro, making his fastball a fringe-average pitch that gets hit frequently despite solid spin rates and vertical break. His slider remains a potential plus pitch in the low 80s with high spin rates and good shape he can land for strikes or get chase swings with. He rarely uses his below-average changeup in the upper 80s and struggles to find a consistent release point. In addition to his loss of velocity, Bednar showed a surprising lack of aggression on the mound and showed fringy control, far from what he showed at Mississippi State.
THE FUTURE: Bednar must regain his fastball velocity to have any future as a starter in the major leagues. Otherwise, he'll have to try to ride his slider to a bullpen role.

BA GRADE: 45/High		Fastball: 45		Slider: 60		Changeup: 40		Control: 45	

Year	Age	Club (League)	Lvl	W	L	ERA	G	GS	IP	H	HR	BB	SO	BB/9	SO/9	WHIP	AVG
2022	22	San Jose (CAL)	LoA	1	3	4.19	12	12	43	25	7	22	51	4.6	10.7	1.09	.167
Minor League Totals				1	3	3.78	16	16	50	31	7	23	57	4.1	10.3	1.08	.174

21 WADE MECKLER, OF

Born: April 21, 2000. **B-T:** L-R. **HT:** 5-10. **WT:** 178.
Drafted: Oregon State, 2022 (8th round). **Signed by:** Larry Casian.
TRACK RECORD: Meckler spent two seasons at Oregon State sandwiched around the coronavirus pandemic and was the starting left fielder and No. 2 hitter on the Beavers team that reached Super Regionals in 2022. The Giants drafted him in the eighth round and signed him for $97,500. Meckler quickly moved to Low-A San Jose after signing and hit .367 overall in a loud pro debut.
SCOUTING REPORT: No one tool in particular stands out in Meckler's game, but has a good feel for contact, a strong knowledge of the strike zone and drew more walks (20) than strikeouts (16) in his pro debut. He manages at-bats well, gets on base and causes havoc with his nearly plus-plus speed. Meckler is purely a contact hitter and has below-average power, but his speed should help him beat out some extra grounders and be an average hitter. The Giants are confident in Meckler's ability to play center field as an average defender but he will likely move around the outfield. His below-average arm strength likely limits

him to left field if he has to move to a corner.

THE FUTURE: Meckler will open 2023 back in the Pacific Northwest with High-A Eugene. He projects to be a versatile fourth outfielder who provides a pinch of offensive impact.

BA GRADE: 45/High		Hit: 50		Power: 40		Speed: 65		Fielding: 50		Arm: 40	

Year	Age	Club (League)	Lvl	AVG	G	AB	R	H	2B	3B	HR	RBI	BB	SO	SB	OBP	SLG
2022	22	Giants Black (ACL)	R	.289	12	38	12	11	4	0	0	6	11	8	1	.460	.395
2022	22	San Jose (CAL)	LoA	.439	11	41	9	18	7	0	1	8	9	8	1	.540	.683
Minor League Totals				.367	23	79	21	29	11	0	1	14	20	16	2	.500	.544

22 NICK SWINEY, LHP

Born: Feb. 12, 1999. **B-T:** L-L. **HT:** 6-3. **WT:** 185.
Drafted: North Carolina State, 2020 (2nd round supplemental). **Signed by:** Mark O'Sullivan.

TRACK RECORD: Swiney spent most of his freshman and sophomore seasons in North Carolina State's bullpen and moved full-time to the rotation as a junior, but he made just four starts before the season was cut short by the coronavirus pandemic. The Giants saw enough in that limited sample to take him in the second supplemental round and sign him for $1,197,500. Swiney made just 12 starts in his pro debut due to a concussion, but he returned to pitch a full season for the first time in 2022. He posted a 3.46 ERA at High-A Eugene while pitching a career-high 89 innings.

SCOUTING REPORT: Swiney's best pitch is his 78-81 mph changeup, which projects as a true plus weapon. He throws the pitch for strikes and gets plenty of chases on it as well to generate whiffs at a rate of nearly 45%. Swiney's changeup would play even better if his 88-91 mph fastball gained more velocity, which is what he and the Giants will work toward in 2023. Swiney rounds out his mix with a mid-70s curveball with low spin but deep break and has a chance to be average. He has struggled with below-average control throughout his career.

THE FUTURE: Swiney needs to improve his fastball velocity and control to reach his ceiling as a No. 5 starter. He'll be tested at Double-A Richmond in 2023.

BA GRADE: 45/High		Fastball: 45		Curveball: 50	Changeup: 60		Control: 40	

Year	Age	Club (League	Lvl	W	L	ERA	G	GS	IP	H	HR	BB	SO	BB/9	SO/9	WHIP	AVG
2022	23	Eugene (NWL)	HiA	4	6	3.84	21	20	89	63	7	45	105	4.6	10.6	1.21	.193
Minor League Totals				4	6	3.04	33	32	121	86	7	63	163	4.7	12.1	1.23	.192

23 BLAKE SABOL, C/OF

Born: Jan. 7, 1998. **B-T:** L-R. **HT:** 6-3. **WT:** 223.
Drafted: Southern California, 2019 (7th round). **Signed by:** Rick Allen (Pirates).

TRACK RECORD: Sabol was a prominent high school player at Aliso Niguel (Calif.) High and turned down Cleveland as a 33rd-round pick to attend Southern California, where he showed good athleticism but struggled to produce over three seasons. The Pirates drafted him in the seventh round in 2019 and he progressively improved as a hitter leading up to a breakout 2022. Sabol set career highs in nearly every offensive category as he rose to Triple-A and helped lead Surprise to the Arizona Fall League championship after the season. The Reds selected him in the Rule 5 draft and traded him to the Giants.

SCOUTING REPORT: Sabol is a long, lanky athlete and has always had a solid feel for the barrel from the left side. He tapped into his above-average power more consistently after spending time with Pirates minor league coaches and learned to more aggressively hunt pitches he can damage on in front of the plate. Sabol has all-fields power and solid bat speed, but his swing can get long and be susceptible to velocity up in the zone. Questions about whether Sabol can stick at catcher have trailed him since high school. He's a good framer and pitchers enjoy working with him, but he's still a fringy defender with a fringe-average arm. He plays mostly left field when he's not behind the plate, where his marginal foot and arm are best suited.

THE FUTURE: Sabol has hit his way into a chance for big league at-bats in 2023. He'll aim to make his debut during the season.

BA GRADE: 45/High		Hit: 50		Power: 55		Speed: 45		Fielding: 45		Arm: 45	

Year	Age	Club (League)	Lvl	AVG	G	AB	R	H	2B	3B	HR	RBI	BB	SO	SB	OBP	SLG
2022	24	Altoona (EL)	AA	.281	98	366	61	103	23	5	14	60	38	107	9	.347	.486
2022	24	Indianapolis (IL)	AAA	.296	25	81	13	24	3	1	5	15	17	22	1	.426	.543
Minor League Totals				.282	246	900	150	254	48	13	34	142	128	274	21	.372	.478

24 WILLIAM KEMPNER, RHP

Born: June 18, 2001. **B-T:** R-R. **HT:** 6-0. **WT:** 222.
Drafted: Gonzaga, 2022 (3rd round). **Signed by:** Larry Casian.
TRACK RECORD: Gonzaga provided a wellspring of talent in the 2022 draft, with its entire starting rotation plus outfielder Nick Morabito all going in the top three rounds. Kempner was the last of the Bulldogs selected when he was drafted in the third round by his hometown team and signed for $522,500. Kempner made only nine starts for Gonzaga during the college season due to a finger injury, so the Giants took it slow and limited him to just nine innings after he signed.
SCOUTING REPORT: Kempner is a thick-bodied righthander who combines power stuff with a funk-filled delivery and sidearm slot. He works with a three-pitch mix, led by a darting, high-spin fastball that sits around 95 mph and touches 100. It's nearly a plus-plus pitch with its velocity, spin and life, but his command of it needs work. Kempner backs up his fastball with a potentially above-average slider with sweeping life and elite spin rates. He finishes his mix with a developing changeup in the high 80s that he threw sparingly in college and not at all as a pro. Kempner's high-effort delivery leads to scattershot control and command that will likely push him to the bullpen. He averaged more than six walks per nine innings at Gonzaga and had similar results in his pro debut.
THE FUTURE: Kempner will start for now but projects to move to the bullpen, where he has a chance to flummox hitters with his fastball and slider. He'll head to High-A Eugene in 2023.

| BA GRADE: 45/High | | Fastball: 65 | | Slider: 55 | | Changeup: 45 | | Control: 40 | | | | |

Year	Age	Club (League)	Lvl	W	L	ERA	G	GS	IP	H	HR	BB	SO	BB/9	SO/9	WHIP	AVG
2022	21	Giants Black (ACL)	R	1	0	2.70	2	0	3	4	0	2	5	5.4	13.5	1.80	.333
2022	21	San Jose (CAL)	LoA	0	0	6.35	3	2	6	6	1	4	6	6.4	9.5	1.76	.273
Minor League Totals				1	0	5.00	5	2	9	10	1	6	11	6.0	11.0	1.78	.294

25 PATRICK BAILEY, C

Born: May 29, 1999. **B-T:** B-R. **HT:** 6-1. **WT:** 210.
Drafted: North Carolina State, 2020 (1st round). **Signed by:** Mark O'Sullivan.
TRACK RECORD: The Giants made Bailey the 13th overall pick of the 2020 draft after a decorated career at North Carolina State and signed him for $3,797,500. Bailey struggled with injuries and underperformance in his pro debut and was sent back to High-A Eugene for a repeat season in 2022. He again struggled to hit with a .225 average but showed flashes of power, patience and defense.
SCOUTING REPORT: Bailey has long stood out for his defense and is easily the best defensive catcher in the Giants system. He's a plus defender with quick, quiet hands behind the plate and is adept in both receiving and blocking. His average arm strength plays up with his sound footwork and quick release and led him to throw out 30% of attempted basestealers in 2022. Bailey's offensive game is more of a work in progress. He's a switch hitter with an inconsistent approach and gets in trouble when he starts chasing power. His swing can be a bit grooved as well, especially from the right side. Bailey is a vastly better hitter from the left side (.252, .851 OPS) than the right (.133, 460 OPS) and may need to scrap switch-hitting.
THE FUTURE: Bailey will move to Double-A in 2023 and try to become more consistent at the plate. He has the ceiling of a defensive-minded backup catcher.

| BA GRADE: 40/High | | Hit: 40 | | Power: 50 | | Speed: 30 | | Fielding: 60 | | Arm: 55 | | |

Year	Age	Club (League)	Lvl	AVG	G	AB	R	H	2B	3B	HR	RBI	BB	SO	SB	OBP	SLG
2022	23	Eugene (NWL)	HiA	.225	83	267	49	60	14	1	12	51	49	72	1	.342	.419
Minor League Totals				.247	165	584	110	144	39	1	21	90	97	163	8	.354	.425

26 MATT MIKULSKI, LHP

Born: May 8, 1999. **B-T:** L-L. **HT:** 6-4. **WT:** 205.
Drafted: Fordham, 2021 (2nd round). **Signed by:** John DiCarlo.
TRACK RECORD: Mikulski pitched four years at Fordham and rose up draft boards as a senior when his velocity spiked to touch triple digits. He led the Atlantic 10 Conference in both ERA and strikeouts and was drafted by the Giants in the second round, and signed for $1,197,500. Mikulski was conservatively assigned to Low-A San Jose to start his full-season debut in 2022 but struggled mightily against younger competition. His fastball lost several ticks of velocity and he got hit around for a 6.95 ERA and a .296/.383/.497 opponent slash line.
SCOUTING REPORT: Mikulski is a strong 6-foot-4 lefthander, but his poor arm action and declining stuff

raise concerns. His fastball sits at 90 mph and touches 95, down 4-5 mph from where he was in college. His low 80s slider with good shape and powerful bite is an average offering, but his soft, slurvy curveball in the low-70s is a below-average and ineffective pitch and his below-average, low-80s changeup needs to make significant strides. Mikulski dealt with nagging knee pain all year and the Giants believe a return to health might help his stuff tick back up. The team also tried to shorten Mikulski's arm action but it got too short and cost him flexibility in his delivery. He throws strikes with average control.

THE FUTURE: Mikulski will attempt to rebound with a clean bill of health in 2023. With no pitch presently better than average, his stuff needs to come back for him to have a major league future.

BA GRADE: 40/High	Fastball: 50	Curveball: 40	Slider: 50	Changeup: 40	Control: 50

Year	Age	Club (League)	Lvl	W	L	ERA	G	GS	IP	H	HR	BB	SO	BB/9	SO/9	WHIP	AVG
2022	23	San Jose (CAL)	LoA	4	5	6.95	22	18	79	94	12	31	96	3.5	10.9	1.58	.296
Minor League Totals				4	5	6.64	26	22	84	98	12	34	101	3.6	10.8	1.57	.293

27 RJ DABOVICH, RHP

Born: Jan. 11, 1999. **B-T:** R-R. **HT:** 6-3. **WT:** 215.
Drafted: Arizona State, 2020 (4th round). **Signed by:** Chuck Hensley.
TRACK RECORD: Dabovich bounced between starting and relieving at Arizona State and in the Cape Cod League but moved to the bullpen full-time after the Giants drafted him in the fourth round of the shortened 2020 draft. Dabovich dominated in his first season as a reliever, but he ran into trouble in 2022 once he reached Triple-A and started facing higher-level hitters.
SCOUTING REPORT: Dabovich is a physical, 6-foot-3 righthander who follows a simple formula—four-seam fastballs up followed by curveballs down for chases. His fastball is an above-average pitch that sits 95-98 mph with carry through the top of the zone at its best, but he pitched through a nagging hamstring injury in 2022 that threw off his mechanics and resulted in less rise. He also struggled to adjust to the Triple-A Pacific Coast League's automatic ball-strike system, which led to fewer strikes with his fastball and an elevated walk rate. Dabovich's curveball is a plus offering in the mid-80s with strong, downward snap that generates whiffs more than half the time he throws it. His control was already fringy and fell to below-average with his injury and the ABS system at Triple-A.
THE FUTURE: Dabovich will head back to Triple-A to begin 2023. He has the potential to reach the majors as a low to mid-leverage relief prospect if his fastball and control rebound.

BA GRADE: 40/High	Fastball: 55	Curveball: 60	Control: 40

Year	Age	Club (League)	Lvl	W	L	ERA	G	GS	IP	H	HR	BB	SO	BB/9	SO/9	WHIP	AVG
2022	23	Richmond (EL)	AA	4	1	2.70	22	0	27	18	1	6	38	2.0	12.8	0.90	.182
2022	23	Sacramento (PCL)	AAA	2	0	4.38	23	1	25	16	1	20	31	7.3	11.3	1.46	.193
Minor League Totals				7	2	3.23	76	1	84	49	5	39	131	4.2	14.1	1.05	.166

28 RANDY RODRIGUEZ, RHP

Born: Sept. 5, 1999. **B-T:** R-R. **HT:** 6-0. **WT:** 166.
Signed: Dominican Republic, 2017. **Signed by:** Gabriel Elias.
TRACK RECORD: Rodriguez signed with the Giants out of the Dominican Republic in 2017 and was mostly a nondescript reliever until 2021, when he broke out at Low-A San Jose and was placed on the Giants 40-man roster. Rodriguez wasn't allowed to contact any team personnel in the offseason because of the lockout and was behind schedule when spring training finally commenced, leading to a middling encore. He began the year as a starter at High-A Eugene but was used exclusively as a reliever in short stints at Double-A and Triple-A and struggled against upper-level hitters.
SCOUTING REPORT: Rodriguez lost fastball velocity and the shape of his slider got too vertical during the lockout, problems he worked to fix throughout the 2022 season. He slowly regained his prior velocity and is now back to sitting at 93-94 mph and touching 98. His slider has begun flashing the sweepy, potentially plus version of itself and remains a swing-and-miss offering in the low-80s. Rodriguez mostly works off his fastball and slider, making their restoration critical, but he also has a firm, below-average changeup in the 87-90 mph range he'll occasionally mix in. Rodriguez has well below-average command and control and threw fewer strikes the higher he climbed in 2022.
THE FUTURE: Rodriguez will need to regain command of the strike zone to last in the big leagues as a reliever. He'll open 2023 in the upper levels with an eye on making his debut.

BA GRADE: 40/High		Fastball: 50		Slider: 60		Changeup: 40		Control: 30			
Year	Age	Club (League)	Lvl	W	L	ERA	G	GS	IP	H	HR	BB	SO	BB/9	SO/9	WHIP	AVG
2022	22	Eugene (NWL)	HiA	2	3	3.38	16	13	51	35	5	24	71	4.3	12.6	1.16	.193
2022	22	Richmond (EL)	AA	0	1	6.30	6	0	10	7	2	8	19	7.2	17.1	1.50	.184
2022	22	Sacramento (PCL)	AAA	0	1	10.50	5	0	6	3	0	11	7	16.5	10.5	2.33	.143
Minor League Totals				11	15	3.63	85	15	181	139	9	91	261	4.5	13.0	1.27	.209

29 JOSE CRUZ, RHP

Born: May 18, 2000. **B-T:** R-R. **HT:** 6-1. **WT:** 178.
Signed: Dominican Republic, 2017. **Signed by:** Gabriel Elias.
TRACK RECORD: Cruz signed with the Giants out of the Dominican Republic in 2017 and was a nondescript relief prospect in the lower levels before a developmental breakthrough in 2022 altered his outlook. Arizona Complex League pitching coach Mario Rodriguez advised Cruz to lower his arm slot and shift from a four-seam fastball to a two-seam fastball, and the resulting changes led to a breakout season at Low-A San Jose. Cruz emerged as the California League's most dominant relief prospect and finished the year with a 2.06 ERA and 86 strikeouts in 52.1 innings.
SCOUTING REPORT: Cruz primarily works with two plus pitches in his two-seam fastball and changeup, the latter of which jumped with Cruz's alterations to his arm slot and pitch mix. Cruz's fastball sits at 95-98 mph and gives hitters fits with its velocity and bite out of his deceptive, lower arm slot. His changeup mirrors the fastball out of his hand but pulls back at 85-87 mph, more than 10 mph of separation from his fastball. Cruz also has a slider, but it's a clear third pitch that will need improvement to be even below-average. Cruz's arsenal plays up because of the low release height in his delivery. He needs to improve his fringy control, but his mix works enough to get grounders and strikeouts.
THE FUTURE: The Giants added Cruz to the 40-man roster after the season. He will open 2023 at High-A Eugene and has a chance to be a middle reliever.

BA GRADE: 40/High		Fastball: 60		Slider: 30		Changeup: 60		Control: 45			
Year	Age	Club (League)	Lvl	W	L	ERA	G	GS	IP	H	HR	BB	SO	BB/9	SO/9	WHIP	AVG
2022	22	San Jose (CAL)	LoA	2	1	2.06	38	0	52	21	3	23	86	4.0	14.8	0.84	.119
Minor League Totals				9	7	3.74	91	3	154	113	8	76	204	4.4	11.9	1.23	.202

30 HAYDEN BIRDSONG, RHP

Born: Aug. 30, 2001. **B-T:** R-R. **HT:** 6-4. **WT:** 200.
Drafted: Eastern Illinois, 2022 (6th round). **Signed by:** Tom Shafer.
TRACK RECORD: Birdsong began his college career at Lake Land (Ill.) JC in 2020 before transferring to Eastern Illinois. He spent the bulk of his time in the Panthers bullpen over the next two years and was drafted by the Giants in the sixth round of the 2022 draft, signing for a below-slot $187,500. Birdsong got into seven games after signing and raised eyebrows with 23 strikeouts in 11.2 innings in his pro debut.
SCOUTING REPORT: Birdsong stands out for his big, 6-foot-4 frame and premium arm strength. His fastball sits 93-96 mph and has room to keep ticking up as he gets stronger to be a potentially plus pitch. He complements his fastball with an above-average, upper-70s curveball with 11-to-5 shape and late finish. Birdsong mostly throws his fastball and curveball, but he also has a fringy slider with similar velocity to his curveball and a rarely-used, low-80s changeup that is well below-average. All of Birdsong's pitches play up with an over-the-top arm slot that helps him create near-ideal spin efficiency, but he struggles to command his secondaries and has below-average control overall.
THE FUTURE: Birdsong is nestled among a host of potential middle-innings reliever prospects in the Giants' system. He'll head to High-A Eugene in 2023.

BA GRADE: 40/High		Fastball: 60		Curveball: 55		Slider: 45		Changeup: 30		Control: 40	
Year	Age	Club (League)	Lvl	W	L	ERA	G	GS	IP	H	HR	BB	SO	BB/9	SO/9	WHIP	AVG
2022	20	Giants Orange (ACL)	R	0	0	1.59	4	0	6	2	0	0	12	0.0	19.1	0.35	.118
2022	20	San Jose (CAL)	LoA	1	0	4.50	3	0	6	8	0	3	11	4.5	16.5	1.83	.320
Minor League Totals				1	0	3.09	7	0	12	10	0	3	23	2.3	17.7	1.11	.238

Seattle Mariners

BY KYLE GLASER

After more than two decades in the wilderness, the Mariners finally made it back to the promised land in 2022.

Led by star rookie center fielder Julio Rodriguez and a dominant pitching staff, the Mariners reached the postseason for the first time in 21 years to end the longest playoff drought in North American professional sports. The Mariners won 90 games and clinched the second American League wild card, securing the franchise's first playoff appearance since 2001

The way they did it was particularly memorable. The Mariners entered July five games under .500 but reeled off 14 consecutive wins going into the all-star break to turn their season around. They used that run to springboard into playoff position and remained there the rest of the year, clinching a postseason on a walkoff home run by catcher Cal Raleigh on Sept. 30.

The Mariners kept the magic going by sweeping the Blue Jays in the Wild Card Series, highlighted by erasing a seven-run deficit in the clinching game. They fell to the eventual champion Astros in the AL Division Series, coming up just short in an epic, 18-inning loss in Game 3.

The Mariners' magical season was the culmination of a four-year rebuild engineered by general manager Jerry Dipoto. Between 2018 and 2022, the Mariners built a premium farm system that yielded Rodriguez, Raleigh and righthanders George Kirby and Logan Gilbert, among other homegrown talents.

Seattle also astutely traded for young players who would eventually play pivotal roles, such as shortstop J.P. Crawford, first baseman Ty France and righthanded reliever Andres Muñoz. Sensing the time to compete was at hand, Dipoto and the Mariners swung trades for veterans in 2022 that helped put them over the top, including righthander Luis Castillo, third baseman Eugenio Suarez and DH Carlos Santana.

After graduating 10 prospects and trading 23 others over the last two years, the Mariners' farm system has been hollowed out. Still, there is frontline talent in the system, led by catcher Harry Ford and shortstop Cole Young, the club's two most recent first-round picks, and the organization's ability to develop pitching continued with righthanders Bryce Miller, Taylor Dollard and Bryan Woo in 2022.

Between a controllable major league roster and talent in the upper levels ready to reinforce it, the Mariners are in good shape to continue competing for the foreseeable future. That will also give the organization time to backfill the farm system and

George Kirby's rookie season demonstrated he can be a rotation fixture for the Mariners.

PROJECTED 2026 LINEUP

Catcher	Cal Raleigh	29
First Base	Ty France	31
Second Base	Cole Young	22
Third Base	Harry Ford	23
Shortstop	J.P. Crawford	31
Left Field	Jarred Kelenic	26
Center Field	Julio Rodriguez	25
Right Field	Gabriel Gonzalez	22
Designated Hitter	Eugenio Suarez	34
No. 1 Starter	Luis Castillo	33
No. 2 Starter	George Kirby	28
No. 3 Starter	Logan Gilbert	29
No. 4 Starter	Robbie Ray	34
No. 5 Starter	Bryce Miller	27
Closer	Andres Muñoz	27

replace its losses, putting the franchise in its best position since its glory years of 1995-2001.

Now that the Mariners have added one long drought, the next step is to end the second. The Mariners remain the only franchise to have never reached a World Series, and getting their will not be an easy task with the Astros looming large,

But with Rodriguez, Castillo, Crawford, France, Raleigh, Kirby, Gilbert, Suarez, Muñoz and lefthanders Marco Gonzales and Robbie Ray all locked up or under team control for at least three more seasons, the Mariners have the talent in place. If they can effectively backfill the farm system, their window to compete will extend well beyond then. ∎

DEPTH CHART

SEATTLE MARINERS

TOP 2023 MLB CONTRIBUTORS	RANK
Bryce Miller, RHP	3
Emerson Hancock, RHP	5
Taylor Dollard, RHP	6
BREAKOUT PROSPECTS	**RANK**
Axel Sanchez, SS	16
Tyler Gough, RHP	22

SOURCE OF TOP 30 TALENT

Homegrown	28	Acquired	2
College	12	Trade	2
Junior college	0	Rule 5 draft	0
High school	6	Independent league	0
Nondrafted free agent	0	Free agent/waivers	0
International	10		

LF
Zach DeLoach (12)
Lazaro Montes (14)
Spencer Packard (21)

CF
Jonatan Clase (11)
Cade Marlowe (15)
Victor Labrada (27)
George Feliz

RF
Gabriel Gonzalez (4)
Alberto Rodriguez (26)
Jack Larsen

3B
Starlin Aguilar (29)
Jose Caballero
Ben Ramirez

SS
Axel Sanchez (16)
Josh Hood (25)
Martin Gonzalez

2B
Cole Young (2)
Michael Arroyo (8)
Kaden Polcovich (26)

1B
Tyler Locklear (9)
Robert Perez Jr. (17)

C
Harry Ford (1)
Freddy Batista

LHP

LHSP
Juan Pinto (30)

LHRP
Jorge Benitez
Brayan Perez

RHP

RHSP
Bryce Miller (3)
Emerson Hancock (5)
Taylor Dollard (6)
Bryan Woo (7)
Walter Ford (13)
Michael Morales (18)
Ashton Izzi (20)
Tyler Gough (22)
Joseph Hernandez (28)
Juan Mercedes
Stephen Kolek
Logan Rinehart

RHRP
Prelander Berroa (10)
Isaiah Campbell (19)
Travis Kuhn (23)
Jean Muñoz
Chris Clarke
Juan Then
Jimmy Joyce
Ty Adcock
Kelvin Nuñez
Luis Curvelo

1 HARRY FORD, C

Born: February 21, 2003. **B-T:** R-R. **HT:** 5-10. **WT:** 200.
Drafted: HS—Kennesaw, GA, 2021 (1st round).
Signed by: John Wiedenbauer.

TRACK RECORD: Ford emerged as the top high school catcher in the 2021 draft class and became known as a "unicorn" due to his plus speed. The Mariners drafted him 12th overall after he wowed team officials, including general manager Jerry Dipoto, during a private batting practice, and they signed him for $4,366,400 to forgo a Georgia Tech commitment. Ford started his first full season slowly at Low-A Modesto as he battled shoulder tightness and a sprained ankle, but he took off once he got healthy. He hit .300 with a .942 OPS from June 1 through the end of the season and finished fourth in the league overall with a .425 on-base percentage. He capped his season by hitting .455 with three home runs for Great Britain, where his parents were born, in the World Baseball Classic qualifier to help the nation qualify for its first WBC.

SCOUTING REPORT: Ford is a rare athlete on the baseball diamond. He is built like a wrestler with a short, strong, compact frame but has the speed and explosiveness of a relay runner, posting plus run times and flying around the bases once he gets underway. Ford's strength and twitchiness serve him well in the batter's box, where he makes frequent contact with a simple, direct swing from the right side. He has a natural feel for driving balls the other way to right-center field and has the hand-eye coordination, barrel feel and patient approach to be an above-average hitter. He works counts and draws walks with his advanced pitch recognition and strike-zone discipline, helping him post a high OBP even when he's slumping. Ford will swing and miss against pitches up in the zone, but when he connects, he has the natural strength to drive balls over the fence from left-center to right-center. He crushes lefthanders in particular and has a chance to reach average power at maturity. Ford's athleticism allows him to make standout plays defensively behind the plate, including chasing popups far down the lines and making quick throws off balls in the dirt. He still has to improve his blocking and receiving, especially when catching good breaking stuff or pitchers with spotty control, but he has the physical traits and work ethic to keep average defense in reach. He has plus arm strength and is adept at throwing from multiple arm angles. Beyond his physical ability, Ford is a benevolent, thoughtful individual who demonstrates that he is invested in his teammates' well-being. He organized rides to the ballpark for

LARRY GOREN/FOUR SEAM IMAGES

BA GRADE	SCOUTING GRADES	
55 Risk: V. High	**Hit:** 55. **Power:** 50. **Run:** 60.	**Field:** 45. **Arm:** 60.

Projected future grades on 20-80 scouting scale

BEST TOOLS

BATTING

Best Hitter for Average	Cole Young
Best Power Hitter	Lazaro Montes
Best Strike-Zone Discipline	Harry Ford
Fastest Baserunner	Jonatan Clase
Best Athlete	Harry Ford

PITCHING

Best Fastball	Bryce Miller
Best Curveball	Juan Pinto
Best Slider	Taylor Dollard
Best Changeup	Emerson Hancock
Best Control	Taylor Dollard

FIELDING

Best Defensive Catcher	Harry Ford
Best Defensive Infielder	Axel Sanchez
Best Infield Arm	Milkar Perez
Best Defensive Outfielder	Cade Marlowe
Best Outfield Arm	Gabriel Gonzalez

teammates who didn't have cars at Modesto and brought a cake for every player who had a birthday during the season.

THE FUTURE: Ford has the foundational skills to catch, but with Cal Raleigh entrenched in Seattle, his athleticism will allow him to move to second or third base. Ford's combination of strength, speed and plate discipline gives him a chance to be an above-average, everyday regular in the Mariners' lineup.

Year	Age	Club (League)	Lvl	AVG	G	AB	R	H	2B	3B	HR	RBI	BB	SO	SB	OBP	SLG
2022	19	Modesto (CAL)	LoA	.274	104	390	89	107	23	4	11	65	88	115	23	.425	.438
Minor League Totals				.276	123	445	101	123	30	4	14	75	97	129	26	.422	.456

2 COLE YOUNG, SS

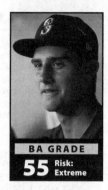

Born: July 29, 2003. **B-T:** L-R. **HT:** 6-3. **WT:** 190.
Drafted: HS—Wexford, PA, 2022 (1st round). **Signed by:** Jackson Laumann.

TRACK RECORD: Young starred on the high school showcase circuit as one of the top hitters in the 2022 draft class and batted .433 during his senior spring at North Allegheny High outside of Pittsburgh. The Mariners drafted him 21st overall and signed him for $3.3 million to forgo a Duke commitment. Young immediately lived up to his reputation as a premium hitter after signing. He hit .367 with as many walks as strikeouts in his pro debut.

SCOUTING REPORT: Young has few peers his age when it comes to pure hitting ability. He has a fast, direct swing from the left side and a preternatural ability to square up almost any pitch. He catches up to high velocity, stays back on secondary pitches and consistently puts himself in a good position to find the barrel. He controls the strike zone and doesn't miss pitches to hit,

BA GRADE

55 Risk: Extreme

making him a universally plus hitter and potentially a plus-plus one. Young primarily hits hard line drives from line to line, but he showed surprising power by hitting balls 20 rows deep at T-Mobile Park during a post-draft batting practice. He has an advanced feel for identifying pitches he can drive and could grow into 15-20 home run power as he gets stronger. Young is a smooth, reliable defender at shortstop who makes all the routine plays with easy actions. He may lose range as he gets bigger and move off the position, but his above-average speed and first-step quickness will allow him to be at least an average second baseman. He moves fluidly around the bag on double plays and makes every throw with above-average arm strength.

THE FUTURE: The Mariners internally compare Young to Daniel Murphy as a hitter and believe he could similarly hit around .300 annually. He'll open his first full season back at Modesto in 2023.

SCOUTING GRADES	Hitting: 60	Power: 45	Speed: 55	Fielding: 50	Arm: 55

Year	Age	Club (League)	Lvl	AVG	G	AB	R	H	2B	3B	HR	RBI	BB	SO	SB	OBP	SLG
2022	18	Mariners (ACL)	R	.333	7	21	6	7	1	1	0	5	4	4	3	.423	.476
2022	18	Modesto (CAL)	LoA	.385	10	39	11	15	0	0	2	9	4	4	1	.422	.538
Minor League Totals				.367	17	60	17	22	1	1	2	14	8	8	4	.423	.517

3 BRYCE MILLER, RHP

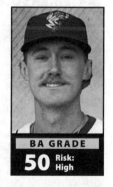

Born: August 23, 1998. **B-T:** R-R. **HT:** 6-2. **WT:** 180.
Drafted: Texas A&M, 2021 (4th round). **Signed by:** Derek Miller.

TRACK RECORD: Miller spent two seasons in the Texas A&M bullpen before moving to the rotation as a senior. He finished third on the team in strikeouts in his lone year as a starter in 2021 and was drafted by the Mariners in the fourth round, signing for $400,000. Miller initially faced questions about whether he would start or relieve in pro ball, but he made a strong case to remain a starter in his full-season debut in 2022. He flew up the Mariners' system to Double-A and led the organization with 163 strikeouts.

SCOUTING REPORT: Miller is an athletic, 6-foot-2 righthander with the best pure stuff in the Mariners' system. His plus-plus fastball sits 95-96 mph and regularly touches 100 with little effort out of a clean, electric delivery. He aggressively challenges hitters in the strike zone with his fastball and frequently

BA GRADE

50 Risk: High

gets swings and misses with his heater's late finish and explosion. Miller holds his velocity and mostly blows hitters away with his fastball, but his secondaries have progressed to become viable weapons. His mid-80s slider with hard break flashes above-average, and he has feel for an average mid-80s changeup with late fade, though it occasionally sails out of his hand. He also has a fringy but usable curveball in the low 80s. Miller streamlined his delivery as a pro and now pounds the strike zone with average control.

THE FUTURE: Miller has the potential to be a midrotation starter but can also slide into high-leverage relief if the Mariners need. He'll see Triple-A Tacoma in 2023 and could make his major league debut.

SCOUTING GRADES:	Fastball: 70	Curveball: 45	Slider: 55	Changeup: 50	Control: 50

Year	Age	Club (League)	Lvl	W	L	ERA	G	GS	IP	H	HR	BB	SO	BB/9	SO/9	WHIP	AVG
2022	23	Modesto (CAL)	LoA	0	0	1.69	1	1	5	5	0	2	3	3.4	5.1	1.31	.238
2022	23	Everett (NWL)	HiA	3	3	3.24	16	15	78	54	7	25	99	2.9	11.5	1.02	.194
2022	23	Arkansas (TL)	AA	4	1	3.20	10	10	51	34	3	19	61	3.4	10.8	1.05	.191
Minor League Totals				7	4	3.27	32	29	143	108	10	48	178	3.0	11.2	1.09	.208

4 GABRIEL GONZALEZ, OF

Born: January 4, 2004. **B-T:** B-R. **HT:** 5-10. **WT:** 180.
Signed: Venezuela, 2021. **Signed by:** Luis Martinez.

TRACK RECORD: Gonzalez signed with the Mariners for $1.3 million out of
Venezuela in 2021 and quickly established himself as one of the organization's
most promising offensive talents. He led the Dominican Summer League in
extra-base hits in his pro debut and continued to produce in his first season
stateside in 2022. Gonzalez hit a team-best .357 in the Arizona Complex
League and earned a promotion as an 18-year-old to Low-A Modesto.

SCOUTING REPORT: Gonzalez is a physical, righthanded power hitter with a
fast, powerful swing. He demolishes pitches in the strike zone with his quick
hands and plus power and is adept at driving balls the other way for opposite-
field home runs. He already posts exit velocities up to 116 mph—the same

BA GRADE

55 Risk: Extreme

maximum exit velocity as Austin Riley and C.J. Cron in the majors in 2022—and has the natural hand-
eye coordination, pitch recognition and contact skills to get to his power in games. Gonzalez doesn't swing
and miss much for a power hitter, but he frequently chases pitches out of the zone for weak contact and
has to improve his pitch selection. His hand speed, strength and natural feel for contact give him a chance
to be a fringy to average hitter if he improves his swing decisions. Gonzalez has a thick, physically mature
body and has already slowed to a fringe-average runner. He is limited to a corner outfield spot defensively,
where he has marginal range but good instincts and plus-plus arm strength. He projects to be a fringy to
average defensive right fielder.

THE FUTURE: Gonzalez has the thump to be a middle-of-the-order power threat, but he'll need to improve
his swing decisions and monitor his conditioning. He should reach High-A Everett in 2023.

SCOUTING GRADES	Hitting: 45	Power: 60	Speed: 40	Fielding: 45	Arm: 70

Year	Age	Club (League)	Lvl	AVG	G	AB	R	H	2B	3B	HR	RBI	BB	SO	SB	OBP	SLG
2022	18	Mariners (ACL)	R	.357	35	126	20	45	9	0	5	17	8	21	5	.421	.548
2022	18	Modesto (CAL)	LoA	.286	32	126	31	36	5	1	2	17	13	21	4	.400	.389
Minor League Totals				.307	121	440	90	135	29	5	14	70	42	78	18	.393	.491

5 EMERSON HANCOCK, RHP

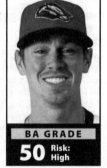

Born: May 31, 1999. **B-T:** R-R. **HT:** 6-4. **WT:** 213.
Drafted: Georgia, 2020 (1st round). **Signed by:** John Wiedenbauer.

TRACK RECORD: A 38th-round pick of the D-backs out of high school,
Hancock became one of the top pitchers in the Southeastern Conference at
Georgia and was drafted sixth overall by the Mariners in the shortened 2020
draft. He pitched just 44.2 innings in his pro debut due to recurring shoulder
soreness and missed the first six weeks of the 2022 season with a lat strain, but
he stayed healthy after he returned in May and became a steady presence in
Double-A Arkansas' rotation. He earned a selection to the Futures Game and
struck out the side in his lone inning.

SCOUTING REPORT: Hancock is a lean, 6-foot-4 righthander who lives on
weak contact rather than swings and misses. His fastball sits 92-94 mph and

BA GRADE

50 Risk: High

touches 96, and he's able to both ride it at the top of the zone or sink it. His mid-80s changeup with late
drop is a plus pitch that pairs particularly well with his sinker and is his go-to out pitch. He is comfortable throwing his changeup in any count to lefthanded and righthanded hitters and uses it to induce a
heavy dose of ground balls. Hancock's low-80s slider is a fringy pitch that lacks power or movement, but
he keeps it off of barrels to avoid damage. Hancock's control is merely average and none of his pitches
is overwhelming, but he's a smart competitor who reads swings and sequences well. Hancock's primary
concern is his health. His short arm action and low arm slot put a lot of strain on his shoulder, leading to
concerns about his durability. He has never pitched more than 100 innings in a season and has completed
six innings just twice in 33 professional starts.

THE FUTURE: The Mariners acknowledge Hancock will likely fall short of his draft status, but they believe
he has a chance to be an effective No. 4 or 5 starter.

SCOUTING GRADES:	Fastball: 55	Slider: 45	Changeup: 60	Control: 50

Year	Age	Club (League)	Lvl	W	L	ERA	G	GS	IP	H	HR	BB	SO	BB/9	SO/9	WHIP	AVG
2022	23	Arkansas (TL)	AA	7	4	3.75	21	21	98	80	16	38	92	3.5	8.4	1.20	.219
Minor League Totals				10	5	3.40	33	33	143	109	17	55	135	3.5	8.5	1.15	.208

422 · Baseball America 2023 Prospect Handbook   **BaseballAmerica**.com

6 TAYLOR DOLLARD, RHP

Born: August 17, 1999. **B-T:** R-R. **HT:** 6-3. **WT:** 195.
Drafted: Cal Poly, 2020 (5th round). **Signed by:** Ryan Holmes.

BA GRADE
50 Risk: High

TRACK RECORD: Dollard spent his first two seasons in Cal Poly's bullpen and starred in the Cape Cod League before moving into the Mustangs' rotation as a junior. He made four starts before the coronavirus pandemic canceled the 2020 season, but that was enough for the Mariners to draft him in the fifth round and sign him for $406,600. Dollard struggled at the Class A levels in his pro debut, but improvements to his stuff and movement led to a breakout 2022 season at Double-A Arkansas. He led the minors with 16 wins.

SCOUTING REPORT: Dollard has long been a smooth athlete with a clean delivery and plus control, but his stuff was a tick light. That changed after he hit the weight room hard after the 2021 season and came back throwing 1-2 mph harder with improved vertical ride. Dollard's fastball now ranges from 91-94 mph with above-average extension that helps it jump on hitters faster than they expect. His primary offspeed pitch is a plus slider that sits 78-82 mph with a long arc and bend. Dollard's slider lacks exceptional power or spin, but he has exquisite command of the pitch and is able to locate it on the corners where hitters can't do anything. He also has an average low-80s split-changeup and a soft, vertical curveball in the high 60s he'll throw to disrupt hitters' timing. Dollard's stuff isn't overwhelming, but he is a fearless competitor who goes right after hitters and quickly gets ahead in counts. He effectively exploits batters' holes with his plus command and has the intelligence and athleticism to make quick adjustments.

THE FUTURE: Dollard projects to be a solid back-of-the-rotation starter who can slide into long relief as needed, similar to Collin McHugh. He'll head to Triple-A Tacoma in 2023.

SCOUTING GRADES:	Fastball: 50	Curveball: 45	Slider: 60	Changeup: 50	Control: 60

Year	Age	Club (League)	Lvl	W	L	ERA	G	GS	IP	H	HR	BB	SO	BB/9	SO/9	WHIP	AVG
2022	23	Arkansas (TL)	AA	16	2	2.25	27	27	144	106	9	31	131	1.9	8.2	0.95	.203
Minor League Totals				25	6	3.47	46	45	249	224	23	55	264	2.0	9.5	1.12	.236

7 BRYAN WOO, RHP

Born: January 30, 2000. **B-T:** R-R. **HT:** 6-2. **WT:** 205.
Drafted: Cal Poly, 2021 (6th round). **Signed by:** Chris Horn.

BA GRADE
50 Risk: High

TRACK RECORD: Woo fell under the radar in high school but pitched so well in the Alaska League after his senior year that teams tried to sign him as a nondrafted free agent. He instead stuck with his commitment to Cal Poly, where his and spent three seasons bouncing between the bullpen and rotation, capped by a breakout junior year that was cut short by Tommy John surgery. The Mariners drafted Woo in the sixth round in 2021, signed him for $318,200 and guided him through the rehab process. Woo zipped up three levels to High-A in 2022, then emerged in the Arizona Fall League with an 0.84 ERA in five starts.

SCOUTING REPORT: Woo is an athletic, 6-foot-2 righthander with an easy, explosive delivery. His plus fastball sits 93-94 mph and touches 96 with above-average ride that helps it miss bats in the zone. He primarily pitches east to west with his fastball, but he has the command to elevate it and get chase swings above the zone. Woo complements his fastball with a sweeping, mid-80s slider that he commands to his glove side and plays well against righthanded hitters. The quality of his slider can be inconsistent, but it generally ranges from average to plus and is consistently competitive. Woo's firm, 87-90 mph changeup has progressed rapidly in a short time and flashes above-average with late drop and run. He is a good athlete with above-average control, though he occasionally gets too much of the plate. His command should sharpen the further he moves away from surgery.

THE FUTURE: Woo has the ingredients to be a mid-to-back-of-the-rotation starter, but he has to show he can maintain his stuff over a full season. That will be his primary goal at Double-A Arkansas in 2023.

SCOUTING GRADES:	Fastball: 60	Slider: 55	Changeup: 50	Control: 55

Year	Age	Club (League)	Lvl	W	L	ERA	G	GS	IP	H	HR	BB	SO	BB/9	SO/9	WHIP	AVG
2022	22	Mariners (ACL)	R	0	0	0.00	3	3	5	3	0	0	9	0.0	17.4	0.64	.176
2022	22	Modesto (CAL)	LoA	0	1	3.98	6	6	20	18	2	6	29	2.7	12.8	1.18	.240
2022	22	Everett (NWL)	HiA	1	3	4.78	7	7	32	32	2	16	46	4.5	12.9	1.50	.254
Minor League Totals				1	4	4.11	16	16	57	53	4	22	84	3.5	13.3	1.32	.243

8 MICHAEL ARROYO, SS

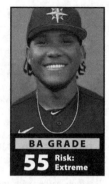

BA GRADE

55 Risk: Extreme

Born: November 3, 2004. **B-T:** R-R. **HT:** 5-10. **WT:** 180.
Signed: Colombia, 2022. **Signed by:** David Brito.

TRACK RECORD: Arroyo spent most of his youth representing Colombia at international tournaments across the globe, including in the United States, Panama, Mexico and the Bahamas, and established himself as one of the top players in the 2022 international class. The Mariners signed him on the first day of the 2022 signing period for $1.375 million, the largest bonus given to a Colombian amateur. Arroyo immediately impressed team officials when he reported to the Mariners' Dominican complex and continued to stand out in his pro debut in the Dominican Summer League. He hit a team-best .314 and had nearly as many walks (27) as strikeouts (33).

SCOUTING REPORT: Arroyo is an exceptionally mature hitter for his age. He has a preternatural feel for the strike zone, is extremely disciplined and quickly adjusts to different velocities and pitch types. He rarely chases out of the zone and does a good job identifying pitches to drive. Arroyo has quick hands and generates a lot of contact with a short, direct swing from the right side. He can manipulate the barrel and covers the entire plate, which gives opponents few zones to attack and helps him project to be a plus hitter. Arroyo doesn't hit the ball overly hard, but he has room to get stronger and his balls carry well off the barrel. Arroyo is firmly a bat-first player. He is a shortstop now, but he's an average runner with fringy range who will be stretched at the position as he matures. He is a reliable defender with solid hands and an average arm and should be an average defensive second baseman.

THE FUTURE: Arroyo's swing mechanics and overall skill set draw frequent comparisons with Howie Kendrick. He projects to be a similarly contact-driven second baseman and will make his U.S. debut in the Arizona Complex League in 2023.

SCOUTING GRADES	Hitting: 60	Power: 40	Speed: 50	Fielding: 50	Arm: 50

Year	Age	Club (League)	Lvl	AVG	G	AB	R	H	2B	3B	HR	RBI	BB	SO	SB	OBP	SLG
2022	17	Mariners (DSL)	R	.314	49	153	46	48	10	2	4	22	27	33	4	.457	.484
Minor League Totals				.314	49	153	46	48	10	2	4	22	27	33	4	.457	.484

9 TYLER LOCKLEAR, 3B

BA GRADE

50 Risk: High

Born: November 24, 2000. **B-T:** R-R. **HT:** 6-3. **WT:** 210.
Drafted: Virginia Commonwealth, 2022 (2nd round). **Signed by:** Jackson Laumann.

TRACK RECORD: A former tight end who was recruited to play college football, Locklear emerged as one of the country's top power hitters at Virginia Commonwealth. He tied for the Cape Cod League lead with nine home runs in 2021 after his sophomore year. He followed by setting VCU's single-season record with 20 home runs as a junior. The Mariners drafted him in the second round in 2022 and signed him for $1,276,500. Locklear quickly moved to Low-A Modesto after signing and caught fire late, bashing seven home runs in his final 16 games.

SCOUTING REPORT: Locklear stands an imposing, muscular 6-foot-3 and is one of the strongest players his age. He crushes balls to all fields with plus-plus raw power—including home runs the opposite way off of right-field scoreboards—and posts elite top-end exit velocities. Locklear has some stiffness to his swing and his bat moves in and out of the zone quickly, but he controls the strike zone. His pitch selection gives him a chance to be a fringy hitter with plus power if he can make swing adjustments against higher-level pitchers. Locklear is a decent athlete for his size and has good hands at third base, but his footwork and actions need to be softened and his arm is a tick below-average. He will likely move to first base and could potentially end up in left field. He has below-average speed but makes up for it with good instincts on the bases.

THE FUTURE: Locklear has a chance to emerge as a power-hitting, everyday first baseman if he makes the necessary swing adjustments. He'll open at High-A Everett in 2023.

SCOUTING GRADES	Hitting: 45	Power: 60	Speed: 40	Fielding: 40	Arm: 50

Year	Age	Club (League)	Lvl	AVG	G	AB	R	H	2B	3B	HR	RBI	BB	SO	SB	OBP	SLG
2022	21	Mariners (ACL)	R	.333	2	6	0	2	1	0	0	2	1	1	0	.556	.500
2022	21	Modesto (CAL)	LoA	.282	29	117	19	33	5	0	7	29	7	29	0	.353	.504
Minor League Totals				.285	31	123	19	35	6	0	7	31	8	30	0	.366	.504

10 PRELANDER BERROA, RHP

Born: April 18, 2000. **B-T:** R-R. **HT:** 5-11. **WT:** 170.
Signed: Dominican Republic, 2016. **Signed by:** Fred Guerrero (Twins).

TRACK RECORD: Berroa initially worked out for teams as an infielder before converting to pitching and signed with the Twins for $200,000 in 2016 on the first day of the 2016 international signing period. The Twins traded Berroa to the Giants as one of three prospects for reliever Sam Dyson at the 2019 trade deadline, and the Giants subsequently flipped Berroa to the Mariners for utility infielder Donnie Walton early in the 2022 season. Berroa took off after the trade and had his best season under the Mariners' tutelage. He finished with a career-low 2.68 ERA, a career-high 150 strikeouts and reached Double-A for the first time.

BA GRADE

50 Risk: High

SCOUTING REPORT: Berroa is undersized at 5-foot-11 but pitches bigger than his stature. His explosive, plus-plus fastball sits 96-99 mph and touches 101-102 with late life to get swings and misses in the strike zone. He began throwing his slider more after joining the Mariners and morphed it into a plus downer in the upper 80s that gets swings over the top. He is able to land his slider for strikes early in counts in addition to putting batters away with it. He also has a firm, well below-average changeup in the low 90s he rarely throws. Berroa gets ugly swings from good hitters, but his control is below-average and he struggles to stay focused for more than a few innings at a time. He no longer throws balls to the backstop as he did in his younger years, but his effortful delivery will always limit his strike-throwing. He pitched fewer than five innings in 21 of his 26 starts even during his breakout 2022 season.

THE FUTURE: Berroa will continue starting, but his size, durability and control will make him a hard-throwing reliever in the majors. He has a chance to be a setup man who pitches seventh and eighth innings if his control improves another tick.

| SCOUTING GRADES: | Fastball: 70 | | Slider: 60 | | | Changeup: 30 | | Control: 40 | |

Year	Age	Club (League)	Lvl	W	L	ERA	G	GS	IP	H	HR	BB	SO	BB/9	SO/9	WHIP	AVG
2022	22	Everett (NWL)	HiA	2	2	2.41	13	13	52	29	2	32	81	5.5	13.9	1.17	.160
2022	22	Eugene (NWL)	HiA	0	0	0.68	4	4	13	5	0	6	16	4.1	10.8	0.83	.122
2022	22	Arkansas (TL)	AA	2	1	4.37	9	9	35	20	3	25	53	6.4	13.6	1.29	.167
Minor League Totals				16	11	3.72	81	72	309	239	24	171	397	5.0	11.6	1.33	.215

11 JONATAN CLASE, OF

Born: May 23, 2002. **B-T:** B-R. **HT:** 5-9. **WT:** 180.
Signed: Dominican Republic, 2018. **Signed by:** Audo Vicente.

TRACK RECORD: Clase signed with the Mariners for $35,000 in 2018 and quickly showed some of the most prolific tools in the system. The coronavirus pandemic and repeated hamstring and quad strains limited him to just 70 games in his first three years as a professional, but he stayed healthy in 2022 and put together a productive season at Low-A Modesto. He led the California League with 11 triples and 55 stolen bases and showed exciting power-speed potential, but he also showed a concerning lack of plate discipline.

SCOUTING REPORT: Clase is the fastest and most electric player in the Mariners system by a fair margin. He is a strong, twitchy athlete with plus-plus speed and can change games with both his power and his legs. He is a switch-hitter who can drive the ball from both sides of the plate and has grown into plus raw power, particularly from the left side. Clase's speed and strength are tantalizing, but he's a wild free swinger who takes big hacks and lacks instincts in the batter's box. He struggles with changing speeds and doesn't make adjustments, limiting him to a well below-average hitter. Clase's speed makes him a threat on the bases even when he gets bad jumps. He covers wide swaths of ground in center field and projects to be an above-average defender with an average arm.

THE FUTURE: Clase has the tools to be an everyday center fielder, but he will have to improve his approach against higher-level pitching to get there. He'll begin 2023 at High-A Everett.

| BA GRADE: 50/Very High | Hit: 30 | | Power: 50 | Speed: 70 | | Fielding: 55 | | Arm: 50 | |

Year	Age	Club (League)	Lvl	AVG	G	AB	R	H	2B	3B	HR	RBI	BB	SO	SB	OBP	SLG
2022	20	Modesto (CAL)	LoA	.267	107	423	91	113	22	11	13	49	65	133	55	.373	.463
Minor League Totals				.276	184	695	167	192	35	18	17	81	122	204	102	.391	.452

12 ZACH DeLOACH, OF

Born: Aug. **18, 1998. B-T:** L-R. **HT:** 6-1. **WT:** 205.
Drafted: Texas A&M, 2020 (2nd round). **Signed by:** Derek Miller.

TRACK RECORD: DeLoach struggled his first two seasons at Texas A&M but parlayed a strong showing in the Cape Cod League into a breakout junior year before the pandemic prematurely ended the season. The Mariners believed in DeLoach's breakout and drafted him in the second round, No. 43 overall, and signed him for $1,729,800. DeLoach rose rapidly to Double-A Arkansas in his pro debut, but he plateaued at the level in 2022. He posted a .258 batting average and .778 OPS for the Travelers, almost exactly league average in both categories.

SCOUTING REPORT: DeLoach is a solid player who does many things well but nothing exceptional. His best trait is his ability to recognize pitches and control the strike zone from the left side. He's a patient hitter who consistently puts together high-quality at-bats and doesn't chase, leading to high walk totals and solid on-base percentages. DeLoach has a sound lefthanded swing that makes a fair amount of contact, especially against fastballs, but he mostly hits the ball on the ground. His power is fringy at best and he'll need to drive the ball more to be an average hitter. He struggles against same-side pitching and fits best as part of a platoon. DeLoach is limited to a corner outfield spot defensively as a fringe-average runner whose range and reads need improvement. His below-average arm fits best in left field.

THE FUTURE: DeLoach projects to be a platoon outfielder with his ability to make contact and get on base against righthanded pitching. He'll open at Triple-A Tacoma in 2023.

| BA Grade: 45/Medium | | Hit: 50 | | | Power: 40 | | Speed: 50 | | | Fielding: 45 | | Arm: 40 | |

Year	Age	Club (League)	Lvl	AVG	G	AB	R	H	2B	3B	HR	RBI	BB	SO	SB	OBP	SLG
2022	23	Arkansas (TL)	AA	.258	114	418	79	108	15	3	14	73	71	119	4	.369	.409
Minor League Totals				.268	221	852	163	228	48	7	28	132	131	240	11	.371	.439

13 WALTER FORD, RHP

Born: December 28, 2004. **B-T:** R-R. **HT:** 6-3. **WT:** 198.
Drafted: HS—Pace, Fla., 2022 (2nd round supplemental). **Signed by:** Rob Mummau.

TRACK RECORD: Originally a top prospect in the 2023 class, Ford reclassified for the 2022 draft after a strong showing on the summer showcase circuit that included pitching three scoreless innings for USA Baseball's 18U National team. He followed with a solid spring at Pace (Fla.) High and was drafted by the Mariners in the supplemental second round, signing for $1.25 million to forgo an Alabama commitment. Ford did not pitch after signing but quickly built a popular public following. He is very active on social media and goes by the nickname "Vanilla Missile", which he has branded on T-shirts, hats and other accessories he sells online.

SCOUTING REPORT: Ford already possesses loud stuff and has room to grow into even more velocity. His fastball sits 92-94 mph and touches 96-97 out of an athletic, powerful delivery. He still has room to get stronger in his 6-foot-3 frame and could touch triple digits as he reaches physical maturity. Ford complements his fastball with a potentially above-average curveball with 11-to-5 shape and big depth. His above-average slider features similar shape but is thrown harder. He also has a low-80s changeup he shows feel for but doesn't throw often. Ford has a lot of moving parts in his delivery, including an arm plunge in the back, and isn't always synced up with his timing and release point. He flashes average control when he's on time and has the ability to miss bats with three different pitches.

THE FUTURE: Ford's arm strength is exciting, but he is very young and has a lot of refinement ahead with his stuff and delivery. He will make his pro debut in 2023.

| BA Grade: 50/Extreme | | Fastball: 60 | | Curveball: 55 | | Slider: 50 | | Changeup: 40 | | Control: 50 | |

Year	Age	Club (League)	Lvl	W	L	ERA	G	GS	IP	H	HR	BB	SO	BB/9	SO/9	WHIP	AVG
2022	17	Did not play															

14 LAZARO MONTES, OF

Born: Oct. **22, 2004. B-T:** L-R. **HT:** 6-3. **WT:** 210.
Signed: Cuba, 2022. **Signed by:** Ismael Rosado.

TRACK RECORD: Montes grew up in Cuba and moved to the Dominican Republic to train with renowned hitting instructor Aldo Ramirez, who famously trained Astros slugger Yordan Alvarez. Montes quickly emerged as a top prospect under Ramirez's tutelage and signed with the Mariners for $2.5 million on the first day of the 2022 international signing period. Montes showcased his power with 10 home runs in his professional debut in the Dominican Summer League after signing, but he also had an alarming 33% strikeout rate against low-quality pitching.

SCOUTING REPORT: Montes is a physical specimen with tremendous strength. He makes loud contact to all fields from the left side and already posts some of the highest exit velocities in the Mariners organization. He destroys balls with true, 80-grade raw power and is a threat to leave the park at any time. Montes' power is mesmerizing, but he has massive holes in his swing that limit his ability to make contact. He crushes fastballs and breaking balls down in the zone but swings through against anything above his waist. He'll have to adjust to pitches up in the zone to be even a below-average hitter. Montes is a well below-average runner, but he's a good athlete with better body control than his speed suggests and has a chance to get faster with the right coaching. His glove, hands and arm have all improved defensively and he has a chance to be an average left fielder, albeit one with limited range.

THE FUTURE: Montes has the potential to be a 30-plus home run threat, but only if he closes the hole in his swing. He will make his stateside debut in the Rookie-level Arizona League in 2023.

BA Grade: 50/Extreme		Hit: 30		Power: 60		Speed: 30			Fielding: 50		Arm: 40	
Year	Age	Club (League)	Lvl	AVG	G	AB	R	H	2B	3B	HR	RBI	BB	SO	SB	OBP	SLG
2022	17	Mariners (DSL)	R	.284	55	176	34	50	13	5	10	41	35	74	3	.422	.585
Minor League Totals				.284	55	176	34	50	13	5	10	41	35	74	3	.422	.585

15 CADE MARLOWE, OF

Born: June 24, 1997. **B-T:** L-R. **HT:** 6-2. **WT:** 220.
Drafted: West Georgia, 2019 (20th round). **Signed by:** John Wiedenbauer.

TRACK RECORD: Marlowe set Division II West Georgia's single-season and career stolen base records and signed with the Mariners for $5,000 as a 20th-round senior sign in 2019. Expected to be organizational depth, Marlowe instead showed some of the best tools and physicality in the system and had a breakout season across the Class A levels in 2021. He proved it wasn't a fluke in 2022, and posted his second consecutive season with at least 20 doubles, 20 home runs, 100 RBIs and 20 stolen bases as he rose from Double-A to Triple-A. The Mariners added him to the taxi squad on their Wild Card Series roster after the season.

SCOUTING REPORT: Marlowe is a strong, athletic lefthanded hitter with impact tools despite being old for a prospect. He has above-average power and drives balls to the middle of the field to rack up doubles and homers. He makes loud contact when he connects and is a threat on the bases with his plus speed and sharp base-stealing acumen. Marlowe has decent strike-zone discipline, but his swing is stiff and he whiffs in the zone too often. His strength and discipline give him a chance to be a below-average hitter, but he'll likely struggle against better arms. Marlowe's speed and instincts make him an above-average defender at all three outfield positions. He has an elite work ethic and is extremely intelligent–he planned to go to medical school before being drafted.

THE FUTURE: Marlowe's speed, strength and ability to play all three outfield spots give him a chance to stick as a reserve outfielder. His major league debut should come in 2023.

BA Grade: 40/Medium		Hit: 40		Power: 50		Speed: 60			Fielding: 55		Arm: 45	
Year	Age	Club (League)	Lvl	AVG	G	AB	R	H	2B	3B	HR	RBI	BB	SO	SB	OBP	SLG
2022	25	Arkansas (TL)	AA	.291	120	447	75	130	18	4	20	86	55	133	36	.380	.483
2022	25	Tacoma (PCL)	AAA	.250	13	52	8	13	3	1	3	16	7	23	6	.350	.519
Minor League Totals				.285	301	1140	199	325	61	18	52	239	149	350	76	.373	.507

16 AXEL SANCHEZ, SS

Born: Dec. 10, 2002. **B-T:** R-R. **HT:** 6-0. **WT:** 170.
Signed: Dominican Republic, 2019. **Signed by:** Audo Vicente/Emilio De Los Santos

TRACK RECORD: Sanchez signed with the Mariners for $290,000 when he was 16 and had to wait two seasons to make his pro debut due to the coronavirus pandemic. He failed to stand out to Mariners officials in his early years, but the organization's coaches raved about his instincts and believed he was on the verge of a breakout. That prediction came true in 2022 as Sanchez rose three levels to High-A in an eye-opening season. He set new career highs in batting average (.285), home runs (10) and OPS (.875) and emerged as the system's best defensive shortstop.

SCOUTING REPORT: Sanchez originally got too heavy after he signed, but after slimming down, he developed a newfound explosiveness. With his trimmer build, he's now a plus defender at shortstop with soft hands, above-average range and a plus, accurate arm that plays up with a quick release. He is adept at making plays up the middle and moves fluidly around the infield despite fringy speed, showing an advanced feel for positioning and taking good angles to the ball. Sanchez swings hard at the plate and makes loud contact when he finds the barrel. He has above-average raw power and flashes the ability to get to it, but his swing drags and his bat path can be overly steep, leading to concerns he'll be a below-average hitter against better pitching.

THE FUTURE: Sanchez's shortstop defense gives him a path to the majors even if his bat falls behind. If he can make the necessary swing adjustments, he has a chance to be an everyday player.

| BA Grade: 45/High | | Hit: 40 | | Power: 45 | | Speed: 45 | | | Fielding: 60 | | Arm: 60 | | |

Year	Age	Club (League)	Lvl	AVG	G	AB	R	H	2B	3B	HR	RBI	BB	SO	SB	OBP	SLG
2022	19	Mariners (ACL)	R	.267	27	86	15	23	5	2	2	9	11	20	9	.354	.442
2022	19	Modesto (CAL)	LoA	.305	33	131	27	40	13	2	8	37	15	42	4	.401	.618
2022	19	Everett (NWL)	HiA	.235	8	34	0	8	1	0	0	1	0	9	0	.235	.265
Minor League Totals				.274	120	413	75	113	26	4	11	76	46	117	28	.362	.436

17 ROBERT PEREZ JR., 1B

Born: June 26, 2000. **B-T:** R-R. **HT:** 6-1. **WT:** 170.
Signed: Venezuela, 2016. **Signed by:** Emilio Carrasquel.

TRACK RECORD: Perez is the son of former Blue Jays outfielder Robert Perez Sr. but wasn't a top prospect as an amateur despite his big league pedigree. The Mariners signed Perez for $75,000 during the 2016 signing period and kept him in short-season ball for almost three years, where he largely failed to distinguish himself. Perez returned from the coronavirus shutdown vastly improved and showed some of the best power in the Low-A California League in 2021. He took another step forward in 2022, and led the Mariners systems in home runs (27), RBIs (114), runs scored (100) and total bases (254) as he rose to High-A Everett and won the Mariners minor league hitter of the year award.

SCOUTING REPORT: Perez is a strong, physical masher with tremendous strength from the right side. He has plus-plus raw power and gets to most of it in games, hitting gargantuan home runs to his pull side and posting exit velocities on par with top major league sluggers. Perez destroys balls when he makes contact, but he is a dead-pull hitter who pulls off the ball and doesn't cover the outer half of the plate. He struggles with top-end velocity and projects to be a below-average hitter who has to feast on mistakes. Perez is a threat offensively but an enormous liability defensively. He is limited to first base and struggles to field routine grounders or make easy scoops with his hard hands and limited athleticism.

THE FUTURE: Perez's power gives him a chance to emerge in the majors despite his shortcomings, likely as a DH. He'll open at Double-A Arkansas in 2023.

| BA Grade: 45/High | | Hit: 30 | | Power: 60 | | Speed: 30 | | | Fielding: 30 | | Arm: 40 | | |

Year	Age	Club (League)	Lvl	AVG	G	AB	R	H	2B	3B	HR	RBI	BB	SO	SB	OBP	SLG
2022	22	Modesto (CAL)	LoA	.270	92	345	78	93	18	1	20	87	48	108	5	.369	.501
2022	22	Everett (NWL)	HiA	.342	35	120	22	41	6	1	7	27	23	34	1	.477	.583
Minor League Totals				.262	399	1501	245	393	78	5	61	290	169	455	14	.353	.442

18 MICHAEL MORALES, RHP

Born: Aug. 13, 2002. **B-T:** R-R. **HT:** 6-2. **WT:** 205.
Drafted: HS—Enola, Pa., 2021 (3rd round). **Signed by:** Dave Pepe.

TRACK RECORD: Morales emerged as an intriguing, projectable pitcher out of cold-weather Pennsylvania in the 2021 draft and signed with the Mariners for an above-slot $1.5 million after they selected him in the third round. He made his pro debut at Low-A Modesto in 2022 and displayed promising traits, but he also showed his stuff wasn't quite ready for full-season ball. Morales posted a 5.91 ERA, worst in the California League among qualified pitchers, and gave up 143 hits, tied for most in the league.

SCOUTING REPORT: Morales has the foundation to be a major league starter despite his poor debut. He has an athletic, 6-foot-2 frame and a polished, repeatable delivery that allows him to pound the strike zone with above-average control. He possesses a unique ability to shape his pitches and can throw four offerings for strikes at any time. Morales' pitchability and control are in place, but he needs to get stronger to improve his stuff. His fastball features below-average velocity at 89-92 mph and his upper-70s curveball needs more power and bite to reach its above-average potential. He added a mid-80s slider to try and give him another power offering, but it's a well below-average pitch that is still developing. His fringy changeup remains a work in progress. Morales is a smart, cerebral individual who actively seeks out information to improve, but his commitment to working out and getting stronger left Mariners officials underwhelmed in his pro debut.

THE FUTURE: Morales has the potential to be a back-of-the-rotation starter, but only if he gets stronger and grows into more velocity. He'll head to High-A Everett in 2023.

BA Grade: 45/Very High	Fastball: 50	Curveball: 55	Slider: 30	Changeup: 45	Control: 55

Year	Age	Club (League)	Lvl	W	L	ERA	G	GS	IP	H	HR	BB	SO	BB/9	SO/9	WHIP	AVG
2022	19	Modesto (CAL)	LoA	5	7	5.91	26	26	120	143	14	50	125	3.7	9.3	1.60	.292
Minor League Totals				5	7	6.01	27	27	121	145	14	51	126	3.8	9.3	1.62	.294

19 ISAIAH CAMPBELL, RHP

Born: August 15, 1997. **B-T:** R-R. **HT:** 6-4. **WT:** 230.
Drafted: Arkansas, 2019 (2nd round supplemental). **Signed by:** Ben Collman.
TRACK RECORD: Campbell struggled with elbow injuries as an underclassman at Arkansas but finally stayed healthy and became the Razorbacks' ace as a redshirt junior in 2019. The Mariners drafted him in the supplemental second round on the strength of that showing and signed him for $850,000. Campbell again ran into health issues after signing and made only five appearances in his pro debut before having season-ending surgery to clean up loose bodies in his right elbow, but he returned in 2022 and thrived with a move to the bullpen. He led all Mariners relief prospects (min. 25 appearances) with a 1.57 ERA and recorded 11 saves as he rose from High-A to Double-A.
SCOUTING REPORT: Previously a four-pitch starter, Campbell has streamlined his arsenal in relief and now throws his fastball and slider exclusively. His above-average fastball sits 94-96 mph and touches 98-99 out of his big, powerful frame and gets swings and misses up in the strike zone. He throws an above-average, 82-84 mph slider more frequently than his fastball and has a good feel for locating it, frequently gets swings and misses and weak contact off the edges of the plate. Campbell doesn't throw a changeup, but his slider is effective against lefties and helps him handle them. He throws strikes with above-average control and walked only three batters in 28 innings of relief.
THE FUTURE: Campbell has a chance to rise as a middle reliever if he can avoid further injuries. He'll see Triple-A Tacoma in 2023.

BA Grade: 40/High	Fastball: 55	Slider: 55	Control: 55

Year	Age	Club (League)	Lvl	W	L	ERA	G	GS	IP	H	HR	BB	SO	BB/9	SO/9	WHIP	AVG
2022	24	Everett (NWL)	HiA	1	0	0.82	19	4	33	18	2	10	35	2.7	9.5	0.85	.159
2022	24	Arkansas (TL)	AA	0	4	3.46	14	0	13	13	2	2	24	1.4	16.6	1.15	.250
Minor League Totals				4	5	1.79	38	4	65	44	6	18	79	2.5	10.9	0.95	.190

20 ASHTON IZZI, RHP

Born: Nov. 18, 2003. **B-T:** R-R. **HT:** 6-3. **WT:** 170.
Drafted: HS—Oswego, Ill., 2022 (4th round). **Signed by:** Joe Saunders.
TRACK RECORD: Izzi emerged as one of the top high school pitching prospects in the 2022 draft class with a breakout showing at the WWBA World Championships in Jupiter, Fla. He teamed with lefthander Noah Schultz to give Oswego (Ill.) East High one of the top high school pitching duos in the nation in the spring and was drafted by the Mariners in the fourth round, signing for an above-slot $1.1 million to forgo a Wichita State commitment. Izzi did not pitch after signing, but he impressed at the Mariners' postseason fall development camp.
SCOUTING REPORT: Izzi has a long, lean build that screams projection and upside. His fastball sits 92-96 mph out of a clean delivery and arm action and should tick up as he adds weight and strength to his frame. His best secondary pitch is an above-average changeup with armside run that sits in the mid-80s. Izzi's breaking balls are targeted areas for growth. His curveball shows good shape and he has added a slider with intriguing spin rates, but both pitches need more power and finish. Izzi is still a gangly, long-limbed teenager and should add the strength and stability to finish pitches as he gets more physical. He throws strikes with average control.
THE FUTURE: Izzi has intriguing rotation potential, but he has years of strength gains ahead. He will make his pro debut in 2023.

BA Grade: 45/Extreme	Fastball: 55	Curveball: 45	Slider: 40	Changeup: 55	Control: 50

Year	Age	Club (League)	Lvl	W	L	ERA	G	GS	IP	H	HR	BB	SO	BB/9	SO/9	WHIP	AVG
2022	18	Did not play															

21 SPENCER PACKARD, OF

Born: Oct. 12, 1997. **B-T:** L-L. **HT:** 6-1. **WT:** 205.
Drafted: Campbell, 2021 (9th round). **Signed by:** Ty Holub.

TRACK RECORD: Packard began his college career at Arizona Western JC before transferring to Campbell, where he started three years in the Camels outfield and led the Big South Conference in hits and RBIs as a senior. The Mariners drafted him in the ninth round and gave him a $25,000 bonus as a senior sign. Packard opened his first full season at High-A Everett in 2022 and quickly asserted himself as a player to watch in the Mariners system. He finished among Everett's leaders in hits, doubles, home runs and RBIs despite missing more than two months with a strained hamstring and finished in the Arizona Fall League.
SCOUTING REPORT: Packard lacks exceptional physicality or tools, but he can hit. He calmly separates balls and strikes with a polished, patient approach from the left side and hits balls where they're pitched, using the whole field with a quick, inside-out swing. He has the power to drive balls out to his pullside and projects to be an average hitter who could reach double digit home runs given enough at-bats. Packard doesn't offer much defensively and will have to hit his way to the majors. He's a well below-average runner with limited athleticism and is a below-average defender in left field.
THE FUTURE: Packard's hitting ability gives him a chance to rise as an extra outfielder or callup option. He'll open at Double-A Arkansas in 2023.

BA Grade: 40/High			Hit: 50		Power: 45		Speed: 30		Fielding: 40		Arm: 40		

Year	Age	Club (League)	Lvl	AVG	G	AB	R	H	2B	3B	HR	RBI	BB	SO	SB	OBP	SLG
2022	24	Mariners (ACL)	R	.417	4	12	1	5	1	0	0	4	1	2	0	.462	.500
2022	24	Everett (NWL)	HiA	.282	69	255	43	72	15	1	12	37	41	47	5	.397	.490
Minor League Totals				.279	104	391	67	109	20	2	15	60	58	69	7	.389	.455

22 TYLER GOUGH, RHP

Born: Aug. 12, 2003. **B-T:** B-R. **HT:** 6-2. **WT:** 205.
Drafted: HS—San Juan Capistrano, Calif., 2022 (12th round). **Signed by:** Ryan Holmes.

TRACK RECORD: Gough began his prep career at remote Heritage (Menifee, Calif.) High before transferring to high-profile JSerra (San Juan Capistrano, Calif.) High. He missed most of his senior spring with biceps tendinitis, but returned to record critical saves in the CIF semifinals and championship game. He struck out all five batters he faced at the draft combine to continue his late momentum and was drafted by the Mariners in the 12th round, signing for an above-slot $250,000.
SCOUTING REPORT: Gough is a cerebral, 6-foot-2 righthander whose stuff keeps ticking up. His high-spin fastball has progressed from 88-91 mph to 92-96 mph and gets swings and misses in the strike zone. He complements his fastball with a plus split-changeup in the low 80s that dives late to keep hitters off-balance. His upper-70s curveball is less refined, but it flashes above-average with downer action to give him a viable third pitch. Gough throws strikes with average control and is fearless in attacking hitters. He is a disciplined, focused individual whose father served in the Air Force.
THE FUTURE: Gough has the ingredients to be a starter, but he has to prove he can maintain his improved stuff over longer stints. He'll try to do that in his pro debut in 2023.

BA Grade: 45/Extreme		Fastball: 55		Curveball: 50		Changeup: 60		Control: 50		

Year	Age	Club (League)	Lvl	W	L	ERA	G	GS	IP	H	HR	BB	SO	BB/9	SO/9	WHIP	AVG
2022	18	Did not play															

23 TRAVIS KUHN, RHP

Born: May 20, 1998. **B-T:** R-R. **HT:** 5-10. **WT:** 195.
Drafted: San Diego, 2019 (19th round). **Signed by:** Gary Patchett.

TRACK RECORD: Kuhn walked on at San Diego and redshirted as a freshman before blossoming into one of the Toreros best relievers. The Mariners drafted him in the 19th round and signed him for $85,000. Kuhn's first full season was delayed by the coronavirus pandemic, but he emerged as a prospect at the Class A levels in 2021 and finished with a strong showing in the Arizona Fall League. Kuhn continued his rise in 2022 at Double-A Arkansas and led the Travelers bullpen with 71 strikeouts.
SCOUTING REPORT: Kuhn is a fearless, aggressive righthander with the stuff and mentality perfectly suited for relief. His fastball sits 95-96 mph with run and sink and gets up to 98-99 mph when he reaches back for more in big spots. His short, mid-80s slider is a plus pitch with late break that ties up hitters and generates awkward, uncomfortable swings. Kuhn keeps the ball on the ground with his fastball and slider

and is hard to elevate against. He allowed only three home runs in 59.1 innings in 2022. Kuhn pitches exclusively from the stretch and frequently spins out of his effortful delivery, leading to balls sailing to his armside. He has below-average control and will need to tighten the direction in his delivery. Kuhn is a tough competitor who rarely backs down and is capable of pitching either one- or two-inning stints.
THE FUTURE: Kuhn has a chance to settle in as a low to mid leverage reliever in the Mariners bullpen. He'll move to Triple-A Tacoma in 2023.

BA Grade: 40/High		Fastball: 55		Slider: 60		Control: 40							
Year	Age	Club (League)	Lvl	W	L	ERA	G	GS	IP	H	HR	BB	SO	BB/9	SO/9	WHIP	AVG
2022	24	Arkansas (TL)	AA	3	3	4.10	50	0	59	43	3	35	71	5.3	10.8	1.31	.203
Minor League Totals				11	7	4.67	95	0	118	96	12	66	146	5.0	11.2	1.38	.220

24 KADEN POLCOVICH, 2B

Born: Feb. 21, 1999. **B-T:** B-R. **HT:** 5-10. **WT:** 185.
Drafted: Oklahoma State, 2020 (3rd round). **Signed by:** Jordan Bley.
TRACK RECORD: Polcovich comes from an athletic family. His dad, Kevin, played shortstop for the Pirates for two seasons and his mom, Lisa, played volleyball at Florida. Polcovich spent two seasons at Northwest Oklahoma JC before transferring to Oklahoma State for the 2020 season, but he played only 18 games for the Cowboys before the coronavirus pandemic ended the year. The Mariners saw enough to draft him in the third round and sign him for $575,000. Polcovich raced to Double-A Arkansas in his first full season and remained at the level in 2022. He finished among the team leaders in doubles (21), home runs (12) and stolen bases (18).
SCOUTING REPORT: Polcovich fits the stereotypical "gamer" profile as an undersized utilityman who does a little bit of everything. A switch-hitter, he is much better from the left side (.263 AVG, .795 OPS) than the right (.196, .588) He's an aggressive hitter who is prone to overswinging, but he knows the strike zone and has sneaky, average raw power from the left side. Polcovich is a plus runner and efficient basestealer with his advanced instincts. His fringy arm limits him to second base, but he can stand at third base and has shown a feel for tracking balls in center field.
THE FUTURE: Polcovich has a chance to surface in the majors as an up-down utilityman. He'll head to Triple-A in 2023.

BA Grade: 40/High		Hit: 30		Power: 40		Speed: 60		Fielding: 45		Arm: 45						
Year	Age	Club (League)	Lvl	AVG	G	AB	R	H	2B	3B	HR	RBI	BB	SO	SB	OBP	SLG
2022	23	Arkansas (TL)	AA	.242	118	451	70	109	21	4	12	60	59	118	18	.345	.386
Minor League Totals				.232	212	793	138	184	37	8	24	121	122	223	38	.349	.390

25 JOSH HOOD, SS

Born: July 21, 2000. **B-T:** R-R. **HT:** 6-2. **WT:** 202.
Drafted: North Carolina State, 2022 (6th round). **Signed by:** Ty Holub.
TRACK RECORD: Hood led Pennsylvania in home runs as a freshman and won the Ivy League's rookie of the year award, but he played only eight games the next two seasons due to the coronavirus pandemic and transferred to North Carolina State for the 2022 season. He started every game for the Wolfpack and starred in the Atlantic Coast Conference tournament in front of Mariners scouting director Scott Hunter, which led the team to draft him in the sixth round and sign him for $250,000.
SCOUTING REPORT: Hood holds promise as a twitchy athlete who hits the ball hard, even if he has some rough edges to his game. He is a well below-average hitter who swings and misses too much, but he impacts the baseball when he connects and posts loud exit velocities. He gets to his power in games and projects to hit double-digit homers. Hood's strengths lie in his secondary tools. He is a plus runner who has the athleticism to stick at shortstop or move all around the diamond. He has a plus arm and is an intelligent, instinctive player who projects to be an above-average defender at every position. He has mostly played shortstop and third base but has the tools to handle second base and all three outfield spots.
THE FUTURE: Hood projects to be a utilityman who hits for power, similar to Chad Pinder. He'll head to the Class A levels in 2023.

BA Grade: 40/High		Hit: 30		Power: 45		Speed: 60		Fielding: 55		Arm: 60						
Year	Age	Club (League)	Lvl	AVG	G	AB	R	H	2B	3B	HR	RBI	BB	SO	SB	OBP	SLG
2022	21	Mariners (ACL)	R	.150	8	20	2	3	0	0	0	2	4	7	2	.280	.150
Minor League Totals				.150	8	20	2	3	0	0	0	2	4	7	2	.280	.150

26 ALBERTO RODRIGUEZ, OF

Born: Oct. 6, 2000. **B-T:** L-L. **HT:** 5-11. **WT:** 180.
Signed: Dominican Republic, 2017. **Signed by:** Sandy Rosario/Lorenzo Perez/Luciano del Rosario (Blue Jays)

TRACK RECORD: Rodriguez signed with the Blue Jays for $500,000 and was acquired by the Mariners in exchange for Taijuan Walker at the 2020 trade deadline. He delivered a breakout season at Low-A Modesto in 2021 and was added to the 40-man roster after the season, but he ballooned out of shape during the lockout and regressed in 2022 at High-A Everett. He ended the year with an underwhelming showing in the Arizona Fall League and was outrighted off the roster.

SCOUTING REPORT: Rodriguez has long struggled with his weight and has enormous peaks and valleys depending on his fitness. He has a busy setup but a sound lefthanded swing that makes loud contact to all fields when he connects. He has good direction at the plate when he's in shape, but he has to open up early to get around his large midsection when he isn't and pulls off balls, as was the case in 2022. He starts expanding the zone to compensate and devolves from there. Rodriguez shows the potential to be an above-average hitter with average power when he's in shape, but he's a non-prospect when he isn't. Rodriguez has slowed to a well below-average runner and is a well below-average defender in right field who doesn't move well. His above-average arm strength is negated by a long arm stroke.

THE FUTURE: Rodriguez has a chance to be a reserve outfielder, but only if he gets back in shape. He'll open at Double-A Arkansas in 2023.

| BA Grade: 40/High | | Hit: 40 | | Power: 50 | | Speed: 30 | | Fielding: 30 | | Arm: 55 | |

Year	Age	Club (League)	Lvl	AVG	G	AB	R	H	2B	3B	HR	RBI	BB	SO	SB	OBP	SLG
2022	21	Everett (NWL)	HiA	.261	119	472	59	123	28	3	10	46	50	138	6	.336	.396
Minor League Totals				.274	327	1267	202	347	81	10	27	174	154	327	55	.356	.418

27 VICTOR LABRADA, OF

Born: Jan. 16, 2000. **B-T:** L-L. **HT:** 5-9. **WT:** 165.
Signed: Cuba, 2019. **Signed by:** Audo Vicente.

TRACK RECORD: Labrada starred as Cuba's leadoff hitter at the 2018 Pan-American championships and briefly played in Cuba's major league, Serie Nacional. He relocated to the Dominican Republic to pursue an MLB career and signed with the Mariners for $350,000. Labrada impressed in his stateside debut with Low-A Modesto in 2021, but he hit a wall offensively at High-A Everett in 2022.

SCOUTING REPORT: Labrada is an undersized sparkplug whose best trait is his high-energy style of play. He slaps the ball around with a quick, compact swing and uses his above-average speed to beat out infield hits and steal bases. He always runs hard, including coming on and off the field, and sets a frenzied tone atop a lineup. Labrada is an aggressive hitter and expands the zone too often, which was exposed against better pitching. He has some pullside power but gets in trouble overswinging, which limits him to a well below-average hitter. Labrada's speed and high motor make him a threat on the bases and help him outrun bad jumps or routes in center field. He projects to be an above-average defender with a below-average arm.

THE FUTURE: Labrada's speed and ability to play center field give him a chance to be an up-down option. He'll move to Double-A Arkansas in 2023.

| BA Grade: 40/High | | Hit: 30 | | Power: 30 | | Speed: 55 | | Fielding: 55 | | Arm: 40 | |

Year	Age	Club (League)	Lvl	AVG	G	AB	R	H	2B	3B	HR	RBI	BB	SO	SB	OBP	SLG
2022	22	Modesto (CAL)	LoA	.400	12	50	13	20	5	0	2	13	9	8	3	.492	.620
2022	22	Everett (NWL)	HiA	.232	111	401	66	93	15	6	10	31	49	134	27	.328	.374
Minor League Totals				.260	222	855	158	222	43	12	19	99	111	265	62	.354	.405

28 JOSEPH HERNANDEZ, RHP

Born: June 15, 2000. **B-T:** R-R. **HT:** 5-11. **WT:** 170.
Signed: Dominican Republic, 2017. **Signed by:** Francisco Rosario/Kelvin Dominguez.

TRACK RECORD: Hernandez signed with the Mariners for $45,000 in 2017 as part of the same signing class as Julio Rodriguez. He spent most of his first three seasons in the complex leagues and missed a year due to the coronavirus pandemic, but he finally made his full-season debut in 2022 and flourished. He led the California League with a 3.39 ERA, 143 strikeouts and a .193 opponent average.

SCOUTING REPORT: Hernandez is an undersized righthander who relies heavily on his above-average, 79-83 mph slider. It's a tight, horizontal pitch he throws nearly 60% of the time and gets righthanded batters reaching as it runs away from their barrels. It also gets in on lefties with hard, sharp break and keeps them in check. Hernandez's fastball is a below-average, 90-93 mph pitch that serves more as a change-of-pace offering for his slider. He also has a below-average, mid-80s changeup he'll occasionally mix in. Hernandez has fringy control and mostly relies on batters chasing his slider out of the zone.

THE FUTURE: Hernandez's slider gives him an out pitch that will play at higher levels if he can land it in the zone more. He projects to be a slider-heavy reliever out of the bullpen.

BA Grade: 40/High		Fastball: 40	Slider: 55				Changeup: 40		Control: 45				

Year	Age	Club (League)	Lvl	W	L	ERA	G	GS	IP	H	HR	BB	SO	BB/9	SO/9	WHIP	AVG
2022	22	Modesto (CAL)	LoA	9	5	3.39	24	22	117	79	10	54	143	4.2	11.0	1.14	.193
Minor League Totals				16	9	4.07	54	33	197	157	18	101	243	4.6	11.1	1.31	.219

29 STARLIN AGUILAR, 3B

Born: Jan. 26, 2004. **B-T:** L-R. **HT:** 5-11. **WT:** 170.
Signed: Dominican Republic, 2021. **Signed by:** Audo Vicente/Rafael Mateo.

TRACK RECORD: Aguilar emerged as a promising hitter from an early age in the Dominican Republic and trained with Rudy Santin, whose program produced Red Sox third baseman Rafael Devers and Rays shortstop Wander Franco. The Mariners signed Aguilar for $1.5 million in 2021 and sent him to the Rookie-level Arizona League for his stateside debut in 2022. Aguilar hit a team-leading .291 in the ACL and showed impressive contact skills, but he also hit zero home runs and scuffled defensively.

SCOUTING REPORT: Aguilar's calling card is his smooth, lefthanded swing. He sees the ball well out of the pitcher's hand and makes a lot of contact with a fluid, compact stroke. Aguilar has no problem making contact, but it's often soft contact. He mostly flares softly-hit singles the other way and makes no attempt to drive the ball. His large body has added the wrong type of weight and he's not particularly strong, leading to concerns he'll top out at 8-10 home runs. Aguilar has a thick, chunky frame and is a bottom of the scale runner with limited athleticism. His slow reactions, hard hands and below-average arm strength make him a well below-average defender at third base and will force an eventual move to first base.

THE FUTURE: Aguilar has to get stronger and tap into more power to profile as a corner infielder. He'll try to make those gains at Low-A Modesto in 2023.

BA Grade: 45/Extreme		Hit: 50		Power: 30		Speed: 20		Fielding: 30		Arm: 40		

Year	Age	Club (League)	Lvl	AVG	G	AB	R	H	2B	3B	HR	RBI	BB	SO	SB	OBP	SLG
2022	18	Mariners (ACL)	R	.291	46	175	13	51	6	1	0	20	8	42	0	.319	.337
Minor League Totals				.268	99	358	51	96	19	2	2	41	37	83	0	.341	.349

30 JUAN PINTO, LHP

Born: Aug. 26, 2004. **B-T:** L-L. **HT:** 6-4. **WT:** 175.
Signed: Venezuela, 2021. **Signed by:** Dan Rovetto/Rafael Santo Domingo.

TRACK RECORD: Pinto was one of the youngest players in the 2020-21 international signing class and signed with the Mariners for $700,000 out of Venezuela. The Mariners held him back from pitching to focus on strength and conditioning in his first year in the organization, and he returned bigger and stronger for his pro debut in the Dominican Summer League in 2022. Pinto showed some of the best stuff in the league once he got on the mound, but he also struggled with his control and had 29 walks, 13 wild pitches and six hit batters in 30 innings.

SCOUTING REPORT: Pinto is a long, lean 6-foot-4 lefthander with enticing stuff and lots of physical projection remaining. His fastball sits 88-90 mph, touches 92 and has room to tick up as he matures and fills out his frame. His fastball plays up with plus life and movement and could be a plus pitch at its peak. Pinto's best pitch is a plus curveball with tight spin, sharp bite and good depth. He also has a nascent changeup that slowly developing. Pinto misses plenty of bats with his fastball and curveball, but his control and command are well below-average. His control could improve as he gets stronger to improve his body control and gains more game experience.

THE FUTURE: Pinto's ability to miss bats from the left side is promising, but his outlook depends on if he can improve his control. He'll move stateside to the Arizona Complex League in 2023.

BA Grade: 45/Extreme		Fastball: 60		Curveball: 60	Changeup: 40		Control: 30				

Year	Age	Club (League)	Lvl	W	L	ERA	G	GS	IP	H	HR	BB	SO	BB/9	SO/9	WHIP	AVG
2022	17	Mariners (DSL)	R	1	2	4.75	10	10	30	24	0	29	33	8.6	9.8	1.75	.224
Minor League Totals				1	2	4.75	10	10	30	24	0	29	33	8.6	9.8	1.75	.224

Tampa Bay Rays

BY J.J. COOPER

For the fourth consecutive season, the Rays were a playoff team. But the 2022 season was a clear step backwards for the organization. Two years after going to the World Series and a year after they won 100 games for the first time, the Rays finished with 86 wins, making the playoffs only because of the expanded wild card format.

The Rays' pitching was once again excellent; the lineup was not. Tampa Bay went from second in the American League in run scored to 11th. In slugging percentage, the Rays dropped from fourth to 13th.

Injuries to Mike Zunino and Brandon Lowe played a part in the Rays' power outage. Those two combined for 72 home runs in 2021. They finished with 13 in 2022, and no one stepped up to replace them. Randy Arozarena and Isaac Paredes led the Rays with 20 home runs apiece. Ji-Man Choi was the only other Ray to reach double digits.

The Rays gave some playing time to rookies Vidal Brujan and Josh Lowe and second-year shortstop Taylor Walls in 2022. All three struggled offensively. While Tampa Bay has further offensive help not far away from St. Petersburg in second baseman Curtis Mead, the farm system overall has taken a slight step backwards. There are not as many pitching prospects as there have been in recent years.

The Rays' vaunted prospect depth has taken a hit because of graduations, attrition and trades mandated by a crowded 40-man roster.

Tampa Bay is a transactional team that continually turns over its roster. The Rays have well-earned confidence that they can get more out of pitchers than many other teams, something that was made clear from success stories like Jeffrey Springs, Jason Adam and Drew Rasmussen in 2022.

What the Rays do as well as anyone is improve pitchers' control. Almost every pitcher the Rays acquire comes to throw more strikes and walk fewer batters, as typified by Tyler Glasnow's instant improvement when he came over from the Pirates in 2018. Young power arms Shane McClanahan and Shane Baz also have shaken their early-career reputations as wild.

Where do the Rays go from here? The path is becoming tougher. The rise of the Orioles adds yet another playoff contender in an American League East full of them. The more balanced scheduling will give every AL East team a boost, but Tampa Bay needs to see some of their promising young players take a further step forward in 2023.

Shortstop Wander Franco has been quite good, but he hasn't yet taken the leap from solid regular to potential superstar. It's easy to forget that he'll

Rookies Josh Lowe (pictured) and Vidal Brujan struggled in their first lengthy MLB exposure.

PROJECTED 2026 LINEUP

Catcher	Francisco Mejia	30
First Base	Kyle Manzardo	25
Second Base	Wander Franco	25
Third Base	Isaac Paredes	27
Shortstop	Carson Williams	22
Left Field	Randy Arozarena	31
Center Field	Josh Lowe	28
Right Field	Brandon Lowe	31
Designated Hitter	Curtis Mead	25
No. 1 Starter	Shane McClanahan	29
No. 2 Starter	Shane Baz	26
No. 3 Starter	Drew Rasmussen	30
No. 4 Starter	Taj Bradley	25
No. 5 Starter	Mason Montgomery	25
Closer	Luis Patiño	26

be just 22 years old for all of the 2023 season. The Rays cannot get back to the World Series without getting more production from their lineup.

Tampa Bay's pitching staff is in better shape. Adding a healthy Glasnow to a staff that already has McClanahan and Rasmussen should give Tampa Bay a pitching staff to compete with anyone, and righthander Taj Bradley isn't far away from adding further depth.

Despite being one of the lowest-spending teams in baseball year after year, the Rays remain in an enviable position with a playoff-caliber MLB roster and a still-solid farm system. But the path in future years looks a little tougher than it did from 2019 to 2021. ■

DOUGLAS P. DEFELICE/GETTY IMAGES

DEPTH CHART

TAMPA BAY RAYS

TOP 2023 MLB CONTRIBUTORS	RANK
Curtis Mead, 2B/3B	2
Jonathan Aranda, 2B/1B	6
Colby White, RHP	20
BREAKOUT PROSPECTS	**RANK**
Willy Vasquez, 3B	15
Santiago Suarez, RHP	17

SOURCE OF TOP 30 TALENT

Homegrown	19	Acquired	11
College	9	Trade	10
Junior college	1	Rule 5 draft	1
High school	5	Independent league	0
Nondrafted free agent	0	Free agent/waivers	0
International	4		

LF
Heriberto Hernandez (18)
Chandler Simpson (22)
Tristan Peters

CF
Mason Auer (7)
Brock Jones (12)
Kameron Misner (16)
Ryan Cermak (21)
Shane Sasaki (24)

RF
Luke Raley

3B
Junior Caminero (8)
Willy Vasquez (15)
Austin Shenton (28)

SS
Carson Williams (4)
Greg Jones (19)
Carlos Colmenarez (23)
Jalen Battles
Odalys Peguero
Narcisco Polanco

2B
Curtis Mead (2)
Osleivis Basabe (11)
Ryan Spikes

1B
Kyle Manzardo (5)
Jonathan Aranda (6)
Xavier Isaac (13)

C
Rene Pinto (14)
Blake Hunt
Dominic Keegan

LHP

LHSP	LHRP
Mason Montgomery (9)	Ian Seymour (30)
	Keyshawn Askew
	Patrick Wicklander

RHP

RHSP	RHRP
Shane Baz (1)	Colby White (20)
Taj Bradley (3)	Marcus Johnson (25)
Cole Wilcox (10)	Calvin Faucher (26)
Santiago Suarez (17)	Kevin Kelly (27)
J.J. Goss	Austin Vernon (29)
Ben Peoples	Evan Reifert (31)
Nick Bitsko	Trevor Martin
Evan McKendry	Trevor Brigden
	Logan Workman
	Alfredo Zarraga

1 SHANE BAZ, RHP

Born: June 17, 1999. **B-T:** R-R. **Ht.:** 6-2. **Wt.:** 190.
Drafted: HS—Tomball, Texas, 2017 (1st round).
Signed by: Wayne Mathis (Pirates).

TRACK RECORD: After a 2021 season full of highlights, Baz's 2022 season never got going. In 2021, he pitched for Team USA's silver medal-winning Olympic team, emerged as one of the best pitching prospects in baseball, earned a late callup to the Rays and started a game in the postseason. In 2022, Baz got off to a late start thanks to surgery to remove loose bodies in his right elbow during spring training. The surgery foreshadowed further problems. Baz returned to action in mid May and joined the Rays rotation in early June. He pitched extremely effectively in his first five starts—2.92 ERA with 28 strikeouts and nine walks in 24.2 innings—but gave up seven runs and three home runs in just 2.1 innings before being lifted with elbow pain in his final start on July 10. He spent the rest of the season on the injured list and had Tommy John surgery in late September. The Rays initially acquired Baz as the player to be named later in the trade that saw Tampa Bay acquire Tyler Glasnow and Austin Meadows from the Pirates for Chris Archer. In hindsight, any one of those prospects would have been a fair trade for Archer, but acquiring all three in the same deal proved to be one of the best trades any MLB team has made this century.

SCOUTING REPORT: When healthy, Baz has some of the best pure stuff in baseball. His 94-99 mph fastball is similar to Gerrit Cole's in terms of velocity and movement. It has well above-average carry at the top of the zone to generate an above-average rate of swings-and-misses. It also has the flat plane that accentuates its liveliness. As importantly, Baz does an excellent job of locating it in and around the strike zone. His plus slider is a hard pitch at 86-89 mph with minimal sweep. It's effective because of its power. Baz has an average 87-88 mph changeup he uses only against lefthanded hitters, and it pairs well with his slider. His fringe-average low-80s curveball is a useful early-count pitch to steal a strike against a hitter geared up for his fastball or slider. His curve moves north-south, so he's comfortable throwing it to both lefties and righties. When Baz was drafted 12th overall out of high school in 2017, evaluators had significant concerns about his control and command, but as he's gotten stronger and matured, he's developed into a much more consistent strike-thrower. His plus control backed up a little in 2022, but that

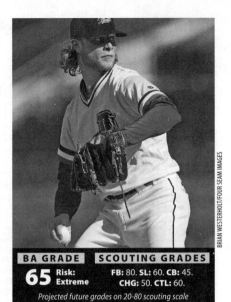

BRIAN WESTERHOLT/FOUR SEAM IMAGES

BA GRADE	SCOUTING GRADES
65 Risk: Extreme	FB: 80. SL: 60. CB: 45. CHG: 50. CTL: 60.

Projected future grades on 20-80 scouting scale

BEST TOOLS

BATTING

Best Hitter For Average	Curtis Mead
Best Power Hitter	Junior Caminero
Best Strike-Zone Discipline	Osleivis Basabe
Fastest Baserunner	Greg Jones
Best Athlete	Mason Auer

PITCHING

Best Fastball	Shane Baz
Best Curveball	Calvin Faucher
Best Slider	Shane Baz
Best Changeup	Austin Vernon
Best Control	Taj Bradley

FIELDING

Best Defensive Catcher	Rene Pinto
Best Defensive Infielder	Carson Williams
Best Infield Arm	Carson Williams
Best Defensive Outfielder	Mason Auer
Best Outfield Arm	Mason Auer

may have been related to his lingering elbow issues.
THE FUTURE: Baz's 2023 season will be spent rehabbing from elbow surgery, but assuming his rehab goes as planned, he should be a valuable part of the Rays' rotation in 2024. In a Tampa Bay system that is thinner in pitching prospects than it has been in years, Baz has the best combination of multiple effective pitches, pure stuff and pitchability. If he makes a full recovery, he could give the Rays another front-of-the-rotation starter to team with lefthander Shane McClanahan and righthander Tyler Glasnow.

Year	Age	Club (League)	Lvl	W	L	ERA	G	GS	IP	H	HR	BB	SO	BB/9	SO/9	WHIP	AVG
2022	23	Durham (IL)	AAA	0	0	1.38	4	4	13	8	1	4	20	2.8	13.8	0.92	.167
2022	23	Tampa Bay (AL)	MLB	1	2	5.00	6	6	27	27	5	9	30	3.0	10.0	1.33	.252
Major League Totals				3	2	4.02	9	9	40	33	8	12	48	2.7	10.7	1.12	.216
Minor League Totals				12	14	3.00	60	60	249	203	20	97	298	3.5	10.8	1.20	.220

2 CURTIS MEAD, 2B/3B

Born: October 26, 2000. **B-T:** R-R. **HT:** 6-2. **WT:** 171. **Signed:** Australia, 2018.
Signed by: Howard Norsetter/Roberto Aquino/Derrick Chung (Phillies).

TRACK RECORD: Acquired from the Phillies for lefthander Cristopher Sanchez, Mead should become the first Australian position player regular of the 21st century. After breaking out in Class A in 2021, Mead again earned a midseason promotion in 2022, but his work to improve his arm strength led to a right elbow strain. He had to be shut down with Triple-A Durham in mid July, and eventually had an injection to help heal the injury and missed the remainder of the season. He is expected to be ready for spring training.
SCOUTING REPORT: Mead is one of the best pure hitters in the minors. He ranked among the best in the minors in average exit velocity (91 mph) and hard-hit rate (over 50%). He is a tinkerer who will adjust his stance and setup to see what works and what doesn't, partly because his hands work so well. Mead's swing is relatively level and conducive to line drives and high batting averages more than massive home run numbers, but he's expected to develop into a 25-plus home run threat as he learns how to better capitalize on hitter's counts. Defensively, Mead's below-average arm limits him. Second base may fit better than third, and the new restrictions on shifting will benefit him. His arm strength would have been stretched on shifts into short right field, but now that positioning is prohibited. At third base, Mead's arm will likely always be a liability, but he has worked on quickening his release. His range is fringe-average at best, but his hands are adequate. He has also played first base.
THE FUTURE: Mead has the best combination of power and hitting ability in the Rays' organization. Despite his persistent defensive limitations, his offensive upside should make him a long-term regular.

BA GRADE
55 Risk: Medium

SCOUTING GRADES	Hitting: 70	Power: 60	Speed: 40	Fielding: 45	Arm: 40

Year	Age	Club (League)	Lvl	AVG	G	AB	R	H	2B	3B	HR	RBI	BB	SO	SB	OBP	SLG
2022	21	Montgomery (SL)	AA	.305	56	210	35	64	21	0	10	36	25	45	6	.394	.548
2022	21	Durham (IL)	AAA	.278	20	72	8	20	6	0	3	14	11	17	1	.376	.486
Minor League Totals				.306	226	857	147	262	77	4	32	138	83	156	22	.376	.517

3 TAJ BRADLEY, RHP

Born: March 20, 2001. **B-T:** R-R. **HT:** 6-2. **WT:** 190.
Drafted: HS—Stone Mountain, GA, 2018 (5th round). **Signed by:** Milt Hill.

TRACK RECORD: A high school outfielder with a strong arm, Bradley immediately became a prospect when he tried pitching as a senior. A 17-year-old at the time of the 2017 draft, Bradley moved slowly with the Rays initially, but since the pandemic he has moved from Low-A to Triple-A in two seasons. Bradley's 1.76 ERA was the lowest among qualifiers in the minor leagues in 2021. He was battling for a repeat ERA crown in 2022 with a 1.70 mark in 16 starts for Double-A Montgomery, but he struggled at times after a promotion to Triple-A Durham.
SCOUTING REPORT: Bradley's fastball and cutter/slider give him a pair of big league-ready pitches. His nearly plus-plus 94-96 mph fastball will touch

BA GRADE
55 Risk: Medium

97-98 and has plenty of life. He throws a plus cutter/slider that is thrown with a cutter grip and a fastball mentality, but he has the ability to make it bigger and sweepier or tighter and harder. It's not a strikeout pitch as much as it is one that hitters struggle to barrel. Bradley's ability to throw both of these pitches for strikes gives hitters problems. When Bradley is on, hitters are usually behind in counts. The question has long been whether he can develop a third pitch to go with them. So far, he's struggled to find the confidence in either his curveball or a changeup. He's tried a variety of changeup grips but has returned to a splitter grip that will flash average. His 76-78 mph, below-average curveball could be an early-count surprise pitch to steal a strike, but he struggles to land it in the zone.
THE FUTURE: Bradley's late-season struggles in Triple-A are useful for his long-term development. His intelligence and athleticism make him a probable midrotation starter after further development.

SCOUTING GRADES:	Fastball: 65	Curveball: 40	Changeup: 45	Cutter: 60	Control: 60

Year	Age	Club (League)	Lvl	W	L	ERA	G	GS	IP	H	HR	BB	SO	BB/9	SO/9	WHIP	AVG
2022	21	Montgomery (SL)	AA	3	1	1.70	16	16	74	50	4	18	88	2.2	10.7	0.91	.189
2022	21	Durham (IL)	AAA	4	3	3.66	12	12	59	55	10	15	53	2.3	8.1	1.19	.240
Minor League Totals				22	16	2.61	73	70	311	238	27	95	345	2.8	10.0	1.07	.209

4 CARSON WILLIAMS, SS

Born: June 24, 2003. **B-T:** R-R. **HT:** 6-2. **WT:** 180.
Drafted: HS—San Diego, 2021 (1st round). **Signed by:** Jaime Jones.
TRACK RECORD: Heading into his senior year of high school, Williams was seen as a smooth defensive shortstop, but one who seemed more interesting as a pitcher. After gaining 10-15 pounds of good weight, his power developed, and he turned into one of the best prep shortstops in a loaded 2021 draft class. Williams was the star for Low-A Charleston's Carolina League champions in 2022. He finished second in the league with 19 home runs.
SCOUTING REPORT: There was little question about Williams' defense, but his bat has proved better than expected. He showed plus power all year in 2022, and when he was locked in, he strung together solid at-bats. Williams doesn't chase pitches at an unusual rate, but he goes through stretches where he will swing and miss at hittable pitches in the strike zone. His 32% strikeout

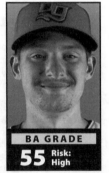

BA GRADE
55 Risk: High

rate will have to improve as he gains more experience. Williams' power is primarily to his pull side, but he's also shown he's comfortable driving the ball out to straightaway center field. He regularly cleared tall batting eyes in Carolina League games. Williams' defense has lived up to expectations. His plus-plus arm is the best in the organization and is extremely accurate. He had just three throwing errors all season. He's a bigger, rangy shortstop who relies on his arm, soft hands and his length. Williams' first-step quickness is only average, but the total package is that of a plus defensive shortstop. The Rays move most of their infielders around, but Williams has played only shortstop.
THE FUTURE: When he heads to High-A Bowling Green in 2023, Williams will work on making more consistent contact, but he has the potential to become a physical shortstop with power and defense.

SCOUTING GRADES	Hitting: 40	Power: 60	Speed: 55	Fielding: 60	Arm: 70

Year	Age	Club (League)	Lvl	AVG	G	AB	R	H	2B	3B	HR	RBI	BB	SO	SB	OBP	SLG
2022	19	Charleston (CAR)	LoA	.252	113	452	81	114	22	10	19	70	57	168	28	.347	.471
Minor League Totals				.255	124	491	89	125	26	11	19	78	63	181	30	.351	.468

5 KYLE MANZARDO, 1B

Born: July 18, 2000. **B-T:** L-R. **HT:** 6-1. **WT:** 205.
Drafted: Washington State, 2021 (2nd round). **Signed by:** James Bonnici.
TRACK RECORD: After Manzardo starred at Washington State, the Rays drafted the first baseman in the second round in 2021, counting on a potent bat to make up for his limited athleticism. He has rewarded their faith. Manzardo climbed further faster than any other Rays prospect in 2022. Tampa Bay generally has players spend a full year at one level in their first full season, but Manzardo torched the High-A South Atlantic League. After a post-trade deadline promotion, he handled the jump to Double-A Montgomery and finished among the top 10 in the minors with a .327 batting average, .426 on-base percentage and .617 slugging.
SCOUTING REPORT: Manzardo's stance and lefthanded swing are simple and

BA GRADE
55 Risk: High

well-timed. He is a pure hitter who presents pitchers with a puzzle: he rarely swings and misses at pitches in the zone, and he knows the zone well enough to rarely swing at pitches off the plate. Manzardo doesn't hit the ball exceptionally hard (88 mph average exit velocity), but he knows how to yank the ball over the fence, and he peppers the gaps with a swing that can drive the ball to all fields. Manzardo posts high batting averages despite the fact that he's a bottom-of-the-scale runner who gets no infield hits. Manzardo was much better at home than on the road in 2022, and his Bowling Green and Montgomery home parks might have boosted his power output. Despite his lack of foot speed, Manzardo is a competent first baseman with good hands and an average arm. He handles what he gets to with few issues, but his range is limited.
THE FUTURE: After a successful half-season in Double-A, Manzardo should spend much of 2023 at Triple-A Durham. He could be an option for the big league club by the end of 2023. Manzardo's lack of athleticism and first base-only profile puts a lot of pressure on his promising bat.

SCOUTING GRADES	Hitting: 65	Power: 55	Speed: 20	Fielding: 50	Arm: 50

Year	Age	Club (League)	Lvl	AVG	G	AB	R	H	2B	3B	HR	RBI	BB	SO	SB	OBP	SLG
2022	21	Bowling Green (SAL)	HiA	.329	63	225	53	74	16	1	17	55	45	46	0	.436	.636
2022	21	Montgomery (SL)	AA	.323	30	99	18	32	10	0	5	26	14	19	1	.402	.576
Minor League Totals				.330	106	367	81	121	31	1	24	89	63	71	1	.427	.616

6 JONATHAN ARANDA, 2B/1B

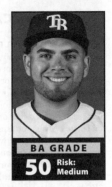

Born: May 23, 1998. **B-T:** R-R. **HT:** 5-10. **WT:** 175.
Signed: Mexico, 2015. **Signed by:** Eddie Diaz.

TRACK RECORD: It took Aranda six pro seasons to reach Double-A, where was honored as Southern League MVP in 2021. In his seventh season, he reached the majors, earning three callups as the Rays attempted to bolster a sagging offense. Aranda started out hot in MLB and was hitting .325/.386/.500 in mid September, but he finished the season on a 2-for-38 slide.

SCOUTING REPORT: The Rays collect players who make plenty of quality contact, and Aranda has long been viewed as one of the organization's best pure hitters. Few minor league hitters have a better plan at the plate. He's comfortable hitting breaking balls and will be selective to get to the pitch he wants to hit, sometimes spitting on a tough-to-hit strike because he trusts his two-strike approach. Aranda rarely swings and misses, and he controls the strike zone. His power is average at best and his bat speed is average, which explains why he can be beaten by top-notch velocity. Aranda's stumbling block is his defensive position. The Rays have tried Aranda at first base, second base and third base as well as left field, but he's a below-average defender at all of them. His hands are adequate, but he has slow feet, limited range and a slow first step. The effort level is there, but often he is a step too slow to make a play, or he gets caught on an in-between hop since he struggles to go in or back quickly enough to create better hops.

THE FUTURE: Aranda's bat is big league ready, but with his defensive limitations his best shot at a regular job in Tampa Bay is to claim a spot as a first baseman/DH who can play elsewhere in a pinch.

BA GRADE: 50 Risk: Medium

SCOUTING GRADES	Hitting: 60	Power: 50	Speed: 30	Fielding: 40	Arm: 50

Year	Age	Club (League)	Lvl	AVG	G	AB	R	H	2B	3B	HR	RBI	BB	SO	SB	OBP	SLG
2022	24	Durham (IL)	AAA	.318	104	403	71	128	26	1	18	85	45	100	4	.394	.521
2022	24	Tampa Bay (AL)	MLB	.192	32	78	10	15	4	0	2	6	8	23	0	.276	.321
Major League Totals				.192	32	78	10	15	4	0	2	6	8	23	0	.276	.321
Minor League Totals				.298	414	1495	249	445	84	18	37	246	165	304	29	.377	.452

7 MASON AUER, OF

Born: March 1, 2001. **B-T:** R-R. **HT:** 6-0. **WT:** 210.
Drafted: San Jacinto (Texas) JC, 2021 (5th round). **Signed by:** Pat Murphy.

TRACK RECORD: A football and baseball star at Kickapoo High in Springfield, Mo., Auer barely played at Missouri State as a two-way freshman in the coronavirus-shortened 2020 season. He transferred to San Jacinto (Texas) JC and blossomed, hitting .373/.525/.627 with 11 home runs in 65 games. In his first full pro season spent at Low-A Charleston and High-A Bowling Green, Auer led the minors with 12 triples and led the Rays organization with 48 steals in 55 attempts. He was sent to the Arizona Fall League to gather additional at-bats.

SCOUTING REPORT: Coming out of the draft, the expectation was that Auer would be a toolsy if somewhat raw hitter, but he's proven to have more polish than expected. He has a smooth, level swing with some adjustability. Auer can be induced to chase, but he has feel for getting the barrel on the ball. He also has plus-plus raw power and flashes above-average game power as well. Auer toned down the leg kick he had used earlier in his career and now relies on a smaller toe tap to help him lock in on his timing. He's managed to combine solid contact ability (20% strikeout rate) with decent plate discipline (10% walk rate) and burgeoning power. Auer needs to polish his reads and routes, but he has the tools to be an above-average defender in center field and a plus defender in the corners. He has a top-of-the-scale arm that has been measured at 98.9 mph on a throw in the Arizona Fall League. He's a plus-plus runner who is a threat to steal any time he reaches.

THE FUTURE: The Rays keep developing athletic center fielders who can also be plus defenders in the corners. Auer is following in the footsteps of Josh Lowe and Kameron Misner, but he is a better pure hitter than either of them, with similar defensive ability and a better arm.

BA GRADE: 55 Risk: High

SCOUTING GRADES	Hitting: 50	Power: 55	Speed: 70	Fielding: 55	Arm: 80

Year	Age	Club (League)	Lvl	AVG	G	AB	R	H	2B	3B	HR	RBI	BB	SO	SB	OBP	SLG
2022	21	Charleston (CAR)	LoA	.293	60	232	46	68	13	9	4	31	31	48	24	.378	.478
2022	21	Bowling Green (SAL)	HiA	.288	55	226	38	65	8	3	11	31	24	62	24	.367	.496
Minor League Totals				.289	126	492	91	142	23	12	15	65	61	117	58	.374	.476

8 JUNIOR CAMINERO, 3B/SS

Born: July 5, 2003. **B-T:** R-R. **HT:** 5-11. **WT:** 155.
Signed: Dominican Republic, 2019. **Signed by:** Amiro Santana (Guardians).

TRACK RECORD: Caminero signed with Cleveland in 2019, but he had to wait until 2021 to make his pro debut thanks to the coronavirus pandemic. Tampa Bay acquired him in November 2021 at the reserve roster deadline in a deal that sent righthander Tobias Myers to the Guardians. It was a typical Rays trade. They took a flier on a high-upside if far-away prospect. The Guardians designated Myers for assignment in July, while Caminero had an impressive U.S. debut, hitting his way into the Low-A Charleston lineup for the final two months of the season.

SCOUTING REPORT: Caminero is more physically mature than many 18-year-olds, but there's likely further strength and power coming as he gets to his early 20s. He's heavier than his listed 155 pounds. Caminero is strong enough and his hands work well enough that he can get fooled and still manage to hit the ball hard. He will get caught out front but keep his hands back. A thinker at the plate, Caminero rarely makes the same mistake twice. He has played second base, third base and shortstop, but he's not a long-term shortstop. Second or third base is a possibility, but his range is limited and he's not particularly rangy or twitchy. His plus arm is an asset at either spot and would fit in right field as well.

THE FUTURE: Caminero will have to keep working on his agility to stay in the dirt, but his hitting ability may handle a move to the outfield one day. Caminero's ceiling is as a 30-plus home run slugger, but he'll have to keep improving as he climbs the ladder. Because he signed in 2019, Caminero will need to be added to the 40-man roster after the 2023 season, which may lead the Rays to speed up his timetable by sending him to High-A Bowling Green to start the season.

BA GRADE
50 Risk: High

SCOUTING GRADES		Hitting: 50		Power: 60		Speed: 45			Fielding: 45		Arm: 60		
Year	**Age**	**Club (League)**	**Lvl**	**AVG**	**G**	**AB**	**R**	**H**	**2B**	**3B**	**HR**	**RBI**	**BB**	**SO**	**SB**	**OBP**	**SLG**
2022	18	Rays (FCL)	R	.326	36	132	18	43	5	1	5	31	15	21	7	.403	.492
2022	18	Charleston (CAR)	LoA	.299	26	107	19	32	2	1	6	20	8	22	5	.359	.505
Minor League Totals				.306	105	385	63	118	15	2	20	84	43	71	14	.382	.512

9 MASON MONTGOMERY, LHP

Born: June 17, 2000. **B-T:** L-L. **HT:** 6-2. **WT:** 200.
Drafted: Texas Tech, 2021 (6th round). **Signed by:** Pat Murphy.

TRACK RECORD: After the Rays drafted him out of Texas Tech in the sixth round in 2021, Montgomery toyed with Florida Complex League hitters. That helped the Rays feel comfortable jumping him to High-A Bowling Green to start 2022. He earned a mid-July promotion to Double-A Montgomery. Montgomery allowed one run or fewer in his last five starts. His 2.10 ERA was fourth best in the minors and his 171 strikeouts ranked sixth, and he allowed more than three runs only once all season.

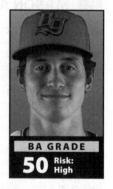

BA GRADE
50 Risk: High

SCOUTING REPORT: Montgomery's plus fastball has carry and the flat approach angle to baffle hitters. His fastball plays above its 89-94 mph velocity because of its movement, and he has the ability to spot it around the strike zone. At times, Montgomery could dominate just relying on that one pitch. He affects hitters' timing by varying his velocity—he can touch 96-97 mph—but will sometimes gear it down as well. Montgomery's 83-85 mph slider is fringe-average at best. It doesn't have exceptional power or movement, but it's been effective because he can throw it for strikes or induce chases. His below-average, low-80s changeup is a pitch he's used rarely so far. He doesn't throw it for strikes nearly as much, but when he does, it gets squared up.

THE FUTURE: Montgomery's profile as a savvy, fastball-heavy lefty with fringe-average secondaries doesn't always work against more advanced hitters. He'll need to better develop his slider and changeup as he climbs the ladder, but his control, command and fastball quality give him a solid shot at being a useful lefty reliever or back-end starter. If the secondaries improve, he could exceed that projection.

SCOUTING GRADES:		Fastball: 60		Slider: 45			Changeup: 40		Control: 55		
Year	**Age**	**Club (League)**	**Lvl**	**W**	**L**	**ERA**	**G**	**GS**	**IP**	**H**	**HR**	**BB**	**SO**	**BB/9**	**SO/9**	**WHIP**	**AVG**
2022	22	Bowling Green (SAL)	HiA	3	2	1.81	16	16	70	49	6	27	118	3.5	15.2	1.09	.194
2022	22	Montgomery (SL)	AA	3	1	2.48	11	11	54	40	5	16	53	2.7	8.8	1.03	.199
Minor League Totals				7	3	2.00	32	31	135	93	11	44	191	2.9	12.8	1.02	.190

10 COLE WILCOX, RHP

Born: July 14, 1999. **B-T:** R-R. **HT:** 6-5. **WT:** 232.
Drafted: Georgia, 2020 (3rd round). **Signed by:** Tyler Stubblefield (Padres).

TRACK RECORD: The Padres drafted Wilcox in the third round as an eligible sophomore out of Georgia in 2020. He signed for $3.3 million, or first-round money. Wilcox never threw an official pitch with the Padres because he was shipped to the Rays in the Blake Snell trade after the 2020 season that also brought Francisco Mejia and Blake Hunt to Tampa Bay. Wilcox was effective in his pro debut in 2021 but was shut down in July with an elbow injury that eventually needed Tommy John surgery. He returned to the mound in August 2022 to make three rehab appearances in the Florida Complex League and four abbreviated starts with Low-A Charleston

BA GRADE
55 Risk: Extreme

SCOUTING REPORT: Getting back on the mound and demonstrating his health was an important milestone for Wilcox, but his velocity didn't fully bounce back in his late-season stint. He touched 98-99 mph and sat 93-95 pre-injury, but he maxed out at 95 and sat 91-93 in 2022. Assuming his arm strength returns to his pre-surgery levels in 2023, Wilcox should profile as a sinker/slider power pitcher. Both are potentially plus pitches. He gets sink and run on his fastball, and it pairs well with his 84-87 mph power slider. He largely shelved his changeup in his briefer return outings, but it's flashed fringe-average. When Wilcox was in high school, teams were highly concerned about his control, but that has proven to be a significant strength rather than a weakness. He has walked fewer than 1.5 batters per nine innings in his final year of college and his first two years of pro ball. His command is not as sharp.

THE FUTURE: The 2023 season will be a big one for Wilcox. He showed his feel and control has returned to where it was before his injury, but he still needs to show he has the same power stuff that has long been his calling card. He should be ticketed for High-A Bowling Green.

SCOUTING GRADES:	Fastball: 60	Slider: 60	Changeup: 45	Control: 60

Year	Age	Club (League)	Lvl	W	L	ERA	G	GS	IP	H	HR	BB	SO	BB/9	SO/9	WHIP	AVG
2022	22	Rays (FCL)	R	0	1	7.20	3	3	5	7	0	2	9	3.6	16.2	1.80	.318
2022	22	Charleston (CAR)	LoA	0	1	2.45	4	4	11	8	1	2	15	1.6	12.3	0.91	.190
Minor League Totals				1	2	2.54	17	17	60	48	2	9	76	1.3	11.3	0.94	.210

11 OSLEIVIS BASABE, 2B/3B

Born: Sept. 13, 2000. **B-T:** R-R. **HT:** 6-1. **WT:** 165.
Signed: Venezuela, 2000. **Signed by:** Carlos Plaza (Rangers).

TRACK RECORD: The Rangers signed Basabe with some of the bonus room they had acquired in their attempt to sign Shohei Ohtani. Texas then traded him to the Rays in a six-player deal that sent Nate Lowe to the Rangers. Basabe has shown an intelligent, heady approach at the plate and in the field, but he's not the twitchy athlete he appeared to be when he signed out of Venezuela.

SCOUTING REPORT: Basabe is a career .316 minor league hitter who didn't look out of place as a teenager playing in the winter Venezuelan League. As one of the youngest players in the Southern League, his .333 batting average was best in the league among hitters with 200 or more plate appearances. Basabe hits the ball hard with a level swing that produces tons of contact and hard line drives, but few lofted fly balls. Unless he revamps his swing, he projects as a plus hitter with below-average power. Basabe rarely misses a hittable pitch in the strike zone. Defensively, he has only average hands and feet and an average arm, but he slows the game down, rarely rushes himself and has a quick release that allows his arm to work at second or third base.

THE FUTURE: It says something for Basabe's development that the Rays added him to the 40-man roster while trading Xavier Edwards to the Marlins. Basabe should compete for a spot with Triple-A Durham in spring training. His baseball IQ and bat-to-ball skills could get him to St. Petersburg before his 23rd birthday.

BA GRADE: 50/High	Hit: 60	Power: 40	Run: 55	Field: 50	Arm: 50

Year	Age	Club (League)	Lvl	AVG	G	AB	R	H	2B	3B	HR	RBI	BB	SO	SB	OBP	SLG
2022	21	Bowling Green (SAL)	HiA	.315	55	216	41	68	16	2	4	22	16	34	7	.370	.463
2022	21	Montgomery (SL)	AA	.333	57	228	39	76	23	3	0	25	24	25	14	.399	.461
Minor League Totals				.316	271	1091	199	345	67	19	8	149	99	150	58	.375	.434

12 BROCK JONES, OF

Born: March 28, 2001. **B-T:** L-L. **HT:** 6-0. **WT:** 197.
Drafted: Stanford, 2022 (2nd round). **Signed by:** Tim Fortugno.

TRACK RECORD: As a freshman at Stanford, Jones played special teams for the Cardinal football team in addition to baseball. He focused full-time on baseball in 2021 and 2022, and helped lead Stanford to the College World Series. He had a three home run game in the super regional and also homered in Omaha. After being drafted in the second round by the Rays, he was sent to Low-A Charleston where he helped them win the Carolina League title.

SCOUTING REPORT: Jones has strength, he glides to balls in the outfield with a graceful gait and plus speed and he seems to embrace being in the spotlight. The big question facing Jones is whether he's going to hit enough for his other tools to play. He's a streaky hitter with a choppy swing, but when he's hot, he can carry a team. He hit 15 of his 21 home runs for Stanford in the final 27 games of the season, including a six-game home run streak. Jones is comfortable working counts and should consistently get on base. Jones is physically mature and maxed out, but he's just started focusing on baseball full-time, so there's some developmental projection remaining. His speed is an asset in center field, where he's a plus defender. His arm is below-average.

THE FUTURE: Jones is yet another in the Rays' large collection of athletic center fielders with power, defense, speed and some hit tool questions. With Shane Sasaki on the same development path, Jones will likely start playing corner outfield spots in 2023 just to ensure the Rays can spread innings around.

BA GRADE: 50/High		Hit: 45		Power: 55		Run: 60			Field: 60			Arm: 40	
Year	Age	Club (League)	Lvl	AVG	G	AB	R	H	2B	3B	HR	RBI	BB	SO	SB	OBP	SLG
2022	21	Rays (FCL)	R	.211	6	19	4	4	0	0	0	2	5	6	2	.375	.211
2022	21	Charleston (CAR)	LoA	.286	13	49	15	14	4	1	4	12	12	21	9	.419	.653
Minor League Totals				.265	19	68	19	18	4	1	4	14	17	27	11	.407	.529

13 XAVIER ISAAC, 1B

Born: December 17, 2003. **B-T:** L-L. **HT:** 6-0. **WT:** 240.
Drafted: HS—Kernersville, NC, 2022 (1st round). **Signed by:** Landon Lassiter.

TRACK RECORD: The Rays made one of the most surprising picks of the 2022 first round when they drafted Isaac with the 29th pick and signed him to the slot-recommended $2.548 million bonus. Isaac had missed the entire 2021 summer showcase circuit because of a broken bone in his foot, meaning MLB teams got very few chances to see him face top-level pitching. The track record of players with Isaac's profile of prep prospects who missed the summer showcase circuit is concerning. Recent other examples among first round picks include Austin Beck, Keonic Cavaco, Connor Scott and Jordyn Adams. All four have been disappointments as pros.

SCOUTING REPORT: The Rays are extremely confident in Isaac's ability to hit for average and power, as that's his standout and carrying tools. He is a massive 6-foot, 240 pound first baseman who is a well below-average runner and currently a below-average fielder at first base. He actually looks more comfortable in the outfield, but with his frame and speed, is unlikely to stick there as a pro. If Isaac hits like the Rays believe, none of that will matter. Isaac has exceptional power potential with top-of-the-scale raw power that matches up with almost anyone. He also has shown bat-to-ball skills and the ability to use the whole field, but that was largely in games against non-competitive pitching.

THE FUTURE: Isaac had just 21 plate appearances with the Rays' Florida Complex League team in his pro debut, so it will be 2023 before evaluators get a feel for what he can do. He's a high-risk prospect, but one with a middle-of-the-lineup, home-run champ ceiling.

BA GRADE: 55/Extreme		Hit: 50		Power: 65		Run: 30			Field: 40			Arm: 45	
Year	Age	Club (League)	Lvl	AVG	G	AB	R	H	2B	3B	HR	RBI	BB	SO	SB	OBP	SLG
2022	18	Rays (FCL)	R	.211	5	19	4	4	3	0	0	5	2	3	0	.286	.368
Minor League Totals				.211	5	19	4	4	3	0	0	5	2	3	0	.286	.368

14 RENE PINTO, C

Born: Nov. 2, 1996. **B-T:** R-R. **HT:** 5-10. **WT:** 195.
Signed: Venezuela, 2013. **Signed by:** William Bergolla/Ronnie Blanco/Marlon Roche.

TRACK RECORD: Pinto made his MLB debut on April 26, 2022. He's also the second-longest employed Ray on the 40-man roster. Pinto signed with the Rays out of Venezuela in 2013. Only 2012 signee Yonny Chrinos has been a Ray longer among players on the current 40-man roster. Because he's a late-bloomer, Pinto was only added to the 40-man roster before the 2022 season, so he used only his first option while shuttling back-and-forth from Durham to Tampa Bay and back.

SCOUTING REPORT: Pinto fits the profile of an MLB backup catcher thanks to arm, power and defense. And he doesn't fit the profile of a starting catcher because of his struggles to consistently make contact. His significant swing-and-miss issues at the plate ensures he gets to that power only sporadically. Pinto should do better than the 42% strikeout rate he showed in his MLB debut, but his modest bat speed and bat-to-ball skills explain why he projects to be a well below-average hitter. He's a solid game-caller, but only an average receiver. Pinto does a good job of shutting down running games with a plus arm.

THE FUTURE: Pinto's 2023 season will largely be determined by the Rays other moves at catcher. Pinto is ready to serve as the Rays' backup catcher, but if the Rays add an external catcher and retain Francisco Mejia, Pinto would likely end up back as the No. 3 catcher for another year thanks to his two remaining options.

BA GRADE: 40/Low		Hit: 30		Power: 55		Run: 40			Field: 50			Arm: 60		

Year	Age	Club (League)	Lvl	AVG	G	AB	R	H	2B	3B	HR	RBI	BB	SO	SB	OBP	SLG
2022	25	Durham (IL)	AAA	.266	73	282	39	75	26	2	14	54	22	82	1	.320	.521
2022	25	Tampa Bay (AL)	MLB	.213	25	80	5	17	3	0	2	10	2	35	0	.241	.325
Major League Totals				.213	25	80	5	17	3	0	2	10	2	35	0	.241	.325
Minor League Totals				.276	521	1921	260	531	132	12	58	299	143	441	17	.330	.448

15 WILLY VASQUEZ, 3B

Born: Sept. 6, 2001. **B-T:** R-R. **HT:** 6-0. **WT:** 191.
Signed: Dominican Republic, 2019. **Signed by:** Remmy Hernandez/Daniel Santana.

TRACK RECORD: Vasquez was one of the Rays' breakout prospects in 2021. He impressed in the Florida Complex League and earned a promotion to Low-A Charleston for the playoffs. Returning to Charleston to start 2022, he struggled at the plate in the first half of the season, but hit .320/.380/.553 from July 1 until the end of the season.

SCOUTING REPORT: Vasquez's aggressiveness at the plate caused him issues in 2022, especially early in the season. But he showed some improvements and adjustments as the season wore on. He has consistently shown plus-plus raw power, and his max exit velocities are top tier (114-115 mph), although he hits a lot of screaming ground balls. He struggles with pitch recognition and chasing sliders away, but his hand-eye coordination is excellent. Defensively, the development of Carson Williams meant Vasquez played much more third base in 2022. That's a better long-term fit for him as he projects as a plus defender with a plus arm at third and a fringe-average defender at shortstop. He's an average runner.

THE FUTURE: Vasquez has clear flaws he needs to improve, but the foundation is there to be an everyday regular in the majors as a third baseman with the power and glove to be a productive player. He impressed in Australia to add further at-bats during the winter. He will jump to Bowling Green in 2023, but with a 40-man roster decision looming after the 2023 season, the pace of his development needs to pick up.

BA GRADE: 50/High		Hit: 40		Power: 60		Run: 50			Field: 60			Arm: 60		

Year	Age	Club (League)	Lvl	AVG	G	AB	R	H	2B	3B	HR	RBI	BB	SO	SB	OBP	SLG
2022	20	Charleston (CAR)	LoA	.256	113	449	78	115	21	9	10	73	36	126	25	.313	.410
Minor League Totals				.271	164	639	110	173	29	13	12	109	57	157	41	.333	.413

16 KAMERON MISNER, OF

Born: Jan. 8, 1998. **B-T:** L-L. **HT:** 6-4. **WT:** 219.
Drafted: Missouri, 2019 (1st round supplemental). **Signed by:** Joe Dunigan (Marlins).

TRACK RECORD: A rough finish to his junior season at Missouri knocked Misner out of the first round in the 2019 draft, but his power and speed meant he still only lasted to the 35th pick. The Marlins traded him to the Rays for infielder Joey Wendle. In his first season as a Ray, Misner led the Southern League with 84 walks and was third with a .384 on-base percentage.

SCOUTING REPORT: Misner is a capable center fielder who has speed and power, but his troubles with strikeouts stand between him and a regular spot in the majors. Misner was too passive in 2022. It did help him pile up walks, but also left him behind in counts. Misner faced two-strike counts three times as often as he saw three-ball counts. Misner has a solid understanding of the strike zone, but his uphill swing path means he has a small window of opportunity to make solid contact. Too often he misses pitches in the strike zone. Misner is a reliable, above-average defender in center field with an above-average arm. An above-average runner from home to first, he shows plus speed underway.

THE FUTURE: The Rays are an excellent fit for Misner, as Tampa Bay has shown it is willing to sacrifice some offense for excellent defense from its outfielders. Misner can play center, but as a Ray, he most likely fits as a plus defender in a corner. The Rays left him unprotected in the Rule 5 draft.

| BA GRADE: 45/High | | Hit: 40 | | Power: 55 | | Run: 60 | | Field: 60 | | Arm: 55 | |

Year	Age	Club (League)	Lvl	AVG	G	AB	R	H	2B	3B	HR	RBI	BB	SO	SB	OBP	SLG
2022	24	Montgomery (SL)	AA	.251	117	415	80	104	25	1	16	62	86	155	32	.384	.431
Minor League Totals				.255	261	973	177	248	63	4	30	145	173	333	69	.373	.420

17 SANTIAGO SUAREZ, RHP

Born: Jan. 11, 2005. **B-T:** R-R. **HT:** 6-2. **WT:** 175.
Signed: Venezuela, 2022. **Signed by:** Manuel Padron/Clifford Nuitter/Tibaldo Hernandez (Marlins).
TRACK RECORD: Suarez was a bit of a late bloomer. The Marlins are one of the more patient teams on the international amateur market, so when Suarez showed quality stuff as a 17-year-old, they were well-positioned to sign him for $385,000. He made his pro debut just 10 days after he signed and quickly established himself as one of the best pitchers in the Dominican Summer League. The Rays acquired him as part of a four-player deal that sent Xavier Edwards and J.T. Chargois to the Marlins.
SCOUTING REPORT: Suarez is an extremely well-rounded pitching prospect with a chance to have three average or better pitches and above-average control and command. Suarez's maturity, clean arm action and athleticism makes it easy for scouts to see him developing as a starting pitcher. He already shows feel for getting ahead of hitters thanks to his ability to land his curveball for strikes and he has a 92-95 mph fastball with the ride to work up in the zone. His changeup is less developed, but has enough promise to project as a future average pitch.
THE FUTURE: As soon as he became a Ray, Suarez became one of the team's best young pitching prospects. It's reasonable to expect further velocity gains as he matures. He projects as a solid back-end starting pitcher.

| BA GRADE: 45/High | | Fastball: 55 | | Curveball: 55 | Changeup: 50 | | Control: 60 | | | | |

Year	Age	Club (League)	Lvl	W	L	ERA	G	GS	IP	H	HR	BB	SO	BB/9	SO/9	WHIP	AVG
2022	17	Miami (DSL)	R	1	1	2.31	11	11	39	36	1	6	38	1.4	8.8	1.08	.250
Minor League Totals				1	1	2.31	11	11	39	36	1	6	38	1.4	8.8	1.08	.250

18 HERIBERTO HERNANDEZ, OF

Born: Dec. 16, 1999. **B-T:** R-R. **HT:** 6-1. **WT:** 180.
Signed: Dominican Republic, 2017. **Signed by:** Willy Espinal (Rangers).
TRACK RECORD: Acquired in the 2020 trade that sent Nate Lowe to the Rangers, Hernandez set the High-A Bowling Green single-season home run record with 24, but he also finished third in the South Atlantic League with 155 strikeouts.
SCOUTING REPORT: Hernandez has hit the ball as hard as nearly anyone in the Rays organization for a couple of years. In 2022 he developed a better ability to lift the ball to hit long home runs rather than just screaming line drives and ground balls. Hernandez is going to have to hit for big power, as he has below-average bat-to-ball skills. He makes solid swing decisions, but trades plenty of swings and misses and strikeouts to hit the ball as hard as he does. A former catcher, Hernandez does not fit the Rays profile for an outfielder thanks to his defensive limitations. He's fringe-average at best in left or right field and isn't capable of playing center field. First base is an option as well, as the Rays haven't regularly played an outfielder who can't play center since Avisail Garcia in 2019.
THE FUTURE: Hernandez was left off the 40-man roster and went unpicked in the Rule 5 draft. He remains an intriguing power prospect, but as he heads to Double-A, he need to make strides defensively and find a little more adjustability to his swing.

| BA GRADE: 45/High | | Hit: 40 | | Power: 60 | | Run: 40 | | Field: 45 | | Arm: 55 | |

Year	Age	Club (League)	Lvl	AVG	G	AB	R	H	2B	3B	HR	RBI	BB	SO	SB	OBP	SLG
2022	22	Bowling Green (SAL)	HiA	.255	119	419	70	107	28	1	24	89	67	155	6	.368	.499
Minor League Totals				.278	305	1051	229	292	75	10	59	231	198	346	24	.402	.537

19 GREG JONES, SS

Born: March 7, 1998. **B-T:** B-R. **HT:** 6-2. **WT:** 175.
Drafted: UNC Wilmington, 2019 (1st round). **Signed by:** Joe Hastings.
TRACK RECORD: A draft-eligible sophomore who broke out at UNC Wilmington in 2019, Jones has long been considered a promising prospect with loud tools, but injuries and inconsistency have hampered his production since being drafted 22nd overall.
SCOUTING REPORT: Jones had struggled in a late-season promotion to Double-A Montgomery in 2021, but that was a month after a strong half season at High-A Bowling Green. His 2022 season was much more troubling for his development. Jones has a level, flat swing that should help him make plenty of

contact, but he swings through hittable pitches. He has a better righthanded swing than lefty with more consistency and more power. Jones has plus raw power (although it doesn't always play in games), a plus arm and plus-plus speed. He makes highlight plays defensively, but also struggles at times to make routine plays. Jones has only played shortstop with the Rays, but some scouts have long believed he could be even better in center field. Jones is a career 86% basestealer. He has battled shoulder, knee and quad injuries. His 79 games played in 2022 was actually a career high.

THE FUTURE: The pandemic did Jones no favors, as he didn't reach full-season ball until he was 23 years old, but he has to start speeding up his development. The Rays demonstrated their continued faith in Jones by adding him to the 40-man roster, protecting him from the major league Rule 5 draft. But Jones will turn 25 before the 2023 season begins. He'll need to make significant strides in his contact ability and his defensive consistency. He could start to add some defensive versatility as well, but his main focus has to be on improving his contact ability.

| BA GRADE: 45/High | | Hit: 30 | | Power: 45 | | Field: 55 | | Run: 70 | | Arm: 60 | |

Year	Age	Club (League)	Lvl	AVG	G	AB	R	H	2B	3B	HR	RBI	BB	SO	SB	OBP	SLG
2022	24	Montgomery (SL)	AA	.238	79	319	54	76	19	3	8	40	27	128	37	.318	.392
Minor League Totals				.273	199	784	149	214	40	11	23	104	82	280	90	.358	.440

20 COLBY WHITE, RHP

Born: July 4, 1998. **B-T:** R-R. **HT:** 6-0. **WT:** 210.
Drafted: Mississippi State, 2019 (6th round). **Signed by:** Rickey Drexler.

TRACK RECORD: While many MLB relievers are starters who move to the bullpen at the big league level, White has been developed to be a closer. He finished games at Pearl River (Miss.) JC for two years, served as a setup man at Mississippi State and then moved right back into serving as a closer in pro ball. He climbed four minor league levels in 2021, and seemed ready to compete for a spot in the Rays bullpen, but he tore his ulnar collateral ligament and had Tommy John surgery in April 2022.

SCOUTING REPORT: White has the stuff to be a moment-of-truth reliever if he returns to his pre-injury form. As a short righthander with an extremely lively 94-98 mph fastball that consistently gets above hitters' bats at the top of the zone, White also mixes in a low-80s plus slider and a developing splitter. His changeup is below-average, but does keep lefties on their toes. White doesn't try to work the corners, but his fringe-average control is enough as he has enough stuff to beat hitters in the zone even if he's not painting the corners.

THE FUTURE: White was expected to be part of the Rays' bullpen in 2022 before his elbow injury caused a delay to those plans. The Rays still added him to the 40-man roster in the offseason, figuring that someone with his back-of-the-bullpen stuff would be nabbed if left to the Rule 5 draft. He should be ready to return by May or June, and could play a factor in the Rays bullpen in the second half of 2023.

| BA GRADE: 50/Extreme | Fastball: 70 | Slider: 60 | Splitter: 45 | Changeup: 40 | Control: 45 |

Year	Age	Club (League)	Lvl	W	L	ERA	G	GS	IP	H	HR	BB	SO	BB/9	SO/9	WHIP	AVG
2022	24	Did not play—Injured															

21 RYAN CERMAK, OF

Born: June 2, 2001. **B-T:** R-R. **HT:** 6-1. **WT:** 205.
Drafted: Illinois State, 2022 (2nd round supplemental). **Signed by:** Tom Couston

TRACK RECORD: Illinois State has had a number of impressive future big leaguers in recent years, led by Paul DeJong and Owen Miller, but it's been quite a while since they had a slugger like Cermak. Cermak hit 19 home runs, which was the most by a Redbird hitter since 1999. A third baseman as a freshman, Cermak quickly found a home in center field. He had a brief stint in the Florida Complex League in his pro debut, showing power and speed in his seven-game cameo.

SCOUTING REPORT: Cermak fits a lot of the attributes the Rays look for in their outfield prospects. He's a center fielder with a plus arm that could capably fit in a corner as well. Cermak has shown a steady knack for making the highlight-caliber play in center, but by Rays standards, he will be competing with a lot of other above-average defenders in center. He has been clocked at 95 mph on the mound. He's also an above-average runner. Cermak has plenty of bat speed and looks to do damage with plus power. He should top 110 mph exit velocities at his best. He can get too aggressive, as he'll need to better lay off sliders off the plate in pro ball.

THE FUTURE: Cermak's seven-game stint in the FCL was largely designed just to get him comfortable with the routine and schedule of pro ball. He'll get a much heavier workload in 2023, and could battle for a spot in High-A Bowling Green. Long-term, he projects as a power-oriented, well-rounded center fielder.

BA GRADE: 45/High		Hit: 45		Power: 55		Run: 55			Field: 55			Arm: 60	
Year	Age	Club (League)	Lvl	AVG	G	AB	R	H	2B	3B	HR	RBI	BB	SO	SB	OBP	SLG
2022	21	Rays (FCL)	R	.273	7	22	5	6	0	1	2	5	1	9	3	.333	.636
Minor League Totals				.273	7	22	5	6	0	1	2	5	1	9	3	.333	.636

22 CHANDLER SIMPSON, OF

Born: Nov. 18, 2000. **B-T:** L-R. **HT:** 6-0. **WT:** 170.
Drafted: Georgia Tech, 2022 (2nd round supplemental). **Signed by:** Milt Mill.
TRACK RECORD: Georgia Tech's single-season batting average leaderboard is a remarkable who's who of future big leaguers. Jay Payton's .434 is the Yellow Jackets' single-season record. Coming into 2022, Mark Teixeira, Nomar Garciaparra, Riccardo Ingram and Jason Varitek were the rest of the top five. But Simpson, a transfer from Alabama-Birmingham, just missed breaking Payton's record with a .433 junior season that led the nation by 22 points.
SCOUTING REPORT: Simpson is a true throwback as a contact hitter who relies heavily on his top-of-the-scale speed. His speed is a true game changer. He scored from second on a sacrifice fly in a college game in 2022 without an error. He also was one of the hardest hitters in college baseball to strike out. Simpson's entire approach is focused around spraying the ball. He has bottom-of-the-scale power and is not expected to ever hit more than five home runs a year. Simpson played second base in college, where his sidearm throwing motion was somewhat stressed and his well below-average arm strength was a clear liability. The Rays moved him to left field immediately, where he has the speed to cover massive amounts of ground. His throwing motion is a little better from the outfield as well.
THE FUTURE: Simpson is the type of player who barely exists in the current pro game. He has bottom-of-the-scale power, but he has the speed to beat out hits on ground balls hit to shortstop or third base. The new pickoff rules, pitch clock and bigger bases all should help Simpson raise havoc on the basepaths.

BA GRADE: 45/High		Hit: 60		Power: 20		Run: 80			Field: 55			Arm: 30	
Year	Age	Club (League)	Lvl	AVG	G	AB	R	H	2B	3B	HR	RBI	BB	SO	SB	OBP	SLG
2022	21	Rays (FCL)	R	.370	8	27	5	10	3	0	0	3	6	4	8	.471	.481
Minor League Totals				.370	8	27	5	10	3	0	0	3	6	4	8	.471	.481

23 CARLOS COLMENAREZ, SS

Born: Nov. 15, 2003. **B-T:** L-R. **HT:** 5-10. **WT:** 185.
Signed: Dominican Republic, 2021. **Signed by:** Daniel Santana.
TRACK RECORD: Colmenarez was the Rays' top target and one of the top prospects in the 2020 international amateur class that got delayed to a Jan 15, 2021 signing date. After an injury-marred 2021 season in the Dominican Summer League, Colmenarez sandwiched two poor months around an excellent July (.302/.413/.453) in his domestic debut in the Florida Complex League.
SCOUTING REPORT: Colmenarez was seen as one of the more advanced hitters in his signing class, but he's struggled with pitch selection and approach at times as a pro. He needs to get better at recognizing and hitting breaking balls. He has yet to show the power development that was expected when he signed, but it is worth remembering that he will play the entire 2023 season as a 20-year-old. Defensively, Colmenarez has lived up to expectations. He has above-average range and a plus arm, and he showed reliability as well, making only three errors in 23 games.
THE FUTURE: Colmenarez's logical next step is Low-A Charleston, but he needs to take more controlled swings and a better approach if he's going to handle the jump to a significantly more advanced level. He still has the potential to be an everyday regular as a lefthanded hitting shortstop who's capable of handling the defensive responsibilities, but he's likely to be a one-level a year prospect.

BA GRADE: 50/Extreme		Hit: 45		Power: 45		Field: 55			Run: 55			Arm: 60	
Year	Age	Club (League)	Lvl	AVG	G	AB	R	H	2B	3B	HR	RBI	BB	SO	SB	OBP	SLG
2022	18	Rays (FCL)	R	.254	35	126	36	32	7	3	1	19	17	41	13	.379	.381
Minor League Totals				.251	61	223	43	56	9	4	1	31	25	71	20	.353	.341

24 SHANE SASAKI, OF

Born: July 1, 2000. **B-T:** R-R. **HT:** 6-0. **WT:** 175.
Drafted: HS—Honolulu, Hawaii, 2019 (3rd round). **Signed by:** Casey Onaga.
TRACK RECORD: Sasaki was the Rays' most improved prospect in 2022. Before the season began, he appeared on track to be an org player as an outfielder who could run and play center field, but didn't hit with enough authority to project as a big leaguer. Before 2022, Sasaki would normally lose weight throughout the season. He added 10-15 pounds of good weight and then maintained it through the season while making better swing decisions. He was one of the best players on Baseball America's 2022 MiLB Team of the Year.
SCOUTING REPORT: Sasaki is a top- or bottom-of-the-order table setter who knows that's what he is. His improved strength now allows him to line balls to the gaps, but he's not a home run threat. Sasaki has also improved his pitch recognition and become more selective, staying in the strike zone. His two-strike approach is now what you want in a contact hitter. He has plus-plus speed that plays on the basepaths. He's an above-average defender in center field with a fringe-average arm. That might not be enough to play center for the Rays, as they are a team that wants top-of-the-scale defenders in center, but it will play for a lot of teams.
THE FUTURE: Sasaki put himself on the prospect radar with his breakout season, but he needs to now build on that.

| BA GRADE: 45/High | | Hit: 50 | | Power: 30 | | Speed: 70 | | Field: 55 | | Arm: 45 | |

Year	Age	Club (League)	Lvl	AVG	G	AB	R	H	2B	3B	HR	RBI	BB	SO	SB	OBP	SLG
2022	21	Charleston (CAR)	LoA	.324	89	346	71	112	27	3	9	57	49	92	47	.410	.497
Minor League Totals				.304	135	514	110	156	33	5	11	74	70	147	70	.390	.451

25 MARCUS JOHNSON, RHP

Born: Dec. 11, 2000. **B-T:** R-R. **HT:** 6-0. **WT:** 200.
Drafted: Duke, 2022 (4th round). **Signed by:** Blake Newsome (Marlins).
TRACK RECORD: Johnson was one of Duke's best relievers in 2021. He moved into the rotation as Duke's Friday night starter for 2022, but he struggled in the new role, even if he continued to show solid stuff and the ability to both miss bats and throw strikes. The Rays acquired him and Santiago Suarez in the November 2022 trade that sent Xavier Edwards and J.T. Chargois to the Marlins.
SCOUTING REPORT: Johnson was hit hard for a pitcher with quality stuff. His average fastball sits at 91-93 mph and touches 95 as a starter and he's touched 97 as a reliever. It doesn't have particularly notable movement characteristics, so it's better as a pitch to set up his secondaries more than it is a bat-misser on its own. His low-80s slider and mid-80s changeup both also have promise to be above-average pitches or better. He will sometimes tip his changeup by slowing his arm speed, but it has tumble and fade when he throws it properly. His slider has plenty of sweep and bat-missing potential.
THE FUTURE: Johnson's success has come as a reliever, not as a starter, but the Rays see Johnson having starter traits, and they will continue to develop him as such.

| BA GRADE: 45/High | | Fastball: 50 | | Slider: 55 | | Changeup: 55 | | Control: 50 | |

Year	Age	Club (League)	Lvl	W	L	ERA	G	GS	IP	H	HR	BB	SO	BB/9	SO/9	WHIP	AVG
2022	21	Marlins (FCL)	R	0	1	8.31	2	2	4	5	0	4	5	8.3	10.4	2.08	.294
2022	21	Jupiter (FSL)	LoA	1	2	5.11	3	2	12	7	2	7	24	5.1	17.5	1.14	.159
Minor League Totals				1	3	5.94	5	4	17	12	2	11	29	5.9	15.7	1.38	.197

26 CALVIN FAUCHER, RHP

Born: Sept. 22, 1995. **B-T:** R-R. **HT:** 6-1. **WT:** 190.
Drafted: UC Irvine, 2017 (10th round). **Signed by:** John Leavitt (Twins).
TRACK RECORD: A $10,000 senior sign as a 2017 Twins 10th-round pick, Faucher's development has been entirely as a reliever. He pitched in the bullpen at Southwestern (Calif.) JC, was the closer for UC Irvine and pitched as a reliever in five seasons in the minors before he made his MLB debut on May 9, 2022. The Rays acquired Faucher along with DH Nelson Cruz for Joe Ryan and Drew Strotman in July 2021.
SCOUTING REPORT: When Faucher was drafted, he threw a low-90s fastball and a low-80s slider. Now, his slider sits in the same velocity range as he fastball did coming out of school. Faucher's hard 88-91 mph slider is a plus pitch with sweep but very modest depth, producing chases and swings and misses from righties. His mid-80s curveball has flashed plus potential, especially against lefthanded hitters, with vertical depth but he seemed to lose confidence in it in 2022. Faucher's mid-90s fastball is only average,

and becomes less effective when he's behind in counts and hitters can hunt for it. Faucher's control and command are only fringe-average and he struggles at times to throw strikes. He searched for a comfortable spot on the pitching rubber all year, going from the first base to third base side of the rubber.
THE FUTURE: Faucher should fit in the Rays' bullpen mix in 2023 as a reliever.

BA GRADE: 40/Medium	Fastball: 50			Curveball: 55		Slider: 60				Control: 45			
Year	Age	Club (League)	Lvl	W	L	ERA	G	GS	IP	H	HR	BB	SO	BB/9	SO/9	WHIP	AVG
2022	26	Durham (IL)	AAA	3	3	3.56	34	4	43	44	7	21	52	4.4	10.9	1.51	.260
2022	26	Tampa Bay (AL)	MLB	2	3	5.48	22	0	21	26	4	10	21	4.2	8.9	1.69	.289
Major League Totals				2	3	5.48	22	0	21	26	4	10	21	4.2	8.9	1.69	.289
Minor League Totals				14	10	4.08	141	7	227	230	22	113	260	4.5	10.3	1.51	.264

27 KEVIN KELLY, RHP

Born: Nov. 28, 1997. **B-T:** R-R. **HT:** 6-2. **WT:** 200.
Drafted: James Madison, 2019 (19th round). **Signed by:** Bob Mayer (Guardians).
TRACK RECORD: Kelly spent two seasons in James Madison's rotation including a year as the school's Friday starter before the Guardians selected him in the 19th round. The Guardians immediately moved him to the bullpen. His lone pro start is as a two-inning opener, but his time as a college starter has helped him battle and show plenty of guile. Even with a crowded 40-man roster, the Rays liked Kelly enough to pay cash to Colorado to get the Rockies to pick him for them in the Rule 5 draft.
SCOUTING REPORT: Kelly is a sidearmer who rarely dominates, but never gets dominated. There's nothing all that flashy about his low-90s sinker, his four-seam fastball or his sweepy above-average slider. But hitters rarely square Kelly up, and more often, they end up hitting a grounder off his sinker or slider for weak contact. Like a number of sinker-slider righthanders, he's deadly to righthanded hitters but more vulnerable against lefties, although he can drop over a curve to try to give them something else to worry about.
THE FUTURE: The Rays love to give hitters different looks when they go to the bullpen. Kelly fits that perfectly, and he was one of the most MLB-ready pitchers available in the Rule 5 draft as a reliever with more than 30 successful outings at Triple-A.

BA GRADE: 40/Medium	Fastball: 50			Slider: 55		Curveball: 45				Control: 55			
Year	Age	Club (League)	Lvl	W	L	ERA	G	GS	IP	H	HR	BB	SO	BB/9	SO/9	WHIP	AVG
2022	24	Akron (EL)	AA	3	2	1.11	16	0	24	14	0	9	32	3.3	11.8	0.95	.157
2022	24	Columbus (IL)	AAA	2	0	2.73	32	1	33	28	1	13	43	3.5	11.7	1.24	.220
Minor League Totals				11	7	3.17	102	1	131	116	9	32	181	2.2	12.5	1.13	.230

28 AUSTIN VERNON, RHP

Born: Feb. 8, 1999. **B-T:** R-R. **HT:** 6-8. **WT:** 265.
Drafted: North Carolina Central, 2021 (10th round). **Signed by:** Joe Hastings.
TRACK RECORD: A massive 6-foot-8 righthander, Vernon is likely to be the last player ever drafted out of North Carolina Central after the school cut its baseball program at the end of 2021, his draft season. He served as a long reliever/spot starter by design in 2022 as it helped him get more innings to work on his delivery.
SCOUTING REPORT: He may have started in 2022, but Vernon's effortful and almost violent delivery and long arm action beckon for a bullpen role. Vernon's success is largely thanks to a devastating plus slider. He often shows better control and command of it than his fastball, and Class A hitters were utterly defenseless when he threw it in advantageous counts. Vernon's fastball gives hitters a second above-average pitch to worry about. His struggles to control it sometimes hindered its effectiveness in 2022, but it has outstanding carry with nearly 20 inches of induced vertical break, bushels of run and he sits 94-96 mph while touching 97-98. He has an average changeup as well. It's his below-average control that is his biggest hurdle.
THE FUTURE: Vernon has the stuff to be a useful reliever, but there's a lot of refinement still to go. He has smoothed out his delivery somewhat compared to what it was in college, but it still is difficult to repeat. But his stuff is top-shelf.

BA GRADE: 45/High	Fastball: 60			Slider: 65		Changeup: 50				Control: 40			
Year	Age	Club (League)	Lvl	W	L	ERA	G	GS	IP	H	HR	BB	SO	BB/9	SO/9	WHIP	AVG
2022	23	Charleston (CAR)	LoA	9	1	1.69	15	1	59	32	6	23	91	3.5	14.0	0.94	.156
2022	23	Bowling Green (SAL)	HiA	0	3	4.50	9	6	20	12	1	18	23	8.1	10.4	1.50	.176
Minor League Totals				11	4	2.20	29	9	90	48	7	45	131	4.5	13.1	1.03	.154

29 AUSTIN SHENTON, 3B

Born: Jan. 22, 1998. **B-T:** R-R. **HT:** 6-0. **WT:** 205.
Drafted: Florida International, 2019 (5th round). **Signed by:** Dan Rovetto (Mariners).
TRACK RECORD: Shenton's a fringy defender who will have to really hit to carve out a big league role, so his 2022 season can only be viewed as a significant setback. Hampered by a hip injury, Shenton never got going in 2022, as his OPS dropped nearly 200 points from his 2021 breakout season that saw him traded to the Rays for Diego Castilo. He spent the second half of the season on the injured list.
SCOUTING REPORT: Shenton has big lefthanded power, although it wasn't nearly as apparent in 2022. He makes solid swing decisions, but he sacrifices contact ability for bat speed and exit velocities. His strikeout rate climbed while his power production dipped. At his best, Shenton can be a lefty power bat with solid on-base percentages and modest batting averages. He's going to have to hit, as he's a below-average defender at third. He can also handle first base adequately. He's a below-average runner.
THE FUTURE: The Rays left Shenton unprotected and he was not picked in the Rule 5 draft. He should get his first taste of Triple-A, as he should be fully ready to go for spring training. But he's going to need to stay healthy and drive the ball more consistently to factor into the Rays' future plans.

BA GRADE: 40/High		Hit: 40		Power: 60		Run: 40		Field: 40		Arm: 50	

Year	Age	Club (League)	Lvl	AVG	G	AB	R	H	2B	3B	HR	RBI	BB	SO	SB	OBP	SLG
2022	24	Montgomery (SL)	AA	.236	52	195	28	46	9	1	8	29	28	70	0	.338	.415
Minor League Totals				.280	185	708	123	198	58	6	29	135	94	201	1	.375	.501

30 IAN SEYMOUR, LHP

Born: Dec. 13, 1998. **B-T:** L-L. **HT:** 6-0. **WT:** 210.
Drafted: Virginia Tech, 2020 (2nd round). **Signed by:** Landon Lassiter.
TRACK RECORD: In 2021, Seymour was a very funky, fascinating lefty with two above-average or better pitches who impressed at two Class A stops and even got a spot start in Triple-A. When the 2022 season began it was clear that something was wrong. His velocity was down several notches and he was hit hard while struggling to find the strike zone. He was eventually diagnosed with a torn elbow ligament that required Tommy John surgery in June.
SCOUTING REPORT: When healthy, Seymour has a plus 90-94 mph fastball whose life and flat plane makes it more effective than his velocity may indicate. In addition, hitters struggle to pick up the ball because of Seymour's unusual delivery that hides the ball well. His 79-83 mph plus changeup is a true bat-misser as well. His below-average slider is not nearly as impressive. He's still really looking for a breaking ball, which is one of the reasons he projects to eventually slide to the pen. He has fringe-average control.
THE FUTURE: Seymour's elbow injury means he'll miss further time in 2023, but if he can get back to his pre-injury form, he's a funky lefty who can get righthanders out as a reliever with a different look that can baffle hitters.

BA GRADE: 45/Extreme		Fastball: 60		Slider: 40		Changeup: 60		Control: 45	

Year	Age	Club (League)	Lvl	W	L	ERA	G	GS	IP	H	HR	BB	SO	BB/9	SO/9	WHIP	AVG
2022	23	Montgomery (SL)	AA	0	2	8.10	5	5	17	22	2	12	23	6.5	12.4	2.04	.319
Minor League Totals				4	2	3.38	19	18	72	48	6	31	110	3.9	13.8	1.10	.188

Texas Rangers

BY JOSH NORRIS

Over the past two offseasons, the Rangers have made one thing abundantly clear: They are willing to spend money to improve their team.

Following the 2021 season, Texas outlaid more than half a billion dollars to add shortstop Corey Seager, second baseman Marcus Semien and right-hander Jon Gray. A year later, they pulled an early stunner and lured ace righthander Jacob deGrom out of New York with a deal that will pay him $185 million over the next five seasons.

They'll need the help, because the American League West got a lot more difficult in 2022 thanks to a long-awaited breakthrough in the Pacific Northwest. The Mariners, led by budding superstar Julio Rodriguez and a homegrown core that also includes righthanders George Kirby and Logan Gilbert, made the playoffs for the first time since 2001.

The AL West crown—and the eventual World Series title—was won by the Astros, whose factory of young pitching does not appear to be near its conclusion.

If the Rangers do overtake one or both of those clubs in the near future, they'll do it under new leadership.

Longtime executive Jon Daniels was let go by the club in August—he caught on with the Rays—and two days prior, Texas fired manager Chris Woodward. He was replaced in the middle of October with veteran skipper Bruce Bochy.

Texas has a fine farm system that started to bear its first fruit late in the season, when 2019 first-rounder Josh Jung made his big league debut. The slugger, who has missed significant development time due to injuries, showed flashes of the potential the team hopes will turn into a middle-of-the-lineup thumper for years to come.

Below the surface, the Rangers' No. 1 prospect—outfielder Evan Carter—continued to look like one of the best hidden gems a team has unearthed in recent draft memory. Carter was deep below the radar, but Texas had connections and took him in the second round of the 2020 draft.

After missing most of his first pro season with a back injury, Carter re-emerged in 2022 and showed uncommon plate discipline and contact skills while playing an excellent center field. If he adds strength, he has all-star potential.

In the draft, the Rangers got creative. With the third overall pick, the team selected Kumar Rocker out of the independent Frontier League. Rocker, who was a teammate of 2021 Texas first-rounder Jack Leiter at Vanderbilt, was a first-rounder in 2021 but failed his physical with the Mets and did not sign.

The Rangers signed Rocker for well below slot

The Rangers graduated three preseason Top 30 Prospects, led by third baseman Ezequiel Duran.

PROJECTED 2026 LINEUP

Catcher	Jonah Heim	31
First Base	Nathaniel Lowe	31
Second Base	Marcus Semien	36
Third Base	Josh Jung	28
Shortstop	Corey Seager	32
Left Field	Ezequiel Duran	27
Center Field	Evan Carter	24
Right Field	Dustin Harris	27
Designated Hitter	Justin Foscue	27
No. 1 Starter	Jacob deGrom	38
No. 2 Starter	Jon Gray	34
No. 3 Starter	Owen White	26
No. 4 Starter	Brock Porter	23
No. 5 Starter	Jack Leiter	26
Closer	Kumar Rocker	26

value and used the savings to nab high school righthander Brock Porter for a record bonus among players selected in the fourth round.

Porter was one of the best high school arms available in the class, so Texas' two-step with Rocker could land the club a pair of impact arms.

Texas has spent big and done a good job putting together a farm system filled with players who not only can eventually supplement the big league roster, but could also be valuable trade chips if the team is chasing a playoff spot, something the team hasn't done in quite a while.

And with their recent free agent signings, the Rangers have proven Texas has room for much more than a lone star. ∎

DEPTH CHART

TEXAS RANGERS

TOP 2023 MLB CONTRIBUTORS	RANK
Owen White, RHP	2
Josh Jung, 3B	3
BREAKOUT PROSPECTS	
Yeison Morrobel, OF	13
Danyer Cueva, SS	18

SOURCE OF TOP 30 TALENT

Homegrown	28	Acquired	2
College	7	Trade	1
Junior college	0	Rule 5 draft	0
High school	13	Independent league	1
Nondrafted free agent	0	Free agent/waivers	0
International	8		

LF
Aaron Zavala (6)
Tommy Specht (28)
Alejandro Osuna

CF
Evan Carter (1)
Anthony Gutierrez (5)
Yeison Morrobel (13)
Jonathan Ornelas (25)
Jojo Blackmon (30)
Daniel Mateo

RF
Dustin Harris (9)
Marcos Torres (24)
Yosy Galan

3B
Gleider Figuereo (16)
Echedry Vargas (29)

SS
Cameron Cauley (15)
Danyer Cueva (18)
Chandler Pollard (23)

2B
Luisangel Acuña (4)
Justin Foscue (11)
Thomas Saggese (22)
Maximo Acosta

1B
Josh Jung (3)
Trevor Hauver
Blaine Crim

C
Cody Freeman
Matt Whatley
Jesus Lopez
Daniel Bruzal
Ian Moller

LHP

LHSP	LHRP
Mitchell Bratt (14)	Grant Wolfram
Cole Ragans (19)	
Cody Bradford (21)	
Larson Kindreich	

RHP

RHSP	RHRP
Owen White (2)	Marc Church
Jack Leiter (7)	Yerry Rodriguez
Brock Porter (8)	Winston Santos
Kumar Rocker (10)	Dane Acker
Cole Winn (12)	Leandro Calderon
Zak Kent (17)	Grant Anderson
Emiliano Teodo (20)	Ricky Vanasco
Luis Ramirez (26)	Fernery Ozuna
Tekoah Roby (27)	Nick Starr
	Tim Brennan

1 EVAN CARTER, OF

Born: Aug. 29, 2002. **B-T:** L-R. **HT:** 6-4. **WT:** 190.
Drafted: HS—Elizabethton, TN, 2020 (2nd round).
Signed by: Derrick Tucker/Ryan Coe.

TRACK RECORD: The Rangers shocked the industry by selecting Carter with their second-round pick in 2020 and signing him away from a commitment to Duke with a bonus of $1.25 million. The combination of not playing in many summer showcase events and the lost 2020 season meant that Carter didn't get as much exposure as typical prep prospects. Area scouts Derrick Tucker and Ryan Coe saw enough to pound the table for Carter, and he has repaid their confidence in spades. The Rangers immediately showed their confidence in Carter by jumping him over extended spring training and the Arizona Complex League to send him to Low-A Down East for his pro debut in 2021. He was the youngest player in the Carolina League when he debuted, and was the third-youngest player on a full-season roster on Opening Day, behind only Oakland's Robert Puason and the Marlins' Eury Perez. Carter showed hints of his potential with Down East before a back injury ended his season after jut 32 games. He arrived in 2022 no worse for wear and showed a tantalizing combination of contact, barrel accuracy, strike-zone discipline and speed in a season spent mostly at High-A Hickory. The staggered minor league schedule allowed Texas to push Carter to Double-A for the season's final week and the Texas League playoffs. He went 9-for-21 in the regular year and helped Frisco claim the TL championship.

SCOUTING REPORT: Carter has all the ingredients to be an impact player at the top of a lineup. His knowledge of the strike zone is extraordinary for someone so young and with such little experience. These traits showed in his outstanding chase and in-zone miss rates of just 17% and 15%, respectively. Overall, he swung and missed just 22% of the time, a figure that places him among the best in the system. He also did an excellent job hitting balls with the ideal combination of exit velocity and launch angle. Now, he needs to get stronger, and the Rangers believe his frame has plenty of room for extra muscle. Internal evaluators point to Carter's large hands and feet as reason to believe that the strength gains will come as he continues to grow into his body, though outside scouts are a little more skeptical based on his narrow frame. Defensively, Carter is athletic enough that he should be able to balance strength gains with the lithe athleticism needed to remain in center

EDDIE KELLY

BA GRADE	SCOUTING GRADES
60 Risk: High	Hit: 60. **Power:** 50. **Run:** 60. Field: 55. **Arm:** 50.

Projected future grades on 20-80 scouting scale

BEST TOOLS

BATTING

Best Hitter for Average	Aaron Zavala
Best Power Hitter	Sam Huff
Best Strike-Zone Discipline	Aaron Zavala
Fastest Baserunner	JoJo Blackmon
Best Athlete	JoJo Blackmon

PITCHING

Best Fastball	Winston Santos
Best Curveball	Owen White
Best Slider	Marc Church
Best Changeup	Fernery Ozuna
Best Control	Tim Brennan

FIELDING

Best Defensive Catcher	Matt Whatley
Best Defensive Infielder	Jonathan Ornelas
Best Infield Arm	Jonathan Ornelas
Best Defensive Outfielder	Evan Carter

in the long term. He already plays an excellent center field, with range in all directions. Carter also blends plus speed with the instincts to swipe plenty of bags as he moves up the ladder. He stole 28 bases in 2022, but the total might have been higher if he hadn't played through a foot injury resulting from a foul ball at the plate.

THE FUTURE: Carter will return to Double-A to begin 2023, when he'll continue his quest to marry his already top-flight plate discipline while also adding a little bit more thump. He has the ceiling of an excellent regular with a few all-star appearances.

Year	Age	Club (League)	Lvl	AVG	G	AB	R	H	2B	3B	HR	RBI	BB	SO	SB	OBP	SLG
2022	19	Hickory (SAL)	HiA	.287	100	376	78	108	18	10	11	66	59	75	26	.388	.476
2022	19	Frisco (TL)	AA	.429	6	21	8	9	3	0	1	7	5	6	2	.536	.714
Minor League Totals				.282	138	503	108	142	29	11	14	85	98	109	40	.406	.467

2 OWEN WHITE, RHP

Born: Aug. 9, 1999. **B-T:** R-R. **HT:** 6-3. **WT:** 199.
Drafted: HS—China Grove, NC, 2018 (2nd round). **Signed by:** Jay Heafner.

TRACK RECORD: Almost since the moment he was drafted, White's development has been stagnated. The Rangers rested him post-draft, he missed the 2019 season with Tommy John surgery and then lost 2020 to the pandemic. His 2021 season was limited to just 35.1 innings by a broken hand suffered during his first start of the season. He made up for lost time by pitching in the Arizona Fall League, where he was named the league's pitcher of the year. The 2022 season was White's fullest yet, but he still missed two months of the second half at Double-A Frisco with fatigue in his pitching arm. White returned for the Texas League playoffs and struck out all six hitters he faced in Frisco's championship-clinching win.

BA GRADE

55 Risk: High

SCOUTING REPORT: Despite pitching just 113.2 innings since being drafted in 2018, White has established himself as the clear top arm in Texas' system. He boasts a full four-pitch complement, led by a mid-90s fastball that peaked at 98 mph and grades as plus despite just average shape. White's best offspeed pitch is a mid-80s slider with excellent spin and shape that got chases at a rate of nearly 39%. His slider is followed closely by a curveball that averages nearly 3,000 rpm of spin and shows powerful downer break in the high 70s. Though his changeup is the fourth pitch in his arsenal, White throws it for plenty of strikes and scouts believe it could get to an average offering. He also throws a low-90s two-seamer, but it isn't a featured part of his mix. White ties everything together with plus control and a fierce competitive streak that draws raves throughout the organization.

THE FUTURE: After closing the year in Double-A, White will likely move to Triple-A Round Rock to begin 2023 and could push for a callup by season's end.

SCOUTING GRADES		Fastball: 55		Curveball: 55		Slider: 60		Changeup: 50		Control: 60					
Year	Age	Club (League)	Lvl	W	L	ERA	G	GS	IP	H	HR	BB	SO	BB/9	SO/9	WHIP	AVG
2022	22	Hickory (SAL)	HiA	6	2	3.99	11	10	59	51	7	19	81	2.9	12.4	1.19	.230
2022	22	Frisco (TL)	AA	3	0	2.49	4	4	22	19	1	4	23	1.7	9.6	1.06	.241
Minor League Totals				13	3	3.42	24	22	116	96	10	35	160	2.7	12.4	1.13	.224

3 JOSH JUNG, 3B

Born: Feb. 12, 1998. **B-T:** R-R. **HT:** 6-2. **WT:** 214.
Drafted: Texas Tech, 2019 (1st round). **Signed by:** Josh Simpson.

TRACK RECORD: When Jung stays healthy, he hits. Unfortunately, he's had serious trouble staying on the field since being drafted eighth overall out of Texas Tech in 2019. After earning co-Big 12 Conference player of the year honors in his draft season, Jung signed for $4.4 million, then spent what would have been his first full season as a pro at the Rangers' alternate training site in 2020. A broken foot limited him to 78 games in 2021 and shoulder surgery delayed the start of his 2022 season until July 28. Nonetheless, he recovered in time to make his MLB debut on Sept. 9.

BA GRADE

55 Risk: High

SCOUTING REPORT: The 2022 season was the first time Jung showed real weakness at the plate. Between Triple-A and the big leagues, he struck out 74 times against just 11 walks. He was extremely aggressive during his time in the minor leagues, swinging nearly half the time and missing on pitches in the zone around 20% of the time. Rangers officials believe Jung was pressing a little bit and expect him to look a bit more like himself with further experience. That's especially true considering injuries and the pandemic have limited him to just 777 plate appearances in three seasons. Jung is mostly steady at third base but struggles on hard shots hit his way. He's got the body control and agility to make accurate throws from a variety of angles, which mitigates his below-average arm strength. He's a below-average runner.

THE FUTURE: The Rangers have the middle infield locked up for a long while, but they have a vacancy at third base. Jung will battle with Ezequiel Duran for the spot, but first base is an option, too.

SCOUTING GRADES		Hitting: 55		Power: 60		Speed: 40		Fielding: 45		Arm: 50					
Year	Age	Club (League)	Lvl	AVG	G	AB	R	H	2B	3B	HR	RBI	BB	SO	SB	OBP	SLG
2022	24	Rangers (ACL)	R	.240	8	25	4	6	0	0	3	5	3	5	0	.345	.600
2022	24	Round Rock (PCL)	AAA	.273	23	99	15	27	7	0	6	24	4	30	1	.321	.525
2022	24	Texas (AL)	MLB	.204	26	98	9	20	4	1	5	14	4	39	2	.235	.418
Major League Totals				.204	26	98	9	20	4	1	5	14	4	39	2	.235	.418
Minor League Totals				.311	153	602	96	187	43	2	30	118	56	143	7	.381	.538

4 LUISANGEL ACUÑA, SS/2B

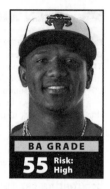

Born: March 12, 2002. **B-T:** R-R. **HT:** 5-10. **WT:** 181.
Signed: Venezuela, 2018. **Signed by:** Rafic Saab.

TRACK RECORD: Acuña is the younger brother of Braves superstar Ronald Acuña Jr. and signed out of Venezuela in 2018. He had a breakout season in 2021 at Low-A, where he was the ninth-ranked prospect in the Carolina League. Acuña's chance at encore was cut short almost immediately when he strained his hamstring in his first at-bat of the season when he stepped on first base awkwardly while trying to leg out an infield hit. He recovered to overwhelm High-A before hitting a speed bump in Double-A. He made up for the early lost at-bats by playing in the Arizona Fall League.

BA GRADE
55 **Risk:** High

SCOUTING REPORT: Acuña's offensive impact will depend on whether he can tone down his aggression. He doesn't swing and miss at an alarming rate, but he swings roughly 46% of the time and hits the ball on the ground at a rate higher than 50%. The Rangers expected Acuña to struggle once he got to Double-A and promoted him to the Texas League to let him find the holes in his game against more experienced pitchers. Acuña makes plenty of impact on contact, with a lot of high-end exit velocities hit at optimal angles. Defensively, there's little chance Acuña sticks at shortstop because of fringy arm strength and an internal clock that doesn't befit the position. He'd be fine at second base and could be an intriguing option in center field. Acuña is an above-average runner, which helped him steal 40 bases in 49 tries.

THE FUTURE: Acuña will return to Double-A in 2023, when he'll attempt to refine his approach and improve his batted ball profile. The Rangers added him to their 40-man roster after the season.

SCOUTING GRADES	Hitting: 40		Power: 55		Speed: 55			Fielding: 50		Arm: 40	

Year	Age	Club (League)	Lvl	AVG	G	AB	R	H	2B	3B	HR	RBI	BB	SO	SB	OBP	SLG
2022	20	Hickory (SAL)	HiA	.317	54	205	45	65	10	0	8	29	34	60	28	.417	.483
2022	20	Frisco (TL)	AA	.224	37	152	21	34	6	2	3	18	17	36	12	.302	.349
Minor League Totals				.286	253	972	204	278	42	8	25	150	134	232	101	.373	.423

5 ANTHONY GUTIERREZ, OF

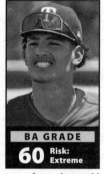

Born: Nov. 25, 2004. **B-T:** R-R. **HT:** 6-3. **WT:** 180.
Signed: Venezuela, 2022. **Signed by:** Rafic Saab/Willy Espinal.

TRACK RECORD: Gutierrez emerged from the Covid shutdown with a stronger, more developed body. He inked with the Rangers for $1.97 million on Jan. 15, 2022, and began his career in the Dominican Summer League but was impressive enough to earn a July 11 promotion to the Arizona Complex League. The Rangers brought Gutierrez with them on their annual instructional league barnstorming trip against college teams in and around Texas.

BA GRADE
60 **Risk:** Extreme

SCOUTING REPORT: Simply by moving Gutierrez to the U.S. in his first pro season, the Rangers made it clear how highly they value him. He has all the hallmarks of a high-end prospect—twitchy athleticism, an advanced idea of the strike zone and the physical projection to buttress his tools with further strength. Now, he needs to combine those gifts with even further strength gains on a frame that could easily take on 20 more pounds of muscle. Gutierrez's offensive profile will likely be power over hit, and his early holes are at the top of the strike zone and against higher quality breaking balls. His high chase rate was counterbalanced by an in-zone miss rate of just 12% and a knack for being on time against fastballs. In center field, Gutierrez uses above-average speed to glide to balls hit in all directions. His throwing arm teeters between above-average and plus and could get to the latter grade if his body takes the requisite strength gains as he matures.

THE FUTURE: After 22 games in the ACL, Gutierrez will likely continue his aggressive move up through the system by heading to Low-A Down East as an 18-year-old. If he develops as the Rangers hope, he could be the system's top prospect in a couple of years.

SCOUTING GRADES	Hitting: 45		Power: 60		Speed: 55			Fielding: 60		Arm: 55	

Year	Age	Club (League)	Lvl	AVG	G	AB	R	H	2B	3B	HR	RBI	BB	SO	SB	OBP	SLG
2022	17	Rangers (ACL)	R	.259	22	81	13	21	5	2	1	8	3	16	6	.299	.407
2022	17	Rangers Red (DSL)	R	.352	23	91	22	32	8	0	3	16	8	18	5	.408	.538
Minor League Totals				.308	45	172	35	53	13	2	4	24	11	34	11	.358	.477

6 AARON ZAVALA, OF

Born: June 24, 2000. **B-T:** L-R. **HT:** 6-0. **WT:** 193.
Drafted: Oregon, 2021 (2nd round). **Signed by:** Gary McGraw.

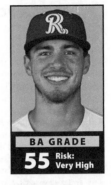

BA GRADE
55 Risk: Very High

TRACK RECORD: Zavala was one of the 2021 draft cycle's highest-rising prospects. He dominated for Oregon as a junior by hitting .392/.526/.628 while his power surged. He hit nine home runs after hitting only one in his previous 58 games. Zavala showed a tremendous batting eye in college, finishing with more walks (75) than strikeouts (68). The Rangers selected him in the second round in 2021, then signed him for a well-below slot bonus of $830,000 after a medical issue popped up during his physical.
SCOUTING REPORT: Zavala's sublime strike-zone discipline is both a blessing and a curse. His discipline is easily the best in the system, but his approach sometimes means he passes on pitches he should impact. Power is in there—Zavala's 90th percentile exit velocity of 103.9 mph was among the better marks in the system—but he swings at one of the lowest rates (37.9%) in the organization. Zavala's numbers, including a significant weakness against lefthanders, translated almost identically during his stops at High-A Hickory and Double-A Frisco. As a right fielder, Zavala will need to adjust his approach to get to the power more often to fit a corner player's profile. Scouts see him as an average defender with below-average arm strength that plays a tick higher because of a short stroke and a quick release. He's an average runner.
THE FUTURE: Zavala has an intriguing mix of skills buoyed by an outstanding batting eye, but his career is also clouded by injuries. He was sent to the Arizona Fall League to make up for lost time, but his stint was limited to five games after suffering a torn ulnar collateral ligament that required surgery.

SCOUTING GRADES	Hitting: 60		Power: 40		Speed: 50		Fielding: 50		Arm: 50		

Year	Age	Club (League)	Lvl	AVG	G	AB	R	H	2B	3B	HR	RBI	BB	SO	SB	OBP	SLG
2022	22	Hickory (SAL)	HiA	.278	81	299	61	83	10	3	11	41	68	79	10	.424	.441
2022	22	Frisco (TL)	AA	.277	30	112	28	31	8	0	5	21	21	29	4	.410	.482
Minor League Totals				.280	133	486	107	136	23	3	17	71	102	128	23	.420	.444

7 JACK LEITER, RHP

Born: April 21, 2000. **B-T:** R-R. **HT:** 6-1. **WT:** 205.
Drafted: Vanderbilt, 2021 (1st round). **Signed by:** Derrick Tucker.

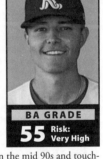

BA GRADE
55 Risk: Very High

TRACK RECORD: The son of longtime big league lefthander Al Leiter, Jack was selected in the 20th round of the 2019 draft out of high school in New Jersey but chose to attend Vanderbilt. He became an eligible sophomore after the 2021 season, which because of the pandemic was his only full season of college. The Rangers selected him second overall and let him rest after a heavy college workload. Texas assigned Leiter to Double-A to begin his pro career in 2022, and he spent the year taking his lumps against advanced hitters in the Texas League.
SCOUTING REPORT: Against upper-level competition, Leiter learned which parts of his arsenal play better and which ones need more refinement. The shape of his fastball backed up considerably and proved hittable despite sitting in the mid 90s and touching 100 mph. To be more successful, he needs to use his fastball in the upper part of the strike zone, where it will play better with the rest of his mix. Leiter's best offspeed pitch is his slider, which sat in the mid 80s and got whiffs and chases at easily the highest rates of his repertoire. Leiter's big-breaking, upper-70s curveball has significant break and would pair well with his fastball if he threw the latter pitch up in the zone more often. His curve is easily recognizable out of his hand, however, and got the lowest rates of strikes, swings and chases of any pitch in his mix. Leiter's mid-80s changeup is his weakest pitch and was used sparingly. Leiter threw strikes just 59% of the time as well, leading to an elevated walk rate of 5.4 per nine innings. Lefthanded batters hit Leiter particularly hard, including eight of the 11 home runs he allowed.
THE FUTURE: If Leiter can tweak his arsenal and improve his control and command, he has a chance to be a midrotation starter. If not, he might fit more toward the back of a rotation.

SCOUTING GRADES	Fastball: 55		Curveball: 50		Slider: 60		Changeup: 45		Control: 40		

Year	Age	Club (League)	Lvl	W	L	ERA	G	GS	IP	H	HR	BB	SO	BB/9	SO/9	WHIP	AVG
2022	22	Frisco (TL)	AA	3	10	5.54	23	22	93	88	11	56	109	5.4	10.6	1.55	.246
Minor League Totals				3	10	5.54	23	22	93	88	11	56	109	5.4	10.6	1.55	.246

8 BROCK PORTER, RHP

Born: June 3, 2003. **B-T:** R-R. **HT:** 6-4. **WT:** 208.
Drafted: HS—Orchard Lake, Mich., 2022 (4th round). **Signed by:** Chris Collias.
TRACK RECORD: After the Rangers took Kumar Rocker at No. 3 overall in 2022, the industry wondered if they had a plan to spend big with their next selection, which came in the fourth round after they'd forfeited their second- and third-round picks by signing free agents Corey Seager and Marcus Semien. That theory proved true with Texas' selection of Porter, whom they signed for $3.7 million. The bonus is far and away the highest for a fourth-round pick, besting Giants righthander Eric Silva's 2021 bonus by roughly $2.2 million. Porter did not pitch during the remainder of the regular season and participated in instructional league without getting into a game.
SCOUTING REPORT: Porter stands out for his mid-90s fastball with heavy sink and a devastating low-80s changeup that rivaled Padres first-rounder Dylan Lesko for the best in the 2022 class. His changeup is effective because it's thrown with excellent conviction, features a velocity separation of roughly 18-20 mph from his fastball and has hard, trapdoor action down and away from righthanded hitters. Porter still has plenty of projection remaining on his 6-foot-4, 208-pound frame and could begin touching triple digits—he has a goal of reaching 103 mph one day—as he adds strength. The next step will be to settle on a breaking ball that best fits his arm action. He currently throws both a curveball and a slider, with the latter a bit ahead of the former. The Rangers are leaning toward a slider or a slurve going forward. Porter's arm action is very long and could stand to be cleaned up to improve his control and command.
THE FUTURE: Porter's first official action is likely to come in the Arizona Complex League in 2023 with a chance at a move to Low-A late in the year. If he can find an ideal breaking ball to complement his fastball and changeup, he'll have a chance as a midrotation starter.

BA GRADE
55 Risk: Extreme

SCOUTING GRADES	Fastball: 60	Curveball: 50	Slider: 55	Changeup: 60	Control: 50

Year	Age	Club (League)	Lvl	W	L	ERA	G	GS	IP	H	HR	BB	SO	BB/9	SO/9	WHIP	AVG
2022	19	Did not pitch															

9 DUSTIN HARRIS, OF/1B

Born: July 8, 1999. **B-T:** L-R. **HT:** 6-2. **WT:** 185.
Drafted: St. Petersburg (Fla.) JC, 2019 (11th round).
Signed by: Trevor Schaeffer (Athletics).
TRACK RECORD: Harris was drafted by the Athletics in the 11th round in 2019 and made it to their short-season affiliate in the New York-Penn League in his first pro season. A year later, with the minor league season lost to the pandemic, Oakland traded him to Texas as part of the two-player package used to obtain Mike Minor. Harris crushed two Class A levels in 2021 and won the Rangers' minor league player of the year award. He had an up-and-down 2022 season, which ended with a sprained right wrist on Aug. 10.
SCOUTING REPORT: When the minor leagues began enforcing the new pitch clock rules, Harris suffered. He was forced to speed up his pre-pitch routine

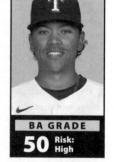

BA GRADE
50 Risk: High

and consequently got out of his rhythm. The result was a difficult May before a strong second half of the season. He also got a bit out of whack with his mechanics, sometimes letting the ball travel too deep and hooking hittable pitches foul to his pull side. Once he tweaked his mechanics and bat path, he started looking more like himself. Harris' under-the-hood numbers were quite good, including a high rate of hitting balls at an optimal mix of exit velocity and launch angle, as well as solid rates of chase and in-zone miss. Drafted as a third baseman and primarily a first baseman as a pro, Harris' transition to the outfield was a bit of a bumpy ride. He has average speed and gets decent jumps on balls, but early on he looked tentative in left field simply trying to catch the ball. Outside evaluators believe he won't be much more than fringe-average.
THE FUTURE: Harris was added to the Rangers' 40-man roster after the season and should head to Triple-A Round Rock to begin 2023. He'll be a bat-first player no matter where he lands on the diamond, but a successful transition to the outfield would give him a lot more value.

SCOUTING GRADES	Hitting: 55	Power: 55	Speed: 45	Fielding: 45	Arm: 45

Year	Age	Club (League)	Lvl	AVG	G	AB	R	H	2B	3B	HR	RBI	BB	SO	SB	OBP	SLG
2022	22	Frisco (TL)	AA	.257	85	331	58	85	16	2	17	66	42	74	19	.346	.471
Minor League Totals				.302	253	944	177	285	49	6	38	177	114	186	53	.382	.487

10 KUMAR ROCKER, RHP

Born: Nov. 22, 1999. **B-T:** R-R. **HT:** 6-5. **WT:** 245.
Drafted: Frontier League, 2022 (1st round). **Signed by:** Tyler Carroll.
TRACK RECORD: Rocker was Freshman of the Year at Vanderbilt in 2019, when he threw a no-hitter with 19 strikeouts against Duke in super regionals. In 2021, he racked up 173 strikeouts, tying him for the most in the nation with Vandy teammate Jack Leiter. The Mets selected Rocker 10th overall that year, but the sides failed to come to terms after a physical turned up something the Mets didn't like. Rocker's only pre-draft action in 2022 came with Tri-City of the MLB Partner Frontier League. The Rangers drafted him with the third overall pick and signed him for $5.2 million, roughly two-thirds of slot value. Rocker did not pitch during the regular season or instructional league but made six starts in the Arizona Fall League.

BA GRADE
55 Risk: **Extreme**

SCOUTING REPORT: When Rocker got to the AFL, the first thing that jumped out was an arm slot noticeably lower than the one he had used in college and with Tri-City. This allowed Rocker to pitch as comfortably as possible while easing the stress on his pitching shoulder. His delivery is upright and rotational, with limited use of his lower half. Scouts in the AFL noticed that he slowed his arm speed on both his slider and changeup. Rocker's fastball in the AFL sat in the mid 90s and showed late darting action. His mid-80s slider, while inconsistent, showed flashes of the wipeout offering that helped make him an elite prospect. Rocker's changeup lags behind his other two offerings, but it does show enough fading action to at least be usable.
THE FUTURE: If Rocker can kick off the rust and find more consistency with his new delivery, he could fit in a rotation. If not, his fastball/slider combination would work out of the bullpen.

SCOUTING GRADES	Fastball: 60	Slider: 60	Changeup: 45	Cutter: 40	Control: 45

Year	Age	Club (League)	Lvl	W	L	ERA	G	GS	IP	H	HR	BB	SO	BB/9	SO/9	WHIP	AVG
2022	22	Did not pitch															

11 JUSTIN FOSCUE, 2B

Born: March 2, 1999. **B-T:** R-R. **HT:** 6-0. **WT:** 205.
Drafted: Mississippi State, 2020 (1st round). **Signed by:** Brian Morrison.
TRACK RECORD: After starring in the Southeastern Conference and earning a spot with USA Baseball's Collegiate National Team after his sophomore season, Foscue was selected by the Rangers in the first-round of the 2020 draft. Despite dealing with injuries, Foscue tore up the lower levels in his official debut in 2021, including 17 home runs in just 62 games. He concluded his season with a turn in the Arizona Fall League. He put together another solid season in 2022, though his home run power didn't show up until late, including five longballs at offensive oasis Amarillo.
SCOUTING REPORT: Nearly all Foscue's value is centered around his offense, which is why the Rangers went to work rescuing his power from an early-season funk. To do so, they tweaked his hitting mechanics to keep him from collapsing on his back side, which had left him hitting with a more handsy approach that promoted contact at the expense of power. Foscue makes excellent decisions, as shown by a chase rate of 22%, a whiff rate of 17.4% and a stellar in-zone miss rate of just 12%. Foscue also makes plenty of impact on contact, as shown by a hard-hit rate of 34.5% and a max exit velocity of 108 mph in 2022. Scouts are intrigued by his pull-side power, but some believe he can be coaxed into weak contact by soft stuff on the outer part of the plate, and internal evaluators note that he's made strides to close a previous hole on hard fastballs near the top of the zone. Defensively, evaluators inside and outside the organization see a player who was already short on quickness and athleticism and lost a few steps this year. There's plenty of doubt he can stick up the middle, and some scouts even believe he might not be a strong enough defender to play first base. There's also plenty of concern given his injury history, which has included a plethora of issues in his midsection, including back soreness entering this year that lingered into the season's early months.
THE FUTURE: After helping Double-A Frisco to a Texas League crown in 2022, Foscue will move to Triple-A in 2023. The Rangers are loaded for bear in the middle infield anyway, so he's likely to dabble at other positions as well. If he stays healthy, he could make his big league debut late in the year.

BA GRADE: 50/High	Hit: 55	Power: 50	Speed: 40	Fielding: 40	Arm: 45

Year	Age	Club (League)	Lvl	AVG	G	AB	R	H	2B	3B	HR	RBI	BB	SO	SB	OBP	SLG
2022	23	Frisco (TL)	AA	.288	101	400	60	115	31	1	15	81	45	66	3	.367	.483
Minor League Totals				.283	163	629	112	178	50	2	32	132	70	138	5	.369	.521

12 COLE WINN, RHP

Born: Nov. 25, 1999. **B-T:** R-R. **HT:** 6-2. **WT:** 190.
Drafted: HS—Orange, Calif., 2018 (1st round). **Signed by:** Steve Flores.

TRACK RECORD: In his draft year, Winn helped lead his Orange Lutheran squad to the National High School Invitational title. He also won BA's High School Player of the Year award and was drafted in the first round. He had a breakout season in 2021 and appeared in the Futures Game but took a step back in 2022. He was the second-youngest pitcher in the Pacific Coast League on Opening Day, but he saw his ERA soar as his walk rate doubled from 3.2 walks per nine in 2021 to 6.4 walks-per nine in 2022.

SCOUTING REPORT: A chunk of Winn's troubles in 2022 stemmed from a line drive he took off his ankle early in the season. He tried to pitch through the injury but struggled to land properly and his timing and command suffered. Even when he was healthy, Winn's fastball command was not ideal. The pitch itself was fine—sitting around 94, touching 98 and showing excellent carry through the zone—but he threw it for strikes the least often of any of his four pitches. Winn's best secondary pitch is his curveball, which is a deep breaker in the low 80s. He finishes his mix with a mid-80s slider and a changeup that comes in a touch hotter. Winn threw his changeup the most frequently of his three offspeed pitches—around 21.5% of the time—and the Rangers would like to see that number decrease a bit.

THE FUTURE: The Rangers added Winn to their 40-man roster and will likely send him back to Triple-A in 2023 for a bit of a reset. He'll pitch all year at 23 years old and will need to focus on refining his control and getting better at getting outs within the strike zone.

BA GRADE: 50/High   **Fastball:** 50   **Curveball:** 55   **Slider:** 50   **Changeup:** 45   **Control:** 40

Year	Age	Club (League)	Lvl	W	L	ERA	G	GS	IP	H	HR	BB	SO	BB/9	SO/9	WHIP	AVG
2022	22	Round Rock (PCL)	AAA	9	8	6.51	28	28	122	125	13	87	123	6.4	9.1	1.74	.265
Minor League Totals				17	15	4.72	67	67	276	227	25	157	295	5.1	9.6	1.39	.223

13 YEISON MORROBEL, OF

Born: Dec. 8, 2003. **B-T:** L-L. **HT:** 6-1. **WT:** 190.
Signed: Dominican Republic, 2021. **Signed by:** Willy Espinal/JC Alvarez.

TRACK RECORD: Morrobel was the biggest target in the Rangers' 2021 international class and has lived up to expectations so far at the lowest levels of the minor leagues. He walked more often than he struck out in the DSL in 2021 and then continued to show solid swing decisions in 2022, when he posted a strikeout-to-walk rate of exactly 2-to-1 in a year spent mostly in the Arizona Complex League. He was one of three Rangers prospects to place among the Top 10 Prospects in the ACL.

SCOUTING REPORT: None of Morrobel's tools jumps off the page, but he's got a solid foundation on which to build and the possibility of plenty of strength gains to come leads evaluators to believe there will be more power throughout his game. He's got a sound lefthanded swing that allows him to handle breaking balls from both righthanders and lefthanders and permitted him an in-zone miss rate of just 14%. Morrobel will continue to play center field but will likely head to a corner outfield spot as his body takes the expected strength gains. External scouts believe he'll have the arm and corresponding power to play in right field. He's an average runner now but might slow down as he matures.

THE FUTURE: Morrobel finished the year at Low-A Down East and will return to the level in 2023. He'll work to continue adding the necessary strength to reach his ceiling of an everyday right fielder.

BA GRADE: 55/Extreme   **Hit:** 55   **Power:** 50   **Speed:** 50   **Fielding:** 50   **Arm:** 60

Year	Age	Club (League)	Lvl	AVG	G	AB	R	H	2B	3B	HR	RBI	BB	SO	SB	OBP	SLG
2022	18	Rangers (ACL)	R	.329	41	152	31	50	13	1	3	21	17	34	5	.405	.487
2022	18	Down East (CAR)	LoA	.231	8	26	3	6	1	0	0	3	3	6	2	.310	.269
Minor League Totals				.292	100	363	67	106	25	7	4	54	50	65	15	.393	.433

14 MITCHELL BRATT, LHP

Born: July 3, 2003. **B-T:** L-L. **HT:** 6-2. **WT:** 205.
Drafted: HS—Statesboro, Ga., 2021 (5th round). **Signed by:** Takeshi Sakurayama.

TRACK RECORD: The Canadian-born Bratt moved to Georgia during the pandemic in order to take advantage of the laxer restrictions that would help him get seen by scouts. The move worked and Bratt was taken in the fifth round of the 2021 draft as the first prep arm in Texas' 2021 class. His $850,000 bonus was tied for the second-most in the round. Bratt got his feet wet in pro ball in the Arizona Complex League after the draft, then spent all of 2022 at Low-A Down East, where he produced a 2.45 ERA in

80.2 innings.

SCOUTING REPORT: Bratt employs an up-tempo delivery and works with a full four-pitch mix led by a low-90s fastball that touched 95 and plays better because of some deception in his delivery as well as run and carry through the zone. He shows feel to land both his mid-70s curveball and low-80s slider for strikes, but needs to do a better job making them look like two disparate pitches. Bratt's mid-80s changeup is a clear fourth pitch in his mix and projects to be below-average. Bratt is one of the system's most athletic pitchers and the organization believes the way his hips move is a sign of more power to come. Bratt's game is also a bit too reliant on chases right now and he'll need to do a better job of getting outs in the strike zone.

THE FUTURE: Bratt will move to High-A in 2023, where he will look to continue to build strength and sharpen his offspeed pitches. He has the upside of a back-end starter.

BA GRADE: 50/High		Fastball: 55		Curveball: 45		Slider: 50		Changeup: 40		Control: 50				
Year	Age	Club (League)	Lvl	W	L	ERA	G	GS	IP	H	HR	BB	SO	BB/9	SO/9	WHIP	AVG
2022	18	Down East (CAR)	LoA	5	5	2.45	19	18	81	66	4	28	99	3.1	11.0	1.17	.218
Minor League Totals				5	5	2.28	23	18	87	70	4	28	112	2.9	11.6	1.13	.215

15 CAMERON CAULEY, SS

Born: Feb. 6, 2003. **B-T:** R-R. **HT:** 5-10. **WT:** 170.
Drafted: HS—Mount Belvieu, Texas, 2021 (3rd round). **Signed by:** Josh Simpson.
TRACK RECORD: Cauley's father Chris played three seasons in the minor leagues with the White Sox and was a member of the staff at Cameron's high school in Texas. The younger Cauley was drafted in the third round in 2021, when he was the first prep player selected in the Rangers' class. He spent all of 2022 at Low-A Down East save for two weeks on the injured list.

SCOUTING REPORT: Cauley is an extraordinary athlete with a swing that whips through the zone and lashes line drives. Despite that, he still is working to learn to pull the ball with authority. He covers the outer half of the plate well but gets tied up on pitches on the inner half. To help alleviate that, the Rangers worked with Cauley at instructional league to tone his lower half a little bit and increase the mobility in his hips. Cauley is a double-plus runner who has the potential to be a plus defender if he can make his actions more consistent. If not, his speed would allow him to slide into center field, where his plus arm strength would also be an asset.

THE FUTURE: Cauley's numbers weren't pretty in 2022, but the Rangers believe with further refinement he has the upside of an everyday player. He'll work on turning his potential into reality when he moves to High-A Hickory.

BA GRADE: 50/Very High		Hit: 45		Power: 40		Speed: 70		Fielding: 60		Arm: 60				
Year	Age	Club (League)	Lvl	AVG	G	AB	R	H	2B	3B	HR	RBI	BB	SO	SB	OBP	SLG
2022	19	Down East (CAR)	LoA	.209	76	287	36	60	11	3	2	21	38	91	38	.306	.289
Minor League Totals				.220	100	381	56	84	15	7	2	38	46	122	48	.307	.312

16 GLEIDER FIGUEREO, 3B

Born: June 27, 2004. **B-T:** L-R. **HT:** 6-0. **WT:** 165.
Signed: Dominican Republic, 2021. **Signed by:** Willy Espinal.
TRACK RECORD: Figuereo wasn't a big-name signing out of the 2021 international class, but he saw big-time strength gains with the help of trainer and former big leaguer Edinson Volquez. Figuereo scorched the ACL with nine home runs, which tied him for second on the circuit. His offensive numbers were all over the league leaderboard and he was one of three Rangers to rank among the league's Top 10.

SCOUTING REPORT: Figuereo's added strength complemented a loose, whippy swing with an excellent bat path to go with sound swing decisions and enough raw juice to produce max exit velos of 106 mph. He also tweaked his setup, becoming more upright to generate even more power and improved leverage. He's also shown the ability to manipulate his barrel and make loud contact on more than just fastballs. Defensively, Figuereo has significant improvements to make. His throwing arm is plenty strong for the hot corner but needs to get much more accurate if he's to stick there in the long term. He's got OK footwork but he has a tendency to rush through plays.

THE FUTURE: Figuereo got a taste of Low-A to end the season and will return there in 2023. His goals for the season will revolve around getting better defensively and maintaining the progress he showed in Arizona. If he does it again, he could shoot up the rankings.

| BA GRADE: 50/Very High | | Hit: 55 | | Power: 50 | | Speed: 40 | | Fielding: 45 | | Arm: 40 | |

Year	Age	Club (League)	Lvl	AVG	G	AB	R	H	2B	3B	HR	RBI	BB	SO	SB	OBP	SLG
2022	18	Rangers (ACL)	R	.280	35	125	29	35	5	5	9	31	15	33	7	.363	.616
2022	18	Down East (CAR)	LoA	.208	6	24	0	5	0	0	0	1	2	8	0	.269	.208
Minor League Totals				.249	89	305	52	76	11	9	11	60	45	72	10	.352	.452

17 ZAK KENT, RHP

Born: Feb. 24, 1998. **B-T:** R-R. **HT:** 6-3. **WT:** 208.
Drafted: Virginia Military Institute, 2019 (9th round). **Signed by:** Brian Matthews.
TRACK RECORD: Kent pitched three successful seasons at Virginia Military Institute and whiffed 132 hitters in his junior year. The Rangers took him in the ninth round and let him get his feet wet in the lower levels of the minor leagues. He reached Double-A in 2021 and ascended to Triple-A by the end of 2022. The Rangers were intrigued enough by the progress Kent made to add him to their 40-man roster and shield him from the Rule 5 draft.
SCOUTING REPORT: Kent dealt with a litany of injuries in 2022 to his hip and back and oblique muscles, which required three separate stays on the injured list. At his best, Kent mixes and matches with a five-pitch repertoire that includes four- and two-seam fastballs with the latter being introduced in the middle of the season as a way to get more grounders. Kent previously threw a split-fingered fastball but had trouble building up the necessary calluses and began throwing a traditional changeup during the season. Scouts outside the organization peg the changeup as fringe-average.
THE FUTURE: Kent struggled at the beginning of the season but rebounded as the season went on in between stints on the IL. His fastball-slider mix could at least make him a nasty reliever but if his other offspeeds comes forward he could have a bit more ceiling. He should make his debut in 2023.

| BA GRADE: 45/High | | Fastball: 60 | | Curveball: 50 | | Slider: 60 | | Changeup: 45 | | Control: 45 | |

Year	Age	Club (League)	Lvl	W	L	ERA	G	GS	IP	H	HR	BB	SO	BB/9	SO/9	WHIP	AVG
2022	24	Frisco (TL)	AA	2	3	4.68	19	19	83	83	11	30	87	3.3	9.5	1.37	.263
2022	24	Round Rock (PCL)	AAA	1	1	1.67	5	5	27	17	2	13	23	4.3	7.7	1.11	.181
Minor League Totals				9	11	3.92	55	46	218	205	29	74	245	3.1	10.1	1.28	.248

18 DANYER CUEVA, SS

Born: May 27, 2004. **B-T:** L-R. **HT:** 6-1. **WT:** 160.
Signed: Venezuela, 2021. **Signed by:** Jhonny Gomez/Rafic Saab.
TRACK RECORD: Cueva was part of what appears to be an excellent 2021 international class that also netted the Rangers outfielder Yeison Morrobel and infielder Gleider Figuereo. The trio was excellent in the Arizona Complex League and could form an exciting pack of position players at Low-A Down East in 2023. Cueva trained in Venezuela with Kander Depablos and was lauded for a smooth swing from the left side.
SCOUTING REPORT: Of the prospects clustered in the ACL, Cueva might have the highest floor but the lowest ceiling. He's a free-swinger at the plate who will have to tone down that aspect of his approach, and his chase rate will have to be reined in as well. Opposing scouts saw a player with enough power potential to produce 12-15 home runs a year while making enough quality contact to get to the majors on the strength of his offense alone. Early in his career it was thought that he might have to move over to second base. His speed and athleticism ticked up, however, and now he has a decent chance of sticking at short-stop. That thought is not unanimous, and some believe he will slide over to second base in the long run.
THE FUTURE: Cueva got a taste of Low-A to end the season and will return to the level in 2023. He'll get a chance to prove his offensive chops against better pitching and will work to keep himself at shortstop. He has the ceiling of an everyday, bat-first middle infielder.

| BA GRADE: 50/Extreme | | Hit: 60 | | Power: 45 | | Speed: 50 | | Fielding: 50 | | Arm: 55 | |

Year	Age	Club (League)	Lvl	AVG	G	AB	R	H	2B	3B	HR	RBI	BB	SO	SB	OBP	SLG
2022	18	Rangers (ACL)	R	.330	44	176	39	58	10	1	5	31	10	40	3	.376	.483
2022	18	Down East (CAR)	LoA	.111	5	18	0	2	0	0	0	0	0	5	0	.111	.111
Minor League Totals				.295	98	396	87	117	21	4	6	56	32	93	12	.364	.414

19 COLE RAGANS, LHP

Born: Dec. 12, 1997. **B-T:** L-L. **HT:** 6-4. **WT:** 190.
Drafted: HS—Tallahassee, Fla., 2016 (1st round). **Signed by:** Brett Campbell.
TRACK RECORD: Ragans' ascent to the big leagues was one of the best stories in the minor leagues in 2022.

After being drafted in the first round in 2016 and debuting the next spring, two Tommy John surgeries and the pandemic kept him off the mound until 2021, when he also made the Futures Game. He made his major league debut on Aug. 4 and made nine starts, working to a mark of 0-3, 5.40.

SCOUTING REPORT: After all the time recovering, it's only natural that Ragans' rust-removal process would be lengthy. More than that, the Rangers also noticed that he learned to better pace himself throughout the season in order to maintain the crispness on his stuff from Opening Day until season's end. Ragans operates with a four-pitch mix led by a 92-95 mph fastball that touched 96. His best offspeed pitch is a potentially plus changeup in the 82-84 mph range that he threw for plenty of strikes both in the zone and for chases. His repertoire also featured a mid-70s curveball of varying quality and a new cutter in the low 90s that he can manipulate to make look like a slider with deeper break. Both the curve and the cutter project to be fringe-average to average, and the Rangers would like to see him add more power to both. He struggled a bit with fastball command down the stretch but overall showed average control.

THE FUTURE: If he continues to add more power to his mix, Ragans could carve out a career as a back-end starter. He'll likely see plenty of big league time in 2023.

BA GRADE: 40/Medium		Fastball: 55		Curveball: 45		Changeup: 60		Cutter: 50		Control: 50			

Year	Age	Club (League)	Lvl	W	L	ERA	G	GS	IP	H	HR	BB	SO	BB/9	SO/9	WHIP	AVG
2022	24	Frisco (TL)	AA	5	3	2.81	10	10	51	41	6	19	65	3.3	11.4	1.17	.219
2022	24	Round Rock (PCL)	AAA	3	2	3.32	8	8	43	34	4	12	48	2.5	10.0	1.06	.211
2022	24	Texas (AL)	MLB	0	3	4.95	9	9	40	43	6	16	27	3.6	6.1	1.48	.272
Major League Totals				0	3	4.95	9	9	40	43	6	16	27	3.6	6.1	1.48	.272
Minor League Totals				15	10	3.67	54	50	240	209	27	106	296	4.0	11.1	1.31	.234

20 EMILIANO TEODO, RHP

Born: Feb. 14, 2001. **B-T:** R-R. **HT:** 6-0. **WT:** 175.
Signed: Dominican Republic, 2020. **Signed by:** JC Alvarez/Jack Marino.

TRACK RECORD: Teodo signed for just $10,000 as a 19-year-old but has already rewarded the Rangers' confidence with some of the system's best pure stuff. Teodo was an off-the-radar prospect who didn't even have a trainer and was identified at a tryout camp the year before he signed. The whippy-armed former position player spent his first pro season in the Arizona Complex League before moving to Low-A, where his 115 strikeouts led the team and placed seventh in the Carolina League.

SCOUTING REPORT: Teodo works with a three-pitch mix led by a mighty four-seam fastball that averaged 96 mph and touched 101. He shows much better command of the pitch, especially up in the zone, when he doesn't try to throw it as hard as he can. Teodo's slider is a sharp-snapper as well. The breaking ball averages around 85 mph and touched 94. He has a below-average changeup that could get better with further repetitions and was thrown just 5% of the time. There's no question that Teodo has an impact arm. Now, the Rangers will have to figure out where it plays. His wiry body and spindly lower half might push him toward the pen, but Teodo stayed at Texas' minor league complex over the winter in an effort to add mass and turn himself into a potential starter who could air it out for five innings.

THE FUTURE: Teodo will head to High-A Hickory in 2023 and will work to sharpen his command and build enough stamina to remain a starter.

BA GRADE: 45/High		Fastball: 70		Slider: 60		Changeup: 40		Control: 40			

Year	Age	Club (League)	Lvl	W	L	ERA	G	GS	IP	H	HR	BB	SO	BB/9	SO/9	WHIP	AVG
2022	21	Down East (CAR)	LoA	3	6	3.09	22	17	84	51	7	44	115	4.7	12.3	1.13	.171
Minor League Totals				7	8	3.17	41	17	114	75	7	62	163	4.9	12.9	1.21	.182

21 CODY BRADFORD, LHP

Born: Feb. 22, 1998. **B-T:** L-L. **HT:** 6-4. **WT:** 197.
Drafted: Baylor, 2019 (6th round). **Signed by:** Josh Simpson.

TRACK RECORD: Bradford was the Big 12 pitcher of the year in 2018 but had surgery for thoracic outlet syndrome the next season. He also spent a summer with Chatham of the Cape Cod League, where he was teammates with future Blue Jays all-star Alek Manoah and future 1-1 pick Spencer Torkelson. The injury limited Bradford to just three starts in his draft year, but the Rangers still popped him in the sixth round. He reached Double-A in his pro debut and spent all of 2022 at the same level.

SCOUTING REPORT: Bradford works with a four-pitch mix led a fastball whose movement helps it play better than its low-90s velocity. The combination of a deceptive delivery and excellent extension makes the fastball extremely difficult to hit at the top of the zone, but he's at his best when he moves it around to all four quadrants. Bradford backs the fastball with a low-80s slider and a high-80s cutter. The latter was introduced because of an inconsistency in Bradford's delivery that allowed hitters to easily tell when the slider was coming. Longer extension meant a fastball and shorter extension signaled a slider. The cutter gave Bradford a similar movement profile—albeit with firmer velocity—that he could achieve with the same delivery as his four-seamer. Bradford's best offspeed, however, is his 82-85 mph changeup, which kills spin effectively and can be a useful weapon in any count.

THE FUTURE: Bradford was inconsistent in the early portion of the season but figured it out later and got back to the best version of himself. He could fit in the back of a rotation if he carries that momentum into 2023.

BA Grade: 45/High		Fastball: 55		Slider: 40		Changeup: 60		Cutter: 50			Control: 55	

Year	Age	Club (League)	Lvl	W	L	ERA	G	GS	IP	H	HR	BB	SO	BB/9	SO/9	WHIP	AVG
2022	24	Frisco (TL)	AA	10	7	5.01	26	26	119	114	18	33	124	2.5	9.4	1.24	.248
Minor League Totals				16	11	4.60	46	46	215	210	28	54	252	2.3	10.5	1.23	.251

22 THOMAS SAGGESE, 2B

Born: April 10, 2002. **B-T:** R-R. **HT:** 6-0. **WT:** 185.
Drafted: HS—Carlsbad, Calif., 2020 (5th round) **Signed by:** Steve Flores.

TRACK RECORD: The Rangers went high school-heavy in the shortened 2020 draft, popping four prep players after taking Justin Foscue out of Mississippi State in the first round. The last player in their class was Saggese, who looks like he could be another pleasant surprise along with second-rounder Evan Carter. His average (.308), slugging percentage (.487) and OPS (.846) each placed among the top 10 in the South Atlantic League, where he was the circuit's third-youngest player on Opening Day.

SCOUTING REPORT: Saggese is a very aggressive hitter who swung 56% of the time but made loud impact on contact. Internal evaluators said he did a good job being more patient as the year wore on but still could stand to improve even further. He chased far too often. He doesn't have the cleanest actions in the field but is nimble enough to make plays on the run thanks to average arm strength despite a throwing stroke with a bit of a hitch that could lead to inconsistency. He's a fringe-average runner who can turn in times closer to average when he gets clean breaks out of the box. The Rangers also love Saggese's baseball rat tendencies and note his intense level of focus during games.

THE FUTURE: Saggese finished 2022 at Double-A Frisco for the last part of the regular season and then the team's run to the Texas League title. He'll return to the level in 2023, when a refined approach married with the league's hitter-friendly atmosphere could lead to a big season.

BA GRADE: 45/High		Hit: 40		Power: 50		Speed: 45		Fielding: 40		Arm: 45	

Year	Age	Club (League)	Lvl	AVG	G	AB	R	H	2B	3B	HR	RBI	BB	SO	SB	OBP	SLG
2022	20	Hickory (SAL)	HiA	.308	98	380	56	117	22	2	14	61	29	94	11	.359	.487
2022	20	Frisco (TL)	AA	.381	5	21	5	8	3	2	1	9	1	3	1	.409	.857
Minor League Totals				.291	176	643	105	187	39	7	25	107	72	182	23	.365	.490

23 CHANDLER POLLARD, SS

Born: May 3, 2004. **B-T:** R-R. **HT:** 6-2. **WT:** 173.
Drafted: HS—College Park, Ga., 2022 (5th round). **Signed by:** Tyler Carroll.

TRACK RECORD: Pollard was the Rangers' fifth-rounder in the 2022 draft and was induced to turn pro instead of heading to Washington State thanks to a signing bonus of $418,500. He got into two games in the Arizona Complex League after signing before heading to instructional league. He was also part of the team's annual instructional league college tour and held his own against older competition.

SCOUTING REPORT: Pollard stands out for his athleticism, which translates in the field and on the bases. He glides around the diamond with ease and stole 59 bases—to go with 11 home runs—in his senior season of high school in Georgia. There's little doubt he sticks at least on the left side of the infield, where his plus arm would fit perfectly. If not, his speed would also fit nicely in center field. He needs plenty of polish offensively and the Rangers have already worked with him to be more consistent in his approach. He tends to get too big with his swing and the Rangers would like to see him stay within himself with a line drive approach geared toward contact up the middle.

THE FUTURE: Pollard has the ceiling of a sparkplug-type of player who causes havoc on the bases.

BA GRADE: 45/Very High		Hit: 40		Power: 40		Speed: 70		Fielding: 60		Arm: 60	

Year	Age	Club (League)	Lvl	AVG	G	AB	R	H	2B	3B	HR	RBI	BB	SO	SB	OBP	SLG
2022	18	Rangers (ACL)	R	.000	2	5	0	0	0	0	0	0	1	2	0	.375	.000
Minor League Totals				.000	2	5	0	0	0	0	0	0	1	2	0	.375	.000

24 MARCOS TORRES, OF

Born: Sept. 30, 2004. **B-T:** L-L. **HT:** 6-3. **WT:** 163.
Signed: Venezuela, 2022. **Signed by:** Rafic Saab/Jhonny Gomez.

TRACK RECORD: Torres was part of the Rangers' most recent international class and began opening eyes thanks to a mature body and present tools. He performed well in the Dominican Summer League and continued impressing evaluators during fall instructional league.

SCOUTING REPORT: Torres' swing is loose and quick and produces excellent natural bat speed thanks to an incredibly strong set of hands. He impressed his organization by taking the skills he displayed during showcases and translating them into game action. He showed sound swing decisions and impact in the DSL but worked at instructional league to optimize his bat path to keep it in the zone longer. Torres will likely get chances in center field as he moves up the ladder but a thickening build could push him to a corner as he matures. Torres was exposed to all three outfield spots in the DSL but predominantly played left field. He ran the 60-yard dash in 6.6 seconds during showcases, giving him potentially plus speed, but he could slow down a tick as he gains muscle.

THE FUTURE: Torres will move stateside in 2023, when he'll try to build on the success he showed in the DSL and instructional league. If everything clicks, he could be an average regular in left field.

BA GRADE: 50/Extreme   **Hit:** 40   **Power:** 55   **Speed:** 55   **Fielding:** 40   **Arm:** 50

Year	Age	Club (League)	Lvl	AVG	G	AB	R	H	2B	3B	HR	RBI	BB	SO	SB	OBP	SLG
2022	17	Rangers Blue (DSL)	R	.282	53	181	34	51	9	3	6	33	26	43	13	.394	.464
Minor League Totals				.282	53	181	34	51	9	3	6	33	26	43	13	.394	.464

25 JONATHAN ORNELAS, SS/OF

Born: May 26, 2000. **B-T:** R-R. **HT:** 6-1. **WT:** 195.
Drafted: HS—Glendale, Ariz., 2018 (3rd round). **Signed by:** Levi Lacey.

TRACK RECORD: After being drafted in the third round in 2018, Ornelas put up solid if unspectacular numbers. Those figures got a bump in 2022, although he also had noticeable splits favoring home games and at-bats against lefthanders. The Rangers added him to the 40-man roster after the season to shield him from the Rule 5 draft.

SCOUTING REPORT: Ornelas doesn't have a standout tool but he hits the ball plenty hard and has enough defensive versatility to move around the diamond with ease. He's an extremely aggressive hitter who has below-average swing decisions and pitch recognition. He made some swing adjustments to help him stay behind the ball better and increase his impact on contact, though the Rangers would still like to see him get the ball in the air more often. Ornelas took most of his defensive reps at shortstop and third base but got four games apiece at second base and center field.

THE FUTURE: After a year bouncing around the diamond for Texas League-champion Frisco, Ornelas will head to Triple-A to try to prove his breakout was real. Better pitch recognition skills and more fly balls will aid that effort. He could make his big league debut in 2023.

BA GRADE: 45/High   **Hit:** 40   **Power:** 45   **Speed:** 45   **Fielding:** 45   **Arm:** 60

Year	Age	Club (League)	Lvl	AVG	G	AB	R	H	2B	3B	HR	RBI	BB	SO	SB	OBP	SLG
2022	22	Frisco (TL)	AA	.299	123	525	84	157	20	2	14	64	45	121	14	.360	.425
Minor League Totals				.278	378	1486	250	413	72	13	31	168	133	352	51	.344	.406

26 LUIS RAMIREZ, RHP

Born: April 6, 2001. **B-T:** R-R. **HT:** 6-2. **WT:** 200.
Drafted: Long Beach State, 2022 (7th round). **Signed by:** Pat Perry.

TRACK RECORD: Ramirez is an alumnus of Salesian High in Los Angeles, which counts two NFL players among its alumni base. He matriculated to Long Beach State and started for three years sandwiched around a stellar turn in the Cape Cod League in 2021, when he tied for the league lead in strikeouts. A shoulder injury ended Ramirez's season on April 22 but the Rangers popped him in the seventh round.

SCOUTING REPORT: At his best, Ramirez operates with a heavy sinking fastball in the low 90s that plays particularly well to his glove side. He also does a fantastic job manipulating the shape of his low-80s, slurvy slider. The next step will be bringing his changeup forward. The pitch flashed above-average in college but was not thrown enough to comfortably project it to reach those heights as a pro. Ramirez has also shown solid control and command with decent feel to move his pitches around all quadrants of the strike zone. The Rangers would like to see that aspect of his game take a step forward.

THE FUTURE: Ramirez did not pitch after signing but was invited to the team's instructional league camp in Arizona. His pedigree should allow him to begin his career at one of the Class A levels. He has a ceiling in the back of a rotation.

BA GRADE: 45/High	Fastball: 55	Slider: 55	Changeup: 45	Control: 55

Year	Age	Club (League)	Lvl	W	L	ERA	G	GS	IP	H	HR	BB	SO	BB/9	SO/9	WHIP	AVG
2022	21	Did not play—Injured															

27 TEKOAH ROBY, RHP

Born: Sept. 18, 2001. **B-T:** R-R. **HT:** 6-1. **WT:** 185.
Drafted: HS—Pensacola, Fla., 2020 (3rd round). **Signed by:** Brian Morrison.
TRACK RECORD: Roby was the Rangers' third-round pick in the shortened draft during the pandemic year of 2020. He was lauded for his ability to post high spin rates as well as his fiery demeanor on the mound. His 2021 season was cut short by an elbow strain, but he made every turn during a full season at High-A Hickory.
SCOUTING REPORT: Roby works with a four-pitch mix led by a low-90s fastball that peaked at 96. He needs to command the pitch better, especially in the lower part of the zone. Roby backs the fastball up with a high-80s curveball with spin rates around 2,800 rpm as well as a changeup in the low 80s. He changed the grip on the pitch during the season to help it play better. The Rangers added a slider to Roby's repertoire near the end of the season to give him something with velocity in between his four-seamer and his curveball/changeup duo, and it holds the same line as his fastball for longer on its way to the plate. Command was Roby's biggest issue this year, and it led to 19 home runs allowed. Scouts were a little surprised by Roby's command issues because his arm action and delivery are fairly clean.
THE FUTURE: Roby will head to Double-A in 2023 and will be severely challenged to improve his command in the hitter-friendly Texas League.

BA GRADE: 45/High	Fastball: 50	Curveball: 50	Slider: 40	Changeup: 50	Control: 40

Year	Age	Club (League)	Lvl	W	L	ERA	G	GS	IP	H	HR	BB	SO	BB/9	SO/9	WHIP	AVG
2022	20	Hickory (SAL)	HiA	3	11	4.64	22	21	105	95	19	35	126	3.0	10.8	1.24	.239
Minor League Totals				5	13	4.26	28	27	127	109	20	42	161	3.0	11.4	1.19	.229

28 TOMMY SPECHT, OF

Born: June 24, 2004. **B-T:** L-R. **HT:** 6-3. **WT:** 200.
Drafted: HS—Dubuque, Iowa, 2022 (6th round). **Signed by:** Dustin Smith.
TRACK RECORD: Specht was the Rangers' sixth-round pick but fourth selection overall because they lost their second- and third-round picks for signing free agents. He drew interest for his lefthanded offense, and Texas bought him out of his commitment to Kentucky with a $450,000 signing bonus. He played in three games in the Rookie-level Arizona Complex League.
SCOUTING REPORT: Specht has a smooth swing from the left side that is geared for more impact than contact. His power is mostly to the gaps now but should turn into home runs as he finishes filling out his frame. The Rangers are especially buying in on Specht's power potential based on strong batting practices and a solid idea of the strike zone. He's an above-average runner who could handle center in a pinch but will likely move over as he gains mass. His plus arm will fit nicely in right field.
THE FUTURE: Specht could head to Low-A Down East or stay back in Arizona for extended spring training and the Arizona Complex League depending on how the rosters shake out in April. He has a chance to be an everyday right fielder with further seasoning and a more refined hit tool.

BA GRADE: 50/Extreme	Hit: 40	Power: 50	Speed: 55	Fielding: 50	Arm: 60

Year	Age	Club (League)	Lvl	AVG	G	AB	R	H	2B	3B	HR	RBI	BB	SO	SB	OBP	SLG
2022	18	Rangers (ACL)	R	.200	3	10	2	2	1	0	0	0	2	6	0	.333	.300
Minor League Totals				.200	3	10	2	2	1	0	0	0	2	6	0	.333	.300

29 ECHEDRY VARGAS, 3B

Born: Feb. 27, 2005. **B-T:** R-R. **HT:** 5-11. **WT:** 170.
Signed: Dominican Republic, 2022. **Signed by:** JC Alvarez.

TRACK RECORD: Vargas was signed in the Rangers' most recent international class for a small bonus of just $10,000. He quickly proved his worth in the Dominican Summer League, where he produced an .878 OPS. His offensive skills mask his lack of a true defensive home or standout athleticism.

SCOUTING REPORT: Vargas' best attribute is his contact ability. He needs to stay in the zone more, but his high rate of chase was mitigated by excellent bat-to-ball skills on pitches in the zone. He reminds some within the organization of an early-stage version of Ezequiel Duran because of his ability to make loud contact despite a bit of a free-swinging approach. The Rangers worked with Vargas at instructional league to try to clean up his bat path. Vargas is not the most athletic player in the world but has the chance to stick on the infield—either at second or third base—and has the arm strength to handle the left side. He's a fringe-average runner who can steal bases on a combination of instincts and aggression rather than being any sort of burner.

THE FUTURE: Vargas will move to the Arizona Complex League in 2023, when he'll try to harness his approach to make the most of his contact ability and try to point himself toward a ceiling as a utility infielder.

BA GRADE: 45/Extreme	Hit: 40	Power: 50	Speed: 45	Fielding: 40	Arm: 50

Year	Age	Club (League)	Lvl	AVG	G	AB	R	H	2B	3B	HR	RBI	BB	SO	SB	OBP	SLG
2022	17	Rangers Blue (DSL)	R	.301	54	196	40	59	19	5	4	27	13	27	13	.368	.510
Minor League Totals				.301	54	196	40	59	19	5	4	27	13	27	13	.368	.510

30 JOJO BLACKMON, OF

Born: March 31, 2003. **B-T:** L-L. **HT:** 5-11. **WT:** 185.
Drafted: HS—Pensacola, Fla., 2021 (11th round). **Signed by:** Brett Campbell.

TRACK RECORD: The Rangers bet on Blackmon's tools in the 11th round of the 2021 draft and signed him for $250,000. Blackmon was a talented wide receiver at Escambia High in Pensacola, Fla., and had football offers to Kentucky, Coastal Carolina and Florida Atlantic, among others. Blackmon chose baseball and already ranks as the fastest runner and best athlete in the system.

SCOUTING REPORT: Blackmon's tools are apparent in every phase of the game. On the bases and on defense, he's an easy double-plus runner. He's a skilled outfield defender whose route-running skills from the gridiron easily translate to center field, where he has a case as the system's best prospect at the position. Perhaps most intriguing, however, is Blackmon's amount of hard contact. His average exit velocity was an outstanding 89.7 mph—the same figure posted by more established minor league power brokers like Dermis Garcia, Will Benson and Jordan Westburg—and his maximum approached 111 mph. He also does an excellent job getting the ball in the air and doesn't have an egregious amount of chase in his game, though his in-zone whiff rates need to come down. His strikeout rates—which were around 38% combined between Rookie ball and Low-A—are an eyesore, but his standout speed and impact potential make him worth at least a flier, especially given he's just starting his baseball-only career. He has a fringe-average arm now that should get better with more coaching.

THE FUTURE: Blackmon will return to Low-A and will work hard to cut down on his strikeouts to let his other standout tools shine.

BA GRADE: 45/Extreme	Hit: 30	Power: 60	Speed: 70	Fielding: 60	Arm: 50

Year	Age	Club (League)	Lvl	AVG	G	AB	R	H	2B	3B	HR	RBI	BB	SO	SB	OBP	SLG
2022	19	Rangers (ACL)	R	.265	38	132	29	35	4	4	8	15	22	60	16	.382	.538
2022	19	Down East (CAR)	LoA	.160	16	50	11	8	0	3	1	9	6	22	2	.250	.340
Minor League Totals				.236	72	237	50	56	5	9	9	30	40	111	26	.354	.447

Toronto Blue Jays

BY GEOFF PONTES

In what proved to be an arms race in the American League East, the Blue Jays finished second in the division and qualified for the playoffs for the first time in a full season since 2016.

They pushed forward around their Golden Generation and continued to fortify their core with veteran talent. While the Blue Jays entered the season with a bottom-tier farm system, strong 2021 and 2022 draft classes, as well as much-needed breakouts on the farm, bolstered the Blue Jays' minor league depth.

Toronto's young core of Vladimir Guerrero Jr., Bo Bichette and Alek Manoah received reinforcements in the form of a top tier-free agent for the second consecutive season when Toronto inked Kevin Gausman to a five-year, $110 million contract. The Blue Jays had signed George Springer for six years and $150 million the year before.

In the days following the ratification of the new Collective Bargaining Agreement in March, the Blue Jays dealt 2021 first-round pick Gunnar Hoglund, shortstop Kevin Smith and lefthanders Zach Logue and Kirby Snead for Gold Glove third baseman Matt Chapman. Chapman's presence provided a plus defender in the infield and much needed thump to the lineup. Toronto also acquired all-star Whit Merrifield at the trade deadline from the Royals, proving up until the last possible moment that the Blue Jays were pushing the chips all-in for 2022.

The Blue Jays finished 92-70 overall and clinched home-field advantage in the first year for the expanded postseason that features a Wild Card Series, but they were swept by the Mariners two games to none.

Righthander Alek Manoah, the 11th overall pick in the 2019 draft, had a breakout season. He was selected to the All-Star Game alongside teammates Guerrero, Springer and fan favorite Alejandro Kirk, a 24-year-old catcher who also solidified himself as a part of the Blue Jays' exciting young core.

On the farm, the Blue Jays saw exciting breakouts from a pair of pitchers led by lefthander Ricky Tiedemann. Their 2021 third-round pick broke out almost immediately upon his debut and ascended to the top half of the Top 100 Prospects list by season's end. Righthander Yosver Zulueta, who signed out of Cuba in 2019, debuted after two injury-plagued years and reached Triple-A by season's end.

No. 1 prospect Gabriel Moreno made his major league debut and looks poised to contribute in 2023. Surprise breakouts like shortstop Addison Barger and 2021 draftee Hayden Juenger helped

Overpowering Alek Manoah has been a big contributor to Toronto's success in 2021 and '22.

PROJECTED 2026 LINEUP

Catcher	Gabriel Moreno	26
First Base	Vladimir Guerrero Jr.	27
Second Base	Addison Barger	26
Third Base	Orelvis Martinez	24
Shortstop	Bo Bichette	28
Left Field	Lourdes Gurriel Jr.	32
Center Field	George Springer	36
Right Field	Gabriel Martinez	23
Designated Hitter	Alejandro Kirk	27
No. 1 Starter	Alek Manoah	28
No. 2 Starter	Jose Berrios	32
No. 3 Starter	Kevin Gausman	36
No. 4 Starter	Ricky Tiedemann	24
No. 5 Starter	Yosver Zulueta	28
Closer	Nate Pearson	30

add depth to a system in flux due to trades in recent seasons.

In the 2022 draft, the Blue Jays added another talented lefthander in Brandon Barriera, from the Florida high school ranks, as well as an intriguing group of hitters in Josh Kasevich and Cade Doughty, both college infielders, and high school shortstop Tucker Toman.

Overall, it was an encouraging season for the Blue Jays and their fans. Toronto fielded one of the best teams in baseball, while another core of young prospects began to take shape down on the farm.

After back-to-back 90-win seasons, the Blue Jays enter 2023 poised to compete for a title despite a very competitive division. ■

DEPTH CHART

TORONTO BLUE JAYS

TOP 2023 MLB CONTRIBUTORS	RANK
Gabriel Moreno, C	1
Yosver Zulueta, RHP	3
Addison Barger, SS	5
BREAKOUT PROSPECTS	**RANK**
Hagen Danner, RHP	18
Kendry Rojas, LHP	21
Manuel Beltre, SS	22

SOURCE OF TOP 30 TALENT

Homegrown	28	Acquired	2
College	7	Trade	2
Junior college	3	Rule 5 draft	0
High school	5	Independent league	0
Nondrafted free agent	0	Free agent/waivers	0
International	13		

LF
Gabriel Martinez (15)
Zach Britton (25)

CF
Dasan Brown (14)
Yhoangel Aponte
Devonte Brown
Roque Salinas

RF
Alan Roden
Cullen Large

3B
Tucker Toman (7)
Cade Doughty (8)
Damiano Palmagiani (26)

SS
Addison Barger (5)
Orelvis Martinez (6)
Josh Kasevich (12)
Leo Jimenez (20)
Manuel Beltre (22)

2B
Otto Lopez (16)
Adrian Pinto (24)
Davis Schneider (37)
Michael Turconi

1B
Spencer Horwitz (19)
Rainer Nuñez (27)

C
Gabriel Moreno (1)
Luis Meza

LHP

LHSP	LHRP
Ricky Tiedemann (2)	Matt Gage
Brandon Barriera (4)	
Adam Macko (11)	
Kendry Rojas (21)	
Johan Simon (32)	
Jimmy Robbins	

RHP

RHSP	RHRP
Yosver Zulueta (3)	Hayden Juenger (9)
Dahian Santos (13)	Nate Pearson (10)
Sem Robberse (17)	Hagen Danner (18)
Alejandro Melean (23)	Troy Watson
Yondrei Rojas (28)	Jackson Rees
C.J. Van Eyk (29)	Adrian Hernandez
Trent Palmer (30)	
Lazaro Estrada	
Irv Carter	
Ryan Jennings	

1 GABRIEL MORENO, C

Born: Feb. 14, 2000. **B-T:** R-R. **HT:** 5-11. **WT:** 195.
Signed: Venezuela, 2016.
Signed by: Francisco Plasencia.

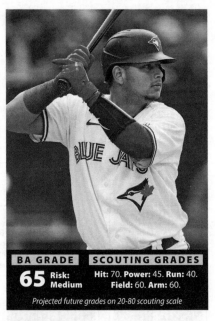

BA GRADE **SCOUTING GRADES**

65 Risk: Medium

Hit: 70. **Power:** 45. **Run:** 40.
Field: 60. **Arm:** 60.

Projected future grades on 20-80 scouting scale

TRACK RECORD: The Blue Jays signed Moreno in 2016 for just $25,000 at the age of 16 out of Venezuela. Since then, he has blossomed into one of the top prospects in baseball. Moreno progressed steadily over his first few seasons in the organization, first displaying advanced plate discipline and defense in consecutive seasons in the Dominican Summer League and the Gulf Coast League. He made adjustments to his swing to tap into more power before his 2019 season with Low-A Lansing, and the changes and resulting production helped cement him as one of the top catching prospects in the low minors. He made further adjustments at Double-A New Hampshire in 2021 to produce additional power and was on his way to a banner season before a fractured thumb in late June put him on the injured list for two months. He returned to finish the year at Triple-A Buffalo and further enhanced his standing with a strong showing in the Arizona Fall League. Moreno began 2022 at Triple-A Buffalo and continued to impress offensively. He hit .315/.386/.420 over 62 games and made his major league debut on June 11. He hit .315/.356/.377 in 25 games with the Blue Jays and made their American League Wild Card Series roster.

SCOUTING REPORT: Always an elite hitter, Moreno continues to make contact at one of the highest rates of any prospect. He possesses superior hand-eye coordination and a discerning eye that he uses to identify spin quickly out of the pitcher's hand. His swing plane has flattened out, and he is naturally comfortable shooting pitches on the outer half of the plate to the opposite field. After showing increased power and more aggressiveness in two-strike counts in previous seasons, Moreno has steadily become a more conservative hitter as he's moved up the ladder. His two-strike swing has become more subdued and controlled, leading to an increase in line drives and ground balls and a corresponding decrease in fly balls and exit velocity numbers. His power production has dropped as a result, but he has the bat control, pitch recognition and strength to make adjustments and get to 12-15 home run power in the future. Moreno faces few questions about his ability to stick at catcher as an above-average defender with a plus arm. He is an adept receiver, gets out of the crouch quickly on throws and is a twitchy, fluid mover behind the

BEST TOOLS

BATTING
Best Hitter For Average	Gabriel Martinez
Best Power Hitter	Orelvis Martinez
Best Strike-Zone Discipline	Spencer Horwitz
Fastest Baserunner	Steward Berroa
Best Athlete	Dasan Brown

PITCHING
Best Fastball	Ricky Tiedemann
Best Curveball	Lazaro Estrada
Best Slider	Dahian Santos
Best Changeup	Adrian Hernandez
Best Control	Sem Robberse

FIELDING
Best Defensive Catcher	Gabriel Moreno
Best Defensive Infielder	Manuel Beltre
Best Defensive Outfielder	Steward Berroa
Best Infield Arm	Addison Barger
Best Outfield Arm	Sebastian Espino

plate. He's a good blocker and pitch-framer and shows the ability to manage games in the moment. **THE FUTURE:** Moreno got a taste of the majors during 2022 season. He made appearances at second base, third base and left field for on-the-job training in order to increase his flexibility, but his future is behind the plate, even if the Blue Jays have enviable depth at that position. He'll have the opportunity to seize a larger share of the catching duties in 2023 and could be on his way to becoming a future all-star.

Year	Age	Club (League	Lvl	AVG	G	AB	R	H	2B	3B	HR	RBI	BB	SO	SB	OBP	SLG
2022	22	Buffalo (IL)	AAA	.315	62	238	35	75	16	0	3	39	24	45	7	.386	.420
2022	22	Toronto (AL)	MLB	.319	25	69	10	22	1	0	1	7	4	8	0	.356	.377
Major League Totals				.319	25	69	10	22	1	0	1	7	4	8	0	.356	.377
Minor League Totals				.310	253	962	145	298	64	9	27	189	73	133	22	.365	.479

2 RICKY TIEDEMANN, LHP

Born: Aug. 18, 2002. **B-T:** L-L. **HT:** 6-4. **WT:** 220.
Drafted: Golden West (Calif.) JC, 2021 (3rd round). **Signed by:** Joey Aversa.

BA GRADE

60 Risk:
High

TRACK RECORD: Tiedemann went unpicked out of high school in the five-round 2020 draft after teams didn't meet his bonus demands. He decommitted from San Diego State and enrolled at Golden West (Calif.) JC to make himself available for the 2021 draft. The Blue Jays drafted him in the third round and signed him for a below-slot $644,800. Tiedemann immediately turned heads with a velocity spike. In 2022, he climbed three levels of the minors to Double-A and led the organization with a 2.17 ERA.

SCOUTING REPORT: A tall, physical specimen whose frame balances strength and athleticism, Tiedemann sets up on the third base side of the rubber and delivers the ball from a low arm slot. This creates a difficult angle for both lefthanded and righthanded hitters and allows him to wear out the armside half of the plate. Tiedemann mixes three pitches, topped by a plus mid-90s four-seam fastball with heavy armside run. His sweepy slider sits 80-82 mph with a foot of horizontal break and is another plus pitch he mostly throws against lefthanded batters. His changeup is a plus-plus mid-80s offering with tumble and fade that plays off his fastball and annihilates righthanded hitters. Tiedemann is a good athlete who shows above-average control of all three of his pitches, which all drive swings and misses. He has the ability to keep hitters off-balance with advanced sequencing.

THE FUTURE: Tiedemann's strong three-pitch mix, unique release characteristics and power from the left side give him the ingredients to develop into a front-of-the-rotation stalwart.

SCOUTING GRADES:	Fastball: 65	Slider: 60	Changeup: 70	Control: 55

Year	Age	Club (League)	Lvl	W	L	ERA	G	GS	IP	H	HR	BB	SO	BB/9	SO/9	WHIP	AVG
2022	19	Dunedin (FSL)	LoA	3	1	1.80	6	6	30	11	1	13	49	3.9	14.7	0.80	.115
2022	19	Vancouver (NWL)	HiA	2	2	2.39	8	8	38	23	2	12	54	2.9	12.9	0.93	.176
2022	19	New Hampshire (EL)	AA	0	1	2.45	4	4	11	5	0	4	14	3.3	11.5	0.82	.147
Minor League Totals				5	4	2.17	18	18	79	39	3	29	117	3.3	13.4	0.86	.149

3 YOSVER ZULUETA, RHP

Born: Jan. 23, 1998 **B-T:** R-R **HT:** 6-1 **WT:** 190.
Signed: Cuba, 2019. **Signed by:** Andrew Tinnish.

BA GRADE

55 Risk:
High

TRACK RECORD: Zulueta signed with the Blue Jays out of Cuba for $1 million in 2019 but had Tommy John surgery shortly after signing. Then he spent the 2020 pandemic rehabbing and faced only one batter in 2021 before he tore the anterior cruciate ligament in his right knee covering first base in his first game for Low-A Dunedin. Finally healthy in 2022, Zulueta began the year in Low-A and rocketed up four levels to Triple-A in a breakout campaign.

SCOUTING REPORT: Zulueta is a high-powered righthander with a fastball that can reach triple digits with ease. His fastball comfortably sits at 96-97 mph as a starter and repeatedly reaches 100 with heavy armside run, making it particularly effective against lefthanded hitters. His fastball can play down at times and be hittable, especially against righthanded batters, but he's able to offset that with a plus mid-80s slider that features a foot of horizontal break. Zulueta throws his slider nearly as often as his fastball against righthanded hitters and commands his slider better. Zulueta's arsenal is built around his fastball and slider. He has a mid-80s changeup that will flash above-average, but he struggles to execute it consistently. His curveball is a softer variation of his slider with greater depth at 78-80 mph. Zulueta has below-average control. He splitt 2022 between starting and relieving, but the Blue Jays say they were just managing his innings.

THE FUTURE: Zulueta's power stuff and feel for sequencing give him a chance to start. His powerful fastball/slider combination gives him a fallback as a high-leverage reliever.

SCOUTING GRADES:	Fastball: 60	Slider: 60	Curveball: 50	Changeup: 50	Control: 40

Year	Age	Club (League)	Lvl	W	L	ERA	G	GS	IP	H	HR	BB	SO	BB/9	SO/9	WHIP	AVG
2022	24	Dunedin (FSL)	LoA	0	0	3.00	3	3	12	9	0	3	23	2.2	17.2	1.00	.205
2022	24	Vancouver (NWL)	HiA	1	3	3.80	6	6	24	18	1	11	31	4.2	11.8	1.23	.209
2022	24	New Hampshire (EL)	AA	1	1	4.11	9	2	15	10	1	14	25	8.2	14.7	1.57	.179
2022	24	Buffalo (IL)	AAA	0	1	3.86	3	1	5	3	0	4	5	7.7	9.6	1.50	.200
Minor League Totals				2	5	3.72	22	13	56	40	2	32	84	5.2	13.6	1.29	.198

4 BRANDON BARRIERA, LHP

Born: March 4, 2004. **B-T:** L-L **HT:** 6-2 **WT:** 180.
Drafted: HS—Plantation, Fla., 2022 (1st round). **Signed by:** Adrian Casanova.

TRACK RECORD: The latest standout from national prep power American Heritage High in South Florida, Barriera pitched for USA Baseball's 12U and 15U national teams and emerged early as one of the top high school pitchers in the 2022 draft class. He entered his senior season with considerable hype and went 5-0, 2.27 in eight starts before deciding to sit out the remainder of the year to prepare for the draft. The Blue Jays drafted Barriera 23rd overall and signed him for a tick under $3.6 million to forgo a Vanderbilt commitment. In his first post-draft interview on MLB Network, Barriera vowed the 22 teams who passed him up were "going to regret this."

BA GRADE

55 Risk: Extreme

SCOUTING REPORT: Barriera is an athletic lefthander with a prototypical pitcher's build, whippy arm speed and lots of physical projection remaining. He mixes four pitches but primarily works off of his fastball and slider. His plus fastball sits 92-95 mph and touches 98-99 with cut and explosive late life. His nearly plus-plus slider is his most dominant pitch as a low-80s sweeper with late bite that elicits ugly swings. Barriera flashes a mid-70s curveball and mid-80s changeup which project to be average pitches, but his fastball and slider combination account for a majority of his usage. The development of Barriera's changeup in the coming years could dictate his ultimate role. It flashed above-average as an amateur, leading many to believe it can develop into a consistent weapon. He throws everything for strikes with average control.

THE FUTURE: Barriera has the stuff and physicality to blossom into a midrotation or better starter if everything clicks. He is set to make his pro debut in 2023.

SCOUTING GRADES:	Fastball: 60	Curveball: 50	Slider: 65	Changeup: 50	Control: 50

Year	Age	Club (League)	Lvl	W	L	ERA	G	GS	IP	H	HR	BB	SO	BB/9	SO/9	WHIP	AVG
2022	18	Did not play															

5 ADDISON BARGER, SS/3B

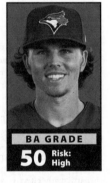

Born: Nov. 12, 1999. **B-T:** L-R. **HT:** 6-0. **WT:** 175.
Drafted: HS—Tampa, 2018 (6th round). **Signed by:** Matt Bishoff.

TRACK RECORD: Barger impressed as one of the top all-around high school players in the 2018 draft class and signed with the Blue Jays for $271,100 as a sixth-round pick. He took time to gel as a professional and spent most of 2019 on the restricted list, but he emerged from the coronavirus shutdown stronger and with a more power-focused swing to begin his ascent. Barger enjoyed an encouraging campaign at Low-A Dunedin in 2021 and broke out loudly in 2022, rising three levels to finish the season at Triple-A Buffalo. He led the Blue Jays organization in multiple categories including hits, runs, RBIs and OPS and earned an assignment to the Arizona Fall League.

BA GRADE

50 Risk: High

SCOUTING REPORT: Barger transformed from a contact hitter to an overly aggressive power hitter before finding a good balance between the two approaches in 2022. Barger has an unorthodox setup at the plate with an upright, open stance and a pronounced leg kick he uses as a timing mechanism. He looks to do damage on the inner half and shoots balls to his pull side, with 24 of his 26 home runs in 2022 going to right field. After previously struggling to control his aggressiveness, Barger has become more subdued to cut down his chase swings and make more contact in the zone. He's still a fringy hitter who doesn't walk much, but he makes enough contact to get to his power. Barger can play multiple positions on the infield. His sound actions and plus arm strength should allow him to stick at shortstop as an average defender, and he can also capably play second base or third base.

THE FUTURE: Barger's power and defense give him a chance to be a regular in the middle infield. He is in position to make his major league debut in 2023.

SCOUTING GRADES	Hitting: 45	Power: 55	Speed: 50	Fielding: 50	Arm: 60

Year	Age	Club (League)	Lvl	AVG	G	AB	R	H	2B	3B	HR	RBI	BB	SO	SB	OBP	SLG
2022	22	Vancouver (NWL)	HiA	.300	69	260	46	78	21	2	14	53	25	76	7	.366	.558
2022	22	New Hampshire (EL)	AA	.313	47	176	26	55	11	0	9	29	18	50	2	.384	.528
2022	22	Buffalo (IL)	AAA	.355	8	31	8	11	1	0	3	9	5	5	0	.444	.677
Minor League Totals				.266	282	1044	175	278	67	6	49	199	114	311	16	.348	.483

6 ORELVIS MARTINEZ, SS/3B

Born: Nov. 19, 2001. **B-T:** R-R. **HT:** 6-1. **WT:** 190.
Signed: Dominican Republic, 2018. **Signed by:** Alexis de la Cruz/Sandy Rosario.

TRACK RECORD: Martinez signed with the Blue Jays out of the Dominican Republic for $3.51 million in 2018 and started his professional career hot. He ranked as the No. 1 prospect in the Rookie-level Gulf Coast League in 2019 and led the Low-A Florida State League in home runs, slugging percentage and OPS in 2021 before receiving a late promotion to High-A Vancouver. Martinez impressed in big league camp in 2022 and received an aggressive assignment to Double-A New Hampshire, where the 20-year-old struggled for the first time in his career. He hit a career-high 30 home runs, but also had the sixth-lowest batting average (.203) and on-base percentage (.286) in the Eastern League.

SCOUTING REPORT: Martinez's game is driven by his tremendous bat speed and plus power. He has the ability to turn around premium velocity and feasts on fastballs, sending them out a long way to all fields with loud exit velocities. Martinez does immense damage on contact, but his hyper-aggressive approach was exposed by higher-level pitching at Double-A in 2022. He has an extreme tendency to chase and expand the strike zone, making him easy prey for pitchers who are happy to let him get himself out. Martinez makes contact on pitches in the zone with a knack for hard contact and steep launch angles, but he's a well below-average hitter who will have to vastly improve his strike-zone discipline and swing decisions to make enough contact at higher levels. Martinez is a fringy defender at both shortstop and third base. His plus arm and average athleticism give him a chance to be playable at third base.

THE FUTURE: A talented but enigmatic player, Martinez requires a lot of polish to make the jump from low minors standout to future major league regular. He'll likely repeat Double-A in 2023.

BA GRADE
55 Risk: Extreme

SCOUTING GRADES	Hitting: 30	Power: 60	Speed: 45	Fielding: 45	Arm: 60

Year	Age	Club (League)	Lvl	AVG	G	AB	R	H	2B	3B	HR	RBI	BB	SO	SB	OBP	SLG
2022	20	New Hampshire (EL)	AA	.203	118	433	57	88	15	0	30	76	40	140	6	.286	.446
Minor League Totals				.237	256	970	143	230	49	7	65	195	97	282	12	.320	.503

7 TUCKER TOMAN, 3B/SS

Born: Nov. 12, 2003. **B-T:** B-R. **HT:** 6-1. **WT:** 190.
Drafted: HS—Columbia, S.C., 2022 (2nd round supplemental). **Signed by:** Mike Tidick.

TRACK RECORD: Toman grew up around the game as the son of longtime college coach Jim Toman, who most recently coached at Middle Tennessee State. Tucker established himself early as one of the top high school hitters for his age and was drafted by the Blue Jays in the supplemental second round with the 77th overall pick in 2022. He signed for an above-slot $2 million to forgo a Louisiana State commitment and made his professional debut with a strong but abbreviated showing in the Florida Complex League.

SCOUTING REPORT: Toman is a gifted switch-hitter with advanced plate discipline and a knack for contact. He's a pure hitter who displays plus bat speed and feel for the barrel from the left side and makes consistent hard contact. His righthanded swing lacks loft and doesn't have much power behind it, but his discerning eye and advanced command of the strike zone allow him to be a threat from both sides of the plate. He projects to be at least an above-average hitter and could grow into average power with physical maturity. While views on Toman's long-term upside were split among amateur evaluators, few questioned Toman's ability to hit with wood in pro ball. The Blue Jays drafted Toman as a shortstop, but he projects to move to second base. He's a fringy runner with fringy arm strength that plays up with a quick release and solid accuracy. He has a chance to be an average defender at the keystone with more development.

THE FUTURE: Toman projects to be a bat-first second baseman who hits for a high average withb the upside for above-average power from the left side. Improvements to his righthanded swing could pay dividends and also hint at untapped upside. Toman will open 2023 at Low-A Dunedin in 2023.

BA GRADE
55 Risk: Extreme

SCOUTING GRADES	Hitting: 55	Power: 50	Speed: 40	Fielding: 45	Arm: 45

Year	Age	Club (League)	Lvl	AVG	G	AB	R	H	2B	3B	HR	RBI	BB	SO	SB	OBP	SLG
2022	18	Blue Jays (FCL)	R	.289	11	38	4	11	3	0	0	5	7	12	0	.391	.368
Minor League Totals				.289	11	38	4	11	3	0	0	5	7	12	0	.391	.368

8 CADE DOUGHTY, 2B/3B

Born: March 26, 2001. **B-T:** R-R. **HT:** 6-1. **WT:** 195.
Drafted: Louisiana State, 2022 (2nd round supplemental). **Signed by:** Chris Curtis.
TRACK RECORD: Doughty was one of the top prospects in the 2019 high school class but fell to the Tigers in the 39th round because of his strong commitment to Louisiana State. His father Richard and older brother Braden both played baseball at LSU, and Doughty joined the family legacy by spending three seasons as a starter in the middle of LSU's lineup. He hit .301 with 30 home runs and .921 OPS in a decorated college career and was drafted 78th overall in the second round by the Blue Jays in 2022, signing for slot value at $833,600. Doughty played primarily second base in college and split his time between second and third base in his pro debut.

BA GRADE
50 Risk: High

SCOUTING REPORT: Doughty is an adept contact hitter who has progressively seen his power grow. He has above-average contact skills from the right side and gets the most out of his average raw power by aggressively attacking pitches throughout his at-bats. Those aggressive tendencies can get him in trouble. He's prone to expanding the strike zone, but his power production keeps increasing. He hit six homers in 26 games for Low-A Dunedin in his pro debut despite modest exit velocities and launch angle data. Doughty is a fringe-average defender at second base with an average arm. He's a fringy runner who isn't a threat to steal bases. Doughty's tools are all roughly average, but he is a savvy player with a high baseball IQ that helps everything play up. He takes advantage of defensive mishaps with smart baserunning and plays hard in all facets.
THE FUTURE: Doughty's contact skills and feel for the game give him a chance to play above his tools and become a solid, if unspectacular, everyday second baseman in the major leagues. He'll see High-A Vancouver during his first full season in 2023.

| SCOUTING GRADES | Hitting: 50 | | Power: 50 | | Speed: 45 | | Fielding: 45 | | Arm: 50 | |

Year	Age	Club (League)	Lvl	AVG	G	AB	R	H	2B	3B	HR	RBI	BB	SO	SB	OBP	SLG
2022	21	Dunedin (FSL)	LoA	.272	26	103	21	28	5	0	6	24	10	29	3	.370	.495
Minor League Totals				.272	26	103	21	28	5	0	6	24	10	29	3	.370	.495

9 HAYDEN JUENGER, RHP

Born: Aug. 9, 2000. **B-T:** R-R. **HT:** 6-0. **WT:** 180.
Drafted: Missouri State, 2021 (6th round). **Signed by:** Matt Huck.
TRACK RECORD: Juenger spent three seasons pitching out of Missouri State's bullpen and was one of the top college relievers available when the Blue Jays selected him in the sixth round of the 2021 draft. He worked as a traditional reliever in his pro debut for High-A Vancouver after signing, but the Blue Jays aggressively pushed him to Double-A to begin his first full season in 2022. Juenger worked three to four innings as an opener for New Hampshire. He flourished with the new arrangement and received a midseason promotion to Triple-A Buffalo, where he worked as a more traditional multi-inning reliever in the second half of the season.

BA GRADE
50 Risk: High

SCOUTING REPORT: A slight but athletic righthander, Juenger mixes three pitches that all play up with unique characteristics. His drop-and-drive delivery and three-quarters arm slot create an unusually low release height, giving his pitches an unfamiliar trajectory for hitters, which creates uncomfortable at-bats. Juenger's plus fastball ranges from 93-97 mph early in outings before dropping to 91-94 in subsequent innings, when he often loses the zone. His 83-84 mph slider with late horizontal break and mid-80s changeup with heavy armside run are both average pitches which give him effective weapons against hitters on both sides of the plate. Juenger leans on his fastball heavily and throws it nearly 60% of the time. His usage for each secondary pitch could be higher, but he often pockets them for long stretches while focusing on attacking with his fastball. Juenger throws all three of his pitches for strikes with average control.
THE FUTURE: Juenger projects best as a multi-inning weapon out of the bullpen, but he is capable of filling a variety of roles. He is in position to make his major league debut in 2023.

| SCOUTING GRADES: | Fastball: 60 | | Slider: 50 | | Changeup: 50 | | Control: 50 | |

Year	Age	Club (League)	Lvl	W	L	ERA	G	GS	IP	H	HR	BB	SO	BB/9	SO/9	WHIP	AVG
2022	21	New Hampshire (EL)	AA	0	5	4.02	20	17	56	40	12	21	67	3.4	10.8	1.09	.196
2022	21	Buffalo (IL)	AAA	3	2	3.31	18	2	33	23	6	16	33	4.4	9.1	1.19	.195
Minor League Totals				5	7	3.56	49	19	109	74	18	41	134	3.4	11.1	1.06	.190

10 NATE PEARSON, RHP

Born: Aug. 20, 1996. **B-T:** R-R. **HT:** 6-6. **WT:** 250.
Drafted: JC of Central Florida, 2017 (1st round). **Signed by:** Matt Bishoff.

TRACK RECORD: Once considered the top prospect in the Blue Jays organization, Pearson has dealt with a litany of injuries that have delayed his path to establishing himself in Toronto. A line drive fractured his right forearm in 2019. Then his MLB debut season in 2020 was interrupted by a flexor strain in his elbow, and then he missed most of 2021 with groin injuries and a sports hernia. As a result, he has pitched a total of 61 innings the past two seasons. Expected to contribute to the Blue Jays in 2022, Pearson instead missed most of the season with a lat strain and remained in the Triple-A Buffalo bullpen after he returned from the injured list in September.

BA GRADE

50 Risk: Very High

SCOUTING REPORT: Pearson is physically imposing at 6-foot-6, 250 pounds with broad shoulders and an extra-large build. His large frame and natural strength translate to easy 99-104 mph fastballs, and he pairs his fastball with an above-average, hard slider in the upper 80s with late horizontal bite. He also has an average power curveball in the mid 80s with 11-to-5 shape and two-plane break and a firm changeup that is a fringe-average pitch. His changeup used to be a bigger part of his arsenal but has backed up in recent years. Pearson has increasingly pitched in relief due to his injuries and fringy control. He primarily focuses on his fastball and slider as a reliever, while mixing in an occasional curveball against lefthanded hitters.

THE FUTURE: At 26 years old and with a long list of injuries, Pearson appears destined for a bullpen role. His raw stuff could allow him to flourish as a high-leverage reliever if he can stay healthy. .

SCOUTING GRADES:	Fastball: 65	Curveball: 50	Slider: 55	Changeup: 45	Control: 45

Year	Age	Club (League)	Lvl	W	L	ERA	G	GS	IP	H	HR	BB	SO	BB/9	SO/9	WHIP	AVG
2022	25	Dunedin (FSL)	LoA	0	0	3.38	2	1	3	1	0	1	1	3.4	3.4	0.75	.125
2022	25	Buffalo (IL)	AAA	2	1	3.55	11	0	13	7	2	7	18	5.0	12.8	1.11	.163
Major League Totals				2	1	5.18	17	5	33	28	7	25	36	6.8	9.8	1.61	.222
Minor League Totals				8	9	2.71	59	41	169	104	15	53	209	2.8	11.1	0.93	.174

11 ADAM MACKO, LHP

Born: Dec. 30, 2000. **B-T:** L-L. **HT:** 6-0. **WT:** 170.
Drafted: HS—Vauxhall, Alberta, 2019 (7th round). **Signed by:** Les McTavish/Alex Ross (Mariners).

TRACK RECORD: Macko was born in Slovakia and was introduced to baseball in first grade. He taught himself to pitch by watching YouTube videos of Justin Verlander and David Price and developed a unique talent for the game, which he honed after his family moved to Ireland and eventually Canada. Macko blossomed with formal baseball instruction and became Canada's top prospect in the 2019 draft, leading the Mariners to draft him in the seventh round and sign him for $250,000. He got off to a solid start at High-A Everett in 2022 but made only eight starts before having season-ending meniscus surgery in his right knee. Seattle traded him to the Blue Jays in November to acquire Teoscar Hernandez.

SCOUTING REPORT: Macko's stuff was inconsistent in 2022 as he lowered his arm slot and dealt with injuries, but it's still plenty potent. His fastball ranges from 91-96 mph out of a low slot and release point from the left side that creates a tough angle for lefthanded hitters. His signature pitch is a plus curveball with tight spin and late drop in the low 70s, but at times it devolves into a sweepy, soft offering in the upper 60s. Macko also has an average horizontal slider in the mid-80s that gives lefties trouble and a fringy, low-80s changeup that is improving. Macko is a good athlete, but he overthrows at times and nibbles at others, which results in below-average control. His biggest concern is health. Macko has pitched only 95 innings in three seasons after missing most of 2021 with shoulder tenderness and most of 2022 with his knee injury.

THE FUTURE: Macko has the arsenal to start, but his control and health point to a likely relief future. His primary goal will be to stay healthy in 2023.

BA GRADE: 50/Very High	Fastball: 55	Curveball: 60	Slider: 50	Changeup: 45	Control: 40

Year	Age	Club (League)	Lvl	W	L	ERA	G	GS	IP	H	HR	BB	SO	BB/9	SO/9	WHIP	AVG
2022	21	Everett (NWL)	HiA	0	2	3.99	8	8	38	33	4	20	60	4.7	14.1	1.38	.234
Minor League Totals				2	7	3.98	26	19	95	81	6	53	148	5.0	14.0	1.41	.228

12 JOSH KASEVICH, SS

Born: Jan. 17, 2001. **B-T:** R-R. **HT:** 6-2. **WT:** 200.
Drafted: Oregon, 2022 (2nd round). **Signed by:** Ryan Fox.
TRACK RECORD: Kasevich hit .310/.383/.445 with seven home runs while striking out far less than he walked in 2022, and earned a spot on the All-Pacific-12 Conference first team. The Blue Jays selected him with the 60th overall pick in the second round and signed him for a below-slot $997,500.
SCOUTING REPORT: A well-rounded contributor on both sides of the ball in college, Kasevich is a sure-handed shortstop with a hit-over-power profile at the plate. He fits in with a Blue Jays system that values high-end bat-to-ball skills and advanced plate discipline. With a simple righthanded swing, Kasevich shows the ability to hit anything thrown inside the zone with little effort, with loose adjustability in his hands and level bat path that generates hard line drives and hard ground balls on his best contact. Kasevich rarely strikes out and shows the ability to avoid chase swings. His game power is below-average, but his exit velocity data hints at average raw power in his lean 6-foot-2 frame. He is a fringe-average runner and not a basestealing threat. Kasevich, while not a slick defender, is instead practical, polished and fundamentally sound. He rarely makes mistakes in the field and shows an above-average arm.
THE FUTURE: Kasevich is a strong defender with above-average contact and on-base skills but little power. He looks like an average shortstop with enough offense and defensive value to play every day.

BA GRADE: 45/High	Hit: 55	Power: 40	Run: 45	Field: 55	Arm: 55

Year	Age	Club (League)	Lvl	AVG	G	AB	R	H	2B	3B	HR	RBI	BB	SO	SB	OBP	SLG
2022	21	Dunedin (FSL)	LoA	.262	25	107	18	28	8	0	0	7	11	9	0	.344	.336
Minor League Totals				.262	25	107	18	28	8	0	0	7	11	9	0	.344	.336

13 DAHIAN SANTOS, RHP

Born: Feb. 26, 2003. **B-T:** R-R. **HT:** 5-11. **WT:** 160.
Signed: Venezuela, 2019. **Signed by:** Francisco Plasencia/Jose Contreras.
TRACK RECORD: Santos signed with the Blue Jays for $150,000 in 2019. Since that time he has blossomed into one of the top young pitchers in the system. With Low-A Dunedin in 2022, Santos made 19 appearances, including 14 starts, and recorded a 3.44 ERA with 120 strikeouts, second most in the Florida State League. He was promoted to High-A Vancouver for four starts.
SCOUTING REPORT: An athletic righthander who oozes projection from his slender frame, Santos employs a true tall-and-fall operation with long whippy arm action and slings the ball from a sidearm slot. This unique arm action and release allows all of Santos' pitches to play up, particularly his sweeping slider. Santos mixes three pitches including a low-90s side-spinning four-seam fastball, a low-80s slider with more than a foot of horizontal break and a mid-80s changeup he shows an innate ability to kill lift and spin on. It's the makings of three average or better pitches with his 2,700-rpm sweeping slider the crown jewel of his arsenal—a future plus-plus pitch. Santos' command has been below-average, and with a unique operation and arm action it's never likely to get to anything more than average.
THE FUTURE: A talented and projectable pitcher who could add strength and velocity in the coming years, Santos projects as a back-of-the-rotation starter with a reliever floor.

BA Grade: 50/Extreme	Fastball: 50	Slider: 70	Changeup: 55	Control: 40

Year	Age	Club (League)	Lvl	W	L	ERA	G	GS	IP	H	HR	BB	SO	BB/9	SO/9	WHIP	AVG
2022	19	Dunedin (FSL)	LoA	4	5	3.44	19	14	73	47	8	35	120	4.3	14.7	1.12	.181
2022	19	Vancouver (NWL)	HiA	0	2	10.66	4	4	13	17	3	9	22	6.4	15.6	2.05	.333
Minor League Totals				5	11	4.84	35	27	126	102	17	60	200	4.3	14.2	1.28	.220

14 DASAN BROWN, OF

Born: Sept. 25, 2001. **B-T:** R-R. **HT:** 6-0. **WT:** 185.
Drafted: HS—Oakville Ontario, 2019 (3rd round). **Signed by:** Kory Lafreniere.
TRACK RECORD: An Ontario native, Brown signed with the Blue Jays for an above-slot $800,000 as a third-round pick in 2019. He began his pro career as a 17-year-old in the Gulf Coast League. Following the 2020 pandemic, Brown was assigned to Low-A Dunedin and returned there in 2022 before earning a promotion to High-A Vancouver after hitting .279/.369/.450 in 38 games.
SCOUTING REPORT: There are few profiles in the amateur space more fraught with fool's gold than a tooled-up, righthanded-hitting prep outfielder from cold-weather climates, but Brown took a sizable step forward in 2022 and solidified his prospect pedigree. A top-of-the-scale athlete, Brown is a 70-grade run-

ner with explosiveness in everything he does. He uses a simple, hands-driven swing that uses little of his lower half and relies on his bat speed and quick-twitch mechanisms. He's a below-average contact hitter with average approach and shows the ability to identify balls and strikes. While his power is below-average at present, he projects to add more strength as he matures. His bat path is fairly level, but he showed the ability to barrel up on his best struck drives. Offensively Brown is work in progress, but one who made strides at the plate in 2022. Brown uses his speed most effectively in the field. Defensively he's one of the better center fielders in Class A and showed gap-closing speed and precision.

THE FUTURE: A standout center fielder who got an early start on his professional career, Brown will be 21 for all of 2023 and should return to Vancouver to begin his season. He has potential for an everyday regular in center with gold glove defense.

| BA GRADE: 50/ Extreme | | Hit: 45 | | Power: 45 | | Run: 70 | | Field: 70 | | Arm: 60 | |

Year	Age	Club (League)	Lvl	AVG	G	AB	R	H	2B	3B	HR	RBI	BB	SO	SB	OBP	SLG
2022	20	Blue Jays (FCL)	R	.188	6	16	5	3	1	0	0	1	2	7	2	.409	.250
2022	20	Dunedin (FSL)	LoA	.279	38	140	35	39	8	2	4	12	17	45	11	.369	.450
2022	20	Vancouver (NWL)	HiA	.298	40	151	25	45	11	0	2	11	14	50	11	.392	.411
Minor League Totals				.253	149	550	106	139	30	5	10	45	62	193	52	.363	.380

15 GABRIEL MARTINEZ, OF

Born: July 24, 2002. **B-T:** R-R. **HT:** 6-0. **WT:** 170.
Signed: Venezuela, 2018. **Signed by:** Francisco Plasencia.

TRACK RECORD: Martinez signed out of Venezuela in 2018 and took a few years to marinate, but popped up during the summer of 2021 after hitting .330 in the Florida Complex League. He made his full-season debut with Low-A Dunedin in 2021 and returned to the level to begin 2022. There Martinez hit .288/.348/.483 with 11 home runs and a 17% strikeout rate across 65 games. He was promoted to High-A Vancouver in early August and finished the season hitting .324/.381/.490 over 28 games.

SCOUTING REPORT: A true bat-first prospect, Martinez combines two key elements that drive his success at the plate. He possesses above-average bat-to-ball skills and above-average power and is capable of hitting a variety of pitch shapes and locations throughout the zone. He's physically strong with loose hands and mighty wrists that allow him to hit well-struck drives all over the field. Where Martinez gets into trouble is when he begins to expand the zone, and at times he is overly aggressive in his plan of attack. Martinez's strong contact skills have kept his strikeouts in check, however. He is limited to an outfield corner, but could end up at first base due to a lack of range.

THE FUTURE: Martinez will go as far as the bat will take him. His tantalizing hit and power combination could allow him to settle in as a hit-first regular in one of the outfield corners.

| BA GRADE: 45/High | | Hit: 55 | | Power: 55 | | Run: 40 | | Field: 40 | | Arm: 50 | |

Year	Age	Club (League)	Lvl	AVG	G	AB	R	H	2B	3B	HR	RBI	BB	SO	SB	OBP	SLG
2022	19	Blue Jays (FCL)	R	.100	3	10	1	1	0	0	0	0	1	2	1	.250	.200
2022	19	Dunedin (FSL)	LoA	.288	65	240	46	69	14	0	11	46	22	45	3	.348	.483
2022	19	Vancouver (NWL)	HiA	.324	28	102	11	33	8	0	3	13	9	17	0	.381	.490
Minor League Totals				.282	188	677	105	191	45	2	16	102	75	112	19	.358	.425

16 OTTO LOPEZ, 2B/SS

Born: Oct. 1, 1998. **B-T:** R-R. **HT:** 5-10. **WT:** 160.
Signed: Dominican Republic, 2016. **Signed by:** Sandy Rosario/Lorenzo Perez/Alexis de la Cruz.

TRACK RECORD: Lopez signed for just $60,000 out of the Dominican Republic in 2016 and since then has been one of the most steady contact hitters in a Blue Jays' system full of strong hit tools. Lopez won back-to-back league batting titles on both sides of the 2020 pandemic. He won the Low-A Midwest League batting title in 2019 and followed with one in the Double-A Eastern League in 2021. He spent the majority of his 2022 season with Triple-A Buffalo and hit .297. Lopez shuttled back and forth from Toronto to Buffalo and appeared in parts of six different series for the Blue Jays.

SCOUTING REPORT: A classic utility player, Lopez can fill in at all three outfield spots in addition to his natural position of second base. He can fill in at shortstop in a pinch but not for any extended period. At the plate, he's a hit-over-power profile who uses the whole field and has plus contact skills and running ability to get on base. Lopez flashes an advanced approach at the plate and rarely expands the zone with consistent, quality at-bats. His game power is poor and unlikely to ever be a large part of his game. He's a plus runner but only an average basestealer and has never eclipsed the 25 stolen base mark in any season. Defensively he's average at a variety of spots and can play all three outfield spots but lacks experience at the positions.

THE FUTURE: A plus contact hitter who knows how to get on-base with the ability to handle four to five positions on the diamond, Lopez has the look of a low-risk utility player.

BA GRADE: 40/Medium		Hit: 55			Power: 20		Run: 60			Field: 50			Arm: 45	

Year	Age	Club (League)	Lvl	AVG	G	AB	R	H	2B	3B	HR	RBI	BB	SO	SB	OBP	SLG
2022	23	Dunedin (FSL)	LoA	.050	5	20	0	1	0	0	0	2	2	4	0	.136	.050
2022	23	Buffalo (IL)	AAA	.297	91	340	53	101	19	6	3	34	41	61	14	.378	.415
2022	23	Toronto (AL)	MLB	.667	8	9	0	6	0	0	0	3	1	1	0	.700	.667
Major League Totals				**.600**	**9**	**10**	**0**	**6**	**0**	**0**	**0**	**3**	**1**	**2**	**0**	**.636**	**.600**
Minor League Totals				**.305**	**426**	**1644**	**271**	**502**	**89**	**24**	**17**	**193**	**163**	**265**	**77**	**.373**	**.420**

17 SEM ROBBERSE, RHP

Born: Oct. 12, 2001. **B-T:** R-R. **HT:** 6-1. **WT:** 180.
Signed: Netherlands, 2019. **Signed by:** Andrew Tinnish.
TRACK RECORD: While baseball is a global game, few legitimate major league prospects have come from Europe. Robberse, who grew up in the Netherlands, is looking to make a name for himself as a true European major leaguer. After signing for $125,000 in 2019, Robberse blossomed into a starting pitching prospect. He spent a majority of his 2022 season at High-A Vancouver and made 17 starts for the Canadians before seeing a late-season promotion to Double-A New Hampshire.
SCOUTING REPORT: A slight righthander with a long arm action and true three-quarters slot, Robberse uses three pitches in his fastball, slider and changeup combination. He sits 89-92 mph on a four-seam fastball that has natural cut and mixes in a low-to-mid-80s slider with moderate sweep. The two pitches account for over 75% of his pitch usage. He shows a mid-to-high-80s changeup to lefthanded hitters that generated high rates of whiffs and chase swings. Robberse lacks power but repeats his delivery well and shows the ability to tunnel both his slider and changeup off his fastball.
THE FUTURE: Robberse has the look of a pitchability back-of-the-rotation starter. If he can add strength, and subsequently velocity, he has a chance to crack a big league rotation.

BA Grade: 45/High		Fastball: 45		Slider: 50		Changeup: 55		Control: 50	

Year	Age	Club (League)	Lvl	W	L	ERA	G	GS	IP	H	HR	BB	SO	BB/9	SO/9	WHIP	AVG
2022	20	Vancouver (NWL)	HiA	4	4	3.12	17	17	87	76	7	24	78	2.5	8.1	1.15	.231
2022	20	New Hampshire (EL)	AA	0	3	3.65	5	5	25	19	4	10	19	3.6	6.9	1.18	.211
Minor League Totals				**11**	**14**	**3.59**	**48**	**44**	**210**	**191**	**18**	**72**	**196**	**3.1**	**8.4**	**1.25**	**.238**

18 HAGEN DANNER, RHP

Born: Sept. 30, 1998. **B-T:** R-R. **HT:** 6-2. **WT:** 210.
Drafted: HS—Huntington Beach, Calif., 2017 (2nd round). **Signed by:** Joey Aversa.
TRACK RECORD: Danner was drafted as a catcher, a position he played for the better part of three seasons before committing to pitching full time prior to the 2020 pandemic. He returned in 2021 and flashed loud power reliever stuff in 25 appearances for High-A Vancouver and earned an addition to the 40-man roster. Danner spent much of 2022 injured and made just four appearances for Double-A New Hampshire. He returned in the Arizona Fall League, where he made eight appearances and flashed his signature stuff. The Blue Jays kept Danner on the 40-man roster despite his injury-riddled season.
SCOUTING REPORT: In AFL play, Danner sat 96-98 mph on his four-seam fastball and touched 99 with ride and cut. His fastball has the ability to overpower hitters no matter where it lands in the zone, with exploding life as it nears the plate. His primary secondary is a high-80s slider with cutter-like shape, and he'll flash a more traditional hammer breaking ball at 78-79 mph with depth and two-plane break. With a violent delivery and injury history, Danner is a high-risk relief prospect with immense, high-leverage relief upside. His strike-throwing has been average in his small professional sample as a pitcher. If he can manage to stay healthy and show his command is average or better, Danner's 2023 season might end in the big league bullpen.
THE FUTURE: A potential fire-breathing dragon at the back end of a bullpen, Danner's future depends heavily on his ability to stay healthy and throw strikes.

BA GRADE: 45/High		Fastball: 70		Curveball: 55		Slider: 50		Control: 45	

Year	Age	Club (League)	Lvl	W	L	ERA	G	GS	IP	H	HR	BB	SO	BB/9	SO/9	WHIP	AVG
2022	23	New Hampshire (EL)	AA	0	0	4.91	4	0	4	5	0	3	1	7.4	2.5	2.18	.312
Minor League Totals				**2**	**1**	**2.29**	**29**	**0**	**39**	**26**	**2**	**15**	**43**	**3.4**	**9.8**	**1.04**	**.187**

19 SPENCER HORWITZ, 1B/OF

Born: Nov. 14, 1997. **B-T:** L-R. **HT:** 6-0. **WT:** 190.
Drafted: Radford, 2019 (24th round). **Signed by:** Coulson Barbiche.

TRACK RECORD: Horwitz signed out of Radford for $100,000 in the 24th round of the 2019 draft. All he has done is hit for the better part of two seasons coming off the pandemic. He hit .294/.400/.462 between High-A and Double-A in 2021 and followed that up with a strong Arizona Fall League performance. Assigned back to Double-A New Hampshire in 2022, Horwitz hit .297/.413/.517 over 70 games before a promotion to Triple-A Buffalo in early July. The Blue Jays added him to the 40-man roster in November.
SCOUTING REPORT: A bat-first prospect with some of the most well-rounded plate skills in the Blue Jays system, Horwitz flashes a strong lefthanded swing that allows him to make hard contact at a high rate. His bat-to-ball skills are average but his plate discipline is elite, as he rarely expands the zone, and works deep into at-bats. While his swing isn't naturally geared for power, he's added loft over the last few seasons which has allowed him to get to more of his above-average raw power. Horwitz is a culmination of good hitter traits that allow his profile to work. He's a well below-average runner, and defensively is best used at first base. He's played some corner outfield but he's limited in the role due to a lack of range.
THE FUTURE: If Horwitz continues to improve as a power hitter without sacrificing his approach, he has a chance to carve out a role as a first base/DH on the strong side of a platoon.

BA GRADE: 40/Medium	Hitting: 55	Power: 50	Run: 30	Field: 40	Arm: 50

Year	Age	Club (League)	Lvl	AVG	G	AB	R	H	2B	3B	HR	RBI	BB	SO	SB	OBP	SLG
2022	24	New Hampshire (EL)	AA	.297	70	232	46	69	19	1	10	39	43	54	3	.413	.517
2022	24	Buffalo (IL)	AAA	.246	44	171	31	42	14	0	2	12	30	41	4	.361	.363
Minor League Totals				.290	283	1056	182	306	82	3	28	169	167	193	16	.390	.453

20 LEO JIMENEZ, SS

Born: May 17, 2001. **B-T:** R-R. **HT:** 6-0. **WT:** 195.
Signed: Panama, 2017. **Signed by:** Alex Zapata/Sandy Rosario.

TRACK RECORD: While Panama isn't a hotbed for prospects, it historically has produced several strong players and numerous major leaguers. When Jimenez signed for $825,000 in 2017, he was considered one of the best Panamanian prospects in recent memory. He broke camp with Low-A Dunedin in 2021 but played just 54 games after dislocating his left shoulder in early July. Jimenez was assigned to High-A Vancouver out of camp in 2022 and played 69 games for the Canadians before he broke his hand in mid-August and missed the remainder of the season.
SCOUTING REPORT: Jimenez has a contact-driven profile with an advanced approach and is capable of filling in at multiple spots around the diamond. His bat-to-ball skills are above-average and he pairs that with a discerning eye that has led to high walk totals as a professional. He utilizes a lofty swing that's geared to ambush fastballs over the plate. While Jimenez is fairly physical already, he's still growing into his frame and shows the ability to backspin the ball, with the potential to develop fringe-average power at peak with natural strength gains. He's just an average runner, likely to slow down as he ages, and baserunning is not a major part of his game. Jimenez shows strong infield actions, has a quick first step and a good internal clock that allows him to handle shortstop with an average arm.
THE FUTURE: Jimenez has upside if he can add power and stay healthy in the coming years, but for now he looks like a utility player with solid contact and approach skills.

BA GRADE: 50/Extreme	Hitting: 55	Power: 40	Run: 45	Field: 55	Arm: 50

Year	Age	Club (League)	Lvl	AVG	G	AB	R	H	2B	3B	HR	RBI	BB	SO	SB	OBP	SLG
2022	21	Vancouver (NWL)	HiA	.230	69	244	45	56	14	3	6	40	27	58	7	.340	.385
Minor League Totals				.272	223	778	133	212	45	7	7	102	118	155	14	.397	.375

21 KENDRY ROJAS, LHP

Born: Nov. 26, 2002. **B-T:** L-L. **HT:** 6-2. **WT:** 190.
Signed: Cuba, 2020. **Signed by:** Erick Ramirez/Luis Natera.

TRACK RECORD: After signing out of Cuba for $215,000 during the 2020 international signing period, Rojas debuted in the Florida Complex League in 2021 and made eight appearances. He was assigned to Low-A Dunedin to begin 2022 and made eight appearances before going down with a lat injury that put him on the shelf for all of June and July. He returned in mid August and made four starts, throwing 11.2 innings with 12 strikeouts and just two walks.

SCOUTING REPORT: Rojas is a low-slot lefthander with an athletic, repeatable operation and projectable ceiling in both his frame and pitch mix. He sits low 90s on a four-seam fastball with average ride that plays up out of his low slot. He pairs his fastball with a low-80s slider and a mid-80s changeup, both of which he sells with arm speed and his deceptive arm slot. Rojas shows the ability to command his secondaries with above-average strike rates. He is still learning to command his fastball and is prone to missing arm side.
THE FUTURE: With added power to his pitch mix and improved fastball command, Rojas could take a step forward into legitimate starting pitching prospect territory in 2023.

BA GRADE: 50/Extreme	Fastball: 45	Slider: 55	Changeup: 50	Control: 50

Year	Age	Club (League)	Lvl	W	L	ERA	G	GS	IP	H	HR	BB	SO	BB/9	SO/9	WHIP	AVG
2022	19	Blue Jays (FCL)	R	0	0	0.00	1	1	1	0	0	0	3	0.0	27.0	0.00	.000
2022	19	Dunedin (FSL)	LoA	2	2	4.08	12	10	40	36	1	19	43	4.3	9.8	1.39	.237
Minor League Totals				2	2	3.36	21	15	64	50	2	24	85	3.4	11.9	1.15	.211

22 MANUEL BELTRE, SS

Born: June 9, 2004. **B-T:** R-R. **HT:** 5-11. **WT:** 165.
Drafted: Dominican Republic, 2021. **Signed by:** Sandy Rosario/Lorenzo Perez.
TRACK RECORD: Beltre signed out of the Dominican Republic in January 2021 for $2.35 million as one of the top players available that year. He debuted in the Dominican Summer League in 2021 a little more than a month after his 17th birthday. He made his U.S. debut in 2022 in the Florida Complex League before he was promoted to Low-A Dunedin in the final week of the season.
SCOUTING REPORT: Beltre is an undersized, righthanded-hitting shortstop with a big swing and natural twitch. He's still a work-in-progress at the plate. He makes a high rate of contact, particularly in-zone, despite a longer bat path. Beltre's game power is well below-average currently, but his bat speed and lift in his swing portend future gains. He's an average runner, but a high-energy player who never dogs it down the line. Defensively, Beltre is an above-average defender with an opportunity to stick at shortstop.
THE FUTURE: Overall, Beltre has a contact-driven profile with some potential for increased power with the actions and range to stick in the dirt long term.

BA GRADE: 50/Extreme	Hit: 50	Power: 45	Run: 50	Field: 55	Arm: 50

Year	Age	Club (League)	Lvl	AVG	G	AB	R	H	2B	3B	HR	RBI	BB	SO	SB	OBP	SLG
2022	18	Blue Jays (FCL)	R	.234	49	171	25	40	8	1	1	23	22	41	9	.351	.310
2022	18	Dunedin (FSL)	LoA	.381	5	21	3	8	1	0	1	3	1	3	0	.409	.571
Minor League Totals				.238	107	374	67	89	19	4	4	55	65	77	19	.374	.342

23 ALEJANDRO MELEAN, RHP

Born: Oct. 11, 2000. **B-T:** R-R. **HT:** 6-0. **WT:** 175.
Signed: Venezuela, 2017. **Signed by:** Francisco Plasencia.
TRACK RECORD: Melean was one of several breakouts for the Blue Jays on the pitching side in 2022. He dominated over his first nine appearances with High-A Vancouver to earn a promotion to Double-A New Hampshire in late July.
SCOUTING REPORT: Melean is a stout righthander with a strong build who throws exclusively from the stretch. He made strides with his strike-throwing late in 2021 and it carried over into 2022. He was mostly limited to 50-60 pitches per start in 2022. A polished strike-thrower with a high aptitude for sequencing, Melean can manipulate his slider to add late depth, and he generates ground balls with all three of his pitches. His pitch mix consists of a four-seam fastball that sits 92-94 mph and touches 95 with ride and heavy armside run. His primary secondary is his 79-81 mph changeup with heavy tumble and fade. Melean is comfortable snapping off right-on-right changeups. His breaking ball is a sweepy slider in the same velocity range as his changeup, giving him the ability to work east to west with his secondaries. Both secondaries generate chases outside the zone and have limited batters to very little hard contact.
THE FUTURE: Melean's three-pitch mix and strike-throwing ability allow him to fit a variety of roles. His best fit long term is as a swingman reliever capable of giving a team multiple innings out of the bullpen.

BA GRADE: 40/ Medium	Fastball: 45	Slider: 55	Changeup: 50	Control: 50

Year	Age	Club (League)	Lvl	W	L	ERA	G	GS	IP	H	HR	BB	SO	BB/9	SO/9	WHIP	AVG
2022	21	Vancouver (NWL)	HiA	2	1	1.69	9	5	32	20	2	8	35	2.2	9.8	0.88	.174
2022	21	New Hampshire (EL)	AA	0	4	5.10	8	8	30	26	5	17	24	5.1	7.2	1.43	.234
Minor League Totals				8	15	4.55	56	40	198	198	26	98	207	4.5	9.4	1.50	.255

24 ADRIAN PINTO, 2B

Born: Sept. 22, 2002. **B-T:** R-R. **HT:** 5-6. **WT:** 156.
Signed: Venezuela, 2019. **Signed by:** Orlando Medina/Rolando Fernandez (Rockies).

TRACK RECORD: The Blue Jays acquired Pinto in the trade that sent Randal Grichuk to the Rockies on the eve of the 2022 season. Pinto was assigned to Low-A Dunedin, where he hit .242/.375/.363 over 47 games before going down with a left hamstring strain that cost him the final three months of 2022. At just 20 years old for the entire 2023 campaign, Pinto should return to Dunedin to begin his season.
SCOUTING REPORT: The Blue Jays target above-average contact hitters with advanced approaches in all possible marketplaces, and Pinto is no exception. He makes contact at a high rate with a simple setup, as he crowds the plate in order to cover the whole plate despite shorter levers. He has well below-average power at present and impact doesn't project to be a major part of his game. Still, Pinto has natural loft to his swing and bat speed that portends at least modest gains to his in-game power in the coming years. Pinto is an above-average runner and shows solid jumps as a basestealer. He's rangy in the infield and can handle shortstop and second base and has also spent time in center field in each of his two professional seasons. He's likely limited to second base and the outfield long term due to his fringe-average arm.
THE FUTURE: Due to injury, the Blue Jays haven't gotten a look at what a full season of Pinto looks like. He is a talented player who can add value on both sides of the ball.

BA Grade: 50/Extreme			Hit: 55			Power: 30			Run: 55			Field: 55			Arm: 45	

Year	Age	Club (League)	Lvl	AVG	G	AB	R	H	2B	3B	HR	RBI	BB	SO	SB	OBP	SLG
2022	19	Dunedin (FSL)	LoA	.242	47	157	36	38	5	4	2	10	24	32	18	.375	.363
Minor League Totals				.304	101	332	100	101	20	8	5	37	62	50	59	.435	.458

25 ZACH BRITTON, OF/C

Born: Sept. 9, 1998. **B-T:** L-R. **HT:** 6-1. **WT:** 200.
Drafted: Louisville, 2020 (5th round). **Signed by:** Nate Murrie.

TRACK RECORD: Britton broke through to the Louisville starting nine as a sophomore and then started all 17 games prior to the 2020 pandemic shutdown, hitting .322/.446/.542. The Blue Jays selected him with the 136th pick in 2020 and signed him for a below-slot $97,500. Britton was assigned to High-A Vancouver out of spring training in 2022 and hit .239/.390/.441 over 57 games before a promotion to Double-A New Hampshire for the final few months. He finished his season with a good run in the Arizona Fall League, where he hit .404/.482/.575 over 14 games.
SCOUTING REPORT: Britton's game is centered on his ability to get on base and backspin the ball to the gaps on his best contact. His bat-to-ball skills are fringy and his heavily flyball-focused swing leads to lots of lazy fly outs. While his bat path and setup are geared toward power, Britton possesses just fringe-average raw power, as his best hit balls tend to play more for doubles than home runs. He has an advanced approach at the plate and rarely expands the zone. He's a fringe-average runner who is limited to an outfielder corner with a tick below-average throwing arm. Britton has played catcher more than any other position as a pro, but he has focused on outfield since reaching Double-A in 2022.
THE FUTURE: Britton has a bat-first corner outfield profile and could be capable of filling in as an up-and-down type of player, especially if viewed as an emergency third catcher.

BA GRADE: 40/High			Hit: 45			Power: 45			Run: 45			Field: 45			Arm: 45	

Year	Age	Club (League)	Lvl	AVG	G	AB	R	H	2B	3B	HR	RBI	BB	SO	SB	OBP	SLG
2022	23	Vancouver (NWL)	HiA	.239	57	188	34	45	15	1	7	25	41	70	10	.390	.441
2022	23	New Hampshire (EL)	AA	.234	19	64	14	15	5	0	3	8	12	17	0	.355	.453
Minor League Totals				.231	155	519	98	120	38	1	17	68	101	189	15	.377	.407

26 DAMIANO PALMEGIANI, 1B/3B

Born: Jan. 24, 2000. **B-T:** R-R. **HT:** 6-1. **WT:** 195.
Drafted: Southern Nevada JC, 2021 (14th round). **Signed by:** Joey Aversa.

TRACK RECORD: Palmegiani was born in Venezuela but grew up in British Columbia rooting for the Blue Jays. Toronto twice drafted Palmegiani, first in the 35th round in 2018 out of high school and again in 2021 out of Southern Nevada JC. He was assigned to Low-A Dunedin to start 2022 and hit .256/.351/.508 in the power-starved Florida State League. He was promoted to High-A Vancouver, where he hit .224/.335/.443 with 13 home runs over 62 games with his hometown Canadians.
SCOUTING REPORT: Palmegiani provides a robust combination of plate skills similar to fellow Blue Jays

prospect Spencer Horwitz. While his profile is slanted towards power, he's shown a unique ability to avoid strikeouts. He's an above-average contact hitter who rarely expands the zone and limits his swing and miss in-zone. While Palmegiani's raw power is just average, his ability to backspin the ball allows his power to play a half grade above his raw power. He can handle third base but as a limited defender overall and below-average runner, his most likely defensive home is first base.

THE FUTURE: A bat-first prospect with a good combination of contact, approach and power, Palmegiani may hit enough to carve out a role as platoon bat or offensive-driven, second-division regular at first base.

BA GRADE: 40/High		Hit: 55			Power: 55		Run: 40			Field: 40			Arm: 50	
Year	Age	Club (League)	Lvl	AVG	G	AB	R	H	2B	3B	HR	RBI	BB	SO	SB	OBP	SLG
2022	22	Dunedin (FSL)	LoA	.256	56	195	30	50	14	1	11	37	23	47	2	.351	.508
2022	22	Vancouver (NWL)	HiA	.224	62	228	44	51	11	0	13	46	31	60	3	.335	.443
Minor League Totals				.247	135	462	85	114	27	1	26	92	61	116	6	.352	.478

27 RAINER NUÑEZ, 1B

Born: Dec. 4, 2000. **B-T:** R-R. **HT:** 6-3. **WT:** 180.
Signed: Dominican Republic, 2017. **Signed by:** Alexis de la Cruz.

TRACK RECORD: Nuñez signed in 2017 out of the Dominican Republic for $350,000 and quickly moved off shortstop to third base as a pro. In 2019, he moved from third base to first base. He spent two seasons in Rookie ball before making his full-season debut with Low-A Dunedin late in 2021. He returned to Dunedin to begin 2022 and hit his way to High-A Vancouver in early August. He finished his season on a high note by hitting .321/.379/.491 with four home runs over 27 games.

SCOUTING REPORT: Nuñez is an offense-oriented prospect with a balance of average bat-to-ball skills and plus power. While his natural strength and ability to punish mistakes in the zone are noteworthy, it's often dragged down by his inability to differentiate balls from strikes. In fact, Nuñez ran one of the highest whiff rates among Blue Jays prospects at a full-season level, and he chased pitches outside of the zone more than 43% of the time in 2022. Nuñez's swing has several moving parts: he has a deep knee bend, a unique hand motion in his load where he extends the fingers on his bottom hand before swinging and a long powerful swing bath that sweeps through the zone. He hits for plus power, and advancements to his pitch recognition skills could go a long way toward tapping into his power ceiling. He is limited to first base only with below-average defensive ability and well-below-average speed.

THE FUTURE: Nuñez has a plus skill in his in-game power hitting ability but will need to refine his over-zealous approach to carry the heavy offensive demands of everyday first baseman.

BA GRADE: 40/High		Hit: 40			Power: 60		Run: 30			Field: 40			Throw: 50	
Year	Age	Club (League)	Lvl	AVG	G	AB	R	H	2B	3B	HR	RBI	BB	SO	SB	OBP	SLG
2022	21	Dunedin (FSL)	LoA	.299	93	361	50	108	19	1	15	63	14	82	0	.328	.482
2022	21	Vancouver (NWL)	HiA	.321	27	106	15	34	6	0	4	19	10	27	0	.379	.491
Minor League Totals				.268	265	990	150	265	54	2	30	167	75	197	2	.322	.417

28 YONDREI ROJAS, RHP

Born: Nov. 22, 2002. **B-T:** R-R. **HT:** 5-10. **WT:** 180. **Signed:** Venezuela, 2021.
Signed by: Miguel Leal.

TRACK RECORD: Rojas signed for just $10,000 in Feb. 2021 out of Venezuela. Over his two seasons in the Blue Jays system, Rojas has blossomed into one of the most intriguing pitchers in the lower minors. He made his professional debut in the summer of 2021 in the Dominican Summer League and struck out 27 batters over 21.1 innings and recorded seven saves in eight opportunities. He made his U.S. debut in 2022 in the Florida Complex League, where he made seven appearances with 31 strikeouts and just six walks across 29.2 innings. He was promoted to Low-A Dunedin in August and made four appearances there.

SCOUTING REPORT: An undersized righthander with a longer arm action and a low three-quarters slot, Rojas utilizes an easy operation with a whippy fast arm and four-pitch mix. His repertoire consists of a four-seam fastball that sits 93-95 mph and touches 96 mph at peak with heavy armside run, a low-80s slider with moderate sweep, a mid-80s changeup that is his best bat-missing pitch, and a low-80s curveball with more depth than his slider. He shows at least average command across his pitch mix, and his fastball command borders on plus.

THE FUTURE: Rojas is a projectable starting pitching prospect with the ability to land all four of his pitches for strikes with at least average power and movement.

| BA GRADE: 45/Extreme | | Fastball: 55 | | Curveball: 45 | | Slider: 45 | | Changeup: 50 | | Control: 55 | | |

Year	Age	Club (League)	Lvl	W	L	ERA	G	GS	IP	H	HR	BB	SO	BB/9	SO/9	WHIP	AVG
2022	19	Blue Jays (FCL)	R	1	3	4.60	7	6	29	20	4	6	31	1.8	9.5	0.89	.190
2022	19	Dunedin (FSL)	LoA	1	1	5.40	4	2	17	16	1	6	12	3.2	6.5	1.32	.258
Minor League Totals				2	5	4.28	27	8	67	61	5	21	70	2.8	9.4	1.22	.243

29 C.J. VAN EYK, RHP

Born: Sept. 15, 1998. **B-T:** R-R. **HT:** 6-1. **WT:** 205.
Drafted: Florida State, 2020 (2nd round). **Signed by:** Brandon Bishoff.
TRACK RECORD: Van Eyk was first drafted by the Mets in the 19th round of the 2017 draft. He honored his commitment to Florida State, where he was a standout for the Seminoles over three years and made the jump to the rotation full-time in 2019. He made four starts prior to the pandemic shutdown his junior season and allowed just three earned runs with 25 strikeouts over 20.2 innings. He was selected in the second round of the 2020 draft by the Blue Jays and signed for $1,797,500. He made his debut the following spring with High-A Vancouver and made 19 starts, where he compiled a 4-6 record, with a 5.83 ERA and 100 strikeouts to 39 walks over 80.1 innings. Following the 2021 season Van Eyk had Tommy John surgery.
SCOUTING REPORT: Van Eyk has never lacked stuff dating back to his days at Florida State—what has plagued Van Eyk is his consistency. From start to start, his fastball velocity and quality will waver and he synchronizes his timing with his arm often late at foot plant. On his best days Van Eyk showed a four-seam fastball at 93-95 mph that touched 97 with an efficient spin axis that translated to ride and late bore. His primary secondary is a low-80s curveball with plus depth that generates swings and misses when he has command of it. He'll mix in a mid-80s slider with tight, classic slider shape and a low-80s changeup he'll execute with arm speed. It's a deep arsenal of pitches, but what pitcher awaits on the other side of Tommy John is anyone's guess.
THE FUTURE: Van Eyk has back-of-the-rotation upside if he can iron out his command. One year removed from TJ, he is likely to return to the mound early in the 2023 season.

| BA GRADE: 45/Extreme | | Fastball: 50 | | Curveball: 55 | | Slider: 45 | | Changeup: 55 | | Control: 40 | | |

Year	Age	Club (League)	Lvl	W	L	ERA	G	GS	IP	H	HR	BB	SO	BB/9	SO/9	WHIP	AVG
2022	23	Did not play—Injured															

30 TRENT PALMER, RHP

Born: April 2, 1999. **B-T:** R-R. **HT:** 6-1. **WT:** 230.
Drafted: Jacksonville, 2020 (3rd round). **Signed by:** Matt O'Brien.
TRACK RECORD: Palmer stood out over the summer of 2019 in the Cape Cod League where he made seven appearances for Wareham and earned an all-star nod that summer. He made just four starts for Jacksonville during the 2020 spring before the season was canceled due to the pandemic. It was enough for the Blue Jays to select Palmer with the 77th overall pick in the third round. Palmer signed for an above-slot bonus of $847,500 and made his professional debut the following spring with Low-A Dunedin, where he made 16 starts and compiled a 4-2 record with a 3.00 ERA—with 83 strikeouts over 63 innings. He broke camp with High-A Vancouver in 2022 and made six starts before he was promoted to Double-A New Hampshire. While there, Palmer made seven starts before he sustained an elbow injury in early July. He had Tommy John surgery in August 2022 and is unlikely to pitch in 2023.
SCOUTING REPORT: Palmer is a large-bodied, low-slot righthander with an unusual operation and long arm action he uses to hide the ball well. His pitch mix consists of three pitches: a sinking fastball at 92-94 mph that touches 97, a low-80s slider that generates ride like a cutter with the horizontal movement of a sweeper, and a high-70s changeup with heavy tumble and fade. Prior to Palmer's injury he possessed one of the best sliders in the minor leagues, though he struggled to command it for spells in 2022.
THE FUTURE: Palmer is likely to return at some point in 2024, and with the clock ticking, he could end up fast-tracked to the bullpen when he is back on the mound.

| BA GRADE: 45/Extreme | | Fastball: 50 | | Slider: 60 | | Changeup: 55 | | Control: 40 | | |

Year	Age	Club (League)	Lvl	W	L	ERA	G	GS	IP	H	HR	BB	SO	BB/9	SO/9	WHIP	AVG
2022	23	Vancouver (NWL)	HiA	1	2	4.18	6	6	24	28	5	8	36	3.0	13.7	1.52	.277
2022	23	New Hampshire (EL)	AA	1	1	3.69	7	7	32	22	3	15	33	4.3	9.4	1.17	.190
Minor League Totals				6	5	3.42	29	29	118	83	8	65	152	4.9	11.6	1.25	.192

Washington Nationals

BY SAVANNAH McCANN

When Nationals manager Davey Martinez coined the phrase "bumpy roads lead to beautiful places," he was referring to starting the 2019 season 19-31 and ending it as World Series champions.

Well, after the 2022 season, Nationals fans might ask: Where do crash landings lead?

On its way to a 107-loss season, Washington made a franchise-altering trade by sending Juan Soto, who has two more seasons of club control, plus Josh Bell to the Padres for five young players, two of whom—shortstop CJ Abrams and lefthander MacKenzie Gore—had big league experience. The other three—outfielders Robert Hassell III and James Wood and righthander Jarlin Susana—were at the lower levels at the time.

While the Nationals' major league performance was historically bad—the club's minus-252 run differential was worst in MLB and 17th worst of the expansion era—the farm system got an immediate boost. The Nationals' system is clearly more talented now than it was a year ago.

However, fans and people around the baseball world want to know what is next.

The top of the Nationals' farm system has been completely overhauled, thanks to the Soto blockbuster and a run of quality first-round picks, including power-speed high school outfielder Elijiah Green in 2022, power-hitting prep shortstop Brady House in 2021 and power-armed college righthander Cade Cavalli in 2020.

In addition, the Nationals may be able to finally cash in on prospects who have grown within the system. Cavalli and second baseman Luis Garcia will start for the big league club in 2023 after gaining major league reps in 2022.

Lower down the minor league ladder, prospects like outfielder TJ White, lefthander Mitchell Parker and catcher Israel Pineda had breakout seasons that put their names on the map.

Outfielders Jeremy De La Rosa and Cristhian Vaquero and righthander Andry Lara all showed growth in 2022 and signal that international signing and developing is still a focus after Soto, Garcia and Victor Robles all played their way from Dominican amateurs to major league regulars.

With so much young talent in the system, the Nationals plan to capitalize. Across every level of Washington's minor league system, TrackMan technology will be installed, and the organization is hiring biomechanists who focus on data-driven player development and data analytics.

DeJon Watson, who was hired in November 2021 to serve as farm director, wants to shift the organization's focus to be more data and statistics-driven. He has full support from general manager

Shortstop CJ Abrams was a key piece of the Nationals' five-player return for Juan Soto.

PROJECTED 2026 LINEUP

Catcher	Keibert Ruiz	27
First Base	TJ White	22
Second Base	Luis Garcia	26
Third Base	Brady House	23
Shortstop	CJ Abrams	25
Left Field	Robert Hassell III	24
Center Field	Elijah Green	22
Right Field	James Wood	23
Designated Hitter	Joey Meneses	34
No. 1 Starter	Cade Cavalli	27
No. 2 Starter	MacKenzie Gore	27
No. 3 Starter	Josiah Gray	28
No. 4 Starter	Jarlin Susana	22
No. 5 Starter	Jackson Rutledge	27
Closer	Jose Ferrer	26

Mike Rizzo, who will oversee baseball operations through at least the 2023 season.

Still, there remains a huge question mark looming over the Nationals. It is rumored that the Lerner family, which 16 years ago purchased the franchise from Major League Baseball, is expected to sell the team before the 2023 season. The hangup remains who will own the television rights and if those can be sold along with the team.

The organization states it is running under normal circumstances. But it's hard to imagine that there is anything normal when the identity of the franchise's future owner or what that owner's philosophy will be is unknown until the team's sale is completed. ∎

DEPTH CHART

WASHINGTON NATIONALS

TOP 2023 MLB CONTRIBUTORS	RANK
Cade Cavalli, RHP	4
BREAKOUT PROSPECTS	
Mitchell Parker, LHP	14
Israel Pineda, C	19
Zach Brzykcy, RHP	21

SOURCE OF TOP 30 TALENT

Homegrown	23	Acquired	7
College	9	Trade	6
Junior college	2	Rule 5 draft	1
High school	4	Independent league	0
Nondrafted free agent	1	Free agent/waivers	0
International	7		

LF
Robert Hassell III (2)
Daylen Lile (27)
Jared McKenzie

CF
Elijiah Green (3)
Cristhian Vaquero (6)
Jeremy De La Rosa (8)

RF
James Wood (1)
Roismar Quintana (17)
Brenner Cox

3B
Brady House (5)
Jake Alu
Sammy Infante
Nathaniel Ochoa Leyva

SS
Armando Cruz (12)
Trey Lipscomb (24)

2B
Darren Baker
J.T. Arruda

1B
TJ White (10)
Will Frizzell (30)
Branden Boissiere

C
Israel Pineda (19)
Drew Millas (25)
Onix Vega

LHP

LHSP	LHRP
Jake Bennett (11)	Matt Cronin (18)
Mitchell Parker (14)	Jose Ferrer (20)
	Evan Lee (23)
	Tim Cate (28)

RHP

RHSP	RHRP
Cade Cavalli (4)	Thaddeus Ward (16)
Jarlin Susana (7)	Zach Brzykcy (21)
Jackson Rutledge (9)	Gerardo Carrillo (26)
Andry Lara (15)	Orlando Ribalta
Jake Irvin (22)	Chance Huff
Aldo Ramirez (29)	
Marquis Grissom	
Kyle Luckham	
Cole Quintanilla	

1 JAMES WOOD, OF

Born: Sept. 17, 2002. **B-T:** L-R. **HT:** 6-7. **WT:** 240.
Drafted: HS—Bradenton, Fla., 2021 (2nd round).
Signed by: John Martin (Padres).

TRACK RECORD: Wood moved away from his hometown in Maryland to attend Florida's IMG Academy and gain greater exposure on the baseball diamond. A standout in basketball as well as baseball, Wood used his first summer on the showcase circuit to his advantage and emerged as one of the most physically impressive players in the 2021 draft class. Despite Wood's elevated strikeout totals his senior spring, the Padres saw his plus-plus raw power and huge upside and drafted him 62nd overall in the second round and signed him for an above-slot $2.6 million to sway him from a Mississippi State commitment. The gamble paid off immediately as Wood emerged as one of the best prospects in the Rookie-level Arizona Complex League after signing. He continued to impress in his full-season debut with Low-A Lake Elsinore in 2022, hitting .337 with 30 extra-base hits in 50 games despite going on the injured list twice with right wrist soreness. The Nationals acquired Wood, along with shortstop CJ Abrams, outfielder Robert Hassell III, lefthander MacKenzie Gore and righthander Jarlin Susana, in the eight-player trade that sent Juan Soto to San Diego. Wood continued to impress in 21 games with Low-A Fredericksburg to close out the season.
SCOUTING REPORT: There is no questioning Wood's athletic ability. His father is Kenny Wood, a former college basketball standout at Richmond, and James was a gifted basketball player before shifting to baseball full-time. At 6-foot-7, 240 pounds, Wood's athleticism and plus-plus raw power flows easily. He hits enormous home runs to all fields and has the strength, leverage and bat speed to demolish any pitch. He catches up to mid-90s velocity with ease and has the balance and pitch recognition to identify and stay back on secondary stuff. There are still questions surrounding Wood's high strikeout numbers, but a widened stance and learning to be less aggressive in early counts has helped him improve his contact ability. Wood's aggressiveness is still a work in progress, but he is improving. Due to his height, he has a longer bat path than most other players. He makes consistent contact in all parts of the zone despite his long levers and should continue to develop as a contact hitter with his widened stance. Wood is a smooth runner with above-average speed in center field and has a chance to stick there, but

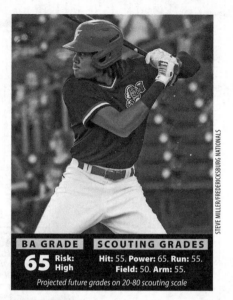

STEVE MILLER/FREDERICKSBURG NATIONALS

BA GRADE	SCOUTING GRADES
65 Risk: High	Hit: 55. **Power:** 65. **Run:** 55. Field: 50. Arm: 55.

Projected future grades on 20-80 scouting scale

BEST TOOLS

BATTING

Best Hitter for Average	Robert Hassell III
Best Power Hitter	Elijah Green
Best Strike-Zone Discipline	Robert Hassell III
Fastest Baserunner	Jacob Young
Best Athlete	Elijah Green

PITCHING

Best Fastball	Jarlin Susana
Best Curveball	Evan Lee
Best Slider	Cade Cavalli
Best Changeup	Jake Bennett
Best Control	Jake Irvin

FIELDING

Best Defensive Catcher	Israel Pineda
Best Defensive Infielder	Jordy Barley
Best Infield Arm	Armando Cruz
Best Defensive Outfielder	Elijah Green
Best Outfield Arm	Elijah Green

that will depend on how he fills out. Most likely he will eventually move to one of the corners as he adds more weight and strength, where he will be a slightly above-average defender with an above-average arm.
THE FUTURE: Wood has a chance to be a game-changing power hitter in the middle of the Nationals' order for years to come. If he can stick with the adjustments made to his stance and flatten out his bat path, he has the upside to hit 30-35 home runs. He is expected to open 2023 at High-A Wilmington and has a chance to reach Washington by 2024.

Year	Age	Club (League)	Lvl	AVG	G	AB	R	H	2B	3B	HR	RBI	BB	SO	SB	OBP	SLG
2022	19	Padres (ACL)	R	.125	5	16	1	2	0	0	0	0	3	7	1	.263	.125
2022	19	Lake Elsinore (CAL)	LoA	.337	50	193	55	65	19	1	10	45	37	42	15	.453	.601
2022	19	Fredericksburg (CAR)	LoA	.293	21	82	14	24	8	0	2	17	10	26	4	.366	.463
Minor League Totals				.326	102	377	88	123	32	1	15	84	63	107	30	.430	.536

2 ROBERT HASSELL III, OF

Born: August 15, 2001. **B-T:** L-L. **HT:** 6-2. **WT:** 195. **Drafted:** HS—Thompson's Station, Tenn., 2020 (1st round). **Signed by:** Tyler Stubblefield (Padres).

TRACK RECORD: The Padres signed Hassell for a below-slot $4.3 million after drafting him eighth overall in 2020. He was invited to big league spring training in 2021 before making his pro debut at Low-A. He reached High-A Fort Wayne that season and began 2022 at the level. He was named to the Futures Game before becoming a key prospect in the blockbuster trade that sent Juan Soto to the Padres and Hassell plus four other young talents to the Nationals. He spent two weeks with High-A Wilmington affiliate before moving to Double-A Harrisburg on Aug. 16 and then the Arizona Fall League in October. Hassell's AFL time was limited to two games when he broke the hamate bone in his right hand.

SCOUTING REPORT: A plus hitter with advanced ball-to-bat skills, Hassell immediately proved why he was dubbed one of the best pure hitters in his draft class. He has an ability to control the zone and sees lefthanders well, in a way that is rare for a young lefthanded hitter. While Hassell doesn't project for more than fringe-average power, his ability to hit for average and get on base makes him a candidate to hit at the top of a batting order. He is an on-base machine with above-average speed and an affinity for stealing bases. His above-average arm gives him the ability to play any outfield position, but has a chance to stay in center field, where he has spent the majority of his minor league career.

THE FUTURE: If Hassell can unlock his 15-20 homer upside, the Nationals are looking at a possible all-star. He heads back to Double-A in 2023 and should see time at Triple-A and possibly Washington.

BA GRADE
60 Risk: High

SCOUTING GRADES	Hitting: 60	Power: 45	Speed: 55	Fielding: 55	Arm: 55

Year	Age	Club (League)	Lvl	AVG	G	AB	R	H	2B	3B	HR	RBI	BB	SO	SB	OBP	SLG
2022	20	Wilmington (SAL)	HiA	.211	10	38	9	8	1	0	0	3	6	12	3	.311	.237
2022	20	Fort Wayne (MWL)	HiA	.299	75	304	49	91	19	1	10	55	38	66	20	.379	.467
2022	20	Harrisburg (EL)	AA	.222	27	108	9	24	5	0	1	12	13	35	1	.311	.296
Minor League Totals				.288	222	893	154	257	58	5	22	146	123	212	58	.375	.438

3 ELIJAH GREEN, OF

Born: December 4 , 2003. **B-T:** R-R. **HT:** 6-3. **WT:** 225. **Drafted:** HS—Bradenton, Fla., 2022 (1st round). **Signed by:** Alex Morales.

TRACK RECORD: Green is one of the most dynamic athletes scouts have seen in years. As an underclassman in 2020, he jumped on the map during the summer showcase circuit. After an impressive stint with USA Baseball's 18U National Team and senior season with IMG Academy, he left no question that he was one of the top prospects in the 2022 draft. The Nationals drafted him fifth overall and signed him for $6.5 million, right at slot value. Green mashed in the Rookie-level Florida Complex League, and hit .302/.404/.535 in 12 games. His .939 OPS was highest among those 18-and-under who batted at least 50 times. Green proved he can do just about everything at an elite level, with strength and power that rival some top MLB sluggers.

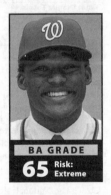

BA GRADE
65 Risk: Extreme

SCOUTING REPORT: The son of NFL tight end Eric Green, Elijah's physicality is rarely seen on the baseball field at his age. The righthanded hitter has already accessed his power at 18 years old. Green has shown the ability to drive the ball to all fields and out of just about any ballpark. He has shown some swing-and-miss—he struck out 40% of the time in the FCL—and has struggled against higher velocity. Not only has Green shown plus-plus power, but he also shows elite speed. He's able to steal bases and cover a ton of ground in center field. It's uncommon to see an MLB center fielder with Green's size, but he is an outlier athlete. He has a plus arm and has a chance to be an above-average defender.

THE FUTURE: Green has rare tools and athleticism and a lot of upside to reach. The biggest question mark surrounding him is his feel to hit and contact ability. His 45% swinging-strike rate was well above average in the swing-happy FCL. Green should make more than enough impact to live with those whiffs, but a full season in 2023 will make that assessment much more clear.

SCOUTING GRADES	Hitting: 50	Power: 70	Speed: 70	Fielding: 55	Arm: 60

Year	Age	Club (League)	Lvl	AVG	G	AB	R	H	2B	3B	HR	RBI	BB	SO	SB	OBP	SLG
2022	18	Nationals (FCL)	R	.302	12	43	9	13	4	0	2	9	6	21	1	.404	.535
Minor League Totals				.302	12	43	9	13	4	0	2	9	6	21	1	.404	.535

4 CADE CAVALLI, RHP

Born: August 14, 1998. **B-T:** R-R. **HT:** 6-4. **WT:** 226.
Drafted: Oklahoma, 2020 (1st round). **Signed by:** Jerad Head.

TRACK RECORD: After leading the minor leagues with 157 strikeouts in 2021 while reaching Triple-A in his pro debut, it seemed like Cavalli was almost MLB ready. The Nationals wanted their 2020 first-round pick to work on his changeup before he made his debut. Cavalli spent nearly the entire 2022 season with Triple-A Rochester before making his MLB debut on Aug. 26. Despite being knocked around by the Reds, he showed flashes of promise. His secondary pitches looked much better and his fastball was exactly as advertised. Cavalli made one start before being shut down with shoulder inflammation. He is expected to be ready to go for spring training.

SCOUTING REPORT: Cavalli has a four-pitch mix headlined by a four-seam fastball that averages 96 mph and tops out at 99-100 mph. Velocity has never been a question for the physical righthander, but his fastball has played down dating back to college because of a lack of deception or standout movement or spin. In 2022, Cavalli began relying more on his promising secondaries. His go-to breaking ball is a hard, mid-80s hammer curveball with 12-to-6 shape. He throws the pitch for strikes less frequently than a firm, upper-80s slider, but the curveball is the better swing-and-miss pitch. His curve is a 65 pitch on the scouting scale and his slider is above-average. Cavalli worked hard to improve a firm, upper-80s changeup, and his ability to consistently command that pitch could help keep hitters off his fastball. Cavalli can be a solid strike-thrower, but he'll need to find a solid balance of aggression and precision with how he attacks the strike zone.

THE FUTURE: The Nationals will rely on Cavalli to join a rebuilding rotation. If he can get outs in the zone, the organization can say that one piece of the rebuilding puzzle is in place.

BA GRADE
60 Risk: High

SCOUTING GRADES:	Fastball: 70	Curveball: 65	Slider: 55	Changeup: 55	Control: 50

Year	Age	Club (League)	Lvl	W	L	ERA	G	GS	IP	H	HR	BB	SO	BB/9	SO/9	WHIP	AVG
2022	23	Rochester (IL)	AAA	6	4	3.71	20	20	97	75	3	39	104	3.6	9.6	1.18	.215
2022	23	Washington (NL)	MLB	0	1	14.54	1	1	4	6	0	2	6	4.2	12.5	1.85	.333
Major League Totals				0	1	14.54	1	1	4	6	0	2	6	4.2	12.5	1.85	.333
Minor League Totals				13	13	3.51	44	44	220	171	8	99	279	4.0	11.4	1.23	.214

5 BRADY HOUSE, SS

Born: June 4, 2003. **B-T:** R-R. **HT:** 6-4. **WT:** 215.
Drafted: HS—Winder, Ga., 2021 (1st round). **Signed by:** Eric Robinson.

TRACK RECORD: When the Nationals drafted House 11th overall in 2021, they got what many believed was one of the top high school prospects in the 2021 draft class. House had loud offensive tools, led by explosive raw power that some scouts projected to double-plus grades. House made frequent quality contact in the Florida Complex League after signing for $5 million. His second season did not go as planned. He hit .303/.386/.420 for Low-A Fredericksburg through his first 30 games but made almost no impact after that—.228 with no homers—while dealing with a back injury and a bout with Covid. The Nationals shut House down in early June and expect him to be ready for minor league spring training in 2023.

SCOUTING REPORT: The loudest tool in House's set is his raw power. He looks and acts the part of a large slugger, standing in at 6-foot-4, 215 pounds. House has shown an ability to hit to all fields with authority since his debut, but he struggled hitting high velocity in 2022. He looked raw at the plate at times, which calls into question his hitting ability, but the Nationals aren't panicking. House has a strong ability to recognize pitches and has a good feel for the zone. House was a 50/50 bet to stick at shortstop even before the Nationals traded for CJ Abrams. House has sure hands, a good internal clock that compensates for ordinary range and impressive natural athleticism. His plus arm will fit at third base if he slides over.

THE FUTURE: House's back injury is a giant mitigating factor when it comes to explaining his low exit velocities in his first full season. A full, healthy season should give House the reps to address the hit tool concerns and regain his power.

BA GRADE
55 Risk: Extreme

SCOUTING GRADES	Hitting: 50	Power: 65	Speed: 50	Fielding: 50	Arm: 60

Year	Age	Club (League)	Lvl	AVG	G	AB	R	H	2B	3B	HR	RBI	BB	SO	SB	OBP	SLG
2022	19	Fredericksburg (CAR)	LoA	.278	45	176	24	49	8	0	3	31	12	59	1	.356	.375
Minor League Totals				.289	61	235	38	68	11	0	7	43	19	72	1	.366	.426

6 CRISTHIAN VAQUERO, OF

Born: September 13, 2004. **B-T:** B-R. **HT:** 6-3. **WT:** 180.
Signed: Cuba, 2022. **Signed by:** Johnny DiPuglia.

TRACK RECORD: The Nationals went all-in on Vaquero and signed him for $4.925 million in January 2021 when the international signing period opened. The switch-hitting Cuban outfielder received the highest bonus of any player in his signing class. The Nationals saw Vaquero as the best position player available that year, with talent well beyond his age. He was a young rising star in the Cuban junior leagues before starting his professional career in the Dominican Summer League in 2022.

SCOUTING REPORT: Vaquero has a high ceiling. He's an explosive player with a quick first step in center field. He then takes long, gliding strides to cover plenty of ground with well above-average speed. His plus arm and double-plus speed indicate that he could stick in center. Vaquero has plenty of time to develop and gain experience at the plate to quiet concerns about his pure hitting ability. He had a reputation as an aggressive hitter while in Cuba, but he showed good feel for the barrel in the DSL with a strikeout rate just south of 18% and a healthy walk rate of 15%. He needs to hit the ball in the air more frequently as he matures to reach his above-average power potential. He is a natural lefthanded hitter who taught himself to bat righthanded shortly before signing with Washington. He will continue to switch-hit in pro ball, but will need to prove that he can be just as aggressive and powerful on his right side.

THE FUTURE: At age 18 in 2023, Vaquero is still very young and is far from the big leagues, but he is ready to be tested in the Florida Complex League.

BA GRADE
55 Risk: Extreme

SCOUTING GRADES	Hitting: 50	Power: 55	Speed: 70	Fielding: 55	Arm: 60

Year	Age	Club (League)	Lvl	AVG	G	AB	R	H	2B	3B	HR	RBI	BB	SO	SB	OBP	SLG
2022	17	Nationals (DSL)	R	.256	55	176	33	45	4	4	1	22	33	38	17	.379	.341
Minor League Totals				.256	55	176	33	45	4	4	1	22	33	38	17	.379	.341

7 JARLIN SUSANA, RHP

Born: March 23, 2004. **B-T:** R-R. **HT:** 6-6. **WT:** 235.
Signed: Dominican Republic, 2022. **Signed by:** Trevor Schumm/Chris Kemp (Padres).

TRACK RECORD: Susana used the Covid shutdown in 2020 to define himself as a pitcher. When international scouting resumed, he emerged with a fastball that touched 96 mph and he was regarded as one of the top pitching prospects in the 2021 international class. With most teams having committed most of their bonus pool money for that signing period already, Susana opted to wait another year to sign with the Padres on Jan. 15, 2022. San Diego sent him directly to the Arizona Complex League in 2022 as an 18-year-old. In just eight appearances, he showed enough promise to become a key piece in the blockbuster that sent Juan Soto to San Diego for Susana plus four other young talents to the Nationals. Washington promoted Susana to Low-A Fredericksburg on Aug. 24.

BA GRADE
55 Risk: Extreme

SCOUTING REPORT: The 6-foot-6, 235-pound Susana added muscle that has immediately manifested into power behind his fastball. He sits 97-98 and has reached 103 mph more than once. He throws an average rate of strikes but doesn't get whiffs commensurate with his velocity. Susana's best pitch is a high-80s power slider that could be plus. It's his top swing-and-miss pitch, more for velocity than wicked movement. His slider and curveball can blend together at times, but the latter is starting to improve. His arsenal rounds out with an 86-89 mph changeup that has sink and fade. While power clearly isn't an issue for the young righthander, command of his extra-large frame and power stuff can be.

THE FUTURE: While Susana is still years away from reaching Washington, he is trending in that direction. With multiple potential plus pitches and a power arsenal, the key will be controlled repetition.

SCOUTING GRADES:	Fastball: 70	Curveball: 45	Slider: 60	Changeup: 45	Control: 45

Year	Age	Club (League)	Lvl	W	L	ERA	G	GS	IP	H	HR	BB	SO	BB/9	SO/9	WHIP	AVG
2022	18	Padres (ACL)	R	0	0	2.45	8	7	29	15	1	11	44	3.4	13.5	0.89	.155
2022	18	Nationals (FCL)	R	0	0	1.69	2	2	5	4	0	4	9	6.8	15.2	1.50	.200
2022	18	Fredericksburg (CAR)	LoA	0	0	2.61	3	3	10	9	1	5	13	4.4	11.3	1.35	.231
Minor League Totals				0	0	2.40	13	12	45	28	2	20	66	4.0	13.2	1.07	.179

8 JEREMY DE LA ROSA, OF

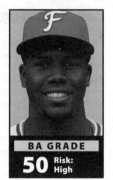

Born: January 16, 2002. **B-T:** L-L. **HT:** 5-11. **WT:** 160.
Signed: Dominican Republic, 2018. **Signed by:** Modesto Ulloa.

TRACK RECORD: De La Rosa was not a highly touted prospect when the Nationals signed him out of the Dominican Republic in 2018. However, the Nationals had a belief in De La Rosa and he quickly showed it was warranted. De La Rosa jumped straight to Rookie-level Gulf Coast League in 2019 to make his pro debut as a 17-year-old. He then joined the Nationals' 60-player pool at the alternate training site in 2020 when the pandemic shut down the sport. De La Rosa struggled in his first full season at Low-A Fredericksburg in 2021, owing to a 34% strikeout rate. One of the Nationals' favorite qualities in De La Rosa is his resilience. The young hitter continued to work and make adjustments, all without ever showing he was disappointed in his slow start.

BA GRADE
50 Risk: High

SCOUTING REPORT: De La Rosa's hard work paid off in a big way in a return to Fredericksburg in 2022. He hit .315/.394/.505 with 10 home runs and 26 stolen bases in 69 games before going up to High-A Wilmington on July 12. A hand injury sapped his power and ended his season on Aug. 27. He had hamate surgery shortly after. De La Rosa has proven to be a capable hitter and well-rounded prospect. The lefthanded hitter is able to get in a good hitting position and has flashed plus raw power. Scouts were impressed with his improved approach in 2022. He cut his strikeout rate to around 26% and showed better pitch selection, with a willingness to use the entire field. As long as he doesn't sell out for power, De La Rosa has a chance to be a tough out with on-base skills and a chance for solid-average power production. He's a plus runner and an above-average center fielder.

THE FUTURE: The Nationals were enthused by De La Rosa's turnaround season. He still has plenty to prove at High-A, but 2022 was a step in the right direction.

SCOUTING GRADES	Hitting: 50		Power: 55		Speed: 60			Fielding: 55			Arm: 45	
Year	**Age**	**Club (League)**	**Lvl**	**AVG**	**G**	**AB**	**R**	**H**	**2B**	**3B**	**HR**	**RBI**	**BB**	**SO**	**SB**	**OBP**	**SLG**
2022	20	Fredericksburg (CAR)	LoA	.315	69	279	56	88	19	2	10	57	36	78	26	.394	.505
2022	20	Wilmington (SAL)	HiA	.195	32	118	10	23	4	1	1	10	12	37	13	.273	.271
Minor League Totals				.246	214	805	114	198	36	9	18	99	90	266	49	.325	.380

9 JACKSON RUTLEDGE, RHP

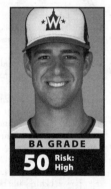

Born: April 1, 1999. **B-T:** R-R. **HT:** 6-8. **WT:** 250.
Drafted: San Jacinto (Texas) JC, 2019 (1st round). **Signed by:** Brandon Larson.

TRACK RECORD: Injuries and battling back are common themes in Rutledge's story. He started his career at Arkansas and suffered a torn hip labrum. He transferred to San Jacinto (Texas) JC in 2019, and the Nationals drafted him 17th overall that spring. Rutledge reached Low-A in his pro debut but suffered a setback at the alternate training site in 2020, with shoulder and blister issues limiting him. He pitched to a 7.68 ERA in 36.1 innings across three lower levels in 2021, adding concern to his ability to be consistent. He responded with a dominant 2022 season at Low-A Fredericksburg, and struck out 99 in 97.1 innings. He ended the season on a high note by delivering eight shutout innings in Game 1 of the Carolina League semifinals.

BA GRADE
50 Risk: High

SCOUTING REPORT: At 6-foot-8, Rutledge can be an intimidating figure on the mound, and he has a fastball to match. He throws both four-seam and two-seam fastballs, with both versions of his heater sit 94-95 mph and touch 97-98. His four-seam has modest carry, and he looks more like a sinker/slider pitcher after inducing ground balls about half the time in 2022. Rutledge's best secondary is an 82-87 mph slider that generated whiffs at a 47% clip and has earned plus grades. He also throws a firm changeup in the upper 80s. Previously a below-average strike-thrower, Rutledge walked just 6.9% of batters with Low-A Fredericksburg in 2022, though scouts wonder about timing issues that stem from a super compact arm action and his ability to sync up his release and foot strike.

THE FUTURE: The Nationals were impressed with the improvements that Rutledge showed in 2022 and believe he still has a chance to be a back-of-the-rotation starter. Still, he has not pitched above High-A as he enters his age-24 season. The 2023 season will be more of a test.

SCOUTING GRADES:	Fastball: 60		Curveball: 50		Slider: 60		Changeup: 50		Control: 50		
Year	**Age**	**Club (League)**	**Lvl**	**W**	**L**	**ERA**	**G**	**GS**	**IP**	**H**	**HR**	**BB**	**SO**	**BB/9**	**SO/9**	**WHIP**	**AVG**
2022	23	Fredericksburg (CAR)	LoA	8	6	4.90	20	20	97	106	7	29	99	2.7	9.2	1.39	.276
Minor League Totals				11	12	5.11	43	43	171	168	11	64	179	3.4	9.4	1.36	.255

10 TJ WHITE, OF

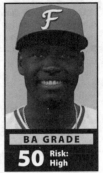

Born: July 23, 2003. **B-T:** B-R. **HT:** 6-2. **WT:** 210.
Drafted: HS—Roebuck, SC, 2021 (5th round). **Signed by:** Eric Robinson.

TRACK RECORD: White did not turn 18 until two weeks after the 2021 draft, making him one of the youngest players in the class. The Nationals liked his power upside and signed him for an over-slot $400,000 in the fifth round. The powerful switch-hitter impressed in the Florida Complex League, hitting four homers and slugging .547 in 15 games. White adapted well to Low-A Fredericksburg in 2022, and put up a .784 OPS that ranked fifth-best among qualified Carolina League teenagers.

BA GRADE
50 Risk: High

SCOUTING REPORT: White did a nice job making adjustments in 2022. His goal was to improve his defensive work in the outfield and also put up better in-game power numbers. Scouts have praised White's swing from both sides of the plate. Most of his power in 2022 came as a lefthanded hitter, with 10 of his 11 home runs coming from that side. White has a solid batting eye, as evidenced by a 11.5% walk rate and respectable chase rate, and has the ability to recognize and punish mistakes from opposing pitchers. White is a good runner, but he has been described as "crude" in the outfield and is regarded as a bat-first player who will need to hit enough for teams to live with his defense. After spending time at both outfield corners in 2021, White played exclusively left field in 2022. He could improve his defense with more reps and better route-running. If he doesn't, he faces a potential move to first base. White has two pro seasons under his belt and is still a teenager, so he has plenty of time for refinement.
THE FUTURE: The organization believes White will improve as he gains experience. He has improved his defense and has gotten better at controlling the strike zone.

SCOUTING GRADES	Hitting: 50	Power: 60	Speed: 40	Fielding: 45	Arm: 45

Year	Age	Club (League)	Lvl	AVG	G	AB	R	H	2B	3B	HR	RBI	BB	SO	SB	OBP	SLG
2022	18	Fredericksburg (CAR)	LoA	.258	92	329	55	85	20	2	11	52	44	104	8	.353	.432
Minor League Totals				.262	107	382	66	100	22	2	15	64	49	118	9	.353	.448

11 JAKE BENNETT, LHP

Born: December 2, 2000. **B-T:** L-L. **HT:** 6-6. **WT:** 234.
Drafted: Oklahoma, 2022 (2nd round). **Signed by:** Cody Staab.

TRACK RECORD: The Nationals originally drafted Bennett as a 39th-round pick in 2019 out of high school. He turned down the offer and headed to Oklahoma, where he pitched with current Nationals top pitching prospect and former high school teammate, Cade Cavalli. Bennett is a lefthander with strong control who attacked the zone in college and was instrumental in the Sooners' 2022 College World Series finals appearance. At 6-foot-6, the southpaw has mastered a smooth and athletic approach on the mound. The Nationals drafted him in the second round in 2022 and signed him for slot value of just over $1.7 million.

SCOUTING REPORT: Bennett pitches with a three-pitch mix that is led by a fastball that sits in the 91-94 mph range. The pitch has played up with good deception and extension out in front. His changeup is his go-to secondary, and for good reason. It's a true plus pitch that sits between 82-85 mph and is especially effective against righthanded hitters. He rounds out his arsenal with his slider, which lacks the consistency of the other two pitches. Bennett is much more effective against righthanded hitters than same-side ones, thanks to his plus changeup. He relies on control to get outs, which allows him to limit walks. He might not be a hard thrower, but he will collect outs and continue to be a workhorse.
THE FUTURE: The southpaw has a chance to become a No. 4 or 5 starter for the Nationals. He will make his pro debut in 2023.

BA GRADE: 50/High	Fastball: 55	Slider: 50	Changeup: 60	Control: 55

Year	Age	Club (League)	Lvl	W	L	ERA	G	GS	IP	H	HR	BB	SO	BB/9	SO/9	WHIP	AVG
2022	21	Did not play															

12 ARMANDO CRUZ, SS

Born: January 16, 2004. **B-T:** R-R. **HT:** 5-10. **WT:** 160.
Signed: Dominican Republic, 2021. **Signed By:** Modesto Ulloa/Ricky Vasquez.

TRACK RECORD: Cruz received the highest bonus by a 16-year-old in the 2020-21 international class when he signed with the Nationals for $3.9 million. In the Dominican Summer League in 2021, he hit

.232 and hoped to show improvement in his first full season. In 2022, he spent the majority of the season in the Florida Complex League. His bat continues to be a work in progress, but his defensive work is starting to shine. Cruz was promoted to Low-A Fredericksburg in September, where he played three games.

SCOUTING REPORT: Scouts raved about Cruz's defensive skills at shortstop before he was signed and dubbed him the best defender in the class. His above-average speed and plus arm allow him to make tough plays look easy. If his defense continues to develop, he could be a Gold Glove-caliber defender. However, he needs to prove that he can hit. While Cruz hasn't shown much power, the organization is pleased with the improvements he made in 2022. The 18-year-old will need to add more strength to improve the quality of his contact, and while he struck out just 17% of the time, he could stand to improve his swing decisions.

THE FUTURE: Cruz's glove will get him far. His ceiling is one of the elite defensive shortstops in baseball. His future on the Nationals' roster, however, will be determined if he can improve at the plate and take advantage of his natural bat-to-ball skills.

| BA GRADE: 50/ Extreme | Hit: 40 | | Power: 30 | Speed: 55 | | Fielding: 65 | | Arm: 60 |

Year	Age	Club (League)	Lvl	AVG	G	AB	R	H	2B	3B	HR	RBI	BB	SO	SB	OBP	SLG
2022	18	Nationals (FCL)	R	.275	52	207	41	57	8	2	2	20	11	39	6	.320	.362
2022	18	Fredericksburg (CAR)	LoA	.267	3	15	3	4	1	0	0	2	2	2	0	.353	.333
Minor League Totals				.256	103	399	66	102	17	3	3	39	29	68	17	.309	.336

13 COLE HENRY, RHP

Born: July 15, 1999. **B-T:** R-R. **HT:** 6-4. **WT:** 214.
Drafted: Louisiana State, 2020 (2nd round). **Signed by:** Brandon Larson.

TRACK RECORD: The Nationals drafted Henry in the second round in 2020 as a sophomore out of Louisiana State. After getting off to a hot start with High-A Wilmington in 2021, he missed the better part of three months with elbow soreness. He returned and joined the team's Arizona Fall League contingent. Henry opened 2022 with seven starts for Double-A Harrisburg before he was quickly promoted to Triple-A Rochester in June. He appeared to be on a fast track to Washington until he had thoracic outlet syndrome surgery in late August.

SCOUTING REPORT: Prior to having TOS surgery, Henry threw both a two-seam and four-seam fastball, with the latter touching the high 90s. His best secondary pitch is his changeup followed closely by his improving curveball, a short breaker that has been an inconsistent offering for him. Both secondaries had flashed plus potential. In addition to his considerable stuff, Henry goes right after hitters, and pitches with moxie and little fear. His reliever risk is enhanced following TOS surgery.

THE FUTURE: Henry joins Stephen Strasburg and Will Harris as Nationals pitchers who had TOS surgery. The future was bright for Henry, but now it's more uncertain. The average recovery time from TOS surgery is six to eight months, and the organization hopes Henry will be back in time for spring training.

| BA GRADE: 50/ Extreme | Fastball: 55 | | Curveball: 50 | Changeup: 55 | | Control: 50 | | |

Year	Age	Club (League)	Lvl	W	L	ERA	G	GS	IP	H	HR	BB	SO	BB/9	SO/9	WHIP	AVG
2022	22	Harrisburg (EL)	AA	0	0	0.76	7	7	24	5	1	9	28	3.4	10.6	0.59	.067
2022	22	Rochester (IL)	AAA	1	0	4.50	2	2	8	9	1	2	6	2.2	6.8	1.38	.281
Minor League Totals				4	5	2.06	20	19	79	42	5	23	104	2.6	11.9	0.83	.155

14 MITCHELL PARKER, LHP

Born: September 27, 1999. **B-T:** L-L. **HT:** 6-4. **WT:** 195.
Drafted: San Jacinto (Texas) JC, 2020 (5th round). **Signed by:** Jimmy Gonzales.

TRACK RECORD: Parker was selected in the 2018 and 2019 drafts but did not sign before the Nationals signed him as a fifth-round pick in 2020. Some of his stats did not reflect how truly productive his 2021 debut season was with Low-A Fredericksburg and High-A Wilmington. He took off in 2022 with Wilmington, where he posted a 2.88 ERA and near 27% strikeout rate, though he also walked 15% clip.

SCOUTING REPORT: Scouts describe Parker as a powerful, high-slot lefthander whose fastball plays up with good carry at the top of the zone. While the fastball sits in the 90-94 mph range, it has elite carry and more than 21 inches of induced vertical break that helped it wrack up more whiffs than any of his other pitches. Mitchell throws a low-80s curveball as his most-used secondary, which is also his biggest emphasis during the offseason. He throws a mid-80s changeup and a low-80s splitter, the former with plus sinking life and the latter with some cutting life. Mitchell has a solid arsenal of pitches but needs to find a way to throw them for more strikes.

THE FUTURE: Parker could have performed at the Double-A level in 2022 if given the chance, so expect to see him start there in 2023. If he continues to improve, he has a chance to stick as a starter despite lacking a legitimate plus pitch. He could move to a bullpen role if he's unable to improve his control and get ahead in counts more frequently.

| BA GRADE: 45/High | | Fastball: 55 | | Curveball: 50 | | Splitter: 55 | | Changeup: 45 | | Control: 40 | | | |

Year	Age	Club (League)	Lvl	W	L	ERA	G	GS	IP	H	HR	BB	SO	BB/9	SO/9	WHIP	AVG
2022	22	Wilmington (SAL)	HiA	6	4	2.88	24	24	100	76	3	67	117	6.0	10.5	1.43	.208
Minor League Totals				10	16	3.88	47	45	202	179	15	105	261	4.7	11.6	1.41	.233

15 ANDRY LARA, RHP

Born: January 6, 2003. **B-T:** R-R. **HT:** 6-5. **WT:** 235.
Signed: Venezuela, 2019. **Signed by:** Ronald Morillo.
TRACK RECORD: Lara was the top player in the Nationals' 2019 international class and signed for a $1.25 million bonus. After spending 2020 at the organization's facility in West Palm Beach, Fla., and struggling at instructional league, his 2021 debut was much more promising. In 2022, he was the youngest pitcher on Low-A Fredericksburg's roster. He struggled in the Carolina League, especially in July where he posted a 7.31 ERA.
SCOUTING REPORT: Lara has a smooth delivery and an all-around athletic operation on the mound, but he needs to continue adding strength to his frame to sustain his mid-90s velocity throughout outings. His fastball sits around 94 mph and has touched 98, while both his secondaries need more refinement and consistency. Lara's slider was his go-to and best secondary in 2022. It's a low-80s slider that has slurve-like shape at times. An upper-80s changeup is his third offering, and he needs to develop more feel for it to become an average third pitch to fully round out his arsenal. It's a key focus of his offseason work. Lara is praised for his maturity and work ethic for his age, and he'll be in just his age-20 season during 2023.
THE FUTURE: Lara's confidence and ability to make adjustments impressed the organization, despite some ugly outings. The Nationals consider the 2022 season a "learning year" and hope he can find a better routine in 2023. If he can develop an average third pitch, he could move quickly.

| BA GRADE: 45/High | | Fastball: 55 | | Slider: 45 | | Changeup: 45 | | Control: 50 | | | |

Year	Age	Club (League)	Lvl	W	L	ERA	G	GS	IP	H	HR	BB	SO	BB/9	SO/9	WHIP	AVG
2022	19	Fredericksburg (CAR)	LoA	3	8	5.51	23	23	101	103	10	44	105	3.9	9.3	1.45	.258
Minor League Totals				6	11	5.23	34	32	150	144	17	65	157	3.9	9.4	1.40	.248

16 THAD WARD, RHP

Born: January 16, 1997. **B-T:** R-R. **HT:** 6-3. **WT:** 192.
Drafted: Central Florida, 2018 (5th round). **Signed by:** Stephen Hargett (Red Sox).
TRACK RECORD: Though Ward pitched mostly as a sinker/slider long reliever in college, the Red Sox believed he had the potential to add to those quality pitches to emerge as a starter. Ward added a four-seamer, cutter and curveball while dominating in two levels of Class A in 2019. But he blew out in early 2021 in Double-A Portland. Tommy John surgery sidelined him into the middle of 2022. Ward made an impressive return, forging a 2.28 ERA across four levels in 13 starts, concluding the year at Portland. The Nationals selected Ward with the first pick in the major league Rule 5 draft.
SCOUTING REPORT: Ward's strength remains his sinker—which was mostly 91-92 mph and topped out at 94 in 2022—and sweeper slider. His cutter plays from the same tunnel, which helped him leave righthanded hitters guessing. They hit .162/.227/.235. Ward's curveball is fringy and his four-seamer was ineffective, and he was hit hard by lefthanded hitters (.290/.389/.419 with 19% strikeouts and nearly 13% walks). Those splits combine with a below-average changeup to make him a safer bet as a reliever than as a starter, though improved four-seam command with a healthy offseason could give him back-of-the-rotation potential.
THE FUTURE: The Nationals believe Ward has another gear to reach as he returns from surgery. He is believed to be a starter long term but must build up his durability. Ward probably will be eased into the rotation by working in relief first. He must remain on Washington's active roster or else be offered back to the Red Sox if he clears waivers first.

| BA GRADE: 45/Medium | | Fastball: 55 | | Curveball: 40 | | Slider: 55 | | Changeup: 40 | | Cutter: 45 | | Control: 45 | | |

Year	Age	Club (League)	Lvl	W	L	ERA	G	GS	IP	H	HR	BB	SO	BB/9	SO/9	WHIP	AVG
2022	25	Red Sox (FCL)	R	0	0	0.00	2	2	5	1	0	0	9	0.0	16.2	0.20	.059
2022	25	Salem (CAR)	LoA	0	0	0.00	2	2	6	2	0	1	10	1.5	15.0	0.50	.100
2022	25	Greenville (SAL)	HiA	0	1	5.14	2	2	7	9	0	4	6	5.1	7.7	1.86	.300
2022	25	Portland (EL)	AA	0	1	2.43	7	7	33	28	3	14	41	3.8	11.1	1.26	.230
Minor League Totals				8	10	2.53	51	51	217	173	11	93	261	3.9	10.8	1.23	.218

17 ROISMAR QUINTANA, OF

Born: February 6, 2003. **B-T:** R-R. **HT:** 6-1. **WT:** 190.
Signed: Venezuela, 2019. **Signed by:** Ronald Morillo.

TRACK RECORD: Along with righthander Andry Lara, Quintana was one of the Nationals' key targets in the 2019 international class. He signed for $820,000. He participated in instructional league after the canceled 2020 season and impressed, but he didn't play much in 2021 because of two hamstring tears. Quintana played just seven games in 2021. Finally healthy, he was a Florida Complex League all-star in 2022.

SCOUTING REPORT: Quintana will sink or swim based on how much he hits. He has plus raw power and got to some of it in games in 2022, hitting five homers in 50 games. He makes good in-zone contact but needs to cut down his chase rate to become even an average hitter. As fills out, Quintana's average speed will likely slow even more. However, it is worth watching his development after the hamstring injuries. At the plate, Quintana will need to be more aggressive and tap into the plus power and strength he has added. He has only played right field as a pro and will likely stick there as a capable defender.

THE FUTURE: Quintana projects as one of the most exciting young hitters in the system, but he needs a lot more reps. He signed in 2019 but has just 57 games under his belt and would benefit from a full season at Low-A. He has shown the Nationals glimpses of ability. They hope to see a breakout in 2023.

BA GRADE: 50/Extreme	Hit: 45	Power: 55	Speed: 45	Fielding: 50	Arm: 50

Year	Age	Club (League)	Lvl	AVG	G	AB	R	H	2B	3B	HR	RBI	BB	SO	SB	OBP	SLG
2022	19	Nationals (FCL)	R	.289	50	180	41	52	10	1	5	28	9	46	3	.342	.439
Minor League Totals				.290	57	193	44	56	12	1	6	33	15	51	3	.361	.456

18 MATT CRONIN, LHP

Born: September 20, 1997. **B-T:** L-L. **HT:** 6-2. **WT:** 195.
Drafted: Arkansas, 2019 (4th round). **Signed by:** Jerad Head.

TRACK RECORD: Cronin was a dominant reliever turned closer over three seasons at Arkansas. The Nationals drafted the lefty in the fourth round in 2019, and he made his debut at Low-A the same year. In 2021, he spent time in the Florida Complex League and High-A Wilmington before earning a jump to Double-A Harrisburg. He pitched lights out to start the 2022 season and allowed just five hits in 16.1 innings before earning a promotion to Triple-A in May. He was added to the 40-man roster in November.

SCOUTING REPORT: Cronin's fastball sits in the 90-91 mph range and touches 93-94. Excellent carry, including more than 22 inches of induced vertical break, helps it play up from that velocity. Cronin pitched heavily off his fastball but also used a trio of secondaries: a 12-to-6 curveball in the upper 70s, a low-80s split-changeup and a mid-80s slider. His curveball previously showed impressive potential, but he struggled to land the pitch for strikes in 2022 and metrics labeled it as Cronin's worst offering. His slider and split-change could wind up being more useful secondaries for him.

THE FUTURE: The Nationals believe that Cronin will be a lefthanded fixture in the bullpen moving forward.

BA GRADE: 45/High	Fastball: 55	Curveball: 40	Slider: 50	Changeup: 45	Control: 45

Year	Age	Club (League)	Lvl	W	L	ERA	G	GS	IP	H	HR	BB	SO	BB/9	SO/9	WHIP	AVG
2022	24	Harrisburg (EL)	AA	1	0	0.00	14	0	16	5	0	7	22	3.9	12.1	0.73	.096
2022	24	Rochester (IL)	AAA	3	1	3.53	34	0	36	30	3	15	34	3.8	8.6	1.26	.229
Minor League Totals				8	2	2.25	88	0	104	66	6	49	147	4.2	12.7	1.11	.184

19 ISRAEL PINEDA, C

Born: April 3, 2000. **B-T:** R-R. **HT:** 5-11. **WT:** 190.
Signed: Venezuela, 2016. **Signed By:** German Robles.

TRACK RECORD: Pineda impressed when he signed out of Venezuela in 2016 for $450,000. However, he took a step back in 2019 and continued to struggle at High-A in 2021. He worked in the offseason to add strength and speed and it paid off in 2022, when he became one of the most improved prospects in the system. After starting the season repeating at High-A Wilmington, Pineda was promoted to Double-A Harrisburg after just 67 games. He thrived in Harrisburg and slashed .280/.340/.538 and showed improved defensive skills. He finished the season with six games for Triple-A Rochester and then made his big league debut.

SCOUTING REPORT: Pineda's defense took a step forward in 2022, especially in the quickness in his hands. His framing still needs some work, but he has the mechanics to be one of the best catchers in the system. His pop times average sub-2.0 seconds—the major league average—on throws to second base and his arm is a true plus tool. He showcased his ability to control the running game. Across three minor league levels, Pineda threw out 38% of basestealers. He has a chance to be a powerful hitter—in the minors in 2022 he hit 16 home runs and 20 doubles while slugging .458— but is aggressive at the plate. If he can slow things down and try to take advantage of mistakes, he could grow into an above-average offensive player.

THE FUTURE: The Nationals were encouraged by Pineda's development in 2022, which culminated in his first callup to Washington in his seventh pro season. If he can continue to grow defensively, he could become Washington's backup catcher of the future.

BA GRADE: 45/High		Hit: 30		Power: 50		Speed: 40			Fielding: 55		Arm: 60	

Year	Age	Club (League)	Lvl	AVG	G	AB	R	H	2B	3B	HR	RBI	BB	SO	SB	OBP	SLG
2022	22	Wilmington (SAL)	HiA	.264	67	246	31	65	16	2	8	45	22	70	2	.325	.443
2022	22	Harrisburg (EL)	AA	.280	26	93	15	26	3	0	7	21	9	18	1	.340	.538
2022	22	Rochester (IL)	AAA	.095	6	21	3	2	1	0	1	5	5	7	0	.269	.286
2022	22	Washington (NL)	MLB	.077	4	13	1	1	0	0	0	0	1	7	0	.143	.077
Major League Totals				.077	4	13	1	1	0	0	0	0	1	7	0	.143	.077
Minor League Totals				.237	340	1251	167	297	55	4	41	190	100	328	4	.298	.386

20 JOSE FERRER, LHP

Born: March 3, 2000. **B-T:** L-L. **HT:** 6-1. **WT:** 215.
Signed: Dominican Republic, 2017. **Signed by:** Moises De La Mota.

TRACK RECORD: The Nationals signed Ferrer out of the Dominican Republic in 2017 for $100,000. The lefty didn't break into full-season ball until 2022—but it was an impressive debut and something of a breakout season. He progressed from Low-A Fredericksburg to Double-A Harrisburg and across three levels posted a 2.48 ERA over 65.1 innings with a 30.5% strikeout rate and just a 4.3% walk rate. He earned an appearance in the Futures Game.

SCOUTING REPORT: Ferrer was known for his curveball when he signed, but in 2022 he developed his fastball and shaped his breaking ball into a slider. The fastball now sits at around 95 mph and has touched 99, with modest carry and spin. His slider sits in the upper 80s and flashes potential, but he needs to throw it for strikes more often. His third pitch is an upper-80s changeup that he lands at a high rate and used to generate whiffs at nearly a 50% clip. Command is still a work in progress for Ferrer, though his overall walk rates have been excellent throughout his stateside career.

THE FUTURE: Ferrer was added to the Nationals' 40-man roster in November to protect him from the Rule 5 draft, and he's seen as a lefty option in the bullpen. He will likely start the 2023 season at Double-A, but with another big year could see an MLB debut quickly.

BA GRADE: 45/ High		Fastball: 65		Slider: 50		Changeup: 50		Control: 60				

Year	Age	Club (League)	Lvl	W	L	ERA	G	GS	IP	H	HR	BB	SO	BB/9	SO/9	WHIP	AVG
2022	22	Fredericksburg (CAR)	LoA	1	0	1.42	13	0	19	12	1	1	24	0.5	11.4	0.68	.171
2022	22	Wilmington (SAL)	HiA	2	1	2.56	28	0	39	32	6	9	43	2.1	10.0	1.06	.225
2022	22	Harrisburg (EL)	AA	0	1	4.70	7	0	8	10	1	1	11	1.2	12.9	1.43	.323
Minor League Totals				6	10	2.83	88	2	153	126	9	44	202	2.6	11.9	1.11	.218

21 ZACH BRZYKCY, RHP

Born: July 12, 1999. **B-T:** R-R. **HT:** 6-2. **WT:** 230.
Signed: Virginia Tech, 2020 (NDFA). **Signed by:** Bobby Myrick.

TRACK RECORD: Brzykcy was named the Cape Cod League reliever of the year in 2019 as a rising junior. It was a small sample compared to his body of work at Virginia Tech, and he went undrafted during the pandemic-shortened five-round draft in 2020. Brzykey signed with the Nationals for $20,000 as a nondrafted free agent and has been dominant out of the bullpen. The reliever started the 2022 season at High-A but after 17 games was promoted to Double-A. He showed electric stuff and improved command—enough to jump three levels and end the year with Triple-A Rochester for two games.

SCOUTING REPORT: Brzykcy attacks the zone and uses his power fastball to get hitters out. His fastball sits in the 95-98 mph range. It has explosive life and excellent carry, by way of more than 22 inches of induced vertical break. He's not afraid to use his secondary pitches either. His curveball is just a tick above-average in the mid 80s, but it has a nice 11-to-5 shape and generated whiffs at a 33% rate. His repertoire is rounded out with a split-changeup that has some sink and sits in the high 80s.

THE FUTURE: Brzykcy has the makeup of a big league reliever, potentially someone who can pitch late innings. He isn't afraid to go after hitters and his command has significantly improved. He will likely start the season at Triple-A, but his MLB debut is imminent.

BA GRADE: 45/High	Fastball: 65		Curveball: 55	Changeup: 45		Control: 50								
Year	Age	Club (League)	Lvl	W	L	ERA	G	GS	IP	H	HR	BB	SO	BB/9	SO/9	WHIP	AVG
2022	22	Wilmington (SAL)	HiA	6	1	1.66	17	0	22	10	2	10	39	4.2	16.2	0.92	.137
2022	22	Harrisburg (EL)	AA	2	1	1.89	32	0	38	21	3	19	54	4.5	12.8	1.05	.162
2022	22	Rochester (IL)	AAA	0	0	0.00	2	0	2	2	0	0	2	0.0	10.8	1.20	.286
Minor League Totals				14	6	3.49	79	1	124	88	13	54	181	3.9	13.2	1.15	.199

22 JAKE IRVIN, RHP

Born: February 18, 1997. **B-T:** R-R. **HT:** 6-6. **WT:** 225.
Drafted: Oklahoma, 2018 (4th round). **Signed by:** Ed Gustafson.

TRACK RECORD: The Oklahoma-to-Nationals pitching pipeline began with Irvin. He was selected by the club in the fourth round of the 2018 draft. He shared a roster with Nationals top pitching prospect Cade Cavalli for one year with the Sooners. Irvin started slow in 2019 at Low-A Hagerstown but finished the season strong. In 2020, during instructional league, he felt some tightness in his elbow and had Tommy John surgery that October. He sat out the entire 2021 season and returned to the mound in 2022, where he split time between High-A Wilmington and Double-A Harrisburg.

SCOUTING REPORT: Irvin has a three-pitch mix led by a fastball that sits around 94 mph and gets up to 97-98 at peak, with mediocre life. His go-to secondary is a low-80s curveball that is described as a power slurve by some scouts. He has good feel for his breaking ball, but a firm, upper-80s changeup remains a work in progress. Irvin has feel to throw all three pitches for strikes and posted a strong 6.6% walk rate.

THE FUTURE: The righthander's pitch quality gives him a chance to profile as a back-of-the-rotation starter, but he will need to build up his arm and get more innings against age-appropriate competition in the upper minors.

BA GRADE: 40/ High	Fastball: 50		Curveball: 55	Changeup: 40		Control: 55								
Year	Age	Club (League)	Lvl	W	L	ERA	G	GS	IP	H	HR	BB	SO	BB/9	SO/9	WHIP	AVG
2022	25	Wilmington (SAL)	HiA	0	0	1.50	9	9	30	24	0	8	29	2.4	8.7	1.07	.222
2022	25	Harrisburg (EL)	AA	0	4	4.79	15	15	73	66	9	20	78	2.5	9.6	1.17	.240
Minor League Totals				9	12	3.64	60	56	252	228	23	73	235	2.6	8.4	1.19	.241

23 EVAN LEE, LHP

Born: June 18, 1997. **B-T:** L-L. **HT:** 6-1. **WT:** 200.
Drafted: Arkansas, 2018 (15th round). **Signed by:** Ed Gustafson.

TRACK RECORD: Lee was selected as a draft-eligible sophomore in the 15th round in 2018. He impressed right away as mainly a reliever in the short-season New York-Penn League and began his work as a starter in 2021. He made his MLB debut in June 2022, his first stint above Double-A. Lee made three appearances out of the bullpen before straining the flexor tendon in his left elbow. He returned in late August and eased back into action. The Nationals needed space on the 40-man roster and outrighted Lee to Triple-A following the season.

SCOUTING REPORT: Lee's fastball has gotten into the mid 90s, but he more typically sits in the 90-91 mph range, with solid spin and carry. His curveball has plus potential and is his most consistent swing-and-miss offering. His low-to-mid-80s changeup had solid results in 2022, but it looks more like a below-average pitch moving forward, while Lee worked to add a hard cutter/slider breaking pitch to his arsenal in the upper 80s that needs more work as well. Lee has fringe-average control.

THE FUTURE: The Nationals still believe that Lee could be a starter once he fully recovers from the elbow injury. However, it is more likely that he becomes a bulk-inning reliever. He had never pitched at Triple-A prior to making his MLB debut. Despite the injury setback, the organization still views him as a reliable lefty option.

BA GRADE: 40/ Medium	Fastball: 45		Curveball: 55	Changeup: 40		Cutter: 45		Control: 45						
Year	Age	Club (League)	Lvl	W	L	ERA	G	GS	IP	H	HR	BB	SO	BB/9	SO/9	WHIP	AVG
2022	25	Nationals (FCL)	R	0	0	0.00	2	2	3	0	0	1	4	3.0	12.0	0.33	.000
2022	25	Wilmington (SAL)	HiA	0	1	4.50	3	3	6	5	0	6	6	9.0	9.0	1.83	.238
2022	25	Harrisburg (EL)	AA	0	3	3.60	7	7	30	25	2	15	37	4.5	11.1	1.33	.229
2022	25	Washington (NL)	MLB	0	1	4.15	4	1	9	9	1	7	7	7.3	7.3	1.85	.257
Major League Totals				0	1	4.15	4	1	9	9	1	7	7	7.3	7.3	1.85	.257
Minor League Totals				7	9	3.74	47	35	152	130	10	75	196	4.5	11.6	1.35	.233

24 TREY LIPSCOMB, 3B

Born: June 14, 2000. **B-T:** R-R. **HT:** 6-1. **WT:** 200.
Drafted: Tennessee, 2022 (3rd round). **Signed by:** Brian Cleary.
TRACK RECORD: The Nationals drafted Lipscomb out of Tennessee in the third round in 2022 and signed him for full slot value of $758,900. In his first three years with the Volunteers, the infielder didn't get a ton of reps, but he made up for it in his senior season. He began his pro career with Low-A Fredericksburg and looked calm, cool and collected during at-bats.
SCOUTING REPORT: Lipscomb looks comfortable at the plate and waits for pitchers to make a mistake. He keeps things simple, trusting his athleticism and hands to drive the ball. Lipscomb has an ability to make changes at the plate, which has turned heads in the organization. His swing follows a flat bat path and his exit velocities in his pro debut were modest, but his 22 home runs with Tennessee during the 2022 season were the second most in a season in the program's history. He has an average arm, which could play well at third base. However, the Nationals' plan is to develop him as a true utility player, despite getting all of his fielding innings at third base in his pro debut. Lipscomb can play all around the infield.
THE FUTURE: Lipscomb is seen as a player who has a little bit of everything, including power, defensive skill and speed. How his bat progresses as he faces more advanced pitching will ultimately determine his future role.

| BA GRADE: 40/ High | | Hit: 40 | | Power: 55 | | Speed: 45 | | Fielding: 50 | | Arm: 50 | |

Year	Age	Club (League)	Lvl	AVG	G	AB	R	H	2B	3B	HR	RBI	BB	SO	SB	OBP	SLG
2022	22	Fredericksburg (CAR)	LoA	.299	23	97	15	29	4	1	1	13	4	19	12	.327	.392
Minor League Totals				.299	23	97	15	29	4	1	1	13	4	19	12	.327	.392

25 DREW MILLAS, C

Born: January 15, 1998. **B-T:** B-R. **HT:** 6-2. **WT:** 205.
Drafted: Missouri State, 2019 (7th round). **Signed by:** Steve Abney (Athletics).
TRACK RECORD: Millas was drafted in the seventh round in 2019 by the Athletics, but his professional career didn't start until two years later. After a sprained ulnar collateral ligament in his right elbow and a blood clotting issue, the catcher impressed at High-A Landing in 2021. The Nationals acquired Millas and two other prospects in July of that year in the deal that sent Yan Gomes and Josh Harrison to Oakland. Millas improved defensively in 2022 and advanced to Double-A Harrisburg, where he struggled offensively, but he played in the Arizona Fall League and slashed .305/.333/.492 in 15 games.
SCOUTING REPORT: Millas is an athletic catcher with a plus arm and very quick hands. He's able to control the running game solidly—he threw out 26% of basestealers in 2022—but he's so excited to throw that he can sometimes make mistakes with his receiving. Millas could also stand to get lower in his stance and improve as a pitch framer—which is the biggest area where the Nationals want to see him improve behind the plate. Offensively, Millas showed solid plate discipline in the lower minors, but his strikeout rates and walk rates went in the wrong directions when he was challenged at Double-A, and he doesn't project for much power or impact.
THE FUTURE: Defense is what will get Millas to the big leagues. He has a real chance to be a backup catcher, but needs to work on being less aggressive at the plate. He'll need more reps against upper level arms, but his glove could give him a big league debut in the near future.

| BA GRADE: 40/ High | | Hit: 40 | | Power: 30 | | Speed: 30 | | Fielding: 55 | | Arm: 60 | |

Year	Age	Club (League)	Lvl	AVG	G	AB	R	H	2B	3B	HR	RBI	BB	SO	SB	OBP	SLG
2022	24	Fredericksburg (CAR)	LoA	.246	18	61	15	15	2	0	2	10	14	13	6	.387	.377
2022	24	Wilmington (SAL)	HiA	.237	25	76	13	18	8	2	1	10	22	20	1	.408	.434
2022	24	Harrisburg (EL)	AA	.211	45	152	12	32	4	0	3	16	15	53	1	.280	.296
Minor League Totals				.245	174	611	89	150	30	3	9	84	105	139	23	.357	.349

26 GERARDO CARRILLO, RHP

Born: September 13, 1998. **B-T:** R-R. **HT:** 6-1. **WT:** 180.
Signed: Mexico, 2016. **Signed by:** Mike Brito/Roman Barinas/Juvenal Soto (Dodgers).
TRACK RECORD: The Dodgers signed Carrillo in 2016 out of Mexico as a 17-year-old for just $75,000. In 2021, he joined the Nationals in the blockbuster that sent Max Scherzer and Trea Turner to Los Angeles and brought Keibert Ruiz and Josiah Gray to Washington. Carrillo quickly became one of the most exciting pitching prospects in the organization. He was sidelined initially in 2022 with a shoulder injury but returned in early July. His velocity was down, but as he got further away from injury his power started to come back.

SCOUTING REPORT: Carrillo's fastball sat 94-97 mph before the injury, but in 2022 he averaged 91-92 mph and peaked around 95. The Nationals are confident that velocity will come back, and his power sinking fastball was previously his calling card. He also has a hard slider/cutter hybrid that could be an above-average secondary pitch and rounds out his arsenal with a mid-80s changeup that could be an average pitch.

THE FUTURE: The 2023 season is going to be important for Carrillo's development and should answer a lot of questions. He needs to prove he can regain his power fastball and that his command can improve enough to compete in the major leagues. His likely MLB role is low-leverage reliever.

| BA GRADE: 40/ High | | Fastball: 55 | | Slider: 55 | | Changeup: 45 | | Control: 40 | |

Year	Age	Club (League)	Lvl	W	L	ERA	G	GS	IP	H	HR	BB	SO	BB/9	SO/9	WHIP	AVG
2022	23	Nationals (FCL)	R	0	0	3.00	2	1	3	5	0	0	1	0.0	3.0	1.67	.385
2022	23	Wilmington (SAL)	HiA	1	0	3.60	9	0	10	7	1	5	10	4.5	9.0	1.20	.189
2022	23	Harrisburg (EL)	AA	1	1	11.32	10	0	10	14	1	8	17	7.0	14.8	2.13	.304
Minor League Totals				19	20	4.18	94	64	314	287	23	145	304	4.2	8.7	1.38	.240

27 DAYLEN LILE, OF

Born: November 30, 2002. **B-T:** L-R. **HT:** 6-0. **WT:** 195.
Drafted: HS—Louisville, 2021 (2nd round). **Signed by:** Brian Cleary.

TRACK RECORD: The Nationals signed Lile in the second round of the 2021 draft for an over-slot $1.75 million bonus. After a lackluster performance at the Florida Complex League in his pro debut, Lile didn't get a chance at an encore because he had Tommy John surgery in March and missed the entire 2022 season.

SCOUTING REPORT: Lile had a strong reputation as an advanced pure hitter in high school, with a long track record of performance. That has not translated yet in the 19 games he has played professionally. He has a quick, easy swing that allows him to make consistent contact and a mature approach that led to a walk rate near 19% in the FCL in 2021. Lile was never projected to generate a ton of power, but there is hope he can reach an average level down the line. His defense is average at best, with fring-average arm strength that makes him fit best in left field.

THE FUTURE: Lile is expected to be full-go for the 2023 season and will still be in his age-20 season. Once he returns, the Nationals will have a better idea of where his skill level is and whether his bat will be enough to allow him to profile as a corner outfielder.

| BA GRADE: 45/ Very High | | Hit: 55 | | Power: 45 | | Speed: 50 | | Fielding: 50 | | Arm: 45 | |

Year	Age	Club (League)	Lvl	AVG	G	AB	R	H	2B	3B	HR	RBI	BB	SO	SB	OBP	SLG
2022	19	Did not play—Injured															

28 TIM CATE, LHP

Born: September 30, 1997. **B-T:** L-L. **HT:** 6-0. **WT:** 185.
Drafted: Connecticut, 2018 (2nd round). **Signed by:** John Malone.

TRACK RECORD: Cate looks like a different pitcher than the one who was named the Nationals' minor league pitcher of the year in 2019. After the Nationals selected him in the second round of the 2018 draft, he excelled. However, he started to struggle when facing higher talent in Double-A in 2021. Cate began the 2022 season repeating High-A and pitched well, but he again struggled against Double-A hitters after a July promotion. He posted a 6.16 ERA in 57 innings with Harrisburg and then got hit around in the Arizona Fall League after the season—where he allowed 25 hits and 20 earned runs in just 10 innings.

SCOUTING REPORT: Cate's curveball remains his lone carrying pitch and it's still an effective breaking ball with high spin and velocity in the upper 70s, but the rest of his arsenal hasn't been quite good enough to help him set it up. Cate throws a fastball in the 88-90 mph range and the pitch tops out around 93 without any unique shape or deception to help it play up. He can cut the pitch at times, but it's solidly below-average, as is a mid-80s changeup that doesn't have much velocity separation from his fastball. Cate has shown solid control, but that backs up against upper level hitters as he's forced to nibble around the zone to try and avoid contact.

THE FUTURE: Considering only Cate's curveball, it still looks like he could find a place in the big league bullpen. However, the Nationals can't and won't overlook his inability to perform at the upper levels of the minors. The 2023 season will be big for Cate to see if he can re-establish his prospect stock.

BA GRADE: 40/High		Fastball: 40		Curveball: 60		Changeup: 40		Control: 50				

Year	Age	Club (League)	Lvl	W	L	ERA	G	GS	IP	H	HR	BB	SO	BB/9	SO/9	WHIP	AVG
2022	24	Wilmington (SAL)	HiA	4	3	2.92	12	10	52	42	2	15	52	2.6	8.9	1.09	.216
2022	24	Harrisburg (EL)	AA	2	5	6.16	11	11	57	62	9	22	51	3.5	8.1	1.47	.271
Minor League Totals				21	33	4.28	83	80	402	406	34	122	368	2.7	8.2	1.31	.259

29 ALDO RAMIREZ, RHP

Born: May 6, 2001. **B-T:** R-R. **HT:** 6-0. **WT:** 180.
Signed: Mexico, 2018. **Signed by:** Sotero Torres/Eddie Romero/Todd Claus (Red Sox).
TRACK RECORD: The Red Sox signed Ramirez out of the Mexican League in 2018 as a 17-year-old. He started his pro career strong before he was sidelined in June 2021 with an elbow injury. A month later, he was traded to the Nationals in the trade that sent Kyle Schwarber to Boston. Ramirez continued to deal with right elbow pain throughout spring training in 2022 and he eventually had Tommy John surgery that kept him out for the entirety of the season.
SCOUTING REPORT: Ramirez's velocity was in the 92-95 mph range before his injury. He had good command and a feel for his secondary pitches, which included a potential above-average curveball that had solid movement and depth and a changeup that looked like it could become an average third pitch. Scouts praised his fastball command when he was healthy, and a career 6% minor league walk rate is evidence of that.
THE FUTURE: Getting healthy is Ramirez's number one priority, because he has never thrown a full season or compiled more than 62 innings in a single year. He has the talent to be a back-of-the-rotation starter, but there's plenty of unknown surrounding him given his injury and lack of exposure to the upper minors.

BA GRADE: 40/ Very High		Fastball: 50		Curveball: 55		Changeup: 50		Control: 55				

Year	Age	Club (League)	Lvl	W	L	ERA	G	GS	IP	H	HR	BB	SO	BB/9	SO/9	WHIP	AVG
2022	21	Did not play—Injured															

30 WILL FRIZZELL, 1B

Born: February 21, 1999. **B-T:** L-R. **HT:** 6-5. **WT:** 225.
Drafted: Texas A&M, 2021 (8th round). **Signed by:** Brandon Larson.
TRACK RECORD: The Nationals drafted Frizzell out of Texas A&M in the eighth round in 2021. He started in the Florida Complex League that season and immediately impressed. He wasn't challenged at all in 2022 and started the season in the FCL before earning a promotion to Low-A Fredericksburg, where he slashed .388/.448/.671 as a 23-year-old. After the season he played in the Arizona Fall League where he hit just .200 in seven games, with nine strikeouts and no walks.
SCOUTING REPORT: Frizzell's offensive production and underlying hitting data is impressive, though it's difficult to take that at face value because 19 or 20 is a more appropriate age for a Carolina League top prospect. Frizzell has shown pure hitting ability, solid zone control and strong exit velocities, with solid home run power versus righthanders, including all 11 of his home runs. Even at first base, Frizzell is a below-average defender who spent all but one game as a DH.
THE FUTURE: With virtually no defensive value, Frizzell's path to the majors is entirely reliant on his bat, and so far he's not faced even High-A competition. While his numbers were impressive in 2022, he needs to be challenged in 2023.

BA GRADE: 40/ High		Hit: 45		Power: 45		Speed: 40		Fielding: 30		Arm: 40		

Year	Age	Club (League)	Lvl	AVG	G	AB	R	H	2B	3B	HR	RBI	BB	SO	SB	OBP	SLG
2022	23	Nationals (FCL)	R	.438	11	32	7	14	4	0	0	14	6	6	0	.538	.563
2022	23	Fredericksburg (CAR)	LoA	.377	34	138	28	52	11	0	11	44	13	35	0	.426	.696
Minor League Totals				.376	54	202	39	76	18	0	12	64	20	47	0	.434	.644

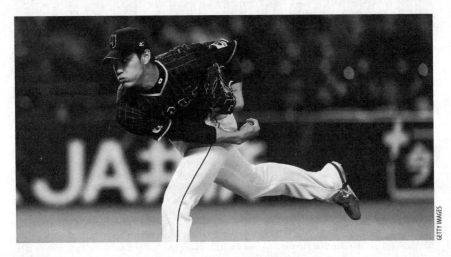

GETTY IMAGES

Kyle Glaser reported on international professionals who were eligible to sign with MLB teams as the Prospect Handbook went to press. This year, three notable players came over from Japan's Nippon Professional Baseball (NPB).

In December, 29-year-old outfielder Masataka Yoshida signed with Red Sox and 30-year-old right-hander Kodai Senga signed with the Mets. But 29-year-old righthander Shintaro Fujinami remained unsigned when this book went to press.

SHINTARO FUJINAMI, RHP

Born: April 12, 1994. **B-T:** R-R. **HT:** 6-6. **WT:** 180.

BA GRADE

45 Risk: Medium

TRACK RECORD: Fujinami entered Japanese baseball lore when he led Osaka Toin to both the spring and summer Koshien tournament championships in 2012, including pitching a two-hitter with 14 strikeouts in his final start. He was drafted by Hanshin in the first round that year and made the NPB All-Star Game as a 19-year-old rookie the following year, the first of four consecutive All-Star selections. Fujinami rivaled Shohei Ohtani for the best pitching prospect in Japan in those early years, but his control suddenly regressed and his star faded rapidly. Hanshin demoted him to the minors during a disastrous 2017 season and he spent the next five years shuttling back and forth between the majors and minors in Japan. He regained some semblance of control in limited action in 2022, leading Hanshin to post him after the season.

SCOUTING REPORT: Fujinami has an appealing pitcher's frame at 6-foot-6, 180 pounds and still possesses the explosive stuff that once left scouts considering him on par with Ohtani as a prospect. His heavy fast-ball sits 94-95 mph and touches 98-99 with little effort out of a clean, easy delivery and jumps on hitters with late explosion and armside bore. He complements it with a 90-92 mph splitter that tunnels well off his fastball and flashes plus when he locates it at the bottom of the zone. Like many Japanese pitchers, Fujinami mostly throws his fastball and splitter, but his slider shows promise at 85-88 mph with tight turn and drop and could become an average pitch with more usage and development in the majors. Fujinami's stuff is explosive, but his delivery lacks deception and he struggles to throw strikes. His strike-throwing issues are more mental than mechanical and have been ingrained for so long they may be difficult to fix.

THE FUTURE: Fujinami will likely get a chance to start in MLB because his stuff is so enticing, but his lack of deception and control will make it difficult to get through a lineup multiple times. He is likely to end up in a bullpen and could pitch in leverage situations.

SCOUTING GRADES	Fastball: 60	Slider: 50	Splitter: 60	Control: 40

Year	Age	Club (League)	Lvl	W	L	ERA	G	GS	IP	H	HR	BB	SO	BB/9	SO/9	WHIP	AVG
2022	28	Hanshin (CL)	NPB	3	5	3.38	16	—	67	58	6	21	65	2.8	8.8	1.19	—
Japanese League Totals				57	54	3.41	189	—	994	886	61	459	1011	4.2	9.2	1.35	—

The major league phase of the Rule 5 draft occurred on Dec. 7, 2022. A few of these players rank in their new organizations' Top 30 Prospects, but since all 15 will be in big league spring training camp in 2023, we provide thumbnail scouting reports for all of them in this space.

Pick	2023 Org	Player	Pos	2022 Org	BA Grade/Risk

1. Nationals — Thad Ward — RHP — Red Sox — 45/Medium

After a breakout 2019 season, Ward missed 2020 to the pandemic and the majority of 2021 and 2022 to Tommy John surgery. After showing increased power and a deep arsenal of pitches pre-injury, Ward emerged in July 2022 with similar power and pitch shapes. Still primarily relying on his two-seam fastball at 91-94 mph, Ward mixes in a sweepy low-80s slider with heavy gloveside break, a mid-to-high-80s cutter, a mid-80s changeup and a four-seam fastball variation.

2. Athletics — Ryan Noda — 1B — Dodgers — 40/Medium

Despite below-average contact skills, Noda manages his whiffs enough that his elite plate discipline (20% chase rate) and plus power still play. His power is notable in that he's slugged 54 home runs combined over the last two seasons and has the exit velocity data to back that up. Noda is one of the better first base defenders in the minor leagues, with the ability to handle a corner outfield spot in a pinch.

3. Pirates — Jose Hernandez — LHP — Dodgers — 40/Medium

Hernandez sits 95-97 mph and touches 100 mph on his four-seam fastball while mixing in a tight mid-80s slider and a changeup. Hernandez's slider generated whiffs at a rate of 60% to go with a 35% chase rate. He has a powerful two-pitch mix that the Pirates believe could slot into their big league bullpen immediately and stick for the entire season.

4. Giants — Blake Sabol — C/OF — Pirates — 45/High

Sabol is a lefthanded hitter with above-average power and a potentially average hit tool who has reached Triple-A. He's limited enough at catcher that it's hard to see him as a regular there or even as a No. 2 catcher, but his lefthanded pop could play in the corner outfield spots and DH and allow him to serve as a No. 3 catcher.

5. Tigers — Mason Englert — RHP — Rangers — 45/High

While Englert lacks powerful stuff, he does use two fastball variations and four secondaries with command. His four-seam and two-seam fastballs sit 91-93 mph and touch 95 with generic shape but with a flat vertical approach angle. Englert has a true starter's profile with a deep arsenal of offerings, strike-throwing skills and a track record of missing bats.

Thad Ward

TOM PRIDDY/FOUR SEAM IMAGES

6. Rays   **Kevin Kelly**   **RHP**   **Guardians**   **40/Medium**

Kelly uses four pitches and two fastball shapes but primarily relies on his sinker/slider mix. His low-90s sinker is his most thrown pitch, driving groundball contact at a high rate and getting average whiffs for a sinker. His slider is a mid-70s sweeper with between 15-17 inches of horizontal break. Kelly throws strikes and generates lots of weak contact.

7. Marlins   **Nic Enright**   **RHP**   **Guardians**   **40/Medium**

Enright was one of the most polished available relievers in this year's Rule 5 class, with plenty of upper-levels experience His low-90s fastball has modest velocity, but it has some of the best carry in the minors, which makes it a bat-misser. His low-80s slider generates plenty of swings-and-misses and serves as an excellent chase pitch when he gets ahead.

8. White Sox   **Nick Avila**   **RHP**   **Giants**   **40/Medium**

Avila uses four different pitch shapes led by a high-ride mid-90s four-seam fastball. He has three secondaries in a cutter, curveball and slider. All of his pitches generated a 30% or higher whiff rate in 2022. He has the look of a pitcher whose stuff could play up out of the bullpen. It's a deep mix of average or better pitches with above-average power.

9. Orioles   **Andrew Politi**   **RHP**   **Red Sox**   **40/Medium**

Politi is an undersized righthander with a high-effort delivery. His fastball sits 93-95 mph and touches 97 with cut and a flatter approach angle. He also throws an upper-80s slider and low-80s curveball with good depth. All of his pitches play as average but he has proven he can miss bats, throw consistent strikes and generate ground balls.

10. Brewers   **Gus Varland**   **RHP**   **Dodgers**   **40/Medium**

While Varland's fastball was sitting 93-95 mph as a starter in April and May, he was sitting 96-97 and touching 98 out of the bullpen in September. His slider jumped from sitting 84-86 mph to sitting 88-90. Over his final 14 appearances, Varland had a 3.44 ERA and 31 strikeouts and five walks over 18.1 innings.

11. Phillies   **Noah Song**   **RHP**   **Red Sox**   **50/Extreme**

Song has not pitched professionally since 2019 and has been instead stashed on the military list while at Naval flight school. There has been no public information surrounding his return to the mound. Drafted in the fourth round in 2019, Song's arsenal included a mid-to-high-90s fastball with two breaking balls and a changeup.

12. Padres   **Jose Lopez**   **LHP**   **Rays**   **40/Medium**

Coming into 2022, Lopez added power and improved the shape of his two primary pitches—his four-seam fastball and slider. His fastball went from sitting 93-95 mph to 95-96 with an added inch of vertical break and a cleaner spin axis, while his slider added a few ticks of velocity and nearly three inches of sweep on average.

13. Mariners   **Chris Clarke**   **RHP**   **Cubs**   **40/Medium**

The 6-foot-7 Clarke has an above-average curveball and two-seam fastball. The Mariners selected Clarke in the Rule 5 for his above-average breaking ball and advanced strike-throwing ability. His ability to generate ground balls at a high rate while throwing strikes and missing bats should allow him to potentially stick out of the pen.

14. Cardinals   **Wilking Rodriguez**   **RHP**   **Yankees**   **40/Low**

The Cardinals had scouted Rodriguez, a 32-year-old who dominated the Mexican League, with the intent of signing him during the season. The Yankees signed him instead, but St. Louis jumped at the opportunity to add Rodriguez in the Rule 5. His three-pitch mix is heavily driven by his mid-to-high-90s fastball and mid-80s breaking ball. He is MLB-ready.

15. Mets   **Zach Greene**   **RHP**   **Yankees**   **40/Medium**

Greene uses four pitches, led by a low-90s four-seam fastball with ride and heavy cut from a low angle of release. He pairs that with a sweeping slider at 78-80 mph to produce a majority of his whiffs. Greene will mix in an occasional changeup and cutter as well. He's a pitcher with high-minors experience and success in the Yankees' system.

Ryan Noda

PROSPECT GRADUATION GRADES

Each October, November and December, Baseball America develops its Top 30 Prospects rankings for the Prospect Handbook.

This year we added a new wrinkle. We evaluated and ranked the top overall graduated prospects from the previous Prospect Handbook. The goal is to give prospects-turned-big leaguers their due before we say farewell and turn our attention to the next wave of talent working its way up the minor league ladder.

Each graduated prospect is listed here with his preseason BA Grade and then his updated BA Grade based on what happened in 2022. Players are ranked by updated end-of-season BA Grade, which gauges each player's realistic upside on the 20-80 scouting scale. A Risk assessment deducts points—10 for High, five for Medium and none for Low—to determine each prospect's Tier.

In the vast majority of cases, these graduated prospects were also top 2022 rookies—but not always. In this ranking, you will find three pitchers—Brewers lefthander Aaron Ashby and relievers Camilo Doval of the Giants and Andres Muñoz of the Mariners—who we classified as prospect-eligible in 2022 even though they were not eligible for Rookie of the Year awards.

Each player's listed age is his baseball age in 2023.

1. JULIO RODRIGUEZ   CF, MARINERS

Preseason: 75/Medium | **Updated:** 75/Low | **Tier:** 75   **Age:** 22 | **Upside Role:** Franchise CF

All-star. Rookie of the Year. Seventh in American League MVP balloting. Rarely is a rookie as productive as Rodriguez was in 2022. His 147 OPS+ ranks 14th among qualified rookies since integration, and the only players as young or younger than Rodriguez were Mike Trout (168) and Albert Pujols (157). Throw in solid defense in center field, a strong throwing arm and better-than-expected speed and Rodriguez is a franchise player, potentially an all-timer.

2. ADLEY RUTSCHMAN   C, ORIOLES

Preseason: 75/Medium | **Updated:** 75/Low | **Tier:** 75   **Age:** 25 | **Upside Role:** Franchise C

Rutschman entered the season ranked as the No. 1 prospect in baseball and is an even a better bet today to be a franchise player. He had one of the best seasons ever for a rookie catcher, batting .254/.362/.445 with 13 home runs and 65 walks in 113 games while playing Gold Glove-caliber defense.

3. MICHAEL HARRIS II   CF, BRAVES

Preseason: 60/High | **Updated:** 65/Low | **Tier:** 65   **Age:** 22 | **Upside Role:** All-star CF

The Braves dipped down to Double-A to call up Harris on May 28 and he helped ignite the club's offense. He hit .297/.339/.514 with 19 homers and 20 steals, backed by Gold Glove-caliber defense in center field. Harris looks like a future all-star.

4. GEORGE KIRBY   RHP, MARINERS

Preseason: 70/High | **Updated:** 70/Medium | **Tier:** 65   **Age:** 25 | **Upside Role:** No. 2 starter

Kirby doesn't have one truly outstanding wipeout pitch, but he throws hard and leans on veteran-level savvy and feel for six pitch types to keep hitters guessing. To that end, Kirby's advanced metrics such as FIP and K-BB% were on par with wily veterans such as Shane Bieber and Zac Gallen.

5. BOBBY WITT JR.   SS, ROYALS

Preseason: 75/Medium | **Updated:** 65/Medium | **Tier:** 60   **Age:** 23 | **Upside Role:** All-star SS

The 2021 Minor League Player of the Year made the Royals' 2022 Opening Day roster and showed a lot of promise by hitting .254/.294/.428 with 20 homers and 30 steals. He thus became the 13th rookie ever to go 20-20. Improved selectivity at the plate and reliability at shortstop can get Witt to occasional all-star status.

PROSPECT GRADUATION GRADES

6. SPENCER STRIDER — RHP, BRAVES

Preseason: 50/High | **Updated:** 65/Medium | **Tier:** 60   **Age:** 24 | **Upside Role:** No. 2 or 3 starter

Strider spent the first two months of 2022 in the Braves' bullpen before seamlessly moving to the rotation on May 30. He was able to map his closer stuff to stints of five or six innings, striking out 38% of batters to establish a new record for rookies with at least 100 innings. In the rotation, Strider recorded a 2.77 ERA and 0.99 WHIP in 107 innings.

7. NICK LODOLO — LHP, REDS

Preseason: 55/High | **Updated:** 60/Medium | **Tier:** 55   **Age:** 25 | **Upside Role:** No. 3 starter

Lodolo showcased present No. 3 starter stuff in his MLB debut season. The 6-foot-6 lefthander threw strikes, worked ahead of hitters and missed bats with a 94 mph four-seam fastball, curveball and changeup. A healthy Lodolo has a No. 3 starter or better future.

8. RILEY GREENE — CF, TIGERS

Preseason: 65/Medium | **Updated:** 60/Medium | **Tier:** 55   **Age:** 22 | **Upside Role:** First-division CF

Greene injured his foot in spring training, which delayed his MLB debut until June 18. He performed at a roughly league-average rate as a 21-year-old big leaguer by hitting .253/.321/.362. Bigger picture: Greene proved himself capable in center field and had some of the best plate discipline markers among rookies. The 2023 season could be big for growth.

9. REID DETMERS — LHP, ANGELS

Preseason: 55/Medium | **Updated:** 55/Low | **Tier:** 55   **Age:** 23 | **Upside Role:** No. 3 or 4 starter

Detmers no-hit the Rays in May but didn't truly shine consistently until after he learned to de-emphasize his fastball and tune up his slider and changeup usage. In his final 13 starts of the season, he recorded a 3.04 ERA with 78 strikeouts, 25 walks and two home runs allowed in 71 innings.

10. JEREMY PEÑA — SS, ASTROS

Preseason: 55/High | **Updated:** 60/Medium | **Tier:** 55   **Age:** 25 | **Upside Role:** First-division SS

Peña was up to the challenge of succeeding franchise icon Carlos Correa. He produced at an average rate during the season, won a Gold Glove at shortstop and delivered a series of key hits in the postseason that made him MVP of both the American League Championship Series and World Series. Improving his chase rate—a fifth-worst 41% as a rookie—and on-base percentage are top priorities.

11. ONEIL CRUZ — SS, PIRATES

Preseason: 65/Medium | **Updated:** 60/Medium | **Tier:** 55   **Age:** 24 | **Upside Role:** First-division SS

Cruz stands out from the pack in Statcast metrics such as max exit velocity, sprint speed, arm strength and barrel rate. At the other extreme, he also struck out 35% of the time—third-highest in MLB at 300 plate appearances—and was graded unfavorably for his fielding at shortstop. Still, Cruz hit .265/.324/.513 with 27% strikeouts versus righthanders and should benefit from the shift ban. That hints at upside that would play at any position.

12. STEVEN KWAN — LF, GUARDIANS

Preseason: 45/High | **Updated:** 55/Low | **Tier:** 55   **Age:** 25 | **Upside Role:** First-division LF

Expectations for Kwan were modest coming into the year, but he showed his upside immediately by hitting .469 in spring training with zero strikeouts in 32 at-bats. He showed a true magic wand-type bat and elite discipline by hitting .298.373/.400 with 62 walks against 60 strikeouts in 147 games. He also won a Gold Glove in left field. Kwan looks like a first-division leadoff hitter who will contend for batting titles.

13. ANDRES MUÑOZ   RP, MARINERS

Preseason: 55/Extreme | **Updated:** 55/Low | **Tier:** 55   **Age:** 24 | **Upside Role:** All-star closer

The Mariners traded for Muñoz in August 2020 while he was rehabbing from Tommy John surgery he had that spring. The wait was worth it. In 2022, Muñoz ranked fourth among qualified relievers with a 38.7% strikeout rate, fifth with a 42% chase rate and second only to Jhoan Duran with an average fastball velocity of 100.2 mph.

14. VINNIE PASQUANTINO   1B, ROYALS

Preseason: 50/High | **Updated:** 55/Low | **Tier:** 55   **Age:** 25 | **Upside** Role: First-division 1B

Pasquantino was ready when the Royals finally looked his way on June 28. It took a while to get rolling, but he showed first-division upside in his final 40-game stretch by hitting .362/.442/.553 with seven of his 10 homers. Pasquantino has a remarkable batting eye and was one of two rookies, along with Steven Kwan, to have more walks than strikeouts.

15. JHOAN DURAN   RP, TWINS

Preseason: 50/High | **Updated:** 50/Medium | **Tier:** 55   **Age:** 25 | **Upside Role:** All-star closer

By the metric win probability added, only girzzled Rockies closer Daniel Bard pitched more effectively in big spots than Duran, a rookie in his MLB debut season. Duran threw the fastest average fastball in MLB at 100.9 mph while also wielding one of the deadliest curveballs in any bullpen. It translated to a 1.82 ERA in 67.2 innings for Duran, who has all-star closer potential.

16. CJ ABRAMS   SS, NATIONALS

Preseason: 65/High | **Updated:** 55/Medium | **Tier:** 50   **Age:** 22 | **Upside Role:** Regular SS

Because of the pandemic, injuries and making the Padres' Opening Day roster, Abrams has just 114 games of minor league experience—and it showed. But his steady defensive play and .303 September batting average hinted at his above-average upside at shortstop.

17. VAUGHN GRISSOM   2B, BRAVES

Preseason: 45/High | **Updated:** 55/Medium | **Tier:** 50   **Age:** 22 | **Upside Role:** Regular 2B

Grissom began the season in High-A and finished it in Atlanta. He had a long run as the club's second baseman as he filled in for the injured Ozzie Albies. Grissom hit .291/.353/.440 with five home runs in 41 games. Given his youth and aptitude, he looks like a potential above-average regular.

18. BRYSON STOTT   SS, PHILLIES

Preseason: 55/High | **Updated:** 50/Low | **Tier:** 50   **Age:** 25 | **Upside** Role: Regular 2B

Stott upped his power in 2021 and made the Phillies' Opening Day roster in 2022. He took his lumps early before finding more of a groove in the second half, hitting .276/.331/.404 and settling in as the everyday shortstop for the eventual National League pennant winners.

19. BRAYAN BELLO   RHP, RED SOX

Preseason: 55/High | **Updated:** 60/High | **Tier:** 50   **Age:** 24 | **Upside Role:** No. 3 or 4 starter

Bello emerged from the lost 2020 throwing harder—he averaged nearly 97 mph in his MLB debut season—which helped his outstanding changeup play up. With an uptick in command, Bello has No. 3 starter upside, which he flashed in his final eight starts, when he compiled a 3.12 ERA, 40 strikeouts and 16 walks in 40 innings.

20. AARON ASHBY   LHP, BREWERS

Preseason: 60/High | **Updated:** 55/Medium | **Tier:** 50   **Age:** 25 | **Upside Role:** No. 3 or 4 starter

Ashby misses bats with four distinct pitch types and keeps the ball on the ground with a 55% ground-ball rate that ranked second among starters with 50 innings. The next step will be throwing more first-pitch strikes so that he can leverage his outstanding slider, changeup and curveball. Ashby has the ability to be a No. 3 or 4 starter if he can harness his stuff.

21. HUNTER GREENE   RHP, REDS

Preseason: 55/High | **Updated:** 50/Medium | **Tier:** 50   **Age:** 23 | **Upside Role:** No. 3 or 4 starter

It was a tale of two seasons for Greene after he made the Reds' Opening Day roster. He ran up a 5.66 ERA in his first 14 starts, allowing 20 homers in 70 innings. In his final 10 turns, Greene tweaked his pitch mix and put up a 2.91 ERA, allowed four homers and a .197 opponent average while logging 76 strikeouts in 55.2 innings. That hints at midrotation upside.

22. JOE RYAN   RHP, TWINS

Preseason: 50/Medium | **Updated:** 50/Low | **Tier:** 50   **Age:** 27 | **Upside Role:** No. 4 starter

Ryan had one of the best seasons by a rookie starter, with a 3.55 ERA and 1.10 WHIP in 147 innings. He struck out a batter per inning despite averaging just 92 mph on his four-seam fastball and not having a positive run value on any secondary pitch. Ryan befuddles hitters with his low arm slot and riding fastball. As he heads into his age-27 season, Ryan is a mature, developed pitcher. That also makes him a lock to operate as at least a No. 4 starter.

23. EDWARD CABRERA   RHP, MARLINS

Preseason: 55/High | **Updated:** 55/Medium | **Tier:** 50   **Age:** 25 | **Upside Role:** No. 3 or 4 starter

Cabrera answered questions about whether his stuff would play in MLB—if not about his durability—by showcasing a 96 mph fastball and three secondary pitches with positive run values. In his final 11 starts, Cabrera recorded a 2.89 ERA with 60 strikeouts and 24 walks in 56 innings. A No. 3 upside is attainable.

24. CAMILO DOVAL   RP, GIANTS

Preseason: 50/High | **Updated:** 50/Low | **Tier:** 50   **Age:** 25 | **Upside Role:** First-division closer

Doval's profile is one of extremes: 99 mph velocity, 56% groundball rate, too many walks and a 1.24 WHIP that was fifth-worst among 20-save closers in 2022. Because of his lower arm slot, Doval has platoon issues and allowed lefthanded hitters to bat .261 and reach base 37% of the time. He already has racked up 30 career saves in two MLB seasons.

25. NOLAN GORMAN   2B, CARDINALS

Preseason: 60/High | **Updated:** 55/High | **Tier:** 45   **Age:** 23 | **Upside Role:** Regular 2B

Drafted as a third baseman out of high school, Gorman's move to second base is complete. He played only third base plus one game in left field in 2022. Gorman earned a callup on May 20 and produced for about a month before tailing off and finishing the season back at Triple-A. Still, there are encouraging signs in Gorman's hard-hit rate and barrel rate for a young power hitter. He needs to tidy up his plate discipline and gain experience versus big league lefthanders.

SIGNING BONUSES

FIRST ROUND

No.	Team: Player, Pos.	Bonus
1.	Orioles: Jackson Holliday, SS	$8,190,000
2.	D-backs: Druw Jones, OF	$8,189,400
3.	Rangers: Kumar Rocker, RHP	$5,200,000
4.	Pirates: Termarr Johnson, SS	$7,219,000
5.	Nationals: Elijah Green, OF	$6,500,000
6.	Marlins: Jacob Berry, 3B	$6,000,000
7.	Cubs: Cade Horton, RHP	$4,450,000
8.	Twins: Brooks Lee, SS	$5,675,000
9.	Royals: Gavin Cross, OF	$5,200,400
10.	Rockies: Gabriel Hughes, RHP	$4,000,000
11.	Mets: Kevin Parada, C	$5,019,735
12.	Tigers: Jace Jung, 2B	$4,590,300
13.	Angels: Zach Neto, SS	$3,500,000
14.	Mets: Jett Williams, SS	$3,900,000
15.	Padres: Dylan Lesko, RHP	$3,900,000
16.	Guardians: Chase DeLauter, OF	$3,750,000
17.	Phillies: Justin Crawford, OF	$3,894,000
18.	Reds: Cam Collier, 3B	$5,000,000
19.	Athletics: Daniel Susac, C	$3,531,200
20.	Braves: Owen Murphy, RHP	$2,556,900
21.	Mariners: Cole Young, SS	$3,300,000
22.	Cardinals: Cooper Hjerpe, LHP	$3,182,200
23.	Blue Jays: Brandon Barriera, LHP	$3,597,500
24.	Red Sox: Mikey Romero, SS	$2,300,000
25.	Yankees: Spencer Jones, OF	$2,880,800
26.	White Sox: Noah Schultz, LHP	$2,800,000
27.	Brewers: Eric Brown, SS	$2,050,000
28.	Astros: Drew Gilbert, OF	$2,497,500
29.	Rays: Xavier Isaac, 1B	$2,548,900
30.	Giants: Reggie Crawford, LHP/1B	$2,297,500
31.	Rockies: Sterlin Thompson, OF	$2,430,500
32.	Reds: Sal Stewart, 3B	$2,100,000

SUPPLEMENTAL FIRST ROUND

No.	Team: Player, Pos.	Bonus
33.	Orioles: Dylan Beavers, OF	$2,200,000
34.	D-backs: Landon Sims, RHP	$2,347,050
35.	Braves: JR Ritchie, RHP	$2,397,500
36.	Pirates: Thomas Harrington, RHP	$2,047,500
37.	Guardians: Justin Campbell, RHP	$1,700,000
38.	Rockies: Jordan Beck, OF	$2,200,000
39.	Padres: Robby Snelling, LHP	$3,000,000

SECOND ROUND

No.	Team: Player, Pos.	Bonus
40.	Dodgers: Dalton Rushing, C	$1,956,890
41.	Red Sox: Cutter Coffey, SS	$1,847,500
42.	Orioles: Max Wagner, 3B	$1,900,000
43.	D-backs: Ivan Melendez, 1B	$1,400,000
44.	Pirates: Hunter Barco, LHP	$1,525,000
45.	Nationals: Jake Bennett, LHP	$1,734,800
46.	Marlins: Jacob Miller, RHP	$1,697,900
47.	Cubs: Jackson Ferris, LHP	$3,005,000
48.	Twins: Connor Prielipp, LHP	$1,825,000
49.	Royals: Cayden Wallace, 3B	$1,697,500

No.	Team: Player, Pos.	Bonus
50.	Rockies: Jackson Cox, RHP	$1,850,000
51.	Tigers: Peyton Graham, SS	$1,800,000
52.	Mets: Blade Tidwell, RHP	$1,850,000
53.	Padres: Adam Mazur, RHP	$1,250,000
54.	Guardians: Parker Messick, LHP	$1,300,000
55.	Reds: Logan Tanner, C	$1,030,500
56.	Athletics: Henry Bolte, OF	$2,000,000
57.	Braves: Cole Phillips, RHP	$1,497,500
58.	Mariners: Tyler Locklear, 3B	$1,276,500
59.	Cardinals: Brycen Mautz, LHP	$1,100,000
60.	Blue Jays: Josh Kasevich, SS	$997,500
61.	Yankees: Drew Thorpe, RHP	$1,187,600
62.	White Sox: Peyton Pallette, RHP	$1,500,000
63.	Brewers: Jacob Misiorowski, RHP	$2,350,000
64.	Astros: Jacob Melton, OF	$1,000,000
65.	Rays: Brock Jones, OF	$1,077,600
66.	Giants: Carson Whisenhunt, LHP	$1,866,220

SUPPLEMENTAL SECOND ROUND

No.	Team: Player, Pos.	Bonus
67.	Orioles: Jud Fabian, OF	$1,026,800
68.	Twins: Tanner Schobel, SS	$1,002,000
69.	Athletics: Clark Elliott, OF	$900,000
70.	Rays: Chandler Simpson, SS	$747,500
71.	Rays: Ryan Cermak, OF	$747,500
72.	Brewers: Robert Moore, SS	$800,000
73.	Reds: Justin Boyd, OF	$847,500
74.	Mariners: Walter Ford, RHP	$1,250,000
75.	Mets: Nick Morabito, OF	$1,000,000
76.	Braves: Blake Burkhalter, RHP	$647,500
77.	Blue Jays: Tucker Toman, SS	$2,000,000
78.	Blue Jays: Cade Doughty, 2B	$831,100
79.	Red Sox: Roman Anthony, OF	$2,500,000
80.	Astros: Andrew Taylor, RHP	$804,700

THIRD ROUND

No.	Team: Player, Pos.	Bonus
81.	Orioles: Nolan McLean, RHP	Did not sign
82.	D-backs: Nate Savino, LHP	$700,000
83.	Pirates: Jack Brannigan, 3B/RHP	$770,700
84.	Nationals: Trey Lipscomb, 3B	$758,900
85.	Marlins: Karson Milbrandt, RHP	$1,497,500
86.	Cubs: Christopher Paciolla, SS	$900,000
87.	Royals: Mason Barnett, RHP	$697,500
88.	Rockies: Carson Palmquist, LHP	$775,000
89.	Angels: Ben Joyce, RHP	$997,500
90.	Mets: Brandon Sproat, RHP	Did not sign
91.	Padres: Henry Williams, RHP	$800,000
92.	Guardians: Joe Lampe, OF	$800,000
93.	Phillies: Gabriel Rincones, OF	$627,500
94.	Reds: Bryce Hubbart, LHP	$522,500
95.	Athletics: Colby Thomas, OF	$750,000
96.	Braves: Drake Baldwin, C	$633,300
97.	Cardinals: Pete Hansen, LHP	$629,800
98.	Blue Jays: Alan Roden, OF	$497,500
99.	Red Sox: Dalton Rogers, LHP	$447,500
100.	Yankees: Trystan Vrieling, RHP	$608,900

2021 DRAFT

FIRST ROUND

No. Team: Player, Pos.	Bonus
1. Pirates: Henry Davis, C	$6,500,000
2. Rangers: Jack Leiter, RHP	$7,922,000
3. Tigers: Jackson Jobe, RHP	$6,900,000
4. Red Sox: Marcelo Mayer, SS	$6,664,000
5. Orioles: Colton Cowser, OF	$4,900,000
6. D-backs: Jordan Lawlar, SS	$6,713,300
7. Royals: Frank Mozzicato, LHP	$3,547,500
8. Rockies: Benny Montgomery, OF	$5,000,000
9. Angels: Sam Bachman, RHP	$3,847,500
10. Mets: Kumar Rocker, RHP	Did not sign
11. Nationals: Brady House, SS	$5,000,000
12. Mariners: Harry Ford, C	$4,366,400
13. Phillies: Andrew Painter, RHP	$3,900,000
14. Giants: Will Bednar, RHP	$3,647,500
15. Brewers: Sal Frelick, OF	$4,000,000
16. Marlins: Kahlil Watson, SS	$4,540,790
17. Reds: Matt McLain, SS	$4,625,000
18. Cardinals: Michael McGreevy, RHP	$2,750,000
19. Blue Jays: Gunnar Hoglund, RHP	$3,247,500
20. Yankees: Trey Sweeney, SS	$3,000,000
21. Cubs: Jordan Wicks, LHP	$3,132,300
22. White Sox: Colson Montgomery, SS	$3,027,000
23. Guardians: Gavin Williams, RHP	$2,250,000
24. Braves: Ryan Cusick, RHP	$2,700,000
25. Athletics: Max Muncy, SS	$2,850,000
26. Twins: Chase Petty, RHP	$2,500,000
27. Padres: Jackson Merrill, SS	$1,800,000
28. Rays: Carson Williams, SS	$2,347,500
29. Dodgers: Maddux Bruns, LHP	$2,197,500
30. Reds: Jay Allen, OF	$2,397,500

SUPPLEMENTAL FIRST ROUND

No. Team: Player, Pos.	Bonus
31. Marlins: Joe Mack, C	$2,500,000
32. Tigers: Ty Madden, RHP	$2,500,000
33. Brewers: Tyler Black, 2B	$2,200,000
34. Rays: Cooper Kinney, 2B	$2,145,600
35. Reds: Mat Nelson, C	$2,093,300
36. Twins: Noah Miller, SS	$1,700,000

SECOND ROUND

No. Team: Player, Pos.	Bonus
37. Pirates: Anthony Solometo, LHP	$2,797,500
38. Rangers: Aaron Zavala, OF	$830,000
39. Tigers: Izaac Pacheco, SS	$2,750,000
40. Red Sox: Jud Fabian, OF	Did not sign
41. Orioles: Connor Norby, 2B	$1,700,000
42. D-backs: Ryan Bliss, SS	$1,250,000
43. Royals: Ben Kudrna, RHP	$2,997,500
44. Rockies: Jaden Hill, RHP	$1,689,500
45. Angels: Ky Bush, LHP	$1,747,500
46. Mets: Calvin Ziegler, RHP	$910,000
47. Nationals: Daylen Lile, OF	$1,750,000
48. Mariners: Edwin Arroyo, SS	$1,650,000
49. Phillies: Ethan Wilson, OF	$1,507,600
50. Giants: Matt Mikulski, LHP	$1,197,500

TOP THREE ROUNDS

51. Brewers: Russell Smith, LHP	$1,000,000
52. Marlins: Cody Morissette, SS	$1,403,200
53. Reds: Andrew Abbott, LHP	$1,300,000
54. Cardinals: Joshua Baez, OF	$2,250,000
55. Yankees: Brendan Beck, RHP	$1,050,000
56. Cubs: James Triantos, 3B	$2,100,000
57. White Sox: Wes Kath, 3B	$1,800,000
58. Guardians: Doug Nikhazy, LHP	$1,200,000
59. Braves: Spencer Schwellenbach, RHP	$997,500
60. Athletics: Zack Gelof, 3B	$1,157,400
61. Twins: Steve Hajjar, LHP	$1,129,700
62. Padres: James Wood, OF	$2,600,000
63. Rays: Kyle Manzardo, 1B	$747,500

SUPPLEMENTAL SECOND ROUND

No. Team: Player, Pos.	Bonus
64. Pirates: Lonnie White Jr., OF	$1,500,000
65. Orioles: Reed Trimble, OF	$800,000
66. Royals: Peyton Wilson, 2B	$1,000,800
67. D-backs: Adrian Del Castillo, C	$1,000,000
68. Rockies: Joe Rock, LHP	$953,100
69. Guardians: Tommy Mace, RHP	$1,100,000
70. Cardinals: Ryan Holgate, OF	$875,000
71. Padres: Robert Gasser, LHP	$884,200

THIRD ROUND

No. Team: Player, Pos.	Bonus
72. Pirates: Bubba Chandler, RHP	$3,000,000
73. Rangers: Cameron Cauley, SS	$1,000,000
74. Tigers: Dylan Smith, RHP	$1,115,000
75. Red Sox: Tyler McDonough, 2B	$828,600
76. Orioles: John Rhodes, OF	$1,375,000
77. D-backs: Jacob Steinmetz, RHP	$500,000
78. Royals: Carter Jensen, C	$1,097,500
79. Rockies: McCade Brown, RHP	$780,400
80. Angels: Landon Marceaux, RHP	$765,300
81. Mets: Dominic Hamel, RHP	$755,300
82. Nationals: Branden Boissiere, OF	$600,000
83. Mariners: Michael Morales, RHP	$1,500,000
84. Phillies: Jordan Viars, OF	$747,500
85. Giants: Mason Black, RHP	$708,200
86. Brewers: Alex Binelas, 3B	$700,000
87. Astros: Tyler Whitaker, OF	$1,500,000
88. Marlins: Jordan McCants, SS	$800,000
89. Reds: Jose Torres, SS	$622,500
90. Cardinals: Austin Love, RHP	$600,000
91. Blue Jays: Ricky Tiedemann, LHP	$644,800
92. Yankees: Brock Selvidge, LHP	$1,500,000
93. Cubs: Drew Gray, LHP	$900,000
94. White Sox: Sean Burke, RHP	$900,000
95. Guardians: Jake Fox, SS	$850,000
96. Braves: Dylan Dodd, LHP	$122,500
97. Athletics: Mason Miller, RHP	$599,100
98. Twins: Cade Povich, LHP	$500,000
99. Padres: Kevin Kopps, RHP	$300,000
100. Rays: Ryan Spikes, SS	$1,097,500
101. Dodgers: Peter Heubeck, RHP	$1,269,500

2020 DRAFT

TOP THREE ROUNDS

FIRST ROUND

No. Team: Player, Pos.	Bonus
1. Tigers: Spencer Torkelson, 3B	$8,416,300
2. Orioles: Heston Kjerstad, OF	$5,200,000
3. Marlins: Max Meyer, RHP	$6,700,000
4. Royals: Asa Lacy, LHP	$6,670,000
5. Blue Jays: Austin Martin, SS	$7,000,825
6. Mariners: Emerson Hancock, RHP	$5,700,000
7. Pirates: Nick Gonzales, SS	$5,432,400
8. Padres: Robert Hassell III, OF	$4,300,000
9. Rockies: Zac Veen, OF	$5,000,000
10. Angels: Reid Detmers, LHP	$4,670,000
11. White Sox: Garrett Crochet, LHP	$4,547,500
12. Reds: Austin Hendrick, OF	$4,000,000
13. Giants: Patrick Bailey, C	$3,797,500
14. Rangers: Justin Foscue, 2B	$3,250,000
15. Phillies: Mick Abel, RHP	$4,075,000
16. Cubs: Ed Howard, SS	$3,745,500
17. Red Sox: Nick Yorke, 2B	$2,700,000
18. D-backs: Bryce Jarvis, RHP	$2,650,000
19. Mets: Pete Crow-Armstrong, OF	$3,359,000
20. Brewers: Garrett Mitchell, OF	$3,242,900
21. Cardinals: Jordan Walker, 3B	$2,900,000
22. Nationals: Cade Cavalli, RHP	$3,027,000
23. Indians: Carson Tucker, SS	$2,000,000
24. Rays: Nick Bitsko, RHP	$3,000,000
25. Braves: Jared Shuster, LHP	$2,197,500
26. Athletics: Tyler Soderstrom, C	$3,300,000
27. Twins: Aaron Sabato, 1B	$2,750,000
28. Yankees: Austin Wells, C	$2,500,000
29. Dodgers: Bobby Miller, RHP	$2,197,500

SUPPLEMENTAL FIRST ROUND

No. Team: Player, Pos.	Bonus
30. Orioles: Jordan Westburg, SS	$2,365,500
31. Pirates: Carmen Mlodzinski, RHP	$2,050,000
32. Royals: Nick Loftin, SS	$3,000,000
33. D-backs: Slade Cecconi, RHP	$2,384,900
34. Padres: Justin Lange, RHP	$2,000,000
35. Rockies: Drew Romo, C	$2,095,800
36. Indians: Tanner Burns, RHP	$1,600,000
37. Rays: Alika Williams, SS	$1,850,000

SECOND ROUND

No. Team: Player, Pos.	Bonus
38. Tigers: Dillon Dingler, C	$1,952,300
39. Orioles: Hudson Haskin, OF	$1,906,800
40. Marlins: Dax Fulton, LHP	$2,400,000
41. Royals: Ben Hernandez, RHP	$1,450,000
42. Blue Jays: C.J. Van Eyk, RHP	$1,797,500
43. Mariners: Zach DeLoach, OF	$1,729,800
44. Pirates: Jared Jones, RHP	$2,200,000
45. Padres: Owen Caissie, OF	$1,200,004
46. Rockies: Chris McMahon, RHP	$1,637,400
47. White Sox: Jared Kelley, RHP	$3,000,000
48. Reds: Christian Roa, RHP	$1,543,600
49. Giants: Casey Schmitt, 3B	$1,147,500
50. Rangers: Evan Carter, OF	$1,250,000

51. Cubs: Burl Carraway, LHP		$1,050,000
52. Mets: J.T. Ginn, RHP		$2,900,000
53. Brewers: Freddy Zamora, SS		$1,150,000
54. Cardinals: Masyn Winn, SS/RHP		$2,100,000
55. Nationals: Cole Henry, RHP		$2,000,000
56. Indians: Logan Allen, LHP		$1,125,000
57. Rays: Ian Seymour, LHP		$1,243,600
58. Athletics: Jeff Criswell, RHP		$1,000,000
59. Twins: Alerick Soularie, OF		$900,000
60. Dodgers: Landon Knack, RHP		$712,500

SUPPLEMENTAL SECOND ROUND

No. Team: Player, Pos.	Bonus
61. Marlins: Kyle Nicolas, RHP	$1,129,700
62. Tigers: Daniel Cabrera, OF	$1,210,000
63. Cardinals: Tink Hence, RHP	$1,115,000
64. Mariners: Connor Phillips, RHP	$1,050,300
65. Reds: Jackson Miller, C	$1,290,000
66. Dodgers: Clayton Beeter, RHP	$1,196,500
67. Giants: Nick Swiney, LHP	$1,197,500
68. Giants: Jimmy Glowenke, SS	$597,500
69. Mets: Isaiah Greene, OF	$850,000
70. Cardinals: Alec Burleson, OF	$700,000
71. Nationals: Sammy Infante, SS	$1,000,000
72. Astros: Alex Santos, RHP	$1,250,000

THIRD ROUND

No. Team: Player, Pos.	Bonus
73. Tigers: Trei Cruz, SS	$900,000
74. Orioles: Anthony Servideo, SS	$950,000
75. Marlins: Zach McCambley, RHP	$775,000
76. Royals: Tyler Gentry, OF	$750,000
77. Blue Jays: Trent Palmer, RHP	$847,500
78. Mariners: Kaden Polcovich, 2B	$575,000
79. Pirates: Nick Garcia, RHP	$1,200,000
80. Padres: Cole Wilcox, RHP	$3,300,000
81. Rockies: Sam Weatherly, LHP	$755,300
82. Angels: David Calabrese, OF	$744,200
83. White Sox: Adisyn Coffey, RHP	$50,000
84. Reds: Bryce Bonnin, RHP	$700,000
85. Giants: Kyle Harrison, LHP	$2,497,500
86. Rangers: Tekoah Roby, RHP	$775,000
87. Phillies: Casey Martin, SS	$1,300,000
88. Cubs: Jordan Nwogu, OF	$678,600
89. Red Sox: Blaze Jordan, 3B	$1,750,000
90. D-backs: Liam Norris, LHP	$800,000
91. Mets: Anthony Walters, SS	$20,000
92. Brewers: Zavier Warren, C	$575,000
93. Cardinals: Levi Prater, LHP	$575,000
94. Nationals: Holden Powell, RHP	$500,000
95. Indians: Petey Halpin, OF	$1,525,000
96. Rays: Hunter Barnhart, RHP	$585,000
97. Braves: Jesse Franklin, OF	$497,500
98. Athletics: Michael Guldberg, OF	$300,000
99. Yankees: Trevor Hauver, 2B	$587,400
100. Dodgers: Jake Vogel, OF	$1,622,500
101. Astros: Tyler Brown, RHP	$577,000

INDEX

D

Dabovich, RJ (Giants) 416
Dalquist, Andrew (White Sox) 113
Dana, Caden (Angels) 218
Danner, Hagen (Blue Jays) 476
Davidson, Logan (Athletics) 336
Davis, Brennen (Cubs) 85
Davis, Henry (Pirates) 357
De Andrade, Danny (Twins) 284
De Avila, Luis (Braves) 46
de Jesus, Randy (Angels) 220
De La Cruz, Carlos (Phillies) 349
De La Cruz, Elly (Reds) 116
De La Cruz, Jose (Tigers) 177
De La Rosa, Jeremy (Nationals) 488
De Los Santos, Anderson (Orioles) 65
De Los Santos, Deyvison (D-backs) 22
De Paula, Juan (Dodgers) 234
DeLauter, Chase (Guardians) 136
DeLoach, Zach (Mariners) 426
DeLuca, Jonny (Dodgers) 236
Denoyer, Noah (Orioles) 62
Devers, Luis (Cubs) 96
Diaz, Joel (Mets) 299
Diaz, Jordan (Athletics) 328
Diaz, Yainer (Astros) 181
Diaz, Yilber (D-backs) 32
Dingler, Dillon (Tigers) 167
Dirden, Justin (Astros) 184
Dodd, Dylan (Braves) 40
Dollard, Taylor (Mariners) 423
Dombroski, Trey (Astros) 189
Dominguez, Jasson (Yankees) 309
Doughty, Cade (Blue Jays) 472
Doyle, Brenton (Rockies) 157
Dubin, Shawn (Astros) 192
Dunham, Elijah (Yankees) 315
Duran, Carlos (Dodgers) 241

E

Eder, Jake (Marlins) 247
Edwards, Xavier (Marlins) 249
Elliott, Clark (Athletics) 332
Encarnacion-Strand, Christian (Reds) 118
Encarnacion, Jerar (Marlins) 254
Englert, Mason (Tigers) 173
Enlow, Blayne (Twins) 286
Enright, Nic (Marlins) 252
Erla, Mason (Angels) 222
Espino, Daniel (Guardians) 132
Estanista, Jaydenn (Phillies) 349
Estes, Joey (Athletics) 331

F

Fabian, Jud (Orioles) 58
Faucher, Calvin (Rays) 447
Felipe, Angel (Padres) 400
Fernandez, Yanquiel (Rockies) 154
Fernandez, Yeiner (Dodgers) 239
Ferrer, Jose (Nationals) 493
Ferris, Jackson (Cubs) 91
Festa, David (Twins) 280
Figuereo, Gleider (Rangers) 459
Fitts, Richard (Yankees) 316
Fletcher, Dominic (D-backs) 27
Fleury, Jose (Astros) 191
Flores, Wilmer (Tigers) 165
Florial, Estevan (Yankees) 313
Ford, Harry (Mariners) 420
Ford, Walter (Mariners) 426
Foscue, Justin (Rangers) 457

Fox, Jake (Guardians) 139
France, J.P. (Astros) 190
Franklin, Jesse (Braves) 43
Franklin, Kohl (Cubs) 97
Frasso, Nick (Dodgers) 234
Freeman, Tyler (Guardians) 137
Frelick, Sal (Brewers) 261
Frizzell, Will (Nationals) 497
Fulton, Dax (Marlins) 248

G

Gaddis, Hunter (Guardians) 143
Garcia, Eduardo (Brewers) 273
Garcia, Maikel (Royals) 199
Garcia, Yhoswar (Phillies) 351
Gasser, Robert (Brewers) 265
Gelof, Zack (Athletics) 325
Genao, Angel (Guardians) 142
Gentry, Tyler (Royals) 199
Gerardo, Jose (Marlins) 253
Gil, Luis (Yankees) 313
Gilbert, Drew (Astros) 181
Ginn, J.T. (Athletics) 330
Gomez, Antonio (Yankees) 319
Gomez, Moises (Cardinals) 380
Gomez, Yoendrys (Yankees) 319
Gonzales, Nick (Pirates) 360
Gonzalez, Gabriel (Mariners) 422
Gonzalez, Omar (Yankees) 318
Gonzalez, Wikelman (Red Sox) 74
Goodman, Hunter (Rockies) 154
Gordon, Colton (Astros) 192
Gorski, Matt (Pirates) 363
Gough, Tyler (Mariners) 430
Graceffo, Gordon (Cardinals) 375
Graham, Peyton (Tigers) 167
Grammes, Conor (D-backs) 33
Green, Elijah (Nationals) 485
Greene, Zach (Mets) 304
Groome, Jay (Padres) 392
Groshans, Jordan (Marlins) 249
Grove, Michael (Dodgers) 237
Guerrero, Juan (Rockies) 158
Guilarte, Daniel (Brewers) 269
Gutierrez, Anthony (Rangers) 454
Guzman, Denzer (Angels) 215

H

Hackenberg, Adam (White Sox) 113
Hall, Anthony (Yankees) 317
Hall, DL (Orioles) 54
Halpin, Petey (Guardians) 143
Hamel, Dominic (Mets) 298
Hamilton, David (Red Sox) 81
Hamilton, Quincy (Astros) 187
Hancock, Emerson (Mariners) 422
Hansen, Pete (Cardinals) 379
Hardman, Tyler (Yankees) 316
Harrington, Thomas (Pirates) 361
Harris, Brett (Athletics) 331
Harris, Dustin (Rangers) 456
Harris, Hogan (Athletics) 330
Harrison, Kyle (Giants) 405
Hartwig, Grant (Mets) 305
Haskin, Hudson (Orioles) 64
Hassell III, Robert (Nationals) 485
Hawkins, Garrett (Padres) 397
Headrick, Brent (Twins) 284
Helman, Michael (Twins) 287
Hence, Tink (Cardinals) 373
Henderson, Gunnar (Orioles) 52
Henderson, Logan (Brewers) 267

Henriquez, Ronny (Twins) 286
Henry, Cole (Nationals) 490
Hensley, David (Astros) 182
Hernaiz, Darell (Orioles) 60
Hernandez, Ben (Royals) 208
Hernandez, Cristian (Cubs) 87
Hernandez, Diego (Royals) 205
Hernandez, Erick (White Sox) 112
Hernandez, Heriberto (Rays) 444
Hernandez, Joseph (Mariners) 432
Herrera, Ivan (Cardinals) 376
Herz, DJ (Cubs) 92
Heubeck, Peter (Dodgers) 240
Hickey, Nathan (Red Sox) 75
Hidalgo, Alejandro (Twins) 285
Hill, Darius (Cubs) 94
Hill, Jaden (Rockies) 155
Hinds, Rece (Reds) 129
Hjerpe, Cooper (Cardinals) 374
Hodge, Porter (Cubs) 94
Hoeing, Bryan (Marlins) 254
Hoffmann, Andrew (Royals) 203
Hoglund, Gunnar (Athletics) 329
Holliday, Jackson (Orioles) 53
Hollowell, Gavin (Rockies) 159
Hood, Josh (Mariners) 431
Horton, Cade (Cubs) 86
Horwitz, Spencer (Blue Jays) 477
House, Brady (Nationals) 486
Howell, Korry (Padres) 394
Hughes, Gabriel (Rockies) 150
Hunter, Cade (Reds) 127
Hurt, Kyle (Dodgers) 240
Hurter, Brant (Tigers) 175

I

Iriarte, Jairo (Padres) 393
Irvin, Jake (Nationals) 494
Isaac, Xavier (Rays) 442
Izzi, Ashton (Mariners) 429

J

Jackson, Jeremiah (Angels) 220
Jacob, Alek (Padres) 398
Jameson, Drey (D-backs) 23
Jarvis, Bryce (D-backs) 32
Jean, Jefferson (Athletics) 335
Jensen, Carter (Royals) 201
Jimenez, Leonardo (Blue Jays) 477
Jobe, Jackson (Tigers) 164
Johnson, Marcus (Rays) 447
Johnson, Seth (Orioles) 59
Johnson, Termarr (Pirates) 357
Jones, Brock (Rays) 442
Jones, Druw (D-backs) 21
Jones, Greg (Rays) 444
Jones, Jared (Pirates) 361
Jones, Nolan (Rockies) 157
Jones, Spencer (Yankees) 311
Jordan, Blaze (Red Sox) 74
Jorge, Carlos (Reds) 123
Jorge, Dyan (Rockies) 158
Joyce, Ben (Angels) 217
Juan, Jorge (Athletics) 335
Juarez, Victor (Rockies) 153
Juenger, Hayden (Blue Jays) 472
Julien, Edouard (Twins) 278
Julks, Corey (Astros) 193
Jung, Jace (Tigers) 165
Jung, Josh (Rangers) 453

K

Karcher, Ricky (Reds) — 126
Kasevich, Josh (Blue Jays) — 474
Kath, Wes (White Sox) — 108
Kavadas, Niko (Red Sox) — 78
Keith, Colt (Tigers) — 166
Keith, Damon (Dodgers) — 240
Kelley, Jared (White Sox) — 106
Kelly, Kevin (Rays) — 448
Kelly, Zack (Red Sox) — 80
Kempner, William (Giants) — 415
Kennedy, Michael (Pirates) — 364
Kent, Zak (Rangers) — 460
Kerkering, Orion (Phillies) — 352
Kilian, Caleb (Cubs) — 89
King Jr., Lamar (Padres) — 395
Kjerstad, Heston (Orioles) — 58
Knack, Landon (Dodgers) — 238
Knehr, Reiss (Padres) — 396
Knorr, Michael (Astros) — 191
Kopp, Ronan (Dodgers) — 235
Kowar, Jackson (Royals) — 204
Kreidler, Ryan (Tigers) — 168
Kudrna, Ben (Royals) — 198
Kuhn, Travis (Mariners) — 430

L

Labrada, Victor (Mariners) — 432
Lacy, Asa (Royals) — 202
Lara, Andry (Nationals) — 491
Lara, Luis (Brewers) — 266
Lavastida, Bryan (Guardians) — 145
Laverde, Dario (Angels) — 225
Lawlar, Jordan (D-backs) — 21
Lee, Brooks (Twins) — 277
Lee, Evan (Nationals) — 494
Lee, Hao Yu (Phillies) — 343
Lee, Korey (Astros) — 183
Legumina, Casey (Reds) — 129
Leiter, Jack (Rangers) — 455
Leon, Pedro (Astros) — 183
Leonard, Eddys (Dodgers) — 235
Lesko, Dylan (Padres) — 389
Lewis, Ian (Marlins) — 252
Lewis, Royce (Twins) — 276
Liberatore, Matthew (Cardinals) — 374
Lile, Daylen (Nationals) — 496
Lin, Yu-Min (D-backs) — 28
Lipcius, Andre (Tigers) — 172
Lipscomb, Trey (Nationals) — 495
Lizarraga, Victor (Padres) — 391
Locklear, Tyler (Mariners) — 424
Loftin, Nick (Royals) — 200
Loperfido, Joey (Astros) — 188
Lopez, Dariel (Pirates) — 366
Lopez, Otto (Blue Jays) — 475
Loutos, Ryan (Cardinals) — 385
Love, Austin (Cardinals) — 381
Lowe, Isaiah (Padres) — 398
Luciano, Marco (Giants) — 404
Lugo, Matthew (Red Sox) — 76
Lugo, William (Mets) — 305

M

Mack, Joe (Marlins) — 249
Macko, Adam (Blue Jays) — 473
Madden, Jake (Angels) — 218
Madden, Ty (Tigers) — 166
Made, Kevin (Cubs) — 93
Maier, Adam (Braves) — 44

Malloy, Justyn-Henry (Tigers) — 169
Mann, Devin (Dodgers) — 238
Manzardo, Kyle (Rays) — 438
Marceaux, Landon (Angels) — 222
Marchan, Rafael (Phillies) — 352
Marlowe, Cade (Mariners) — 427
Marsee, Jakob (Padres) — 396
Marsh, Alec (Royals) — 202
Marte, Noelvi (Reds) — 117
Martin, Austin (Twins) — 282
Martinez, Angel (Guardians) — 136
Martinez, Gabriel (Blue Jays) — 475
Martinez, Justin (D-backs) — 30
Martinez, Orelvis (Blue Jays) — 471
Martorella, Nathan (Padres) — 397
Mata, Bryan (Red Sox) — 72
Matijevic, JJ (Astros) — 190
Matos, Luis (Giants) — 406
Mauricio, Ronny (Mets) — 296
Mautz, Brycen (Cardinals) — 378
Mayer, Marcelo (Red Sox) — 68
Mayo, Coby (Orioles) — 57
Mazur, Adam (Padres) — 391
McCabe, David (Braves) — 48
McCambley, Zach (Marlins) — 256
McCollum, Tommy (Phillies) — 353
McCray, Grant (Giants) — 406
McDermott, Chayce (Orioles) — 62
McDougal, Tanner (White Sox) — 107
McFarlane, Alex (Phillies) — 345
McGarry, Griff (Phillies) — 341
McGowan, Christian (Phillies) — 348
McGreevy, Michael (Cardinals) — 376
McIntosh, Paul (Marlins) — 257
McLain, Matt (Reds) — 122
Mead, Curtis (Rays) — 437
Meadows, Parker (Tigers) — 170
Mears, Joshua (Padres) — 395
Meckler, Wade (Giants) — 413
Mederos, Victor (Angels) — 225
Medina, Luis (Athletics) — 329
Meidroth, Chase (Red Sox) — 80
Mejia, Jonathan (Cardinals) — 377
Melean, Alejandro (Blue Jays) — 478
Melendez, Ivan (D-backs) — 25
Melendez, Jaime (Astros) — 190
Melton, Jacob (Astros) — 182
Melton, Troy (Tigers) — 173
Mena, Cristian (White Sox) — 103
Mendez, Hendry (Brewers) — 269
Mercedes, Yasser (Twins) — 282
Merrill, Jackson (Padres) — 388
Mervis, Matt (Cubs) — 86
Messick, Parker (Guardians) — 140
Meyer, Max (Marlins) — 245
Mieses, Luis (White Sox) — 109
Mikulski, Matt (Giants) — 415
Milbrandt, Karson (Marlins) — 251
Millas, Drew (Nationals) — 495
Miller, Bobby (Dodgers) — 229
Miller, Bryce (Mariners) — 421
Miller, Erik (Phillies) — 343
Miller, Jacob (Marlins) — 250
Miller, Mason (Athletics) — 325
Miller, Noah (Twins) — 283
Mills, Zane (Cardinals) — 384
Misiorowski, Jacob (Brewers) — 263
Misner, Kameron (Rays) — 443
Mitchell, Garrett (Brewers) — 262
Mlodzinski, Carmen (Pirates) — 366
Montes, Lazaro (Mariners) — 426
Montgomery, Benny (Rockies) — 151
Montgomery, Colson (White Sox) — 100

Montgomery, Mason (Rays) — 440
Mooney, Sean (Twins) — 288
Moore, Robert (Brewers) — 266
Morabito, Nick (Mets) — 301
Morales, Francisco (Phillies) — 346
Morales, Michael (Mariners) — 428
Moreno, Gabriel (Blue Jays) — 468
Moreno, Luis (Mets) — 303
Morris, Cody (Guardians) — 140
Morrobel, Yeison (Rangers) — 458
Morton, Kadon (Braves) — 48
Mozzicato, Frank (Royals) — 198
Muller, Kyle (Braves) — 36
Muncy, Max (Athletics) — 326
Muñoz, Roddery (Braves) — 47
Murphy, Chris (Red Sox) — 74
Murphy, Luke (Angels) — 224
Murphy, Owen (Braves) — 37
Murphy, Ryan (Giants) — 412
Mushinski, Parker (Astros) — 192
Muzziotti, Simon (Phillies) — 344

N

Nastrini, Nick (Dodgers) — 232
Naylor, Bo (Guardians) — 133
Nelson, Ryne (D-backs) — 23
Neto, Zach (Angels) — 213
Nicolas, Kyle (Pirates) — 362
Nikhazy, Doug (Guardians) — 144
Noda, Ryan (Athletics) — 333
Noel, Jhonkensy (Guardians) — 141
Nolasco, Rodolfo (Pirates) — 368
Norby, Connor (Orioles) — 55
Nowlin, Jaylen (Twins) — 289
Nuñez, Malcolm (Pirates) — 365
Nuñez, Nasim (Marlins) — 250
Nuñez, Rainer (Blue Jays) — 480

O

O'Hoppe, Logan (Angels) — 212
O'Rae, Dylan (Brewers) — 271
Olson, Reese (Tigers) — 169
Ornelas, Jonathan (Rangers) — 463
Ornelas, Tirso (Padres) — 401
Ortiz, Jhailyn (Phillies) — 350
Ortiz, Joey (Orioles) — 56
Ortiz, Luis (Pirates) — 358
Orze, Eric (Mets) — 304
Osorio, Javier (Tigers) — 176
Ottenbreit, Micah (Phillies) — 349
Outman, James (Dodgers) — 233
Ovalles, Layonel (Mets) — 300

P

Pacheco, Alberto (Rockies) — 160
Pacheco, Freddy (Cardinals) — 382
Pacheco, Izaac (Tigers) — 171
Packard, Spencer (Mariners) — 430
Pages, Andy (Dodgers) — 231
Painter, Andrew (Phillies) — 340
Palacios, Richie (Guardians) — 143
Palencia, Daniel (Cubs) — 90
Pallette, Peyton (White Sox) — 103
Palmegiani, Damiano (Blue Jays) — 479
Palmer, Trent (Blue Jays) — 481
Palmquist, Carson (Rockies) — 159
Paniagua, Inohan (Cardinals) — 379
Parada, Kevin (Mets) — 294
Paris, Kyren (Angels) — 219
Parker, Mitchell (Nationals) — 490
Patiño, Wilderd (D-backs) — 26

U

Ullola, Miguel (Astros) 185
Urbina, Misael (Twins) 285
Ureña, Engelth (Yankees) 315
Ureña, Walbert (Angels) 218
Uribe, Abner (Brewers) 266

V

Valdez, Enmanuel (Red Sox) 77
Valera, George (Guardians) 134
Valerio, Felix (Brewers) 268
Van Eyk, C.J. (Blue Jays) 481
Vaquero, Cristhian (Nationals) 487
Vargas, Carlos (D-backs) 30
Vargas, Echedry (Rangers) 465
Vargas, Jordy (Rockies) 152
Vargas, Marco (Marlins) 253
Vargas, Miguel (Dodgers) 229
Varland, Louie (Twins) 280
Vasil, Mike (Mets) 298
Vasquez, Randy (Yankees) 312
Vasquez, Willy (Rays) 443
Vavra, Terrin (Orioles) 60
Vazquez, Daniel (Royals) 209
Veen, Zac (Rockies) 149
Vela, Noel (Padres) 396
Ventura, Jordany (Mets) 299
Vera, Arol (Angels) 223
Vera, Norge (White Sox) 104
Veras, Wilfred (White Sox) 108
Verdugo, Rosman (Padres) 393
Vernon, Austin (Rays) 448
Viars, Jordan (Phillies) 347
Vientos, Mark (Mets) 295
Vines, Darius (Braves) 39
Virbitsky, Kyle (Athletics) 337

Vivas, Jorbit (Dodgers) 237
Vodnik, Victor (Braves) 43
Volpe, Anthony (Yankees) 308
Vrieling, Trystan (Yankees) 317
Vukovich, A.J. (D-backs) 25

W

Waddell, Luke (Braves) 48
Wagner, Max (Orioles) 61
Wagner, Will (Astros) 188
Waites, Cole (Giants) 412
Waldichuk, Ken (Athletics) 326
Walker, Jordan (Cardinals) 372
Wallace, Cayden (Royals) 197
Wallner, Matt (Twins) 279
Walsh, Jake (Cardinals) 382
Walston, Blake (D-backs) 24
Walter, Brandon (Red Sox) 73
Ward, Thad (Nationals) 491
Warren, Will (Yankees) 311
Waters, Drew (Royals) 197
Watson, Kahlil (Marlins) 251
Way, Beck (Royals) 202
Weissert, Greg (Yankees) 319
Wells, Austin (Yankees) 310
Wentz, Joey (Tigers) 171
Wesneski, Hayden (Cubs) 88
Westburg, Jordan (Orioles) 55
Whisenhunt, Carson (Giants) 408
White Jr., Lonnie (Pirates) 368
White, Colby (Rays) 445
White, Owen (Rangers) 453
White, TJ (Nationals) 489
Whitley, Forrest (Astros) 193
Wicks, Jordan (Cubs) 89
Wiemer, Joey (Brewers) 261
Wilcox, Cole (Rays) 441

Williams, Carson (Rays) 438
Williams, Gavin (Guardians) 133
Williams, Henry (Padres) 394
Williams, Jett (Mets) 295
Williamson, Brandon (Reds) 121
Willis, Alec (Cardinals) 380
Wilson, Brooks (Braves) 44
Wilson, Ethan (Phillies) 345
Wilson, Peyton (Royals) 207
Winn, Cole (Rangers) 458
Winn, Keaton (Giants) 410
Winn, Masyn (Cardinals) 373
Wong, Connor (Red Sox) 77
Woo, Bryan (Mariners) 423
Wood, James (Nationals) 484
Wood, Matt (Brewers) 270
Woods Richardson, Simeon (Twins) 281
Workman, Gage (Tigers) 176
Wrobleski, Justin (Dodgers) 241

Y

Yeager, Justin (Braves) 47
Yorke, Nick (Red Sox) 71
Yoshida, Masataka (Red Sox) 70
Young, Cole (Mariners) 421

Z

Zamora, Freddy (Brewers) 273
Zavala, Aaron (Rangers) 455
Zavala, Samuel (Padres) 390
Zerpa, Angel (Royals) 200
Ziegler, Calvin (Mets) 297
Zobac, Steven (Royals) 208
Zulueta, Yosver (Blue Jays) 469
Zuniga, Guillermo (Cardinals) 385